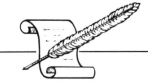

HISTORIC DOCUMENTS OF 1978

Cumulative Index 1974-78

Congressional Quarterly, Inc.

Historic Documents of 1978

Major Contributors: Michael J. Glennon, James R. Ingram, Barbara L. Risk

Other Contributors: Mary Costello, Howard Fields, John L. Moore, Margaret C. Thompson, Susan E. Tifft
Cumulative Index: Diane Huffman
Production Manager: I. D. Fuller
Assistant Production Manager: Maceo Mayo

Copyright 1979 by Congressional Quarterly Inc.
1414 22nd Street N.W., Washington, D.C. 20037

Library of Congress Cataloging in Publication Data

Historic documents. 1972—
    Washington. Congressional Quarterly Inc.

    1. United States—Politics and government—1945— —Yearbooks.
2. World politics—1945— —Yearbooks. I. Congressional Quarterly Inc.

E839.5.H57   917.3'03'9205   72-97888
ISBN 0-87187-140-8

FOREWORD

Publication of *Historic Documents of 1978* carries through a seventh year the project launched by Congressional Quarterly with *Historic Documents 1972*. The purpose of this continuing series of volumes is to give students, scholars, librarians, journalists and citizens convenient access to documents of basic importance in the broad range of public affairs.

To place the documents in perspective, each entry is preceded by a brief introduction containing background materials, in some cases a short summary of the document itself and, where necessary, relevant subsequent developments. We believe these introductions will prove increasingly useful in future years when the events and questions now covered are less fresh in one's memory and the documents may be difficult to find or unobtainable.

The year 1978 saw intense negotiations and diplomatic moves on a variety of fronts. As had happened in 1977, the world was again stunned by a major breakthrough in the Middle East negotiations. President Carter met in September with Egyptian President Anwar Sadat and Israeli Prime Minister Menachem Begin for 13 days of grueling negotiations. The resulting accords held out the promise of a peace treaty between Egypt and Israel within three months but at year's end there were still issues to be resolved.

A strategic arms limitation agreement between the United States and the Soviet Union also remained elusive in 1978, despite two years of negotiations and prior agreement on a basic framework for the treaty. But not all diplomatic efforts were frustrated in 1978. President Carter won a hard campaign for Senate ratification of the Panama Canal treaties. And the White House made the surprise announcement in December that the United States and the People's Republic of China would establish full diplomatic relations.

Economic issues—spiraling inflation and the declining value of the dollar—continued to cause concern at home and abroad in 1978. To back up pledges made at several international meetings, President Carter in late October announced a new anti-inflation plan, and then eight days later revealed a monetary package aimed at bolstering the dollar.

These developments added substantially to the usual outpouring of presidential statements, court decisions, committee reports, special studies and speeches of national or international importance. We have selected for inclusion in this book as many as possible of the documents that in our judgment will be of more than transitory interest. Where space limitations prevented reproduction of the full texts, the excerpts used were chosen to set forth the essentials and, at the same time, to preserve the flavor of the materials.

Patricia Ann O'Connor
Editor

Washington, D.C.
February, 1979

174916

How to Use This Book

The documents are arranged in chronological order. If you know the approximate date of the report, speech, statement, court decision or other document you are looking for, glance through the titles for that month in the Table of Contents below.

If the Table of Contents does not lead you directly to the document you want, make a double check by turning to the subject Index at the end of the book. There you may find references not only to the particular document you seek but also to other entries on the same or a related subject. The Index in this volume is a **five-year cumulative index** of Historic Documents covering the years 1974-1978.

The introduction to each document is printed in italic type. The document itself, printed in roman type, follows the spelling, capitalization and punctuation of the original or official copy. Where the full text is not given, omissions of material are indicated by the customary ellipsis points.

TABLE OF CONTENTS

February

March

April

May

June

July

August

September

October

November

December

HISTORIC
DOCUMENTS
OF
1978

 **HISTORIC DOCUMENTS OF 1978**

January

MONDALE'S EULOGY OF HUMPHREY

January 15, 1978

*An outpouring of public and private tributes by former political sup-
porters and adversaries alike followed the death Jan. 13 of Sen. Hubert H.
Humphrey. Sen. Humphrey died at his home in Waverly, Minn., after a
courageous fight against cancer.*

*The former vice president's body was flown to Washington, D.C., where
it lay in state in the rotunda of the U.S. Capitol. A memorial service for
Humphrey was held Jan. 15 in the Capitol; a second service was held Jan.
16 at House of Hope Presbyterian Church, St. Paul, Minn. President
Jimmy Carter and Vice President Walter Mondale delivered eulogies at
both services.*

*Among those present at the service in the Capitol were former Presi-
dents Gerald R. Ford and Richard M. Nixon, Mrs. Lyndon B. Johnson and
former Vice President Nelson A. Rockefeller. It was the first time that
Nixon had visited Washington since his resignation from the presidency in
1974.*

*Humphrey's political career spanned 30 years. After first gaining nation-
al attention at the 1948 Democratic Convention when, as mayor of Minneapolis, he fought for a civil rights plank in the party platform, Humphrey
was elected to the Senate in 1949 where he continued to champion civil
rights. He was credited with the establishment of the Arms Control and
Disarmament Agency, the Peace Corps and the Food for Peace program.
In 1964 he left the Senate to serve as Johnson's vice president. Four years
later he was the Democratic Party's nominee for president, losing to Richard Nixon in a close race. In 1971 Humphrey returned to the Senate. Seeking the Democratic presidential nomination in 1972, he lost to Sen. George*

3

*McGovern of South Dakota. In the 1976 presidential race, he let it be
known that he was available for nomination, but he did not campaign actively. Later in 1976, after dropping out of a contest with West Virginia
Sen. Robert C. Byrd for election as Senate majority leader, he was appointed to a specially created office, deputy president pro tempore of the
Senate. As deputy president pro tempore, Humphrey often met with President Carter and developed into one of the president's strongest supporters
on Capitol Hill.*

*Humphrey's impact on public policy over the years was enormous. Yet
his most remarkable achievement was in gaining the special affection of
the American people. His stature grew as passions over old political battles faded. To blacks and other minorities he symbolized the nation's commitment to equal rights.*

*His enthusiasm was infectious, and legendary. Known for his bouncy,
garrulous nature, Humphrey had an optimistic, almost old-fashioned faith
in people and the country. His ideology was "the politics of joy," his sobri-
quet "the Happy Warrior." Even near the end of his life, with his body
wasted by disease and chemotherapy, his optimism was irrepressible.*

*Speaking of his friend and mentor of 31 years, Mondale delivered a mov-
ing eulogy at the Jan. 15 service. "Hubert will be remembered by all of us
who served with him as one of the greatest legislators in our history,"
Mondale said. "He will be remembered as one of the most loved men of
his times. And even though he failed to realize his greatest goal, he
achieved something much more rare and valuable than the nation's highest office. He became his country's conscience."*

*In his remarks at the Capitol, Carter said that Humphrey's was "the
first voice I ever heard, a lone voice, persistently demanding basic human
rights for all Americans." Carter gratefully acknowledged Humphrey's
support in the Senate and concluded by asserting that "Hubert Humphrey
was the most beloved of all Americans, and . . . his family encompassed
not just the people of the United States but . . . all people everywhere."*

*Following is the text of Vice President Mondale's eulogy of
Sen. Humphrey at the Capitol Jan. 15, 1978:*

Dear Muriel, the Humphrey family and guests:
There is a natural impulse at a time like this to dwell on the many
accomplishments of Hubert Humphrey's remarkable life, by listing a cata-
logue of past events as though there were some way to quantify what he
was all about. But I don't want to do that because Hubert didn't want it
and neither does Muriel. Even though this is one of the saddest moments
of my life and I feel as great a loss as I have ever known, we must remind
ourselves of Hubert's last great wish:

That this be a time to celebrate life and the future, not to mourn the past and his death. I hope you will forgive me if I don't entirely succeed in looking forward and not backward. Because I must for a moment. Two days ago as I flew back from the West over the land that Hubert loved to this city that he loved I thought back over his life and its meaning and I tried to understand what it was about this unique person that made him such an uplifting symbol of hope and joy for all people. And I thought of the letter that he wrote to Muriel 40 years ago when he first visited Washington.

He said in that letter:

"Maybe I seem foolish to have such vain hopes and plans, but Bucky, I can see how some day, if you and I just apply ourselves and make up our minds to work for bigger things, how we can some day live here in Washington and probably be in government, politics or service. I intend to set my aim at Congress."

Hubert was wrong only in thinking that his hopes and plans might be in vain. They were not, as we all know. Not only did he succeed with his beloved wife at his side, he succeeded gloriously and beyond even his most optimistic dreams.

Hubert will be remembered by all of us who served with him as one of the greatest legislators in our history. He will be remembered as one of the most loved men of his times. And even though he failed to realize his greatest goal, he achieved something much more rare and valuable than the nation's highest office. He became his country's conscience.

Today the love that flows from everywhere enveloping Hubert flows also to you, Muriel, and the presence today here, where America bids farewell to her heroes, of President and Mrs. Carter, of former Presidents Ford and Nixon, and your special friend and former first lady, Mrs. Johnson, attest to the love and the respect that the nation holds for both of you. That letter to Bucky, his Muriel, also noted three principles by which Hubert defined his life: work, determination and high goals. They were a part of his life's pattern when I first met him 31 years ago. I was only 18, fresh out of high school, and he was the mayor of Minneapolis. He had then all the other sparkling qualities he maintained throughout his life: boundless good humor, endless optimism and hope, infinite interests, intense concern for people and their problems, compassion without being patronizing, energy beyond belief, and a spirit so filled with love there was no room for hate or bitterness.

He was simply incredible. When he said that life was not meant to be endured but rather to be enjoyed, you knew what he meant. You could see it simply by watching him and listening to him.

When Hubert looked at the lives of black Americans in the '40s, he saw endurance and not enjoyment, and his heart insisted that it was time for Americans to walk forthrightly into the bright sunshine of human rights.

When Hubert looked at the young who could not get a good education, he saw endurance and not enjoyment. When Hubert saw old people in ill health, he saw endurance and not enjoyment. When Hubert saw middle-

5

class people striving to survive, and working people without jobs and decent homes, he saw endurance and not enjoyment.

Hubert was criticized for proclaiming the politics of joy. But he knew that joy is essential to us and is not frivolous. He loved to point out that ours is the only nation in the world to officially declare the pursuit of happiness as a national goal. But he was also a sentimental man and that was part of his life, too. He cried in public and without embarrassment. In his last major speech in his beloved Minnesota he wiped tears from his eyes and said, "A man without tears is a man without a heart." If he cried often, it was not for himself, but for others.

Above all, Hubert was a man with a good heart. And on this sad day it would be good for us to recall Shakespeare's words: "A good leg will fall. A straight back will stoop. A black beard will turn white. A curled pate will grow bald. A fair face will wither. A full eye will wax hollow. But a good heart is the sun and the moon, for it shines bright and never changes, but keeps its course truly." Hubert's heart kept its course truly.

He taught us all how to hope and how to love, how to win and how to lose, he taught us how to live, and finally, he taught us how to die.

STATE OF THE UNION ADDRESS, ACCOMPANYING MESSAGE

January 19, 1978

President Carter stressed domestic affairs, especially problems of the economy, in a State of the Union address which he delivered in person to a joint session of Congress Jan. 19. For the first time, the State of the Union address was accompanied by a longer written message which the president did not deliver. While the speech itself took only 30 minutes for Carter to deliver, the written message was 50 pages in length and outlined in considerably greater detail the president's 1978 legislative agenda.

In his address, the president claimed that his foreign policy had achieved three basic objectives: national security, world peace and world economic stability. He said that because of his campaign in support of human rights "there has been significant movement toward greater freedom and humanity in several parts of the world." He asserted that at home unemployment and inflation had both been reduced, the economy had grown and the standard of living had risen.

Emphasis on Limits

In tone, however, the address was subdued and cautious, emphasizing the limits of government to intervene successfully in some of the most vexing problems facing the nation. "We need patience and good will, but we really need to realize that there is a limit to the role and the function of government," he said. The president also said, "Government cannot eliminate poverty, or provide a bountiful economy or reduce inflation or save our cities or cure illiteracy or provide energy, and government cannot

7

mandate goodness. Only a true partnership between government and the people can ever hope to reach these goals."

Still, the president pointed to the "risk of inaction" in times such as the present "when there is no single overwhelming crisis." He later said, "For the first time in a generation, we are not haunted by a major international crisis or by domestic turmoil, and we now have a rare and priceless opportunity to address the persistent problems which burden us as a nation and which became quietly and steadily worse over the years."

The Economy

Chief among the "persistent problems," Carter indicated, were the sluggish economy and diminishing energy resources. The two, he said, were inextricably linked. "Every day we spend more than $120 million for foreign oil," Carter asserted. "This slows our economic growth, lowers the value of the dollar overseas, and aggravates unemployment and inflation at home."

Abandoning his earlier predictions of a balanced federal budget by the end of his term, Carter merely said that with the right steps the nation "can move rapidly toward a balanced budget." His first full budget, he said, was "lean and tight." (Carter Budget Message, see p. 95.)

He sketched his recommendations for stimulus tax cuts, which were separately announced in a Jan. 21 message to Congress. "Almost $17 billion in income tax cuts will go to individuals," he said. "Ninety-six per cent of American taxpayers will see their taxes go down. For a typical family of four this will mean an annual saving of more than $250. . . ." His proposed tax reductions, with tax cuts for business included, reached $24.5 billion.

The centerpiece of his economic proposals was a program "to encourage businesses to hire young and disadvantaged Americans." The program was designed to provide for the voluntary creation of new jobs by local businesses, with the federal government paying for the required on-the-job training. The president also saw a voluntary program as the best way to curb inflation. He said, "I do not believe in wage and price controls. A sincere commitment to voluntary constraint provides a way — perhaps the only way — to fight inflation without government interference."

Few New Initiatives

The State of the Union address and the written message which accompanied it contained only a few new initiatives. To familiar proposals in the economic, energy and foreign relations areas, Carter added reform of the civil service, a continued reduction in government red tape and a new Cabinet-level Department of Education. He called again for ratification of the Panama Canal treaties, pledged to work toward peace in the Middle East and emphasized the importance of negotiating a strategic arms accord with the Soviet Union.

Reaction

Carter's statements stressing the limits to the ability of government to bring about change were greeted by applause in the House chamber. Frequently that applause was led by Republicans. But many Democrats, too, found the limited government theme attractive. Sen. Alan Cranston, D-Calif., said that he believed the address "responded to a feeling which I frequently encounter in California, that the government cannot be the manager of everything, but must call forth the resources of the people to solve some problems."

Much of the reaction in Congress to the speech, however, followed partisan lines. House Speaker Thomas P. O'Neill Jr., D-Mass., said that the address "was excellently received by members." House Minority Leader John J. Rhodes, R-Ariz., said that it "lacked focus or direction." But Sen. Daniel Patrick Moynihan, D-N.Y., voiced intense disappointment over what he saw as Carter's failure to address himself to urban needs.

Following are the texts of President Jimmy Carter's first State of the Union address delivered to a nationally televised joint session of Congress Jan. 19, 1978, and of the written message which accompanied it. (Boldface headings in brackets have been added by Congressional Quarterly to highlight the organization of the text.):

STATE OF THE UNION ADDRESS

Mr. President, Mr. Speaker, Members of the 95th Congress, ladies and gentlemen:

Two years ago today we had the first Caucus in Iowa and one year ago tomorrow, I walked from here to the White House to take up the duties of President of the United States. I didn't know it then when I walked, but I have been trying to save energy ever since. [Laughter] I return tonight to fulfill one of those duties of the Constitution: To "give to the Congress" — and to the nation — "information on the state of the Union."

Militarily, politically, economically and in spirit, the state of our Union is sound.

We are a great country, a strong country, a vital and a dynamic country — and so we will remain.

We are a confident people and a hard-working people, a decent and a compassionate people — and so we will remain.

I want to speak to you tonight about where we are and where we must go, about what we have done and what we must do. And I want to pledge to you my best efforts and ask you to pledge yours.

Each generation of Americans has to face circumstances not of its own choosing, but by which its character is measured and its spirit is tested.

There are times of emergency, when a nation and its leaders must bring their energies to bear on a single urgent task. That was a duty Abraham Lincoln faced when our land was torn apart by conflict in the War Between the States. That was the duty faced by Franklin Roosevelt when he led America out of an economic depression and again when he led America to victory in war.

There are other times when there is no single overwhelming crisis — yet profound national interests are at stake.

At such times the risk of inaction can be equally great. It becomes the task of leaders to call forth the vast and restless energies of our people to build for the future.

That is what Harry Truman did in the years after the Second World War, when we helped Europe and Japan rebuild themselves and secured an international order that has protected freedom from aggression.

[Sense of Unity]

We live in such time now — and we face such duties.

We have come through a long period of turmoil and doubt, but we have once again found our moral course and with a new spirit, we are striving to express our best instincts to the rest of the world.

There is all across our land, a growing sense of peace and a sense of common purpose. This sense of unity cannot be expressed in programs or in legislation, or in dollars.

It is an achievement that belongs to every individual American. This unity ties together and it towers over all our efforts here in Washington, and it serves as an inspiring beacon for all of us who are elected to serve. This new atmosphere demands a new spirit, a partnership between those of us who lead and those who elect. The foundations of this partnership are truth, the courage to face hard decisions; concern for one another and the common good over special interests; and a basic faith and trust in the wisdom and strength and judgment of the American people.

For the first time in a generation, we are not haunted by a major international crisis or by domestic turmoil, and we now have a rare and a priceless opportunity to address persistent problems and burdens which come to us as a Nation — quietly and steadily getting worse over the years.

As President, I have had to ask you — the Members of Congress, and you, the American people — to come to grips with some of the most difficult and hard questions facing our society.

We must make a maximum effort — because if we do not aim for the best, we are very likely to achieve little.

I see no benefit to the country if we delay because the problems will only get worse.

We need patience and good will, but we really need to realize that there is a limit to the role and the function of government.

Government cannot solve all our problems, it can't set our goals, it cannot define our vision. Government cannot eliminate poverty, or provide a bountiful economy or reduce inflation or save our cities or cure illiteracy or provide energy, and government cannot mandate goodness. Only a true partnership between government and the people can ever hope to reach these goals.

Those of us who govern can sometimes inspire, and we can identify needs and marshal resources, but we simply cannot be the managers of everything and everybody.

We here in Washington must move away from crisis management, and we must establish clear goals for the immediate future and the distant future which will let us work together and not in conflict.

[Energy Program Needed]

Never again should we neglect a growing crisis like the shortage of energy, where further delay will only lead to more harsh and painful solutions.

Everyday we spend more than $120 million for foreign oil. This slows our economic growth. It lowers the value of the dollar overseas, and it aggravates unemployment and inflation here at home.

Now we know what we must do, increase production.

We must cut down on waste. And we must use more of those fuels which are plentiful and more permanent.

We must be fair to people and we must not disrupt our Nation's economy and our budget.

Now that sounds simple. But I recognize the difficulties involved. I know that it is not easy for the Congress to act. But the fact remains that on the energy legislation, we have failed the American people. Almost five years after the oil embargo dramatized the problem for us all, we still do not have a national energy program.

Not much longer can we tolerate this stalemate. It undermines our national interest both at home and abroad. We must succeed, and I believe we will.

Our main task at home this year, with energy a central element, is the Nation's economy. We must continue the recovery and further cut unemployment and inflation.

Last year was a good one for the United States. We reached all of our major economic goals for 1977. Four million new jobs were created — an all-time record — and the number of unemployed dropped by more than a million. Unemployment right now is the lowest it has been since 1974, and not since World War II has such a high percentage of American people been employed.

The rate of inflation went down. There was a good growth in business profits and investments, the source of more jobs for our workers, and a higher standard of living for all our people. After taxes and inflation, there was a healthy increase in workers' wages.

This year, our country will have the first two trillion dollar economy in the history of the world.

Now we are proud of this progress the first year, but we must do even better in the future.

[Economic Problems]

We still have serious problems on which all of us must work together. Our trade deficit is too large. Inflation is still too high, and too many Americans still do not have a job. Now, I didn't have any simple answers for all these problems. But we have developed an economic policy that is working, because it is simple, balanced and fair. It is based on four principles:

First, the economy must keep on expanding to produce new jobs and better income which our people need. The fruits of growth must be widely shared. More jobs must be made available to those who have been by-passed until now, and the tax system must be made fairer and simpler.

Secondly, private business and not the government must lead the expansion in the future.

Third, we must lower the rate of inflation and keep it down. Inflation slows down economic growth, and it is the most cruel to the poor and also to the elderly and others who live on fixed incomes.

And fourth, we must contribute to the strength of the world economy.

I will announce detailed proposals for improving our tax system later this week. We can make our tax laws fairer, we can make them simpler and easier to understand; and at the same time, we can — and we will — reduce the tax burden on American citizens by $25 billion.

The tax reforms and the tax reductions go together. Only with the long overdue reforms will the full tax cut be advisable.

Almost $17 billion in income tax cuts will go to individuals. Ninety-six per cent of all American taxpayers will see their taxes go down. For a typical family of four, this means an annual saving of more than $250 a year, or a tax reduction of about 20 per cent.

A further $2 billion cut in excise taxes will give more relief and also contribute directly to lowering the rate of inflation.

We will also provide strong additional incentives for business investment and growth through substantial cuts in the corporate tax rates and improvement in the investment tax credit.

These tax proposals will increase opportunity everywhere in the Nation. But additional jobs for the disadvantaged deserve special attention.

We have already passed laws to assure equal access to the voting booth, and to restaurants, and to schools, to housing; and laws to permit access to jobs. But job opportunity — the chance to earn a decent living — is also a basic human right which we cannot and will not ignore.

A major priority for our Nation is the final elimination of the barriers that restrict the opportunities available to women, and also to black people, Hispanics and other minorities. We have come a long way toward that goal. But there is still more to do.

What we inherited from the past must not be permitted to shackle us in the future.

I will be asking you for a substantial increase in funds for public jobs for our young people, and I also am recommending that the Congress continue the Public Service Employment Programs at more than twice the level of a year ago.

When welfare reform is completed, we will have more than a million additional jobs so that those on welfare who are able to work can work.

However, again, we know that in our free society, private business is still the best source of new jobs.

Therefore, I will propose a new program to encourage businesses to hire young and disadvantaged Americans. Those people only need skills and a chance, in order to take their place in our economic system. Let's give them the chance they need.

A major step in the right direction would be the early passage of a greatly improved Humphrey-Hawkins Bill.

My budget for 1979 addresses these national needs, but it is lean and tight. I have cut waste wherever possible.

I am proposing an increase of less than 2 per cent after adjusting for inflation — the smallest increase in the Federal budget in four years.

Lately, Federal spending has taken a steadily increasing portion of what Americans produce. Our new budget reverses that trend, and later I hope to bring the Government's toll down even further. And with your help, we will do that.

In time of high employment and a strong economy, deficit spending should not be a feature of our budget.

As the economy continues to gain strength and as our unemployment rates continue to fall, revenues will grow. With careful planning, efficient management and proper restraint on spending, we can move rapidly toward a balanced budget — and we will.

Next year the budget deficit will be only slightly less than this year. But one-third of the deficit is due to the necessary tax cuts that I have proposed. This year the right choice is to reduce the burden on taxpayers and provide more jobs for our people.

The third element in our program is a renewed attack on inflation. We have learned the hard way that high unemployment will not prevent or cure inflation. Government can help us by stimulating private investment and by maintaining a responsible economic policy. Through a new top level review process, we will do a better job of reducing government regulation that drives up costs and drives up prices.

But again, government alone cannot bring down the rate of inflation. When a level of high inflation is expected to continue, then companies raise prices to protect their profit margins against the prospective increases in wages and other costs; while workers demand higher wages as protection against the expected price increases. It's like an escalation in the arms race, and understandably, no one wants to disarm alone.

[Voluntary Anti-inflation Program]

No one firm or a group of workers can halt this process. It is an effort that we must all make together. I am therefore asking government, business, labor, and other groups to join in a voluntary program to moderate inflation by holding wage and price increases in each sector of the economy during 1978 below the average increases of the last two years.

I do not believe in wage and price controls. A sincere commitment to voluntary constraint provides a way, perhaps the only way to fight inflation without government interference.

As I came into the Capitol tonight, I saw the farmers, my fellow farmers, standing out in the snow. I am familiar with their problem and I know from Congress' action that you are, too. When I was running Carter's Warehouse, we had spread on our own farms five, ten, fifteen fertilizers for about $40 a ton. The last time I was home, the price was about $100 a ton. The cost of nitrogen has gone up 150 per cent, and the price of products that farmers sell has either stayed the same or gone down a little. Now this past year in 1977, you the Congress and I together passed a new Agricultural Act. It went into effect October 1. It will have its first impact on the 1978 crops. It will help a great deal. It will add $8.5 billion or more to help the farmers with their price supports and target prices.

Last year we had the highest level of exports of farm products in the history of our country, $24 billion. We expect to have more this year. We will be working together. But I think it is incumbent on us to monitor very carefully the farm situation and continue to work harmoniously with the farmers of our country. What is best for the farmer, the farm families, in the long run is best for the consumers of our country.

Economic success at home is also the key to success in our international economic policy. An effective energy program, strong investment and productivity and controlled inflation will provide [improve] our trade balance and balance it, and it will help to protect the integrity of the dollar overseas.

By working closely with our friends abroad, we can promote the economic health of the whole world. With fair and balanced agreements lowering the barriers to trade.

Despite the inevitable pressures that build up when the world economy suffers from high unemployment, we must firmly resist the demands for self-defeating protectionism. But free trade must also be fair trade. And I am determined to protect the American industry and American workers against the foreign trade practices which are unfair or illegal.

In a separate written message to Congress, I have outlined other domestic initiatives, such as welfare reform, consumer protection, basic education skills, urban policy, reform of our labor laws and national health care later on this year. I will not repeat those tonight. But there are several other points that I would like to make directly to you.

During these past years, Americans have seen our government grow far from us.

[Government Reorganization]

For some citizens the government has almost become like a foreign country, so strange and distant that we have often had to deal with it through trained ambassadors who have sometimes become too powerful and too influential — lawyers, accountants and lobbyists. This cannot go on.

We must have what Abraham Lincoln wanted, a government for the people.

We have made progress toward that kind of government. You have given me the authority requested to reorganize the Federal bureaucracy. And I am using that authority.

We have already begun a series of reorganization plans which will be completed over a period of three years. We have also proposed abolishing almost 500 Federal advisory and other commissions and boards. But I know that the American people are still sick and tired of Federal paperwork and red tape. Bit by bit we are chopping down the thicket of unnecessary Federal regulations by which government too often interferes in our personal lives and our personal business. We have cut the public's Federal paperwork load by more than 12 per cent in less than a year. And we are not through cutting.

We have made a good start on turning the gobbledygook of Federal regulations into plain English that people can understand. But we know that we still have a long way to go. We have brought together parts of eleven government agencies to create a new Department of Energy. And now it is time to take another major step by creating a separate Department of Education.

But even the best-organized government will only be as effective as the people who carry out its policies. For this reason, I consider Civil Service reform to be absolutely vital. Worked out with the civil servants themselves, this reorganization plan will restore the merit principle to a system which has grown into a bureaucratic maze. It will provide greater management flexibility and better rewards for better performance without compromising job security.

Then and only then can we have a government that is efficient, open, and truly worthy of our people's understanding and respect. I have promised that we will have such a government and I intend to keep that promise.

In our foreign policy, the separation of people from government has been in the past a source of weakness and error. In a democratic system like ours, foreign policy decisions must be able to stand the test of public examination and public debate. If we make a mistake in this Administration, it will be on the side of frankness and openness with the American people.

In our modern world when the deaths of literally millions of people can result from a few terrifying seconds of destruction, the path of national strength and security is identical to the path of peace. Tonight, I am happy to report that because we are strong, our Nation is at peace with the world.

[Human Rights and Defense]

We are a confident Nation. We have restored a moral basis for our foreign policy. The very heart of our identity as a Nation is our firm commitment to human rights.

We stand for human rights because we believe that government has as a purpose, to promote the well-being of its citizens. This is true in our domestic policy, it is also true in our foreign policy. The world must know that in support of human rights, the United States will stand firm.

We expect no quick or easy results, but there has been significant movement toward greater freedom and humanity in several parts of the world.

Thousands of political prisoners have been freed. The leaders of the world — even our ideological adversaries — now see that their attitude toward fundamental human rights affects their standing in the international community and it affects their relations with the United States.

To serve the interests of every American, our foreign policy has three major goals. The first and prime concern is and will remain the security of our country.

Security is based on our national will and security is based on the strength of our armed forces. We have the will, and militarily, we are very strong. Security also comes through the strength of our alliances. We have reconfirmed our commitment to the defense of Europe, and this year, we will demonstrate that commitment by further modernizing and strengthening our military capabilities there.

Security can also be enhanced by agreements with potential adversaries which reduce the threat of nuclear disaster while maintaining our own relative strategic capability.

In areas of peaceful competition with the Soviet Union, we will continue to more than hold our own.

At the same time, we are negotiating with quiet confidence, without haste, with careful determination, to ease the tension between us and to ensure greater stability and security.

The Strategic Arms Limitation Talks have been long and difficult. We want a mutual limit on both the quality and quantity of the giant nuclear arsenals of both nations — and then we want actual reductions in strategic arms as a major step toward the ultimate elimination of nuclear weapons from the face of the earth.

If those talks result in an agreement this year — and I trust they will — I pledge to you that the agreement will maintain and enhance the stability of the world's strategic balance and the security of the United States.

For 30 years, concerted but unsuccessful efforts have been made to ban the testing of atomic explosives — both military weapons and peaceful nuclear devices.

We are hard at work with Great Britain and the Soviet Union on an agreement which will stop testing and will protect our national security and provide for adequate verification of compliance.

We are now making progress, I believe good progress, toward this comprehensive ban on nuclear explosions.

We are also working vigorously to halt the proliferation of nuclear weapons among the nations of the world which do not now have them and to reduce the deadly global traffic in conventional arms sales. Our stand for peace is suspect if we are also the principal arms merchant of the world. So we have decided to cut down our arms transfers abroad on a year-by-year basis, and to work with other major arms exporters to encourage their similar restraint.

Every American has a stake in our second major goal — a world at peace. In a nuclear age, each of us is threatened when peace is not secured everywhere. We are trying to promote harmony in those parts of the world where major differences exist among other nations and threaten international peace.

In the Middle East, we are contributing our good offices to maintain the momentum of the current negotiations — and to keep open the lines of communication among the Middle Eastern leaders. The whole world has a great stake in the success of these efforts. This is a precious opportunity for a historic settlement of a longstanding conflict — an opportunity which may never come again in our lifetime.

Our role has been difficult and sometimes thankless and controversial. But it has been constructive and it has been necessary, and it will continue.

Our third major foreign policy goal is one that touches the life of every American citizen everyday: world economic growth and stability.

This requires strong economic performance by the industrialized democracies like ourselves and progress in resolving the global energy crisis. Last fall, with the help of others, we succeeded in our vigorous efforts to maintain the stability of the price of oil. But as many foreign leaders have emphasized to me personally, and I am sure to you, the greatest future contribution that America can make to the world economy would be an effective energy conservation program here at home.

We will not hesitate to take the actions needed to protect the integrity of the American dollar.

We are trying to develop a more just international system. And in this spirit, we are supporting the struggle for human development; in Africa, in Asia, and in Latin America.

[Panama Canal Treaties]

Finally, the world is watching to see how we act on one of our most important and controversial items of business: approval of the Panama Canal Treaties.

The treaties now before the Senate are the result of the work of four Administrations — two Democratic, two Republican.

They guarantee that the Canal will be open always for unrestricted use by the ships of the world. Our ships have the right to go to the head of the line for priority of passage in times of emergency or need.

We retain the permanent right to defend the Canal with our own military forces, if necessary, to guarantee its openness and its neutrality.

The treaties are to the clear advantage of ourselves, the Panamanians, and the other users of the Canal. Ratifying the Panama Canal Treaties will demonstrate our good faith to the world, discourage the spread of hostile ideologies in this hemisphere and directly contribute to the economic well-being and the security of the United States. [Applause]

I have to say that that is very welcome applause. [Laughter]

There were two moments on my recent journey which, for me, confirmed the final aims of our foreign policy and what it always must be.

One was a little village in India, where I met a people as passionately attached to their rights and liberties as we are — but whose children have a far smaller chance for good health or food or education or human fulfillment than a child born in this country.

The other moment was in Warsaw, capital of a nation twice devastated by war in this century. Their people have rebuilt the city which war's destruction took from them; but what was new only emphasized clearly what was lost.

What I saw in those two places crystalized for me the purposes of our own Nation's policy: to ensure economic justice, to advance human rights, to resolve conflicts without violence, and to proclaim in our great democracy our constant faith in the liberty and dignity of human beings everywhere.

We Americans have a great deal of work to do together. In the end, how well we do that work will depend on the spirit in which we approach it.

We must seek fresh answers, unhindered by the stale prescriptions of the past.

It has been said that our best years are behind us. But I say again that America's best is still ahead. We have emerged from bitter experiences chastened but proud, confident once again, ready to face challenges once again, and united once again.

[A Solemn Time]

We come together tonight at a solemn time. Last week the Senate lost a good and honest man, Lee Metcalf of Montana.

And today, the flag of the United States flew at half-mast from this Capitol and from American installations and ships all over the world, in mourning for Senator Hubert Humphrey.

Because he exemplified so well the joy and the zest of living, his death reminds us not so much of our own mortality but of the possibilities offered to us by life. He always looked to the future with a special American kind of confidence, of hope and enthusiasm.

The best way that we can honor him is by following his example. Our task — to use the words of Senator Humphrey — is "reconciliation, rebuilding, and rebirth."

Reconciliation of private needs and interests into a higher purpose.

Rebuilding the old dreams of justice and liberty, and country and community.

Rebirth of our faith in the common good.

Each of us here tonight — and all who are listening in their homes — must rededicate ourselves to serving the common good.

We are a community, a beloved community, all of us; our individual fates are linked; our futures intertwined; and if we act in that knowledge and in that spirit, together, as the Bible says, we can move mountains.

Thank you very much.

ACCOMPANYING MESSAGE

To the Congress of the United States:

Tonight's State of the Union Address concentrates on this year's highest priorities — a strong energy bill; a coordinated economic program of job creation, tax reduction, tax reform and anti-inflation measures; making the government more effective and efficient; maintaining the peace through a strong national defense; and ratifying both the Panama Canal Treaties and, if completed, the SALT II treaty.

It is important that the Congress and the Nation also understand what our other important initiatives and goals will be for 1978. I am therefore sending to Congress this separate, more detailed State of the Union Message, which describes Administration priorities in the areas not fully covered in the Address.

DOMESTIC AFFAIRS

A number of serious domestic problems faced the Nation when I took office one year ago. The economy had not yet fully recovered from the recession; our country had no sound energy policy; the Federal government was operating inefficiently and ineffectively in many areas; concerns about the openness and integrity of our government remained in the aftermath of Watergate; and many of our most pressing social problems had not been addressed.

In 1977, my Administration did not solve all of those problems. But Congress joined us in tackling many of these issues, and together we made progress. Now that a year has passed, I believe we are a more confident people, with more trust in our institutions. We are a country on the move again, prepared to address our problems with boldness and confidence, at home and abroad. We have reasserted our concern for the problems of people here at home and reaffirmed our position of moral leadership in the world.

This year, my domestic goals will continue to reflect those concerns that guided my actions in 1977: restoring economic prosperity; meeting our Nation's human needs; making the government more efficient and more responsive; and developing and protecting our natural resources.

RESTORING ECONOMIC PROSPERITY

I am devoting a substantial part of my State of the Union Address to the need for a comprehensive economic program, and I will devote the bulk of my Economic Report to Congress, to be delivered tomorrow, to a complete description of my Administration's economic goals and objectives. In this Message, therefore, I will not repeat those statements but I want to set forth briefly the key elements of those proposals:

—a $23 billion income tax cut in 1979, with $17 billion going to individuals and their families and $6 billion going to businesses;

—a tax reform program designed to make our tax laws fairer and simpler;

—an anti-inflation program, designed to reduce annual increases in wages and prices, with the cooperation of labor and business and with the Federal government setting an example; reductions of $2 billion in excise and payroll taxes will also make a contribution to reducing inflation;

—an extension of the funding for 725,000 public service (CETA) jobs, and a $700 million increase in spending for our youth employment efforts;

—a major new $400 million private sector jobs initiative, designed primarily to encourage businesses to hire unemployed minorities and youth.

I plan to work very closely with Congress to secure prompt action on these economic proposals. Their adoption will help achieve the kind of economic prosperity for our Nation that all of us want. Along with a sound energy bill, enactment of these economic proposals will be my highest domestic priority for 1978.

Energy

There can be no higher priority than prompt enactment of comprehensive energy legislation along the lines submitted to the Congress last spring.

Huge oil price increases in 1973-74 contributed to the double-digit inflation of 1974, and to the worst recession in 40 years. These price hikes were also the principal cause of our foreign trade deficit, which has contributed to the weakness of the dollar abroad.

Unless we act now, our energy problems will rapidly get worse. Failure to act will fuel inflation, erode the value of the dollar, render us vulnerable to disruptions in our oil supply, and limit our economic progress in the years to come.

I am confident that the Congress will respond to the Nation's clear need, by enacting responsible and balanced energy legislation early this year.

Employment

Last year we made considerable progress in our efforts to reduce unemployment. The unemployment rate decreased from 7.8 per cent to 6.4 per cent. During the year, 4.1 million new jobs were created. Unemployment fell by 1.1 million workers. The actions we took as part of our $21 billion economic stimulus package substantially helped us achieve these favorable results.

In 1978, the Administration will continue its efforts to reduce unemployment still further and to increase employment opportunities for all Americans. As part of the budget I will propose:

—additional funds to increase youth programs 260 per cent above the 1976 level, providing $2.3 billion in outlays and 450,000 man-years of employment and training for young workers;

—a $400 million private sector employment program focused on youth and other disadvantaged workers and aimed at mobilizing private industry to work with government in finding jobs. It will be implemented through business councils established throughout the country;

—maintenance of the 725,000 CETA jobs through 1979, while tying them in future years to national unemployment rates;

—beginning of a demonstration program for the jobs component of the Better Jobs and Income Program.

Humphrey-Hawkins Legislation

The Administration will seek passage of the Humphrey-Hawkins Full Employment and Balanced Growth Act.

This Act will help the Administration and the Congress in planning our efforts to reduce unemployment and to create jobs, while maintaining reasonable price stability. Its enactment would serve as a living memorial to the late Senator Hubert Humphrey.

Private Sector Jobs

The Administration plans a major $400 million effort to involve business and labor in the training and hiring of the hard-core unemployed.

The program will closely tie the Federal employment system with the private sector, through the use of business councils. I am confident that the private sector will respond positively to the call to help the Nation solve one of its most serious problems — the employment of our youth and minorities.

Inflation

Although inflation is lower now than in the recent past, we still must do more to keep it down. The steps my Administration will take include:

—incentives for business investment, contained in our tax proposals, which will increase production investment, and thereby help us hold down prices and costs;

—reduction in excise and unemployment taxes, proposed in the new budget;

—continuing reductions in needlessly complex Federal regulations. We have established a high-level inter-agency committee to review the effects of regulation in our economy, and we will continue our efforts for regulatory reform in the airline industry and elsewhere;

—a special effort to hold down the soaring costs of health care, through enactment of the Hospital Cost Containment Act.

But the government cannot solve this problem alone — especially once business, labor, and consumers have accepted inflation as a fact of life, and adjusted their behavior accordingly. I have therefore asked business and labor to undertake, voluntarily, a new program to reduce inflation. I will ask each industry to aim for smaller price and wage increases in 1978 than it averaged over the last two years. As a major employer the Federal government should take the lead in this effort. Voluntary cooperation is one way — perhaps the only way — to reduce inflation without unacceptable government interference and coercion.

Urban Assistance and Community Development

The Administration and Congress took major steps last year to meet the needs of our cities. We increased funding for Community Development Block Grants by $2.7 billion over three years, and provided an alternative formula for allocating funds that was more responsive to the needs of distressed urban areas. Next year we will recommend an increase of $150 million over the 1978 level for the Community Development Block Grant program. We enacted a new program of Urban Development Action Grants at an annual level of $400 million, and extended and expanded Anti-Recession Fiscal Assistance (ARFA).

I am proposing that the ARFA program, which expires September 30, 1978, be extended. We are evaluating possible revisions in programs and funding, and will make our recommendations to the Congress within two months.

The Administration is also studying closely the possible need for extended Federal lending to New York City. The current legislation expires on June 30, 1978. We are committed, along with the State and City, to preserving the City's solvency. If such extended lending is necessary for that purpose, we will propose it. However, all the interested parties must contribute to a permanent solution.

This spring I will submit to Congress a message outlining this Administration's urban policy, based on the work of the Urban and Regional Policy Group, chaired by the Secretary of Housing and Urban Development. It will be designed to make existing Federal programs more effective, and will involve new initiatives and resources to address our urban needs. The longstanding problems of our cities are structural in nature and cannot be corrected by short-term or one-time efforts. This Administration is committed to a long-term and continuing effort to meet stubborn problems and changing needs. Our urban policy proposals will:

—build a more effective partnership between the Federal government, State and local governments, the private sector, neighborhood groups and concerned citizens;

—be sufficiently flexible to meet the diverse needs of our urban areas and to respond to particular problems of distressed areas;

—address the fiscal needs of hard-pressed urban governments, as well as the economic and social needs of city residents;

—improve the urban physical environment and strengthen urban communities;

—use Federal assistance to stimulate job-creating investments by the private sector and to encourage innovative actions by the State and local governments.

Agriculture and Rural Development

Decent farm income and a strong family farm system are vital to our national economic stability and strength. For too long farm prices for many commodities have been severely depressed. Working with the Congress in the past year, we have adopted new programs and policies designed to strengthen farm income and to ensure abundant, reasonably priced food for consumers. Partially as a result of these policies and programs, farm prices are now improving. Nevertheless, we cannot be satisfied with the economic condition of many American farmers today. We will continue to monitor our agricultural economy and to work with Congressional and farm leaders to make certain that Federal programs and policies are carried out effectively.

Food and Agriculture Act

In the past year we have worked with the Congress to enact a new comprehensive Food and Agriculture Act, which will protect producers and consumers. We have also exercised set-aside authority for wheat and feed grains, which will protect farm income. This year we expect to pay farmers $7.3 billion for all price support programs. The new farm bill which became effective October 1, 1977, achieves long-needed changes in our agricultural policies, including:

—minimal governmental intervention in markets and in the decisions farmers make;

—price support loans for major commodities that permit us to remain competitive in world markets;

—a grain reserve designed to remove excess products from the market and hold them until supplies are short;

—income support levels based on cost-of-production.

Grain Reserve

Last year we initiated a plan to place 30-35 million metric tons of food and feed grains in reserve. Establishing this reserve will add further strength and stability to the market and provide a hedge against export control on grain. Most of this grain will be owned and controlled by farmers. To strengthen farmer control of the grain and to help keep the grain out of government ownership, terms of the farmer storage facility loan program were liberalized. In 1978, the Administration will propose an international emergency grain reserve of up to 6 million metric tons to help us meet our food aid commitments abroad.

Agricultural Disaster and Drought Aid

Because of the record droughts in 1977, I worked with Congress to pass an $844 million Emergency Drought Assistance Program. This year we will ask Congress to eliminate the many inconsistencies and inequities in existing disaster aid programs, and we will continue to give high priority to addressing the effects of the drought, which has begun to abate.

We are taking other steps to improve life in rural America. I recently signed a law to encourage better delivery of health services in rural communities. We will continue to expand the assignment of the National Health Service Corps' doctors, dentists and other health professionals to underserved rural areas. We will shortly be announcing methods to improve the effectiveness of rural housing programs with greater emphasis on home ownership for rural Americans.

Agricultural Exports

I want to increase our agricultural exports. To do so we need competitive prices, high quality products, and reserve supplies to meet all contingencies. We must remove unnecessary barriers to exports. And we must have an affirmative export policy. In 1977, the Administration more than doubled (to $1.7 billion) the short-term export credit program, increased Soviet grain purchase authorization to 15 million tons, developed a risk assurance program, and expanded efforts to develop export markets around the world.

This year we will continue these efforts, especially to reduce barriers to agricultural trade.

Sugar

To stabilize world sugar prices and to protect domestic sugar-producers, we negotiated an international sugar agreement this year with the major sugar-producing countries. We will seek Congressional ratification of the agreement early in 1978. The sugar program required by the 1977 Food and Agricultural Act will protect the domestic sugar industry in the meantime.

Rural Development and Credit Policy

In fiscal year 1977, the Farmers Home Administration provided nearly $7 billion in loans in four areas: farming, housing, community facilities and business and industrial development. We expect to provide at least $1 billion more in the current fiscal year.

Small Business

This Administration took several steps in 1977 to strengthen small business. The Small Business Administration expanded its financial and management assistance to these firms and developed an advocacy program to represent small business interests before all Federal departments and agencies. In 1978, we will continue efforts to support small business through tax cuts and special tax incentives, reduced regulations and other programmatic reforms, and expanded SBA loan authority.

MEETING OUR NATION'S HUMAN NEEDS

The Administration's constant concern has been with meeting the human needs of all Americans. Over the past year, we have moved on a number of fronts to make certain our citizens will be well housed, better educated, and properly cared for when they are in need. This year we will pursue our current initiatives in these areas and launch new ones.

Health

This past year we were very active in the effort to improve the health of our citizens and to restrain skyrocketing health care costs, through:

—establishment of a Mental Health Commission to help develop a national mental health program. The Commission will issue its final report later this year, and I expect to carefully consider the Commission's findings.

—a campaign to immunize the more than 20 million children not yet protected against communicable childhood diseases.

—reorganization of part of HEW to allow more efficient delivery of Medicare/Medicaid services. The cost savings from the reorganizations will be realized more fully this year.

—signing legislation to attack fraud and abuse in Medicare/Medicaid programs.

—signing legislation to make Medicare/Medicaid reimbursement available to physician extenders in rural clinics. The beneficial effects of that bill will be felt in our Nation's rural areas for the first time this year.

In 1978, the Administration will continue these and other efforts to bring us better and less costly health care.

Hospital Cost Containment

One of my main legislative goals for this year is the Hospital Cost Containment Bill. That bill, which would save hospital users more than $7 billion in the first two years after enactment, is our principal weapon in the effort to decrease health care costs, which now double every five years.

National Health Insurance

I will submit to Congress later this year a National Health Insurance proposal. While Congress will not have the time to complete action on this proposal in 1978, it is important to begin the national debate on the many complex issues involved in National Health Insurance.

National Health Insurance will not solve all our health problems. A sensible national health policy also requires more effective delivery of preventive services, better nutrition, vigorous abatement of environmental and occupational threats to health, and efforts to change individual lifestyles that endanger health.

But National Health Insurance is a crucial step. It will protect our people from ruinous medical bills and provide each citizen with better access to sound and balanced health insurance coverage.

Medicaid Improvements for Children

Last year I proposed the Child Health Assessment Program to improve the early and preventive screening, diagnosis and treatment program for lower-income children under Medicaid. The Administration will press for enactment of this measure, and will urge its expansion to make an additional 1.7 million lower-income children eligible.

Teenage Pregnancy Proposal

I will propose legislation to establish networks of community based services to prevent unwanted adolescent pregnancies. We need and will urge expansion of existing family planning services to reach an additional 280,-000 teenagers.

Drug Abuse

Drug abuse threatens the health and safety of our children, here and abroad. We will continue the efforts begun last year to make our drug abuse prevention and control programs more effective and efficient.

World Health

This year I will present a strategy for working directly with other nations and through international organizations to raise the standards of health and nutrition around the world.

Education

Last year the Congress adopted with our cooperation a 15 per cent increase in education funding — the largest increase since enactment of the Elementary and Secondary Education Act.

This year we will continue to demonstrate our commitment to improving the Nation's education programs. HEW's education budget expenditures will be increased by 14 per cent, with the most significant increases coming in education of the disadvantaged, assistance to State programs for education of the handicapped, and college student financial aid.

The Administration will also work with the Congress for the creation of a separate Cabinet-level Department of Education, and for legislation to replace and reform expiring Federal education acts.

These legislative proposals will concentrate on:

—increasing basic literacy;

—ensuring that students are prepared for jobs;

—supporting post-secondary education and lifelong learning; and,

—strengthening the partnership between Federal, State, and local governments.

To augment existing programs, I will propose legislation to help low-and middle-income families meet rising college tuition costs, and will also support a significant expansion of student aid programs.

Income Assistance

Over the past year we have made many far-reaching improvements in the programs that provide income assistance to the needy. My Administration will continue to assign great importance to this area in 1978.

Welfare Reform

I proposed last year a reform of the Nation's welfare system, through the Better Jobs and Income Act. This Act would fundamentally reform current programs to assist the poor by:

—consolidating the Aid to Families with Dependent Children, Supplemental Security Income and Food Stamps programs into a single consolidated cash assistance program that provides a basic nationally uniform Federal benefit;

—improving efforts to find jobs for the poor in the private sector, and creating up to 1.4 million public service jobs for heads of families who cannot be placed in unsubsidized employment; and

—improving work incentives by expanding the Earned Income Tax Credit.

We will work actively with the Congress in the coming year to pass the Better Jobs and Income Act, and we will provide in this year's budget for pilot employment programs so we will be ready to implement the welfare reform program.

Family and Children

My Administration will continue its strong commitment to strengthening the American family and to expanding programs for children.

The Administration will propose this year that the school breakfast program be made mandatory in schools with high concentrations of needy children. Further, we will propose a major expansion in special supplemental food programs for women, infants, and children.

Among other major actions in 1978 will be:

—convening a White House Conference on Families;

—pressing for enactment of our proposed reforms in foster care programs including new financial assistance to aid in the adoption of hard-to-place children;

—more than doubling the budget outlays for child welfare services, with an emphasis on services that help keep families together;

—continuing $200 million in special funding for day care under Title XX of the Social Security Act.

We will also depend upon the revitalized Community Services Administration to develop new approaches to assist the poor.

The Elderly

Last year saw the enactment of Social Security financing legislation that will assure the system's financial integrity into the next century. This year the Administration will continue to work for strengthened legislation against unwarranted age discrimination in the Federal and private sector. We will propose legislation to extend and strengthen the Older Americans Act and we will seek a 13 per cent increase in funding for programs providing daily meals to the elderly, raising the total of daily meals served to 385,000. In addition, the Administration will work to assure that the contributions of older Americans are sought in our efforts to meet national needs.

Housing

Last year we made progress toward our national goal of a decent home in a suitable environment for every American family. 1977 was a good year for housing, generally, with total new starts exceeding two million. And we have renewed the Federal government's commitment to housing for the needy.

Early last year, the Administration proposed major new initiatives to meet the housing needs of low- and moderate-income Americans — initiatives which are central to our urban development strategy. We had about 118,000 starts under section 8 and public housing subsidized programs in 1977. We look forward to another 30 per cent increase in subsidized housing starts in these programs for 1978, and 92,000 starts in the Assisted Housing Rehabilitation Loan Programs. We will reassess our national housing needs and goals and our current housing and credit policies designed to meet those needs.

In 1978, the Administration will strengthen its commitment to meet the housing needs of all communities with a variety of expanded programs and new initiatives:

—rental housing assistance to an additional 400,000 low-income families, and help to enable an additional 50,000 moderate-income families to own their own homes. The total number of families receiving housing assistance will increase from 2.6 million in 1977 to 3.1 million in 1979.

—more funds for the rehabilitation loan program under section 312, with an expansion of existing programs for substantial renovations and the creation of a new moderate rehabilitation program under section 8.

—a major new operating subsidy program for 1979. This new program, coupled with improved management controls and the monitoring of troubled projects, is intended to reduce the inventory of defaulted projects and aid in restoring distressed urban areas. The Department of Housing and Urban Development has made substantial progress in 1977 in reducing the stock of defaulted projects. This new program will give the Department additional tools. Outlays for this program are estimated to total $52 million in 1979.

—a Federal financing mechanism for assisted housing projects through use of the GNMA [Government National Mortgage Assn.] Tandem program.

—a targeted GNMA Tandem program which will provide subsidies designed to bring middle-income families back to the cities.

—targeting of rural housing programs to lower-income residents, including a special program to help very poor families own their own homes.

—continuing high levels of production of housing for the elderly and handicapped.

Transportation

This year we will build on the efforts we made last year to strengthen the Nation's transportation system by decreasing consumer costs, pursuing increased energy efficiency, and improving safety:

—negotiation of a new US-UK bilateral air services agreement;

—approval of new international air routes from a number of American cities;

—requiring passive restraint systems on all new automobiles by 1984;

—setting new fuel efficiency standards for 1981-1984 model automobiles;

—beginning work on the Northeast Corridor Railroad Improvement Program;

—passing an all-cargo airline deregulation bill.

We will also continue our policy of increasing competition and reducing airfares in international flights, and pursue additional bilateral agreements. Consumers have already benefited from reduced international fares and improved service.

Highway and Transit Programs

We will soon propose a comprehensive highway and transit program, which will provide more than $45 billion in total authorizations in the 1979-1982 period. The program will give states and localities more flexibility in planning and programming their highway and transit funding, by reducing the number of narrow, categorical accounts and by using consolidated accounts for a wider range of potential transportation projects.

In addition, we will make funding of transportation programs more uniform and give localities more control over highway and mass transit funds in large urban areas.

Highway Safety

The Administration will propose legislation to strengthen our efforts for highway safety and to reduce restrictions on the states' use of Federal highway safety grant funds. That legislation will earmark funds for the Department of Transportation to support important highway safety projects, such as the 55 mile per hour speed limit program.

Inland Waterway User Fees

Users of Federal inland waterways should pay fees which will pay a substantial part of the cost of constructing, operating and maintaining those waterways. My Administration will continue to work closely with Congress toward passage of a bill that will, for the first time, establish inland waterway user fees.

Aircraft Noise Abatement

My Administration will again seek passage of legislation to control aircraft noise.

No-Fault Automobile Insurance

We continue to support legislation to establish Federal minimum standards for no-fault automobile insurance.

Veterans

In 1977, we took a number of steps to make certain that the country continues to meet the special needs of our millions of veterans. Legislation was passed to increase compensation benefits for service-connected disabilities, benefits under the G.I. Bill, and veterans pension benefits. Millions of veterans will feel the effects of these increases this year.

In 1978, we will further improve our veterans programs by:

—initiating a government-wide review of the problems of Vietnam veterans and the means by which current programs can be made more effective in meeting their needs;

—beginning new programs to deal with problems of alcohol, drug abuse and psychological readjustment;

—proposing increased benefits for service-connected disabilities, and improvements in the veterans pension program;

—continuing special employment programs for Vietnam-era veterans.

Arts and Humanities

Americans are increasingly aware that the arts and humanities preserve and transmit our heritage, enrich our lives, and contribute significantly to the social and economic well-being of our Nation. This Administration is committed to fostering the highest standards of creativity and scholarship in an open partnership between public and private sectors — and we believe that the products of this commitment must be available to the many Americans who wish to share in them. This year's substantial increases in the budgets for the Arts and Humanities Endowments demonstrate my strong belief in the value of these programs.

MAKING THE GOVERNMENT MORE EFFICIENT AND MORE RESPONSIVE

Government Employees

Civil Service Reform

The Civil Service System is too often a bureaucratic maze which stifles the initiative of our dedicated Government employees while inadequately protecting their rights. Our 2.8 million civil servants are governed by outdated rules and institutions that keep them from being as efficient as they would like to be. No one is more frustrated by this system than hardworking public servants. Therefore, one of my major priorities in 1978 will be to ensure passage of the first comprehensive reform of the system since its creation nearly a century ago — reforms developed with the direct involvement of civil servants. Early this year, Congress will receive legislation and a reorganization plan to:

—restructure the institutions that run the Civil Service;

—increase safeguards against abuses of official power;

—provide greater incentives for managers to improve the Government's efficiency and responsiveness;

—reduce the system's red tape and delays;

—speed the procedures for dealing with employee grievances and disciplinary actions;

—make equal employment opportunities more effective.

Last year the Administration acted to protect Federal employees from the loss of a job due to reorganization. Such protection will be maintained.

Hatch Act Reform

I will continue to support reform of the Hatch Act, which would restore the right of most Civil Service employees to participate in the political process.

Part-time and Flexi-time Employment

To help obtain Federal jobs for the elderly, the handicapped, women, and others with family responsibilities, all Federal agencies will carry forward renewed efforts to increase part-time and flexi-time employment opportunities.

Reorganization, Management and Regulatory Reform

The Government Reorganization Project will keep working to make the Government more responsive and efficient. Last year we combined parts of 11 agencies into one Department of Energy, streamlined the Executive Office of the President and reduced the White House Staff, and proposed the abolition of nearly 500 advisory committees and small agencies.

In addition to the upcoming Civil Service and education reform efforts, we will soon submit proposals:

—to restructure our equal employment programs to provide better protection for the rights of minorities and women, and to ease the burden of compliance on State and local government as well as business;

—to improve the administration of justice; and

—to reorganize our disaster assistance programs.

Additional studies are under way in many other areas, and several of these will result in reorganization proposals later this year. Efforts to improve Federal cash management continue.

We are also vigorously pursuing the effort begun last year to reduce the burden of outdated, ineffective, and nit-picking regulations. For example, the Department of Health, Education and Welfare eliminated 5 per cent of their regulations, the Federal Trade Commission rescinded 111 outdated sets of rules on trade practices and both the Civil Aeronautics Board and the Interstate Commerce Commission have moved to allow more competition, which has led to lower prices. In 1978, we will continue these efforts.

Worker Health and Safety

The Occupational Health and Safety Administration has already slashed its paperwork requirements by 50 per cent and eliminated 1,100 unnecessary regulations, while improving its capacity to protect workers. This spring the Task Force on Worker Safety will make further recommendations to increase protection for workers and minimize employer cost.

Airline Regulatory Reform

Last year, I signed legislation deregulating all cargo air transportation. This year, I will continue to work for passage of the airline regulatory reform bill for passengers. That bill will allow air carriers to compete through lower fares, new services, and new markets, without excessive government interference or disruption of service to small communities.

Trucking Regulatory Reform

Forty years of tight government controls have not done enough to bring us competitive prices, good services, and efficient use of fuel. We will consider measures to bring more competition into the motor carrier area.

Drugs

We will propose legislation to reform regulation of the drug industry, which will protect the consumer and make regulations fairer and less burdensome.

Regulatory Process

Early in 1978, I will issue an Executive Order to improve the regulatory process. This Order will require officials responsible for regulations to sign them; assure that policy-level officials are fully involved in the process; require that regulations be written in plain English; make it easier for the public to participate in the process; increase coordination between agencies with overlapping responsibilities; require a closer look at the cost of regulations before they are issued; and require "sunset" reviews of existing regulations.

I have also set up an interagency committee to help regulatory agencies review the economic effects of major regulations, so that we can be sure that the costs of each proposed regulation have been fully considered. In this way we will be able to identify the least costly means of achieving our regulatory goals.

Paperwork Reduction

In 1977, my Administration decreased by 12 per cent the paperwork burden that the Government imposes on the people. This was done by eliminating, consolidating, simplifying, and decreasing the frequency of reports. That savings is the equivalent of 50,000 full-time workers filling out Federal forms for a full year. All departments and agencies are currently setting goals for further substantial reductions in 1978. All reporting requirements associated with grant-in-aid programs will be subject to "sunset" reviews, and ended unless they are found necessary. In addition, we are reviewing the recommendations of the Commission on Federal Paperwork.

Labor Law Reform

Last year we proposed legislation to reform our Nation's labor laws, in order to streamline the conduct of elections for employee representation and strengthen the enforcement powers of the National Labor Relations Board. We will work closely with Congress to ensure early passage of this bill, which is one of my highest legislative goals this year.

Election Reform

Last year, I supported proposals to make our elections fairer and more honest. These included public financing of Congressional campaigns, amendments to the Federal Election Campaign Act and other election reforms. The Administration will continue to support Congressional action on these measures.

Consumer Reform

We have taken many actions to benefit consumers by reducing the costs and improving the quality and safety of products. But one consumer initiative merits separate emphasis — the creation of the Office of Consumer Representation. We supported legislation last year to create such an Office, so that the interests of consumers could be represented in one government agency. The Office would not require additional government employees or expenditures since it would merely consolidate the consumer offices that already exist throughout the government. I am strongly committed to this legislation, and regard its enactment as one of the year's primary legislative priorities.

Public Broadcasting Reform

I proposed legislation last year to strengthen the public broadcasting service by providing increased long-term Federal support, insulation from political pressure, better coordination among the national organizations that run public broadcasting, and more opportunity for citizens to participate at the local level. My Administration will work with Congress this year to pass these reforms.

Openness and Integrity

One of our primary goals is to make certain that the government's ethical standards are high, and they they are fully observed. And we must ensure that our government is open and responsive to the American people.

Last year, I took steps in that direction by requiring that the senior officials of my Administration publicly disclose their income and assets and pledge not to do business with their agencies for two years after leaving government service. To increase the government's openness, we took steps to make certain that the spirit as well as the letter of the Freedom of Information Act was observed. And we tried to bring the Presidency to the people with citizen forums and discussion panels throughout the country.

This year, we will continue these efforts, concentrating our primary attention on these areas:

Lobby Reform

The Administration will press for legislation requiring registration of lobbyists and thorough public disclosure of their lobbying activities. This long-overdue legislation will help reestablish confidence and trust in government.

Ethics

I applaud the strong ethical codes adopted last year by the House and Senate. I believe those codes and the standards established for my

Administration's officials should be made law, so that they will clearly apply to public officials in the future. I urge Congress to pass the Public Officials Integrity Act this year.

Classification

We are completing a study of classification systems for government documents and I will shortly issue an Executive Order designed to eliminate improper and unnecessary classification and to ensure that documents are declassified more rapidly.

Justice

Civil Rights and Equal Opportunity

All Americans have fundamental civil rights requiring government protection, and all must be afforded equal opportunities to participate as full members in our society. In 1977, this principle guided my Administration in numerous areas, and I plan to make certain that this year our efforts on behalf of civil rights and equal opportunities continue unabated. Our Nation's concern for human rights must be heard as clearly at home as abroad.

Educational Opportunities

In 1977, my Administration vigorously attacked educational discrimination on the elementary, secondary and higher education levels. A major suit was pursued to ensure non-discrimination at the university level. At the same time, we recognized and reaffirmed the importance of affirmative action programs to ensure equal opportunities at educational institutions through our brief in the *Bakke* case. Our efforts to eliminate discrimination and promote affirmative action programs, relying on flexible goals rather than on quotas, will continue in full force.

Handicapped

HEW issued regulations and guidelines to implement legislation guaranteeing equal access to programs receiving financial assistance from HEW. This year the other Cabinet Departments will issue similar regulations, so that the rights of handicapped Americans will begin to be fully observed. We are providing a $50 million loan fund to States and institutions to enable them to comply with these regulations and to eliminate barriers which prevent access by our handicapped citizens to federally assisted programs and activities. We are proposing a major increase in funding under the Education of all Handicapped Children Act.

Equal Opportunity

This past year the Administration reaffirmed Executive Order 11375, which prohibits discrimination on the basis of sex in Federal employment. In addition, I voluntarily placed the Executive Office of the President under Title VII of the Civil Rights Act. This year, as part of our effort to eliminate sex discrimination in unemployment [sic] and education, I will continue to urge the ratification of the Equal Rights Amendment to the Constitution.

This past year the Equal Employment Opportunity Commission was reorganized to increase its efficiency. As a result, the Commission made substantial progress on reducing its backlog of complaints. With the more than 40 per cent increase in funding that will be proposed in the 1979 budget, the EEOC will be able to further reduce its backlog. Early this year I will propose to Congress a reorganization plan concerning equal opportunity enforcement which will strengthen the EEOC.

Anti-Foreign Boycott

I strongly supported, and signed, legislation to prohibit American participation in secondary economic boycotts by foreign countries. That law will be strictly enforced by my Administration this year through the regulations just issued by the Department of Commerce.

Minority Business

Last year, we started a number of programs to make more opportunities available for minority-owned businesses. That effort will be continued and strengthened this year:

—We are half way toward our two-year goal of $2 billion in Federal purchases of services and goods from minority-owned firms. We will reach that goal by the end of the year.

—We will raise the goal for Federal deposits in minority-owned banks above the 1977 level of $100 billion.

—We will continue to enforce the $400 million minority business set-aside provision in the local public works act, and may exceed that target.

—We will continue to implement the minority business set-aside policy established for contracts let in the Northeast Corridor Railroad Improvement Program.

Undocumented Aliens

Last year, I proposed legislation to impose sanctions on employers who hire undocumented aliens and to change the legal status of the many undocumented aliens now residing in this country. That legislation would afford undocumented aliens residing here continuously since before 1970 the opportunity to apply for permanent resident status. It would create a new five-year temporary resident status for those undocumented aliens who resided here continuously from 1970 to January 1, 1977. I want to work with Congress this year toward passage of an undocumented aliens bill, for this social and economic problem can no longer be ignored.

Native Americans

The Administration has acted consistently to uphold its trusteeship responsibility to Native Americans. We also have elevated the post of Commissioner of Indian Affairs to the level of Assistant Secretary of Interior. In 1978, the Administration will review Federal Native American policy and will step up efforts to help Indian tribes assess and manage their natural resources.

Legal and Judicial Reform

Last year, my Administration began a number of major efforts to improve our Nation's legal and judicial system, and we intend to pursue those and related efforts fully this year.

Criminal Code Reform

We have worked closely with members of Congress to develop a proposed revision of the Nation's Criminal Code. That revision will codify in one part of the U.S. Code all Federal crime laws and will reform many outdated and inconsistent criminal laws. My Administration will work closely with Congress this year to seek passage of the first complete codification of the Nation's criminal laws.

Judicial Reform

The Federal judicial system has suffered for many years from an inadequate number of judges, and we will continue to work with Congress on an Omnibus Judgeship Bill to correct this problem. We will also continue our efforts to use our judges more effectively, through legislation which we have proposed to expand significantly the authority of magistrates, to increase the use of arbitration, and to tighten Federal jurisdiction. We will work this year to complete Congressional action on these bills.

Wiretap Reform

Last year we proposed legislation reforming our approach to electronic surveillance for foreign intelligence purposes, and affording greater protection to our citizens. Essentially, that legislation would require the government to obtain a court order before beginning any foreign intelligence wiretaps in this country. My Administration supports early passage of this much needed legislation.

Anti-trust Enforcement and Competition

Our Nation's anti-trust laws must be vigorously enforced. Therefore, I recently established a Presidential Commission to review Federal anti-trust enforcement, and to make its recommendations this year.

Last year, we initiated a new program, administered by the Department of Justice, to provide grant funds to State Attorneys General in order to strengthen anti-trust enforcement at the State level. We expect to see the results of this program this year.

By reducing government regulation, we can increase competition and thereby lower consumer costs. This year we will continue our deregulatory efforts in the legislative and administrative areas in order to reduce anti-competitive practices and abuses.

Crime Reduction and Criminal Justice

This past year the Reorganization Project and the Justice Department have been developing proposals to reorganize and to improve our Nation's criminal justice system, in order to strengthen enforcement and ensure equal justice. This year I will be sending a Message to Congress on criminal justice and crime reduction. My Message will include proposals to:

—reorganize the Federal Law Enforcement Assistance Administration;

—improve our criminal research efforts;

—develop better law enforcement methods against organized crime, white collar crime, drug abuse, and public corruption; and

—develop minimum standards for Federal correctional institutions.

FBI and Intelligence Agencies' Charters

I plan to issue a comprehensive Executive Order to govern the intelligence activities of the FBI, CIA, NSA [National Security Agency] and the Defense Department. That Executive Order will be the basis for the Administration's recommendations on legislative charters governing the activities of the FBI and various intelligence agencies.

Privacy

The Privacy Protection Study Committee recently proposed an extensive list of new legislative and regulatory safeguards. My Administration is analyzing these recent proposals and will develop this year a program to ensure that personal privacy is adequately protected.

District of Columbia

We proposed last year a series of reforms, including full voting representation in Congress, designed to give the residents of the District significantly greater control over their local affairs. My Administration will continue to work for the passage of those reforms this year.

DEVELOPING AND PROTECTING
OUR NATURAL RESOURCES

National Energy Policy

In April 1977, I proposed to the Nation a comprehensive national energy policy. That policy is based on three principles, which will continue to guide our progress in 1978:

—we must learn to use energy more efficiently and more carefully, through conservation measures, including retrofitting our buildings, factories and homes;

—we must shift from oil and natural gas, which are becoming more scarce, to coal and renewable sources of energy which we have in abundance;

—we must provide fair prices to producers of energy, so as to encourage development of new supplies without permitting windfall profits.

The debate on this comprehensive policy has been long and arduous. A number of difficult, contentious issues remain to be settled. I am confident, however, that the Congress recognizes the seriousness of our energy problem and will act expeditiously on this program early this year. Securing passage of an acceptable energy bill — one which is fair to consumers, provides needed energy savings, and is prudent from a fiscal and budgetary standpoint — will continue as our highest and most urgent national priority in 1978.

Energy Statutes and Actions

We have already begun to lay a strong foundation for implementation of a national energy policy. In 1977 we took steps to put in place important policies and structural reforms needed to meet our energy goals:

—Creation of a new Department of Energy which combines, for the first time, major governmental functions of energy research, regulation, pricing policy, information collection and dissemination, and overall policy development. Without a strong organization, we would not hope to implement a comprehensive national policy.

—Congress has approved our proposed route for a pipeline to bring natural gas from the North Slope of Alaska to the lower 48 states.

—Passage of the Emergency Natural Gas Act to cope with the hardships of last winter's freeze and assure that high priority gas users were not cut off during supply emergencies.

—Funding of more than $4 billion to store the first 500 million barrels of oil in a strategic petroleum reserve. We have already begun to fill that reserve, and we remain committed to a 1 billion barrel strategic reserve by 1985.

Outer Continental Shelf Legislation

Legislation to improve the management of the Outer Continental Shelf for oil and gas development is a major item of unfinished business pending before Congress. Prompt passage is necessary so that we can have the benefit of the new law as we move to open more offshore areas to development and production. This bill mandates long-needed reforms in the leasing program to provide for the necessary development of offshore oil and gas while enhancing competition among oil companies, assuring that the public receives a fair return for the sale of the public's oil and gas resources, and protecting our marine and coastal resources.

39

Nuclear Energy

The United States has also advanced a policy to prevent the proliferation of nuclear weapons around the world. An International Nuclear Fuel Cycle Evaluation has been established with wide international participation to examine alternatives to existing proliferation-prone technologies. In addition, legislation was proposed last year to establish better controls on export of nuclear fuels and technologies. We will work with Congress to secure passage of that legislation early in 1978.

Our commitment to preventing the spread of nuclear weapons has led us to reorient our own domestic nuclear policies. I have deferred indefinitely the commercial reprocessing of spent nuclear fuel and plutonium recycling.

The Clinch River Plant itself would waste more than $2 billion while teaching us little that we do not already know, or cannot learn from our existing nuclear research and development program. I have recommended that the Clinch River Breeder Project be stopped, because it represents a premature and unwise commitment to commercialization of technology that we do not now need.

However, we intend to continue to develop the nuclear energy the Nation needs.

We will continue to move forward with a major research program on breeder technology.

We will begin to implement our program for government management of spent fuel from nuclear reactors.

In 1978, my Administration will work towards a policy for safe, permanent disposal of nuclear wastes.

In 1978 and beyond, we will carry on a vigorous nuclear research and development program designed to give us safe technologies that will reduce the danger of nuclear proliferation and will be environmentally responsible. We will also seek to improve the current system of licensing nuclear power reactors in order to cut bureaucratic delays, while firmly maintaining and strengthening health, safety and environmental requirements. I will propose nuclear licensing legislation to the Congress this year.

Environment

One of my deepest personal commitments is to a clean, healthy environment for all of our citizens. Last May, I outlined this Administration's environmental priorities and policies in a comprehensive Environmental Message. Working closely with the Congress, we have made good progress on many of the measures contained in that Message; it will continue to guide our administrative and legislative actions in 1978. Overall, we will:

—increase our environmental outlays by more than 10 per cent, and provide the new staff resources necessary to ensure that the Nation's environmental laws are obeyed;

—determine the best way of enforcing the landmark environmental statutes enacted in 1977, taking considerations of science and public policy into account;

—pursue several important initiatives, including a National Heritage program and designation of national interest lands in Alaska, to manage our precious natural resources better and to preserve our heritage.

Environmental Statutes

In 1977, we worked closely with Congress to enact three of the most significant environmental statutes in recent years:

—The Surface Mining Control and Reclamation Act establishes a joint Federal-State program to make sure we use economically and environmentally sound strip-mining practices. It also sets up a fund to reclaim lands which have been ravaged by uncontrolled, careless mining, and provides clear, stable policy direction for operators.

—The Clean Air Act Amendments establish strict but achievable standards for auto emissions and ensure continued progress in reducing pollution from stationary air pollution sources.

—The Clean Water Act authorizes many of our most important water clean-up programs and will protect our Nation's wetlands without unnecessary Federal requirements. The Act also reforms the sewage treatment construction grant program and gives strong emphasis to the control of toxic chemicals in our environment.

We will provide the leadership and the funding necessary to carry out these new laws.

Water Policy

In 1977, an effort was begun to ensure that Federal programs and policies provide sound and fair management of our limited and valuable water resources. We began a complete review of Federal water policy, which will be completed this year. After close consultation with the Congress, the States, and the public, we will propose measures needed to carry out the recommendations of that study.

We will also continue with the strong dam safety inspection program which was initiated late last year to make sure our dams, public or private, are safe.

Alaska Lands

Last year, I sent Congress a proposal for use of Federal lands in Alaska. This proposal will protect 92 million acres for the public, will create or expand 13 national parks and reserves, 13 national wildlife refuges, and will confer wild and scenic river status on 33 waterways. I hope Congress will adopt these measures, which are needed this year to preserve the unique natural treasures of Alaska and, at the same time, permit the orderly development of Alaskan resources.

Redwood National Park

Redwood National Park contains some of the Nation's largest and oldest trees. Last year, to protect these trees from destruction by commercial logging at the edges of the Park, legislation was proposed to expand its boundaries. We will press for Congressional action on this bill in 1978.

National Heritage Program

We will shortly be proposing a Federal-State program to preserve unique elements of our natural and cultural heritage. This program, modeled after successful ones in several states, will be administered by the Department of the Interior. Although many of the necessary steps can be taken administratively, we will seek some new legislative authority in 1978.

Federal Compliance with Environmental Laws

My Administration is committed to the principle that the Federal government must set a good example of compliance with those environmental laws and regulations which have been established for the private sector. So far, unfortunately, the Federal record has been found wanting. My 1979 budget includes money to bring Federal facilities into compliance with existing environmental laws and regulations.

Federal Reclamation

In 1977, we began a thorough review of the 1902 Reclamation Act. After the study has been completed and reviewed this year, I will propose to Congress any changes needed to modernize the law.

Mining Law Reform

Last year the Administration proposed legislation to replace the archaic 1872 Mining Law with a modern leasing system for publicly-owned mineral resources. The 1872 system has resulted in withdrawal of large areas of land from mineral exploration as the only tool for environmental protection. The Administration's proposal would establish a balanced system where the public interests in mineral development, environmental protection and revenue to the U.S. Treasury will all be accomplished. Special provisions would minimize burdens on small operators and provide incentives for exploration.

Oil Spills

Last year I proposed to Congress legislation which would establish strict liability standards for oil tanker spills and would improve regulations aimed at preventing future oil spills. That legislation is still needed.

Science and Technology

The health of American science and technology and the creation of new knowledge is important to our economic well-being, to our national security, to our ability to help solve pressing national problems in such areas as energy, environment, health, natural resources. I am recommending a program of real growth of scientific research and other steps that will strengthen the Nation's research centers and encourage a new surge of technological innovation by American industry. The budget increase of 11 per cent for basic research will lead to improved opportunities for young scientists and engineers, and upgraded scientific equipment in the Nation's research centers. I am determined to maintain our Nation's leadership role in science and technology.

We will continue America's progress in the field of space exploration with continued development of the space shuttle system and procurement of four shuttle orbiters for operations from both East and West coasts, development of a spacecraft to study for the first time the polar regions of the Sun, and increased outlays for demonstrations of the practical applications of space-based systems and development of space technology.

FOREIGN AFFAIRS

A year ago I set five goals for United States foreign policy in the late 1970s and early 1980s: to reassert America's moral leadership; to strengthen our traditional ties with friends and allies; to work toward a more just international system; to promote regional reconciliation; and to preserve peace through preparedness and arms control. These goals continue to underlie my agenda for 1978.

Moral Leadership

During the past year, we have placed American foreign policy on a new course consistent with the values and highest ideals of the American people. We are trying to limit the worldwide sale of arms; we are trying to prevent nuclear explosives — and the ability to make them — from spreading to more countries; we are building a new relationship with the developing countries, and we are promoting human rights throughout the world.

Human Rights

Virtually everywhere, human rights have become an important issue — especially in countries where they are systematically violated. There has been real progress, and for that the United States can take some credit.

We have taken the lead among Western nations at the Belgrade Review Conference on Security and Cooperation in Europe. Working closely with our Allies, and with neutral and non-aligned nations, our delegation — led by Ambassador Arthur Goldberg — has conducted a thorough review of implementation of the Helsinki Final Act, in all its aspects. We have made clear the United States is committed to the full implementation of the Final Act in this and other areas. We will seek a further Review Conference in two years; meanwhile, we will press for better implementation of the Helsinki Final Act.

43

Non-Proliferation

We must not ignore the enormous dangers posed by the unrestrained spread of nuclear weapons technology. We recognize the benefits of commercial nuclear power, but we also must acknowledge the risks. We believe that all countries can enjoy the benefits, while the risks are minimized, by developing safer technologies and creating new institutions to manage and safeguard all phases of the nuclear fuel cycle. Meanwhile, we have decided to postpone a premature commitment to technologies we cannot yet safely manage on a commercial scale; and we are seeking to persuade others that there are sound economic and energy reasons for them to do likewise.

Arms Sales

The world is threatened by the spiraling increase in trade of conventional arms. Not only do these arms increase the likelihood of conflict, they also divert resources from other human needs. It will not be easy to slow this spiral. We will begin to cut back on our own sales in recognition of the fact that, as the world's principal seller, we have a duty to take the first step. But we know that our efforts can only succeed if other major arms suppliers and recipients cooperate.

Ties With Friends and Allies

The energy crisis has underscored the reality of interdependence among nations and the need for a stable international financial and trading system. Our own actions reflect the belief that consultations with traditional friends and dialogue with developing nations are the only way that the United States can provide the economic and political leadership which the world expects of us.

Working with the Allies

During the past year, the United States restored our traditional friends and allies to the center of our foreign policy. Within days after his inauguration, the Vice President visited Brussels, Rome, Bonn, Paris, Reykjavik, and Tokyo. I met frequently in Washington with European and Japanese leaders. I participated in the Economic Summit in London, the 1977 NATO Summit, and a Four-Power Summit with leaders of Britain, Germany, and France. At the beginning of 1978, I visited France and Belgium — and while in Brussels, made the first visit by an American President to the headquarters of the European Community. We have also consulted with our European Allies on such diverse subjects as SALT, MBFR [Mutual and Balanced Force Reductions], the Middle East, Africa, human rights, the Belgrade Conference, energy, non-proliferation, the global economy, and North-South relations. We will intensify these efforts this year, expanding the list to include close consultations with the Allies on major arms control issues.

On May 30-31, we will host a NATO Summit in Washington, and we are also planning another Economic Summit this year.

We have shown in our dealing with Japan that close allies can find solutions to shared problems. Early in the year, we were concerned about nuclear reprocessing in Japan, but through flexibility and goodwill on both sides a suitable accommodation was reached on the building of a nuclear reprocessing plant there. Most recently, we reached agreement with the Japanese on ways to deal with their large current account surplus. Our trade and economic talks are another example of constructive action.

International Economic Cooperation

We are working to improve and extend the international economic system, to strengthen international economic institutions, and to ensure that international economic competition takes place in an orderly fashion. We will seek to improve cooperation among nations in the IMF, the GATT [General Agreement on Tariffs and Trade], the World Bank, the OECD [Organization for Economic Cooperation and Development], and other international organizations which have enabled us to maintain an open, liberal, trade and payments system.

The American economy remains strong. Our competitive position in international trade is excellent. In 1977 our merchandise exports exceeded imports (except for oil) by a large amount. Our inflation rate is among the lowest in the industrial world.

But our balance of trade and payments incurred a large and worrisome deficit. There were two main causes:

—In 1977, $45 billion flowed out to pay for imported oil. This wiped out what would otherwise have been a trade surplus.

—The demand here for foreign goods was much greater than the demand for American goods abroad. In 1977, American GNP [gross national product] increased roughly twice as fast in real terms as the GNP of our main trading partners.

Against this background, the exchange rate of the dollar declined relative to the currencies of Japan, Germany, Switzerland, and other European countries. These developments led to disorderly conditions in the exchange markets. In December I made clear that the United States would intervene to counter these disorders, and we have done so.

To assure the integrity of the dollar we must act now:

—We need a healthy and growing United States economy, with adequate investment, a prudent budget, and declining inflation. This will make us more competitive and more attractive to foreign investors.

—We need to conserve energy and develop alternative sources of supply. This will reduce our dependence on imported oil, and cut the outflow of dollars.

—We need to see a more vigorous world economy. Stronger growth, particularly in countries like Germany, Japan, Switzerland, and the Netherlands, can help reduce our own deficits and bring stability to international payments.

Factors already at work will reduce our trade deficit. Economic activity in Europe and elsewhere should rise. Our oil imports should level off this year. The effect of new exchange rates that have already occurred will, when their full effect is realized, improve our trade balance by several billions of dollars. While our trade and payments deficit in 1978 will be large, our external position should show some improvement.

We must also augment our capacity to deal with possible strains and pressures by strengthening our international trade and monetary system. I urge the Congress to act promptly to approve United States participation in the IMF's Supplementary Financing Facility.

The trading nations of the world are engaged in negotiations to reduce barriers and improve the international trading system by a reciprocal and balanced opening of markets. Freer trade will enable us all to use the world's resources more efficiently and will contribute to economic growth.

We will also attempt to strengthen the rules that have regulated international trade during the last 30 years. International competition must take place within a framework of agreed rules that are recognized as appropriate and fair.

The Developing Countries

One of the most critical issues facing the United States is our economic and political relationship with developing countries. Our economy has become visibly dependent on the developing world for supplies and markets.

North-South Dialogue

Throughout 1975 and 1976 the United States and other developed countries worked with a group of developing nations in the Conference of International Economic Cooperations (CIEC). That "North-South Dialogue" reached agreement on some issues in June 1977, but there remain a number of unresolved questions. The United States will continue to consult and negotiate with developing countries on questions like commodity price stabilization, technology, and a common fund for international buffer stocks. We will pursue the North-South dialogue in the months ahead, confident that the developed nations and the developing nations can agree upon measures that will let all nations participate more fully in the management of the world economy.

Africa

Our relations with Africa involve energy, human rights, economic development, and the North-South dialogue. The Maputo and Lagos Conferences demonstrated that African countries can discuss difficult problems with us, to mutual advantage. Our relations with Nigeria have improved dramatically.

The Administration's FY 79 budget substantially increases development assistance to Africa, including continued support for the African Development Fund, and other programs to help African governments meet their people's basic human needs. The growth of African regional institutions like the Sahel Development Fund is important to African development.

Latin America/Caribbean

The Administration's approach to Latin America and the Caribbean recognizes this region's diversity. We have placed great importance on the protection and defense of human rights, on halting the proliferation of nuclear weapons capabilities, on restraining conventional arms sales, on contributing to the settlement of disputes, and on engaging Latin governments in global economic negotiations.

We are now seeking Senate ratification of Protocol I of the Treaty of Tlatelolco, and the American Convention on Human Rights. Through the Caribbean Group, we are trying to promote regional development. And we intend to help several nations develop alternative energy sources.

Panama

General Torrijos and I signed the two Panama Canal Treaties on September 9, 1977. These treaties meet the legitimate interests of Panama and the United States and guarantee our permanent right to protect and defend the Canal. They will contribute importantly to regional stability.

Asia

The United States has sought to underline our desire for a close relationship with the developing countries of Asia through my visit to that continent and through regular contacts with the member countries of the Association of Southeast Asian Nations. We welcome the cooperation with ASEAN of the developed countries of the region, such as Japan and Australia.

Promoting Regional Reconciliation

The greatest danger to world peace and stability is not war among the great powers, but war among small nations. During the past year, the United States has helped to promote productive negotiations in two troubled regions: the Middle East and Southern Africa. We have also tried to settle conflicts in the Horn of Africa and on Cyprus. And we have negotiated two Panama Canal Treaties that will enhance our country's relations with all the nations of Latin America.

The Middle East

In an effort to break with the rigid approaches of the past and bring about an overall peace settlement, I have looked to three basic principles: normalization of political, economic and cultural relations through peace treaties; withdrawal of armed forces from occupied territory to recognized and secure borders and the establishment of effective security measures; and a resolution of the Palestinian question.

Significant progress toward peace in the Middle East was made last year; we particularly applaud President Sadat's courageous initiative, reciprocated by Prime Minister Begin, in launching direct negotiations. The United States will continue this year to encourage all parties to resolve this deep-seated conflict.

Southern Africa

The entering Administration inherited problems in Rhodesia, Namibia, and South Africa.

—With the British, the United States launched new Rhodesian discussions last year. The Anglo-American Plan of September 1 sets forth fair and workable principles for majority rule: a transition period leading to free elections, a UN presence, a constitution with a judicially protected bill of rights, and a Zimbabwe Development Fund.

—The five-power Contact Group, in which the United States participates, has held discussions with South Africa and with the Southwest Africa Peoples Organization and other interested parties on an internationally acceptable settlement for an independent Namibia under majority rule. This effort has produced wide agreement, including provisions for a substantial UN presence.

—The United States has told the South African Prime Minister that unless his nation begins a progressive transformation toward full political participation for all its people, our relations will suffer. We supported a United Nations arms embargo on South Africa, prohibited "gray area" sales, and began a review of US/South African economic relations.

The Horn of Africa

Arms supplied by the Soviet Union now fuel both sides of a conflict in the Horn of Africa between Somalia and Ethiopia. There is a danger that the Soviet Union and Cuba will commit their own soldiers in this conflict, transforming it from a local war to a confrontation with broader strategic implications.

We deplore the fact that disagreements in this region have grown — with the assistance of outside powers — into bloody conflict. We have made clear to both sides that we will supply no arms for aggressive purposes. We will not recognize forcible changes in boundaries. We want to see the fighting end and the parties move from the battlefield to the negotiating table.

Cyprus

We hope that the groundwork was laid in 1977 for a permanent settlement in Cyprus and we are encouraging movement in that direction.

Preserving Peace

During the past year, the Administration has assessed the threats to our own and our Allies' security, as well as our collective strength to combat these threats. We have sought to promote responsible arms control efforts and to reduce competition in arms. Recognizing that a strong defense is the foundation of our security, we have made certain that our defense spending will be sufficient and used to maximum effect.

Arms Control

The fundamental purposes of our arms limitations efforts are to promote our own national security and to strengthen international stability, thereby enhancing the prospects for peace everywhere.

—We are trying to move the Strategic Arms Limitation Talks toward more ambitious objectives. We want to reduce, not just contain, the competition in the number of strategic weapons possessed by the United States and the Soviet Union, and to limit qualitative improvements in weapons which merely raise the risks to all of us. Precisely because of our determination to obtain both of these objectives negotiations have been difficult and prolonged. However, I am confident that the agreement that we will present to the Congress will meet them.

—We have also made solid progress toward an objective that the United States has pursued for many years: a comprehensive treaty banning all nuclear explosions. This treaty will be open to all nations of the world. It will be a major step toward reduced reliance on these weapons and toward halting their further spread in the world.

—At the same time we are seeking arms limitations agreements with the Soviet Union that will contribute to security and stability in various regions of the world. In Europe we and our NATO Allies are seeking a mutual and balanced force reductions agreement that will achieve greater stability and balance at lower levels of forces. In the Indian Ocean, where neither we nor the Soviet Union has yet deployed military power on a large scale, we are working for an agreement to prevent a major military competition.

—For the first time, we have begun to negotiate with the Soviet Union the outlines of a treaty banning chemical warfare.

—An essential element of American security is the maintenance of stability in the Western Pacific, where the United States plays a major role in maintaining a balance of power. We are seeking to readjust our military presence in Korea by reducing our ground forces on the Peninsula and undertaking compensatory measures to ensure that an adequate balance of forces remain. We are talking with the Filipino government about the future of our military bases there.

—We are continuing the process of normalization of our relations with the People's Republic of China within the framework of the Shanghai Communiqué.

—In the last year, we have sought to halt the worldwide spread of nuclear weapons capacity. Nearly 40 nations have joined with us in an effort to find nuclear power sources that cannot be readily used for building nuclear weapons.

Defense Posture/Budget

The defense budget that I am recommending to Congress will fulfill our most pressing defense needs. I am requesting increases in defense spending that more than compensate for inflation. They are needed to maintain an adequate military balance in the face of continued Soviet military efforts.

—As we negotiate with the Soviets over strategic arms, we are continuing to preserve essential equivalence in strategic nuclear strength. Here our technological advantage over the Soviet Union is most apparent. We are building cruise missiles, which together with upgraded B-52s will assure the capability of this element of our Triad. We are continuing to develop the M-X missile system in case we need to deploy them. In this budget, I am requesting funds for continued increase in our Trident submarine force, which is our most important strategic program because submarines are so hard for any enemy to destroy.

—With our NATO Allies we are trying to improve the initial combat capability of NATO forces. We will improve the readiness of critical combat units, enhance American capability to send ground and tactical air forces reinforcements, and increase our permanent forces there. To lay the foundation for future improvements, the budget I propose requests 18 per cent increases in the procurement of equipment for the Army. The United States is not taking these steps alone; we are participating in a mutual effort.

—The importance of sea forces to United States national security is undisputed. The Navy receives the largest share of the defense budget, and I am requesting funds to continue its modernization. But, we need to examine the appropriate size and mix of United States naval forces in the future. Therefore, I have deferred spending for new aircraft carriers until a current Defense Department study is completed early this year. While we maintain our naval strength, we should have the capability to deploy rapidly a light but effective combat force worldwide, if necessary, without overseas base support. To this end, I am requesting funds for a vigorous airlift enhancement program.

In these and other ways, we are seeking to develop a foreign policy which is wider in scope; a foreign policy which recognizes global diversity; and a foreign policy which builds a more just and stable international system.

JIMMY CARTER

The White House,
January 19, 1978

JUSTICE DEPARTMENT INQUIRY
INTO MARSTON DISMISSAL
January 19-23, 1978

The removal of David W. Marston as U.S. attorney in Philadelphia created a serious political problem for the Carter administration. The decision to replace the Republican appointee with a Democrat brought charges that he was fired because he was pressing an investigation involving two Democratic members of the U.S. House of Representatives from Pennsylvania. His dismissal also cast a shadow on Jimmy Carter's June 19, 1976, campaign pledge to appoint federal judges and prosecutors "strictly on the basis of merit and without any consideration of political aspects or influence."

Since his appointment in June 1976 by President Gerald R. Ford, Marston had successfully prosecuted several prominent Pennsylvania Democrats, including the speaker of the Pennsylvania House of Representatives and the chairman of the state Senate Appropriations Committee. Marston had previously worked as an aide to Sen. Richard S. Schweiker, R-Pa.

Eilberg Message

Questioned about Marston at a Jan. 12 news conference, President Carter first replied that his removal was being handled by Attorney General Griffin Bell and that he (Carter) had "not interfered in it at all." When asked if he was aware of Marston's investigations of members of Congress and if he had been contacted by any representatives regarding the investigation, the president disclosed that he had received a telephone call in November 1977 from Rep. Joshua Eilberg, D-Pa., asking him to "expedite" Marston's removal. He added, "As far as any investigation of Members of

Congress, however, I'm not familiar with that at all, and it was never men-tioned to me." Carter passed along Eilberg's concerns to the attorney gen-eral and said that Bell's decision to fire Marston had been made months before he had ever heard of the Philadelphia attorney.

It was later confirmed that Eilberg was indeed one of the Democratic representatives under investigation by Marston's office. The other subject of the investigation was Rep. Daniel J. Flood. The inquiry centered on fed-eral financing for a wing added to Hahnemann Hospital in Philadelphia. Eilberg's law firm represented the hospital and the construction project was overseen by an engineering firm allegedly favored by Flood.

Despite criticism from Republicans and other supporters, Bell fired Marston Jan. 20. Marston emerged from his meeting with the attorney general in Washington, D.C., to charge that his removal was "purely polit-ical." "He said we have a system and he has to accept that system," Marston was quoted as saying of Bell. He added, "They had a system in Philadelphia too . . . and I didn't accept that system. I threw it out and eliminated politics. . . ."

Justice Investigation

Because of the controversy created by Marston's dismissal, the Justice Department began an investigation into possible obstruction of justice. The inquiry sought to determine if Marston's ouster had been caused by pressure from Eilberg or any other congressional source. According to the materials gathered by Michael Shaheen, head of the Office of Professional Responsibility, neither Carter nor Bell knew at the time Carter spoke with Eilberg that the Pennsylvania Democrat was the subject of an investiga-tion. The president said in a statement he submitted to Shaheen that he first learned Eilberg was "of investigative interest" immediately prior to the Jan. 12 news conference.

Marston charged that he was being removed for political reasons; specif-ically, because he was investigating Democratic representatives. He fur-ther charged that in November 1977 he had informed a Justice Depart-ment official, Russell T. Baker, deputy assistant attorney general, about his investigation of Eilberg. Baker swore in an affidavit that he relayed the information to his superior, Benjamin R. Civiletti, then assistant attorney general in the criminal division, "some time on or after Nov. 25, 1977. . . ." Civiletti, who subsequently became deputy attorney general, however, swore that he had no knowledge of Marston's investigations whatsoever.

At his Jan. 30 news conference, the president was asked about the ap-pearance of conflict between his statement submitted to the Justice De-partment and his remarks on Jan. 12 that he was not aware of any investi-

gations of congressmen. Carter replied that his Jan. 12 answer was "obviously related" to the time of his telephone conversations with Eilberg and Bell. He insisted there was "nothing improper" in the handling of the case and added, "This was a routine matter for me and I did not consider my taking the telephone call from Congressman Eilberg nor relaying his request to the attorney general to be ill-advised at all."

Soon after his dismissal, Marston announced he would seek the Republican nomination for governor of Pennsylvania. Although he enjoyed widespread recognition throughout the state, he finished fourth in a field of seven candidates in the May 16 primary election.

The House Committee on Standards of Official Conduct Sept. 13, 1978, accused Eilberg of illegally accepting more than $100,000 in legal fees to help Hahnemann Hospital obtain a federal grant. Eilberg was indicted Oct. 24 by a Philadelphia grand jury on a conflict of interest charge in the hospital grant case. Flood, who was not charged in that indictment, had already been indicted in other cases on 13 counts of bribery, perjury and conspiracy to influence federal officials in exchange for bribes. Both Eilberg and Flood pleaded innocent. [In February 1979 Eilberg changed his plea to guilty and was placed on probation and fined; Flood's trial ended in a mistrial and the Justice Department announced he would be retried.]

Following are texts of the letter from President Carter and affidavits received by the Justice Department's Office of Professional Responsibility:

CARTER STATEMENT

To Michael Shaheen

I am writing this letter to you in response to your inquiry. On Thursday, January 12, 1978, I first heard that Congressman Eilberg of Pennsylvania was of investigative interest to the Department of Justice or the U.S. Attorney in Philadelphia.

I heard this from my Congressional Liaison Assistant, Mr. Frank Moore, a few minutes before the press conference which I held on that day in the Old Executive Office Building in Washington.

I was advised by Frank that he himself had heard of this matter for the first time on the same morning.

Sincerely,
(Signed): Jimmy Carter

The White House
January 20, 1978

BELL AFFIDAVIT

Michael E. Shaheen Jr., Counsel, Office of Professional Responsibility, has asked that I prepare an affidavit indicating when I first learned that Congressman Joshua Eilberg was or was alleged to be under investigation.

I am absolutely certain that prior to noon on January 10, 1978, when I spoke before the National Press Club, I had no knowledge that Congressman Eilberg was either under investigation in any manner, or that there had been press accounts speculating about any such investigation. It is my best recollection that I learned about the possibility of such an investigation either on Tuesday, January 10, or Wednesday, January 11, 1978. Such knowledge was conveyed to me either by Michael J. Egan, the Associate Attorney General, one of the members of my personal staff, or from my reading of press accounts speculating about such an investigation. Even at this time, however, I had no knowledge that there was in fact an investigation involving Congressman Eilberg. I only knew that the press had speculated that such an investigation existed and that there was a possibility that his name had come up in an investigation involving a transaction in Philadelphia. Subsequent to learning of this speculation about an investigation relating to Congressman Eilberg, I asked Mike Egan, the Associate Attorney General, to determine the exact facts and details regarding the truth of such speculation.

Also, I am absolutely certain that prior to my learning of the possibility of such an investigation as described above, I did not discuss such an investigation or even the possibility of the existence of such an investigation with the President or with anyone at the White House or with anyone else.

> Griffin B. Bell
> Attorney General

January 19, 1978

CIVILETTI AFFIDAVIT

I have been asked by Michael Shaheen to prepare an affidavit concerning any knowledge that I have relating to an investigative interest in Joshua Eilberg by the Department of Justice or the United States Attorney's Office in Philadelphia.

I have no knowledge of any investigation relating to or concerning in any way Joshua Eilberg conducted or being conducted by the U.S. Attorney's Office in Philadelphia.

In connection with the issue of grand jury reform, and legislation pending in Congress on this subject about which I testified before the "Eilberg Committee" in May or June of 1977, I had approximately a 30-second conversation with someone in the Criminal Division of the Department of Justice in which I was advised that there either had been a complaint made against Congressman Eilberg in the past which had been investigated and proven to be unsubstantial, or that there was an assertion against Eilberg which might have to be looked into if it was significant.

The conversation as [sic] an aside and my clear impression was that there was no investigation pending anywhere and that there was no likely investigation but it was a routine assertion to be reviewed preliminarily. My only comment was that it seemed immaterial and irrelevant to the issue before me which was grand jury reform. During this breif [sic] conversation, neither Mr. Marston's name nor the United States Attorney's Office in Philadelphia was mentioned, nor was I even aware at the time what congressional district Eilberg represented.

Because of the nature of the comment, and [sic] aside, and its insignificance, I did not communicate it to anyone. Neither the Deputy Attorney General, the Associate Attorney General, the Attorney General nor anyone else inside or outside the Department.

I have never heard anything more concerning the matter, and I do not now know anything about the Philadelphia U.S. Attorney Office's investigation of any matters, subjects or persons.

Benjamin R. Civiletti
[Assistant Attorney General]

[January 19, 1978]

BAKER AFFIDAVIT

Russell T. Baker, Jr., being duly sworn, deposes and says as follows:

On August 17, 1977, I met with Assistant United States Attorney Alan M. Lieberman in my office in Washington on matters entirely unrelated to the subject of this affidavit. At the end of our meeting we casually discussed the proposed grand jury "reform" legislation for a few minutes, and Lieberman mentioned the fact that his political corruption unit in Philadelphia had recently started an investigation of a transaction that might involve Congressman Eilberg, one of the sponsors of that legislation. As I understood it, Lieberman had no evidence, allegations, or even intelligence that Congressman Eilberg had committed a criminal offense, and Lieberman was not reporting that Congressman Eilberg was a target or even a subject of the investigation.

I mentioned that information to Benjamin R. Civiletti, Assistant Attorney General for the Criminal Division, shortly thereafter, but since Congressman Eilberg was not a subject of the investigation, which was at a very preliminary stage, the information was not reported to the Attorney General or anyone else.

In September, 1977, I was in Philadelphia for two days to review the Philadelphia Strike Force. While I was there I had discussions with United States Attorney David Marston and Neil Welch, the Special Agent-in-Charge of the Federal Bureau of Investigation in Philadelphia. Welch urged me to report back to Washington that Philadelphia was a "cesspool" of political corruption, that Marston was doing an excellent job, and that it was important to retain him. I reported that to Mr. Civiletti and Associate Attorney General [Michael J.] Egan upon my return. While in Philadelphia I did not ask and was not told anything about the investigation that Lieberman had mentioned to me in August.

I next heard about the investigation on Wednesday, November 16, 1977, during the United States Attorneys' Conference. Marston came to my office late that afternoon to discuss with me several matters, principally the question of whether he would be replaced as United States Attorney. He had just come from a meeting with Mr. Egan. Near the end of that conversation he told me that the investigation which Lieberman had mentioned to me in August was still active, and he reminded me that the investigation involved Congressman Eilberg. I was not advised of any change in Congressman Eilberg's status, however, and I came away from that conversation with the understanding that Lieberman's inquiry was, with respect to Congressman Eilberg, still in a very preliminary stage.

My notes indicate that I reported my conversation with Marston to Mr. Civiletti sometime on or after November 25, 1977, and told him that the investigation that involved Eilberg was still active but that there was no change in status. My best recollection is that he told me that I should advise Mr. Egan. I never did so. Nor did I tell anyone else.

> Russell T. Baker, Jr.
> Deputy Assistant Attorney General
> Criminal Division
> Department of Justice

[January 18, 1978]

EGAN AFFIDAVIT

On Tuesday, January 10th, as I was leaving a luncheon at the National Press Club a reporter asked me if I knew that Representative Joshua Eilberg was under investigation. That was the first indication I had that Eilberg might be under investigation. At about 3 p.m. of that same day, John Russell of our Public Information Office showed me something off of the UPI wire which stated that Eilberg was under investigation by the Department of Justice. I asked Russell to check that with United States Attorney Marston. Russell reported back to me that he had talked to Marston and that Marston would neither confirm nor deny the report. I asked Phil Modlin, Deputy Associate Attorney General, to check with the Criminal Division. Modlin reported back to me that he had talked to Jack Keeney, Deputy Assistant Attorney General in the Criminal Division, and that Keeney had told him that the Criminal Division had no knowledge that Eilberg was under investigation. I told Modlin to check with Tom Henderson, head of the Public Integrity Section of the Criminal Division. He told me that Keeney had already done so, and that Henderson knew nothing of any investigation of Eilberg. On Wednesday morning, January 11th, I called Marston to find out what he knew. Marston told me that Eilberg was of investigatory interest to his office. I told him that I had checked with Keeney and Henderson, and neither of them knew anything about it. He told me to check with Tim Baker, another Deputy Assistant Attorney General in the Criminal Division. I checked with Baker, and he confirmed what Marston told me.

My phone call to Marston and my conversation with Baker provided the first knowledge that I had of the Department's investigatory interest in Joshua Eilberg.

Michael J. Egan
Associate Attorney General

January 17, 1978

DOWD AFFIDAVIT

1. I have been requested by Michael E. Shaheen, Jr., Counsel, Office of Professional Responsibility to submit an affidavit concerning my knowledge regarding an investigation of Congressman Joshua Eilberg.

2. I am Attorney-in-Charge of Strike Force 18, Organized Crime and Racketeering Section, Criminal Division, United States Department of Justice, and am responsible for a number of investigations being jointly conducted with United States Attorneys and Organized Crime Strike Forces throughout the United States.

3. In the course of my duties I participated in the gathering of information as part of the investigation of Hahnemann Hospital in Philadelphia, Pennsylvania.

4. Based upon my examinations of the files and my questioning of attorneys and agents participating in the investigation of Hahnemann Hospital, I am not aware of any information concerning the conduct and activities of Congressman Eilberg uncovered in the investigation of Hahnemann Hospital prior to December 19, 1977.

5. By mutual arrangement, the information concerning the conduct of Congressman Eilberg obtained on or after December 19, 1977, was conveyed to the United States Attorney's Office in Philadelphia on January 4, 1978.

6. No information concerning the conduct of Congressman Eilberg in the Hahnemann Hospital investigation was communicated by me to any superior official within the Department of Justice in Washington, D.C., until January 11, 1978, and again on January 16, 1978.

7. I am not aware of any communication, act, endeavor or attempt by any official of the Department of Justice or the Executive Branch to in any way impede, frustrate, obstruct the investigation or the gathering of information concerning any person or entity involved in the Hahnemann Hospital investigation.

John M. Dowd

[January 20, 1978]

KELLY AFFIDAVIT

I have been asked by Michael E. Shaheen Jr., Counsel, Office of Professional Responsibility, to prepare an affidavit concerning my first knowledge regarding any investigation of Congressman Joshua Eilberg. On January 10, 1978, I attended a National Press Club luncheon where the Attorney General addressed those present. I am absolutely certain that prior to that time I had no knowledge that Congressman Eilberg was either under investigation in any manner whatsoever or that there had been press accounts speculating about the existence of any such investigation. To the best of my knowledge, I learned that such an investigation might exist and that the press was reporting the existence of such an investigation on either late Tuesday, January 10, or Wednesday, January 11, 1978. I cannot recall how that information first came to my attention. I believe that it was passed on to me either by someone from the Public Information Office or another member of Judge Bell's personal staff who had learned about the possibility of such an investigation from press accounts. Even at this time, however, and for several days thereafter, I had no knowledge that there was in fact an investigation in existence involving Congressman Eilberg. I only knew that the press had speculated that such an investigation existed and there was a possibility that his name had come up in an investigation involving a transaction in Philadelphia.

Also, I am absolutely certain that prior to learning of the possibility of such an investigation as described above, I had never discussed such an investigation or even the possibility of the existence of such an investigation with anyone.

J. Michael Kelly
Counselor to the Attorney General

January 19, 1978

ADAMSON AFFIDAVIT

I have been asked by Michael E. Shaheen Jr., Counsel, Office of Professional Responsibility, to submit an affidavit stating when I first learned that Congressman Joshua Eilberg was or was alleged to be under investigation.

I traveled to the National Press Club Building with the Attorney General at about noon, Tuesday, January 10, 1978. I knew absolutely nothing of such an investigation or the possibility of such an investigation at that time. The Attorney General received a question during the course of this event about the decision to replace Mr. Marston. His answer reflected the facts as I perceived them to be at the time, and discussed as well the overall policy of attempting to replace United States Attorneys with persons of equal or better calibre and ability than the incumbent. As he and I left the room afterwards, another television crew from Philadelphia attempted to ask the Attorney General what he had said about Mr. Marston during the meeting. I heard then no mention of the possibility of such an investigation. Shortly after I returned to the Department of Justice that afternoon, I heard from either Mr. Michael J. Egan, the Associate Attorney General, or one of the press officers, or from one of the other members of the Attorney General's personal staff, that there was some press account that alleged Congressman Eilberg was under federal investigation. I also then heard that Mr. Egan was attempting to ascertain whether there was some factual basis for this report. I did not hear the results of Mr. Egan's inquiry that day. Some time early the next morning, I heard from Mr. Egan a statement that Mr. Marston had told him that there was such an investigation and that he had heard that Tim Baker had said that there was not. I also heard that prior to calling Mr. Marston himself, Mr. Egan said he had asked press officer John Russell to call Mr. Marston to see if such an investigation was being conducted. Mr. Egan stated that he was told by Mr. Russell that Mr. Marston would not answer the question asked him and hung up the phone. I believe I communicated on Wednesday this discrepancy and information to the Attorney General and my understanding that Mr. Egan was still attempting to locate the true facts. I was particularly interested because that morning I was expecting a telephone call from Congressman Eilberg or his chief counsel on the House Immigration Subcommittee concerning the planned parole on January 11, 1978, of 7,000 Indochinese refugees. As it developed, I did not hear other than reading press accounts during this week until Monday night, January 16, 1978, whether Congressman Eilberg was in fact under investigation. Prior to this time, and not until Tuesday afternoon, January 10, 1978, I personally only knew that the press had reported that such an investigation existed and that there was a possibility that Congressman Eilberg's name had come up involving a transaction in Philadelphia.

I am absolutely certain that prior to my learning during the week of the National Press Club speech of the possibility of such an investigation, I had no indication or information there was even the possibility of such an investigation of Congressman Eilberg going on. Prior to the week of the National Press Club speech I did not discuss such an investigation or even the possibility of the existence of such with the Attorney General, or others on the Attorney General's staff, or other employees of the Department of

Justice, or with anyone at the White House, or the President, or with anyone else whosoever.

> Terrence B. Adamson
> Special Assistant
> to the Attorney General

[January 19, 1978]

BARON AFFIDAVIT

I have been asked by Michael E. Shaheen, Counsel, Office of Professional Responsibility, to prepare an affidavit concerning my first knowledge regarding any investigation of Congressman Joshua Eilberg.

On January 10, 1978, I attended a National Press Club luncheon where the Attorney General addressed those present. Prior to that time I had no knowledge either that Congressman Eilberg was under investigation or that there had been allegations in the press or elsewhere to that effect.

Prior to January 12, I had heard no information to suggest that such an investigation existed. My first knowledge that there was even speculation about the possibility that Congressman Eilberg might be under investigation came on January 12. At some point on January 12 I believe I was in a meeting with the Attorney General in which he mentioned that he had no information that Congressman Eilberg was under investigation but he had read a newspaper article which speculated that there was such an investigation. That was the first information I received that there was even speculation to that effect. Between January 12 and January 18, when I left Washington, D.C., I attended several meetings in which the status of David Marston as U.S. Attorney was discussed. At these meetings I heard discussion of the question of whether Congressman Eilberg was under investigation. This discussion has left me with the present impression that an investigation is being conducted of an incident involving Congressman Eilberg's former law firm and the funding of an addition to a Philadelphia hospital, but that the investigation has not yet connected Congressman Eilberg with the alleged illegalities and thus, as far as I know, even now Congressman Eilberg could not be considered the target of an investigation. Between January 18 and today, I have been in St. Louis and involved in other matters and I cannot recall any precise remarks between January 12 and 18 which led to my present impression.

> Frederick D. Baron
> [Special Assistant to the Attorney General]

[January 23, 1978]

JARDINE STATEMENT

January 16, 1978

To the best of my recollection, I first heard reports that Congressman Joshua Eilberg was allegedly under investigation by the Philadelphia U.S. Attorney's office toward the end of the week of January 9 through 13, 1978. I heard these allegations as a result of their report in newspapers during that week, although I do not recall whether I first learned of the allegations through reading newspaper clips or through discussions with other members of the Attorney General's staff as a result of those newspaper reports.

James S. Jardine

[Special Assistant to the Attorney General]

JORDAN AFFIDAVIT

I have been asked by Michael E. Shaheen, Counsel, Office of Professional Responsibility, to prepare an affidavit concerning my first knowledge regarding any investigation of Congressman Joshua Eilberg.

On January 10, 1978 I attended a National Press Club luncheon where the Attorney General addressed those present. Prior to that time I had no knowledge either that Congressman Eilberg was under investigation or that there had been allegations in the press or elsewhere to that effect.

I left the National Press Club with Michael Egan at approximately 1:45 p.m. to return to the Department of Justice. On the way out of the Press Club, Mike Egan mentioned in my presence that just prior to his leaving the Department for the Press Club, he had been shown a UPI wire report either alleging or speculating that a criminal investigation of Congressman Eilberg was underway in the United States Attorneys Office in Philadelphia. This was my first knowledge of the possibility that Congressman Eilberg might be under investigation.

Prior to learning of the possibility of such an investigation on Tuesday, January 10, I had never discussed the possibility of the existence of such an investigation with anyone.

Upon returning to the Department of Justice on January 10, I may have mentioned to Mike Kelly [Counselor to the Attorney General] or one or more of the other Special Assistants that Mr. Egan had mentioned the UPI story to me. I did not tell Judge Bell because I understood from Mr. Egan that he would look into the story and discuss it at the appropriate time with Judge Bell. For the remainder of the week I heard from Mike Egan, other members of Judge Bell's staff, and the members of the Public Information Office that efforts were underway to determine whether there was an investigation of Congressman Eilberg. I am certain that prior to the President's news conference on Thursday, January 12, I had heard no information to suggest that such an investigation existed, except for newspaper speculation.

On Friday, January 13, I was present in a meeting at which Tim Baker stated that Congressman Eilberg was under investigation because "the scent was on his trail." He gave no facts that justified to me a statement that Congressman Eilberg was under investigation.

I first learned facts that justified an assertion that Congressman Eilberg "was under investigation" late Monday afternoon, January 16.

J. Phillip Jordan
[Special Assistant to the Attorney General]

[January 19, 1978]

MARSTON AFFIDAVIT

I, David W. Marston, United States Attorney in and for the Eastern District of Pennsylvania, do swear and aver that the following information is true and correct to the best of my knowledge, information and belief:

On the evening of November 13, 1977, while attending the opening reception at the United States Attorney's Conference in Washington, D.C., I had the following conversation with Assistant Attorney General Michael J. Egan, in the presence of my wife.

Mr. Egan advised me that by late spring 1978 I might have to be replaced as United States Attorney because Congressman Joshua Eilberg had called the President of the United States; he had not reached him, but the President returned his call, and Congressman Eilberg pushed for my replacement, reportedly saying something to the effect of "I recognize I can't have Glancey or my nominee, but it has to be anybody but Marston." Mr. Egan told me the President then called the Attorney General and the Attorney General then called Mr. Egan and asked him why it was taking so long to replace me.

I said to Mr. Egan and I hoped if I were being replaced solely for political reasons, they would not make a political mistake, citing the fact that a number of prominent Democratic public officials, including former United States Senator Joseph Clark and Congressman [Peter H.] Kostmayer [D-Pa.] and [Robert W.] Edgar [D-Pa.] had supported my retention.

I told him I thought there was political danger for the Administration in relying solely on a Congressman with close ties to [Philadelphia Mayor Frank L.] Rizzo, and I advised him that Philadelphia's newly-elected District Attorney had taken on the Rizzo organization in the spring primary, beat them 2 to 1, and that the D.A. had campaigned heavily on the issue of my being retained in office. Mr. Egan said that was a fair point, but stated that "when the pressure comes from on high, it must be relieved." After further discussion he suggested that the "pressure" might be relieved by firing the other two United States Attorneys in Pennsylvania (who were already slated for removal and had not been invited to the U.S. Attorney's Conference) promptly at the first of the year.

It occurred to me during this conversation that this office had an open investigation involving Hahnemann Hospital and preliminary indications were that Congressman Eilberg might be a subject of that investigation. I knew that the Eilberg law firm represented Hahnemann Hospital, but I did not know precisely what involvement by Congressman Eilberg had been indicated by the investigation to that point; since I was uncertain of this, and did not want to give Mr. Egan the impression that anyone favoring my removal would automatically be investigated, I did not mention the Hahnemann investigation to him on November 13.

However, after returning to my hotel I became concerned about the implications of such a phone call from someone potentially the subject of a federal investigation and I felt that someone in the Justice Department should be aware of both Mr. Egan's description of the Eilberg phone call and the President's phone call to the Attorney General, together with relevant facts of the Hahnemann investigation which might involve Eilberg. Therefore, on the afternoon of Wednesday, November 16, when I was called to the office of Deputy Assistant Attorney General T. Russell Baker on other matters, I relayed the Egan conversation to him in the same detail as stated above, together with the substance of the Hahnemann investigation, the possible Eilberg involvement, and my reason for not having told that to Mr. Egan. Mr. Baker made some notes during the conversation, but did not say to me at that time what action he would take.

Subsequently, during the week of January 8, 1978, I believe on either Wednesday the 11th or Thursday the 12th, Mr. Baker advised me by telephone that he remembered our November 16 conversation clearly and that he had subsequently relayed the information I gave him to then Assistant Attorney General in charge of the Criminal Division, Benjamin Civiletti.

On Friday, January 13, 1978, I had another conversation with Mr. Baker. At that point I was concerned because I had seen a press report quoting the Attorney General as saying that he did not know of the existence of any investigation implicating Eilberg until the day before, and that if there was in fact such an investigation, I had been "negligent" in not telling him. Mr. Baker told me that he had been asked that morning to tell the Attorney General all he knew about the situation. I responded by saying in substance, I hope that you told him that I told you and you told Mr. Civiletti, so that the Attorney General knows that I was not negligent. Mr. Baker indicated to me that he had so advised the Attorney General, and he further made a statement to the effect that if anyone was negligent perhaps he was, because he might not have put sufficient urgency into his communication with Mr. Civiletti.

On Wednesday, January 11, I received a telephone call from Associate Attorney General Egan. He advised me that he was concerned because he was reading a UPI wire story, the last paragraph of which stated that my office had Eilberg and Congressman Flood under investigation, and he had checked thoroughly in the Justice Department as of two or three days previously, and found no evidence of any such investigation. He asked if I did in fact have any such investigation in progress.

I reminded him of the conversation we had had on November 13, 1977, in detail, and I further advised him of my concern following that conversation, which resulted in my recounting that conversation, the description of our Hahnemann investigation and Eilberg's possible implication, to Deputy Assistant Attorney General T. Russell Baker on the following Wednesday afternoon, November 16, 1977. I further stated that information concerning the investigation was being developed by John Dowd [Deputy Assistant Attorney General in the Criminal Division] during the debriefing of Steven Elko [former administrative assistant to Rep. Flood], which had been conducted in the Justice Department in Washington for at least the previous several weeks. Mr. Egan then stated that he had checked with Jack Keeney [Attorney-in-Charge of Strike Force 18, Organized Crime and Racketeering Section, Criminal Division] and had not been able to discover any evidence of a case involving Eilberg. He asked again who was debriefing Mr. Elko and I told him it was John Dowd.

He then asked me if I considered Eilberg to be a "target" at that point, stating that he recognized target was a word of art. I replied that the word target was not a designation that I used, but that I would consider Eilberg a person likely to be indicted and Flood a person certain to be indicted if this investigation were to continue unimpeded. He thanked me for that information and hung up.

On Thursday morning, January 12, Mr. Baker called me. He said he had talked to Mr. Egan and would like to know all of the facts as I knew them concerning the Hahnemann investigation and Eilberg's possible implication. I told him that Mr. Egan had made essentially the same request to me the previous afternoon and Mr. Baker advised me that he was aware of that, but that Mr. Egan thought he (Baker) and I "spoke the same language" and therefore was making the present request. I called Assistant United States Attorney Alan M. Lieberman into my office with the case file, and we both spoke to Mr. Baker at some length to give him the background concerning this case.

> David W. Marston
> United States Attorney
> Eastern District of Pennsylvania

[January 16, 1978]

PRESIDENT'S ECONOMIC REPORT, ECONOMIC ADVISERS' REPORT
January 20, 27, 1978

President Carter reported to Congress on the state of the U.S. economy Jan. 20, recommending an overall economic program which was generally cautious and departed but little from policies already in effect. Pointing to the persistent problems of structural unemployment and inflation, the president reiterated his belief that the government should be only a partner in efforts to ameliorate them. "Government programs can provide valuable assistance to the unemployed," he said. "In the end, however, we must turn to the private sector for the bulk of permanent job opportunities for the disadvantaged." And speaking of the stubborn inflation, he said, "No one group — neither business, nor labor, nor government — can stop this spiral on its own. What is needed is a joint effort."

Carter's economic message, which accompanied the annual report of the Council of Economic Advisers, also stressed his preference for stimulating the economy through a reduction of taxes rather than through increases in federal spending. One tax cut, he said, should take place later in 1978, and a second should perhaps come a little later than that. (Budget message, p. 95)

The president also stressed the importance he placed on careful management of federal expenditures. His administration, he said, had "given high priority to making more effective use of limited Federal expenditures." He added, "In formulating my recommendations for the 1979 budget, I have exercised very strict controls over spending. Adjusted for inflation, the increase in outlays has been held to less than 2 percent and the share of federal expenditures in GNP [gross national product] will fall to 22.0 percent. I intend to continue prudent expenditure controls in the future. With good management, we can, I believe, achieve our Nation's important social goals and still reduce over time the share of gross national product committed to federal expenditures to about 21 percent." (In fiscal 1976 federal outlays had amounted to 22.5 percent of the gross national product.)

Carter strongly tied enactment of an energy program by Congress to the health of the economy. Describing at some length the harmful effect on the economy of the "new era of expensive energy," he called for adoption of legislation which would reduce consumption of diminishing supplies and be consistent with the administration's overall economic strategy.

The report of the Council of Economic Advisers retreated slightly from Carter's earlier numerical goals for reducing unemployment and inflation and for accelerating economic growth. But the president remained optimistic. "I have begun from the premise," he said, "that our economy is basically healthy, but that well-chosen Government policies will assure continued progress toward our economic goals." He added, "Last year, more than four million new jobs were created in our country — an all-time record — and unemployment was reduced by more than one million persons."

Council's Forecasts

The Council of Economic Advisers predicted that — if Carter's proposed tax cut were approved by Congress — the economy would grow by between 4.5 and 5 percent during 1978. The rate of expansion should increase employment in 1978, the council said, by nearly 3 percent. It predicted that the unemployment rate would be between 6 and 6.25 percent by the end of 1978 and drop to between 5.5 and 6 percent by the end of 1979. Moreover, if the president's appeal to business and labor to cooperate in a voluntary program were successful, the council said, the rate of inflation could be trimmed half a percentage point a year off the basic 6.5 percent rate which then prevailed.

Further surveying the economy, the economic advisers forecast a 7 to 8 percent increase in real terms in business fixed investment over the course of 1978. They said that plans for plant and equipment outlays would be raised as the dimensions of the U.S. energy program became more certain and as the new tax proposals influenced business expectations. Consumption during the year, the council said, should grow somewhat more slowly than disposable income — increasing about 4.5 percent in real terms. Housing starts would remain at high levels early in 1978, but some reduction in single family starts was expected by the end of the year.

The council called a 4 percent unemployment rate in 1983, the goal of the Full Employment and Balanced Growth Act of 1978, "a very ambi-

tious objective." "The major unanswered question regarding this target," the council said, "is whether it can be achieved without creating pressures in labor and product markets that would touch off a new round of inflation." The council added, "Responsible policy, however, requires not that we abandon efforts to reach the 1983 unemployment goal, but that we work steadily to reduce the conflict between low unemployment and inflation by developing structural measures to improve the functioning of markets."

> *Following are excerpts from the Jan. 20, 1978, Economic Report of the President and the Annual Report of the Council of Economic Advisers issued Jan. 27, 1978. (Bold-face headings in brackets have been added by Congressional Quarterly to highlight the organization of the text.):*

ECONOMIC REPORT OF THE PRESIDENT

To the Congress of the United States:

I will be working closely with the Congress in 1978 to enact a program addressed to the immediate and the long-term needs of our economy. I am proposing tax reductions and reforms to continue our strong economic recovery, to encourage increased investment by American businesses, and to create a simpler and fairer tax system. I am seeking legislation to address the special problems of the disadvantaged and the unemployed. And I am taking new steps to combat inflation.

This report to the Congress on the condition of the economy sets forth the overall framework within which my economic proposals were formulated. It outlines, for you and for the Nation, my economic priorities for the years ahead and my strategies for achieving them.

I have begun from the premise that our economy is basically healthy, but that well-chosen Government policies will assure continued progress toward our economic goals.

Last year more than four million new jobs were created in our country — an all-time record — and unemployment was reduced by more than one million persons. Output rose by almost 6 percent, and the benefits of this large increase were widely shared. The after-tax income of consumers, adjusted for inflation, rose substantially during 1977. Wages of the typical American worker increased by more than the rise of prices, and business profits also advanced.

The American economy is completing three years of recovery from the severe recession of 1974-75. Recovery in most other nations has lagged far behind our own. In the economies of our six major trading partners, seven million persons were unemployed at year's end — more than at the depths of the 1974-75 recession. Our inflation rate is also lower than in most other nations around the world. We have a great many accomplishments. But much progress remains to be made, and there are problems to be dealt with along the way.

The recession of 1974-75 was the worst in 40 years, and the substantial increase in output over the past three years still leaves the economy operating below its productive potential. We cannot be content when almost 6½ million people actively seeking jobs cannot find work, when 3¼ million workers take part-time jobs because they cannot find fulltime employment, and when one million people have stopped looking for a job because they have lost hope of finding one. We cannot be content when a substantial portion of our industrial plant stands idle, as it does today.

We cannot be satisfied with an economic recovery that bypasses significant segments of the American people. Unemployment among minorities is more than twice as high as that among whites — and unemployment among minority teenagers is tragically high. Women have fewer satisfying job opportunities than men, and older Americans often find their access to the job market blocked. Farm incomes have dropped precipitously.

We must also address other problems if we are to assure full restoration of prosperity. Inflation is a serious economic concern for all Americans. The inflation rate is too high and must be brought down. Moreover, a residue of unease and caution about the future still pervades the thinking of some of our people. Businesses are still hesitant in their long-term investment planning, and the stock market remains depressed despite the substantial increase in business profits.

The economic difficulties that we face in the United States also confront most nations around the world. Our mutual problems are the legacy of the trauma suffered by the world economy during the early 1970s. The massive escalation of oil prices since 1973 continues to impose great burdens on the world economy. Oil imports drain away the purchasing power of oil-importing nations and upset the international balance of payments.

Many foreign governments have been reluctant to adopt policies needed to stimulate economic growth because they are concerned that inflationary pressures might be renewed or that their balance of international payments might be worsened. Abroad, as well as at home, concerns about the future have deterred business investment in new plants and equipment. As a consequence, economic growth has stagnated in many countries, and the rise in the capital stock needed to increase productivity, raise standards of living, and avoid future inflationary bottlenecks is not occurring.

The problems we face today are more complex and difficult than those of an earlier era. We cannot concentrate just on inflation, or just on unemployment, or just on deficits in the Federal budget or our international payments. Nor can we act in isolation from other countries. We must deal with all of these problems simultaneously and on a worldwide basis.

Our problems cannot be solved overnight. But we can resolve them if we fix our sights on long-term objectives, adopt programs that will help us to realize our goals, and remain prepared to make adjustments as basic circumstances change.

[Economic Objectives]

In making my decisions on tax and budget policies for fiscal 1979, and in planning more generally for our Nation's future, I have been guided by four objectives for our economy that I believe our Nation should pursue.

We must continue to move steadily toward a high-employment economy in which the benefits of prosperity are widely shared. Progress in reducing unemployment of our labor and capital resources must be sure and sustainable. Over the next several years I believe we can increase our real output by 4½ to 5 percent per year, and reduce unemployment by about one-half of a percentage point each year. An especially high priority is to increase job opportunities for the disadvantaged, particularly for black and Spanish-speaking Americans, and to deal more effectively with local pockets of unemployment, such as those in urban areas. We should eliminate unfair advantages through reform of the tax system, and restructure our welfare system to assure that the fruits of economic growth are enjoyed by all Americans.

We should rely principally on the private sector to lead the economic expansion and to create new jobs for a growing labor force. Five out of every six new jobs in the economy are created in the private sector. There are good reasons for continuing to rely mainly on the private sector in the years ahead. By emphasizing the creation of private jobs, our resources will be used more efficiently, our future capacity to produce will expand more rapidly, and the standard of living for our people will rise faster. Reliance upon the private sector does not mean neglecting the tasks that government can and must perform. The Federal Government can be an active partner to help achieve progress toward meeting national needs and, through competent management, still absorb a declining portion of the Nation's output.

We must contain and reduce the rate of inflation as we move toward a more fully employed economy. Inflation extracts a heavy toll from all Americans, and particularly from the poor and those on fixed incomes. Reducing inflation would benefit us all. A more stable price environment would make it easier for business firms and consumers to plan for the future. Thus, reduced inflation would substantially enhance our chances to maintain a strong economic expansion and return to a high employment economy. In the years ahead we must seek to unwind the inflation we have inherited from the past and take the steps necessary to prevent new inflationary pressures as we approach high employment.

We must act in ways that contribute to the health of the world economy. As the strongest economy in the world, the United States has unique responsibilities to improve the international economic climate. The well-being of the United States depends on the condition of other nations around the world. Their economic destiny is, in turn, shaped by ours. The United States can retain its stature in the world only by pursuing policies that measure up to its role as a leader in international economic affairs.

These four economic objectives are sufficiently ambitious to constitute a serious challenge, but sufficiently realistic to be within our reach. A well-designed program will permit us to achieve them. The principal elements of my economic strategy are:

- Adopting promptly an effective national energy program;
- Managing Federal budget expenditures carefully and prudently, so that we can meet national needs while gradually reducing the share of our national output devoted to Federal spending;
- Using tax reductions to ensure steady growth of the private economy and reforming the tax system to make it fairer, simpler, and more progressive;
- Working to reduce the Federal deficit and balance the budget as rapidly as the developing strength of the economy allows;
- Improving existing programs and developing new ones to attack the problem of structural unemployment among the disadvantaged;
- Promoting greater business capital formation in order to enhance productivity gains, increase standards of living, and reduce the chances that capacity shortages would inhibit expansion later on;
- Adopting more effective programs to reduce the current rate of inflation and prevent a reacceleration of inflation as we approach high employment; and
- Pursuing international economic policies that promote economic recovery throughout the world, encourage an expansion of world trade, and maintain a strong international monetary system.

[Prompt Adoption of an Energy Plan]

It has now been over four years since our economy was buffeted by the oil embargo and its aftermath of sharply increased oil prices. The massive oil price increase in 1973-74 contributed to the double-digit inflation of 1974 and to the worst recession in 40 years. It is a primary factor today behind the large deficit in our international balance of payments. Yet the United States still has not enacted a comprehensive and effective energy policy.

Our dependence on imported oil is sapping the strength of the American economy. Last year our imports of oil reached a total of about $45 billion, compared with $8½ billion in 1973. The increased expenditures on those imports have been like a sudden and massive tax imposed on the American people. Only part of the revenues have been returned to the United States in the form of higher exports of American goods to oil-producing countries. As a consequence, that "tax" has become a major obstacle to economic growth.

The huge deficit in foreign trade arising from our oil imports has contributed to the fall in the value of the dollar abroad. The dollar's decline has raised the cost of the goods we import and contributed to inflation. Our deficit also has unsettled international monetary markets, with adverse consequences for our international trading partners. Our response to the energy crisis is therefore a central element in our international and domestic economic policy. The energy program will not solve our problems at once, but it will pave the way for a balanced foreign trade position and a strong and sound dollar....

Dealing with the energy problem is a difficult test for our Nation. It is a test of our economic and political maturity. Our people would surely react if there were an immediate crisis. But I am asking them to undertake sacrifices to *prevent* a crisis. If we fail to act today, we will bring a crisis upon ourselves and our children in years to come.

[Federal Budget Expenditures]

My Administration has given high priority to making more effective use of limited Federal resources. In fiscal 1976, Federal outlays amounted to 22½ percent of the Nation's gross national product. This is considerably higher than the share devoted to government spending that prevailed for many years. To some degree, the recent higher share reflects the fact that the economy is still performing below its capacity, and that Federal programs to support the unemployed and the needy are larger than they would be in a high-employment economy. But it also stems from very rapid growth in a number of Federal programs instituted over the past 10 to 15 years.

Most of our Federal expenditure programs are designed to achieve important national goals that the private sector of the economy cannot accomplish. Only the government can provide for the national defense, and government resources are essential to cushion the hardships created by economic recession, to preserve our national resources, to protect the environment, and to meet other critical needs.

The Federal Government has a particular obligation to provide assistance to those who remain in need even during good times. Last year I presented to the Congress a program to reform the welfare system — the Better Jobs and Income Act of 1977 — that is a concrete example of our commitment to devote resources to the most pressing national needs. My program will cost money. But it also will establish a more easily understood welfare system that is less costly to administer, less subject to abuse, and more responsive to the true needs of those who receive a helping hand from government. This program will create up to 1.4 million jobs for those able to work, and it will replace the patchwork of Federal, State, and local programs with a consistent income-support system that will relieve much of the enormous burden now placed on State and local governments.

In the management of a business enterprise, efficiency is enforced by the discipline of the market place. The collective judgments of millions of consumers establish an environment in which waste and efficiency are eventually penalized. The government, however, is not subject to that discipline. We in government must therefore impose stringent controls on ourselves to ensure greater efficiency and to make better choices among the possible uses of the taxpayers' money.

To assist us in this endeavor, I have adopted methods of budgetary control that have been tested in the business community. Early last year I asked the Office of Management and Budget to inaugurate a system of zero-based budgeting throughout the Federal Government. Within this budgetary system, every Federal program is given careful scrutiny — no matter how large or how small it may be, no matter how long it has been in existence or how recently established....

In formulating my recommendations for the 1979 budget, I have exercised very strict controls over spending. Adjusted for inflation, the increase in outlays has been held to less than 2 percent. I intend to continue prudent expenditure controls in the future. With good management we can, I believe, achieve our Nation's important social goals and still reduce over time the share of gross national product committed to Federal expenditures to about 21 percent.

[Tax Reductions]

I propose to rely principally upon growth in the private sector of the economy to reduce unemployment and raise incomes. Special Federal efforts will, of course, be necessary to deal with such problems as structural unemployment, but tax reductions will be the primary means by which Federal budget policy will promote growth. Careful management of budget outlays and a growing economy should permit substantial reductions in the years ahead. Tax reductions will be needed to strengthen consumer purchasing power and expand consumer markets. Stable growth in markets, together with added tax incentives for business, will lead to rising business investment and growing productivity.

As inflation and real economic growth raise the incomes of most Americans, they are pushed into higher income tax brackets. The tax burden on individuals is raised just as if higher rates had been enacted. The payroll taxes levied on workers and business firms for social security and unemployment insurance will also increase substantially over the year ahead. These are very large increases, but they are needed to keep our social security and unemployment insurance systems soundly financed.

Between 1977 and 1979, taxes on businesses and individuals will rise very sharply as a result of these several factors. Even though our economy is basically healthy, this increasingly heavy tax burden would exert a mounting drag on economic growth. It must, therefore, be counteracted by tax reductions. The magnitude and timing of the reductions should be designed to maintain economic growth at a steady pace, taking into account the effects both of the growing tax burden and of other factors at work in the economy.

Consistent with this strategy, I am proposing a $25 billion program of net tax reductions accompanied by substantial tax reforms.

Individual income taxes will be reduced primarily through across-the-board reductions in personal tax rates, with special emphasis on low- and middle-income taxpayers. Personal taxes also will be simplified by my proposal to replace the existing personal exemption and credit with a tax credit of $240 for each person in the taxpayer's family.

There also will be important reforms that will improve the individual income tax system and raise substantial revenues, enabling me to recommend larger personal tax reductions.

Overall, I am proposing personal tax reductions of $24 billion, offset by $7 billion in tax reforms. These tax cuts, which will take effect next October 1, will significantly improve the progressivity of the tax system. The typical four-person family with $15,000 in income will receive a tax cut of $258 — or more than 19 percent. As a result of the changes I am recommending, filling out tax returns will be simpler for many people.

Individuals also will benefit from reductions I have proposed in the Federal excise tax on telephone bills, and in the Federal payroll tax for unemployment insurance. These two proposals will add about $2 billion to consumers' purchasing power that will be realized principally through lower prices.

Business taxes will be reduced by more than $8 billion in 1979 under my tax program, offset partially by more than $2 billion in business tax reforms for a net tax reduction of nearly $6 billion. I have recommended that the overall corporate tax rate be reduced on October 1 from the current 48 percent to 45 percent, and be cut further to 44 percent in 1980. I also recommend that the existing 10-percent investment tax credit be made permanent, and that the benefits of this credit be extended to investments in industrial and utility structures. My proposal will enable businesses to use the investment tax credit to offset up to 90 percent of their Federal tax liability, compared with the 50-percent limit now imposed.

Important new tax reforms also will affect businesses. I am, for example, proposing to reduce the deductibility of a large class of business entertainment expenses. I have also proposed changes in the tax status of international business transactions that are of significant cost to taxpayers but that benefit the public insufficiently.

Because tax reform measures will raise $9 billion in revenue, it has been possible for me to recommend $34 billion in overall tax reductions while keeping the net loss in revenues to $25 billion, the level I believe is appropriate given the state of our economy and the size of the budget deficit....

These tax reductions are essential to healthy economic recovery during 1978 and 1979. Prospects for continuation of that recovery in the near term are favorable. Consumers have been spending freely, and many other economic indicators recently have been moving up strongly. Without the tax reductions I have proposed, however, the longer-term prospects for economic growth would become increasingly poor. Because of the fiscal drag imposed by rising payroll taxes and inflation, economic growth would slow substantially in late 1978, and fall to about 3½ percent in 1979. The unemployment rate would stop declining and might begin to rise again, and the growth of investment outlays for new plant and equipment would slow significantly.

With the reductions in taxes I have proposed, on the other hand, the economy should grow by 4½ to 5 percent in both 1978 and 1979. Nearly one million new jobs would be created. Unemployment would therefore continue to fall and by late 1979 should be down to around 5½ to 6 percent. Capacity utilization and after-tax business profits would both improve, and thus the rate of investment in new plants and equipment should increase significantly....

[Structural Unemployment]

Meaningful job opportunities ought to be available for all Americans who wish to work. But overall fiscal and monetary policy alone will not provide employment to many in our Nation. If we are to reduce unemployment satisfactorily, we must do more.

Eleven percent of adult American workers from minority groups are now jobless — close to the rate a year ago, and over twice as high as the unemployment rate for white adults. About 17 percent of our teenagers are unemployed today; among black teenagers the unemployment rate is nearly 40 percent. These intolerably high rates of unemployment must be brought down. This is an important goal, but achieving it will be a difficult task.

A generally healthy and growing economy is a prerequisite for dealing effectively with structural unemployment, but it is not enough. Even in good times some groups suffer from very high unemployment, which adds to the difficulty of achieving low unemployment and low inflation simultaneously. As the economy moves toward high employment, employers try to fill job vacancies from those groups of workers with substantial training and experience. Wage rates are bid up and prices follow, while large numbers from other groups are still looking unsuccessfully for work. Efforts to reduce unemployment among the unskilled and otherwise disadvantaged can be frustrated by inflationary pressures set off in those sectors of the labor market already fully employed.

To reach high levels of employment while maintaining reasonable price stability, we must take effective and adequate measures now to increase the employment opportunities of the disadvantaged. This principle is a key element of the Humphrey-Hawkins Bill — The Full Employment and Balanced Growth Act. I support this legislation and hope the Congress will enact it.

We have already taken several significant steps in this direction. Last year I proposed and the Congress appropriated $8.4 billion to expand the Public Service Employment Program to 725,000 jobs. These jobs are more sharply targeted on the long-term unemployed and the poor than previous programs under the Comprehensive Employment and Training Act. Direct opportunities for youth also have been expanded. The Youth Employment and Demonstration Projects Act of 1977, which is providing job experience and training in skills to unemployed youths, also was proposed by my Administration and enacted in 1977, providing 166,000 work and training positions for unemployed youths....

[Capital Formation]

Over a broad expanse of years, improvement of the standard of living in this Nation depends primarily on growth in the productivity of the American work force. During the first two decades of the postwar period, the productivity of American labor increased at an average annual rate of about 3 percent. Over the past ten years, however, productivity growth has slowed markedly — to about 2 percent or less a year.

The reasons for this break with past trends are complex, but one factor that clearly stands out is the relatively slow growth in the stock of business plant and equipment. Historically, improvements in productivity have been linked closely to investment in plant and equipment. Investment in new facilities has embodied new and more productive technology and has provided our work force with more and better tools.

Business investment has lagged during the recovery for several reasons. Some of the fears engendered by the steep recession and severe inflation of 1973-75 have remained and have reduced the incentive for business to invest. Uncertainties about energy supplies and energy prices have also been a deterrent to investment, and so have concerns about governmental regulations in a variety of areas. Finally, high costs of capital goods and a depressed stock market have diminished the incentives and raised the costs to businesses of investment in new plant and equipment....

[Rate of Inflation]

We cannot achieve full prosperity unless we deal effectively with inflation. We must take steps to reduce the high rate of inflation inherited from the past and to guard against a renewed outbreak of inflation as we regain a high-employment economy.

Our economy is not suffering at present from excess demand. Monetary growth in recent years has not been excessive, and Federal budget deficits have occurred in an economy with high unemployment and excess capacity. Yet prices continue to rise as a result of an inflationary process that has been under way for a decade.

Our present inflation began back in the late 1960s and accelerated sharply in the early years of the 1970s. Since 1974 the rate of consumer price inflation has decline substantially — from 12 percent to between 6 and 6½ percent at present. But that improvement is due largely to the termination of special influences affecting prices during 1974 — the sharp rise of food and fuel prices, and the bulge in prices following the removal of wage and price controls.

Recent experience has demonstrated that the inflation we have inherited from the past cannot be cured by policies that slow growth and keep unemployment high. Since 1975, inflation has persisted stubbornly at a 6 to 6½ percent rate — even though unemployment went as high as 9 percent and still stands above 6 percent, and even though a substantial proportion of our industrial capacity has been idle. The human tragedy and waste of resources associated with policies of slow growth are intolerable,

and the impact of such policies on the current inflation is very small. Moreover, by discouraging investment in new capacity, slow growth sows the
seeds of future inflationary problems when the economy does return to
high employment. Economic stagnation is not the answer to inflation....

Government regulations also add to costs and raise prices. To some
extent, this is the inevitable cost of much needed improvements in the
environment and in the health and safety of workers and consumers. But
there is no question that the scope of regulation has become excessive and
that too little attention is given to its economic costs. We should not, and
will not, give up our efforts to achieve cleaner air and water and a safer
workplace. But, wherever possible, the extent of regulation should be reduced. We have eliminated hundreds of unneeded regulations already and
will continue to pare down the remainder.

I also intend to put a high priority on minimizing the adverse effects of
governmental regulations on the economy....

I have given special attention to reducing the runaway cost of health
care. The cost of a day in the hospital has more than doubled since 1970.
Continuing escalation in the charges for hospital care can no longer be tol-
erated. I have submitted legislation, the Hospital Cost Containment Act
of 1977, that would limit sharply the rate of growth in hospital spending,
and I urge the Congress to enact this legislation in 1978....

Government alone cannot unwind the current inflation, however.
Today's inflationary process is largely the consequence of self-fulfilling expectations. Businessmen, expecting inflation to continue, are less resistant
to cost increases than they might be, since they have come to believe that,
with all prices rising, their own increased costs can be passed on to consumers through higher prices. Wage increases are based on the expectation
that prices will continue to rise. Wage gains in one sector spur similar
demands in others.

There are gainers and losers in this process, since some groups in the
economy are more successful than others at defending themselves against
inflation. On the whole, however, the main result is continued inflation.
No one group — neither business, nor labor, nor government — can stop
this spiral on its own. What is needed is a joint effort.

Since the current inflation has developed strong momentum, it cannot
be brought to a sudden halt. But we can achieve a gradual but sustained
deceleration — having each succeeding year's inflation lower than the previous one. The benefits of slower growth of prices and wages would be
broadly shared. Everyone would be better off. A conscious effort should be
made by those who make wage and price decisions to take the individual
actions necessary to bring about an economy-wide deceleration of
inflation.

*I am therefore asking the business community and American workers
to participate in a voluntary program to decelerate the rate of price and
wage increase....*

I have chosen this approach after reviewing extensively all of the available options. There is no guarantee that establishing a voluntary decelera-

tion standard will unwind the current inflation. I believe, however, that with the cooperation of business and labor, this proposal will work....

In this message I have outlined my fundamental economic goals and the strategy for attaining them. It is an ambitious, but I believe a realistic, agenda for the future. It calls for a broad range of actions to improve the health and fairness of the American economy. And it calls upon the American people to participate actively in many of these efforts.

I ask the Congress and the American people to join with me in a sustained effort to achieve a lasting prosperity. We all share the same fundamental goals. We can work together to reach them.

Jimmy Carter

January 20, 1978.

THE ANNUAL REPORT OF THE COUNCIL OF ECONOMIC ADVISERS

Chapter 1

Progress During 1977 — The Third Year of Recovery

As the new administration took office at the beginning of 1977, the economy was turning up strongly from a period of very slow real growth during the latter part of 1976. With the unemployment rate hovering near 8 percent and with inflation still a serious problem, however, the Nation was far from the goals of "maximum employment, production, and purchasing power" established in the Employment Act of 1946. Progress toward these goals was essential to the achievement of rising living standards and greater equality of income and of opportunity. Strong and steady growth in the U.S. economy was also needed to help sustain the pace of economic expansion among the nations of the Western world. An economic stimulus program was therefore designed by the new Administration to keep the economy on a path of recovery at a pace sufficient to reduce the unemployment of labor and capital resources significantly.

In the course of the year, continuing progress was made in closing the substantial gap between actual and potential real output that existed at the beginning of 1977. Real gross national product (GNP) expanded in each quarter at a pace above its long-term potential growth, and the gain in 1977 as a whole amounted to 4.9 percent. By the fourth quarter, real GNP was 5.7 percent higher than it had been a year earlier.

This increase in real output made possible a 4.1-million increase in employment between the end of 1976 and the end of 1977. A temporary slack-

ening in the rate of expansion around midyear limited the midyear reduction in unemployment, but unemployment fell significantly early in
the year and again in the later months. The unemployment rate fell to 7.0
percent for 1977 as a whole and reached 6.4 percent at year-end.

The expansion in total output was large enough to permit a substantial
improvement in living standards. Real per capita disposable income rose
by 4.9 percent during the year. At the same time, the increase in industrial
production of 5.6 percent lifted capacity utilization in manufacturing from
81 percent at the end of 1976 to 83 percent at the end of 1977. This increase played an important role in the 9.5-percent advance of corporate
profits for the year as a whole.

DEVELOPMENTS DURING THE YEAR

The pace of economic expansion was exceptionally strong during the
early part of 1977. As the year opened, businesses were increasing their
production schedules in an effort to rebuild stocks depleted by the
unexpectedly sharp rise of consumer spending in the latter months of 1976.
The rate of nonfarm inventory investment rose from near zero in the
fourth quarter of 1976 to 1 percent of real GNP by the second quarter of
1977, accounting for almost 30 percent of the expansion in real output during the first half of the year. The rise in consumer spending that began in
late 1976 continued in the opening months of 1977. With final sales and inventory accumulation both moving up briskly, real GNP in the first quarter increased at an annual rate of 7½ percent....

The pace of advance in economic activity early in the year was so rapid
that an abnormally cold winter had only a mild transitory effect on overall
economic performance. January temperatures were as much as 20 percent
below normal in some parts of the country, causing shortages of natural
gas and numerous plant shutdowns. Plant closings typically lasted only
one to a few days, however, and most of the loss in output was made up
before the end of the first quarter.

Construction activity was significantly depressed by the winter weather
but rebounded in the second quarter. Government spending also rose
sharply. The strength of these two sectors offset a developing weakness in
consumer spending, and growth of real GNP in the second quarter remained at a relatively rapid 6-percent annual rate.

During these 2 quarters of large gains in real output substantial progress
was made in reducing unemployment. From December to April total civilian employment rose by almost 1½ million, and the unemployment rate
fell by 0.7 percentage point. Job gains were widespread among manufacturing, construction, retail trade, services, and other industries. The
length of the workweek in manufacturing also increased.

The rapid pace of expansion in the first half could not have been expected to continue since it was based, in part, on a rebuilding of stocks and a
restoration of inventory investment to a more normal relationship with
GNP. The slowdown in the rate of expansion during the middle of the year

was more widespread and prolonged, however, than could be accounted for solely by patterns of inventory accumulation.

The rise of consumer spending slowed abruptly in the second quarter when the personal saving rate rose substantially. During the first 2 years of the recovery, consumers' purchases of goods and services had risen much faster than their after-tax incomes, so that by early 1977 the fraction of disposable income devoted to saving had fallen to the lowest level in 25 years. Restoration of a more normal allocation of consumer incomes between consumption and saving was inevitable, and the major part of the adjustment took place in the second quarter.

As retail sales faltered, manufacturers adjusted their production schedules promptly to avoid an undesired buildup of inventories — as they had in 1976, when consumer spending also slowed temporarily. As a consequence, demands for labor moderated, and the unemployment rate stopped declining. Total hours worked in nonfarm establishments, which had been rising strongly in the first 4 months of the year, topped out and remained essentially unchanged from May through September; the rise of industrial output during this period slowed to about half the pace recorded in the first 5 months of the year.

The caution exhibited by business in their inventory policies was even more evident in their willingness to make longer-term investment commitments. Plans for business capital outlays normally gain increasing strength as rates of capacity utilization and profits rise during the course of an economic recovery. For a time in late 1976 and early 1977 it appeared that the usual cyclical processes were occurring: the real value of contracts and orders for plant and equipment was improving vigorously. Around the middle of the year, however, the rise of this indicator of business fixed investment slowed, and production of business equipment, though continuing to advance, increased at a more moderate pace than earlier in the year.

The hesitancy of business capital spending (which is examined later in this chapter) was singularly disappointing. These outlays, in real terms, have yet to recover their peak levels reached in late 1973 and early 1974. Industrial capacity has therefore been expanding at a very sluggish pace — and at a time when the labor force is increasing rapidly. Over the long run, continuing growth of real output and a stronger rise of productivity will depend heavily on restoring a more vigorous rate of expansion in business outlays for new plant and equipment.

Developments in the foreign sector also restrained the rate of economic expansion. Imports of oil rose substantially early in the year, partly as a consequence of the effects of the cold winter on fuel consumption; and other imports increased more than would have been anticipated on the basis of historical relationships between growth of real output and these imports. U.S. exports meanwhile increased scarcely at all in real terms because of the very slow rate of economic expansion among most of our major trading partners.

The midyear slowdown of economic expansion would have been more serious had it not been for the effects of the Administration's stimulus programs. These programs began to increase government spending and disposable personal incomes by midyear, and their stimulative effects continued to build over the remainder of 1977. Fiscal policy was thus instrumental in the quickening tempo of activity late in 1977.

Signs of an emergence from the pause of 1977 first became evident late in the fall, when new retail sales figures indicated that consumers had begun to increase their purchases of goods in the third quarter. A combination of factors led to a further strengthening of consumer spending during the fourth quarter. Growth in personal income was sustained by rising output and employment in other sectors and was further bolstered by the Federal pay raise in October and by the growing effects of the stimulus programs. With consumer prices increasing at a relatively moderate rate during this period, gains in nominal income were translated into greater purchasing power and rising consumer spending. In the fourth quarter, consumer outlays for durable and nondurable goods, adjusted for inflation, rose at an annual rate of over 10 percent.

This surge of consumer buying — coupled as it was with some improvement in the pace of fixed investment — was not fully anticipated by businesses, whose production schedules were still geared to the slower pace of retail sales that had prevailed earlier. The rate of inventory accumulation therefore declined steeply in the fourth quarter, holding down overall GNP growth to an annual rate of 4.2 percent. It is clear, however, that activity was strengthening as the year came to a close. Employment in the final 2 months rose rapidly, and the unemployment rate fell to 6.4 percent in December.

Failure to make any significant progress on the inflation front in 1977 was a disappointment. . . . Consumer prices of goods and services other than food and energy, a measure of the underlying rate of inflation, increased by 6.4 percent in the 12 months ending in December 1977, about the same rate as in 1976.

An underlying inflation rate of 6 to 6½ percent has persisted since mid-1975 and is deeply embedded in the wage-cost-price structure. In the nonfarm business sector, compensation per hour — which includes both wages and fringes — in the fourth quarter of 1977 was about 8½ percent more than a year earlier. This increase in labor cost exceeded productivity gains by about 6 percent and therefore put strong upward pressures on prices. These price increases, in turn, wiped out most of the rise in workers' nominal earnings.

Changes in food and fuel prices during 1977 caused substantial variation in the overall rate of price change from the underlying rate of inflation. In the first half, both food and energy prices were rising rapidly, reflecting the cold winter and the increasing prices of imported foods (particularly coffee, tea, and cocoa). Overall consumer prices increased during this period at an annual rate of 9 percent. As food supplies improved, the rise of consumer prices slowed materially to an annual rate of around 4½ percent in the second half of 1977.

[MAJOR SECTORS OF DEMAND]

The sources of economic expansion shifted somewhat during 1977. During the first 2 years of the current economic recovery, household spending for personal consumption and new housing were the principal dynamic elements. In turn, the increase in final demand stemming from these sources prompted a pronounced swing from decumulation to rebuilding of inventories during the first year of the upturn. As the rise of consumer spending moderated last year, growth in business fixed investment and particularly accelerated government spending assumed more important roles in determining the pace of expansion.

PERSONAL CONSUMPTION

The saving rate during 1977 rose considerably, marking a reversal of the pattern of the preceding 3 years. This reversal and the pronounced mid-year weakness of consumer spending were due to a number of causes. Some of them have their roots in the forces that had disturbed the economy generally, and the household sector in particular, earlier in the 1970s. High inflation rates eroded the real value of household wealth held in savings at depository institutions and in other nominally denominated forms. Employment growth in the early 1970s was also less steady than during most of the 1960s. These two developments may well have prompted somewhat more cautious consumer behavior and caused higher saving rates. The saving rate reached an exceptionally high level in 1973 — the cyclical peak year, which was marked by accelerating inflation and a sharp and largely unanticipated rise in farm income. In the following year of recession, households held the real value of consumption of nondurables and services level while the real value of both durable purchases and saving declined in the face of falling real incomes.

By late 1975 the economy was moving up again, the pace of inflation had abated somewhat from double-digit rates, and household income had been bolstered by tax cuts. As confidence was renewed, consumers were apparently attempting to regain previously planned consumption levels and to rebuild their stocks of durable goods. Although spending for durable goods rose somewhat erratically during 1976, the overall gain was strong, and the saving rate dropped sharply further from its recession level, reaching a 25-year low in the first quarter of 1977. By then, real per capita consumption was almost 8 percent higher than its cyclical peak in the third quarter of 1973. Once consumption levels had been brought more closely into balance with individuals' plans and anticipated earnings, it became natural for households to resume a historically more normal balance between current consumption and saving for future needs.

A number of nonrecurring factors contributed to the final phase of decline in the saving rate in the first quarter of last year: deferred automobile purchases because of the strike at the Ford Motor Company late in 1976, unusually large estate and gift tax payments, and exceptionally large home heating expenses. The extent of the decline during 1976 and in the first quarter of 1977 was underestimated, however, in preliminary data. More complete data becoming available later in the year made it more apparent that the slowing in consumption growth, which began in the spring, was an inevitable result of the restoration of more customary spending and saving patterns.

The saving rate rose abruptly in the second quarter and more gradually in the following quarters. Surveys of consumers' attitudes showed only a small reduction in consumer confidence in this period. . . .

The slower rise in the saving rate in the fourth quarter was coupled with resumption of strong growth in disposable income. These forces led to a vigorous increase in consumption.

HOUSING

The pace of single-family homebuilding was at a record level last year, although the rate of increase of aggregate residential construction expenditures slowed to 15 percent from 22 percent in 1976. Housing starts for the year came to almost 2 million units. Single-family starts totaled a record 1½ million — 150,000 more than in any previous year — and the rate was higher at year-end. The demographic determinants of housing demand are increasingly favoring a high rate of single-family home construction as the post-World War II baby boom population is reaching the childbearing age. Furthermore the demand for single-family homes, which are predominantly owner-occupied, appears to reflect the belief that homeownership is valuable as an investment. The rate of increase of new home prices, exclusive of changes due to quality or size differences, is currently about 11 percent annually, or about 5 percentage points greater than the average increase of other prices. Although part of this price pattern is a temporary response of the prices of new construction materials to strong demand, land prices have also been rising substantially.

In California particularly, and to a lesser extent elsewhere in the country, there was an element of speculation in the housing markets in the early part of the year. An increasing number of homes were being bought by individuals who could not indefinitely carry the mortgages, but who anticipated a speculative profit from a near-term resale. In some areas of Southern California the inflation in new home prices reached a 25-percent annual rate. At first, lenders' willingness to grant mortgages in such cases fueled the speculative surge of construction that was evident early in 1977. The Federal Home Loan Bank of San Francisco, however, took effective steps to dampen the expansion of mortgage credit, and lenders were encouraged to require a commitment from home purchasers to occupy the homes they bought. By midyear both price increases for new homes and new housing starts had slowed in the West.

New starts of multi-family units last year came to 535,000, up 43 percent from 1976 but still well below the 1972 peak of 1 million units. The lower level of unsubsidized multi-unit building in recent years results, in part, from the overbuilding that occurred in some regions of the country from 1971 to 1973. Since 1976, multi-family construction has turned up in most of the country as vacancy rates have declined. The Northeast was an exception as outmigration and the prevalence of rent controls have curbed expansion.

INVENTORIES

Inventory accumulation contributed substantially to growth of real GNP in the first quarter of 1977. The rate of accumulation in nonfarm inventories, in 1972 dollars, rose from near zero in the last quarter of 1976 to about $10 billion. Thereafter the rate of nonfarm inventory accumulation rose only moderately further in the second and third quarters and then declined sharply at year-end.

Business continued in 1977 to follow the very cautious inventory policies that have typified this expansion. Book values of inventories of nondurable goods rose slightly more rapidly than sales in the second quarter as consumption of nondurable goods slackened. In the summer months, new orders and the growth of production slowed sharply, preventing substantial undesired accumulation of stocks during a period of sluggish sales. . . .

GOVERNMENT SPENDING

Spending by both the Federal and State and local governments was a particularly important source of economic expansion in mid-1977 when the contribution of other sectors to continued growth of output was moderating. The real value of Federal Government purchases had been essentially unchanged during 1976, and in the fourth quarter of that year was only 1 percent above its level at the cyclical trough 7 quarters earlier. In contrast, the real value of Federal purchases rose by 7.2 percent in 1977; the most significant increases occurred in the second and third quarters.

Both the defense and nondefense components of Federal purchases accelerated sharply. The upswing in real defense purchases marked the end of the decline that began in 1969. While defense procurement rose strongly, however, the number of military personnel remained about constant.

The increase of nondefense Federal purchases at midyear was significantly affected by Commodity Credit Corporation (CCC) transactions. Steep declines of farm crop prices led to a large increase from a year earlier in CCC purchases for crops under loan agreements. CCC purchases added about $4½ billion, at an annual rate, to the value of Federal purchases by the third quarter; the pace leveled off in the fourth quarter. These acquisitions represent a transfer from private inventory accumulation to government purchases and do contribute directly to expanded output. Other Federal nondefense purchases from the private sector, however, also rose in real terms during 1977.

State and local government purchases grew at an annual rate of only 1.4 percent, in real terms, from the recession trough through the end of 1976; but these purchases increased by 3.2 percent during 1977. Earlier in the current cyclical upswing, States and localities were recovering from substantial operating account deficits that had accumulated during the previous downturn. Fiscal positions improved as the recovery proceeded, reflecting increased revenues generated by rising incomes and adjustments in both tax rates and spending patterns. These lagged adjustments moved budgets into substantial surplus by mid-1976.

Beginning in 1977, real purchases by State and local governments rose notably as a result of their stronger fiscal positions. The fiscal situations were further improved during the year by significant increases in Federal grants as part of the Administration's stimulus package. This package included an expansion of public service jobs from about 310,000 in the spring to 615,000 positions at the end of the year. About 80 percent of these jobs were with State and local government units. At the same time there were indications that State and local capital formation, which dropped off sharply in 1975 and 1976, was reviving. Construction of educational facilities continued to decline, as children born in the late stages of the baby boom reached adulthood and left school, but housing and redevelopment building, and sewer and water supply construction rose vigorously during the second half of last year. Many of these projects were assisted by an increase in Federal grants for local public works.

EMPLOYMENT AND UNEMPLOYMENT

Growth in economic activity over the 4 quarters of 1977 was sufficient to generate over 4 million new jobs. Employment increased rapidly in the first half of the year as a result of the strong growth in total output; but as the pace of expansion moderated in the third quarter, employment growth slackened. The midyear slowdown was also evident in total hours of work at nonagricultural establishments in the private goods-producing business sector, which declined during the third quarter when manufacturing production and employment flattened out temporarily. Strong expansion of employment resumed again late in the year.

Gains in employment in the first half of the year lowered the unemployment rate from 7.9 percent in the last quarter of 1976 to 7.1 percent in the second quarter of 1977. Only moderate further progress was made until the fourth quarter, when unemployment began declining again, reaching a 3-year low of 6.4 percent in December.

A major disappointment with respect to our economic performance in 1977 was the unemployment situation of black Americans. Total black employment increased by 4.8 percent from the fourth quarter of 1976 to the fourth quarter of 1977, exceeding the 4.4-percent increase in white employment, but the black unemployment rate remained unchanged at 13.4 percent as the labor force grew rapidly. The unemployment rate for black teenagers rose, however, from 36.6 percent to 38.3 percent. Although labor force growth explains the failure of these unemployment rates to fall, it does not dispel the problem of high unemployment among minorities. Furthermore, the problem for teenagers in particular is unlikely to be corrected merely by expansion of the total economy. Effective structural measures are needed as the recovery continues. . . .

Employment in the government sector grew 2.6 percent during 1977, considerably less rapidly than in the private sector. Federal employment has accounted for a dwindling share of total employment in the past decade and was virtually unchanged during the year. State and local employment, on the other hand, has been the fastest growing major sector of the economy for the past two decades. From 1953 to 1973 the average annual rate of growth was 4.8 percent. This growth rate declined to 3.3 percent from 1973 to 1976, when the expansion of State and local expenditures was relatively slow. State and local employment grew by 3.1 percent, or 392,-000 jobs, in 1977; much of the increase was in the second half of the year. Over 200,000 of the additional jobs on State and local payrolls were financed under the expansion of Comprehensive Employment and Training Act (CETA) jobs that was part of the Administration's stimulus package. . . .

The labor force grew very rapidly during 1977, rising by 3.1 percent or 3 million persons between the fourth quarter of 1976 and the fourth quarter of 1977. The number of adult men in the labor force increased 1.9 percent, closely in line with the long-term trend. Unemployment for this group fell from 6.0 percent to 4.8 percent. Employment developments for adult women were sharply different. As their number in the labor force increased by 4.5 percent, the unemployment rate of adult women fell by only 0.7 percentage point to 6.8 percent in the fourth quarter. The teenage labor force grew by 4.6 percent; the unemployment rate of teenagers fell during 1977, but remained a distressingly high 16.7 percent in the fourth quarter.

The role of high labor force participation in rapid labor force growth and slower decline in aggregate unemployment is shown by the rising ratio of employment to the total civilian noninstitutional population of working age — up 1.7 percentage points during 1977 to 58 percent in December. This is a post-World War II record. At the cyclical peak in the fourth quarter of 1973, this ratio was 57.3 percent, when unemployment was 4.8 percent. In 1968, when the unemployment rate was 3.6 percent, the employment to population ratio was considerably lower than in either 1977 or 1973. Hence, given the income and career aspirations of broad segments of the population, the economy is confronted with a challenge not only to create jobs but to match workers to employment opportunities.

PRICES AND WAGES IN 1977

The pace of inflation last year was essentially unchanged from 1976, excluding the effects of a few especially volatile factors. The rise in the consumer price index accelerated to 9 percent in the first half of the year, from a 4.8-percent rate during 1976, in response to short supplies of food and strong demands for energy caused by the harsh winter weather. In the second half, however, these forces were absent. Indeed, as the new spring crops came in, wholesale prices of food and farm products declined sharply. As the benefits were passed on to consumers, the rise in consumer prices slowed to an annual rate of 4½ percent in the second half.

Farm supplies are subject to disturbances from weather and these show up in volatile price movements because of relatively inelastic demand for food products. Other prices may also be subjected to shocks that have little to do with the overall balance of supply and demand in the economy. Energy prices are a current example of this phenomenon. For this reason, it is important to look at the movements of price indexes after these special factors have been removed — that is, to look at the "underlying rate" of inflation. This underlying rate, measured by the consumer price index exclusive of food and energy prices, has remained relatively steady in the range of 6 to 6½ percent during almost the entire 3 years of expansion.

The stability of the underlying inflation rate reflects, on the one hand, the continued high levels of unemployment and excess capacity, which have forestalled the acceleration of inflation that has often occurred in the course of extended cyclical expansion. On the other hand, inflationary expectations and institutional characteristics of modern economies have kept the inflation rate from declining. . . .

WAGES, PRODUCTIVITY, AND UNIT LABOR COSTS

During the first year of the recovery, productivity rose faster than its long-run trend, as it typically does in such periods. Since businesses tend to calculate costs on the basis of secular trends in productivity and set their prices accordingly, the rise in prices exceeded that of unit labor costs, and profits per unit of output improved markedly. Since then, the growth of productivity has slowed, and the movements of prices and unit labor costs have been more nearly parallel.

On a year-over-year basis, the rate of change in hourly compensation was essentially the same last year as in 1976. Compensation per hour in the private nonfarm sector showed an 8.5 percent increase, about 0.2 percent less than in 1976. The rate of growth of private nonfarm productivity, however, slowed substantially to 2 percent. The rise in labor cost per unit of output therefore increased to about 6½ percent.

Hourly compensation increased about 1 percentage point faster than the index of average hourly earnings during the year. The latter measure shows the change in wages exclusive of the effects of shifts of employment among industries and changes in manufacturing overtime; it is often used as a measure of the basic rate of wage increases, though it is only an approximation. About one-half of the difference in 1977 between hourly compensation and average hourly earnings was accounted for by the shift of employment toward high-wage industries. The remaining difference was primarily due to the increase of fringe benefits, included in compensation but not counted in the earnings index. Fringe benefits per hour have risen more rapidly than wages but rose at about the same rate last year as in 1976. . . .

New collective bargaining agreements concluded last year generally provided for wage increases greater than the 1977 rate of increase of average hourly earnings. Those that were concluded in the first 9 months of last year and included cost-of-living adjustment clauses provided an average annual basic wage increase of 5.0 percent, plus the augmentation from the escalators. If inflation continues at a 6 percent rate, the total annual wage increase would be about 8 percent. Wage increases in contracts without escalator clauses averaged 6.9 percent annually over the life of the contract. These data, however, omit increases in fringe benefits. The data on combined changes in wages and fringe benefits, which are limited to agreements covering 5,000 or more workers, suggest that total labor compensation under collective bargaining agreements probably continued to rise more rapidly than compensation for all nonfarm employees. First-year negotiated adjustments of wages and benefits averaged 9.6 percent last year. . . .

FOOD PRICES IN 1977

Movements of food prices exerted a major effect on the overall rate of price change during the past year. Between the fourth quarter of 1976 and the fourth quarter of 1977 the consumer price index for food increased 7.7 percent.

The severe freeze in July 1975 that reduced the 1976-77 Brazilian coffee crop by 60 percent was reflected in U.S. food prices in early 1977. Reduced supplies from Brazil, normally the world's largest coffee producer, caused world supplies to decline 17 percent and average retail coffee prices in the United States to increase 54 percent during the first 6 months of last year.

During the middle of last January temperatures in Florida were below freezing for several days, reducing the fruit crop and heavily damaging the vegetable crop. Prices of these commodities escalated rapidly until supplies became available from other areas. Fruit and vegetable prices increased at an annual rate of 24 percent in the first quarter but declined in the third quarter. . . .

Abundant supplies of all food products helped to restrain price changes over the year. Food grain prices declined throughout the year as U.S. farmers harvested a third consecutive large crop. The lower food grain prices were reflected in the modest 4-percent increase from the fourth quarter of 1976 to the fourth quarter of 1977 in the cereal and bakery component of the consumer price index.

Declining feed grain prices prompted significantly increased cattle feeding in the latter months of the year. Total beef and veal production nonetheless declined 4 percent in 1977. The decline would have been larger if the drought conditions in the West and Southwest had not encouraged more rapid slaughtering. Last year marked the third consecutive year of a cyclical reduction in the U.S. cattle herd that has been the deepest in history.

Total meat production, however, was unchanged from 1976, as production of competing meat and poultry products rose to offset declines in beef output. Consumers substituted more abundant pork and poultry for beef products during 1977; as a result there were only modest increases in prices for meat products in general. From the fourth quarter of 1976 to the final quarter of 1977, beef prices rose only 4 percent, pork prices rose 6 percent, and poultry prices increased by 7 percent. Retail prices of dairy products increased 5 percent, largely reflecting the March increase in the support price of milk. . . .

OTHER PRICE DEVELOPMENTS

Prices in 1977 for most goods and services other than food and agricultural products moved in a fairly homogeneous fashion. A few exceptions should be mentioned.

At the retail level, energy prices again posed a special problem early in the year, as noted above, although the pace of increase in energy prices slowed slightly later in the year. Prices of houses, both new and old, rose sharply. On the other hand, prices of apparel and household appliances lagged behind the aggregate indexes.

Medical costs, led by physicians' fees and hospital charges, continued to rise at rates substantially above those of other items, and insurance costs have also risen rapidly. This Administration has proposed to try to reduce inflation in hospital costs by negotiation between representatives of hospitals and physicians, insurers, and the government, which now pays more than half of all hospital charges. The initial goal is to reduce cost increases per admission to 9 percent in fiscal 1978.

At the wholesale level, costs of construction materials rose rapidly during most of the year as prices of lumber and other building materials, especially insulation, moved up sharply. These, of course, contributed to the rise in the price of houses. The rise in lumber prices seem clearly associated with the strength in single-family construction activity, which is particularly lumber intensive. Wholesale and retail fuel prices rose significantly early in the year. Paralleling the moderate rise in retail prices of apparel, textile prices rose less rapidly than the overall average, possibly as a consequence of weak consumer demand and strong worldwide competition as well as of good cotton crops. The pace of inflation has also been relatively moderate for nonpetroleum chemicals, rubber, scrap metals, and most internationally traded commodities. Although many raw industrial commodity prices rose early in the year, possibly as a result of speculation occasioned by fears that inflation would accelerate, increases tapered off and some prices fell in the latter half of 1977. Excess world capacity undoubtedly helped to keep these prices in check.

[FISCAL POLICY]

Soon after the new Administration came into office, it proposed a series of measures intended to raise the rate of growth in real output in 1977 and 1978 to a pace that would lead to significant reductions in the unemployment rate. The package of stimulative measures that was proposed would have had a 20-year budgetary impact of $31 billion.

Given the lags inherent in the implementation of fiscal policy, however, the new measures did not have an effect until early summer. Indeed, in the first quarter of 1977, fiscal policy was actually contractionary by almost any measure because of the unusually slow growth in Federal spending in combination with a sharp upturn in receipts. For the rest of 1977, however, fiscal policy was more expansive, as expenditures resumed their normal growth and the initiatives in the stimulus package began to take effect. . . .

Total Federal Government expenditures rose by 9½ percent in 1977 . . . , up slightly from the growth in 1976. As noted earlier, beginning in the second quarter, growth in real Federal defense and nondefense purchases was the most rapid since the mid-1960s and was an important factor in sustaining real growth in the economy during the year.

Grants to State and local governments grew somewhat less rapidly than purchases. Most of the growth in grants occurred in the second half of the year, in part as a result of the expenditure components of the President's stimulus program. The growth in Federal transfer payments in 1977 was slowed by declining outlays for unemployment insurance; other social insurance expenditures rose enough for benefits to keep pace with the increase in the general price level. . . .

Federal receipts rose by $41.6 billion in 1977, a somewhat smaller increase than occurred in 1976. The growth was unevenly distributed over the year, with a very large increase in the first quarter and much smaller ones in subsequent quarters. The abnormally large $20.4-billion (annual rate) increase in the first quarter was due to an extra $4 billion in payroll tax increases and a nonrecurring $5.5-billion increase in estate and gift taxes. The additional payroll taxes were the result of the temporary 0.2 percentage point increase in the Federal unemployment insurance (UI) tax rate mandated by the Unemployment Compensation Amendments of 1976, increases in State unemployment insurances taxes — which are counted in the Federal sector — to meet the higher costs of unemployment benefits paid during the recession, and an automatic rise in the taxable wage base for social security. The increase in estate and gift tax collections occurred in response to the revisions made in the Tax Reform Act of 1976. Since gifts were treated more liberally under the old law, there was an incentive to cluster gifts at the very end of 1976, before the new law came into effect. The receipts were collected in early 1977.

The reduction in the rate of increase in receipts during the remainder of the year reflected the personal and corporate tax cuts enacted as part of the stimulus package. For the year as a whole personal taxes and contributions for social insurance grew the most rapidly. Together they now account for 77 percent of total Federal receipts, compared with 60 percent in 1957. Most of this increase results from legislated increases in social insurance taxes. Periodic tax reductions have maintained the share of personal taxes in total Federal receipts at a fairly constant 45 percent over the past 20 years, offsetting the rise that would have resulted otherwise because of the progressivity of this tax. The total Federal tax share of GNP rose from 19.5 percent in 1976 to 19.8 percent in 1977.

The Federal deficit on a national income and products accounts (NIPA) basis declined in 1977 for the second year in a row, falling to $49.6 billion for the year. This was $9.5 billion smaller than the deficit projected in February, even after adjusting for withdrawal of portions of the stimulus package. . . .

MONETARY POLICY

Short-term interest rates rose fairly sharply from April through October of last year, following an unusual period of downward drift during the first 2 years of the current expansion. Nonetheless, financial markets showed few signs of stress during 1977. Deposit flows to thrift institutions remained fairly high, although some slowing was apparent late in the year. Mortgage credit rose rapidly and there were few signs of tightening of mortgage terms. The volume of new corporate bond issues was down slightly from the preceding year as businesses shifted somewhat toward mortgages and shorter-term borrowing. The yields on new corporate bonds and on long-term Treasury issues rose in the first quarter but then remained stable until late in the year, when a further increase occurred. State and local bond yields drifted slightly lower in 1977, despite a considerable increase in offerings. On balance, the strong liquidity positions and ample cash flow of major lending institutions early in the year limited the upward movement of long-term rates and accommodated substantial credit flows, though at rising costs to many borrowers.

The sharp increase of almost 2 percentage points in the Federal funds rate between April and October was unsettling, however, both because of its speed and because of uncertainties about its implications for the future of interest rates. From March through October the narrowly defined money supply (M_1, the sum of demand deposits and currency) grew erratically but rapidly, averaging a 10-percent annual rate. This was substantially faster than the 6½ percent upper limit of the target growth range announced by the Federal Reserve at the end of 1976 for the year ahead. Consequently, the Federal Reserve moved to tighten the availability of bank reserves, which led to increases in the Federal funds rate and other short-term interest rates.

The unusually rapid growth of M_1 in 1977 was sharply at variance with the pattern of growth during the first 2 years of the current expansion. During that earlier period money growth had been unusually slow relative to nominal GNP. The resulting rapid rise in velocity (the ratio of GNP to M_1) was accompanied by stable or slightly declining interest rates, indicating that the private sector was developing new means for economizing on cash balances. . . . Questions arose during the year concerning the possibility that the unusual velocity pattern would not continue. If velocity growth were returning to a historically more normal pattern, further increases in interest rates would be required to hold growth of the monetary aggregates within the Federal Reserve's target ranges. . . .

Movements of virtually all short-term interest rates tended to follow the Federal funds rate during the year, rising from late spring through early fall and then leveling out through December. During the year as a whole the rate on 3-month Treasury bills rose from 4.5 to 6.1 percent. The prime rate charged by banks on short-term business loans followed, rising from 6¼ percent to 7¾ percent. There were, however, reports of shading of the prime rate, as banks sought to expand their business loans.

Long-term interest rates were relatively stable during the year, after declining rapidly in the preceding 2 years. The yield on newly issued Aaa-rated utility bonds averaged 8.2 percent, compared with an average 8.5 percent during 1976. The yield for 20-year Treasury securities rose unevenly from a January low of 7.5 to 7.9 percent in December, but averaged 7.7 percent for the year, compared with 7.9 percent in 1976.

Corporations had no apparent difficulties in marketing new debt issues, for there was ample demand from both financial institutions and individuals wary of common stocks. Although the yield curve became substantially flatter, as short rates rose relative to long, the curve remained positively sloped particularly within the 1-year range. This resulted in part from the fact that bond market participants expected some further rise in short rates.

Interest rates on municipal bonds were an exception to the general pattern of interest rates: yields on lower-rated tax exempt bonds continued to fall. Yields on Baa-rated municipal bonds fell from 6.7 percent in December 1976 to 5.8 percent in December 1977, as investors' fears of municipal bankruptcies abated. Inflation also pushed more incomes into the range where the tax exemption is valuable, and the growth of tax exempt mutual funds offered individuals greater access to the municipal bond market. This downward movement of yields was not shared by the more highly rated municipals: the yield on Aaa bonds fluctuated in a narrow band of 5.1 to 5.3 percent. . . .

Business credit availability remained ample at commercial banks, insurance companies, and pension funds. The latter two classes of institutions have been active lenders in the new issues markets, as the funds available to them rose during 1977.

Although new corporate long-term bond issues were down slightly from 1976, the rise in new commercial mortgages offset this decline. Short-term corporate borrowing from commercial banks and finance companies rose more rapidly in 1977 than earlier in the recovery. Nevertheless, total business borrowing needs remained moderate.

While M_1 growth rates rose during the course of 1977, the growth rate of time and savings deposits at commercial banks (other than negotiable certificates of deposit at large commercial banks) fell. For the 6 months ending in March 1977, the growth rate of these deposits was 15.8 percent, at an annual rate. For the 9 months ending in December the growth rate slowed to 9.3 percent. There was some outflow from State and local savings accounts and growth in personal savings accounts slowed. The rate of savings flows at thrift institutions slowed late in the year, falling from a 14.8 percent annual rate through October to about 11 percent in the final 2 months of the year. It might have slowed earlier but for the success of the thrift institutions in capturing funds previously held at banks in the "wild card" certificates that were issued in 1973 and matured last summer. As a consequence of continued inflows during the major part of the year, mortgage credit remained readily available.

The continuation of strong savings flows at thrift institutions during most of the year was attributable to several causes. Short-term rates remained below the levels of the previous business cycle peak in November 1973 and were generally below the regulatory ceilings on deposits until late in the year. The response of the public to changes in relative interest rates is likely to be gradual at first and then to gain momentum when interest rates approach or surpass previous peaks.

It is also important that the deposit and liability structure of financial intermediaries has changed substantially since 1973, the last period of credit market tightness. On the deposit side, the institutions rely less on passbook accounts, and more on long-term certificates of deposit. At savings and loan associations, for example, passbook accounts fell from over 50 percent of deposits in late 1972 to under 40 percent in 1977. At the other end of the maturity range, long-term certificates have become more important. . . .

Although the total Federal deficit of $45 billion in fiscal 1977, on a unified budget basis, was down from the $61 billion of fiscal 1976, the Federal Government remained a large borrowing sector. This large Federal deficit was substantially offset, however, by the $27-billion surplus of State and local governments (including both operating and social insurance funds) during the same 4 quarters. The total government deficit (on a NIPA basis) was $18 billion for fiscal 1977. In addition, about $25 billion of Federal debt was purchased for foreign official accounts. . . .

[THE ECONOMY AT YEAR-END]

Prospects for continued expansion were favorable as 1977 came to a close. The sectors of the economy were relatively lean, and the balance sheets of business and financial institutions were strong. Nevertheless much remains to be accomplished to achieve the Nation's economic goals. The great resources of the U.S. economy are still incompletely utilized. Since the cyclical peak in the fourth quarter of 1973, growth in real output has averaged 2.3 percent per year. This is an abnormally slow rate of growth for a 4-year period. Capacity utilization in manufacturing still hovers 4 to 5 percentage points below levels that, in the past, have been consistent with high employment, and its low level is contributing significantly to lagging profit growth and a rate of investment that is too low to meet long-run needs.

The unemployment problem remains one of the most critical facing the Nation. Not only is the aggregate rate too high, but the composition of unemployment implies that recovery is bypassing some segments of society. Young people and minorities, in particular, continue to account for a disproportionate share of the unemployed, and continued rapid growth of demand may make only small inroads into this problem. It is important to identify and correct the imperfections in labor markets that limit the employment opportunities of these groups if prosperity is to be equitably shared.

Progress in curbing inflation has also been painfully slow because it has proved difficult to reverse the momentum that develops when past inflation comes to be expected. Stabilizing the rate of inflation is an important first step. Reducing the rate further remains a challenging goal.

Continued and accelerated growth in productivity is also required both as a major contributor to the reduction of inflation, and in order to sustain or enhance the U.S. position in international trade. Stronger growth of investment will be required to achieve this objective, as well as to avoid capacity bottlenecks at future levels of high employment, to accommodate needs for environmental control equipment, and to adapt to changing technological and cost conditions affecting particular areas and industries.

A critical challenge remaining at the end of 1977 is a successful shift toward greater energy self-sufficiency. This must entail both conservation of existing resources of oil and gas and conversion to more abundant alternative energy sources. Passage of the Administration's National Energy Plan and the help of all sectors of our economy in its implementation are the first steps in laying the foundation for secure economic growth over the coming decades. . . .

CARTER'S BUDGET MESSAGE

January 23, 1978

Stressing fiscal restraint and prudent management, President Carter sent his 1979 budget requests to Congress Jan. 23 asking $500.2 billion in expenditures for the fiscal year starting Oct. 1, 1978. The budget anticipated a deficit for the year of $60.6 billion. Together with a proposal for a $24.5 billion net tax reduction, which Carter had sent Congress two days earlier, the budget was designed both to sustain the economic recovery and to resist the rising rate of inflation.

The fiscal 1979 budget had been awaited with particular interest as it was the first that was truly Carter's. The previous year's budget had been written basically by President Ford, and the new president had been able to make only a few revisions. (Historic Documents of 1977, p. 57) *The fiscal 1979 budget had been expected to reveal the direction Carter wished to take the country in the economic sphere. It was a direction, it turned out, not very different from that of his two Republican predecessors.*

In his budget message, President Carter made plain his conviction that there were limits to what government could do to cure social problems. "In formulating this budget," he said, "I have been made acutely aware once more of the overwhelming number of demands upon the budget and of the finite nature of our resources." He added, "Public needs are critically important; but private needs are equally valid, and the only resources the government has are those it collects from the taxpayer. . . . The span of government is not infinite." As for Carter's goal of balancing the budget by 1981, however, the administration acknowledged that its chances of being achieved were fading. The goal might have to be "deferred," the

*budget said, if the president decided the economy needed additional stim-
ulus.*

*Praise for the budget came quickly from the chairmen of the two con-
gressional budget committees. Sen. Edmund S. Muskie, D-Maine, chairman of the Senate Budget Committee, said that Carter had used "sound
economic reasoning" in developing overall economic strategy. Similarly,
Rep. Robert N. Giaimo, D-Conn., chairman of the House Budget Committee, said that the budget moved "in the right direction on two counts —
first, by working to maintain our economic growth, and, second, by calling
for restraints on the growth in federal spending." The fiscal 1979 budget
was the fourth to face the full effect of the procedures established by the
Congressional Budget and Impoundment Control Act of 1974 (PL 93-433).*

*The proposed budget projected a $38 billion spending increase, which
represented an 8 percent rate of federal spending growth. That was a little
more than half the 15 percent rate of growth in the preceding year. In only
three years since 1968 had the growth of federal spending been less than 8
percent. Most of the growth in fiscal 1979 resulted from continuing current
policies with adjustments for inflation and demographic changes. Only
$7.8 billion of the spending increase, the administration estimated, re-
sulted from new spending initiatives. That amount represented a growth
rate of only 1.6 percent.*

Spending Proposals

*The largest increases in the fiscal 1979 budget were proposed in the
areas of income security ($12.4 billion, or 8.3 percent); national defense
($10.1 billion, or 9.4 percent); health ($5.4 billion, or 12.2 percent); interest ($5.1 billion, or 11.7 percent); education ($2.9 billion, or 10.7 percent);
energy ($1.8 billion, or 23 percent); and international affairs ($944 million,
or 14 percent). The income security increase included a $9.8 billion, or 10.1
percent, rise in Social Security.*

*The most substantial decline in projected outlays was in agriculture, for
which the administration projected a $3.6 billion, or 40 percent, spending
reduction. Much of the spending on agriculture, however, would depend
on the weather and the harvest. The budget gave no sign that the administration was responding to farmers who were demonstrating in Washington,
D.C., and elsewhere.*

*Carter listed several "new priorities" in his budget message. They
included:*

*● Energy — with special emphasis on conservation and non-nuclear
research development, accelerated acquisition of a strategic petroleum reserve, resolution of problems of nuclear waste management, and research
into alternatives to the plutonium-fueled liquid metal fast breeder reactor.*

● *Human needs — especially a beginning to Carter's welfare reform program, health care for low-income mothers and children, major increases in education assistance at all levels, jobs programs and a start on a program to prevent unwanted adolescent pregnancies.*

● *National defense — especially an increase in spending for the North Atlantic Treaty Organization (NATO).*

● *Research and development, which was earmarked for a 5 percent real growth in spending.*

Tax Reduction

The most controversial and innovative part of President Carter's fiscal plan for 1979 was his proposal for a $33.9 billion reduction in revenues, partially offset by $9.4 billion in revenue-raising recommendations. Carter's tax program included provisions to reduce personal taxes by $23.5 billion while implementing "reforms" in the personal tax system that would raise $8.4 billion; to reduce business taxes by $8.4 billion while introducing changes to raise $1.1 billion; and to reduce individual and business taxes by an additional $2 billion by eliminating the excise tax on telephone service and reducing the federal unemployment compensation payroll tax.

The president said that the net $24.5 billion tax reduction would stimulate the economy to grow at a rate between 4.5 and 5 percent through 1979, as compared to a relatively poor 3.5 percent growth rate without it. The tax reduction was also seen by the administration as offsetting to a degree the Social Security payroll tax increases enacted late in 1977.

Congressional Reaction

Congressional reaction to the first Carter budget divided for the most part along party lines. A number of Republicans challenged the president's claim that the proposed budget was "restrained." Rep. John J. Rhodes, R-Ariz., the House minority leader, said that the budget included a number of "phony cuts" to "understate" the likely growth in spending. A liberal Democrat, Rep. Abner J. Mikva of Illinois, said that the spending total "leaves some chores on the economic agenda undone, but realistically there is no way they could be done." He added, "This year is almost a test of our capacity to run government. The people sense that a government that keeps running a deficit year after year doesn't know how to run its own ship." But another liberal, Rep. Parren J. Mitchell, D-Md., chairman of the Congressional Black Caucus, called Carter "dead wrong" in proposing as large an increase in defense spending as he did. "If $10 billion is to be added, it should be for economic stimulus," Mitchell said, "and the Department of Defense does not stimulate the economy."

Following is the text of President Carter's fiscal 1979 budget message, sent to Congress on Jan. 23, 1978. (Boldface headings in brackets have been added by Congressional Quarterly to highlight the organization of the text):

To the Congress of the United States:

The first complete budget of any new administration is its most important. It is the administration's first full statement of its priorities, policies, and proposals for meeting our national needs. Last February, after just one month in office, I submitted a revised budget to the Congress. That revision changed the direction of the prior administration's budget, but was — of necessity — based upon a review of limited scope. I promised then that future budgets would reflect detailed, zero-based reviews of federal spending programs, reform of the tax system, and reorganization of the government. This budget is my first major step in meeting that promise. It reflects, I believe, a determination to face and make difficult decisions in a manner that places the common good above that of any particular interest.

This budget represents a careful balancing of several considerations:

—The importance of a fiscal policy that provides for a continuing recovery of the nation's economy from the 1974-75 recession;

—The obligation of the government to meet the critical needs of the nation and its people;

—The fact that resources are limited and that government must discipline its choices and its scope; and

—The need for careful and prudent management of the taxpayers' resources.

My budget provides for total outlays of $500 billion, an increase of $38 billion, or 8 percent, over the 1978 target, and receipts of $440 billion. This budget total is a restrained one that:

—Meets essential national needs;

—Imposes strict priorities upon federal expanditures; and

—Decreases the share of the nation's gross national product taken by the federal government from 22.6 percent to 22.0 percent. This budget places us on a path that will permit a balanced budget in the future if the private economy continues its recovery over the coming years.

At the same time, my budget embodies a fiscal policy that will strengthen the economic recovery. I propose a progressive tax reduction of $25 billion to help assure continued economic recovery and reduction in unemployment. An integral part of this tax reduction proposal is a set of recommendations for tax reform that will make the tax system simpler and more equitable. Without the reduction, I would have been able to announce a decline in the deficit of $15 to $20 billion between 1978 and 1979. With the reduction, the budget deficit will still decline slightly, because of careful restraints on expenditures. But I judged that the most important priority this year was to reduce the burdens on taxpayers. Only in this way can we ensure a vigorous economy, a declining unemployment rate, a strong expansion of private investment, and a stable budget balance in future years.

While the expenditures I recommend in this budget are restrained, they are, nevertheless, directed toward overcoming our nation's crucial problems. I have looked carefully at existing approaches to these problems and improved those approaches where possible. The spending priorities of the past are now being shifted toward long-neglected areas. These new priorities are based on the following judgments:

[Energy Plan]

—An effective national energy plan is essential to reduce our increasingly critical dependence upon diminishing supplies of oil and gas, to encourage conservation of scarce energy resources, to stimulate conversion to more abundant fuels, and to reduce our large trade deficit.

The national energy plan I proposed last spring defined these goals. This budget includes the programs and initiatives designed to meet those objectives. Included are increased emphases on conservation and non-nuclear research and development, energy grants and technical assistance to states and localities, accelerated acquisition of the strategic petroleum reserve, and greater emphases on nuclear waste management. I continue in the unswerving belief that the nation's leaders have the obligation to plan for the future, and that the national energy plan is essential to the future health and vigor of the American economy. The United States also must take the lead in minimizing the risks of nuclear weapons proliferation as we advance nuclear power technology. Thus, this budget increases research and development funding for systems that present fewer risks than the plutonium-fueled liquid metal fast breeder reactor.

[Human Needs]

—The essential human needs of our citizens must be given high priority.

In the spring of 1977 I proposed a long-overdue reform of the nation's welfare system. This reform recognizes that this is a nation of men and women who do not wish to be wards of the government but who want to work and to be self-sufficient. It includes a combination of employment opportunities and incentives for those who should work, and a basic income for those who cannot. This budget anticipates that Congress will pass the program for better jobs and income, and begins the process of careful planning for the implementation of an efficient and equitable system.

The budget also recognizes that ensuring the opportunity to compete and excel remains very important to our people. To give all children the healthiest possible start in life, I propose major expansion of medical care and nutritional supplements for low-income expectant mothers and infants. In addition, I propose major increases in educational assistance at all levels. Because of the continued high level of unemployment, particularly among minorities, I believe public employment programs should be continued at high levels for another year. Major increases in programs stressing employment for unemployed youth are recommended. A new effort will be mounted to place more disadvantaged persons in private sector jobs by increasing the involvement of the business community in local employment and training programs.

I view a workable urban strategy as an important link in a well-articulated domestic program and essential to the continuing recovery of the national economy. This budget includes increases for many programs benefiting urban areas and supports several efforts to improve these programs. I anticipate sending to the Congress early in the spring a set of further proposals dealing with the nation's urban problems.

[Defense]

—The nation's armed forces must always stand sufficiently strong to deter aggression and to assure our security.

My request for defense provides for the steady modernization of our strategic forces, and for substantial improvements in the combat readiness of our tactical forces. To parallel commitments made by our European allies, I am proposing significant increases in our overall defense effort, with special emphasis on those forces and capabilities most directly related to our NATO commitments. The defense budget I recommend also emphasizes modernization and research and development to meet future challenges to our security. But at the same time, I am restraining defense expenditures by introducing important efficiencies and by placing careful priorities upon our defense needs. The 1979 defense budget is prudent and tight, but consists of a real growth in outlays of 3 percent above the current year's budget. Consistent with campaign pledges to the American people, it is $8 billion below the defense budget projected for 1979 by the previous administration.

[Environment]

—The Federal Government has an obligation to nurture and protect our environment — the common resource, birthright and sustenance of the American people.

This budget provides for substantially increased emphasis on protection of all our environmental resources, for new attention to our common heritage, and for substantial additions to our system of public lands. Planned use of our natural resources has been designed so that the most important of our unspoiled areas can remain forever in the hands of the people.

[Technology]

—The Federal Government must lead the way in investing in the nation's technological future.

Shortly after taking office, I determined that investment in basic research on the part of the federal government had fallen far too low over the past decade. Accordingly, I directed that a careful review be undertaken of appropriate basic research opportunities. As a result of that review, this budget proposes a real rate of growth of almost 5 percent for basic research in 1979. I believe this emphasis is important to the continued vitality of our economy.

[Government Operations]

—This budget also reflects this administration's commitment to two important approaches to making government work more efficiently and responsively: reorganization and zero-base budgeting.

The reorganization effort I have launched seeks more than just a streamlining of organization structure and the elimination of overlaps and duplication. It seeks to make our government more responsive, more efficient, and more clearly focused on the most pressing needs of our society. In 1977 I proposed — and the Congress accepted — a Cabinet-level Department of Energy, a streamlined Executive Office of the President, and a consolidation of our international information activities. In 1978 I will propose further reorganizations in such areas as the federal government's civil rights activities and the federal civil service system to make it more responsive and effective.

As I promised during my campaign, zero-base budgeting systems have been applied throughout the federal government. This budget is the product of a comprehensive zero-base review of all federal programs, both existing and new. In reviewing each agency's proposals, I have used zero-base budget alternatives and agency rankings to compare and evaluate the many requests competing for resources. As a result of the first year's effort, we have gained a better understanding of federal programs and have made better, more evenhanded judgments. Because of this system the budget includes dollar savings, and improvements in the way programs are operated. With experience, zero-based budgeting should be even more effective in future years.

Other significant changes in the budget process are reflected in this document. First: I have directed the Office of Management and Budget to establish a multi-year budget planning system using longer range budget projections. This will ensure that budget decisions are made with full awareness of their longer range implications. Second: We are using better techniques for estimating outlays so as to avoid the chronic "shortfalls" of recent years. Third: We have explicitly related the classification of the budget in terms of functions performed by government programs to the national needs and agency missions served, as called for in the Congressional Budget Act of 1974.

In formulating this budget I have been made acutely aware once more of the overwhelming number of demands upon the budget and of the finite nature of our resources. Public needs are critically important; but private needs are equally valid, and the only resources the government has are those it collects from the taxpayer. The competition for these resources and my belief and commitment that we must firmly limit what the government taxes and expends have led me to the premises on which my first budget is based.

—Critical national needs exist — particularly human and social ones — to which resources must be directed.

—Government resources are scarce; their use must be planned with the full awareness that they come from the earnings of workers and profits of business firms.

—The span of government is not infinite. Priorities must be set and some old priorities changed. If we are to meet adequately the most critical needs, some demands must also be deferred. Government action must be limited to those areas where its intervention is more likely to solve problems than to compound them.

—We have an obligation to manage with excellence, and to maintain proper priorities within the $500 billion proposed in this budget. We all know that in a budget of this scale — larger than the gross national product of all but three nations in the world — there are dollars wasted and dollars misspent. These must be minimal.

These premises are unexceptionable in general, but difficult and controversial to apply. They have guided my actions in formulating this budget and they will continue to do so in the future. But to be successful I will need, and will work for, the help and cooperation of the Congress. Both the Congress and the Executive have a clear, joint interest in an approach that helps us to meet the demands of the future. In recent years the Congress has taken important steps — through the establishment of the congressional budget process — to improve its own means of establishing priorities. This administration has worked closely with the congressional appropriations and budget committees and has found them invaluable sources of advice. We will continue in this spirit of cooperation, and I look forward to working with the Congress and its leadership to obtain adoption of my budget for fiscal year 1979.

Jimmy Carter.

January 20, 1978

February

CARTER ARMS SALES POLICY
February 1, November 29, 1978

Responding to growing concern over the burgeoning world arms traffic and following up on a campaign pledge, President Carter announced Feb. 1 that the administration would impose an $8.6 billion ceiling on sales of weapons to non-allied countries for the 1978 fiscal year, an 8 percent cut from fiscal 1977.

But the administration projected that overall foreign military sales would rise in 1978, despite the proposed reduction in sales to the largest category of clientele for U.S. arms — primarily Middle Eastern countries. Sales to allies — NATO countries, Australia, New Zealand and Japan — were excluded from the ceiling. Also exempted were certain types of transfers to the so-called "ceiling countries."

Later in the year, on Nov. 29, Carter said that the fiscal 1978 ceiling had been a success and would be lowered another 8 percent for fiscal 1979 — to $8.434 billion — after taking into account a projected inflation rate of 7.2 percent. But he indicated that the United States' unilateral effort to slow down world arms sales would be halted or relaxed unless other nations joined in showing restraint.

In announcing the initial reduction on Feb. 1, Carter said that "a larger cut in the ceiling would violate commitments already made, including our historic interest in the security of the Middle East. . . . A smaller reduction would neglect our responsibility to set an example of restraint that others might follow." The announcement immediately prompted criticism on Capitol Hill from supporters of arms sales restraints, who asserted that the president, in allowing total exports to rise, had abandoned his pledge to reduce the arms trade.

Administration officials responded that these critics misinterpreted the president's aims and ignored other elements of the policy, including the administration's commitment to slow the spread of advanced weapons into new regions and to cut out development of systems designed solely for export.

Controversy surrounding the administration's arms sales policy was further fanned by the Feb. 14 announcement of plans to sell $4.8 billion worth of jet warplanes to Egypt, Saudi Arabia and Israel. The decision, which ultimately was approved by Congress, was aimed at maintaining the existing military balance in the Middle East and at advancing the cause of peace in the region, the Carter administration said. (Mideast jet sales, p. 125)

Previous Statements

"We cannot be both the world's leading champion of peace and the world's leading supplier of weapons of war," said Carter on numerous occasions throughout his campaign for the presidency.

Soon after his election, Carter ordered a review of U.S. military sales practices. Outlining the new administration's arms sales policy May 19, 1977, Carter announced that "the United States will henceforth view arms transfers as an exceptional foreign policy implement.... The burden of persuasion will be on those who favor a particular arms sale rather than on those who oppose it."

But despite that statement by Carter, his administration in the ensuing four months submitted 45 sales proposals to Congress for a total cost of $4.1 billion. Included were more than $2 billion in sales to Iran and Saudi Arabia, which, along with Israel, accounted for more than half of U.S. exports. (South Korea, Australia and Jordan were the next largest purchasers.)

And according to figures released by the Pentagon Oct. 2, the United States sold a record $13.6 billion worth of military weapons and services to foreign nations in fiscal 1978, compared with $11.4 billion in fiscal 1977.

However, Carter said in his Nov. 29 statement that fiscal 1978 sales to the ceiling countries totaled $8.540 billion, well within the $8.551 billion ceiling. He said the ceiling would be cut another $733 million for fiscal 1979, measured in constant dollars. As for fiscal 1980, he said his decision would "depend on the degree of cooperation we receive in the coming year *from other nations, particularly in the area of specific achievements and evidence of concrete progress on arms transfer restraint."*

Issues Involved

The United States is responsible for about 50 percent of the world arms trade and the Soviet Union for a third, although some analysts believe the Soviet share is larger than it appears because all relevant data is not available. Britain and France each have about 5 percent of the world arms market.

Many observers have said that the fivefold increase in U.S. arms exports since 1970 was not simply the result of bureaucratic momentum or better salesmanship by the defense industry; rather, it reflected changing patterns of world power, particularly the new wealth of the oil-producing nations and the increasing reluctance of the United States to become involved in regional conflicts. Another major factor was the Nixon administration's heavy use of arms sales to help developing nations become self-sufficient.

Critics of arms sales pointed to the adverse economic implications. They argued that arms sales pushed up oil prices, which affected the economies of all nations. Middle East governments bought arms in part to protect their oil, the higher oil prices inflated the cost of the imported weapons, and oil-exporting countries boosted oil prices to cover added costs of the weapons.

The White House, the Defense Department and the State Department have offered several reasons for continued arms sales abroad. These can be summed up as an argument that weapons sales are an essential tool of U.S. foreign policy and a vital means of exercising U.S. influence overseas. A National Security Council study released in July 1977 predicted that a U.S. policy of reducing arms sales was not likely to diminish worldwide traffic in conventional weapons unless other countries could be persuaded to adopt similar restraints. But, "the prospect that other countries will voluntarily and spontaneously . . . [practice] restraint is unlikely," the report said.

Following are the texts of statements by President Carter, issued Feb. 1 and Nov. 29, 1978, announcing reductions in the ceiling on arms sales abroad:

Feb. 1 Statement

The United States Government, the Executive Branch and the Congress, are pledged to bring about a reduction in the trade in conventional arms.

Last year, I promised to begin reducing U.S. arms sales as a necessary first step. I will continue that policy this year.

In the last fiscal year, the previous Administration and my Administration made sales commitments totaling many billions of dollars. While high, however, the total was considerably less than it would have been in the absence of new restraints we introduced, particularly in sales commitments to the developing countries of the world. Between January 20 and the close of the fiscal year, I approved and sent to Congress arms sales totaling $5.7 billion, which is less than half the total approved during the same period in 1976.

Today, I am announcing that arms transfer agreements covered by the ceiling which I have established will be reduced by $740 million in Fiscal Year 1978. This means that for the fiscal year which began on October 1, 1977, and which will end on September 30, 1978, new commitments under the Foreign Military Sales and Military Assistance programs for weapons and weapons-related items to all countries except NATO, Japan, Australia and New Zealand will not exceed $8.6 billion. The comparable figure for Fiscal Year 1977 was $9.3 billion. This is a reduction of 8 percent, figured on constant Fiscal Year 1976 dollars.

A larger cut in the ceiling would violate commitments already made, including our historic interest in the security of the Middle East, and would ignore the continuing realities of world politics and risk the confidence and security of those nations with whom the United States has vital and shared foreign policy and security interests. A smaller reduction would neglect our responsibility to set an example of restraint that others might follow.

I intend to make further reductions in the next fiscal year. The extent of next year's reduction will depend upon the world political situation and upon the degree of cooperation and understanding of other nations.

I want to emphasize that the restraint policy I announced on May 19, 1977, was not aimed exclusively at the volume of arms transfers. Equally important is restraint in the sophistication of arms being transferred and on the spreading capability to produce armaments. Therefore, in addition to the ceiling, I established five specific controls applicable to all transfers except those to our NATO allies, Japan, Australia, and New Zealand. These controls included: (1) a control on the first introduction of certain advanced systems into an area; (2) a prohibition on advanced systems for export only; (3) a prohibition on various types of coproduction arrangements; (4) tighter controls on retransfer; and (5) special controls on sales promotions.

These guidelines are at the heart of my decisions to approve or disapprove an arms transfer.

As I stated in my October 4 speech to the United Nations, genuine progress in this area will require multilateral efforts. But, we are committed to taking the first steps alone to stop the spiral of increasing arms transfers. I call upon suppliers and recipients alike to join us in a determined effort to make the world a safer place in which to live.

Nov. 29 Statement

Conventional arms transfer restraint is an important objective of this Administration and the Congress. To insure U.S. leadership and to supplement existing legislation, I established for the first time a set of quantitative and qualitative standards by which arms transfer requests considered by this government would be judged. The principal consideration in the application of those standards is whether the transfer in question promotes our security and the security of our close friends.

I am pleased to announce that this government has kept its pledge to take the leadership in restraining arms sales. Under the ceiling I established, U.S. government transfers of weapons and related items to countries other than NATO, Japan, Australia and New Zealand, which totaled $8.54 billion in Fiscal 1978, were reduced by 8% (or approximately $700 million measured in constant dollars) from the comparable Fiscal 1977 level. When I set this goal last year, I said that I would make further reductions in the next fiscal year. Today, I am announcing an additional cut of approximately $733 million* or 8% for Fiscal 1979 measured in constant dollars. This means that for the fiscal year that began on Oct. 1, 1978, and which will end on Sept. 30, 1979, new commitments under the Foreign Military Sales (FMS) and Military Assistance (MAP) programs for weapons and weapons-related items to all countries except NATO, Japan, Australia, and New Zealand will not exceed $8.43 billion. This cut is consistent with our national security interests, including our historic interest in the security of the Middle East.

When I addressed the United Nations General Assembly in October 1977, I emphasized that the U.S. had taken the first steps at conventional arms restraint, but that we could not go very far alone. Multilateral cooperation remains essential to the achievement of meaningful restraint measures. We continue to believe that all nations have an interest in restraining transfers of conventional weaponry which threaten the stability of various regions of the world and divert recipient resources from other worthy objectives without necessarily enhancing national security. We are making a maximum effort to achieve multilateral cooperation on the arms restraint issue.

My decision on U.S. arms transfer levels for Fiscal 1980 depend on the degree of cooperation we receive in the coming year from other nations, particularly in the areas of specific achievements and evidence of concrete progress on arms transfer restraint.

---

*FY 1979 Ceiling on Conventional Arms Transfers *(in $ millions)*

Fiscal year 1978 ceiling..$8,551
Inflation (7.2 percent) ....+616

Fiscal year 1978 ceiling in fiscal year 1979 dollars 9,167
Policy reduction ....−733

Fiscal year 1979 ceiling 8,434

CARTER ON COAL STRIKE
February 11–March 25, 1978

A 109-day strike of the United Mine Workers (UMW) union against coal mine operators represented one of the most troublesome domestic issues faced by President Carter since his inauguration. Until mid-February the administration remained aloof from the negotiations. Government intervention, however, failed to produce a settlement and the president was finally compelled in March to invoke the practically unenforceable provisions of the Taft-Hartley Act. As the strike dragged on through the winter, fears rose that sections of the country, particularly the Midwest and East, would face drastic reductions of energy supplies as coal surpluses dwindled. Though some regions did suffer hardships because of a shortage of coal, an emergency reallocation of energy resources averted major problems. Conservation measures adopted by industrial energy users prevented mass layoffs of employees.

The 160,000 coal miners in the UMW, led by Arnold Miller, the union president, walked off their jobs Dec. 6, 1977, when their three-year contract expired. At the same time, the 10,000 mine construction workers represented by the UMW also went out on strike. Negotiations between the UMW and the mine operators, represented by the Bituminous Coal Operators Association (BCOA), were held up on several issues, the chief of which were the imposition of penalties for those who participated in wildcat strikes; the end of automatic cost-of-living pay increases; establishment of partial payment for medical care previously provided to the miners without charge; and the restructuring of the miners' pension system to guarantee equity of benefits for all retired miners. (The 1974 Pension Reform Act raised benefits for miners retiring after 1975 to levels above

111

those for miners who had retired before 1975.) While talks progressed between the miners and the BCOA, negotiations were underway between the striking construction workers and the Association of Bituminous Contractors, the bargaining unit for mine construction contractors. Agreement between these two groups was reached shortly after the end of the coal miners' strike.

First Contract

In early February, the UMW and BCOA negotiators, aided by mediators from the Federal Mediation and Conciliation Service, reached agreement on a pact that would have given the miners a 37 percent increase in wages and benefits over three years. The agreement, however, also provided for wildcat strike penalties, provisions on medical payments and other features sought by the mine operators. It did not contain provisions for equalizing the pension system.

Miller, the UMW president, presented the proposed contract to the union's bargaining council, a 37-member board (two more members were added after the first contract proposal) that must vote on all contracts before they can be presented to the rank-and-file membership for approval. The bargaining council Feb. 12 voted overwhelmingly against the negotiated contract. The rejection did little for Miller's falling esteem within the union.

Shortly before the rejection of the first contract, President Carter issued a statement outlining steps the administration was preparing to take to alleviate the effects of a prolonged strike. Carter emphasized that he continued to rely on collective bargaining to resolve the differences between the two sides but added that he had "instructed members of my Cabinet to accelerate planning and preparation for any contingencies that arise from continuation of the strike." Plans were being readied, Carter said, for the transfer of energy supplies to sections of the country running low on fuel, conservation measures in federal facilities, the possible relaxation of air pollution rules, and preserving the peace in mining regions.

Government Measures

After the bargaining council's rejection of the first contract, the BCOA negotiators showed little enthusiasm for returning to the talks with the union. It was at this point that the Carter administration officially intervened in the negotiating process. The president Feb. 14, again stressing his belief in the collective bargaining process, sent a plea to both sides to resume "serious negotiations" at the White House and the Department of Labor as a "final opportunity for this bargaining process to work." If the renewed negotiations failed, the president warned, ". . . then I will have no choice but to resort to stronger measures." Asked by a reporter if he would invoke the Taft-Hartley Act to force the miners back to work, the president responded, "That's one of the options available to me, yes."

Reacting to the administration pressure, industry representatives returned to the negotiations. Labor Secretary F. Ray Marshall participated in most of the negotiating sessions and was able to inform Carter Feb. 24 that agreement had been reached on a second contract.

In the interim between the first and second contracts the UMW had negotiated a separate contract with the Pittsburg and Midway Coal Co., an independent company that was not a member of the BCOA. The UMW subsequently proposed the Pittsburg contract as a model for negotiations, a move the BCOA initially rejected. But the industry later bowed to government pressure to reach an agreement and accepted a modified version of the Pittsburg contract. It included less severe language detailing penalties for wildcat strikers and a 37 percent increase in benefits and wages over three years. The agreement was reached Feb. 24 just a few hours after the administration announced that the president was prepared to take "drastic steps" to end the coal strike. It was widely reported in the press that the steps Carter contemplated included both the invoking of the Taft-Hartley Act and government seizure of the mines. In announcing the settlement, the president praised the efforts of the negotiators and the Labor Department mediators. He also talked directly to the striking miners, saying if they did not ratify the proposed contract, "time will have run out for all of us, and I will have to take the drastic and unsatisfactory legal action which I would have announced tonight."

Taft-Hartley

The rank and file of the UMW voted down the contract by a 2-1 margin over the weekend of March 3-5. The president March 6 invoked the Taft-Hartley Act despite the likelihood that it would be widely ignored by the miners as generally had been the case in the past. In his statement, Carter predicted that unless the strike ended, one million workers would be forced out of work within 30 days. He instructed the attorney general to prepare a back-to-work order and appointed a three-member board of inquiry. "These steps are absolutely necessary," he declared, "if our Nation is not to be the innocent victim of a total breakdown of the collective bargaining process."

The board of inquiry submitted its report to President Carter March 9. In it, the board reviewed the course of the negotiations, reported on the hearings it had conducted March 8 and concluded that "this dispute has reached a critical impasse." The government sought and received a temporary injunction March 9 from U.S. District Court Judge Aubrey E. Robinson Jr. that ordered that the mines be opened and that no one be allowed to interfere with miners wishing to return to work. Few miners chose to work and the administration, anxious to avoid potentially violent confrontations with the miners, did little to enforce the order. When government lawyers March 17 requested that the injunction be extended to its full, 80-day limit, Judge Robinson refused, arguing that the government had failed to prove the existence of a national emergency.

Although the Taft-Hartley injunction ordering the miners back to work was disregarded by a majority of strikers, it did provide a degree of added pressure on the union and the operators. Administration officials began to suggest company-by-company or regional settlements, actions that would have threatened the industry's united bargaining front and further weakened the UMW leadership. Faced with mounting pressure, the two sides, without direct government involvement, resumed negotiations March 10 and reached agreement on a pact March 14. The terms of the new settlement included: a 39 percent increase in wages and benefits over three years, an annual maximum charge of $200 for the formerly free medical care, an increase in monthly pension payments for pre-1974 retirees, the elimination of language referring to disciplinary procedures for wildcat strikers, company takeover of the health care system and some production bonuses.

The onset of warmer weather, the increased productivity of non-union mines (which produce about one-half of the nation's coal) and the financial burden carried by the miners for more than three months had lessened the impact of the strike. A majority of miners had ratified the pact by March 25. President Carter expressed his satisfaction at the end of the strike and said that the contract "upholds the important principle of industrywide bargaining between the coal operators and the UMW."

The settlement's potential impact on inflation provoked reactions from various sectors; Edison Electric Institute, an association of electric utilities, warned that electric rates would rise 5 to 6 percent. The Council on Wage and Price Stability estimated that the cost of steel production would rise 1 percent. And some administration officials feared that other unions would seek equally generous settlements when their contracts expired.

Following are President Carter's Feb. 11, Feb. 14, Feb. 24 and March 25, 1978, statements on the strike; excerpts from his Feb. 17, March 9 and March 17 news conferences; and his March 6 announcement of the invocation of the Taft-Hartley Act:

FEBRUARY 11 STATEMENT

In recent weeks I have been following closely developments in the coal strike. Earlier this week it appeared that the impasse might be over when the bargainers reached a tentative agreement on a new contract.

Recent events, however, have slowed and, perhaps, threatened ratification of that contract. At the same time, the situation in some areas of the country has become a matter of increasing concern.

Voluntary power cutbacks have become widespread in the east-central region, centering in Ohio, and several utilities have ordered mandatory cutbacks to industrial customers. More such cutbacks will follow even if the strike is settled soon, and employment impacts will be felt shortly.

In view of the uncertainties of the current situation, I have instructed members of my Cabinet to accelerate planning and preparation for any contingencies that may arise from continuation of the strike.

—I have asked the Secretary of Labor, working in close cooperation with the Federal Mediation and Conciliation Service, to continue efforts to facilitate the collective bargaining process.

—I have asked the Secretary of Energy (1) to identify and plan for possible movements of coal to points of critical shortage, and (2) to continue his efforts to ensure maximum possible electric power transfer into the affected region from other electric utility systems not affected by the coal strike.

—I have asked the Administrator of General Services to ensure that all Federal facilities in the affected region reduce their power consumption to minimum necessary levels, effective immediately.

—I have instructed the Administrator of the Environmental Protection Agency to provide expedited review of any requests for temporary relaxation of the Clean Air Act regulations that may be needed.

—I have instructed the Attorney General, working in close cooperation with the Governors of the affected States, to review and plan for any Federal measures that may be needed to ensure continued peace and lawfulness in the areas most affected by the strike.

—In addition, I have requested formation of a Federal/State task force, with headquarters in Canton, Ohio, to coordinate efforts to ensure that employment and human need consequences of power cutbacks are minimized, and that power brought into the affected region is shared equitably. This task force, to be composed of Governors, representatives of Federal agencies, State public utilities and industrial users, will be established immediately and will convene initial meetings within the next few days.

I continue to believe that the solution to the strike must be worked out in free collective bargaining by the parties. I hope that all those involved in the strike will abide by the law and act responsibly in all respects. I urge all parties to respect the principles of fairness and cooperation during the days ahead.

Those in areas most affected by the strike have already made great sacrifices. Before the strike is over, and for several weeks thereafter until the normal flow of coal is restored, even greater hardship will occur. I urge all those in areas threatened by power cutbacks to conserve energy, so that these sacrifices are shared equally and so that no one will suffer unfairly or unnecessarily.

FEBRUARY 14 STATEMENT

The present stalemate in the coal strike inflicts continuing and increasing hardships on this country and also on the miners, both active and retired. It cannot be allowed to continue.

I have just directed the Secretary of Labor to convey to negotiators for management and for the mineworkers my personal and most urgent request that serious negotiations be resumed immediately here in the White House.

I've also instructed the Secretary of Labor to participate personally in these negotiations and to give me a report, at least daily, on progress that is being made in resolving the present stalemate.

I continue to support the collective bargaining process. However, the welfare of this country must be my overriding concern. Renewed negotiations here in the White House must be viewed as a final opportunity for this bargaining process to work. If it does not, then I will have no choice but to resort to stronger measures.

While law enforcement is a primary responsibility of State and local governments, I've also asked the Attorney General to give me a complete assessment of the powers available to ensure protection of life and property in these extraordinary circumstances.

Reporter. Mr. President, would you invoke the Taft-Hartley Act if they failed to negotiate?

The President. That's one of the options available to me, yes.

FEBRUARY 17 NEWS CONFERENCE

The President. It's nice to be here in New England, in Rhode Island, and I'm very proud to have a press conference here for the Nation.

I've just talked to the Secretary of Labor about progress on the settlement of the coal strike. They are making good progress. No final agreement has been reached.

I've been in coal mines in Pennsylvania and other places to see the miners at work. I know that they are hard-working and patriotic Americans. They and the industry leaders both recognize that there is a tremendous responsibility on their shoulders because the future of the unions, the future of an effective collective bargaining process, the future of the coal industry, and the welfare of our Nation depends upon the success of these negotiations.

They've been bargaining now, steadily, since they began at the White House a day and a half ago. They continued in their discussions until 2 o'clock this morning, and then after that, management with the Secretary of Labor from 2:30 until 5 in the morning. And I've asked them to stay at the bargaining table until a final agreement is reached.

I have confidence that they will be successful because they and I want to avoid the necessity for me, as President, to take more serious action if the bargaining process is not effective. The whole Nation is looking to them with hope and with confidence. . . .

Q. Mr. President, without asking you to announce a deadline for a coal settlement, can you give us any clue as to the extent of your patience with the situation?

The President. Well, the country is suffering already from the consequences of the coal strike. I have asked the Secretary of Labor and I've asked the negotiators from the workers and from the coal operators to stay at the bargaining table in constant sessions until they reach an agreement. There has been some progress made to date.

As you know, there is a division within the labor union itself. But the bargaining council, which consists of 39 members, is being kept as close as possible to the negotiating team that represents labor. We hope that when an agreement is reached that this will be in such a form and with close enough consultations ahead of time that it will be presented immediately to the membership of the United Mine Workers for approval.

So, I think that all of us are determined. I've met personally at the White House with labor and management in the coal industry, and I can testify to you that they are sincere in wanting to reach an agreement.

Q. Would you be willing to see it going on for another week?

The President. No. I don't think we could afford another week of negotiations. I would hope that they could conclude their negotiations within the next few hours or a day or so. . . .

The President. Mr. Bradley [Ed Bradley] with CBS.

Q. Mr. President, back on the subject of the coal talks,...that deadline Secretary Marshall talked about yesterday — is [it] still in effect? If at the end of that period they have not reached an agreement, you can invoke the Taft-Hartley Act, but the miners have said they will not mine the coal and the Army can't. If you do invoke those provisions and they refuse to mine coal, what can you do, sir?

The President. That's all spelled out in the law. The miners, the coal operators, the Secretary of Labor, I, the Attorney General, the Governors all would like, if possible, to avoid an invocation of the Taft-Hartley law and to let the coal dispute, through collective bargaining, lead to a new and acceptable contract. So there's no rigid time limit.

If it's obvious to me that progress is being made, then my preference would be to keep the bargaining process going.

In the last 24 hours I have detected progress, and we have not yet been able to get a final settlement. Even after a settlement is reached at the Labor Department, even after the bargaining council, who represents the coal miners, approve the terms that have been derived with the negotiating team, it would still have to be submitted to the union members back home for their approval. So that would take 2, 3 weeks. And I think it would probably take an additional week or so before coal could start flowing to its destination after it has been mined.

So we still face a substantial delay. And I recognize that it's one of the most serious problems that I've faced as President. And I believe that the negotiators do, too. But I am not trying, and don't want to predict exactly what will happen in the future. And I don't want to set a rigid time limit on anyone. But I have had the urgency of this question imparted by me personally and constantly by the Secretary of Labor during negotiating times. . . .

Q. Mr. President, as you know, the coal strike has passed all records in length.

The President. Yes.

Q. Do you feel that the negotiators have really reached a point of being irresponsible in not reaching a settlement?

The President. No, I don't ascribe irresponsibility to the negotiators.

When the negotiations broke down, when the bargaining council refused to accept for presentation to the miners the first agreement, that's the point at which I decided to intercede.

I invited both sides to come to the White House, which they did, and the union expanded their negotiating team from six members to nine members to try to bring in some of those who did not agree with the first settlement, to more closely assure that if a new settlement was reached the miners would accept it. Now we are keeping the bargaining council in an adjacent room to the negotiators themselves, and there's a constant interrelationship of communications with them.

But I believe that all the negotiators and the bargaining council, on behalf of the union, are negotiating in good faith. . . .

FEBRUARY 24 STATEMENT

I've just talked on the telephone with the representatives of the Bituminous Coal Operators and also the United Mine Workers. And I'm glad to announce that the United Mine Workers and the coal operators have agreed to a negotiated settlement of their contract dispute.

This is the outcome toward which all of us have been working so hard, especially Secretary of Labor Ray Marshall. We've been devoted to this; it's one on which our country should feel both gratitude and pride. It was because we believed in the free process of collective bargaining that I have been so determined to give that process every chance to work. It has worked. And the settlement it has produced is better for everyone involved — for the mine workers, the mine owners, and the public — than would have been the drastic steps that I was prepared to take this evening if the negotiating process had failed.

Although a settlement has been reached, it will not be final until it is studied and democratically ratified by the members of the United Mine Workers. Before I close, I would like to speak directly to them.

The work you do in the mines is sometimes dangerous and always difficult. No one can visit a coal mine, even for a short time, as I have, without coming away with a vivid sense of respect and appreciation for the job you do. Yours is a historic struggle. Whenever there has been progress in the mines, whenever there have been improvements in pay or in safety conditions or in health conditions, it's been because you fought for it. Your dedication to justice in the mines has been matched only by your dedication to your country whenever it needed you, whether in war or in peacetime. The agreement that has been reached today is no different. You struggled for it, and it is a significant achievement.

The choice is now yours to make. But I hope that you will follow the lead of your bargaining council and ratify the negotiated settlement. This agreement serves the national interest, as well as your own interests and those of your families. If it is not approved without delay, time will have run out for all of us, and I will have to take the drastic and unsatisfactory legal action which I would have announced tonight.

The miners and the operators share with the public one overriding interest, which is to resolve the long-term problems of your industry.

I will now appoint a Presidential commission, which has already been discussed with you, to work with unions and management to find answers to the basic questions of health, safety, and stable productivity. In the meantime, I offer my congratulations and my sincere thanks to those who have made the collective bargaining process work.

Thank you very much.

INVOCATION OF TAFT-HARTLEY ACT

A majority of the United Mine Workers have now rejected the negotiated coal contract. I'm disappointed that this agreement was not approved. But I recognize that the United Mine Workers' system of collective bargaining requires approval by union members before a contract can take effect.

My policy has been to do everything possible to help the collective bargaining process produce a settlement. But this rejection by the United Mine Workers' collective bargaining is now at an impasse.

The coal strike is 3 months old. The country cannot afford to wait any longer.

Coal supplies have been reduced to a critical level throughout the Midwest. Tens of thousands of people are already out of work because factories have laid off workers to conserve fuel. Power curtailments have reached 50 percent in Indiana, 30 percent in West Virginia, and critical levels in other parts of the Midwest. One month from now, at least a million more Americans would be unemployed if the coal strike continued.

My responsibility is to protect the health and safety of the American public, and I intend to do so.

I've ordered the Attorney General, under the Taft-Hartley Act, to prepare for an injunction to require the miners to return to work and the mine owners to place the mines back into production.

I've appointed a Board of Inquiry and asked it to report back to me as soon as possible to begin the emergency dispute-settling procedure under the Taft-Hartley Act.

In addition, I've asked the Attorney General and the Governors of the affected States to make certain that the law is obeyed, that violence is prevented, and that lives and property are fully protected.

The Department of Energy will use, as necessary, its allocation powers to minimize the effects of fuel shortage on regions which are most dependent on coal by moving energy resources to places where they are most urgently needed. We will depend on the free and voluntary distribution of energy whenever possible.

I have not taken this action lightly. These steps are absolutely necessary if our Nation is not to be the innocent victim of a total breakdown of the collective bargaining process.

I expect that all parties affected by these actions will cooperate fully and abide completely by the law. Under a Taft-Hartley injunction, miners ordinarily are required by law to return to work under the existing contract, unless more acceptable terms can be negotiated nationwide between management and labor.

During recent negotiations, both mine workers and operators agreed on new wages to begin in 1978. When the Taft-Hartley injunction takes effect, we will seek to permit any company to offer this new wage settlement to those who return to work under the injunction.

The new 1978 wage package is a generous one which reflects the special conditions of coal mining. And I must say quite frankly that I do not support and would personally oppose any more liberal and inflationary wage settlement.

The best permanent solution to this dispute is a settlement reached through collective bargaining. While the Taft-Hartley injunction is in effect, I will take steps to see that all parties resume negotiations as rapidly as possible. Whenever negotiated coal contracts are ratified by the UMW membership, the Taft-Hartley injunction will be lifted.

The difficult and dangerous work of coal miners has helped America prosper and grow strong. For too many years in the past, the miners, their parents, and their grandparents paid an unfair and bitter price for working in the mines. They often did not have the safety protection they needed. And they did not receive compensation for black lung disease and other hazards that they encounter daily.

More improvements are still needed in these working conditions for miners. But we have made important progress. I recently signed legislation, passed by Congress, that will significantly improve both black lung benefits and the enforcement of Federal health and safety standards in the coal mines.

As Americans, we all share the responsibility for preserving the health and safety of our country, which is now in danger. The labor laws of our country, of the United States, have been written to protect our Nation and at the same time to protect the rights of workers.

In times of crisis, the law binds us together. It allows us to make decisions openly and peacefully, and it gives us, through the courts and legal procedures, means to resolve disputes fairly. Respect for the rule of law ensures the strength of our Nation. The law will be enforced.

As President, I call on the mine workers, the coal mine operators, and all Americans to join in a common effort under the law to protect our country, to preserve the health and safety of our people, and to resolve fairly the differences which have already caused so much suffering and division in our land.

Thank you very much.

MARCH 9 NEWS CONFERENCE

The President. Good afternoon. . . .

Three days ago, I appointed a Board of Inquiry whose purpose under the Taft-Hartley Act was to investigate the negotiating stalemate, and we know that this has closed our Nation's coal mines.

This morning, the Board presented its report to me. Its finding was that an impasse does exist and that the situation is serious. This morning, using the authority of the Taft-Hartley Act, I directed the Attorney General to seek this afternoon a court injunction which will order the miners to return to work and the operators to open the mines during the 80-day cooling off period, during which time negotiations will proceed.

The welfare of our Nation requires this difficult step, and I expect that all parties will obey the law. The Federal Government will use its resources to minimize the national economic and social dislocations caused by this labor dispute.

The Department of Energy and the State Governors will improve the distribution of energy resources by moving our supplies of coal to places where the need is most urgent. The relief agencies of the Federal Government are prepared, if necessary, to act in a coordinated fashion to assist local areas which are particularly hard hit.

This is a time for cooling off. We will do everything in our power to be sure that it does not become a time of confrontation. The law must be enforced.

I have met this afternoon with the Attorney General and have asked him to assume personal direction of Federal law enforcement activities in this area.

The Secretary of Labor just informed me that he has asked the Board of Inquiry, as an extension of their duties, to go into the coal mining areas and consult with the miners, to encourage compliance with the law and to return to the negotiating area.

There is no easy solution to this problem. What is required from all of us now is reason, patience, and a willingness to cooperate with one another and to obey the laws of the United States.

I'm confident that with the support of the miners and the coal owners, the mine operators, and the American people, and all public officials, that we can resolve this dispute without further damage to the well-being of our Nation. . . .

Q. Mr. President, there seem to be conflicting signals on what you would do if miners do not return to work. Would you consider seeking legislation to seize the mines, or do you have any other alternatives?

The President. My firm belief and my firm commitment is that the Taft-Hartley Act will be enforced, that this will be adequate to assure supplies of coal to our country to avoid an additional crisis, and that it will also be an adequate incentive to bring the bargaining parties back to the negotiating table for successful resolution.

I have absolutely no plans to seek congressional action authorizing seizure of the coal mines. . . .

Q. Mr. President, do you agree with the position of the coal operators as stated in the latest contract on both the issues of the right to strike and pension benefits? And can you explain why or why not?

The President. Well, I would rather not single out any particular aspect of the contract for my approbation or rejection. There are issues of that kind that have been in deep contention. The coal operators want to eliminate the possibility of wildcat strikes and to increase production. The coal miners want the security of their retirement funds, and they want to have continuation of health benefits without contributing to the fund out of their salaries. Those have been the major items in contention. And I don't want to comment on the degree of my approval of them.

One item on which there has been general and early agreement is the wage package, and this, I think, would be a basis for a resolution of the differences. But I don't want to comment as a President on my approval or disapproval of individual items.

Q. One followup: Do you think the miners should have gone along with the contract as it was last submitted?

The President. Well, I was hoping that they would. As you know, there have been two contracts negotiated between the mine leaders and the coal operators. One was rejected by the bargaining council. The other contract was approved by the bargaining council — 39 members, ostensibly representing all the miners throughout the country — and rejected by the membership.

But I was hoping that those contracts would be accepted. I've never gotten involved in saying that a particular provision should be in or out of the contract, but one that's freely negotiated. I was obviously hoping that it would be approved. . . .

Q. Mr. President, what are your plans if the coal miners refuse to obey Taft-Hartley and return to work? What do you do then?

The President. Well, the injunction, if it is granted — and the hearing for a temporary restraining order is commencing now, about 3:30 — it's a far-reaching injunction. It prevents the interference of any law violators with those who want to go back to work. It prevents a picketing against those who are complying with the law and mining coal. It requires the coal mine owners and the mine workers to recommence negotiation efforts. It prevents the interference with the transportation of coal in any form, and it provides a legal mechanism by which the Federal law enforcement officials and the State and local law enforcement officials can provide for the protection of lives and property.

I believe the coal miners to be law-abiding and patriotic citizens. And I believe that a substantial portion of them, an adequate proportion of them, will comply with the law. We also have modified the historic provisions of the Taft-Hartley law by encouraging the operators and the mine workers to negotiate during this period regional settlements based on the wage package which was in general agreement from the very beginning weeks of the negotiations themselves. So, I believe that the law will be obeyed.

I might say one other thing. We've got about, I think, 82 percent of the mine workers who are not now working. We are still producing about 50 percent as much coal, and the reserve supplies of coal are down below, December 5, only about 45 percent. So, I believe that if we can get a moderate number — hopefully all, but a moderate number — of coal miners to go back to work, that we can prevent a crisis evolving in our country.

The distribution of existing energy supplies — electricity, oil, natural gas, and coal — will also help to alleviate the problem. The injunction has broad coverage, and I think the sum total of all I've described will be adequate. . . .

MARCH 17 NEWS CONFERENCE

The President. I've just got a few minutes, and I thought I'd take a few questions from the local press. . . .

Q. Mr. President, now that it is apparent that the Taft-Hartley Act isn't working, what are your options?

The President. Well, the Taft-Hartley Act is working. There's nothing in the Taft-Hartley Act that compels an individual miner to go into a mine and produce coal. But we have seen a rapid increase in coal production in recent days. We have no interruptions now with the nonunion miners producing coal. They were interrupted before.

We have an increase every day in the number of union miners who are going back into the mines. There's been no disruption recently, since the Taft-Hartley injunction, in the transfer of coal from one place to another when it is needed. And we are continuing to produce a substantial amount of coal additionally each day.

So, although the miners have not yet gone back to work, the Taft-Hartley Act is working. It's also brought to the bargaining table, without Federal mediators, which is good, the representatives of the operators and the miners. And they'd [sic] now worked out a third contract, which we hope will be accepted. So the Taft-Hartley Act is working. . . .

MARCH 25 STATEMENT

I am pleased that the members of the United Mine Workers have voted to approve the latest coal contract. Miners will now be returning to work early next week, and full coal production will resume shortly.

From the outset, we have known that the only satisfactory conclusion to this strike would be a collectively bargained agreement, acceptable to both sides. Over the past 6 weeks, our efforts have been directed toward that end.

With Friday's vote, we have achieved that goal. This Nation has endured a long strike without widespread unemployment or drastic reductions in electric power. Despite many predictions to the contrary, there has been no serious violence.

The contract which was approved on Friday upholds the important principle of industrywide bargaining between the coal operators and the UMW.

The Governors of the States most affected by the strike have displayed great leadership and cooperation in dealing with its consequences.

I particularly wish to thank the people of the affected regions. Through their conservation efforts, coal demand was reduced and far worse coal shortages averted.

The work of three Federal departments also greatly aided the resolution of this problem. The Department of Labor and the Federal Mediation and Conciliation Service were even handed as they facilitated collective bargaining, and the Department of Energy showed great ingenuity and organization as it coordinated the movement of coal to the areas which needed it most.

However, the Government's interest in the coal industry does not end with this contract agreement. I will soon appoint a Presidential Commission on the Coal Industry, a panel which will address the industry's long-term problems.

Friday's agreement, coupled with the work of this Commission, will enable the coal industry to take its rightful place as one of the foundations of our long-term energy strategy.

MIDEAST WARPLANE SALES
February 14;   May 12, 15, 18, 1978

The Senate on May 15 sustained a key element in the Carter administration's policy toward the Middle East by refusing to block a controversial plan to sell highly sophisticated jet fighter planes to Saudi Arabia. President Carter had proposed the sale of the fighters to Saudi Arabia as part of a "package deal" which also included the sale of warplanes to Egypt and Israel. Moreover, he had vowed to cancel the sale of planes to Israel if Congress prohibited the sales to Saudi Arabia and Egypt. Under arms sales law, contracts went into effect automatically unless they were disapproved by a majority in both chambers of Congress within 30 days.

The Senate's 44-54 decision to turn down a resolution blocking the sales was preceded by 10 hours of emotional debate on the Senate floor and two months of intense lobbying. The vote marked a bitter first defeat in Congress for Israel and for U.S. Jewish organizations which had fought the weapons package.

The sale was first proposed in a Feb. 14 statement by Secretary of State Cyrus R. Vance in which Vance outlined the administration's justification for selling warplanes to adversaries in the Middle East.

Sale Terms

The terms of the sale as announced by Vance were 15 F-15s and 75 F-16s for Israel, 50 F-5Es for Egypt and 60 F-15s for Saudi Arabia. Anticipating criticism from supporters of Israel, Vance declared, "Our commitment to

125

Israel's security has been and remains firm." However, he said that "Egypt, too, must have reasonable assurance of its ability to defend itself if it is to continue the peace negotiations with confidence." Vance said that Egypt had lost its "major source of military equipment" when the government ended its friendship with the Soviets in 1976 and, consequently, "we have a basic interest in responding to Egypt's legitimate needs." Concerning the sale to Saudi Arabia of F-15s, the most sophisticated of all the planes in the package, the secretary said the Saudis were "of immense importance in promoting a course of moderation" in the Middle East. He also noted that the Saudis had vast influence over "petroleum and financial policy." The Saudi government, he added, "has a legitimate requirement to modernize its very limited air defenses."

Formal notification of the proposed sales was not sent to Congress until April 28 to allow the Senate time to conclude debate on the Panama Canal treaties. (See p. 177) In the interim, opponents of the sale geared up their lobbying efforts and the president faced frequent questions on the merits of the sales. Little opposition was raised to the sale of jets to Egypt because the F-5Es were almost entirely defensive craft with a limited range; the major issue was the sale of F-15s to Saudi Arabia. The planes, considered to be the world's finest fighters, had a fairly extensive range and could be equipped for bomber missions. Carter and other administration spokesmen emphasized that the Saudis intended to use the planes only for national defense, especially against their radical neighbors in Iraq and South Yemen. In one of several moves to deflate criticism, the administration sought and received assurances from Saudi Arabia that it would not base the F-15s at the airfield at Tabuk, 250 miles from Jerusalem.

Lobbying

Pro-Israeli lobbyists contended that the sales not only would imperil Israel's national security but also would mark the end of the "special relationship" the country enjoyed with the United States. Opponents of the sales also circulated reports, later vehemently denied by the administration, that White House aides viewed the issue as an opportunity to "break" the so-called Israeli lobby, traditionally one of the strongest and most influential in Washington.

Discussion of the sales continued through April and May. Secretary of Defense Harold Brown defended the sales at a Senate Foreign Relations Committee hearing, saying, "I believe it is fair to say that Saudi Arabia can be expected only to use these aircraft in defense of its territory." Persistent criticism of the proposed sales forced the administration to offer a compromise on May 11 that would allow Israel to purchase an additional 20 F-15s in 1983-84. The compromise appeared to help assure Senate approval of the sales to the three Middle East countries.

The administration had hoped to avoid full Senate consideration of the sales by a majority vote against a resolution of disapproval in the Foreign

Relations Committee. The committee on May 11, however, deadlocked on the issue 8-8 and, in an unusual move, decided to send the resolution to disallow the sales to the Senate floor without recommendation.

President Carter May 12 sent every member of the Senate a letter urging approval of the sales package. "The choice," the president wrote, "is stark and fundamental. Shall we support and give confidence to those in the Middle East who work for moderation and peace? Or shall we turn them aside, shattering their confidence in us and serving the cause of radicalism?" Rejection of the airplane sales, he said, would breach the trust Egyptian President Anwar el-Sadat had placed in the United States and would cause the administration to lose an opportunity to "enhance its relationship with the Saudis as they take these vital steps to defend themselves against their radical neighbors armed by the Soviet Union."

The Senate refused to block the sales after a lengthy debate May 15. Opponents warned that the sale would create an imbalance of military power in the region. Sen. Jacob Javits, R-N.Y., said, "What do we want to do with the Israelis? Sap their vitality? Sap their morale? Cut the legs out from under them? That's what this is all about." Added Sen. Clifford P. Case, R-N.J., "Will we risk destroying Israel by gradually eroding our support?"

Commitment to Israel

Immediately following the vote, administration officials, including the president, began a series of actions designed to lessen its negative political impact. Phone calls to Jewish leaders and to senators who had opposed the sales stressed the administration's continuing commitment to Israel's security. In a statement released after the Senate vote, Carter stressed that the "action reaffirms our historic and unshakable commitment to the security of Israel — a commitment which will continue to have the unwavering support of this administration and the American people." Carter added that the vote also "strengthens our ties with moderate Arab nations who share our goal of peace and stability" in the Middle East.

The administration's efforts to reassure Israel of a continuing U.S. commitment were capped May 18 when Vice President Walter F. Mondale addressed the annual meeting of the American Jewish Committee in New York. Admitting the probability of disagreement on the several issues to be resolved in the Middle East, Mondale said, however, that "there is no room in such a dialogue for an atmosphere which is poisoned by recriminations — by the questioning of one another's good faith. And," he added, "we will never reach the goal [of peace] if every step demands new proof — not of the rightness of our cause or the rationality of our judgment — but rather of the purity of our intentions."

"No one issue," the vice president declared, would "ever deflect the strength" of the U.S. commitment to Israel. "So long as America believes in its own professed ideals there will always be a special relationship between

the United States and Israel." The United States would continue to fulfill its commitment, he said, "because the strength and prosperity of Israel — and all that it represents — are a fundamental reflection of our deepest principles.... And we would never forsake that commitment — not for the trappings of office — not for a hundred planes — and not for thousands of barrels of oil."

Following are Secretary of State Vance's Feb. 14 statement; the texts of President Carter's May 12 letter to the members of the Senate and his May 15 statement following Senate approval of the warplane sales; and excerpts from Vice President Mondale's May 18 speech to the American Jewish Committee:

VANCE STATEMENT

Consistent with our policy that arms transfers will be used to promote our national security and that of our close friends, I have recommended to the President and he has approved sales of certain aircraft to Israel, Egypt and Saudi Arabia, subject to the usual Congressional review. Next week we will begin the official process of informing and consulting with the Congress. The formal notifications will not be submitted until after the Easter recess in order to give Congress an opportunity to review fully the proposed sales. These sales will be undertaken over a period of several years. Deciding to make the sales was a very complex decision, and I want to share our views on this matter with the American people.

Any new aircraft sales to this region must be seen in the context of both the negotiating process and our objective of a peace settlement. We have considered carefully this aspect of the matter and concluded that our interests in Middle East peace and security will be best served if we go forward with some part of the aircraft sales requested by these countries.

Our commitment to Israel's security has been and remains firm. Israel must have full confidence in its ability to assure its own defense. In particular, this means Israel must be able to plan for the continued modernization of its air force. The President's decision gives particular emphasis to these points.

Egypt, too, must have reasonable assurance of its ability to defend itself if it is to continue the peace negotiations with confidence. When President Sadat made his decision several years ago to follow a course in foreign affairs that involved a change in his country's relations with the Soviet Union, he lost his major source of military equipment. This was particularly the case in Egyptian defensive aircraft capability. We believe we have a basic interest in responding to Egypt's legitimate needs.

Saudi Arabia is of immense importance in promoting a course of moderation in the Middle East—with respect to peacemaking and other regional initiatives—and more broadly in world affairs, as in petroleum and financial policy. The Saudi Government has a legitimate requirement to modernize its very limited air defenses. For several years, we and they have recognized the need to modernize their air force with an advanced interceptor. They have asked for a limited number of F-15s, the first of which would not be delivered for several years. We believe their request is reasonable and in our interest to fulfill.

We have concluded, therefore, that the sales of these aircraft to the countries in question will help to meet their legitimate security requirements, will not alter the basic military balance in the region, and will be consistent with the overriding objective of a just and lasting peace.

Accordingly, the Administration plans to notify Congress of our intent to make the following sales:

- For Israel, 15 F-15s, in addition to the 25 previously sold, and 75 F-16s.
- For Egypt, 50 F-5s.
- For Saudi Arabia, 60 F-15s.

We will be signing contracts for these aircraft over the next several years. These sales will be consistent with the President's global arms transfer policy and will be within the dollar volume ceiling that he has established. The details will be reported to Congress when the statutory notifications are provided.

All of these sales are directly supportive of our overall objectives in the Middle East. Members of the Administration will be testifying before a number of Congressional committees in support of this package so that Congress will have full opportunity to make its judgment during the period of its review.

CARTER LETTER

Letter to Members of Congress.   *May 12, 1978*

The motion in the Senate next Monday to block all of the proposed aircraft sales to Israel, Egypt, and Saudi Arabia presents a vital test of our national purpose. In the hours before the Senate votes, it is my duty as President to draw attention to the powerful reasons supporting each of the sales and the dire consequences of rejecting them.

Our basic goal is to secure peace, stability, and harmonious relations among the nations of the Middle East. Since becoming President, I and my chief foreign policy advisers have spent more of our time and effort on this subject than any other foreign policy issue.

The number of aircraft proposed for each of the countries has been carefully considered to insure a regional balance, but the decision before the Senate transcends the particular transactions.

The choice is stark and fundamental. Shall we support and give confidence to those in the Middle East who work for moderation and peace? Or shall we turn them aside, shattering their confidence in us and serving the cause of radicalism?

It is my considered judgment that the aircraft sales to Egypt are essential to enable President Sadat to continue his efforts for peace. At great personal and political risk, President Sadat has taken an initiative which has created the best prospects for peace in the Middle East in three decades. With similar risks, he has turned away from a relationship with the Soviet Union and placed his trust in the United States.

To reject the proposed aircraft sale to Egypt would be a breach of that trust. Such a rejection would be a devastating blow to President Sadat, to the military forces of Egypt, to the people of Egypt, and to the forces of moderation in the Middle East.

Saudi Arabia has become a firm friend of the United States. As its influence dramatically expands in the world, Saudi Arabia has been not only a firm supporter of the peace process but a moderating and conciliatory force on a wide range of global issues.

It is beyond challenge that the Saudi air defense system must be modernized and augmented. The United States has an opportunity through these proposed sales to enhance its relationship with the Saudis as they take these vital steps to defend themselves against their radical neighbors armed by the Soviet Union. But I must tell you with great gravity that it is an opportunity that we will quickly lose if we do not grasp it immediately.

If the Saudis are forced to turn elsewhere to meet their defense needs, it will unquestionably impair the peace process. Moreover, the erosion of confidence will inevitably have a far broader — and adverse — impact on the wide range of issues on which we have been working in close harmony.

The aircraft sales to Israel are a reflection of our strong and unshakeable commitment to the security of Israel. The American people fully understand that our commitment to Israel's survival and security is total, unequivocal, and firmly fixed in our national policy.

The long-term interests of Israel are served by the proposed sales to Egypt and Saudi Arabia. It is in Israel's interest to encourage the forces of moderation in the Middle East, and to promote their close relationship with the United States. It would not serve Israel's interest if we were to fail to keep bi-partisan commitments, made by the prior Administration as well as by mine, to provide aircraft for the defense of Saudi Arabia. It would be against Israel's interest if moderate nations are brushed aside by the United States, opening vast possibilities for the intrusion of hostile influences.

In the end, the national interest of the United States is the issue. On the basis of the most careful and serious analysis of all factors, I am convinced that the proposed sales will enhance U.S. national objectives, contribute to our national security, and promote peace in the Middle East.

JIMMY CARTER

CARTER STATEMENT

I am deeply gratified by the Senate's decision today which will permit the proposed arms sales to Israel, Egypt, and Saudi Arabia. That action reaffirms our historic and unshakable commitment to the security of Israel — a commitment which will continue to have the unwavering support of this administration and the American people.

At the same time, the Senate vote strengthens our ties with moderate Arab nations who share our goal of peace and stability in the region. We also honor bipartisan pledges made by the previous administration as well as my own to help our friends in the Middle East meet their legitimate needs for self-defense.

The approval of these sales will not violate the arms limitation policy of this administration, which I announced last May. That pledge to limit arms sales will be met. If and when other nations are willing to join with us in mutual restraint on the sale of conventional weapons, even greater reductions will be possible.

In the meantime, the Senate's action makes it clear that the United States stands ready to provide needed assistance when unrestrained arms sales by other nations pose a threat to the security of our friends and allies.

With this issue resolved, the sharp debate over the proposed sales can now be put behind us. That debate has been among friends who share the same goals. All of us can now concentrate our full attention on finding a sound and just basis for permanent peace.

The United States will continue to play a responsible and active role in the search for peace in the Middle East. We will intensify our effort to help the parties narrow their differences. Our own national interest and moral values permit us to do no less.

MONDALE SPEECH

...There is in this distinguished gathering an unmistakable message: That the great principles and objectives of the American Jewish Committee are alive and well in New York City.

And I come here this evening to assure you that they are also very much alive and well in Washington. I'd accepted this invitation to speak at this banquet some weeks ago. Since that time, developments have occurred which I know have hurt many of you in this room. And I'm very pleased that I have this chance to be with you this evening, to speak to you from the heart, and as honestly and frankly as I can, about the hopes and the objectives of your Administration in Washington, which I think are shared by the people of this country.

The last few days have been very difficult for all of us who care deeply about the future of Israel — and the prospect for peace in the Middle East. Some of us have found ourselves on different sides of that question for the first time in our history. And that division has been painful....

We meet tonight at a time of celebration — of the birth of Israel thirty years ago. And we do so in the context of very difficult negotiation — on the tangible attributes of peace in the Middle East. Sometimes the larger purpose gets clouded by the issues of the moment. And at a time of celebration

— a time of hope and memory — it serves us well to remember what that purpose is.

There's an old saying that change is not made in the midst of despair. Rather it is born out of the rising crest of growing expectations. If the chances for peace were slight tonight, there would be no occasion for disagreement. If the future promised only more conflict and more destruction, we might all unite in the solace of our despondency.

But these are not such times. These are times when peace *might* become a reality. The barriers are unmistakable — the course ahead uncertain. But still in many ways the prize is closer now than it has ever been before. And it stares at us not from notebooks filled with sterile formulas — but from the hard reality of face-to-face negotiations. It beckons us not in the glaring light of ideology — but in the hazier shadows of compromise. It invites us to accede as well as demand — to give as well as take — because the prize is so precious — and its attainment so tangibly promising.

In such a context there will inevitably be disagreement. And there should be. There should be active, forceful, intelligent debate. But there is no room in such a dialogue for an atmosphere which is poisoned by recriminations — by the questioning of one another's good faith. And we will never reach the goal if every step demands new proof — not of the rightness of our cause or the rationality of our judgment — but rather of the purity of our intentions....

...At times the air is filled with voices which question the motives of Americans who care enough about their own country to champion the cause of another. They fail to recognize that a deep and abiding love for Israel reflects a still broader commitment — to the basic democratic principles we cherish most at home. In a thousand different forums — in a thousand different ways — that commitment has helped to shape the domestic priorities of this nation. No one issue — and no single loss on a single question — will ever deflect the strength of that commitment.

Almost three decades ago, a President of this organization, one of its most distinguished — Jacob Blaustein — wrote to David Ben-Gurion as follows: "To American Jews, America is home. There exist their thriving roots; there is the country which they have helped to build; and there they will always share its fruits and its destiny." The most eloquent proof of that conviction — and the most forceful rebuttal to any contrary slander — has always been the integrity and the patriotism of the Jewish people themselves.

And by the same token, it is equally slanderous for any person — or nation — to mistake a temporal disagreement over a discrete question — with a fundamental disagreement over a common goal. In 1971, this Committee sponsored a seminar in Washington — on the need for fairness and perspective in public discourse. And the basic assumption of that dialogue was that friendship comes easy when the issues are simple and the answers clear. But the true test comes with the hard questions, and the complex solutions, and the differences which must surround the fine lines of judgment. The true measure of friendship is the freedom to express those differences. And that is a lesson for our time as well....

The arms sales question was not an easy one — especially in the atmosphere with which it was charged. It yielded no clear choices or obvious wisdom. It invoked in microcosm all the intricate complexities surrounding the Middle East.

In the face of those complexities, we made a difficult choice. It was a choice of policy — a choice on the merits — a choice which reflected the considered belief in the rightness of our course.

We believe it is necessary to work with the moderate forces in the Arab world if a peaceful and stable Middle East is to evolve. We believe that our support for Egypt and Saudi Arabia will help promote that objective — *without* threatening the security of Israel. And we believe that these actions are taken in the best interests of peace.

We may differ in that judgment, and freely express our disagreement. The recent debate in the Senate was useful and constructive. It helped to clarify our policy in some important respects. But we must not cloud the issue with questions of sincerity or good faith. They can only deflect our purpose and degrade our course.

Let no one doubt this nation's commitment to the strength and survival of Israel. It was forged in thirty years of partnership under seven American Presidents. It is a *special* partnership. I've heard some people say it is no longer a special relationship. So long as America believes in its own professed ideals, there will *always* be a special relationship between the United States and Israel....

Throughout Israel's history, we have given tangible meaning to this special relationship — in the form of substantial support. In the last four years alone, the United States has allocated $10 billion in military and economic assistance to Israel — more than any nation in the world.

The proportions of the figures are staggering. Of all American security assistance proposed in next year's budget, 42% of our supporting assistance — 48% of our military sales credits — and 56% of our military grants — are distributed to a single nation — the nation of Israel. And repayment on half of those credits — totalling a billion dollars — is systematically waived by the United States.

That support is not given grudgingly. It has been asked by the President of the United States and by this Administration. It has been adopted by this Congress, because it is the belief of the American people that that kind of support is warranted and deserved and needed by the State of Israel.

And that military assistance to that country will continue regardless of any negotiating differences. It will continue not as a lever to force accommodation, but as a fundamental commitment to the strength and survival of a free democracy.... It reflects a special relationship — which will always remain special....

And in an age of great sophistication — when every politician's statement is qualified by a dozen conditions — we cannot doubt the sincerity of a President who speaks of a "total" and "absolute commitment" to Israel — not for another thirty years, but "forever." I've served in the White House for sixteen months. And there is no question in my mind that President Carter will fulfill the letter and the spirit of that promise.

We intend to fulfill our historic commitment — and not only in memory of a tragic history or in partnership with a strong ally. We intend to fulfill it because the strength and prosperity of Israel — and all that it represents — are a fundamental reflection of our deepest principles.

For seventy years, the American Jewish Committee has helped to move this nation toward the fulfillment of those principles. I've been proud to stand with you. I've fought for the strength and the survival of Israel all my life. And we would never forsake that commitment — not for the trappings of office — not for a hundred planes — and not for thousands of barrels of oil....

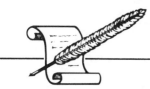

March

CIVIL SERVICE REFORM
March 2; May 23, 1978

President Carter signed into law Oct. 13 a modified version of his blueprint for reforming the civil service system. Although Congress extensively reworked Carter's plan, the final bill still contained all but one of the basic changes he had proposed for injecting merit into the civil service pay systems and giving federal managers more flexibility to fire incompetent employees. It was the most extensive revamping of the federal employment system since the civil service system was established in 1883.

Enactment was a significant victory for Carter, who in his election campaign and after taking office had strongly urged governmental reorganization. In a March 2 message to Congress spelling out his proposals, Carter said the civil service system "has become a bureaucratic maze which neglects merit, tolerates poor performance, permits abuse of legitimate employee rights and mires every personnel action in red tape, delay and confusion.

"Civil service reform will be the centerpiece of governmental reorganization during my term in office."

The bill had been in danger several times in the seven months the House and Senate spent working on it. The administration and congressional backers fought off filibuster threats, vehement opposition from federal employees' unions and other perils that seemed to pop up every time it appeared the bill had clear sailing. When the measure did reach the floor, the support in both chambers was overwhelming, passing the Senate Aug. 24 by an 87-1 vote and the House Sept. 13 by a 385-10 vote. The final version approved by House and Senate conferees cleared easily Oct. 6.

The bill contained Carter's plan for a Senior Executive Service (SES) of top federal employees, a merit pay system for middle-level management, increased management flexibility in firing incompetent workers and statutory labor rights for federal employees. It did not contain Carter's proposals for curtailing veterans' preference in federal hiring.

Background

In 1880 Chicago lawyer Charles Julius Guiteau went to Washington to seek a political patronage job as an American consul in France. When the unhappy Guiteau didn't get the job, he took drastic action. He shot and killed President James A. Garfield.

In shocked response, Congress finally heeded the arguments of a growing reform movement that advocated selecting federal employees on the basis of merit instead of political connections. The Pendleton Civil Service Act, passed in 1883, ended the era of the spoils system and replaced it with a merit system for choosing government workers. The act set up a bipartisan Civil Service Commission to help federal agencies fill jobs by open, competitive examination.

Nearly a century later, President Carter charged there was not enough merit in the merit system. He proposed to abolish the Civil Service Commission, contending that over the years the commission had "assumed additional and inherently conflicting responsibilities.... It is a manager, rulemaker, prosecutor and judge. Consequently, none of these jobs are being done as effectively as they should be."

The president's package of civil service change had been developed from a study by a team of 110 civil servants and business and academic representatives. The Personnel Management Project's year-long study resulted in a two-part administration proposal, Carter's Reorganization Plan No. 2 of 1978. The first part, submitted March 2, outlined legislation needed to implement the plan. The second part, sent to Congress May 23, automatically took effect Aug. 11 under the president's reorganization authority, after Congress passed up its opportunity to block the plan within 60 days.

What It Does

As signed into law, the reorganization plan contained these major features:

● New Agencies
Two new agencies were created to replace the Civil Service Commission — the Office of Personnel Management (OPM), which took over personnel management functions, and the Merit Systems Protection Board (MSPB), the new board of appeals for employee grievances.

● Merit System, Banned Practices

Merit system principles and prohibited personnel practices were defined. The bill also spelled out procedures for investigating and punishing prohibited personnel practices, including reprisals against employees who blow the whistle on government wrongdoing.

● Incompetent Workers

Federal managers were given slightly more flexibility in firing incompetent employees. However, the final bill did not give management nearly as much leeway as Carter had requested in firings based either on incompetency or misconduct. The appeals process spelled out for adverse actions — such as a firing or suspension — retained substantial protections for employees who challenge agency actions.

● New Senior Corps

A new Senior Executive Service (SES) was authorized, to consist of about 8,000 top federal managers and policy-makers. Carter had proposed an elite corps of about 9,200 top employees, but Congress exempted several intelligence agencies from the SES.

Employees in the new service would be eligible for substantial cash bonuses. They would have less tenure than civil service employees, and they could be transferred more easily within an agency or between agencies.

● Merit Pay

Merit pay was established for federal employees at civil service levels GS-13 through GS-15. Although employees at those levels were still entitled to some of the automatic comparability raise given to all civil servants each year, other raises would be based on detailed evaluation of individual performance. In addition, those in the merit pay system were entitled to some cash bonuses not available to other civil service employees.

● Labor Practices

A Federal Labor Relations Authority — comparable to the National Labor Relations Board for private sector employees — was established to hear complaints about unfair labor practices.

● Employee Limit

A ceiling on the total number of federal employees was established for 1979-81. However, the bill gave the president some flexibility in exceeding the ceiling.

● Unions

The rights of federal employees to join labor unions and bargain collectively on certain personnel practices and policies were established in law. Previously, those rights were granted only by executive order, subject to change by the president with no congressional review.

The bill did not give federal employees the right to strike to negotiate for pay or fringe benefits or to require agency shops where employees would have to pay union dues regardless of whether they belonged to the union representing their unit.

Federal employee unions had wanted those more sweeping rights, but all were opposed by the administration and rejected by Congress. Although the unions attacked the reform bill as far too management-oriented, it still gave them something they had sought for years — statutory protection of federal employee rights to organize and bargain collectively.

The only major Carter proposal rejected by Congress was curtailment of veterans' preference in federal hiring.

Following are the texts of President Carter's March 2, 1978, and May 23, 1978, messages to Congress on reorganization of the federal civil service system:

MARCH 2 MESSAGE

To the Congress of the United States:

I am transmitting to the Congress today a comprehensive program to reform the Federal Civil Service system. My proposals are intended to increase the government's efficiency by placing new emphasis on the quality of performance of Federal workers. At the same time, my recommendations will ensure that employees and the public are protected against political abuse of the system.

Nearly a century has passed since enactment of the first Civil Service Act—the Pendleton Act of 1883. That Act established the United States Civil Service Commission and the merit system it administers. These institutions have served our Nation well in fostering development of a Federal workforce which is basically honest, competent, and dedicated to constitutional ideals and the public interest.

But the system has serious defects. It has become a bureaucratic maze which neglects merit, tolerates poor performance, permits abuse of legitimate employee rights, and mires every personnel action in red tape, delay and confusion.

Civil Service reform will be the centerpiece of government reorganization during my term in office.

I have seen at first hand the frustration among those who work within the bureaucracy. No one is more concerned at the inability of government to deliver on its promises than the worker who is trying to do a good job.

Most Civil Service employees perform with spirit and integrity. Nevertheless, there is still widespread criticism of Federal government performance. The public suspects that there are too many government workers, that they are underworked, overpaid, and insulated from the consequences of incompetence.

Such sweeping criticisms are unfair to dedicated Federal workers who are conscientiously trying to do their best, but we have to recognize that the only way to restore public confidence in the vast majority who work well is to deal effectively and firmly with the few who do not.

For the past 7 months, a task force of more than 100 career civil servants has analyzed the Civil Service, explored its weaknesses and strengths and suggested how it can be improved.

The objectives of the Civil Service reform proposals I am transmitting today are:

—To strengthen the protection of legitimate employee rights;

—To provide incentives and opportunities for managers to improve the efficiency and responsiveness of the Federal Government;

—To reduce the red tape and costly delay in the present personnel system;

—To promote equal employment opportunity;

—To improve labor-management relations.

My specific proposals are these:

1. Replacing the Civil Service Commission with an Office of Personnel Management and a Merit Protection Board

Originally established to conduct Civil Service examinations, the Civil Service Commission has, over the years, assumed additional and inherently conflicting responsibilities. It serves simultaneously both as the protector of employee rights and as the promoter of efficient personnel management policy. It is a manager, rulemaker, prosecutor and judge. Consequently, none of these jobs are being done as effectively as they should be.

Acting under my existing reorganization authority, I propose to correct the inherent conflict of interest within the Civil Service Commission by abolishing the Commission and replacing it with a Merit Protection Board and Office of Personnel Management.

The Office of Personnel Management will be the center for personnel administration (including examination, training, and administration of pay and benefits); it will not have any prosecutorial or adjudicative powers against individuals. Its Director will be appointed by the President and confirmed by the Senate. The Director will be the government's management spokesman on Federal employee labor relations and will coordinate Federal personnel matters, except for Presidential appointments.

The Merit Protection Board will be the adjudicatory arm of the new personnel system. It will be headed by a bipartisan board of three members, appointed for 7 years, serving non-renewable overlapping terms, and removable only for cause. This structure will guarantee independent and impartial protection to employees. I also propose to create a Special Counsel to the Board, appointed by the President and confirmed by the Senate, who will investigate and prosecute political abuses and merit system violations. This will help safeguard the rights of Federal employees who "blow the whistle" on violations of laws or regulations by other employees, including their supervisors.

In addition, these proposals will write into law for the first time the fundamental principles of the merit system and enumerate prohibited personnel practices.

2. A Senior Executive Service

A critical factor in determining whether Federal programs succeed or fail is the ability of the senior managers who run them. Throughout the Executive Branch, these 9,200 top administrators carry responsibilities that are often more challenging than comparable work in private industry. But under the Civil Service system, they lack the incentives for first-rate performance that managers in private industry have. The Civil Service system treats top managers just like the 2.1 million employees whose activities they direct. They are equally insulated from the risks of poor performance, and equally deprived of tangible rewards for excellence.

To help solve these problems I am proposing legislation to create a Senior Executive Service affecting managers in grades GS-16 through non-Presidentially appointed Executive Level IV or its equivalent. It would allow:

—Transfer of executives among senior positions on the basis of government need;

—Authority for agency heads to adjust salaries within a range set by law with the result that top managers would no longer receive automatic pay increases based on longevity;

—Annual performance reviews, with inadequate performance resulting in removal from the Senior Executive Service (back to GS-15) without any right of appeal to the Merit Protection Board.

Agency heads would be authorized to distribute bonuses for superior performance to not more than 50 percent of the senior executives each year. These would be allocated according to criteria prescribed by the Office of Personnel Management, and should average less than five percent of base salary per year. They would not constitute an increase in salary but rather a one-time payment. The Office of Personnel Management also would be empowered to award an additional stipend directly to a select group of senior executives, approximately five percent of the total of the Senior Executive Service, who have especially distinguished themselves in their work. The total of base salary, bonus, and honorary stipend should in no case exceed 95 percent of the salary level for an Executive Level II position.

No one now serving in the "supergrade" managerial positions would be required to join the Senior Executive Service. But all would have the opportunity to join. And the current percentage of non-career supergrade managers—approximately 10 percent—would be written into law for the first time, so that the Office of Personnel Management would not retain the existing authority of the Civil Service Commission to expand the proportion of political appointees.

This new Senior Executive Service will provide a highly qualified corps of top managers with strong incentives and opportunities to improve the management of the Federal government.

3. Incentive Pay for Lower Level Federal Managers and Supervisors

The current Federal pay system provides virtually automatic "step" pay increases as well as further increases to keep Federal salaries comparable to those in private business. This may be appropriate for most Federal employees, but performance—not merely endurance—should determine the compensation of Federal managers and supervisors. I am proposing legislation to let the Office of Personnel Management establish an incentive pay system for government managers, starting with those in grades GS-13 through GS-15. Approximately 72,000 managers and supervisors would be affected by such a system which could later be extended by Congress to other managers and supervisors.

These managers and supervisors would no longer receive automatic "step" increases in pay and would receive only 50 percent of their annual comparability pay increase. They would, however, be eligible for "performance" pay increases of up to 12 percent of their existing salary. Such a change would not increase payroll costs, and it should be insulated against improprieties through the use of strong audit and performance reviews by the Office of Personnel Management.

4. A Fairer and Speedier Disciplinary System

The simple concept of a "merit system" has grown into a tangled web of complicated rules and regulations.

Managers are weakened in their ability to reward the best and most talented people—and to fire those few who are unwilling to work.

The sad fact is that it is easier to promote and transfer incompetent employees than to get rid of them.

It may take as long as 3 years merely to fire someone for just cause, and at the same time the protection of legitimate rights is a costly and time-consuming process for the employee.

A speedier and fairer disciplinary system will create a climate in which managers may discharge non-performing employees — using due process — with reasonable assurance that their judgment, if valid, will prevail.

At the same time, employees will receive a more rapid hearing for their grievances.

The procedures that exist to protect employee rights are absolutely essential.

But employee appeals must now go through the Civil Service Commission, which has a built-in conflict of interest by serving simultaneously as rule-maker, prosecutor, judge, and employee advocate.

The legislation I am proposing today would give all competitive employees a statutory right of appeal. It would spell out fair and sensible standards for the Merit Protection Board to apply in hearing appeals. Employees would be provided with attorneys' fees if they prevail and the agency's action were found to have been wholly without basis. Both employees and managers would have, for the first time, subpoena power to ensure witness participation and document submission. The subpoena power would expedite the appeals process, as would new provisions for prehearing discovery. One of the three existing appeal levels would be eliminated.

These changes would provide both employees and managers with speedier and fairer judgments on the appeal of disciplinary actions.

5. Improved Labor-Management Relations

In 1962, President John F. Kennedy issued Executive Order 10988, establishing a labor-management relations program in the Executive Branch. The Executive Order has demonstrated its value through five Administrations. However, I believe that the time has come to increase its effectiveness by abolishing the Federal Labor Relations Council created by Executive Order 10988 and transferring its functions, along with related functions of the Assistant Secretary of Labor for Labor Relations, to a newly established Federal Labor Relations Authority. The Authority will be composed of three full-time members appointed by the President with the advice and consent of the Senate.

I have also directed members of my Administration to develop, as part of Civil Service reform, a Labor-Management Relations legislative proposal by working with the appropriate Congressional Committees, Federal employees and their representatives. The goal of this legislation will be to make Executive Branch labor relations more comparable to those of private business, while recognizing the special requirements of the Federal Government and the paramount public interest in the effective conduct of the public's business. This will facilitate Civil Service reform of the managerial and supervisory elements of the Executive Branch, free of union involvement, and, at the same time, improve the collective bargaining process as an integral part of the personnel system for Federal workers.

It will permit the establishment through collective bargaining of grievance and arbitration systems, the cost of which will be borne largely by the parties to the dispute. Such procedures will largely displace the multiple appeals systems which now exist and which are unanimously perceived as too costly, too cumbersome and ineffective.

6. Decentralized Personnel Decisionmaking

Examining candidates for jobs in the career service is now done almost exclusively by the Civil Service Commission, which now may take as long as six or eight months to fill important agency positions.

In addition, many routine personnel management actions must be submitted to the Civil Service Commission for prior approval. Much red tape and delay are generated by these requirements; the public benefits little, if at all. My legislative proposals would authorize the Office of Personnel Management to delegate personnel authority to departments and agencies.

The risk of abuse would be minimized by performance agreements between agencies and the Office of Personnel Management, by requirements for reporting, and by follow-up evaluations.

7. Changes in the Veterans Preference Law

Granting preference in Federal employment to veterans of military service has long been an important and worthwhile national policy. It will remain our policy because of the debt we owe those who have served our nation. It is especially essential for disabled veterans, and there should be no change in current law which would adversely affect them. But the Veterans Preference Act of 1944 also conferred a *lifetime benefit* upon the non-disabled veteran, far beyond anything provided by other veterans readjustment laws like the GI Bill, the benefits of which are limited to 10 years following discharge from the service. Current law also severely limits agency ability to consider qualified applicants by forbidding consideration of all except the three highest-scoring applicants — the so-called rule of three. As a result of the 5-point lifetime preference and the "rule of three," women, minorities and other qualified non-veteran candidates often face insuperable obstacles in their quest for Federal jobs.

Similarly, where a manager believes a program would benefit from fewer employees, the veterans preference provides an absolute lifetime benefit to veterans. In any Reduction in Force, all veterans may "bump" all non-veterans, even those with far greater seniority. Thus women and minorities who have recently acquired middle management positions are more likely to lose their jobs in any cutback.

Therefore I propose:

—Limiting the 5-point veterans preference to the 10 year period following their discharge from the service, beginning 2 years after legislation is enacted;

—Expanding the number of applicants who may be considered by a hiring agency from three to seven, unless the Office of Personnel Management should determine that another number or category ranking is more appropriate;

—Eliminating the veterans preference for retired military officers of field grade rank or above and limiting its availability for other military personnel who have retired after at least 20 years in service to 3 years following their retirement;

—Restricting the absolute preference now accorded veterans in Reductions in Force to their first 3 years of Federal employment, after which time they would be granted 5 extra years of seniority for purposes of determining their rights when Reduction in Force occurs.

These changes would focus the veterans preference more sharply to help disabled veterans and veterans of the Viet Nam conflict. I have already proposed a 2-year extension of the Veterans Readjustment Appointment Authority to give these veterans easier entry into the Federal workforce; I support amendments to waive the educational limitation for disabled veterans and to expand Federal job openings for certain veterans in grades GS-5 to GS-7 under this authority. I propose that veterans with 50 percent or higher disability be eligible for non-competitive appointments.

These changes are intended to let the Federal Government meet the needs of the American people more effectively. At the same time, they would make the Federal work place a better environment for Federal employees. I ask the Congress to act promptly on Civil Service Reform and the Reorganization Plan which I will shortly submit.

JIMMY CARTER

The White House
March 2, 1978

MAY 23 MESSAGE

To the Congress of the United States:

On March 2 I sent to Congress a Civil Service reform proposal to enable the Federal Government to improve its service to the American people.

Today I am submitting another part of my comprehensive proposal to reform the Federal personnel management system through Reorganization Plan No. 2 of 1978. The plan will reorganize the Civil Service Commission and thereby create new institutions to increase the effectiveness of management and strengthen the protection of employee rights.

The Civil Service Commission has acquired inherently conflicting responsibilities: to help manage the Federal Government and to protect the rights of Federal employees. It has done neither job well. The plan would separate the two functions.

Office of Personnel Management

The positive personnel management tasks of the government — such as training, productivity programs, examinations, and pay and benefits administration — would be the responsibility of an Office of Personnel Management. Its director, appointed by the President and confirmed by the Senate, would be responsible for administering federal personnel matters except for presidential appointments. The director would be the government's principal representative in federal labor relations matters.

Merit Systems Protection Board

The adjudication and prosecution responsibilities of the Civil Service Commission will be performed by the Merit Systems Protection Board. The board will be headed by a bipartisan panel of three members appointed to 6-year, staggered terms. This board would be the first independent and institutionally impartial federal agency solely for the protection of federal employees.

The plan will create, within the board, a Special Counsel to investigate and prosecute political abuses and merit system violations. Under the civil service reform legislation now being considered by the Congress, the counsel would have power to investigate and prevent reprisals against employees who report illegal acts — the so-called "whistle-blowers." The counsel would be appointed by the President and confirmed by the Senate.

Federal Labor Relations Authority

An Executive Order now vests existing labor-management relations in a part-time Federal Labor Relations Council, comprised of three top government managers; other important functions are assigned to the Assistant Secretary of Labor for Labor-Management Relations. This arrangement is defective because the Council members are part-time, they come exclusively from the ranks of management and their jurisdiction is fragmented.

The plan I submit today would consolidate the central policymaking functions in labor-management relations now divided between the Council and the Assistant Secretary into one Federal Labor Relations Authority. The Authority would be composed of three full-time members appointed by the President with the advice and consent of the Senate. Its General Counsel, also appointed by the President and confirmed by the Senate, would present unfair labor practice complaints. The plan also provides for the continuance of the Federal Service Impasses Panel within the Authority to resolve negotiating impasses between federal employee unions and agencies.

The cost of replacing the Civil Service Commission can be paid by our present resources. The reorganization itself would neither increase nor decrease the costs of personnel management throughout the government. But taken together with the substantive reforms I have proposed, this plan will greatly improve the government's ability to manage programs, speed the delivery of federal services to the public, and aid in executing other reorganizations I will propose to the Congress, by improving federal personnel management.

Each of the provisions of this proposed reorganization would accomplish one or more of the purposes set forth in 5 U.S.C. 901 (a). No functions are abolished by the plan, but the offices referred to in 5 U.S.C. 5109 (b) and 5 U.S.C. 1103 (d) are abolished. The portions of the plan providing for the appointment and pay for the head and one or more officers of the Office of Personnel Management, the Merit Systems Protection Board, the Federal Labor Relations Authority and the Federal Service Impasses Panel, are necessary to carry out the reorganization. The rates of compensation are comparable to those for similar positions within the executive branch.

I am confident that this plan and the companion civil service reform legislation will both lead to more effective protection of federal employees' legitimate rights and a more rewarding workplace. At the same time the American people will benefit from a better managed, more productive and more efficient federal government.

JIMMY CARTER

The White House
May 23, 1978

RHODESIA'S 'INTERNAL AGREEMENT'
March 3, 1978

Rhodesian Prime Minister Ian D. Smith probably had little choice. Beset by an intensification of the six-year-old guerrilla war against his government, increasing pressure from the United States and Britain for a transition to black majority rule, a deteriorating economic situation and the condemnation of the world community, Smith and three black leaders — Bishop Abel Muzorewa, the Rev. Ndabanigi Sithole and Senator Jeremiah Chirau — signed on March 3 an "internal agreement," a plan for the transition to black majority rule.

The agreement created an Executive Council, the first biracial executive authority in the nation's history, to draft a constitution and prepare for elections "by universal suffrage" by the end of 1978. The Council was composed of Smith and the three black leaders who signed the agreement.

Considerable protection was provided to the white minority. The "internal agreement" stipulated that a 100-member parliament was to be elected and, although there were fewer than 250,000 whites compared to 6.8 million blacks in Rhodesia, 28 of those 100 seats were reserved for whites. It was announced in late November 1978 that any party winning more than five seats in the election would be entitled to proportional representation in the cabinet. This assured Rhodesian whites of about 28 percent of the cabinet posts. The parliamentary election was originally scheduled for December 1978 but in November it was postponed until the following April to allow more time to complete the new constitution.

The agreement also provided that any constitutional amendment en-

*acted during the next 10 years must be approved by 78 parliamentary
votes, thereby virtually ruling out any change opposed by the whites.
Property and civil rights as well as the jobs and pensions of civil servants
were guaranteed. Most of the property and the government jobs in
Rhodesia were held by whites.*

'Black Rule'

*Smith and his supporters argued that he had at last accepted the
principle of black rule in Rhodesia. Smith had rejected that principle since
becoming prime minister in 1964, and Britain's insistence on "unimpeded
progress toward majority rule" caused him to issue Rhodesia's "Unilateral
Declaration of Independence" from Britain in November 1965. But by
1978, Smith's concessions in the "internal agreement" were widely viewed
as too little and too late.*

*Robert Mugabe and Joshua Nkomo, the leaders of the two major black
nationalist guerrilla groups in the Patriotic Front, rejected the "internal
agreement" immediately and vowed to continue their war against the
Smith government. Some 10,000 Rhodesians — black and white — had
already been killed in that war. The five so-called "front line" African
states of Zambia, Tanzania, Mozambique, Angola and Botswana also
rejected the agreement and promised to continue or increase their support
to the Patriotic Front. For entirely different reasons, conservative white
Rhodesians criticized the agreement and accused Smith of selling out the
white cause.*

'All Parties Conference'

*The United States and Britain, while refusing to endorse or reject the
"internal agreement," continued to insist on the convocation of an "all
parties conference," which would include the Patriotic Front. Smith was
apparently unsuccessful in his effort to convince U.S. officials to exclude
the guerrillas from any settlement during a visit to the United States in
October 1978. Smith, pointing to Soviet and Cuban support for the
Patriotic Front, labeled the guerrillas "communists."*

*The United States and Britain seemed convinced that no settlement
excluding the black nationalists opposed to Smith could succeed. Both
feared that without a swift and peaceful transition to black majority rule,
an all-out civil war was likely. Such a conflict might involve not only
blacks against whites but competing black factions against each other and
possibly the entanglement of other African countries and even the Soviet
Union and Cuba.*

> *Following is the text of the agreement signed on March 3 in
> Salisbury, Rhodesia, by Prime Minister Ian D. Smith,*

RHODESIA'S 'INTERNAL AGREEMENT'

Bishop Abel Muzorewa, the Rev. Ndabanigi Sithole and Senator Jeremiah Chirau:

Whereas the present constitutional situation in Rhodesia has led to the imposition of economic and other sanctions by the international community against Rhodesia and to armed conflict within Rhodesia and from neighboring territories;

And whereas it is necessary in the interests of our country that an agreement should be reached that would lead to the termination of such sanctions and the cessation of the armed conflict;

And whereas, in an endeavor to reach such an agreement, delegates from the Rhodesian government, African National Council (Sithole), United African National Council and Zimbabwe United People's Organization have met during the last two months in Salisbury and, having discussed fully the proposals put forward by the various delegations, have reached agreement on certain fundamental principles to be embodied in a new constitution that will lead to the termination of the aforementioned sanctions and the cessation of the armed conflict.

Now, therefore:

A.

It is hereby agreed that a constitution will be drafted and enacted which will provide for majority rule on the basis of universal adult suffrage on the following terms:

[1]

There will be a legislative assembly consisting of 100 members and the following provisions will apply thereto:

(a) There will be a common voters' roll, with all citizens of 18 years and over being eligible for registration as voters, subject to certain recognized disqualifications.

(b) 72 of the seats in the legislative assembly will be reserved for blacks who will be elected by voters who are enrolled on the common roll.

(c) 28 of the seats in the legislative assembly will be reserved for whites (i.e., Europeans as defined in the 1969 Constitution) who will be elected as follows:

(i.) 20 will be elected on a preferential voting system by white voters who are enrolled on the common roll.

(ii.) Eight will be elected by voters who are enrolled on the common roll from 16 candidates who will be nominated, in the case of the first parliament, by an electoral college composed of the white members of the present House of Assembly and, in the case of any subsequent parliament, by an electoral college composed of the 28 whites who are members of the parliament dissolved immediately prior to the general election.

(d) The reserved seats referred to in (c) above shall be retained for a period of at least 10 years or of two parliaments, whichever is the longer, and shall be reviewed at the expiration of that period, at which time a commission shall be appointed, the chairman of which shall be a judge of the High Court, to undertake this review. If that commission recommends that the arrangements regarding the said reserved seats should be changed:

(i.) An amendment to the constitution to effect such change may be made by a bill which receives the affirmative votes of not less than 51 members.

(ii.) The said bill shall also provide that the 72 seats referred to in (b) above shall not be reserved for blacks.

(e) The members filling the seats referred to in (c) above will be prohibited from forming a coalition with any single minority party for the purpose of forming a government.

[2]

There will be a just declaration of rights which will protect the rights and freedoms of individuals and, inter alia, will provide for protection from deprivation of property unless adequate compensation is paid promptly, and for protection of pension rights of persons who are members of pension funds.

[3]

The independence and qualifications of the judiciary will be entrenched and judges will have security of tenure.

[4]

There will be an independent public services board, the members of which will have security of tenure. The board will be responsible for appointments to, promotions in and discharges from the public service.

[5]

The public service, police force, defense forces and prison service will be maintained in a high state of efficiency and free from political interference.

[6]

Pensions which are payable from the consolidated revenue fund will be guaranteed and charged on the consolidated revenue fund and will be remittable outside the country.

[7]

Citizens who at present are entitled to dual citizenship will not be deprived of their present entitlement.

[8]

The above-mentioned provisions will be set out or provided for in the constitution and will be regarded as specially entrenched provisions which may only be amended by a bill which receives the affirmative votes of not less than 78 members.

B.

It is hereby also agreed that, following the agreement set out above, the next step will be the setting up of a transitional government. The prime function of the transitional government will be:

(a) To bring about a cease-fire, and

(b) To deal with related matters such as:

(i.) The composition of the future military forces, including those members of the nationalist forces who wish to take up a military career, and the rehabilitation of others:

(ii) The rehabilitation of those affected by the war.

C.

It is also hereby agreed that it will be the duty of the transitional government to determine and deal with the following matters:

(a) The release of detainees;

(b) The review of sentences for offenses of a political character;

(c) The further removal of discrimination;

(d) The creation of a climate conducive to the holding of free and democratic elections;

(e) The drafting of the new constitution in terms of this agreement;

(f) Procedures for registration of voters with a view to the holding of a general election at the earliest possible date.

D.

It is also hereby agreed that the transitional government will comprise an executive council and a ministerial council, and the following provisions will apply thereto:

[1]
Executive Council

(a) Composition:

The executive council will be composed of the prime minister and three black ministers, being the heads of those delegations engaged in the negotiations. The members will take turns in presiding as chairman of the executive council in such sequence and for such period as that council may determine. Decision of the executive council will be by consensus.

(b) Functions:

(i.) The executive council will be responsible for insuring that the functions given to and the duties imposed on the transitional government by the constitutional agreement are dealt with as expeditiously as possible. It will take policy decisions in connection with the preparation and drafting of the new constitution and the other matters set out in sections B and C of this agreement and with any other matters which may arise.

(ii.) The executive council may refer the matters set out in sections B and C of this agreement, or any other matter, to the ministerial council for examination and recommendation.

(iii.) The executive council will review decisions or recommendations of the ministerial council and may confirm such decisions or recommendations or refer them back to the ministerial council for further consideration.

[2]
Ministerial Council

(a) Composition:

The ministerial council will be composed of equal numbers of black and white ministers. The black ministers will be nominated in equal proportions by the heads of those delegations engaged in the negotiations. The white ministers will be nominated by the prime minister. The chairmanship of the ministerial council will alternate between black and white ministers. The prime minister will nominate which white minister shall take the chair, and the heads of those delegations engaged in the negotiations will nominate which of the black ministers shall take the chair in the sequence and for the period determined by the ministerial council.

(b) Functions:

(i.) The ministerial council will operate on the cabinet system. For each portfolio, or group of portfolios, there will be a black and a white minister who will share responsibility.

(ii.) The ministerial council will be responsible for initiating legislation and for supervising the preparation of such legislation as may be directed by the executive council.

(iii.) The ministerial council will make recommendations to the executive council on all matters referred to it by the executive council and on any other matter it thinks fit.

(iv.) Decisions of the ministerial council will be by majority vote and subject to review by the executive council.

[3]
Parliament

(a) Parliament will continue to function during the life of the transitional government and will meet for the following purposes as and when the executive council considers it should be summoned:

(i.) To pass a constitution amendment act enabling ministers who have not been elected to parliament to serve for periods in excess of four months;

(ii.) To pass legislation for the registration of voters;

(iii.) To pass the 1978-79 budget;

(iv.) To enact any legislation or deal with any other matter brought forward by the transitional government (e.g. for the further removal of discrimination);

(v.) To enact the new constitution;

(vi.) To nominate 16 whites for election by voters on the common roll to eight of the seats reserved for whites.

(b) The work of the various select committees and of the Senate Legal Committee will proceed as normal.

E.

It is also hereby agreed that independence day shall be Dec. 31, 1978.

Signed at Salisbury,
this third day of March 1978.

CHINESE CONSTITUTION
March 5, 1978

Meeting in Peking Feb. 26-March 5, the National People's Congress, China's nominal parliament, adopted a new constitution for the People's Republic. The constitution, which replaced a charter adopted in 1975, was based largely on the 1954 constitution, China's first as a communist state. (1975 constitution, 1975 Historic Documents, p. 43)

Other highlights of the first session of the Fifth National People's Congress included the reappointment of Hua Kuo-feng as premier. The Congress also named Marshal Yeh Chien-ying as chairman of its Standing Committee, a ceremonial post equivalent to head of state. Although First Deputy Premier Teng Hsiao-ping remained the third-ranking member of the Communist Party hierarchy, his apparent predominance in the government was indicated by the Congress' selection of 13 deputy premiers and a new State Council (cabinet) that was weighted toward Teng's political allies and programs.

In another action, the Congress March 5 adopted a 10-year economic program for the country. In submitting his report on the work of the government at the opening session Feb. 26, Hua said that suppression of radicals had brought "order" to the country and that the economy "once in a state of stagnation or even decline and retrogression . . . has turned the corner and is now on the path of steady growth and healthy development." Hua stressed the "decisive importance" of rapid economic development in order to make China a "modern, powerful socialist country by the end of the century."

Provisions of Constitution

The constitution consisted of a preamble and 60 articles, double the number in the previous 1975 charter. Several articles from the 1954 document were revived and a number of provisions of the 1975 constitution were dropped. The right to defense in a trial was restored, and ethnic minorities were given back their rights to "preserve or reform their own customs and ways." The new constitution appeared to strengthen the role of the legislature in affirming that it was the highest organ of state power, while deleting the 1975 words "under the leadership of the Communist Party."

For the first time, the constitution included a commitment to encourage birth control in the world's most populous nation. According to article 53, "The state advocates and encourages family planning." In his speech to the parliament, Communist Party Chairman Hua had called for a population growth rate of "less than one percent within three years." He called birth control "a very significant matter . . . conducive to the planned development of the national economy."

The new constitution also encouraged citizen complaints about inefficiency and arrogance among state officials.

In a reference to the Taiwan issue, the preamble asserted, "Taiwan is China's sacred territory. We are determined to liberate Taiwan and accomplish the great cause of unifying our motherland." (Following the establishment of diplomatic relations between the United States and the People's Republic, Secretary of State Cyrus R. Vance said Dec. 17 that the United States did not expect China to use force to regain Taiwan, although Peking gave Washington no such pledge in the agreement to establish diplomatic ties. See p. 781)

> *Following is the text of the Constitution of the People's Republic of China, adopted on March 5, 1978, by the Fifth National People's Congress of the People's Republic of China at its first session:*

PREAMBLE

After more than a century of heroic struggle the Chinese people, led by the Communist Party of China headed by our great leader and teacher Chairman Mao Tsetung, finally overthrew the reactionary rule of imperialism, feudalism and bureaucrat-capitalism by means of people's revolutionary war, winning complete victory in the new democratic revolution, and in 1949 founded the People's Republic of China.

The founding of the People's Republic of China marked the beginning of the historical period of socialism in our country. Since then, under the leadership of Chairman Mao and the Chinese Communist Party, the people of all our nationalities have carried out Chairman Mao's proletarian revolutionary line in the political, economic, cultural and military fields and in foreign affairs and have won great victories in socialist revolution and socialist construction through repeated struggles against enemies both at home and abroad and through the Great Proletarian Cultural Revolution. The dictatorship of the proletariat in our country has been consolidated and strengthened, and China has become a socialist country with the beginnings of prosperity.

Chairman Mao Tsetung was the founder of the People's Republic of China. All our victories in revolution and construction have been won under the guidance of Marxism-Leninism-Mao Tsetung Thought. The fundamental guarantee that the people of all our nationalities will struggle in unity and carry the proletarian revolution through to the end is always to hold high and staunchly to defend the great banner of Chairman Mao.

The triumphant conclusion of the first Great Proletarian Cultural Revolution has ushered in a new period of development in China's socialist revolution and socialist construction. In accordance with the basic line of the Chinese Communist Party for the entire historical period of socialism, the general task for the people of the whole country in this new period is: To persevere in continuing the revolution under the dictatorship of the proletariat, carry forward the three great revolutionary movements of class struggle, the struggle for production and scientific experiment, and make China a great and powerful socialist country with modern agriculture, industry, national defence and science and technology by the end of the century.

We must persevere in the struggle of the proletariat against the bourgeoisie and in the struggle for the socialist road against the capitalist road. We must oppose revisionism and prevent the restoration of capitalism. We must be prepared to deal with subversion and aggression against our country by social-imperialism and imperialism.

We should consolidate and expand the revolutionary united front which is led by the working class and based on the worker-peasant alliance, and which unites the large numbers of intellectuals and other working people, patriotic democratic parties, patriotic personages, our compatriots in Taiwan, Hongkong and Macao, and our countrymen residing abroad. We should enhance the great unity of all the nationalities in our country. We should correctly distinguish and handle the contradictions among the people and those between ourselves and the enemy. We should endeavour to create among the people of the whole country a political situation in which there are both centralism and democracy, both discipline and freedom, both unity of will and personal ease of mind and liveliness, so as to help bring all positive factors into play, overcome all difficulties, better consolidate the proletarian dictatorship and build up our country more rapidly.

Taiwan is China's sacred territory. We are determined to liberate Taiwan and accomplish the great cause of unifying our motherland.

In international affairs, we should establish and develop relations with other countries on the basis of the Five Principles of mutual respect for sovereignty and territorial integrity, mutual non-aggression, non-interference in each other's internal affairs, equality and mutual benefit, and peaceful coexistence. Our country will never seek hegemony, or strive to be a superpower. We should uphold proletarian internationalism. In accordance with the theory of the three worlds, we should strengthen our unity with the proletariat and the oppressed people and nations throughout the world, the socialist countries, and the third world countries, and we should unite with all countries subjected to aggression, subversion, interference, control and bullying by the social- imperialist and imperialist superpowers to form the broadest possible international united front against the hegemonism of the superpowers and against a new world war, and strive for the progress and emancipation of humanity.

Chapter One

GENERAL PRINCIPLES

Article 1

The People's Republic of China is a socialist state of the dictatorship of the proletariat led by the working class and based on the alliance of workers and peasants.

Article 2

The Communist Party of China is the core of leadership of the whole Chinese people. The working class exercises leadership over the state through its vanguard, the Communist Party of China.

The guiding ideology of the People's Republic of China is Marxism-Leninism-Mao Tsetung Thought.

Article 3

All power in the People's Republic of China belongs to the people. The organs through which the people exercise state power are the National People's Congress and the local people's congresses at various levels.

The National People's Congress, the local people's congresses at various levels and all other organs of state practise democratic centralism.

Article 4

The People's Republic of China is a unitary multi-national state.

All the nationalities are equal. There should be unity and fraternal love among the nationalities and they should help and learn from each other. Discrimination against, or oppression of, any nationality, and acts which undermine the unity of the nationalities are prohibited. Big-nationality chauvinism and local-nationality chauvinism must be opposed.

All the nationalities have the freedom to use and develop their own spoken and written languages, and to preserve or reform their own customs and ways.

Regional autonomy applies in an area where a minority nationality lives in a compact community. All the national autonomous areas are inalienable parts of the People's Republic of China.

Article 5

There are mainly two kinds of ownership of the means of production in the People's Republic of China at the present stage: socialist ownership by the whole people and socialist collective ownership by the working people.

The state allows non-agricultural individual labourers to engage in individual labour involving no exploitation of others, within the limits permitted by law and under unified arrangement and management by organizations at the basic level in cities and towns or in rural areas. At the same time, it guides these individual labourers step by step onto the road of socialist collectivization.

Article 6

The state sector of the economy, that is, the socialist sector owned by the whole people, is the leading force in the national economy.

Mineral resources, waters and those forests, undeveloped lands and other marine and land resources owned by the state are the property of the whole people.

The state may requisition by purchase, take over for use, or nationalize land under conditions prescribed by law.

Article 7

The rural people's commune sector of the economy is a socialist sector collectively owned by the masses of working people. At present, it generally takes the form of three-level ownership, that is, ownership by the commune, the production brigade and the production team, with the production team as the basic accounting unit. A production brigade may become the basic accounting unit when its conditions are ripe.

Provided that the absolute predominance of the collective economy of the people's commune is ensured, commune members may farm small plots of land for personal needs, engage in limited household side-line production, and in pastoral areas they may also keep a limited number of livestock for personal needs.

Article 8

Socialist public property shall be inviolable. The state ensures the consolidation and development of the socialist sector of the economy owned by the whole people and of the socialist sector collectively owned by the masses of working people.

The state prohibits any person from using any means whatsoever to disrupt the economic order of the society, undermine the economic plans of the state, encroach upon or squander state and collective property, or injure the public interest.

Article 9

The state protects the right of citizens to own lawfully earned income, savings, houses and other means of livelihood.

Article 10

The state applies the socialist principles: "He who does not work, neither shall he eat" and "from each according to his ability, to each according to his work."

Work is an honourable duty for every citizen able to work. The state promotes socialist labour emulation, and, putting proletarian politics in command, it applies the policy of combining moral encouragement with material reward, with the stress on the former, in order to heighten the citizens' socialist enthusiasm and creativeness in work.

Article 11

The state adheres to the general line of going all out, aiming high and achieving greater, faster, better and more economical results in building socialism, it undertakes the planned, proportionate and high-speed development of the national economy, and it continuously develops the productive forces, so as to consolidate the country's independence and security and improve the people's material and cultural life step by step.

In developing the national economy, the state adheres to the principle of building our country independently, with the initiative in our own hands and through self-reliance, hard struggle, diligence and thrift, it adheres to the principle of taking agriculture as the foundation and industry as the leading factor, and it adheres to the principle of bringing the initiative of both the central and local authorities into full play under the unified leadership of the central authorities.

The state protects the environment and natural resources and prevents and eliminates pollution and other hazards to the public.

Article 12

The state devotes major efforts to developing science, expands scientific research, promotes technical innovation and technical revolution and adopts advanced techniques wherever possible in all departments of the national economy. In scientific and technological work we must follow the practice of combining professional contingents with the masses, and combining learning from others with our own creative efforts.

Article 13

The state devotes major efforts to developing education in order to raise the cultural and scientific level of the whole nation. Education must serve proletarian politics and be combined with productive labour and must enable everyone who receives an education to develop morally, intellectually and physically and become a worker with both socialist consciousness and culture.

Article 14

The state upholds the leading position of Marxism-Leninism-Mao Tsetung Thought in all spheres of ideology and culture. All cultural undertakings must serve the workers, peasants and soldiers and serve socialism.

The state applies the policy of "letting a hundred flowers blossom and a hundred schools of thought contend" so as to promote the development of the arts and sciences and bring about a flourishing socialist culture.

Article 15

All organs of state must constantly maintain close contact with the masses of the people, rely on them, heed their opinions, be concerned for their weal and woe, streamline administration, practise economy, raise efficiency and combat bureaucracy.

The leading personnel of state organs at all levels must conform to the requirements for successors in the proletarian revolutionary cause and their composition must conform to the principle of the three-in-one combination of the old, the middle-aged and the young.

Article 16

The personnel of organs of state must earnestly study Marxism-Leninism-Mao Tsetung Thought, wholeheartedly serve the people, endeavour to perfect their professional competence, take an active part in collective productive labour, accept supervision by the masses, be models in observing the Constitution and the law, correctly implement the policies of the state, seek the truth from facts, and must not have recourse to deception or exploit their position and power to seek personal gain.

Article 17

The state adheres to the principle of socialist democracy, and ensures to the people the right to participate in the management of state affairs and of all economic and cultural undertakings, and the right to supervise the organs of state and their personnel.

Article 18

The state safeguards the socialist system, suppresses all treasonable and counter-revolutionary activities, punishes all traitors and counter-revolutionaries, and punishes new-born bourgeois elements and other bad elements.

The state deprives of political rights, as prescribed by law, those landlords, rich peasants and reactionary capitalists who have not yet been reformed, and at the same time it provides them with the opportunity to earn a living so that they may be reformed through labour and become law-abiding citizens supporting themselves by their own labour.

Article 19

The Chairman of the Central Committee of the Communist Party of China commands the armed forces of the People's Republic of China.

The Chinese People's Liberation Army is the workers' and peasants' own armed force led by the Communist Party of China; it is the pillar of the dictatorship of the proletariat. The state devotes major efforts to the revolutionization and modernization of the Chinese People's Liberation Army, strengthens the building of the militia and adopts a system under which our armed forces are a combination of the field armies, the regional forces and the militia.

The fundamental task of the armed forces of the People's Republic of China is: To safeguard the socialist revolution and socialist construction, to defend the sovereignty, territorial integrity and security of the state, and to guard against subversion and aggression by social-imperialism, imperialism and their lackeys.

Chapter Two

THE STRUCTURE OF THE STATE

Section I

THE NATIONAL PEOPLE'S CONGRESS

Article 20

The National People's Congress is the highest organ of state power.

Article 21

The National People's Congress is composed of deputies elected by the people's congresses of the provinces, autonomous regions, and municipalities directly under the Central Government, and by the People's Liberation Army. The deputies should be elected by secret ballot after democratic consultation.

The National People's Congress is elected for a term of five years. Under special circumstances, its term of office may be extended or the succeeding National People's Congress may be convened before its due date.

The National People's Congress holds one session each year. When necessary, the session may be advanced or postponed.

Article 22

The National People's Congress exercises the following functions and powers:

(1) to amend the Constitution;

(2) to make laws;

(3) to supervise the enforcement of the Constitution and the law;

(4) to decide on the choice of the Premier of the State Council upon the recommendation of the Central Committee of the Communist Party of China;

(5) to decide on the choice of other members of the State Council upon the recommendation of the Premier of the State Council;

(6) to elect the President of the Supreme People's Court and the Chief Procurator of the Supreme People's Procuratorate;

(7) to examine and approve the national economic plan, the state budget and the final state accounts;

(8) to confirm the following administrative divisions: provinces, autonomous regions, and municipalities directly under the Central Government;

(9) to decide on questions of war and peace; and

(10) to exercise such other functions and powers as the National People's Congress deems necessary.

Article 23

The National People's Congress has the power to remove from office the members of the State Council, the President of the Supreme People's Court and the Chief Procurator of the Supreme People's Procuratorate.

Article 24

The Standing Committee of the National People's Congress is the permanent organ of the National People's Congress. It is responsible and accountable to the National People's Congress.

The Standing Committee of the National People's Congress is composed of the following members:

the Chairman;

the Vice-Chairmen;

the Secretary-General; and
other members.

The National People's Congress elects the Standing Committee of the National People's Congress and has the power to recall its members.

Article 25

The Standing Committee of the National People's Congress exercises the following functions and powers:

(1) to conduct the election of deputies to the National People's Congress;

(2) to convene the sessions of the National People's Congress;

(3) to interpret the Constitution and laws and to enact decrees;

(4) to supervise the work of the State Council, the Supreme People's Court and the Supreme People's Procuratorate;

(5) to change and annul inappropriate decisions adopted by the organs of state power of provinces, autonomous regions, and municipalities directly under the Central Government;

(6) to decide on the appointment and removal of individual members of the State Council upon the recommendation of the Premier of the State Council when the National People's Congress is not in session;

(7) to appoint and remove Vice-Presidents of the Supreme People's Court and Deputy Chief Procurators of the Supreme People's Procuratorate;

(8) to decide on the appointment and removal of plenipotentiary representatives abroad;

(9) to decide on the ratification and abrogation of treaties concluded with foreign states;

(10) to institute state titles of honour and decide on their conferment;

(11) to decide on the granting of pardons;

(12) to decide on the proclamation of a state of war in the event of armed attack on the country when the National People's Congress is not in session; and

(13) to exercise such other functions and powers as are vested in it by the National People's Congress.

Article 26

The Chairman of the Standing Committee of the National People's Congress presides over the work of the Standing Committee; receives foreign diplomatic envoys; and in accordance with the decisions of the National People's Congress or its Standing Committee promulgates laws and decrees, dispatches and recalls plenipotentiary representatives abroad, ratifies treaties concluded with foreign states and confers state titles of honour.

The Vice-Chairmen of the Standing Committee of the National People's Congress assist the Chairman in his work and may exercise part of the Chairman's functions and powers on his behalf.

Article 27

The National People's Congress and its Standing Committee may establish special committees as deemed necessary.

Article 28

Deputies to the National People's Congress have the right to address inquiries to the State Council, the Supreme People's Court, the Supreme People's Procuratorate, and the ministries and commissions of the State Council, which are all under obligation to answer.

Article 29

Deputies to the National People's Congress are subject to supervision by the units which elect them. These electoral units have the power to replace at any time the deputies they elect, as prescribed by law.

Section II

THE STATE COUNCIL

Article 30

The State Council is the Central People's Government and the executive organ of the highest organ of state power; it is the highest organ of state administration.

The State Council is responsible and accountable to the National People's Congress, or, when the National People's Congress is not in session, to its Standing Committee.

Article 31

The State Council is composed of the following members:
the Premier;
the Vice-Premiers;
the ministers; and
the ministers heading the commissions.

The Premier presides over the work of the State Council and the Vice-Premiers assist the Premier in his work.

Article 32

The State Council exercises the following functions and powers:

(1) to formulate administrative measures, issue decisions and orders and verify their execution, in accordance with the Constitution, laws and decrees;

(2) to submit proposals on laws and other matters to the National People's Congress or its Standing Committee;

(3) to exercise unified leadership over the work of the ministries and commissions and other organizations under it;

(4) to exercise unified leadership over the work of local organs of state administration at various levels throughout the country;

(5) to draw up and put into effect the national economic plan and the state budget;

(6) to protect the interests of the state, maintain public order and safeguard the rights of citizens;

(7) to confirm the following administrative divisions: autonomous prefectures, counties, autonomous counties, and cities;

(8) to appoint and remove administrative personnel according to the provisions of the law; and

(9) to exercise such other functions and powers as are vested in it by the National People's Congress or its Standing Committee.

Section III

THE LOCAL PEOPLE'S CONGRESSES AND THE LOCAL REVOLUTIONARY COMMITTEES AT VARIOUS LEVELS

Article 33

The administrative division of the People's Republic of China is as follows:

(1) The country is divided into provinces, autonomous regions, and municipalities directly under the Central Government;

(2) Provinces and autonomous regions are divided into autonomous prefectures, counties, autonomous counties, and cities; and

(3) Counties and autonomous counties are divided into people's communes and towns.

Municipalities directly under the Central Government and other large cities are divided into districts and counties. Autonomous prefectures are divided into counties, autonomous counties, and cities.

Autonomous regions, autonomous prefectures and autonomous counties are all national autonomous areas.

Article 34

People's congresses and revolutionary committees are established in provinces, municipalities directly under the Central Government, counties, cities, municipal districts, people's communes and towns.

People's congresses and revolutionary committees of the people's communes are organizations of political power at the grass-roots level, and are also leading organs of collective economy.

Revolutionary committees at the provincial level may establish administrative offices as their agencies in prefectures.

Organs of self-government are established in autonomous regions, autonomous prefectures and autonomous counties.

Article 35

Local people's congresses at various levels are local organs of state power.

Deputies to the people's congresses of provinces, municipalities directly under the Central Government, counties, and cities divided into districts are elected by people's congresses at the next lower level by secret ballot after democratic consultation; deputies to the people's congresses of cities not divided into districts, and of municipal districts, people's communes and towns are directly elected by the voters by secret ballot after democratic consultation.

The people's congresses of provinces and municipalities directly under the Central Government are elected for a term of five years. The people's congresses of counties, cities and municipal districts are elected for a term of three years. The people's congresses of people's communes and towns are elected for a term of two years.

Local people's congresses at various levels hold at least one session each year which is to be convened by revolutionary committees at the corresponding levels.

The units and electorates which elect the deputies to the local people's congresses at various levels have the power to supervise, remove and replace their deputies at any time according to the provisions of the law.

Article 36

Local people's congresses at various levels, in their respective administrative areas, ensure the observance and enforcement of the Constitution, laws and decrees; ensure the implementation of the state plan; make plans for local economic and cultural development and for public utilities; examine and approve local economic plans, budgets and final accounts; protect public property; maintain public order; safeguard the rights of citizens and the equal rights of minority nationalities; and promote the development of socialist revolution and socialist construction.

Local people's congresses may adopt and issue decisions within the limits of their authority as prescribed by law.

Local people's congresses elect, and have the power to recall, members of revolutionary committees at the corresponding levels. People's congresses at county level and above elect, and have the power to recall, the presidents of the people's courts and the chief procurators of the people's procuratorates at the corresponding levels.

Deputies to local people's congresses at various levels have the right to address inquiries to the revolutionary committees, people's courts, people's procuratorates and organs under the revolutionary committees at the corresponding levels, which are all under obligation to answer.

Article 37

Local revolutionary committees at various levels, that is, local people's governments, are the executive organs of local people's congresses at the corresponding levels and they are also local organs of state administration.

A local revolutionary committee is composed of a chairman, vice-chairmen and other members.

Local revolutionary committees carry out the decisions of people's congresses at the corresponding levels as well as the decisions and orders of the organs of state administration at higher levels, direct the administrative work of their respective areas, and issue decisions and orders within the limits of their authority as prescribed by law. Revolutionary committees at county level and above appoint or remove the personnel of organs of state according to the provisions of the law.

Local revolutionary committees are responsible and accountable to people's congresses at the corresponding levels and to the organs of state administration at the next higher level, and work under the unified leadership of the State Council.

Section IV

THE ORGANS OF SELF-GOVERNMENT
OF NATIONAL AUTONOMOUS AREAS

Article 38

The organs of self-government of autonomous regions, autonomous prefectures and autonomous counties are people's congresses and revolutionary committees.

The election of the people's congresses and revolutionary committees of national autonomous areas, their terms of office, their functions and powers and also the establishment of their agencies should conform to the basic principles governing the organization of local organs of state as specified in Section III, Chapter Two, of the Constitution.

In autonomous areas where a number of nationalities live together, each nationality is entitled to appropriate representation in the organs of self-government.

Article 39

The organs of self-government of national autonomous areas exercise autonomy within the limits of their authority as prescribed by law, in addition to exercising the functions and powers of local organs of state as specified by the Constitution.

The organs of self-government of national autonomous areas may, in the light of the political, economic and cultural characteristics of the nationality or nationalities in a given area, make regulations on the exercise of autonomy and also specific regulations and submit them to the Standing Committee of the National People's Congress for approval.

In performing their functions, the organs of self-government of national autonomous areas employ the spoken and written language or languages commonly used by the nationality or nationalities in the locality.

Article 40

The higher organs of state shall fully safeguard the exercise of autonomy by the organs of self-government of national autonomous areas, take into full consideration the characteristics and needs of the various minority nationalities, make a major effort to train cadres of the minority nationalities, and actively support and assist all the minority nationalities in their socialist revolution and construction and thus advance their socialist economic and cultural development.

Section V

THE PEOPLE'S COURTS AND THE PEOPLE'S PROCURATORATES

Article 41

The Supreme People's Court, local people's courts at various levels and special people's courts exercise judicial authority. The people's courts are formed as prescribed by law.

In accordance with law, the people's courts apply the system whereby representatives of the masses participate as assessors in administering justice. With regard to major counter-revolutionary or criminal cases, the masses should be drawn in for discussion and suggestions.

All cases in the people's courts are heard in public except those involving special circumstances as prescribed by law. The accused has the right to defence.

Article 42

The Supreme People's Court is the highest judicial organ.

The Supreme People's Court supervises the administration of justice by local people's courts at various levels and by special people's courts; people's courts at the higher levels supervise the administration of justice by people's courts at the lower levels.

The Supreme People's Court is responsible and accountable to the National People's Congress and its Standing Committee. Local people's courts at various levels are responsible and accountable to local people's congresses at the corresponding levels.

Article 43

The Supreme People's Procuratorate exercises procuratorial authority to ensure observance of the Constitution and the law by all the departments under the State Council, the local organs of state at various levels, the personnel of organs of state and the citizens. Local people's procuratorates and special people's procuratorates exercise procuratorial authority within the limits prescribed by law. The people's procuratorates are formed as prescribed by law.

The Supreme People's Procuratorate supervises the work of local people's procuratorates at various levels and of special people's procuratorates; people's procuratorates at the higher levels supervise the work of those at the lower levels.

The Supreme People's Procuratorate is responsible and accountable to the National People's Congress and its Standing Committee. Local people's procuratorates at various levels are responsible and accountable to people's congresses at the corresponding levels.

Chapter Three

THE FUNDAMENTAL RIGHTS AND DUTIES OF CITIZENS

Article 44

All citizens who have reached the age of eighteen have the right to vote and to stand for election, with the exception of persons deprived of these rights by law.

Article 45

Citizens enjoy freedom of speech, correspondence, the press, assembly, association, procession, demonstration and the freedom to strike, and have the right to "speak out freely, air their views fully, hold great debates and write big-character posters."

Article 46

Citizens enjoy freedom to believe in religion and freedom not to believe in religion and to propagate atheism.

Article 47

The citizens' freedom of person and their homes are inviolable.

No citizen may be arrested except by decision of a people's court or with the sanction of a people's procuratorate, and the arrest must be made by a public security organ.

Article 48

Citizens have the right to work. To ensure that citizens enjoy this right, the state provides employment in accordance with the principle of overall consideration, and, on the basis of increased production, the state gradually increases payment for labour, improves working conditions, strengthens labour protection and expands collective welfare.

Article 49

Working people have the right to rest. To ensure that working people enjoy this right, the state prescribes working hours and systems of vacations and gradually expands material facilities for the working people to rest and recuperate.

Article 50

Working people have the right to material assistance in old age, and in case of illness or disability. To ensure that working people enjoy this right, the state gradually expands social insurance, social assistance, public health services, co-operative medical services, and other services.

The state cares for and ensures the livelihood of disabled revolutionary armymen and the families of revolutionary martyrs.

Article 51

Citizens have the right to education. To ensure that citizens enjoy this right, the state gradually increases the number of schools of various types and of other cultural and educational institutions and popularizes education.

The state pays special attention to the healthy development of young people and children.

Article 52

Citizens have the freedom to engage in scientific research, literary and artistic creation and other cultural activities. The state encourages and assists the creative endeavours of citizens engaged in science, education, literature, art, journalism, publishing, public health, sports and other cultural work.

Article 53

Women enjoy equal rights with men in all spheres of political, economic, cultural, social and family life. Men and women enjoy equal pay for equal work.

Men and women shall marry of their own free will. The state protects marriage, the family, and the mother and child.

The state advocates and encourages family planning.

Article 54

The state protects the just rights and interests of overseas Chinese and their relatives.

Article 55

Citizens have the right to lodge complaints with organs of state at any level against any person working in an organ of state, enterprise or institution for transgression of law or neglect of duty. Citizens have the right to appeal to organs of state at any level against any infringement of their rights. No one shall suppress such complaints and appeals or retaliate against persons making them.

Article 56

Citizens must support the leadership of the Communist Party of China, support the socialist system, safeguard the unification of the motherland and the unity of all nationalities in our country and abide by the Constitution and the law.

Article 57

Citizens must take care of and protect public property, observe labour discipline, observe public order, respect social ethics and safeguard state secrets.

Article 58

It is the lofty duty of every citizen to defend the motherland and resist aggression.

It is the honourable obligation of citizens to perform military service and to join the militia according to the law.

Article 59

The People's Republic of China grants the right of residence to any foreign national persecuted for supporting a just cause, for taking part in revolutionary movements or for engaging in scientific work.

Chapter Four

THE NATIONAL FLAG, THE NATIONAL EMBLEM AND THE CAPITAL

Article 60

The national flag of the People's Republic of China has five stars on a field of red.

The national emblem of the People's Republic of China is: Tien An Men in the centre, illuminated by five stars and encircled by ears of grain and a cogwheel.

The capital of the People's Republic of China is Peking.

SENATE RATIFICATION
OF PANAMA CANAL TREATIES
March 16; April 18, 1978

A foreign policy issue fraught with political hazards for President Carter came to a head in March and April during Senate debates on ratification of the Panama Canal treaties. The treaties — one passing control of the 51-mile waterway to Panama by the year 2000, the other allowing the United States to have a major role in guaranteeing the neutrality of the canal after 2000 — had been signed Sept. 8, 1977, in Washington, D.C., by President Carter and the Panamanian head of state, Brig. Gen. Omar Torrijos Herrera. But the treaties ran into a stumbling block in October 1977 when members of the Senate Foreign Relations Committee informed the White House that the pacts could not be ratified without clarification of the part of the neutrality treaty stating that the United States and Panama "agree to maintain the regime of neutrality." Committee members were concerned about the type of U.S. response the treaty allowed if, for example, political upheaval in Panama closed the canal. This sticking point prompted Carter and Torrijos to meet again, on Oct. 14, 1977, to issue a Statement of Understanding clarifying the terms of the neutrality pact. (For background, see Historic Documents of 1977, p. 591.) The question of U.S. participation in guaranteeing the neutrality of the canal would continue to trouble members of the Senate throughout the ratification process.

Heavy pressure was exerted on senators by both opponents and proponents of the treaties. Undecided senators were barraged with mail from groups interested in the issue. Conservative political groups declared that the treaties represented a public test of conservative principles and vowed to work for the defeat of senators who voted for ratification. A prominent leader of the anti-treaty forces was former Governor Ronald Reagan of California whose attacks on the treaties during his unsuccessful 1976 primary campaign for the Republican presidential nomination brought the issue wide public attention. The administration sent various officials on speaking tours across the country to rally support for the treaties. On the other hand, treaty opponents in Congress formed a "truth squad" of 20 conservative lawmakers who visited several cities to argue that the canal pacts would harm the United States in terms of both economics and national security.

Fireside Chat

President Carter entered the fight directly with a Feb. 1 "fireside chat" on the Panama Canal treaties. In the talk, the president forcefully laid out his reasons for ratification. "The most important reason — the only reason — to ratify the treaties is that they are in the highest national interest of the United States and will strengthen our position in the world. Our security interests will be stronger," he continued. "Our trade opportunities will be improved. We will demonstrate that as a large and powerful country, we are able to deal fairly and honorably with a proud but smaller sovereign nation. We will honor our commitment to those engaged in world commerce that the Panama Canal will be open and available for use by their ships — at a reasonable and competitive cost — both now and in the future."

The president went on to dispute most of the major criticisms voiced by opponents of the treaties. He said, for example, that the United States would always have the right to "take whatever military action is necessary" to ensure the continued safe operation of the canal. Responding to assertions that the canal was U.S. property bought with U.S. tax dollars, Carter asserted, "We do not own the Panama Canal. We have never had sovereignty over it. We have only had the right to use it." Concerning relations with other Latin American countries, Carter declared that ratification of the treaties would "increase our Nation's influence in this hemisphere, will help to reduce any mistrust and disagreement and they will remove a major source of anti-American feeling." He added that the treaties represented "not merely the surest way to protect and save the canal; it's a strong, positive act of a people who are still confident, still creative, still great."

The Senate Foreign Relations Committee finished its work on the treaties Jan. 30, and debate began on the Senate floor Feb. 8.

Intense Lobbying

As the initial vote on the treaties approached, the lobbying efforts of opponents and supporters grew more intense. Conservative groups, led by the American Conservative Union and the Conservative Caucus, spread their anti-treaty arguments through newspaper advertisements, a 30-minute videotape television program and thousands of letters to senators. Two groups established solely to fight ratification, the Committee to Save the Panama Canal and the Emergency Coalition to Save the Panama Canal, also stepped up their activities.

To win public support for ratification, canal supporters emulated the tactics of their opponents. The Committee of Americans for the Canal Treaties Inc., whose membership included former President Gerald R. Ford, Mrs. Lyndon B. Johnson and AFL-CIO President George Meany, and the Committee for Ratification of the Panama Canal Treaties were established to promote the treaties with advertisements and public speaking tours. In addition, the White House arranged a series of meetings with "opinion leaders" from across the country to point out the merits of ratification.

The consideration of the treaties was complicated by charges in February that Torrijos and members of his family were involved in narcotics dealing. In two lengthy closed sessions Feb. 21-22, the Senate examined charges against the Panamanian leader. Revelations concerning the Torrijos family included "no evidence that would stand up in a court of law," Senate Majority Leader Robert C. Byrd, D-W.Va., told reporters following the session.

Neutrality Treaty

The Senate approved the neutrality pact March 16 by a 68-32 vote, one vote over the two-thirds margin necessary for ratification. The alterations to the approved pact included the terms of the Carter-Torrijos understanding that gave the United States the right to defend the canal if it were threatened and granted "head of the line" privileges for U.S. ships during emergencies. In addition, the administration and Senate leadership accepted two conditions to win the votes of previously undecided senators. Sponsored by Georgia Democrats Herman E. Talmadge and Sam Nunn, one condition allowed the two countries to work out an agreement to station U.S. troops in Panama after 1999 if both parties desired such an arrangement. The other, more controversial condition gave the United States the right to use "military force in the Republic of Panama" to keep the canal open. Sponsored by Dennis DeConcini, D-Ariz., the condition was accepted by the administration in return for DeConcini's vote for ratification. Immediately preceding the final vote, the Senate tabled a proposal by treaty opponent Robert P. Griffin, R-Mich., to send the treaty back to the president for renegotiation.

The approved neutrality pact also contained reservations and understandings dealing with the maintenance of U.S. citizens' graves in the Canal Zone, the use of operating revenues, the manner in which tolls may be adjusted, the determination of "need or emergency" to allow a Panamanian or U.S. vessel to go to the "head of the line," the limit to financial responsibility incurred by the United States and instructions that all amendments, conditions, reservations and understandings be included in the "instrument of ratification."

In an attempt to push for the ratification of the basic treaty while simultaneously trying to assuage Panamanian fears, Carter, in a statement issued at the White House March 16, emphasized that the neutrality treaty ratified by the Senate allowed the United States to take "whatever actions are necessary to make sure the canal remains open and safe." He added, however, that this "does not mean there is a right of intervention, nor do we want a right of intervention by the United States in the internal affairs of Panama." And Carter praised the Panamanians and their leaders, saying "General Torrijos and the Panamanian people have been patient and forbearing during the negotiations and during the Senate debate. They've earned the confidence and respect of the American people."

Despite Carter's disclaimer concerning American intervention in Panama, soon after Senate ratification of the neutrality pact Panama let it be known at the United Nations that it would not accept the terms of the DeConcini Reservation. The problem surrounded the phrase "military force in Panama" which the administration had agreed to and the Senate ratified. A compromise in the form of a reservation added to the basic treaty was worked out between the Senate leadership and DeConcini. The reservation, which also received the approval of the Panamanian government, stated that the United States would not intervene in the "internal affairs of the Republic of Panama" or interfere with its "political independence or sovereign integrity" in the course of keeping the canal open, neutral and secure.

Basic Treaty

After more intense debate, similar to that which preceded the vote on the neutrality pact, the basic treaty that will turn over control of the canal to the Panamanians Dec. 31, 1999, was ratified by the Senate April 18. The Senate approved the reservation designed to reduce the impact of the DeConcini Reservation and several other reservations dealing with, among other issues, the construction of another canal in Panama, interest payments on original U.S. investments in the canal and the schedule for the exchange of instruments of ratification. Near the end of the historic debate, the Senate again rejected a proposal by Sen. Griffin to send the treaties back to the president for renegotiation.

In his remarks made April 18 after ratification of the basic treaty, President Carter said, "This is a day of which Americans can always feel proud, *for now we have reminded the world and ourselves of the things that we stand for as a nation." The ratification of the treaties, Carter said, was an indication "that what is best and noblest in our national spirit will prevail. Today we've shown that we are still builders, with our face still turned confidently to the future."*

Torrijos appeared on Panamanian television April 18 to say that if the treaties had not been ratified "[w]e would have started another struggle for liberation," and perhaps closed the canal by force. "Today the canal was placed within two votes of being destroyed," he added. Torrijos said that he accepted the final language approved by the Senate and he termed the passage of the treaties "the greatest, the most-awaited and most discussed triumph" of his country.

> *Following are the texts of President Carter's Feb. 1 "fireside chat" and his March 16 and April 18 statements on ratification of the treaties; the treaties as signed by Carter and Torrijos in 1977 and as altered by the Senate in 1978: [The treaties, as signed, were included in* Historic Documents of 1977. *They are being repeated in this volume because of the Senate alterations.] (Boldface headings in brackets have been added by Congressional Quarterly to highlight the organization of the text):*

FIRESIDE CHAT
February 1, 1978

Good evening.

Seventy-five years ago, our Nation signed a treaty which gave us rights to build a canal across Panama, to take the historic step of joining the Atlantic and Pacific Oceans. The results of the agreement have been of great benefit to ourselves and to other nations throughout the world who navigate the high seas.

The building of the canal was one of the greatest engineering feats of history. Although massive in concept and construction, it's relatively simple in design and has been reliable and efficient in operation. We Americans are justly and deeply proud of this great achievement.

The canal has also been a source of pride and benefit to the people of Panama — but a cause of some continuing discontent. Because we have controlled a 10-mile-wide strip of land across the heart of their country and because they considered the original terms of the agreement to be unfair, the people of Panama have been dissatisfied with the treaty. It was drafted here in our country and was not signed by any Panamanian. Our own Secretary of State who did sign the original treaty said it was "vastly advantageous to the United States and . . . not so advantageous to Panama."

In 1964, after consulting with former Presidents Truman and Eisenhower, President Johnson committed our Nation to work towards a new treaty with the Republic of Panama. And last summer, after 14 years of negotiation under two Democratic Presidents and two Republican Presidents, we reached and signed an agreement that is fair and beneficial to both countries. The United States Senate will soon be debating whether these treaties should be ratified.

Throughout the negotiations, we were determined that our national security interests would be protected; that the canal would always be open and neutral and available to ships of all nations; that in time of need or emergency our warships would have the right to go to the head of the line for priority passage through the canal; and that our military forces would have the permanent right to defend the canal if it should ever be in danger. The new treaties meet all of these requirements.

[Terms of Agreement]

Let me outline the terms of the agreement. There are two treaties — one covering the rest of this century, and the other guaranteeing the safety, openness, and neutrality of the canal after the year 1999, when Panama will be in charge of its operation.

For the rest of this century, we will operate the canal through a nine-person board of directors. Five members will be from the United States and four will be from Panama. Within the area of the present Canal Zone, we have the right to select whatever lands and waters our military and civilian forces need to maintain, to operate, and to defend the canal.

About 75 percent of those who now maintain and operate the canal are Panamanians; over the next 22 years, as we manage the canal together, this percentage will increase. The Americans who work on the canal will continue to have their rights of employment, promotion, and retirement carefully protected.

We will share with Panama some of the fees paid by shippers who use the canal. As in the past, the canal should continue to be self-supporting.

This is not a partisan issue. The treaties are strongly backed by President Gerald Ford and by Former Secretaries of State Dean Rusk and Henry Kissinger. They are endorsed by our business and professional leaders, especially those who recognize the benefits of good will and trade with other nations in this hemisphere. And they were endorsed overwhelmingly by the Senate Foreign Relations Committee which, this week, moved closer to ratification by approving the treaties, although with some recommended changes which we do not feel are needed.

And the treaties are supported enthusiastically by every member of the Joint Chiefs of Staff — General George Brown, the Chairman, General Bernard Rogers, Chief of Staff of the Army, Admiral James Holloway, Chief of Naval Operations, General David Jones, Chief of Staff of the Air Force, and General Lewis Wilson, Commandant of the Marine Corps —

responsible men whose profession is the defense of this Nation and the preservation of our security.

The treaties also have been overwhelmingly supported throughout Latin America, but predictably, they are opposed abroad by some who are unfriendly to the United States and who would like to see disorder in Panama and a disruption of our political, economic, and military ties with our friends in Central and South America and in the Caribbean.

I know that the treaties also have been opposed by many Americans. Much of that opposition is based on misunderstanding and misinformation. I've found that when the full terms of the agreement are known, most people are convinced that the national interests of our country will be served best by ratifying the treaties.

Tonight, I want you to hear the facts. I want to answer the most serious questions and tell you why I feel the Panama Canal treaties should be approved.

[U.S. National Interest]

The most important reason — the only reason — to ratify the treaties is that they are in the highest national interest of the United States and will strengthen our position in the world. Our security interests will be stronger. Our trade opportunities will be improved. We will demonstrate that as a large and powerful country, we are able to deal fairly and honorably with a proud but smaller sovereign nation. We will honor our commitment to those engaged in world commerce that the Panama Canal will be open and available for use by their ships — at a reasonable and competitive cost — both now and in the future.

Let me answer specifically the most common questions about the treaties.

Will our Nation have the right to protect and defend the canal against any armed attack or threat to the security of the canal or of ships going through it?

The answer is yes, and is contained in both treaties and also in the statement of understanding between the leaders of our two nations.

The first treaty says, and I quote: "The United States of America and the Republic of Panama commit themselves to protect and defend the Panama Canal. Each Party shall act, in accordance with its constitutional processes, to meet the danger resulting from an armed attack or other actions which threaten the security of the Panama Canal or [of] ships transiting it."

The neutrality treaty says, and I quote again: "The United States of America and the Republic of Panama agree to maintain the regime of neutrality established in this Treaty, which shall be maintained in order that the Canal shall remain permanently neutral. . . ."

And to explain exactly what that means, the statement of understanding says, and I quote again: "Under (the Neutrality Treaty), Panama and the United States have the responsibility to assure that the Panama Canal will remain open and secure to ships of all nations. The correct interpretation of this principle is that each of the two countries shall, in accordance with their respective constitutional processes, defend the Canal against any threat to the regime of neutrality, and consequently [shall] have the right to act against the Canal or against the peaceful transit of vessels through the Canal."

It is obvious that we can take whatever military action is necessary to make sure that the canal always remains open and safe.

Of course, this does not give the United States any right to intervene in the internal affairs of Panama, nor would our military action ever be directed against the territorial integrity or the political independence of Panama.

Military experts agree that even with the Panamanian Armed Forces joined with us as brothers against a common enemy, it would take a large number of American troops to ward off a heavy attack. I, as President, would not hesitate to deploy whatever armed forces are necessary to defend the canal, and I have no doubt that even in a sustained combat, that we would be successful. But there is a much better way than sending our sons and grandsons to fight in the jungles of Panama.

We would serve our interests better by implementing the new treaties, an action that will help to avoid any attack on the Panama Canal.

What we want is the permanent right to use the canal — and we can defend this right through the treaties — through real cooperation with Panama. The citizens of Panama and their government have already shown their support of the new partnership, and a protocol to the neutrality treaty will be signed by many other nations, thereby showing their strong approval.

The new treaties will naturally change Panama from a passive and sometimes deeply resentful bystander into an active and interested partner, whose vital interests will be served by a well-operated canal. This agreement leads to cooperation and not confrontation between our country and Panama.

[Question of Ownership]

Another question is: Why should we give away the Panama Canal Zone? As many people say, "We bought it; we paid for it; it's ours."

I must repeat a very important point: We do not own the Panama Canal Zone. We have never had sovereignty over it. We have only had the right to use it.

The Canal Zone cannot be compared with United States territory. We bought Alaska from the Russians, and no one has ever doubted that we own it. We bought the Louisiana Purchases — Territories from France, and that's an integral part of the United States.

From the beginning, we have made an annual payment to Panama to use their land. You do not pay rent on your own land. The Panama Canal Zone has always been Panamanian territory. The U.S. Supreme Court and previous American Presidents have repeatedly acknowledged the sovereignty of Panama over the Canal Zone.

We've never needed to own the Panama Canal Zone, any more than we need to own a 10-mile-wide strip of land all the way through Canada from Alaska when we build an international gas pipeline.

The new treaties give us what we do need — not ownership of the canal but the right to use it and to protect it. As the Chairman of the Joint Chiefs of Staff has said, "The strategic value of the canal lies in its use."

There's another question: Can our naval ships, our warships, in time of need or emergency, get through the canal immediately instead of waiting in line?

The treaties answer that clearly by guaranteeing that our ships will always have expeditious transit through the canal. To make sure that there could be no possible disagreement about what these words mean, the joint statement says that expeditious transit, and I quote, "is intended . . . to assure the transit of such vessels through the Canal as quickly as possible, without any impediment, with expedited treatment, and in case of need or emergency, to go to the head of the line of vessels in order to transit the Canal rapidly."

Will the treaties affect our standing in Latin America? Will they create a so-called power vacuum, which our enemies might move in to fill? They will do just the opposite. The treaties will increase our Nation's influence in this hemisphere, will help to reduce any mistrust and disagreement, and they will remove a major source of anti-American feeling.

The new agreement has already provided vivid proof to the people of this hemisphere that a new era of friendship and cooperation is beginning and that what they regard as the last remnant of alleged American colonialism is being removed.

Last fall, I met individually with the leaders of 18 countries in this hemisphere. Between the United States and Latin America there is already a new sense of equality, a new sense of trust and mutual respect that exists because of the Panama Canal treaties. This opens up a fine opportunity for us in good will, trade, jobs, exports, and political cooperation.

If the treaties should be rejected, this would all be lost, and disappointment and despair among our good neighbors and traditional friends would be severe.

In the peaceful struggle against alien ideologies like communism, these treaties are a step in the right direction. Nothing could strengthen our competitors and adversaries in this hemisphere more than for us to reject this agreement.

What if a new sea-level canal should be needed in the future? This question has been studied over and over throughout this century, from before the time the canal was built up through the last few years. Every study has reached the same conclusion — that the best place to build a sea-level canal is in Panama.

The treaties say that if we want to build such a canal, we will build it in Panama, and if any canal is to be built in Panama, that we, the United

States, will have the right to participate in the project.

This is a clear benefit to us, for it ensures that, say, 10 or 20 years from now, no unfriendly but wealthy power will be able to purchase the right to build a sea-level canal, to bypass the existing canal, perhaps leaving that other nation in control of the only usable waterway across the isthmus.

Are we paying Panama to take the canal? We are not. Under the new treaty, any payments to Panama will come from tolls paid by ships which use the canal.

[Panamanian Government]

What about the present and the future stability and the capability of the Panamanian Government? Do the people of Panama themselves support the agreement?

Well, as you know, Panama and her people have been our historical allies and friends. The present leader of Panama has been in office for more than 9 years, and he heads a stable government which has encouraged the development of free enterprise in Panama. Democratic elections will be held this August to choose the members of the Panamanian Assembly, who will in turn elect a President and a Vice President by majority vote. In the past, regimes have changed in Panama, but for 75 years, no Panamanian government has ever wanted to close the canal.

Panama wants the canal open and neutral — perhaps even more than we do. The canal's continued operation is very important to us, but it is much more than that to Panama. To Panama, it's crucial. Much of her economy flows directly or indirectly from the canal. Panama would be no more likely to neglect or to close the canal than we would be to close the Interstate Highway System here in the United States.

In an open and free referendum last October, which was monitored very carefully by the United Nations, the people of Panama gave the new treaties their support.

The major threat to the canal comes not from any government of Panama, but from misguided persons who may try to fan the flames of dissatisfaction with the terms of the old treaty.

There's a final question — about the deeper meaning of the treaties themselves, to us and to Panama.

Recently, I discussed the treaties with David McCullough, author of "The Path Between the Seas," the great history of the Panama Canal. He believes that the canal is something that we built and have looked after these many years; it is "ours" in that sense, which is very different from just ownership.

So, when we talk of the canal, whether we are old, young, for or against the treaties, we are talking about very deep and elemental feelings about our own strength.

Still, we Americans want a more humane and stable world. We believe in good will and fairness, as well as strength. This agreement with Panama is something we want because we know it is right. This is not merely the surest way to protect and save the canal; it's a strong, positive act of a people who are still confident, still creative, still great.

This new partnership can become a source of national pride and self-respect in much the same way that building the canal was 75 years ago. It's the spirit in which we act that is so very important.

Theodore Roosevelt, who was President when America built the canal, saw history itself as a force, and the history of our own time and the changes it has brought would not be lost on him. He knew that change was inevitable and necessary. Change is growth. The true conservative, he once remarked, keeps his face to the future.

But if Theodore Roosevelt were to endorse the treaties, as I'm quite sure he would, it would be mainly because he could see the decision as one by which we are demonstrating the kind of great power we wish to be.

"We cannot avoid meeting great issues," Roosevelt said. "All that we can determine for ourselves is whether we shall meet them well or ill."

The Panama Canal is a vast, heroic expression of that age-old desire to bridge the divide and to bring people closer together. This is what the treaties are all about.

We can sense what Roosevelt called "the lift toward nobler things which marks a great and generous people."

In this historic decision, he would join us in our pride for being a great and generous people, with the national strength and wisdom to do what is right for us and what is fair to others.

Thank you very much.

CARTER STATEMENT
March 16, 1978

I have a brief statement to make.

The people of our Nation owe a debt of thanks to the Members of the United States Senate for their courageous action taken today in voting for the Panama Canal neutrality treaty.

I add my sincere personal congratulations to the entire Senate, and especially to the three men who have led their colleagues with bipartisan statesmanship and wisdom through this long debate — Senator Robert Byrd, the majority leader, Senator Howard Baker, the minority leader, and Senator John Sparkman, chairman of the Senate Foreign Relations Committee.

As a nation, we also owe our gratitude and admiration to former President Ford and to Democratic and Republican leaders who have served in previous administrations who, by giving the treaties their support, gave us the opportunity to judge the treaties on their merits and not on a partisan, political basis.

This vote today is, of course, only the first step in the process of ratification, but I am confident that the Senate will show the same courage and foresight when it considers the second treaty. This is a promising step toward a new era in our relationships with Panama and with all of Latin America.

General Torrijos and the Panamanian people have been patient and forbearing during the negotiations and during the Senate debate. They've earned the confidence and respect of the American people. Their actions during the last few months is proof of their willingness to form a partnership with us, to join in cooperation rather than confrontation.

It's been more than 14 years since negotiations began with Panama, and we've been through many months of discussion and debate about the two treaties that the Senate has considered. This has been a long debate, but all of us have learned from it.

The basic purpose and the underlying principles of the treaty have been affirmed and strengthened by the actions of the Senate. Under the treaty as approved, the United States and Panama will have joint responsibility to assure that the canal after the year 2000 will remain neutral and secure, open and accessible.

The United States can take whatever actions are necessary to make sure the canal remains open and safe. The vessels of war and auxiliary vessels of the United States and Panama are assured of transit through the canal as quickly as possible and can go to the head of the line in time of emergency or need.

While the right of the United States and Panama to act against any threat to the regime of neutrality is assured by this treaty, it does not mean that there is a right of intervention, nor do we want a right of intervention by the United States in the internal affairs of Panama.

But perhaps the most encouraging lesson of all in these last long months is that in a full and open debate, even in a very controversial and difficult issue, in our foreign policy objectives, we can still reach the decisions that are in our Nation's long-term, best interests.

I congratulate again the Senators for their decision and give them, on behalf of the Nation, my sincere thanks.

CARTER STATEMENT
April 18, 1978

THE PRESIDENT. This is a day of which Americans can always feel proud, for now we have reminded the world and ourselves of the things that we stand for as a nation. The negotiations that led to these treaties began 14 years ago, and they continued under four administrations, four Presidents. I'm proud that they reached their conclusion while I was President. But I'm far prouder that we, as a people, have shown that in a full and open debate about difficult foreign policy objectives, that we will reach the decisions that are in the best interest of our Nation.

The debate has been long and hard. But in the end, it's given our decision a firm base in the will of the American people. Over the last 8 months, millions of Americans have studied the treaties, have registered their views and, in some cases, have changed their minds. No matter which side they took in this debate, most Americans have acted out of sincere concern about our Nation's interest.

I would like to express my thanks to a few for the job they've done. Under the leadership of Senators Byrd and Baker and Sparkman and others, the Senate has carried out its responsibility of advice and consent with great care. All of us owe them our thanks. I feel a special gratitude and admiration for those Senators who have done what was right, because it was right, despite tremendous pressure and, in some cases, political threats.

The loyal employees of the Panama Canal Zone and the Canal Zone Government also deserve our gratitude and our admiration for their performance during these months of great uncertainty.

And General Torrijos and the people of Panama, who have followed this debate closely and through every stage, have been willing partners and cooperative and patient friends. There is no better indication of the prospect for friendly relations between us in the future than their conduct during the last few months.

We now have a partnership with Panama to maintain and to operate and to defend the canal. We have the clear right to take whatever action is necessary to defend the canal and to keep it open and neutral and accessible. We do not have the right to interfere in Panama's internal affairs. That is a right we neither possess nor desire.

These treaties can mark the beginning of a new era in our relations not only with Panama but with all the rest of the world. They symbolize our determination to deal with the developing nations of the world, on the basis of mutual respect and partnership. But the treaties also reaffirm a spirit that is very strong, constant, and old in the American character.

Sixty-four years ago when the first ship traveled through the canal, our people took legitimate pride in what our ingenuity, our perserverance, and our vision had brought about. We were a nation of builders, and the canal was one of our greatest glories.

And today we have shown that we remain true to that determination, that ingenuity, and most of all, that vision. Today we've proven that what is best and noblest in our national spirit will prevail. Today we've shown that we are still builders, with our face still turned confidently to the future. That is why I believe all Americans should share the pride I feel in the accomplishments which we registered today.

When I was coming in to make this announcement, the Ambassador of Panama, Gabriel Lewis, informed me that General Torrijos has accepted the terms of the treaty that passed the Senate this afternoon. And I want to reaffirm my thanks and my commitment to a true partnership with General Torrijos and the people of a great nation, Panama.

Thank you.

REPORTER. Mr. President, are you going down to Panama now?

THE PRESIDENT. Now?

Q. With these treaties in a few weeks, for formal ceremonies?

THE PRESIDENT. I have been invited by General Torrijos to come to

Panama. I would like very much to accept his invitation.
Q. Thank you.
THE PRESIDENT. Thank you.

PANAMA CANAL TREATY

[Reservations, Understandings, p. 213]

The United States of America and the Republic of Panama,

Acting in the spirit of the Joint Declaration of April 3, 1964, by the Representatives of the Governments of the United States of America and the Republic of Panama, and of the Joint Statement of Principles of February 7, 1974, initialed by the Secretary of State of the United States of America and the Foreign Minister of the Republic of Panama, and

Acknowledging the Republic of Panama's sovereignty over its territory,

Have decided to terminate the prior Treaties pertaining to the Panama Canal and to conclude a new Treaty to serve as the basis for a new relationship between them and, accordingly, have agreed upon the following:

ARTICLE I

Abrogation of Prior Treaties
and Establishment
of a New Relationship

1. Upon its entry into force, this Treaty terminates and supersedes:

(a) The Isthmian Canal Convention between the United States of America and the Republic of Panama, signed at Washington, November 18, 1903;

(b) The Treaty of Friendship and Cooperation signed at Washington, March 2, 1936, and the Treaty of Mutual Understanding and Cooperation and the related Memorandum of Understandings Reached, signed at Panama, January 25, 1955, between the United States of America and the Republic of Panama;

(c) All other treaties, conventions, agreements and exchanges of notes between the United States of America and the Republic of Panama, concerning the Panama Canal which were in force prior to the entry into force of this Treaty; and

(d) Provisions concerning the Panama Canal which appear in other treaties, conventions, agreements and exchanges of notes between the United States of America and the Republic of Panama which were in force prior to the entry into force of this Treaty.

2. In accordance with the terms of this Treaty and related agreements, the Republic of Panama, as territorial sovereign, grants to the United States of America, for the duration of this Treaty, the rights necessary to regulate the transit of ships through the Panama Canal, and

to manage, operate, maintain, improve, protect and defend the Canal. The Republic of Panama guarantees to the United States of America the peaceful use of the land and water areas which it has been granted the rights to use for such purposes [pursuant] to this Treaty and related agreements.

3. The Republic of Panama shall participate increasingly in the management and protection and defense of the Canal, as provided in this Treaty.

4. In view of the special relationship established by this Treaty, the United States of America and the Republic of Panama shall cooperate to assure the uninterrupted and efficient operation of the Panama Canal.

ARTICLE II

Ratification, Entry into Force, and Termination

1. This Treaty shall be subject to ratification in accordance with the constitutional procedures of the two Parties. The instruments of ratification of this Treaty shall be exchanged at Panama at the same time as the instruments of ratification of the Treaty Concerning the Permanent Neutrality and Operation of the Panama Canal, signed this date, are exchanged. This Treaty shall enter into force, simultaneously with the Treaty Concerning the Permanent Neutrality and Operation of the Panama Canal, six calendar months from the date of the exchange of the instruments of ratification.

2. This Treaty shall terminate at noon, Panama time, December 31, 1999.

ARTICLE III

Canal Operation and Management

1. The Republic of Panama, as territorial sovereign, grants to the United States of America the rights to manage, operate, and maintain the Panama Canal, its complementary works, installations and equipment and to provide for the orderly transit of vessels through the Panama Canal. The United States of America accepts the grant of such rights and undertakes to exercise them in accordance with this Treaty and related agreements.

2. In carrying out the foregoing responsibilities, the United States of America may:

(a) Use for the aforementioned purposes, without cost except as provided in this Treaty, the various installations and areas (including the Panama Canal) and waters, described in the Agreement in Implementation of this Article, signed this date, as well as such other areas and installations as are made available to the United States of America under this Treaty and related agreements, and take the measures necessary to ensure sanitation of such areas;

(b) Make such improvements and alterations to the aforesaid installations and areas as it deems appropriate, consistent with the terms of this Treaty;

(c) Make and enforce all rules pertaining to the passage of vessels through the Canal and other rules with respect to navigation and maritime matters, in accordance with this Treaty and related agreements. The Republic of Panama will lend its cooperation, when necessary, in the enforcement of such rules;

(d) Establish, modify, collect and retain tolls for the use of the Panama Canal, and other charges, and establish and modify methods of their assessment;

(e) Regulate relations with employees of the United States Government;

(f) Provide supporting services to facilitate the performance of its responsibilities under this Article;

(g) Issue and enforce regulations for the effective exercise of the rights and responsibilities of the United States of America under this Treaty and related agreements. The Republic of Panama will lend its cooperation, when necessary, in the enforcement of such rules; and

(h) Exercise any other right granted under this Treaty, or otherwise agreed upon between the two Parties.

3. Pursuant to the foregoing grant of rights, the United States of America shall, in accordance with the terms of this Treaty and the provisions of United States law, carry out its responsibilities by means of a United States Government agency called the Panama Canal Commission, which shall be constituted by and in conformity with the laws of the United States of America.

(a) The Panama Canal Commission shall be supervised by a Board composed of nine members, five of whom shall be nationals of the United States of America, and four of whom shall be Panamanian nationals proposed by the Republic of Panama for appointment to such positions by the United States of America in a timely manner.

(b) Should the Republic of Panama request the United States of America to remove a Panamanian national from membership on the Board, the United States of America shall agree to such a request. In that event, the Republic of Panama shall propose another Panamanian national for appointment by the United States of America to such position in a timely manner. In case of removal of a Panamanian member of the Board at the initiative of the United States of America, both Parties will consult in advance in order to reach agreement concerning such removal, and the Republic of Panama shall propose another Panamanian national for appointment by the United States of America in his stead.

(c) The United States of America shall employ a national of the United States of America as Administrator of the Panama Canal Commission, and a Panamanian national as Deputy Administrator, through December 31, 1989. Beginning January 1, 1990, a Panamanian national shall be employed as the Administrator and a national of the United States of America shall occupy the position of Deputy Administrator. Such Panamanian nationals shall be proposed to the United States of America by the Republic of Panama for appointment to such positions by the United States of America.

(d) Should the United States of America remove the Panamanian national from his position as Deputy Administrator, or Administrator, the Republic of Panama shall propose another Panamanian national for appointment to such position by the United States of America.

4. An illustrative description of the activities the Panama Canal Commission will perform in carrying out the responsibilities and rights of the United States of America under this Article is set forth at the Annex. Also set forth in the Annex are procedures for the discontinuance or transfer of those activities performed prior to the entry into force of this Treaty by the Panama Canal Company or the Canal Zone Government which are not to be carried out by the Panama Canal Commission.

5. The Panama Canal Commission shall reimburse the Republic of Panama for the costs incurred by the Republic of Panama in providing the following public services in the Canal operating areas and in housing areas set forth in the Agreement in Implementation of Article III of this Treaty and occupied by both United States and Panamanian citizen employees of the Panama Canal Commission: police, fire protection, street maintenance, street lighting, street cleaning, traffic management and garbage collection. The Panama Canal Commission shall pay the Republic of Panama the sum of ten million United States dollars ($10,000,000) per annum for the foregoing services. It is agreed that every three years from the date that this Treaty enters into force, the costs involved in furnishing said services shall be reexamined to determine whether adjustment of the annual payment should be made because of inflation and other relevant factors affecting the cost of such services.

6. The Republic of Panama shall be responsible for providing, in all areas comprising the former Canal Zone, services of a general jurisdictional nature such as customs and immigration, postal services, courts and licensing, in accordance with this Treaty and related agreements.

7. The United States of America and the Republic of Panama shall establish a Panama Canal Consultative Committee, composed of an equal number of high-level representatives of the United States of America and the Republic of Panama, and which may appoint such subcommittees as it may deem appropriate. This Committee shall advise the United States of America and the Republic of Panama on matters of policy affecting the Canal's operation. In view of both Parties' special interest in the continuity and efficiency of the Canal operation in the future, the Committee shall advise on matters such as general tolls policy, employment and training policies to increase the participation of Panamanian nationals in the operation of the Canal, and international policies on matters concerning the Canal. The Committee's recommendations shall be transmitted to the two Governments, which shall give such recommendations full consideration in the formulation of such policy decisions.

8. In addition to the participation of Panamanian nationals at high management levels of the Panama Canal Commission, as provided for in paragraph 3 of this Article, there shall be growing participation of Panamanian nationals at all other levels and areas of employment in the aforesaid Commission, with the objective of preparing, in an orderly and efficient fashion, for the assumption by the Republic of Panama of full responsibility for the management, operation and maintenance of the Canal upon the termination of this Treaty.

9. The use of the areas, waters and installations with respect to which the United States of America is granted rights pursuant to this Article, and the rights and legal status of United States Government agencies and employees operating in the Republic of Panama pursuant to this Article, shall be governed by the Agreement in Implementation of this Article, signed this date.

10. Upon entry into force of this Treaty, the United States Government agencies known as the Panama Canal Company and the Canal Zone Government shall cease to operate within the territory of the Republic of Panama that formerly constituted the Canal Zone.

ARTICLE IV

Protection and Defense

1. The United States of America and the Republic of Panama commit themselves to protect and defend the Panama Canal. Each Party shall act, in accordance with its constitutional processes, to meet the danger resulting from an armed attack or other actions which threaten the security of the Panama Canal or of ships transiting it.

2. For the duration of this Treaty, the United States of America shall have primary responsibility to protect and defend the Canal. The rights of the United States of America to station, train, and move military forces within the Republic of Panama are described in the Agreement in Implementation of this Article, signed this date. The use of areas and installations and the legal status of the armed forces of the United States of America in the Republic of Panama shall be governed by the aforesaid Agreement.

3. In order to facilitate the participation and cooperation of the armed forces of both Parties in the protection and defense of the Canal, the United States of America and the Republic of Panama shall establish a Combined Board comprised of an equal number of senior military representatives of each Party. These representatives shall be charged by their respective governments with consulting and cooperating on all matters pertaining to the protection and defense of the Canal, and with planning for actions to be taken in concert for that purpose. Such combined protection and defense arrangements shall not inhibit the identity or lines of authority of the armed forces of the United States of America or the Republic of Panama. The Combined Board shall provide for coordination and cooperation concerning such matters as:

(a) The preparation of contingency plans for the protection and defense of the Canal based upon the cooperative efforts of the armed forces of both Parties;

(b) The planning and conduct of combined military exercises; and

(c) The conduct of United States and Panamanian military operations with respect to the protection and defense of the Canal.

4. The Combined Board shall, at five-year intervals throughout the duration of this Treaty, review the resources being made available by the two Parties for the protection and defense of the Canal. Also, the Combined Board shall make appropriate recommendations to the two Governments respecting projected requirements, the efficient utilization of available resources of the two Parties, and other matters of mutual interest with respect to the protection and defense of the Canal.

5. To the extent possible consistent with its primary responsibility for the protection and defense of the Panama Canal, the United States of America will endeavor to maintain its armed forces in the Republic of Panama in normal times at a level not in excess of that of the armed forces of the United States of America in the territory of the former Canal Zone immediately prior to the entry into force of this Treaty.

ARTICLE V

Principle of Non-Intervention

Employees of the Panama Canal Commission, their dependents and designated contractors of the Panama Canal Commission, who are nationals of the United States of America, shall respect the laws of the Republic of Panama and shall abstain from any activity incompatible with the spirit of this Treaty. Accordingly, they shall abstain from any political activity in the Republic of Panama as well as from any intervention in the internal affairs of the Republic of Panama. The United States of America shall take all measures within its authority to ensure that the provisions of this Article are fulfilled.

ARTICLE VI

Protection of the Environment

1. The United States of America and the Republic of Panama commit themselves to implement this Treaty in a manner consistent with the protection of the natural environment of the Republic of Panama. To this end, they shall consult and cooperate with each other in all appropriate ways to ensure that they shall give due regard to the protection and conservation of the environment.

2. A Joint Commission on the Environment shall be established with equal representation from the United States of America and the Republic of Panama, which shall periodically review the implementation of this Treaty and shall recommend as appropriate to the two Governments ways

to avoid or, should this not be possible, to mitigate the adverse environmental impacts which might result from their respective actions pursuant to the Treaty.

3. The United States of America and the Republic of Panama shall furnish the Joint Commission on the Environment complete information on any action taken in accordance with this Treaty which, in the judgment of both, might have a significant effect on the environment. Such information shall be made available to the Commission as far in advance of the contemplated action as possible to facilitate the study by the Commission of any potential environmental problems and to allow for consideration of the recommendation of the Commission before the contemplated action is carried out.

ARTICLE VII

Flags

1. The entire territory of the Republic of Panama, including the areas the use of which the Republic of Panama makes available to the United States of America pursuant to this Treaty and related agreements, shall be under the flag of the Republic of Panama, and consequently such flag always shall occupy the position of honor.

2. The flag of the United States of America may be displayed, together with the flag of the Republic of Panama, at the headquarters of the Panama Canal Commission, at the site of the Combined Board, and as provided in the Agreement in Implementation of Article IV of this Treaty.

3. The flag of the United States of America also may be displayed at other places and on some occasions, as agreed by both Parties.

ARTICLE VIII

Privileges and Immunities

1. The installations owned or used by the agencies or instrumentalities of the United States of America operating in the Republic of Panama pursuant to this Treaty and related agreements, and their official archives and documents, shall be inviolable. The two Parties shall agree on procedures to be followed in the conduct of any criminal investigation at such locations by the Republic of Panama.

2. Agencies and instrumentalities of the Government of the United States of America operating in the Republic of Panama pursuant to this Treaty and related agreements shall be immune from the jurisdiction of the Republic of Panama.

3. In addition to such other privileges and immunities as are afforded to employees of the United States Government and their dependents pursuant to this Treaty, the United States of America may designate up to twenty officials of the Panama Canal Commission who, along with their dependents, shall enjoy the privileges and immunities accorded to diplomatic agents and their dependents under international law and prac-

tice. The United States of America shall furnish to the Republic of Panama a list of the names of said officials and their dependents, identifying the positions they occupy in the Government of the United States of America, and shall keep such list current at all times.

ARTICLE IX

Applicable Laws and
Law Enforcement

1. In accordance with the provisions of this Treaty and related agreements, the law of the Republic of Panama shall apply in the areas made available for the use of the United States of America pursuant to this Treaty. The law of the Republic of Panama shall be applied to matters or events which occurred in the former Canal Zone prior to the entry into force of this Treaty only to the extent specifically provided in prior treaties and agreements.

2. Natural or juridical persons who, on the date of entry into force of this Treaty, are engaged in business or non-profit activities at locations in the former Canal Zone may continue such business or activities at those locations under the same terms and conditions prevailing prior to the entry into force of this Treaty for a thirty-month transition period from its entry into force. The Republic of Panama shall maintain the same operating conditions as those applicable to the aforementioned enterprises prior to the entry into force of this Treaty in order that they may receive licenses to do business in the Republic of Panama subject to their compliance with the requirements of its law. Thereafter, such persons shall receive the same treatment under the law of the Republic of Panama as similar enterprises already established in the rest of the territory of the Republic of Panama without discrimination.

3. The rights of ownership, as recognized by the United States of America, enjoyed by natural or juridical private persons in buildings and other improvements to real property located in the former Canal Zone shall be recognized by the Republic of Panama in conformity with its laws.

4. With respect to buildings and other improvements to real property located in the Canal operating areas, housing areas or other areas subject to the licensing procedure established in Article IV of the Agreement in Implementation of Article III of this Treaty, the owners shall be authorized to continue using the land upon which their property is located in accordance with the procedures established in that Article.

5. With respect to buildings and other improvements to real property located in areas of the former Canal Zone to which the aforesaid licensing procedure is not applicable, or may cease to be applicable during the lifetime or upon termination of this Treaty, the owners may continue to use the land upon which their property is located, subject to the payment of a reasonable charge to the Republic of Panama. Should the Republic of Panama decide to sell such land, the owners of the buildings or other improvements located thereon shall be offered a first option to purchase such

land at a reasonable cost. In the case of non-profit enterprises, such as churches and fraternal organizations, the cost of purchase will be nominal in accordance with the prevailing practice in the rest of the territory of the Republic of Panama.

6. If any of the aforementioned persons are required by the Republic of Panama to discontinue their activities or vacate their property for public purposes, they shall be compensated at fair market value by the Republic of Panama.

7. The provisions of paragraphs 2-6 above shall apply to natural or juridical persons who have been engaged in business or non-profit activities at locations in the former Canal Zone for at least six months prior to the date of signature of this Treaty.

8. The Republic of Panama shall not issue, adopt or enforce any law, decree, regulation, or international agreement or take any other action which purports to regulate or would otherwise interfere with the exercise on the part of the United States of America of any right granted under this Treaty or related agreements.

9. Vessels transiting the Canal, and cargo, passengers and crews carried on such vessels shall be exempt from any taxes, fees, or other charges by the Republic of Panama. However, in the event such vessels call at a Panamanian port, they may be assessed charges incident thereto, such as charges for services provided to the vessel. The Republic of Panama may also require the passengers and crew disembarking from such vessels to pay such taxes, fees and charges as are established under Panamanian law for persons entering its territory. Such taxes, fees and charges shall be assessed on a nondiscriminatory basis.

10. The United States of America and the Republic of Panama will cooperate in taking such steps as may from time to time be necessary to guarantee the security of the Panama Canal Commission, its property, its employees and their dependents, and their property, for Forces of the United States of America and the members thereof, the civilian component of the United States Forces, the dependents of members of the Forces and the civilian component, and their property, and the contractors of the Panama Canal Commission and of the United States Forces, their dependents, and their property. The Republic of Panama will seek from its Legislative Branch such legislation as may be needed to carry out the foregoing purposes and to punish any offenders.

11. The Parties shall conclude an agreement whereby nationals of either State, who are sentenced by the courts of the other State, and who are not domiciled therein, may elect to serve their sentences in their State of nationality.

ARTICLE X

Employment with the
Panama Canal Commission

1. In exercising its right and fulfilling its responsibilities as the employer, the United States of America shall establish employment and

labor regulations which shall contain the terms, conditions and prerequisites for all categories of employees of the Panama Canal Commission. These regulations shall be provided to the Republic of Panama prior to their entry into force.

2. (a) The regulations shall establish a system of preference when hiring employees, for Panamanian applicants possessing the skills and qualifications required for employment by the Panama Canal Commission. The United States of America shall endeavor to ensure that the number of Panamanian nationals employed by the Panama Canal Commission in relation to the total number of its employees will conform to the proportion established for foreign enterprises under the law of the Republic of Panama.

(b) The terms and conditions of employment to be established will in general be no less favorable to persons already employed by the Panama Canal Company or Canal Zone Government prior to the entry into force of this Treaty, than those in effect immediately prior to that date.

3. (a) The United States of America shall establish an employment policy for the Panama Canal Commission that shall generally limit the recruitment of personnel outside the Republic of Panama to persons possessing requisite skills and qualifications which are not available in the Republic of Panama.

(b) The United States of America will establish training programs for Panamanian employees and apprentices in order to increase the number of Panamanian nationals qualified to assume positions with the Panama Canal Commission, as positions become available.

(c) Within five years from the entry into force of this Treaty, the number of United States nationals employed by the Panama Canal Commission who were previously employed by the Panama Canal Company shall be at least twenty percent less than the total number of United States nationals working for the Panama Canal Company immediately prior to the entry into force of this Treaty.

(d) The United States of America shall periodically inform the Republic of Panama, through the Coordinating Committee, established pursuant to the Agreement in Implementation of Article III of this Treaty, of available positions within the Panama Canal Commission. The Republic of Panama shall similarly provide the United States of America any information it may have as to the availability of Panamanian nationals claiming to have skills and qualifications that might be required by the Panama Canal Commission, in order that the United States of America may take this information into account.

4. The United States of America will establish qualification standards for skills, training and experience required by the Panama Canal Commission. In establishing such standards, to the extent they include a requirement for a professional license, the United States of America, without prejudice to its right to require additional professional skills and qualifications, shall recognize the professional licenses issued by the Republic of Panama.

5. The United States of America shall establish a policy for the periodic rotation, at a maximum of every five years, of United States citizen employees and other non-Panamanian employees, hired after the entry into force of this Treaty. It is recognized that certain exceptions to the said policy of rotation may be made for sound administrative reasons, such as in the case of employees holding positions requiring certain non-transferable or non-recruitable skills.

6. With regard to wages and fringe benefits, there shall be no discrimination on the basis of nationality, sex, or race. Payments by the Panama Canal Commission of additional remuneration, or the provision of other benefits, such as home leave benefits, to United States nationals employed prior to entry into force of this Treaty, or to persons of any nationality, including Panamanian nationals who are thereafter recruited outside of the Republic of Panama and who change their place of residence, shall not be considered to be discrimination for the purpose of this paragraph.

7. Persons employed by the Panama Canal Company or Canal Zone Government prior to the entry into force of this Treaty, who are displaced from their employment as a result of the discontinuance by the United States of America of certain activities pursuant to this Treaty, will be placed by the United States of America, to the maximum extent feasible, in other appropriate jobs with the Government of the United States in accordance with United States Civil Service regulations. For such persons who are not United States nationals, placement efforts will be confined to United States Government activities located within the Republic of Panama. Likewise, persons previously employed in activities for which the Republic of Panama assumes responsibility as a result of this Treaty will be continued in their employment to the maximum extent feasible by the Republic of Panama. The Republic of Panama shall, to the maximum extent feasible, ensure that the terms and conditions of employment applicable to personnel employed in the activities for which it assumes responsibility are no less favorable than those in effect immediately prior to the entry into force of this Treaty. Non-United States nationals employed by the Panama Canal Company or Canal Zone Government prior to the entry into force of this Treaty who are involuntarily separated from their positions because of the discontinuance of an activity by reason of this Treaty, who are not entitled to an immediate annuity under the United States Civil Service Retirement System, and for whom continued employment in the Republic of Panama by the Government of the United States of America is not practicable, will be provided special job placement assistance by the Republic of Panama for employment in positions for which they may be qualified by experience and training.

8. The Parties agree to establish a system whereby the Panama Canal Commission may, if deemed mutually convenient or desirable by the two Parties, assign certain employees of the Panama Canal Commission, for a limited period of time, to assist in the operation of activities transferred to the responsibility of the Republic of Panama as a result of this Treaty or

related agreements. The salaries and other costs of employment of any such persons assigned to provide such assistance shall be reimbursed to the United States of America by the Republic of Panama.

9. (a) The right of employees to negotiate collective contracts with the Panama Canal Commission is recognized. Labor relations with employees of the Panama Canal Commission shall be conducted in accordance with forms of collective bargaining established by the United States of America after consultation with employee unions.

(b) Employee unions shall have the right to affiliate with international labor organizations.

10. The United States of America will provide an appropriate early optional retirement program for all persons employed by the Panama Canal Company or Canal Zone Government immediately prior to the entry into force of this Treaty. In this regard, taking into account the unique circumstances created by the provisions of this Treaty, including its duration, and their effect upon such employees, the United States of America shall, with respect to them:

(a) determine that conditions exist which invoke applicable United States law permitting early retirement annuities and apply such law for a substantial period of the duration of the Treaty;

(b) seek special legislation to provide more liberal entitlement to, and calculation of, retirement annuities than is currently provided for by law.

ARTICLE XI

Provisions for the
Transition Period

1. The Republic of Panama shall reassume plenary jurisdiction over the former Canal Zone upon entry into force of this Treaty and in accordance with its terms. In order to provide for an orderly transition to the full application of the jurisdictional arrangements established by this Treaty and related agreements, the provisions of this Article shall become applicable upon the date this Treaty enters into force, and shall remain in effect for thirty calendar months. The authority granted in this Article to the United States of America for this transition period shall supplement, and is not intended to limit, the full application and effect of the rights and authority granted to the United States of America elsewhere in this Treaty and in related agreements.

2. During this transition period, the criminal and civil laws of the United States of America shall apply concurrently with those of the Republic of Panama in certain of the areas and installations made available for the use of the United States of America pursuant to this Treaty, in accordance with the following provisions:

(a) The Republic of Panama permits the authorities of the United States of America to have the primary right to exercise criminal jurisdiction over United States citizen employees of the Panama Canal Commission and their dependents, and members of the United States Forces and civilian component and their dependents, in the following cases:

(i) for any offense committed during the transition period within such areas and installations, and

(ii) for any offense committed prior to that period in the former Canal Zone.

The Republic of Panama shall have the primary right to exercise jurisdiction over all other offenses committed by such persons, except as otherwise provided in this Treaty and related agreements or as may be otherwise agreed.

(b) Either Party may waive its primary right to exercise jurisdiction in a specific case or category of cases.

3. The United States of America shall retain the right to exercise jurisdiction in criminal cases relating to offenses committed prior to the entry into force of this Treaty in violation of the laws applicable in the former Canal Zone.

4. For the transition period, the United States of America shall retain police authority and maintain a police force in the aforementioned areas and installations. In such areas, the police authorities of the United States of America may take into custody any person not subject to their primary jurisdiction if such person is believed to have committed or to be committing an offense against applicable laws or regulations, and shall promptly transfer custody to the police authorities of the Republic of Panama. The United States of America and the Republic of Panama shall establish joint police patrols in agreed areas. Any arrests conducted by a joint patrol shall be the responsibility of the patrol member or members representing the party having primary jurisdiction over the person or persons arrested.

5. The courts of the United States of America and related personnel, functioning in the former Canal Zone immediately prior to the entry into force of this Treaty, may continue to function during the transition period for the judicial enforcement of the jurisdiction to be exercised by the United States of America in accordance with this Article.

6. In civil cases, the civilian courts of the United States of America in the Republic of Panama shall have no jurisdiction over new cases of a private civil nature, but shall retain full jurisdiction during the transition period to dispose of any civil cases, including admiralty cases, already instituted and pending before the courts prior to the entry into force of this Treaty.

7. The laws, regulations, and administrative authority of the United States of America applicable in the former Canal Zone immediately prior to the entry into force of this Treaty shall, to the extent not inconsistent with this Treaty and related agreements, continue in force for the purpose of the exercise by the United States of America of law enforcement and judicial jurisdiction only during the transition period. The United States of America may amend, repeal or otherwise change such laws, regulations and administrative authority. The two Parties shall consult concerning

procedural and substantive matters relative to the implementation of this Article, including the disposition of cases pending at the end of the transition period and, in this respect, may enter into appropriate agreements by an exchange of notes or other instrument.

8. During this transition period, the United States of America may continue to incarcerate individuals in the areas and installations made available for the use of the United States of America by the Republic of Panama pursuant to this Treaty and related agreements, or to transfer them to penal facilities in the United States of America to serve their sentences.

ARTICLE XII

A Sea-Level Canal or
a Third Lane of Locks

1. The United States of America and the Republic of Panama recognize that a sea-level canal may be important for international navigation in the future. Consequently, during the duration of this Treaty, both Parties commit themselves to study jointly the feasibility of a sea-level canal in the Republic of Panama, and in the event they determine that such a waterway is necessary, they shall negotiate terms, agreeable to both Parties, for its construction.

2. The United States of America and the Republic of Panama agree on the following:

(a) No new interoceanic canal shall be constructed in the territory of the Republic of Panama during the duration of this Treaty, except in accordance with the provisions of this Treaty, or as the two Parties may otherwise agree; and

(b) During the duration of this Treaty, the United States of America shall not negotiate with third States for the right to construct an interoceanic canal on any other route in the Western Hemisphere, except as the two Parties may otherwise agree.

3. The Republic of Panama grants to the United States of America the right to add a third lane of locks to the existing Panama Canal. This right may be exercised at any time during the duration of this Treaty, provided that the United States of America has delivered to the Republic of Panama copies of the plans for such construction.

4. In the event the United States of America exercises the right granted in paragraph 3 above, it may use for that purpose, in addition to the areas otherwise made available to the United States of America pursuant to this Treaty, such other areas as the two Parties may agree upon. The terms and conditions applicable to Canal operating areas made available by the Republic of Panama for the use of the United States of America pursuant to Article III of this Treaty shall apply in a similar manner to such additional areas.

5. In the construction of the aforesaid works, the United States of America shall not use nuclear excavation techniques without the previous consent of the Republic of Panama.

ARTICLE XIII

Property Transfer and Economic Participation by the Republic of Panama

1. Upon termination of this Treaty, the Republic of Panama shall assume total responsibility for the management, operation, and maintenance of the Panama Canal, which shall be turned over in operating condition and free of liens and debts, except as the two Parties may otherwise agree.

2. The United States of America transfers, without charge, to the Republic of Panama all right, title and interest the United States of America may have with respect to all real property, including non-removable improvements thereon, as set forth below:

(a) Upon the entry into force of this Treaty, the Panama Railroad and such property that was located in the former Canal Zone but that is not within the land and water areas the use of which is made available to the United States of America pursuant to this Treaty. However, it is agreed that the transfer on such date shall not include buildings and other facilities, except housing, the use of which is retained by the United States of America pursuant to this Treaty and related agreements, outside such areas;

(b) Such property located in an area or a portion thereof at such time as the use by the United States of America of such area or portion thereof ceases pursuant to agreement between the two Parties.

(c) Housing units made available for occupancy by members of the Armed Forces of the Republic of Panama in accordance with paragraph 5(b) of Annex B to the Agreement in Implementation of Article IV of this Treaty at such time as such units are made available to the Republic of Panama.

(d) Upon termination of this Treaty, all real property, and non-removable improvements that were used by the United States of America for the purposes of this Treaty and related agreements, and equipment related to the management, operation and maintenance of the Canal remaining in the Republic of Panama.

3. The Republic of Panama agrees to hold the United States of America harmless with respect to any claims which may be made by third parties relating to rights, title and interest in such property.

4. The Republic of Panama shall receive, in addition, from the Panama Canal Commission a just and equitable return on the national resources which it has dedicated to the efficient management, operation, maintenance, protection and defense of the Panama Canal, in accordance with the following:

(a) An annual amount to be paid out of Canal operating revenues computed at a rate of thirty hundredths of a United States dollar ($0.30) per Panama Canal net ton, or its equivalence, for each vessel transiting the Canal, after the entry into force of this Treaty, for which tolls are charged. The rate of thirty hundredths of a United States dollar ($0.30) per Panama Canal net ton, or its equivalency, will be adjusted to reflect changes in the United States wholesale price index for total manufactured goods during biennial periods. The first adjustment shall take place five years after entry into force of this Treaty, taking into account the changes that occurred in such price index during the preceding two years. Thereafter successive adjustments shall take place at the end of each biennial period. If the United States of America should decide that another indexing method is preferable, such method shall be proposed to the Republic of Panama and applied if mutually agreed.

(b) A fixed annuity of ten million United States dollars ($10,000,-000) to be paid out of Canal operating revenues. This amount shall constitute a fixed expense of the Panama Canal Commission.

(c) An annual amount of up to ten million United States dollars ($10,000,000) per year, to be paid out of Canal operating revenues to the extent that such revenues exceed expenditures of the Panama Canal Commission including amounts paid pursuant to this Treaty. In the event Canal operating revenues in any year do not produce a surplus sufficient to cover this payment, the unpaid balance shall be paid from operating surpluses in future years in a manner to be mutually agreed.

ARTICLE XIV

Settlement of Disputes

In the event that any question should arise between the Parties concerning the interpretation of this Treaty or related agreements, they shall make every effort to resolve the matter through consultation in the appropriate committees established pursuant to this Treaty and related agreements, or, if appropriate, through diplomatic channels. In the event the Parties are unable to resolve a particular matter through such means, they may, in appropriate cases, agree to submit the matter to reconciliation, mediation, arbitration, or such other procedure for the peaceful settlement of the dispute as they may mutually deem appropriate.

ANNEX

Procedures for the Cessation or Transfer of Activities Carried out by the Panama Canal Company and the Canal Zone Government and Illustrative List of the Functions that may be Performed by the Panama Canal Commission

1. The laws of the Republic of Panama shall regulate the exercise of private economic activities within the areas made available by the

Republic of Panama for the use of the United States of America pursuant to this Treaty. Natural or juridical persons who, at least six months prior to the date of signature of this Treaty, were legally established and engaged in the exercise of economic activities in the former Canal Zone, may continue such activities in accordance with the provisions of paragraphs 2-7 of Article IX of this Treaty.

2. The Panama Canal Commission shall not perform governmental or commercial functions as stipulated in paragraph 4 of this Annex, provided, however, that this shall not be deemed to limit in any way the right of the United States of America to perform those functions that may be necessary for the efficient management, operation and maintenance of the Canal.

3. It is understood that the Panama Canal Commission, in the exercise of the rights of the United States of America with respect to the management, operation and maintenance of the Canal, may perform functions such as are set forth below by way of illustration:

a. Management of the Canal enterprise.

b. Aids to navigation in Canal waters and in proximity thereto.

c. Control of vessel movement.

d. Operation and maintenance of the locks.

e. Tug service for the transit of vessels and dredging for the piers and docks of the Panama Canal Commission.

f. Control of the water levels in Gatun, Alajuela (Madden) and Miraflores Lakes.

g. Non-commercial transportation services in Canal waters.

h. Meteorological and hydrographic services.

i. Admeasurement.

j. Non-commercial motor transport and maintenance.

k. Industrial security through the use of watchmen.

l. Procurement and warehousing.

m. Telecommunications.

n. Protection of the environment by preventing and controlling the spillage of oil and substances harmful to human or animal life and of the ecological equilibrium in areas used in operation of the Canal and the anchorages.

o. Non-commercial vessel repair.

p. Air conditioning services in Canal installations.

q. Industrial sanitation and health services.

r. Engineering design, construction and maintenance of Panama Canal Commission installations.

s. Dredging of the Canal channel, terminal ports and adjacent waters.

t. Control of the banks and stabilizing of the slopes of the Canal.

u. Non-commercial handling of cargo on the piers and docks of the Panama Canal Commission.

v. Maintenance of public areas of the Panama Canal Commission, such as parks and gardens.

w. Generation of electric power.

x. Purification and supply of water.

y. Marine salvage in Canal waters.

z. Such other functions as may be necessary or appropriate to carry out, in conformity with this Treaty and related agreements, the rights and responsibilities of the United States of America with respect to the management, operation and maintenance of the Panama Canal.

4. The following activities and operations carried out by the Panama Canal Company and the Canal Zone Government shall not be carried out by the Panama Canal Commission, effective upon the dates indicated herein:

(a) Upon the date of entry into force of this Treaty:

(i) Wholesale and retail sales, including those through commissaries, food stores, department stores, optical shops and pastry shops;

(ii) The production of food and drink, including milk products and bakery products;

(iii) The operation of public restaurants and cafeterias and the sale of articles through vending machines;

(iv) The operation of movie theaters, bowling alleys, pool rooms and other recreational and amusement facilities for the use of which a charge is payable;

(v) The operation of laundry and dry cleaning plants other than those operated for official use;

(vi) The repair and service of privately owned automobiles or the sale of petroleum or lubricants, including the operation of gasoline stations, repair garages and tire repair and recapping facilities, and the repair and service of other privately owned property, including appliances, electronic devices, boats, motors, and furniture;

(vii) The operation of cold storage and freezer plants other than those operated for official use;

(viii) The operation of freight houses other than those operated for official use;

(ix) Commercial services to and supply of privately owned and operated vessels, including the construction of vessels, the sale of petroleum and lubricants and the provision of water, tug services not related to the Canal or other United States Government operations, and repair of such vessels, except in situations where repairs may be necessary to remove disabled vessels from the Canal;

(x) Printing services other than for official use;

(xi) Maritime transportation for the use of the general public;

(xii) Health and medical services provided to individuals, including hospitals, leprosariums, veterinary, mortuary and cemetery services;

(xiii) Educational services not for professional training, including schools and libraries;

(xiv) Postal services;

(xv) Immigration, customs and quarantine controls, except those measures necessary to ensure the sanitation of the Canal;

(xvi) Commercial pier and dock services, such as the handling of cargo and passengers; and

(xvii) Any other commercial activity of a similar nature, not related to the management, operation or maintenance of the Canal.

(b) Within thirty calendar months from the date of entry into force of this Treaty, governmental services such as:

(i) Police;

(ii) Courts; and

(iii) Prison system.

5. (a) With respect to those activities or functions described in paragraph 4 above, or otherwise agreed upon by the two Parties, which are to be assumed by the Government of the Republic of Panama or by private persons subject to its authority, the two Parties shall consult prior to the discontinuance of such activities or functions by the Panama Canal Commission to develop appropriate arrangements for the orderly transfer and continued efficient operation or conduct thereof.

(b) In the event that appropriate arrangements cannot be arrived at to ensure the continued performance of a particular activity or function described in paragraph 4 above which is necessary to the efficient management, operation or maintenance of the Canal, the Panama Canal Commission may, to the extent consistent with the other provisions of this Treaty and related agreements, continue to perform such activity or function until such arrangements can be made.

AGREED MINUTE TO THE PANAMA CANAL TREATY

1. With reference to paragraph 1(c) of Article I (Abrogation of Prior Treaties and Establishment of a New Relationship), it is understood that the treaties, conventions, agreements and exchanges of notes, or portions thereof, abrogated and superseded thereby include:

(a) The Agreement delimiting the Canal Zone referred to in Article II of the Interoceanic Canal Convention of November 18, 1903, signed at Panama on June 15, 1904.

(b) The Boundary Convention signed at Panama on Sept. 2, 1914.

(c) The Convention regarding the Colon Corridor and certain other corridors through the Canal Zone signed at Panama on May 24, 1950.

(d) The Trans-Isthmian Highway Convention signed at Washington on March 2, 1936, the Agreement supplementing that Convention entered into through an exchange of notes signed at Washington on August 31 and September 6, 1940, and the arrangement between the United States of America and Panama respecting the Trans-Isthmian Joint Highway Board, entered into through an exchange of notes at Panama on October 19 and 23, 1939.

(e) The Highway Convention between the United States and Panama signed at Panama on September 14, 1950.

(f) The Convention regulating the transit of alcoholic liquors through the Canal Zone signed at Panama on March 14, 1932.

(g) The Protocol of an Agreement restricting use of Panama and Canal Zone waters by belligerents signed at Washington on October 10, 1914.

(h) The Agreement providing for the reciprocal recognition of motor vehicle license plates in Panama and the Canal Zone entered into through an exchange of notes at Panama on December 7 and December 12, 1950, and the Agreement establishing procedures for the reciprocal recognition of motor vehicle operator's licenses in the Canal Zone and Panama entered into through an exchange of notes at Panama on October 31, 1960.

(i) The General Relations Agreement entered into through an exchange of notes at Washington on May 18, 1942.

(j) Any other treaty, convention, agreement or exchange of notes between the United States and the Republic of Panama, or portions thereof, concerning the Panama Canal which was entered into prior to the entry into force of the Panama Canal Treaty.

2. It is further understood that the following treaties, conventions, agreements and exchanges of notes between the two Parties are not affected by paragraph 1 of Article I of the Panama Canal Treaty:

(a) The Agreement confirming the cooperative agreement between the Panamanian Ministry of Agriculture and Livestock and the United States Department of Agriculture for the prevention of foot-and-mouth disease and rinderpest in Panama, entered into by an exchange of notes signed at Panama on June 21 and October 5, 1972, and amended May 28 and June 12, 1974.

(b) The Loan Agreement to assist Panama in executing public marketing programs in basic grains and perishables, with annex, signed at Panama on September 10, 1975.

(c) The Agreement concerning the regulation of commercial aviation in the Republic of Panama, entered into by an exchange of notes signed at Panama on April 22, 1929.

(d) The Air Transport Agreement signed at Panama on March 31, 1949, and amended May 29 and June 3, 1952, June 5, 1967, December 23, 1974, and March 6, 1975.

(e) The Agreement relating to the establishment of headquarters in Panama for a civil aviation technical assistance group for the Latin American area, entered into by an exchange of notes signed at Panama on August 8, 1952.

(f) The Agreement relating to the furnishing by the Federal Aviation Agency of certain services and materials for air navigation aids, entered into by an exchange of notes signed at Panama on December 5, 1967, and February 22, 1968.

(g) The Declaration permitting consuls to take note in person, or by authorized representatives, of declarations of values of exports made by shippers before customs officers, entered into by an exchange of notes signed at Washington on April 17, 1913.

(h) The Agreement relating to customs privileges for consular officers, entered into by an exchange of notes signed at Panama on January 7 and 31, 1935.

(i) The Agreement relating to the sale of military equipment, materials, and services to Panama, entered into by an exchange of notes signed at Panama on May 20, 1959.

(j) The Agreement relating to the furnishing of defense articles and services to Panama for the purpose of contributing to its internal security, entered into by an exchange of notes signed at Panama on March 26 and May 23, 1962.

(k) The Agreement relating to the deposit by Panama of ten percent of the value of grant military assistance and excess defense articles furnished by the United States, entered into by an exchange of notes signed at Panama on April 4 and May 9, 1972.

(l) The Agreement concerning payment to the United States of net proceeds from the sale of defense articles furnished under the military assistance program, entered into by an exchange of notes signed at Panama on May 20 and December 6, 1974.

(m) The General Agreement for Technical and Economic Cooperation, signed at Panama on December 11, 1961.

(n) The Loan Agreement relating to the Panama City water supply system, with annex, signed at Panama on May 6, 1969, and amended September 30, 1971.

(o) The Loan Agreement for rural municipal development in Panama, signed at Panama on November 28, 1975.

(p) The Loan Agreement relating to a project for the modernization, restructuring and orientation of Panama's educational programs, signed at Panama on November 19, 1975.

(q) The Treaty providing for the extradition of criminals, signed at Panama on May 25, 1904.

(r) The Agreement relating to legal tender and fractional silver coinage by Panama, entered into by an exchange of notes signed at Washington and New York on June 20, 1904, and amended March 26 and April 2, 1930, May 28 and June 6, 1931, March 2, 1936, June 17, 1946, May 9 and 24, 1950, September 11 and October 22, 1953, August 23 and October 25, 1961, and September 26 and October 23, 1962.

(s) The Agreement for enlargement and use by Canal Zone of sewerage facilities in Colon Free Zone Area, entered into by an exchange of notes signed at Panama on March 8 and 25, 1954.

(t) The Agreement relating to the construction of the inter-American highway, entered into by an exchange of notes signed at Panama on May 15 and June 7, 1943.

(u) The Agreement for cooperation in the construction of the Panama segment of the Darien Gap highway, signed at Washington on May 6, 1971.

(v) The Agreement relating to investment guaranties under sec. 413(b) (4) of the Mutual Security Act of 1954, as amended, entered into by an exchange of notes signed at Washington on January 23, 1961.

(w) The Informal Arrangement relating to cooperation between the American Embassy, or Consulate, and Panamanian authorities when American merchant seamen or tourists are brought before a magistrate's court, entered into by an exchange of notes signed at Panama on September 18 and October 15, 1947.

(x) The Agreement relating to the mutual recognition of ship measurement certificates, entered into by an exchange of notes signed at Washington on August 17, 1937.

(y) The Agreement relating to the detail of a military officer to serve as adviser to the Minister of Foreign Affairs of Panama, signed at Washington on July 7, 1942, and extended and amended February 17, March 23, September 22 and November 6, 1959, March 26 and July 6, 1962, and September 20 and October 8, 1962.

(z) The Agreement relating to the exchange of official publications, entered into by an exchange of notes signed at Panama on November 27, 1941 and March 7, 1942.

(aa) The Convention for the Prevention of Smuggling of Intoxicating Liquors, signed at Washington on June 6, 1924.

(bb) The Arrangement providing for relief from double income tax on shipping profits, entered into by an exchange of notes signed at Washington on January 15, February 8, and March 28, 1941.

(cc) The Agreement for withholding of Panamanian income tax from compensation paid to Panamanians employed within Canal Zone by the canal, railroad, or auxiliary works, entered into by an exchange of notes signed at Panama on August 12 and 30, 1963.

(dd) The Agreement relating to the withholding of contributions for educational insurance from salaries paid to certain Canal Zone employees, entered into by an exchange of notes signed at Panama on September 8 and October 13, 1972.

(ee) The Agreement for radio communications between amateur stations on behalf of third parties, entered into by an exchange of notes signed at Panama on July 19 and August 1, 1956.

(ff) The Agreement relating to the granting of reciprocal authorizations to permit licensed amateur radio operators of either country to operate their stations in the other country, entered into by an exchange of notes signed at Panama on November 16, 1966.

(gg) The Convention facilitating the work of traveling salesmen, signed at Washington on February 8, 1919.

(hh) The Reciprocal Agreement for gratis nonimmigrant visas, entered into by an exchange of notes signed at Panama on March 27 and May 22 and 25, 1956.

(ii) The Agreement modifying the Agreement of March 27 and May 22 and 25, 1956 for gratis nonimmigrant visas, entered into by an exchange of notes signed at Panama on June 14 and 17, 1971.

(jj) Any other treaty, convention, agreement or exchange of notes, or portions thereof, which does not concern the Panama Canal and which is in force immediately prior to the entry into force of the Panama Canal Treaty.

3. With reference to paragraph 2 of Article X (Employment with the Panama Canal Commission), concerning the endeavor to ensure that the number of Panamanian nationals employed in relation to the total number of employees will conform to the proportion established under Panamanian law for foreign business enterprises, it is recognized that progress in this regard may require an extended period in consonance with the concept of a growing and orderly Panamanian participation, through training programs and otherwise, and that progress may be affected from time to time by such actions as the transfer or discontinuance of functions and activities.

4. With reference to paragraph 10(a) of Article X, it is understood that the currently applicable United States law is that contained in Section 8336 of Title 5, United States Code.

5. With reference to paragraph 2 of Article XI (Transitional Provisions), the areas and installations in which the jurisdictional arrangements therein described shall apply during the transition period are as follows:

(a) The Canal operating areas and housing areas described in Annex A to the Agreement in Implementation of Article III of the Panama Canal Treaty.

(b) The Defense Sites and Areas of Military Coordination described in the Agreement in Implementation of Article IV of the Panama Canal Treaty.

(c) The Ports of Balboa and Cristobal described in Annex B of the Agreement in Implementation of Article III of the Panama Canal Treaty.

6. With reference to paragraph 4 of Article XI, the areas in which the police authorities of the Republic of Panama may conduct joint police patrols with the police authorities of the United States of America during the transition period are as follows:

(a) Those portions of the Canal operating areas open to the general public, the housing areas and the Ports of Balboa and Cristobal.

(b) Those areas of military coordination in which joint police patrols are established pursuant to the provisions of the Agreement in Implementation of Article IV of this Treaty, signed this date. The two police authorities shall develop appropriate administrative arrangements for the scheduling and conduct of such joint police patrols.

DONE at Washington, this 7th day of September, 1977, in duplicate, in the English and Spanish languages, both texts being equally authentic.

RESERVATIONS AND UNDERSTANDINGS
TO BASIC CANAL TREATY

Reservations

(1) Pursuant to its adherence to the principle of nonintervention, any action taken by the United States of America in the exercise of its rights to assure that the Panama Canal shall remain open, neutral, secure, and accessible, pursuant to the provisions of the Panama Canal Treaty, the Treaty Concerning the Permanent Neutrality and Operation of the Panama Canal, and the resolutions of ratification thereto, shall be only for the purpose of assuring that the Canal shall remain open, neutral, secure, and accessible, and shall not have as its purpose or be interpreted as a right of intervention in the internal affairs of the Republic of Panama or interference with its political independence or sovereign integrity.

(2) The instruments of ratification of the Panama Canal Treaty to be exchanged by the United States of America and the Republic of Panama shall each include provisions whereby each Party agrees to waive its rights and release the other Party from its obligations under paragraph 2 of Article XII of the Treaty.

(3) Notwithstanding any provision of the Treaty, no funds may be drawn from the Treasury of the United States of America for payments under paragraph 4 of Article XIII without statutory authorization.

(4) Any accumulated unpaid balance under paragraph 4(c) of Article XIII of the Treaty at the date of termination of the Treaty shall be payable only to the extent of any operating surplus in the last year of the duration of the Treaty, and that nothing in such paragraph may be construed as obligating the United States of America to pay, after the date of the termination of the Treaty, any such unpaid balance which shall have accrued before such date.

(5) Exchange of the instruments of ratification of the Panama Canal Treaty and of the Treaty Concerning the Permanent Neutrality and Operation of the Panama Canal shall not be effective earlier than March 31, 1979, and such Treaties shall not enter into force prior to October 1, 1979, unless legislation necessary to implement the provisions of the Panama Canal Treaty shall have been enacted by the Congress of the United States of America before March 31, 1979.

(6) After the date of entry into force of the Treaty, the Panama Canal Commission shall, unless otherwise provided by legislation enacted by the Congress of the United States of America, be obligated to reimburse the Treasury of the United States of America, as nearly as possible, for the interest cost of the funds or other assets directly invested in the Commission by the Government of the United States of America and for the interest cost of the funds or other assets directly invested in the predecessor Panama Canal Company by the Government of the United States of America and not reimbursed before the date of entry into force of the

Treaty. Such reimbursement for such interest costs shall be made at a rate determined by the Secretary of the Treasury of the United States of America and at annual intervals to the extent earned, and if not earned, shall be made from subsequent earnings. For purposes of this reservation, the phrase "funds or other assets directly invested" shall have the same meaning as the phrase "net direct investment" has under section 62 of title 2 of the Canal Zone Code.

Understandings

(1) Before the first day of the three-year period beginning on the date of entry into force of the Treaty and before each three-year period following thereafter, the two parties shall agree upon the specific levels and quality of services, as are referred to in paragraph 5 of Article III of the Treaty, to be provided during the following three-year period and, except for the first three-year period, on the reimbursement to be made for the costs of such services, such services to be limited to such as are essential to the effective functioning of the Canal operating areas and the housing areas referred to in paragraph 5 of Article III. If payments made under paragraph 5 of Article III for the preceding three-year period, including the initial three-year period, exceed or are less than the actual costs to the Republic of Panama for supplying, during such period, the specific levels and quality of services agreed upon, then the Panama Canal Commission shall deduct from or add to the payment required to be made to the Republic of Panama for each of the following three years one-third of such excess or deficit, as the case may be. There shall be an independent and binding audit, conducted by an auditor mutually selected by both Parties, of any costs of services disputed by the two Parties pursuant to the reexamination of such costs provided for in this understanding.

(2) Nothing in paragraph 3, 4, or 5 of Article IV of the Treaty may be construed to limit either the provisions of the first paragraph of Article IV providing that each Party shall act, in accordance with its constitutional processes, to meet danger threatening the security of the Panama Canal, or the provisions of paragraph 2 of Article IV providing that the United States of America shall have primary responsibility to protect and defend the Canal for the duration of the Treaty.

(3) Nothing in paragraph 4(c) of Article XIII of the Treaty shall be construed to limit the authority of the United States of America, through the United States Government agency called the Panama Canal Commission, to make such financial decisions and incur such expenses as are reasonable and necessary for the management, operation, and maintenance of the Panama Canal. In addition, toll rates established pursuant to paragraph 2(d) of Article III need not be set at levels designed to produce revenues to cover the payment to the Republic of Panama described in paragraph 4(c) of Article XIII.

(4) Any agreement concluded pursuant to paragraph 11 of Article IX of the Treaty with respect to the transfer of prisoners shall be concluded in

accordance with the constitutional processes of both Parties.

(5) Nothing in the Treaty, in the Annex or Agreed Minute relating to the Treaty, or in any other agreement relating to the Treaty obligates the United States of America to provide any economic assistance, military grant assistance, security supporting assistance, foreign military sales credits, or international military education and training to the Republic of Panama.

(6) The President shall include all reservations and understandings incorporated by the Senate in this resolution of ratification in the instrument of ratification to be exchanged with the Government of the Republic of Panama.

TREATY
CONCERNING THE PERMANENT NEUTRALITY AND OPERATION OF THE PANAMA CANAL

*[Conditions, Reservations, Understandings, p. 220;
Amendments in italics in text of treaty]*

The United States of America and the Republic of Panama have agreed upon the following:

ARTICLE I

The Republic of Panama declares that the Canal, as an international transit waterway, shall be permanently neutral in accordance with the regime established in this Treaty. The same regime of neutrality shall apply to any other international waterway that may be built either partially or wholly in the territory of the Republic of Panama.

ARTICLE II

The Republic of Panama declares the neutrality of the Canal in order that both in time of peace and in time of war it shall remain secure and open to peaceful transit by the vessels of all nations on terms of entire equality, so that there will be no discrimination against any nation, or its citizens or subjects, concerning the conditions or charges of transit, or for any other reason, and so that the Canal, and therefore the Isthmus of Panama, shall not be the target of reprisals in any armed conflict between other nations of the world. The foregoing shall be subject to the following requirements:

(a) Payment of tolls and other charges for transit and ancillary services, provided they have been fixed in conformity with the provisions of Article III (c);

(b) Compliance with applicable rules and regulations, provided such rules and regulations are applied in conformity with the provisions of Article III;

(c) The requirement that transiting vessels commit no acts of hostility while in the Canal; and

(d) Such other conditions and restrictions as are established by this Treaty.

ARTICLE III

1. For purposes of the security, efficiency and proper maintenance of the Canal the following rules shall apply:

(a) The Canal shall be operated efficiently in accordance with conditions of transit through the Canal, and rules and regulations that shall be just, equitable and reasonable, and limited to those necessary for safe navigation and efficient, sanitary operation of the Canal;

(b) Ancillary services necessary for transit through the Canal shall be provided;

(c) Tolls and other charges for transit and ancillary services shall be just, reasonable, equitable and consistent with the principles of international law;

(d) As a pre-condition of transit, vessels may be required to establish clearly the financial responsibility and guarantees for payment of reasonable and adequate indemnification, consistent with international practice and standards, for damages resulting from acts or omissions of such vessels when passing through the Canal. In the case of vessels owned or operated by a State or for which it has acknowledged responsibility, a certification by that State that it shall observe its obligations under international law to pay for damages resulting from the act or omission of such vessels when passing through the Canal shall be deemed sufficient to establish such financial responsibility;

(e) Vessels of war and auxiliary vessels of all nations shall at all times be entitled to transit the Canal, irrespective of their internal operation, means of propulsion, origin, destination or armament, without being subjected, as a condition of transit, to inspection, search or surveillance. However, such vessels may be required to certify that they have complied with all applicable health, sanitation and quarantine regulations. In addition, such vessels shall be entitled to refuse to disclose their internal operation, origin, armament, cargo or destination. However, auxiliary vessels may be required to present written assurances, certified by an official at a high level of the government of the State requesting the exemption, that they are owned or operated by that government and in this case are being used only on government non-commercial service.

2. For the purposes of this Treaty, the terms "Canal," "vessel of war," "auxiliary vessel," "internal operation," "armament" and "inspection" shall have the meanings assigned them in Annex A to this Treaty.

ARTICLE IV

The United States of America and the Republic of Panama agree to maintain the regime of neutrality established in this Treaty, which shall be maintained in order that the Canal shall remain permanently neutral, notwithstanding the termination of any other treaties entered into by the two Contracting Parties.

A correct and authoritative statement of certain rights and duties of the Parties under the foregoing is contained in the Statement of Understanding issued by the Government of the United States of America on October 14, 1977, and by the Government of the Republic of Panama on October 18, 1977, which is hereby incorporated as an integral part of this Treaty, as follows:

"Under the Treaty Concerning the Permanent Neutrality and Operation of the Panama Canal (the Neutrality Treaty), Panama and the United States have the responsibility to assure that the Panama Canal will remain open and secure to ships of all nations. The correct interpretation of this principle is that each of the two countries shall, in accordance with their respective constitutional processes, defend the Canal against any threat to the regime of neutrality, and consequently shall have the right to act against any aggression or threat directed against the Canal or against the peaceful transit of vessels through the Canal.

"This does not mean, nor shall it be interpreted as, a right of intervention of the United States in the internal affairs of Panama. Any United States action will be directed at insuring that the Canal will remain open, secure, and accessible, and it shall never be directed against the territorial integrity or political independence of Panama."

ARTICLE V

After the termination of the Panama Canal Treaty, only the Republic of Panama shall operate the Canal and maintain military forces, defense sites and military installations within its national territory.

ARTICLE VI

1. In recognition of the important contributions of the United States of America and of the Republic of Panama to the construction, operation, maintenance, and protection and defense of the Canal, vessels of war and auxiliary vessels of those nations shall, notwithstanding any other provisions of this Treaty, be entitled to transit the Canal irrespective of their internal operation, means of propulsion, origin, destination, armament or cargo carried. Such vessels of war and auxiliary vessels will be entitled to transit the Canal expeditiously.

In accordance with the Statement of Understanding mentioned in Ar-

ticle IV above: "The Neutrality Treaty provides that the vessels of war and auxiliary vessels of the United States and Panama will be entitled to transit the Canal expeditiously. This is intended, and it shall so be interpreted, to assure the transit of such vessels through the Canal as quickly as possible, without any impediment, with expedited treatment, and in the case of need or emergency, to go to the head of the line of vessels in order to transit the Canal rapidly."

2. The United States of America, so long as it has responsibility for the operation of the Canal, may continue to provide the Republic of Colombia toll-free transit through the Canal for its troops, vessels and materials of war. Thereafter, the Republic of Panama may provide the Republic of Colombia and the Republic of Costa Rica with the right of toll-free transit.

ARTICLE VII

1. The United States of America and the Republic of Panama shall jointly sponsor a resolution in the Organization of American States opening to accession by all States of the world the Protocol to this Treaty whereby all the signatories will adhere to the objectives of this Treaty, agreeing to respect the regime of neutrality set forth herein.

2. The Organization of American States shall act as the depository for this Treaty and related instruments.

ARTICLE VIII

This Treaty shall be subject to ratification in accordance with the constitutional procedures of the two Parties. The instruments of ratification of this Treaty shall be exchanged at Panama at the same time as the instruments of ratification of the Panama Canal Treaty, signed this date, are exchanged. This Treaty shall enter into force, simultaneously with the Panama Canal Treaty, six calendar months from the date of the exchange of the instruments of ratification.

DONE at Washington, this 7th day of September, 1977, in duplicate, in the English and Spanish languages, both texts being equally authentic.

ANNEX A

1. "Canal" includes the existing Panama Canal, the entrances thereto and the territorial seas of the Republic of Panama adjacent thereto, as defined on the map annexed hereto (Annex B), and any other inter-oceanic waterway in which the United States of America is a participant or in which the United States of America has participated in connection with the construction or financing, that may be operated wholly or partially within the territory of the Republic of Panama, the entrances thereto and the territorial seas adjacent thereto.

2. "Vessel of war" means a ship belonging to the naval forces of a

State, and bearing the external marks distinguishing warships of its nationality, under the command of an officer duly commissioned by the government and whose name appears in the Navy List, and manned by a crew which is under regular naval discipline.

3. "Auxiliary vessel" means any ship, not a vessel of war, that is owned or operated by a State and used, for the time being, exclusively on government non-commercial service.

4. "Internal operation" encompasses all machinery and propulsion systems, as well as the management and control of the vessel, including its crew. It does not include the measures necessary to transit vessels under the control of pilots while such vessels are in the Canal.

5. "Armament" means arms, ammunitions, implements of war and other equipment of a vessel which possesses characteristics appropriate for use for warlike purposes.

6. "Inspection" includes on-board examination of vessel structure, cargo, armament and internal operation. It does not include those measures strictly necessary for admeasurement, nor those measures strictly necessary to assure safe, sanitary transit and navigation, including examination of deck and visual navigation equipment, nor in the case of live cargoes, such as cattle or other livestock, that may carry communicable diseases, those measures necessary to assure that health and sanitation requirements are satisfied.

PROTOCOL

TO THE TREATY CONCERNING THE PERMANENT NEUTRALITY AND OPERATION OF THE PANAMA CANAL

Whereas the maintenance of the neutrality of the Panama Canal is important not only to the commerce and security of the United States of America and the Republic of Panama, but to the peace and security of the Western Hemisphere and to the interests of world commerce as well;

Whereas the regime of neutrality which the United States of America and the Republic of Panama have agreed to maintain will ensure permanent access to the Canal by vessels of all nations on the basis of entire equality;

Whereas the said regime of effective neutrality shall constitute the best protection for the Canal and shall ensure the absence of any hostile act against it;

The Contracting Parties to this Protocol have agreed upon the following:

ARTICLE I

The Contracting Parties hereby acknowledge the regime of permanent neutrality for the Canal established in the Treaty Concerning the Permanent Neutrality and Operation of the Panama Canal and associate themselves with its objectives.

ARTICLE II

The Contracting Parties agree to observe and respect the regime of permanent neutrality of the Canal in time of war as in time of peace, and to ensure that vessels of their registry strictly observe the applicable rules.

ARTICLE III

This Protocol shall be open to accession by all states of the world, and shall enter into force for each State at the time of deposit of its instrument of accession with the Secretary General of the Organization of American States.

CONDITIONS, RESERVATIONS AND UNDERSTANDINGS TO NEUTRALITY TREATY

Conditions

(1) Notwithstanding the provisions of Article V or any other provision of the Treaty, if the Canal is closed, or its operations are interfered with, the United States of America and the Republic of Panama shall each independently have the right to take such steps as each deems necessary, in accordance with its constitutional processes, including the use of military force in the Republic of Panama, to reopen the Canal or restore the operations of the Canal, as the case may be.

(2) The instruments of ratification of the Treaty shall be exchanged only upon the conclusion of a Protocol of Exchange, to be signed by authorized representatives of both Governments, which shall constitute an integral part of the Treaty documents and which shall include the following:

"Nothing in the Treaty shall preclude the Republic of Panama and the United States of America from making, in accordance with their respective constitutional processes, any agreement or arrangement between the two countries to facilitate performance at any time after December 31, 1999, of their responsibilities to maintain the regime of neutrality established in the Treaty, including agreements or arrangements for the stationing of any United States military forces or the maintenance of defense sites after that date in the Republic of Panama that the Republic of Panama and the United States of America may deem necessary or appropriate."

Reservations

(1) Before the date of entry into force of the Treaty, the two Parties shall begin to negotiate for an agreement under which the American Battle

Monuments Commission would, upon the date of entry into force of such agreement and thereafter, administer, free of all taxes and other charges and without compensation to the Republic of Panama and in accordance with the practices, privileges, and immunities associated with the administration of cemeteries outside the United States of America by the American Battle Monuments Commission, including the display of the flag of the United States of America, such part of Corozal Cemetery in the former Canal Zone as encompasses the remains of citizens of the United States of America.

(2) The flag of the United States of America may be displayed, pursuant to the provisions of paragraph 3 of Article VII of the Panama Canal Treaty, at such part of Corozal Cemetery in the former Canal Zone as encompasses the remains of citizens of the United States of America.

(3) The President —

(A) shall have announced, before the date of entry into force of the Treaty, his intention to transfer, consistent with an agreement with the Republic of Panama, and before the date of termination of the Panama Canal Treaty, to the American Battle Monuments Commission the administration of such part of Corozal Cemetery as encompasses the remains of citizens of the United States of America; and

(B) shall have announced, immediately after the date of exchange of instruments of ratification, plans, to be carried out at the expense of the Government of the United States of America, for —

(i) removing, before the date of entry into force of the Treaty, the remains of citizens of the United States of America from Mount Hope Cemetery to such part of Corozal Cemetery as encompasses such remains, except that the remains of any citizen whose next of kin objects in writing to the Secretary of the Army not later than three months after the date of exchange of the instruments of ratification of the Treaty shall not be removed; and

(ii) transporting to the United States of America for reinterment, if the next of kin so requests, not later than thirty months after the date of entry into force of the Treaty, any such remains encompassed by Corozal Cemetery and, before the date of entry into force of the Treaty, any remains removed from Mount Hope Cemetery pursuant to subclause (i); and

(C) shall have fully advised, before the date of entry into force of the Treaty, the next of kin objecting under clause (B)(i) of all available options and their implications.

(4) To carry out the purposes of Article III of the Treaty of assuring the security, efficiency, and proper maintenance of the Panama Canal, the United States of America and the Republic of Panama, during their respective periods of responsibility for Canal operation and maintenance, shall, unless the amount of the operating revenues of the Canal exceeds the amount needed to carry out the purposes of such Article, use such revenues of the Canal only for purposes consistent with the purposes of Article III.

Understandings

(1) Paragraph 1(c) of Article III of the Treaty shall be construed as requiring, before any adjustment in tolls for use of the Canal, that the effects of any such toll adjustment on the trade patterns of the two Parties shall be given full consideration, including consideration of the following factors in a manner consistent with the regime of neutrality:

(A) the costs of operating and maintaining the Panama Canal;

(B) the competitive position of the use of the Canal in relation to other means of transportation;

(C) the interests of both Parties in maintaining their domestic fleets;

(D) the impact of such an adjustment on the various geographical areas of each of the two Parties; and

(E) the interests of both Parties in maximizing their international commerce.

The United States of America and the Republic of Panama shall cooperate in exchanging information necessary for the consideration of such factors.

(2) The agreement 'to maintain the regime of neutrality established in this Treaty' in Article IV of the Treaty means that either of the two Parties to the Treaty may, in accordance with its constitutional processes, take unilateral action to defend the Panama Canal against any threat, as determined by the Party taking such action.

(3) The determination of 'need or emergency' for the purpose of any vessel of war or auxiliary vessel of the United States of America or the Republic of Panama going to the head of the line of vessels in order to transit the Panama Canal rapidly shall be made by the nation operating such vessel.

(4) Nothing in the Treaty, in Annex A or B thereto, in the Protocol relating to the Treaty, or in any other agreement relating to the Treaty, obligates the United States of America to provide any economic assistance, military grant assistance, security supporting assistance, foreign military sales credits, or international military education and training to the Republic of Panama.

(5) The President shall include all amendments, conditions, reservations, and understandings incorporated by the Senate in this resolution of ratification in the instrument of ratification to be exchanged with the Government of the Republic of Panama.

CARTER ON U.S. POLICY TOWARD THE SOVIET UNION
March 17; June 7, 1978

President Carter issued stern warnings to the Soviet Union in speeches at Wake Forest University in Winston-Salem, N.C., on March 27 and at the United States Naval Academy in Annapolis, Md., on June 7. In a major address on American defense policy at Wake Forest, Carter alluded to the tremendous "increase in Soviet military power" over the past decade but maintained that "we will not allow any other nation to gain military superiority over us." To the graduating class at his alma mater, the Naval Academy, Carter warned, "The Soviet Union can choose either confrontation or cooperation. The United States is adequately prepared to meet either choice."

The president told his audience at Wake Forest that the United States had "recently completed a major reassessment of our national defense strategy." The principles that emerged from that reassessment called for: (1) "maintaining strategic nuclear balance," (2) working closely "with our NATO allies to strengthen and modernize our defenses in Europe," and (3) developing forces to counter any threats to friends and allies in Asia, the Middle East and "other regions of the world."

Arms Limitation

Admitting that the Soviet Union had achieved "functional equivalence in strategic forces with the United States," Carter called for improving and modernizing American nuclear capabilities. Referring to the strategic arms limitation talks (SALT) in Geneva, the President pledged that "before I sign any SALT agreement on behalf of the United States, I will make sure that it preserves the strategic balance, that we can independently verify Soviet compliance and that we will be at least as strong relative to the Soviet Union as we would be without an agreement."

The president was critical of what he called the "excessive Soviet buildup" of forces in Europe. As a result of this buildup, he said, "we and our NATO allies have had to take important steps to cope with short-term vulnerabilities and respond to long-term threats." Carter also voiced administration concern about Soviet and Cuban interference in other areas, particularly in Ethiopia. "There has been an ominous inclination on the part of the Soviet Union to use its military power to intervene in local conflicts with advisers, with equipment and with full logistical support and encouragement for mercenaries from other communist countries, as we can observe today in Africa," he said.

The president stressed that the United States was prepared "to cooperate with the Soviet Union toward common social, scientific and economic goals," but he warned that unless the Russians exercised restraint in their strategic and conventional arms buildup or in their interference in other areas of the world, "popular support in the United States for such cooperation with the Soviets will certainly erode."

'Cooperation or Confrontation'

President Carter, in a hard-hitting speech on June 7 to the 128th class to graduate from the Naval Academy, said that the Soviet Union could choose cooperation or confrontation with the United States. "Our long-term objective," he said, "must be to convince the Soviet Union of the advantages of cooperation and the cost of disruptive behavior."

The president's remarks to the graduating midshipmen represented the strongest criticism he had expressed of Soviet policies and the Soviet system. The Russian military buildup throughout the world "appears to be excessive far beyond any legitimate requirements to defend themselves or to defend their allies," Carter asserted. "The Soviet Union apparently sees military power and military assistance as the best means of expanding their influence abroad. Obviously, areas of instability in the world provide a tempting target for this effort. And all too often they seem ready to exploit any such opportunity."

Soviet System

Carter attacked not only the Soviet military buildup and arms transfers but the Soviet system as well. The Russians had demonstrated, he said, that "the Soviet system cannot tolerate freely expressed ideas or notions of loyal opposition and the free movement of people." As a result, the president said, "outside their tightly controlled bloc, the Soviet Union has difficult political relations with other nations. Their cultural bonds with others are few and frayed. Their form of government is becoming increasingly unattractive to other nations."

With respect to U.S.-Soviet relations, Carter called for mutual restraint *"in troubled areas and in troubled times,"* meticulous adherence to agreements that have already been reached between the two countries, nuclear arms limitation and the protection of human rights. The president called upon the Russians to join with the United States in seeking a peaceful solution in southern Africa, Eritrea and Angola. *"Let us all work not to divide and to seek domination in Africa but to help those nations to fulfill their great potential."*

Carter stressed the *"fundamental importance"* of a new strategic arms limitation treaty and reported that the *"prospects for a SALT II agreement are good."* He warned against overestimating Soviet nuclear capability, noting that *"the military capability of the United States and its allies is adequate to meet any foreseeable threat."*

President Carter denied that the United States was trying to link a SALT agreement with Soviet conduct at home or around the world. *"In a democratic society, however, we do recognize that tensions, sharp disputes or threats to peace will complicate the quest for a successful agreement,"* he warned. (SALT Negotiations, p. 549)

Soviet Reaction

The Soviet Union lost no time in responding to Carter's March 17 speech. The official Soviet press agency Tass complained that the speech *"actually means a shift in American foreign policy from the earlier proclaimed course toward ensuring national security of the U.S. through negotiations, through limiting the arms race and deepening detente to a course of threats and buildup of tension."*

In reaction to the June 7 Annapolis speech, the Communist Party newspaper Pravda suggested that the Carter administration was reverting to Cold War tactics. The Soviet press agency Tass referred to the president's remark that *"the Soviet Union can choose either confrontation or cooperation"* by stating, *"Carter knows very well that the Soviet Union has once and for all chosen the road of peaceful coexistence, of strengthening detente and it promotes these goals consistently and unswervingly."*

Following are the texts of President Carter's speeches at Wake Forest University on March 17, 1978 and at the United States Naval Academy on June 7, 1978. (Boldface headings in brackets have been added by Congressional Quarterly to highlight the organization of the texts.):

WAKE FOREST SPEECH

As someone who comes from a great tobacco-producing state, it is an honor for me to be here in the capital of the greatest tobacco state in the world. (Applause) What you do here means a lot to Georgia. And we have always found that the people in Winston-Salem and throughout North Carolina share with us common purposes, a common heritage, and a common future. You have always received me with open arms. You expressed your confidence in me during the campaign for President. And I am indeed honored to come here to Wake Forest, to Winston-Salem, and North Carolina, our neighbor state, to make a speech of major importance.

It is a pleasure to be with your great Senator, Bob Morgan, who cast a courageous vote yesterday, and who is extremely knowledgeable about the subject that I will talk about. He is on the Armed Forces Committee, as you know — the Armed Services Committee is responsible for our nation's defense. He is on the special committee, a highly selective committee on our nation's intelligence, and he has been one of the staunch protectors of our nation and is a great man and a great statesman.

Bob, I am very glad to be with you. (Applause)

It is also good to renew my friendship with your great Governor, Jim Hunt. I first met him before he was Governor and before I was President. We formed an instant personal friendship and his leadership of your State has brought credit to you and the admiration of the rest of the nation. And I am particularly grateful to be here with Steve Neal. (Applause)

The first time I came here was to join with him in his campaign in 1974, when the prospects were not very bright. But because of the confidence in him, expressed by the people of the Fifth District, he was successful.

He has now assumed a leadership position in the Congress. He is a man, also, who believes in the strong defense of our country. His voting record proves this. In addition, he is on the Science and Technology Committee, which is responsible for advancing our purposes in the future. And he is honored by being the Chairman of that portion of the Banking and Finance Committee responsible for international trade. This means a great deal to us because the exporting of our products and the protection of our textile industry, our tobacco industry, our farm products, is very crucial and Steve has now worked himself up to a seniority position so he can be exceptionally effective now and in the future.

I would like to also acknowledge the presence of two of the members of my Cabinet, Secretary of Defense Harold Brown, and your own Juanita Kreps, Secretary of Commerce. (Applause)

To Georgia and to North Carolina, the most important, perhaps, Member in the Congress is the Chairman of the Senate Agriculture Committee. He takes care of tobacco farmers; he takes care of peanut farmers, important to both Georgia and North Carolina, and I am very honored to have with us my own United States Senator, Herman Talmadge. (Applause)

I won't acknowledge the presence of every distinguished guest here today, but I would like to say I am pleased that several of North Carolina's great Members of Congress have chosen to come to honor me by their presence, Charlie Whitley, Richardson Preyer, Bill Hefner, and Lamar Gudger. Would you stand up? (Applause)

Charlie, I believe that you and Bob Morgan are alumni of Wake Forest. Is that not correct? I know Wake Forest people are glad to have you back.

Well, I would like to say that this is a remarkably great honor for me. This is a great college, and it is a time in our nation's history when we need to stop and assess our past, our present, and our future.

I have noticed the statistics in North Carolina that show that under my own Administration, because of your work, not mine, there has been remarkable economic progress.

In the State of North Carolina, the unemployment rate, for instance, last year, dropped 2.3 percent. You now have an extraordinarily low rate of only 4-1/2 percent. This shows not only that our nation is strong, but the North Carolina people want to work and when they are given a chance, they do work. And I thank you for that. (Applause)

[Military Heritage]

One hundred ninety-eight years ago, in the southern part of your State, 400 North Carolina militiamen took up arms in our own war of independence. Against a force of 1,300 British soldiers, the North Carolinians prevailed — and their battle at Ramsour's Mill became a step on the road to victory at Yorktown one year later.

Your ancestors in North Carolina and mine in Georgia and their neighbors throughout the 13 Colonies earned our freedom in combat. That is a sacrifice which Americans have had to make time and time again in our Nation's history. We have learned that strength is the final protector of liberty.

This is a commitment and a sacrifice that I understand well, for the tradition of military service has been running deep for generations in my own family. My first ancestor to live in Georgia, James Carter, who moved there from North Carolina, fought in the Revolution. My father was a First Lieutenant in the Army in World War I. My oldest son volunteered to go to Vietnam. And I spent 11 years of my life as a professional military officer in the United Sates Navy. This is typical of American families.

Down through the generations,the purposes of our armed forces have always been the same, no matter what generation it was: to defend our security when it is threatened and through demonstrated strength, to reduce the chances that we will have to fight again.

These words of John Kennedy will still guide our actions, and I quote him, "The purpose of our arms is peace, not war — to make certain that they will never have to be used."

That purpose is unchanged. But the world has been changing and our responses as a Nation must change with it.

This morning I would like to talk to you about our national security — where we now stand, what new circumstances we face, and what we are going to do in the future.

[Dispelling Myths]

Let me deal at the beginning with some myths. One myth is that this country somehow is pulling back from protecting its interests and its friends around the world. That is not the case, as will be explained and demonstrated in our actions as a Nation.

Another myth is that our defense budget is too burdensome, and consumes an undue part of our Federal revenues. National defense is, of course, a large and important item of expenditures, but it represents only about five percent of our gross national product, and about a quarter of our current Federal budget. It also is a mistake to believe that our country's defense spending is mainly for intercontinental missiles or nuclear weapons. Only about ten percent of our defense budget goes for strategic forces or for nuclear deterrence. More than 50 percent is simply to pay for and support the services of the men and women in our armed forces.

Finally, some believe that because we do possess nuclear weapons of great destructive power, that we need do nothing more to guarantee our Nation's security.

Unfortunately, it is not that simple. Our potential adversaries have now built up massive forces armed with conventional weapons — tanks, aircraft, infantry, mechanized units.

These forces could be used for political blackmail, and they could threaten our vital interests unless we and our allies and friends have our own military strength and conventional forces as a counterbalance.

Of course, our national security rests on more than just military power. It depends partly on the productive capacity of our factories and our farms, on an adequate supply of natural resources with which God has blessed us, on an economic system which values human freedom above centralized control, on the creative ideas of our best minds, on the hard work, cohesion, moral strength and determination of the American people, and on the friendship of our neighbors to the north and south.

Our security depends on strong bonds with our allies, and on whether other nations seek to live in peace and refrain from trying to dominate those who live around them.

But adequate and capable military forces are still an essential element of our national security. We, like our ancestors, have the obligation to maintain strength equal to the challenges of the world in which we live, and we Americans will continue to do so. (Applause)

[World Changes]

Let us review briefly how national security issues have changed over the past decade or two.

The world has grown both more complex and more interdependent. There is now a division among the Communist powers; the old colonial empires have fallen, and many new nations have risen in their place; old ideological labels have lost some of their meaning. There have also been changes in the military balance among nations. Over the past 20 years, the military forces of the Soviets have grown substantially, both in absolute numbers and relative to our own.

There also has been an ominous inclination on the part of the Soviet Union to use its military power — to intervene in local conflicts with advisors, with equipment, and with full logistical support and encouragement for mercenaries from other Communist countries, as we can observe today in Africa.

This increase in Soviet military power has been going on for a long time. Discounting inflation, since 1960, Soviet military spending has doubled, rising steadily in real terms by three or four percent a year, while our own military budget is actually lower now than it was in 1960.

The Soviets, who traditionally were not a significant naval power, now rank number two in world naval forces.

In its balanced strategic nuclear capability, the United States retains important advantages. But over the past decade, the steady Soviet buildup has achieved functional equivalence in strategic forces with the United States.

These changes demand that we maintain adequate responses — diplomatic, military and economic; and we will. (Applause)

As President and as Commander-in-Chief, I am responsible, along with the Congress, for modernizing, expanding and improving our armed forces whenever our national security requires it. We have recently completed a major reassessment of our national defense strategy. And out of this process have come some overall principles designed to preserve our national security during the years ahead.

[Will Not Lose Superiority]

We will match, together with our allies and friends, any threatening power through a combination of military forces, political efforts and economic programs. We will not allow any other nation to gain military superiority over us. (Applause)

We shall seek the cooperation of the Soviet Union and other nations in reducing areas of tension. We do not desire to intervene militarily in the internal domestic affairs of other countries, nor to aggravate regional conflicts. And we shall oppose intervention by others.

While assuring our own military capabilities, we shall seek security through dependable, verifiable arms control agreements wherever possible.

We shall use our great economic, technological and diplomatic advantages to defend our interests and to promote American values. We are prepared, for instance, to cooperate with the Soviet Union toward common social, scientific and economic goals — but if they fail to demonstrate in missile programs and other force levels or in the projection of Soviet or proxy forces into other lands and continents, then popular support in the United States for such cooperation with the Soviets will certainly erode.

These principles mean that, even as we search for agreement in arms control, we will continue to modernize our strategic systems and to revitalize our conventional forces. And I have no doubt that the Congress shares my commitment in this respect.

We shall implement this policy that I have outlined so briefly in three different ways: by maintaining strategic nuclear balance, by working closely with our NATO allies to strengthen and modernize our defenses in Europe; and by maintaining and developing forces to counter any threats to our allies and friends in our vital interests in Asia, the Middle East, and other regions of the world.

Let me take up each of these three in turn.

[Maintaining Nuclear Balance]

Our first and most fundamental concern is to prevent nuclear war. (Applause) The horrors of nuclear conflict, and our desire to reduce the world's arsenals of fearsome nuclear weapons, do not free us from the need to analyze the situation objectively and to make sensible choices about our purposes and means.

Our strategic forces must be — and must be known to be — a match for the capabilities of the Soviets. They will never be able to use their nuclear forces to threaten, to coerce, or to blackmail us or our friends. (Applause)

Our continuing major effort in the SALT talks taking place every day in Geneva are one means toward a goal of strategic nuclear stability.

We and the Soviets have already reached agreement on some basic points, although still others remain to be resolved. We are making good progress. We are not looking for a one-sided advantage.

Before I sign any SALT agreement on behalf of the United States, I will make sure that it preserves the strategic balance, that we can independently verify Soviet compliance, and that we will be at least as strong relative to the Soviet Union as we would be without any agreement.

But in addition to the limits and reductions of a SALT II agreement, we must take other steps to protect the strategic balance. During the next decade, improvements in the Soviet missiles can make our land-based missile forces and silos increasingly vulnerable to a Soviet first strike. Such an attack would amount to national suicide for the Soviet Union. But however remote, it is a threat against which we must constantly be on guard.

We have a superb submarine fleet which is relatively invulnerable to attack when it is at sea, and we have under construction new Trident submarines and missiles which give our submarine ballistic missile force even greater range and security.

I have ordered rapid development and deployment of cruise missiles to reinforce the strategic value of our bombers. We are working on the M-X intercontinental ballistic missile and a Trident II submarine-launched ballistic missile to give us more options to respond to Soviet strategic deployments. If it becomes necessary to guarantee the clear invulnerability of our strategic deterrent, I shall not hesitate to take actions for full-scale development and deployment of these systems.

Our strategic defense forces, our nuclear forces, are a triad — land-based missiles, sea-based missiles and air-breathing systems such as bombers and cruise missiles. Through the plans I have described, all three legs of this triad will be modernized and improved. Each will retain the ability, on its own, to impose devastating retaliation upon an aggressor.

[Working With NATO Allies]

For thirty years and more we have been committed to the defense of Europe, bound by the knowledge that Western Europe security is vital to our own. We continue to cooperate with our NATO allies in a strategy for flexible response, combining conventional forces and nuclear forces so that no aggressor can threaten the territory of Europe or its freedom which in the past we have fought together to defend.

For several years we and our allies have been trying to negotiate mutual and balanced reductions in military forces in Europe with the Soviets and with the Warsaw Pact nations who are their allies. But in the meantime, the Soviets have continued to increase and to modernize their forces beyond a level necessary for defense. In the face of this excessive Soviet buildup, we and our NATO allies have had to take important steps to cope with short-term vulnerabilities and respond to long-term threats. We are significantly strengthening U.S. forces stationed in Western Europe and improving our ability to speed additional ground and air forces to the defense of Europe in a time of crisis.

Our European allies, who supply the major portion of NATO's conventional combat strength, are also improving their readiness and their reinforcement capabilities and their antitank defenses. The heads of the NATO governments will be here in our country attending a summit meeting in May, where we will address a long-term defense program which will expand and integrate more closely allied defense plans.

[Protecting U.S. Interests]

For many years, the United States has been a major world power. Our longstanding concerns encompass our own security interests and those of our allies and friends far beyond our own shores and Europe.

We have important historical responsibilities to enhance peace in East Asia, in the Middle East, in the Persian Gulf, and throughout our own hemisphere. Our preference in all these areas is to turn first to international agreements that reduce the overall level of arms and minimize the threat of conflict. But we have the will, and we will also maintain the capacity, to honor our commitments and to protect our interests in those critical areas.

In the Pacific, our effective security is enhanced by mutual defense treaties with our allies and by our friendship and cooperation with other Pacific nations.

Japan and South Korea, closely linked with the United States, are located geographically where the vital interests of great powers converge. It is imperative that Northeast Asia remain stable. We will maintain and even enhance our military strength in this area, improving our air strength, and reducing our ground forces, as the South Korean army continues to modernize and to increase its own capabilities.

In the Middle East and the region of the Indian Ocean, we seek permanent peace and stability. The economic health and well-being of the United States, Western Europe, Japan, depend upon continued access to the oil from the Persian Gulf.

In all these situations, the primary responsibility for preserving peace and military stability rests with the countries of the region. We shall continue to work with our friends and allies to strengthen their ability to prevent threats to their interests and to ours.

In addition, however, we will maintain forces of our own which can be called upon, if necessary, to support mutual defense efforts. The Secretary of Defense at my direction is improving and will maintain quickly deployable forces — air, land and sea — to defend our interests throughout the world.

Arms control agreements are a major goal as instruments of our national security, but this will be possible only if we maintain appropriate military force levels. Reaching balanced, verifiable agreements with our adversaries can limit the cost of security and reduce the risk of war. But even then, we must — and we will — proceed efficiently with whatever arms programs our own security requires.

When I leave this auditorium, I shall be going to visit with the crew aboard one of our most modern nuclear powered aircraft carriers in the Atlantic Ocean. The men and women of our own armed forces remain committed as able professionals and as patriotic Americans, to our common defense. They must stand constantly ready to fight, in the hope that through strength, combat will be prevented. We as Americans will always support them in their courageous vigil. (Applause)

['No Cause for Pessimism']

This has been a serious and a sober talk, but there is no cause for pessimism. We face a challenge and we will do whatever is necessary to meet it. We will preserve and protect our country and continue to promote and to maintain peace around the world.

This means that we shall have to continue to support strong and efficient military forces.

For most of human history, people have wished vainly that freedom and the flowering of the human spirit, which freedom nourishes, did not finally have to depend upon the force of arms. We, like our forebears, live in a time when those who would destroy liberty are restrained less by their respect for freedom itself than by their knowledge that those of us who cherish freedom are strong.

We are a great Nation made up of talented people. We can readily afford the necessary costs of our military forces, as well as an increased level, if needed, to prevent any adversary from destabilizing the peace of the world. The money we spend on defense is not wasted any more than is the cost of maintaining a police force in a local community to keep the peace. This investment purchases our freedom to fulfill the worthy goals of our Nation.

Southerners, whose ancestors a hundred years ago knew the horrors of a homeland devastated by war, are particularly determined that war shall never come to us again. All Americans understand the basic lesson of history: that we need to be resolute and able to protect ourselves, to prevent threats and domination by others.

No matter how peaceful and secure and easy the circumstances of our lives now seem, we have no guarantee that the blessings will endure. That is why we will always maintain the strength which, God willing, we shall never need to use.

Thank you very much. (Applause)

NAVAL ACADEMY ADDRESS

Admiral McKee, Governor Lee, distinguished guests, members of the graduating class and friends:

We do have many distinguished guests here today. I invited my old boss, Adm. Hyman Rickover, to come and join us. He sent word back that he would, of course, comply with my order as commander in chief, but he thought his work for the Navy in Washington was more important than listening to my speech. I was not surprised.

I am glad to be back for the Naval Academy graduation, although I return with a different rank.

I remember that 32 years ago I had the same experience that most of you are sharing today. I was not a midshipman officer. Most of you are not officers. I was thinking more about leave and marriage than I was about world events or a distant future. I would guess there are some among you who would feel the same.

I was quite disappointed with my first appointment. We drew lots for assignments and I had requested a new destroyer in the Pacific. I was assigned to the oldest ship in the Atlantic, the U.S.S. Wyoming, which was so dilapidated that because of safety purposes it was not permitted to come into Norfolk harbor alongside a pier, but had to anchor in isolation in Hampton Roads.

We had a distinguished speaker, Adm. Chester Nimitz. As will be the case with you, I don't remember a word he said.

My one hope was that the graduation services would be brief. As will be the case with you, I was disappointed. And I have to confess to you in confidence that at the time I did not expect to come back here later as President of the United States.

Seven years later I reluctantly left the Navy. But I can say in retrospect the Naval Academy and my service in the U.S. Navy was good preparation for the career which I eventually chose.

I congratulate the members of the Class of 1978. Although your education from the perspective of an older person has just begun, you have laid the foundation for a career that can be as rewarding and as challenging as any in the world.

[Role of Modern Naval Officers]

As officers in the modern Navy you will be actors in a worldwide political and military drama. You will be called upon not only to master the technicalities of military science and military leadership but also to have a sensitive understanding of the international community within which the Navy operates.

Today I want to discuss one of the most important aspects of that international context — the relationship between the world's two greatest powers, the United States of America and the Soviet Union.

We must realize that for a very long time our relationship with the Soviet Union will be competitive. That competition is to be constructive if we are successful. Instead it could be dangerous and politically disastrous.

Then our relationship must be cooperative as well. We must avoid excessive swings in the public mood in our country from euphoria, when things are going well, to despair, when they are not; from an exaggerated sense of compatibility with the Soviet Union to open expression of hostility.

[Détente Termed Central to Peace]

Détente between our two countries is central to world peace. It is important for the world, for the American public and for you as future leaders of the Navy to understand its complex and sensitive nature.

The word "détente" can be simplistically defined as the easing of tension between nations. The word is in practice, however, further defined by experience as those nations evolve new means by which they can live with each other in peace. To be stable, to be supported by the American people and to be a basis for widening the scope of cooperation, détente must be broadly defined and truly reciprocal.

Both nations must exercise restraint in troubled areas and in troubled times. Both must honor meticulously those agreements which have already been reached to widen cooperation, naturally, and mutually limit nuclear arms production, permit the free movement of people and expression of ideas and to protect human rights.

Neither of us should entertain the notion that military supremacy can be attained or that transient military advantage can be politically exploited.

Our principal goal is to help shape a world which is more responsive to the desire of people everywhere for economic well-being, social justice, political self-determination and basic human rights. We seek a world of peace but such a world must accommodate diversity — social, political and ideological. Only then can there be a genuine cooperation among nations and among cultures.

We desire to dominate no one. We will continue to widen our cooperation with the positive new forces in the world. We want to increase our collaboration with the Soviet Union, but also with the emerging nations, with the nations of Eastern Europe and with the People's Republic of China.

We are particularly dedicated to genuine self-determination and majority rule in those areas of the world where these goals have not yet been attained.

[Advantages of Cooperation]

Our long-term objectives must be to convince the Soviet Union of the advantages of cooperation and of the cost of disruptive behavior.

We remember that the United States and the Soviet Union were allies in the Second World War. One of the great historical accomplishments of the U.S. Navy was to guide and protect the tremendous shipments of armament and supplies from our country to Murmansk and to other Soviet ports in support of a joint effort to meet the Nazi threat.

In the agony of that massive conflict, 20 million Soviet lives were lost. Millions more who live in the Soviet Union still recall the horror and the hunger of that time. I'm convinced that the people of the Soviet Union want peace. I cannot believe that they could possibly want war.

Through the years our nation has sought accommodation with the Soviet Union, as demonstrated by the Austrian Peace Treaty, the Quadripartite Agreement concerning Berlin, the termination of nuclear testing in the atmosphere, joint scientific explorations in space, trade agreements, the antiballistic missile treaty, the interim agreement on strategic offensive armaments and the limited test-ban agreement.

[Efforts on Arms Treaty Continue]

Efforts still continue with negotiations toward a SALT II agreement, a comprehensive test ban against nuclear explosives, reductions in conventional arms transfers to other countries, the prohibition against attack on satellites in space, an agreement to stabilize the level of force deployment in the Indian Ocean, and increased trade and scientific and cultural exchange.

We must be willing to explore such avenues of cooperation despite the basic issues which divide us. The risks of nuclear war alone propel us in this direction.

The numbers and destructive potential of nuclear weapons has been increasing at an alarming rate. That is why a SALT agreement, which enhances the security of both nations, is of fundamental importance.

We and the Soviet Union are negotiating in good faith almost every day because we both know that a failure to succeed would precipitate a resumption of a massive nuclear arms race.

I'm glad to report to you today that the prospects for a SALT II agreement are good.

[Significant Differences]

Beyond this major effort, improved trade and technological and cultural exchange are among the immediate benefits of cooperation between our two countries. However, these efforts to cooperate do not erase the significant differences between us.

What are these differences? To the Soviet Union, détente seems to mean a continuing aggressive struggle for political advantage and increased influence in a variety of ways. The Soviet Union apparently sees military power and military assistance as the best means of expanding their influence abroad. Obviously, areas of instability in the world provide a tempting target for this effort. And all too often they seem ready to exploit any such opportunity.

As became apparent in Korea, in Angola, and also, as you know, in Ethiopia more recently, the Soviets prefer to use proxy forces to achieve their purposes.

[Buildup Is Considered Excessive]

To other nations throughout the world, the Soviets' military buildup appears to be excessive far beyond any legitimate requirements to defend themselves or to defend their allies. For more than 15 years they have maintained this program of military growth, investing almost 15 percent of their total gross national product in armaments, and this sustained growth continues.

The abuse of basic human rights in their own country, in violation of the agreement which was reached at Helsinki, has earned them the condemnation of people everywhere who love freedom. By their actions they have demonstrated that the Soviet system cannot tolerate freely expressed ideas or notions of loyal opposition and the free movement of people. The Soviet Union attempts to export a totalitarian and repressive form of government resulting in a closed society.

Some of these characteristics and goals create problems for the Soviet Union. Outside their tightly controlled bloc, the Soviet Union has difficult political relations with other nations. Their cultural bonds with others are few and frayed. Their form of government is becoming increasingly unattractive to other nations so that even Marxist-Leninist groups no longer look on the Soviet Union as a model to be imitated.

Many countries are becoming very concerned that the nonaligned movement is being subverted by Cuba, which is obviously closely aligned with the Soviet Union and dependent upon the Soviets for economic sustenance and for military and political guidance and direction.

Although the Soviet Union has the second largest economic system in the world, its growth is slowing greatly and its standard of living does not compare favorably with that of other nations at the same equivalent stage of economic development.

[Soviet Agricultural Lag]

Agricultural production still remains a serious problem for the Soviet Union so that in times of average or certainly adverse conditions for crop production, they must turn to us or turn to other nations for food supplies.

We in our country are in a much more favorable position. Our industrial base and our productivity are unmatched. Our scientific and technological capability is superior to all others. Our alliances with other free nations are strong and growing stronger, and our military capability is now and will be second to none.

In contrast to the Soviet Union, we are surrounded by friendly neighbors and wide seas. Our social structure is stable and cohesive and our foreign policy enjoys bipartisan public support, which gives it continuity. We are also strong because of what we stand for as a nation — the realistic chance for every person to build a better life, protection by both law and custom from arbitrary exercise of government power, the right of every individual to speak out, to participate fully in government and to share political power.

[U.S. Social System Praised]

Our philosophy is based on personal freedom, the most powerful of all ideas, and our democratic way of life warrants the admiration and emulation by other people throughout the world.

Our work for human rights makes us part of an international tide growing in force. We are strengthened by being part of it.

Our growing economic strength is also a major political factor, a potential influence for the benefit of others.

Our gross national product exceeds that of all nine nations combined in the European Economic Community and it is twice as great as that of the Soviet Union.

Additionally we are now learning how to use our resources more wisely, creating a new harmony between our people and our environment.

Our analysis of American military strength also furnishes a basis for confidence. We know that neither the United States nor the Soviet Union can launch a nuclear assault on the other without suffering a devastating counterattack which could destroy the aggressor nation.

[Missile Strength Compared]

Although the Soviet Union has more missile launchers, greater throw-weight and more continental air defense capabilities, the United States has more warheads, generally greater accuracy, more heavy bombers, a more balanced nuclear force, better missile submarines and superior antisubmarine warfare capabilities.

A successful SALT II agreement will give both nations equal but lower ceilings on missile launchers and also on missiles with multiple warheads.

We envision in SALT III an even greater mutual reduction in nuclear weapons. With essential nuclear equivalents, relative conventional force strength has now become more important. The fact is that the military capability of the United States and its allies is adequate to meet any foreseeable threat. It is possible that each side tends to exaggerate the military capability of the other.

Accurate analyses are important as a basis for making decisions for the future. False or excessive estimates of Soviet strength or American weakness contribute to the effectiveness of the Soviet propaganda effort.

For example, recently, alarming news reports of the military budget proposals for the U.S. Navy ignored the fact that we have the highest defense budget in history and the largest portion of this will go to the Navy.

You men are joining a long tradition of superior leadership, seamanship and ship design. And I am confident that the U.S. Navy has no peer nor equal on the high seas today, and you, I and others will always keep the Navy strong.

Let there be no doubt about our present and future strength. This brief assessment, which I have just made, shows that we need not be overly concerned about our ability to compete and to compete successfully. Certainly there is no cause for alarm. The healthy self-criticism and the free debate which are essential in a democracy should never be confused with weakness or despair or lack of purpose.

[U.S. Foreign Policy]

What are the principal elements of American foreign policy to the Soviet Union. Let me outline them very briefly:

We will continue to maintain equivalent nuclear strength because we believe that, in the absence of worldwide nuclear disarmament, such equivalency is the least threatening and the most stable situation for the world.

We will maintain a prudent and sustained level of military spending keyed to a stronger NATO, more mobile forces and undiminished presence in the Pacific.

We and our allies must and will be able to meet any foreseeable challenge to our security from either strategic nuclear forces or from conventional forces.

America has the capability to honor this commitment without excessive sacrifice on the part of our citizens and that commitment to military strength will be honored.

Looking beyond our alliances we will support worldwide and regional organizations which are dedicated to enhancing international peace, like the United Nations, the Organization of American States and the Organization for African Unity.

[Attitudes on African Issue]

In Africa we and our African friends want to see a continent that is free of the dominance of outside powers, free of the bitterness of racial injustice, free of conflict and free of the burdens of poverty and hunger and disease.

We are convinced that the best way to work toward these objectives is through affirmative policies that recognize African realities and that recognize African aspirations.

The persistent and increasing military involvement of the Soviet Union and Cuba in Africa could deny this hopeful vision.

We are deeply concerned about the threat to regional peace and to the autonomy of countries within which these foreign troops seem permanently to be stationed. That is why I have spoken out on this subject today and that is why I and the American people will support African efforts to contain such intrusions as we have done recently in Zaire.

I urge again that all other powers join us in emphasizing works of peace rather than the weapons of war.

[Wider Exchange With Soviets Sought]

In their assistance to Africa, let the Soviet Union now join us in seeking a peaceful and a speedy transition to majority rule in Rhodesia and in Namibia. Let us see efforts to resolve peacefully the disputes in Eritrea and in Angola. Let us all work not to divide and to seek domination in Africa but to help those nations to fulfill their great potential.

We will seek peace, better communication and understanding, cultural and scientific exchange and increased trade with the Soviet Union and with other nations.

We will attempt to prevent the proliferation of nuclear weapons among those nations not now having this capability. We will continue to negotiate constructively and persistently for a fair strategic arms limitation agreement.

We know that no ideological victories can be won by either side by the use of nuclear weapons. We have no desire to link the negotiation for a SALT agreement with other competitive relationships nor to impose other special conditions on the process.

In a democratic society, however, where public opinion is an integral factor in the shaping and implementation of foreign policy, we do recognize that tensions, sharp disputes or threats to peace will complicate the quest for a successful agreement.

This is not a matter of our preference but a simple recognition of fact. The Soviet Union can choose either confrontation or cooperation. The United States is adequately prepared to meet either choice. We would prefer cooperation through a détente that increasingly involves similar restraints for both sides, similar readiness to resolve disputes by negotiation and not by violence, similar willingness to compete peacefully and not militarily.

Anything less than that is likely to undermine detente and this is why I hope that no one will underestimate the concerns which I have expressed today.

A competition without restraint and without shared rules will escalate into graver tensions and our relationship as a whole with the Soviet Union will suffer.

I do not wish this to happen and I do not believe that Mr. Brezhnev desires it. And this is why it is time for us to speak frankly and to face the problems squarely. By a combination of adequate American strength, of quiet self-restraint in the use of it, of a refusal to believe in the inevitability of war and of a patient and persistent development of all the peaceful alternatives, we hope eventually to lead international society into a more stable, more peaceful and a more hopeful future.

[Role to be Played by Midshipmen]

You and I leave here today to do our common duty — protecting our nation's vital interests by peaceful means if possible, by resolute action if necessary. We go forth sobered by these responsibilities but confident of our strength. We go forth knowing that our nation's goals — peace, security, liberty for ourselves and for others — will determine our future and that we together can prevail.

To attain these goals, our nation will require exactly those qualities of courage, self-sacrifice, idealism and self-discipline which you as midshipmen have learned here at Annapolis so well. That is why your nation expects so much of you and that is why you have so much to give.

I leave you now with my congratulations and with a prayer to God that both you and I will prove worthy of the task that is before us and the nation which we have sworn to serve.

Thank you very much.

CARTER'S URBAN MESSAGE
March 27, 1978

Stressing a "new partnership" of government, the private sector and neighborhood and voluntary groups, President Carter sent Congress March 27 his proposals for a series of programs aimed at invigorating the nation's ailing cities.

Emerging after a year of jurisdictional battles, false starts and other delays, the administration's plan was the result of an effort to involve Congress, non-federal groups and virtually the entire range of government agencies in a probing examination of federal programs affecting cities. Despite this broad consultation, by October adjournment Congress had failed to pass any major component of the urban package. Supporters of Carter's plan, however, said that they had anticipated that many of the proposals would be left for action by the new Congress in 1979.

The underlying theme of Carter's proposal was efficiency in the use of federal dollars. Characterized by one observer as marking the end of "the day of federal government largesse," the administration's policy proposed only modest increases in federal aid for new programs and substantial "retargeting" of government dollars in existing programs.

This approach signaled a major shift in urban policy from the massive infusions of federal funds in the "Great Society" programs of the 1960s, constituting what Patricia Roberts Harris, secretary of housing and urban development, called a "targeting of need, not of cities." In his message to Congress, Carter maintained that while some new federal money was needed to fill "gaps," the long-term answer to urban problems lay in making existing programs work more efficiently. "For those of us who live in our urban areas, the gravest flaw in past federal policy was not that we failed to spend money. It was that too many programs were ineffective, and too many that did work had their benefits canceled out by other federal and state activities," the president declared.

New Initiatives

To "target" existing programs, the president proposed more than 160 changes in 38 federal programs already in operation to make them more sensitive to urban needs. In addition, the plan called for 30 initiatives requiring new legislation, ranging from creation of a National Development Bank to grants for urban parks, social service programs and the arts. The major proposals were:

● National Development Bank — to stimulate business expansion in both urban and rural "distressed" areas through grants and $11 billion in loan guarantees.
● Urban impact statement — required before any new federal program could be implemented to determine negative impact on cities.
● Fiscal assistance — targeted to aid governments in cities with unusually high unemployment.
● Tax credits — to employers hiring Comprehensive Employment Training Act (CETA) workers between 18 and 24, and to businesses investing in "distressed" areas.
● Community and human development — increased low-cost loans for housing rehabilitation; grants to build inner-city health clinics, to improve day care and "meals on wheels" programs and to create an "urban volunteer corps" made up of professionals to help neighborhood renewal programs.
● Incentive grants — to states to encourage new urban planning and redirection of state programs toward urban areas.
● Inter-Agency Coordinating Council — to facilitate the administration of major urban projects considered too large or complex to be handled by one agency.

Policy Development

The administration proposal was developed by many hands in a complex process over a 12-month period. The "open" way in which it was drafted appeared to be a response to criticism of the closed-door approach taken in framing Carter's energy package. However, the broad consultation put President Carter in a tight time squeeze which forced him to make billion-dollar decisions about the shape of his urban policy in the last 48 hours before its announcement.

Decisions on major components of the plan for the cities were delayed partly because of jurisdictional disputes between the Department of Housing and Urban Development (HUD) and the Commerce Department. The most visible object of the vying between the two departments was the placement of the proposed National Development Bank. In the end, Carter chose tripartite administration of the bank by the Treasury, Commerce and HUD departments.

Reaction

The administration was widely praised for the open manner in which the urban policy was developed and for the policy's delicate balancing of political practicality and fiscal restraint. However, those most affected by the proposal offered reactions ranging from cautious approval to disappointment, with criticism most often centered on restraints on federal spending.

Vernon E. Jordan, president of the National Urban League, described the policy as "disheartening" and a "missed opportunity." He urged the administration to remake the program into a "domestic urban Marshall Plan" for the cities. Many governors and mayors were pleased by their inclusion in the program, but they too called for higher spending. Some urban experts criticized the plan for spreading money thinly over a multiplicity of federal agencies and programs.

On the other hand, a number of observers extolled the program for its "modest" and "reasonable" goals, citing its goal of easing inner-city crises in the short-term and helping cities adapt to their evolving roles in the long-term.

Following is the text of President Carter's March 27, 1978, message to Congress proposing major changes in urban policy:

To the Congress of the United States:

I submit today my proposals for a comprehensive national urban policy. These proposals set a policy framework for actions my Administration has already taken, for proposed new initiatives, and for our efforts to assist America's communities and their residents in the years to come. The policy represents a comprehensive, long-term commitment to the Nation's urban areas.

The urban policy I am announcing today will build a *New Partnership* involving all levels of government, the private sector, and neighborhood and voluntary organizations in a major effort to make America's cities better places in which to live and work. It is a comprehensive policy aimed both at making cities more healthy and improving the lives of the people who live in them.

The major proposals will:

• Improve the effectiveness of existing Federal programs by coordinating these programs, simplifying planning requirements, reorienting resources, and reducing paperwork. And the proposals will make Federal actions more supportive of the urban policy effort and develop a process for analyzing the urban and community impact of all major Federal initiatives.

• Provide employment opportunities, primarily in the private sector, to the long-term unemployed and the disadvantaged in cities. This will be done through a labor-intensive public works program and tax and other incentives for business to hire the long-term unemployed.

• Provide fiscal relief to the most hard-pressed communities.

• Provide strong incentives to attract private investment to distressed communities, including the creation of a National Development Bank, expanded grant programs and targeted tax incentives.

• Encourage states to become partners in assisting urban areas through a new incentive grant program.

• Stimulate greater involvement by neighborhood organizations and voluntary associations through funding neighborhood development projects and by creating an Urban Volunteer Corps. These efforts will be undertaken with the approval of local elected officials.

• Increase access to opportunity for those disadvantaged by economic circumstance or a history of discrimination.

• Provide additional social and health services to disadvantaged people in cities and communities.

• Improve the urban physical environment and the cultural and aesthetic aspects of urban life by providing additional assistance for housing rehabilitation, mass transit, the arts, culture, parks and recreation facilities.

America's communities are an invaluable national asset. They are the center of our culture, the incubators of new ideas and inventions, the centers of commerce and finance, and the homes of our great museums, libraries and theatres. Cities contain trillions of dollars of public and private investments — investments which we must conserve, rehabilitate and fully use.

The New Partnership I am proposing today will focus the full energies of my Administration on a comprehensive, long-term effort. It will encourage States to redirect their own resources to support their urban areas more effectively. It will encourage local governments to streamline and coordinate their own activities. It will offer incentives to the private sector to make new investments in economically depressed communities. And it will involve citizens and neighborhood and voluntary organizations in meeting the economic and social needs of their communities.

The New Partnership will be guided by these principles:

• Simplifying and improving programs and policy at all levels of government.

- Combining the resources of federal, state and local government, and using them as a lever to involve the even greater strength of our private economy to conserve and strengthen our cities and communities.
- Being flexible enough to give help where it is most needed and to respond to the particular needs of each community.
- Increasing access to opportunity for those disadvantaged by economic circumstances or history of discrimination.
- And above all, drawing on the sense of community and voluntary effort that I believe is alive in America, and on the loyalty that Americans feel for their neighborhoods.

The need for a New Partnership is clear from the record of the last fifteen years. During the 1960s, the federal government took a strong leadership role in responding to the problems of the cities. The federal government attempted to identify the problems, develop the solutions and implement the programs. State and local governments and the private sector were not sufficiently involved. While many of these programs were successful, we learned an important lesson: that the federal government alone has neither the resources nor the knowledge to solve all urban problems.

An equally important lesson emerged from the experience of the early 1970s. During this period, the federal government retreated from its responsibilities, leaving states and localities with insufficient resources, interest or leadership to accomplish all that needed to be done. We learned that states and localities cannot solve the problems by themselves.

These experiences taught us that a successful urban policy must build a partnership that involves the leadership of the federal government and the participation of all levels of government, the private sector, neighborhood and voluntary organizations and individual citizens.

Prior Actions

The problems of our Nation's cities are complex and deep-seated. They have developed gradually over a generation as a result of private market and demographic forces and inadvertent government action; and the problems worsened markedly during the early 1970s.

These problems will not be solved immediately. They can be solved only by the long-term commitment which I offer today, and by the efforts of all levels of government, the private sector and neighborhood and voluntary organizations.

For my Administration, this commitment began on the day I took office and it will continue throughout my Presidency. With the cooperation of Congress, my Administration has already provided substantial increases in funding in many of the major urban assistance programs. Total assistance to state and local governments has increased by 25 percent, from $68 billion in FY 1977 to $85 billion in FY 1979. These increases are the direct result of actions we have taken during the past 14 months. They are as much a part of my Administration's urban policy as the initiatives which I am announcing today. Some of the most important programs have already been enacted into law or proposed to the Congress. These include:

• A $2.7 billion increase over three years in the Community Development Block Grant Program, accompanied by a change in the formula to provide more assistance to the older and declining cities.

• A $400 million a year Urban Development Action Grant Program providing assistance primarily to distressed cities.

• An expansion of youth and training programs and an increase in the number of public service employment jobs, from 325,000 to 725,000. Expenditures for employment and training doubled from FY '77 to FY '79 to over $12 billion.

• A $400 million private sector jobs proposal has been included in my proposal to reauthorize the CETA legislation. This initiative will encourage private businesses to hire the long-term unemployed and the disadvantaged.

• A sixty-five percent increase in grants provided by the Economic Development Administration to urban areas.

• A thirty percent increase in overall federal assistance to education, including a $400 million increase in the Elementary and Secondary Education Act, targeted in substantial part to large city school systems with a concentration of children from low-income families.

• An economic stimulus package enacted last year, (Anti-Recession Fiscal Assistance, Local Public Works and CETA) which provided almost $9 billion in additional aid to states and cities.

• A welfare reform proposal which, upon passage, will provide immediate fiscal relief to state and local governments.

• A doubling of outlays for the Section 312 housing rehabilitation loan program.

• Creation of a consumer cooperative bank which would provide financing assistance to consumer cooperatives which have difficulty obtaining conventional financing.

Improvements in Existing Programs

The Administration's Urban and Regional Policy Group (URPG) has examined all of the major urban assistance programs and proposed improvements. It also has worked with agencies traditionally not involved in urban policy, such as the Defense Department, the General Services Administration, and the Environmental Protection Agency, and has developed proposals to make their actions more supportive of urban areas. As a result of this massive effort, the federal government has become more sensitive to urban problems and more committed to their solutions.

The review of existing federal programs has resulted in more than 150 improvements in existing programs. Most of these improvements can be undertaken immediately through administrative action. Some will require legislation. None will increase the federal budget.

A few examples of the improvements are:

- All agencies will develop goals and timetables for minority participation in their grants and contracts — five major agencies have already begun.
- The Defense Department will set up a new program to increase procurement in urban areas.
- EPA will modify its water and sewer program to discourage wasteful sprawl.
- HUD has retargeted the Tandem Mortgage Assistance Program to provide greater support for urban housing.
- The existing countercyclical fiscal assistance program will be retargeted to help governments with unemployment rates above the national average.
- HUD and EDA are developing common planning and application requirements.
- The General Services Administration will attempt to locate federal facilities in cities whenever such a location is not inconsistent with the agency's mission.
- The Department of Transportation has proposed legislation to consolidate many categories of urban highway and transit grants, and to standardize the local matching share. These steps will provide local governments with greater flexibility to develop transportation systems suited to their needs.
- The Environmental Protection Agency will amend its regulations to accommodate new economic development in high pollution areas. Localities will be permitted to "bank" reductions in pollution which result from firms going out of business. These reductions then can be transferred to new firms locating in the community.

The effect of all these changes may be greater than even the substantial new initiatives which I have proposed in this message.

New Initiatives

The new initiatives which I am announcing today address five major urban needs:

1) Improving the operation of federal, state and local governments
2) Employment and Economic Development
3) Fiscal assistance
4) Community and Human Development
5) Neighborhoods and Voluntary Associations

These initiatives require $4.4 billion in budget authority, $1.7 billion in new tax incentives, and $2.2 billion in guaranteed loan authority in FY 1979. For FY 1980 the budget authority will be $6.1 billion, the tax incentives $1.7 billion and the guaranteed loan authority $3.8 billion.

I. Improving the Operation of Federal, State and Local Governments

Federal Programs

Over the long run, reorganization of the economic and community development programs may be necessary. Last June, I directed my reorganization project staff in the Office of Management and Budget to begin exploring the reorganization options. They have completed the first stages of this work. During the next several months, they will consult with the Congress, state and local officials and the public to develop the best solution.

There are several actions I will take immediately.

• **Urban and Community Impact Analysis.** I am implementing a process through my Domestic Policy Staff (DPS) and Office of Management and Budget (OMB) to ensure that we do not inadvertently take actions which contradict the goals of the urban policy. Each agency submitting a major domestic initiative must include its own urban and community impact analysis. DPS and OMB will review these submissions and will ensure that any anti-urban impacts of proposed federal policies will be brought to my attention.

• **Interagency Coordinating Council.** To improve program coordination, I will form an Interagency Coordinating Council, composed of the Assistant Secretaries with major program responsibilities in the key urban departments. The Council will have two functions:

It will serve as a catalyst for operational improvements which cut across Departments (for example, instituting uniform grant applications); and it will encourage interagency cooperation on projects which are too large or too complex to be funded by one agency. This Council will, for the first time, provide a coordinated federal response to communities which develop comprehensive and multi-year projects. It will have direction from the Executive Office of the President.

• **Consolidating Planning Requirements and Other Management Improvements.** We soon will announce the consolidation of intra-agency planning requirements. I have asked the Director of the Office of Management and Budget to direct an interagency task force to improve the management of federal grant-in-aid programs and consolidate the numerous planning requirements in the community and economic development grant programs.

• **Improved Data and Information.** I have asked the Secretary of Commerce, in her capacity as Chair of the Statistical Policy Coordination Committee, to design an improved urban data and information system. At the present time much of this data is inadequate or out of date.

The Role of State Governments

State government policies, even more than federal policies, are important to the fiscal and economic health of cities. States affect their cities in a number of ways, including setting taxation and annexation powers, determining the placement of major development investments and apportioning the financial responsibility for welfare and education expenditures.

The federal government has little or no control over these developments, all of which clearly affect the economic and fiscal health of cities and communities.

These state responsibilities underscore the need for an urban policy which includes the states as full and equal partners. The effectiveness of our urban policy will be enhanced if the states can be encouraged to complement the federal effort.

To encourage states to support their urban areas, I will offer a new program of state incentive grants. These grants will be provided, on a discretionary basis, to states which adopt approved plans to help their cities and communities. The plans must be developed with the participation and approval of communities within the state. The grants will be provided to the states to finance a portion of the plan. The State Incentive Grant Program will be administered by HUD and will provide $400 million over two years.

Local Government Role

Many communities and cities can improve management and planning improvements by reforming fiscal management practices, streamlining local regulatory procedures, and coordinating local community and economic development activities.

The federal government provides planning and technical assistance to communities through HUD and Commerce to help cities improve their management and planning practices. These funds will be used increasingly to build the local government's capacity to undertake the necessary fiscal and management reforms.

The federal government will offer special consideration in discretionary programs to cities which achieve coordinated action at the local level.

II. Employment and Economic Development

There is a serious shortage of jobs for many residents of our urban areas and a lack of investment to build the tax base of our cities.

The urban policy will address this issue in two ways.

In the short run, it will provide additional employment opportunities through a labor-intensive public works program, a target employment tax credit, and a private sector training and jobs initiative to encourage businesses to hire the hardcore unemployed, together with the extension I have already proposed in employment and training opportunities under the CETA Act.

In the long run, the policy attempts to rebuild the private sector economic base of these communities through a National Development Bank, a special tax incentive, an increase in economic development grants and other incentives.

Labor-intensive Public Works

I ask Congress for $1 billion a year for a program of labor-intensive public works, targeted on communities with high unemployment. Half of the estimated 60,000 full-time equivalent jobs created annually by this program will be reserved for the disadvantaged and the long-term unemployed. These workers will be paid at Davis-Bacon trainee wage levels.

This program will enable cities to make needed repairs on buildings, streets, parks, and other public facilities.

In contrast to the Local Public Works program — which involves projects requiring large equipment, material expenditures and a prolonged planning period — more of the funds under this labor-intensive program will go to job creation.

Targeted Employment Tax Credit

I also propose a Targeted Employment Tax Credit to encourage business to hire disadvantaged young workers between the ages of 18 and 24 who suffer the highest unemployment rates in the Nation.

Under my proposal, private employers of young and disadvantaged, or handicapped, workers would be entitled to claim a $2,000 tax credit for each eligible worker during the first year of employment and a $1,500 credit for each eligible worker during the second year.

I am proposing this Targeted Employment Tax Credit as a substitute for the expiring Employment Tax Credit. The current program costs $2.5 billion a year and has had little influence on hiring decisions. The Administration's targeted program will cost approximately $1.5 billion a year, with far greater impact.

Location of Federal Facilities

I will sign a new Executive Order directing the General Services Administration to give first priority to cities in locating new federal facilities or consolidating or relocating existing facilities. Under my Administration, federal facilities will be located in cities, unless such a location is inconsistent with the agency's mission.

Federal buildings and facilities can be an important source of jobs and of rental payments and, in many cities, a principal stabilizing force preventing decline.

The federal government should set an example for the private sector to invest in urban areas.

Federal Government Procurement

To assure that federal procurement is used to strengthen the economic base of our Nation's cities and communities, I will:

● strengthen the implementation of the existing procurement set-aside program for labor surplus areas, by directing the General Services Administration to work with each agency to develop specific procurement targets and to monitor their implementation. GSA will report to me every six months on the progress of each Agency;

• direct the Defense Department to implement an experimental program to target more of its procurement to high unemployment areas.

National Development Bank

I propose the creation of a National Development Bank, which would encourage businesses to locate or expand in economically distressed urban and rural areas. The Bank would be authorized to guarantee investments totaling $11 billion through 1981.

To lower operating costs in urban areas, the Bank would provide long-term, low-cost financing which, in conjunction with expanded grant programs administered by HUD and EDA, will reduce a firm's financing costs by up to 60 percent.

The Bank uses four major financing tools:

• Grants of up to 15 percent of a firm's total capital cost, to a maximum $3 million, for fixed assets of a project. The grants, which would be made under expanded EDA and HUD authorities, would cover expenditures for land assembly, site preparation, rehabilitation, and equipment.

• Loan guarantees, provided by the Bank to cover three-quarters of the remaining capital costs up to a maximum of $15 million per project. The Bank could, at its discretion, reduce the interest rate down to two and one-half percent for particularly desirable projects. Bank financing would be conditioned on obtaining 21 percent of the project's total costs from private lenders.

• The ceiling for industrial reserve bonds in economically distressed areas would be increased from $5 to $20 million with the approval of the Bank. A business which used this financing for a project could also receive a grant.

• The Bank also will provide a secondary loan market for private loans in eligible areas to finance capital expenditures. This will be particularly beneficial to small businesses.

Bank projects will require the approval of state or local government economic development entities, which would be responsible to the elected local leadership. Distressed urban and rural areas would be eligible. Additional employment would be a key test of project eligibility.

The Bank will be an interagency corporation, governed by a Board composed of the Secretaries of HUD, Commerce and the Treasury. This will ensure coordination between the major economic, community development and urban finance agencies of the government.

The Office of Management and Budget is currently assessing the organization of the federal economic and community development activities. The Bank will function on an interagency basis pending recommendations in this area.

Economic Development Grants

I propose substantial increases of $275 million each in the UDAG grant program and the EDA Title I program. These increases will be used in conjunction with the financing incentives available from the National Development Bank.

Taken together these major increases will help leverage substantial new private sector investment in urban areas and address the long-term economic deterioration experienced by certain urban and rural areas.

Differential Investment Tax Credit

I propose that firms that locate or expand in economically distressed areas be eligible for a differential 5 percent investment tax credit, to a total of 15 percent for both structures and equipment. The credit would be available only to firms awarded "Certificates of Necessity" by the Commerce Department based on financing need and employment potential.

Commerce will be authorized to issue up to $200 million in certificates for each of the next two years.

Air Quality Planning Grants

I propose a $25 million planning grant program to help cities and communities comply with the Clean Air Act without limiting severely new, private sector investment within their areas.

I have also asked EPA, HUD and EDA to provide technical assistance to help local governments reconcile potential conflicts between air pollution and economic development goals.

Minority Business

Minority businesses are a critical part of the private sector economic base of many cities, communities and neighborhoods, and provide important employment opportunities to city residents.

I propose today two important initiatives which will increase the role of minority businesses in our economy. First, in comparison with FY 1977 levels, we will triple federal procurement from minority businesses by the end of FY 1979 — an increase over our earlier commitment to double minority procurement.

In addition, I intend to ask all federal agencies to include goals for minority business participation in their contract and grant-in-aid programs. Five agencies — HUD, Commerce, EPA, Interior and DOT — already have proposed improvements in minority business programs. These programs all build on our successful experience with the Local Public Works Program.

Finally, I intend to facilitate greater interaction between the minority business community and the leaders of our Nation's largest corporations.

Community Development Corporations

I propose that an additional $20 million be appropriated to the Community Services Administration as venture capital for the most effective

Community Development Corporations. This assistance will help them have a substantial impact on their designated areas.

The funding will be made available for projects that receive support from local elected officials, involve leveraging private sector funds and are coordinated with HUD, EDA or the Small Business Administration.

Role of Private Financial Institutions

An effective urban strategy must involve private financial institutions. I am asking the independent financial regulatory agencies to develop appropriate actions, consistent with safe, sound and prudent lending practices, to encourage financial institutions to play a greater role in meeting the credit needs of their communities.

First, I am requesting that financial regulatory agencies determine what further actions are necessary to halt the practice of redlining — the refusal to extend credit without a sound economic justification. I will encourage those agencies to develop strong, consistent and effective regulations to implement the Community Reinvestment Act.

Second, I propose the creation of an Institute for Community Investment, under the Federal Home Loan Bank Board. The Institute will bring together appraisers, realtors, lenders, building and insurance companies to develop a consistent approach toward urban lending and to train urban lending specialists.

Third, I propose a pilot program to create Neighborhood Commercial Reinvestment Centers under the Comptroller of the Currency. This proposal is an adaptation of the highly successful Urban Reinvestment Task Force housing credit concept to the commercial credit area. Neighborhood Commercial Reinvestment Centers will be local organizations, comprised of merchants and neighborhood residents, local government officials, and commercial banks which will provide business credit in urban neighborhoods. SBA, EDA and HUD will work with the financial regulatory agencies to revitalize specific commercial areas.

Finally, I have asked the Secretary of Housing and Urban Development to chair an interagency task force to evaluate the availability of credit in urban areas and recommend appropriate further action. I have asked the task force to examine and make recommendations with respect to the following areas:

• The availability of mortgage and commercial credit in urban areas, and the impacts of the activities of federal agencies on such credit;

• Existing mortgage insurance, casualty insurance and business credit insurance programs;

• The full range of urban credit and insurance risk reduction techniques.

III. Fiscal Assistance

While the fiscal condition of many state and local governments has improved dramatically over the last three years, many cities and communities still are experiencing severe problems. These cities and communities require fiscal assistance from the federal government, if they are to avoid severe service cutbacks or tax increases.

Supplemental Fiscal Assistance

Cities and communities currently receive fiscal assistance through the Anti-Recession Fiscal Assistance Act (ARFA), which expires on September 30, 1978. This program has been an effective tool for helping states and local governments withstand the fiscal impact of high unemployment.

Current unemployment projections, however, suggest that even if the ARFA program were extended in its current form, it would phase out by mid-FY 1979, when unemployment is expected to drop below six percent. If the program is permitted to phase out, many cities and communities will experience severe fiscal strain.

I propose today that ARFA be replaced with a Supplemental Fiscal Assistance Program, which will provide $1 billion of fiscal assistance annually for the next two fiscal years to local governments experiencing significant fiscal strain. Further extension of this program will be considered together with General Revenue Sharing.

Fiscal Relief in Welfare Proposal

In addition, I propose to phase in the fiscal relief component of the Better Jobs and Income Act as soon as Congress passes this legislation, rather than in 1981 as originally planned.

IV. Community and Human Development

A comprehensive program to revitalize America's cities must provide for community and human needs. This involves both physical facilities, such as parks, recreation facilities, housing and transportation systems, and the provision of health and social services.

Housing Rehabilitation

The conservation and upgrading of our housing stock is important to maintaining the strength of urban areas. Housing and rehabilitation improves the quality of community life and provides construction jobs in areas of high unemployment.

I propose an additional $150 million in FY 1979 for the Section 312 rehabilitation loan program, which will more than double the existing program. This expanded effort will permit the rehabilitation of small multi-family housing projects in distressed neighborhoods, for which financing presently is inadequate. In addition, expanded Section 312 funding will be used to strengthen the Urban Homesteading program.

Urban Transportation

In many cities, public transportation is inadequately financed. The federal government has begun to make substantial investments to rehabilitate, revitalize and construct urban transportation systems.

I have already submitted to Congress my proposals to extend and strengthen the highway and mass transit programs.

To supplement these efforts I today propose an additional $200 million for capital investments in intermodal urban transportation projects. These funds will be used to link existing transportation facilities in selected cities.

Resource Recovery Planning

Solid waste disposal is a growing problem in the many urban areas which face a shortage of landfill sites. At the same time, techniques to recover valuable resources and energy from solid waste have emerged.

I will request $15 million for the EPA to provide grants of $300,000 to $400,000 to cities for feasibility studies of solid waste recovery systems.

Arts and Culture

Cities are centers of culture and art, which thrive on the vitality of the urban environment.

To help renew and develop this artistic and cultural spirit, I propose a new Livable Cities program administered by the Department of Housing and Urban Development, with the participation of the National Endowment for the Arts. This program will provide up to $20 million in grants to states and communities for neighborhood- and community-based arts programs, urban design and planning, and the creation and display of art in public spaces. Historic preservation of buildings should also be encouraged.

Urban Parks and Recreation

The quality of life in urban areas is critically affected by the availability of open spaces and recreation facilities. Yet hard pressed communities often lack the resources to maintain and invest adequately in these amenities.

To address this problem, I propose a major new federal grant program. Urban communities will compete for funds to revive and rebuild parks and recreation facilities. Challenge grants totalling $150 million will be provided for construction and major rehabilitation of urban recreation systems, such as parks, tennis and basketball courts, swimming pools, bicycle paths, and other facilities. Cities will be awarded grants based on the quality of their planning, the degree of need and their ability to match the federal funds with private and local contributions.

Social Services

Urban revitalization efforts must be accompanied by efforts to help those in need to improve their own lives. A variety of income support and social service programs are designed to do this. Since 1974, however, the support given to state social service programs by the federal government has declined in real terms.

I propose an additional $150 million of new budget authority for the Title programs. These funds will be used to improve the delivery of social services in urban areas — ranging from Meals on Wheels for the elderly to day care for children of working mothers — and to develop greater coordination between local, public and private agencies.

Health Services

Nearly 50 million Americans live in areas without adequate health services. These areas, many of which are in inner cities, suffer from higher infant mortality rates, greater poverty and shortages of health care personnel.

In underserved areas, emergency room and outpatient departments of city hospitals are used as the routine source of medical care by the poor, primarily due to the lack of private physicians. As these departments were not designed to provide comprehensive medical care, the hospital resources are strained and the poor often go without adequate care.

To help meet the primary health care needs of the urban poor and reduce the strain on city hospitals, I propose to expand federally-supported Community Health Centers and to fund city-sponsored programs which provide comprehensive, but less costly, primary care services. The city-sponsored programs will enroll the medically indigent in existing health systems, such as HMOs. They also will help expand locally-supported centers, reform hospital outpatient departments and provide comprehensive health services.

Education

Schools are the focus of community activities in many places. Yet they are seldom fully used or linked to other community and social services.

I intend to provide $1.5 million to expand the experimental Cities in Schools program which seeks to bridge the gap by uniting a number of social services within schools to better serve both students and their families. We intend to expand this promising new program to 10 pilot schools.

In addition, I urge the Congress to enact the $600 million increase in the Title I program of the Elementary and Secondary Education Act, which I recently proposed, including my recommendation that $400 million of these funds be targeted to cities and other areas with high concentrations of low-income families.

V. Neighborhoods and Volunteer Organizations

No resource of our urban communities is more valuable than the commitment of our citizens.

Volunteer groups, which gain strength from the selfless efforts of many individuals, make an indispensable contribution to their cities.

Urban Volunteer Corps

I propose a $40 million program in ACTION to increase the effectiveness of voluntary activities at the local level. With the agreement of local government, the program will create a corps of volunteers at the local level and match their skills with the needs of local governments and community and neighborhood organizations.

It also will provide small grants averaging $5,000 for voluntary improvement and beautification projects.

ACTION would select, with the concurrence of local government, a lead agency in each city to administer the Urban Volunteer Corps.

Self-Help Development Program

Neighborhood associations are playing a key role in housing and neighborhood revitalization. We must strengthen that role.

I will request $15 million in FY 1979 for a self-help development program to be administered by the Office for Neighborhoods in HUD.

This new program will provide funds for specific housing and revitalization projects in poor and low-income areas. Each project would involve the participation of local residents, the private sector and local government and would require the concurrence of the mayor.

Crime Prevention

Street crime is a serious problem in America's cities and communities. Over the last few years a number of promising initiatives have been undertaken by community groups and local law enforcement agencies to combat street crime. Escort services for the elderly, centers to help the victims of crime, and neighborhood watchers are examples of promising developments.

I propose a program which will add $10 million in new resources to existing efforts in the Law Enforcement Assistance Administration for the program operated jointly by ACTION and LEAA. Under this program, mayors and local neighborhood groups will develop community crime prevention programs based on successful pilot models. My reorganization proposals for LEAA and the legislation I will submit to extend the Law Enforcement Assistance Act will strengthen our efforts at crime prevention.

Community Development Credit Unions

Some urban communities are not served by any financial institutions. Community Development Credit Unions address this problem by investing their assets in the communities in which they are established. This type of credit union was first established under the poverty programs in the 1960s. About 225 exist today, and many are the only financial institutions in their communities.

I am proposing a $12 million program to provide $200,000 seed capital for new Community Development Credit Unions, to provide them with an operating subsidy for staff, training and technical assistance.

The job of revitalizing the urban communities of our country will not be done overnight. Problems which have accumulated gradually over generations cannot be solved in a year or even in the term of a President.

But I believe that a New Partnership — bringing together in a common effort all who have a stake in the future of our communities — can bring us closer to our long-term goals. We can make America's cities more attractive places in which to live and work; we can help the people of urban America lead happier and more useful lives. But we can only do it together.

JIMMY CARTER

The White House,
March 27, 1978

COURT ON JUDICIAL IMMUNITY

March 28, 1978

The Supreme Court March 28 upheld the century-old tradition of judicial immunity that protects judges against suits brought as a result of their judicial actions. In a 5-3 decision, the court ruled in Stump v. Sparkman *that Judge Harold D. Stump of DeKalb County, Ind., could not be sued for damages in a case that flowed from his 1971 approval of a mother's petition for the sterilization of her 15-year-old daughter.*

The daughter, Linda Kay Spitler Sparkman, was told at the time that she had to enter the hospital to undergo an appendectomy and did not discover the true nature of the operation until she had married and attempted to become pregnant. She and her husband, Leo Sparkman, then brought suit against her mother, the doctors, the hospital and Judge Stump, seeking damages for alleged violations of their rights.

The mother's petition said that her daughter was "somewhat retarded," although she attended school and had been promoted each year. The petition also said that the girl had been associating with "older youth or young men" and had stayed out overnight with them on several occasions. It stated that it would be in the daughter's best interest if she underwent a tubal ligation "to prevent unfortunate circumstances. . . ." Stump approved the mother's petition without holding a hearing, without appointing a guardian for the daughter's interests and without leaving a public record.

First expressed in Bradley v. Fisher *(1872), judicial immunity allows judges to perform without fear for personal consequences, even if their actions are beyond their jurisdictions or appear malicious or corrupt. The federal district judge who first heard the Stump case held Stump immune from the damage suit, but the 7th U.S. Circuit Court of Appeals reversed the lower court ruling. Stump appealed to the Supreme Court.*

Justice Byron R. White wrote the majority opinion, joined by Chief Justice Warren E. Burger and Justices Harry A. Blackmun, William H. Rehnquist and John Paul Stevens. Justice Potter Stewart wrote a sharp dissent in which he was joined by Justices Thurgood Marshall and Lewis F. Powell Jr. Powell also filed a separate dissenting opinion. Justice William J. Brennan Jr. did not participate.

Majority Opinion

Quoting from Bradley, *White noted in the majority opinion that a judge is subject to liability only when it is determined that he has acted in the "clear absence of all jurisdiction." Consequently, he wrote, "We cannot agree that there was a 'clear absence of all jurisdiction' in the DeKalb County Circuit Court to consider the petition presented by Mrs. McFarlin," the mother of Linda Kay Spitler Sparkman. "As an Indiana circuit judge, Judge Stump had 'original exclusive jurisdiction in all cases at law and in equity whatsoever . . . ,' jurisdiction over the settlement of estates and over guardianships, appellate jurisdiction as conferred by law, and jurisdiction over 'all other causes, matters and proceedings where exclusive jurisdiction thereof is not conferred by law upon some other court, board or officer.' " White added that the court agreed with the judgment of the District Court that "neither by statute or case law has the broad jurisdiction granted to the circuit courts of Indiana been circumscribed to foreclose consideration of a petition for authorization of a minor's sterilization."*

Objecting to the finding by the Court of Appeals that Stump was not eligible for immunity because he not only acted outside his jurisdiction but also failed to follow procedural due process, White asserted that this "misconceives the doctrine of judicial immunity. A judge is absolutely immune from liability for his judicial acts even if his exercise of authority is flawed by the commission of grave procedural errors."

Judicial Act

The majority opinion further held that Stump's action constituted a judicial act despite the fact that the petition submitted "was not given a docket number, was not placed on file with the clerk's office, and was approved in an ex parte (only one party represented) proceeding without notice to the minor, without a hearing and without the appointment of a guardian ad litem," as had been argued by the respondents. The opinion added, "We find no merit to respondents' argument that the informality with which he (Stump) proceeded rendered his action nonjudicial and deprived him of his absolute immunity."

White added that the court's judgment in the case must not be affected by the nature of the judicial action. "Disagreement with the action taken by the judge, however, does not justify depriving that judge of his immunity," even though the result is sometimes "unfairness to litigants." White concluded: "The fact that the issue before the judge is a controversial one is all the more reason that he should be able to act without fear of suit."

Dissents

In his dissent, Justice Stewart asserted that "the scope of judicial immunity is limited to liability for 'judicial acts' and I think that what Judge Stump did . . . was beyond the pale of anything that could sensibly be called a judicial act." Stewart claimed that the court's finding that Stump's action was normal was "factually untrue" and that its judgment that he was acting in his judicial capacity was "legally unsound." Stewart added that the "conduct of a judge surely does not become a judicial act merely on his say-so. A judge is not free, like a loose cannon, to inflict indiscriminate damage whenever he announces that he is acting in his judicial capacity."

In a concurring dissent, Justice Powell declared that the court's decision left the respondents with none of the normal means of legal recourse and, therefore, the judge's act could not be considered judicial. He wrote: "But where a judicial officer acts in a manner that precludes all resort to appellate or other judicial remedies that otherwise would be available, the underlying assumption of the Bradley doctrine is inoperative."

Following are excerpts from the majority and dissenting opinions in the Supreme Court's March 28, 1978, decision on judicial immunity:

No. 76-1750

Harold D. Stump et al., Petitioners,	On Writ of Certiorari to
v.	the United States
Linda Kay Sparkman and	Court of Appeals for
Leo Sparkman.	the Seventh Circuit.

[March 28, 1978]

MR. JUSTICE WHITE delivered the opinion of the court. [MR. JUSTICE BRENNAN took no part in the consideration or decision of this case.]

This case requires us to consider the scope of a judge's immunity from damages liability. . . .

I

The relevant facts underlying respondents' suit are not in dispute. On July 9, 1971, Ora Spitler McFarlin, the mother of respondent Linda Kay Sparkman, presented to Judge Harold D. Stump of the Circuit Court of DeKalb County, Ind., a document captioned "Petition To Have Tubal Ligation Performed on Minor and Indemnity Agreement."... In this petition Mrs. McFarlin stated under oath that her daughter was 15 years of age and was "somewhat retarded," although she attended public school and had been promoted each year with her class. The petition further stated that Linda had been associating with "older youth or young men" and had stayed out overnight with them on several occasions. As a result of this behavior and Linda's mental capabilities, it was stated that it would be in the daughter's best interest if she underwent a tubal ligation in order "to prevent unfortunate circumstances...."....

The petition was approved by Judge Stump on the same day. He affixed his signature as "Judge, DeKalb Circuit Court," to the statement that he did "hereby approve the above Petition by affidavit form on behalf of Ora Spitler McFarlin, to have Tubal Ligation performed upon her minor daughter, Linda Spitler, subject to said Ora Spitler McFarlin covenanting and agreeing to indemnify and keep indemnified Dr. John Hines and the DeKalb Memorial Hospital from any matters or causes of action arising therefrom.". . .

Approximately two years after the operation, Linda Spitler was married to respondent Leo Sparkman. Her inability to become pregnant led her to discover that she had been sterilized during the 1971 operation. As a result of this revelation, the Sparkmans filed suit in the United States District Court for the Northern District of Indiana against Mrs. McFarlin, her attorney, Judge Stump, the doctors who had performed and assisted in the tubal ligation, and the DeKalb Memorial Hospital. . . .

Ruling upon the defendants' various motions to dismiss the complaint, the District Court concluded that each of the constitutional claims asserted by respondents required a showing of state action and that the only state action alleged in the complaint was the approval by Judge Stump, acting as circuit court judge, of the petition presented to him by Mrs. McFarlin. The Sparkmans sought to hold the private defendants liable on a theory that they had conspired with Judge Stump to bring about the allegedly unconstitutional acts. The District Court, however, held that no federal action would lie against any of the defendants because Judge Stump, the only state agent, was absolutely immune from suit under the doctrine of judicial immunity. The court stated that "whether or not Judge Stump's 'approval' of the petition may in retrospect appear to have been premised on an erroneous view of the law, Judge Stump surely had jurisdiction to consider the petition and to act thereon." *Sparkman* v. *McFarlin* . . . (1976). Accordingly, under *Bradley v. Fisher* . . . (1872), Judge Stump was entitled to judicial immunity.

On appeal, the Court of Appeals for the Seventh Circuit reversed the judgment of the District Court, holding that the "crucial issue" was "whether Judge Stump acted within his jurisdiction" and concluding that he had not. . . . He was accordingly not immune from damages liability under the controlling authorities. The Court of Appeals also held that the judge had forfeited his immunity "because of his failure to comply with elementary principles of procedural due process.". . .

We granted certiorari . . . to consider the correctness of this ruling. We reverse.

II

The governing principle of law is well established and is not questioned by the parties. As early as 1872, the Court recognized that it was "a general principle of the highest importance to the proper administration of justice that a judicial officer, in exercising the authority vested in him, [should] be free to act upon his own convictions, without apprehension of personal consequences to himself...." *Bradley* v. *Fisher*.... For that reason the Court held that "judges of courts of superior or general jurisdiction are not liable to civil actions for their judicial acts, even when such acts are in excess of their jurisdiction, and are alleged to have been done maliciously or corruptly." . . . Later we held that this doctrine of judicial immunity was applicable in suits under § 1 of the Civil Rights Act of 1871 . . . for the legislative record gave no indication that Congress intended to abolish this long-established principle. *Pierson* v. *Ray*...(1967).

The Court of Appeals correctly recognized that the necessary inquiry in determining whether a defendant judge is immune from suit is whether at the time he took the challenged action he had jurisdiction over the subject matter before him. Because "some of the most difficult and embarrassing questions which a judicial officer is called upon to consider and determine relate to his jurisdiction...," *Bradley* . . ., the scope of the judge's jurisdiction must be construed broadly where the issue is the immunity of the judge. A judge will not be deprived of immunity because the action he took was in error, was done maliciously, or was in excess of his authority; rather, he will be subject to liability only when he has acted in the "clear absence of all jurisdiction.". . .

We cannot agree that there was a "clear absence of all jurisdiction" in the DeKalb County Circuit Court to consider the petition presented by Mrs. McFarlin. As an Indiana circuit court judge, Judge Stump had "original exclusive jurisdiction in all cases at law and in equity whatsoever . . . ," jurisdiction over the settlement of estates and over guardianships, appellate jurisdiction as conferred by law, and jurisdiction over "all other causes, matters and proceedings where exclusive jurisdiction thereof is not conferred by law upon some other court, board or officer." Ind[iana] Code. . .(1975). This is indeed a broad jurisdictional grant; yet the Court of Appeals concluded that Judge Stump did not have jurisdiction over the petition authorizing Linda Sparkman's sterilization.

In so doing, the Court of Appeals noted that the Indiana statutes provided for the sterilization of institutionalized persons under certain circumstances . . . but otherwise contained no express authority for judicial approval of tubal ligations. It is true that the statutory grant of general jurisdiction to the Indiana circuit courts does not itemize types of cases those courts may hear and hence does not expressly mention sterilization petitions presented by the parents of a minor. But in our view, it is more significant that there was no Indiana statute and no case law in 1971 prohibiting a circuit court, a court of general jurisdiction, from considering a petition of the type presented to Judge Stump. . . . The District Court concluded that Judge Stump had jurisdiction . . . to entertain and act upon Mrs. McFarlin's petition. We agree with the District Court, it appearing that neither by statute or case law has the broad jurisdiction granted to the circuit courts of Indiana been circumscribed to foreclose consideration of a petition for authorization of a minor's sterilization.

The Court of Appeals also concluded that support for Judge Stump's actions could not be found in the common law of Indiana. . . .

Perhaps realizing the broad scope of Judge Stump's jurisdiction, the Court of Appeals stated that, even if the action taken by him was not foreclosed under the Indiana statutory scheme, it would still be "an illegitimate exercise of his common law power because of his failure to comply with elementary principles of procedural due process." . . . This misconceives the doctrine of judicial immunity. A judge is absolutely immune from liability for his judicial acts even if his exercise of authority is flawed by the commission of grave procedural errors. The Court made this point clear in *Bradley* . . . where it stated that "this erroneous manner in which [the court's] jurisdiction was exercised, however it may have affected the validity of the act, did not make the act any less a judicial act; nor did it render the defendant liable to answer in damages for it at the suit of the plaintiff, as though the court had proceeded without having any jurisdiction whatever...."

We conclude that the Court of Appeals, employing an unduly restrictive view of the scope of Judge Stump's jurisdiction, erred in holding that he was not entitled to judicial immunity. Because the court over which Judge Stump presides is one of general jurisdiction, neither the procedural errors he may have committed nor the lack of a specific statute authorizing his approval of the petition in question rendered him liable in damages for the consequences of his actions.

The respondents argue that even if Judge Stump had jurisdiction to consider the petition presented to him by Mrs. McFarlin, he is still not entitled to judicial immunity because his approval of the petition did not constitute a "judicial" act. It is only for acts performed in his "judicial" capacity that a judge is absolutely immune, they say. We do not disagree with this statement of the law, but we cannot characterize the approval of the petition as a nonjudicial act.

Respondents themselves stated in their pleadings before the District Court that Judge Stump was "clothed with the authority of the state" at the time that he approved the petition and that "he was acting as a county circuit court judge." Plaintiffs' Reply Brief to the Memorandum Filed on Behalf of Harold D. Stump in Support of His Motion to Dismiss. . . . They nevertheless now argue that Judge Stump's approval of the petition was not a judicial act because the petition was not given a docket number, was not placed on file with the clerk's office, and was approved in an *ex parte* proceeding without notice to the minor, without a hearing, and without the appointment of a *guardian ad litem.*

This Court has not had occasion to consider, for purposes of the judicial immunity doctrine, the necessary attributes of a judicial act; but it has previously rejected the argument, somewhat similar to the one raised here, that the lack of formality involved in the Illinois Supreme Court's consideration of a petitioner's application for admission to the state bar prevented it from being a "judicial proceeding" and from presenting a case or controversy that could be reviewed by this Court. . . .

. . . [T]he factors determining whether an act by a judge is a "judicial" one relate to the nature of the act itself, *i.e.,* whether it is a function normally performed by a judge, and to the expectations of the parties, *i.e.,* whether they dealt with the judge in his judicial capacity. Here, both factors indicate that Judge Stump's approval of the sterilization petition was a judicial act. State judges with general jurisdiction not infrequently are called upon in their official capacity to approve petitions relating to the affairs of minors, as for example, a petition to settle a minor's claim. Furthermore, as even respondents have admitted, at the time he approved the petition presented to him by Mrs. McFarlin, Judge Stump was "acting as a county circuit court judge."... [Plaintiffs' Reply Brief] We may infer from the record that it was only because Judge Stump served in that position that Mrs. McFarlin, on the advice of counsel, submitted the petition to him for his approval. Because Judge Stump performed the type of act normally performed only by judges and because he did so in his capacity as a circuit court judge, we find no merit to respondents' argument that the informality with which he proceeded rendered his action nonjudicial and deprived him of his absolute immunity.

Both the Court of Appeals and the respondents seem to suggest that, because of the tragic consequences of Judge Stump's actions, he should not be immune. For example, the Court of Appeals noted that "[t]here are actions of purported judicial character that a judge, even when exercising general jurisdiction, is not empowered to take," . . . and respondents argue that Judge Stump's action was "so unfair" and "so totally devoid of judicial concern for the interests and well-being of the young girl involved" as to disqualify it as a judicial act. . . . Disagreement with the action taken by the judge, however, does not justify depriving that judge of his immunity. Despite the unfairness to litigants that sometimes results, the doctrine of judicial immunity is thought to be in the best interests of "the proper administration of justice . . . [, for it allows] a judicial officer, in exercising the authority vested in him [to] be free to act upon his own convictions, without apprehension of personal consequences to himself." *Bradley* v.

Fisher. . . . The fact that the issue before the judge is a controversial one is all the more reason that he should be able to act without fear of suit. . . .

The Indiana law vested in Judge Stump the power to entertain and act upon the petition for sterilization. He is, therefore, under the controlling cases, immune from damages liability even if his approval of the petition was in error. Accordingly, the judgment of the Court of Appeals is reversed and the case is remanded for further proceedings consistent with this opinion.

It is so ordered.

MR. JUSTICE STEWART, with whom MR. JUSTICE MARSHALL and MR. JUSTICE POWELL join, dissenting.

It is established federal law that judges of general jurisdiction are absolutely immune from monetary liability "for judicial acts, even when such acts are in excess of their jurisdiction, and are alleged to have been done maliciously or corruptly." *Bradley* v. *Fisher*.... It is also established that this immunity is in no way diminished in a proceeding under 42 U.S.C. §1983 [deprivation of rights]. *Pierson* v. *Ray*.... But the scope of judicial immunity is limited to liability for "judicial acts," and I think that what Judge Stump did on July 9, 1971, was beyond the pale of anything that could sensibly be called a judicial act.

Neither in *Bradley* v. *Fisher* nor in *Pierson* v. *Ray* was there any claim that the conduct in question was not a judicial act, and the Court thus had no occasion in either case to discuss the meaning of that term. Yet the proposition that judicial immunity extends only to liability for "judicial acts" was emphasized no less than seven times in Mr. Justice Field's opinion for the Court in the *Bradley* case. . . . And if the limitations inherent in that concept have any realistic meaning at all, then I cannot believe that the action of Judge Stump in approving Mrs. McFarlin's petition is protected by judicial immunity.

The Court finds two reasons for holding that Judge Stump's approval of the sterilization petition was a judicial act. First, the Court says, it was "a function normally performed by a judge." Second, the Court says, the act was performed in Judge Stump's "judicial capacity." With all respect, I think that the first of these grounds is factually untrue and that the second is legally unsound.

When the Court says that what Judge Stump did was an act "normally performed by a judge," it is not clear to me whether the Court means that a judge "normally" is asked to approve a mother's decision to have her child given surgical treatment generally, or that a judge "normally" is asked to approve a mother's wish to have her daughter sterilized. But whichever way the Court's statement is to be taken, it is factually inaccurate. In Indiana, as elsewhere in our country, a parent is authorized to arrange for and consent to medical and surgical treatment of his minor child. . . . And when a parent decides to call a physician to care for his sick child or arranges to have a surgeon remove his child's tonsils, he does not, "normally" or otherwise, need to seek the approval of a judge. On the other hand, Indiana did in 1971 have statutory procedures for the sterilization of certain people who were *institutionalized.* But these statutes provided for *administrative proceedings* before a board established by the superintendent of each public hospital. Only if, after notice and an evidentiary hearing, an order of sterilization was entered in these proceedings could there be review in a circuit court. . . .

In sum, what Judge Stump did on July 9, 1971, was in no way an act "normally performed by a judge." Indeed, there is no reason to believe that such an act has ever been performed by *any* other Indiana judge, either before or since.

When the Court says that Judge Stump was acting in "his judicial capacity" in approving Mrs. McFarlin's petition, it is not clear to me whether the Court means that Mrs. McFarlin submitted the petition to him only because he was a judge, or that, in approving it, he *said* that he was acting as a judge. But however the Court's test is to be understood, it is, I think demonstrably unsound.

It can safely be assumed that the Court is correct in concluding that Mrs. McFarlin came to Judge Stump with her petition because he was a county circuit court judge. But false illusions as to a judge's power can hardly convert a judge's response to those illusions into a judicial act. In short, a judge's approval of a mother's petition to lock her daughter in the attic would hardly be a judicial act simply because the mother had submitted her petition to the judge in his official capacity.

If, on the other hand, the Court's test depends upon the fact that Judge Stump *said* he was acting in his judicial capacity, it is equally invalid. It is true that Judge Stump affixed his signature to the approval of the petition as "Judge, DeKalb Circuit Court." But the conduct of a judge surely does not become a judicial act merely on his own say-so. A judge is not free, like a loose cannon, to inflict indiscriminate damage whenever he announces that he is acting in his judicial capacity.

If the standard adopted by the Court is invalid, then what is the proper measure of a judicial act? Contrary to implications in the Court's opinion, my conclusion that what Judge Stump did was not a judicial act is not based upon the fact that he acted with informality, or that he may not have been "in his judge's robes," or "in the courtroom itself." . . . And I do not reach this conclusion simply "because the petition was not given a docket number, was not placed on file with the clerk's office, and was approved in an *ex parte* proceeding without notice to the minor, without a hearing, and without the appointment of a *guardian ad litem.*". . .

It seems to me, rather, that the concept of what is a judicial act must take its content from a consideration of the factors that support immunity from liability for the performance of such an act. . . .

Not one of the considerations . . . summarized in the *Pierson* opinion was present here. There was no "case," controversial or otherwise. There were no litigants. There was and could be no appeal. And there was not even the pretext of principled decision-making. The total absence of *any* of these normal attributes of a judicial proceeding convinces me that the conduct complained of in this case was not a judicial act.

The petitioners' brief speaks of "an aura of deism which surrounds the bench . . . essential to the maintenance of respect for the judicial institution." Though the rhetoric may be overblown, I do not quarrel with it. But if aura there be, it is hardly protected by exonerating from liability such lawless conduct as took place here. And if intimidation would serve to deter its recurrence, that would surely be in the public interest.

MR. JUSTICE POWELL, dissenting.

While I join the opinion of MR. JUSTICE STEWART, I wish to emphasize what I take to be the central feature of this case — petitioner's preclusion of any possibility for the vindication of respondent's rights elsewhere in the judicial system.

Bradley v. *Fisher*...(1872), which established the absolute judicial immunity at issue in this case, recognized that the immunity was designed to further the public interest in an independent judiciary, sometimes at the expense of legitimate individual grievances. . . . The *Bradley* Court accepted those costs to aggrieved individuals because the judicial system itself provided other means for protecting individual rights. . . . Underlying the *Bradley* immunity, then, is the notion that private rights can be sacrificed in some degree to the achievement of the greater public good deriving from a completely independent judiciary, because there exist alternative forums and methods for vindicating those rights.

But where a judicial officer acts in a manner that precludes all resort to appellate or other judicial remedies that otherwise would be available, the underlying assumption of the *Bradley* doctrine is inoperative. . . . In this case, as MR. JUSTICE STEWART points out, . . . petitioner's unjudicial conduct insured that "[t]here was and could be no appeal." The complete absence of normal judicial process foreclosed resort to any of the "numerous remedies" that "the law has provided for private parties." *Bradley*. . . .

In sum, I agree with MR. JUSTICE STEWART that respondent's actions were not "judicial," and that he is entitled to no judicial immunity from suit. . . .

CARTER WORLD TRIP, PART II —
SOUTH AMERICA AND AFRICA
March 28-April 3, 1978

President Jimmy Carter left Washington, D.C., March 28 for state visits to four third world nations. In seven days the presidential party, which included Carter's wife Rosalynn, their daughter Amy, Secretary of State Cyrus R. Vance, Zbigniew Brzezinski, the president's national security adviser, approximately 45 aides and a press contingent of about 200, made stops in Venezuela, Brazil, Nigeria and Liberia. The trip was the second half of Carter's world tour originally scheduled for the fall of 1977. That trip was postponed and then divided into two parts, the first of which took place in December 1977 and January 1978. (Historic Documents of 1977, p. 897)

The itineraries, administration spokesmen said, would reflect the diversity of world economic, political and military power which exists beyond the traditional relations among the superpowers, the Western European countries and Japan. On the first half of the tour, Carter had visited Poland, Iran, India, Saudi Arabia, Egypt, France and Belgium in nine days. The second trip was designed to emphasize U.S. efforts to establish and reinforce ties with developing nations, a move Brzezinski called "long overdue." The pace of the second trip was considerably more relaxed than the earlier one; the itinerary allowed for a one-day rest stop in Rio de Janiero, Brazil.

Latin America

The first stop on the president's tour was in Venezuela, a member of the Organization of Petroleum Exporting Countries (OPEC) and considered

Latin America's strongest democracy. In his remarks welcoming Carter, Venezuelan President Carlos Andres Perez urged quick approval by the U.S. Senate of the second Panama Canal Treaty (Panama Canal Treaties, p. 177). *In his toast at a state dinner March 28, Perez urged an increase in measures of practical cooperation between developed and developing nations. Carter replied in his speech before the Venezuelan Congress in Caracas March 29, "The industrial nations must provide long-term capital and reduced trade barriers. The developing nations must assume the obligations that accompany responsible participation in an evolving world economy." President Carter promised increased U.S. activity in these areas and unveiled vague plans for a foundation to promote technological cooperation among nations and a fund for the education of Latin American students in schools in the United States.*

Relations with Brazil, historically one of the United States' closest allies in Latin America, soured in 1977 when the Carter administration criticized the government for violations of human rights and sought to reverse its decision to purchase a nuclear reprocessing plant from West Germany. In a somewhat formal welcoming ceremony in Brasilia, the modern capital city, Brazilian President Ernesto Geisel remarked that he hoped Carter's visit would contribute to "forming a fair opinion on the Brazilian reality."

In his public statements, Carter did not avoid mention of the conflicts between the two countries but attempted to place greater emphasis on areas of agreement. In a news conference March 30 in Brasilia, the president called attention to "the major factors which bind us in harmony with Brazil." They were, he said, "more important than the differences that have been published between our approach to human rights, for instance, and the subject of nonproliferation [of] weapons." Carter added, "We do have a sharp difference of opinion, however, on how the human rights issue should be addressed, how specific allegations should be investigated, and what actions can be taken to correct any defects that exist in your country or mine."

Africa

In Nigeria, an OPEC member, the second largest supplier of crude oil to the United States and an influential power in African affairs, Carter on April 1 made what was billed as a major policy address to an audience of government officials at Lagos' National Arts Theatre. The general theme of the president's speech was similar to the one he presented in South America: the necessity for greater cooperation between the developed and developing nations. The president's visit marked the first state visit of an American president to a sub-Sahara nation.

Concerning the persistent problem of majority rule in Zimbabwe (Rhodesia) and Namibia (South-West Africa), the president forcefully warned that "the hour is late.... The parties must choose." He also urged that South Africa change over to majority rule "progressively and peacefully, with assured respect for the rights of all." Carter objected to the role of Cuba and the Soviet Union in African affairs, particularly in the Horn of Africa, and called for an end to the "military intervention of outside powers or their proxies in such disputes."

Lt. Gen. Olusego Obasanjo, the Nigerian strongman, used his toast at a state dinner April 2 to point to his country's concern about foreign economic and military "collaboration with the South African regime" and pressed for greater economic sanctions against South Africa. "Your country's little gestures of disengagement in this regard are welcome," Obasanjo said, "and we hope, Mr. President, that they mark the beginning of a realization that, put together, Black Africa as a whole offers wider economic possibilities as an alternative choice than South Africa alone, and that without a peaceful change of policy of apartheid now, any investment in South Africa is a risky and insecure investment."

Referring to relations between developed and developing nations, Obasanjo asserted that the problems of development "are of such immense dimensions that they demand global perspectives and strategies because . . . the conventional and piecemeal approach of donors and receivers of aid and technical assistance has proved itself totally inadequate." In their statements, neither Carter nor Obasanjo disclosed any concrete plans for cooperation between poorer and richer nations.

The final stop on the tour was a five-hour, primarily ceremonial call in Liberia, the tiny West African nation, a democracy, originally settled by former U.S. slaves. In contrast to the other stops, Carter was greeted by enthusiastic crowds which lined the 40-mile route from the airport to Monrovia, the capital. President William R. Torbert Jr. declared a national holiday to mark Carter's visit, the first official visit of an American president to Liberia. (Franklin D. Roosevelt stopped in Liberia briefly on his return from the 1943 Casablanca Conference.) While reaffirming the close ties between the two countries, Carter in his remarks at Roberts International Airport took time to reiterate his theme: "Only three decades ago, many nations of these continents [Africa, Asia and Latin America] were largely colonies of foreign powers. Their rise to independence means a world in which we must treat each other as equals, and one of the purposes of these trips has been to demonstrate the genuine respect my Nation feels for its partners around the world and our opposition to the continuation or reestablishment of colonialism in any form whatsoever."

On his return to Washington, D.C., the president remarked that "the trip was designed to show our great Nation's adaptation to a changing world. And in that way it has been a great success, I think, for the United States." He added, "the day of the so-called ugly American is over."

Following are the texts of Carter's March 30, 1978, press conference in Brasilia; his April 1 address at the National Arts Theatre in Lagos, Nigeria; and excerpts from Lt. Gen. Obasanjo's toast at the state dinner in Lagos April 3. (Bold-face headings in brackets have been added by Congressional Quarterly to highlight the organization of the text.):

BRASILIA PRESS CONFERENCE

THE PRESIDENT: Good morning, ladies and gentlemen. I am very delighted to be here in Brasilia to participate in a live press conference, and I will alternate questions from the Brazilian and the American press.

I will begin with Mr. Bonfim.

[U.S.-Brazil Relations]

Q: Mr. President, at the beginning of your Administration there was a clear tendency to isolate and treat Brazil coldly in favor of democratically-elected governments, elected by the people.

Yesterday at the airport you stressed the need for cooperation between Brazil and the United States as equal partners. Who has changed; Brazil or you?

P: I certainly have not changed. The experience that I have had in Brazil as Governor of Georgia before I became President made Brazil the most important country to me. I and my wife visited it frequently. We had a partnership arrangement between my own State and the State of Pernambuco.

We studied the background, the history, the culture and the government of Brazil and there has not ever been any inclination on my part or the part of my Administration to underestimate the extreme importance of Brazil as a major world power, nor to underestimate the extreme importance of very close and harmonious relationships between the United States and Brazil.

There are some differences of opinion between ourselves and Brazil which have been very highly publicized.

But on the long scale of things, both in the past history and in the future, the major factors which bind us in harmony with Brazil far transcend — are much more important than the differences that have been published between our approach to human rights, for instance, and the subject of nonproliferation weapons. But our commitment to Brazil as a friend, our need for Brazil as a partner and a friend has always been the case and is presently very important to us and will always be that important in the future.

Helen?

[Airplane Sales]

Q: Regarding the use of American military supplies to invade a country and to cause untold suffering to hundreds of thousands, some say it is a violation of U.S. law. In view of the facts that you have before you, is it a violation; and two, what would cause you to reassess your war plane package to the Middle East?

P: Are you referring to the Lebanon question?

Q: Yes.

P: As you know, when the terrorist attack in Israel precipitated the counter-move by Israel into Lebanon which has been a haven for the Palestinian terrorists the United States took the initiative in the United Nations, I might say, without the approval of Israel, to initiate United Nations action there to expedite the removal of Israeli forces from Lebanon.

We have obviously attempted to comply with the law and this is a matter that we are still addressing. The other part of your question?

Q: What would cause you to reassess your war plane package to the Middle East and how do you think you have attempted to comply with the law?

P: We are attempting to terminate as rapidly as possible the military presence of Israel in Southern Lebanon through United Nations action. I believe this is the proper way to do it rather than unilateral action on our part which would probably be unsuccessful in any case to get Israel to withdraw. The presence of United Nation forces, the French, Swedes, and others, I believe is the preferable way and it marshals the opinion of the entire world through the United Nations against the Israeli presence being retained in Lebanon.

This has not caused me to reassess the American position on the sale of war planes and other equipment to the Middle East. This is a very well balanced package. It emphasizes our interest in military security of the Middle East. It does not change at all the fact that Israel still retains a predominant air capability and military capability. There is no threat to their security. But it also lets the nations involved and the world know that our friendship, our partnership, our sharing of military equipment with the moderate Arab nations is an important permanent force of our foreign policy.

[Loans and Human Rights]

Q: The American commerical banks are the main Brazilian source of external credit. It seems to some people in Washington that sooner or later a Congressman may try to establish a link between commercial banking loans and the human rights policy. I would like to know your opinion about this subject.

P: Brazil is a major trading partner of the United States, in commercial goods and also in loans and I might say timely repayments. The debt of

Brazil is very manageable. The loans of the American banks to Brazil are sound. Additional loans are being pursued by the American banks as an excellent advantage for their future investments in Brazil based on the strength of your country. It would be inconceivable to me that any act of Congress would try to restrict the lending of money by American private banks to Brazil under any circumstance.

This would violate the principles of our own free enterprise system and if such an act was passed by Congress, I would not approve it.

Q: What is in the first place for you: the private enterprise and the private system or the human rights policy?

P: They are both important to us. And I don't see any incompatability between a belief in a free enterprise system where government does not dominate the banks or the production of agricultural products or commercial products on the one hand and a deep and consistent and permanent and strong belief in enhancing human rights around the world.

I might say that the American business community, the Congress of the United States, the general populace of the United States supports completely a commitment of our Nation to human rights. It is a basic element of our national consciousness that is not a violation at all or no conflict between human rights on the one hand and the free enterprise system on the other.

[Namibia Compromise]

Q: Mr. President, tomorrow you fly to Africa. What can you tell us today about the revised five-power proposal?

P: As you know, under the auspices of the United Nations, our own country, Canada, Britain, France and the Federal Republic of Germany have been working jointly to present to South Africa and to the so-called SWAPO Organization, Southwest Africa Political [sic] Organization, a compromise solution to restoring majority rule in Namibia.

We have presented this proposal this week to the South African government, which now controls Namibia, and also to the SWAPO leaders. We are hopeful that if the proposal is not completely acceptable to both those parties, that it will at least be acceptable enough to prevent unilateral action on the part of South Africa to hold elections in complete violation of the United Nations resolutions and in complete violation of the principle of restoring majority rule to Namibia.

I cannot tell you what the outcome of those consultations will be. I will get a more complete report when I arrive in Lagos. Ambassador Young has been in Africa now for about a week. This is one of the reasons that he is there. And I will be glad to give you a more detailed report after I get additional information.

[Brazil and Nuclear Weapons]

Q: Mr. President, now that you have a broad nonproliferation act in your hands, do you expect you can persuade Brazil to give up reprocessing and enrichment technology being acquired from Germany? And in that case, what are the carrots you might specifically use to further the power of your arguments in your meeting with President Geisel?

P: We strongly favor the right of any country to have part of its energy supplies come from nuclear power. As you know, our country has been the leader in the evolution of atomic power for peaceful uses and we would do nothing to prevent this trend from continuing both in Brazil and in other countries around the world.

Our own nuclear nonproliferation policy, however, tries to draw a distinction between the right and the meeting of needs of countries to produce energy from atomic power on the one hand, and the right of the country to evolve weapons-grade nuclear materials through either enrichment processes or through reprocessing.

We have no authority over either West Germany or Brazil, nor do we want any. But as a friend of both countries, we reserve the right to express our opinion to them that it would be very good to have, and possible to have a complete nuclear fuel system throughout a country without having the ability to reprocess spent fuel from the power reactors. In the United States, for instance, in the last 25 years or so, on several occasions major investments, multi-billion-dollar investments in all, have been made in reprocessing plants. So far as I know, for the civilian nuclear technology, all those plants have now been abandoned as being non-economical.

So this is a difference that does exist between Brazil and the United States. The right of Brazil and West Germany to continue with their agreement is one that we do not challenge, but we have reserved the right and have used the right to express our concern both to the Brazilian government and to the West German government.

I think it is accurate to say that the European nations have now announced that in the future, they will not make reprocessing plants part of their overseas sales inventory. And we are very deeply concerned about this. Of course, Brazil has announced that they have no intention of producing nuclear explosives. Brazil is the signatory to the Treaty of Tlatalolco. So far, however, Brazil has retained a caveat that it will not apply to them until all other nations sign it. And Argentina, Cuba, France, Russia have not yet signed the Tlatalolco Treaty.

We would hope that every effort would be made by Brazil and other countries as it is on the part of our own country to prevent the spread of nuclear explosive capability to any nation which does not presently have it.

Q: Mr. President, what are the carrots?

P: We have no specific carrots to offer except that we are making available to countries and now in a much more predictable way with the new Congressional law enriched uranium which is suitable for production of power but not suitable for explosives and technological advice and counsel, both in the use of uranium with which Brazil is not blessed as a natural resource, and also thorium which we have in our own country and which Brazil already has.

The new thorium technology is a much safer one to provide power without going to plutonium. Recently Brazil, I think very wisely, signed an additional agreement with West Germany which would open up advice and technological ability to use thorium. But the right of Brazil and the advisability of Brazil to have a very advanced nuclear power capability is one that we don't dispute, but on the other hand, approve.

I might add one other point, and that is that we see a clear need for all nations to sign the non-proliferation treaty. We are signatories of it. So are the Soviet Union, the Germans, most of the countries in the world, and this combined with international atomic agency safeguards is a good guarantee within a country and throughout the developed and developing world that there will not be a trend in the future toward other nations developing nuclear explosive capability.

[Trying to Oust Begin?]

Q: Mr. President, have you or any other top U.S.-officials — Dr. Brzezinski, for instance — suggested that Prime Minister Begin may not be the right man to head that government in the present circumstances? And apart from what may or may not have been said, do you now think that the Begin government can make the hard decisions necessary to move the peace process forward?

P: I can say unequivocally that no one in any position of responsibility in the United States Administration has ever insinuated that Prime Minister Begin is not qualified to be Prime Minister or that he should be replaced. This report, the origin of which I do not know, is completely false.

I think that Prime Minister Begin and his government are able to negotiate in an adequately flexible way to reach an agreement with Egypt, later Jordan and other of the neighboring countries. This is our hope and this is our belief.

We have not given up on the possibility of a negotiated peace settlement in the Middle East.

Under the Begin government with him as Prime Minister, recently arrangements have been made between Israel and Egypt for Ezer Weizman to go to Egypt again which will be a continuation of the probing for compatability. I think it is obvious now that with the issues so sharply drawn that key differences remain that must be addressed on the side of Israel. The things that are of deepest concern is Israel's refusal to acknowledge that United Nations Resolution 242 as applies clearly to the West Bank, their unwillingness to grant to the West Bank Palestinians, the Palestinian Arabs, a right to participate in the determination of their own future by voting at the end of a five-year period and so forth for the kind of affiliation they would have with Israel or Jordan or under a joint administration, and this is a problem for which I have no clear solution yet. But I believe that the Begin government is completely capable of negotiating an agreement with Egypt.

I promised this gentleman right here.

[Future Visits]

Q: I am from Channel 13, Argentina. Excuse me, my colleague.

In connection with your visit now in Latin America, do you expect in the future — do you consider the possibility of another visit to the other countries of Latin America — like in my case, Argentina, and do you have an eventual visit date for this?

P: We have not yet set any date, nor made any plans for future visits. As you may know, I have visited Argentina in the past. So has my wife. And this year, this past year, Secretary of State — our Secretary of State, Cyrus Vance, visited Argentina, too, and your own leader, Videla [Lt. Gen. Jorge Rafael Videla, Argentine president], came to visit us in Washington. I have no plans now for any additional trips anywhere after I return to Washington.

Yes, sir?

[Meeting With Cardinal]

Q: What is the purpose of this meeting that you are having in Rio with [Archbishop Paulo Evaristo] Cardinal Arns and five other people? I mean what specifically are you intending to discuss with them, and —

P: I don't have any agenda prepared for my visit with Cardinal Arns and the others. In a diverse society like you have here in Brazil, it is important for me to visit with different persons who represent different views. I will have thorough discussions, as you know, with President Geisel and his Administration and I want to meet with as many other people as I can. I have, by the way, met and talked to Cardinal Arns previously in the United States. I think this is typical of leaders who visit other countries. I noticed, for instance, with some interest that when President Geisel visited the Federal Republic of Germany recently, he not only met with Chancellor Schmidt, but he met with the leaders of the opposition parties.

And as a leader of a nation, I reserve the right to meet with whom I please. And I think this is a constructive thing, which will give me a much better overall understanding of what exists in Brazil, and I think the right of people to speak to me as a foreign visitor is one that is important to Brazil to preserve and to cherish, and I am thankful that I have that right when I visit your country.

[Inflation Program]

Q: Mr. President, when you return from this Latin American and African trip, do you have any plans to combat the number one concern of the American people? I refer to inflation. Specifically, do you have any changes in mind in your up-to-now voluntary program of price and wage restraints?

P: Yes. My Administration, during the last couple of weeks, has been evolving a complete analysis of what we can do, both through administrative action, through public statements, through working with the business community and the labor community, and through Congressional action to control inflation, which is becoming an increasingly important problem for us.

I think the consumer price index figures that were released this week, the day we left Washington, were much better than we had anticipated, but still a cause for concern.

So when I get home, one of the first acts that I shall take is to make public the decisions that we are now putting together.

Q: Will they change the voluntary nature of the program, Mr. President?

P: I will address the details when I get back home.

Yes, I will get you next.

[Brazil Government—1]

Q: I would like to know whether in your meeting with General Figueiredo yesterday you discussed the program of the general political opening up of the Brazilian Government and the implementation of that plan?

P: I did not have an opportunity to discuss any matters of importance with General Figueiredo. I only met him very briefly in a larger group of people, thirty or forty people, and in the receiving line when I came into the airport. So I have not had a chance to discuss this with him.

Ann?

[Steel Price Hike]

Q: Mr. President, despite some jawboning pressure from your Administration, U.S. Steel has raised its prices again. How does that fit in with your overall plans on inflation that is going to have some substantial impact nationwide?

P: It fits in very poorly. (Laughter) I think the prices announced by U.S. Steel, as their plans, are excessive, and although I have not been thoroughly briefed on what the Council on Wage and Price Stability has recommended, I will get that report today, but I think any such increase as I have heard, approximately $10 a ton, is excessive and does cause additional, very serious inflationary pressures in our country, and I think is much greater than would be warranted by the recent coal settlement.

Yes, ma'am?

[Brazil Government—2]

Q: I am from the State of Sao Paulo. My basic question was the same as he asked, but I would like to know how you view the succession here in

Brazil and how do you view the problem of political and civil rights in Brazil?

P: I think the type of succession and the process through which you choose your leaders, or your leaders are chosen, is one to be decided in Brazil. I am not here to tell you how to form your government. I have no inclination to do that. The Brazilian people are completely aware of the process and that is a judgment for you to make.

Brazil, like the United States, is struggling with the very difficult question of identifying human rights and civil rights violations, enhancing the Democratic processes and also encouraging confidence among the people in my government in the United States and in the government here in Brazil and other countries.

The differences that have arisen on the human rights issue is not based upon the lack of commitment to enhance human rights. I think great progress has been made in your country and also in ours. We do have a sharp difference of opinion, however, on how the human rights issue should be addressed, how specific allegations should be investigated, and what action can be taken to correct any defects that exist in your country or mine or others.

We believe that this is an international problem, that the focusing of world attention and world pressure on us and other countries is a very beneficial factor, that high publicity should be given to any proven violation of human rights. It is a commitment that our nation has that I want not to abandon but to enhance and to strengthen.

Brazil, on the other hand, also struggling with the same problem trying to give greater human rights does not believe that the international organizations and multi-national opinions should be marshaled. However, I do note that recently Brazil did vote for an increase in the financing of the Inter-American Human Rights Commission.

[Inter-American Commission]

We think that when an allegation is made in our own country, in Brazil, in the European countries, wherever, that some responsible delegation from the Inter-American Human Rights Commission or the United Nations should go in, get the facts, make the facts public. If there is an actual violation, there would be a great incentive to the government involved, ours or yours or others, to correct the defect.

If the allegation is false, then the exposition of the error, or the false allegation, would be good for the world to know.

So I think this is a very deep and important consideration. One of the best things about the development on human rights in the last year or so has been the worldwide attention to it. It was kind of a dormant issue for too long. Now I doubt that there is a world leader who exists that doesn't constantly feel the pressure of considering the human rights question — to analyze one's own Administration, one's own country, what the rest of the world thinks about us and how we can correct any defects and prevent allegations in the future either true or false.

[Middle East Visit]

Q: Mr. President, with the new movement which is now apparent in the Middle East question, is there any possibility of a Middle East stop on your way back home?

P: No. No. I have no intention to stop in the Middle East. I will go from here to Nigeria, from there to Liberia, and then back home.

Maybe one more question.

[Human Rights in Brazil]

Q: The restraint of your public words until now, your specific desire to meet with the new President, all these facts amount to a virtual blessing of the Brazilian mission. Is your interest in civil rights and political dissidents fading away, or are American economic interests in this country so strong that Brazil is already a special case?

P: I might say that the history, the culture, the common defense requirements, trade, common purpose bind, the people of Brazil, all bind the people of Brazil and the people of the United States together in an unbreakable commitment regardless of the identity of the leaders in our own country or yours. The people of Brazil and the United States are bound together. There is no lessening of our commitment to the principles that you described. The basic freedoms to democratic government, to the protection of human rights, to the prevention of nuclear proliferation, these commitments are also very deep for us.

[Conclusion]

Obviously, the overwhelming responsibility when I come to a foreign country, no matter where it is, is to meet with the leaders who are in office. But I also will be visiting the Congress this morning. I am sure that I will be meeting with the Chairman of a Foreign Relations Committee who is also a candidate for President.

We have already pointed out I will be meeting with religious leaders and I hope that in this process that I will have a chance to get views from all elements, at least some of the major elements of the Brazilian society. But I am not endorsing any candidates, and I think that the overwhelming sense of my visit already has been that the strength of our friendship and the mutuality of our purposes now and in the future far override any sharply expressed differences of opinion on even the major and very important issues of human rights, non-proliferation, trade, and so forth.

MR. CORMIER (AP): Thank you, Mr. President.

CARTER SPEECH IN LAGOS

Director [Bolaji] Akinyemi [director general, Nigerian Institute of International Affairs], Commissioner [for External Affairs Joseph Nanven] Garba, distinguished officials of the Government of Nigeria and of the United States, distinguished guests from other countries, and my friends, the Nigerian people:

I come from a great nation to visit a great nation. When my voice speaks words, they are not the words of a personal person but the words of a country.

It's no coincidence that I come here to this institute, where free and open discussions and debate contribute to the comprehension and understanding and the reaching of agreements that solve problems that have separated people one from another.

It is no coincidence that I come to Nigeria to talk about our bilateral relationships and the problems of Africa. And it is no coincidence that our Nation has now turned in an unprecedented way toward Africa — not to give you our services but to share with you a common future, combining our strengths and yours, correcting our weaknesses and correcting yours. And this departure from past aloofness by the United States is not just a personal commitment of my own, but I represent the deep feelings and the deep interest of all the people of my country.

I'm proud and deeply moved to be the first American President to make an official visit to your country. And I'm especially grateful for the warmth and the generosity of my reception by the Government and by the people of Nigeria.

I don't know who's doing the work, but many Nigerians are standing beside the roadway to make me and my family feel welcome, and I thank you for it.

[U.S.-Nigeria Cooperation]

During my first year as President of the United States, I've been pleased to work closely with General Obasanjo, learning from him and from other African leaders. Our cooperation has had a special meaning for me, since Africa has been so much in my thoughts during the past 15 months.

Our countries have much in common. Nigeria and the United States are vast and diverse nations seeking to use our great resources for the benefit of all our people. That's the way it is now; that's the way it will continue to be in the future.

Americans admire the energy, the wisdom, the hard work, the sense of optimism of the Nigerian people, for these are exactly the same qualities which we admire in my country.

The Nigerian Government has shown these qualities in your own national accomplishments and in your efforts for worldwide peace and economic progress — in the Organization for African Unity, in the United Nations, and in other councils where nations seek common ground so as to resolve differences and to work together.

We admire also the humane and the creative way which Nigeria has come through a divisive time in your own history. Through public debate and far-reaching planning, you are designing a democratic future for a new "One Nigeria," and we're grateful and excited about this prospect.

[History of Friendship]

Our bonds of friendship go back many years. Nigerian students first came to the United States in the 19th century. Your first President, Nnamdi Azikiwe, studied in our country. In applying to Lincoln University, he wrote that he believed in education for service and service for humanity.

Tens of thousands of young Nigerians have followed him to America to prepare themselves for service here in their homeland. Many are present or future teachers, who will help you achieve your goal of universal primary education.

We in the United States are learning from you as well, for we are enriched by our ties and heritage in Africa, just as we hope to contribute to the realization of African hopes and African expectations.

Our nations and our continents are bound together by strong ties that we inherit from our histories. We also share three basic commitments to the future of Africa.

We share with you a commitment to majority rule and individual human rights. In order to meet the basic needs of the people, we share with you a commitment to economic growth and to human development. We share with you a commitment to an Africa that is at peace, free from colonialism, free from racism, free from military interference by outside nations, and free from the inevitable conflicts that can come when the integrity of national boundaries are not respected. We share these things with you as well.

These three common commitments shape our attitude toward your continent. You have been among the leaders of international efforts to bring the principles of majority rule and individual rights into reality in southern Africa.

[Majority Rule]

During the past year, we've worked closely with your Government and the other frontline states in the quest to achieve these goals in Namibia [South-West Africa] and in Zambabwe [Rhodesia].

Our efforts have now reached a critical stage. On Namibia, there has been some progress, with the parties showing some degree of flexibility. It is important that accommodation be now reached. This past week, we and the other Western members of the United Nations Security Council have presented to the disputing parties our proposals for an internationally acceptable agreement based on free elections.

These proposals provide the best hope for a fair and peaceful solution that will bring independence to Namibia in a manner consistent with Security Council Resolution 385. No group is favored at the expense of another. They protect the rights of all. They should be accepted without further delay.

The tragic assassination [March 27] of Chief [Clemens] Kapuuo [president of the Democratic Turnhalle Alliance, a rival of the South-West Africa Peoples Organization, the main black nationalist group] should not lead to an era of violence and recrimination, but to an internationally supervised choice by the people of Namibia to elect leadership that will unite their country in peace and not divide it in war.

On Rhodesia, or Zimbabwe, Great Britain and the United States have put forward a plan for the solution, based on three fundamental principles: first, fair and free elections; secondly, an irreversible transition to genuine majority rule and independence; and third, respect for the individual rights of all the citizens of an independent Zimbabwe.

This plan provides the best basis for agreement. It is widely supported within the international community and by the Presidents of the frontline nations who surround Zimbabwe itself. Its principles must be honored. Let there be no question of the commitment of the United States to these principles or our determination to pursue a just settlement which brings a cease-fire and an internationally recognized legal government.

The present challenge to our diplomacy and to yours is to help all the parties get together, based on the Anglo-American plan, and build on areas of agreement. Only a fair arrangement with broad support among the parties can endure.

The transition to independence of a new Zimbabwe must ensure an opportunity for all parties to compete in the democratic process on an equal footing. The past must lead irrevocably to majority rule and a future in which the rights of each citizen of Zimbabwe are protected, regardless of tribal or ethnic origin or race. That is our Nation's position. We will not depart from it.

The hour is late with regard both to Zimbabwe and to Namibia. The parties must choose. They can choose a path of agreement and be remembered as men of vision and courage who created new nations, born in peace, or they can insist on rigid postures that will produce new political complications, generating new conflicts, growing additional bloodshed, and delay the fulfilment of their hopes.

We in the United States remain committed, as do the people of Nigeria, to the path of genuine progress and fairness, for the sake of all the nations of the region and for the sake of international peace.

In the name of justice, we also believe that South African society should and can be transformed progressively and peacefully, with assured respect for the rights of all. We've made it clear to South Africa that the nature of our relations will depend on whether there is progress towards full participation for all her people, in every respect of the social and economic life of the nation, and an end to discrimination, an end to apartheid, based on race or ethnic origin. We stand firm in that message as well.

I grew up in a society struggling to find racial harmony through racial justice. Though our problems were different, I know that progress can best be found if the determination to see wrongs righted is unmatched by an understanding that the prisoners of injustice include the privileged as well as the powerless.

I believe we should therefore combine our determination to support the rights of the oppressed people in South Africa with a willingness to hold out our hands to the white minority if they decide to transform their society and to do away with apartheid and the crippling burdens of past injustices.

I also believe that progress can be made. As Andrew Young said here in Lagos last August, a belief in dreams for the future is not naive if we are ready to work to realize those dreams.

Our concern for human rights extends throughout this continent and throughout the world. Whatever the ideology or the power or the race of a government that abuses the rights of its people, we oppose those abuses.

We in America welcome the real progress in human rights that is being made in many countries, in Africa as well as in other regions.

Americans were particularly encouraged that the African group at the United Nations Human Rights Commission moved this year to consider the oppressive policies of two of its own member nations.

We are encouraged, too, by the movement towards democracy being made by many nations. Nigeria is an outstanding example. The free and fair elections that you held in the past year leave no doubt that your Government is determined to pursue its decision to establish civilian rule in 1979. This action will be an inspiration to all those in the world who love democracy and who love freedom. And we congratulate you on this.

Each country must, of course, adapt the instruments of democracy to fit its own particular needs, a process now being completed by your constituent assembly. The basic elements are participation by individuals in the decisions that affect their lives, respect for civil liberties through the rule of law, and thus, protection of the dignity of all men and women.

Wherever these fundamental principles exist, a government can accommodate to necessary change without breaking, and its people can demand such change without being broken.

These principles are necessary for democracy, and they sustain development as well. For in a democracy, the people themselves can best ensure that their government will promote their economic rights, as well as their political and civil liberties.

I believe, as I know you do as well, that every person also has a right to education, to health care, to nutrition, to shelter, to food, and to employment. These are the foundations on which men and women can build better lives.

[Economic Development]

This is our second great, common goal between the United States and Nigeria — human development made possible by fair and equitable economic progress.

My country is ready to do its fair share in support of African development, both because it's in our own interest and also because it's right. More and more, the economic well-being of Americans depends on the growth of the developing nations here in Africa and in other parts of the world. A good example is our relationship with Nigeria, which is marked by respect for each other's independence and a growing recognition of our interdependence.

Nigeria, for instance, is the United States' second largest supplier of imported crude oil. The United States is the largest market for Nigeria's petroleum, and thus the largest source of the revenue which is so vital to Nigeria's dynamic economic development program.

But the scope of our commerce is much broader than in petroleum alone. Our growing trade serves the interests of both countries. When we purchase Nigerian products, we contribute to Nigerian development. But unless we can also share our technology and share our productive capacity with you, our own economy slows down, American workers lose their jobs, and the resulting economic sluggishness means that we can buy less from you.

Financial encouragement to developing nations is therefore in our interest, because a world of prosperous, developing economies is a world in which America's economy can prosper.

We are increasing our bilateral development assistance to Africa, and on my return to Washington, I will recommend to the Congress that the United States contribute $125 million to the second replenishment of the African Development Fund.

I'm happy to announce, also, that just before leaving Washington, I authorized our Corps of Engineers to offer to participate, as requested by you, in the comprehensive development of the Niger River System.

We are giving new priority to cooperating in international efforts to improve health around the world. We would like to study with you how we can best work with Nigeria and other nations of Africa to deal with the killing and the crippling diseases that still afflict this continent.

Three days ago I spoke in Caracas, Venezuela, about our commitment to international economic growth and equity. All of us can gain if we act fairly toward one another.

Nigeria acted on this principle in helping to negotiate the Lomé Convention and the birth of the Economic Community of West African States.

All nations can act on this principle by making world trade increasingly free and fair. Private investment can help, under arrangements benefiting both the investors and also the host countries like your own. And sharing technology can make a crucial difference. We are especially pleased that Nigeria is sending so many of your young people to the United States for training in the middle-level technical skills.

There must be fair international agreements on such issues as stabilizing commodity prices, the creation of a Common Fund, and relieving the debt burden of the poorest nations.

Every government has the obligation to promote economic justice within its own nation, as well as among nations. American development assistance will go increasingly to those areas where it can make the greatest contribution to the economic rights of the poor.

[Peace in Africa]

Progress towards economic development requires the pursuit of our third goal as well — again which we share with you — a peaceful Africa, free of military intervention, for economic progress is best pursued in times of peace.

Africans themselves can best find peaceful answers to African disputes through the Organization of African Unity and, when needed, with the help of the United Nations.

We support your efforts to strengthen the peacemaking role of the Organization of African Unity, and we share Nigeria's belief in the practical contributions the United Nations can make.

U.N. peacekeeping forces are already, today, playing a crucial role in the Middle East. They can help bring independence and majority rule, in peace, to Namibia and to Zimbabwe.

The military intervention of outside powers or their proxies in such disputes too often makes local conflicts even more complicated and dangerous and opens the door to a new form of domination or colonialism. We oppose such intervention by outside military forces. We must not allow great power rivalries to destroy our hopes for an Africa at peace.

This is one reason we applaud the leading role of Nigeria in seeking to find peaceful solutions to such tragedies as the recent struggle between Ethiopia and Somalia in the Horn of Africa.

We are concerned that foreign troops are already planning for military action inside Ethiopia against the Eritreans, which will result in greatly increased bloodshed among those unfortunate peoples. Although I will remain careful to see that our friends are not put at a disadvantage, I am working to curb our own role as a supplier of arms, and we urge others to show similar restraint.

We prefer to seek good relations with African and other nations through the works of peace, not war. America's contribution will be to life and development and not to death or destruction.

Plainly, military restraint by outsiders can best be brought about if all nations, including those who buy weapons, actively seek that constraint. We would welcome and support voluntary regional agreements among African leaders to reduce the purchase of weapons as a major step towards peace and away from the economic deprivation of the poor, when badly needed money that could give them a better life goes to purchase weapons to take lives.

I've talked about many subjects this afternoon, very briefly, but in one way or another, I've been talking about change in the world that we all share. Sometimes we grow impatient or cynical about that change, thinking that it's too slow, that it may not come at all.

I know something about social change. In my own lifetime, I've seen the region of my birth, the southern part of the United States, changed from a place of poverty and despair and racial division to a land of bright promise and opportunity and increasing racial harmony.

I've seen the towering wall between the races taken down, piece by piece, until the whites and the blacks of my country could reach across it to each other.

I know that our own society is different from any other, and I know that we still have much to do in the United States. But nothing can shake my faith that in every part of the world, peaceful change can come and bless the lives of human beings. Nothing can make me doubt that this continent will win its struggle for freedom — freedom from racism and the denial of human rights, freedom from want and suffering, and freedom from the destruction of war and foreign intervention.

Nigeria is a great and influential nation, a regional and an international leader. We stand by you in your work. We know that Africans will always take the lead in shaping the destiny of your own people. And we know that this continent will enjoy the liberation that can come to those who put racial division and injustice behind them.

I believe that this day is coming for Africa. And on that day, blacks and whites alike will be able to say, in the words of a great man from my own State, Dr. Martin Luther King, Jr., "Free at last, free at last, great God Almighty, we are free at last."

Thank you very much.

OBASANJO TOAST

. . . On the political plane, Mr. President, one outstanding and most welcome development in contemporary relations between Nigeria and your great country, particularly since the inception of your administration, as I had occasion to say when I welcomed you in Dodan Barracks, is the growing contact and consultation between us.

As a result of this development, you are now, no doubt, better equipped to understand the reason for our persistent reference to the grave threat to international peace and security caused by the explosive situation in the southern part of Africa.

For obvious reasons, and by virtue of our position, we cannot remain indifferent while the racists in southern Africa oppress, repress, and subject to inhuman degradation, the overwhelming majority of the indigenous people of the area and deny them the most basic human rights and elementary freedoms.

You will, no doubt, understand and appreciate, therefore, our uncompromising insistence on dismantling the present inhuman systems in southern Africa in favor of a fair and just society.

From all indications our two Governments share identical views in this regard, which I believe is perfectly understandable, judging by your own country's great struggles, soon after its foundation, for the attainment of these same ideals.

In our endeavors to achieve these goals, our choice of means and methods and our precision of timing may differ. But from our exchange of views from this visit, we are convinced that our common desires and dedication to the task cannot be called in doubt. On our part, we shall therefore continue to extend all necessary moral and material assistance to the victims of injustice, oppression, and apartheid in southern Africa.

I believe, also, that it is pertinent to mention our deep concern about the present level of foreign collaboration with the South African regime, particularly in economic and military matters which tend to sustain the apartheid machinery of repression and persecution of the majority indigenous African population. Your country's little gestures of disengagement in this regard are welcome, and we hope, Mr. President, that they mark the beginnings of a realization that, put together, Black Africa as a whole offers wider economic possibilities as an alternative choice than South Africa alone, and that without a peaceful change of policy of apartheid now, any investment in South Africa is a risky and insecure investment.

In Zimbabwe, your country and the British colonial authority have, over the past 1 year, embarked together on a search for a durable, just, and acceptable settlement, leading to an early transfer of power to the majority population of the land.

We have joined those who believe that the Anglo-American proposals for a peaceful settlement ought to be given a chance, and we were quick to say so. This we have done because we believe that these proposals contain sufficient positive elements to serve as bases for bringing about true independence in Zimbabwe, and we think it will not be wise to throw away the baby with the bath water.

We expressed our concern when it appeared to us that these proposals were not being pursued with as much candor and enthusiasm as Africa had hoped. With total rejection of the so-called internal settlement of Ian Smith by the world community, and your personal continued support for the Anglo-American proposals, we are gratified to note that the proposals are back on the rails once again.

We assure you of our positive support in the search for an early establishment of unqualified democracy in a truly independent Zimbabwe. Similarly, in Namibia, we are encouraged to note the positive role which the United States of America is playing in collaboration with other Western powers to usher in an era of independence and so end South Africa's illegal military occupation.

We stand firmly by SWAPO [South-West Africa People's Organization] in their struggles for the freedom of their fatherland, and we also pledge to work ceaselessly to see that peace and justice return to that part of our continent in the context of true independence.

We believe that a truly independent Namibia and a South Africa, rid of the inhuman policy of apartheid, can live together as good neighbors in harmony and cooperation.

As you will be fully aware, our newly independent states in Africa have not been spared the ordeal of spending their meager resources in the prosecution of fratricidal and often futile wars, in many cases with encouragement by powers from ideological camps outside the continent who are seeking ideological, economic, and strategic spheres of inference [sic].

It is Africa's desire to settle her own disputes our own way, if necessary under the auspices of the Organization of African Unity.

While we are naturally preoccupied with peace and security in the African continent in the first instance, I believe the point is worth emphasizing here that Africa is equally interested in the current efforts at detente between East and West, as this is the only dependable means of ensuring peace and stability in the world and development all around, especially in new states. For the same reasons, we are vitally interested in an early restoration of just and durable peace in the Middle East.

On the question of world peace, Mr. President, what applies to Africa in terms of congenial atmosphere and conditions for development applies equally to the rest of the developing world generally. The problems of development of these countries are of such immense dimensions that they demand global perspectives and strategies because, as we have all seen, the conventional and piecemeal approach of donors and receivers of aid and technical assistance has proved itself totally inadequate. A completely fresh approach, therefore, may serve to emphasize the interdependence of our resources and, hopefully, also stem the tide of deep frustration that now pervades the underprivileged half of the world and which the developed world sees as lack of opposition of their efforts.

We believe in this regard that what we require is a fundamental restructuring of the international economic system to modify drastically and modernize the rules governing international trade, access to markets and development capital, the unimpeded flow of technology, and a demonstration of a greater sense of commitment and political will on the part of all concerned to concretize the demands of a new international economic order.

Unfortunately, there has so far been no demonstrable evidence of that sense of commitment, or even of concern, at international forums, where discussions are currently proceeding on relief for the least developed countries, or agreement on an acceptable form of common fund to provide a mechanism for insuring uninterrupted and regular flow of earnings for the exports of the Third World.

Your country, Mr. President, has the necessary capacity and the influence and is well placed to play a leading role in this regard. We can bring the developed and developing worlds together in the harmonious cooperation to inspire reforms and to adopt new development initiatives.

We share your concern about the dangerous, high level of armament and about the enormous economic resources consumed by the armament race.

We continue to follow the progress of the strategic arms limitation talks, and we hope that there will be an early agreement that will lead to a reduction in the production and stockpiling of armaments and subsequent freeing of more resources of the world for social programs that will directly lead to improvement of quality of life, especially in developing countries.

Mr. President, let me end by saying once again what a great pleasure it has been for the Nigerian Government and people to welcome you and Mrs. Carter. We hope that even in spite of its brevity, your visit has nevertheless offered you some closer personal insight into our conditions and our way of life.

As you leave our shores after this historic visit to Africa, you do so, Mr. President, with the sincere good wishes of the Government and people of Nigeria and the appreciation of the value of your memorable visit here. . . .

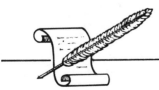
April

COURT ON PENSIONS
FOR MEN AND WOMEN
April 25, 1978

Despite the fact that they can expect to live longer than the average man, women do not have to pay higher amounts into employer-operated pension plans, the Supreme Court ruled April 25. The justices voted 6-2.

The court based its opinion on the 1964 Civil Rights Act, which prohibits discrimination in employment on the basis of sex. The act also forbids a differential between wages paid to men and women performing identical tasks. Justice John Paul Stevens, writing for the majority, said that the larger amount women were forced to pay into the pension funds constituted such a difference in the wages for men and women.

Stevens was joined in the majority by Justices Potter Stewart, Byron R. White, Lewis F. Powell Jr., Thurgood Marshall and Harry A. Blackmun. Chief Justice Warren E. Burger and Justice William H. Rehnquist dissented. Justice William J. Brennan Jr. did not participate in the case. In the same case the court ruled, 7-1, that employers did not have to compensate women for past pay discrimination resulting from higher pension payments.

The case, Los Angeles v. Manhart, rose out of a suit brought against the Los Angeles Department of Water and Power. The suit charged the department discriminated against its 2,000 female employees because they were forced to pay 14.84 percent more than their male counterparts into the department-operated pension plan. The rate of payment was based on actuarial studies that indicated that women, on the average, live longer than men and, therefore, would be likely to draw a larger amount from the pension fund.

Majority Opinion

While admitting the validity of this generalization, Stevens wrote that the department's practice discriminated against women as individuals who may or may not live longer than the average man. This, he said, was a violation of the 1964 Civil Rights Act. Further, Stevens rejected the department's argument that equal contributions would force the men to subsidize the women participants. He declared, "when insurance risks are grouped, the better risks always subsidize the poorer risks. Healthy persons subsidize medical benefits for the less healthy; unmarried workers subsidize the pensions of married workers; persons who eat, drink, or smoke to excess may subsidize pension benefits for persons whose habits are more temperate. Treating different classes of risks as though they were the same for purposes of group insurance is a common practice which had never been considered inherently unfair."

The court, however, refused to approve the lower court's decision to award retroactive payments to the women who had paid the larger amount into the pension plan. A ruling that ordered reimbursement, Stevens said, could be devastating if applied to the private retirement plan industry that holds $400 billion in trust for the retirement security of 50 million Americans.

In Dissent

In his dissent, Chief Justice Burger defended the use of actuarial tables for gauging the rates paid to insurance and pension plans by men and women. Employers who, in order to "operate economically workable group pension programs," Burger wrote, must be allowed to "rely on statistically sound and proven disparities in longevity between men and women." He added that the effect of the court's decision on pension plans was "revolutionary" and "favorable to women at the expense of men. . . ."

Justice Marshall argued in his opinion in favor of reimbursement of the women employees. Basing his argument on former court decisions, he wrote: "Respondents in this case cannot be 'made whole' unless they receive a refund of the money that was illegally withheld from their paychecks. . . ."

In a separate concurring opinion, Justice Blackmun warned that the court's decision could undermine the effect of its 1976 ruling that employers who excluded pregnancy from disability benefit programs did not discriminate against women. (General Electric v. Gilbert; see Supreme Court on Pregnancy Benefits, Historic Documents of 1976, p. 891)

Following are excerpts from Justice Stevens' majority opinion delivered April 25, 1978, that forbade employers to compel women to make larger contributions to pension funds than men who earn the same salary; Chief Justice Burger's dissent; Justice Marshall's opinion arguing for reimbursement for the women; and Justice Blackmun's opinion concurring with the majority opinion:

No. 76-1810

City of Los Angeles, Department of Water and Power, et al., Petitioners, *v.* Marie Manhart et al.	On Writ of Certiorari to the United States Court of Appeals for the Ninth Circuit.

[April 25, 1978]

MR. JUSTICE STEVENS delivered the opinion of the Court. [MR. JUSTICE BRENNAN took no part in the consideration or decision of this case.]

As a class, women live longer than men. For this reason, the Los Angeles Department of Water and Power required its female employees to make larger contributions to its pension fund than its male employees. We granted certiorari to decide whether this practice discriminated against individual female employees because of their sex in violation of § 703(a)(1) of the Civil Rights Act of 1964, as amended.

For many years the Department has administered retirement, disability, and death benefit programs for its employees. Upon retirement each employee is eligible for a monthly retirement benefit computed as a fraction of his or her salary multiplied by years of service. The monthly benefits for men and women of the same age, seniority, and salary are equal. Benefits are funded entirely by contributions from the employees and the Department, augmented by the income earned on those contributions. No private insurance company is involved in the administration or payment of benefits.

Based on a study of mortality tables and its own experience, the Department determined that its 2,000 female employees, on the average, will live a few years longer than its 10,000 male employees. The cost of a pension for the average retired female is greater than for the average male retiree because more monthly payments must be made for the average woman. The Department therefore required female employees to make monthly contributions to the fund which were 14.84% higher than the contributions required of comparable male employees. Because employee contributions were withheld from pay checks, a female employee took home less pay than a male employee earning the same salary.

Since the effective date of the Equal Employment Opportunity Act of 1972, the Department has been an employer within the meaning of Title VII of the Civil Rights Act of 1964. . . . In 1973, respondents brought this suit in the United States District Court for the Central District of California on behalf of a class of women employed or formerly employed by the Department. They prayed for an injunction and restitution of excess contributions.

While this action was pending, the California Legislature enacted a law prohibiting certain municipal agencies from requiring female employees to make higher pension fund contributions than males. The Department therefore amended its plan, effective January 1, 1975. The current plan draws no distinction, either in contributions or in benefits, on the basis of sex. On a motion for summary judgment, the District Court held that the contribution differential violated § 703 (a)(1) and ordered a refund of all excess contributions made before the amendment of the plan. The United States Court of Appeals for the Ninth Circuit affirmed.

The Department and various *amici curiae* contend that: (1) the differential in take-home pay between men and women was not discrimination within the meaning of § 703 (a)(1) because it was offset by a difference in the value of the pension benefits provided to the two classes of employees; (2) the differential was based on a factor "other than sex" within the meaning of the Equal Pay Act and was therefore protected by the so-called Bennett Amendment; (3) the rationale of *General Electric Co.* v. *Gilbert* . . . [1976] requires reversal; and (4) in any event, the retroactive monetary recovery is unjustified. We consider these contentions in turn.

I

There are both real and fictional differences between women and men. It is true that the average man is taller than the average woman; it is not true that the average woman driver is more accident-prone than the average man. Before the Civil Rights Act of 1964 was enacted, an employer could fashion his personnel policies on the basis of assumptions about the differences between men and women, whether or not the assumptions were valid.

. . .This case does not, however, involve a fictional difference between men and women. It involves a generalization that the parties accept as unquestionably true: women, as a class, do live longer than men. The Department treated its women employees differently from its men employees because the two classes are in fact different. It is equally true, however, that all individuals in the respective classes do not share the characteristic which differentiates the average class representatives. Many women do not live as long as the average man and many men outlive the average woman. The question, therefore, is whether the existence or nonexistence of "discrimination" is to be determined by comparison of class characteristics or individual characteristics. A "stereotyped" answer to that question may not be the same as the answer which the language and purpose of the statute command.

The statute makes it unlawful "to discriminate against any *individual* with respect to his compensation, terms, conditions or privileges of employment, because of such *individual's* race, color, religion, sex, or national origin." . . . (emphasis added). The statute's focus on the individual is unambiguous. It precludes treatment of individuals as simply components of a racial, religious, sexual, or national class. If height is required for a job, a tall woman may not be refused employment merely because, on the average, women are too short. Even a true generalization about the class is an insufficient reason for disqualifying an individual to whom the generalization does not apply.

That proposition is of critical importance in this case because there is no assurance that any individual woman working for the Department will actually fit the generalization on which the Department's policy is based. Many of those individuals will not live as long as the average man. While they were working, those individuals received smaller paychecks because of their sex, but they will receive no compensating advantage when they retire.

It is true, of course, that while contributions are being collected from the employees, the Department cannot know which individuals will predecease the average woman. Therefore, unless women as a class are assessed an extra charge, they will be subsidized, to some extent, by the class of male employees. It follows, according to the Department, that fairness to its class of male employees justifies the extra assessment against all of its female employees.

But the question of fairness to various classes affected by the statute is essentially a matter of policy for the legislature to address. Congress has decided that classifications based on sex, like those based on national origin or race, are unlawful. . . .

Even if the statutory language were less clear, the basic policy of the statute requires that we focus on fairness to individuals rather than fairness to classes. Practices which classify employees in terms of religion, race, or sex tend to preserve traditional assumptions about groups rather than thoughtful scrutiny of individuals. . . .

Finally, there is no reason to believe that Congress intended a special definition of discrimination in the context of employee group insurance coverage. It is true that insurance is concerned with events that are individually unpredictable, but that is characteristic of many employment decisions. Individual risks, like individual performance, may not be predicted by resort to classifications proscribed by Title VII. Indeed, the fact that this case involves a group insurance program highlights a basic flaw in the department's fairness argument. For when insurance risks are grouped, the better risks always subsidize the poorer risks. Healthy persons subsidize medical benefits for the less healthy; unmarried workers subsidize the pensions of married workers; persons who eat, drink, or smoke to excess may subsidize pension benefits for persons whose habits are more temperate. Treating different classes of risks as though they were the same for purposes of group insurance is a common practice which has never been considered inherently unfair. To insure the flabby and the fit as though they were equivalent risks may be more common than treating men and women alike; but nothing more than habit makes one "subsidy" seem less fair than the other.

An employment practice which requires 2,000 individuals to contribute more money into a fund than 10,000 other employees simply because each of them is a woman, rather than a man, is in direct conflict with both the language and the policy of the Act. Such a practice does not pass the simple test of whether the evidence shows "treatment of a person in a manner which but for the person's sex would be different." It constitutes discrimination and is unlawful unless exempted by the Equal Pay Act or some other affirmative justification.

II

Shortly before the enactment of Title VII in 1964, Senator [Wallace F.] Bennett [R-Utah, 1951-74] proposed an amendment providing that a compensation differential based on sex would not be unlawful if it was authorized by the Equal Pay Act, which had been passed a year earlier. The Equal Pay Act requires employers to pay members of both sexes the same wages for equivalent work, except when the differential is pursuant to one of four specified exceptions. The Department contends that the fourth exception applies here. That exception authorizes a "differential based on any other factor other than sex."

The Department argues that the different contributions exacted from men and women were based on the factor of longevity rather than sex. It is plain, however, that any individual's life expectancy is based on a number of factors, of which sex is only one. The record contains no evidence that any factor other than the employee's sex was taken into account in calculating the 14.84% differential between the respective contributions by men and women. We agree with Judge Duniway's observation that one cannot "say that an actuarial distinction based entirely on sex is 'based on any other factor other than sex'. Sex is exactly what it is based on. . . ."

We are also unpersuaded by the Department's reliance on a colloquy between Senator [Jennings] Randolph [D-W.Va.] and Senator [Hubert H.] Humphrey [D-Minn., 1949-64, 1971-78] during the debate on the Civil Rights Act of 1964. Commenting on the Bennett Amendment, Senator Humphrey expressed his understanding that it would allow many differences in the treatment of men and women under industrial benefit plans, including earlier retirement options for women. Though he did not address differences in employee contributions based on sex, Senator Humphrey apparently assumed that the 1964 Act would have little, if any, impact on existing pension plans. His statement cannot, however, fairly be made the sole guide to interpreting the Equal Pay Act, which had been adopted a year earlier; and it is the 1963 statute, with its exceptions, on which the Department ultimately relies. We conclude that Senator Humphrey's isolated comment on the Senate floor cannot change the effect of the plain language of the statute itself.

III

The Department argues that reversal is required by *General Electric Co. v. Gilbert*. . . . We are satisfied, however, that neither the holding nor the reasoning of *Gilbert* is controlling.

In *Gilbert* the Court held that the exclusion of pregnancy from an employer's disability benefit plan did not constitute sex discrimination within the meaning of Title VII. Relying on the reasoning in *Geduldig* v. *Aiello* . . . [1974], the Court first held that the General Electric plan did not involve "discrimination based upon gender as such." The two groups of potential recipients which that case concerned were pregnant women and nonpregnant persons. "While the first group is exclusively female, the second includes members of both sexes." . . .In contrast, each of the two groups of employees involved in this case is composed entirely and exclusively of members of the same sex. On its face, this plan discriminates on the basis of sex whereas the General Electric plan discriminated on the basis of a special physical disability.

In *Gilbert* the Court did note that the plan as actually administered had provided more favorable benefits to women as a class than to men as a class. This evidence supported the conclusion that not only had plaintiffs failed to establish a prima facie case by proving that the plan was discriminatory on its face, but they had also failed to prove any discriminatory effect.

In this case, however, the Department argues that the absence of a discriminatory effect on women as a class justifies an employment practice which, on its face, discriminated against individual employees because of their sex. But even if the Department's actuarial evidence is sufficient to prevent plaintiffs from establishing a prima facie case on the theory that the effect of the practice on women as a class was discriminatory, that evidence does not defeat the claim that the practice, on its face, discriminated against every individual woman employed by the department. . . .

Although we conclude that the Department's practice violated Title VII, we do not suggest that the statute was intended to revolutionize the insurance and pension industries. All that is at issue today is a requirement that men and women make unequal contributions to an employee-operated pension fund. Nothing in our holding implies that it would be unlawful for an employer to set aside equal retirement contributions for each employee and let each retiree purchase the largest benefit which his or her accumulated contributions could command in the open market. Nor does it call into question the insurance industry practice of considering the composition of an employer's work force in determining the probable cost of a retirement or death benefit plan. Finally, we recognize that in a case of this kind it may be necessary to take special care in fashioning appropriate relief.

IV

The Department challenges the District Court's award of retroactive relief to the entire class of female employees and retirees. Title VII does not require a district court to grant any retroactive relief. A court that finds unlawful discrimination "may enjoin [the discrimination] and order such affirmative action as may be appropriate, which may include, but is not limited to, reinstatement . . . with or without back pay . . . or any other equitable relief as the court deems appropriate.". . . To the point of redundancy, the statute stresses that retroactive relief "may" be awarded if it is "appropriate."

In *Albemarle Paper Co.* v. *Moody* . . . [1975], the Court reviewed the scope of a district court's discretion to fashion appropriate remedies for a Title VII violation and concluded that "back pay should be denied only for reasons which, if applied generally, would not frustrate the central statutory purposes of eradicating discrimination throughout the economy and making persons whole for injuries suffered through past discrimination.". . . Applying that standard, the Court ruled that an award of backpay should not be conditioned on a showing of bad faith. . . . But the *Albemarle* Court also held that backpay was not to be awarded automatically in every case.

The *Albemarle* presumption in favor of retroactive liability can seldom be overcome, but it does not make meaningless the district courts' duty to determine that such relief is appropriate. For several reasons, we conclude that the District Court gave insufficient attention to the equitable nature of Title VII remedies. Although we now have no doubt about the application of the statute in this case, we must recognize that conscientious and intelligent administrators of pension funds, who did not have the benefit of the extensive briefs and arguments presented to us, may well have assumed that a program like the Department's was entirely lawful. The courts had been silent on the question, and the administrative agencies had conflicting views. The Department's failure to act more swiftly is a sign, not of its recalcitrance, but of the problem's complexity. As commentators have noted, pension administrators could reasonably have thought it unfair — or even illegal — to make male employees shoulder more than their "actuarial share" of the pension burden. There is no reason to believe that the threat of a backpay award is needed to cause other administrators to amend their practices to conform to this decision.

Nor can we ignore the potential impact which changes in rules affecting insurance and pension plans may have on the economy. Fifty million Americans participate in retirement plans other than Social Security. The assets held in trust for these employees are vast and growing — more than $400 billion were reserved for retirement benefits at the end of 1977 and reserves are increasing by almost $50 billion a year. These plans, like other forms of insurance, depend on the accumulation of large sums to cover contingencies. . . . Risks that the insurer foresees will be included in the calculation of liability, and the rates or contributions charged will reflect that calculation. The occurrence of major unforeseen contingencies, however, jeopardizes the insurer's solvency and, ultimately, the insureds' benefits. Drastic changes in the legal rules governing pension and insurance funds should not be applied retroactively unless the legislature has plainly commanded that result. The EEOC [Equal Employment Opportunity Commission] itself has recognized that the administrators of retirement plans must be given time to adjust gradually to Title VII's demands. Courts have also shown sensitivity to the special dangers of retroactive Title VII awards in this field. . . .

There can be no doubt that the prohibition against sex-differentiated employee contributions represents a marked departure from past practice. Although Title VII was enacted in 1964, this is apparently the first litigation challenging contribution differences based on valid actuarial tables. Retroactive liability could be devastating for a pension fund. . . . If, as the courts below apparently contemplated, the plaintiffs' contributions are recovered from the pension fund, the administrators of the fund will be forced to meet unchanged obligations with diminished assets. If the reserve proves inadequate, either the expectations of all retired employees will be disappointed or current employees will be forced to pay not only for their own future security but also for the unanticipated reduction in the contributions of past employees.

Without qualifying the force of the *Albemarle* presumption in favor of retroactive relief, we conclude that it was error to grant such relief in this case. Accordingly, although we agree with the Court of Appeals' analysis of the statute, we vacate its judgment and remand the case for further proceedings consistent with this opinion. . . .

MR. CHIEF JUSTICE BURGER, with whom MR. JUSTICE REHNQUIST joins, concurring in part and dissenting in part.

I join Part IV of the Court's opinion; as to Parts I, II, and III, I dissent.

Gender-based actuarial tables have been in use since at least 1843, and their statistical validity has been repeatedly verified. The vast life insurance, annuity and pension plan industry is based on these tables. As the Court recognizes. . ., it is a fact that "women, as a class, do live longer than men." It is equally true that employers cannot know in advance when individual members of the classes will die. . . . Yet, if they are to operate economically workable group pension programs, it is only rational to permit them to rely on statistically sound and proven disparities in longevity between men and women. Indeed, it seems to me irrational to assume Congress intended to outlaw use of the fact that, for whatever reasons or combination of reasons, women as a class outlive men.

The Court's conclusion that the language of the civil rights statute is clear, admitting of no advertence to the legislative history, such as there was, is not soundly based. An effect upon pension plans so revolutionary and discriminatory — this time favorable to women at the expense of men — should not be read into the statute without either a clear statement of that intent in the statute, or some reliable indication in the legislative history that this was Congress' purpose. The Court's casual dismissal of Senator Humphrey's apparent assumption that the "Act would have little, if any, impact on existing pension plans," . . . is to dismiss a significant manifestation of what impact on industrial benefit plans was contemplated. It is reasonably clear there was no intention to abrogate an employer's right, in this narrow and limited context, to treat women differently from men in the face of historical reliance on mortality experience statistics. . . .

The reality of differences in human mortality is what mortality experience tables reflect. . . . But categorizing people on the basis of sex, the one acknowledged immutable difference between men and women, is to take into account all of the unknown reasons, whether biologically or culturally based, or both, which give women a significantly greater life expectancy than men. It is therefore true as the Court says, "that any individual's life expectancy is based on a number of factors, of which sex is only one."
. . .But it is not true that by seizing upon the only constant, "measurable" factor, no others were taken into account. All other factors, whether known but variable — or unknown — are the elements which automatically account for the actuarial disparity. And all are accounted for when the constant factor is used as a basis for determining the costs and benefits of a group pension plan.

Here, of course, petitioners are discriminating in take-home pay between men and women. . . . The practice of petitioners, however, falls squarely under the exemption provided by the Equal Pay Act . . . incorporated into Title VII by the so-called Bennett Amendment. . . . That exemption tells us that an employer may not discriminate between employees on the basis of sex by paying one sex lesser compensation than the other "except where such payment is made pursuant to . . . a differential based on any other factor other than sex. . . ." The "other factor other than sex" is longevity; sex is the umbrella-constant under which all of the elements leading to differences in longevity are grouped and assimilated, and the only objective feature upon which an employer — or anyone else, including insurance companies — may reliably base a cost differential for the "risk" being insured.

This is in no sense a failure to treat women as "individuals" in violation of the statute, as the Court holds. It is to treat them as individually as it is possible to do in the face of the unknowable length of each individual life. Individually, every woman has the same statistical possibility of outliving men. . . .

Of course, women cannot be disqualified from, for example, heavy labor just because the generality of women are thought not as strong as men — a proposition which perhaps may sometime be statistically demonstrable, but will remain individually refutable. When, however, it is impossible to tailor a program such as a pension plan to the individual, nothing should prevent application of reliable statistical facts to the individual, for whom the facts cannot be disproved until long after planning, funding, and operating the program has been undertaken.

I find it anomalous, if not contradictory, that the Court's opinion tells us, in effect . . . that the holding is not really a barrier to responding to the complaints of men employees, as a group. The Court states that employers may give each employee precisely the same dollar amount and require them to secure their own annuities directly from an insurer, who, of course, is under no compulsion to ignore 135 years of accumulated, recorded longevity experience.

MR. JUSTICE MARSHALL, concurring in part and dissenting in part.

I agree that Title VII of the Civil Rights Act of 1964, as amended, forbids petitioners' practice of requiring female employees to make larger contributions to a pension fund than do male employees. I therefore join all of the Court's opinion except Part IV.

I also agree with the Court's statement in Part IV that, once a Title VII violation is found, *Albemarle Paper Co.* v. *Moody* . . . (1975), establishes a "presumption in favor of retroactive liability" and that this presumption "can seldom be overcome.". . . . But I do not agree that the presumption should be deemed overcome in this case, especially since the relief was granted by the District Court in the exercise of its discretion and was upheld by the Court of Appeals. . . .

In *Albemarle Paper Co.* v. *Moody* . . . this Court made clear that, subject to the presumption in favor of retroactive relief, the District Court retains its "traditional" equitable discretion "to locate 'a just result,' " with appellate review limited to determining "whether the District Court was 'clearly erroneous' in its factual findings and whether it 'abused' its . . . discretion.". . . . The Court here does not assert that any findings of the District Court were clearly erroneous, nor does it conclude that there was any abuse of discretion. Instead, it states merely that the District Court gave "insufficient attention" to certain factors in striking the equitable balance. . . .

The first such factor mentioned by the Court relates to the "complexity" of the issue presented here, which may have led some pension fund administrators to assume that "a program like the Department's was entirely lawful," and that the alternative of equal contributions was perhaps unlawful because of a preconceived "unfair[ness]" to men. . . . The District Court found, however, that petitioners "should have been placed on notice" of the illegality of requiring larger contributions from women on April 5, 1972, when the Equal Employment Opportunity Commission amended its regulations to make this illegality clear. The retroactive relief ordered by the District Court ran from April 5, 1972, through December 31, 1974, after which date petitioners changed to an equal contribution program. . . . Even if the April 1972 beginning date were too early, as the Court contends. . . , during the nearly three-year period involved there surely was some point at which "conscientious and intelligent administrators" . . . should have responded to the EEOC's guidelines. Yet the Court today denies all retroactive relief, without even knowing whether petitioners made any efforts to ascertain their particular plan's legality.

The other major factor relied on by the Court involves "the potential impact . . . on the economy" that might result from retroactive changes in "the rules" applying to pension and insurance funds. According to the

Court, such changes could "jeopardize[] [an] insurer's solvency and, ultimately, the insureds' benefits." . . .As with the first factor, however, little reference is made by the Court to the situation in this case. No claim is made by either petitioners or the Court that the relief granted here would in any way have threatened the plan's solvency, or indeed that risks of this nature were not "foresee[n]" and thus "included in the calculation of liability" and reflected in "the rates or contributions charged.". . . No one has suggested, moreover, that the relatively modest award at issue — involving a small percentage of the amounts withheld from respondents' paychecks for pension purposes over a 33-month period . . . could in any way be considered "devastating.". . . And if a "devastating" award were made in some future case, this Court would have ample opportunity to strike it down at that time.

The necessarily speculative character of the Court's analysis in Part IV is underscored by its suggestion that the retroactive relief in this case would have led to a reduction in the benefits paid to retirees or an increase in the contributions paid by current employees. . . . It states that taking the award out of the pension fund was "apparently contemplated" by the court below . . . but the District Court gave no indication of where it thought the recovery would come from. The Court of Appeals listed a number of ultimate sources of the money here involved, including increased employer contributions to the fund or one lump sum payment from the Department. . . .Indeed, the Department itself contemplated that the money for the award would come from city revenues . . . with the Department thereby paying for this Title VII award in the same way that it would have to pay for any ordinary backpay award arising from its discriminatory practices. Hence the possibility of "harm" falling on "innocent" retirees or employees . . . is here largely chimerical.

There are thus several factors mentioned by the Court that might be important in some other case but that appear to provide little cause for concern in the case presently before us. To the extent that the Court believes that these factors were not adequately considered when the award of retroactive relief was made, moreover, surely the proper course would be a remand to the District Court for further findings and a new equitable assessment of the appropriate remedy. When the District Court was found to have abused its discretion by denying backpay in *Albemarle*, this Court did not take it upon itself to formulate an award; it remanded to the District Court for this purpose. . . . There is no more reason for the Court here to deny all retroactive relief on its own; once the relevant legal considerations are established, the task of finding the facts and applying the law to those facts is best left to the District Court, particularly when an equitable search for a " 'just result' " is involved. . . .

In this case, however, I do not believe that a remand is necessary. The District Court considered the question of when petitioners could be charged with knowledge of the state of the law . . . and petitioners do not challenge the particular date selected or claim that they needed time to adjust their plan. As discussed above, moreover, no claim is made that the Department's or the plan's solvency would have been threatened, and it appears unlikely that either retirees or employees would have paid any part of the award. There is every indication, in short, that the factors which the Court thinks might be important in some hypothetical case are of no concern to the petitioners who would have had to pay the award in this case.

The Court today reaffirms "the force of the *Albemarle* presumption in favor of retroactive relief," . . . yet fails to give effect to the principal reason why the presumption exists. In *Albemarle* we emphasized that a "central" purpose of Title VII is "making persons whole for injuries suffered through past discrimination.". . . Respondents in this case cannot be "made whole" unless they receive a refund of the money that was illegally withheld from their paychecks by petitioners. . . . Here, as the Court of Appeals observed, respondents "actually earned the amount in question, but then had it taken from them in violation of Title VII.". . . In view of the strength of respondents' "restitution"-like claim . . . and in view of the statute's "central" make-whole purpose . . . I would affirm the judgment of the Court of Appeals.

MR. JUSTICE BLACKMUN, concurring in part and concurring in the judgment.

MR. JUSTICE STEWART wrote the opinion for the Court in *Geduldig* v. *Aiello* . . . (1974), and joined the Court's opinion in *General Electric Co.* v. *Gilbert* . . . (1976). MR. JUSTICE WHITE and MR. JUSTICE POWELL joined both *Geduldig* and *General Electric*. MR. JUSTICE STEVENS, who writes the opinion for the Court in the present case, dissented in *General Electric*. . . . MR. JUSTICE MARSHALL, who joins the Court's opinion in large part here, dissented in both *Geduldig* and *General Electric*. . . . My own discomfort with the latter case was apparent, I believe, from my separate concurrence there. . . .

These "line-ups" surely are not without significance. The participation of my Brothers STEWART, WHITE and POWELL in today's majority opinion *should* be a sign that the decision in this case is not in tension with *Geduldig* and *General Electric* and, indeed, is wholly consistent with them. I am not at all sure that this is so; the votes of MR. JUSTICE MARSHALL and MR. JUSTICE STEVENS would indicate quite the contrary.

Given the decisions in *Geduldig* and *General Electric* — the one constitutional, the other statutory — the present case just cannot be an easy one for the Court. I might have thought that those decisions would have required the Court to conclude that the critical difference in the Department's pension payments was based on life expectancy, a nonstigmatizing factor that demonstrably differentiates females from males and that is not measurable on an individual basis. I might have thought, too, that there is nothing arbitrary, irrational, or "discriminatory" about recognizing the objective and accepted . . . disparity in female-male life expectancies in computing rates for retirement plans. Moreover, it is unrealistic to attempt to force, as the Court does, an individualized analysis upon what is basically an insurance context. . . .

The Court's rationale, of course, is that Congress, by Title VII of the Civil Rights Act of 1964, as amended, intended to eliminate, with certain exceptions, "race, color, religion, sex, or national origin," . . . as factors upon which employers may act. A program such as the one challenged here does exacerbate gender consciousness. But the program under consideration in *General Electric* did exactly the same thing and yet was upheld against challenge.

The Court's distinction between the present case and *General Electric* — that the permitted classes there were "pregnant women and nonpregnant persons," both female and male . . . seems to me to be just too easy. It is probably the only distinction that can be drawn. For me, it does not serve to distinguish the case on any principled basis. I therefore must conclude that today's decision cuts back on *General Electric,* and inferentially on *Geduldig,* the reasoning of which was adopted there . . . and, indeed, makes the recognition of those cases as continuing precedent somewhat questionable. I do not say that this is necessarily bad. If that is what Congress has chosen to do by Title VII — as the Court today with such assurance asserts — so be it. I feel, however, that we should meet the posture of the earlier cases head-on and not by thin rationalization that seeks to distinguish but fails in its quest.

I therefore join only Part IV of the Court's opinion, and concur in its judgment.

COURT ON CORPORATE SPENDING
IN REFERENDUM CAMPAIGNS
April 26, 1978

The Supreme Court ruled April 26 that states could not prevent corporations from spending money to try to influence the outcome of referendums. The 5-4 decision struck down a Massachusetts law that made it a crime for banks and corporations in the state to mount propaganda campaigns aimed at influencing the public on issues not "materially affecting" the property, business or assets of the corporation.

Justice Lewis F. Powell Jr. wrote the majority opinion in which he was joined by Chief Justice Warren E. Burger and Justices Potter Stewart, Harry A. Blackmun and John Paul Stevens. The chief justice also filed a concurring opinion. A dissent filed by Justice Byron R. White was joined by Justices William J. Brennan Jr. and Thurgood Marshall. Justice William H. Rehnquist filed a separate dissent.

The case was initiated in 1976 when Massachusetts voters were asked to decide in a referendum if the legislature should pass a law enacting a graduated income tax. Two banks and three other corporations in Massachusetts declared that they wanted to spend money to publicize their opposition to the income tax. The attorney general of Massachusetts informed the businesses, however, that they would be prosecuted under a state law that forbade information campaigns by corporations on issues not affecting them materially. The law specifically mentioned taxes on an individual's income as an issue that did not materially affect a corporation. The banks and corporations went to court, seeking to have the law declared unconstitutional. Lawyers for the concerns argued that the state law violated the First Amendment and the due process and equal protection clauses of the Fourteenth Amendment. The Supreme Judicial Court of Massachusetts upheld the law; the concerns then asked the U.S. Supreme Court to review the state court decision.

Majority Opinion

For the majority, Justice Powell asserted that the state court had incorrectly based its decision on the question of whether corporations were entitled to First Amendment rights. "The proper question," Powell wrote, "is not whether corporations 'have' First Amendment rights and, if so, whether they are co-extensive with those of natural persons. Instead, the question must be whether...[the statute] abridges the expression that the First Amendment was meant to protect. We hold that it does."

Powell disputed the argument that corporate speech can be limited in a way that personal speech is not: "If the speakers here were not corporations, no one would suggest that the State could silence their proposed speech. It is the type of speech indispensable to decisionmaking in a democracy and this is no less true because the speech comes from a corporation rather than an individual. The inherent worth of the speech in terms of its capacity for informing the public does not depend upon the identity of its source, whether corporation, association, union, or individual." Powell declared that media businesses do "not have a monopoly on either the First Amendment or the ability to enlighten.... Similarly, the Court's decisions involving corporations in the business of communication or entertainment are based not only on the role of the First Amendment in fostering individual self-expression but also on its role in affording the public access to discussion, debate, and the dissemination of information and ideas."

Justice Powell also warned that if a state legislature is allowed to restrict certain types of business communication, "it also may limit other corporations — religious, charitable, civic — to their respective 'business' when addressing the public. Such power in government to channel the expression of views is unacceptable under the First Amendment."

In response to arguments that corporations, because of their size and wealth, could exert undue influence on public opinion and create suspicions about the validity of democratic processes, Powell said, "The risk of corruption perceived in cases involving candidate elections...simply is not present in a popular vote on a public issue...the fact that advocacy may persuade the electorate is hardly a reason to suppress it...." Powell added that if stockholders did not agree with public positions taken by a corporation, a possibility raised by the Massachusetts attorney general, they had ample opportunity to voice their dissatisfaction "through the procedures of corporate democracy...."

Burger Opinion

In his concurring opinion, the chief justice argued that the limitations placed on corporations by the Massachusetts law could lead to "similar restraints on media conglomerates with their vastly greater influence." He added, "Because the First Amendment was meant to guarantee freedom to express and communicate ideas, I can see no difference between the right of those who seek to disseminate ideas by way of a newspaper and those who give lectures or speeches and seek to enlarge the audience by publication and wide dissemination....

"...In short, the First Amendment does not 'belong' to any definable category of persons or entities: it belongs to all who would exercise its freedoms."

Dissenting Opinions

Warning that the court's decision "not only invalidates a statute which has been on the books in one form or another for many years, but also casts considerable doubt upon the constitutionality of legislation passed by some 31 States restricting corporate political activity as well as upon the Federal Corrupt Practices Act," Justice White argued in his dissent that corporate communications are not closely connected to individual self-expression. "Ideas," he wrote, "which are not a product of individual choices are entitled to less First Amendment protection." Confining corporate comment to areas directly related to business, he said, increases the individual's protection under the terms of the First Amendment.

Stressing his concern that the court's decision might lead to the return of legal corporate campaign contributions and expenditures on behalf of candidates, Justice White said, "As I understand the view that has now become part of First Amendment jurisprudence, the use of corporate funds, even for causes irrelevant to the corporation's business, may be no more limited than that of individual funds. Hence corporate contributions to and expenditures on behalf of political candidates may be no more limited than those of individuals. Individual contributions under federal law are limited but not entirely forbidden, and under Buckley v. Valeo, expenditures may not constitutionally be limited at all. Most state corrupt practices acts, like the federal Act, forbid any contributions or expenditures by corporations to or for a political candidate."

"The electoral process, of course, is the essence of our democracy," White concluded. "It is an arena in which the public interest in preventing corporate domination and the coerced support by shareholders of causes with which they disagree is at its strongest and any claim that corporate expenditures ar. integral to the economic functioning of the corporation is at its weakest."

In a separate dissent, Justice Rehnquist said that his "views of the limited application of the First Amendment to the States" compelled him to uphold the Massachusetts statute. After briefly reviewing the rights generally granted to corporations, Rehnquist asserted, "It cannot be so readily concluded that the right of political expression is equally necessary to carry out the functions of a corporation organized for commercial purposes."

*Following are excerpts from the Supreme Court's ruling,
delivered April 26, 1978, on corporate spending in referendum campaigns.*

No. 76-1172

First National Bank of Boston et al., Appellants, *v.* Francis X. Bellotti, Etc., et al.	On Appeal from the Supreme Judicial Court of Massachusetts.

[April 26, 1978]

MR. JUSTICE POWELL delivered the opinion of the Court.

In sustaining a state criminal statute that forbids certain expenditures by banks and business corporations for the purpose of influencing the vote on referendum proposals, the Massachusetts Supreme Judicial Court held that the First Amendment rights of a corporation are limited to issues that materially affect its business, property, or assets. The court rejected appellants' claim that the statute abridges freedom of speech in violation of the First and Fourteenth Amendments. The issue presented in this context is one of first impression in this Court. We postponed the question of jurisdiction to our consideration of the merits.... We now reverse.

I

The statute at issue, Massachusetts General Laws ch. 55, § 8, prohibits appellants, two national banking associations and three business corporations, from making contributions or expenditures "for the purpose of...influencing or affecting the vote on any question submitted to the voters, other than one materially affecting any of the property, business or assets of the corporation." The statute further specifies that "[n]o question submitted to the voters solely concerning the taxation of the income, property or transactions of individuals shall be deemed materially to affect the property, business or assets of the corporation." A corporation that violates § 8 may receive a maximum fine of $50,000; a corporate officer, director, or agent who violates the section may receive a maximum fine of $10,000 or imprisonment for up to one year, or both.

Appellants wanted to spend money to publicize their views on a proposed constitutional amendment that was to be submitted to the voters as a ballot question at a general election on November 2, 1976. The amendment would have permitted the legislature to impose a graduated tax on the income of individuals. After appellee, the Attorney General of Massachusetts, informed the appellants that he intended to enforce § 8 against them, they brought this action seeking to have the statute declared unconstitutional. On April 26, 1976, the case was submitted to a single Justice of the Supreme Judicial Court on an expedited basis and upon agreed facts, in order to settle the question before the upcoming election. Judgment was reserved and the case referred to the full court that same day.

Appellants argued that § 8 violates the First Amendment, the Due Process and Equal Protection Clauses of the Fourteenth Amendment, and similar provisions of the Massachusetts Constitution. They prayed that the statute be declared unconstitutional on its face and as it would be applied to their proposed expenditures. The parties' statement of agreed facts reflected their disagreement as to the effect that the adoption of a personal income tax would have on appellants' business; it noted that "[t]here is a division of opinion among economists as to whether and to what extent a graduated income tax imposed solely on individuals would affect the business and assets of corporations."... Appellee did not dispute that appellants' management believed that the tax would have a significant effect on their businesses.

On September 22, 1976, the full bench directed the single justice to enter judgment upholding the constitutionality of § 8....

II

Because the 1976 referendum has been held, and the proposed constitutional amendment defeated, we face at the outset a question of mootness. As the case falls within the class of controversies "capable of repetition, yet evading review," *Southern Pacific Terminal Co.* v. *ICC* ...(1911), we conclude that it is not moot....

III

The court below framed the principal question in this case as whether and to what extent corporations have First Amendment rights. We believe that the court posed the wrong question. The Constitution often protects interests broader than those of the party seeking their vindication. The First Amendment, in particular, serves significant societal interests. The proper question therefore is not whether corporations "have" First Amendment rights and, if so, whether they are coextensive with those of natural persons. Instead, the question must be whether §8 abridges expression that the First Amendment was meant to protect. We hold that it does.

A

The speech proposed by appellants is at the heart of the First Amendment's protection.... In appellants' view, the enactment of a graduated personal income tax, as proposed to be authorized by constitutional amendment, would have a serious adverse effect on the economy of the State.... The importance of the referendum issue to the people and government of Massachusetts is not disputed. Its merits, however, are the subject of sharp disagreement.

As the Court said in *Mills* v. *Alabama*... (1966), "there is practically universal agreement that a major purpose of [the First] Amendment was to protect the free discussion of governmental affairs." If the speakers here were not corporations, no one would suggest that the State could silence their proposed speech. It is the type of speech indispensable to decision-making in a democracy, and this is no less true because the speech comes from a corporation rather than an individual. The inherent worth of the speech in terms of its capacity for informing the public does not depend upon the identity of its source, whether corporation, association, union, or individual.

The court below nevertheless held that corporate speech is protected by the First Amendment only when it pertains directly to the corporation's business interests. In deciding whether this novel and restrictive gloss on the First Amendment comports with the Constitution and the precedents of this Court, we need not survey the outer boundaries of the Amendment's protection of corporate speech, or address the abstract question whether corporations have the full measure of rights that individuals enjoy under the First Amendment. The question in this case, simply put, is whether the corporate identity of the speaker deprives this proposed speech of what otherwise would be its clear entitlement to protection. We turn now to that question.

B

The court below found confirmation of the legislature's definition of the scope of a corporation's First Amendment rights in the language of the Fourteenth Amendment. Noting that the First Amendment is applicable to the States through the Fourteenth, and seizing upon the observation that corporations "cannot claim for themselves the liberty which the Fourteenth Amendment guarantees," *Pierce* v. *Society of Sisters*...(1925), the court concluded that a corporation's First Amendment rights must derive from its property rights under the Fourteenth.

This is an artificial mode of analysis, untenable under decisions of this Court.... Freedom of speech and the other freedoms encompassed by the First Amendment always have been viewed as fundamental components of the liberty safeguarded by the Due Process Clause...and the Court has not identified a separate source for the right when it has been asserted by corporations.... In *Grosjean* v. *American Press Co.*...(1936), the Court rejected the very reasoning adopted by the Supreme Judicial Court and did not rely on the corporation's property rights under the Fourteenth Amendment in sustaining its freedom of speech.

Yet appellee suggests that First Amendment rights generally have been afforded only to corporations engaged in the communications business or through which individuals express themselves, and the court below apparently accepted the "materially affecting" theory as the conceptual common denominator between appellee's position and the precedents of this Court. It is true that the "materially affecting" requirement would have been satisfied in the Court's decisions affording protection to the speech of media corporations and corporations otherwise in the business of communication or entertainment, and to the commercial speech of business corporations.... In such cases, the speech would be connected to the corporation's business almost by definition. But the effect on the business of the corporation was not the governing rationale in any of these decisions. None of them mentions, let alone attributes significance to the fact, that the subject of the challenged communication materially affected the corporation's business.

The press cases emphasize the special and constitutionally recognized role of that institution in informing and educating the public, offering criticism, and providing a forum for discussion and debate.... But the press does not have a monopoly on either the First Amendment or the ability to enlighten.... Similarly, the Court's decisions involving corporations in the business of communication or entertainment are based not only on the role of the First Amendment in fostering individual self-expression but also on its role in affording the public access to discussion, debate, and the dissemination of information and ideas.... Even decisions seemingly based exclusively on the individual's right to express himself acknowledge that the expression may contribute to society's edification....

Nor do our recent commercial speech cases lend support to appellee's business interest theory. They illustrate that the First Amendment goes beyond protection of the press and the self-expression of individuals to prohibit government from limiting the stock of information from which members of the public may draw. A commercial advertisement is constitutionally protected not so much because it pertains to the seller's business as because it furthers the societal interest in the "free flow of commercial information." *Virginia State Bd. of Pharmacy* v. *Virginia Citizens Consumer Council, Inc.*...(1976)....

C

We thus find no support in the First or Fourteenth Amendments, or in the decisions of this Court, for the proposition that speech that otherwise would be within the protection of the First Amendment loses that protection simply because its source is a corporation that cannot prove, to the satisfaction of a court, a material effect on its business or property. The "materially affecting" requirement is not an identification of the boundaries of corporate speech etched by the Constitution itself. Rather, it amounts to an impermissible legislative prohibition of speech based on the identity of the interests that spokesmen may represent in public debate over controversial issues and a requirement that the speaker have a sufficiently great interest in the subject to justify communication....

In the realm of protected speech, the legislature is constitutionally disqualified from dictating the subjects about which persons may speak and the speakers who may address a public issue.... If a legislature may direct business corporations to "stick to business," it also may limit other corporations — religious, charitable, or civic — to their respective "business" when addressing the public. Such power in government to channel the expression of views is unacceptable under the First Amendment. Especially where, as here, the legislature's suppression of speech suggests an attempt to give one side of a debatable public question an advantage in expressing its views to the people, the First Amendment is plainly offended. Yet the State contends that its action is necessitated by governmental interests of the highest order. We next consider these asserted interests.

IV

The constitutionality of § 8's prohibition of the "exposition of ideas" by corporations turns on whether it can survive the exacting scrutiny necessitated by a state-imposed restriction of freedom of speech. Especially where, as here, a prohibition is directed at speech itself, and the speech is intimately related to the process of governing, "the State may prevail only upon showing a subordinating interest which is compelling," *Bates* v. *City of Little Rock*...(1960)..., "and the burden is on the government to show the existence of such an interest." *Elrod* v. *Burns*...(1976). Even then, the State must employ means "closely drawn to avoid unnecessary abridgment...." *Buckley* v. *Valeo*...(1976)....

A

Preserving the integrity of the electoral process, preventing corruption, and "sustain[ing] the active, alert responsibility of the individual citizen in a democracy for the wise conduct of government" are interests of the highest importance. *Buckley*.... Preservation of the individual citizen's confidence in government is equally important....

Appellee advances a number of arguments in support of his view that these interests are endangered by corporate participation in discussion of a referendum issue. They hinge upon the assumption that such participation would exert an undue influence on the outcome of a referendum vote, and — in the end — destroy the confidence of the people in the democratic process and the integrity of government. According to appellee, corporations are wealthy and powerful and their views may drown out other points of view.... But there has been no showing that the relative voice of corporations has been overwhelming or even significant in influencing referenda in Massachusetts, or that there has been any threat to the confidence of the citizenry in government....

B

Finally, the State argues that § 8 protects corporate shareholders, an interest that is both legitimate and traditionally within the province of state law.... The statute is said to serve this interest by preventing the use of corporate resources in furtherance of views with which some shareholders may disagree. This purpose is belied, however, by the provisions of the statute, which are both under- and over-inclusive.

The under-inclusiveness of the statute is self-evident. Corporate expenditures with respect to a referendum are prohibited, while corporate activity with respect to the passage or defeat of legislation is permitted...even though corporations may engage in lobbying more often than they take positions on ballot questions submitted to the voters. Nor does § 8 prohibit a corporation from expressing its views, by the expenditure of corporate funds, on any public issue until it becomes the subject of a referendum, though the displeasure of disapproving shareholders is unlikely to be any less.

The fact that a particular kind of ballot question has been singled out for special treatment undermines the likelihood of a genuine state interest in protecting shareholders. It suggests instead that the legislature may have been concerned with silencing corporations on a particular subject. Indeed, appellee has conceded that "the legislative and judicial history of the statute indicates...that the second crime was 'tailor-made' to prohibit corporate campaign contributions to oppose a graduated income tax amendment."...

V

Because § 8 prohibits protected speech in a manner unjustified by a compelling state interest, it must be invalidated. The judgment of the Supreme Judicial Court is

Reversed.

MR. CHIEF JUSTICE BURGER, concurring.

I join the opinion and judgment of the Court but write separately to raise some questions likely to arise in this area in the future.

A disquieting aspect of Massachusetts' position is that it may carry the risk of impinging on the First Amendment rights of those who employ the corporate form — as most do — to carry on the business of mass communications, particularly the large media conglomerates. This is so because of the difficulty, and perhaps impossibility, of distinguishing, either as a matter of fact of constitutional law, media corporations from corporations such as the appellants in this case.

Making traditional use of the corporate form, some media enterprises have amassed vast wealth and power and conduct many activities, some directly related — and some not — to their publishing and broadcasting activities. See *Miami Herald Publishing Co.* v. *Tornillo*...(1974). Today, a corporation might own the dominant newspaper in one or more large metropolitan centers, television and radio stations in those same centers and others, a newspaper chain, news magazines with nationwide circulation, national or worldwide wire news services, and substantial interests in book publishing and distribution enterprises. Corporate ownership may extend, vertically, to pulp mills and pulp timber lands to insure an adequate, continuing supply of newsprint and to trucking and steamship lines for the purpose of transporting the newsprint to the presses. Such activities would be logical economic auxiliaries to a publishing conglomerate. Ownership also may extend beyond to business activities unrelated to the task of publishing newspapers and magazines or broadcasting radio and television programs. Obviously, such far-reaching ownership would not be possible without the state-provided corporate form and its "special rules relating to such matters as limited liability, perpetual life, and the accumulation, distribution, and taxation of assets...." [Quote from Justice White's dissenting opinion]....

In terms of "unfair advantage in the political process" and "corporate domination of the electoral process,"... it could be argued that such media conglomerates as I describe pose a much more realistic threat to valid interests than do appellants and similar entities not regularly concerned with shaping popular opinion on public issues.... In *Tornillo,* for example, we noted the serious contentions advanced that a result of the growth of modern media empires "has been to place in a few hands the power to inform the American people and shape public opinion."...

In terms of Massachusetts' other concern, the interests of minority shareholders, I perceive no basis for saying that the managers and directors of the media conglomerates are more or less sensitive to the views and desires of minority shareholders than are corporate officers generally. Nor can it be said, even if relevant to First Amendment analysis — which it is not — that the former are more virtuous, wise or restrained in the exercise of corporate power than are the latter.... Thus, no factual distinction has been identified as yet that would justify government restraints on the right of appellants to express their views without, at the same time, opening the door to similar restraints on media conglomerates with their vastly greater influence.

Despite these factual similarities between media and nonmedia corporations, those who view the Press Clause as somehow conferring special and extraordinary privileges or status on the "institutional press" — which are not extended to those who wish to express ideas other than by publishing a newspaper — might perceive no danger to institutional media corporations flowing from the position asserted by Massachusetts. Under this narrow reading of the Press Clause, government could perhaps impose on nonmedia corporations restrictions not permissible with respect to "media" enterprises.... The Court has not yet squarely resolved whether the Press Clause confers upon the "institutional press" any freedom from government restraint not enjoyed by all others.

I perceive two fundamental difficulties with a narrow reading of the Press Clause. First, although certainty on this point is not possible, the history of the Clause does not suggest that the authors contemplated a "special" or "institutional" privilege.... The common 18th century understanding of freedom of the press is suggested by Andrew Bradford, a colonial American newspaperman. In defining the nature of the liberty, he did not limit it to a particular group.... Indeed most pre-First Amendment commentators "who employed the term 'freedom of speech' with great frequency, used it synonomously with freedom of the press." L. Levy, Legacy of Suppression: Freedom of Speech and Press in Early American History 174 (1963).

Those interpreting the Press Clause as extending protection only to, or creating a special role for, the "institutional press" must either (a) assert such an intention on the part of the Framers for which no supporting evidence is available...; (b) argue that events after 1791 somehow operated to "constitutionalize" this interpretation...; or (c) candidly acknowledging the absence of historical support, suggest that the intent of the Framers is not important today....

To conclude that the Framers did not intend to limit the freedom of the press to one select group is not necessarily to suggest that the Press Clause is redundant. The Speech Clause standing alone may be viewed as a protection of the liberty to express ideas and beliefs, while the Press Clause focuses specifically on the liberty to disseminate expression broadly and "comprehends every sort of publication which affords a vehicle of information and opinion." *Lovell* v. *Griffin...*(1938). Yet there is no fundamental distinction between expression and dissemination. The liberty encompassed by the Press Clause, although complementary to and a natural extension of Speech Clause liberty, merited special mention simply because it had been more often the object of official restraints. Soon after the invention of the printing press, English and continental monarchs, fearful of the power implicit in its use and the threat to Establishment thought and order — political and religious — devised restraints, such as licensing, censors, indices of prohibited books, and prosecutions for seditious libel, which generally were unknown in the pre-printing press era. Official restrictions were the official response to the new, disquieting idea that this invention would provide a means for mass communication.

The second fundamental difficulty with interpreting the Press Clause as conferring special status on a limited group is one of definition.... The very task of including some entities within the "institutional press" while excluding others, whether undertaken by legislature, court or administrative agency, is reminiscent of the abhorred licensing system of Tudor and Stuart England — a system the First Amendment was intended to ban from this country.... Further, the officials undertaking that task would be required to distinguish the protected from the unprotected on the basis of such variables as content of expression, frequency or fervor of expression, or ownership of the technological means of dissemination. Yet nothing in this Court's opinions supports such a confining approach to the scope of Press Clause protection....

The meaning of the Press Clause, as a provision separate and apart from the Speech Clause, is implicated only indirectly by this case. Yet Massachusetts' position poses serious questions. The evolution of traditional newspapers into modern corporate conglomerates in which the daily dissemination of news by print is no longer the major part of the whole enterprise suggests the need for caution in limiting the First Amendment rights of corporations as such. Thus, the tentative probings of this brief inquiry are wholly consistent, I think, with the Court's refusal to sustain §8's serious and potentially dangerous restriction on the freedom of political speech.

Because the First Amendment was meant to guarantee freedom to express and communicate ideas, I can see no difference between the right of those who seek to disseminate ideas by way of a newspaper and those who give lectures or speeches and seek to enlarge the audience by publication and wide dissemination....

In short, the First Amendment does not "belong" to any definable category of persons or entities: it belongs to all who exercise its freedoms.

MR. JUSTICE WHITE, with whom MR. JUSTICE BRENNAN and MR. JUSTICE MARSHALL join, dissenting.

The Massachusetts statute challenged here forbids the use of corporate funds to publish views about referenda issues having no material effect on the business, property or assets of the corporation. The legislative judgment that the personal income tax issue, which is the subject of the referendum out of which this case arose, has no such effect was sustained by the Supreme Judicial Court of Massachusetts and is not disapproved by this Court today. Hence, as this case comes to us, the issue is whether a State may prevent corporate management from using the corporate treasury to propagate views having no connection with the corporate business. The Court commendably enough squarely faces the issue but unfortunately errs in deciding it. The Court invalidates the Massachusetts statute and holds that the First Amendment guarantees corporate managers the right to use not only their personal funds, but also those of the corporation, to circulate fact and opinion irrelevant to the business placed in their charge and necessarily representing their own personal or collective views about political and social questions. I do not suggest for a moment that the First Amendment requires a State to forbid such use of corporate funds, but I do strongly disagree that the First Amendment forbids state interference with managerial decisions of this kind.

By holding that Massachusetts may not prohibit corporate expenditures or contributions made in connection with referenda involving issues having no material connection with the corporate business, the Court not only invalidates a statute which has been on the books in one form or another for many years, but also casts considerable doubt upon the constitutionality of legislation passed by some 31 States restricting corporate political activity, as well as upon the Federal Corrupt Practices Act.... The Court's fundamental error is its failure to realize that the state regulatory interests in terms of which the alleged curtailment of First Amendment rights accomplished by the statute must be evaluated are themselves derived from the First Amendment. The question posed by this case, as approached by the Court, is whether the State has struck the best possible balance, *i.e.,* the one which it would have chosen, between competing First Amendment interests. Although in my view the choice made by the State would survive even the most exacting scrutiny, perhaps a rational argument might be made to the contrary. What is inexplicable, is for the Court to substitute its judgment as to the proper balance for that of Massachusetts where the State has passed legislation reasonably designed to further First Amendment interests in the context of the political arena where the expertise of legislators is at its peak and that of judges is at its very lowest. Moreover, the result reached today in critical respects marks a drastic departure from the Court's prior decisions which have protected against governmental infringement the very First Amendment interests which the Court now deems inadequate to justify the Massachusetts statute.

I

There is now little doubt that corporate communications come within the scope of the First Amendment. This, however, is merely the starting point of analysis, because an examination of the First Amendment values that corporate expression furthers and the threat to the functioning of a free society it is capable of posing reveals that it is not fungible with communications emanating from individuals and is subject to restrictions which individual expression is not. Indeed, what some have considered to be the principal function of the First Amendment, the use of communication as a means of self-expression, self-realization and self-fulfillment, is not at all furthered by corporate speech. It is clear that the communications of profitmaking corporations are not "an integral part of the development of ideas, of mental exploration and of the affirmation of self." They do not represent a manifestation of individual freedom or choice. Undoubtedly, as this Court has recognized...there are some corporations formed for the express purpose of advancing certain ideological causes shared by all their members, or, as in the case of the press, of disseminating information and ideas. Under such circumstances, association in a corporate form may be viewed as merely a means of achieving effective self-expression. But this is hardly the case generally with corporations operated for the purpose of making profits. Shareholders in such entities do not share a common set of political or social views, and they certainly have not invested their money for the purpose of advancing political or social causes or in an enterprise engaged in the business of disseminating news and opinion. In fact, as discussed *infra,* the government has a strong interest in assuring that investment decisions are not predicated upon agreement or disagreement with the activities of corporations in the political arena....

The self-expression of the communicator is not the only value encompassed by the First Amendment. One of its functions, often referred to as the right to hear or receive information, is to protect the interchange of ideas. Any communication of ideas, and consequently any expenditure of funds which makes the communication of ideas possible, it can be argued, furthers the purposes of the First Amendment. This proposition does not establish, however, that the right of the general public to receive communications financed by means of corporate expenditures is of the same dimension as that to hear other forms of expression. In the first place, as discussed *supra,* corporate expenditures designed to further political causes lack the connection with individual self-expression which is one of the principal justifications for the constitutional protection of speech provided by the First Amendment. Ideas which are not a product of individual choice are entitled to less First Amendment protection. Secondly, the restriction of corporate speech concerned with political matters impinges much less severely upon the availability of ideas to the general public than do restrictions upon individual speech. Even the complete curtailment of corporate communications concerning political or ideological questions not integral to day-to-day business functions would leave individuals, including corporate shareholders, employees, and customers, free to communicate their thoughts. Moreover, it is unlikely that any significant communication would be lost by such a prohibition. These individuals would remain perfectly free to communicate any ideas which could be conveyed by means of the corporate form. Indeed, such individuals could even form associations for the very purpose of promoting political or ideological causes.

I recognize that there may be certain communications undertaken by corporations which could not be restricted without impinging seriously upon the right to receive information. In the absence of advertising and similar promotional activities, for example, the ability of consumers to obtain information relating to products manufactured by corporations would be significantly impeded. There is also a need for employees, customers, and shareholders of corporations to be able to receive communications about matters relating to the functioning of corporations. Such communications are clearly desired by all investors and may well be viewed as an associational form of self-expression.... It is for such reasons that the Court has extended a certain degree of First Amendment protection to activities of this kind. None of the considerations, however, are implicated by a prohibition upon corporate expenditures relating to referenda concerning questions of general public concern having no connection with corporate business affairs....

The governmental interest in regulating corporate political communications, especially those relating to electoral matters, also raises considerations which differ significantly from those governing the regulation of individual speech. Corporations are artificial entities created by law for the purpose of furthering certain economic goals. In order to facilitate the achievement of such ends, special rules relating to such matters as limited liability, perpetual life, and the accumulation, distribution, and taxation of assets are normally applied to them. States have provided corporations with such attributes in order to increase their economic viability and thus strengthen the economy generally. It has long been recognized, however, that the special status of corporations has placed them in a position to control vast amounts of economic power which may, if not regulated, dominate not only the economy but also the very heart of our democracy, the electoral process. Although *Buckley* v. *Valeo*...(1976) provides support for the position that the desire to equalize the financial resources available to candidates does not justify the limitation upon the expression of support which a restriction upon individual contributions entails, the interest of Massachusetts and the many other States which have restricted corporate political activity is quite different. It is not one of equalizing the resources of opposing candidates or opposing positions but rather of preventing institutions which have been permitted to amass wealth as a result of special advantages extended by the State for certain economic purposes from using that wealth to acquire an unfair advantage in the political process, especially where, as here, the issue involved has no material connection with the business of the corporation. The State need not permit its own creation to consume it. Massachusetts could permissibly conclude that not to impose limits upon the political activities of corporations would have placed it in a position of departing from neutrality and indirectly assisting the propagation of corporate views because of the advantages its laws give to the corporate acquisition of funds to finance such activities. Such expenditures may be viewed as seriously threatening the role of the First Amendment as a guarantor of a free marketplace of ideas....

This Nation has for many years recognized the need for measures designed to prevent corporate domination of the political process. The Corrupt Practices Act, first enacted in 1907, has consistently barred corporate contributions in connection with federal elections. This Court has repeatedly recognized that one of the principal purposes of this prohibition is "to avoid the deleterious influences on federal elections resulting from the use of money by those who exercise control over large aggregations of capital." *United States* v. *Auto Workers*...(1957).... Although this Court has never adjudicated the constitutionality of the Act, there is no suggestion in its cases construing it, cited *supra,* that this purpose is in any sense illegitimate or deserving of other than the utmost respect; indeed, the thrust of its opinions, until today, has been to the contrary....

II

There is an additional overriding interest related to the prevention of corporate domination which is substantially advanced by Massachusetts' restrictions upon corporate contributions: assuring that shareholders are not compelled to support and financially further beliefs with which they disagree where, as is the case here, the issue involved does not materially affect the business, property, or other affairs of the corporation. The State has not interfered with the prerogatives of corporate management to communicate about matters that have material impact on the business affairs entrusted to them, however much individual stockholders may disagree on economic or ideological grounds. Nor has the State forbidden management from formulating and circulating its views at its own expense or at the expense of others, even where the subject at issue is irrelevant to corporate business affairs. But Massachusetts *has* chosen to forbid corporate management from spending corporate funds in referenda elections absent some demonstrable effect of the issue on the economic life of the company....

This is not only a policy which a State may adopt consistent with the First Amendment but one which protects the very freedoms that this Court has held to be guaranteed by the First Amendment....

Finally, even if corporations developed an effective mechanism for rebating to shareholders that portion of their investment used to finance political activities with which they disagreed, a State may still choose to restrict corporate political activity irrelevant to business functions on the grounds that many investors would be deterred from investing in corporations because of a wish not to associate with corporations propagating certain views. The State has an interest not only in enabling but also in eliminating the danger that investment decisions will be significantly influenced by the ideological views of corporations. While the latter concern may not be of the same constitutional magnitude as the former, it is far from trivial....

The Court today purports not to foreclose the possibility that the Corrupt Practices Act and state statutes which prohibit corporate expenditures only in the context of elections to public office may survive constitutional scrutiny because of the interest in preventing the corruption of elected representatives through the creation of political debts.... It does not choose to explain or even suggest, however, why the state interests which it so cursorily dismisses are less worthy than the interest in preventing corruption or the appearance of it. More importantly, the analytical framework employed by the Court clearly raises great doubt about the Corrupt Practices Act. The question in the present case, as viewed by the Court, "is whether the corporate identity of the speaker deprives this proposed speech of what otherwise would be its clear entitlement to protection,"...which it answers in the negative. But the Court has previously held in *Buckley* v. *Valeo*...that the interest in preventing corruption is insufficient to justify restrictions upon individual expenditures relative to candidates for political office. If the corporate identity of the speaker makes no difference, all the Court has done is to reserve the formal interment of the Corrupt Practices Act and similar state statutes for another day. As I understand the view that has now become part of First Amendment jurisprudence, the use of corporate funds, even for causes irrelevant to the corporation's business, may be no more limited than that of individual funds. Hence, corporate contributions to and expenditures on behalf of political candidates may be no more limited than those of individuals. Individual contributions under federal law are limited but not entirely forbidden, and under *Buckley* v. *Valeo,* expenditures may not constitutionally be limited at all. Most state corrupt practices acts, like the federal Act, forbid *any* contributions or expenditures by corporations to or for a political candidate.

...[T]he interests in protecting a system of freedom of expression...are sufficient to justify any incremental curtailment in the volume of expression which the Massachusetts statute might produce. I would hold that apart from corporate activities, such as those discussed in Part I...and exempted from regulation in [*United States* v.] *CIO*[1948], which are integrally related to corporate business operations, a State may prohibit corporate expenditures for political or ideological purposes. There can be no doubt that corporate expenditures in connection with referenda immaterial to corporate business affairs fall clearly into the category of corporate activities which may be barred. The electoral process, of course, is the essence of our democracy. It is an arena in which the public interest in preventing corporate domination and the coerced support by shareholders of causes with which they disagree is at its strongest and any claim that corporate expenditures are integral to the economic functioning of the corporation is at its weakest.

I would affirm the judgment of the Supreme Judicial Court for the Commonwealth of Massachusetts.

MR. JUSTICE REHNQUIST, dissenting.

This Court decided at an early date, with neither argument nor discussion, that a business corporation is a "person" entitled to the protection of the Equal Protection Clause of the Fourteenth Amendment. *Santa Clara County* v. *Southern Pacific R. Co.*...(1886). Likewise, it soon became accepted that the property of a corporation was protected under the Due Process Clause of that same amendment. See, *e.g., Smyth* v. *Ames*...(1898). Nevertheless, we concluded soon thereafter that the liberty protected by that amendment "is the liberty of natural, not artificial persons." *Northwestern Nat'l Life Ins. Co.* v. *Riggs*...(1906). Before today, our only considered and explicit departures from that holding have been that a corporation engaged in the business of publishing or broadcasting enjoys the same liberty of the press as is enjoyed by natural persons. *Grosjean* v. *American Press Co.*...(1936), and that a non-profit membership corporation organized for the purpose of "achieving...equality of treatment by all government, federal, state and local, for the...Negro community" enjoys certain liberties of political expression. *NAACP* v. *Button*...(1963)

The question presented today, whether business corporations have a constitutionally protected liberty to engage in political activities, has never been squarely addressed by any previous decision of this Court. However, the General Court of the Commonwealth of Massachusetts, the Congress of the United States, and the legislatures of 30 other States of this Republic have considered the matter, and have concluded that restrictions upon the political activity of business corporations are both politically desirable and constitutionally permissible. The judgment of such a broad consensus of governmental bodies expressed over a period of many decades is entitled to considerable deference from this Court. I think it quite probable that their judgment may properly be reconciled with our controlling precedents, but I am certain that under my views of the limited application of the First Amendment to the States, which I share with the two immediately preceding occupants of my seat on the Court, but not with my present colleagues, the judgment of the Supreme Judicial Court of Massachusetts should be affirmed....

...The appellants herein either were created by the Commonvealth or were admitted into the Commonwealth only for the limited purposes described in their charters and regulated by state law. Since it cannot be disputed that the mere creation of a corporation does not invest it with all the liberties enjoyed by natural persons,...(corporations do not enjoy the privilege against self-incrimination), our inquiry must seek to determine which constitutional protections are "incidental to its very existence." *Dartmouth College* [v. *Woodward* (1819)]....

There can be little doubt that when a State creates a corporation with the power to acquire and utilize property, it necessarily and implicitly guarantees that the corporation will not be deprived of that property absent due process of law. Likewise, when a State charters a corporation for the purpose of publishing a newspaper, it necessarily assumes that the corporation is entitled to the liberty of the press essential to the conduct of its business. *Grosjean* so held, and our subsequent cases have so assumed....

Until recently, it was not thought that any persons, natural or artificial, had any protected right to engage in commercial speech.... Although the Court has never explicitly recognized a corporation's right of commercial speech, such a right might be considered necessarily incidental to the business of a commercial corporation.

It cannot be so readily concluded that the right of political expression is equally necessary to carry out the functions of a corporation organized for commercial purposes. A State grants to a business corporation the blessings of potentially perpetual life and limited liability to enhance its efficiency as an economic entity. It might reasonably be concluded that those properties, so beneficial in the economic sphere, pose special dangers in the political sphere. Furthermore, it might be argued that liberties of political expression are not at all necessary to effectuate the purposes for which States permit commercial corporations to exist. So long as the Judicial Branches of the State and Federal Governments remain open to protect the corporation's interest in its property, it has no need, though it may have the desire, to petition the political branches for similar protection. Indeed, the States might reasonably fear that the corporation would use its economic power to obtain further benefits beyond those already bestowed. I would think that any particular form of organization upon which the State confers special privileges or immunities different from those of natural persons would be subject to like regulation, whether the organization is a labor union, a partnership, a trade association, or a corporation.

One need not adopt such a restrictive view of the political liberties of business corporations to affirm the judgment of the Supreme Judicial Court in this case. That court reasoned that this Court's decisions entitling the property of a corporation to constitutional protection should be construed as recognizing the liberty of a corporation to express itself on political matters concerning that property. Thus, the Court construed the statute in question not to forbid political expression by a corporation "when a general political issue materially affects a corporation's business, property or assets."...

I can see no basis for concluding that the liberty of a corporation to engage in political activity with regard to matters having no material effect on its business is necessarily incidental to the purposes for which the Commonwealth permitted these corporations to be organized or admitted within its boundaries. Nor can I disagree with the Supreme Judicial Court's factual finding that no such effect has been shown by these appellants. Because the statute as construed provides at least as much protection as the Fourteenth Amendment requires, I believe it is constitutionally valid.

It is true, as the Court points out...that recent decisions of this Court have emphasized the interest of the public in receiving the information offered by the speaker seeking protection. The free flow of information is in no way diminished by the Commonwealth's decision to permit the operation of business corporations with limited rights of political expression. All natural persons...remain as free as before to engage in political activity....

I would affirm the judgment of the Supreme Judicial Court.

▼▼▼

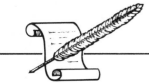

May

CARTER ON LAWYERS, DOCTORS
MAY 4, 5, 1978

President Carter used a western tour to call attention to what he indicated were the shortcomings of two of the most prestigious professions in the United States. In a speech in California May 4 he sharply criticized the legal profession, charging that "90 percent of our lawyers serve 10 percent of our people. We are over-lawyered, and under-represented." A day later, in remarks in Washington, he continued the populist theme by attacking the medical profession.

In a speech delivered at the 100th anniversary meeting of the Los Angeles Bar Association, the president asserted that four challenges must be met in order to improve justice: make criminal justice fairer, faster and more sensible; hold law to the highest standards of impartiality, honesty and fairness; ensure that access to the legal system does not depend on political influence or political power; reduce reliance on litigation and increase the pace of cases that are litigated.

To help make the administration of justice more efficient, Carter suggested that crimes such as drunkenness be removed from the courts, that the federal criminal code be streamlined and that sentencing standards for federal offenses be made uniform. He urged the selection of judges on a merit basis and the appointment of more women and minority judges.

To reduce economic impediments to the judicial system, the president said his administration had expanded the Legal Services Corporation and had supported "efforts to broaden the use of class action, and to expand the definitions of standing to sue." He asked that lawyers join in the administration's efforts to fight inflation by *"decelerating the rise in legal fees."*

Carter told the lawyers, *"One of the greatest failings of the organized bar in the past century since the American Bar Association was founded is that it has fought innovations. When greater competition has come to the legal profession, when no-fault systems have been adopted, when lawyers have begun to advertise or compete — in short, when the profession has accommodated the interests of the public — it has done so only when forced to."*

The president expressed his support for speedy appeals, national standards for no-fault automobile insurance, an end to the *"regulatory burden,"* greater reliance on small claims courts and experiments with alternative systems for resolving disputes.

Doctors' 'Interests'

The speech admonishing the legal profession was delivered in the middle of a three-day tour by the president through four western states. The day after the Los Angeles speech, Carter participated in a town meeting in Spokane. In his remarks in Spokane, Carter turned his attention to the medical profession. He declared that *"when you let doctors organize into the American Medical Association, their interest is to protect the interests, not of patients, but of doctors. And they have been the major obstacle to progress in our country in having a better health care system in years gone by."*

In response to a question about national health insurance Carter said, *"We need to get away from the commitment of medical doctors, hospital administrators, even patients, to go into a hospital for treatment when they could get adequate treatment in an outpatient clinic. . . . We now spend about $600 or $700 — I am not sure of the exact figure — for every man, woman and child in this country for health care and we don't nearly have the best health care in the world. . . . "*

Reaction

The president of the American Bar Association, William B. Spann Jr., said he was *"surprised"* by Carter's charge that lawyers resist change. Spann added that the president's attack was *"particularly astonishing"* because the organization was preparing to meet with Carter to discuss the establishment of a legal center to help poor people. In an editorial decrying Carter's comments about doctors, the Medical World News declared that *"Carter has never made much of a secret of his intense dislike of physicians"* and warned that the president could lose the support of the medical profession for a national health insurance plan.

Following are the text of President Carter's May 4 speech on the legal profession and excerpts from his May 5 comments on the medical profession. (Boldface headings in brackets have been added by Congressional Quarterly to highlight the organization of the text.):

CARTER SPEECH ON LAWYERS

Governor [Edmund G. (Jerry)] *Brown,* [Jr.], *Mayor* [Tom] *Bradley, President* [Samuel L.] *Williams, President-Elect* [John D.] *Taylor, distinguished members of the Los Angeles County Bar, ladies and gentlemen:*

For the last half an hour, I have been sitting in a room nearby listening to the report on the background of this tremendous organization and also listening to the report on the future of the organization. And I have been thrilled with your past accomplishments and I have been touched by some of the struggles that you have experienced in your own history.

I congratulate you on your 100th Anniversary.

I would like to begin my speech with a quote from a book published in 1852.

"Jarndyce and Jarndyce drones on. This scarecrow of a suit has, in the course of time, become so complicated that no man alive knows what it means — innumerable children have been born into the case; innumerable old people have died out of it; whole families have inherited legendary hatreds with the suit — there are not three Jarndyces left upon the earth, perhaps since old Tom Jarndyce in despair blew his brains out at a coffee house in Chancery, but Jarndyce and Jarndyce still drags its dreary length before the court."

This quotation comes from the novel "Bleak House," and although Charles Dickens, who by the way was a court reporter himself, was writing about a chancery suit in London long ago, he could have been writing about a modern anti-trust suit in Federal Court. His subject was the same that should preoccupy you and me, lawyers, mayors, governors and the President of the United States; that is, insuring that our legal system serves the ends of justice without delay.

I am not a lawyer, but there is no question that has concerned me more throughout my adult life than that of human justice — striving to alleviate the inequalities, the unfairness, the chance differences of fortune that exist among people and to help ensure that all people possess the basic material and political rights that they need for full participation in the life of our society.

I grew up in a community in Georgia that often did not provide simple justice for a majority of our citizens because of the divisions of privilege between those who owned land and property, and those who did not, the divisions of power between those who controlled the political system and those who were controlled by it, the wall of discrimination that separated blacks and whites.

As a Governor and as a President, I have learned that, as Reinhold Niebuhr said, "It is the sad duty of politics to establish justice in a sinful world." I am trying now as your President to carry our Nation's message of basic justice and human rights to other nations.

But I know that we cannot speak of human rights in other countries unless we are going to do our utmost to protect the rights of our own people here at home.

[Excessive Delays, Litigation]

Let me tell you about some of the things that concern me.

On the last day of the Administration of Lyndon Johnson, the government filed an anti-trust suit against a major computer company. Nine years have passed; three new presidential administrations have taken office; hundreds of millions of dollars have been spent on legal fees. But still the trial is not nearly over, and it has been speculated that the judge who has supervised it for the last nine years may die or retire before the trial is completed, in which case it would start all over again. Generations of computers have come and gone, there is not a single computer now being sold that was being sold when the case began — but still the case goes on.

I am worried about a legal system in which expensive talent on both sides produces interminable delay — especially when delay itself can often mean victory for one side.

Justice should not be forced to obey the timetables of those who seek to avoid it.

As a public official, I have inspected many prisons and I know that nearly all inmates are drawn from the ranks of the powerless and the poor. A child of privilege frequently receives the benefit of the doubt; a child of poverty seldom does.

In many courts, plea bargaining serves the convenience of the judge and the lawyers, not the ends of justice, because the courts simply lack the time to give everyone a fair trial.

We have the heaviest concentration of lawyers on earth — one for every 500 Americans: three times as many as are in England; four times as many as are in West Germany; twenty-one times as many as there are in Japan. We have more litigation; but I am not sure that we have more justice. No resources of talent and training in our own society, even including the medical care, is more wastefully or unfairly distributed than legal skills.

Ninety percent of our lawyers serve ten percent of our people. We are over-lawyered, and under-represented.

Excessive litigation and legal featherbedding are encouraged. Non-contested divorces become major legal confrontations in many states. Complete title searches on the same property are unnecessarily repeated with each sale. Routine automobile accidents, the cases clog our courts while no-fault automobile insurance is opposed.

The number of medical malpractice suits skyrockets. Mahatma Gandhi, who himself was a very successful lawyer, said of his profession, and I quote, "Lawyers will as a rule advance quarrels rather than repress them." We do not serve justice when we encourage disputes in our society, rather than resolving them.

In my own region of the country, perhaps even yours as well, lawyers of great influence and prestige led the fight against civil rights and economic justice. They were paid lavish fees by their states and heaped with honors for their efforts. They knew all the maneuvers, and for too long they kept the promises of the Constitution of the United States from coming true.

The basic right to vote, to hold a job, to own a home, to be informed of one's legal rights when arrested, to have legal counsel if an indigent — these rights have been denied for generations, in our country, and are being recently won only after intense struggle.

I think about these things when I come to speak with you. What I think about most, however, is the enormous potential for good within an aroused legal profession, and how often that potential has not been and is not used. More than any other nation on earth, ours was created out of respect for the law. We had the first written Constitution — it is the oldest; we proclaimed ours a government of laws, not of men; we put our faith in interpretations of the laws to resolve our most basic disputes.

None of us would change our system of laws and justice for any other in the world. From the beginning, it made the citizens the masters of the state, and not the other way around, and it has extended increasing protection to the poor and the victims of discrimination.

It is because of the enormous power of the law, and of the position of great influence and privilege which lawyers occupy within our society, that lawyers bear such a heavy obligation to serve the ends of true justice, and through dynamic effort, individually and collectively through organizations such as this, search for those ends of justice. I know that you understand these obligations.

During the last generation, many of our most important advances toward racial integration and protection of our people against government and its abuse have been made through the courts.

[Four Challenges]

I heard the comments a few minutes ago about Chief Justice Earl Warren who has been an inspiration to all of us who serve in government. But let me mention briefly four challenges that we should face in order to improve justice in America.

First, in making criminal justice fairer, faster, more sensible, and more certain; second, in holding the law to the highest standards of impartiality, honesty, and fairness; third, in ensuring that access to the legal systems does not depend on political influence or economic power, and fourth, in reducing our over-reliance on litigation, and speeding up those cases that are litigated.

[Fairer Criminal Justice] Our starting point in ensuring justice is to reduce crime through measures that are effective and fair.

There was encouraging progress in this direction last year, when the volume of crime fell for the first time in many years by four percent below the previous year's level. It is a welcome development, but it does not change the urgent need to control crime. States and local governments must take the lead in this effort, but the federal government must do its part.

We should streamline the Federal Criminal Code, which now contains many provisions which overlap, duplicate one another, are inconsistent and need upgrading. With the leadership of Senator [James O.] Eastland and Senator [Edward M.] Kennedy and the late Senator [John L.] McClellan, a twelve-year effort recently culminated in the Senate passage of this new comprehensive criminal code. I hope the House will pass it this year without delay.

We are working with congressional leaders to reorganize the Law Enforcement Assistance Agency, to gear our funding system to our most pressing needs, and to provide better support for state and local governments, and to concentrate our help on improving the criminal justice system and reducing crime. I will propose a consolidation and a reorganization of many of the functions now performed by more than 110 different federal agencies that have direct responsibility for law enforcement.

We can reduce the tremendous overload on our criminal justice system by removing such crimes as drunkenness, and vagrancy from the courts, thereby freeing the courts to deal with serious offenses and enabling us to treat these social illnesses in ways that offer a greater hope of success than conviction and incarceration.

I am supporting uniform sentencing standards for federal offenses, which will make the punishment for crimes more rational and fair and will help ensure that the rich and the poor are treated alike, no matter what court might convict them.

Powerful white-collar criminals cheat consumers of millions of dollars; public officials who abuse their high rank damage the integrity of our nation in profound and long-lasting ways. But too often these big-shot crooks escape the full consequences of their acts. Justice must be blind to rank power and position. The Justice Department is now undertaking a major new effort on white-collar crime.

I have directed the Justice Department also to review our prison policy alternatives to incarceration, such as station house citations, supervised release, work-release programs and other community-based facilities.

I urge all judges and all lawyers to use your enormous influence to make these efforts a success.

[Adherence to Standards] Our second challenge is to see that our legal system lives up to its noblest tradition of honesty and impartiality, so that all people stand equal before the bar of justice.

One of the most important steps that we can take is to restore public confidence in our system of justice, to assure that government decisions are thoroughly impartial, and that personal interests and influence have no part. I have required all major appointees of mine, as a condition of accepting office, to disclose their personal financial interests. I have also required them to pledge that, after their term of public service is over, they would forego all contacts with their former agency in government for one year.

Last year I proposed legislation to make these standards a permanent part of the American law. In its current form, this ethics legislation would extend similar standards to the Legislative and Judicial Branches of our government. It has already passed the Senate and cleared the Rules Committee in the House and is ready for floor action without delay.

Last week the House passed a bill I supported requiring those organizations which do significant lobbying of Congress to disclose their activities to the public. Although lobbying is a constitutionally protected activity, the American people have a right to know what major forces are affecting the legislative process. It is time now for the Senate to follow the lead of the House and pass a lobby reform bill.

Law enforcement agencies must set a clear example for their respect for the law. Recently, as the number of undocumented aliens has grown, there has been a disturbing trend particularly in your part of the country toward routine police harassment of our Mexican-American families. I know that your own bar association has studied this problem.

Last month, the Justice Department intervened in a harassment case in Texas where three policemen had been convicted for the death of a Mexican-American prisoner. In filing for a review of the one-year jail terms given to the convicted men, the Justice Department said, and I quote, "The public perception of inequality and the belief that the life of a Mexican-American citizen has little value can only do damage to respect for the laws and belief in justice."

This kind of harassment must stop, and my administration, working with you, will do what it can to see that it does. Moreover, we have submitted legislation to Congress now which will stop the flow of illegal immigration while fully protecting the rights of our Hispanic citizens.

When I was Governor of Georgia, I appointed judges on the basis of merit alone. And one of my first acts as President was to create a nominating commission to recommend candidates to me for all appointments as Federal Circuit Judges. I am pleased that many Senators, including those from California, have now set up similar commissions at the District Court level.

The passage of the Omnibus Judgeship Act, now pending in a House-Senate Conference Committee, will provide a test for the concept of merit selection. The conferees have recently agreed that the President should set "standards and guidelines" governing the selection of District Judges, and I intend to use this authority to encourage establishment of more merit panels and to open the selection process.

The passage of this act — which will create 152 Federal judgeships — offers a unique opportunity to make our judiciary more fully representative of our population. We have an abominable record to date. Of the 525 Federal judges, only 20 are black or Hispanic, and only six, about one percent, are women.

While the Federal Bench in Southern California has become more representative, this is not true elsewhere in the nation. My Executive Order on the Circuit Court Nominating Commission specifically requires special efforts to identify qualified minority and female candidates.

During too many of the struggles for equal justice, just in the lifetimes of you and me — the questions of one-man, one-vote, voting rights for blacks, representation for indigent clients, and others — much of the organized bar sat on the sidelines or actually opposed these efforts. In today's struggle for women's rights, the passage of the Equal Rights Amendment and the full participation of women and minorities at all levels of society, I hope that lawyers throughout the country will follow the actions that your bar association has already taken here in Los Angeles County.

[Remove Economic Barriers] The third challenge is suggested by the American Bar Association's theme for this year "Access to Justice." Too often the amount of justice that a person gets depends on the amount of money that he or she can pay. Access to justice must not depend on economic status, and it must not be thwarted by arbitrary procedural rules.

Overcoming these procedural barriers means that groups with distinct interests to defend — in civil rights, economic questions, environmental causes and so forth — must be able to defend them fully. We are supporting efforts to broaden the use of class action, and to expand the definitions of standing to sue. My administration supports bills before Congress that would empower citizens to participate in the proceedings of federal agencies — a right that has too often been reserved for the large and the powerful corporations which have the legal resources to express their view forcefully.

We must remove the economic barriers to justice. When a poor family is cheated by a merchant, unfairly threatened with eviction, falsely accused of a crime, it can very rarely take advantage of the skilled legal talent at reasonable rates.

In the City of New York there are 35,000 lawyers — one for every 200 citizens. But only a handful of these lawyers are available for service to the city's poor — one lawyer for every 5,000 poor people. That is why we have now expanded the Legal Services Corporation; in fiscal year 1979, its budget will be more than twice as large as it was when my administration took office about a year ago.

But you know and I know that legal help is often beyond the reach of most of the middle class Americans as well. Here, too, I believe that the bar has an obligation to accommodate those with modest incomes. Free and open competition is the best way to bring legal services within the reach of average citizens. Another solution, which my administration supports, is the expansion of pre-paid legal plans, legal clinics, and other low cost alternatives, such as those pioneered by the United Auto Workers.

The Neighborhood Justice Center near here in Venice and Marvista is a good example of what we are trying to do.

I also ask that lawyers join the effort to stop inflation by following the example we have asked of every other group in our society and join in decelerating the rise in legal fees. This morning new inflation figures were published in Washington that caused me grave concern. How can we, the privileged members of American society, call upon the working people, the men and women of our country, to make a financial sacrifice to deal with inflation unless attorneys, doctors, accountants and other professionals, Presidents, assume the same responsibility to assist in our efforts to keep a lid on inflation?

One of the greatest failings of the organized bar in the past century since the American Bar Association was founded is that it has fought innovations. When greater competition has come to the legal profession, when no-fault systems have been adopted, when lawyers have begun to advertise or compete — in short, when the profession has accommodated the interests of the public — it has done so only when forced to.

Constructive work is now under way and as the second century of the Bar Association begins, the people of this country are beginning to see leadership from the members of the bar.

[Reduce Litigation] But as we make litigation more accessible, our fourth challenge is to make the adversary system less necessary for the daily lives of most Americans — and more difficult when it must be used. By resorting to litigation at the drop of a hat, by regarding the adversary system as an end in itself, we have made justice more cumbersome, more expensive and less equal than it ought to be.

This is a phenomenon more and more widely recognized — I know — among members of the bar.

One answer is to be sure that other pathways to justice do exist.

Many suggestions have already been made for making litigation less necessary, and my administration will work with you and other members of the bar to implement them.

In the great number of cases there is no sound reason for a lawyer to be involved in land transfers or title searches. Simplified procedures and use of modern computer technology can save consumers needless legal fees.

We must eliminate from our judicial system cases which can be resolved in other ways. No-fault automobile insurance systems, adopted by many states, are a step in the right direction; national standards for no-fault will have a much greater impact. We support no-fault divorce laws, like those passed when I was Governor of Georgia and the ones passed here in California, that can reduce litigation that is unnecessary and also the bitterness that litigation brings. We must look for ways to reduce the tremendous burden of medical malpractice costs.

Delays in our courts because of the excessive litigation are matched by the interminable delays in many federal regulatory agencies.

In trying to solve society's problems, our regulators have proposed unnecessarily detailed specifications, and written regulations in the kind of gobbledygook that could employ a generation of law school graduates just to interpret them.

I have pledged to reduce this regulatory burden for the first time on American citizens and we have taken some steps toward change. A few weeks ago, I signed an Executive Order that will be carried out which requires the heads of departments and agencies personally to approve the regulatory agendas of their organizations; that regulations be signed by the one who wrote them; that regulations be gone over rigorously in "sunset" reviews to terminate them when they have served their purpose; that they be simply written; and that they are the most cost effective rules possible to devise.

Where the free marketplace can do a better job than regulations — as in the setting of airline fares — I will work hard to deregulate that industry, and to encourage free and effective competition.

The Senate has passed a superb airline deregulation bill. I predict that next week it will come out of the House subcommittee and we expect success on the floor of the House.

We must also find a way to remove the vested interests in over-litigation and delay. Last year, corporations spent $24 billion on legal services — 12 times as much as we spent on all federal, state and local courts combined. We must ask whether this is the right way or the best way to conserve our legal resources or to ensure justice.

We are reviewing suggestions for reducing litigation, including more arbitration, greater reliance on small claims courts and experiments with alternative systems for resolving disputes, such as the experimental arbitration systems now in existence in San Francisco, and in Philadelphia, and in other parts of our country.

But even with all of these steps, much litigation will of course still be necessary. There are a variety of steps that can be taken together to make necessary litigation more efficient and to reduce unnecessary delays.

I support legislation now in Congress to expand the functions and the jurisdiction of federal magistrates, to reduce the burden on federal judges.

I support a speedy appeals act to reduce the delay between sentencing and appeal; and I have directed Attorney General [Griffin B.] Bell to study whether we can also apply strict time limits to civil trials and to regulatory proceedings.

[Timeless Responsibility]

Those of us — Presidents and lawyers — who enjoy privilege, power and influence in our society can be called to a harsh account for the ways we are using this power. Our hierarchy of privilege in this nation, based not on birth but on social and economic status, tends to insulate some of us from the problems faced by the average American. The natural tendency for all of us is to ignore what does not touch us directly. The natural temptation when dealing with the law is to assure that whatever is legal is just.

But if our nation is to thrive, if we are to fulfill the vision and promise of our founding fathers, if we are truly to serve the ends of justice, we must look beyond these comfortable insulations of privilege.

I have too much respect for the potential of the law to believe that this leadership is not possible from you.

I hope that lawyers throughout the country will take up the challenges I have made today. I know you understand the responsibility to serve justice. You have dedicated your very lives to this task.

This responsibility is older than our Constitution, older than the Bill of Rights, older even than the tradition of the common law.

It comes from the roots of our western heritage, with the prophet Amos, who said, "Let justice roll down like waters, and righteousness like an ever flowing stream."

Thank you very much.

CARTER COMMENTS ON DOCTORS

. . .I know that doctors care very seriously about their patients. But when you let doctors organize into the American Medical Association, their interest is to protect the interests, not of patients, but of doctors. And they have been the major obstacle to progress in our country in having a better health care system in years gone by.

So I look upon myself as a spokesman for the client and the medical patient and the student in a classroom, the elderly person, the mentally ill person. And I think this sense that I am that person would be the greatest achievement that I could derive for myself on the domestic scene. . . .

Q: Mr. President, my name is Kyra Coffey. I know what I want to say, first of all, is really unprofessional and un — what am I trying to say? — not really related, but I think you are really cute. I do. (Laughter)

P: You are the first questioner that has made me blush. (Laughter)

Q: Now I would like to ask my question. If you are going to reduce the government interference in the lives of the American people as you said, why then are you pushing for a national health care plan which will only increase our income tax, and increase our national debt, just as it has in England and Sweden? Thank you.

P: Thank you. If that was the result of a national health plan, just to increase the burden on the American people financially, I of course would never consider it. Beginning with President Truman's Administration, there has been a growing interest and desire among the American people to have a more far-reaching or comprehensive health plan for our nation.

There would be several emphases in the new plan that don't presently exist and I will just mention a few of them.

One is the prevention of disease, and not just a commitment to treat an affliction or disease, after it occurs in the human body. Fifteen months ago the immunization program for children, for instance, had almost been completely forgotten. Now with our new CHAPS Program, so-called, we are trying to test people at an early age, four or five years old, to see what defects they have, immunize them against prospective diseases for a change as did occur in my childhood, perhaps in yours, and make sure that the emphasis is on prevention.

The second thing we want to do is let Americans prepay through a routine monthly payment, for instance, for this kind of care and not just depend upon a concerted and very expensive care after they become ill.

We need to get away from the commitment of medical doctors, hospital administrators, even patients, to go into a hospital for treatment when they could get adequate treatment in an outpatient clinic. As you know, many hospital insurance policies won't pay off unless you are admitted to the hospital as a patient.

Obviously, this is more convenient for the doctors perhaps. It is much more profitable for those who own, operate hospitals. You are quite often given services or treatment that you don't need and of course it makes the expense of hospital care in our country far greater per person than any other nation on earth, including Sweden, Canada, England, where they do have a more comprehensive health care program. . . .

We have seen in recent years an unbelievable explosion in health care costs. Last year, for instance, the hospital costs went up in our country 16 percent. The inflation rate went up about 6 percent. This has been typical of the last few years. . . .

We now spend about $600 or $700 — I am not sure of the exact figure — for every man, woman and child in this country for health care and we don't nearly have the best health care in the world. . . .

COURT ON SAFETY INSPECTIONS
May 23, 1978

Inspectors for the Occupational Safety and Health Administration (OSHA), a Department of Labor agency, can no longer make spot checks of work places without a search warrant unless the business owners agree to the inspection, the Supreme Court ruled May 23. The potentially disruptive effect of the 5-3 ruling was partially offset, however, by the court's loosening of the legal requirements for a warrant. The majority opinion further held that the warrants could be issued without the knowledge of the employer and OSHA thereby could retain the element of surprise that Labor Department lawyers had argued was essential to the inspection process.

The case rose out of a routine inspection of an electrical and plumbing contractor's firm in Pocatello, Idaho, on Sept. 11, 1975. The contractor, Ferrol G. Barlow, refused to allow an OSHA inspector to enter the working area of his business without a search warrant, arguing that the search constituted a violation of his Fourth Amendment protection against unreasonable searches. Barlow refused again when the inspector returned with a court order; he then went to court to seek an injunction against further attempts to inspect his business. A three-judge district court ruled in Barlow's favor and the Labor Department appealed to the Supreme Court.

Majority Opinion

Writing for the majority, Justice Byron White declared, "This court has already held that warrantless searches are generally unreasonable, and that this rule applies to commercial premises as well as homes." White was joined in the majority by Chief Justice Warren E. Burger and Justices Potter Stewart, Thurgood Marshall and Lewis F. Powell Jr.

In defense of the warrantless search, the Labor Department had argued that many sectors of the business community are subject to government regulation that includes the warrantless search; issuing warrants would remove some of the element of surprise deemed helpful in inspections; warrants would create more bureaucratic problems and reduce the effectiveness of the inspection program; and, a ruling against the OSHA searches would put in jeopardy other kinds of searches allowed by other regulatory agencies.

White said that government regulation that includes inspection is the exception rather than the rule and cited its use in specialized concerns such as liquor and gun businesses. Furthermore, he wrote, employees are free to report any unsafe or unhealthful conditions they observe. "The Government inspector, however, is not an employee. Without a warrant," White continued, "he stands in no better position than a member of the public. What is observable by the public is observable, without a warrant, by the Government inspector as well. The owner of a business has not, by the necessary utilization of employees in his operation, thrown open the areas where employees alone are permitted to the warrantless scrutiny of Government agents."

Similarly, White held that the element of surprise would not be gravely affected by the ruling. The majority of business owners, he said, usually allowed the inspection to proceed; those who did not might be visited again by an inspector with a warrant. That process was not significantly different from previous procedure, he wrote, which required a court order to compel the employer to allow the inspection. And to ensure that OSHA would receive warrants with little trouble, White declared the agency would not have to show probable cause to believe that the business intended for inspection contained violations of the agency's regulations. "Probable cause in the criminal law sense is not required," and, for this reason, White said he doubted that "consumption of enforcement energies in the obtaining of such warrants will exceed manageable proportions."

Finally, the majority opinion said that the court's finding was meant to apply only to the warrantless searches conducted by OSHA and did not affect enforcement measures taken by other regulatory agencies.

Dissent

In his dissent, Justice John Paul Stevens wrote that the OSHA inspections were "reasonable" under the terms of the Fourth Amendment. He also warned that the court's ruling would weaken the warrant power. Stevens was joined in the dissent by Justices Harry A. Blackmun and William

H. Rehnquist. Justice William J. Brennan Jr. did not participate in the case.

Stevens declared that the court was substituting "its judgment for that of Congress" in deciding what type of inspection OSHA was allowed to employ. The inspection warrant, he said, "adds little to the protections already afforded by the statute and pertinent regulations, and the slight additional benefit it might provide is insufficient to identify a constitutional violation or to justify overriding Congress' judgment that the power to conduct warrantless inspections is essential."

The inspection warrant, he continued, is "essentially a formality" whose provisions were covered by existing OSHA procedures. The court's ruling, he added, requires "formalities which merely place an additional strain on already overtaxed federal resources."

Following are excerpts from the Supreme Court's majority opinion, delivered May 23, 1978, mandating a search warrant for OSHA inspections when business owners refuse to allow inspectors to enter freely and excerpts from Justice Stevens' dissent:

No. 76-1143

Ray Marshall,
Secretary of Labor,
el al., Appellants,
v.
Barlow's, Inc.

On Appeal from the United States District Court for the District of Idaho.

[May 23, 1978]

MR. JUSTICE WHITE delivered the opinion of the Court. [MR. JUSTICE BRENNAN took no part in the consideration or decision of this case.]. . . .

I

The Secretary [of Labor] urges that warrantless inspections to enforce OSHA are reasonable within the meaning of the Fourth Amendment. Among other things, he relies on § 8 (a) of the Act . . . which authorizes inspection of business premises without a warrant and which the Secretary urges represents a congressional construction of the Fourth Amendment that the courts should not reject. Regretfully, we are unable to agree.

The Warrant Clause of the Fourth Amendment protects commercial buildings as well as private homes. To hold otherwise would belie the origin of that Amendment, and the American colonial experience. An important forerunner of the first 10 Amendments to the United States Constitution, the Virginia Bill of Rights, specifically opposed "general warrants, whereby an officer or messenger may be commanded to search suspected places without evidence of a fact committed." The general warrant was a recurring point of contention in the colonies immediately preceding the Revolution. The particular offensiveness it engendered was acutely felt by the merchants and businessmen whose premises and products were inspected for compliance with the several Parliamentary revenue measures that most irritated the colonists. Against this background, it is untenable that the ban on warrantless searches was not intended to shield places of business as well as of residence.

This Court has already held that warrantless searches are generally unreasonable, and that this rule applies to commercial premises as well as homes.

These same cases also held that the Fourth Amendment prohibition against unreasonable searches protects against warrantless intrusions during civil as well as criminal investigations. *See* v. *City of Seattle* [1967]. . . . The reason is found in the "basic purpose of this Amendment . . . [which] is to safeguard the privacy and security of individuals against arbitrary invasions by governmental officials." *Camara* [v. *Municipal Court*, (1967)]. . . . If the government intrudes on a person's property, the privacy interest suffers whether the government's motivation is to investigate violations of criminal laws or breaches of other statutory or regulatory standards. It therefore appears that unless some recognized exception to the warrant requirement applies, *See* v. *City of Seattle* . . . would require a warrant to conduct the inspection sought in this case.

The Secretary urges that an exception from the search warrant requirement has been recognized for "pervasively regulated business[es]," *United States* v. *Biswell* . . . (1972), and for "closely regulated" industries "long subject to close supervision and inspection." *Colonnade Catering Corp.* v. *United States* . . . (1970). These cases are indeed exceptions, but they represent responses to relatively unique circumstances. Certain industries have such a history of government oversight that no reasonable expectation of privacy could exist for a proprietor over the stock of such an enterprise. Liquor (*Colonnade*) and firearms (*Biswell*) are industries of this type; when an entrepreneur embarks upon such a business, he has voluntarily chosen to subject himself to a full arsenal of governmental regulation.

Industries such as these fall within the "certain carefully defined classes of cases," referenced in *Camara*. . . . The element that distinguishes these enterprises from ordinary businesses is a long tradition of close government supervision. . . .

The clear import of our cases is that the closely regulated industry of the type involved in *Colonnade* and *Biswell* is the exception. The Secretary would make it the rule. Invoking the Walsh-Healy Act of 1936 . . . , the Secretary attempts to support a conclusion that all businesses involved in interstate commerce have long been subjected to close supervision of employee safety and health conditions. But the degree of federal involvement in employee working circumstances has never been of the order of specificity and pervasiveness that OSHA mandates. It is quite unconvincing to argue that the imposition of minimum wages and maximum hours on employers who contracted with the government under the Walsh-Healy Act prepared the entirety of American interstate commerce for regulation of working conditions to the minutest detail. Nor can any but the most fictional sense of voluntary consent to later searches be found in the single fact that one conducts a business affecting interstate commerce; under current practice and law, few businesses can be conducted without having some effect on interstate commerce.

The Secretary also attempts to derive support for a *Colonnade-Biswell*-type exception by drawing analogies from the field of labor law. In *Republic Aviation Corp.* v. *NLRB* . . . (1945), this Court upheld the rights of employees to solicit for a union during nonworking time where efficiency was not compromised. By opening up his property to employees, the employer had yielded so much of his private property rights as to allow those employees to exercise § 7 rights under the National Labor Relations Act. But this Court also held that the private property rights of an owner prevailed over the intrusion of nonemployee organizers, even in nonworking areas of the plant and during nonworking hours. *NLRB* v. *Babcock & Wilcox Co.* . . . (1956).

The critical fact in this case is that entry over Mr. Barlow's objection is being sought by a Government agent. Employees are not being prohibited from reporting OSHA violations. What they observe in their daily functions is undoubtedly beyond the employer's reasonable expectation of privacy. The Government inspector, however, is not an employee. Without a warrant he stands in no better position than a member of the public. What is observable by the public is observable, without a warrant, by the Government inspector as well. The owner of a business has not, by the necessary utilization of employees in his operation, thrown open the areas where employees alone are permitted to the warrantless scrutiny of Government agents. That an employee is free to report, and the Government is free to use, any evidence of noncompliance with OSHA that the employee observes furnishes no justification for federal agents to enter a place of business from which the public is restricted and to conduct their own warrantless search.

II

The Secretary nevertheless stoutly argues that the enforcement scheme of the Act requires warrantless searches, and that the restrictions on search discretion contained in the Act and its regulations already protect as much privacy as a warrant would. The Secretary thereby asserts the actual reasonableness of OSHA searches, whatever the general rule against warrantless searches might be. Because "reasonableness is still the ultimate standard," . . . the Secretary suggests that the Court decide whether a warrant is needed by arriving at a sensible balance between the administrative necessities of OSHA inspections and the incremental protection of privacy of business owners a warrant would afford. He suggests that only a decision exempting OSHA inspections from the Warrant Clause would give "full recognition to the competing public and private interests here at stake." *Camara* v. *Municipal Court.* . . .

The Secretary submits that warrantless inspections are essential to the proper enforcement of OSHA because they afford the opportunity to inspect without prior notice and hence to preserve the advantages of surprise. While the dangerous conditions outlawed by the Act include structural defects that cannot be quickly hidden or remedied, the Act also regulates a myriad of safety details that may be amenable to speedy alteration or disguise. The risk is that during the interval between an inspector's initial request to search a plant and his procuring a warrant following the owner's refusal of permission, violations of this latter type could be corrected and thus escape the inspector's notice. To the suggestion that warrants may be issued *ex parte* and executed without delay and without prior notice, thereby preserving the element of surprise, the Secretary expresses concern for the administrative strain that would be experienced by the inspection system, and by the courts, should *ex parte* warrants issued in advance become standard practice.

We are unconvinced, however, that requiring warrants to inspect will impose serious burdens on the inspection system or the courts, will prevent inspections necessary to enforce the statute, or will make them less effective. In the first place, the great majority of businessmen can be expected in normal course to consent to inspection without warrant; the Secretary has not brought to this Court's attention any widespread pattern of refusal. In those cases where an owner does insist on a warrant, the Secretary argues that inspection efficiency will be impeded by the advance notice and delay. The Act's penalty provisions for giving advance notice of a search . . . and the Secretary's own regulations . . . indicate that surprise searches are indeed contemplated. However, the Secretary has also promulgated a regulation providing that upon refusal to permit an inspector to enter the property or to complete his inspection, the inspector shall attempt to ascertain the reasons for the refusal and report to his superior, who shall "promptly take appropriate action, including compulsory process, if necessary.". . . The regulation represents a choice to proceed by process where entry is refused; and on the basis of evidence available from present practice, the Act's effectiveness has not been crippled by providing those owners who wish to refuse an initial requested entry with a time lapse while the inspector obtains the necessary process. Indeed, the kind of process sought in this case and apparently anticipated by the regulation provides notice to the business operator. If this safeguard endangers the efficient administration of OSHA, the Secretary should never have adopted it, particularly when the Act does not require it. Nor is it immediately apparent why the advantages of surprise would be lost if, after being refused entry, procedures were available for the Secretary to seek an *ex parte* warrant and to reappear at the premises without further notice to the establishment being inspected.

Whether the Secretary proceeds to secure a warrant or other process, with or without prior notice, his entitlement to inspect will not depend on his demonstrating probable cause to believe that conditions in violation of OSHA exist on the premises. Probable cause in the criminal law sense is not required. For purposes of an administrative search such as this, probable cause justifying the issuance of a warrant may be based not only on specific evidence of an existing violation but also on a showing that "reasonable legislative or administrative standards for conducting an . . . inspection are satisfied with respect to a particular [establishment]." *Camara* v. *Municipal Court*. . . . A warrant showing that a specific business has been chosen for an OSHA search on the basis of a general administrative plan for the enforcement of the Act derived from neutral sources such as, for example, dispersion of employees in various types of industries across a given area, and the desired frequency of searches in any of the lesser divisions of the area, would protect an employer's Fourth Amendment rights. We doubt that the consumption of enforcement energies in the obtaining of such warrants will exceed manageable proportions.

Finally, the Secretary urges that requiring a warrant for OSHA inspectors will mean that, as a practical matter, warrantless search provisions in other regulatory statutes are also constitutionally infirm. The reasonableness of a warrantless search, however, will depend upon the specific enforcement needs and privacy guarantees of each statute. Some of the states cited apply only to a single industry, where regulations might already be so pervasive that a *Colonnade-Biswell* exception to the warrant requirement could apply. Some statutes already envision resort to federal court enforcement when entry is refused, employing specific language in some cases and general language in others. In short, we base today's opinion on the facts and law concerned with OSHA and do not retreat from a holding appropriate to that statute because of its real or imagined effect on other, different administrative schemes.

Nor do we agree that the incremental protections afforded the employer's privacy by a warrant are so marginal that they fail to justify the administrative burdens that may be entailed. The authority to make warrantless searches devolves almost unbridled discretion upon executive and administrative officers, particularly those in the field, as to when to search and whom to search. A warrant, by contrast, would provide assurances from a neutral officer that the inspection is reasonable under the Constitution, is authorized by statute, and is pursuant to an administrative plan containing specific neutral criteria. Also, a warrant would then and there advise the owner of the scope and objects of the search, beyond which limits the inspector is not expected to proceed. These are important functions for a warrant to perform, functions which underlie the Court's prior decisions that the Warrant Clause applies to inspections for compliance with regulatory statutes. . . . We conclude that the concerns expressed by the Secretary do not suffice to justify warrantless inspections under OSHA or vitiate the general constitutional requirement that for a search to be reasonable a warrant must be obtained.

III

We hold that Barlow was entitled to a declaratory judgment that the Act is unconstitutional insofar as it purports to authorize inspections without warrant or its equivalent and to an injunction enjoining the Act's enforcement to that extent. The judgment of the District Court is therefore affirmed.

So ordered.

MR. JUSTICE STEVENS, with whom MR. JUSTICE BLACKMUN and MR. JUSTICE REHNQUIST join, dissenting.

Congress enacted the Occupational Safety and Health Act to safeguard employees against hazards in the work areas of businesses subject to the Act. To ensure compliance, Congress authorized the Secretary of Labor to conduct routine, non-consensual inspections. Today the Court holds that the Fourth Amendment prohibits such inspections without a warrant. The Court also holds that the constitutionally required warrant may be issued without any showing of probable cause. I disagree with both of these holdings.

The Fourth Amendment contains two separate clauses, each flatly prohibiting a category of governmental conduct. The first clause states that the right to be free from unreasonable searches "shall not be violated"; the second unequivocally prohibits the issuance of warrants except "upon probable cause." In this case the ultimate question is whether the category of warrantless searches authorized by the statute is "unreasonable" within the meaning of the first clause.

In cases involving the investigation of criminal activity, the Court has held that the reasonableness of a search generally depends upon whether it was conducted pursuant to a valid warrant. . . . There is, however, also a category of searches which are reasonable within the meaning of the first clause even though the probable cause requirement of the Warrant Clause cannot be satisfied. . . . The regulatory inspection program challenged in this case, in my judgment, falls within this category.

I

The warrant requirement is linked "textually . . . to the probable-cause concept" in the Warrant Clause. *South Dakota* v. *Opperman* [1976]. . . . The routine OSHA inspections are, by definition, not based on cause to believe there is a violation on the premises to be inspected. Hence, if the inspections were measured against the requirements of the Warrant Clause, they would be automatically and unequivocally unreasonable.

Because of the acknowledged importance and reasonableness of routine inspections in the enforcement of federal regulatory statutes such as OSHA, the Court recognizes that requiring full compliance with the Warrant Clause would invalidate all such inspection programs. Yet, rather than simply analyzing such programs under the "reasonableness" clause of the Fourth Amendment, the Court holds the OSHA program invalid under the Warrant Clause and then avoids a blanket prohibition on all routine, regulatory inspections by relying on the notion that the "probable cause" requirement in the Warrant Clause may be relaxed whenever the Court believes that the governmental need to conduct a category of "searches" outweighs the intrusion on interests protected by the Fourth Amendment.

The Court's approach disregards the plain language of the Warrant Clause and is unfaithful to the balance struck by the Framers of the Fourth Amendment — "the one procedural safeguard in the Constitution that grew directly out of the events which immediately preceded the revolutionary struggle with England." This preconstitutional history includes the controversy in England over the issuance of general warrants to aid enforcement of the seditious libel laws and the colonial experience with writs of assistance issued to facilitate collection of the various import duties imposed by Parliament. The Framers' familiarity with the abuses attending the issuance of such general warrants provided the principal stimulus for the restraints on arbitrary governmental intrusions embodied in the Fourth Amendment. . . .

Since the general warrant, not the warrantless search, was the immediate evil at which the Fourth Amendment was directed, it is not surprising that the Framers placed precise limits on its issuance. The requirement that a warrant only issue on a showing of particularized probable cause was the means adopted to circumscribe the warrant power. While the subsequent course of Fourth Amendment jurisprudence in this Court emphasizes the dangers posed by warrantless searches conducted without probable cause, it is the general reasonableness standard in the first clause, not the Warrant Clause, that the Framers adopted to limit this category of searches. It is of course true that the existence of a valid warrant normally satisfies the reasonableness requirement under the Fourth Amendment. But we should not dilute the requirements of the Warrant Clause in an effort to force every kind of governmental intrusion which satisfies the Fourth Amendment definition of a "search" into a judiciary developed, warrant-preference scheme.

Fidelity to the original understanding of the Fourth Amendment, therefore, leads to the conclusion that the Warrant Clause has no application to routine, regulatory inspections of commercial premises. If such inspections are valid, it is because they comport with the ultimate reasonableness standard of the Fourth Amendment. If the Court were correct in its view that such inspections, if undertaken without a warrant, are unreasonable in the constitutional sense, the issuance of a "new-fangled warrant" — to use Mr. Justice Clark's characteristically expressive term — without any true showing of particularized probable cause would not be sufficient to validate them.

II

Even if a warrant issued without probable cause were faithful to the Warrant Clause, I could not accept the Court's holding that the Government's inspection program is constitutionally unreasonable because it fails to require such a warrant procedure. In determining whether a warrant is a necessary safeguard in a given class of cases, "the Court has weighed the public interest against the Fourth Amendment interest of the individual. . . ." *United States* v. *Martinez-Fuerte* [1976]. . . . Several considerations persuade me that this balance should be struck in favor of the routine inspections authorized by Congress.

Congress has determined that regulation and supervision of safety in the work place furthers an important public interest and that the power to conduct warrantless searches is necessary to accomplish the safety goals of the legislation. In assessing the public interest side of the Fourth Amendment balance, however, the Court today substitutes its judgment for that of Congress on the question of what inspection authority is needed to effectuate the purposes of the Act. The Court states that if surprise is truly an important ingredient of an effective, representative inspection program, it can be retained by obtaining *ex parte* warrants in advance. The Court assures the Secretary that this will not unduly burden enforcement resources because most employers will consent to inspection.

The Court's analysis does not persuade me that Congress' determination that the warrantless inspection power is a necessary adjunct of the exercise of the regulatory power is unreasonable. It was surely not unreasonable to conclude that the rate at which employers deny entry to inspectors would increase if covered businesses, which may have safety violations on their premises, have a right to deny warrantless entry to a compliance inspector. The Court is correct that this problem could be avoided by requiring inspectors to obtain a warrant prior to every inspection visit. But the adoption of such a practice undercuts the Court's explanation of why a warrant requirement would not create undue enforcement problems. For, even if it were true that many employers would not exercise their right to demand a warrant, it would provide little solace to those charged with administration of OSHA; faced with an increase in the rate of refusals and the added costs generated by futile trips to inspection sites where entry is denied, officials may be compelled to adopt a general practice of obtaining warrants in advance. While the Court's prediction of the effect a warrant requirement would have on the behavior of covered employers may turn out to be accurate, its judgment is essentially empirical. On such an issue, I would defer to Congress' judgment regarding the importance of a warrantless search power to the OSHA enforcement scheme.

The Court also appears uncomfortable with the notion of second-guessing Congress and the Secretary on the question of how the substantive goals of OSHA can best be achieved. Thus, the Court offers an alternative explanation for its refusal to accept the legislative judgment. We are told that, in any event, the Secretary, who is charged with enforcement of the Act, has indicated that inspections without delay are not essential to the enforcement scheme. The Court bases this conclusion on a regulation prescribing the administrative response when a compliance inspector is denied entry. . . . The Court views this regulation as an admission by the Secretary that no enforcement problem is generated by permitting employers to deny entry and delaying the inspection until a warrant has been obtained. I disagree. The regulation was promulgated against the background of a statutory right to immediate entry, of which covered employers are presumably aware and which Congress and the Secretary obviously thought would keep denials of entry to a minimum. In these circumstances, it was surely not unreasonable for the Secretary to adopt an orderly procedure for dealing with what he believed would be the occasional denial of entry. The regulation does not imply a judgment by the Secretary that delay caused by numerous denials of entry would be administratively acceptable.

Even if a warrant requirement does not "frustrate" the legislative purpose, the Court has no authority to impose an additional burden on the Secretary unless that burden is required to protect the employer's Fourth Amendment interests. The essential function of the traditional warrant requirement is the interposition of a neutral magistrate between the citizen and the presumably zealous law enforcement officer so that there might be an objective determination of probable cause. But this purpose is not served by the new-fangled inspection warrant. . . . [T]he only question for the magistrate's consideration is whether the contemplated inspection deviates from an inspection schedule drawn up by higher-level agency officials.

Unlike the traditional warrant, the inspection warrant provides no protection against the search itself for employers whom the government has no reason to suspect are violating OSHA regulation. The Court plainly accepts the proposition that random health and safety inspections are reasonable. It does not question Congress' determination that the public interest in work places free from health and safety hazards outweighs the employer's desire to conduct his business only in the presence of permittees, except in those rare instances when the government has probable cause to suspect that the premises harbor a violation of the law.

What purposes, then, are served by the administrative warrant procedure? The inspection warrant purports to serve three functions: to inform the employer that the inspection is authorized by the statute, to advise him of the lawful limits of the inspection, and to assure him that the person demanding entry is an authorized inspector. . . . An examination of these functions in the OSHA context reveals that the inspection warrant adds little to the protections already afforded by the statute and pertinent regulations, and the slight additional benefit it might provide is insufficient to identify a constitutional violation or to justify overriding Congress' judgment that the power to conduct warrantless inspections is essential.

The inspection warrant is supposed to assure the employer that the inspection is in fact routine, and that the inspector has not improperly departed from the program of representative inspections established by responsible officials. But to the extent that harassment inspections would be reduced by the necessity of obtaining a warrant, the Secretary's present enforcement scheme would have precisely the same effect. . . . If, under the present scheme, entry to covered premises is denied, the inspector can gain entry only by informing his administrative superiors of the refusal and seeking a court order requiring the employer to submit to the inspection. The inspector who would like to conduct a nonroutine search is just as likely to be deterred by the prospect of informing his superiors of his intention and of making false representations to the court when he seeks compulsory process as by the prospect of having to make bad-faith representations in an *ex parte* warrant proceeding.

The other two asserted purposes of the administrative warrant are also adequately achieved under the existing scheme. If the employer has doubts about the official status of the inspector, he is given adequate opportunity to reassure himself in this regard before permitting entry. The OSHA inspector's statutory right to enter the premises is conditioned upon the presentation of appropriate credentials. . . . These credentials state the inspector's name, identify him as an OSHA compliance officer, and contain his photograph and signature. If the employer still has doubts, he may make a toll free call to verify the inspector's authority . . . or simply deny entry and await the presentation of a court order.

The warrant is not needed to inform the employer of the lawful limits of an OSHA inspection. The statute expressly provides that the inspection may enter all areas in a covered business. . . . While it is true that the inspection power granted by Congress is broad, the warrant procedure required by the Court does not purport to restrict this power but simply to ensure that the employer is appraised of its scope. Since both the statute and the pertinent regulations perform this informational function, a warrant is superfluous.

Requiring the inspection warrant, therefore, adds little in the way of protection to that already provided under the existing enforcement scheme. In these circumstances, the warrant is essentially a formality. In view of the obviously enormous cost of enforcing a health and safety scheme of the dimensions of OSHA, this Court should not, in the guise of construing the Fourth Amendment, require formalities which merely place an additional strain on already overtaxed federal resources.

Congress, like this Court, has an obligation to obey the mandate of the Fourth Amendment. In the past the "Court has been particularly sensitive to the amendment's broad standard of 'reasonableness' where . . . authorizing statutes permitted the challenged searches." *Almeida-Sanchez* v. *United States* [1937]. . . . In *United States* v. *Martinez-Fuerte* . . . , for example, respondents challenged the routine stopping of vehicles to check for aliens at permanent checkpoints located away from the border. The checkpoints were established pursuant to statutory authority and their location and operation were governed by administrative criteria. The Court rejected respondents' argument that the constitutional reasonableness of the location and operation of the fixed checkpoints should be reviewed in a *Camara* warrant proceeding. The Court observed that the reassuring purposes of the inspection warrant were adequately served by the visible manifestations of authority exhibited at the fixed checkpoints.

Moreover, although the location and method of operation of the fixed checkpoints were deemed critical to the constitutional reasonableness of the challenged stops, the Court did not require Border Patrol officials to obtain a warrant based on a showing that the checkpoints were located and operated in accordance with administrative standards. Indeed, the Court observed that "[t]he choice of checkpoint locations must be left largely to the discretion of Border Patrol officials to be exercised in accordance with statutes and regulations that may be applicable . . . [and] [m]any incidents of checkpoint operation also must be committed to the discretion of such officials.". . . The Court had no difficulty assuming that those officials responsible for allocating limited enforcement resources would be "unlikely to locate a checkpoint where it bears arbitrarily or oppressively on motorists as a class.". . .

The Court's recognition of Congress' role in balancing the public interest advanced by various regulatory statutes and the private interest in being free from arbitrary governmental intrusion has not been limited to situations in which, for example, Congress is exercising its special power to exclude aliens. Until today we have not rejected a congressional judgment concerning the reasonableness of a category of regulatory inspections of commercial premises. While businesses are unquestionably entitled to Fourth Amendment protection, we have "recognized that a business, by its special nature and voluntary existence, may open itself to intrusions that would not be permissible in a purely private context." *G. M. Leasing Corp.* v. *United States* [1947]. . . . Thus, in *Colonnade Catering Corp.* v. *United States* . . . , the Court recognized the reasonableness of a statutory authorization to inspect the premises of a caterer dealing in alcoholic beverages, noting that "Congress has broad authority to design such powers of inspection under the liquor laws it deems necessary to meet the evils at hand.". . . And in *United States* v. *Biswell* . . . the Court sustained the authority to conduct warrantless searches of firearm dealers under the Gun Control Act of 1968 primarily on the basis of the reasonableness of the congressional evaluation of the interests at stake.

The Court, however, concludes that the deference accorded Congress in *Biswell* and *Colonnade* should be limited to situations where the evils addressed by the regulatory statute are peculiar to a specific industry and that industry is one which has long been subject to government regulation. The Court reasons that only in those situations can it be said that a person who engages in business will be aware of and consent to routine, regulatory inspections. I cannot agree that the respect due the congressional judgment should be so narrowly confined.

In the first place, the longevity of a regulatory program does not, in my judgment, have any bearing on the reasonableness of routine inspections necessary to achieve adequate enforcement of that program. Congress' conception of what constitute urgent federal interests need not remain static. The recent vintage of public and congressional awareness of the dangers post by health and safety hazards in the work place is not a basis for according less respect to the considered judgment of Congress. Indeed, in *Biswell*, the Court upheld an inspection program authorized by a regulatory statute enacted in 1968. Thus, the critical fact is the congressional determination that federal regulation would further significant public interests, not the date that determination was made.

In the second place, I see no basis for the Court's conclusion that a congressional determination that a category of regulatory inspections is reasonable need only be respected when Congress is legislating on an industry-by-industry basis. The pertinent inquiry is not whether the inspection program is authorized by a regulatory statute directed at a single industry but whether Congress has limited the exercise of the inspection power to those commercial premises where the evils at which the statute is directed are to be found. Thus, in *Biswell*, if Congress had authorized inspections of all commercial premises as a means of restricting the illegal traffic in firearms, the Court would have found the inspection program unreasonable; the power to inspect was upheld because it was tailored to the subject matter of Congress' proper exercise of regulatory power. Similarly, OSHA is directed at health and safety hazards in the work place, and the inspection power granted the Secretary extends only to those areas where such hazards are likely to be found.

Finally, the Court would distinguish the respect accorded Congress' judgment in *Colonnade* and *Biswell* on the ground that businesses engaged in the liquor and firearms industry "accept the burdens as well as the benefits of their trade. . . ." In the Court's view, such businesses consent to the restrictions placed upon them, while it would be fiction to conclude that a businessman subject to OSHA consented to routine safety inspections. In fact, however, consent is fictional in both contexts. Here, as well as in *Biswell*, businesses are required to be aware of and comply with regulations governing their business activities. In both situations, the validity of the regulations depends not upon the consent of those regulated but on the existence of a federal statute embodying a congressional determination that the public interest in the health of the Nation's work force or the limitation of illegal firearms traffic outweighs the businessman's interest in preventing a government inspector from viewing those areas of his premises which relate to the subject matter of the regulation.

The case before us involves an attempt to conduct a warrantless search of the working area of an electrical and plumbing contractor. The statute authorizes such an inspection during reasonable hours. The inspection is limited to those areas over which Congress has exercised its proper legislative authority. The area is also one to which employees have regular access without any suggestion that the work performed or the equipment used has any special claim to confidentiality. Congress has determined that industrial safety is an urgent federal interest requiring regulation and supervision, and further, that warrantless inspections are necessary to accomplish the safety goals of the legislation. While one may question the wisdom of pervasive governmental oversight of industrial life, I decline to question Congress' judgment that the inspection power is a necessary enforcement device in achieving the goals of a valid exercise of regulatory power.

I respectfully dissent.

COURT ON NEWSROOM SEARCHES

May 31, 1978

Newspaper offices enjoy no special protection from searches by police officers for information or evidence they expect to find if the officers have a warrant, the Supreme Court ruled May 31. Further, the court said that a person who is not involved in a crime in any way may not resist a search of his home for evidence of a crime related to someone else, if, again, the police officers have a warrant.

The 5-3 decision rejected the contention of the press generally that the issuance of a subpoena, not a warrant, was the proper method for the government to use in obtaining information held by, say, a newspaper. Under a subpoena journalists, for example, might be ordered to produce material that police believed was related to an investigation. If a newspaper believed that the material should not be given to the police, it could oppose the subpoena in a court hearing. A search warrant, on the other hand, could be issued without the knowledge of the subjects of the search.

The majority opinion was written by Justice Byron R. White; he was joined by Chief Justice Warren E. Burger and Justices Harry A. Blackmun, Lewis F. Powell Jr. and William H. Rehnquist. Dissenting were Justices Potter Stewart, Thurgood Marshall and John Paul Stevens. Justice William J. Brennan Jr. did not participate in the case because of illness.

The Case

The case arose in 1971 when police searched the offices of The Stanford Daily, *the student newspaper at Stanford University. The search took place after a campus antiwar demonstration developed into a melee between police and students. Several police officers were injured, and when the* Daily *carried photographs of the incident the police sought a warrant to search the* Daily *offices for photographs and other materials to help them identify the students who had assaulted the policemen. The newspaper later filed suit against the police, charging that the search, though fruitless, had violated constitutional rights, particularly those guaranteed by the First Amendment.*

The district court ruling, which was upheld by the U.S. Court of Appeals for the Ninth Circuit, said that the police should have first used a subpoena in an attempt to obtain the materials because no employee at the Daily *was suspected of having participated in a crime and because the search involved the constitutional protections guaranteed to the press.*

Majority Opinion

In his decision overturning the lower court's finding, Justice White dwelt on the applicability of warrants to an innocent "third party." He wrote, "Under existing law, valid warrants may be issued to search any *property, whether or not occupied by a third party, at which there is probable cause to believe that fruits, instrumentalities, or evidence of a crime will be found. . . . In situations where the State does not seek to seize 'persons' but only those 'things' which there is probable cause to believe are located on the place to be searched, there is no apparent basis in the language of the [Fourth] Amendment for also imposing the requirements for a valid arrest — probable cause to believe that the third party is implicated in the crime."*

White criticized the lower court ruling as an impediment to police investigative work: "Forbidding the warrant and insisting on the subpoena instead when the custodian of the object of the search is not then suspected of crime involves hazards to criminal investigation much more serious than the District Court believed. . . ."

The majority opinion rejected the argument that unannounced searches disrupted the functions of news businesses and concluded, "Properly administered, the preconditions for a warrant — probable cause, specificity with respect to the place to be searched and the things to be seized, and overall reasonableness — should afford sufficient protection against the harms that are assertedly threatened by warrants for searching newspaper offices."

In a concurring opinion, Justice Powell asserted that the men who wrote the Constitution meant that the Fourth Amendment applied to the press as well as citizens. And he predicted that abuses of warrants to search newsrooms would be "minimal" if the magistrates petitioned to issue warrants applied "reasonableness and particularity requirements."

Dissenting Opinions

"It seems to me self-evident," wrote Justice Stewart in his dissent, "that police searches of newspaper offices burden the freedom of the press." This is so, he said, because a search disrupts the operation of a newspaper and threatens the confidentiality of reporters' sources. Unannounced policy searches of newsrooms, Stewart argued, would result in "a diminishing flow of potentially important information to the public." He urged greater reliance on subpoenas duces tecum [Latin for "bring it with you"] as a means for gaining access to materials in the possession of a newspaper, except in cases in which there is cause to believe that the custodians of the subpoenaed materials are likely to destroy the materials or are themselves suspected of participation in criminal activity.

Justice Stevens based his separate dissenting opinion on the rights of the "innocent third party." He wrote, "In this case, the warrant application set forth no facts suggesting that respondent [The Stanford Daily] was involved in any wrongdoing or would destroy the desired evidence if given notice of what the police desired." Justice Stevens concluded, therefore, that the search was not reasonable under the terms of the First Clause of the Fourth Amendment.

Criticism of Decision

Protesting the court's ruling, Jack C. Landau, director of the Reporters Committee for Freedom of the Press, called it "a constitutional outrage to the First Amendment rights of every news organization and to the citizens they serve." He said that the police search of the Stanford newsroom had not been an isolated incident in the country.

In an editorial, The Washington Post said that the decision "threatens the privacy of every home and office in the country. . . ." Calling the possible abuses under the ruling "legion," the newspaper urged Congress to eliminate them "by passing legislation denying to federal judges the authority to issue warrants of this kind." By approving such a measure, The Washington Post said, Congress "would be sending a message to the Supreme Court that its whittling away of the Fourth Amendment has gone too far."

Following are excerpts from the Supreme Court's majority opinion, delivered May 31, 1978, upholding the right of police officers to search newsrooms and other places even if the persons therein were not suspected of criminal activity; Justice Powell's concurring opinion; Justice Stewart's dissent; and Justice Stevens' concurring dissent:

Nos. 76-1484 and 76-1600

James Zurcher, Etc., et al., Petitioners,
76-1484   v.
          The Stanford Daily et al.

Louis P. Bergna, District Attorney,
     and Craig Brown, Petitioners,
76-1600   v.
          The Stanford Daily et al.

On Writs of Certio-
rari to the United
States Court of
Appeals for the
Ninth Circuit.

[May 31, 1978]

MR JUSTICE WHITE delivered the opinion of the Court. [MR. JUS-
TICE BRENNAN took no part in the consideration or decision of this
case.]

The terms of the Fourth Amendment, applicable to the States by virtue
of the Fourteenth Amendment, are familiar:

"The right of the people to be secure in their persons, houses,
papers, and effects, against unreasonable searches and seizures, shall
not be violated, and no Warrants shall issue, but upon probable
cause, supported by Oath or affirmation, and particularly describing
the place to be searched, and the persons or things to be seized."

As heretofore understood, the Amendment has not been a barrier to
warrants to search property on which there is probable cause to believe that
fruits, instrumentalities, or evidence of crime is located, whether or not the
owner or possessor of the premises to be searched is himself reasonably
suspected of complicity in the crime being investigated. We are now asked
to reconstrue the Fourth Amendment and to hold for the first time that
when the place to be searched is occupied by a person not then a suspect, a
warrant to search for criminal objects and evidence reasonably believed to
be located there should not issue except in the most unusual circumstances,
and that except in such circumstances, a subpoena *duces tecum* must be
relied upon to recover the objects or evidence sought.

I

Late in the day on Friday, April 9, 1971, officers of the Palo Alto Police
Department and of the Santa Clara County Sheriff's Department
responded to a call from the director of the Stanford University Hospital requesting the removal of a large group of demonstrators who had seized the
hospital's administrative offices and occupied them since the previous
afternoon. After several futile efforts to persuade the demonstrators to leave
peacefully, more drastic measures were employed. The demonstrators had
barricaded the doors at both ends of a hall adjacent to the administrative
offices. The police chose to force their way in at the west end of the corridor.

As they did so, a group of demonstrators emerged through the doors at the east end and, armed with sticks and clubs, attacked the group of nine police officers stationed there. One officer was knocked to the floor and struck repeatedly on the head; another suffered a broken shoulder. All nine were injured. There were no police photographers at the east doors, and most bystanders and reporters were on the west side. The officers themselves were able to identify only two of their assailants, but one of them did see at least one person photographing the assault at the east doors.

On Sunday, April 11, a special edition of the Stanford Daily (Daily), a student newspaper published at Stanford University, carried articles and photographs devoted to the hospital protest and the violent clash between demonstrators and police. The photographs carried the byline of a Daily staff member and indicated that he had been at the east end of the hospital hallway where he could have photographed the assault on the nine officers. The next day, the Santa Clara County District Attorney's Office secured a warrant from the municipal court for an immediate search of the Daily's offices for negatives, film and pictures showing the events and occurrences at the hospital on the evening of April 9. The warrant issued on a finding of "just, probable and reasonable cause for believing that: Negatives and photographs and films, evidence material and relevant to the identification of the perpetrators of felonies, to wit, Battery on a Peace Officer, and Assault with a Deadly Weapon, will be located [on the premises of the Daily]." The warrant affidavit contained no allegation or indication that members of the Daily staff were in any way involved in unlawful acts at the hospital.

The search pursuant to the warrant was conducted later that day by four police officers and took place in the presence of some members of the Daily staff. The Daily's photographic laboratories, filing cabinets, desks, and waste paper baskets were searched. Locked drawers and rooms were not opened. The officers apparently had opportunity to read notes and correspondence during the search; but contrary to claims of the staff, the officers denied that they had exceeded the limits of the warrant. They had not been advised by the staff that the areas they were searching contained confidential materials. The search revealed only the photographs that had already been published on April 11, and no materials were removed from the Daily's office.

A month later the Daily and various members of its staff, respondents here, brought a civil action in the United States District Court for the Northern District of California seeking declaratory and injunctive relief under 42 U. S. C. § 1983 against the police officers who conducted the search, the chief of police, the district attorney and one of his deputies, and the judge who had issued the warrant. The complaint alleged that the search of the Daily office had deprived respondents under color of state law of rights secured to them by the First, Fourth, and Fourteenth Amendments of the United States Constitution.

The District Court denied the request for an injunction but on respondents' motion for summary judgment, granted . . . declaratory relief. The court did not question the existence of probable cause to believe that a crime had been committed and to believe that relevant evidence would be found on the Daily's premises. It held, however, that the Fourth and Fourteenth Amendments forbade the issuance of a warrant to search for materials in possession of one not suspected of crime unless there is probable cause to believe, based on facts presented in a sworn affidavit, that a subpoena *duces tecum* would be impracticable. Moreover, the failure to honor a subpoena would not alone justify a warrant; it must also appear that the possessor of the objects sought would disregard a court order not to remove or destroy them. The District Court further held that where the innocent object of the search is a newspaper, First Amendment interests are also involved and that such a search is constitutionally permissible "only in the rare circumstance where there is a *clear showing* that (1) important materials will be destroyed or removed from the jurisdiction; *and* (2) a restraining order would be futile." . . . Since these preconditions to a valid warrant had not been satisfied here, the search of the Daily's offices was declared to have been illegal. The Court of Appeals affirmed *per curiam,* adopting the opinion of the District Court. . . . We issued the writs of certiorari requested by petitioners. . . . We reverse.

II

The issue here is how the Fourth Amendment is to be construed and applied to the "third party" search, the recurring situation where state authorities have probable cause to believe that fruits, instrumentalities, or other evidence of crime is located on identified property but do not then have probable cause to believe that the owner or possessor of the property is himself implicated in the crime that has occurred or is occurring. Because under the District Court's rule impracticability can be shown only by furnishing facts demonstrating that the third party will not only disobey the subpoena but will also ignore a restraining order not to move or destroy the property, it is apparent that only in unusual situations could the State satisfy such a severe burden and that for all practical purposes the effect of the rule is that fruits, instrumentalities, and evidence of crime may be recovered from third parties only by subpoena, not by search warrant. At least, we assume that the District Court did not intend its rule to be toothless and anticipated that only subpoenas would be available in many cases where without the rule a search warrant would issue.

It is an understatement to say that there is no direct authority in this or any other federal court for the District Court's sweeping revision of the Fourth Amendment. Under existing law, valid warrants may be issued to search *any* property, whether or not occupied by a third party, at which there is probable cause to believe that fruits, instrumentalities, or evidence of a crime will be found. Nothing on the face of the Amendment suggests that a third-party search warrant should not normally issue. The warrant clause speaks of search warrants issued on "probable cause" and "particularly describing the place to be searched and the persons or things to be seized." In situations where the State does not seek to seize "persons" but only those "things" which there is probable cause to believe are located on the place to be searched, there is no apparent basis in the language of the Amendment for also imposing the requirements for a valid arrest — probable cause to believe that the third party is implicated in the crime.

As the Fourth Amendment has been construed and applied by this Court, "when the State's reason to believe incriminating evidence will be found becomes sufficiently great, the invasion of privacy becomes justified and a warrant to search and seize will issue." *Fisher* v. *United States* . . . (1976). In *Camera* v. *Municipal Court* . . . (1967), we indicated that in applying the "probable cause" standard "by which a particular decision to search is tested against the constitutional standard of reasonableness," it is necessary "to focus upon the governmental interest which allegedly justifies the official intrusion" and that in criminal investigations, a warrant to search for recoverable items is reasonable "only when there is 'probable cause' to believe they will be uncovered in a particular dwelling." Search warrants are not directed at persons; they authorize the search of "places" and the seizure of "things," and as a constitutional matter they need not even name the person from whom the things will be seized. *United States* v. *Kahn* . . . (1974).

Because the State's interest in enforcing the criminal law and recovering evidence is the same whether the third party is culpable or not, the premise of the District Court's holding appears to be that State entitlement to a search warrant depends on the culpability of the owner or possessor of the place to be searched and on the State's right to arrest him. The cases are to the contrary. Prior to *Camara* v. *Municipal Court* . . . and *See* v. *City of Seattle* . . . (1967), the central purpose of the Fourth Amendment was seen to be the protection of the individual against official searches for evidence to convict him of a crime. Entries upon property for civil purposes, where the occupant was suspected of no criminal conduct whatsoever, involved a more peripheral concern and the less intense "right to be secure from intrusion into personal privacy." *Frank* v. *Maryland* . . . (1959); *Camara* v. *Municipal Court.* . . . Such searches could proceed without warrant, as long as the State's interest was sufficiently substantial. Under this view, the Fourth Amendment was *more* protective where the place to be searched was occupied by one suspected of crime and the search was for evidence to use against him. *Camara* and *See,* disagreeing with *Frank* to this extent, held that a warrant *is* required where entry is sought for *civil* purposes, as well as when criminal law enforcement is involved. Neither case, however, suggested that to secure a search warrant the owner or occupant of the place to be inspected or searched must be suspected of criminal involvement. Indeed, both cases held that a less stringent standard of probable cause is acceptable where the entry is not to secure evidence of crime against the possessor.

We have suggested nothing to the contrary since *Camara* and *See.* . . .

The critical element in a reasonable search is not that the owner of the property is suspected of crime but that there is reasonable cause to believe that the specific "things" to be searched for and seized are located on the property to which entry is sought. . . .

Rule 41 of the Federal Rules of Criminal Procedure . . . authorizes warrants to search for contraband, fruits or instrumentalities of crime or "any . . . property that constitutes evidence of the commission of a criminal offense. . . ." Upon proper showing, the warrant is to issue "identifying the property and naming or describing the person or place to be searched." Probable cause for the warrant must be presented, but there is nothing in the Rule indicating that the officers must be entitled to arrest the owner of the "place" to be searched before a search warrant may issue and the "property" may be searched for and seized. The Rule deals with warrants to search, and is unrelated to arrests. Nor is there anything in the Fourth Amendment indicating that absent probable cause to arrest a third party, resort must be had to a subpoena.

The Court of Appeals for the Sixth Circuit expressed the correct view of Rule 41 and of the Fourth Amendment when, disagreeing with the decisions of the Court of Appeals and the District Court in the present case, it ruled that "[o]nce it is established that probable cause exists to believe a federal crime has been committed a warrant may issue for the search of any property which the magistrate has probable cause to believe may be the place of concealment of evidence of the crime.". . .

The net of the matter is that "[s]earches and seizures, in a technical sense, are independent of, rather than ancillary to, arrest and arraignment." American Law Institute, A Model Code of Pre-Arraignment Procedure, Commentary 491 (1975). The Model Code provides that the warrant application "shall describe with particularity the individuals or places to be searched and the individuals or things to be seized, and shall be supported by one or more affidavits particularly setting forth the facts and circumstances tending to show that such individuals or things are or will be in the places, or the things are or will be in possession of the individuals, to be searched.". . . There is no suggestion that the occupant of the place to be searched must himself be implicated in misconduct.

Against this background, it is untenable to conclude that property may not be searched unless its occupant is reasonably suspected of crime and is subject to arrest. And if those considered free of criminal involvement may nevertheless be searched or inspected under civil statutes, it is difficult to understand why the Fourth Amendment would prevent entry onto their property to recover evidence of a crime not committed by them but by others. As we understand the structure and language of the Fourth Amendment and our cases expounding it, valid warrants to search property may be issued when it is satisfactorily demonstrated to the magistrate that fruits, instrumentalities, or evidence of crime is located on the premises. The Fourth Amendment has itself struck the balance between privacy and public need, and there is no occasion or justification for a court to revise the Amendment and strike a new balance by denying the search warrant in the circumstances present here and by insisting that the investigation proceed by subpoena *duces tecum*, whether on the theory that the latter is a less intrusive alternative, or otherwise.

This is not to question that "reasonableness" is the overriding test of compliance with the Fourth Amendment or to assert that searches, however or whenever executed, may never be unreasonable if supported by a warrant issued on probable cause and properly identifying the place to be searched and the property to be seized. We do hold, however, that the courts may not, in the name of Fourth Amendment reasonableness, forbid the States from issuing warrants to search for evidence simply because the owner or possessor of the place to be searched is not then reasonably suspected of criminal involvement.

III

In any event, the reasons presented by the District Court and adopted by the Court of Appeals for arriving at its remarkable conclusion do not withstand analysis. First, we have said, it is apparent that whether the third-party occupant is suspect or not, the State's interest in enforcing the criminal law and recovering the evidence remains the same; and it is the seeming innocence of the property owner that the District Court relied on to foreclose the warrant to search. But as respondents themselves now concede, if the third party knows that contraband or other illegal materials are on his property, he is sufficiently culpable to justify the issuance of a search warrant. Similarly, if his ethical stance is the determining factor, it seems to us that whether or not he knows that the sought-after articles are secreted on his property and whether or not he knows that the articles are in fact the fruits, instrumentalities, or evidence of crime, he will be so informed when the search warrant is served, and it is doubtful that he should then be permitted to object to the search, to withhold, if it is there, the evidence of crime reasonably believed to be possessed by him or secreted on his property, and to forbid the search and insist that the officers serve him with a subpoena *duces tecum*.

Second, we are unpersuaded that the District Court's new rule denying search warrants against third parties and insisting on subpoenas would substantially further privacy interests without seriously undermining law enforcement efforts. Because of the fundamental public interest in implementing the criminal law, the search warrant, a heretofore effective and constitutionally acceptable enforcement tool, should not be suppressed on the basis of surmise and without solid evidence supporting the change. As the District Court understands it, denying third-party search warrants would not have substantial adverse effects on criminal investigations because the nonsuspect third party, once served with a subpoena, will preserve the evidence and ultimately lawfully respond. The difficulty with this assumption is that search warrants are often employed early in an investigation, perhaps before the identity of any likely criminal and certainly before all the perpetrators are or could be known. The seemingly blameless third party in possession of the fruits or evidence may not be innocent at all; and if he is, he may nevertheless be so related to or so sympathetic with the culpable that he cannot be relied upon to retain and preserve the articles that may implicate his friends, or at least not to notify those who would be damaged by the evidence that the authorities are aware of its location. In any event, it is likely that the real culprits will have access to the property, and the delay involved in employing the subpoena *duces tecum,* offering as it does the opportunity to litigate its validity, could easily result in the disappearance of the evidence, whatever the good faith of the third party.

Forbidding the warrant and insisting on the subpoena instead when the custodian of the object of the search is not then suspected of crime, involves hazards to criminal investigation much more serious than the District Court believed; and the record is barren of anything but the District Court's assumptions to support its conclusions. At the very least, the burden of justifying a major revision of the Fourth Amendment has not been carried.

We are also not convinced that the net gain to privacy interests by the District Court's new rule would be worth the candle. In the normal course of events, search warrants are more difficult to obtain than subpoenas, since the latter do not involve the judiciary and do not require proof of probable cause. Where, in the real world, subpoenas would suffice, it can be expected that they will be employed by the rational prosecutor. On the other hand, when choice is available under local law and the prosecutor chooses to use the search warrant, it is unlikely that he has needlessly selected the more difficult course. His choice is more likely to be based on the solid belief, arrived at through experience but difficult, if not impossible, to sustain in a specific case, that the warranted search is necessary to secure and to avoid the destruction of evidence.

IV

The District Court held, and respondents assert here, that whatever may be true of third-party searches generally, where the third party is a newspaper, there are additional factors derived from the First Amendment that justify a nearly *per se* rule forbidding the search warrant and permitting only the subpoena *duces tecum.* The general submission is that searches of newspaper offices for evidence of crime reasonably believed to be on the premises will seriously threaten the ability of the press to gather, analyze, and disseminate news. This is said to be true for several reasons: first, searches will be physically disruptive to such an extent that timely publication will be impeded. Second, confidential sources of information will dry up, and the press will also lose opportunities to cover various events because of fears of the participants that press files will be readily available to the authorities. Third, reporters will be deterred from recording and preserving their recollections for future use if such information is subject to seizure. Fourth, the processing of news and its dissemination will be chilled by the prospects that searches will disclose internal editorial deliberations. Fifth, the press will resort to self-censorship to conceal its possession of information of potential interest to the police.

It is true that the struggle from which the Fourth Amendment emerged "is largely a history of conflict between the Crown and the press," *Stanford* v. *Texas* . . . (1965), and that in issuing warrants and determining the reasonableness of a search, state and federal magistrates should be aware that "unrestricted power of search and seizure could also be an instrument for stifling liberty of expression." *Marcus* v. *Search Warrant* . . . (1961). Where the materials sought to be seized may be protected by the First Amendment, the requirements of the Fourth Amendment must be applied with "scrupulous exactitude." *Stanford* v. *Texas.* . . . "A seizure reasonable as to one type of material in one setting may be unreasonable in a different setting or with respect to another kind of material." *Roaden* v. *Kentucky,* . . . (1973). Hence, in *Stanford* v. *Texas,* the Court invalidated a warrant authorizing the search of a private home for all books, records, and other materials relating to the Communist Party, on the ground that whether or not the warrant would have been sufficient in other contexts, it authorized the searchers to rummage among and make judgments about books and papers and was the functional equivalent of a general warrant, one of the principal targets of the Fourth Amendment. Where presumptively protected materials are sought to be seized, the warrant requirement should be administered to leave as little as possible to the discretion or whim of the officer in the field. . . .

Neither the Fourth Amendment nor the cases requiring consideration of First Amendment values in issuing search warrants, however, call for imposing the regime ordered by the District Court. Aware of the long struggle between Crown and press and desiring to curb unjustified official intrusions, the Framers took the enormously important step of subjecting searches to the test of reasonableness and to the general rule requiring search warrants issued by neutral magistrates. They nevertheless did not forbid warrants where the press was involved, did not require special showings that subpoenas would be impractical, and did not insist that the owner of the place to be searched, if connected with the press, must be shown to be implicated in the offense being investigated. Further, the prior cases do no more than insist that the courts apply the warrant requirements with particular exactitude when First Amendment interests would be endangered by the search. As we see it, no more than this is required where the warrant requested is for the seizure of criminal evidence reasonably believed to be on the premises occupied by a newspaper. Properly administered, the preconditions for a warrant — probable cause, specificity with respect to the place to be searched and the things to be seized, and overall reasonableness — should afford sufficient protection against the harms that are assertedly threatened by warrants for searching newspaper offices.

There is no reason to believe, for example, that magistrates cannot guard against searches of the type, scope, and intrusiveness that would actually interfere with the timely publication of a newspaper. Nor, if the requirements of specificity and reasonableness are properly applied, policed, and observed, will there be any occasion or opportunity for officers to rummage at large in newspaper files or to intrude into or to deter normal editorial and publication decisions. The warrant issued in this case authorized nothing of this sort. Nor are we convinced, anymore than we were in *Branzburg* v. *Hayes* . . . (1972), that confidential sources will disappear and that the press will suppress news because of fears of warranted searches. Whatever incremental effect there may be in this regard if search warrants, as well as subpoenas, are permissible in proper circumstances, it does not make a constitutional difference in our judgment.

The fact is that respondents and *amici* have pointed to only a very few instances in the entire United States since 1971 involving the issuance of warrants for searching newspaper premises. This reality hardly suggests abuse; and if abuse occurs, there will be time enough to deal with it. Furthermore, the press is not only an important, critical, and valuable asset to society, but it is not easily intimidated — nor should it be.

Respondents also insist that the press should be afforded opportunity to litigate the State's entitlement to the material it seeks before it is turned over or seized and that whereas the search warrant procedure is defective in this respect, resort to the subpoena would solve the problem. The Court has held that a restraining order imposing a prior restraint upon free expression is invalid for want of notice and opportunity for a hearing, *Carroll* v. *Princess Anne* . . . (1968), and that seizures not merely for use as evidence but entirely removing arguably protected materials from circulation may be effected only after an adversary hearing and a judicial finding of obscenity. *A Quantity of Books* v. *Kansas* . . . (1964). But presumptively protected materials are not necessarily immune from seizure under warrant for use at a criminal trial. Not every such seizure, and not even most, will impose a prior restraint. . . . And surely a warrant to search newspaper premises for criminal evidence such as the one issued here for news photographs taken in a public place carries no realistic threat of prior restraint or of any direct restraint whatsoever on the publication of the Daily or on its communication of ideas. The hazards of such warrants can be avoided by a neutral magistrate carrying out his responsibilities under the Fourth Amendment, for he has ample tools at his disposal to confine warrants to search within reasonable limits.

We note finally that if the evidence sought by warrant is sufficiently connected with the crime to satisfy the probable cause requirement, it will very likely be sufficiently relevant to justify a subpoena and to withstand a motion to quash. Further, Fifth Amendment and state shield law objections that might be asserted in opposition to compliance with a subpoena are largely irrelevant to determining the legality of a search warrant under the Fourth Amendment. Of course, the Fourth Amendment does not prevent or advise against legislative or executive efforts to establish nonconstitutional protections against possible abuses of the search warrant procedure, but we decline to reinterpret the Amendment to impose a general constitutional barrier against warrants to search newspaper premises, to require resort to subpoenas as a general rule, or to demand prior notice and hearing in connection with the issuance of search warrants.

V

We accordingly reject the reasons given by the District Court and adopted by the Court of Appeals for holding the search for photographs at the *Stanford Daily* to have been unreasonable within the meaning of the Fourth Amendment and in violation of the First Amendment. Nor has anything else presented here persuaded us that the Amendments forbade this search. It follows that the judgment of the Court of Appeals is reversed.

So ordered. . . .

MR. JUSTICE POWELL, concurring.

I join the opinion of the Court, and I write simply to emphasize what I take to be the fundamental error of MR. JUSTICE STEWART'S dissenting opinion. As I understand that opinion, it would read into the Fourth Amendment, as a new and *per se* exception, the rule that any search of an entity protected by the Press Clause of the First Amendment is unreasonable so long as a subpoena could be used as a substitute procedure. Even aside from the difficulties involved in deciding on a case-by-case basis whether a subpoena can serve as an adequate substitute. I agree with the Court that there is no constitutional basis for such a reading.

If the Framers had believed that the press was entitled to a special procedure, not available to others, when government authorities required evidence in its possession, one would have expected the terms of the Fourth Amendment to reflect that belief. . . .

This is not to say that a warrant which would be sufficient to support the search of an apartment or an automobile necessarily would be reasonable in supporting the search of a newspaper office. As the Court's opinion makes clear . . ., the magistrate must judge the reasonableness of every warrant in light of the circumstances of the particular case, carefully considering the description of the evidence sought, the situation of the premises, and the position and interests of the owner or occupant. While there is no justification for the establishment of a separate Fourth Amendment procedure for the press, a magistrate asked to issue a warrant for the search of press offices can and should take cognizance of the independent values protected by the First Amendment — such as those highlighted by MR. JUSTICE STEWART — when he weighs such factors. If the reasonableness and particularity requirements are thus applied, the dangers are likely to be minimal. . . .

In any event, considerations such as these are the province of the Fourth Amendment. There is no authority either in history or in the Constitution itself for exempting certain classes of persons or entities from its reach.

MR. JUSTICE STEWART, with whom MR. JUSTICE MARSHALL joins, dissenting.

Believing that the search by the police of the offices of The Stanford Daily infringed the First and Fourteenth Amendments' guarantee of a free press, I respectfully dissent.

I

It seems to me self-evident that police searches of newspaper offices burden the freedom of the press. The most immediate and obvious First Amendment injury caused by such a visitation by the police is physical disruption of the operation of the newspaper. Policemen occupying a newsroom and searching it thoroughly for what may be an extended period of time will inevitably interrupt its normal operations, and thus impair or even temporarily prevent the processes of newsgathering, writing, editing, and publishing. By contrast, a subpoena would afford the newspaper itself an opportunity to locate whatever material might be requested and produce it.

But there is another and more serious burden on a free press imposed by an unannounced police search of a newspaper office: the possibility of disclosure of information received from confidential sources, or of the identity of the sources themselves. Protection of those sources is necessary to ensure that the press can fulfill its constitutionally designated function of informing the public; because important information can often be obtained only by an assurance that the source will not be revealed. *Branzburg* v. *Hayes* [1972] . . . (dissenting opinion). And the Court has recognized that " 'without some protection for seeking out the news, freedom of the press could be eviscerated.' " *Pell* v. *Procunier* [1974] . . . .

A search warrant allows police officers to ransack the files of a newspaper, reading each and every document until they have found the one named in the warrant, while a subpoena would permit the newspaper itself to produce only the specific documents requested. A search, unlike a subpoena, will therefore lead to the needless exposure of confidential information completely unrelated to the purpose of the investigation. The knowledge that police officers can make an unannounced raid on a newsroom is thus bound to have a deterrent effect on the availability of confidential news sources. The end result, wholly inimical to the First Amendment, will be a diminishing flow of potentially important information to the public.

One need not rely on mere intuition to reach this conclusion. The record in this case includes affidavits not only from members of the staff of The Stanford Daily but from many professional journalists and editors, attesting to precisely such personal experience. Despite the Court's rejection of this uncontroverted evidence, I believe it clearly establishes that unannounced police searches of newspaper offices will significantly burden the constitutionally protected function of the press to gather news and report it to the public.

II

In *Branzburg* v. *Hayes* . . . the more limited disclosure of a journalist's sources caused by compelling him to testify was held to be justified by the necessity of "pursuing and prosecuting those crimes reported to the press by informants and in thus deterring the commission of such crimes in the future.". . .The Court found that these important societal interests would be frustrated if a reporter were able to claim an absolute privilege for his confidential sources. In the present case, however, the respondents do not claim that any of the evidence sought was privileged from disclosure; they claim only that a subpoena would have served equally well to produce that evidence. Thus, we are not concerned with the principle, central to *Branzburg*, that " 'the public . . . has a right to every man's evidence,' " . . . but only with whether any significant societal interest would be impaired if the police were generally required to obtain evidence from the press by means of a subpoena rather than a search.

It is well to recall the actual circumstances of this case. The application for a warrant showed only that there was reason to believe that photographic evidence of assaults on the police would be found in the offices of The Stanford Daily. There was no emergency need to protect life or property by an immediate search. The evidence sought was not contraband, but material obtained by the Daily in the normal exercise of its journalistic function. Neither the Daily nor any member of its staff was suspected of criminal activity. And there was no showing the Daily would not respond to a subpoena commanding production of the photographs, or that for any other reason a subpoena could not be obtained. Surely, then, a subpoena *duces tecum* would have been just as effective as a police raid in obtaining the production of the material sought by the Santa Clara County District Attorney.

The District Court and the Court of Appeals clearly recognized that *if* the affidavits submitted with a search warrant application should demonstrate probable cause to believe that a subpoena would be impractical, the magistrate must have the authority to issue a warrant. In such a case, by definition, a subpoena would not be adequate to protect the relevant societal interest. But they held, and I agree, that a warrant should issue only after the magistrate has performed the careful "balanc[ing] of these vital constitutional and societal interests." *Branzburg* v. *Hayes* . . . (concurring opinion of MR. JUSTICE POWELL).

The decisions of this Court establish that a prior adversary judicial hearing is generally required to assess in advance any threatened invasion of First Amendment liberty. A search by police officers affords no timely opportunity for such a hearing, since a search warrant is ordinarily issued *ex parte* upon the affidavit of a policeman or prosecutor. There is no opportunity to challenge the necessity for the search until after it has occurred and the constitutional protection of the newspaper has been irretrievably invaded.

On the other hand, a subpoena would allow a newspaper, through a motion to quash, an opportunity for an adversary hearing with respect to the production of any material which a prosecutor might think is in its possession. This very principle was emphasized in the *Branzburg* case. . . .

If, in the present case, The Stanford Daily had been served with a subpoena, it would have had an opportunity to demonstrate to the court what the police ultimately found to be true — that the evidence sought did not exist. The legitimate needs of government thus would have been served without infringing the freedom of the press.

III

Perhaps as a matter of abstract policy a newspaper office should receive no more protection from unannounced police searches than, say, the office of a doctor or the office of a bank. But we are here to uphold a Constitution. And our Constitution does not explicitly protect the practice of medicine or the business of banking from all abridgment by government. It does explicitly protect the freedom of the press.

For these reasons I would affirm the judgment of the Court of Appeals.

MR. JUSTICE STEVENS, dissenting.

The novel problem presented by this case is an outgrowth of the profound change in Fourth Amendment law that occurred in 1967, when *Warden* v. *Hayden* . . . was decided. The question is what kind of "probable cause" must be established in order to obtain a warrant to conduct an unannounced search for documentary evidence in the private files of a person not suspected of involvement in any criminal activity. The Court holds that a reasonable belief that the files contain relevant evidence is a sufficient justification. This holding rests on a misconstruction of history and of the Fourth Amendment's purposely broad language.

The Amendment contains two clauses, one protecting "persons, houses, papers, and effects, against unreasonable searches and seizures," the other regulating the issuance of warrants: "no Warrants shall issue, but upon probable cause, supported by Oath or affirmation, and particularly describing the place to be searched, and the persons or things to be seized." When these words were written, the procedures of the Warrant Clause were not the primary protection against oppressive searches. It is unlikely that the authors expected private papers ever to be among the "things" that could be seized with a warrant, for only a few years earlier, in 1765, Lord Camden had delivered his famous opinion denying that any magistrate had power to authorize the seizure of private papers. Because all such seizures were considered unreasonable, the Warrant Clause was not framed to protect against them.

Nonetheless, the authors of the Clause used words that were adequate for situations not expressly contemplated at the time. . . . Today, for the first time, the Court has an opportunity to consider the kind of showing that is necessary to justify the vastly expanded "degree of intrusion" upon privacy that is authorized by the opinion in *Warden* v. *Hayden*. . . .

In the pre-*Hayden* era warrants were used to search for contraband, weapons and plunder, but not for "mere evidence." The practical effect of the rule prohibiting the issuance of warrants to search for mere evidence was to narrowly limit not only the category of objects, but also the category of persons and the character of the privacy interests that might be affected by an unannounced police search.

Just as the witnesses who participate in an investigation or a trial far outnumber the defendants, the persons who possess evidence that may help to identify an offender, or explain an aspect of a criminal transaction, far outnumber those who have custody of weapons or plunder. Countless law abiding citizens — doctors, lawyers, merchants, customers, bystanders — may have documents in their possession that relate to an ongoing criminal investigation. The consequences of subjecting this large category of persons to unannounced police searches are extremely serious. The *ex parte* warrant procedure enables the prosecutor to obtain access to privileged documents that could not be examined if advance notice gave the custodian an opportunity to object. The search for the documents described in a warrant may involve the inspection of files containing other private matter. The dramatic character of a sudden search may cause an entirely unjustified injury to the reputation of the persons searched.

Of greatest importance, however, is the question whether the offensive intrusion on the privacy of the ordinary citizen is justified by the law enforcement interest it is intended to vindicate. Possession of contraband or the proceeds or tools of crime gives rise to two inferences: that the custodian is involved in the criminal activity, and that, if given notice of an intended search, he will conceal or destroy what is being sought. The probability of criminal culpability justifies the invasion of his privacy; the need to accomplish the law enforcement purpose of the search justifies acting without advance notice and by force, if necessary. By satisfying the probable cause standard appropriate for weapons or plunder, the police effectively demonstrate that no less intrusive method of investigation will succeed.

Mere possession of documentary evidence, however, is much less likely to demonstrate that the custodian is guilty of any wrongdoing or that he will not honor a subpoena or informal request to produce it. In the pre-*Hayden* era, evidence of that kind was routinely obtained by procedures that presumed that the custodian would respect his obligation to obey subpoenas and to cooperate in the investigation of crime. These procedures had a constitutional dimension. For the innocent citizen's interest in the privacy of his papers and possessions is an aspect of liberty protected by the Due Process Clause of the Fourteenth Amendment. Notice and an opportunity to object to the deprivation of the citizen's liberty are, therefore, the constitutionally mandated general rule. An exception to that rule can only be justified by strict compliance with the Fourth Amendment. That Amendment flatly prohibits the issuance of any warrant unless justified by probable cause.

A showing of probable cause that was adequate to justify the issuance of a warrant to search for stolen goods in the 18th century does not automatically satisfy the new dimensions of the Fourth Amendment in the post-*Hayden* era. In *Hayden* itself, the Court recognized that the meaning of probable cause should be reconsidered in the light of the new authority it conferred on the police. The only conceivable justification for an unannounced search of an innocent citizen is the fear that, if notice were given, he would conceal or destroy the object of the search. Probable cause to believe that the custodian is a criminal, or that he holds a criminal's weapons, spoils, or the like, justifies that fear, and therefore such a showing complies with the Clause. But if nothing said under oath in the warrant application demonstrates the need for an unannounced search by force, the probable cause requirement is not satisfied. In the absence of some other showing of reasonableness, the ensuing search violates the Fourth Amendment.

In this case, the warrant application set forth no facts suggesting that respondent was involved in any wrongdoing or would destroy the desired evidence if given notice of what the police desired. I would therefore hold that the warrant did not comply with the Warrant Clause and that the search was unreasonable within the meaning of the First Clause of the Fourth Amendment.

I respectfully dissent.

CARTER'S NATO SPEECH
May 31, 1978

Addressing the heads of government of the 15-member North Atlantic Treaty Organization (NATO) May 31, President Carter pledged that the United States "is prepared to use all the forces necessary" — including the use of nuclear weapons — "for the defense of the NATO area."

The president's remarks came at the conclusion of a two-day NATO summit conference in Washington, during which the Western leaders agreed on a comprehensive set of guidelines for the alliance's defense over a 10- 15-year period. Carter praised the Long-Term Defense Program as "an unprecedented attempt by NATO to look across a longer span of years than ever before." At the same time, however, he noted that "no procedures have yet been devised for ensuring that [the program] is carried out. We must avoid bold programs heartily endorsed — then largely ignored."

The cost of the long-range program was estimated at $60 billion to $80 billion. The plan emphasized a buildup of anti-tank weapons in central Europe and an integrated allied air defense. The guidelines also focused on increased defenses against chemical, nuclear and biological warfare; on a "coherent alliance command control and communications capability over time"; on provisions for more rapid reinforcement of U.S. troops in the event of an attack by Warsaw Pact forces; and on efforts to increase ammunition stocks to allow soldiers to fight longer.

In remarks at the opening session of the conference May 30, the president had noted that "in the past year, the United States has increased its conventional combat strength in Europe and is enhancing its capability for rapid deployment to the continent. U.S. theater nuclear forces are being modernized, and the United States will maintain strategic nuclear equivalence with the Soviet Union."

Concern with Africa

Much of the discussion during the two-day conference concerned the growing Soviet penetration in Africa and how NATO should respond to it. Carter emphasized the African problem in his May 30 speech, warning that "as members of the world's greatest alliance, we cannot be indifferent" to the activities of the Soviet Union and Cuba in Africa.

However, there appeared to be divisions among the NATO leaders on the nature of the alliance's response to the African situation. In their final communiqué, which did not refer directly to Soviet involvement in Africa, the heads of government warned the USSR that its actions "cannot but jeopardize the further improvement of East-West relations." The statement also cited "repeated instances in which the Soviet Union and some of its allies have exploited situations of instability and regional conflict in the developing worlds."

> *Following are the texts of President Carter's remarks at the Washington, D.C., NATO conference May 31 and the final communiqué summarizing the Long-Term Defense Program endorsed at the conference:* (Boldface headings in brackets have been added by Congressional Quarterly to highlight the organization of the text of Carter's speech.)

CARTER MAY 31 SPEECH

Thank you, Mr. Secretary General.

These briefings illustrate the magnitude of the challenges we face. They do not justify alarm, but they should strengthen our resolve.

When I took office 16 months ago, I reviewed the condition of U.S. defenses. I found them strong, although needing improvement. In particular, I concluded that the United States should give top priority to Europe, especially the conventional defenses needed in the initial stages of a conflict.

I reached this conclusion for two reasons. First, the Warsaw Pact countries, especially the Soviet Union, have steadily expanded and modernized their conventional forces beyond any legitimate requirement for defense. They are now able to attack with large armored forces more rapidly than we previously believed. Second, although U.S. nuclear forces remain strong and are fundamental to deterrence, the long-recognized role of conventional forces in deterrence of war is increasingly important.

As a result, I directed the Secretary of Defense to strengthen initial conventional defense capacity in Europe. Of course, such efforts would amount to little unless accompanied by improvements in the conventional capacity of our NATO allies. European NATO countries, not the United States, provide the bulk of our military forces in Europe. Also, the competing demands of our free societies limit the portion of our resources we can use for defense. Therefore, we must coordinate our defense planning to make the best use of these limited resources.

From our discussions in London last year, I know that you share my view of the challenges we face. The answers we have developed together are impressive. We are all making significant real increases in our defense budgets. We are strengthening our national forces — and we will do more. Finally, we have designed a bold Long-Term Defense Program to pull together a more effective collective defense during the years ahead.

[Nuclear Forces]

As we improve our conventional defenses, we must remember that the strength of our strategic and theater nuclear forces is also necessary for deterrence and defense. These forces are — and will be — fully adequate. Arms control can make deterrence more stable and perhaps less burdensome — but it will not, in the foreseeable future, eliminate the need for nuclear forces.

For years, the Alliance has relied principally on American strategic forces for deterring nuclear attack on Europe. This coupling of American strategic forces to Europe is critical, for it means that an attack on Europe would have the full consequences of an attack on the United States. Let there be no misunderstanding. The United States is prepared to use *all* the forces necessary for the defense of the NATO area.

As an Alliance, we must continue to review our nuclear deterrence needs in light of developments in Soviet nuclear and conventional forces. As one result of the Long-Term Defense Program, the Nuclear Planning Group is examining in detail the modernizing of our theater nuclear forces, including the question of long-range nuclear systems. We need also to consider jointly the relation of long-range theater nuclear systems to arms control.

This will require considering the full scope of political and military issues, and being sure that we maintain the coupling of American strategic forces to the defense of Europe. As we examine this together, I assure you that the United States will protect the options before us as the SALT II negotiations move toward completion.

[Conventional Forces]

Let me now turn to conventional forces — the bulk of the Long-Term Defense Program. After all, our largest expenditures are for conventional, not nuclear, forces.

We must prepare to fight more effectively together as an Alliance. We must markedly improve our ability to work together on the battlefield. We should overcome unnecessary duplication in our national programs, thus buying more security for the same money.

That is what the Long-Term Defense Program is all about. It is an unprecedented attempt by NATO to look across a longer span of years than ever before. It seeks a more cooperative course, as the only sensible way to improve our defenses without unnecessary increases in defense spending. It lays out specific measures of Alliance cooperation. It is the blueprint we need, and we must carry it out vigorously.

[Legislative Approval Necessary]

Of course, each of us depends on legislative approval for particular programs and projects within the Long-Term Defense Program. Because we lead democracies, we cannot bind our people by fiat. We can, however, pledge to do what is necessary to secure this approval and make this program work.

The United States is already responding to many Long-Term Defense Program recommendations, particularly in the field of reinforcement. And the recommendations will receive the highest priority in our own national defense programming. In short, we will do our part in adapting or modifying U.S. programs to support the NATO Long-Term Defense Program. I am confident that you will take similar action.

[Follow-Through]

Finally, I want to mention the one remaining unresolved aspect of the Long-Term Defense Program. Although the program calls for new and unprecedented Alliance cooperation, no procedures have yet been devised for ensuring that it is carried out. We must avoid bold programs heartily endorsed — then largely ignored. The Report before us directs the Secretary General to present for national review what changes are essential for vigorous follow-through.

Both the NATO Task Forces and we Americans have made several specific proposals to this end. For example, we favor explicitly recognizing NATO's new focus on logistics. One way is to create a new Assistant Secretary General for Logistics. We also favor clear assignment of responsibility for each program to one NATO body. Where appropriate, we would prefer a major NATO command. But I do not ask that you discuss our proposals today. Instead, I ask that all Alliance leaders here today join me in calling for vigorous follow-through of the program.

In conclusion, let me state that we confront a unique opportunity to bring our national defense programs closer together. The result will be a more effective defense. The consequences will be greater security for our people. It is our responsibility not to let this opportunity pass.

LONG-TERM DEFENSE PROGRAM SUMMARY

Introduction

1. At the meeting of Heads of State and Government held in Washington on 30 and 31 May, the leaders of States participating in the integrated defence structure of the Alliance gave their endorsement to a wide range of measures as an action programme designed to help adapt the defence posture of the Alliance to the challenges of the 1980s.[1]

2. This Long-Term Defence Programme has been developed, in response to directives given at the Summit Meeting held in London in May 1977, as a means of strengthening the ongoing NATO force planning and national programmes in the face of the challenge to Alliance security posed by the continuing momentum of the Warsaw Pact military build-up. The programme marks a significant milestone for NATO through its projection of Alliance defence planning into a longer term framework and its emphasis on co-operative efforts to strengthen the defences of the Alliance.

The Political and Military Background

3. The enhancement of NATO's security must be assured not only by strengthening the Alliance's deterrent and defence posture but also by continued pursuit of detente and, as a key part of that process equitable and meaningful arms control and disarmament agreements. However, trends in the military balance, which in the conventional area are moving strongly to NATO's disadvantage, could, if left unchecked, undermine deterrence and stability. NATO is determined to meet this challenge by maintaining a credible deterrent and defence posture. NATO's capabilities will continue to be designed to support the concept of forward defence based on adequate conventional, theatre nuclear and strategic nuclear forces through the 1980s.

4. NATO also recognises the challenge to its collective defence planning arising from the fact that members of the Alliance are sovereign states. Therefore increased Alliance-wide co-ordination of national planning is required to strengthen NATO's defense capabilities by achieving a greater degree of co-operation and rationalization.

The Programme

5. The Long-Term Defence Programme is designed to meet these challenges. It provides for force improvements in certain selected areas and for a far greater degree of Alliance co-operation, leading to an increase in

---

[1] In this connection, Turkey pointed out the importance to her participation of sufficient support from her Allies as well as of the complete removal of existing restrictions on the procurement of defence equipment.

overall defensive capability from the national resources already made available or planned for the Alliance. Further improvements are to be made to the readiness and combat capabilities of NATO's military forces and in the capability to reinforce those forces. The programme recommends a series of detailed actions to improve NATO capabilities in certain priority areas: readiness; reinforcement; reserve mobilization; maritime posture; air defence; communications, command and control; electronic warfare; logistics; rationalization and theatre nuclear forces. In all these areas particular emphasis will be placed on co-operation between member countries.

The Action Areas

Readiness

6. The ability of Warsaw Pact forces to attack with less preparation than in the past challenges NATO forces to be ready to respond rapidly with the maximum possible combat capability. NATO forces thus require improvements to a wide range of defence capabilities, especially anti-armour units, modern air-to-surface weapons and defence against chemical warfare. In-place forces must be ready within the minimum warning time. Arrangements for maximum support from the civil sector are essential. Programmes include increases in the national holdings of tanks, anti-armour weapons and missiles and armed helicopters. It has also been agreed to pursue co-operative or co-ordinated development of the next-generation anti-armour weapons. A programme for substantially increasing national holdings of modern air-to-surface weapons will also be introduced, along with the pursuit of a common family of these types of weapons. Protective equipment against chemical warfare will be provided to meet NATO standards. The ability of combat forces to upload ammunition at short notice will be increased. In addition, a number of nations have agreed to increase the degree of commitment of their forces to NATO, which will enhance readiness in time of crisis. Multilateral discussions to shorten the reaction time of the 1st Netherlands Corps are continuing.

Reinforcement

7. The imbalance of conventional forces in Europe is such that, in periods of rising tension or crisis, deterrence could be put at risk without a capability for rapid and effective reinforcement of Allied Command Europe as a whole. Improvements are now necessary to enhance the Alliance capabilities for rapid reinforcement. This involves the commitment of civil air, sea, land and national infrastructure resources to the reinforcement task and the establishment of effective arrangements to co-ordinate the flow of reinforcements. An essential element is the use of existing European facilities, with improvements where necessary, to receive and move forward external reinforcements with minimum delay. In addition measures will be taken to accelerate the movement of significant fighting units to the forward areas in the critical early phase. A major feature is the prepositioning by the United States of the heavy equipment for three

additional U.S. divisions in the Central Region by 1982, recognising the need for European Allies to provide the necessary support and other facilities. For some Allies modifications to civil aircraft are proposed to carry equipment which cannot be prepositioned. The amphibious lift for the United Kingdom/Netherlands Marine Force is to be improved.

Reserve Mobilization

8. Since reservists comprise a significant proportion of NATO's total ground forces, timely deployment of reserve units is critical, especially in Allied Command Europe. It is therefore necessary to take additional measures to ensure that reservists and reserve formations are properly equipped, trained and capable of being rapidly deployed to locations where they are required. Programmes are designed to bring national reserve forces up to NATO standards and to seek to upgrade and improve the operational readiness of certain reserve units. In addition a number of European countries will consider providing additional reserve brigades over the longer term. This would increase the effective use of individual reservists and make available additional combat units for initial reinforcement.

Maritime Posture

9. A number of maritime programmes have been agreed upon to provide for greatly increased capabilities in maritime command, control and communications and for air defence of naval units. The programmes also include measures to achieve improved anti-submarine capabilities, better anti-missile surface defence and greater mine warfare capabilities. Co-operative or co-ordinated development of key weapon systems will be pursued. It has been recognised that the most serious deficiency lies in shortages in the number of ships, submarines and aircraft and that specific remedies for these shortfalls should be sought under established NATO planning procedures.

Air Defence

10. Agreement has been reached on a basic Alliance-wide co-operative programme to improve air defence capabilities recognising the need for subsequent detailed planning and refinement. It includes measures designed to improve the identification of hostile aircraft and to enhance the control of NATO's own combat aircraft. Provision is to be made for improvements to fighter aircraft, acquisition of improved surface-to-air weaponry, to provide the Alliance with a significantly enhanced capability for engaging Warsaw Pact aircraft penetrating at all levels.

Communications, Command and Control

11. A number of co-operative efforts were agreed which will make important contributions to the overall capabilities of the Alliance for communications, command and control which are essential to political consultation in times of crisis and for the political direction of forces and which will also achieve a high level of interoperability in the area of tactical communications. These include the implementation of the second phase of the NATO Integrated Communications System and co-operation and co-ordinated efforts in the fields of maritime communications, tactical trunk

network, single-channel radio access, NATO/national area interconnection, strategic automatic data processing and war headquarters improvements.

Electronic Warfare

12. All NATO nations have agreed that urgent action is required to cope with this important dimension of modern conflict. Programmes provide for important improvements in NATO's capability to counter the sophisticated electronic warfare threat posed by the Warsaw Pact. They cover land, air and maritime forces, together with improvements in NATO's organization and procedures in this field, including closer co-operation in research and development.

Rationalization

13. The objective is to achieve economic savings and enhanced military efficiency through increased standardization and interoperability. Programmes include development of new procedures for systematic long-range armaments planning, new procedures for the improved formulation and utilization of Standardization Agreements, and continuation of the work being undertaken by the Conference of National Armaments Directors in the field of intellectual property rights. In the development and acquisition of the equipment recommended in the Long-Term Defence Programme, co-operative programmes will be pursued to the greatest extent possible. Nations have also endorsed the need for the transfer of technology between member countries where such transfers contribute to the furtherance of standardization/interoperability of NATO defence equipment.

Logistics

14. Policy and organizational improvements have been agreed to harmonize and co-ordinate arrangements in the rear areas and thereby improve the logistic support of combat forces. The logistics support responsibilities between NATO Commanders and member nations will be more clearly defined, and improved logistics structures provided within NATO military commands. A logistics master planning system is to be developed to provide for better planning and management of NATO logistic functions. There are also to be increased war reserve stocks and ways are being sought to improve flexibility in the use of ammunition stocks in war and to build up stocks of primary fuels with improved storage facilities.

Theatre Nuclear Modernization

15. Measures are being developed to ensure that NATO's theatre nuclear forces continue to play their essential role in NATO's deterrence and defence posture.

Implementation

16. There is to be a vigorous and sustained follow-through on the details of these recommendations. To this end Heads of State and Government have pledged their full support for the intensive civil and military planning and development efforts needed at national and NATO level. Arrange-

ments will be made for ensuring an effective follow-through for the measures approved under the Long-Term Defence Programme, including a study on strengthening of international machinery. There will be further action on related low cost/no cost recommendations and provision for periodic monitoring and review of progress.

June

CARTER WATER POLICY
June 6, 1978

In an effort to regain executive branch control over federal spending for dams, canals and other expensive water management projects, President Carter sent to Congress June 6 his long-delayed national water policy. The attempt was to take some of the control from a Congress that traditionally authorized and funded the projects on a piecemeal, pork-barrel basis.

The policy originally had been scheduled to be completed the previous fall, but attempts to rework it to lessen criticism delayed its transmittal until both houses were well into the appropriations process for the projects. Original intentions had been to make water conservation and long-range planning programs mandatory and to redraw the formula for figuring project costs. Opposition came primarily from the western states.

Carter's message envisioned water conservation as a key component of his policy and he wanted to place the emphasis on projects that were "cost-effective, safe and environmentally sound." The policy also proposed that the states not only assume a larger role in the decision-making process, but that they also shoulder a greater share of the cost burden. And he wanted much of the decision-making switched from the U.S. Army's Corps of Engineers to the Water Resources Council headed by the Interior secretary.

Carter's policy would establish criteria for setting priorities each year for authorizing or funding projects. Those given the highest priority would be the ones that:

- *Offered widely distributed benefits.*

- *Stressed water conservation and considered non-structural solutions.*

● *Had no significant safety problems either in design, construction or operation.*

● *Could show evidence of active public support, including that of state and local officials.*

● *Had the state governments sharing more of the costs than already required.*

● *Had no significant international or inter-governmental problems.*

● *Planned for recovery of some costs through sale of water or power provided by the project.*

● *Were up-to-date and considered current conditions.*

● *Complied with relevant environmental statutes.*

● *Provided funds for fish and wildlife damages at the same time the project was constructed and in equal proportions.*

Background

The water policy issue was one of the greatest sources of tension between Congress and the administration since Carter became president in 1977. The feud began when Carter issued his own version of the budget after only a month in office, proposing to kill 19 irrigation and flood control projects that Congress previously had authorized. The reaction from Congress to what became known as Carter's "hit-list" was immediate and vituperative and represented an early spat in the usual honeymoon between a new administration and a Congress controlled by the president's own party.

After weeks of wrangling, Congress ended up restoring all but 10 of the projects. Carter threatened a veto but didn't follow through. Congress returned in 1978 with proposals to revive eight of the remaining 10, all of which Carter had thought were killed forever in 1977.

1978 Action

Carter wanted to get his water policy in shape before Congress began acting in 1978, but it wasn't ready until June 6, after the House Appropriations Committee had voted to restore funding for the eight projects. Three days later Carter threatened to veto any bill that contained the disputed eight and that did not conform to his new policy. At the same time, he offered his own list of water projects he wanted authorized or funded.

Carter's new policy was largely ignored on Capitol Hill, and six of the hit-list projects ended up in a bill Congress finally passed and sent to Carter. On Oct. 5, Carter vetoed the bill, saying it "would hamper the nation's ability to control inflation, eliminate waste and make the government more efficient."

The same day the House, with the support of the Democratic leadership, attempted to override the veto, but failed on a 223-190 vote that required two-thirds approval for passage. Congress later passed, and Carter signed, a compromise public works bill that omitted funding for the six disputed water projects.

A last-minute try to get the projects onto a highway repair bill. But the bill died in the House several hours later for lack of a quorum on the last vote of the 95th Congress.

Following is the text of President Carter's June 6, 1978, message to Congress outlining his new water policy:

To the Congress of the United States:

I am today sending to Congress water policy initiatives designed to:

—improve planning and efficient management of Federal water resource programs to prevent waste and to permit necessary water projects which are cost-effective, safe and environmentally sound to move forward expeditiously;

—provide a new, national emphasis on water conservation;

—enhance Federal-State cooperation and improved State water resources planning; and

—increase attention to environmental quality.

None of the initiatives would impose any new federal regulatory program for water management.

Last year, I directed the Water Resources Council, the Office of Management and Budget and the Council on Environmental Quality, under the chairmanship of [Interior] Secretary Cecil Andrus, to make a comprehensive review of Federal water policy and to recommend proposed reforms.

This new water policy results from their review, the study of water policy ordered by the Congress in Section 80 of the Water Resources Planning Act of 1974 and our extensive consultations with members of Congress, State, county, city and other local officials and the public.

Water is an essential resource, and over the years, the programs of the Bureau of Reclamation, the Corps of Engineers, the Soil Conservation Service and the Tennessee Valley Authority have helped permit a dramatic improvement in American agriculture, have provided irrigation water essential to the development of the West, and have developed community flood protection, electric power, navigation and recreation throughout the Nation.

I ordered this review of water policies and programs because of my concern that while Federal water resources programs have been of great benefit to our Nation, they are today plagued with problems and inefficiencies. In the course of this water policy review we found that:

—Twenty-five separate Federal agencies spend more than $10 billion per year on water resources projects and related programs.

—These projects often are planned without a uniform, standard basis for estimating benefits and costs.

—States are primarily responsible for water policy within their boundaries, yet are not integrally involved in setting priorities and sharing in Federal project planning and funding.

—There is a $34 billion backlog of authorized or uncompleted projects.

—Some water projects are unsafe or environmentally unwise and have caused losses of natural streams and rivers, fish and wildlife habitat and recreational opportunities.

The study also found that water conservation has not been addressed at a national level even though we have pressing water supply problems. Of 106 watershed subregions in the country, 21 already have severe water shortages. By the year 2000 this number could increase to 39 subregions. The Nation's cities are also beginning to experience water shortage problems which can only be solved at very high cost. In some areas, precious groundwater supplies are also being depleted at a faster rate than they are replenished. In many cases an effective water conservation program could play a key role in alleviating these problems.

These water policy initiatives will make the Federal government's water programs more efficient and responsive in meeting the Nation's water-related needs. They are designed to build on fundamentally sound statutes and on the Principles and Standards which govern the planning and development of Federal water projects, and also to enhance the role of the States, where the primary responsibilities for water policy must lie. For the first time, the Federal government will work with State and local governments and exert needed national leadership in the effort to conserve water. Above all, these policy reforms will encourage water projects which are economically and environmentally sound and will avoid projects which are wasteful or which benefit a few at the expense of many.

Across the Nation there is remarkable diversity in the role water plays. Over most of the West, water is scarce and must be managed carefully — and detailed traditions and laws have grown up to govern the use of water. In other parts of the country, flooding is more of a problem than drought, and in many areas, plentiful water resources have offered opportunities for hydroelectric power and navigation. In the urban areas of our Nation, water supply systems are the major concern — particularly where antiquated systems need rehabilitation in order to conserve water and assure continued economic growth.

Everywhere, water is fundamental to environmental quality. Clean drinking water, recreation, wildlife and beautiful natural areas depend on protection of our water resources.

Given this diversity, Federal water policy cannot attempt to prescribe water use patterns for the country. Nor should the Federal government preempt the primary responsibility of the States for water management and allocation. For those reasons, these water policy reforms will not preempt State or local water responsibilities. Yet water policy is an important national concern, and the Federal government has major responsibilities to exercise leadership, to protect the environment and to develop and maintain hydroelectric power, irrigated agriculture, flood control and navigation.

The primary focus of the proposals is on the water resources programs of the Corps of Engineers, the Bureau of Reclamation, the Soil Conservation Service and the Tennessee Valley Authority, where annual water program budgets total approximately $3.75 billion. These agencies perform the federal government's water resource development programs. In addition, a number of Federal agencies with water-related responsibilities will be affected by this water policy.

I am charging Secretary Andrus with the lead responsibility to see that these initiatives are carried out promptly and fully. With the assistance of the Office of Management and Budget and the Council on Environmental Quality, he will be responsible for working with the other Federal agencies, the Congress, State and local governments and the public to assure proper implementation of this policy and to make appropriate recommendations for reform in the future.

Specific Initiatives Improving Federal Water Resource Programs

The Federal government has played a vital role in developing the water resources of the United States. It is essential that Federal water programs be updated and better coordinated if they are to continue to serve the nation in the best way possible. The reforms I am proposing are designed to modernize and improve the coordination of federal water programs. In addition, in a few days, I will also be sending to the Congress a Budget amendment proposing funding for a number of new water project construction and planning starts. These projects meet the criteria I am announcing today. This is the first time the Executive Branch has proposed new water project starts since Fiscal Year 1975, four years ago.

The actions I am taking include:

• A directive to the Water Resources Council to improve the implementation of the Principles and Standards governing the planning of Federal water projects. The basic planning objectives of the Principles and Standards — national economic development and environmental quality — should be retained and given equal emphasis. In addition, the implementation of the Principles and Standards should be improved by:

—adding water conservation as a specific component of both the economic and environmental objectives;

—requiring the explicit formulation and consideration of a primarily non-structural plan as one alternative whenever structural water projects or programs are planned;

—instituting consistent, specific procedures for calculating benefits and costs in compliance with the Principles and Standards and other applicable planning and evaluation requirements. Benefit-cost analyses have not been uniformly applied by Federal agencies, and in some cases benefits have been improperly recognized, "double-counted" or included when inconsistent with federal policy or sound economic rationale. I am directing the Water Resources Council to prepare within 12 months a manual which ensures that benefits and costs are calculated using the best techniques and provides for consistent application of the Principles and Standards and other requirements;

—ensuring that water projects have been planned in accordance with the Principles and Standards and other planning requirements by creating, by Executive Order, a project review function located in the Water Resources Council. A professional staff will ensure an impartial review of pre-construction project plans for their consistency with established planning and benefit-cost analysis procedures and applicable requirements. They will report on compliance with these requirements to agency heads, who will include their report, together with the agency recommendations, to the Office of Management and Budget. Project reviews will be completed within 60 days, before the Cabinet officer makes his or her Budget request for the coming fiscal year. Responsibility will rest with the Cabinet officer for Budget requests to the Office of Management and Budget, but timely independent review will be provided. This review must be completed within the same budget cycle in which the Cabinet Officer intends to make Budget requests so that the process results in no delay.

—The manual, the Principles and Standards requirements and the independent review process will apply to all authorized projects (and separable project features) not yet under construction.

• Establishment of the following criteria for setting priorities each year among the water projects eligible for funding or authorization, which will form the basis of my decisions on specific water projects:

—Projects should have net national economic benefits unless there are environmental benefits which clearly more than compensate for any economic deficit. Net adverse environmental consequences should be significantly outweighed by economic benefits. Generally, projects with higher benefit/cost ratios and fewer adverse environmental consequences will be given priority within the limits of available funds.

—Projects should have widely distributed benefits.

—Projects should stress water conservation and appropriate nonstructural measures.

—Projects should have no significant safety problems involving design, construction or operation.

—There should be evidence of active public support including support by State and local officials.

—Projects will be given expedited consideration where State governments assume a share of costs over and above existing cost-sharing.

—There should be no significant international or inter-governmental problems.

—Where vendible outputs are involved preference should be given to projects which provide for greater recovery of Federal and State costs, consistent with project purposes.

—The project's problem assessment, environmental impacts, costs and benefits should be based on up-to-date conditions (planning should not be obsolete).

—Projects should be in compliance with all relevant environmental statutes.

—Funding for mitigation of fish and wildlife damages should be provided concurrently and proportionately with construction funding.

• Preparation of a legislative proposal for improving cost-sharing for water projects. Improved cost-sharing will allow States to participate more actively in project decisions and will remove biases in the existing system against non-structural flood control measures. These changes will help assure project merit. This proposal, based on the study required by Section 80 of P.L. 93-251, has two parts:

—participation of States in the financing of federal water project construction. For project purposes with vendible outputs (such as water supply or hydroelectric power), States would contribute 10% of the costs, proportionate to and phased with federal appropriations. Revenues would be returned to the States proportionate to their contribution. For project purposes without vendible outputs (such as flood control), the State financing share would be 5%. There would be a cap on State participation per project per year of 1/4 of 1% of the State's general revenues so that a small State would not be precluded from having a very large project located in it. Where project benefits accrue to more than one State, State contributions would be calculated accordingly, but if a benefiting State did not choose to participate in cost-sharing, its share could be paid by other participating States. This State cost-sharing proposal would apply on a mandatory basis to projects not yet authorized. However, for projects in the authorized backlog, States which voluntarily enter into these cost-sharing arrangements will achieve expedited Executive Branch consideration and priority for project funding, as long as other project planning requirements are met. Soil Conservation Service projects will be completely exempt from this State cost-sharing proposal.

—equalizing cost-sharing for structural and non-structural flood control alternatives. There is existing authority for 80%-20% Federal/non-Federal cost-sharing for non-structural flood control measures (including in-kind contributions such as land and easements). I will begin approving non-structural flood control projects with this funding arrangement and will propose that a parallel cost-sharing requirement (including in-kind contributions) be enacted for structural flood control measures, which currently have a multiplicity of cost-sharing rules.

Another policy issue raised in Section 80 of P.L. 93-251 is that of the appropriate discount rate for computing the present value of future estimated economic benefits of water projects. After careful consideration of a range of options I have decided that the currently legislated discount rate formula is reasonable, and I am therefore recommending that no change be made in the current formula. Nor will I recommend retroactive changes in the discount rate for currently authorized projects.

Water Conservation

Managing our vital water resources depends on a balance of supply, demand and wise use. Using water more efficiently is often cheaper and less damaging to the environment than developing additional supplies. While increases in supply will still be necessary, these reforms place emphasis on water conservation and make clear that this is now a national priority.

In addition to adding the consideration of water conservation to the Principles and Standards, the initiatives I am taking include:

• Directives to all Federal agencies with programs which affect water supply or consumption to encourage water conservation, including:

—making appropriate community water conservation measures a condition of the water supply and wastewater treatment grant and loan programs of the Environmental Protection Agency, the Department of Agriculture and the Department of Commerce;

—integrating water conservation requirements into the housing assistance programs of the Department of Housing and Urban Development, the Veterans Administration and the Department of Agriculture;

—providing technical assistance to farmers and urban dwellers on how to conserve water through existing programs of the Department of Agriculture, the Department of Interior and the Department of Housing and Urban Development;

—requiring development of water conservation programs as a condition of contracts for storage or delivery of municipal and industrial water supplies from federal projects;

—requiring the General Services Administration, in consultation with affected agencies, to establish water conservation goals and standards in Federal buildings and facilities;

—encouraging water conservation in the agricultural assistance programs of the Department of Agriculture and the Department of Interior which affect water consumption in water-short areas: and

—requesting all Federal agencies to examine their programs and policies so that they can implement appropriate measures to increase water conservation and re-use.

•A directive to the Secretary of the Interior to improve the implementation of irrigation repayment and water service contract procedures under existing authorities of the Bureau of Reclamation. The Secretary will:

—require that new and renegotiated contracts include provisions for recalculation and renegotiation of water rates every five years. This will replace the previous practice of 40-year contracts which often do not reflect inflation and thus do not meet the beneficiaries' repayment obligations;

—under existing authority add provisions to recover operation and maintenance costs when existing contracts are renegotiated, or earlier where existing contracts have adjustment clauses;

—more precisely calculate and implement the "ability to pay" provision in existing law which governs recovery of a portion of project capital costs.

● Preparation of legislation to allow States the option of requiring higher prices for municipal and industrial water supplies from Federal projects in order to promote conservation, provided that State revenues in excess of Federal costs would be returned to municipalities or other public water supply entities for use in water conservation or rehabilitation of water supply systems.

Federal--State Cooperation

States must be the focal point for water resource management. The water reforms are based on this guiding principle. Therefore, I am taking several initiatives to strengthen Federal-State relations in the water policy area and to develop a new, creative partnership. In addition to proposing that States increase their roles and responsibilities in water resources development through cost-sharing, the actions I am taking include:

● Proposing a substantial increase from $3 million to $25 million annually in the funding of State water planning under the existing 50%-50% matching program administered by the Water Resources Council. State water planning would integrate water management and implementation programs which emphasize water conservation and which are tailored to each State's needs including assessment of water delivery system rehabilitation needs and development of programs to protect and manage groundwater and instream flows.

● Preparation of legislation to provide $25 million annually in 50%-50% matching grant assistance to States to implement water conservation technical assistance programs. These funds could be passed through to counties and cities for use in urban or rural water conservation programs. This program will be administered by the Water Resources Council in conjunction with matching grants for water resources planning.

● Working with Governors to create a Task Force of Federal, State, county, city and other local officials to continue to address water-related problems. The administrative actions and legislative proposals in this Message are designed to initiate sound water management policy at the national level. However, the Federal government must work closely with the States, and with local governments as well, to continue identifying and examining water-related problems and to help implement the initiatives I am announcing today. This Task Force will be a continuing guide as we implement the water policy reforms and will ensure that the State and local role in our Nation's water policy is constant and meaningful.

● An instruction to Federal Agencies to work promptly and expeditiously to inventory and quantify Federal reserved and Indian water rights. In several areas of the country, States have been unable to allocate water because these rights have not been determined. This quantification effort should focus first on high priority areas, should involve close consultation with the States and water users and should emphasize negotiations rather than litigation wherever possible.

Environmental Protection

Water is a basic requirement for human survival, is necessary for economic growth and prosperity, and is fundamental to protecting the natural environment. Existing environmental statutes relating to water and water projects generally are adequate, but these laws must be consistently applied and effectively enforced to achieve their purposes. Sensitivity to environmental protection must be an important aspect of all water-related planning and management decisions. I am particularly concerned about the need to improve the protection of instream flows and to evolve careful management of our nation's precious groundwater supplies, which are threatened by depletion and contamination.

My initiatives in this area include the following:

● A directive to the Secretary of the Interior and other Federal agency heads to implement vigorously the Fish and Wildlife Coordination Act, the Historic Preservation Act and other environmental statutes. Federal agencies will prepare formal implementing procedures for the Fish and Wildlife Coordination Act and other statutes where appropriate. Affected agencies will prepare reports on compliance with environmental statutes on a project-by-project basis for inclusion in annual submissions to the Office of Management and Budget.

● A directive to agency heads requiring them to include designated funds for environmental mitigation in water project appropriation requests to provide for concurrent and proportionate expenditure of mitigation funds.

● Accelerated implementation of Executive Order No. 11988 on floodplain management. This Order requires agencies to protect floodplains and to reduce risks of flood losses by not conducting, supporting or allowing actions in floodplains unless there are no practicable alternatives. Agency implementation is behind schedule and must be expedited.

● A directive to the Secretaries of Army, Commerce, Housing and Urban Development and Interior to help reduce flood damages through acquisition of flood-prone land and property, where consistent with primary program purposes.

● A directive to the Secretary of Agriculture to encourage more effective soil and water conservation through watershed programs of the Soil Conservation Service by:

—working with the Fish and Wildlife Service to apply fully the recently-adopted stream channel modification guidelines;

—encouraging accelerated land treatment measures prior to funding of structural measures on watershed projects, and making appropriate land treatment measures eligible for Federal cost-sharing;

—establishing periodic post-project monitoring to ensure implementation of land treatment and operation and maintenance activities specified in the work plan and to provide information helpful in improving the design of future projects.

● A directive to Federal agency heads to provide increased cooperation with States and leadership in maintaining instream flows and protecting groundwater through joint assessment of needs, increased assistance in the gathering and sharing of data, appropriate design and operation of Federal water facilities, and other means. I also call upon the Governors and the Congress to work with Federal agencies to protect the fish and wildlife and other values associated with adequate instream flows. New and existing projects should be planned and operated to protect instream flows, consistent with State law and in close consultation with States. Where prior commitments and economic feasibility permit, amendments to authorizing statutes should be sought in order to provide for streamflow maintenance.

Conclusion

These initiatives establish the goals and the framework for water policy reform. They do so without impinging on the rights of States and by calling for a closer partnership among the Federal, State, county, city and other local levels of government. I want to work with the Congress, State and local governments and the public to implement this policy. Together we can protect and manage our nation's water resources, putting water to use for society's benefit, preserving our rivers and streams for future generations of Americans, and averting critical water shortages in the future through adequate supply, conservation and wise planning.

JIMMY CARTER

The White House,
June 6, 1978

CALIFORNIA'S PROPOSITION 13
June 6, 8, 1978

California voters approved Proposition 13, a state constitutional amendment sharply reducing property taxes, by an almost 2 to 1 margin on June 6. The amendment, which went into effect July 1, limited property tax collections by local governments to 1 percent of "full cash value" as determined by the 1975-76 assessments. Property taxes in California had averaged about 3 percent. Proposition 13 allowed reassessments only when property was sold. It also required a two-thirds vote of both houses of the state legislature to levy new taxes and prohibited local governments from imposing new property taxes.

The initiative, which was cosponsored by Republican businessmen Howard A. Jarvis and Paul Gann, slashed property taxes by almost 60 percent and reduced annual property tax revenues from about $12 billion to $5 billion. In California, all property tax revenue went to local governments and schools, and it was estimated that those recipients would face an overall spending cut of approximately 22 percent.

Speech by Brown

The day after voters approved Proposition 13, California Gov. Edmund G. Brown Jr. imposed an immediate freeze on the hiring of state employees. Brown on June 8 went before a joint session of the state legislature in a crisis atmosphere to urge that the state's entire surplus of almost $5 billion be used in the next fiscal year to help schools, cities and counties offset their loss of revenue.

Brown had strongly opposed Proposition 13 in the weeks before the election. But in his speech to the legislature and in later statements he appeared more and more to ally himself with what he perceived to be the dominant mood of the voters. "Over 4 million of our fellow citizens have sent a message to city hall, Sacramento and to all of us. The message is that the property tax must be sharply curtailed and that government spending, wherever it is, must be held in check," Brown told the joint session.

'Taxpayers' Revolt'

Proposition 13 was a reflection of what became known in 1978 as a "taxpayers' revolt." In the Nov. 7 election, referenda resembling Proposition 13 dotted the ballots. But unlike the clear cry for tax relief sent out by Californians in June, the message from around the country in November was more muted.

"Proposition 13 fever" accelerated in the immediate aftermath of the California vote. John Shannon of the Advisory Commission on Intergovernmental Relations, however, cited a number of factors that made property tax reduction as dramatic as California's unlikely in many other states. These factors included: (1) California's $5 billion surplus which could be used to soften the impact of Proposition 13; (2) the state's increasingly high property tax burden and skyrocketing property values; (3) substantially higher state and local taxes than in most other states and (4) an initiative process that made it relatively easy to enact constitutional amendments limiting taxes.

In the wake of Proposition 13, legislators on both the federal and state levels focused attention on measures to curb spending and to reduce taxes. Federal spending had climbed steadily from about 18.7 percent of the gross national product (GNP) in 1958 to an estimated 22.6 percent 20 years later. Federal taxes had increased as well — from 18.4 percent of the GNP in 1976 to an estimated 19.6 percent in 1978. State and local spending and taxes had also been rising — from 8.2 percent of the GNP in 1959 to an estimated 10.6 percent in 1977. State and local taxes had risen from 7.25 percent of GNP in 1966 to 9.66 percent in 1976.

Public Employees

The American Federation of State, County and Municipal Employees, the fastest growing union in the AFL-CIO, in June began to devise a strategy to try to head off the spread of initiatives similar to Proposition 13. Jerry Wurf, union president, told The New York Times *that rational tax reform would not hurt the public employee unions. "If other unions make the mistake of trying to preserve the status quo, the taxpayers will tread on us with the scorn we deserve," he said.*

The union at a convention in Las Vegas, Nevada, June 27 adopted a resolution stating, "The real targets of the initiative campaigns and public referenda, supported by the New Right, are public employees and the services they perform." But some delegates to the convention said that in California many public employees had joined other voters in voting for Proposition 13.

November Election

Tax-cutting proposals modeled on Proposition 13 passed easily in Idaho and Nevada but were defeated in Michigan and Oregon in the Nov. 7 election. In about 12 other states, voters decided on other tax measures that either emphasized a tight control on tax increases or a limitation on state spending. Most of those measures won, but there were notable exceptions. Spending limitation plans were rejected by voters in Colorado and Nebraska; in Arkansas a proposal to repeal the sales tax on food and drugs was defeated.

Many observers believed that the message that came through in November was that voters generally were demanding more efficiency in government but were refusing to risk large and unpredictable cutbacks in services.

> *Following are the texts of Proposition 13 as it appeared on California ballots on June 6, 1978, and of Gov. Edmund G. Brown Jr.'s address before a joint session of the state legislature on June 8, 1978:*

PROPOSITION 13

Section 1: a. The maximum amount of any ad valorem tax on real property shall not exceed one percent (1%) of the full cash value of such property. The one percent (1%) tax to be collected by the counties and apportioned according to law to the districts within the counties.

b. The limitation shall not apply to ad valorem taxes or special assessments to pay the interest and redemption charges on any indebtedness approved by the voters prior to the time this section becomes effective.

Section 2: a. The full cash value means the County Assessors valuation of real property as shown on the 1975-76 tax bill under "full cash value," or thereafter, the appraised value of real property when purchased, newly constructed or a change in ownership has occured [*sic*] after the 1975 assessment. All real property not already assessed up to the 1975-76 tax levels may be reassessed to reflect that valuation.

c. The fair market value base may reflect from year to year the inflationary rate not to exceed 2 percent (2%) for any given year or reduction as shown in the consumer price index or comparable data for the area under taxing jurisdiction.

Section 3: a. From and after the effective date of this article, any changes in State taxes enacted for the purpose of increasing revenues collected pursuant thereto whether by increased rates or changes in methods of computation must be imposed by an act passed by not less than two-thirds of all members elected to each of the two houses of the Legislature, except that no new ad valorem taxes on real property, or sales or transaction taxes on the sales of real property, may be imposed.

Section 4: Cities, Counties and special districts, by a two-thirds vote of the qualified electors of such district, may impose special taxes on such district, except ad valorem taxes on real property or a transaction tax or sales tax on the sale of real property within such City, County or special district.

Section 5: This article shall take effect for the tax year beginning on July 1 following the passage of this Amendment, except Section 3, which shall become effective upon the passage of this article.

Section 6: If any section, part, clause or phrase hereof is for any reason held to be invalid or unconstitutional, the remaining sections shall not be affected but will remain in full force and effect.

GOVERNOR BROWN'S ADDRESS

Mr. Speaker, Mr. Senate Pro Tem, Members of the Legislature, friends, visitors, people of California.

Over 4 million of our fellow citizens have sent a message to City Hall, Sacramento, and to all of us. The message is that the property tax must be sharply curtailed and that government spending, wherever it is, must be held in check. We must look forward to lean and frugal budgets. It is a great challenge and we will meet it. We must do everything possible to minimize the human hardship and maximize the total number of state jobs created in our economy. Prop. 13 takes place on July 1. We have only three weeks to act — three weeks to decide multi-billion dollars of fiscal questions; to set a new direction for the five thousand units of government throughout our state. It is time to put aside partisan differences. The vote represented Democrats, Republicans, people from the north and the south, old and young in all parts of our wonderful state. We must follow three basic principles — no new state taxes. Voters have told us they want a tax cut, they don't want a shell game.

No. 2. The state must share the burden. We must adopt a thoughtful, austere budget. Already I have imposed a hiring freeze. There will be no new hiring and when someone leaves state service he or she will not be replaced unless it is an emergency or unless there is extraordinary reason. We must keep the uncertainty to a minimum.

I will propose budget cuts of at least $300 million. The more money we can save at the state level the more we can share with local governments, fire, police, schools, cities, counties and all those who carry out the people's wish. During the next several days, no later than the next two to three weeks, I will recommend legislation to accomplish six specific tasks.

No. 1. A law is needed to allocate the remaining property tax, that which is left after the 1 percent limit now imposed by Prop. 13.

No. 2. We must commit the entire state surplus to meet the urgent needs of our public schools and local governments. I recommend for this year, and this year only, $4 billion in direct aid and $1 billion in an emergency loan fund. I recommend this for the first year because of the uncertainties that local government will face. Loan money must be made available so that the budgets that will be formed in the next few weeks can be written with as much dispatch and human compassion as we know how to make it [sic]. The current surplus is not ongoing. It has been built up out of tight fiscal management here in Sacramento and by a booming state economy.

For the following year we should have approximately $2 billion to share with local governments and with the funds that will be returned from the loan fund we can make, hopefully, another billion dollars available to share with local governments in the very difficult and painful transition. We need a temporary one-year formula for allocating the surplus where it is most needed. There is no time in the next three weeks for a comprehensive overhaul of a series of complex formulas. We need a bill that commends itself to two thirds of the people in these Chambers, Republicans and Democrats, and we need it soon. People across the state are looking to us for leadership.

Should we need a special contingency fund for emergency situations, we need that because no matter what the formula is, and especially if it is simple, there will be arbitrary impact and we must be able to meet them [sic]. The $1 billion emergency loan fund must be established so that the traditional units of local government can meet their cash flow needs that in some cases will be coming due in the next couple of weeks.

Finally, the legislature itself must adopt a lean and frugal state budget. Certainly that is the message which we hear and to the extent that we do that we not only respond to the people's will but we share with all the people of the state at whatever level of government the very difficult challenge that faces us ahead.

After July 1 I will offer additional suggestions. Plans to limit government spending, examining and overhauling the confusing local jurisdictions, the special districts that now dot our state to the number of over 5,000. I will ask the federal government to reexamine its priorities. Now, when property taxes are cut, the federal government will enjoy a $2 billion windfall. The incentive should be the other way around. Where people have spoken to protect their homes the federal government should assist not by reaping a windfall but by providing assistance to those who face troubled times here in state government.

Finally, a very important point. There are many hardworking people in state and local government. They are not faceless bureaucrats, they have families, they pay taxes, they have the same lives as all the rest of us, and they have to also make plans for their future and for that reason I appeal to you to rise above the partisan temptations, to work together as a body, to fashion a bill that keeps faith with our fiscal realities and with the mood and the philosophy of the people which we serve. Major human tragedies will occur unless we do all that we can, unless we continuously scrutinize every element of our budget, every possibility of our surplus and lay out a plan that will carry us through this first year of transition and will provide opportunities in the second year and beyond to smooth the path for an orderly government both at the state level and at local levels.

As for business, business will reap savings in the order of $3 billion. Many individual businesses will save tens of millions of dollars. These people, these corporate presidents, have a moral obligation to invest that money in California, to create jobs, to create the possibilities of a continuing boom and buoyant economy. It is only through that method will we be able to shelter and smooth the shock in the disruption that can occur.

We have a very monumental task. There is not much time. The people are waiting for us to act.

Thank you very much.

SOLZHENITSYN ON WESTERN DECLINE
June 8, 1978

Alexander I. Solzhenitsyn delivered a stern warning to the West in a June 8 commencement address at Harvard University. "A decline in courage may be the most striking feature which an outside observer notices in the West today," the exiled Russian author said. "The Western world has lost its civic courage, both as a whole and separately, in each country, in each government, in each political party and of course in the United Nations."

"We have placed too much hope in political and social reforms, only to find out," he added, "that we were being deprived of our most precious possession: our spiritual life."

Titled "A World Split Apart," it was Solzhenitsyn's first speech in three years. Forced out of Russia in 1974 for writings critical of the communist state, he lived in Switzerland for a year before settling with his wife in Cavendish, Vt. The commander of an artillery battery and twice decorated for bravery in World War II, Solzhenitsyn in 1945 was sentenced to eight years in a forced labor camp. For another four years, until 1957, he was in exile in Siberia. Among his works, all acclaimed internationally, are The First Circle, Cancer Ward, One Day in the Life of Ivan Denisovich *and* Gulag Archipelago. *He received the Nobel Prize in Literature in 1970.*

Western Weakness

The root of Western weakness, Solzhenitsyn said, may be found in the Renaissance and the Enlightenment when "we recoiled from the Spirit and embraced all that is material, excessively and incommensurately." Up to 50 years earlier, he argued, freedom was granted to people because they were creatures of God, provided the individual maintained "constant religious responsibility." In contemporary society, however, "a total emancipation occurred from the moral heritage of Christian centuries with their great reserves of mercy and sacrifice."

The result was the death of spiritual life, Solzhenitsyn said. "On the way from the Renaissance to our days we have enriched our experience but we have lost the concept of a Supreme Complete Entity which used to restrain our passions and our irresponsibility. . . ." Spiritual life, he continued, "is trampled by the party mob in the East, by the commercial one in the West. This is the essence of the crisis: the split in the world is less terrifying than the similarity of the disease afflicting its main sections."

Despite his strong criticism of Western democracies, Solzhenitsyn denied that communism presented an attractive alternative. He said, however, that the suffering undergone by the inhabitants of communist states had resulted in some "spiritual development" that contrasted with the "spiritual exhaustion" of the West.

"The forces of evil have begun their decisive offensive, you can feel their pressure," he declared, "yet your screens and publications are full of prescribed smiles and raised glasses. What is the joy about?"

Moral Criteria

Solzhenitsyn said that the only weapons left to Western nations to fight communism were moral criteria. He belittled those U.S. policymakers who argue that moral criteria do not apply to international politics, saying, "If you only knew how the youngest of the officials in Moscow's Old Square roar with laughter at your political wizards!"

The "most cruel mistake" of American public opinion, he said, was the "failure to understand the Vietnam war." Opponents of that war, according to Solzhenitsyn, "became accomplices in the betrayal of Far Eastern nations, in the genocide and in the suffering today imposed on 30 million people there. Do these convinced pacifists now hear the moans coming from there? Do they understand their responsibility today?" During the war, he said, the "American intelligentsia lost its nerve, and as a consequence, the danger has come much closer to the United States. But there is no awareness of this." Solzhenitsyn's comments on the Vietnam War evoked scattered boos from the audience.

To survive an attack from the East, Western countries must restore their will power, he said. "To defend oneself, one must also be ready to die; there is little such readiness in a society raised in the cult of material well-being." Another large-scale war, he warned, "may well bury Western civilization forever."

Legalistic Society

Solzhenitsyn warned of the dangers inherent in a society guided only by adherence to legal structures. "I have spent all my life under a communist regime," he said, "and I will tell you that a society without any objective legal scale is a terrible one indeed. But a society with no other scale but the legal one is also less than worthy of man." Reliance on broad legal concepts, he charged, has brought about a "tilt of freedom toward evil."

Criticism of U.S. Press

The news media have also contributed to the weakening of Western society, Solzhenitsyn said. News organizations rely on "guesswork, rumors and suppositions" which their audiences accept as facts. "Hastiness and superficiality — these are the psychic diseases of the 20th century," he charged, "and more than anywhere else this disease is manifested in the press." He also inveighed against the "generally accepted patterns of judgment" which, he said, give rise to "fashionable trends of thoughts and ideas." The trends create, he said, "dangerous herd instincts that block successful development."

Solzhenitsyn was awarded an honorary degree of doctor of letters at the commencement exercises. In his citation, Derek C. Bok, Harvard president, described Solzhenitsyn as the "contemporary voice of a great literary tradition, like his heroic predecessors a courageous exponent of the unfettered human spirit."

> *Following is the text of Alexander I. Solzhenitsyn's June 8, 1978, address at the Harvard University commencement exercises (World copyright ©Alexander Solzhenitsyn 1978):*

I am sincerely happy to be here with you on the occasion of the 327th commencement of this old and illustrious University. My congratulations and best wishes to all of today's graduates.

Harvard's motto is "Veritas." Many of you have already found out and others will find out in the course of their lives that truth eludes us as soon as our concentration begins to flag, all the while leaving the illusion that we are continuing to pursue it. This is the source of much discord. Also, truth seldom is sweet; it is almost invariably bitter. A measure of bitter truth is included in my speech today, but I offer it as a friend, not as an adversary.

Three years ago in the United States I said certain things that were rejected and appeared unacceptable. Today, however, many people agree with what I then said. . . .

The split in today's world is perceptible even to a hasty glance. Any of our contemporaries readily identifies two world powers, each of them quite capable of utterly destroying the other. However, the understanding of the split too often is limited to this political conception: the illusion according to which danger may be abolished through successful diplomatic negotiations or by achieving a balance of armed forces. The truth is that the split is both more profound and more alienating, that the rifts are more numerous than one can see at first glance. These deep manifold splits bear the danger of equally manifold disaster for all of us, in accordance with the ancient truth that a kingdom — in this case, our Earth — divided against itself cannot stand.

Contemporary Worlds

There is the concept of the Third World: thus, we already have three worlds. Undoubtedly, however, the number is even greater; we are just too far away to see. Every ancient and deeply rooted self-contained culture, especially if it is spread over a wide part of the earth's surface, constitutes a self-contained world, full of riddles and surprises to Western thinking. As a minimum, we must include in this category China, India, the Muslim world and Africa, if indeed we accept the approximation of viewing the latter two as uniform. For one thousand years Russia belonged to such a category, although Western thinking systematically committed the mistake of denying its special character and therefore never understood it, just as today the West does not understand Russia in communist captivity. And while it may be that in past years Japan has increasingly become, in effect, a Far West, drawing ever closer to Western ways (I am no judge here), Israel, I think, should not be reckoned as part of the West, if only because of the decisive circumstance that its state system is fundamentally linked to religion.

How short a time ago, relatively, the small world of modern Europe was easily seizing colonies all over the globe, not only without anticipating any real resistance, but usually with contempt for any possible values in the conquered peoples' approach to life. It all seemed an overwhelming success, with no geographic limits. Western society expanded in a triumph of human independence and power. And all of a sudden the twentieth century brought the clear realization of this society's fragility. We now see that the conquests proved to be shortlived and precarious, and this, in turn, points to defects in the Western view of the world which led to these conquests. Relations with the former colonial world now have switched to the opposite extreme and the Western world often exhibits an excess of obsequiousness, but it is difficult yet to estimate the size of the bill which former colonial countries will present to the West and it is difficult to predict whether the surrender not only of its last colonies, but of everything it owns will be sufficient for the West to clear this account.

Convergence

But the persisting blindness of superiority continues to hold the belief that all the vast regions of our planet should develop and mature to the level of contemporary Western systems, the best in theory and the most attractive in practice; that all those other worlds are but temporarily prevented by wicked leaders or by severe crises or by their own barbarity and incomprehension from pursuing Western pluralistic democracy and adopting the Western way of life. Countries are judged on the merit of their progress in that direction. But in fact such a conception is a fruit of Western incomprehension of the essence of other worlds, a result of mistakenly measuring them all with a Western yardstick. The real picture of our planet's development bears little resemblance to all this.

The anguish of a divided world gave birth to the theory of convergence between the leading Western countries and the Soviet Union. It is a soothing theory which overlooks the fact that these worlds are not at all evolving toward each other and that neither one can be transformed into the other without violence. Besides, convergence inevitably means acceptance of the other side's defects, and this can hardly suit anyone.

If I were today addressing an audience in my country, in my examination of the overall pattern of the world's rifts I would have concentrated on the calamities of the East. But since my forced exile in the West has now lasted four years and since my audience is a Western one, I think it may be of greater interest to concentrate on certain aspects of the contemporary West, such as I see them.

A Decline in Courage

may be the most striking feature which an outside observer notices in the West today. The Western world has lost its civic courage, both as a whole and separately, in each country, in each government, in each political party and, of course, in the United Nations. Such a decline in courage is particularly noticeable among the ruling and intellectual elites, causing an impression of a loss of courage by the entire society. There remain many courageous individuals, but they have no determining influence on public life. Political and intellectual functionaries exhibit this depression, passivity and perplexity in their actions and in their statements, and even more so in their self-serving rationales as to how realistic, reasonable and intellectually and even morally justified it is to base state policies on weakness and cowardice. And the decline in courage, at times attaining what could be termed a lack of manhood, is ironically emphasized by occasional outbursts of boldness and inflexibility on the part of those same functionaries when dealing with weak governments and with countries that lack support, or with doomed currents which clearly cannot offer any resistance. But they get tongue-tied and paralyzed when they deal with powerful governments and threatening forces, with aggressors and international terrorists.

Must one point out that from ancient times a decline in courage has been considered the beginning of the end?

Well-Being

When the modern Western states were being formed, it was proclaimed as a principle that governments are meant to serve man and that man lives in order to be free and pursue happiness. (See, for example, the American Declaration of Independence.) Now at last during past decades technical and social progress has permitted the realization of such aspirations: the welfare state. Every citizen has been granted the desired freedom and material goods in such quantity and of such quality as to guarantee in theory the achievement of happiness, in the debased sense of the word which has come into being during those same decades. (In the process, however, one psychological detail has been overlooked: the constant desire to have still more things and a still better life and the struggle to this end imprint many Western faces with worry and even depression, though it is customary to carefully conceal such feelings. This active and tense competition comes to dominate all human thought and does not in the least open a way to free spiritual development.) The individual's independence from many types of state pressure has been guaranteed; the majority of the people have been granted well-being to an extent their fathers and grandfathers could not even dream about; it has become possible to raise young people according to these ideals, preparing them for and summoning them toward physical bloom, happiness, possession of material goods, money and leisure, toward an almost unlimited freedom in the choice of pleasures. So who should now renounce all this, why and for the sake of what should one risk one's precious life in defense of the common good and particularly in the nebulous case when the security of one's nation must be defended in an as yet distant land.

Even biology tells us that a high degree of habitual well-being is not advantageous to a living organism. Today, well-being in the life of Western society has begun to reveal its pernicious mask.

Legalistic Life

Western society has chosen for itself the organization best suited to its purposes and one I might call legalistic. The limits of human rights and rightness are determined by a system of laws; such limits are very broad. People in the West have acquired considerable skill in using, interpreting and manipulating law (though laws tend to be too complicated for an average person to understand without the help of an expert). Every conflict is solved according to the letter of the law and this is considered to be the ultimate solution. If one is right from a legal point of view, nothing more is required, nobody may mention that one could still not be entirely right, and urge self-restraint or a renunciation of these rights, call for sacrifice and selfless risk: this would simply sound absurd. Voluntary self-restraint is almost unheard of: everybody strives toward further expansion to the extreme limit of the legal frames. (An oil company is legally blameless when it buys up an invention of a new type of energy in order to prevent its use. A food product manufacturer is legally blameless when he poisons his produce to make it last longer: after all, people are free not to purchase it.)

I have spent all my life under a communist regime and I will tell you that a society without any objective legal scale is a terrible one indeed. But a society with no other scale but the legal one is also less than worthy of man. A society based on the letter of the law and never reaching any higher fails to take advantage of the full range of human possibilities. The letter of the law is too cold and formal to have a beneficial influence on society. Whenever the tissue of life is woven of legalistic relationships, this creates an atmosphere of spiritual mediocrity that paralyzes man's noblest impulses.

And it will be simply impossible to bear up to the trials of this threatening century with nothing but the supports of a legalistic structure.

The Direction of Freedom

Today's Western society has revealed the inequality between the freedom for good deeds and the freedom for evil deeds. A statesman who wants to achieve something important and highly constructive for his country has to move cautiously and even timidly; thousands of hasty (and irresponsible) critics cling to him at all times; he is constantly rebuffed by parliament and the press. He has to prove that his every step is well-founded and absolutely flawless. Indeed an outstanding, truly great person who has unusual and unexpected initiatives in mind does not get any chance to assert himself; dozens of traps will be set for him from the beginning. Thus mediocrity triumphs under the guise of democratic restraints.

It is feasible and easy everywhere to undermine administrative power and it has in fact been drastically weakened in all Western countries. The defense of individual rights has reached such extremes as to make society as a whole defenseless against certain individuals. It is time, in the West, to defend not so much human rights as human obligations.

On the other hand, destructive and irresponsible freedom has been granted boundless space. Society has turned out to have scarce defense against the abyss of human decadence, for example against the misuse of liberty for moral violence against young people, such as motion pictures full of pornography, crime and horror. This is all considered to be part of freedom and to be counterbalanced, in theory, by the young people's right not to look and not to accept. Life organized legalistically has thus shown its inability to defend itself against the corrosion of evil.

And what shall we say about the dark realms of overt criminality? Legal limits (especially in the United States) are broad enough to encourage not only individual freedom but also certain individual crimes. The culprit can go unpunished or obtain undeserved leniency — all with the support of thousands of defenders in the society. When a government earnestly undertakes to root out terrorism, public opinion immediately accuses it of violating the terrorists' civil rights. There is quite a number of such cases.

This tilt of freedom toward evil has come about gradually, but it evidently stems from a humanistic and benevolent concept according to which man — the master of this world — does not bear any evil within himself, and all the defects of life are caused by misguided social systems which must therefore be corrected. Yet strangely enough, though the best social conditions have been achieved in the West, there still remains a great deal of crime, there even is considerably more of it than in the destitute and lawless Soviet society. (There is a multitude of prisoners in our camps who are termed criminals, but most of them never committed any crime; they merely tried to defend themselves against a lawless state by resorting to means outside of the legal framework.)

The Direction of the Press

The press, too, of course, enjoys the widest freedom. (I shall be using the word press to include all the media.) But what use does it make of it?

Here again, the overriding concern is not to infringe the letter of the law. There is no moral responsibility for distortion or disproportion. What sort of responsibility does a journalist or a newspaper have to the readership or to history? If they have misled public opinion by inaccurate information or wrong conclusions, even if they have contributed to mistakes on a state level, do we know of any case of open regret voiced by the same journalist or the same newspaper? No, this would damage sales. A nation may be the worse for such a mistake, but the journalist always gets away with it. It is most likely that he will start writing the exact opposite to his previous statements with renewed aplomb.

Because instant and credible information is required, it becomes necessary to resort to guesswork, rumors and suppositions to fill in the voids, and none of them will ever be refuted, they settle into the readers' memory. How many hasty, immature, superficial and misleading judgments are expressed every day, confusing readers, and are then left hanging. The press can act the role of public opinion or miseducate it. Thus we may see terrorists heroized, or secret matters pertaining to the nation's defense publicly revealed, or we may witness shameless intrusion into the privacy of well-known people according to the slogan that "everyone is entitled to know everything." (But this is a false slogan of a false era: far greater in value is the forfeited right of people *not to know*, not to have their divine souls stuffed with gossip, nonsense, vain talk. A person who works and leads a meaningful life has no need for this excessive and burdening flow of information.)

Hastiness and superficiality — these are the psychic diseases of the 20th century and more than anywhere else this is manifested in the press. In-depth analysis of a problem is anathema to the press, it is contrary to its nature. The press merely picks out sensational formulas.

Such as it is, however, the press has become the greatest power within the Western countries, exceeding that of the legislature, the executive and the judiciary. Yet one would like to ask: according to what law has it been elected and to whom is it responsible? In the communist East, a journalist is frankly appointed as a state official. But who has voted Western journalists into their positions of power, for how long a time and with what prerogatives?

There is yet another surprise for someone coming from the totalitarian East with its rigorously unified press: one gradually discovers a common trend of preferences within the Western press as a whole (the spirit of the time), generally accepted patterns of judgment and maybe common corporate interests, the sum effect being not competition but unification. Unrestrained freedom exists for the press, but not for the readership because newspapers mostly transmit in a forceful and emphatic way those opinions which do not too openly contradict their own and that general trend.

A Fashion in Thinking

Without any censorship in the West, fashionable trends of thought and ideas are fastidiously separated from those which are not fashionable and the latter, without ever being forbidden, have little chance of finding their way into periodicals or books or be heard in colleges. Your scholars are free in the legal sense, but they are hemmed in by the idols of the prevailing fad. There is no open violence as in the East; however a selection dictated by fashion and the need to accommodate mass standards frequently prevent the most independent-minded persons from contributing to public life and give rise to dangerous herd instincts that block successful development. In America, I have received letters from highly intelligent persons, maybe a teacher in a far away small college, who could do much for the renewal and salvation of his country, but the country cannot hear him because the media will not provide him with a forum. This gives birth to strong mass prejudices, to a blindness which is perilous in our dynamic era. An example is the self-deluding interpretation of the state of affairs in the contemporary world that functions as a sort of a petrified armor around people's minds, to such a degree that human voices from 17 countries of Eastern Europe and Eastern Asia cannot pierce it. It will be broken only by the inexorable crowbar of events.

I have mentioned a few traits of Western life which surprise and shock a new arrival to this world. The purpose and scope of this speech will not allow me to continue such a survey, in particular to look into the impact of these characteristics on important aspects of a nation's life such as elementary education, advanced education in the humanities and art.

Socialism

It is almost universally recognized that the West shows all the world the way to successful economic development, even though in past years it has been sharply offset by chaotic inflation. However, many people living in the West are dissatisfied with their own society. They despise it or accuse it of no longer being up to the level of maturity attained by mankind. And this causes many to sway toward socialism, which is a false and dangerous current.

I hope that no one present will suspect me of expressing my partial criticism of the Western system in order to suggest socialism as an alternative. No, with the experience of a country where socialism has been realized, I shall certainly not speak for such an alternative. The mathematician Igor Shafarevich, a member of the Soviet Academy of Science, has written a brilliantly argued book entitled *Socialism*; this is a penetrating historical analysis demonstrating that socialism of any type and shade leads to a total destruction of the human spirit and to a levelling of mankind into death. Shafarevich's book was published in France almost two years ago and so far no one has been found to refute it. It will shortly be published in English in the U.S.

Not A Model

But should I be asked, instead, whether I would propose the West, such as it is today, as a model to my country, I would frankly have to answer negatively. No, I could not recommend your society as an ideal for the transformation of ours. Through deep suffering, people in our country have now achieved a spiritual development of such intensity that the Western system in its present state of spiritual exhaustion does not look attractive. Even those characteristics of your life which I have just enumerated are extremely saddening.

A fact which cannot be disputed is the weakening of human personality in the West while in the East it has become firmer and stronger. Six decades for our people and three decades for the people of Eastern Europe; during that time we have been through a spiritual training far in advance of Western experience. The complex and deadly crush of life has produced stronger, deeper and more interesting personalities than those generated by standardized Western well-being. Therefore, if our society were to be transformed into yours, it would mean an improvement in certain aspects, but also a change for the worse on some particularly significant points. Of course, a society cannot remain in an abyss of lawlessness as is the case in our country. But it is also demeaning for it to stay on such a soulless and smooth plane of legalism as is the case in yours. After the suffering of decades of violence and oppression, the human soul longs for things higher, warmer and purer than those offered by today's mass living habits, introduced as by a calling card by the revolting invasion of commercial advertising, by TV stupor and by intolerable music.

All this is visible to numerous observers from all the worlds of our planet. The Western way of life is less and less likely to become the leading model.

There are telltale symptoms by which history gives warning to a threatened or perishing society. Such are, for instance, a decline of the arts or a lack of great statesmen. Indeed sometimes the warnings are quite explicit and concrete. The center of your democracy and of your culture is left without electric power for a few hours only, and all of a sudden crowds of American citizens start looting and creating havoc. The smooth surface film must be very thin, then, the social system quite unstable and unhealthy.

But the fight for our planet, physical and spiritual, a fight of cosmic proportions, is not a vague matter of the future; it has already started. The forces of Evil have begun their decisive offensive[,] you can feel their pressure, yet your screens and publications are full of prescribed smiles and raised glasses. What is the joy about?

Shortsightedness

Very well known representatives of your society, such as George Kennan, say: "we cannot apply moral criteria to politics." Thus we mix good and evil, right and wrong and make space for the absolute triumph of absolute Evil in the world. On the contrary, only moral criteria can help the West against communism's well planned world strategy. There are no other criteria. Practical or occasional considerations of any kind will inevitably be swept away by strategy. After a certain level of the problem has been reached, legalistic thinking induces paralysis; it prevents one from seeing the scale and the meaning of events.

In spite of the abundance of information, or maybe partly because of it, the West has great difficulty in finding its bearings amid contemporary events. There have been naive predictions by some American experts who believed that Angola would become the Soviet Union's Vietnam or that the impudent Cuban expeditions in Africa would best be stopped by special U.S. courtesy to Cuba. Kennan's advice to his own country — to begin unilateral disarmament — belongs to the same category. If you only knew how the youngest of the officials in Moscow's Old Square* roar with laughter at your political wizards! As to Fidel Castro, he openly scorns the United States, boldly sending his troops to distant adventures from his country right next to yours.

However, the most cruel mistake occurred with the failure to understand the Vietnam war. Some people sincerely wanted all wars to stop just as soon as possible; others believed that the way should be left open for national, or communist, self-determination in Vietnam (or in Cambodia, as we see today with particular clarity). But in fact members of the U.S. anti-war movement became accomplices in the betrayal of Far Eastern nations, in the genocide and the suffering today imposed on 30 million people there. Do these convinced pacifists now hear the moans coming from there? Do they understand their responsibility today? Or do they prefer not to hear? The American intelligentsia lost its nerve and as a

* The Old Square in Moscow (Staraya Ploshchad') is the place where the Headquarters of the Central Committee of the CPSU are located; it is the real name of what in the West is conventionally referred to as the Kremlin.

consequence the danger has come much closer to the United States. But there is no awareness of this. Your shortsighted politician who signed the hasty Vietnam capitulation seemingly gave America a carefree breathing pause; however, a hundredfold Vietnam now looms over you. That small Vietnam had been a warning and an occasion to mobilize the nation's courage. But if the full might of America suffered a full-fledged defeat at the hands of a small communist half-country, how can the West hope to stand firm in the future?

I have said on another occasion that in the 20th century Western democracy has not won any major war by itself; each time it shielded itself with an ally possessing a powerful land army, whose philosophy it did not question. In World War II against Hitler, instead of winning the conflict with its own forces, which would certainly have been sufficient, Western democracy raised up another enemy, one that would prove worse and more powerful, since Hitler had neither the resources nor the people, nor the ideas with broad appeal, nor such a large number of supporters in the West — a fifth column — as the Soviet Union possessed. Some Western voices already have spoken of the need of a protective screen against hostile forces in the next world conflict; in this case, the shield would be China. But I would not wish such an outcome to any country in the world. First of all it is again a doomed alliance with Evil; it would grant the United States a respite, but when at a later date China with its billion people would turn around armed with American weapons, America itself would fall victim to a Cambodia-style genocide.

Loss of Will

And yet — no weapons, no matter how powerful, can help the West until it overcomes its loss of willpower. In a state of psychological weakness, weapons even become a burden for the capitulating side. To defend oneself, one must also be ready to die; there is little such readiness in a society raised in the cult of material well-being. Nothing is left, in this case, but concessions, attempts to gain time and betrayal. Thus at the shameful Belgrade conference free Western diplomats in their weakness surrendered the line of defense for which enslaved members of the Helsinki Watch Groups are sacrificing their lives.

Western thinking has become conservative: the world situation must stay as it is at any cost, there must be no changes. This debilitating dream of a status quo is the symptom of a society that has ceased to develop. But one must be blind in order not to see that the oceans no longer belong to the West, while the land under its domination keeps shrinking. The two so-called world wars (they were by far not on a world scale, not yet) constituted the internal self-destruction of the small progressive West which has thus prepared its own end. The next war (which does not have to be an atomic one, I do not believe it will be) may well bury Western civilization forever.

In the face of such a danger, with such historical values in your past, with such a high level of attained freedom and, apparently, of devotion to it, how is it possible to lose to such an extent the will to defend oneself?

Humanism and Its Consequences

How has this unfavorable relation of forces come about? How did the West decline from its triumphal march to its present debility? Have there been fatal turns and losses of direction in its development? It does not seem so. The West kept advancing steadily in accordance with its proclaimed social intentions, hand in hand with a dazzling progress in technology. And all of a sudden it found itself in its present state of weakness.

This means that the mistake must be at the root, at the very foundation of thought in modern times. I refer to the prevailing Western view of the world which was born in the Renaissance and has found political expression since the Age of Enlightenment. It became the basis for political and social doctrine and could be called rationalistic humanism or humanistic autonomy: the proclaimed and practiced autonomy of man from any higher force above him. It could also be called anthropocentricity, with man seen as the center of all.

The turn introduced by the Renaissance was probably inevitable historically: the Middle Ages had come to a natural end by exhaustion, having become an intolerable despotic repression of man's physical nature in favor of the spiritual one. But then, we recoiled from the Spirit and embraced all that is material, excessively and incommensurately. The humanistic way of thinking, which had proclaimed itself our guide, did not admit the existence of intrinsic evil in man nor did it see any task higher than the attainment of happiness on earth. It started modern Western civilization on the dangerous trend of worshipping man and his material needs. Everything beyond physical well-being and the accumulation of material goods, all other human requirements and characteristics of a subtler and higher nature were left outside the area of attention of state and social systems, as if human life did not have any higher meaning. Thus, gaps were left open for evil and its drafts blow freely today. Mere freedom per se does not in the least solve all the problems of human life and even adds a number of new ones.

And yet, in early democracies, as in American democracy at the time of its birth, all individual human rights were granted on the ground that man is God's creature. That is, freedom was given to the individual conditionally, in the assumption of his constant religious responsibility. Such was the heritage of the preceding one thousand years. Two hundred or even fifty years ago, it would have seemed quite impossible, in America, that an individual be granted boundless freedom with no purpose, simply for the satisfaction of his whims. Subsequently, however, all such limitations were eroded everywhere in the West; a total emancipation occurred from the moral heritage of Christian centuries with their great reserves of mercy and sacrifice. State systems were becoming ever more materialistic.

The West has finally achieved the rights of man, and even to excess, but man's sense of responsibility to God and society has grown dimmer and dimmer. In the past decades, the legalistic selfishness of the Western approach to the world has reached its peak and the world found itself in a harsh spiritual crisis and a political impasse. All the celebrated technological achievements of Progress, including the conquest of outer space, do not redeem the twentieth century's moral poverty, which no one could have imagined even as late as the nineteenth century.

An Unexpected Kinship

As humanism in its development was becoming more and more materialistic, it also increasingly allowed its concepts to be used first by socialism and then by communism. So that Karl Marx was able to say, in 1844, that "communism is naturalized humanism."

This statement has proved to be not entirely unreasonable. One does see the same stones in the foundations of an eroded humanism and of any type of socialism: boundless materialism; freedom from religion and religious responsibility (which under communist regimes attain the stage of anti-religious dictatorship); concentration on social structures with an allegedly scientific approach. (This last is typical of both the Age of Enlightenment and of marxism.) It is no accident that all of communism's rhetorical vows revolve around Man (with a capital M) and his earthly happiness. At first glance it seems an ugly parallel: common traits in the thinking and way of life of today's West and today's East? But such is the logic of materialistic development.

The interrelationship is such, moreover, that the current of materialism which is farthest to the left, and is hence the most consistent, always proves to be stronger, more attractive and victorious. Humanism that has lost its Christian heritage cannot prevail in this competition. Thus during the past centuries and especially in recent decades, as the process became more acute, the alignment of forces was as follows: liberalism was inevitably pushed aside by radicalism, radicalism had to surrender to socialism and socialism could not stand up to communism. The communist regime in the East could endure and grow due to the enthusiastic support from an enormous number of Western intellectuals who (feeling the kinship!) refused to see communism's crimes, and when they no longer could do so, they tried to justify these crimes. The problem persists: in our Eastern countries, communism has suffered a complete ideological defeat, it is zero and less than zero. And yet Western intellectuals still look at it with considerable interest and empathy, and this is precisely what makes it so immensely difficult for the West to withstand the East.

Before the Turn

I am not examining the case of a disaster brought on by a world war and the changes which it would produce in society. But as long as we wake up every morning under a peaceful sun, we must lead an everyday life. Yet there is a disaster which is already very much with us. I am referring to the calamity of an autonomous, irreligious humanistic consciousness.

It has made man the measure of all things on earth — imperfect man who is never free of pride, self-interest, envy, vanity and dozens of other defects. We are now paying for the mistakes which had not been properly appraised at the beginning of the journey. On the way from the Renaissance to our days we have enriched our experience but we have lost the concept of a Supreme Complete Entity which used to restrain our passions and our irresponsibility. We have placed too much hope in politics and social reforms, only to find out that we were being deprived of our most precious possession: our spiritual life. It is trampled by the party mob in the East, by the commercial one in the West. This is the essence of the crisis: the split in the world is less terrifying than the similarity of the disease afflicting its main sections.

If, as claimed by humanism, man were born only to be happy, he would not be born to die. Since his body is doomed to death, his task on earth evidently must be more spiritual: not a total engrossment in everyday life, not the search for the best ways to obtain material goods and then their carefree consumption. It has to be the fulfillment of a permanent, earnest duty so that one's life journey may become above all an experience of moral growth: to leave life a better human being than one started it. It is imperative to reappraise the scale of the usual human values; its present incorrectness is astounding. It is not possible that assessment of the President's performance should be reduced to the question of how much money one makes or to the availability of gasoline. Only by the voluntary nurturing in ourselves of freely accepted and serene self-restraint can mankind rise above the world stream of materialism.

Today it would be retrogressive to hold on to the ossified formulas of the enlightenment. Such social dogmatism leaves us helpless before the trials of our times.

Even if we are spared destruction by war, life will have to change in order not to perish on its own. We cannot avoid reassessing the fundamental definitions of human life and human society. Is it true that man is above everything? Is there no Superior Spirit above him? Is it right that man's life and society's activities should be ruled by material expansion above all? Is it permissible to promote such expansion to the detriment of our integral spiritual life?

If the world has not approached its end, it has reached a major watershed in history, equal in importance to the turn from the Middle Ages to the Renaissance. It will demand from us a spiritual blaze, we shall have to rise to a new height of vision, to a new level of life where our physical nature will not be cursed as in the Middle Ages, but, even more importantly, our spiritual being will not be trampled upon as in the Modern Era.

This ascension will be similar to climbing onto the next anthropologic stage. No one on earth has any other way left but — upward.

COURT ON MEDIA OWNERSHIP
June 12, 1978

The Supreme Court voted unanimously June 12 to uphold a Federal Communications Commission (FCC) regulation which prohibits, in the future, co-ownership of a newspaper and a radio station or television station in the same community. The court also affirmed the FCC's decision not to make its ruling retroactive, except in those cases in which the only local newspaper owned the only local radio or television outlet. The decision, encompassing six cases, allowed most extant joint ownership arrangements to continue, provided there is no change in the ownership.

After the FCC decision in 1975, which was promulgated in the hope that diversity of ownership would result in a diversity of viewpoints, the National Association of Broadcasters, the National Citizens Committee for Broadcasting, newspaper publishers and others asked the U.S. Circuit Court of Appeals for Washington, D.C., to review the FCC order. The court of appeals upheld the FCC order concerning future co-ownership and found that the rule should apply to existing co-ownership arrangements as well. The FCC's decision to "grandfather" the rules, the lower court said, was arbitrary, capricious and without a rational basis.

Justice Thurgood Marshall wrote the opinion for the court. Justice William J. Brennan Jr. did not participate in the consideration of the cases.

Justice Marshall rejected the argument that the FCC rule violated the rights of free speech and a free press guaranteed by the First Amendment. Using a quotation from a former Supreme Court decision, Red Lion Broadcasting Co. v. FCC, Marshall said that "this argument ignores the fundamental proposition that there is no 'unabridgeable First Amendment right to broadcast comparable to the right of every individual to speak, write, or publish.' " He continued, "The regulations are a reasonable means of promoting the public interest in diversified mass communications; thus they do not violate the First Amendment rights of those who will be denied broadcast licenses pursuant to them."

'Grandfather' Decision

The FCC's decision to grandfather the regulations was sound, Marshall asserted; if the commission had ordered divestiture of all co-ownership arrangements, the opinion said, the results would include the loss of "the stability and continuity of meritorious service provided by newspaper owners," the onset of "economic dislocations" that could prevent new owners from "obtaining sufficient working capital to maintain the quality of local programming" and a decrease in local ownership of broadcast outlets.

In the 16 instances in which the FCC ordered divestiture, Marshall said, it did so for the same reasons that it forbade co-ownership in the future: "The greater the number of owners in a market, the greater the possibility of achieving diversity of program and service viewpoints." The lower court, he declared, had wrongfully assumed that the FCC had chosen these markets for divestiture only because "divestiture would be more harmful in the grandfathered markets."

> Following are excerpts from the Supreme Court's unanimous June 12 decision to uphold the Federal Communication Commission's order prohibiting ownership of both a local newspaper and a local radio or television station:

Nos. 76-1471, 76-1521, 76-1595, 76-1604, 76-1624, & 76-1685

Federal Communications
Commission, Petitioner,
76-1471   v.
National Citizens
Committee for Broadcasting
et al.

On Writs of Certiorari to the United States Court of Appeals for the District of Columbia Circuit.

Channel Two Television
Company et al., Petitioners,
76-1521   v.
National Citizens
Committee for Broadcasting
et. al.

National Association of
Broadcasters, Petitioner,
76-1595　　　*v.*
Federal Communications
Commission et al.

American Newspaper
Publishers Association,
Petitioner,
76-1604　　　*v.*
National Citizens
Committee for Broadcasting
et al.

Illinois Broadcasting
Company, Inc., et al.,
Petitioners,
76-1624　　　*v.*
National Citizens
Committee for Broadcasting
et al.

Post Company et al.,
Petitioners,
76-1685　　　*v.*
National Citizens
Committee for Broadcasting
et al.

[June 12, 1978]

MR. JUSTICE MARSHALL delivered the opinion of the Court. [MR.
JUSTICE BRENNAN took no part in the consideration or decision of
these cases.]

At issue in these cases are Federal Communications Commission regulations governing the permissibility of common ownership of a radio or television broadcast station and a daily newspaper located in the same community. . . . The regulations, adopted after a lengthy rulemaking proceeding, prospectively bar formation or transfer of co-located newspaper broadcast combinations. Existing combinations are generally permitted to continue in operation. However, in communities in which there is common
ownership of the only daily newspaper and the only broadcast station, or
(where there is more than one broadcast station) of the only daily newspaper and the only television station, divestiture of either the newspaper or
the broadcast station is required within five years, unless grounds for
waiver are demonstrated.

The questions for decision are whether these regulations either exceed
the Commission's authority under the Communications Act of 1934 . . . or

violate the First or Fifth Amendment rights of newspaper owners; and whether the lines drawn by the Commission between new and existing newspaper-broadcast combinations, and between existing combinations subject to divestiture and those allowed to continue in operation, are arbitrary or capricious within the meaning of § 10 (e) of the Administrative Procedure Act. . . . For the reasons set forth below, we sustain the regulations in their entirety.

I

. . .[T]he Commission began the instant rulemaking proceedings in 1970 to consider the need for a more restrictive policy toward newspaper ownership of radio and television broadcast stations. . . . Citing studies showing the dominant role of television stations and daily newspapers as sources of local news and other information . . . the notice of rulemaking proposed adoption of regulations that would eliminate all newspaper-broadcast combinations serving the same market, by prospectively banning formation or transfer of such combinations and requiring dissolution of all existing combinations within five years. . . . The Commission suggested that the proposed regulations would serve "the purpose of promoting competition among the mass media involved, and maximizing diversification of service sources and viewpoints." [Notice of Proposed Rulemaking]. . . . At the same time, however, the Commission expressed "substantial concern" about the disruption of service that might result from divestiture of existing combinations. . . . Comments were invited on all aspects of the proposed rules.

The notice of rulemaking generated a considerable response. Nearly 200 parties, including the Antitrust Division of the Justice Department, various broadcast and newspaper interests, public interest groups, and academic and research entities, filed comments on the proposed rules. In addition, a number of studies were submitted, dealing with the effects of newspaper-broadcast cross-ownership on competition and station performance, the economic consequences of divestiture, and the degree of diversity present in the mass media. In March 1974, the Commission requested further comments directed primarily to the core problem of newspaper-television station cross-ownership . . . and close to 50 sets of additional comments were filed. In July 1974, the Commission held three days of oral argument, at which all parties who requested time were allowed to speak.

The regulations at issue here were promulgated and explained in a lengthy report and order released by the Commission on January 31, 1975. The Commission concluded, first, that it had statutory authority to issue the regulations under the Communications Act . . . and that the regulations were valid under the First and Fifth Amendments to the Constitution. . . . In addition, the Commission rejected the suggestion that it lacked the power to order divestiture, reasoning that the statutory requirement of license renewal every three years necessarily implied authority to order divestiture over a five-year period. . . .

After reviewing the comments and studies submitted by the various parties during the course of the proceeding, the Commission then turned to an explanation of the regulations and the justifications for their adoption. The prospective rules, barring formation of new broadcast-newspaper combinations in the same market, as well as transfers of existing combinations to new owners, were adopted without change from the proposal set forth in the notice of rulemaking. While recognizing the pioneering contributions of newspaper owners to the broadcast industry, the Commission concluded that changed circumstances made it possible, and necessary, for all new licensing of broadcast stations to "be expected to add to local diversity." [Memorandum Opinion and Order]. . . .

With respect to the proposed across-the-board divestiture requirement, however, the Commission concluded that "a mere hoped for gain in diversity" was not a sufficient justification. [Order]. . . . Characterizing the divestiture issues as "the most difficult" presented in the proceeding, the Order explained that the proposed rules, while correctly recognizing the central importance of diversity considerations, "may have given too little weight to the consequences which could be expected to attend a focus on the abstract goal alone.". . . Forced dissolution would promote diversity, but it would also cause "disruption for the industry and hardship for individual owners," "resulting in losses or diminution of service to the public.". . .

The Commission concluded that in light of these countervailing considerations divestiture was warranted only in "the most egregious cases," which it identified as those in which a newspaper-broadcast combination has an "effective monopoly" in the local "marketplace of ideas as well as economically." [Order]. . . . The Commission recognized that any standards for defining which combinations fell within that category would necessarily be arbitrary to some degree. . . . It thus decided to require divestiture only where there was common ownership of the sole daily newspaper published in a community and either (1) the sole broadcast station providing that entire community with a clear signal, or (2) the sole television station encompassing the entire community with a clear signal. . . .

The Order identified eight television-newspaper and 10 radio-newspaper combinations meeting the divestiture criteria. . . . Waivers of the divestiture requirement were granted . . . to one television and one radio combination, leaving a total of 16 stations subject to divestiture. The Commission explained that waiver requests would be entertained in the latter cases, but, absent waiver, either the newspaper or the broadcast station would have to be divested by January 1, 1980. . . .

On petitions for reconsideration, the Commission reaffirmed the rules in all material respects.

II

Petitioners NAB [National Association of Broadcasters] and ANPA [American Newspaper Publishers Association] contend that the regulations promulgated by the Commission exceed its statutory rulemaking authority and violate the constitutional rights of newspaper owners. We turn first to the statutory, and then to the constitutional, issues.

A

(1)

Section 303 (r) of the Communications Act . . . provides that "the Commission from time to time, as public convenience, interest, or necessity requires, shall . . . [m]ake such rules and regulations and prescribe such restrictions and conditions, not inconsistent with law, as may be necessary to carry out the provisions of [the Act].". . . . As the Court of Appeals recognized. . . , it is now well established that this general rulemaking authority supplies a statutory basis for the Commission to enact regulations codifying its view of the public interest licensing standard, so long as that view is based on consideration of permissible factors and is otherwise reasonable. If a license applicant does not qualify under standards set forth in such regulations, and does not proffer sufficient grounds for waiver or change of those standards, the Commission may deny the application without further inquiry. . . .

This Court has specifically upheld this rulemaking authority in the context of regulations based on the Commission's policy of promoting diversification of ownership. In *United States* v. *Storer Broadcasting Co.* ...[1956], we sustained the portion of the Commission's multiple ownership rules placing limitations on the total number of stations in each broadcast service a person may own or control. . . . And in *National Broadcasting Co.* v. *United States* . . . [1943], we affirmed regulations that, *inter alia*, prohibited broadcast networks from owning more than one AM radio station in the same community, and from owning " 'any standard broadcast station in any locality where the existing standard broadcast stations are so few or of such unequal desirability . . . that competition would be substantially restrained by such licensing.' ". . .

Petitioner NAB attempts to distinguish these cases on the ground that they involved efforts to increase diversification within the boundaries of the broadcasting industry itself, whereas the instant regulations are concerned with diversification of ownership in the mass communications media as a whole. NAB contends that, since the Act confers jurisdiction on the Commission only to regulate "communication by wire or radio". . . , it is impermissible for the Commission to use its licensing authority with respect to broadcasting to promote diversity in an overall communications market which includes, but is not limited to, the broadcasting industry.

This argument undersells the Commission's power to regulate broadcasting in the "public interest." In making initial licensing decisions between competing applicants, the Commission has long given "primary significance" to "diversification of control of the media of mass communications," and has denied licenses to newspaper owners on the basis of this policy in appropriate cases. . . . As we have discussed on several occasions, see, *e.g., National Broadcasting Co.* v. *United States.* . . ; *Red Lion Broadcasting Co.* v. *FCC* . . . (1969), the physical scarcity of broadcast frequencies, as well as problems of interference between broadcast signals, led Congress to delegate broad authority to the Commission to allocate broadcast licenses in the "public interest." And "[t]he avowed aim of the Communications Act of 1934 was to secure the maximum benefits of radio to all the people of the United States." *National Broadcasting Co.* v. *United States.* . . . It was not inconsistent with the statutory scheme, therefore, for the Commission to conclude that the maximum benefit to the "public interest" would follow from allocation of broadcast licenses so as to promote diversification of the mass media as a whole.

Our past decisions have recognized, moreover, that the First Amendment and antitrust values underlying the Commission's diversification policy may properly be considered by the Commission in determining where the public interest lies. "[T]he 'public interest' standard necessarily invites reference to First Amendment principles," *Columbia Broadcasting System, Inc.* v. *Democratic National Committee* . . . (1973), and, in particular, to the First Amendment goal of achieving "the widest possible dissemination of information from diverse and antagonistic sources," *Associated Press* v. *United States* [1945]. . . . And, while the Commission does not have power to enforce the antitrust laws as such, it is permitted to take antitrust policies into account in making licensing decisions pursuant to the public interest standard. . . .

(2)

It is thus clear that the regulations at issue are based on permissible public interest goals and, so long as the regulations are not an unreasonable means for seeking to achieve these goals, they fall within the general rulemaking authority recognized in the *Storer Broadcasting* and *National Broadcasting* cases. Petitioner ANPA contends that the prospective rules are unreasonable in two respects: first, the rulemaking record did not conclusively establish that prohibiting common ownership of co-located newspapers and broadcast stations would in fact lead to increases in the diversity of viewpoints among local communications media; and second, the regulations were based on the diversification factor to the exclusion of other service factors considered in the past by the Commission in making initial licensing decisions regarding newspaper owners. . . . With respect to the first point, we agree with the Court of Appeals that, notwithstanding the inconclusiveness of the rulemaking record, the Commission acted rationally in finding that diversification of ownership would enhance the possibility of achieving greater diversity of viewpoints. As the Court of Appeals observed, "[d]iversity and its effects are . . . elusive concepts, not easily defined let alone measured without making qualitative judgments objectionable on both policy and First Amendment grounds.". . . Moreover, evidence of specific abuses by common owners is difficult to compile; "the possible benefits of competition do not lend themselves to detailed forecast." *FCC* v. *RCA Communications, Inc.* . . . (1953). In these circumstances, the Commission was entitled to rely on its judgment, based on experience, that "it is unrealistic to expect true diversity from a commonly owned station-newspaper combination. The divergency of their viewpoints cannot be expected to be the same as if they were antagonistically run.". . .

As to the Commission's decision to give controlling weight to its diversification goal in shaping the prospective rules, the Order makes clear that this change in policy was a reasonable administrative response to changed circumstances in the broadcasting industry. . . . The Order explained that, although newspaper owners had previously been allowed, and even encouraged, to acquire licenses for co-located broadcast stations because of the shortage of qualified license applicants, a sufficient number of qualified and experienced applicants other than newspaper owners was now available. In addition, the number of channels open for new licensing had diminished substantially. It had thus become both feasible and more urgent for the Commission to take steps to increase diversification of ownership, and a change in the Commission's policy toward new licensing offered the possibility of increasing diversity without causing any disruption of existing service. In light of these considerations, the Commission clearly did not take an irrational view of the public interest when it decided to impose a prospective ban on new licensing of co-located newspaper-broadcast combinations.

B

Petitioners NAB and ANPA also argue that the regulations, though designed to further the First Amendment goal of achieving "the widest possible dissemination of information from diverse and antagonistic sources," *Associated Press* v. *United States* . . . , nevertheless violate the First Amendment rights of newspaper owners. We cannot agree, for this argument ignores the fundamental proposition that there is no "unabridgeable First Amendment right to broadcast comparable to the right of every individual to speak, write, or publish." *Red Lion Broadcasting Co.* v. *FCC.* . . .

NAB and ANPA contend, however, that it is inconsistent with the First Amendment to promote diversification by barring a newspaper owner from owning certain broadcasting stations. In support, they point to our statement in *Buckley* v. *Valeo* . . . (1976), to the effect that "government may [not] restrict the speech of some elements of our society in order to enhance the relative voice of others.". . . As *Buckley* also recognized, however, " 'the broadcast media pose unique and special problems not present in the traditional free speech case.' " . . . [*Buckley*] quoting *Columbia Broadcasting System* v. *Democratic National Committee.* . . . Thus efforts to " 'enhanc[e] the volume and quality of coverage' of public issues" through regulation of broadcasting may be permissible where similar efforts to regulate the print media would not be. . . . [*Buckley*] quoting

Red Lion Broadcasting Co. v. *FCC.* . . . Requiring those who wish to obtain a broadcast license to demonstrate that such would serve the "public interest" does not restrict the speech of those who are denied licenses; rather, it preserves the interests of the "people as a whole . . . in free speech." *Red Lion Broadcasting Co.* . . . As we stated in *Red Lion*, "to deny a station license because 'the public interest' requires it 'is not a denial of free speech.' " . . . [*Red Lion*] quoting *National Broadcasting Co.* v. *United States.* . . .

Relying on cases such as *Speiser* v. *Randall* . . . (1958), and *Elrod* v. *Burns* . . . (1976), NAB and ANPA also argue that the regulations unconstitutionally condition receipt of a broadcast license upon forfeiture of the right to publish a newspaper. Under the regulations, however, a newspaper owner need not forfeit anything in order to acquire a license for a station located in another community. More importantly, in the cases relied on by petitioners, unlike the instant case, denial of a benefit had the effect of abridging freedom of expression, since the denial was based solely on the content of constitutionally protected speech; in *Speiser* veterans were deprived of a special property-tax exemption if they declined to subscribe to a loyalty oath, while in *Elrod* certain public employees were discharged or threatened with discharge because of their political affiliation. As we wrote in *National Broadcasting* . . . , "the issue before us would be wholly different" if "the Commission [were] to choose among applicants upon the basis of their political, economic or social views.". . . Here the regulations are not content-related; moreover, their purpose and effect is to promote free speech, not to restrict it.

Finally, petitioners argue that the Commission has unfairly "singled out" newspaper owners for more stringent treatment than other license applicants. But the regulations treat newspaper owners in essentially the same fashion as other owners of the major media of mass communications were already treated under the Commission's multiple ownership rules; . . . owners of radio stations, television stations, and newspapers alike are now restricted in their ability to acquire licenses for co-located broadcast stations. . . .

In the instant case, far from seeking to limit the flow of information, the Commission has acted, in the Court of Appeals' words, "to enhance the diversity of information heard by the public without on-going government surveillance of the content of speech.". . . The regulations are a reasonable means of promoting the public interest in diversified mass communications; thus they do not violate the First Amendment rights of those who will be denied broadcast licenses pursuant to them. . . .

III

After upholding the prospective aspect of the Commission's regulations, the Court of Appeals concluded that the Commission's decision to limit divestiture to 16 "egregious cases" of "effective monopoly" was arbitrary and capricious within the meaning of the Administrative Procedure Act

(APA). . . . We agree with the Court of Appeals that regulations promulgated after informal rulemaking, while not subject to review under the "substantial evidence" test of the APA, . . . may be invalidated by a reviewing court under the "arbitrary or capricious" standard if they are not rational and based on consideration of the relevant factors. *Citizens to Preserve Overton Park* v. *Volpe* . . . (1971). Although this review "is to be searching and careful," "[t]he court is not empowered to substitute its judgment for that of the agency.". . .

In the view of the Court of Appeals, the Commission lacked a rational basis, first, for treating existing newspaper-broadcast combinations more leniently than combinations that might seek licenses in the future; and, second, even assuming a distinction between existing and new combinations had been justified, for requiring divestiture in the "egregious cases" while allowing all other existing combinations to continue in operation. We believe that the limited divestiture requirement reflects a rational weighing of competing policies, and we therefore reinstate the portion of the Commission's order that was invalidated by the Court of Appeals.

A

(1)

The Commission was well aware that separating existing newspaper-broadcast combinations would promote diversification of ownership. It concluded, however, that ordering widespread divestiture would not result in "the best practicable service to the American public," . . . a goal that the Commission has always taken into account and that has been specifically approved by this Court, *FCC* v. *Sanders Bros. Radio Station* . . . (1940). . . . In particular, the Commission expressed concern that divestiture would cause "disruption for the industry" and "hardship to individual owners," both of which would result in harm to the public interest. . . . Especially in light of the fact that the number of co-located newspaper-broadcast combinations was already on the decline as a result of natural market forces, and would decline further as a result of the prospective rules, the Commission decided that across-the-board divestiture was not warranted. . . .

The Order identified several specific respects in which the public interest would or might be harmed if a sweeping divestiture requirement were imposed: the stability and continuity of meritorious service provided by the newspaper owners as a group would be lost; owners who had provided meritorious service would unfairly be denied the opportunity to continue in operation; "economic dislocations" might prevent new owners from obtaining sufficient working capital to maintain the quality of local programming; and local ownership of broadcast stations would probably decrease. . . . We cannot say that the Commission acted irrationally in concluding that these public interest harms outweighed the potential gains that would follow from increasing diversification of ownership. . . .

In the instant proceeding, the Commission specifically noted that the existing newspaper-broadcast cross-owners as a group had a "long record of service" in the public interest; many were pioneers in the broadcasting industry and had established and continued "[t]raditions of service" from the outset. . . . Notwithstanding the Commission's diversification policy, all were granted initial licenses upon findings that the public interest would be served thereby, and those that had been in existence for more than three years had also had their licenses renewed on the ground that the public interest would be furthered. The Commission noted, moreover, that its own study of existing co-located newspaper-television combinations showed that in terms of percentage of time devoted to several categories of local programming, these stations had displayed "an undramatic but nonetheless statistically significant superiority" over other television stations. . . . An across-the-board divestiture requirement would result in loss of the services of these superior licensees, and — whether divestiture caused actual losses to existing owners, or just denial of reasonably anticipated gains — the result would be that future licensees would be discouraged from investing the resources necessary to produce quality service.

At the same time, there was no guarantee that the licensees who replaced the existing cross-owners would be able to provide the same level of service or demonstrate the same long-term commitment to broadcasting. And even if the new owners were able in the long run to provide similar or better service, the Commission found that divestiture would cause serious disruption in the transition period. . . .

The Commission's fear that local ownership would decline was grounded in a rational prediction, based on its knowledge of the broadcasting industry and supported by comments in the record, . . . that many of the existing newspaper-broadcast combinations owned by local interest would respond to the divestiture requirement by trading stations with out-of-town owners. It is undisputed that roughly 75% of the existing co-located newspaper-television combinations are locally owned . . . and these owners' knowledge of their local communities and concern for local affairs, built over a period of years, would be lost if they were replaced with outside interests. Local ownership in and of itself has been recognized to be a factor of some — if relatively slight — significance even in the context of initial licensing decisions. . . . It was not unreasonable, therefore, for the Commission to consider it as one of several factors militating against divestiture of combinations that have been in existence for many years.

In light of these countervailing considerations, we cannot agree with the Court of Appeals that it was arbitrary and capricious for the Commission to "grandfather" most existing combinations, and to leave opponents of these combinations to their remedies in individual renewal proceedings. In the latter connection we note that, while individual renewal proceedings are unlikely to accomplish any "overall restructuring" of the existing ownership patterns, the Order does make clear that existing combinations will be subject to challenge by competing applicants in renewal proceedings, to the same extent as they were prior to the instant rulemaking proceedings. . . .

(2)

In concluding that the Commission acted unreasonably in not extending its divestiture requirement across-the-board, the Court of Appeals apparently placed heavy reliance on a "presumption" that existing newspaper-broadcast combinations "do not serve the public interest.". . . The Court derived this presumption primarily from the Commission's own diversification policy, as "reaffirmed" by adoption of the prospective rules in this proceeding, and secondarily from "[t]he policies of the First Amendment," . . . and the Commission's statutory duty to "encourage the larger and more effective use of radio in the public interest.". . . As explained in Part II above, we agree that diversification of ownership furthers statutory and constitutional policies, and, as the Commission recognized, separating existing newspaper-broadcast combinations would promote diversification. But the weighing of policies under the "public interest" standard is a task that Congress has delegated to the Commission in the first instance, and we are unable to find anything in the Communications Act, the First Amendment, or the Commission's past or present practices that would require the Commission to "presume" that its diversification policy should be given controlling weight in all circumstances.

Such a "presumption" would seem to be inconsistent with the Commission's longstanding and judicially approved practice of giving controlling weight in some circumstances to its more general goal of achieving "the best practicable service to the public." Certainly, as discussed in Part III-A (1) above, the Commission through its license renewal policy has made clear that it considers diversification of ownership to be a factor of less significance when deciding whether to allow an existing licensee to continue in operation than when evaluating applicants seeking initial licensing. Nothing in the language or the legislative history of § 303 (g) indicates that Congress intended to foreclose all differences in treatment between new and existing licensees, and indeed, in amending § 307 (d) of the Act in 1952. Congress appears to have lent its approval to the Commission's policy of evaluating existing licensees on a somewhat different basis than new applicants. Moreover, if enactment of the prospective rules in this proceeding itself were deemed to create a "presumption" in favor of divestiture, the Commission's ability to experiment with new policies would be severely hampered. . . .

The Court of Appeals also relied on its perception that the policies militating against divestiture were "lesser policies" to which the Commission had not given as much weight in the past as its divestiture policy. . . . The Commission's past concern with avoiding disruption of existing service is amply illustrated by its license renewal policies. In addition, it is worth noting that in the past when the Commission has changed its multiple ownership rules it has almost invariably tailored the changes so as to operate wholly or primarily on a prospective basis. For example, the regulations adopted in 1970 prohibiting common ownership of a VHF television station and a radio station serving the same market were made to apply only to new licensing decisions; no divestiture of existing combinations was required. . . .

The Court of Appeals apparently reasoned that the Commission's concerns with respect to disruption of existing service, economic dislocations, and decreases in local ownership necessarily could not be very weighty since the Commission has a practice of routinely approving voluntary transfers and assignments of licenses. . . . But the question of whether the Commission should compel proven licensees to divest their stations is a different question from whether the public interest is served by allowing transfers by licensees who no longer wish to continue in the business. . . .

The Court of Appeals' final basis for concluding that the Commission acted arbitrarily in not giving controlling weight to its divestiture policy was the Court's finding that the rulemaking record did not adequately "disclose the extent to which divestiture would actually threaten" the competing policies relied upon by the Commission. . . . However, to the extent that factual determinations were involved in the Commission's decision to grandfather most existing combinations, they were primarily of a judgmental or predictive nature — e.g., whether a divestiture requirement would result in trading of stations with out-of-town owners; whether new owners would perform as well as existing cross-owners, either in the short run or in the long run; whether losses to existing owners would result from forced sales; whether such losses would discourage future investment in quality programming; and whether new owners would have sufficient working capital to finance local programming. In such circumstances complete factual support in the record for the Commission's judgment or prediction is not possible or required; "a forecast of the direction in which future public interest lies necessarily involves deductions based on the expert knowledge of the agency." *Federal Power Commission* v. *Transcontinental Gas Pipe Line Corp.* [1961]. . . .

B

We also must conclude that the Court of Appeals erred in holding that it was arbitrary to order divestiture in the 16 "egregious cases" while allowing other existing combinations to continue in operation. The Commission's decision was based not — as the Court of Appeals may have believed . . . — on a conclusion that divestiture would be more harmful in the grandfathered markets than in the 16 affected markets, but rather on a judgment that the need for diversification was especially great in cases of local monopoly. This policy judgment was certainly not irrational . . . and indeed was founded on the very same assumption that underpinned the diversification policy itself and the prospective rules upheld by the Court of Appeals and now by this Court — that the greater the number of owners in a market, the greater the possibility of achieving diversity of program and service viewpoints.

As to the Commission's criteria for determining which existing newspaper-broadcast combinations have an "effective monopoly" in the "local

marketplace of ideas as well as economically," we think the standards settled upon by the Commission reflect a rational legislative-type judgment.
Some line had to be drawn, and it was hardly unreasonable for the Commission to confine divestiture to communities in which there is common
ownership of the only daily newspaper and either the only television
station or the only broadcast station of any kind encompassing the entire
community with a clear signal. . . . It was not irrational, moreover, for the
Commission to disregard media sources other than newspapers and broadcast stations in setting its divestiture standards. The studies cited by the
Commission in its notice of rulemaking unanimously concluded that newspapers and television are the two most widely utilized media sources for
local news and discussion of public affairs; and, as the Commission noted
in its Order, . . . "aside from the fact that [magazines and other periodi-
cals] often had only a tiny fraction in the market, they were not given real
weight since they often dealt exclusively with regional or national issues
and ignored local issues." Moreover, the differences in treatment between
radio and television stations . . . were certainly justified in light of the far
greater influence of television than radio as a source for local news. . . .

The judgment of the Court of Appeals is affirmed in part and reversed
in part.

It is so ordered.

COURT ON ENDANGERED SPECIES

June 15, 1978

A little fish, a three-inch member of the perch family, was the victor over the mighty Tennessee Valley Authority (TVA) in a ruling handed down by the Supreme Court June 15. In a 6-3 decision, the court said that the TVA must halt work on its $120 million Tellico Dam project because the reservoir to be created would probably destroy the only known habitat of the fish, called the snail darter.

The court based its decision on the Endangered Species Act of 1973 which prohibited actions by federal agencies jeopardizing the existence or habitat of species designated as endangered by the secretary of the interior.

The paradox of the small snail darter bringing work on a huge dam to a standstill was not lost on Chief Justice Warren E. Burger, who wrote the majority opinion. "It may seem curious to some," he wrote, "that the survival of a relatively small number of three-inch fish among all the countless millions of species extant would require the permanent halting of a virtually completed dam for which Congress has expended more than $100 million. . . ." Burger also said, "We conclude, however, that the explicit provisions of the Endangered Species Act require precisely that result. One would be hard pressed to find a statutory provision whose terms were any plainer. . . ."

The majority opinion affirmed an injunction granted by the U.S. Court of Appeals for the Sixth Circuit that stopped work on the dam. Burger was joined in the majority by Justices William J. Brennan Jr., Potter Stewart, Byron White, Thurgood Marshall and John Paul Stevens. The dissenting

*opinion, written by Justice Lewis F. Powell Jr., was joined by Justice Harry
A. Blackmun. Justice William H. Rehnquist dissented in a separate
opinion.*

The Case

*The TVA began work on the Tellico Dam project in 1967. The plan called
for a dam on the Little Tennessee River in Tennessee that would have
created a 16,500 acre reservoir. The purpose of the dam and reservoir was
to stimulate shoreline development, provide water recreation, enhance
flood control and generate electric power to heat 20,000 homes. It was not
until 1973, when the project was 80 percent complete, that an ichthyologist
from the University of Tennessee discovered in the Tennessee River a
previously unknown species of perch, the snail darter,* Percina Imostoma
tanasi. *It was estimated that there were from 10,000 to 15,000 snail darters
in existence. Four months after the discovery of the snail darter, Congress
passed the Endangered Species Act of 1973 and, in January 1975, conservationists petitioned the secretary of the interior to designate the snail
darters as endangered. In November 1975 the secretary complied.*

*Conservationists in February 1976 filed a suit in federal district court,
seeking to halt completion of the dam and the impoundment of the
reservoir. The court dismissed the complaint; that action was overturned
by the appellate court and the gates of the dam remained open, leaving the
river free-flowing.*

Majority Opinion

*After reviewing the history of the Tellico Dam and the unbroken series of
appropriations voted by Congress for the project after it was determined
that the reservoir would possibly eradicate the snail darters, the chief
justice asserted that the project must be halted under the terms of the
Endangered Species Act. "Concededly," he wrote, "this view of the Act
will produce results requiring the sacrifice of the anticipated benefits of the
project and of many millions of dollars in public funds. But examination of
the language, history and structure of the legislation under review here
indicates beyond doubt that Congress intended endangered species to be
afforded the highest of priorities."*

*Taken together, Burger said, congressional actions concerning endan-
gered species "makes it abundantly clear" that snail darters deserved
protection. "The plain intent of Congress," he said, "in enacting this
statute was to halt and reverse the trend toward species extinction,
whatever the cost." The importance to Congress of preserving endangered
species is "incalculable," he said, adding, "Quite obviously, it would be
difficult for a court to balance the loss of a sum certain — even $100 million
— against a congressionally declared 'incalculable' value, even assuming*

we had the power to engage in such a weighing process, which we emphatically do not."

Dissenting Opinions

Justice Powell disputed the majority's interpretation of the Endangered Species Act and congressional action regarding Tellico Dam. The court's reading of the act, Powell said, "gives it a retroactive effect and disregards 12 years of consistently expressed congressional intent to complete the Tellico Project." The court's mistake, he continued, was its belief that the "actions" referred to in the act as not allowed by federal agencies are "all actions that an agency can ever take. . . ." On the contrary, Powell argued, "these words reasonably may be read as applying only to prospective actions . . . actions not yet carried out." Since Tellico Dam was 80 percent finished when the act became law, it should not reasonably fall under the law's provisions. Powell also argued that congressional appropriations for the project in light of the known dangers to the snail darter population indicated Congress' intent to complete to project. He concluded by suggesting that Congress would soon take actions allowing the project to go ahead. "There will be little sentiment to leave this dam standing before an empty reservoir," he said, "serving no purpose other than a conversation piece for incredulous tourists."

In a separate dissenting opinion, Justice Rehnquist argued briefly that the district court was not compelled, under the terms of the Act, to issue an injunction to stop work on the dam.

> *Following are excerpts from the Supreme Court's majority opinion, delivered June 15, 1978, that prohibited completion of the Tellico Dam project, and excerpts from the two dissenting opinions:*

No. 76-1701

Tennessee Valley Authority, Petitioner, *v.* Hiram G. Hill, Jr., et al.	On Writ of Certiorari to the United States Court of Appeals for the Sixth Circuit.

[June 15, 1978]

MR. CHIEF JUSTICE BURGER delivered the opinion of the Court.

The questions presented in this case are (a) whether the Endangered Species Act of 1973 requires a court to enjoin the operation of a virtually completed federal dam — which had been authorized prior to 1973 — when, pursuant to authority vested in him by Congress, the Secretary of the Interior has determined that operation of the dam would eradicate an endangered species; and (b) whether continued congressional appropriations for the dam after 1973 constituted an implied repeal of the Endangered Species Act, at least as to the particular dam.

I

...In January 1975, the respondents in this case and others petitioned the Secretary of the Interior to list the snail darter as an endangered species. After receiving comments from various interested parties, including TVA and the State of Tennessee, the Secretary formally listed the snail darter as an endangered species on November 10, 1975.... More important for the purposes of this case, the Secretary determined that the snail darter apparently lives only in that portion of the Little Tennessee River which would be completely inundated by the reservoir created as a consequence of the Tellico Dam's completion.... Subsequent to this determination, the Secretary declared the area of the Little Tennessee which would be affected by the Tellico Dam to be the "critical habitat" of the snail darter.... Using these determinations as a predicate, and notwithstanding the near completion of the dam, the Secretary declared that pursuant to § 7 of the Act, "all Federal agencies must take such action as is necessary to insure that actions authorized, funded, or carried out by them do not result in the destruction or modification of this critical habitat area."... This notice, of course, was pointedly directed at TVA and clearly aimed at halting completion or operation of the dam.

During the pendency of these administrative actions, other developments of relevance to the snail darter issue were transpiring. Communication was occurring between the Department of the Interior's Fish and Wildlife Service and TVA with a view toward settling the issue informally. These negotiations were to no avail, however, since TVA consistently took the position that the only available alternative was to attempt relocating the snail darter population to another suitable location. To this end, TVA conducted a search of alternate sites which might sustain the fish, culminating in the experimental transplantation of a number of snail darters to the nearby Hiwassee River. However, the Secretary of the Interior was not satisfied with the results of these efforts, finding that TVA had presented "little evidence that they have carefully studied the Hiwassee to determine whether or not" there were "biological and other factors in this river that [would] negate a successful transplant."...

Meanwhile, Congress had also become involved in the fate of the snail darter. Appearing before a Subcommittee of the House Committee on Appropriations in April 1975 — some seven months before the snail darter was listed as endangered — TVA representatives described the discovery of the fish and the relevance of the Endangered Species Act to the Tellico Project.... At that time TVA presented a position which it would advance in successive forums thereafter, namely, that the Act did not prohibit the completion of a project authorized, funded, and substantially constructed before the Act was passed. TVA also described its efforts to transplant the snail darter, but contended that the dam should be finished regardless of the experiment's success.... Congress then approved the TVA general budget, which contained funds for construction of the Tellico Project. In December 1975, one month after the snail darter was declared an endangered species, the President signed the bill into law....

In February 1976, pursuant to § 11 (g) of the Endangered Species Act..., respondents filed the case now under review, seeking to enjoin completion of the dam and impoundment of the reservoir on the ground that those actions would violate the Act by directly causing the extinction of the species *Percina Imostoma tanasi.* The District Court denied respondent's request for a preliminary injunction and set the matter for trial. Shortly thereafter the House and Senate held appropriations hearings which would include discussions of the Tellico budget.

At these hearings, TVA Chairman Wagner reiterated the agency's position that the Act did not apply to a project which was over 50% finished by the time the Act became effective and some 70 to 80% complete when the snail darter was officially listed as endangered. It also notified the Committees of the recently filed lawsuit's status and reported that TVA's efforts to transplant the snail darter had "been very encouraging."...

Trial was held in the District Court on April 29 and 30, 1976, and on May 25, 1976, the court entered its memorandum opinion and order denying respondents their requested relief and dismissing the complaint. The District Court found that closure of the dam and the consequent impoundment of the reservoir would "result in the adverse modification, if not complete destruction, of the snail darter's critical habitat," making it "highly probable" that "the continued existence of the snail darter" would be "jeopardize[d]." *Hill* v. *Tennessee Valley Authority*...(1976). Despite these findings, the District Court declined to embrace the plaintiffs' position on the merits: that once a federal project was shown to jeopardize an endangered species, a court of equity is compelled to issue an injunction restraining violation of the Endangered Species Act.

In reaching this result, the District Court stressed that the entire project was then about 80% complete and, based on available evidence, "there [were] no alternatives to impoundment of the reservoir, short of scrapping the entire project."... The District Court also found that if the Tellico Project was permanently enjoined, "some $53 million would be lost in nonrecoverable obligations,"...meaning that a large portion of the $78 million already expended would be wasted. The court also noted that the Endangered Species Act of 1973 was passed some seven years after construction on the dam commenced and that Congress had continued appropriations for Tellico, with full awareness of the snail darter problem.... To accept the plaintiffs' position, the District Court argued, would inexorably lead to what it characterized as the absurd result of requiring "a court to halt impoundment of water behind a fully completed dam if an endangered species were discovered in the river on the day before such impoundment was scheduled to take place. We cannot conceive that Congress intended such a result."...

Less than a month after the District Court decision, the Senate and House Appropriations Committees recommended the full budget request of $9 million for continued work on Tellico.... On June 29, 1976, both Houses of Congress passed TVA's general budget, which included funds for Tellico; the President signed the bill on July 12, 1976....

Thereafter, in the Court of Appeals, respondents argued that the District Court had abused its discretion by not issuing an injunction in the face of "a blatant statutory violation." *Hill* v. *Tennessee Valley Authority*...(1977). That court agreed, and on January 31, 1977, it reversed, remanding "with instructions that a permanent injunction issue halting all activities incident to the Tellico Project which may destroy or modify the critical habitat of the snail darter."... The Court of Appeals directed that the injunction "remain in effect until Congress, by appropriate legislation, exempts Tellico from compliance with the Act or the snail darter has been deleted from the list of endangered species or its critical habitat materially redefined."...

The Court of Appeals accepted the District Court's finding that closure of the dam would result in the known population of snail darters being "significantly reduced if not completely extirpated." ...[T]he Court of Appeals held that the record revealed a prima facie violation of § 7 of the Act, namely that TVA had failed to take "such action necessary to insure" that its "actions" did not jeopardize the snail darter or its critical habitat.

The reviewing court thus rejected TVA's contention that the word "actions" in § 7 of the Act was not intended by Congress to encompass the terminal phases of ongoing projects. Not only could the court find no "positive reinforcement" for TVA's argument in the Act's legislative history, but such an interpretation was seen as being "inimical to...its objectives." ...By way of illustration, that court pointed out that "the detrimental impact of a project upon an endangered species may not always be clearly perceived before construction is well underway." ...Given such a likelihood, the Court of Appeals was of the opinion that TVA's position would require the District Court, sitting as a chancellor, to balance the worth of an endangered species against the value of an ongoing public works measure, a result which that court was not willing to accept....

As far as the Court of Appeals was concerned, it made no difference that Congress had repeatedly approved appropriations for Tellico, referring to such legislative approval as an "advisory opinion" concerning the proper application of an existing statute. In that court's view, the only relevant legislation was the Act itself, "the meaning and spirit" of which was "clear on its face."...

Turning to the question of an appropriate remedy, the Court of Appeals ruled that the District Court had erred by not issuing an injunction. While recognizing the irretrievable loss of millions of dollars of public funds which would accompany injunctive relief, the court nonetheless decided that the Act explicitly commanded precisely that result....

Following the issuance of the permanent injunction, members of TVA's Board of Directors appeared before Subcommittees of the House and Senate Appropriations Committees to testify in support of continued appropriations for Tellico. The subcommittees were apprised of all aspects of Tellico's status, including the Court of Appeal's decision. TVA reported that the dam stood "ready for the gates to be closed and the reservoir filled,"...and requested funds for completion of certain ancillary parts of the project, such as public use areas, roads and bridges. As to the snail darter itself, TVA commented optimistically on its transplantation efforts, expressing the opinion that the relocated fish were "doing well and ha[d] reproduced."...

Both appropriations committees subsequently recommended the full amount requested for completion of the Tellico Project.... As a solution to the problem, the House [Appropriations] Committee advised that TVA should cooperate with the Department of the Interior "to relocate the endangered species to another suitable habitat so as to permit the project to proceed as rapidly as possible."... Toward this end, the committee recommended a special appropriation of $2 million to facilitate relocation of the snail darter and other endangered species which threatened to delay or stop TVA projects. Much the same occurred on the Senate side, with its Appropriations Committee recommending both the amount requested to complete Tellico and the special appropriation for transplantation of endangered species....

TVA's budget, including funds for completion of Tellico and relocation of the snail darter, passed both Houses of Congress and was signed into law on August 7, 1977....

II

We begin with the premise that operation of the Tellico Dam will either eradicate the known population of snail darters or destroy their critical habitat. Petitioner does not now seriously dispute this fact. In any event, under § 4 (a)(1) of the Act, 16 U.S.C. § 1533 (D), the Secretary of the Interior is vested with exclusive authority to determine whether a species such as the snail darter is "endangered" or "threatened" and to ascertain the factors which have led to such a precarious existence. By § 4 (d) Congress has authorized — indeed commanded — the Secretary to "issue such regulations as he deems necessary and advisable to provide for the conservation of such species."... As we have seen, the Secretary promulgated regulations which declared the snail darter an endangered species whose critical habitat would be destroyed by creation of the Tellico Reservoir. Doubtless petitioner would prefer not to have these regulations on the books, but there is no suggestion that the Secretary exceeded his authority or abused his discretion in issuing the regulations. Indeed, no judicial review of the Secretary's determinations has ever been sought and hence the validity of his actions are not open to review in this Court.

Starting from the above premise, two questions are presented: (a) would

TVA be in violation of the Act if it completed and operated the Tellico Dam as planned?; (b) if TVA's actions would offend the Act, is an injunction the appropriate remedy for the violation? For the reasons stated hereinafter, we hold that both questions must be answered in the affirmative.

(A)

It may seem curious to some that the survival of a relatively small number of three-inch fish among all the countless millions of species extant would require the permanent halting of a virtually completed dam for which Congress has expended more than $100 million. The paradox is not minimized by the fact that Congress continued to appropriate large sums of public money for the project, even after congressional appropriations committees were apprised of its apparent impact upon the survival of the snail darter. We conclude, however, that the explicit provisions of the Endangered Species Act require precisely that result.

One would be hard pressed to find a statutory provision whose terms were any plainer than those in § 7 of the Endangered Species Act. Its very words affirmatively command all federal agencies "to *insure* that actions *authorized, funded,* or *carried out* by them do not *jeopardize* the continued existence" of an endangered species or "*result* in the destruction or modification of habitat of such species".... (Emphasis added.) This language admits of no exception. Nonetheless, petitioner urges, as do the dissenters, that the Act cannot reasonably be interpreted as applying to a federal project which was well under way when Congress passed the Endangered Species Act of 1973. To sustain that position, however, we would be forced to ignore the ordinary meaning of plain language. It has not been shown, for example, how TVA can close the gates of the Tellico Dam without "carrying out" an action that has been "authorized" and "funded" by a federal agency. Nor can we understand how such action will *"insure"* that the snail darter's habitat is not disrupted. Accepting the Secretary's determinations, as we must, it is clear that TVA's proposed operation of the dam will have precisely the opposite effect, namely the *eradication* of an endangered species.

Concededly, this view of the Act will produce results requiring the sacrifice of the anticipated benefits of the project and of many millions of dollars in public funds. But examination of the language, history and structure of the legislation under review here indicates beyond doubt that Congress intended endangered species to be afforded the highest of priorities.

When Congress passed the Act in 1973, it was not legislating on a clean slate. The first major congressional concern for the preservation of the endangered species had come with passage of the Endangered Species Act of 1966.... In that legislation Congress gave the Secretary power to identify "the names of the species of native fish and wildlife found to be threatened with extinction,"...as well as authorization to purchase land for the conservation, protection, restoration, and propogation of "selected species" of "native fish and wildlife" threatened with extinction....

In 1969 Congress enacted the Endangered Species Conservation Act...which continued the provisions of the 1966 Act while at the same time broadening federal involvement in the preservation of endangered species. Under the 1969 legislation, the Secretary was empowered to list species "threatened with worldwide extinction," ...in addition, the importation of any species so recognized into the United States was prohibited.... An indirect approach to the taking of endangered species was also adopted in the Conservation Act by way of a ban on the transportation and sale of wildlife taken in violation of any federal, state, or foreign law....

Despite the fact that the 1966 and 1969 legislation represented "the most comprehensive of its type to be enacted by any nation" up to that time, Congress was soon persuaded that a more expansive approach was needed if the newly declared national policy of preserving endangered species was to be realized. By 1973, when Congress held hearings on what would later become the Endangered Species Act of 1973, it was informed that species were still being lost at the rate of about one per year,...and "the pace of disappearance of species" appeared to be accelerating."...

The legislative proceedings in 1973 are, in fact, replete with expressions of concern over the risk that might lie in the loss of *any* endangered species.... Congress was concerned about the *unknown* uses that endangered species might have and about the *unforeseeable* place such creatures may have in the chain of life on this planet.

In shaping legislation to deal with the problem thus presented, Congress started from the finding that "[t]he two major causes of extinction are hunting and destruction of natural habitat."... Of these twin threats, Congress was informed that the greatest was destruction of natural habitats....

As it was finally passed, the Endangered Species Act of 1973 represented the most comprehensive legislation for the preservation of endangered species ever enacted by any nation. Its stated purposes were "to provide a means whereby the ecosystems upon which endangered species and threatened species depend may be conserved," and "to provide a program for the conservation of such ... species".... In furtherance of these goals, Congress expressly stated in § 2 (c) that "all Federal departments and agencies *shall* seek *to conserve endangered species* and threatened species".... (Emphasis added.) Lest there be any ambiguity as to the meaning of this statutory directive, the Act specifically defined "conserve" as meaning "to use and the use of *all methods and procedures which are necessary* to bring *any endangered species* to the point at which the measures provided pursuant to this Act are no longer necessary." ... (Emphasis added.) Aside from § 7, other provisions indicated the seriousness with which Congress viewed this issue: virtually all dealings with endangered species, including taking, possession, transportation and sale, were prohibited ... except in extremely narrow circumstances.... The

Secretary was also given extensive powers to develop regulations and programs for the preservation of endangered and threatened species.... Citizen involvement was encouraged by the Act, with provisions allowing interested persons to petition the Secretary to list a species as endangered or threatened,...and bring civil suits in United States District Courts to force compliance with any provision of the Act....

It is against this legislative background that we must measure TVA's claim that the Act was not intended to stop operation of a project which, like Tellico Dam, was near completion when an endangered species was discovered in its path. While there is no discussion in the legislative history of precisely this problem, the totality of congressional action makes it abundantly clear that the result we reach today is wholly in accord with both the words of the statute and the intent of Congress. The plain intent of Congress in enacting this statute was to halt and reverse the trend toward species extinction, whatever the cost. This is reflected not only in the stated policies of the Act, but in literally every section of the statute. All persons, including federal agencies, are specifically instructed not to "take" endangered species, meaning that no one is "to harass, harm, pursue, hunt, shoot, wound, kill, trap, capture, or collect" such life forms.... Agencies in particular are directed by §§ 2 (c) and 3 (2) of the Act to "use *all methods* and procedures which are necessary" to preserve endangered species...(emphasis added). In addition, the legislative history undergirding § 7 reveals an explicit congressional decision to require agencies to afford first priority to the declared national policy of saving endangered species. The pointed omission of the type of qualifying language previously included in endangered species legislation reveals a conscious decision by Congress to give endangered species priority over the "primary missions" of federal agencies.

It is not for us to speculate, much less act, on whether Congress would have altered its stance had the specific events of this case been anticipated. In any event, we discern no hint in the deliberations of Congress relating to the 1973 Act that would compel a different result than we reach here. Indeed, the repeated expressions of congressional concern over what it saw as the potentially enormous danger presented by the eradication of *any* endangered species suggests how the balance would have been struck had the issue been presented to Congress in 1973.

Furthermore, it is clear Congress foresaw that § 7 would, on occasion, require agencies to alter ongoing projects in order to fulfill the goals of the Act.... [T]he plain language of the Act, buttressed by its legislative history, shows clearly that Congress viewed the value of endangered species as "incalculable." Quite obviously, it would be difficult for a court to balance the loss of a sum certain — even $100 million — against a congressionally declared "incalculable" value, even assuming we had the power to engage in such a weighing process, which we emphatically do not.

In passing the Endangered Species Act of 1973, Congress was also aware of certain instances in which exceptions to the statute's broad sweep would be necessary. Thus, § 10, 16 U.S.C. § 1539, creates a number of limited "hardship exemptions," none of which would even remotely apply to the Tellico Project. In fact, there are no exemptions in the Endangered Species Act for federal agencies, meaning that under the maxim *expressio unius est exclusio alterius,* we must presume that these were the only "hardship cases" Congress intended to exempt....

Notwithstanding Congress' expression of intent in 1973, we are urged to find that the continuing appropriations for Tellico Dam constitute an implied repeal of the 1973 Act, at least insofar as it applies to the Tellico Project. In support of this view, TVA points to the statements found in various House and Senate appropriations committees' reports; as described in Part I, *supra,* those reports generally reflected the attitude of the *committees* either that the Act did not apply to Tellico or that the dam should be completed regardless of the provisions of the Act. Since we are unwilling to assume that these latter committee statements constituted advice to ignore the provisions of a duly enacted law, we assume that these committees believed that the Act simply was not applicable in this situation. But even under this interpretation of the committees' actions, we are unable to conclude that the Act has been in any respect amended or repealed.

There is nothing in the appropriations measures, as passed, which state that the Tellico Project was to be completed irrespective of the requirements of the Endangered Species Act. These appropriations, in fact, represented relatively minor components of the lump sum amounts for the *entire* TVA budget. To find a repeal of the Endangered Species Act under these circumstances would surely do violence to the "cardinal rule...that repeals by implication are not favored." *Morton v. Mancari...*(1974), quoting *Posadas* v. *National City Bank...*(1936)....

The doctrine disfavoring repeals by implication "applies with full vigor when...the subsequent legislation is an *appropriations* measure." *Committee for Nuclear Responsibility* v. *Seaborg...* (1971) (emphasis added); *Environmental Defense Fund* v. *Froehlke...*(1972). This is perhaps an understatement since it would be more accurate to say that the policy applies with even *greater* force when the claimed repeal rests solely on an appropriations act. We recognize that both substantive enactments and appropriations measures are "acts of Congress," but the latter have the limited and specific purpose of providing funds for authorized programs. When voting on appropriations measures, legislators are entitled to operate under the assumption that the funds will be devoted to purposes which are lawful and not for any purpose forbidden....

...Expressions of committees dealing with requests for appropriations cannot be equated with statutes enacted by Congress, particularly not in the circumstances presented by this case. First, the appropriations committees had no jurisdiction over the subject of endangered species, much less did they conduct the type of extensive hearings which preceded passage of the earlier endangered species acts, especially the 1973 Act. We venture to suggest that the House Committee on Merchant Marine and Fisheries and the Senate Committee on Commerce would be somewhat surprised to learn that their careful work on the substantive legislation had been undone by the simple — and brief — insertion of some inconsistent language in appropriations committees' reports.

Second, there is no indication that Congress as a whole was aware of TVA's position, although the appropriations committees apparently agreed with petitioner's views. Only recently, in *SEC* v. *Sloan*...(1978), we declined to presume general congressional acquiesence in a 34-year-old practice of the SEC, despite the fact that the Senate committee *having jurisdiction over the Commission's activities* had long expressed approval of the practice. MR. JUSTICE REHNQUIST, speaking for the Court, observed that we should be "extremely hesitant to presume general congressional awareness of the Commission's construction based only upon a few isolated statements in the thousands of pages of legislative documents."... *A fortiori*, we should not assume that petitioner's views — and the appropriations committees' acceptance of them — were any better known, especially when the TVA is not the agency with primary responsibility for administering the Endangered Species Act.

Quite apart from the foregoing factors, we would still be unable to find that in this case "the earlier and later statutes are irreconcilable," *Mancari...;* here it is entirely possible "to regard each as effective."... The starting point in this analysis must be the legislative proceedings leading to the 1977 appropriations since the earlier funding of the dam occurred prior to the listing of the snail darter as an endangered species. In all successive years, TVA confidently reported to the appropriations committees that efforts to transplant the snail darter appeared to be successful; this surely gave those committees some basis for the impression that there was no direct conflict between the Tellico Project and the Endangered Species Act. Indeed, the special appropriation for 1978 of $2 million for transplantation of endangered species supports the view that the committees saw such relocation as the means whereby collision between Tellico and the Endangered Species Act could be avoided. It should also be noted that the reports issued by the Senate and House Appropriations Committees in 1976 came within a month of the District Court's decision in this case, which hardly could have given the Members cause for concern over the possible applicability of the Act. This leaves only the 1978 appropriations, the reports for which issued after the Court of Appeals' decision now before us. At that point very little remained to be accomplished on the project; the committees understandably advised TVA to cooperate with the Department of the Interior "to relocate the endangered species to another suitable habitat so as to permit the project to proceed as rapidly as possible."... It is true that the *committees* repeated their earlier expressed "view" that the Act did not prevent completion of the Tellico project. Considering these statements in context, however, it is evident that they "represent only the personal views of these legislators," and "however explicit, cannot serve to change the legislative intent of Congress expressed before the Act's passage." *Regional Rail Reorganization Cases*...(1974).

(B)

Having determined that there is an irreconcilable conflict between operation of the Tellico Dam and the explicit provisions of § 7 of the Endangered Species Act, we must now consider what remedy, if any, is appropriate. It is correct, of course, that a federal judge sitting as a chancellor is not mechanically obligated to grant an injunction for every violation of law. This Court made plain in *Hecht Co.* v. *Bowles*...(1944), that "[a] grant of *jurisdiction* to issue compliance orders hardly suggests an absolute duty to do so under any and all circumstances." As a general matter it may be said that "[s]ince all or almost all equitable remedies are discretionary, the balancing of equities and hardships is appropriate in almost any case as a guide to the chancellor's discretion." Dobbs, Remedies 52 (1973). Thus, in *Hecht* the Court refused to grant an injunction when it appeared from the District Court findings that "the issuance of an injunction would have 'no effect by way of insuring better compliance in the future' and would [have been] 'unjust' to [the] petitioner and not 'in the public interest.' "...

But these principles take a court only so far. Our system of government is, after all, a tripartite one, with each Branch having certain defined functions delegated to it by the Constitution. While "[it] is emphatically the province and duty of the judicial department to say what the law is," *Marbury* v. *Madison*...(1803), it is equally — and emphatically — the exclusive province of the Congress not only to formulate legislative policies, mandate programs and projects, but also to establish their relative priority for the Nation. Once Congress, exercising its delegated powers, has decided the order of priorities in a given area, it is for the Executive to administer the laws and for the courts to enforce them when enforcement is sought.

Here we are urged to view the Endangered Species Act "reasonably," and hence shape a remedy "that accords with some modicum of commonsense and the public weal." [Powell dissent]. But is that our function? We have no expert knowledge on the subject of endangered species, much less do we have a mandate from the people to strike a balance of equities on the side of the Tellico Dam. Congress has spoken in the plainest of words, making it abundantly clear that the balance has been struck in favor of affording endangered species the highest of priorities, thereby adopting a policy which it described as "institutionalized caution."

Our individual appraisal of the wisdom or unwisdom of a particular course consciously selected by the Congress is to be put aside in the process of interpreting a statute. Once the meaning of an enactment is discerned and its constitutionality determined, the judicial process comes to an end. We do not sit as a committee of review, nor are we vested with the power of veto....

We agree with the Court of Appeals that in our constitutional system the commitment to the separation of powers is too fundamental for us to pre-empt congressional action by judicially decreeing what accords with "commonsense and the public weal." Our Constitution vests such responsibilities in the political Branches.   *Affirmed.*

MR. JUSTICE POWELL, with whom MR. JUSTICE BLACKMUN joins, dissenting.

The Court today holds that § 7 of the Endangered Species Act requires a federal court, for the purpose of protecting an endangered species or its habitat, to enjoin permanently the operation of any federal project, whether completed or substantially completed. This decision casts a long shadow over the operation of even the most important projects, serving vital needs of society and national defense, whenever it is determined that continued operation would threaten extinction of an endangered species or its habitat. This result is said to be required by the "plain intent of Congress" as well as by the language of the statute.

In my view § 7 cannot reasonably be interpreted as applying to a project that is completed or substantially completed when its threat to an endangered species is discovered. Nor can I believe that Congress could have intended this Act to produce the "absurd result" — in the words of the District Court — of this case. If it were clear from the language of the Act and its legislative history that Congress intended to authorize this result, this Court would be compelled to enforce it. It is not our province to rectify policy or political judgments by the Legislative Branch, however egregiously they may disserve the public interest. But where the statutory language and legislative history, as in this case, need not be construed to reach such a result, I view it as the duty of this Court to adopt a permissible construction that accords with some modicum of commonsense and the public weal.

I

Although the Court has stated the facts fully, and fairly presented the testimony and action of the Appropriations Committees relevant to this case, I now repeat some of what has been said. I do so because I read the total record as compelling rejection of the Court's conclusion that Congress *intended* the Endangered Species Act to apply to completed or substantially completed projects such as the dam and reservoir project that today's opinion brings to an end — absent relief by Congress itself.

In 1966, Congress authorized and appropriated initial funds for the construction by the Tennessee Valley Authority (TVA) of the Tellico Dam and Reservoir Project on the Little Tennessee River in eastern Tennessee. The project is a comprehensive water resource and regional development project designed to control flooding, provide water supply, promote industrial and recreational development, generate some additional electric power within the TVA system, and generally improve economic conditions in an economically depressed area....

Construction began in 1967, and Congress has voted funds for the project in every year since. In August 1973, when the Tellico Project was half completed, a new species of fish known as the snail darter was discovered in the portion of the Little Tennessee River that would be impounded behind Tellico Dam. The Endangered Species Act was passed the following December.... More than a year later in January 1975, respondents joined others in petitioning the Secretary of the Interior to list the snail darter as an endangered species. On November 10, 1975, when the Tellico Project was 75% completed, the Secretary placed the snail darter on the endangered list and concluded that the "proposed impoundment of water behind the proposed Tellico Dam would result in total destruction of the snail darter's habitat." 40 Fed. Reg. 47506 (1975).... TVA nevertheless determined to continue with the Tellico Project in accordance with the prior authorization by Congress. In February 1976, respondents filed the instant suit to enjoin its completion. By that time the Project was 80% completed.

In March 1976, TVA informed the House and Senate Appropriations Committees about the Project's threat to the snail darter and about respondents' lawsuit. Both committees were advised that TVA was attempting to preserve the fish by relocating them to the Hiwassee River, which closely resembles the Little Tennessee. It stated explicitly, however, that the success of those efforts could not be guaranteed.

In a decision of May 25, 1976, the District Court for the Eastern District of Tennessee held that "the Act should not be construed as preventing completion of the project."... Observing that respondents' argument, carried to its logical extreme, would require a court to enjoin the impoundment of water behind a fully completed dam if an endangered species were discovered in the river on the day before the scheduled impoundment, the District Court concluded that Congress could not have intended such a result. Accordingly, it denied the prayer for an injunction and dismissed the action.

In 1975, 1976, and 1977 Congress, with full knowledge of the Tellico Project's effect on the snail darter and the alleged violation of the Endangered Species Act, continued to appropriate money for the completion of the Project. In doing so, the Appropriations Committees expressly stated that the Act did not prohibit the Project's completion, a view that Congress presumably accepted in approving the appropriations each year.... The appropriations bill was passed by Congress and approved by the President.

The Court of Appeals for the Sixth Circuit nevertheless reversed the District Court in January 1977.... It remanded with instructions to issue a permanent injunction halting all activities incident to the Tellico Project that would modify the critical habitat of the snail darter.

In June 1977, and after being informed of the decision of the Court of Appeals, the Appropriations Committees in both Houses of Congress again recommended approval of TVA's full budget request for the Tellico Project. Both Committees again stated unequivocally that the Endangered Species Act was not intended to halt projects at an advanced stage of completion.... Once again, the appropriations bill was passed by both Houses and signed into law.

II

Today the Court, like the Court of Appeals below, adopts a reading of § 7 of the Act that gives it a retroactive effect and disregards 12 years of consistently expressed congressional intent to complete the Tellico Project. With all due respect, I view this result as an extreme example of a literalist construction, not required by the language of the Act and adopted without regard to its manifest purpose. Moreover, it ignores established canons of statutory construction.

A

The starting point in statutory construction is, of course, the language of § 7 itself. *Blue Chip Stamps*. v. *Manor Drug Store*...(1975) (POWELL, J., concurring). I agree that it can be viewed as a textbook example of fuzzy language, which can be read according to the "eye of the beholder." The critical words direct all federal agencies to take "such action [as may be] necessary to insure that actions authorized, funded or, carried out by them do not jeopardize the continued existence of...endangered species...or result in the destruction or modification of [a critical] habitat of such species...." Respondents — as did the Sixth Circuit — read these words as sweepingly as possible to include all "actions" that any federal agency ever may take with respect to any federal project, whether completed or not.

The Court today embraces this sweeping construction.... Under the Court's reasoning, the Act covers every existing federal installation, including great hydroelectric projects and reservoirs, every river and harbor project, and every national defense installation — however essential to the Nation's economic health and safety. The "actions" that an agency would be prohibited from "carrying out" would include the continued operation of such projects or any change necessary to preserve their continued usefulness. The only pre-condition, according to respondents, to thus destroying the usefulness of even the most important federal project in our country would be a finding by the Secretary of the Interior that a continuation of the project would threaten the survival or critical habitat of a newly discovered species of water spider or amoeba.

"[F]requently words of general meaning are used in a statute, words broad enough to include an act in question, and yet a consideration of the whole legislation, or of the circumstances surrounding its enactment, or of the absurd results which follow from giving such broad meaning to the words, makes it unreasonable to believe that the legislator intended to include the particular act." *Church of the Holy Trinity* v. *United States*...(1892). The result that will follow in this case by virtue of the Court's reading of § 7 makes it unreasonable to believe that Congress intended that reading. Moreover, § 7 may be construed in a way that avoids an "absurd result" without doing violence to its language.

The critical word in § 7 is "actions" and its meaning is far from "plain." It is part of the phrase: "actions authorized, funded or carried out." In terms of planning and executing various activities, it seems evident that the "actions" referred to are not all actions that an agency can ever take, but rather actions that the agency is *deciding whether* to authorize, to fund, or to carry out. In short, these words reasonably may be read as applying only to *prospective actions, i.e.,* actions with respect to which the agency has reasonable decisionmaking alternatives still available, actions *not yet* carried out. At the time respondents brought this lawsuit, the Tellico Project was 80% complete at a cost of more than $78 million. The Court concedes that as of this time and for the purpose of deciding this case, the Tellico dam project is "completed" or "virtually completed and the dam is essentially ready for operation".... Thus, under a prospective reading of § 7, the action already has been "carried out" in terms of any remaining reasonable decisionmaking power....

This is a reasonable construction of the language and also is supported by the presumption against construing statutes to give them a retroactive effect. As this Court stated in *United States Fidelity & Guaranty Co.* v. *Struthers Wells Co...*(1908), the "presumption is very strong that a statute was not meant to act retrospectively, and it ought never to receive such a construction if it is susceptible of any other." This is particularly true where a statute enacts a new regime of regulation. For example, the presumption has been recognized in cases under the National Environmental Policy Act...holding that the requirement of filing an environmental impact statement cannot reasonably be applied to projects substantially completed.... Similarly under § 7 of the Endangered Species Act, at some stage of a federal project, and certainly where a project has been completed, the agency no longer has a reasonable choice simply to abandon it. When that point is reached, as it was in this case, the presumption against retrospective interpretation is at its strongest. The Court today gives no weight to that presumption.

B

The Court recognizes that the first purpose of statutory construction is to ascertain the intent of the legislature.... The Court's opinion reviews at length the legislative history, with quotations from Committee reports and statements by Members of Congress. The Court then ends this discussion with curiously conflicting conclusions.

It finds that the "totality of congressional action makes it abundantly clear that the result we reach today [justifying the termination or abandonment of any federal project] is wholly in accord with both the words of the statute and the intent of Congress."... Yet, in the same paragraph, the Court acknowledges that "there is no discussion in the legislative history of precisely this problem." The opinion nowhere makes clear how the result it reaches can be "abundantly" self-evident from the legislative history when the result was never discussed. While the Court's review of the legislative history establishes that Congress intended to require governmental agencies to take endangered species into account in the planning and execution of their programs, there is not even a hint in the legislative history that Congress intended to compel the undoing or abandonment of any project or program later found to threaten a newly discovered species.

If the relevant Committees that considered the Act, and the Members of Congress who voted on it, had been aware that the Act could be used to terminate major federal projects authorized years earlier and nearly completed, or to require the abandonment of essential and long-completed federal installations and edifices, we can be certain that there would have been hearings, testimony, and debate concerning consequences so wasteful, so inimical to purposes previously deemed important, and so likely to arouse public outrage. The absence of any such consideration by the Committees or in the floor debates indicates quite clearly that no one participating in the legislative process considered these consequences as within the intendment of the Act.

As indicated above, this view of legislative intent at the time of enactment is abundantly confirmed by the subsequent congressional actions and expressions. We have held, properly, that post-enactment statements by individual Members of Congress as to the meaning of a statute are entitled to little or no weight.... The Court also has recognized that subsequent appropriation acts themselves are not necessarily entitled to significant weight in determining whether a prior statute has been superseded.... But these precedents are inapposite. There was no effort here to "bootstrap" a post-enactment view of prior legislation by isolated statements of individual congressmen. Nor is this a case where Congress, without explanation or comment upon the statute in question, merely has voted apparently inconsistent financial support in subsequent appropriations acts. Testimony on this precise issue was presented before congressional committees, and the committee reports for three consecutive years addressed the problem and affirmed their understanding of the original congressional intent. We cannot assume — as the Court suggests — that Congress, when it continued each year to approve the recommended appropriations, was unaware of the contents of the supporting committee reports. All this amounts to strong corroborative evidence that the interpretation of § 7 as not applying to completed or substantially completed projects reflects the initial legislative intent....

III

I have little doubt that Congress will amend the Endangered Species Act to prevent the grave consequences made possible by today's decision. Few, if any, Members of that body will wish to defend an interpretation of the Act that requires the waste of at least $53 million...and denies the people of the Tennessee valley area the benefits of the reservoir that Congress intended to confer. There will be little sentiment to leave this dam standing before an empty reservoir, serving no purpose other than a conversation piece for incredulous tourists.

But more farreaching than the adverse effect on the people of this economically depressed area is the continuing threat to the operation of every federal project, no matter how important to the Nation. If Congress acts expeditiously, as may be anticipated, the Court's decision probably will have no lasting adverse consequences. But I had not thought it to be the province of this Court to force Congress into otherwise unnecessary action by interpreting a statute to produce a result no one intended.

MR. JUSTICE REHNQUIST, *dissenting.*

...[T]he very difficulty and doubtfulness of the correct answer to this legal question convinces me that the Act did *not* prohibit the District Court from refusing, in the exercise of its traditional equitable powers, to enjoin petitioner from completing the Dam. Section 11 (g)(1) of the Act . . . merely provides that "any person may commence a civil suit on his own behalf to enjoin any person, including the United States and any other governmental instrumentality or agency, who is alleged to be in violation of any provision of this chapter." It also grants the district courts "jurisdiction, without regard to the amount in controversy or the citizenship of the parties, to enforce any such provision."

This Court had occasion in *Hecht Co.* v. *Bowles,...*(1944), to construe language in an Act of Congress that lent far greater support to a conclusion that Congress intended an injunction to issue as a matter of right than does the language just quoted....

But in *Hecht* this Court refused to find even in such language an intent on the part of Congress to require that a district court issue an injunction as a matter of course without regard to established equitable considerations....

Only if we were to sharply retreat from the principle of statutory construction announced in *Hecht* could we agree with the Court of Appeals' holding in this case that the judicial enforcement provisions contained in § 11 (g)(1) of the Act require automatic issuance of an injunction by the district courts once a violation is found....

Since the District Court possessed discretion to refuse injunctive relief even though it had found a violation of the Act, the only remaining question is whether this discretion was abused in denying respondents' prayer for an injunction.... The District Court denied respondents injunctive relief because of the significant public and social harms that would flow from such relief and because of the demonstrated good faith of petitioner. As the Court recognizes..., such factors traditionally have played a central role in the decisions of equity courts whether to deny an injunction.... This Court has specifically held that a federal court can refuse to order a federal official to take specific action, even though the action might be required by law, if such an order "would work a public injury or embarrassment" or otherwise "be prejudicial to the public interest." *United States* v. *Dern...*(1933). Here the District Court, confronted with conflicting evidence of congressional purpose, was on even stronger ground in refusing the injunction.

Since equity is "the instrument for nice adjustment and reconciliation between the public interest and private needs," *Hecht*..., a decree in one case will seldom be the exact counterpart of a decree in another.... Here the District Court recognized that Congress when it enacted that Endangered Species Act made the preservation of the habitat of the snail darter an important public concern. But it concluded that this interest on one side of the balance was more than outweighed by other equally significant factors. These factors...satisfy me that the District Court's refusal to issue an injunction was not an abuse of its discretion. I therefore dissent from the Court's opinion holding otherwise.

COURT ON HISTORIC PRESERVATION
June 26, 1978

The Supreme Court ruled June 26 that states and municipalities could protect historic buildings and sites by designating them as landmarks despite the financial burden such designation might place on the owners. In a 6-3 decision, the court said that landmark laws were a reasonable exercise of a state's police power.

Justice William J. Brennan Jr. wrote the majority opinion in which he was joined by Justices Harry A. Blackmun, Thurgood Marshall, Lewis F. Powell Jr., Potter Stewart and Byron R. White. The dissenting opinion, written by Justice William H. Rehnquist, was joined by Chief Justice Warren E. Burger and Justice John Paul Stevens.

Background

The case, Penn Central Transportation Co. v. City of New York, *concerned Penn Central's plans to construct a skyscraper office building atop Grand Central Terminal. The railroad terminal was named a landmark in 1968. The following year, Penn Central, the terminal's owner, leased the air rights above the building to UMP Properties Inc., a British firm. The company proposed to construct an office tower above the terminal and pay Penn Central $1 million each year during construction and $3 million each year thereafter. The New York Landmarks Commission rejected two versions of the planned office tower because they would have altered the design of the terminal. The railroad company went into the state's Supreme Court and charged that the law, the city's Landmarks Preservation Law, violated its constitutional rights. The state Supreme Court granted an injunction* *against the city's use of the landmarks law to halt construction of the tower. The decision was reversed, however, by both the appellate division of the state Supreme Court and the state's Court of Appeals; the Court of Appeals found that the city had not "taken" the property and that Penn Central had had adequate access to due process of law.*

Opened in 1913, Grand Central Terminal is considered by many to be an outstanding example of Beaux Arts architecture. Active in the fight to save the building from being capped by an office tower were dozens of persons prominent in the arts, politics and society.

Majority Opinion

Affirming the lower court decision, Justice Brennan rejected Penn Central's argument that the cost of maintaining historic sites should be borne by the public at large rather than by the owner of the property. He also noted that if the court overturned New York's landmark law, similar legislation in all of the 50 states and more than 500 municipalities would also be invalidated. Brennan wrote, "Stated baldly, appellants' position appears to be that the only means of ensuring that selected owners are not singled out to endure financial hardship for no reason is to hold that any restriction imposed on individual landmarks pursuant to the New York scheme is a 'taking' requiring the payment of 'just compensation.' ...We find no merit in it."

Brennan added, "It is of course true that the Landmark Law has a more severe impact on some landowners than on others, but that in itself does not mean that the law effects a 'taking.' Legislation designed to promote the general welfare commonly burdens some more than others."

Finally, Brennan wrote, the New York City law does not prevent Penn Central from receiving a profit from its operation of the terminal, though it may not be as great as the income the company expected to receive from development of the office tower. The landmark law, he said, does not prevent Penn Central from using the terminal for its primary purpose and allows "Penn Central not only to profit from the Terminal but to obtain a 'reasonable return' on its investment."

Dissenting Opinion

Justice Rehnquist's dissenting opinion held that the city had indeed "taken" the property of the Penn Central without offering just compensation. "Penn Central," Rehnquist wrote, "is prevented from further developing its property basically because it did too good of a job in designing and building it. The City of New York, because of its unadorned admiration for the design, had decided that the owners of the building must preserve it unchanged for the benefit of sightseeing New Yorkers and tourists."

Rehnquist added that if the costs of maintaining Grand Central Terminal were spread across the entire population of the city, "the burden per person would be in cents per year." Instead, he continued, the city "would impose the entire cost of several million dollars per year on Penn Central. But it is precisely this sort of discrimination that the Fifth Amendment prohibits." Further, he argued, the transfer of development rights allowed under the New York law fails to justly compensate Penn Central for the losses imposed by the landmark law.

> *Following are excerpts from Justice Brennan's majority opinion delivered June 26, 1978, that upheld New York City's landmark law, and excerpts from Justice Rehnquist's dissent:*

No. 77-444

| Penn Central Transportation Company et al., Appellants, *v.* City of New York et al. | On Appeal from the Court of Appeals of New York. |

[June 26, 1978]

MR. JUSTICE BRENNAN delivered the opinion of the Court.

The question presented is whether a city may, as part of a comprehensive program to preserve historic landmarks and historic districts, place restrictions on the development of individual historic landmarks — in addition to those imposed by applicable zoning ordinances — without effecting a "taking" requiring the payment of "just compensation." Specifically, we must decide whether the application of New York City's Landmarks Preservation law to the parcel of land occupied by Grand Central Terminal has "taken" its owners' property in violation of the Fifth and Fourteenth Amendments.

I

A

Over the past 50 years, all 50 States and over 500 municipalities have enacted laws to encourage or require the preservation of buildings and areas with historic or aesthetic importance. These nationwide legislative efforts have been precipitated by two concerns. The first is recognition that, in recent years, large numbers of historic structures, landmarks, and areas have been destroyed without adequate consideration of either the values represented therein or the possibility of preserving the destroyed properties for use in economically productive ways. The second is a widely shared belief that structures with special historic, cultural, or architectural significance enhance the quality of life for all. Not only do these buildings and their workmanship represent the lessons of the past and embody

precious features of our heritage, they serve as examples of quality for today....

New York City, responding to similar concerns and acting pursuant to a
New York State enabling act, adopted its Landmarks Preservation Law in
1965....

The New York City law is typical of many urban landmark laws in that
its primary method of achieving its goals is not by acquisitions of historic
properties, but rather by involving public entities in land use decisions affecting these properties and providing services, standards, controls, and incentives that will encourage preservation by private owners and users.
While the law does place special restrictions on landmark properties as a
necessary feature to the attainment of its larger objectives, the major theme
of the Act is to ensure the owners of any such properties both a "reasonable
return" on their investments and maximum latitude to use their parcels for
purposes not inconsistent with the preservation goals....

...[T]he primary responsibility for administering the Act is vested in the
Landmarks Preservation Commission (Commission), a broad based, 11-
member agency assisted by a technical staff....

Although the designation of a landmark and landmark site restricts the
owner's control over the parcel, designation also enhances the economic position of the landmark owner in one significant respect. Under New York
City's zoning laws, owners of real property who have not developed their
property to the full extent permitted by the applicable zoning laws are
allowed to transfer development rights to contiguous parcels on the same
city block.... In 1969, the law governing the conditions under which
transfers from landmark parcels could occur was liberalized...apparently to
ensure that the Landmark Law would not unduly restrict the development
options of the owners of Grand Central Terminal.... The class of recipient
lots was expanded to include lots "across a street and opposite to another
lot or lots which except for the intervention of streets or street intersections
form a series extending to the lot occupied by the landmark building
[provided that] all lots [are] in the same ownership." New York City Zoning
Resolution.... In addition, the 1969 amendment permits, in highly commer-
cialized areas like midtown Manhattan, the transfer of all unused development rights to a single parcel....

B

This case involves the application of New York City's Landmark Preservation Law to Grand Central Terminal (Terminal). The Terminal, which is
owned by the Penn Central Transportation Company and its affiliates
(Penn Central), is one of New York City's most famous buildings. . . .

II

The issues presented by appellants are (1) whether the restrictions imposed by New York City's law upon appellants' exploitation of the Terminal
site effect a "taking" of appellants' property for a public use within the

meaning of the Fifth Amendment, which of course is made applicable to the States through the Fourteenth Amendment, see *Chicago B. & Q. R. Co.* v. *Chicago*...(1897) and, (2) if so, whether the transferable development rights afforded appellants constitute "just compensation" within the meaning of the Fifth Amendment. We need only address the question whether a "taking" has occurred.

A

Before considering appellants' specific contentions, it will be useful to review the factors that have shaped the jurisprudence of the Fifth Amendment injunction "nor shall private property be taken for public use, without just compensation." The question of what constitutes a "taking" for purposes of the Fifth Amendment has proved to be a problem of considerable difficulty. While this Court has recognized that the "Fifth Amendment's guarantee [is] designed to bar Government from forcing some people alone to bear public burdens which, in all fairness and justice, should be borne by the public as a whole," *Armstrong* v. *United States*...(1960), this Court, quite simply, has been unable to develop any "set formula" for determining when "justice and fairness" require that economic injuries caused by public action be compensated by the Government, rather than remain disproportionately concentrated on a few persons....

...[I]n instances in which a state tribunal reasonably concluded that "the health, safety, morals or general welfare" would be promoted by prohibiting particular contemplated uses of land, this Court has upheld land use regulations that destroyed or adversely affected recognized real property interests.... Zoning laws are of course the classic example...which have been viewed as permissible governmental action even when prohibiting the most beneficial use of the property....

Zoning laws generally do not affect existing uses of real property, but taking challenges have also been held to be without merit in a wide variety of situations when the challenged governmental actions prohibited a beneficial use to which individual parcels had previously been devoted and thus caused substantial individualized harm....

Pennsylvania Coal Co. v. *Mahon*...(1922) is the leading case for the proposition that a state statute that substantially furthers important public policies may so frustrate distinct investment-backed expectations as to amount to a "taking." There the claimant had sold the surface rights to particular parcels of property, but expressly reserved the right to remove the coal thereunder. A Pennsylvania statute, enacted after the transactions, forbade any mining of coal that caused the subsidence of any house, unless the house was the property of the owner of the underlying coal and was more than 150 feet from the improved property of another. Because the statute made it commercially impracticable to mine the coal...and thus had nearly the same effect as the complete destruction of rights claimant had purchased from the owners of the surface land..., the Court held that the statute was invalid as effecting a "taking" without just compensation....

Finally, Government actions that may be characterized as acquisitions of resources to permit or facilitate uniquely public functions have often been held to constitute "takings." *United States* v. *Causby* [(1946)]...is illustrative. In holding that direct overflights above the claimant's land, that destroyed the present use of the land as a chicken farm, constituted a "taking," *Causby* emphasized that Government had not "merely destroyed property [but was] using a part of it for the flight of its planes."...

B

In contending that the New York City law has "taken" their property in violation of the Fifth and Fourteenth Amendments, appellants make a series of arguments, which, while tailored to the facts of this case, essentially urge that any substantial restriction imposed pursuant to a landmark law must be accompanied by just compensation if it is to be constitutional. Before considering these, we emphasize what is not in dispute. Because this Court has recognized, in a number of settings, that States and cities may enact land use restrictions or controls to enhance the quality of life by preserving the character and desirable aesthetic features of a city..., appellants do not contest that New York City's objective of preserving structures and areas with special historic, architectural, or cultural significance is an entirely permissible governmental goal. They also do not dispute that the restrictions imposed on its parcel are appropriate means of securing the purposes of the New York City law. Finally, appellants do not challenge any of the specific factual premises of the decision below. They accept for present purposes both that the parcel of land occupied by Grand Central Terminal must, in its present state, be regarded as capable of earning a reasonable return, and that the transferable development rights afforded appellants by virtue of the Terminal's designation as a landmark are valuable, even if not as valuable as the rights to construct above the Terminal. In appellants' view none of these factors derogate from their claim that New York City's law has effected a "taking."

They first observe that the air space above the Terminal is a valuable property interest, citing *United States* v. *Causby*.... They urge that the Landmark Law has deprived them of any gainful use of their "air rights" above the Terminal and that, irrespective of the value of the remainder of their parcel, the city has "taken" their right to this superjacent air space, thus entitling them to "just compensation" measured by the fair market value of these air rights.

Apart from our own disagreement with appellants' characterization of the effect of the New York law..., the submission that appellants may establish a "taking" simply by showing that they have been denied the ability to exploit a property interest that they heretofore had believed was available for development is quite simply untenable. Were this the rule, this Court would have erred not only in upholding laws restricting the development of air rights...but also in approving those prohibiting both the subjacent...and the lateral development...of particular parcels. "Taking" jurisprudence does not divide a single parcel into discrete segments and attempt to determine whether rights in a particular segment have been entirely abrogated. In deciding whether a particular governmental action has effected a taking, this Court focuses rather both on the character of the action and on the nature and extent of the interference with rights in the parcel as a whole, here, the city tax block designated as the "landmark site."

Secondly, appellants, focusing on the character and impact of the New York City law, argue that it effects a "taking" because its operation has significantly diminished the value of the Terminal site. Appellants concede that the decisions sustaining other land use regulations, which, like the New York law, are reasonably related to the promotion of the general welfare, uniformly reject the proposition that diminution in property value, standing alone, can establish a taking...and that the taking issue...is resolved by focusing on the uses the regulations permit.... Appellants, moreover, also do not dispute that a showing of diminution in property value would not establish a taking if the restriction had been imposed as a result of historic district legislation..., but appellants argue that New York City's regulation of individual landmarks is fundamentally different from zoning or from historic district legislation because the controls imposed by New York City's law apply only to individuals who own selected properties.

Stated baldly, appellants' position appears to be that the only means of ensuring that selected owners are not singled out to endure financial hardship for no reason is to hold that any restriction imposed on individual landmarks pursuant to the New York scheme is a "taking" requiring the payment of "just compensation." Agreement with this argument would of course invalidate not just New York City's law, but all comparable landmark legislation in the Nation. We find no merit in it.

It is true, as appellants emphasize, that both historic district legislation and zoning laws regulate all properties within given physical communities whereas landmark laws apply only to selected parcels. But, contrary to appellants' suggestions, landmark laws are not like discriminatory, or "reverse spot," zoning: that is, a land use decision which arbitrarily singles out a particular parcel for different, less favorable treatment than the neighboring ones.... In contrast to discriminatory zoning, which is the antithesis of land use control as part of some comprehensive plan, the New York City law embodies a comprehensive plan to preserve structures of historic or aesthetic interest wherever they might be found in the city....

Equally without merit is the related argument that the decision to designate a structure as a landmark "is inevitably arbitrary or at least subjective because it basically is a matter of taste"...thus unavoidably singling out individual landowners for disparate and unfair treatment. The argument has a particularly hollow ring in this case. For appellants not only did not seek judicial review of either the designation or of the denials of the certificates of appropriateness and of no exterior effect, but do not even now suggest that the Commission's decisions concerning the Terminal were in any sense arbitrary or unprincipled. But in any event, a landmark owner has a right to judicial review of any Commission decision, and, quite simply, there is no basis whatsoever for a conclusion that courts will have any greater difficulty identifying arbitrary or discriminatory action in the context of landmark regulation than in the context of classic zoning or indeed in any other context.

Next, appellants observe that New York City's law differs from zoning laws and historic district ordinances in that the Landmark Law does not impose identical or similar restrictions on all structures located in particular physical communities. It follows, they argue, that New York City's law is inherently incapable of producing the fair and equitable distribution of benefits and burdens of governmental action which is characteristic of zoning laws and historic district legislation and which they maintain is a constitutional requirement if "just compensation" is not to be afforded. It is of course true that the Landmark Law has a more severe impact on some landowners than on others, but that in itself does not mean that the law effects a "taking." Legislation designed to promote the general welfare commonly burdens some more than others....

In any event, appellants' repeated suggestions that they are solely burdened and unbenefited is factually inaccurate. This contention overlooks the fact that the New York City law applies to vast numbers of structures in the city in addition to the Terminal — all the structures contained in the 31 historic districts and over 400 individual landmarks, many of which are close to the Terminal. Unless we are to reject the judgment of the New York City Council that the preservation of landmarks benefit all New York citizens and all structures, both economically and by improving the quality of life in the city as a whole — which we are unwilling to do — we cannot conclude that the owners of the Terminal have in no sense been benefited by the Landmark Law....

...The Landmarks Law's effect is simply to prohibit appellants or anyone else from occupying portions of the airspace above the Terminal, while permitting appellants to use the remainder of the parcel in a gainful fashion. This is no more an appropriation of property by Government for its own uses than is a zoning law prohibiting for "aesthetic" reasons, two or more adult theatres within a specified area, see *Young* v. *American Mini Theatres, Inc.* [(1976)]...or a safety regulation prohibiting excavations below a certain level. See *Goldblatt* v. *City of Hempstead* [(1962)]....

C

Rejection of appellants' broad arguments is not however the end of our inquiry, for all we thus far have established is that the New York law is not rendered invalid by its failure to provide "just compensation" whenever a landmark owner is restricted in the exploitation of property interests, such as air rights, to a greater extent than provided for under applicable zoning laws. We now must consider whether the interference with appellants' property is of such a magnitude that "There must be an exercise of eminent domain and compensation to sustain [it]." *Pennsylvania Coal Co.* v. *Mahon* [(1922)].... That inquiry may be narrowed to the question of the severity of the impact of the law on appellants' parcel, and its resolution in turn requires a careful assessment of the impact of the regulation on the Terminal site....

...Its designation as a landmark not only permits but contemplates that appellants may continue to use the property precisely as it has for the past 65 years: as a railroad terminal containing office space and concessions. So the law does not interfere with what must be regarded as Penn Central's primary expectation concerning the use of the parcel. More importantly, on this record, we must regard the New York City law as permitting Penn Central not only to profit from the Terminal but to obtain a "reasonable return" on its investment.

Appellants, moreover, exaggerate the effect of the Act on its ability to make use of the air rights above the Terminal in two respects. First, it simply cannot be maintained, on this record, that appellants have been prohibited from occupying *any* portion of the airspace above the Terminal. While the Commission's actions in denying applications to construct an office building in excess of 50 stories above the Terminal may indicate that it will refuse to issue a certificate of appropriateness for any comparably sized structure, nothing the Commission has said or done suggests an intention to prohibit *any* construction above the Terminal. The Commission's report emphasized that whether any construction would be allowed depended upon whether the proposed addition "would harmonize in scale, material, and character with [the Terminal]."... Since appellants have not sought approval for the construction of a smaller structure, we do not know that appellants will be denied any use of any portion of the airspace above the Terminal.

Second, to the extent appellants have been denied the right to build above the Terminal, it is not literally accurate to say that they have been denied *all* use of even those pre-existing air rights. Their ability to use these rights has not been abrogated; they are made transferable to at least eight parcels in the vicinity of the Terminal, one or two of which have been found suitable for the construction of new office buildings. Although appellants and others have argued that New York City's transferable development rights program is far from ideal, the New York courts here supportably found that, at least in the case of the Terminal, the rights afforded are valuable. While these rights may well not have constituted "just compensation" if a "taking" had occurred, the rights nevertheless undoubtedly mitigate whatever financial burdens the law has imposed on appellants and, for that reason, are to be taken into account in considering the impact of regulation....

On this record we conclude that the application of New York City's Landmark Preservation Law has not effected a "taking" of appellants' property. The restrictions imposed are substantially related to the promotion of the general welfare and not only permit reasonable beneficial use of the landmark site but afford appellants opportunities further to enhance not only the Terminal site proper but also other properties.

Affirmed.

MR. JUSTICE REHNQUIST, with whom THE CHIEF JUSTICE and MR. JUSTICE STEVENS join, dissenting....

...The question in this case is whether the cost associated with the city of New York's desire to preserve a limited number of "landmarks" within its borders must be borne by all of its taxpayers or whether it can instead be imposed entirely on the owners of the individual properties.

Only in the most superficial sense of the word can this case be said to involve "zoning." Typical zoning restrictions may, it is true, so limit the prospective uses of a piece of property as to diminish the value of that property in the abstract because it may not be used for the forbidden purposes. But any such abstract decrease in value will more than likely be at least partially offset by an increase in value which flows from similar restrictions as to use on neighboring properties. All property owners in a designated area are placed under the same restrictions, not only for the benefit of the municipality as a whole but for the common benefit of one another....

Where a relatively few individual buildings, all separated from one another, are singled out and treated differently from surrounding buildings, no such reciprocity exists. The cost to the property owner which results from the imposition of restrictions applicable only to his property and not that of his neighbors may be substantial — in this case, several million dollars — with no comparable reciprocal benefits. And the cost associated with landmark legislation is likely to be of a completely different order of magnitude than that which results from the imposition of normal zoning restrictions. Unlike the regime affected by the latter, the landowner is not simply prohibited from using his property for certain purposes, while allowed to use it for all other purposes. Under the historic landmark preservation scheme adopted by New York, the property owner is under an affirmative duty to *preserve* his property *as a landmark* at his own expense. To suggest that because traditional zoning results in some limitation of use of the property zoned, the New York landmark preservation scheme should likewise be upheld, represents the ultimate in treating as alike things which are different....

I

The Fifth Amendment provides in part: "nor shall private property be taken for public use, without just compensation." In a very literal sense, the actions of appellees violated this constitutional prohibition.... Because the taking clause of the Fifth Amendment has not always been read literally, however, the constitutionality of appellees' actions requires a closer scrutiny of this Court's interpretation of the three key words in the Taking Clause — "property," "taken," and "just compensation."

A

Appellees do not dispute that valuable property rights have been destroyed. And the Court has frequently emphasized that the term "property" as used in the Taking Clause includes the entire "group of rights inhering in the citizen's [ownership.]" *United States* v. *General Motors* [*Corp.*] ...(1945).... While neighboring landowners are free to use their land and "air rights" in any way consistent with the broad boundaries of New York zoning, Penn Central, absent the permission of appellees, must forever maintain its property in its present state. The property has been thus subjected to a nonconsensual servitude not borne by any neighboring or similar properties.

B

Appellees have thus destroyed — in a literal sense, "taken" — substantial property rights of Penn Central. While the term "taken" might have been narrowly interpreted to include only physical seizures of property rights, "the construction of the phrase has not been so narrow. The courts have held that the deprivation of the former owner rather than the accretion of a right or interest to the sovereign constitutes a taking." *United States* v. *General Motors....* Because "not every destruction or injury to property by governmental action has been held to be a 'taking' in the constitutional sense," *Armstrong* v. *United States...*(1960), however, this does not end our inquiry. But an examination of the two exceptions where the destruction of property does *not* constitute a taking demonstrates that a compensable taking has occurred here.

1

As early as 1887, the Court recognized that the government can prevent a property owner from using his property to injure others without having to compensate the owner for the value of the forbidden use....

Appellees are not prohibiting a nuisance. The record is clear that the proposed addition to the Grand Central Terminal would be in full compliance with zoning, height limitations, and other health and safety requirements. Instead, appellees are seeking to preserve what they believe to be an outstanding example of Beaux Arts architecture. Penn Central is prevented from further developing its property basically because it did *too good* of a job in designing and building it. The city of New York, because of its unadorned admiration for the design, has decided that the owners of the building must preserve it unchanged for the benefit of sightseeing New Yorkers and tourists.

Unlike in the case of land use regulations, appellees are not *prohibiting* Penn Central from using its property in a narrow set of noxious ways. Instead, appellees have placed an *affirmative* duty on Penn Central to maintain the Terminal in its present state and in "good repair." Appellants are not free to use their property as they see fit within broad outer boundaries but must strictly adhere to their past use except where appellees conclude that alternative uses would not detract from the Landmark. While Penn Central may continue to use the Terminal as it is presently designed, appellees otherwise "exercise complete dominion and control over the surface of the land," *United States* v. *Causby...*(1946), and must compensate the owner for his loss.... "Property is taken in the constitutional sense when inroads are made upon an owner's use of it to an extent that, as between private parties, a servitude has been acquired." *United States* v. *Dickinson* ...(1947).

2

Even where the government prohibits a noninjurious use, the Court has ruled that a taking does not take place if the prohibition applies over a broad cross section of land and thereby "secure[s] an average reciprocity of advantage." *Pennsylvania Coal Co.* v. *Mahon*...(1922). It is for this reason that zoning does not constitute a "taking." While zoning at times reduces *individual* property values, the burden is shared relatively evenly and it is reasonable to conclude that on a whole an individual who is harmed by one aspect of the zoning will be benefited by another.

Here, however, a multimillion dollar loss has been imposed on appellants; it is uniquely felt and is not offset by any benefits flowing from the preservation of some 500 other "Landmarks" in New York. Appellees have imposed a substantial cost on less than one one-tenth of one percent of the buildings in New York for the general benefit of all its people. It is exactly this imposition of general costs on a few individuals at which the "taking" protection is directed....

As Justice Holmes pointed out in *Pennsylvania Coal Co.* v. *Mahon* [(1922)], "the question at bottom" in an eminent domain case "is upon whom the loss of the changes desired should fall." ...The benefits that appellees believe will flow from preservation of the Grand Central Terminal will accrue to all the citizens of New York. There is no reason to believe that appellants will enjoy a substantially greater share of these benefits. If the cost of preserving Grand Central Terminal were spread evenly across the entire population of the city of New York, the burden per person would be in cents per year — a minor cost appellees would surely concede for the benefit accrued. Instead, however, appellees would impose the entire cost of several million dollars per year on Penn Central. But it is precisely this sort of discrimination that the Fifth Amendment prohibits.

Appellees in response would argue that a taking only occurs where a property owner is denied *all* reasonable value of his property. The Court has frequently held that, even where a destruction of property rights would not *otherwise* constitute a taking, the inability of the owner to make a reasonable return on his property requires compensation under the Fifth Amendment.... But the converse is not true. A taking does not become a noncompensable exercise of police power simply because the government in its grace allows the owner to make some "reasonable" use of his property....

C

Appellees, apparently recognizing that the constraints imposed on a Landmark site constitute a taking for Fifth Amendment purposes, do not leave the property owner empty handed. As the Court notes...the property owner may theoretically "transfer" his previous right to develop the Landmark property to adjacent properties if they are under his control. Appellees have coined this system "Transfer Development Rights," or TDRs.

Of all the terms used in the Taking Clause, "just compensation" has the strictest meaning. The Fifth Amendment does not allow simply an approximate compensation but requires "a full and perfect equivalent for the property taken." *Monongahela Navigation Co.* v. *United States...*(1893).... And the determination of whether a "full and perfect equivalent" has been awarded is a "judicial function." *United States* v. *New River Collieries Co...*(1923). The fact that *appellees* may believe that TDRs provide full compensation is irrelevant....

Appellees contend that, even if they have "taken" appellants' property, TDRs constitute "just compensation." Appellants, of course, argue that TDRs are highly imperfect compensation. Because the lower courts held that there was no "taking" they did not have to reach the question of whether or not just compensation has already been awarded.... And in other cases the Court of Appeals has noted that TDRs have an "uncertain and contingent market value" and do "not adequately preserve" the value lost when a building is declared to be a Landmark. *Fred F. French Investing Co.* v. *City of New York...*(1976). On the other hand, there is evidence in the record that Penn Central has been offerred substantial amounts for its TDRs. Because the record on appeal is relatively slim, I would remand to the Court of Appeals for a determination of whether TDRs constitute a "full and perfect equivalent for the property taken."

II

Over 50 years ago, Justice Holmes, speaking for the Court, warned that the courts were "in danger of forgetting that a strong public desire to improve the public condition is not enough to warrant achieving the desire by a shorter cut than the constitutional way of paying for the change." *Pennsylvania Coal Co.* v. *Mahon* [(1922)].... The Court's opinion in this case demonstrates that the danger thus foreseen has not abated. The city of New York is in a precarious financial state, and some may believe that the costs of landmark preservation will be more easily borne by corporations such as Penn Central than the overburdened individual taxpayers of New York. But these concerns do not allow us to ignore past precedents construing the Eminent Domain Clause to the end that the desire to improve the public condition is, indeed, achieved by a shorter cut than the constitutional way of paying for the damage.

COURT ON UNIVERSITY AFFIRMATIVE ACTION PROGRAMS
June 28, 1978

In what was widely regarded as the most important civil rights case since Brown v. Board of Education (1954), the Supreme Court ruled June 28 that universities may not reserve a quota of seats for minority students for which white applicants cannot compete. In the same case, Regents of the University of California v. Bakke, the court also held that it was constitutionally permissible for universities to consider race as one of a group of factors to be taken into account for admissions decisions.

Admissions Program

The case arose after Allan Bakke, a 38-year-old white engineer, was twice rejected for admission by the medical school of the University of California at Davis. In an attempt to increase the number of minority physicians, the school had instituted an affirmative action program that set aside 16 places in a class of 100 for minority applicants. Under the terms of the program, white applicants competed for 84 seats while minority applicants competed for all 100 places. Bakke filed suit against the university in 1974, charging that the medical school's admissions policy that reserved 16 seats for minority candidates violated the equal protection guarantees of the Fourteenth Amendment. He alleged (and the university later admitted) that some of the minority applicants who were accepted at Davis had scores below his and demanded that the court order the university to accept his application. The California Supreme Court ruled in favor of Bakke; it found that the university's affirmative action program was unconstitutional because it discriminated against whites and ordered that Bakke be admitted to the medical school in September 1977. The university appealed to the Supreme Court.

Split Decision

On the issue of the admissions program, the court ruled 5-4 that the program was illegal and thus opened the way for Bakke's admission to Davis. The majority consisted of Chief Justice Warren E. Burger and Justices William Rehnquist, Potter Stewart, John Paul Stevens and Lewis F. Powell Jr. The minority on this issue, Justices William J. Brennan Jr., Thurgood Marshall, Byron R. White and Harry A. Blackmun, said that the Davis admissions program should be allowed to continue since its purpose was to compensate for past societal discrimination against minorities.

While one majority of justices struck down the particular affirmative action program in operation at the Davis medical school, a second majority, composed of Brennan, Marshall, White, Blackmun and Powell, upheld consideration of race in the review of students' applications. Powell was the only justice to join both majorities. The decision included six separate opinions.

Powell Opinion

For the majority ordering Bakke's admission to Davis, Powell wrote, "The guarantee of equal protection cannot mean one thing when applied to one individual and something else when applied to a person of different color.... Preferring members of one group for no reason other than race or ethnic origin is discrimination for its own sake. This the Constitution forbids."

Powell termed the university's "disregard of individual rights" guaranteed by the Fourteenth Amendment, the "fatal flaw" of its special admissions program. "Such rights are not absolute," he added. "But when a state's distribution of benefits or imposition of burdens hinges on the color of a person's skin or ancestry, that individual is entitled to a demonstration that the challenged classification is necessary to promote a substantial state interest."

He rejected as unproven the university's arguments that the program would result in an increase in the number of minority doctors but accepted the school's interest in achieving a diverse student population. The rigid program at Davis, however, would "hinder rather than further attainment of genuine diversity," Powell wrote. He recommended that admissions officers study the undergraduate admissions program at Harvard University in which "race or ethnic background may be deemed a 'plus' in a particular applicant's file, yet it does not insulate the individual from comparison with *all other candidates for the available seats." In this way, Powell reasoned, race can be legally considered in admissions.*

Separate Opinions

Justice Brennan, writing for himself and Justices White, Blackmun and Marshall, agreed with Powell on the legality of some affirmative action and went further, arguing that quota systems such as the one at Davis enjoyed constitutional protection. He insisted that neither the Civil Rights Act of 1964 nor the Fourteenth Amendment forbade preferential use of race to remedy past societal discrimination. "We cannot...let color blindness become myopia which masks the reality that many 'created equal' have been treated within our lifetime as inferior both by the law and by their fellow citizens." Brennan and his colleagues added that special considera- tion based on race was justifiable even at institutions that had not previous- ly practiced discrimination: "Properly construed...our prior cases une- quivocally show that a state government may adopt race-conscious programs if the purpose of such programs is to remove the disparate racial impact its actions might otherwise have and if there is reason to believe that the disparate impact is itself the product of past discrimination, whether its own or society at large. There is no question that Davis' program is valid un- der this test."

In Justice Stevens' opinion, which joined Justice Powell's in ordering Bakke's admission to medical school and overturning the Davis admissions program, Stevens viewed the case as a "controversy between two specific litigants" which could be settled by application of the 1964 Civil Rights Act and therefore did not raise constitutional questions. "The question whether race can ever be used as a factor in an admissions decision is not an issue in this case, and...discussion of that issue is inappropriate," Stevens wrote. He was joined in his opinion by Chief Justice Burger and Justices Rehnquist and Stewart.

Justice Blackmun wrote in a separate opinion, "It is somewhat ironic to have us so deeply disturbed over a program where race is an element of con- sciousness, and yet to be aware of the fact that institutions of higher learn- ing...have given conceded preferences up to a point to those possessed of athletic skills, to the children of alumni, to the affluent who may bestow their largess on the institutions, and to those having connections with celebrities, the famous, and the powerful." He added, "I yield to no one in my earnest hope that the time will come when an 'affirmative action' program is unnecessary and is, in truth, only a relic of the past.... At some time, however, beyond any period of what some would claim is only tran- sitional inequality, the United States must and will reach a stage of maturity where action along this line is no longer necessary."

In a bitter separate opinion, Justice Marshall, the only black member of the court, wrote, "During most of the past 200 years, the Constitution as in-

terpreted by this Court did not prohibit the most ingenious and pervasive forms of discrimination against the Negro. Now, when a state acts to remedy the effects of that legacy of discrimination, I cannot believe that this same Constitution stands as a barrier." He added, "The experience of Negroes in America has been different in kind, not just in degree, from that of other ethnic groups. The dream of America as the great melting pot has not been realized for the Negro; because of his skin color he never even made it into the pot."

In a brief, separate opinion, Justice White addressed the issue of whether Title VI of the Civil Rights Act of 1964 — the statute involved — "provides for a private cause of action."

Reaction

Most of the groups and individuals interested in the Bakke case appeared satisfied with the court's decision immediately after it was handed down. Attorney General Griffin B. Bell said he regarded the ruling as "a great gain for affirmative action." Benjamin L. Hooks, executive director of the National Association for the Advancement of Colored People, called the decision "a clear-cut victory for voluntary affirmative action." Arnold Foster, general counsel of the Anti-Defamation League of the B'nai B'rith, said that he was "comforted that, once and for all, the United States Supreme Court has held that racial quotas are flatly illegal." Bakke himself told reporters that he was "pleased" with the decision and would enter medical school in the fall.

Some black leaders, however, were concerned that as a result of the Bakke decision affirmative action programs might not be pressed as vigorously as before. At the end of a three-day symposium on the implications of the ruling, the NAACP on July 22 announced that it would ask President Carter to convene a White House conference on affirmative action and that it would lead a major lobbying effort to impress members of the Cabinet and Congress with the importance of continuing affirmative action.

> Following are excerpts from Justice Powell's decision that ordered Allan Bakke's admission to the medical school of the University of California at Davis, struck down that university's rigid program of special admissions but ruled that some consideration of race is allowable in the admissions procedure; and excerpts from the opinions filed by Justices Brennan, White, Marshall, Blackmun and Stevens:

No. 76-811

Regents of the University of California, Petitioner, | On Writ of Certiorari to
v. | the Supreme Court of
Allan Bakke. | California.

[June 28, 1978]

MR. JUSTICE POWELL announced the judgment of the Court.

This case presents a challenge to the special admissions program of the petitioner, the Medical School of the University of California at Davis, which is designed to assure the admission of a specified number of students from certain minority groups. The Superior Court of California sustained respondent's challenge.... The court enjoined petitioner from considering respondent's race or the race of any other applicant in making admissions decisions. It refused, however, to order respondent's admission to the Medical School.... The Supreme Court of California affirmed those portions of the trial court's judgment declaring the special admissions program unlawful and enjoining petitioner from considering the race of any applicant. It modified that portion of the judgment denying respondent's requested injunction and directed the trial court to order his admission.

For the reasons stated in the following opinion, I believe that so much of the judgment of the California court as holds petitioner's special admissions program unlawful and directs that respondent be admitted to the Medical School must be affirmed. For the reasons expressed in a separate opinion, my Brothers THE CHIEF JUSTICE, MR. JUSTICE STEWART, MR. JUSTICE REHNQUIST, AND MR. JUSTICE STEVENS concur in this judgment.

I also conclude for the reasons stated in the following opinion that the portion of the court's judgment enjoining petitioner from according any consideration to race in its admissions process must be reversed. For reasons expressed in separate opinions, my Brothers MR. JUSTICE BRENNAN, MR. JUSTICE WHITE, MR. JUSTICE MARSHALL, and MR. JUSTICE BLACKMUN concur in this judgment.

Affirmed in part and reversed in part.

I

The Medical School of the University of California at Davis opened in 1968 with an entering class of 50 students. In 1971, the size of the entering class was increased to 100 students, a level at which it remains. No admissions program for disadvantaged or minority students existed when the school opened, and the first class contained three Asians but no blacks, no Mexican-Americans, and no American Indians. Over the next two years, the faculty devised a special admissions program to increase the representation of "disadvantaged" students in each medical school class. The special program consisted of a separate admissions system operating in coordination with the regular admissions process....

Allan Bakke is a white male who applied to the Davis Medical School in both 1973 and 1974. In both years Bakke's application was considered by the general admissions program, and he received an interview.... Despite a strong benchmark score of 468 out of 500, Bakke was rejected. His application had come late in the year, and no applicants in the general admissions process with scores below 470 were accepted after Bakke's application was completed.... There were four special admissions slots unfilled at that time, however, for which Bakke was not considered....

...In both years, applicants were admitted under the special program with grade point averages, MCAT scores, and bench mark scores significantly lower than Bakke's.

After the second rejection, Bakke filed the instant suit in the Superior Court of California. He sought mandatory, injunctive, and declaratory relief compelling his admission to the Medical School. He alleged that the Medical School's special admissions program operated to exclude him from the school on the basis of his race, in violation of his rights under the Equal Protection Clause of the Fourteenth Amendment, Art. I, § 21 of the California Constitution, and § 601 of Title VI of the Civil Rights Act of 1964, 42 U.S.C. § 2000d. The University cross-complained for a declaration that its special admissions program was lawful. The trial court found that the special program operated as a racial quota, because minority applicants in the special program were rated only against one another..., and 16 places in the class of 100 were reserved for them.... Declaring that the University could not take race into account in making admissions decisions, the trial court held the challenged program violative of the Federal Constitution, the state constitution and Title VI. The court refused to order Bakke's admission, however, holding that he had failed to carry his burden of proving that he would have been admitted but for the existence of the special program.

Bakke appealed from the portion of the trial court judgment denying him admission, and the University appealed from the decision that its special admissions program was unlawful and the order enjoining it from considering race in the processing of applications. The Supreme Court of California transferred the case directly from the trial court, "because of the importance of the issues involved."... Although the court agreed that the goals of integrating the medical profession and increasing the number of physicians willing to serve members of minority groups were compelling state interests..., it concluded that the special admissions program was not the least intrusive means of achieving those goals. Without passing on the state constitutional or the federal statutory grounds cited in the trial court's judgment, the California court held that the Equal Protection Clause of the Fourteenth Amendment required that "no applicant may be rejected because of his race, in favor of another who is less qualified, as measured by standards applied without regard to race."...

Turning to Bakke's appeal, the court ruled that since Bakke had established that the University had discriminated against him on the basis of his race, the burden of proof shifted to the University to demonstrate that he would not have been admitted even in the absence of the special admissions program.... [T]he University conceded its inability to carry that burden.... The California court thereupon amended its opinion to direct that the trial court enter judgment ordering Bakke's admission to the medical school....

II

In this Court the parties neither briefed nor argued the applicability of Title VI of the Civil Rights of 1964. Rather, as had the California court, they focused exclusively upon the validity of the special admissions program under the Equal Protection Clause. Because it was possible, however, that a decision on Title VI might obviate resort to constitutional interpretation, see *Ashwander* v. *TVA*...(1936), we requested supplementary briefing on the statutory issue.

A

At the outset we face the question whether a right of action for private parties exists under Title VI....

B

The language of § 601, like that of the Equal Protection Clause, is majestic in its sweep:

> "No person in the United States shall, on the ground of race, color, or national origin, be excluded from participation in, be denied the benefits of, or be subjected to discrimination under any program or activity receiving Federal financial assistance."

The concept of "discrimination," like the phrase "equal protection of the laws," is susceptible to varying interpretations.... Examination of the voluminous legislative history of Title VI reveals a congressional intent to halt federal funding of entities that violate a prohibition of racial discrimination similar to that of the Constitution....

In view of the clear legislative intent, Title VI must be held to proscribe only those racial classifications that would violate the Equal Protection Clause of the Fifth Amendment.

III

A

...[T]he parties fight a sharp preliminary action over the proper characterization of the special admissions program. Petitioner prefers to view it as establishing a "goal" of minority representation in the medical school. Respondent, echoing the courts below, labels it a racial quota.

This semantic distinction is beside the point: the special admissions program is undeniably a classification based on race and ethnic background. To the extent that there existed a pool of at least minimally qualified minority applicants to fill the 16 special admissions seats, white applicants could compete only for 84 seats in the entering class, rather than the 100 open to minority applicants. Whether this limitation is described as a quota or a goal, it is a line drawn on the basis of race and ethnic status.

The guarantees of the Fourteenth Amendment extend to persons. Its language is explicit: "No state shall...deny to any person within its jurisdiction the equal protection of the laws."... The guarantee of equal protection cannot mean one thing when applied to one individual and something else when applied to a person of another color. If both are not accorded the same protection, then it is not equal....

...Racial and ethnic distinctions of any sort are inherently suspect and thus call for the most exacting judicial examination.

B

This perception of racial and ethnic distinctions is rooted in our Nation's constitutional and demographic history....

Over the past 30 years, this Court has embarked upon the crucial mission of interpreting the Equal Protection Clause with the view of assuring to all persons "the protection of equal laws," *Yick Wo [v. Hopkins* (1886)]...in a Nation confronting a legacy of slavery and racial discrimination.... Because the landmark decisions in this area arose in response to the continued exclusion of Negroes from the mainstream of American society, they could be characterized as involving discrimination by the "majority" white race against the Negro minority. But they need not be read as depending upon that characterization for their results. It suffices to say that "[o]ver the years, this Court consistently repudiated '[d]istinctions between citizens solely because of their ancestry' as being 'odious to a free people whose institutions are founded upon the doctrine of equality.'" *Loving* v. *Virginia...*(1967)....

Petitioner urges us to adopt for the first time a more restrictive view of the Equal Protection Clause and hold that discrimination against members of the white "majority" cannot be suspect if its purpose can be characterized as "benign." The clock of our liberties, however, cannot be turned back to 1868.... It is far too late to argue that the guarantee of equal protection to *all* persons permits the recognition of special wards entitled to a degree of protection greater than that accorded others....

...The concepts of "majority" and "minority" necessarily reflect temporary arrangements and political judgments. As observed above, the white "majority" itself is composed of various minority groups, most of which can lay claim to a history of prior discrimination at the hands of the state and private individuals. Not all these groups can receive preferential treatment and corresponding judicial tolerance of distinctions drawn in terms of race and nationality, for then the only "majority" left would be a new minority of White Anglo-Saxon Protestants....

Moreover, there are serious problems of justice connected with the idea of preference itself. First, it may not always be clear that a so-called preference is in fact benign. Courts may be asked to validate burdens imposed upon individual members of particular groups in order to advance the group's general interest.... Nothing in the Constitution supports the notion that individuals may be asked to suffer otherwise impermissible burdens in order to enhance the societal standing of their ethnic groups. Second, preferential programs may only reinforce common stereotypes holding that certain groups are unable to achieve success without special protection based on a factor having no relationship to individual worth....

Third, there is a measure of inequity in forcing innocent persons in respondent's position to bear the burdens of redressing grievances not of their making.

By hitching the meaning of the Equal Protection Clause to these transitory considerations, we would be holding, as a constitutional principle, that judicial scrutiny of classifications touching on racial and ethnic background may vary with the ebb and flow of political forces....

If it is the individual who is entitled to judicial protection against classifications based upon his racial or ethnic background because such distinctions impinge upon personal rights, rather than the individual only because of his membership in a particular group, then constitutional standards may be applied consistently. Political judgments regarding the necessity for the particular classification may be weighed in the constitutional balance *Korematsu* v. *United States*...(1944), but the standard of justification will remain constant. This is as it should be, since those political judgments are the product of rough compromise struck by contending groups within the democratic process. When they touch upon an individual's race or ethnic background, he is entitled to a judicial determination that the burden he is asked to bear on that basis is precisely tailored to serve a compelling governmental interest. The Constitution guarantees that right to every person regardless of his background....

C

Petitioner contends that on several occasions this Court has approved preferential classifications without applying the most exacting scrutiny. Most of the cases upon which petitioner relies are drawn from three areas: school desegregation, employment discrimination, and sex discrimination. Each of the cases cited presented a situation materially different from the facts of this case.

In this case...there has been no determination...that the University engaged in a discriminatory practice requiring remedial efforts. Moreover, the operation of petitioner's special admissions program is quite different from the remedial measures approved in those cases. It prefers the designated minority groups at the expense of other individuals who are totally foreclosed from competition for the 16 special admissions seats in every medical school class. Because of that foreclosure, some individuals are excluded from enjoyment of a state-provided benefit — admission to the medical school — they otherwise would receive. When a classification denies an individual opportunities or benefits enjoyed by others solely because of his race or ethnic background, it must be regarded as suspect. *E.g., McLaurin* v. *Oklahoma State Regents*...(1950).

IV

We have held that in "order to justify the use of a suspect classification, a State must show that its purpose or interest is both constitutionally permissible and substantial, and that its use of the classification is 'necessary...to the accomplishment' of its purpose or the safeguarding of its interest." *In re Griffiths*...(1973)....

A

If petitioner's purpose is to assure within its student body some specified percentage of a particular group merely because of its race or ethnic origin, such a preferential purpose must be rejected...as facially invalid. Preferring members of any one group for no reason other than race or ethnic origin is discrimination for its own sake. This the Constituion forbids. *E.g., Loving* v. *Virginia...; McLaughlin* v. *Florida* [1964]...; *Brown* v. *Board of Education*...(1954).

B

...[T]he purpose of helping certain groups whom the faculty of the Davis Medical School perceived as victims of "societal discrimination" does not justify a classification that imposes disadvantages upon persons like respondent, who bear no responsibility for whatever harm the beneficiaries of the special admissions program are thought to have suffered. To hold otherwise would be to convert a remedy heretofore reserved for violations of legal rights into a privilege that all institutions throughout the Nation could grant at their pleasure to whatever groups are perceived as victims of societal discrimination. That is a step we have never approved. Cf. *Pasadena City Board of Education* v. *Spangler*...(1976).

C

Petitioner identifies, as another purpose of its program, improving the delivery of health care services to communities currently underserved. It may be assumed that in some situations a State's interest in facilitating the health care of its citizens is sufficiently compelling to support the use of a suspect classification. But there is virtually no evidence in the record indicating that petitioner's special admissions program is either needed or geared to promote that goal....

Petitioner simply has not carried its burden of demonstrating that it must prefer members of particular ethnic groups over all other individuals in order to promote better health care delivery to deprived citizens....

D

The fourth goal asserted by petitioner is the attainment of a diverse student body....

Ethnic diversity, however, is only one element in a range of factors a university properly may consider in attaining the goal of a heterogeneous student body. Although a university must have wide discretion in making the sensitive judgments as to who should be admitted, constitutional limitations protecting individual rights may not be disregarded. Respondent urges — and the courts below have held — that petitioner's dual admissions program is a racial classification that impermissibly infringes his rights under the Fourteenth Amendment. As the interest of diversity is compelling in the context of a university's admissions program, the question remains whether the program's racial classification is necessary to promote this interest. *In re Griffiths*...(1973).

V

A

It may be assumed that the reservation of a specified number of seats in each class for individuals from the preferred ethnic groups would contribute ⁺o the attainment of considerable ethnic diversity in the student body. But petitioner's argument that this is the only effective means of serving the interest of diversity is seriously flawed.... The diversity that furthers a compelling state interest encompasses a far broader array of qualifications and characteristics of which racial or ethnic origin is but a single though important element. Petitioner's special admissions program, focused *solely* on ethnic diversity, would hinder rather than further attainment of genuine diversity....

The experience of other university admissions programs, which take race into account in achieving the educational diversity values by the First Amendment, demonstrates that the assignment of a fixed number of places to a minority group is not a necessary means toward that end. An illuminating example is found in the Harvard College program [in which]...race or ethnic background may be deemed a "plus" in a particular applicant's file, yet it does not insulate the individual from comparison with all other candidates for the available seats. The file of a particular black applicant may be examined for his potential contribution to diversity without the factor of race being decisive when compared, for example, with that of an applicant identified as an Italian-American if the latter is thought to exhibit qualities more likely to promote beneficial educational pluralism. Such qualities could include exceptional personal talents, unique work or service experience, leadership potential, maturity, demonstrated compassion, a history of overcoming disadvantage, ability to communicate with the poor, or other qualifications deemed important. In short, an admissions program operated in this way is flexible enough to consider all pertinent elements of diversity in light of the particular qualifications of each applicant, and to place them on the same footing for consideration, although not necessarily according them the same weight. Indeed, the weight attributed to a particular quality may vary from year to year depending upon the "mix" both of the student body and the applicants for the incoming class.

This kind of program treats each applicant as an individual in the admissions process. The applicant who loses out on the last available seat to another candidate receiving a "plus" on the basis of ethnic backgeound will not have been foreclosed from all consideration for that seat simply because he was not the right color or had the wrong surname. It would mean only that his combined qualifications, which may have included similar nonobjective factors, did not outweigh those of the other applicant. His qualifications would have been weighed fairly and competitively, and he would have no basis to complain of unequal treatment under the Fourteenth Amendment....

B

In summary it is evident that the Davis special admission program involves the use of an explicit racial classification never before countenanced by this Court. It tells applicants who are not Negro, Asian, or "Chicano" that they are totally excluded from a specific percentage of the seats in an entering class. No matter how strong their qualifications, quantitative and extracurricular, including their own potential for contribution to educational diversity, they are never afforded the chance to compete with applicants from the preferred groups for the special admission seats. At the same time, the preferred applicants have the opportunity to compete for every seat in the class.

The fatal flaw in petitioner's preferential program is its disregard of individual rights as guaranteed by the Fourteenth Amendment. *Shelley* v. *Kraemer*...(1948). Such rights are not absolute. But when a State's distribution of benefits or imposition of burdens hinges on the color of a person's skin or ancestry, that individual is entitled to a demonstration that the challenged classification is necessary to promote a substantial state interest. Petitioner has failed to carry this burden. For this reason, that portion of the California court's judgment holding petitioner's special admissions program invalid under the Fourteenth Amendment must be affirmed.

C

In enjoining petitioner from ever considering the race of any applicant, however, the courts below failed to recognize that the State has a substantial interest that legitimately may be served by a properly devised admissions program involving the competitive consideration of race and ethnic origin. For this reason, so much of the California court's judgment as enjoins petitioner from any consideration of the race of any applicant must be reversed.

VI

With respect to respondent's entitlement to an injunction directing his admission to the Medical School, petitioner has conceded that it could not carry its burden of proving that, but for the existence of its unlawful special admissions program, respondent still would not have been admitted. Hence, respondent is entitled to the injunction, and that portion of the judgment must be affirmed....

Opinion of MR. JUSTICE BRENNAN, MR. JUSTICE WHITE, MR. JUSTICE MARSHALL, and MR. JUSTICE BLACKMUN, concurring in the judgment in part and dissenting.

The Court today, in reversing in part the judgment of the Supreme Court of California, affirms the constitutional power of Federal and State Government to act affirmatively to achieve equal opportunity for all. The difficulty of the issue presented — whether Government may use race-conscious programs to redress the continuing effects of past discrimination — and the mature consideration which each of our Brethren has brought to it have resulted in many opinions, no single one speaking for the Court. But this should not and must not mask the central meaning of today's opinions: Government may take race into account when it acts not to demean or insult any racial group, but to remedy disadvantages cast on minorities by past racial prejudice, at least when appropriate findings have been made by judicial, legislative, or administrative bodies with competence to act in this area.

THE CHIEF JUSTICE and our Brothers STEWART, REHNQUIST, and STEVENS, have concluded that Title VI of the Civil Rights Act of 1964...prohibits programs such as that at the Davis Medical Scool. On this statutory theory alone, they would hold that respondent Allan Bakke's rights have been violated and that he must, therefore, be admitted to the Medical School. Our Brother POWELL, reaching the Constitution, concludes that, although race may be taken into account in university admissions, the particular special admissions program used by petitioner, which resulted in the exclusion of respondent Bakke, was not shown to be necessary to achieve petitioner's stated goals. Accordingly, these Members of the Court form a majority of five affirming the judgment of the Supreme Court of California insofar as it holds that respondent Bakke "is entitled to an order that he be admitted to the University." Bakke v. Regents of the University of California...(1976).

We agree with MR. JUSTICE POWELL that, as applied to the case before us, Title VI goes no further in prohibiting the use of race than the Equal Protection Clause of the Fourteenth Amendment itself.... Since we conclude that the affirmative admissions program at the Davis Medical School is constitutional, we would reverse the judgment below in all respects. MR. JUSTICE POWELL agrees that some use of race in university admissions are permissible and, therefore, he joins with us to make five votes reversing the judgment below insofar as it prohibits the University from establishing race-conscious programs in the future.

I

Our Nation was founded on the principle that "all men are created equal." Yet candor requires acknowledgement that the Framers of our Constitution, to forge the Thirteen Colonies into one Nation, openly compromised this principle of equality with its antithesis: slavery....

The Fourteenth Amendment, the embodiment in the Constitution of our abiding belief in human equality, has been the law of our land for only slightly more than half its 200 years. And for half of that half, the Equal Protection Clause of the Amendment was largely moribund.... Worse than desuetude, the Clause was early turned against those whom it was intended to set free, condemning them to a "separate but equal" status before the law, a status always separate but seldom equal. Not until 1954 — only

24 years ago — was this odious doctrine interred by our decision in *Brown* v. *Board of Education,*...and its progeny, which proclaimed that separate schools and public facilities of all sorts were inherently unequal and forbidden under our Constitution....

Against this background, claims that law must be "colorblind" or that the datum of race is no longer relevant to public policy must be seen as aspiration rather than as description of reality. This is not to denigrate aspiration; for reality rebukes us that race has too often been used by those who would stigmatize and oppress minorities. Yet we cannot — and as we shall demonstrate, need not under our Constitution or Title VI, which merely extends the constraints of the Fourteenth Amendment to private parties who receive federal funds — let color blindness become myopia which masks the reality that many "created equal" have been treated within our lifetimes as inferior both by the law and by their fellow citizens.

II

The threshold question we must decide is whether Title VI of the Civil Rights Act of 1964 bars recipients of federal funds from giving preferential consideration to disadvantaged members of racial minorities as part of a program designed to enable such individuals to surmount the obstacles imposed by racial discrimination....

In our view, Title VI prohibits only those uses of racial criteria that would violate the Fourteenth Amendment if employed by a State or its agencies; it does not bar the preferential treatment of racial minorities as a means of remedying past societal discrimination to the extent that such action is consistent with the Fourteenth Amendment....

A

The history of Title VI...reveals one fixed purpose: to give the Executive Branch of Government clear authority to terminate federal funding of private programs that use race as a means of disadvantaging minorities in a manner that would be prohibited by Constitution if engaged in by government....

Of course it might be argued that the Congress which enacted Title VI understood the Constitution to require strict racial neutrality or color blindness, and then enshrined that concept as a rule of statutory law. Later interpretation and clarification of the Constitution to permit remedial use of race would then not dislodge Title VI's prohibition upon race-conscious action. But there are three compelling reasons to reject such an hypothesis.

First, no decision of this Court has ever adopted the proposition that the Constitution must be colorblind....

Second, even if it could be argued in 1964 that the Constitution might conceivably require color blindness, Congress surely would not have chosen to codify such a view unless the Constitution clearly required it. The legislative history of Title VI, as well as the statute itself, reveals a desire to induce voluntary compliance with the requirement of nondiscriminatory treatment.... It is inconceivable that Congress intended to encourage voluntary efforts to eliminate the evil of racial discrimination while at the same time forbidding the voluntary use of race-conscious remedies to cure acknowledged or obvious statutory violations.... Surely Congress did not intend to prohibit the use of racial criteria when constitutionally required or to terminate the funding of any entity which implemented such a remedy. It clearly desired to encourage all remedies, including the use of race, necessary to eliminate racial discrimination in violation of the Constitution rather than requiring the recipient to await a judicial adjudication of unconstitutionality and the judicial imposition of a racially oriented remedy.

Third, the legislative history shows that Congress specifically eschewed any static definition of discrimination in favor of broad language that could be shaped by experience, administrative necessity, and evolving judicial doctrine....

In sum, Congress' equating of Title VI's prohibition with the commands of the Fifth and Fourteenth Amendments, its refusal precisely to define that racial discrimination which it intended to prohibit, and its expectation that the statute would be administered in a flexible manner, compel the conclusion that Congress intended the meaning of the statute's prohibition to evolve with the interpretation of the commands of the Constitution. Thus any claim that the use of racial criteria is barred by the plain language of the statute must fail in light of the remedial purpose of Title VI and its legislative history....

B

Section 602 of Title VI...instructs federal agencies to promulgate regulations interpreting Title VI. These regulations, which, under the terms of the statute, require Presidential approval, are entitled to considerable deference in construing Title VI. See, e.g., *Lau* v. *Nichols*...(1964); *Mourning* v. *Family Publications Service, Inc.*...(1973); *Red Lion Broadcasting Co.* v. *FCC*...(1965). Consequently, it is most significant that the Department of Health, Education, and Welfare (HEW), which provides much of the federal assistance to institutions of higher education, has adopted regulations requiring affirmative measures designed to enable racial minorities which have been previously discriminated against by a federally funded institution or program to overcome the effects of such actions and *authorizing* the voluntary undertaking of affirmative action programs by federally funded institutions that have not been guilty of prior discrimination in order to overcome the effects of conditions which have adversely affected the degree of participation by persons of a particular race....

III

The assertion of human equality is closely associated with the proposition that differences in color or creed, birth or status, are neither significant nor relevant to the way in which persons should be treated. Nonetheless, the position that such factors must be "[c]onstitutionally in irrelevance," *Edwards* v. *California*...(1941)...summed up by the short-hand phrase "[o]ur Constitution is color-blind," *Plessy* v. *Ferguson*...(1896) has never been adopted by this Court as the proper meaning of the Equal Protection Clause. Indeed, we have expressly rejected this proposition on a number of occasions.

Our cases have always implied that an "overriding statutory purpose," *McLaughlin* v. *Florida*...(1964) could be found that would justify racial classifications....

We conclude, therefore that racial classifications are not *per se* invalid under the Fourteenth Amendment. Accordingly, we turn to the problem of articulating what our role should be in reviewing state action that expressly classifies by race....

In sum, because of the significant risk that racial classifications established for ostensibly benign purposes can be misused, causing effects not unlike those created by invidious classifications, it is inappropriate to inquire only whether there is any conceivable basis that might sustain such a classification. Instead, to justify such a classification an important and articulated purpose for its use must be shown. In addition, any statute must be stricken that stigmatizes any group or that singles out those least well represented in the political process to bear the brunt of a benign program....

IV

Davis' articulated purpose of remedying the effects of past societal discrimination is, under our cases, sufficiently important to justify the use of race-conscious admissions programs where there is a sound basis for concluding that minority underrepresentation is substantial and chronic, and that the handicap of past discrimination is impeding access of minorities to the medical school....

A

...[O]ur cases under Title VII of the Civil Rights Act have held that, in order to achieve minority participation in previously segregated areas of public life, Congress may require or authorize preferential treatment for those likely disadvantaged by societal racial discrimination. Such legislation has been sustained even without a requirement of findings of intentional racial discrimination by those required or authorized to accord preferential treatment, or a case-by-case determination that those to be benefited suffered from racial discrimination. These decisions compel the conclusion that States also may adopt race-conscious programs designed to overcome substantial, chronic minority underrepresentation where there is reason to believe that the evil addressed is a product of past racial discrimination.

Title VII was enacted pursuant to Congress' power under the Commerce Clause and § 5 of the Fourteenth Amendment. To the extent that Congress acted under the Commerce Clause power, it was restricted in the use of race in governmental decisionmaking by the equal protection component of the Due Process Clause of the Fifth Amendment precisely to the same extent as are the States by § 1 of the Fourteenth Amendment. Therefore, to the extent that Title VII rests on the Commerce Clause power, our decisions...implicitly recognize that the affirmative use of race is consistent with the equal protection component of the Fifth Amendment and therefore of the Fourteenth Amendment. To the extent that Congress acted pursuant to § 5 of the Fourteenth Amendment, those cases impliedly recognize that Congress was empowered under that provision to accord preferential treatment to victims of past discrimination in order to overcome the effects of segregation, and we see no reason to conclude that the States cannot voluntarily accomplish under § 1 of the Fourteenth Amendment what Congress under § 5 of the Fourteenth Amendment validly may authorize or compel either the States or private persons to do.... Nothing whatever in the legislative history of either the Fourteenth Amendment or the Civil Rights Acts even remotely suggests that the States are foreclosed from furthering the fundamental purpose of equal opportunity to which the Amendment and those Acts are addressed.... We therefore conclude that Davis' goal of admitting minority students disadvantaged by the effects of past discrimination is sufficiently important to justify use of race-conscious admissions criteria.

B

Properly construed, therefore, our prior cases unequivocally show that a state government may adopt race-conscious programs if the purpose of such programs is to remove the disparate racial impact its actions might otherwise have and if there is reason to believe that the disparate impact is itself the product of past discrimination, whether its own or that of society at large. There is no question that Davis' program is valid under this test. Certainly, on the basis of the undisputed factual submissions before this Court, Davis had a sound basis for believing that the problem of underrepresentation of minorities was substantial and chronic and that the problem was attributable to handicaps imposed on minority applicants by past and present racial discrimination. Until at least 1973, the practice of medicine in this country was, in fact, if not in law, largely the prerogative of whites....

Moreover, Davis had very good reason to believe that the national pattern of underrepresentation of minorities in medicine would be perpetuated if it retained a single admissions standard. For example, the entering classes in 1968 and 1969, the years in which such a standard was used, included only one Chicano and two Negroes out of 100 admittees....

C

The second prong of our test — whether the Davis program stigmatizes any discrete group or individual and whether race is reasonably used in light of the program's objectives — is clearly satisfied by the Davis program.

It is not even claimed that Davis' program in any way operates to stigmatize or single out any discrete and insular, or even any identifiable, nonminority group. Nor will harm comparable to that imposed upon racial minorities by exclusion or separation on grounds of race be the likely result of the program. It does not, for example, establish an exclusive preserve for minority students apart from and exclusive of whites. Rather, its purpose is to overcome the effects of segregation by bringing the races together....

Nor was Bakke in any sense stamped as inferior by the Medical School's rejection of him.... Unlike discrimination against racial minorities, the use of racial preferences for remedial purposes does not inflict a pervasive injury upon individual whites in the sense that wherever they go or whatever they do there is a significant likelihood that they will be treated as second-class citizens because of their color. This distinction does not mean that the exclusion of a white resulting from the preferential use of race is not sufficiently serious to require justification; but it does mean that the injury inflicted by such a policy is not distinguishable from disadvantages caused by a wide range of government actions, none of which has ever been thought impermissible for that reason alone.

In addition, there is simply no evidence that the Davis program discriminates intentionally or unintentionally against any minority group which it purports to benefit. The program does not establish a quota in the invidious sense of a ceiling on the number of minority applicants to be admitted. Nor can the program reasonably be regarded as stigmatizing the program's beneficiaries or their race as inferior. The Davis program does not simply advance less qualified applicants; rather, it compensates applicants, whom it is uncontested are fully qualified to study medicine, for educational disadvantage which it was reasonable to conclude was a product of state-fostered discrimination. Once admitted, these students must satisfy the same degree requirements as regularly admitted students; they are taught by the same faculty in the same classes; and their performance is evaluated by the same standards by which regularly admitted students are judged....

D

We disagree with the lower courts' conclusion that the Davis program's use of race was unreasonable in light of its objectives. First, as petitioner argues, there are not practical means by which it could achieve its ends in the foreseeable future without the use of race-conscious measures....

Second, the Davis admissions program does not simply equate minority status with disadvantage. Rather, Davis considers on an individual basis each applicant's personal history to determine whether he or she has likely been disadvantaged by racial discrimination....

E

Finally, Davis' special admissions program cannot be said to violate the Constitution simply because it has set aside a predetermined number of places for qualified minority applicants rather than using minority status as a positive factor to be considered in evaluating the applications of disadvantaged minority applicants. For purposes of constitutional adjudication, there is no difference between the two approaches. In any admissions program which accords special consideration to disadvantaged racial minorities, a determination of the degree of preference to be given is unavoidable, and any given preference that results in the exclusion of a white candidate is no more or less constitutionally acceptable than a program such as that at Davis. Furthermore, the extent of the preference inevitably depends on how many minority applicants the particular school is seeking to admit in any particular year so long as the number of qualified minority applicants exceeds that number. There is no sensible, and certainly no constitutional distinction between, for example, adding a set number of points to the admissions rating of disadvantaged minority applicants as an expression of the preference with the expectation that this will result in the admission of an approximately determined number of qualified minority applicants and setting a fixed number of places for such appliants as was done here....

...It may be that the Harvard plan is more acceptable to the public than is the Davis "quota." If it is, any State, including California, is free to adopt it in preference to a less acceptable alternative, just as it is generally free, as far as the Constitution is concerned, to abjure granting any racial preferences in its admissions program. But there is no basis for preferring a particular preference program simply because in achieving the same goals that the Davis Medical School is pursuing, it proceeds in a manner that is not immediately apparent to the public.

IV

Accordingly, we would reverse the judgment of the Supreme Court of California holding the Medical School's special admissions program unconstitutional and directing respondent's admission, as well as that portion of the judgment enjoining the Medical School from according any consideration to race in the admissions process.

Separate opinion of MR. JUSTICE WHITE.

I write separately concerning the question of whether Title VI of the Civil Rights Act of 1964... provides for a private cause of action. Four Justices are apparently of the view that such a private cause of action exists, and four Justices assume it for purposes of this case. I am unwilling merely to assume an affirmative answer. If in fact no private cause of action exists, this Court and the lower courts as well are without jurisdiction to consider respondent's Title VI claim. As I see it, if we are not obliged to do so, it is at least advisable to address this threshold jurisdictional issue. See *United States* v. *Griffin*...(1938). Furthermore, just as it is inappropriate to address constitutional issues without determining whether statutory grounds urged before us are dispositive, it is at least questionable practice to adjudicate a novel and difficult statutory issue without first considering whether we have jurisdiction to decide it. Consequently, I address the question of whether respondent may bring suit under Title VI.

A private cause of action under Title VI would, in terms both of the Civil Rights Act as a whole and that title, not be "consistent with the underlying purposes of the legislative scheme" and contrary to the legislative intent. *Cort* v. *Ash*...(1975). Title II...dealing with public accommodations, and Title VII...dealing with employment, proscribe private discriminatory conduct that as of 1964 neither the Constitution nor other federal statutes had been construed to forbid. Both titles carefully provided for private actions as well as for official participation in enforcement. Title III...and Title IV...dealing with public facilities and public education, respectively, authorize suits by the Attorney General to eliminate racial discrimination in these areas. Because suits to end discrimination in public facilities and public education were already available...it was, of course, unnecessary to provide for private actions under Titles III and IV. But each title carefully provided that its provisions for public actions would not adversely affect pre-existing private remedies....

The role of Title VI was to terminate federal financial support for public and private institutions or programs that discriminated on the basis of race.... [T]here is no express provision for private actions to enforce Title VI, and it would be quite incredible if Congress, after so carefully attending to the matter of private actions in other titles of the Act, intended silently to create a private cause of action to enforce Title VI....

Termination of funding was regarded by Congress as a serious enforcement step, and the legislative history is replete with assurances that it would not occur until every possibility for conciliation had been exhausted. To allow a private individual to sue to cut off funds under Title VI would compromise these assurances and short circuit the procedural preconditions provided in Title VI. If the Federal Government may not cut off funds except pursuant to an agency rule, approved by the President, and presented to the appropriate committee of Congress for a layover period, and after voluntary means to achieve compliance have failed, it is inconceivable that Congress intended to permit individuals to circumvent these administrative prerequisites themselves.

Furthermore, although Congress intended Title VI to end federal financial support for racially discriminatory policies of not only public but also private institutions and programs, it is extremely unlikely that Congress, without a word indicating that it intended to do so, contemplated creating an independent, private statutory cause of action against all private as well as public agencies that might be in violation of the section. There is no doubt that Congress regarded private litigation as an important tool to attack discriminatory practices. It does not at all follow, however, that Congress anticipated new private actions under Title VI itself....

For those who believe, contrary to my views, that Title VI was intended to create a stricter standard of color blindness than the Constitution itself requires, the result of no private cause of action follows even more readily. In that case Congress must be seen to have banned degrees of discrimination, as well as types of discriminators, not previously reached by law. A Congress careful enough to provide that existing private causes of action would be preserved (in Titles III and IV) would not leave for inference a vast new extension of private enforcement power. And a Congress so exceptionally concerned with the satisfaction of procedural preliminaries before confronting fund recipients with the choice of a cut-off or of stopping discriminating would not permit private parties to pose precisely that same dilemma in a greatly widened category of cases with no procedural requirements whatsoever.

Significantly, in at least three instances legislators who played a major role in the passage of Title VI explicitly stated that a private right of action under Title VI does not exist.

As an "indication of legislative intent, explicit or implicit, either to create such a remedy or to deny one," *Cort* v. *Ash*...(1975), clearer statements cannot be imagined, and under *Cort*, "an explicit purpose to deny such cause of action [is] controlling."... If private suits to enjoin conduct allegedly violative of § 601 were permitted, recipients of federal funds would be presented with the choice of either ending what the court, rather than the agency, determined to be a discriminatory practice within the meaning of Title VI or refusing federal funds and thereby escaping from the statute's jurisdictional predicate. This is precisely the same choice which would confront recipients if suit was brought to cut off funds. Both types of actions would equally jeopardize the administrative processes so carefully structured into the law.

This Court has always required "that the inference of such a private cause of action not otherwise authorized by statute must be consistent with the evident legislative intent and, of course, with the effectuation of the purposes intended to be served by the Act." *National Railroad Passenger Corp.* v. *National Association of Railroad Passengers*...(1974).... A private cause of action under Title VI is unable to satisfy either prong of this test.

Because each of my colleagues either has a different view or assumes a private cause of action, however, the merits of the Title VI issue must be addressed. My views in that regard, as well as my views with respect to the equal protection issue, are included in the joint opinion of BRENNAN, WHITE, MARSHALL, and BLACKMUN, JJ.

MR. JUSTICE MARSHALL.

I agree with the judgment of the Court only insofar as it permits a university to consider the race of an applicant in making admissions decisions. I do not agree that petition's admissions program violates the Constitution. For it must be remembered that, during most of the past 200 years, the Constitution as interpreted by this Court did not prohibit the most ingenious and pervasive forms of discrimination against the Negro. Now, when a State acts to remedy the effects of that legacy of discrimination, I cannot believe that this same Constitution stands as a barrier....

II

The position of the Negro today in America is the tragic but inevitable consequence of centuries of unequal treatment. Measured by any benchmark of comfort or achievement, meaningful equality remains a distant dream for the Negro.

A Negro child today has a life expectancy which is shorter by more than five years than that of a white child. The Negro child's mother is over three times more likely to die of complications in childbirth, and the infant mortality rate for Negroes is nearly twice that for whites. The median income of the Negro family is only 60% that of the median of a white family, and the percentage of Negroes who live in families with incomes below the poverty line is nearly four times greater than that of whites.

When the Negro child reaches working age, he finds that America offers him significantly less than it offers his white counterpart. For Negro adults, the unemployment rate is twice that of whites, and the unemployment rate for Negro teenagers is nearly three times that of white teenagers. A Negro male who completes four years of college can expect a median annual income of merely $110 more than a white male who has only a high school diploma. Although Negroes represent 11.5% of the population, they are only 1.2% of the lawyers and judges, 2% of the physicians, 2.3% of the dentists, 1.1% of the engineers and 2.6% of the college and university professors.

The relationship between those figures and the history of unequal treatment afforded to the Negro cannot be denied. At every point from birth to death the impact of the past is reflected in the still disfavored position of the Negro.

In light of the sorry history of discrimination and its devastating impact on the lives of Negroes, bringing the Negro into the mainstream of American life should be a state interest of the highest order. To fail to do so is to ensure that America will forever remain a divided society.

III

I do not believe that the Fourteenth Amendment requires us to accept that fate. Neither its history nor our past cases lend any support to the conclusion that a University may not remedy the cumulative effects of society's discrimination by giving consideration to race in an effort to increase the number and percentage of Negro doctors....

IV

While I applaud the judgment of the Court that a university may consider race in its admissions process, it is more than a little ironic that, after several hundred years of class-based discrimination against Negroes, the Court is unwilling to hold that a class-based remedy for that discrimination is permissible. In declining to so hold, today's judgment ignores the fact that for several hundred years Negroes have been discriminated against, not as individuals, but rather solely because of the color of their skins. It is unnecessary in 20th century America to have individual Negroes demonstrate that they have been victims of racial discrimination; the racism of our society has been so pervasive that none, regardless of wealth or position, has managed to escape its impact. The experience of Negroes in America has been different in kind, not just in degree, from that of other ethnic groups. It is not merely the history of slavery alone but also that a whole people were marked as inferior by the law. And that mark has endured. The dream of America as the great melting pot has not been realized for the Negro; becaue of his skin color he never even made it into the pot.

These differences in the experience of the Negro make it difficult for me to accept that Negroes cannot be afforded greater protection under the Fourteenth Amendment where it is necessary to remedy the effects of past discrimination....

It is because of a legacy of unequal treatment that we now must permit the institutions of this society to give consideration to race in making decisions about who will hold the positions of influence, affluence and prestige in America. For far too long, the doors to those positions have been shut to Negroes. If we are ever to become a fully integrated society, one in which the color of a person's skin will not determine the opportunities available to him or her, we must be willing to take steps to open those doors. I do not believe that anyone can truly look into America's past and still find that a remedy for the effects of that past is impermissible....

I fear that we have come full circle. After the Civil War our government started several "affirmative action" programs. This Court in the *Civil Rights Cases* and *Plessy* v. *Ferguson* destroyed the movement toward complete equality. For almost a century no action was taken, and this nonaction was with the tacit approval of the courts. Then we had *Brown* v. *Board of Education* and the Civil Rights Acts of Congress, followed by numerous affirmative action programs. *Now,* we have this Court again stepping in, this time to stop affirmative action programs of the type used by the University of California.

MR. JUSTICE BLACKMUN.

I participate fully, of course, in the opinion...that bears the names of my Brothers BRENNAN, WHITE, MARSHALL, and myself. I add only some general observations that hold particular significance for me, and then a few comments on equal protection.

At least until the early 1970s, apparently only a very small number, less than 2%, of the physicians, attorneys, and medical and law students in the United States were members of what we now refer to as minority groups. In addition, approximately three-fourths of our Negro physicians were trained at only two medical schools. If ways are not found to remedy that situation, the country can never achieve its professed goal of a society that is not race conscious.

I yield to no one in my earnest hope that the time will come when an "affirmative action" program is unnecessary and is, in truth, only a relic of the past. I would hope that we could reach this stage within a decade at the most. But the story of *Brown* v. *Board of Education*...(1954), decided almost a quarter of a century ago, suggests that that hope is a slim one. At some time, however, beyond any period of what some would claim is only transitional inequality, the United States must and will reach a stage of maturity where action along this line is no longer necessary. Then persons will be regarded as persons, and discrimination of the type we address today will be an ugly feature of history that is instructive but that is behind us....

It is somewhat ironic to have us so deeply disturbed over a program where race is an element of consciousness, and yet to be aware of the fact, as we are, that institutions of higher learning, albeit more on the undergraduate than the graduate level, have given conceded preferences up to a point to those possessed of athletic skills, to the children of alumni, to the affluent who may bestow their largess on the institutions, and to those having connections with celebrities, the famous and the powerful.

Programs of admission to institutions of higher learning are basically a responsibility for academicians and for administrators and the specialists they employ. The judiciary, in contrast, is ill-equipped and poorly trained for this.... For me, therefore, interference by the judiciary must be the rare exception and not the rule....

It is worth noting, perhaps, that governmental preference has not been a stranger to our legal life. We see it in veterans' preferences. We see it in the aid-to-the-handicapped programs. We see it in the progressive income tax. We see it in the Indian programs. We may excuse some of these on the ground that they have specific constitutional protection or, as with Indians, that those benefited are wards of the Government. Nevertheless, these preferences exist and may not be ignored. And in the admissions field, as I have indicated, educational institutions have always used geography, athletic ability, anticipated financial largess, alumni pressure, and other factors of that kind....

...It is gratifying to know that the Court at least finds it constitutional for an academic institution to take race and ethnic background into consideration as one factor, among many, in the administration of its admissions program. I presume that that factor always has been there, though perhaps not conceded or even admitted. It is a fact of life, however, and a part of the real world of which we are all a part. The sooner we get down the road toward accepting and being a part of the real world, and not shutting it out and away from us, the sooner will these difficulties vanish from the scene.

I suspect that it would be impossible to arrange an affirmative action program in a racially neutral way and have it successful. To ask that this be so is to demand the impossible. In order to get beyond racism, we must first take account of race. There is no other way. And in order to treat some persons equally, we must treat them differently. We cannot — we dare not — let the Equal Protection Clause perpetrate racial supremacy....

MR. JUSTICE STEVENS, with whom THE CHIEF JUSTICE, MR. JUSTICE STEWART, and MR. JUSTICE REHNQUIST join, concurring in the judgment in part and dissenting in part.

It is always important at the outset to focus precisely on the controversy before the Court. It is particularly important to do so in this case because correct identification of the issues will determine whether it is necessary or appropriate to express any opinion about the legal status of any admissions program other than petitioner's.

I

...[T]he question whether race can ever be used as a factor in an admissions decision is not an issue in this case, and...discussion of that issue is inappropriate.

II

Both petitioner and respondent have asked us to determine the legality of the University's special admissions program by reference to the Constitution. Our settled practice, however, is to avoid the decision of a constitutional issue if a case can be fairly decided on a statutory ground....

III

Section 601 of the Civil Rights Act of 1964 provides:

"No person in the United States shall, on the ground of race, color, or national origin, be excluded from participation in, be denied the benefits of, or be subjected to discrimination under any program or activity receiving Federal financial assistance."

The University, through its special admissions policy, excluded Bakke from participation in its program of medical education because of his race. The University also acknowledges that it was, and still is, receiving federal financial assistance. The plain language of the statute therefore requires affirmance of the judgment below....

...The statutory prohibition against discrimination in federally funded projects contained in § 601 is more than a simple paraphrasing of what the Fifth or Fourteenth Amendment would require.... As a distillation of what the supporters of the Act believed the Constitution demanded of State and Federal Government, § 601 has independent force, with language and emphasis in addition to that found in the Constitution....

...[W]e need not decide the congruence — or lack of congruence — of the controlling statute and the Constitution since the meaning of the Title VI ban on exclusion is crystal clear: Race cannot be the basis of excluding anyone from participation in a federally funded program....

...We are dealing with a distinct statutory prohibition, enacted at a particular time with particular concerns in mind; neither its language nor any prior interpretation suggests that its place in the Civil Rights Act, won after long debate, is simply that of a constitutional appendage. In unmistakable terms the Act prohibits the exclusion of individuals from federally funded programs because of their race. As succinctly phrased during the Senate debate, under Title VI it is not "permissible to say 'yes' to one person, but to say 'no' to another person, only because of the color of his skin."

...The University's special admissions program violated Title VI of the Civil Rights Act of 1964 by excluding Bakke from the medical school because of his race. It is therefore our duty to affirm the judgment ordering Bakke admitted to the University.

Accordingly, I concur in the Court's judgment insofar as it affirms the judgment of the Supreme Court of California. To the extent that it purports to do anything else, I respectfully dissent.

July

COURT ON CAPITAL PUNISHMENT
July 3, 1978

On July 3, the Supreme Court struck down Ohio's death penalty law because it limited too strictly the factors that a judge might consider in deciding whether to impose a death sentence on a particular defendant. The court's rulings continued a pattern that had begun six years earlier of narrowing a state's application of the death penalty.

In June of 1972, the Supreme Court invalidated virtually all the nation's existing death penalty laws with its finding that they left so much discretion to the judge or jury that they allowed death to be used as a cruel and unusual punishment. One justice wrote that the existing laws allowed death to be imposed in such a "freakish" way that it was "cruel and unusual in the same way that being struck by lightning is cruel and unusual." (Furman v. Georgia) (Historic Documents of 1972, p. 499)

Four years later, in July 1976, the court reviewed the two types of death penalty laws adopted by the states in the wake of the 1972 decision. The court upheld some laws, but struck down those that made death the mandatory penalty for first degree murder. Those laws, held the court, were unconstitutional because they precluded fair consideration of the individual crime and defendant — and any mitigating circumstances that might exist. (Gregg v. Georgia, Woodson v. North Carolina) (Historic Documents of 1976, p. 489)

The Case

The court struck down the Ohio death penalty by 7-1 votes in the cases of 21-year-old Sandra Lockett and 16-year-old Willie Lee Bell, both

*convicted and sentenced to die for murders they did not personally commit
— or even witness. The murders had been committed by others in the
course of unrelated crimes, an armed robbery and a kidnapping, in which
Lockett and Bell participated. Both were convicted of "aggravated murder." Ohio law allows a sentence less severe than death for that crime only
if it is shown that: The victim provoked the crime, the crime was
committed only because the defendant was under duress, and/or the crime
was primarily the result of the defendant's psychosis or mental deficiency.
In neither Bell's nor Lockett's case was such a finding made; both were
sentenced to die. (Lockett v. Ohio, Bell v. Ohio)*

*Chief Justice Warren E. Burger wrote the opinions in both cases; Justice
William J. Brennan Jr. did not participate; Justice William H. Rehnquist
dissented.*

*Lockett challenged her sentence — and the procedure leading to it —
because the judge was not permitted to consider her character, prior
record, age, lack of intent to cause death or her relatively minor part in the
crime, before deciding her sentence.*

*The court agreed with her challenge. Conceding that "the signals from
this court have not . . . always been easy to decipher" on the subject of
capital punishment, Chief Justice Burger wrote that "the states now
deserve the clearest guidance that the court can provide" on the issue.*

The Opinion

*The Eighth Amendment bans cruel and unusual punishments; the 14th
Amendment guarantees that one will not be deprived of life without due
process of law. Under these constitutional provisions, the sentencing
authority, wrote Chief Justice Burger, "in all but the rarest kind of capital
case, [may] not be precluded from considering, as a mitigating factor, any
aspect of a defendant's character of record and any of the circumstances of
the offense that the defendant proffers as a basis for a sentence less than
death."*

*"An individualized decision," continued the Chief Justice, "is essential
in capital cases. The need for treating each defendant in a capital case with
that degree of respect due the uniqueness of the individual is far more
important than in non-capital cases. A variety of flexible techniques —
probation, parole, work furloughs, to name a few — and various post-
conviction remedies, may be available to modify an initial sentence of
confinement in non-capital cases. The non-availability of corrective or
modifying mechanisms with respect to an executed capital sentence
underscores the need for individualized consideration as a constitutional
requirement in imposing the death sentence."*

*(As in previous decisions on the subject, the court left open the
possibility that it might approve mandatory death sentences — and thus*

little individualized consideration — for certain crimes — such as murder by a person already sentenced to life in prison.)

A law like the Ohio one, which severely restricts the mitigating factors that the judge can consider before imposing sentence, "creates the risk that the death penalty will be imposed in spite of factors which may call for a less severe penalty. When the choice is between life and death, that risk is unacceptable and incompatible with the commands of the Eighth and 14th Amendments," concluded Burger.

An 'About-Face'?

Although he agreed with the judgment of the court that the death sentences in these cases were improperly imposed and the law unconstitutional for not requiring a finding that Lockett or Bell intended to cause the victim's death, Justice Byron R. White criticized the court for "its about-face since Furman v. Georgia." The court had returned, White argued, to a position of encouraging the "exercise of unguided discretion" by the sentencing judge, precisely the point that had caused the court in Furman to strike down the pre-1972 capital punishment laws.

"By requiring as a matter of constitutional law that sentencing authorities must be permitted to consider and in their discretion to act upon any and all mitigating circumstances, the court permits them to refuse to impose the death penalty no matter what the circumstances of the crime. This invites a return to the pre-Furman days when the death penalty was generally reserved for those very few for whom society has least consideration," White continued. He disagreed with that portion of the court's holding, adhering to his view that in some circumstances it is constitutional for the death penalty to be mandatory for persons found guilty of a deliberate and unjustified killing.

The Dissent

Dissenting from the court's decision to set aside the death sentences imposed under Ohio law and to strike down the law as unconstitutional, Justice Rehnquist described the court as going "from pillar to post" in its effort to deal with the issue of capital punishment.

Rehnquist expressed doubt that the decision would have much practical effect, "since I would suspect that it has been the practice of most trial judges to permit a defendant to offer virtually any sort of evidence in his own defense as he wished."

But the "new constitutional doctrine" adopted in the case, he continued, "will not eliminate arbitrariness or freakishness in the imposition of sentences, but will codify and institutionalize it. By encouraging defen-

dants in capital cases, and presumably sentencing judges and juries, to take into consideration anything under the sun as a 'mitigating circumstance,' it will not guide sentencing discretion but will totally unleash it."

"I am frank to say that I am uncertain whether today's opinion represents the seminal case in the exposition by this court of the Eighth and 14th Amendments as they apply to capital punishment, or whether instead it represents the third false start in this direction within the past six years," Rehnquist concluded.

Following are excerpts from the Supreme Court rulings in Lockett v. State of Ohio, *and* Bell v. State of Ohio, *delivered July 3, 1978, overturning the Ohio death penalty statute:*

LOCKETT V. STATE OF OHIO

No. 76-6997

Sandra Lockett, Petitioner,	On Writ of Certiorari to the
v.	Supreme Court of Ohio.
State of Ohio.	

[July 3, 1978]

MR. CHIEF JUSTICE BURGER delivered the opinion of the Court with respect to the constitutionality of petitioner's conviction (Parts I and II), together with an opinion (Part III), in which MR. JUSTICE STEWART, MR. JUSTICE POWELL, and MR. JUSTICE STEVENS, joined, on the constitutionality of the statute under which petitioner was sentenced to death and announced the judgment of the Court. [MR. JUSTICE BRENNAN took no part in consideration or decision of this case.]

We granted certiorari in this case to consider, among other questions, whether Ohio violated the Eighth and Fourteenth Amendments by sentencing Sandra Lockett to death pursuant to a statute that narrowly limits the sentencer's discretion to consider the circumstances of the crime and the record and character of the offender as mitigating factors.

I

Lockett was charged with aggravated murder with the aggravating specifications (1) that the murder was "committed for the purpose of escaping detection, apprehension, trial, or punishment" for aggravated robbery, and (2) that the murder was "committed . . . while committing, attempting to commit, or fleeing immediately after committing or attempting to commit aggravated robbery." That offense was punishable by death in Ohio. . . . She was also charged with aggravated robbery. The State's case against her depended largely upon the testimony of a coparticipant, one Al Parker, who gave the following account of her participation in the robbery and murder.

Lockett became acquainted with Parker and Nathan Earl Dew while she and a friend, Joanne Baxter, were in New Jersey. Parker and Dew then accompanied Lockett, Baxter, and Lockett's brother back to Akron, Ohio, Lockett's home town. After they arrived in Akron, Parker and Dew needed money for the trip back to New Jersey. Dew suggested that he pawn his ring. Lockett overheard his suggestion, but felt that the ring was too beautiful to pawn, and suggested instead that they could get some money by robbing a grocery store and a furniture store in the area. She warned that the grocery store's operator was a "big guy" who carried a "45" and that they would have "to get him real quick." She also volunteered to get a gun from her father's basement to aid in carrying out the robberies, but by that time, the two stores had closed and it was too late to proceed with the plan to rob them.

Someone, apparently Lockett's brother, suggested a plan for robbing a pawn shop. He and Dew would enter the shop and pretend to pawn a ring. Next Parker, who had some bullets, would enter the shop, ask to see a gun, load it, and use it to rob the shop. No one planned to kill the pawnshop operator in the course of the robbery. Because she knew the owner, Lockett was not to be among those entering the pawnshop, though she did guide the others to the shop that night.

The next day Parker, Dew, Lockett, and her brother gathered at Baxter's apartment. Lockett's brother asked if they were "still going to do it," and everyone, including Lockett, agreed to proceed. The four then drove by the pawnshop several times and parked the car. Lockett's brother and Dew entered the shop. Parker then left the car and told Lockett to start it again in two minutes. The robbery proceeded according to plan until the pawnbroker grabbed the gun when Parker announced the "stickup." The gun went off with Parker's finger on the trigger, firing a fatal shot into the pawnbroker.

Parker went back to the car where Lockett waited with the engine running. While driving away from the pawnshop, Parker told Lockett what had happened. She took the gun from the pawnshop and put it into her purse. Lockett and Parker drove to Lockett's aunt's house and called a taxicab. Shortly thereafter, while riding away in a taxicab, they were stopped by the police, but by this time Lockett had placed the gun under the front seat. Lockett told the police that Parker rented a room from her mother and lived with her family. After verifying this story with Lockett's parents, the police released Lockett and Parker. Lockett hid Dew and Parker in the attic when the police arrived at the Lockett household later that evening.

Parker was subsequently apprehended and charged with aggravated murder with specifications, an offense punishable by death, and aggravated robbery. Prior to trial, he pleaded guilty to the murder charge and agreed to testify against Lockett, her brother, and Dew. In return, the prosecutor dropped the aggravated robbery charge and the specifications to the murder charge, thereby eliminating the possibility that Parker could receive the death penalty.

Lockett's brother and Dew were later convicted of aggravated murder with specifications. Lockett's brother was sentenced to death, but Dew received a lesser penalty because it was determined that his offense was "primarily the product of mental deficiency," one of the three mitigating circumstances specified in the Ohio death penalty statute.

Two weeks before Lockett's separate trial, the prosecutor offered to permit her to plead guilty to voluntary manslaughter and aggravated robbery (offenses which each carried a maximum penalty of 25 years imprisonment and a maximum fine of $10,000 . . .) if she would cooperate with the State, but she rejected the offer. Just prior to her trial, the prosecutor offered to permit her to plead guilty to aggravated murder without specifications, an offense carrying a mandatory life penalty, with the understanding that the aggravated robbery charge and an outstanding forgery charge would be dismissed. Again she rejected the offer.

At trial, the opening argument of Lockett's defense counsel summarized what appears to have been Lockett's version of the events leading to the killing. He asserted the evidence would show that, as far as Lockett knew, Dew and her brother had planned to pawn Dew's ring for $100 to obtain money for the trip back to New Jersey. Lockett had not waited in the car while the men went into the pawnshop but had gone to a restaurant for lunch and had joined Parker, thinking the ring had been pawned, after she saw him walking back to the car. Lockett's counsel asserted that the evidence would show further that Parker had placed the gun under the seat in the taxicab and that Lockett had voluntarily gone to the police station when she learned that the police were looking for the pawnbroker's killers.

Parker was the State's first witness. His testimony related his version of the robbery and shooting, and he admitted to a prior criminal record of breaking and entering, larceny, and receiving stolen goods, as well as bond-jumping. He also acknowledged that his plea to aggravated murder had eliminated the possibility of the death penalty, and that he had agreed to testify against Lockett, her brother, and Dew as part of his plea agreement with the prosecutor. At the end of the major portion of Parker's testimony, the prosecutor renewed his offer to permit Lockett to plead guilty to aggravated murder without specifications and to drop the other charges against her. For the third time Lockett refused the option of pleading guilty to a lesser offense.

Lockett called Dew and her brother as defense witnesses but they invoked their Fifth Amendment rights and refused to testify. In the course of the defense presentation, Lockett's counsel informed the court, in the presence of the jury, that he believed Lockett was to be the next witness and requested a short recess. After the recess, Lockett's counsel told the judge that Lockett wished to testify but had decided to accept her mother's advice to remain silent, despite her counsel's warning that, if she followed that advice, she would have no defense except the cross-examination of the State's witnesses. Thus, the defense did not introduce any evidence to rebut the prosecutor's case.

The Court instructed the jury that, before it could find Lockett guilty, it had to find that she purposely had killed the pawnbroker while committing or attempting to commit aggravated robbery. The jury was further charged that one who

"purposely aids, helps, associates himself or herself with another for the purpose of committing a crime is regarded as if he or she were the principal offender and is just as guilty as if the person performed every act constituting the offense. . . ."

Regarding the intent requirement, the court instructed:

"[A] person engaged in a common design with others to rob by force and violence an individual or individuals of their property is presumed to acquiesce in whatever may reasonably be necessary to accomplish the object of their enterprise. . . .

"If the conspired robbery and the manner of its accomplishment would be reasonably likely to produce death, each plotter is equally guilty with the principal offender as an aider and abettor in the homicide. . . . An intent to kill by an aider and abettor may be found to exist beyond a reasonable doubt under such circumstances."

The jury found Lockett guilty as charged.

Once a verdict of aggravated murder with specifications had been returned, the Ohio death penalty statute required the trial judge to impose a death sentence unless, after "considering the nature and circumstances of the offense" and Lockett's "history, character, and condition," he found by a preponderance of the evidence that (1) the victim had induced or facilitated the offense, (2) it was unlikely that Lockett would have committed the offense but for the fact that she "was under duress, coercion, or strong provocation," or (3) the offense was "primarily the product of [Lockett's] psychosis or mental deficiency.". . .

In accord with the Ohio statute, the trial judge requested a presentence report as well as psychiatric and psychological reports. The reports contained detailed information about Lockett's intelligence, character, and background. The psychiatric and psychological reports described her as a 21-year-old with low average or average intelligence, and not suffering from a mental deficiency. One of the psychologists reported that "her prognosis for rehabilitation" if returned to society was favorable. The presentence report showed that Lockett had committed no major offenses although she had a record of several minor ones as a juvenile and two minor offenses as an adult. It also showed that she had once used heroin but was receiving treatment at a drug abuse clinic and seemed to be "on the road to success" as far as her drug problem was concerned. It concluded that Lockett suffered no psychosis and was not mentally deficient.

After considering the reports and hearing argument on the penalty issue, the trial judge concluded that the offense had not been primarily the product of psychosis or mental deficiency. Without specifically addressing the other two statutory mitigating factors, the judge said that he had "no alternative, whether [he] like[d] the law or not" but to impose the death penalty. He then sentenced Lockett to death.

II

A

At the outset, we address Lockett's various challenges to the validity of her conviction. Her first contention is that the prosecutor's repeated references in his closing remarks to the State's evidence as "unrefuted" and "uncontradicted" constituted a comment on her failure to testify and violated her Fifth and Fourteenth Amendment rights. See *Griffin* v. *California* . . . (1965). We conclude, however, that the prosecutor's closing comments in this case did not violate constitutional prohibitions. Lockett's own counsel had clearly focused the jury's attention on her silence first by outlining her contemplated defense in his opening statement and, second, by stating to the court and jury near the close of the case, that Lockett would be the "next witness." When viewed against this background, it seems clear that the prosecutor's closing remarks added nothing to the impression that had already been created by Lockett's refusal to testify after the jury had been promised a defense by her lawyer and told that Lockett would take the stand.

B

Lockett also contends that four prospective jurors were excluded from the venire in violation of her Sixth and Fourteenth Amendment rights under the principles established in *Witherspoon* v. *Louisiana* . . . (1968), and *Taylor* v. *Louisiana* . . . (1975). We do not agree.

On *voir dire,* the prosecutor told the venire that there was a possibility that the death penalty might be imposed, but that the judge would make the final decision as to punishment. He then asked whether any of the prospective jurors were so opposed to capital punishment that "they could not sit, listen to the evidence, listen to the law, [and] make their determination solely upon the evidence and the law without considering the fact that capital punishment" might be imposed. Four of the venire responded affirmatively. The trial judge then addressed the following question to those four veniremen:

"[D]o you feel that you could take an oath to well and truely [*sic*] try this case . . . and follow the law, or is your conviction so strong that you cannot take an oath, knowing that a possibility exists in regard to capital punishment?"

Each of the four specifically stated twice that he or she would not "take the oath." They were excused.

In *Witherspoon,* persons generally opposed to capital punishment had been excluded for cause from the jury that convicted and sentenced the petitioner to death. We did not disturb the conviction that we held that "a sentence of death cannot be carried out if the jury that imposed or recommended it was chosen by excluding veniremen for cause simply because they voiced general objections to the death penalty or expressed conscientious or religious scruples against its infliction.". . .

Each of the excluded veniremen in this case made it "unmistakably clear" that they could not be trusted to "abide by existing law" and "to follow conscientiously the instructions" of the trial judge, *Boulden* v. *Holman* . . . (1969). They were thus properly excluded under *Witherspoon,* even assuming *arguendo* that *Witherspoon* provides a basis for attacking the conviction as well as the sentence in a capital case. . . .

C

Lockett's final attack on her conviction, as distinguished from her sentence, merits only brief attention. Specifically she contends that the Ohio Supreme Court's interpretation of the complicity provision of the statute under which she was convicted . . . was so unexpected that it deprived her of fair warning of the crime with which she was charged. The opinion of the Ohio Supreme Court belies this claim. It shows clearly that the construction given the statute by the Ohio court was consistent with both prior Ohio law and with the legislative history of the statute. In such circumstances, any claim of inadequate notice under the Due Process Clause must be rejected.

III

Lockett challenges the constitutionality of Ohio's death penalty statute on a number of grounds. We find it necessary to consider only her contention that her death sentence is invalid because the statute under which it was imposed did not permit the sentencing judge to consider, as mitigating factors, her character, prior record, age, lack of specific intent to cause death, and her relatively minor part in the crime. To address her contention from the proper perspective, it is helpful to review the developments in our recent cases where we have applied the Eighth and Fourteenth Amendments to death penalty statutes. We do not write on a "clean slate."

A

Prior to *Furman* v. *Georgia* . . . (1972), every State that authorized capital punishment had abandoned mandatory death penalties, and instead permitted the jury unguided and unrestrained discretion regarding the imposition of the death penalty in a particular capital case. Mandatory death penalties had proven unsatisfactory, as the plurality noted in *Wooden* v. *North Carolina* . . . (1976), in part because juries "with some regularity disregarded their oaths and refused to convict defendants where a death sentence was the automatic consequence of a guilty verdict."

This Court had never intimated prior to *Furman* that discretion in sentencing offended the Constitution. . . .

The constitutional status of discretionary sentencing in capital cases changed abruptly, however, as a result of the separate opinions supporting the judgment in *Furman*. The question in *Furman* was whether "the imposition and carrying out of the death penalty [in the cases before the Court] constituted cruel and unusual punishment in violation of the Eighth and Fourteenth Amendments.". . . Two Justices concluded that the Eighth Amendment prohibited the death penalty altogether and on that ground voted to reverse the judgments sustaining the death penalties. . . . Three Justices were unwilling to hold the death penalty *per se* unconstitutional under the Eighth and Fourteenth Amendments, but voted to reverse the judgments on other grounds. In separate opinions, the three concluded that discretionary sentencing, unguided by legislatively defined standards, violated the Eighth Amendment because it was "pregnant with discrimination," . . . because it permitted the death penalty to be "wantonly" and "freakishly" imposed . . . and because it imposed the death penalty with "great infrequency" and afforded "no meaningful basis for distinguishing the few cases in which it [was] imposed from the many cases in which it [was] not.". . .

Predictably, the variety of opinions supporting the judgment in *Furman* engendered confusion as to what was required in order to impose the death penalty in accord with the Eighth Amendment. Some States responded to what was thought to be the command of *Furman* by adopting mandatory death penalties for a limited category of specific crimes thus eliminating all discretion from the sentencing process in capital cases. Other States attempted to continue the practice of individually assessing the culpability of each individual defendant convicted of a capital offense and, at the same time, to comply with *Furman,* by providing standards to guide the sentencing decision.

Four years after *Furman,* we considered Eighth Amendment issues posed by five of the post-*Furman* death penalty statutes. Four Justices took the position that all five statutes complied with the Constitution; two Justices took the position that none of them complied. Hence, the disposition of each case varied according to the votes of a plurality of three Justices who delivered a joint opinion in each of the five cases upholding the constitutionality of the statutes of Georgia, Florida, and Texas, and holding those of North Carolina and Louisiana unconstitutional.

The plurality reasoned that to comply with *Furman,* sentencing procedures should not create "a substantial risk that the death penalty [will] be inflicted in an arbitrary and capricious manner." *Gregg* v. *Georgia* . . . [1976]. In the view of the plurality, however, *Furman* did not require that all sentencing discretion be eliminated, but only that it be "directed and limited,". . . so that the death penalty would be imposed in a more consistent and rational manner and so that there would be a "meaningful basis for distinguishing . . . cases in which it is imposed from . . . the cases in which it is not.". . . The plurality also concluded, in the course of invalidating North Carolina's mandatory death penalty statute, that the sentencing process must permit consideration of the "character and record of the individual offender and the circumstances of the particular offense as a constitutionally indispensable part of the process of inflicting the penalty of death," *Woodson* v. *North Carolina* . . . in order to ensure the reliability, under Eighth Amendment standards, of the determination that "death is the appropriate punishment in a specific case.". . .

In the last decade, many of the States have been obliged to revise their death penalty statutes in response to the various opinions supporting the judgments in *Furman* . . . and *Gregg* . . . and its companion cases. The signals from this Court have not, however, always been easy to decipher. The States now deserve the clearest guidance that the Court can provide; we have an obligation to reconcile previously differing views in order to provide that guidance.

B

With that obligation in mind we turn to Lockett's attack on the Ohio statute. Essentially she contends that the Eighth and Fourteenth Amendments require that the sentencer be given a full opportunity to consider mitigating circumstances in capital cases and that the Ohio statute does not comply with that requirement. . . .

We begin by recognizing that the concept of individualized sentencing in criminal cases generally, although not constitutionally required, has long been accepted in this country. . . . Consistent with that concept, sentencing judges traditionally have taken a wide range of factors into account. That States have authority to make aiders and abettors equally responsible, as a matter of law, with principals, or to enact felony murder statutes is beyond constitutional challenge. But the definition of crimes generally has not been thought automatically to dictate what should be the proper penalty. . . . And where sentencing discretion is granted, it generally has been agreed that the sentencing judge's "possession of the fullest information possible concerning the defendant's life and characteristics" is "[h]ighly relevant — *if not essential* — [to the] selection of an appropriate sentence. . . ." *Williams* v. *New York* [1949]. . . .

We are now faced with those questions [of which factors are relevant] and we conclude that the Eighth and Fourteenth Amendments require that the sentencer, in all but the rarest kind of capital case, not be precluded from considering *as a mitigating factor,* any aspect of a defendant's character or record and any of the circumstances of the offense that the defendant proffers as a basis for a sentence less than death. We recognize that, in noncapital cases, the established practice of individualized sentences rests not on constitutional commands but public policy enacted into statutes. The considerations that account for the wide acceptance of individualization of sentences in noncapital cases surely cannot be thought less important in capital cases. Given that the imposition of death by public authority is so profoundly different from all other penalties, we cannot avoid the conclusion that an individualized decision is essential in capital cases. The need for treating each defendant in a capital case with that degree of respect due the uniqueness of the individual is far more important than in noncapital cases. A variety of flexible techniques — probation, parole, work furloughs, to name a few — and various post conviction remedies, may be available to modify an initial sentence of confinement in noncapital cases. The nonavailability of corrective or modifying mechanisms with respect to an executed capital sentence underscores the need for individualized consideration as a constitutional requirement in imposing the death sentence.

There is no perfect procedure for deciding in which cases government authority should be used to impose death. But a statute that prevents the sentencer in all capital cases from giving independent mitigating weight to aspects of the defendant's character and record and to circumstances of the offense proferred in mitigation creates the risk that the death penalty will be imposed in spite of factors which may call for a less severe penalty. When the choice is between life and death, that risk is unacceptable and incompatible with the commands of the Eighth and Fourteenth Amendments.

C

The Ohio death penalty statute does not permit the type of individualized consideration of mitigating factors we now hold to be required by the Eighth and Fourteenth Amendments in capital cases. . . .

[Under the Ohio statute,] once a defendant is found guilty of aggravated murder with at least one of seven specified aggravating circumstances, the death penalty must be imposed unless, considering "the nature and circumstances of the offense and the history, character, and conditions of the offender," the sentencing judge determines that at least one of the following mitigating circumstances is established by a preponderance of the evidence:

"(1) The victim of the offense induced or facilitated it,

"(2) It is unlikely that the offense would have been committed but for the fact that the offender was under duress, coercion, or strong provocation.

"(3) The offense was primarily the product of the offender's psychosis or mental deficiency, though such condition is insufficient to establish the defense of insanity.". . .

. . .We see, therefore, that once it is determined that the victim did not induce or facilitate the offense, that the defendant did not act under duress or coercion, and that the offense was not primarily the product of the defendant's mental deficiency, the Ohio statute mandates the sentence of death. The absence of direct proof that the defendant intended to cause the death of the victim is relevant for mitigating purposes only if it is determined that it sheds some light on one of the three statutory mitigating factors. Similarly, consideration of a defendant's comparatively minor role in the offense, or age, would generally not be permitted, as such, to affect the sentencing decision.

The limited range of mitigating circumstances which may be considered by the sentencer under the Ohio statute is incompatible with the Eighth and Fourteenth Amendments. To meet constitutional requirements, a death penalty statute must not preclude consideration of relevant mitigating factors.

Accordingly, the judgment under review is reversed to the extent that it sustains the imposition of the death penalty; the case is remanded for further proceedings. . . .

MR. JUSTICE MARSHALL, concurring in the judgment.

I continue to adhere to my view that the death penalty is, under all circumstances, a cruel and unusual punishment prohibited by the Eighth Amendment. . . . The cases that have come to this Court since its 1976 decisions permitting imposition of the death penalty have only persuaded me further of that conclusion. . . .

When a death sentence is imposed under the circumstances presented here, I fail to understand how any of my Brethren — even those who believe that the death penalty is not wholly inconsistent with the Constitution — can disagree that it must be vacated. Under the Ohio death penalty statute, this 21-year-old Negro woman was sentenced to death for a killing that she did not actually commit or intend to commit. She was convicted under a theory of vicarious liability. The imposition of the death penalty for this crime totally violates the principle of proportionality embodied in the Eighth Amendment's prohibition, . . . it makes no distinction between a wilful and malicious murderer and an accomplice to an armed robbery in which a killing unintentionally occurs. . . .

Permitting imposition of the death penalty solely on proof of felony-murder, moreover, necessarily leads to the kind of "lightning bolt," "freakish," and "wanton" executions that persuaded other Members of the Court to join MR. JUSTICE BRENNAN and myself in *Furman* v. *Georgia* . . . in holding Georgia's death penalty statute unconstitutional. . . .

As the plurality points out, petitioner was sentenced to death under a statutory scheme that precluded any effective consideration of her degree of involvement in the crime, her age, or her prospects for rehabilitation. Achieving the proper balance between clear guidelines that assure relative equality of treatment, and discretion to consider individual factors whose weight cannot always be preassigned, is no easy task in any sentencing system. Where life itself is what hangs in the balance, a fine precision in the process must be insisted upon. The Ohio statute, with its blunderbuss, virtually mandatory approach to imposition of the death penalty for certain crimes, wholly fails to recognize the unique individuality of every criminal defendant who comes before its courts. . . .

Accordingly, I join in the Court's judgment insofar as it affirms petitioner's conviction and vacates her death sentence. I do not, however, join in the Court's assumption that the death penalty may ever be imposed without violating the command of the Eighth Amendment that no "cruel and unusual punishments" be imposed.

MR. JUSTICE BLACKMUN, concurring in part and concurring in the judgment.

I join the Court's judgment, but only Parts I and II of its opinion. I, too, would reverse the judgment of the Supreme Court of Ohio insofar as it upheld the imposition of the death penalty on petitioner Sandra Lockett, but I would do so for a reason more limited than that which the plurality espouses, and for an additional reason not relied upon by the plurality. . . .

The first reason is that in my view, the Ohio judgment in this case improperly provided the death sentence for a defendant who only aided and abetted a murder, without permitting any consideration by the sentencing authority of the extent of her involvement, or the degree of her *mens rea,* in the commission of the homicide. The Ohio capital statute, together with that State's aiding and abetting statute, and its statutory definition of "purposefulness" as including reckless endangerment, allow for a particularly harsh application of the death penalty to any defendant who has aided or abetted the commission of an armed robbery in the course of which a person is killed, even though accidentally. . . .

The more manageable alternative, in my view, is to follow a proceduralist tack, and require, as Ohio does not, in the case of a nontriggerman such as Lockett, that the sentencing authority have discretion to consider the degree of the defendant's participation in the acts leading to the homicide and the character of the defendant's *mens rea.* That approach does not interfere with the State's individual statutory categories for assessing legal guilt, but merely requires that the sentencing authority be permitted to weigh any available evidence, adduced at trial or at the sentencing hearing, concerning the defendant's degree of participation in the homicide and the nature of his *mens rea* in regard to the commission of the homicidal act. A defendant would be permitted to adduce evidence, if any be available, that he had little or no reason to anticipate that a gun would be fired, or that he played only a minor part in the course of events leading to the use of fatal force. . . .

This approach is not too far off the mark already used by many States in assessing the death penalty. Of 34 States that now have capital statutes, 18 specify that a minor degree of participation in a homicide may be considered by the sentencing authority, and, of the remaining 16 States, nine allow consideration of any mitigating factor. . . .

MR. JUSTICE WHITE, dissenting in part and concurring in the judgments of the Court.

I concur in Parts I and II of the Court's opinion in No. 76-6997, *Lockett* v. *Ohio,* and Part I of the Court's opinion in No. 76-6513, *Bell* v. *Ohio,* and in the judgments. I cannot, however, agree with Part III of the Court's opinion in *Lockett* and Part II of the Court's opinion in *Bell* and to that extent respectfully dissent.

I

The Court has not completed its about-face since *Furman* v. *Georgia*. . . . Today the Court holds, again through a plurality, that the sentencer may constitutionally impose the death penalty only as an exercise of his unguided discretion after being presented with all circumstances which the defendant might believe to be conceivable relevant to the appropriateness of the penalty for the individual offender.

With all due respect, I dissent. I continue to be of the view . . . that it does not violate the Eighth Amendment for a State to impose the death penalty on a mandatory basis when the defendant has been found guilty beyond a reasonable doubt of committing a deliberate, unjustified killing. Moreover, I greatly fear that the effect of the Court's decision today will be to constitutionally compel a restoration of the state of affairs at the time *Furman* was decided, where the death penalty is imposed so erratically and the threat of execution is so attenuated for even the most atrocious murders that "its imposition would then be the pointless and needless extinction of life with only marginal contributions to any discernible social or public purposes." *Furman* v. *Georgia*. . . . By requiring as a matter of constitutional law that sentencing authorities must be permitted to consider and in their discretion to act upon any and all mitigating circumstances, the Court permits them to refuse to impose the death penalty no matter what the circumstances of the crime. This invites a return to the pre-*Furman* days when the death penalty was generally reserved for those very few for whom society has least consideration. . . .

II

I nevertheless concur in the judgment of the Court reversing the imposition of the death sentences because I agree with the contention of the petitioners, ignored by the plurality, that it violates the Eighth Amendment to impose the penalty of death without a finding that the defendant possessed a purpose to cause the death of the victim.

It is now established that a penalty constitutes cruel and unusual punishment if it is excessive in relation to the crime for which it is imposed. . . .

The value of capital punishment as a deterrent to those lacking a purpose to kill is extremely attenuated. Whatever questions may be raised concerning the efficacy of the death penalty as a deterrent to intentional murders — and that debate rages on — its function in deterring individuals from becoming involved in ventures in which death may unintentionally result is even more doubtful. Moreover, whatever legitimate purposes the imposition of death upon those who do not intend to cause death might serve if inflicted with any regularity is surely dissipated by society's apparent unwillingness to impose it upon other than an occasional and erratic basis. . . .

Under those circumstances the conclusion is unavoidable that the infliction of death upon those who had no intent to bring about the death of the victim is not only grossly out of proportion to the severity of the crime but also fails to significantly contribute to acceptable or, indeed, any perceptible goals of punishment. . . .

MR. JUSTICE REHNQUIST, concurring in part and dissenting.

I join Parts I and II of THE CHIEF JUSTICE'S opinion for the Court, but am unable to join Part III of his opinion or in the judgment of reversal.

. . .It seems to me indisputably clear from today's opinion that, while we may not be writing on a clean slate, the Court is scarcely faithful to what has been written before. Rather, it makes a third distinct effort to address the same question, an effort which derives little support from any of the various opinions in *Furman* or from the prevailing opinions in the *Woodson* cases. As a practical matter, I doubt that today's opinion will make a great deal of difference in the manner in which trials in capital cases are conducted, since I would suspect that it has been the practice of most trial judges to permit a defendant to offer virtually any sort of evidence in his own defense as he wished. . . . If a defendant as a matter of constitutional law is to be permitted to offer as evidence in the sentencing hearing any fact, however bizarre, which he wishes, even though the most sympathetically disposed trial judge could conceive of no basis upon which the jury might take it into account in imposing a sentence, the new constitutional doctrine will not eliminate arbitrariness or freakishness in the imposition of sentences, but will codify and institutionalize it. By encouraging defendants in capital cases, and presumably sentencing judges and juries, to take into consideration anything under the sun as a "mitigating circumstance," it will not guide sentencing discretion but will totally unleash it. . . .

. . .I am frank to say that I am uncertain whether today's opinion represents the seminal case in the exposition by this Court of the Eighth and Fourteenth Amendments as they apply to capital punishment, or whether instead it represents the third false start in this direction within the past six years. . . .

I finally reject the proposition urged by my Brother WHITE in his separate opinion, which the Court finds it unnecessary to reach. That claim is that the death penalty, as applied to one who participated in this murder as Lockett did, is "disproportionate" and therefore violative of the Eighth and Fourteenth Amendments. I know of no principle embodied in those amendments, other than perhaps one's personal notion of what is a fitting punishment for a crime, which would allow this Court to hold the death penalty imposed upon her unconstitutional because under the judge's charge to the jury the latter were not required to find that she intended to cause the death of her victim. As my Brother WHITE concedes, approximately half of the States "have not legislatively foreclosed the possibility of imposing the death penalty upon one who did not intend to cause death.". . . Centuries of common-law doctrine establishing the felony-murder doctrine, dealing with the relationship between aiders and abettors and principals, would have to be rejected to adopt this view. Just as surely as many thoughtful moralists and penologists would reject the Biblical notion of "an eye for an eye, a tooth for a tooth," as a guide for minimum sentencing, there is nothing in the prohibition against cruel and unusual punishments contained in the Eighth Amendment which sets that injunction as a limitation on the maximum sentence which society may impose.

Since all of petitioner's claims appear to me to be without merit, I would affirm the judgment of the Supreme Court of Ohio.

BELL V. STATE OF OHIO

No. 76-6513

Willie Lee Bell, Petitioner,
v.
State of Ohio.

On Writ of Certiorari to the Supreme Court of Ohio.

[July 3, 1978]

THE CHIEF JUSTICE delivered the opinion of the Court with respect to the facts of the case and the proceedings below (Part I), together with an opinion (Part II) in which MR. JUSTICE STEWART, MR. JUSTICE POWELL, and MR. JUSTICE STEVENS joined, on the constitutionality of the statute under which petitioner was sentenced to death, and announced the judgment of the Court. [MR. JUSTICE BRENNAN took no part in the consideration or decision of this case.]

We granted certiorari in this case to consider whether the imposition of the death penalty upon Willie Lee Bell pursuant to Ohio [law] . . . violated the Eighth and Fourteenth Amendments.

I

Bell was convicted of aggravated murder with the specification that the murder occurred in the course of a kidnapping. He was sentenced to death.

On October 16, 1974, Bell, who was then 16 years old, met a friend, Samuel Hall, who was then 18, at a youth center in Cincinnati, Ohio. They left the center and went to Hall's home where Hall borrowed a car and proceeded to drive Bell around the area. They followed a car driven by 64-year-old Julius Graber into a parking garage, and Hall, armed with a "sawed off" shotgun, forced Graber to surrender his car keys. Graber was placed, unharmed, into the trunk of his own car. Hall then drove Graber's car and Bell followed in Hall's car to the latter's home. There, Bell got into Graber's car with Hall and, following Hall's directions, drove to a nearby cemetery.

A resident of an apartment near the cemetery saw Graber's car parked on the service road of the cemetery with its parking lights on. He heard two car doors close and then a voice screaming. "Don't shoot me, don't shoot me," followed by two shots. He saw someone return to Graber's car and slide from the passenger's seat into the driver's seat. After observing Graber's car proceed away — with lights off — he called the police.

The police found Graber lying face down in the cemetery with a massive wound on the back of his head and another on his right cheek. He died en route to the hospital.

Although Bell did not testify at his trial, he gave his version of the killing to the police after his arrest in a statement that was recorded and introduced at trial. Bell denied any intention to participate in a killing. He said that after he and Hall had parked in the cemetery, he had asked Hall what they were going to do next, and that Hall had replied, "We'll see, give me the keys." Hall then, according to Bell, released Graber from the trunk and marched him into a forested area to the rear of the cemetery out of Bell's sight. Bell then heard Graber pleading for his life and heard a gunshot. According to Bell, Hall then came back to the car, reloaded the gun, and returned to the wooded area. Bell said he heard a second shot and Hall returned to the car and drove to Dayton, where they spent the night with friends of Hall.

The next day, with Bell driving Graber's car, Bell and Hall stopped at a service station in Dayton. Hall used the shotgun to obtain the keys to the attendant's car, and forced the attendant into the trunk. Hall then drove the attendant's car away from the station with Bell following in Graber's car. A patrolman stopped the car that Hall was driving for a defective muffler and discovered the attendant in the trunk. Bell drove past Hall and the officer and returned to Cincinnati where he abandoned Graber's car.

After his arrest and indictment, Bell waived his right to a trial by jury and requested a trial by a three-judge panel. The panel unanimously found him guilty of aggravated murder and of the specification that the murder occurred in the course of a kidnapping. That offense required the death penalty under Ohio [law] . . . which is set forth in the Appendix to our opinion in *Lockett* v. *Ohio*. No. 76-6997, decided today.

Pursuant to Ohio law, the panel ordered a presentence investigation and psychiatric examination of Bell. The psychiatrists' report was directed specifically to the three mitigating factors and concluded that none of them were present. It also noted, however, that Bell claimed not to have been aware of what Hall was doing when he shot Graber.

The presentence report contained detailed information about the offense and about Bell's background, intelligence, prior offenses, character, and habits. It noted that Hall had accused Bell of actually firing the shotgun at Graber. In addition to describing Bell as having "low average or dull normal intellectual capacity," it noted that Bell had been cited in juvenile court for a series of prior offenses and had allegedly been using mescaline on the night of the offense.

The three-judge panel permitted both sides the opportunity to introduce evidence and make arguments regarding the proper penalty. Bell testified that he had been under the influence of drugs virtually every day for three years prior to his arrest on the night of the killing. He also said that he had viewed Hall as a "big brother" and had followed Hall's instructions because he had been "scared." Several of Bell's teachers testified that Bell had a drug problem and was emotionally unstable and immature for his age.

The defense argued that Bell had acted out of fear and coercion and that the offense was due to Bell's mental deficiency. In support of his contention that Bell was mentally deficient, defense counsel argued that Bell's minority established mental deficiency as a matter of law; he also argued that Bell was mentally deficient compared to other teenagers because of his drug problem and emotional instability and that Bell's mental deficiency contributed to his passive part in the crime.

Prior to sentencing, Bell moved that the Ohio death penalty be declared unconstitutional under the Eighth and Fourteenth Amendments, contending that the Ohio death penalty statute, which had been enacted after *Furman* v. *Georgia* . . . (1972), severely limited the factors that would support an argument for mercy. Bell contended that his youth, the fact that he cooperated with the police, and the lack of proof that he had participated in the actual killing strongly supported an argument for a penalty less than death in this case. He also contended that Ohio's post-*Furman* death penalty statute precluded him from requesting a lesser sentence on the basis of those factors.

After considering the presentence and psychiatric reports as well as other evidence and the arguments of counsel, the panel concluded that none of the mitigating circumstances defined by the Ohio statute had been established. Accordingly, Bell was sentenced to death.

In the Ohio Supreme Court, Bell unsuccessfully renewed his contention that the Ohio death penalty violated the Eighth and Fourteenth Amendments. He also contended, among other things, that the evidence was insufficient to sustain his conviction for aggravated murder because there was no proof that he had intended to kill or that he had aided and abetted Hall with the intent that Graber be killed. That court rejected these arguments and held that the evidence that Bell had aided and abetted was sufficient to sustain the conviction because, under Ohio law, an aider and abettor could be prosecuted and punished as if he were the principal offender. Alternatively, the court concluded that the trial panel might have reasonably concluded that Bell either committed or actively assisted in the murder.

II

Bell contends that the Ohio death penalty statute violated his rights under the Eighth and Fourteenth Amendments because it prevented the sentencing judges from considering the particular circumstances of his crime and aspects of his character and record as mitigating factors. For the reasons stated in Part III of our opinion in *Lockett* v. *Ohio* . . . , we have concluded that "the Eighth and Fourteenth Amendments require that the sentencer, in all but the rarest kind of capital case, not be precluded from considering, *as a mitigating factor,* any aspect of a defendant's character or record and any aspect of the offense that the defendant proffers." We also concluded that "the Ohio death penalty statute does not permit the type of individualized consideration of mitigating factors" that is required by the Eighth and Fourteenth Amendments. We therefore agree with Bell's contention.

Accordingly, the judgment of the Ohio Supreme Court is reversed to the extent that it upholds the imposition of the death penalty and the case is remanded for further proceedings. . . .

MR. JUSTICE BLACKMUN, concurring in part and concurring in the judgment.

I join Part I of the Court's opinion and concur in the judgment. In accord with my views stated separately in *Lockett* v. *Ohio* . . . , I would reverse the judgment of the Ohio Supreme Court insofar as it upheld the imposition of the death penalty on petitioner Bell. Petitioner was charged, *inter alia,* as an aider and abettor in the murder of Julius Graber, and the trial court's verdict was sustained on that basis by the Ohio Supreme Court. . . . Accordingly, I would find the Ohio capital penalty statute deficient in failing to allow consideration of the degree of petitioner's involvement, and the character of his *mens rea,* in the crime.

MR. JUSTICE MARSHALL, concurring in the judgment.

I continue to believe that the death penalty is, under all circumstances, a cruel and unusual punishment prohibited by the Eighth and Fourteenth Amendments, *Furman* v. *Georgia* . . . (1972) (MARSHALL, J., concurring); *Gregg* v. *Georgia* . . . (1976) (MARSHALL, J., dissenting), and thus disagree with the Court's assumption to the contrary. *See Lockett* v. *Ohio* . . . (1978) (MARSHALL, J., concurring and dissenting). I join in the Court's judgment insofar as it requires that petitioner's death sentence be vacated.

MR. JUSTICE REHNQUIST, dissenting.

For the reasons stated in my concurring and dissenting opinion in No. 76-6997, *Lockett* v. *Ohio,* I would affirm the judgment of the Supreme Court of Ohio in this case. I therefore dissent from the Court's judgment reversing it.

COURT ON 'INDECENT' BROADCASTS
July 3, 1978

The Supreme Court July 3 upheld the power of the Federal Communications Commission (FCC) to limit the hours during which radio stations may broadcast certain material which, although offensive to many listeners, is not obscene.

Five of the justices, divided in their reasoning, upheld the FCC's authority, relying primarily upon the "uniquely pervasive presence" of the broadcast media in American life and upon its easy accessibility to children. Justice John Paul Stevens wrote the court's opinion, joined in part by Chief Justice Warren E. Burger, Justices William H. Rehnquist, Lewis F. Powell Jr., and Harry A. Blackmun.

Four of the justices dissented, arguing that the FCC lacked authority to restrict the broadcast of any material that was not actually obscene. Justices Potter Stewart, Byron R. White, William J. Brennan Jr. and Thurgood Marshall held this view.

The Case

About two o'clock on a Tuesday afternoon in October 1973, a New York radio station owned by the Pacifica Foundation aired a monologue by humorist George Carlin. Entitled "Filthy Words," the monologue satirizes society's attitude toward certain words, in particular those seven that are generally banned from use on radio and television programs. The monologue, given before a live audience, was recorded. The recording was played over the radio station. In the monologue Carlin lists the seven "dirty words" (shit, piss, fuck, cunt, cocksucker, motherfucker and tits) and then uses them in various forms throughout the recording.

After receiving a parent's complaint that his young son had heard the monologue, the FCC issued an order to the station, restricting the hours at which such an "offensive" program could be broadcast. Pacifica Foundation challenged the order as in conflict with the Communications Act's prohibition on censorship, and in violation of the First Amendment.

The Opinion

The Supreme Court rejected both challenges. The FCC order was not censorship, wrote Stevens. The censorship prohibition, he continued, consistently has been interpreted to forbid the FCC to edit or excise material from a program before a broadcast, but not to curtail the FCC's review of a program once it has been aired. Furthermore, the court rejected the Pacifica argument that the law's ban on censorship limited the adjacent provision which prohibits the use of indecent, obscene or profane language over the radio.

Pacifica further argued that only obscene material could be regulated by the FCC in this manner. The court again disagreed. Material could be indecent — in conflict with accepted standards of morality — without being obscene, yet both were subject to regulation under the Communications Act.

On the First Amendment question, Pacifica argued that the FCC was regulating this program because of its content. This was a violation of the guarantee of free speech, it continued, because that guarantee forbids government to regulate any speech just because of its content.

"No such absolute rule is mandated by the Constitution," responded Stevens. "Both the content and the context of speech are critical elements of First Amendment analysis." While "some users of even the most offensive words are unquestionably protected" by the First Amendment, "the constitutional protection accorded to . . . such patently offensive . . . language [as used in this case] need not be the same in every context. . . . Words that are commonplace in one setting are shocking in another."

And the context of this broadcast justified the FCC's regulation, held the court, emphasizing that the broadcast media are subject to governmental restriction impermissible if imposed on the print media or on individuals.

"First, the broadcast media have established a uniquely pervasive presence in the lives of all Americans," wrote Justice Stevens. "Patently offensive, indecent material presented over the airwaves confronts the citizen . . . in the privacy of the home. . . . To say that one may avoid further offense by turning off the radio when he hears indecent language is like saying that the remedy for an assault is to run away after the first blow. . . .

"Second, broadcasting is uniquely accessible to children, even those too

young to read," explained Stevens. "Pacifica's broadcast could have enlarged a child's vocabulary in an instant." The court has ruled in a number of earlier cases, he continued, that speech otherwise protected by the First Amendment may be regulated to protect the welfare of young people and their parents' authority in their home.

In this context, the Carlin monologue was a nuisance and could properly be regulated as such without a finding that it was obscene, concluded Stevens, emphasizing the narrowness of the court's ruling.

A nuisance, Stevens wrote, quoting an earlier court decision, " 'may be merely a right thing in the wrong place — like a pig in the parlor instead of the barnyard.' We simply hold that when the Commission finds that a pig has entered the parlor, the exercise of its regulatory power does not depend on proof that the pig is obscene."

Although they agreed with the majority's ruling and with most of Stevens' opinion, Justices Powell and Blackmun wrote separately to disagree with Stevens' theory that "the Justices of this court are free generally to decide on the basis of its content which speech protected by the First Amendment is most 'valuable,' and hence deserving of most protection, and which is less 'valuable' and hence deserving of less protection." The context, not the content, of the monologue was critical to this case, they wrote.

The Dissent

The majority could — and should — have avoided dealing with the constitutional issue in this case, wrote Justices Stewart, White, Brennan and Marshall, by simply holding that the Communications Act allowed the FCC to ban or restrict the broadcast only of obscene materials.

Justice Brennan, joined by Justice Marshall, wrote an additional dissenting opinion, sharply critical of the majority's "misguided . . . attempt to impose its notions of propriety on the whole of the American people." Taking the majority's rationale to its logical extreme, Brennan argued, would result in FCC restrictions on or banning of radio broadcasts of Shakespearean plays, many political speeches, the Nixon tapes and even portions of the Bible.

"I would place the responsibility and the right to weed worthless and offensive communications from the public airways where it belongs," Brennan wrote, "in a public free to choose those communications worthy of its attention from a marketplace unsullied by the censor's hand."

> *Following are excerpts from the Supreme Court's opinion, handed down July 3, 1978, backing the power of the Federal Communications Commission to order that certain "dirty words" not be broadcast during hours when children were likely to be listening:*

No. 77-528

Federal Communications Commission, Petitioner, *v.* Pacifica Foundation.	On Writ of Certiorari to the United States Court of Appeals for the District of Columbia Circuit.

[July 3, 1978]

MR. JUSTICE STEVENS delivered the opinion of the Court (Parts I, II, III, and IV-C) and an opinion in which THE CHIEF JUSTICE and MR. JUSTICE REHNQUIST joined (Parts IV-A and IV-B).

This case requires that we decide whether the Federal Communications Commission has any power to regulate a radio broadcast that is indecent but not obscene.

A satiric humorist named George Carlin recorded a 12-minute monologue entitled "Filthy Words" before a live audience in a California theater. He began by referring to his thoughts about "the words you couldn't say on the public, ah, airwaves, um, the ones you definitely wouldn't say, ever." He proceeded to list those words and repeat them over and over again in a variety of colloquialisms. The transcript of the recording . . . indicates frequent laughter from the audience.

At about 2 o'clock in the afternoon on Tuesday, October 30, 1973, a New York radio station owned by respondent, Pacifica Foundation, broadcast the "Filthy Words" monologue. A few weeks later a man, who stated that he had heard the broadcast while driving with his young son, wrote a letter complaining to the Commission. He stated that, although he could perhaps understand the "record's being sold for private use, I certainly cannot understand the broadcast of same over the air that, supposedly, you control."

The complaint was forwarded to the station for comment. In its response, Pacifica explained that the monologue had been played during a program about contemporary society's attitude toward language and that immediately before its broadcast listeners had been advised that it included "sensitive language which might be regarded as offensive to some." Pacifica characterized George Carlin as "a significant social satirist" who "like Twain and Sahl before him, examines the language of ordinary people. . . . Carlin is not mouthing obscenities, he is merely using words to satirize as harmless and essentially silly our attitudes towards those words." Pacifica stated that it was not aware of any other complaints about the broadcast.

On February 21, 1975, the Commission issued a Declaratory Order granting the complaint and holding that Pacifica "could have been the subject of administrative sanctions.". . . The Commission did not impose formal sanctions, but it did state that the order would be "associated with the station's license file, and in the event that subsequent complaints are received, the Commission will then decide whether it should utilize any of the available sanctions it has been granted by Congress."

In its Memorandum Opinion the Commission stated that it intended to "clarify the standards which will be utilized in considering" the growing number of complaints about indecent speech on the airwaves. . . . Advancing several reasons for treating broadcast speech differently from other forms of expression, the Commission found a power to regulate indecent broadcasting in two statutes: 18 U.S.C. § 1464, which forbids the use of "obscene, indecent, or profane language by means of radio communications," and 47 U.S.C. § 303 (g), which requires the Commission to "encourage the larger and more effective use of radio in the public interest."

The Commission characterized the language used in the Carlin monologue as "patently offensive," though not necessarily obscene, and expressed the opinion that it should be regulated by principles analogous to those found in the law of nuisance where the "law generally speaks to *channeling* behavior more than actually prohibiting it. . . . [T]he concept of 'indecent' is intimately connected with the exposure of children to language that describes, in terms patently offensive as measured by contemporary community standards for the broadcast medium, sexual or excretory activities and organs, at times of the day when there is a reasonable risk that children may be in the audience." . . .

Applying these considerations to the language used in the monologue as broadcast by respondent, the Commission concluded that certain words depicted sexual and excretory activities in a patently offensive manner, noted that they "were broadcast at a time when children were undoubtedly in the audience (*i.e.*, in the early afternoon)," and that the prerecorded language, with these offensive words "repeated over and over," was "deliberately broadcast." . . . In summary, the Commission stated: "We therefore hold that the language as broadcast was indecent and prohibited by 18 U.S.C. 1464."

After the order issued, the Commission was asked to clarify its opinion by ruling that the broadcast of indecent words as part of a live newscast would not be prohibited. The Commission issued another opinion in which it pointed out that it "never intended to place an absolute prohibition on the broadcast of this type of language, but rather sought to channel it to times of day when children most likely would not be exposed to it." . . . The Commission noted that its "declaratory order was issued in a specific factual context," and declined to comment on various hypothetical situations presented by the petition. . . . It relied on its "long standing policy of refusing to issue interpretive rulings or advisory opinions when the critical facts are not explicitly stated or there is a possibility that subsequent events will alter them." . . .

The United States Court of Appeals for the District of Columbia reversed, with each of the three judges on the panel writing separately. . . . Judge Tamm concluded that the order represented censorship and was expressly prohibited by § 326 of the Communications Act.* Alternatively, Judge Tamm read the Commission opinion as the functional equivalent of a rule and concluded that it was "overbroad." . . .

Chief Judge Bazelon's concurrence rested on the Constitution. He was persuaded that § 326's prohibition against censorship is inapplicable to broadcasts forbidden by §1464. However, he concluded that § 1464 must be narrowly construed to cover only language that is obscene or otherwise unprotected by the First Amendment. . . . Judge Leventhal, in dissent, stated that the only issue was whether the Commission could regulate the language "as broadcast." . . . Emphasizing the interest in protecting children, not only from exposure to indecent language, but also from exposure to the idea that such language has official approval . . . he concluded that the Commission had correctly condemned the daytime broadcast as indecent.

Having granted the Commission's petition for certiorari, — U.S. —, we must decide: (1) whether the scope of judicial review encompasses more than the Commission's determination that the monologue was indecent "as broadcast"; (2) whether the Commission's order was a form of censorship forbidden by § 326; (3) whether the broadcast was indecent within the meaning of § 1464; and (4) whether the order violates the First Amendment of the United States Constitution.

I

The general statements in the Commission's memorandum opinion do not change the character of its order. . . . The order "was issued in a special factual context"; questions concerning possible action in other contexts were expressly reserved for the future. The specific holding was carefully confined to the monologue "as broadcast." . . . Accordingly, the focus of our review must be on the Commission's determination that the Carlin monologue was indecent as broadcast.

II

The relevant statutory questions are whether the Commission's action is forbidden "censorship" within the meaning of 47 U.S.C. § 326 and whether speech that concededly is not obscene may be restricted as "indecent" under the authority of 18 U.S.C. § 1464. The questions are not unrelated, for the two statutory provisions have a common origin. Nevertheless, we analyze them separately.

Section 29 of the Radio Act of 1927 provided:

---

* Nothing in this Act shall be understood or construed to give the Commission the power of censorship over the radio communications or signals transmitted by any radio station, and no regulation or condition shall be promulgated or fixed by the Commission which shall interfere with the right of free speech by means of radio communication." 48 Stat. 1091; 47 U.S.C. § 326.

"Nothing in this Act shall be understood or construed to give the licensing authority the power of censorship over the radio communications or signals transmitted by any radio station, and no regulation or condition shall be promulgated or fixed by the licensing authority which shall interfere with the right of free speech by means of radio communications. No person within the jurisdiction of the United States shall utter any obscene, indecent, or profane language by means of radio communication." 44 Stat. 1172-1173.

The prohibition against censorship unequivocally denies the Commission any power to edit proposed broadcasts in advance and to excise material considered inappropriate for the airwaves. The prohibition, however, has never been construed to deny the Commission the power to review the content of completed broadcasts in the performance of its regulatory duties.

During the period between the original enactment of the provision in 1927 and its re-enactment in the Communications Act of 1934, the courts and the Federal Radio Commission held that the section deprived the Commission of the power to subject "broadcasting matter to scrutiny prior to its release," but they concluded that the Commission's "undoubted right" to take note of past program content when considering a licensee's renewal application "is not censorship."

Not only did the Federal Radio Commission so construe the statute prior to 1934; its successor, the Federal Communications Commission, has consistently interpreted the provision in the same way ever since. . . .

Entirely apart from the fact that the subsequent review of program content is not the sort of censorship at which the statute was directed, its history makes it perfectly clear that it was not intended to limit the Commission's power to regulate the broadcast of obscene, indecent, or profane language. A single section of the 1927 Act is the source of both the anticensorship provision and the Commission's authority to impose sanctions for the broadcast of indecent or obscene language. Quite plainly, Congress intended to give meaning to both provisions. Respect for that intent requires that the censorship language be read as inapplicable to the prohibition on broadcasting obscene, indecent, or profane language.

There is nothing in the legislative history to contradict this conclusion. . . .

We conclude, therefore, that § 326 does not limit the Commission's authority to impose sanctions on licensees who engage in obscene, indecent, or profane broadcasting.

III

The only other statutory question presented by this case is whether the afternoon broadcast of the "Filthy Words" monologue was indecent within the meaning of § 1464. Even that question is narrowly confined by the arguments of the parties.

The Commission identified several words that referred to excretory or sexual activities or organs, stated that the repetitive, deliberate use of those words in an afternoon broadcast when children are in the audience was patently offensive, and held that the broadcast was indecent. Pacifica takes issue with the Commission's definition of indecency, but does not dispute the Commission's preliminary determination that each of the components of its definition was present. Specifically, Pacifica does not quarrel with the conclusion that this afternoon broadcast was patently offensive. Pacifica's claim that the broadcast was not indecent within the meaning of the statute rests entirely on the absence of prurient appeal.

The plain language of the statute does not support Pacifica's argument. The words "obscene, indecent, or profane" are written in the disjunctive, implying that each has a separate meaning. Prurient appeal is an element of the obscene, but the normal definition of "indecent" merely refers to nonconformance with accepted standards of morality.

Pacifica argues, however, that this Court has construed the term "indecent" in related statutes to mean "obscene.". . .

Because neither our prior decisions nor the language or history of § 1464 supports the conclusion that prurient appeal is an essential component of indecent language, we reject Pacifica's construction of the statute. When that construction is put to one side, there is no basis for disagreeing with the Commission's conclusion that indecent language was used in this broadcast.

IV

Pacifica makes two constitutional attacks on the Commission's order. First, it argues that the Commission's construction of the statutory language broadly encompasses so much constitutionally protected speech that reversal is required even if Pacifica's broadcast of the "Filthy Words" monologue is not itself protected by the First Amendment. Second, Pacifica argues that inasmuch as the recording is not obscene, the Constitution forbids any abridgment of the right to broadcast it on the radio.

A

The first argument fails because our review is limited to the question whether the Commission has the authority to proscribe this particular broadcast. As the Commission itself emphasized, its order was "issued in a specific factual context.". . . That approach is appropriate for courts as well as the Commission when regulation of indecency is at stake, for indecency is largely a function of context — it cannot be adequately judged in the abstract. . . .

It is true that the Commission's order may lead some broadcasters to censor themselves. At most, however, the Commission's definition of indecency will deter only the broadcasting of patently offensive references to excretory and sexual organs and activities. While some of these references may be protected, they surely lie at the periphery of First Amendment concern. . . .

B

When the issue is narrowed to the facts of this case, the question is whether the First Amendment denies government any power to restrict the public broadcast of indecent language in any circumstances. For if the government has any such power, this was an appropriate occasion for its exercise.

The words of the Carlin monologue are unquestionably "speech" within the meaning of the First Amendment. It is equally clear that the Commission's objections to the broadcast were based in part on its content. The order must therefore fall if, as Pacifica argues, the First Amendment prohibits all governmental regulation that depends on the content of speech. Our past cases demonstrate, however, that no such absolute rule is mandated by the Constitution.

The classic exposition of the proposition that both the content and the context of speech are critical elements of First Amendment analysis is Mr. Justice Holmes' statement for the Court in *Schenk* v. *United States:*

> "We admit that in many places and in ordinary times the defendants in saying all that was said in the circular would have been within their constitutional rights. But the character of every act depends upon the circumstances in which it is done. . . . The most stringent protection of free speech would not protect a man in falsely shouting fire in a theater and causing a panic. It does not even protect a man from an injunction against uttering words that may have all the effect of force. . . . The question in every case is whether the words used are used in such circumstances and are of such a nature as to create a clear and present danger that they will bring about the substantive evils that Congress has a right to prevent.". . .

The question in this case is whether a broadcast of patently offensive words dealing with sex and excretion may be regulated because of its content. Obscene materials have been denied the protection of the First Amendment because their content is so offensive to contemporary moral standards. . . . But the fact that society may find speech offensive is not a sufficient reason for suppressing it. Indeed, if it is the speaker's opinion that gives offense, that consequence is a reason for according it constitutional protection. For it is a central tenet of the First Amendment that the government must remain neutral in the marketplace of ideas. If there were any reason to believe that the Commission's characterization of the Carlin monologue as offensive could be traced to its political content — or even to the fact that it satirized contemporary attitudes about four letter words — First Amendment protection might be required. But that is simply not this case. These words offend for the same reasons that obscenity offends. Their place in the hierarchy of First Amendment values was aptly sketched by Mr. Justice Murphy when he said, "such utterances are no essential part of any exposition of ideas, and are of such slight social value as a step to truth that any benefit that may be derived from them is clearly outweighed by the social interest in order and morality.". . .

Although these words ordinarily lack literary, political, or scientific value, they are not entirely outside the protection of the First Amendment. Some uses of even the most offensive words are unquestionably protected. . . . Indeed, we may assume, *arguendo,* that this monologue would be protected in other contexts. Nonetheless, the constitutional protection accorded to a communication containing such patently offensive sexual and excretory language need not be the same in every context. It is a characteristic of speech such as this that both its capacity to offend and its "social value," to use Mr. Justice Murphy's term, vary with the circumstances. Words that are commonplace in one setting are shocking in another. To paraphrase Mr. Justice Harlan, one occasion's lyric is another's vulgarity. . . .

In this case it is undisputed that the content of Pacifica's broadcast was "vulgar," "offensive," and "shocking." Because content of that character is not entitled to absolute constitutional protection under all circumstances, we must consider its context in order to determine whether the Commission's action was constitutionally permissible.

C

We have long recognized that each medium of expression presents special First Amendment problems. . . . And of all forms of communication, it is broadcasting that has received the most limited First Amendment protection. Thus, although other speakers cannot be licensed except under laws that carefully define and narrow official discretion, a broadcaster may be deprived of his license and his forum if the Commission decides that such an action would serve "the public interest, convenience, and necessity." Similarly, although the First Amendment protects newspaper publishers from being required to print the replies of those whom they criticize, . . . it affords no such protection to broadcasters; on the contrary, they must give free time to the victims of their criticism.

The reasons for these distinctions are complex, but two have relevance to the present case. First, the broadcast media have established a uniquely pervasive presence in the lives of all Americans. Patently offensive, indecent material presented over the airwaves confronts the citizen, not only in public, but also in the privacy of the home, where the individual's right to be let alone plainly outweighs the First Amendment rights of an intruder. . . . Because the broadcast audience is constantly tuning in and out, prior warnings cannot completely protect the listener or viewer from unexpected program content. To say that one may avoid further offense by turning off the radio when he hears indecent language is like saying that the remedy for an assault is to run away after the first blow. One may hang up on an indecent phone call, but that option does not give the caller a constitutional immunity or avoid a harm that has already taken place.

Second, broadcasting is uniquely accessible to children, even those too young to read. Although. . .[an indecent] written message might have been incomprehensible to a first grader, Pacifica's broadcast could have en-larged a child's vocabulary in an instant. Other forms of offensive expression may be withheld from the young without restricting the expression at its source. Bookstores and motion picture theaters, for example, may be prohibited from making indecent material available to children. . . .

It is appropriate, in conclusion, to emphasize the narrowness of our holding. This case does not involve a two-way radio conversation between a cab driver and a dispatcher, or a telecast of an Elizabethan comedy. We have not decided that an occasional expletive in either setting would justify any sanction or, indeed, that this broadcast would justify a criminal prosecution. The Commission's decision rested entirely on a nuisance rationale under which context is all-important. The concept requires consideration of a host of variables. The time of day was emphasized by the Commission. The content of the program in which the language is used will also affect the composition of the audience, and differences between radio, television, and perhaps closed-circuit transmission, may also be relevant. As Mr. Justice Sutherland wrote, a "nuisance may be merely a right thing in the wrong place — like a pig in the parlor instead of the barnyard.". . . We simply hold that when the Commission finds that a pig has entered the parlor, the exercise of its regulatory power does not depend on proof that the pig is obscene.

The judgment of the Court of Appeals is reversed.

MR. JUSTICE POWELL, with whom MR. JUSTICE BLACKMUN joins, concurring.

I join Parts I, II, III, and IV (C) of MR. JUSTICE STEVENS' opinion. The Court today reviews only the Commission's holding that Carlin's monologue was indecent "as broadcast" at two o'clock in the afternoon, and not the broad sweep of the Commission's opinion. . . . In addition to being consistent with our settled practice of not deciding constitutional issues unnecessarily . . . this narrow focus also is conducive to the orderly development of this relatively new and difficult area of law, in the first instance by the Commission, and then by the reviewing courts. . . .

I also agree with much that is said in Part IV of MR. JUSTICE STEVENS' opinion, and with its conclusion that the Commission's holding in this case does not violate the First Amendment. Because I do not subscribe to all that is said in Part IV, however, I state my views separately.

I

It is conceded that the monologue at issue here is not obscene in the constitutional sense. . . . I do not think Carlin, consistently with the First Amendment, could be punished for delivering the same monologue to a live audience composed of adults who, knowing what to expect, chose to attend his performance. . . . And I would assume that an adult could not constitutionally be prohibited from purchasing a recording or transcript of the monologue and playing or reading it in the privacy of his own home. . . .

But it also is true that the language employed is, to most people, vulgar and offensive. It was chosen specifically for this quality, and it was repeated over and over as a sort of verbal shock treatment. The Commission did not err in characterizing the narrow category of language used here as "patently offensive" to most people regardless of age.

The issue, however, is whether the Commission may impose civil sanctions on a licensee radio station for broadcasting the monologue at two o'clock in the afternoon. The Commission's primary concern was to prevent the broadcast from reaching the ears of unsupervised children who were likely to be in the audience at that hour. In essence, the Commission sought to "channel" the monologue to hours when the fewest unsupervised children would be exposed to it. . . . In my view, this consideration provides strong support for the Commission's holding. . . .

II

As the foregoing demonstrates, my views are generally in accord with what is said in Part IV (C) of MR. JUSTICE STEVENS' opinion. . . . I therefore join that portion of his opinion. I do not join Part IV (B), however, because I do not subscribe to the theory that the Justices of this Court are free generally to decide on the basis of its content which speech protected by the First Amendment is most "valuable" and hence deserving of the most protection, and which is less "valuable" and hence deserving of less protection. . . . In my view, the result in this case does not turn on whether Carlin's monologue, viewed as a whole, or the words that comprise it, have more or less "value" than a candidate's campaign speech. This is a judgment for each person to make, not one for the judges to impose upon him.

The result turns instead on the unique characteristics of the broadcast media, combined with society's right to protect its children from speech generally agreed to be inappropriate for their years, and with the interest of unwilling adults in not being assaulted by such offensive speech in their homes. Moreover, I doubt whether today's decision will prevent any adult who wishes to receive Carlin's message in Carlin's own words from doing so, and from making for himself a value judgment as to the merit of the message and words. . . .

MR. JUSTICE BRENNAN, with whom MR. JUSTICE MARSHALL joins, dissenting.

I agree with MR. JUSTICE STEWART that . . . the word "indecent" in 18 U.S.C. § 1464 must be construed to prohibit only obscene speech. I would, therefore, normally refrain from expressing my views on any constitutional issues implicated in this case. However, I find the Court's misapplication of fundamental First Amendment principles so patent, and its attempt to impose *its* notions of propriety on the whole of the American people so misguided, that I am unable to remain silent.

I

For the second time in two years, . . . the Court refuses to embrace the notion, completely antithetical to basic First Amendment values, that the degree of protection the First Amendment affords protected speech varies with the social value ascribed to that speech by five Members of this Court. . . . Yet despite the Court's refusal to create a sliding scale of First Amendment protection calibrated to this Court's perception of the worth of a communication's content, and despite our unanimous agreement that the Carlin monologue is protected speech, a majority of the Court nevertheless finds that, on the facts of this case, the FCC is not constitutionally barred from imposing sanctions on Pacifica for its airing of the Carlin monologue. This majority apparently believes that the FCC's disapproval of Pacifica's afternoon broadcast of Carlin's "Dirty Words" recording is a permissible time, place, and manner regulation. . . . Both the opinion of my Brother STEVENS and the opinion of my Brother POWELL rely principally on two factors in reaching this conclusion: (1) the capacity of a radio broadcast to intrude into the unwilling listener's home, and (2) the presence of children in the listening audience. Dispassionate analysis, removed from individual notions as to what is proper and what is not, starkly reveals that these justifications, whether individually or together, simply do not support even the professedly moderate degree of governmental homogenization of radio communications — if, indeed, such homogenization can ever be moderate given the pre-eminent status of the right of free speech in our constitutional scheme — that the Court today permits.

A

Without question, the privacy interests of an individual in his home are substantial and deserving of significant protection. In finding these interests sufficient to justify the content regulation of protected speech, however, the Court commits two errors. First, it misconceives the nature of the privacy interests involved where an individual voluntarily chooses to admit radio communications into his home. Second, it ignores the constitutionally protected interests of both those who wish to transmit and those who desire to receive broadcasts that many — including the FCC and this Court — might find offensive. . . .

Whatever the minimal discomfort suffered by a listener who inadvertently tunes into a program he finds offensive during the brief interval before he can simply extend his arm and switch stations or flick the "off" button, it is surely worth the candle to preserve the broadcaster's right to send, and the right of those interested to receive, a message entitled to full First Amendment protection. . . .

The Court's balance, of necessity, fails to accord proper weight to the interests of listeners who wish to hear broadcasts the FCC deems offensive. It permits majoritarian tastes completely to preclude a protected message from entering the homes of a receptive, unoffended minority. No decision of this Court supports such a result. Where the individuals comprising the offended majority may freely choose to reject the material being offered, we have never found their privacy interests of such moment to warrant the suppression of speech on privacy grounds. . . .

B

Most parents will undoubtedly find understandable as well as commendable the Court's sympathy with the FCC's desire to prevent offensive broadcasts from reaching the ears of unsupervised children. Unfortunately, the facial appeal of this justification for radio censorship masks its constitutional insufficiency. Although the government unquestionably has a special interest in the well-being of children and consequently "can adopt more stringent controls on communicative materials available to youths than on those available to adults," . . . the Court has accounted for this societal interest by adopting a "variable obscenity" standard that permits the prurient appeal of material available to children to be assessed in terms of the sexual interests of minors. . . .

Because the Carlin monologue is obviously not an erotic appeal to the prurient interests of children, the Court, for the first time, allows the government to prevent minors from gaining access to materials that are not obscene, and are therefore protected, as to them. It thus ignores our recent admonition that "[s]peech that is neither obscene as to youths nor subject to some other legitimate proscription cannot be suppressed solely to protect the young from ideas or images that a legislative body thinks unsuitable for them.". . .

In concluding that the presence of children in the listening audience provides an adequate basis for the FCC to impose sanctions for Pacifica's broadcast of the Carlin monologue, the opinions of my Brother POWELL . . . and my Brother STEVENS, . . . both stress the time-honored right of a parent to raise his child as he sees fit — a right this Court has consistently been vigilant to protect. . . . Yet this principle supports a result directly contrary to that reached by the Court . . . that parents, *not* the government, have the right to make certain decisions regarding the upbringing of their children. As surprising as it may be to individual Members of this Court, some parents may actually find Mr. Carlin's unabashed attitude towards the seven "dirty words" healthy, and deem it desirable to expose their children to the manner in which Mr. Carlin defuses the taboo surrounding the words. Such parents may constitute a minority of the American public, but the absence of great numbers willing to exercise the right to raise their children in this fashion does not alter the right's nature or its existence. Only the Court's regrettable decision does that.

C

As demonstrated above, neither of the factors relied on by both the opinion of my Brother POWELL and the opinion of my Brother STEVENS — the intrusive nature of radio and the presence of children in the listening audience — can, when taken on its own terms, support the FCC's disapproval of the Carlin monologue. These two asserted justifications are further plagued by a common failing: the lack of principled limits on their use as a basis for FCC censorship. No such limits come readily to mind, and neither of the opinions comprising the Court serve to clarify the extent to which the FCC may assert the privacy and children-in-the-audience rationales as justification for expunging from the airways protected communications the Commission finds offensive. Taken to their logical extreme, these rationales would support the cleansing of public radio of any "four-letter words" whatsoever, regardless of their context. The rationales could justify the banning from radio of a myriad of literary works, novels, poems, and plays by the likes of Shakespeare, Joyce, Hemingway, Ben Jonson, Henry Fielding, Robert Burns, and Chaucer; they could support the suppression of a good deal of political speech, such as the Nixon tapes; and they could even provide the basis for imposing sanctions for the broadcast of certain portions of the Bible.

In order to dispel the spectre of the possibility of so unpalatable a degree of censorship, and to defuse Pacifica's overbreadth challenge, the FCC insists that it desires only the authority to reprimand a broadcaster on facts analogous to those present in this case, which it describes as involving "broadcasting for nearly twelve minutes a record which repeated over and over words which depict sexual or excretory activities and organs in a manner patently offensive by its community's contemporary standards in the early afternoon when children were in the audience.". . . The opinions of both my Brother POWELL and my Brother STEVENS take the FCC at its word, and consequently do no more than permit the Commission to censor the afternoon broadcast of the "sort of verbal shock treatment," . . . , involved here. To insure that the FCC's regulation of protected speech does not exceed these bounds, my Brother POWELL is content to rely upon the judgment of the Commission while my Brother STEVENS deems it prudent to rely on this Court's ability accurately to assess the worth of various kinds of speech. For my own part, even accepting that this case is limited to its facts, I would place the responsibility and the right to weed worthless and offensive communications from the public airways where it belongs and where, until today, it resided: in a public free to choose those communications worthy of its attention from a marketplace unsullied by the censor's hand.

II

The absence of any hesitancy in the opinions of my Brothers POWELL and STEVENS to approve the FCC's censorship of the Carlin monologue on the basis of two demonstrably inadequate grounds is a function of their perception that the decision will result in little, if any, curtailment of communicative exchanges protected by the First Amendment. Although the extent to which the Court stands ready to countenance FCC censorship of protected speech is unclear from today's decision, I find the reasoning by which my Brethren conclude that the FCC censorship they approve will not significantly infringe on First Amendment values both disingenuous as to reality and wrong as a matter of law. . . .

. . .Both those desiring to receive Carlin's message over the radio and those wishing to send it to them are prevented from doing so by the Commission's actions. Although, as my Brethren point out, Carlin's message may be disseminated or received by other means, this is of little consolation to those broadcasters and listeners who, for a host of reasons, not least among them financial, do not have access to, or cannot take advantage of, these other means.

Moreover, it is doubtful that even those frustrated listeners in a position to follow my Brother POWELL'S gratuitous advice and attend one of Carlin's performances or purchase one of his records would receive precisely the same message Pacifica's radio station sent its audience. The airways are capable not only of carrying a message, but also of transforming it. A satirist's monologue may be most potent when delivered to a live audience; yet the choice whether this will in fact be the manner in which the message is delivered and received is one the First Amendment prohibits the government from making.

III

It is quite evident that I find the Court's attempt to unstitch the warp and woof of First Amendment law in an effort to reshape its fabric to cover the patently wrong result the Court reaches in this case dangerous as well as lamentable. Yet there runs throughout the opinions of my Brothers POWELL and STEVENS another vein I find equally disturbing: a depressing inability to appreciate that in our land of cultural pluralism, there are many who think, act, and talk differently from the Members of this Court, and who do not share their fragile sensibilities. It is only an acute ethnocentric myopia that enables the Court to approve the censorship of communications solely because of the words they contain. . . .

Today's decision will thus have its greatest impact on broadcasters desiring to reach, and listening audiences comprised of, persons who do not share the Court's view as to which words or expressions are acceptable and who, for a variety of reasons, including a conscious desire to flout majoritarian conventions, express themselves using words that may be regarded as offensive by those from different socio-economic backgrounds. In this context, the Court's decision may be seen for what, in the broader perspective, it really is: another of the dominant culture's inevitable efforts to force those groups who do not share its mores to conform to its way of thinking, acting, and speaking. . . .

MR. JUSTICE STEWART, with whom MR. JUSTICE BRENNAN,

MR. JUSTICE WHITE, and MR. JUSTICE MARSHALL join, dissenting.

The Court today recognizes the wise admonition that we should "avoid the unnecessary decision of [constitutional] issues.". . . But it disregards one important application of this salutary principle — the need to construe an Act of Congress so as to avoid, if possible, passing upon its constitutionality. It is apparent that the constitutional questions raised by the order of the Commission in this case are substantial. Before deciding them, we should be certain that it is necessary to do so.

The statute pursuant to which the Commission acted, 18 U.S.C. § 1464, makes it a federal offense to utter "any obscene, indecent, or profane language by means of radio communication." The Commission held, and the Court today agrees, that "indecent" is a broader concept than "obscene" . . . because language can be "indecent" although it has social, political or artistic value and lacks prurient appeal. . . . But this construction of § 1464 while perhaps plausible, is by no means compelled. To the contrary, I think that "indecent" should properly be read as meaning no more than "obscene." Since the Carlin monologue concededly was not "obscene," I believe that the Commission lacked statutory authority to ban it. Under this construction of the statute, it is unnecessary to address the difficult and important issue of the Commission's constitutional power to prohibit speech that would be constitutionally protected outside the context of electronic broadcasting.

I would hold . . . that Congress intended, by using the word "indecent" in § 1464, to prohibit nothing more than obscene speech. Under that reading of the statute, the Commission's order in this case was not authorized, and on that basis I would affirm the judgment of the Court of Appeals.

BONN ECONOMIC SUMMIT
July 17, 1978

U.S. pledges to curtail oil imports, German promises to spur economic growth, Japanese commitments to reduce a trade surplus and a joint agreement to combat international air piracy were the major results of the fourth annual economic summit in Bonn, West Germany, July 16 and 17. Attended by leaders of seven of the world's richest nations — the United States, West Germany, Japan, Great Britain, France, Canada and Italy — the conference concluded on a note of international economic cooperation, with modest pledges to promote growth without stimulating inflation.

The meeting took place in an atmosphere of concern over the weak dollar, inflation, and President Carter's energy program which was mired in Congress. In addition, the Bonn summit was held at a time when none of the leaders was in position of political strength at home, with the possible exception of French President Valery Giscard d'Estaing who had just survived a recent election test. President Carter, German Chancellor Helmut Schmidt and Japanese Prime Minister Takeo Fukuda faced eroding support from their own parties and legislative bodies. British Prime Minister James Callaghan and Canadian Prime Minister Pierre Elliott Trudeau both anticipated difficult election contests in the fall. The Italian political situation was chronically changeable.

These political exigencies, coupled with the gravity of the economic agenda, prompted one observer to describe the summit as "doomed to success" because none of the leaders could afford its failure. The specific and limited agreements emerging from Bonn reflected each leader's recognition that problems once considered merely domestic must be thought of as common to all the industrialized countries. The "comprehen-

533

sive strategy" adopted at the conference was seen by several observers as more useful and reasonable than the far-reaching but unrealized goals established at previous economic summits.

The joint declaration issued at the conclusion of the meeting said, "We are dealing with long-term problems, which will only yield to sustained efforts. This [comprehensive] strategy is a coherent whole, whose parts are interdependent. To this strategy, each of our countries can contribute; from it, each can benefit."

Economic Growth

The centerpiece of the summit was a joint commitment by Chancellor Schmidt and Prime Minister Fukuda to take steps to strengthen their nations' economies. In a general statement of intent, Schmidt pledged his country to "strengthening demand . . . and a higher rate of growth" through unspecified proposals which would add to the German economy about $6 billion in expansionary programs. To reduce Japan's large trade surplus, Fukuda set detailed goals to assure increased growth rates by accelerating domestic demand and voluntarily controlling the sale of exports.

Prior to the Bonn meeting, Germany and Japan had been far more concerned with the problem of inflation than with economic expansion. Neither country had attained the growth goals established in the economic summit which had been held in London in 1976. Arriving at the conference with a record of controlling inflation and maintaining low unemployment, Schmidt in particular was reluctant to endanger a stable — and politically advantageous — economic situation in his own country with unrealistic promises. Schmidt's pledge to accelerate growth was greeted by cautious expressions of relief from other leaders, who had feared more serious economic problems if Germany declined a partnership with the United States in encouraging economic expansion.

The agreements — and indeed, the summit — hinged on the leadership of Schmidt and Carter, whose relationship had been characterized as cordial but cool. Schmidt conditioned his promise to strengthen the German economy on Carter's agreement to move strongly to conserve energy and reduce inflation. That compromise, as well as visibly warmer relations between the two men, was crucial to the consensus on the "limited goals" established at Bonn.

Carter's Pledge

Recognizing the United States' "particular responsibility in the energy field," President Carter agreed to establish mechanisms by the end of 1978 that would result in oil import savings of 2.5 million barrels a day by 1985. He also promised to maintain an oil reserve of one million barrels and to step up coal production by two-thirds.

However, Carter did not specify how he intended to meet his oil price target nor what steps he would take if Congress did not pass his controversial energy package, including the import equalization tax. The president's goals were seen as achievable though through either his extension of existing price controls or executive imposition of fees on oil imports.

Terrorism Statement

The leaders also reached agreement on the international problem of terrorism and air piracy. In a separate statement, they pledged to "intensify . . . joint efforts to combat international terrorism" through cessation of flights to and from countries which refused to extradite or prosecute air hijackers.

President Carter, in remarks made at the conclusion of the conference, called the statement "worth the entire preparation and conduct of the summit" and underscored the need for other nations to "join with us in this substantive and . . . adequate move to prevent air hijacking in the future."

Following are the texts of the Bonn Economic Summit Conference joint declaration and the joint statement on international terrorism issued July 17, 1978:

SUMMIT JOINT DECLARATION

The Heads of State and Government of Canada, the Federal Republic of Germany, France, Italy, Japan, the United Kingdom of Great Britain and Northern Ireland and the United States of America met in Bonn on 16th and 17th July 1978. The European Community was represented by the President of the European Council and by the President of the European Commission for discussion of matters within the Community's competence.

1. We agreed on a comprehensive strategy covering growth, employment and inflation, international monetary policy, energy, trade and other issues of particular interest to developing countries. We must create more jobs and fight inflation, strengthen international trading, reduce payments imbalances, and achieve greater stability in exchange markets. We are dealing with long-term problems, which will only yield to sustained efforts. This strategy is a coherent whole, whose parts are interdependent. To this strategy, each of our countries can contribute; from it, each can benefit.

Growth, Employment and Inflation

2. We are concerned, above all, about world-wide unemployment because it has been at too high a level for many years, because it hits hardest at the most vulnerable sections of the population, because its economic

cost is high and its human cost higher still. We will act, through measures to assure growth and develop needed skills, to increase employment.

In doing this, we will build on the progress that has already been made in the fight against inflation and will seek new successes in that fight. But we need an improvement in growth where that can be achieved without rekindling inflation in order to reduce extremes of balance of payments surpluses and deficits. This will reduce destabilizing exchange rate movements. Improved growth will help to reduce protectionist pressures. We need it also to encourage the flow of private investment, on which economic progress depends; we will seek to reduce impediments to private investment, both domestically and internationally. Better growth is needed to ensure that the free world is able to develop to meet the expectations of its citizens and the aspirations of the developing countries.

3. A program of different actions by countries that face different conditions is needed to assure steady non-inflationary growth. In countries whose balance of payments situation and inflation rate does not impose special restrictions, this requires a faster rise in domestic demand. In countries where rising prices and costs are creating strong pressures, this means taking new measures against inflation.

—Canada reaffirmed its intention, within the limits permitted by the need to contain and reduce inflation, to achieve higher growth of employment and an increase in output of up to 5%.

—As a contribution to avert the worldwide disturbances of economic equilibrium the German Delegation has indicated that by the end of August it will propose to the legislative bodies additional and quantitatively substantial measures up to 1 p.c. of GNP, designed to achieve a significant strengthening of demand and a higher rate of growth. The order of magnitude will take account of the absorptive capacity of the capital market and the need to avoid inflationary pressures.

—The President of the French Republic has indicated that, while pursuing its policy of reduction of the rate of inflation, the French Government agrees, as a contribution to the common effort, to increase by an amount of about 0.5% of G.N.P. the deficit of the budget of the State for the year 1978.

—The Italian Prime Minister has indicated that the Government undertakes to raise the rate of economic growth in 1979 by 1.5 percentage points with respect to 1978. It plans to achieve this goal by cutting public current expenditure while stimulating investments with the aim of increasing employment in a non-inflationary context.

—The Prime Minister of Japan has referred to the fact that his Government is striving for the attainment of the real growth target for fiscal year 1978, which is about 1.5 percentage points higher than the performance of the previous year, mainly through the expansion of domestic demand. He has further expressed his determination to achieve the said target by taking appropriate measures as necessary. In August or September he will determine whether additional measures are needed.

—The United Kingdom, having achieved a major reduction in the rate of inflation and improvement in the balance of payments has recently given a fiscal stimulus equivalent to rather over 1% of G.N.P. The Government intends to continue the fight against inflation so as to improve still further the prospects for growth and employment.

—The President of the United States stated that reducing inflation is essential to maintaining a healthy U.S. economy and has therefore become the top priority of U.S. economic policy. He identified the major actions that have been taken and are being taken to counter inflation in the United States: Tax cuts originally proposed for fiscal year 1979 have now been reduced by $10 billion; government expenditure projections for 1978 and 1979 have been reduced; a very tight budget is being prepared for 1980; steps are being taken to reduce the direct contribution by government regulations or restrictions to rising costs and prices, and a voluntary programme has been undertaken to achieve deceleration of wages and prices.

—The meeting took note with satisfaction that the common approach of the European Community already agreed at Bremen [state of northern West Germany, consisting of the cities of Bremen and Bremerhaven] would reinforce the effectiveness of this programme.

Energy

4. In spite of some improvement, the present energy situation remains unsatisfactory. Much more needs to be done.

5. We are committed to reduce our dependence on imported oil.

6. We note that the European Community has already agreed at Bremen the following objectives for 1985: to reduce the Community's dependence on imported energy to 50 percent, to limit net oil imports, and to reduce to 0.8 the ratio between the rate of increase in energy consumption and the rate of increase in gross domestic product.

7. Recognizing its particular responsibility in the energy field, the United States will reduce its dependence on imported oil. The U.S. will have in place by the end of the year a comprehensive policy framework within which this effort can be urgently carried forward. By year end, measures will be in effect that will result in oil import savings of approximately 2.5 million barrels per day by 1985. In order to achieve these goals, the U.S. will establish a strategic oil reserve of 1 billion barrels; it will increase coal production by two-thirds; it will maintain the ratio between growth in gross national product and growth in energy demand at or below 0.8; and its oil consumption will grow more slowly than energy consumption. The volume of oil imported in 1978 and 1979 should be less than that imported in 1977. In order to discourage excessive consumption of oil and to encourage the movement toward coal, the U.S. remains determined that the prices paid for oil in the U.S. shall be raised to the world level by the end of 1980.

8. We hope that the oil exporting countries will continue to contribute to a stable world energy situation.

9. Looking to the longer term, our countries will review their national energy programs with a view to speeding them up. General energy targets can serve as useful measures of the progress achieved.

10. Private and public investment to produce energy and to use it more efficiently within the industrial world should be increased. This can contribute significantly to economic growth.

11. The further development of nuclear energy is indispensable, and the slippage in the execution of nuclear power programmes must be reversed. To promote the peaceful use of nuclear energy and reduce the risk of nuclear proliferation, the nuclear fuel cycle studies initiated at the London Summit should be pursued. The President of the United States and the Prime Minister of Canada have expressed their firm intention to continue as reliable suppliers of nuclear fuel within the framework of effective safeguards. The President intends to use the full powers of his office to prevent any interruption of enriched uranium supply and to ensure that existing agreements will be respected. The Prime Minister intends that there shall be no interruption of Canadian uranium supply on the basis of effective safeguards.

12. Coal should play an increasing important role in the long term.

13. Joint or co-ordinated energy research and development should be carried out to hasten the development of new, including renewable, energy sources and the more efficient use of existing sources.

14. In energy development, the environment and human safety of the population must be safeguarded with greatest care.

15. To help developing countries, we will intensify our national development assistance programs in the energy field and we will develop a co-ordinated effort to bring into use renewable energy technologies and to elaborate the details within one year. We suggest that the OECD [Organization for Economic Cooperation and Development] will provide the medium for cooperation with other countries.

16. We stress the need for improvement and co-ordination of assistance for developing countries in the energy field. We suggest that the World Bank explore ways in which its activities in this field can be made increasingly responsive to the needs of the developing countries, and to examine whether new approaches, particularly to financing hydrocarbon exploration, would be useful.

Trade

17. We reaffirm our determination to expand international trade one of the driving forces for more sustained and balanced economic growth. Through our joint efforts we will maintain and strengthen the open international trade system. We appreciate and support the progress as set forth in the Framework of Understanding on the Tokyo Round of Multilateral Trade Negotiations made public in Geneva, July 13th, 1978, even though within this Framework of understanding some difficult and important issues remain unresolved.

The successful conclusion of these negotiations, the biggest yet held, would mean not just a major trade liberalisation programme extending over the 1980s but the most important progress yet made in the GATT [General Agreement on Tariffs and Trade] in relation to non-tariff measures. Thus the GATT rules would be brought more closely into line with the requirements of the next decade — particularly in relation to safeguards — in ways which could avoid any weakening of the world trading system and be of benefit to all trading countries developed and developing alike. A substantially higher degree of equity and discipline in the international trading system would be achieved by the creation of new mechanisms in many fields for consultation and dispute settlement. Uniform application of the GATT rules is vital and we shall move in that direction as soon as possible.

In all areas of the negotiations the Summit countries look forward to working even more closely with the developing countries. We seek to ensure for all participants a sound and balanced result, which adequately takes into account the needs of developing countries, for example, through special and differential treatment, and which bring about their greater participation in the benefits and obligations of the world trading system.

At last year's Downing Street Summit we rejected a protectionist course for world trade. We agreed to give a new impetus to the Tokyo Round. Our negotiators have fulfilled that commitment. Today we charge them, in co-operation with the other participants, to resolve the outstanding issues and to conclude successfully the detailed negotiations by December 15, 1978.

18. We note with satisfaction the renewal of the pledge to maintain an open market oriented economic system made by the OECD Council of Ministers last month. Today's world economic problems cannot be solved by relapsing into open or concealed protectionism.

19. We welcome the statement on positive adjustment policy made by the OECD Ministers. There must be a readiness over time, to accept and facilitate structural change. Measures to prevent such change perpetuate economic inefficiency, place the burden of structural change on trading partners and inhibit the integration of developing countries into the world economy. We are determined in our industrial, social, structural and regional policy initiatives to help sectors in difficulties, without interfering with international competition and trade flows.

20. We note the need for countries with large current accounts deficits to increase exports and for countries with large current accounts surpluses to facilitate increases in imports. In this context, the United States is firmly committed to improve its export performance and is examining measures to this end. The Prime Minister of Japan has stated that he wishes to work for the increase of imports through the expansion of domestic demand and various efforts to facilitate imports. Furthermore, he has stated that in order to cope with the immediate situation of unusual surplus, the Government of Japan is taking a temporary and extraordinary step of calling for moderation in exports with the aim of keeping the total volume of Japan's exports for the fiscal year of 1978 at or below the level of fiscal year 1977.

21. We underline our willingness to increase our co-operation in the field of foreign private investment flows among industrialized countries and between them and developing countries. We will intensify work for further agreements in the OECD and elsewhere.

22. In the context of expanding world economic activity, we recognize the requirement for bettter access to our countries' markets for the products of the developing countries. At the same time we look to increasing readiness on the part of the more advanced developing countries to open their markets to imports.

Relations with Developing Countries

23. Success in our efforts to strengthen our countries' economies will benefit the developing countries, and their economic progress will benefit us. This calls for joint action on the basis of shared responsibility.

24. In the years ahead the developing countries, particularly those most in need, can count on us for an increased flow of financial assistance and other resources for their development. The Prime Minister of Japan has stated that he will strive to double Japan's official development assistance in three years.

We deeply regret the failure of the COMECON [Council for Mutual Economic Assistance] countries to take their due share in the financial assistance to developing countries and invite them once more to do so.

25. The poorer developing countries require increased concessional aid. We support the soft loan funds of the World Bank and the three regional development banks. We pledge our governments to support replenishment of the International Development Association on a scale that would permit its lending to rise annually in real terms.

26. As regards the more advanced developing countries, we renew our pledge to support replenishment of the multilateral development banks' resources, on the scale needed to meet the growing needs for loans on commercial terms. We will encourage governmental and private co-financing of development projects with these banks.

The co-operation of the developing countries in creating a good investment climate and adequate protection for foreign investment is required if foreign private investment is to play its effective role in generating economic growth and in stimulating the transfer of technology.

We also refer to our efforts with respect to developing countries in the field of energy as outlined in paragraph 15 and 16.

27. We agreed to pursue actively the negotiations on a Common Fund to a successful conclusion and to continue our efforts to conclude individual commodity agreements and to complete studies of various ways of stabilizing export earnings.

International Monetary Policy

28. The erratic fluctuations of the exchange markets in recent months have had a damaging effect on confidence, investment and growth through-

out the world. Essentially, exchange rate stability can only be achieved by attacking the fundamental problems which have contributed to the present large balance of payments deficits and surpluses. Implementation of the policies described above in the framework of a concerted program will help to bring about a better pattern of world payments balances and lead to greater stability in international exchange markets. This stability will in turn improve confidence and the environment for sustained economic growth.

29. Although exchange rates need to respond to changes in underlying economic and financial conditions among nations, our monetary authorities will continue to intervene to the extent necessary to counter disorderly conditions in the exchange markets. They will maintain extensive consultation to enhance these efforts' effectiveness. We will support surveillance by the International Monetary Fund, to promote effective functioning of the international monetary system.

30. The representatives of the European Community informed the meeting of the decision of the European Council at Bremen on 6/7 July to consider a scheme for a closer monetary co-operation. The meeting welcomed the report and noted that the Community would keep the other participants informed.

Conclusion

31. It has been our combined purpose to attack the fundamental economic problems that our countries confront.

The measures on which we have agreed are mutually reinforcing. Their total effect should thus be more than the sum of their parts. We will now seek parliamentary and public support for these measures.

We cannot hope to achieve our purposes alone. We shall work closely together with other countries and within the appropriate international institutions; those among us whose countries are members of the European Community intend to make their efforts within this framework.

We have instructed our representatives to convene by the end of 1978 in order to review this Declaration.

We also intend to have a similar meeting among ourselves at an appropriate time next year.

INTERNATIONAL TERRORISM STATEMENT

The heads of state and government, concerned about terrorism and the taking of hostages, declare that their governments will intensify their joint efforts to combat international terrorism.

To this end, in cases where a country refuses extradition or prosecution of those who have hijacked an aircraft and/or do not return such aircraft, the heads of state and government are jointly resolved that their governments should take immediate action to cease all flights to that country.

At the same time, their governments will initiate action to halt all incoming flights from that country or from any country by the airlines of the country concerned. The heads of state and government urge other governments to join them in this commitment.

CARTER 'PRINCIPLES'
FOR NATIONAL HEALTH PLAN
July 29, 1978

President Carter moved on July 29 toward redeeming one of the most far-reaching and difficult promises of his campaign: to press for enactment of a comprehensive national health insurance system. The president directed Joseph A. Califano Jr., secretary of health, education and welfare (HEW), to develop a national health insurance plan to serve as the basis for legislation which he said he would submit to Congress in 1979. In a letter to Califano, Carter listed 10 principles to which a tentative plan must conform.

Although specifics were lacking in Carter's statement of principles, it did offer a broad outline of the president's thinking on national health insurance. In his directive to Califano, Carter said that the plan should assure that all Americans have comprehensive health care coverage with freedom to choose their own doctors and hospitals. He said that the plan should include "aggressive" cost-containment measures and should be designed to strengthen competitive forces within the health care system. It should be "phased in," the president said, as the economy permitted, be financed by multiple sources and include a "significant role" for the private insurance industry.

Risks for Carter

The launching of a comprehensive national health plan posed for President Carter especially difficult economic and political problems. Carter's own timetable for drafting legislative recommendations repeatedly slipped as his advisers considered the risks that were involved. On the one hand, the realities of the economy, inflation, burgeoning health-care costs and slower economic growth, seemed, in the view of a number of administration officials, to argue against the adoption of any new and vastly expensive program. On the other hand, Sen. Edward M. Kennedy, D-Mass., the most vocal advocate of a comprehensive health plan in Congress, and his allies in organized labor were prodding Carter to make good on his campaign promise. Kennedy contended that Congress must act on the health insurance issue "within two years" or wait "another generation."

In edging toward the drafting of his own proposal, Carter also faced the possibility that the constituency for a comprehensive plan was far smaller than previously thought. If that were true, it was because the growth of third-party payments (by insurance companies and the federal government), the existence of federal programs for the aged and the poor and the availability of health benefits for many workers tended to weaken the demand for a comprehensive system. Or perhaps there was a "hidden constituency" in the so-called working poor, Americans with wages too low to permit them to buy private insurance but too high to allow them to participate in Medicaid.

Background

Although by 1978 most of the other industrialized Western nations had comprehensive health insurance systems, the United States for more than 40 years had repeatedly turned away from enactment of such a program. In 1935 President Franklin D. Roosevelt decided not to link a national health system with social security. He reportedly had been persuaded by a physician's argument that a program could not work without the "good will" of the American Medical Association (AMA).

The AMA continued to make its strength in opposition to what it called "socialized medicine" felt until enactment in the Kennedy and Johnson administrations of Medicare and Medicaid, representing health care for the aged and the poor. President Nixon in 1971 outlined a plan that relied heavily on the private insurance industry. But the following year Nixon sent his proposal back to the Department of HEW and it never again came to life. President Ford briefly supported enactment of a national health insurance plan but by 1975 was saying that poor economic conditions ruled out new federal programs.

Meanwhile, numerous health insurance plans originated in Congress. During the 95th Congress four major plans were introduced. For the most part, with minor updating, they duplicated bills of earlier years. By 1978 Sen. Kennedy had become the leading congressional advocate of universal, publicly financed health care. He was chairman of the Health Subcommittee of the Senate Committee on Human Resources.

Kennedy-Labor Plan

In the drafting of Carter's statement of principles some attempt had been made to accommodate the position of Sen. Kennedy and his allies in the AFL-CIO and United Auto Workers (UAW). Indeed, last-minute objections from Kennedy and labor had delayed by one day the announcement of the president's directive to Califano. But, in the end, the president's 10 principles did not go far enough for Kennedy and the AFL-CIO and UAW. On the afternoon of July 28, the day before Carter was to announce his directive to Califano, Kennedy called a press conference to denounce what he called the president's "failure of leadership" on the health issue.

Kennedy and his allies in labor contended that the only way to control health care costs was to control all sources of payment through a unitary national system. They argued that Carter's proposal to trigger in full coverage over a period of years would cause the program to "self-destruct" before it could be fully implemented. They also criticized Carter's suggestion that "many consumers . . . share a moderate portion of the cost of their care."

On Oct. 9, Kennedy and the AFL-CIO and UAW launched a new drive for their plan. They said that "once cost-containment takes effect, the nation will pay less for health care under national health insurance" than if nothing at all were done. The Kennedy-labor forces set up a timetable which envisioned enactment of their plan in 1979, most of the benefits in place two years later and a complete program in place by 1985.

> *Following is the text of President Carter's July 29, 1979, letter directing Joseph A. Califano Jr., secretary of health, education and welfare, to draft a national health insurance plan:*

July 29, 1978

Presidential Directive/DPS-3
TO: The Secretary of Health,
**   Education and Welfare**
SUBJECT: National Health Plan

I have consistently expressed my support for the goal of a universal, comprehensive national health plan to contain skyrocketing health costs and to provide all Americans with coverage for basic health services and with protection from catastrophic expenses.

Such a plan would be the cornerstone of a broader national health policy designed to improve the health of Americans by reducing environmental and occupational hazards and encouraging health enhancing personal behavior, as well as by improving the effectiveness of our medical care system.

The current health care system has significant defects which must be remedied:

● The health care system is highly inflationary. Spending in the health care industry — the nation's third largest industry — has been rising at an annual rate of 12% with little improvement in the health of Americans. These expenditures cannot be successfully contained under current health delivery and financing methods, which produce unnecessary hospitalization, over-reliance on expensive technology and inadequate preventive care.

● At least 20 million Americans have no health insurance.

● Another 65 million Americans face potential bankruptcy because they lack insurance protecting them against catastrophic medical expenses.

● Health resources are unevenly distributed across the country resulting in significant gaps in vital medical services for many residents of rural and inner city areas.

In pursuing the goal of a comprehensive national health plan, I also wish to draw on the strengths of the American health care system:

● American health care professionals and hospitals are among the finest in the world and deliver dedicated, high quality medical care.

● A growing number of Americans have private health insurance. American business increasingly is paying for health coverage for its employees.

● Various government programs have provided an opportunity for millions of elderly, poor and geographically isolated Americans to obtain quality health care.

In past months you and other members of my Administration have been exploring the most effective means of fulfilling my commitment to a comprehensive national health plan. You have considered a broad range of options. However, before I submit legislation to the Congress, I want to be certain that the plan is consistent with our efforts to control inflation in the health care sector and the general economy. Before you send me final recommendations for a national health plan, you should analyze the issues of cost control and health system reform in greater depth. The American people would not accept, and I will not propose, any health care plan which is inflationary.

At the same time, the American people must recognize that if we fail to act, health expenditures will continue to soar. In 1977, health expenditures were $162 billion; they are expected to reach $320 billion by 1983. A comprehensive national health plan will provide a critical opportunity to mount a national effort to bring the system under control.

I am directing you to address these concerns as you proceed to develop in greater detail a national health plan for the American people. The plan must improve the health care system, and combat inflation by controlling spiralling health care costs. To achieve these objectives, the plan, when fully implemented, should conform to the following principles.

1. The plan should assure that all Americans have comprehensive health care coverage, including protection against catastrophic medical expenses.

2. The plan should make quality health care available to all Americans. It should seek to eliminate those aspects of the current health system that often cause the poor to receive substandard care.

3. The plan should assure that all Americans have freedom of choice in the selection of physicians, hospitals, and health delivery systems.

4. The plan must support our efforts to control inflation in the economy by reducing unnecessary health care spending. The plan should include aggressive cost containment measures and should also strengthen competitive forces in the health care sector.

5. The plan should be designed so that additional public and private expenditures for improved health benefits and coverage will be substantially offset by savings from greater efficiency in the health care system.

6. The plan will involve no additional federal spending until FY 1983, because of tight fiscal constraints and the need for careful planning and implementation. Thereafter, the plan should be phased in gradually. As the plan moves from phase to phase, consideration should be given to such factors as the economic and administrative experience under prior phases. The experience of other government programs, in which expenditures far exceeded initial projections, must not be repeated.

The plan should be financed through multiple sources, including government funding and contributions from employers and employees. Careful consideration should be given to the other demands on government budgets, the existing tax burdens on the American people, and the ability of many consumers to share a moderate portion of the cost of their care.

8. The plan should include a significant role for the private insurance industry, with appropriate government regulation.

9. The plan should provide resources and develop payment methods to promote such major reforms in delivering health care services as substantially increasing the availability of ambulatory and preventive services, attracting personnel to underserved rural and urban areas, and encouraging the use of prepaid health plans.

10. The plan should assure consumer representation throughout its operation.

I am directing you to develop a tentative plan as soon as possible which embodies these principles and which will serve as the basis for in-depth consultation with the Congress, State and local officials, interest groups, and consumer representatives. You should then provide me with detailed recommendations so that I can make final decisions on the legislation I will submit to the Congress next year. To respond fully to my economic and budgetary concerns, you should develop alternative methods for phased implementation of the plan.

Jimmy Carter

U.S.-SOVIET STRATEGIC ARMS LIMITATION TALKS

July; December 14, 1978

Early in his administration, President Carter had signaled his intention to move "quickly and aggressively" to conclude new strategic arms limitation talks (SALT) with the Soviet Union. But conclusion of a new SALT agreement proved to be elusive. Despite two years of negotiations and agreement on a basic framework for a treaty, last-minute Soviet reservations in December 1978 delayed completion of a SALT II agreement. In the meantime, the United States and Soviet Union had pledged to adhere to the terms of the 1972 SALT I accord. (1972 SALT treaty, Historic Documents of 1972, p. 431; 1977 negotiations, Historic Documents of 1977, p. 243)

In addition to the military and political complexity of the negotiations themselves, there appeared to be a number of reasons for the slow progress. One of them was the growing opposition in Congress to several proposed weapons limitations being negotiated. Another was the harsh Soviet reaction to Carter's human rights stand and his outspoken support for Russian dissidents — although the president maintained that his stand should have no effect on the SALT negotiations.

The president, however, issued a warning to the Soviet Union in a strong speech on defense at Wake Forest University March 17. "We are not looking for a one-sided advantage, but before I sign a SALT agreement on behalf of the United States, I will make sure that it preserves the strategic balance, that we can independently verify Soviet compliance and that we will be at least as strong relative to the Soviet Union as we would be without an agreement," Carter said. (Wake Forest speech, p. 223)

Issues Involved

The difficulty facing the arms negotiators was whether it was possible to reduce strategic arms levels in the face of strong opposition in both countries to the destruction of existing weapons and curbs on the development of new ones. Other problems included the asymmetries of the two systems and the need for reliable methods of verification (although the Carter administration reported in February 1978 that the USSR had adhered, albeit narrowly, to the terms of the 1972 pact and said that the United States could monitor any SALT agreement satisfactorily).

The agreements toward which the two countries were reportedly moving were modest in terms of slowing the military programs of each side. The basic numerical limits of the agreement would be contained in a treaty that would run until 1985. The treaty would set limits on launchers rather than on missiles because any limit on missiles would be too hard to verify. Restrictions on mobile missiles and cruise missiles would be contained in a separate protocol that would run only through 1981.

As the campaign against the emerging SALT II agreements intensified in late 1977 and 1978, opponents laid heavy emphasis on the argument that the administration was not taking measures to protect the U.S. intercontinental ballistic missiles (ICBMs). Leading SALT opponents had urged development of a new U.S. mobile missile (called M-X) that would nullify improvements in Soviet missile accuracy by deception. However, SALT supporters who fought the mobile missile project argued that it undermined a basic premise of the SALT negotiations — that the number of nuclear launchers on either side be readily apparent.

Another recurrent theme in the opponents' campaign to defeat SALT II was the treaties' potential adverse effect on the U.S. cruise missile program. A third theme in the anti-SALT campaign was the exclusion of the Soviet Backfire bomber from the weapons ceilings to be set by the treaty. The administration countered that the United States retained the right under the SALT agreements to build new bombers similar to the Backfire.

Supporters, Critics Speak Out

Early in December, the Carter administration made a concerted effort to rally support for a SALT II accord. In a speech Dec. 20, the president's national security adviser Zbigniew Brzezinski insisted that the treaty would "maintain the stability of the strategic balance between the United States and the Soviet Union" rather than jeopardizing it. Brzezinski said the administration "will never constrain our ability to meet our national security needs" and that the need to modernize U.S. ICBMs would not be overlooked.

Brzezinski's remarks were in part a response to a Dec. 5 speech by Paul Nitze, former deputy secretary of defense (1967-69), and a leading member *of the Committee on the Present Danger, a private citizens' organization formed in November 1976 to lobby against what its members perceived as a weakening of national security. Nitze charged that the United States would be vulnerable by the early 1980s to a Soviet first strike.*

The committee's arguments against the proposed SALT II treaty were contained in a Dec. 14 paper prepared by Nitze entitled "Considerations Bearing on the Merits of an Agreement." The report criticized the administration for failing to ensure that a U.S. system for protecting its land-based missiles would be permitted by the terms of a new SALT treaty.

An administration assessment of the arms limitations talks and arguments in support of the agreements tentatively reached had been contained in a State Department special report on the SALT negotiations issued in July. "The choice the United States now faces is between a good agreement protecting and enhancing our national security, and no agreement at all," the report stated. "It is against this standard that what has been achieved at SALT should be measured — not against some ideal agreement that as a practical matter, given the relationship between the two countries, cannot be concluded at this time."

> *Following is the text of the Department of State special report on "The Strategic Arms Limitation Talks" released in July 1978, and the Dec. 14, 1978, report on "Considerations Bearing on the Merits of an Agreement" prepared by Paul H. Nitze for the Committee on the Present Danger:*

STATE DEPARTMENT REPORT
THE STRATEGIC ARMS LIMITATION TALKS
Introduction

The Strategic Arms Limitation Talks (SALT) are continuing negotiations between the United States and the Soviet Union on the subject of limiting and reducing strategic nuclear weapons. From the perspective of the security interests of the United States and its allies, there are two fundamental objectives in pursuing the SALT process with the Soviets. First, any SALT agreement must permit the United States to maintain strategic forces which are at least equal to those of the Soviet Union. Second, it should maintain and, if possible, enhance the stability of the strategic balance, thereby reducing the possibility of nuclear war. In addition, an agreement should support and give substance to a political relationship with the Soviets which reduces tension and controls competition and, hence, expenditures for strategic forces.

Since the negotiations for a SALT TWO agreement are still under way, the discussion of this agreement in this paper is necessarily preliminary and tentative pending completion and review of the final agreement.

STRATEGIC FORCE EQUIVALENCE

Any SALT agreement must be consistent with the security interests of the United States and its allies. This means that any agreement must: (1) leave the United States and its allies at least as strong relative to the Soviet Union as they would be in the absence of an agreement, (2) insure that the Soviet Union does not obtain an advantage in strategic forces, and (3) permit the United States necessary flexibility to respond to Soviet challenges not constrained by the agreement. This objective is achieved by insisting that the limitations in the agreement provide for equality in the strategic force levels, and for "essential equivalence" in the strategic forces, of the two sides.

STABILITY

At present the strategic balance is relatively stable. This means that the forces on both sides are sufficiently large, diverse, and survivable that neither side has an incentive to strike first in a crisis situation. However, new weapons which threaten the other side's forces can undermine the stability of the balance, and could give one side the illusion of a temporary advantage. A goal of SALT, therefore, is to restrain arms improvements which threaten the balance, and to encourage actions on each side to preserve stability.

POLITICAL RELATIONSHIP

In addition to these fundamental objectives concerning the security of the United States and its allies, the SALT process has an important role in U.S./Soviet and overall East/West relations. The negotiations themselves have laid the foundation for an improved political relationship with the Soviets and have set some boundaries to the military competition between the sides. Besides protecting and preserving our essential strategic and security interests in an agreement, the ongoing SALT process contributes to these important policy objectives.

WHAT SALT CANNOT DO

To fully understand SALT and the SALT process, it is necessary to understand its limitations, and recognize what SALT cannot realistically be expected to accomplish. In recent years there have been many unrealistic expectations for SALT. It has sometimes been seen as a way of sharply reducing defense spending, or as a means by which all threats against U.S. forces could be eliminated. Some have hoped that SALT would usher in a new era of U.S./Soviet cooperation and do away with military rivalry across the board.

Such hopes are legitimate, but given the nature of the relationship between the United States and the Soviet Union, they are unlikely to be quickly realized. Neither side is ready at this point for far-reaching disarmament schemes. SALT agreements, while they can reduce strategic forces on both sides and restrict the introduction of new strategic weapons, cannot substitute for prudent U.S. efforts to maintain forces which meet our strategic objectives.

The choice the United States now faces is between a good agreement protecting and enhancing our national security, and no agreement at all. It is against this standard that what has been achieved at SALT should be measured — not against some ideal agreement that as a practical matter, given the relationship between the two countries, cannot be concluded at this time.

U.S. Strategic Policies

Underlying U.S. strategic force planning is the concept of deterrence. By maintaining powerful strategic nuclear forces, the United States seeks to dissuade any adversary from a nuclear attack by threatening catastrophic retaliation in response. Because of its unique role in the collective security system of the West, the United States also has a special obligation to deter nuclear attacks on its allies and friends. In addition, the United States and its allies must be free from any coercion and intimidation that could result from perceptions of an overall imbalance or particular asymmetries in nuclear forces. The strategic forces, in conjunction with U.S. and allied theater nuclear and conventional forces, also have a role to play in deterring non-nuclear attacks — particularly large-scale conventional attacks on NATO.

The Soviets also maintain powerful strategic forces. Since deterrence of nuclear war is the most fundamental defense objective of the United States, Soviet perceptions must be taken into account. What the United States considers sufficient forces to deter attack and preserve security may not be perceived the same way by the Soviet Union. To avoid any misunderstanding, the United States insists upon essential equivalence, real and perceived, with the Soviet Union in strategic nuclear forces.

Essential equivalence means insuring that:

—The U.S. posture is in fact, and is seen as, at least equal to the strategic nuclear forces of the Soviet Union.
—Any advantages in certain force characteristics enjoyed by the Soviets are offset by U.S. advantages in other characteristics.

These conditions exist today, and, as cited above, one of the U.S. objectives in SALT TWO is to maintain them in the future. Unless one side or the other allows a major imbalance to develop, or makes serious miscalculations, a condition of mutual deterrence is likely to prevail in the future.

It is also U.S. policy to maintain strategic forces of sufficient strength, diversity, and survivability that the Soviets will not have an incentive to strike first in a crisis. Consistent with this view, it is our policy not to deploy forces which so threaten the Soviet retaliatory capability that they would have an incentive to strike first to avoid losing their deterrent force. However, this policy is contingent on similar Soviet restraint. In sum, it is the U.S. view the strategic balance should be so stable that it cannot be upset in a crisis and will not be undermined over the longer term by strategic force modernization and improvement.

U.S. STRATEGIC FORCES

U.S. strategic offensive forces consist of three main elements: land-based intercontinental ballistic missiles (ICBMs), submarine-launched ballistic missiles (SLBMs), and heavy bombers.

The U.S. ICBM force is composed of 54 Titan and 1,000 Minuteman missiles, the latter consisting of 550 Minuteman III's with up to 3 multiple independently targetable re-entry vehicles (MIRVs) per missile, and 450 Minuteman II's with single warheads. Presently only the ICBM combines the yield, accuracy, range, short flight time, and high readiness which permit it to be effective against the entire range of Soviet targets. ICBMs have the additional advantages of secure and timely command, control, and communications, and have operating costs which are markedly lower than those of bombers or SLBMs.

It is widely recognized that both U.S. and Soviet ICBM forces are becoming increasingly vulnerable to attack, as technological advances produce improvements in missile accuracy. This situation would develop with or without SALT limitations. The MX mobile ICBM program is being pursued as a hedge against growing ICBM vulnerability.

The second element of the U.S. strategic triad is the submarine-launched ballistic missile. The U.S. SLBM force is composed of 41 nuclear submarines equipped with a total of 160 Polaris and 496 Poseidon missiles. Each of the Poseidon missiles can carry up to 14 MIRV warheads. In the near future, 12 Poseidon submarines will be fitted with the longer range Trident I missile (the first deployment of these missiles is planned for October 1979). Deployment of these missiles will enhance survivability by increasing the available in-range ocean operating area for the submarines. Eventually the Poseidon submarines will be replaced by a fleet of much larger Trident submarines, each carrying 24 missiles. The Trident program is designed to provide a survivable sea-based strategic deterrent through the 1990's.

The SLBM force is the most survivable element of the triad both now and in the foreseeable future. Because nuclear submarines (SSBNs) are deployed in vast ocean areas, SLBMs are highly survivable in a first strike attack and thus assure retaliatory capability. The nature of the SLBM force contributes to crisis stability, since the existence of a survivable, at-sea ballistic missile force decreases Soviet incentives to plan attacks on the United States or U.S. ICBMs since such attacks would not eliminate our ability to retaliate. This survivability also insures a secure reserve force which can threaten the postwar recovery of any power, thereby preventing nuclear blackmail.

The third element of the U.S. strategic force triad consists of the heavy bombers, the B-52's. There are currently 420 operational B-52's, about 100 of which are kept on alert at high readiness. These aircraft can be airborne within a matter of minutes after warning of an impending attack. The substantial payload capacity of the bomber force adds significantly to the total retaliatory power of U.S. strategic forces, and each bomber can carry a variety of missiles and bombs, providing flexibility for attacking Soviet targets. B-52's initially took their place in U.S. strategic forces over two decades ago. Successive programs for modernizing these aircraft, such as the integration of modern electronic equipment, have insured their continued effectiveness.

Unlike ballistic missiles, bombers must penetrate defenses which are not constrained by SALT. Consequently, we will have to plan to equip our strategic bombers with improved weapons to counter improvements in Soviet air defenses. There remains the possibility of negotiating air defense limitations in SALT THREE.

Although the B-52 is still a highly effective penetrating bomber, the United States has studied various alternatives for modernizing the heavy bomber leg of the strategic triad. After extensive review of all alternatives, the decision has been made to retain the B-52's, and to equip a portion of them with modern air-launched cruise missiles to penetrate the Soviet air defenses we project for the 1980's.

SOVIET STRATEGIC FORCES

Over the past decade, Soviet strategic offensive forces have expanded substantially. They have placed great emphasis on land-based missiles in their strategic planning, and now have approximately 1,400 ICBMs. The fourth generation of Soviet ICBMs, each capable of carrying several MIRV warheads, is now being deployed. These missiles include the SS-17, SS-18, and SS-19. The SS-18's are replacing older SS-9 missiles, and SS-17's and SS-19's are replacements for the older SS-11.

Although the Soviet SS-18 missile has attracted much public attention because of its great size and throw weight, the smaller SS-19, because of its combination of high accuracy and yield, is also a highly capable ICBM. Both the SS-19 and SS-17 are substantially larger than the U.S. Minuteman ICBMs. In addition, the Soviets have completed development of a fourth new ICBM, the SS-16, designed to be launched from either fixed or mobile launchers.

The Soviets now have a fifth generation of ICBMs under development. Flight testing of some of these new missiles could begin at any time.

The Soviet SLBM force continues to expand and is being modernized. The Soviets now have about 950 SLBMs. In addition to the older YANKEE-class submarines, built in the late 1960's and early 1970's, the

Soviets are now deploying newer DELTA-class submarines. The DELTA I's and II's carry the SS-N-8, a single warhead missile. Both the SS-N-8 and SS-N-18, a very long-range missile capable of carrying MIRVs, will permit the Soviets to cover targets in the U.S. from patrol areas in the Arctic and the waters of the North Pacific.

The Soviet heavy bomber force is currently less than half the size of that of the United States. Some of these bombers are equipped with shorter range cruise missiles. The U.S. expects a prototype of a new modern heavy bomber to be tested in the future. If deployed, this aircraft would replace the aging Bears and Bisons. The Backfire bomber, a new plane whose characteristics and capabilities lie between those of current heavy and medium bombers, is being deployed with medium bomber and naval aviation units at a steady pace. Although the Soviets are probably developing longer range, air-launched cruise missiles (ALCMs), there is no evidence that they could develop within the next five years ALCMs as small and sophisticated as those under development in the United States.

The Salt Process

Those agencies which have a direct interest in national security affairs — the Department of Defense, the Joint Chiefs of Staff, the State Department, the Central Intelligence Agency, and the Arms Control and Disarmament Agency — are involved in advising the President on SALT matters.

The Special Coordination Committee [SCC] of the National Security Council meets regularly to discuss SALT issues and U.S. policy for SALT. This Committee is chaired by the Assistant to the President for National Security Affairs, and includes the Secretaries of State and Defense, the Director of the Arms Control and Disarmament Agency, the Chairman of the Joint Chiefs of Staff, and the Director of Central Intelligence. The U.S. position in the SALT negotiations is reviewed and approved by the President and implemented by the U.S. SALT Delegation in Geneva. Day-to-day guidance for the Delegation is provided by the SALT Backstopping Committee. The SALT Working Group provides in-depth analysis of SALT issues for the Special Coordination Committee. All of these groups include representatives from all of the agencies on the SCC.

SALT ONE

The Strategic Arms Limitation Talks, which formally opened in 1969, are a continuing process. The SALT ONE negotiations, the first step in this process, began in November 1969, and culminated in May 1972, with the signing of the ABM Treaty and the Interim Agreement on Strategic Offensive Arms.

The ABM Treaty

The ABM Treaty sharply limits Anti-Ballistic Missile systems. Each side is permitted only one site for ABM deployment,[1] with tight restrictions on the ABM launchers and radars at that site. The ABM Treaty has prevented an expensive, potentially dangerous, and unnecessary competition in ABM deployment. In addition, deployment of ABM systems on one side would have stimulated expansion of the offensive forces on the other to offset it. The ABM Treaty therefore represents a major step in reducing competition in strategic arms and enhancing stability.

Interim Agreement

The Interim Agreement on Strategic Offensive Arms froze the number of fixed ICBM and SLBM launchers then operational or under construction for five years. During the five-year freeze, the sides would negotiate on a more comprehensive agreement of longer duration. The United States had 1,054 ICBMs and 656 SLBM launchers; the Soviet Union, 1,607 ICBMs and 740 SLBMs. The sides were permitted to expand their SLBM forces up to 710 and 950, respectively, but only by dismantling an equal number of older ICBM launchers or launchers of SLBMs on older submarines. Although under the terms of the agreement the Soviet Union was permitted a numerical advantage in ICBM and SLBM launchers, significant U.S. advantages in heavy bombers and MIRVs compensated for the disparity in missile numbers. These two agreements were approved by wide margins in the U.S. Congress. When the agreements were approved, however, the Congress also passed a resolution urging the President to assure that future SALT agreements provide for U.S. levels which are not inferior to those permitted to the Soviets.

Compliance with the SALT ONE Agreements

The SALT ONE agreements specifically state that each Party shall use national technical means of verification to insure compliance with the agreements. The agreements also ban interference with national technical means of verification and deliberate concealment which impedes verification of compliance with the provisions of the agreements.

The SALT ONE agreements created a special standing body to deal with questions of implementation of agreements which might be concluded, including questions which might arise concerning compliance. This reflected early recognition and agreement that such matters would require special attention.

Since the conclusion of the 1972 SALT agreements, procedures have been established within the U.S. Government for monitoring Soviet performance and for dealing with matters related to compliance. If analysis of intelligence information indicates that there could be a question

---

[1] Under the Treaty, each side was permitted two ABM sites, but this number was subsequently reduced to one site for each side by the ABM Protocol of July 1974.

concerning compliance, the President reviews the available information and decides whether to raise the issue with the Soviet Union.

The United States and the Soviet Union have both raised questions in the Standing Consultative Commission regarding the activities of the other side under the provisions of the ABM Treaty and the Interim Agreement. Raising a topic for discussion does not necessarily constitute a charge of violation of the agreements, but rather can indicate that a side desires clarification of ambiguous activity which has given rise to concern. In each case we have raised, the activity in question has ceased or additional information has allayed our concern. We continue to monitor Soviet actions related to these matters to insure that those of concern do not recur, and that our intelligence analysis of these issues remains valid.

The United States and the Soviet Union have had over five years' experience handling issues in the Standing Consultative Commission. This experience has proven that the SCC is a viable forum for discussion of matters related to compliance with SALT agreements. . . .

SALT TWO

In accordance with Article VII of the Interim Agreement in which the sides committed themselves to continue active negotiations on strategic offensive arms, the SALT TWO negotiations began in November 1972. The primary goal of SALT TWO was to replace the Interim Agreement with a long-term comprehensive treaty providing broad limits on strategic offensive weapon systems. The principal U.S. objectives as the SALT TWO negotiations began were to provide for equal numbers of strategic nuclear delivery vehicles for the sides, to begin the process of reduction of these delivery vehicles, and to impose restraints on qualitative developments which could threaten future stability.

Early discussion between the sides focused on the weapon systems to be included, factors involved in providing for equality in numbers of strategic nuclear delivery vehicles taking into account the important differences between the forces of the two sides, bans on new systems, qualitative limits, and a Soviet proposal to include U.S. forward-based systems. The positions of the sides differed widely on many of these issues.

A major breakthrough occurred at the Vladivostok meeting in November 1974, between President Ford and General Secretary [Leonid I] Brezhnev. At this meeting, the sides agreed to a basic framework for the SALT TWO agreement. Basic elements of the Aide-Memoire, which codified this agreement, included:

—2,400 equal aggregate limit on strategic nuclear delivery vehicles (ICBMs, SLBMs, and heavy bombers) of the sides;

—1,320 equal aggregate limit on MIRV systems;

—ban on construction of new fixed ICBM launchers and on conversion of older fixed launchers from light to heavy ICBMs;

—limits on deployment of new types of strategic offensive arms; and

—important elements of the Interim Agreement (e.g., relating to verification) would be incorporated in the new agreement.

In addition, the Aide-Memoire stated that the duration of the new agreement would be through 1985.

In early 1975, the delegations in Geneva resumed negotiations, working toward an agreement based on this general framework. It was during this time that a Joint Draft Text was first prepared and many limitations were agreed. During the negotiations, however, it became clear that there was fundamental disagreement between the two sides on two major issues: whether cruise missiles were to be limited, and whether the new Soviet bomber known as Backfire would be considered a heavy bomber and therefore counted in the 2,400 aggregate. While there was disagreement on other issues such as MIRV verification provisions, restrictions on new systems, and missile throw weight ceilings, progress was made in these areas. However, no progress was made on the issues of cruise missiles or Backfire.

Description of Elements

When the new Administration took office in 1977, renewed emphasis was placed on the Strategic Arms Limitation Talks. A comprehensive interagency review of SALT was undertaken. Building on the work of the previous Administration, particularly the Vladivostok accord and the subsequent agreement on many issues in Geneva, the United States made a comprehensive proposal which was presented to the Soviets by Secretary of State Vance in March 1977. This proposal would have added significant reductions and qualitative constraints to the ceilings which were agreed to at Vladivostok. At the same time, the United States also presented an alternative proposal for a SALT TWO agreement based on the framework agreed to at Vladivostok, with the Backfire and cruise missile issues deferred until SALT THREE.

Both proposals were rejected by the Soviets as inconsistent with their understanding of the Vladivostok accord.

In subsequent negotiations, the sides agreed on a general framework for SALT TWO which accommodated both the Soviet desire to retain the Vladivostok framework for an agreement, and the U.S. desire for more comprehensive limitations in SALT TWO. The agreement would consist of three parts:

—A Treaty which would be in force through 1985 based on the Vladivostok accord;

—A Protocol of about three years' duration which would cover certain issues such as cruise missile constraints, mobile ICBM limits, and qualitative constraints on ICBMs, while deferring further negotiations on those issues to SALT THREE;

—A Joint Statement of Principles which would be an agreed set of guidelines for future negotiations.

Within this framework, negotiations to resolve the remaining differences have continued on several levels. President Carter, Secretary Vance, and Soviet Foreign Minister [Andrei A.] Gromyko met in Washington in September 1977. Secretary Vance returned to Moscow in April 1978, for further meetings with General Secretary Brezhnev and Foreign Minister Gromyko, and Minister Gromyko met again with President Carter and Secretary Vance in Washington in late May 1978. Significant progress toward completion of a SALT agreement has been made in these meetings. In addition, the SALT Delegation in Geneva has been in session nearly continuously since the 1974 Vladivostok meeting to work out agreed Treaty language on those issues where agreement in principle has been reached. The SALT TWO Treaty will provide for:

—an equal aggregate limit on the number of strategic nuclear delivery vehicles — ICBMs, SLBMs, heavy bombers, and ASBMs [air-to-surface ballistic missiles]. Initially this ceiling will be 2,400, as agreed at Vladivostok. The ceiling will subsequently be lowered to 2,250;
—an equal aggregate limit of 1,320 on the total number of MIRVed ballistic missiles and heavy bombers with long-range cruise missiles;
—a limit of 1,200 on the total number of MIRVed ballistic missiles;
—a limit of 820 on MIRVed ICBMs;
—a ban on construction of additional fixed ICBM launchers, and on any increase in the number of fixed heavy ICBM launchers;
—a ban on certain new types of strategic offensive systems such as ballistic missiles on surface ships;
—an agreement to exchange data on number of constrained weapons systems; and
—advance notification of certain ICBM test launches.

The Treaty will also include detailed definitions of limited systems, provisions to enhance verification, counting rules to facilitate verification of the MIRV limits, a ban on circumvention of the provisions of the agreement, and a provision outlining the duties of the SCC in connection with the SALT TWO Treaty. The duration of the Treaty will be through 1985.

The Protocol will place temporary limits on cruise missiles, mobile ICBMs, and new types of strategic ballistic missiles. We have proposed that the Protocol expire at the end of 1980. The Protocol will permit flight testing and deployment of cruise missiles with a range of up to 2,500 km, while banning the deployment of ground- and sea-launched cruise missiles with a range greater than 600 km. It will also ban deployment (but not development) of mobile ICBM launchers, and ban the testing and deployment of long-range, air-launched ballistic missiles. The sides are presently negotiating the restrictions which would be placed on the introduction of new types of ICBMs and SLBMs.

The limitations in the Protocol in no way prejudice the manner in which these systems will be dealt with in SALT THREE. Any future limits on the issues covered in the Protocol for the period after 1980 would require U.S. agreement and congressional approval.

The third element of the SALT TWO agreement is a Joint Statement of Principles and Guidelines for SALT THREE. The sides have agreed to pursue further reductions in the ceilings and further qualitative limitations on strategic systems as well as resolution of the issues covered by the Protocol. In addition, each side may bring up any other pertinent topic it wishes to discuss.

Effects of the Agreement

The SALT TWO agreement will require the Soviets to dismantle approximately 250-300 strategic offensive systems which are presently deployed. In addition, new Soviet strategic missiles and bombers could be deployed only as replacements for older systems. It will also place a ceiling on the deployment of Soviet MIRVed ICBMs.

The agreement would hold down the total number of Soviet warheads and the throw weight of their strategic forces to a level well below that which it is estimated they would have in the absence of an agreement. The agreement would also reduce our uncertainty concerning the nature of Soviet strategic forces in the 1980's, which would simplify the task of maintaining equivalence in strategic forces.

The agreement would have relatively smaller impact on U.S. forces. No existing U.S. forces would have to be dismantled. The agreement will require the United States to phase out older systems after the first six or seven Trident submarines are deployed. Research and development on a new U.S. mobile ICBM, the MX, can continue on schedule since testing of the MX missile and deployment of a mobile MX would not have begun in any case during the time that the Protocol would be in force. Other planned U.S. programs for modernizing the Minuteman ICBM force will be permitted under the agreement. Testing of long-range cruise missiles and their deployment on B-52's can go forward as planned. Deployment of the Trident submarine and missiles can proceed as planned.

Allied security will also be preserved and enhanced by the SALT TWO agreement. The U.S. has consulted closely with its NATO allies through-out the course of the negotiations, and has taken into account allied security concerns in its negotiating positions.

VERIFICATION

Verification is the process of determining, to the extent necessary to safeguard our national security, that the other side is complying with the SALT TWO agreement. The United States insists that SALT agreements be adequately verified. Verification is one of the most important consider-ations in strategic arms limitation, and has been the subject of intensive negotiations with the Soviets.

Present SALT agreements are verified by "national technical means" (NTM), that is, various technical intelligence techniques which operate outside the territory of the other side. Interference with NTM is prohibited, as are deliberate concealment measures which impede verification by these systems. The SALT agreements have therefore increased our confidence in our continuing ability to monitor Soviet forces compared to the situation that could otherwise exist. Soviet compliance with the ABM Treaty and the Interim Agreement has been closely monitored. As noted previously, the U.S.-Soviet Standing Consultative Commission, created by the SALT agreements, provides a mechanism for working out procedures to implement the agreements, and for clarification of the agreement.

The process of judging the adequacy of verification must take into account the capabilities of existing and future intelligence collection systems and the ability of the other side to evade detection if it should attempt to do so. Equally important is the U.S. ability to respond to Soviet cheating, should it occur. The U.S. technological base, our research and development programs, and the substantial capabilities of our strategic forces provide this hedge.

Since monitoring will always be subject to some degree of uncertainty, the United States must also assess the likelihood that the Soviets would cheat, taking into account the benefits that would accrue to them from such cheating, as well as the risks of their being detected. As a matter of prudence, therefore, the United States analyzes scenarios involving altered or covert Soviet practices that could adversely affect U.S. confidence in Soviet compliance. The following considerations are some that the Soviets must take into account before making a decision to cheat or not to cheat: (1) their uncertainty about overall U.S. capability to monitor and analyze their activities; (2) the potential U.S. reaction to discovered cheating; and (3) the possible strategic gains from cheating.

It must be stressed that the United States does not rely on trust, on Soviet intentions, or on political incentives for the Soviets to comply in assessing whether verification of a SALT agreement is adequate. Such judgments are based most heavily on U.S. monitoring capabilities, especially with regard to potentially significant Soviet noncompliance and on the U.S. ability to respond in a timely manner to possible Soviet cheating.

A primary U.S. objective for the SALT TWO agreement is that it be adequately verifiable. This judgment has to be based on an assessment of the verifiability of the individual provisions of the agreement and of the agreement as a whole. Every effort is being made to insure that, although the possibility of some undetected cheating will always exist, such cheating would not alter the strategic balance, and cheating on a scale large enough to alter the strategic balance would be discovered in time to make an appropriate response.

WITHOUT SALT

In judging the value of the SALT TWO agreement, it is important to look not only at what the agreement accomplishes but also at the situation that would exist in the absence of any agreement.

The U.S.S.R. already has deployed substantially more than 2,250 nuclear delivery vehicles and could deploy many more by the mid-1980's. Further, they could deploy substantially more MIRVed missiles than the 1,200 permitted by the agreement. Numbers of warheads and total missile throw weight would both be significantly greater. There would be no constraints on new missiles, and no constraints of any kind on Backfire.

The United States would not sit idle in the face of such a Soviet weapons buildup, but would do whatever is necessary to retain equivalent forces of its own. There would, however, be substantial costs involved, and the security of the United States at such higher force levels (with comparable high Soviet forces) would be no greater than it is today. Since neither side would allow the other to attain strategic superiority, failure in SALT would likely lead to another spiral in the strategic arms race, with the attendant threat to security which unconstrained expansion and improvement in strategic forces would bring.

It is difficult to predict all the negative political consequences of a failure in SALT. Given the fact, however, that SALT is seen by both sides as a barometer of the overall relationship between the two countries, a failure would also have serious consequences for the broader issues of East-West relations.

In sum, a failure in SALT would bring about increased political insecurity, no increase in military security, and the inherent instability of an unrestrained, and more costly, strategic arms competition.

Conclusion

The United States is under no illusion that progress in SALT can be easily achieved. The importance and complexity of the issues involved have meant a lengthy, difficult negotiating process. However, the progress which has been made is significant.

In the first stage of the SALT process, SALT ONE, the sides agreed to limit ABM systems to a very low level. Deployment of ABM systems would have added impetus to the strategic arms race as the sides attempted both to expand their own ABM systems and to build weapons capable of overcoming such strategic defenses on the other side. In SALT ONE, the sides also agreed to the first quantitative limits on strategic offensive arms, freezing the numbers of SLBM and ICBM launchers permitted each side.

Several significant steps in the process of limiting strategic offensive arms are being taken in SALT TWO. For the first time, the sides have agreed to equal aggregate limits on strategic delivery vehicles and certain subcategories of such vehicles such as MIRVed ballistic missiles. They have also agreed to impose qualitative, as well as quantitative, limits on their strategic offensive arsenals. The process of reduction in numbers of strategic offensive weapons will begin with the SALT TWO agreement as the Soviets dismantle systems to comply with the equal numerical limits imposed by the Treaty. SALT TWO will establish a framework for further reductions in the sides' strategic arsenals in future negotiations, and also for further qualitative restraints on weapons systems.

Fundamental differences in economic, social, and political structure define a basic adversary relationship between the United States and the Soviet Union. Nevertheless, the two sides share the common goal of reducing the risk of nuclear war. The SALT negotiations are an attempt to exploit this common interest and to maintain a stable strategic relationship despite our serious differences on other questions.

The ultimate test of each stage of SALT is whether the agreement reached represents a measurable advance in improving this country's security by maintaining equivalence in strategic forces, while at the same time taking steps to slow the arms race and curb the danger of nuclear war. The last four Presidents have judged SALT vital to our national security interest. An agreement that meets these stated SALT objectives will serve that interest and the interest of all mankind.

Perspectives on Selected Issues

BACKFIRE

The Soviets have developed a modern, swing-wing bomber which bears the NATO designation "Backfire." This aircraft, first observed in 1969, is now being operationally deployed. Its characteristics (e.g., length, weight, wingspan, range, and payload) fall between the characteristics generally attributed to existing heavy bombers and those of medium bombers (tactical aircraft and medium bombers on both sides are not covered by the SALT ceilings).

The Backfire can reach a significant number of targets in the United States on one-way, high-altitude unrefueled missions. However, close observation over a period of years indicates that this bomber is currently being deployed for use in a theater or naval strike role and is a replacement for older Soviet medium bombers.

In this regard, it should be noted that the United States has a number of aircraft which, when deployed in the theater, are capable of striking targets in the Soviet Union. The United States has refused to include these aircraft in SALT because they are theater systems and the Soviet forces which they face are not covered by the SALT limits.

The United States has taken the position that Backfire can be excluded from the aggregate if the Soviets undertake commitments which will inhibit Backfire from assuming an intercontinental role in the future, as well as impose limits on its production rate. These commitments would have the same status as the agreement, binding the Soviets to the commitments contained therein. It should be noted that there are no assurances that will insure that Backfire would not be used against the United States in time of conflict. Instead, they are designed to inhibit Backfire from being given an operational intercontinental role and to limit its overall strategic potential.

MINUTEMAN SURVIVABILITY

With or without a SALT TWO agreement, the U.S. Minuteman force will become increasingly vulnerable to attack by Soviet ICBMs. This situation is the result of the rapid advance in Soviet missile technology, particularly in the area of missile accuracy.

The possibility of eventual vulnerability was foreseen at the time the United States originally deployed a fixed ICBM force. This potential vulnerability of fixed ICBMs is one major reason why U.S. strategic planners determined that deployment of a triad of strategic nuclear delivery systems, each having its own advantages and each posing unique defensive problems for the other side, would be the best way for the United States to maintain a viable strategic deterrent. In recognition of the Minuteman vulnerability problem, the United States is examining the possibility of U.S. deployment of a mobile and more survivable basing mode for ICBMs under the MX program. This program, which will not be affected by the SALT TWO agreement, provides the United States with a response to the increased threat to Minuteman.

In spite of the very real problems associated with maintenance of a survivable land-based missile force, the issue must be viewed in perspective. The uncertainties faced by the Soviets in planning an attack on the Minuteman force are substantial and in themselves may have a deterring effect. Doubts the Soviets might have about the reliability and accuracy of their own missiles, about their ability to avoid fratricide effects (i.e., the possibility that detonation of one RV [re-entry vehicle] may degrade the effectiveness of subsequent RVs), about the precise hardness of U.S. missile silos, or about whether the United States would launch its own ICBMs once the United States verified that a massive Soviet ICBM attack was under way, contribute to these uncertainties. In any case, the Minuteman missiles form only a portion of U.S. retaliatory forces. Any Soviet planner must realize that even a successful attack on Minuteman would leave the Soviet Union exposed to massive response by U.S. SLBMs and heavy bombers.

HEAVY MISSILES AND THROW WEIGHT

The Soviet Union currently has approximately 300 heavy missiles (SS-9's and SS-18's) and an aggregate ICBM throw weight total which significantly exceeds that of U.S. ICBMs. The U.S.S.R. has consistently emphasized land-based missile forces in its strategic planning, and its ICBM throw weight advantage is in part a reflection of that emphasis. The United States, on the other hand, has deliberately chosen to develop smaller, more accurate land-based ICBMs and to diversify its strategic nuclear delivery forces, dividing its capability in a more balanced way among ICBMs, SLBMs, and heavy bombers. (The United States leads the Soviets in total SLBM throw weight and in bomber payload.) Any advantage in one indicator of strategic potential must be put in the perspective of the overall picture in order not to give a misleading impression of the strategic balance. The Soviet advantage in ICBM throw weight is currently compensated by significant U.S. advantages in numbers of nuclear warheads, missile accuracy, numbers and capability of heavy bombers, and other factors.

The United States intends to address the issue of further limitations on heavy missiles in SALT THREE.

GROUND-LAUNCHED AND
SEA-LAUNCHED CRUISE MISSILES
(GLCMs AND SLCMs)

A provision banning deployment of ground- and sea-launched cruise missiles with ranges over 600 km is included in the Protocol. Under current development programs, U.S. ground- and sea-launched land-attack cruise missiles would not be available for deployment until the early 1980s. Under the terms of the Protocol, the United States will be permitted to continue its development and flight test programs for these systems. The United States has preserved the option of deploying such systems in the post-Protocol period, if we decide in consultation with our NATO allies that it would be to our advantage to do so. We have also resisted Soviet pressure for a ban on transfer of cruise missile and other sophisticated technology.

ALCM/HEAVY BOMBER LIMITS

In order to maintain the effectiveness of the heavy bomber leg of the strategic triad, the United States will modernize its bomber force by modifying some B-52's to carry long-range, air-launched cruise missiles (ALCMs). Several alternatives were examined before this option was chosen, including acquiring the new B-1 bomber. It was determined that keeping the penetrating B-52 force, supplemented with standoff ALCMs, provided a cost-effective means of upgrading the bomber force to enable it to penetrate the defenses it may face in the 1980's.

Although the cruise missile is a weapon which has existed since World War II, recent U.S. technological advances in the areas of miniaturization and guidance systems have made the modern cruise missile a particularly effective means of enhancing the effectiveness of the heavy bomber force. Because of its small size and its ability to fly close to the ground, the modern cruise missile presents a difficult target for Soviet air defense systems.

U.S. defense planners have determined that a combination of standoff and penetration bombers will offer the targeting flexibility and greater payload of manned aircraft plus the cruise missile's ability to saturate defenses, and at the same time insure that U.S. bomber force improvements can stay ahead of improvements in Soviet air defense.

Under the terms of the SALT TWO Treaty, the total number of ALCM-carrying heavy bombers and MIRV missiles may not exceed 1,320. Cruise missiles on heavy bombers would be limited to ranges up to 2,500 km for the period of the Protocol. Such a range would permit coverage of most of the Soviet Union with cruise missiles launched outside Soviet air defenses, and will be adequate against Soviet air defenses projected for the early 1980's. To aid verification of SALT provisions regarding ALCMs, the sides have agreed that ALCM-carrying aircraft will be distinguishable from non-ALCM-carrying aircraft.

NITZE REPORT

CONSIDERATIONS BEARING
ON THE MERITS OF AN AGREEMENT
Such as that Foreshadowed by the SALT II
Negotiating Positions of the Sides in Mid-November
and Currently Projected U.S. and
USSR Defense Programs

1. U.S. SALT II OBJECTIVES AND THE CONSTRAINTS WITHIN WHICH THOSE OBJECTIVES HAVE HAD TO BE SOUGHT

The SALT II negotiations began six years ago. The U.S. objective was a treaty of indefinite duration, limiting offensive nuclear forces, to match the treaty limiting ABM defenses which had just been ratified. It was intended that the SALT II treaty should provide equal limitations on the two sides such that essential equivalence in offensive nuclear capabilities would be assured and such that "crisis stability" could and would be maintained. "Crisis stability" was the phrase used to describe a situation in which neither side could hope to gain in relative capabilities from initiating the use of nuclear weapons in a crisis. It was hoped that, if these two objectives had been met, a foundation would have been laid for a reduction in the resources both sides would consider necessary to devote to their offensive nuclear armaments.

It was recognized that there were four constraining considerations which must be taken into account in achieving the primary U.S. objectives. One constraint was that the limitations strategically important to the U.S. should be verifiable. The second was that the legitimate interests of our allies must be taken into account and the terms of the agreement reasonably acceptable to them. The third constraint was that the limitations be such that it would be economically and politically practicable for the United States to deploy those permitted forces necessary to maintain essential equivalence and crisis stability. The fourth was that the terms of an agreement be negotiable; that is, be acceptable to the Soviet side and also be ratifiable by the Congress.

Early in the SALT II negotiations it was evident that there were potential conflicts among these objectives and constraints, and that difficult choices would have to be made in finding an optimum solution. One such conflict was between the objective of maintaining crisis stability and the constraint of verifiability. It had long been recognized that limiting the number and quality of missiles was much more important than limiting the number of launchers. But it would require cooperative measures to monitor the production and storage of missiles; satellite sensors would be inadequate. The Soviets refused to agree to cooperative measures. ICBM silos, however, could be photographed from satellites, and counted and their size estimated. It was also recognized that it was more important to limit the aggregate throw-weight of a force than the number and size of its launchers. This proved to be impossible to negotiate. Verifiable and negotiable controls over missile accuracy also proved to be unattainable. The basic and primary currency of the negotiations thus became limits on the number of launchers, not limits on missiles or their characteristics. This has proven to be the wrong currency.

During the course of the six years of the SALT II negotiation, the originally formulated three U.S. primary objectives and the first three of the constraints have been progressively compromised so as to accommodate one aspect of the fourth constraint — that the terms of the agreements be acceptable to the Soviet side, thereby facilitating their negotiability. At the same time, the U.S. side has been inhibited in publicizing Soviet recalcitrance in the negotiations because of the other aspect of the fourth constraint — that the agreements be ratifiable by the Congress.

The first casualty among our original objectives was that of achieving a treaty of indefinite duration. That objective was given up in the summer of 1974 in order to announce a negotiating breakthrough at the Moscow conference which otherwise would have been without result. Each negotiating "breakthrough" since the Moscow conference has involved a further retreat from our original objectives.

What we have gained from these concessions has been a series of relatively unimportant adjustments in what otherwise would have been the Soviet program for deployments over the next six years, in part, balanced by even less significant adjustments in our programs for future deployments. In essence, most of the negotiating process has been one of trading marginal adjustments to their large strategic program versus marginal adjustments to our much smaller one.

The following sections deal with the principal considerations involved in arriving at a judgment on the merits of the agreements as they appear to be emerging from that process and from the differential strategic nuclear programs of the two sides.

2. THE ICBM BALANCE TO BE EXPECTED BY 1985

a. The MIRVed ICBM Balance

This component of the overall balance is of particular significance. It is likely that if deterrence fails, this component, because of its power and accuracy, its short time of flight, the greater reliability of its command and control, and its known location, would be the key element in an initial strike and any initial counterforce response. This exchange could well determine the military outcome of the war.

(1) The U.S. has closed down the MINUTEMAN III production line and has delayed the initial operating capability (IOC) date of a follow-on missile to 1986 or beyond. Therefore, there is essentially no possibility of the U.S. having any deployed MIRVed ICBM launchers by the expiration date of the Treaty in 1985 other than the 550 MINUTEMAN III silos currently deployed. The accuracy of the MINUTEMAN III has recently been significantly upgraded and it is planned to substitute MARK-12A warheads (with approximately double the yield) for the MARK-12 warheads currently deployed on the MINUTEMAN III. No other significant changes in MINUTEMAN III are now planned. The useful payload of the MINUTEMAN III is approximately 2,200 pounds. The maximum number of reentry vehicles on the MINUTEMAN III is three RVs. The aggregate useful payload (throw-weight) of the U.S. MIRVed ICBM force in 1985 will therefore not exceed $500 \times 2,200$ which equals approximately a million and a quarter pounds. The aggregate number of MIRVed ICBM warheads in the U.S. force will not exceed 550×3, which equal 1,650 RVs.

(2) The USSR is permitted by the proposed terms of the agreement to deploy in excess of 300 SS-18s and approximately 500 SS-19s and -17s. The SS-18s have a useful payload approximating 16,000 pounds, the SS-17s and -19s have a useful payload approximately 7 to 8,000 pounds respectively. The SS-18s have been flight tested with as many as ten RVs, the SS-17s four RVs, the SS-19s six RVs. It can therefore be anticipated that the aggregate throw-weight of the Soviet Union's MIRVed ICBM force will approximate eight to nine million pounds of throw-weight by 1985, and that the number of RVs deployed on those MIRVed missiles will approximate six thousand, each RV having a yield several times that of the U.S. RVs. There is no reason to believe that the accuracy of the Soviet MIRVed RVs by 1985 will be significantly less than that of the improved accuracy of the MINUTEMAN III RVs. The U.S. is developing its more radical accuracy improvement, the Advanced Inertial Reference System (AIRS), for incorporation in a new follow-on missile to be deployed after 1985.

(3) If current accuracy is no better than approximately a fifth of a mile, it would be difficult for them to eliminate more than 70 percent of our MINUTEMAN silos in an initial strike, assuming that they target two of their RVs on each silo. If their accuracy approximates fifteen hundredths of a mile, around 90 percent of our silos would be vulnerable to such a two-on-one attack. A two-on-one attack would require less than half of the MIRVed ICBM RVs they are expected to have available by 1985. When their accuracy approximates a tenth of a mile, around 90 percent of our silos will become vulnerable to an attack by a single RV against each silo, provided that additional RVs are programmed to substitute for missiles that fail during their launch phase.

(4) If we were to use all our MINUTEMEN III, taking account of their improved accuracy and the substitution of MARK-12A for MARK-12

RVs, it is unlikely we could destroy more than 65 percent of the Soviet ICBM silos.

b. The UnMIRVed ICBM Balance

The utility of large single RV unMIRVed ICBMs, which can have very high megatonnage and thus very high fallout potential, is largely as terror weapons to deter the other side from using its surviving deterrent in a second strike.

(1) Until 1985 or beyond the U.S. is expected to have 450 MINUTE-MAN II, each with a throw-weight of less than 2,000 pounds and carrying a single RV in the megaton range. These would give us approximately a million pounds of throw-weight and 550 megatons of yield in our unMIRVed MINUTEMAN ICBM force. In addition, we may choose to maintain the 54 TITAN missiles which were deployed prior to 1965. They have an aggregate yield of some 450 megatons.

(2) In coming down to the 2,250 limit, the Soviet side can be expected to retain at least 360 non-MIRVed ICBMs during the life of the Treaty. It now being agreed that each side will be allowed to test and deploy one new type of ICBM (MIRVed or non-MIRVed) during the period of the Treaty, it is likely that the Soviet side, having little need for a new MIRVed ICBM, will test and then deploy a new non-MIRVed ICBM with a throw-weight of approximately 8,000 pounds and a warhead yield of 15 to 20 megatons, and substitute it for approximately 360 of the currently deployed SS-11s. The aggregate throw-weight of such an unMIRVed ICBM force could be in excess of two and one-half million pounds, and its megatonnage approximately six thousand megatons.

3. THE SLBM BALANCE BY 1985

SLBM forces at-sea are particularly difficult to find and destroy. They can be expected to endure beyond the initial exchanges. They should, therefore, be prime candidates for being held back as strategic reserve forces to influence the latter phases of a war or influence the period of war termination and beyond. It is not expected that SLBMs will achieve high accuracy by 1985. The reliability of SLBM communications constitutes a continuing problem.

a. MIRVed SLBMs

The U.S. is scheduled to have the following MIRVed SLBMs by 1985:

- 21 POSEIDON boats, each with 16 missiles, each missile carrying eight to ten RVs, the yield of each RV being 40 kilotons;
- 10 POSEIDON boats, each "backfitted" with 16 TRI-DENT I missiles, each carrying approximately eight RVs, each missile with a substantially longer range (4,000 miles), and each RV with more than double the yield of the 40 kiloton POSEIDON RV;
- 10 TRIDENT boats, each with 24 TRIDENT I missiles.

It was thus expected that we would, by 1985, have 41 nuclear-propelled SLBM submarines with some 736 tubes and approximately 6,000 RVs. Some 60 percent of these might be at-sea at any given time, giving us some 3,600 RVs at-sea. Assuming a reliability rate of 80 percent, this amounts to approximately 2,900 at-sea reliable RVs, representing an aggregate yield of approximately 200 megatons. In the event of a crisis, it should be possible, in a number of days, to increase the at-sea force by some 25 percent. It now appears, however, that delays in the TRIDENT shipbuilding program make the above target virtually unattainable.

The Soviet side, if they deploy close to the full 820 MIRVed ICBM launchers permitted under the MIRVed ICBM limit, will be able to deploy close to 400 MIRVed SLBM launchers and still stay within the 1,200 limit on MIRVed missile launchers. It is expected that the new Soviet TYPHOON submarine will be significantly larger than the present Soviet SLBM submarines and will carry 20 to 24 missiles each with up to 14 RVs; their smaller MIRVed SLBMs, the SSN8s, are expected to have no more than half that number of MIRVs. The TYPHOON missile could have the throw-weight of the projected U.S. TRIDENT II missile, development of which has not yet been authorized. The TRIDENT II missile is planned to be approximately twice the size (volume) of the TRIDENT I missile, but not be deployed prior to 1985.

It is probable, nevertheless, that the U.S. will continue to have a lead in the number of MIRVed SLBM tubes and RVs into the 1985 time period. However, the accuracy and yield of the U.S. SLBM RVs are substantially less than that of our ICBMs. The U.S. SLBM force does not now, and is not expected by 1985 to, add significantly to our capability against Soviet hard targets, such as hardened silos.

b. UnMIRVed SLBMs

The U.S. is expected to phase out its unMIRVed POLARIS force by about 1985 and thus to have no unMIRVed SLBMs by that time.

The Soviet Union, on the other hand, can be expected to retain over 600 unMIRVed SLBM tubes. Some of these may carry MRVs as our POLARIS missiles do today. Such missiles may be useful as MIRVed missiles against small area targets that are not very hard, such as airfields.

4. THE BOMBER/CRUISE MISSILE BALANCE IN 1985

The essential characteristic of the bomber/cruise missile forces is that while — particularly on the U.S. side — they have great potential power, it is only that portion of the force that is on alert prior to the initial attack that can be expected to survive, and the bulk of even that portion of the force must be used within the initial eight hours of a nuclear war or it too runs the danger of being lost.

The B-1 issue was incorrectly stated by the administration to be a choice between relatively cheap cruise missiles and expensive B-1s. Cruise missiles have to be launched from some kind of survivable platform, preferably one that can endure in a nuclear war environment for more than a few hours. The Executive Branch's position is that this preferably should be an aircraft. Thus, one requires a bomber/cruise misile system consisting of bombers and tankers so based as to give a high probability of prelaunch survivability for those that are on alert, whose take-off is sufficiently rapid and which are so hardened against nuclear effects that it becomes difficult to barrage their escape routes; bombers that are able to penetrate close enough to the target to launch cruise missiles to destroy or suppress defenses; and cruise missiles able to penetrate area and terminal defenses and accurate enough to kill the targets they are aimed at. The cruise missile is thus only part of a multifaceted system. The bomber that launches it and the tankers that refuel the bombers are equally essential parts of the system. The system is greatly improved and the enemy's defensive problem greatly increased, if some of the bombers have the capability for rapid take-off, are hardened against radiation, are more confidently able to penetrate Soviet defenses and thus to launch SRAMs, other types of missiles, or gravity bombs, close to the target.

The B-1 program having been cancelled, the 1985 bomber/cruise missile balance depends critically on whether a Soviet barrier defense around the northern perimeter, and of the eastern and western flanks, of the Soviet Union against the B-52s is possible, upon the number of cruise missiles that will be able to penetrate new Soviet terminal defenses, upon the number of B-52s equipped with cruise missiles that we deploy, the prelaunch and escape survivability of our B-52s and their tankers, and the extent to which a portion of the bomber force can be reconstituted, after it is flushed on warning, so as to endure in a war environment protracted for more than a few hours.

Without limitations on air defense systems, including both forwardly deployed and area or terminal defenses, the effectiveness of U.S. cruise missiles may be degraded during the mid to late 1980s. Limitations on air defenses are not to be included as a part of the SALT II agreement and there is a question as to the Soviet's willingness even to discuss this issue as part of the SALT III negotiations.

The U.S. contemplates deploying some 120 to 150 aircraft equipped with intermediate range ALCMs. The majority of these aircraft are planned to be B-52s; however, some type of transport aircraft carrying a larger number of ALCMs than does a B-52 is also being considered. If an aircraft is equipped to carry more than an agreed maximum number of ALCMs per aircraft, it will be counted as being an appropriate multiple of one "heavy bomber" under the 1,320 limit.

As it now stands, if we maintain 550 MINUTEMAN III launchers, plus our 496 POSEIDON launch tubes, and were to deploy our planned 240 TRIDENT tubes, this would total 1,286 MIRVed missile launchers. This number would exceed the 1,200 limit on MIRVed missile launchers. Therefore, unless there is a delay in the TRIDENT program, we will, in any case, have to phase out some 86 POSEIDON or MINUTEMAN III launchers. If we propose to deploy more than 120 ALCM-carrying planes, we will have to phase out additional POSEIDON or MINUTEMAN III launchers to stay within the 1,320 limit. It is uncertain that the Navy would recommend phasing out POSEIDONs or the Air Force the MINUTEMEN III.

Even if we assume 120 to 150 deployed ALCM-carrying aircraft, it would be unlikely that more than some 50 percent would be on continuous alert or that more than some 90 percent could be brought to readiness under conditions calling for fully generated strategic forces.

The Soviet Union faces a much simpler problem. The U.S. has no substantial air defenses and the Soviet BACKFIRE is not to be counted under any of the proposed limits. Even if BACKFIRE production is limited to current production rates, the number deployed will grow to significant numbers, they can be dispersed to a larger number of fields than our B-52s and their chances of surviving an initial exchange are thus enhanced. In view of our limited defense, BACKFIRE carried cruise missiles would not need to have a range greater than 600 kilometers. If the Soviets exploit their current technology, they could deploy a significant number of such short-range ALCMs on BACKFIREs prior to 1985. The potential of the BACKFIRE to survive the initial exchanges of a nuclear war coupled with its capability to penetrate very limited U.S. defenses would contribute significantly to a greater possibility of Soviet domination of the subsequent phases of such a war.

Whether the FB-111H (which is 40 percent the size of the BACKFIRE) can penetrate depends, among other things, on whether U.S. tankers can survive in sufficient numbers for the required multiple inflight refuelings of the FB-111Hs. If the FB-111H were to carry ALCMs with a range greater than 600 kilometers, they would have to be counted under both the 1,320 ceiling and the 1,200 ceiling.

5. THE DEFINITION AND VERIFICATION PROBLEM

It is impossible to verify compliance unless what is to be limited and the nature of the limitation have been clearly defined and the definition agreed in depth between the parties.

As can be seen from the current state of the negotiation, difficult problems in definition are evident. What the range of a cruise missile is and how it is to be measured have proven to be conceptually difficult to define — not merely difficult to negotiate. What is the permitted production rate of BACKFIRE bombers? Presumably the current rate; the Soviet side will not say what that is, but it is reported that we estimate the rate at approximately 40 per year. What is the permitted "useful payload" of a "small" missile; i.e., exceeding what number of pounds of "useful payload" could cause it to be classed as an MLBM [modern large ballistic missile]? Apparently the "throw-weight" of an SS-19, which term we define as the maximum useful payload an SS-19-type missile booster has put, or can put, into an intercontinental trajectory. But the Soviets will not define "type," will not tell us how they measure useful payload, nor tell us what they assess the useful payload of an SS-19 to be. Etcetera.

Even where the limitations are clearly defined, compliance is in many cases difficult to verify. How do you verify the range of the other side's cruise missile, no matter how precisely "range" is defined? How do you distinguish an ALCM from a GLCM or SLCM, or assure that an ALCM cannot be launched from a sea- or land-based launcher? How do you determine whether it is conventionally armed or nuclear armed? How do you determine that a new missile having the throw-weight of an SS-19 and carrying a bus similar to an SS-19 bus, but with a single RV, is not capable of being deployed as a MIRVed missile? How do you determine that a missile tested both from land-based launchers and SLBM submarines is an SLBM and cannot be used as an ICBM? How do you determine that retired missiles or missiles taken out of retired launchers or extra, newly produced missiles are not being stockpiled to be available for relatively prompt deployment on soft pads or for reload in surviving launchers?

Now that the Soviet side has taken firm action to demonstrate that it does not intend to be bound by any commitment not to deny us information by encrypting the telemetry from their test ranges, we can no longer count on having as much information as we have had in the past to assist in the task of monitoring compliance with SALT limitations.

Quite clearly, in many instances unambiguous verification of the SALT II limitations will not be possible. For this reason the arms control community now uses the phrase "adequately verifiable." It is correct that "verifiability" is not an absolute requirement; it is a means toward the end of a good agreement. A wholly verifiable bad agreement would still be a bad agreement. If those provisions of an agreement which are strategically significant to us are adequately verifiable, the agreement might be a good agreement, even if its less important provisions are not confidently verifiable. The difficulty, however, rests in determining which provisions are "strategically significant" to us and what is meant by the word "adequate." Both phrases lend themselves to subjective judgments.

6. THE ACTIVE AND CIVIL DEFENSE ASPECTS OF THE PROBLEM

The United States has over the last twenty years phased out most of its continental air defense capabilities. The Congress has forced the virtual deactivation of the U.S. ABM defenses permitted under the ABM treaty. In the mid-sixties the U.S. Navy was told that it was not to ask for equipment, men or funds for the purpose of developing ASW [antisubmarine warfare] capabilities designed to attack Soviet SLBMs; as far as we know that order has never been rescinded.

The USSR has persistently put relatively more emphasis on active defensive capabilities than has the United States.

The Soviet Union has devoted a truly enormous effort to air defenses. It has deployed 12,000 surface-to-air missile launchers and approximately 2,700 interceptor fighters. It has deployed thousands of inter-netted air defense radars and ground-control-interceptor centers. It is apparently ready to deploy a new high capability mobile phased-array radar/missile system called the SAX-10. It has recently been reported that the SAX-10 is being deployed on surface ships, thus affording the Soviets the beginnings of a capability to deploy a forward barrier defense against our bomber aircraft.

The Soviet Union has maintained and somewhat improved those ABM capabilities it had earlier deployed in the Moscow area. It is significantly increasing the capabilities of its phased-array ABM "early warning" radars around the periphery of the USSR. This is permitted under the ABM Treaty on the assumption that, in the event of war, such a network, being close to the periphery, could be destroyed. It is also assumed that the even more powerful radars in the Moscow area could, with greater effort, be destroyed. However, the large Soviet phased-array radar deployments, when coupled with the development of a transportable phased ABM radar and high acceleration interceptor combination, could give the USSR a reasonably rapid break-out toward an important "damage limiting" ABM capability, particularly against U.S. SLBM RVs.

Even more important are the civil defense aspects of the problem. Many who have carefully studied the problem concur that a well executed civil defense program — to evacuate most of the population of Moscow and Leningrad would take several days — can reduce fatalities by a factor of five to ten as well as substantially reducing industrial damage and the time necessary for economic recovery. There is now little doubt that the Soviet Union is working on civil defense much harder than was realized as recently as two years ago.

It has recently been announced that the Executive Branch will request an expansion of the U.S. civil defense program to include work to enable more rapid evacuation of our urban population in the event of a crisis. Approval of such a program could be of major importance. It should be noted, however, that after such expansion our program would cost about one-tenth of what the Executive Branch estimates the Soviets are spending on civil defense.

7. THE NUMBER AND HARDNESS OF TARGETS PROBLEM

The potential effectiveness of offensive nuclear forces should be judged in the light of the target structure they might be called upon to strike. From the standpoint of the military outcome of war, were deterrence to fail, the most important targets are hard targets (silos, launch control facilities, command, control and communication bunkers, nuclear storage facilities, and the like). It is because of their strategic significance that they have been hardened. The list of Soviet hard targets is larger than ours, and the targets are generally harder. Their list is growing while ours is not. The Soviets will, by the mid-1980s, have twice as many hard targets as the United States and on the average they will be twice as hard.

Against soft targets the important criteria are soft target (area) potential EMT [equivalent megatons], megatonnage, number of warheads, and the relative effectiveness of the civil defense measures on the two sides.

8. THE BREAK-OUT PROBLEM

The essential effort in the ABM Treaty negotiation was to assure that neither side could break-out of the agreement and thereafter rapidly deploy a significant ABM defense. That was why the main emphasis was put on preventing the deployment of a widespread ABM-capable radar network, the element requiring the longest leadtime.

In the early SALT II negotiations the break-out problem with respect to offensive systems was given much attention by the U.S. side. This effort has had to be put to one side in the interest of negotiability. This has resulted in provisions that leave rapid break-out by the Soviet Union entirely feasible.

For instance, the proposed provisions designed to limit Soviet ability to reload their silos cannot be counted on to be effective for any extended period of time.

The agreements appear to involved such phrases as "cruise missiles can be carried only by heavy bombers." Those who actually have worked on and designed cruise missiles say that any bomber with hard points on its wings can rapidly be converted to carry cruise missiles and that any cruise missile operable from a plane can rapidly be adapted to be launched from ground- or sea-based launchers.

There seems to be no concern with the potential conversion to a damage-limiting ABM role of new air defense systems, designed to counter the U.S. SRAM/cruise missiles.

9. THE COMMAND, CONTROL, COMMUNICATION AND PRE- AND POST-ATTACK INTELLIGENCE PROBLEM

Second strike deterrent forces will fail in their purpose if responsible civil authority is not able effectively to command and control them. This requires that responsible civil authority survive an attack, have time for a considered and intelligent decision, and be able to communicate with those in immediate control of the launching of surviving forces. For these decisions to be intelligent and effective, continuing information, both as to the status of our own forces and those of the enemy, is essential.

Neither those in the Executive Branch, nor those outside it, have confidence in the current status of what is called our $C^3 + I$. In fact, improving its effectiveness and survivability is given the highest priority by most analysts of our strategic posture. There is little doubt that the Soviet Union has put a vastly greater effort than has the U.S. into providing themselves with redundant and survivability $C^3 + I$ systems capable of enduring, if necessary, through a protracted nuclear war. They have also been developing antisatellite and other capabilities which could deny us pre- and post-attack intelligence.

It was hoped that the SALT II provision obligating each side not to interfere with the other side's national technical means of verification would give useful protection to our pre-attack technical intelligence capabilities. With the Soviet Union's demonstration of its determination to protect its right to encrypt test range telemetry much of our technical intelligence capability becomes dependent on unilateral Soviet decisions.

The diminishing survivability and endurance potential of our strategic forces to be expected during the Treaty period sharpen the need for improved U.S. post-attack $C^3 + I$.

10. THE RELATION OF THE STRATEGIC NUCLEAR BALANCE TO THE THEATER BALANCE, CONVENTIONAL AND NUCLEAR

At all times since World War II the Soviet Union has had superior non-nuclear forces on the European central front and on its northern and southern flanks. This has, in part, been due to geography, the USSR enjoying the central position and interior lines, and, in part, to the greater effort that has been made by the USSR and the Warsaw Pact than by NATO.

In the years up to the early 1950s this was offset by the U.S. nuclear monopoly. Later the conventional deficiency was in large measure offset by U.S. superiority in theater nuclear weapons. Today that theater nuclear superiority has disappeared and it has proved necessary to assign a number of our POSEIDON submarines to cover targets of interest to NATO, and thus maintain a theater balance. It has been estimated that the Soviet Union has two to three times as many theater nuclear weapons, with six times the area destructive potential, ten times the throw-weight, and twenty-five times the megatonnage as we. As the Soviets deploy increasing numbers of SS-20 MIRVed missiles, BACKFIRE and other high performance theater bombers, maintaining a theater nuclear balance will become increasingly difficult. More and more of our surviving strategic nuclear forces will be called upon for assignment to offset that imbalance. This consideration is rarely taken into account when the strategic nuclear balance is being examined; it should be.

Moreover, the SALT II agreement could have a serious negative effect upon the evolution of the conventional balance. The European NATO countries have hoped to exploit cruise missile technology in its theater conventional weapon applications. Agreement that armed cruise missiles with a range greater than 600 kilometers are to be limited in SALT would favor the Soviet side. It would support the erroneous Soviet claim that nuclear ballistic missiles deployed in the Soviet Union for peripheral area missions, with medium or intermediate ranges, which under SALT II can be up to 5,500 kilometers, are not "strategic," while cruise missiles deployed in NATO Europe, if over 600 kilometers in range, whether nuclear or conventionally armed, are "strategic."

In specific terms, the SALT II agreements, particularly if the Soviet position that conventionally armed cruise missiles as well as nuclear armed are to be limited is accepted, may prevent the United States from transferring technology important to the conventional defense of Europe because of limitations on the transfer of weapons, components, or technical information relating to weapons limited by the SALT Treaty, as well as prohibiting the deployment by the U.S. of conventionally armed cruise missiles with ranges greater than 600 kilometers.

These limitations could also result in the U.S. Navy being limited to cruise missiles less than 600 kilometers in range, while countries not party to the agreement would not be so limited, and could then significantly out-range it.

11. THE IMPACT OF THE AGREEMENT UPON THE UNITED STATES' ABILITY TO REVERSE CURRENT TRENDS

The Vladivostok Accord did not restrict the USSR from deploying those new weapon systems it planned to deploy, but neither did it restrict us from deploying those weapon systems necessary to maintain stability and rough equivalence, and thus reversing then current trends. It did not restrict the ability of the United States to deploy the B-1, the MINUTE-MAN III and the MX missile in a survivable deployment mode, TRIDENT II, ALCMs, GLCMs, and SLCMs of any range, continental air defense, more durable and reliable command and control, or enhanced civil defense preparations.

U.S. program decisions and delays in making decisions since Vladivostok, plus the terms of the probable SALT agreement now make it difficult, if not impossible, to maintain crisis stability and rough equivalence.

It is argued by some that the restrictions in the agreements, as they apply to the United States, are of little significance; they do not keep us from doing anything we now should, or would want to, do during the period of the agreements. Whether this is so or not depends in large measure on whether or not the agreements permit the deployment of a multiple aimpoint system (MAPS). Under this concept the U.S. would construct a large number of vertical protective shelters or silos, each capable of holding a cannister containing an ICBM (a MINUTEMAN III or a follow-on missile such as the MX) and its launch mechanism; or, alternatively, a cannister which would contain no missile or launch mechanism but which would be indistinguishable from those that did. The cannisters containing the missile and launch mechanism would periodically and randomly be moved and substituted among those that did not. The U.S. is reported to have told the Soviets that it considered that such a system was permitted under the Treaty. The Soviet side is reported to have expressed its most serious reservations about any such interpretation.

If it is agreed by both sides that a MAP deployment is permitted, it is conceivable that the U.S. could deploy such a system rapidly enough to maintain crisis stability. If not so agreed, there does not appear to be any feasible, alternate way to do so within the next decade.

Under the now most likely provisions of a SALT II agreement, it is difficult, if not impossible, to see how we can reverse recent adverse trends. Beginning in the early to mid-1980s, we would have to rely on an ICBM force useful, if deterrence fails, only if the President decides to launch it from under an attack in the few minutes he may have available to do so, a bomber force capable of enduring no more than a few hours, if not earlier used, and an SLBM force at-sea of less than 25 boats, each boat constituting four percent of our "enduring" deterrent power and thus worth enormous Soviet efforts to negate.

12. THE SITUATION IN THE ABSENCE OF AN AGREEMENT

The proponents of ratification of the treaty emphasize that whereas the USSR now has some 2,500 strategic launchers, under SALT II they will have to reduce these to 2,400 some months after entry into force of the agreements, and to 2,250 some three years thereafter. They assert that in the absence of an agreement, the Soviet side may not make any such reductions and may well add some 400, or even more, new strategic launchers to those they would be limited to under SALT II.

Based upon past experience, this is unlikely. The most careful student of Soviet past defense budgets and programs, William Lee [private consultant], tells us that he can identify little if any modification in the general magnitude of Soviet defense budgets and therefore of defense programs in response to international events or changes in U.S. programs. Whereas it is generally said that the increased Soviet emphasis on expanding its intercontinental strategic capabilities was in direct response to the Cuban missile crisis, Lee finds no evidence that this is so. The Soviet five-year planning process is so interrelated and complex, that anything beyond marginal adjustments is extremely disruptive and, in the past, has rarely occurred. He also notes the difficulty the Soviets would have in increasing the percentage of their GNP devoted to defense, which he estimates has now risen to approximately 18 percent.

Nevertheless, the possibility cannot be excluded that the Soviet side, in the absence of SALT II, would not decrease the number of its strategic launchers to 2,250 and, instead, would increase them.

It should be noted, however, that the 300 launchers they are expected to phase out to reach 2,250 are obsolete ICBMs and SLBMs which add little to their capability. Their presently programmed forces, largely composed of new missiles, will provide them with such an excess of MIRVed hard target kill capability, of unMIRVed megatonnage, and of RVs needed for target coverage, that it is hard to see what strategic benefit more of the same would give them. Increased intermediate range systems to cover requirements against China are not limited by SALT.

It is now anticipated that, as the Soviet side completes its deployment of new ICBMs and SLBMs, they will concentrate more heavily on adding to their defensive capabilities. This is where the principal gaps in their warmaking potential now lie. In particular, they are expected to add more attack submarines designed for an ASW role, and aircraft with improved look-down/shoot-down radar capabilities, and to deploy improved antiaircraft systems such as their SAX-10 mobile antiaircraft batteries, etc. For the Soviet Union to shift resources back to offensive forces from a contemplated strengthening of their defenses may not be disadvantageous to the United States.

The more important question is what the United States can be expected to do under the SALT II agreements — and in the absence of such agreements — to reverse currently unfavorable strategic nuclear trends.

13. THE QUESTION OF STRATEGY

Fundamental to the debate over SALT II and over our strategic nuclear program is the question of what strategy to follow, if deterrence were to fail, and the relationship of strategy to deterrence.

Some start from the assumption that a nuclear war is "unthinkable"; that those who do think about it must be Dr. Strangeloves; that deterrence has nothing to do with the military strategy either side intends to follow in the event deterrence were to fail; that, regardless of strategy and of the probable balance of the initially surviving and then enduring nuclear forces, there could be no meaningful winner or loser in a nuclear war.

Others believe that a nuclear war is thinkable, that the United States can best avoid a nuclear war, while preserving its independence and honor, by thinking seriously about nuclear war and taking prudent and timely actions to forestall it. They view the quality of deterrence to be importantly affected by the strategy we intend to follow and could effectively implement, if deterrence were to fail. They question the wisdom and credibility of a so-called minimum deterrence strategy. Under such a strategy, deterrence would depend on the United States' ability and will to launch, in response to a Soviet attack, some limited number of warheads against Soviet cities and industry protected by extensive active and passive defenses. The fact that the remaining U.S. military forces and U.S. population and industry would then be defenseless against ten thousand megatons or more of a Soviet third and fourth strike capability would be ignored.

Few now overtly support the minimum deterrence approach. They are more apt to describe their position with such phrases as "sufficiency" or "flexibility." This leads to the question of how much of what is enough? That judgment in turn must rest importantly upon the relative emphasis placed on the counterforce aspects of nuclear strategy and the countervalue aspects. Neither aspect can be ignored. If our counterforce capabilities, survivable after an initial Soviet strike, were sufficient to out-fight Soviet residual forces, while our other forces were capable of holding Soviet population and industry in reciprocal danger to our own, the quality of deterrence would be high because the Soviets would know we were in a position to implement a credible military strategy in the event deterrence were to fail.

If our strategy were restricted to a revenge attack on, for instance, the 200 largest Soviet cities, the military forces required to support such a strategy would be relatively small. Such a strategy, however, would be suicidal if implemented, vastly more destructive to us than to the Soviet Union, and militarily hopeless. One could, therefore, have only limited confidence in deterrence based upon an implied determination to execute such a strategy to defend vital U.S. interests.

Those that claim that we are stronger than the Soviet Union now and will continue to be so during our lifetimes, more or less regardless of what we do, must equate forces designed to support such a minimum deterrence strategy with superiority.

14. THE CONTINUING NEGOTIATION PROBLEM

It has been characteristic of the SALT negotiation process that the U.S. Executive Branch, in justifying existing agreements, has stressed its hope that their deficiencies will be corrected in future agreements. This argument characterized the justification of the SALT I Interim Agreement. That agreement specified that its terms were not to prejudice, in any way, the scope or terms of the long term comprehensive agreement contemplated for its replacement, the negotiation of which both sides had agreed should begin immediately after entry into force of the Interim Agreement. Despite the best efforts of the U.S. side, the terms of the Interim Agreement have, in fact, prejudiced the terms of SALT II. The nature of the continuing programs of the two sides and the political and psychological pressures on the U.S. made it difficult to achieve any other result.

As one looks into the future, SALT III negotiations are contemplated to begin shortly after SALT II is ratified and enters into force. Two hurdles must be met by the U.S. negotiators during those negotiations. The first is the expiration of the Protocol around January 1, 1982; the second will be the expiration of the Treaty at the end of 1985. It is likely that negotiations will concern themselves with both subjects and that the Soviet side will press for the extension of those provisions of the Protocol which they would have preferred to see in the Treaty, and link that pressure to the SALT III treaty negotiation. The question of whether the U.S. can expect to prevail with respect to its hopes for SALT III will largely depend on the relative bargaining position of the two sides during the negotiations. The evolution of the relative strength of the two sides in the strategic nuclear arena is almost certain to be negative during the entire period prior to expiration of the SALT II Treaty. If the MX and TRIDENT II versions of the "largely-common missile" are then close to their IOCs, this could have a favorable bearing on the negotiations. The impending deployment of the MX version could, however, be destabilizing if a basing mode capable of assuring its survivability and endurance were not concurrently available.

If the SALT II Treaty were to expire in 1985 without replacement and without a survivable and durable U.S. ICBM component, the U.S. could face unprecedented dangers. We would then have to take seriously both existing Soviet nuclear strategic superiority and a superior Soviet breakout potential. To avoid these risks, we would be under pressure to agree to a SALT III less favorable than SALT II, rather than hold out for a more favorable one.

15. THE POLITICAL AND DIPLOMATIC CONSEQUENCES OF A SHIFT IN THE STRATEGIC NUCLEAR BALANCE

Some proponents, rather than taking exception to the main thrust of the analysis contained in the preceding sections, argue a different series of points along the following line:

a. The United States' March 1977 comprehensive proposal leaned over backward in attempting to be fair to the Soviet Union. It offered them complete assurance against any significant counterforce threat from the United States while not assuring comparable protection for the United States.

b. That proposal was wholly unacceptable to the USSR, and any proposal which would in fact assure stability and rough equivalence at lower levels of nuclear armaments would be even more unnegotiable.

c. To insist on such an equitable agreement would assure that there would be no success, at least in the next few years, in negotiating a SALT II set of agreements. Such a delay would risk a breakdown of detente.

d. Rather than risk such a breakdown, it is wiser to negotiate the best deal that is now reachable, preserve at least the outward forms of detente, and open the way to follow-on negotiations for a better deal in the future.

e. And in any case, a deterioration in the state of the strategic nuclear balance will have no adverse political or diplomatic consequences.

To some of us who lived through the Berlin crisis in 1961, the Cuban crisis in 1962, or the Middle East crisis in 1973, the last and key judgment in this chain of reasoning — that an adverse shift in the strategic nuclear balance will have no political or diplomatic consequences — comes as a shock. In the Berlin crisis of 1961 our theater position was clearly unfavorable; we relied entirely on our strategic nuclear superiority to face down Chairman Khrushchev's ultimatum. In Cuba, the Soviet Union faced a position of both theater inferiority and strategic inferiority; they withdrew the missiles they were deploying. In the 1973 Middle East crisis, the theater and the strategic nuclear balances were more balanced; both sides compromised.

It is hard to see what factors in the future are apt to disconnect international politics and diplomacy from a consideration of the underlying real power balances. The nuclear balance is only one element in the overall power balance. But in the Soviet view, it is the fulcrum upon which all other levers of influence — military, economic, or political — rest.

How confident can we be that there is not at least a measure of validity to that viewpoint?

August

CHINA-JAPAN PEACE TREATY

August 12, 1978

Six years after Japan and the People's Republic of China established diplomatic relations and ended a long state of war, the neighboring Asian nations cemented their bonds with a 1978 treaty of "perpetual peace and friendship."

Signing of the brief document Aug. 12 marked an important step in the rapid opening of China to increased trade and cultural exchanges with other nations, after three decades of virtual isolation under communist rule. The treaty signing preceded by four months the related, surprise action by the United States to shift its recognition from the nationalist government on Taiwan to the communist regime — a move actively encouraged by the post-Mao leadership in Peking. (Normalization of U.S.-China relations, p. 781)

Just as it sought to gain technological and economic benefits from its new ties to the United States, China clearly hoped that the stability offered by the treaty with Japan would improve the People's Republic's chances of obtaining sophisticated Japanese plants and machinery needed for industrial modernization on the mainland. For its part, Japan stood to gain a huge new market for its goods and access to China's abundant natural resources.

The Japan-China treaty became effective Oct. 23, when ratifications were exchanged in Tokyo by Chinese Deputy Premier Teng Hsiao-ping and Japanese Prime Minister Takeo Fukuda. Teng, then emerging as the architect of China's modernization policy, was the highest ranking People's Republic leader to visit Japan since 1949.

"Anti-Hegemony" Clause

Terms of the peace and friendship treaty had been agreed upon earlier by representatives of the two countries, after four years of negotiations that frequently bogged down over Japanese reluctance to sign an "anti-hegemony" clause aimed at China's arch-rival, the Soviet Union. The Soviets, contending they had a legitimate right to wield influence in the Pacific region, repeatedly warned the Japanese that signing of an anti-hegemony pledge would strain relations with their Soviet ally.

In the final compromise, China and Japan mutually agreed that neither should seek hegemony in the Asia-Pacific area and that both should oppose any attempted dominance by a third country. However, a phrase was added stating that the treaty would not affect either nation's relations with third countries, and Japanese officials insisted that the anti-hegemony language did not single out any particular foreign power.

At the Tokyo ceremonies marking exchange of the treaty, Fukuda noted that since Sept. 29, 1972, when China and Japan opened diplomatic relations, affairs between the two countries had "developed smoothly." He said the pact was intended to place those relations "on a more stable basis and promises their further extensive development." (1972 joint communiqué, Historic Documents of 1972 p. 827)

> *Following is the text (unofficial translation) of the peace treaty signed Aug. 12, 1978, by representatives of Japan and the People's Republic of China:*

Japan and the People's Republic of China,

Recalling with satisfaction that since the government of Japan and the government of the People's Republic of China issued a joint communiqué in Peking on September 29, 1972, the friendly relations between the two governments and the peoples of the two countries have developed greatly on a new basis,

Confirming that the above-mentioned joint communiqué constitutes the basis of the relations of peace and friendship between the two countries and that the principles enunciated in the joint communiqué should be strictly observed,

Confirming that the principles of the charter of the United Nations should be fully respected,

Hoping to contribute to peace and stability in Asia and in the world,

For the purpose of solidifying and developing the relations of peace and friendship between the two countries,

Have resolved to conclude a treaty of peace and friendship and for that purpose have appointed as their plenipotentiaries:

Japan: Minister for Foreign
              Affairs Sunao Sonoda

People's Republic of China: Minister of Foreign
Affairs Huang Hua

Who, having communicated to each other their full powers, found to be in good and due form, have agreed as follows:

Article I

1. The contracting parties shall develop relations of perpetual peace and friendship between the two countries on the basis of the principles of mutual respect for sovereignty and territorial integrity, mutual non-aggression, non-interference in each other's internal affairs, equality and mutual benefit and peaceful co-existence.
2. The contracting parties confirm that, in conformity with the foregoing principles and the principles of the charter of the United Nations, they shall in their mutual relations settle all disputes by peaceful means and shall refrain from the use or threat of force.

Article II

The contracting parties declare that neither of them should seek hegemony in the Asia-Pacific region or in any other region and that each is opposed to efforts by any other country or group of countries to establish such hegemony.

Article III

The contracting parties shall, in the good-neighborly and friendly spirit and in conformity with the principles of equality and mutual benefit and non-interference in each other's internal affairs, endeavor to further develop economic and cultural relations between the two countries and to promote exchanges between the peoples of the two countries.

Article IV

The present treaty shall not affect the position of either contracting party regarding its relations with third countries.

Article V

1. The present treaty shall be ratified and shall enter into force on the date of the exchange of instruments of ratification which shall take place at Tokyo. The present treaty shall remain in force for ten years and thereafter shall continue to be in force until terminated in accordance with the provisions of paragraph 2.

2. Either contracting party may, by giving one year's written notice to the other contracting party, terminate the present treaty at the end of the initial ten-year period or at any time thereafter.

In witness whereof the respective plenipotentiaries have signed the present treaty and have affixed thereto their seals.

Done in duplicate, in the Japanese and Chinese languages, both texts being equally authentic, at Peking, this Twelfth Day of August, 1978.

For Japan:

For the People's Republic of China:

DISTRICT OF COLUMBIA
VOTING AMENDMENT
August 22, 1978

The Senate, in a cliff-hanging roll-call vote Aug. 22, approved a constitutional amendment that, if ratified by the states, would give voting representation in Congress for the first time to residents of the District of Columbia. The proposed amendment, requiring a two-thirds majority in both chambers, had been approved by the House of Representatives on March 2 by a vote of 289-127 (an 11-vote margin). But its approval by the Senate was by no means certain until the vote was actually taken. When the roll call was completed, the vote was 67-32, just one more than the required two-thirds.

The joint resolution (H J Res 554) passed by Congress included an article proposed as an amendment to the Constitution. The article stated that for purposes of voting representation in Congress the District of Columbia "shall be treated as though it were a state." That is, if the amendment were ratified, the District of Columbia would have two senators and one or two representatives, depending on the district's population.

Earlier consideration of the proposed amendment had focused to a large extent on the constitutional issue, that is, in the view of supporters, whether fundamental rights were to be provided citizens of all races who happened to live in the District of Columbia. But from the moment the bill came to the Senate floor, the fact of the large black population in the District of Columbia permitted a more volatile civil rights issue to be brought into the debate. Indeed, lobbying for the amendment were some of the leaders of the nation's civil rights movement, including Coretta Scott King, widow of the Rev. Martin Luther King Jr., and the Rev. Martin Luther King Sr., the assassinated civil rights leader's father.

Background

Residents of the District of Columbia had not voted for senators or representatives since 1801 when the district had been created and Congress assumed the job of governing it. In the view of many historians, the framers of the Constitution had never intended to disenfranchise residents of the Federal City. In fact, James Madison wrote in Federalist Paper No. 43 that residents of the District of Columbia "will have their voice in the election of the government which is to exercise authority over them." Successive Congresses, however, willed otherwise.

Between 1915 and 1921 numerous resolutions were introduced calling for constitutional amendments to allow District of Columbia residents to vote for president and vice president and to have representation in Congress. They went nowhere. Indeed, it was not until 1961 that residents were granted under the 23rd Amendment to the Constitution the right to vote for president. In 1970 they won the right to send a non-voting delegate to the House, and four years later, with the granting of "home rule," they were able to elect a mayor and other city officials.

Senate Debate

The civil rights emphasis of the debate in the Senate was pointed up by Sen. Edward M. Kennedy, D-Mass., leader of the amendment's supporters, who said that opposition seemed "to arise from . . . the fear that senators elected from the District of Columbia may be too liberal, too urban, too black or too Democratic."

Following the roll call, however, Kennedy said that "strong bipartisan support was able to raise what is a fundamental issue of justice and equality — that people who have fought in our wars and have a population greater than that of seven states ought to have voting representation in Congress. . . ."

The amendment's opponents in the Senate were led by Senators William L. Scott, R-Va., Orrin G. Hatch, R-Utah, Jesse Helms, R-N.C., Paul Laxalt, R-Nev., and James A. McClure, R-Idaho. For the most part, opponents stressed what they said was the unconstitutionality of the proposed amendment. Some conservative Republicans, including Sen. Barry Goldwater, R-Ariz., and Sen. Strom Thurmond, R-S.C., supported the proposal.

While most Democrats favored the bill, some, particularly those from less urban western states, opposed it, arguing that the addition of two senators would dilute their states' power in the Senate. A number also agreed with Sen. John Stennis, D-Miss., who contended that the amendment would give District of Columbia residents "not equal representation but representation far beyond what they deserve."

Ratification Process

The article approved by Congress would become a constitutional amendment only when ratified by the legislatures of three-fourths (38) of the states within a period of seven years.

The first state to ratify the amendment was New Jersey; both houses of the legislature approved it on Sept. 12. By year's end, two other states, Ohio and Michigan, had ratified. Also by the end of the year, one state, Pennsylvania, had rejected the amendment.

Following is the text of the joint resolution (H J Res 554) approved by the House on March 2 and the Senate on Aug. 22:

Resolved by the Senate and House of Representatives of the United States of America in Congress assembled (two-thirds of each House concurring therein), That the following article is proposed as an amendment to the Constitution of the United States, which shall be valid to all intents and purposes as part of the Constitution when ratified by the legislatures of three-fourths of the several States within seven years from the date of its submission by the Congress:

"Article —

"SECTION 1. For purposes of representation in the Congress, election of the President and Vice President, and Article V of this Constitution, the District constituting the seat of government of the United States shall be treated as though it were a State.

"SEC. 2. The exercise of the rights and powers conferred under this article shall be by the people of the District constituting the seat of government, and as shall be provided by the Congress.

"SEC. 3. The twenty-third article of amendment to the Constitution of the United States is hereby repealed.

"SEC. 4. This article shall be inoperative, unless it shall have been ratified as an amendment to the Constitution by the legislatures of three-fourths of the several States within seven years from the date of its submission.".

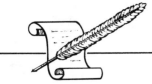
September

PAPAL SUCCESSION

September 3; October 22, 1978

The election Oct. 16 of Cardinal Karol Wojtyla of Poland as the 263rd successor to St. Peter as the bishop of Rome and head of the Roman Catholic Church was hailed by the world's Roman Catholics still grieving over the deaths of Pope Paul VI and Pope John Paul I. Paul VI had died on Aug. 6, after a papal reign of 15 years, and John Paul I on Sept. 28, after a reign of only 34 days, one of the shortest in history.

The sudden death of John Paul I so soon after his installation Sept. 3 had deeply affected millions of Americans of many creeds. A Washington Post *reporter wrote, "Paul was ailing, almost 81, and had finished the course. But John Paul I was only 65, his papacy off to a glowing start." Albino Luciani, the archbishop of Venice, had chosen the double name of John Paul I in honor of his two predecessors in the papacy, Pope John XXIII and Pope Paul VI.*

The dramatic election of Pope John Paul II was seen by many as signaling a sharper break with the past than the choice of John Paul I six weeks earlier. John Paul II was the first pope in 456 years who was not an Italian, and at 58 he was the youngest pope since 1846 when Pius IX was elected at 54. Moreover, for many years he had been engaged in the long struggle over religious freedom between the Catholic Church in Poland and that country's communist government. Early speculation that described his selection as a political statement later seemed overdrawn. But the relationship of his church and atheist regimes was sure to be a central issue of Pope John Paul II's reign.

Pope Paul VI

Pope Paul VI, who had been in rather poor health for some time, died Aug. 6 after a heart attack. From his predecessor, John XXIII, Pope Paul VI had inherited Vatican Council II, and his 15-year papacy was described by a close observer as "a pontifical bridge between old forms that had outlived their usefulness and new ones that were struggling to be born."

Under Paul VI, the Roman Catholic Church began to say Mass in local languages rather than in the traditional Latin. He established policies designed to bring the bishops closer to church decision-making, and he abolished some forms of penance, such as "meatless" Fridays. Moreover, he simplified the procedures for annulment of marriages. Pope Paul VI followed the traditional Church positions on such issues as abortion, artificial birth control and divorce. His encyclical, "Humanae Vitae" (On Human Life), was perhaps his most controversial.

He traveled widely and frequently spoke out on the necessity for world peace and social justice. As Pope he made nine trips outside Italy: to the Holy Land, India, New York City, Portugal, Turkey, Colombia, Switzerland, Uganda and the Far East. Speaking at the United Nations in 1965, Paul VI made an emotional appeal for an end to all war. "Jamais plus la guerre!" ("Never again war!") he declared in French. In more recent years he expressed his abhorrence of political terrorism, offering himself as hostage in the 1978 kidnapping of Aldo Moro, a former Italian prime minister.

Pope John Paul I

The choice of Cardinal Luciani by the conclave on Aug. 26 as successor to Paul VI had been unforeseen. A quiet man who enjoyed reading (including Dickens' novels), John Paul I once told a reporter, "I am a little man accustomed to little things and to silence." He had filled a pastoral role for many years, and his ambition as Pope was to become the Good Shepherd of Christendom.

Pope John Paul I had been in somewhat poor health for many years. In a ceremonial blessing of the sick, during his short reign, John Paul I said, "I wish you to know that your Pope understands and loves you very much. You perhaps do not know that your Pope has been eight times to the hospital and has undergone four operations."

The church's sorrow at John Paul I's sudden death was expressed by Cardinal Carlo Confalonieri, dean of the Sacred College of Cardinals, at a funeral Mass in St. Peter's Square. "Why so soon?" asked Confalonieri. "He passed as a meteor that unexpectedly lights up the heavens and then disappears, leaving us amazed and astonished. We did not have time to know him. Yet one month was enough for him to have conquered our hearts."

Pope John Paul II

The choice of Cardinal Wojtyla to succeed John Paul I astonished the world. That the cardinals — sequestered in a conclave in Rome for the second time in less than two months — would choose a non-Italian was considered unlikely. Yet Italians were in a minority in the College of Cardinals, partly because of a rule established by Paul VI that excluded cardinals over 80 years old from the electoral process. After the election of John Paul II, it was speculated that the cardinals had been unable to unite behind a single Italian candidate. John Paul II's rugged health and relatively young age also appeared to have been factors in his selection. Not long after he became Pope, he was photographed accepting a pair of skis, grasping them with obvious delight.

The fact that John Paul II was Polish and had served as a cardinal in a communist country had an obvious impact on the communist world. A broadcast on Moscow television reporting his election was unprecedented. Polish authorities, departing from their usual policy of banning any recognition of religious events, permitted the broadcast of John Paul II's installation and permitted 3,000 of his countrymen to travel to Rome for the ceremonies.

Moreover, Polish President Henryk Jablonski was among the political figures from many countries who attended John Paul II's installation. The new pope addressd the throng in St. Peter's Square in Italian and made additional remarks in 10 other languages.

Following are the texts of the homilies given by Pope John Paul I at his installation in St. Peter's Square in Rome Sept. 3, 1978, and by Pope John Paul II at his installation in St. Peter's Square Oct. 22.

POPE JOHN PAUL I'S INSTALLATION HOMILY

In this sacred celebration inaugurating the ministry of the supreme pastor of the church, which has been placed on our shoulders, we begin by turning our mind in adoration and prayer to the infinite and eternal God, who has raised us to the chair of blessed Peter by his own design which human reasoning cannot explain, and by his benign graciousness. The words of St. Paul the apostle come spontaneously to our lips: "O the depth of the riches and wisdom and knowledge of God! How unsearchable are his judgments and how inscrutable his ways!" (Rom. 11:33).

Next we embrace in thought and greet with paternal affection the whole church of Christ. We greet this assembly, representing as it were the whole church, which is gathered in this place — a place filled with works of piety, religion and art, which is the attentive custodian of the tomb of the chief of the apostles. We then greet the church that is watching us and listening to us at this moment through the modern media of social communication.

We greet all the members of the people of God: the cardinals, bishops, priests, men and women religious, missionaries, seminary students, lay people engaged in the apostolate and in various professions, people involved in the fields of politics, culture, art and business, fathers and mothers of families, workers, migrants, young people, children, the sick, the suffering, the poor.

We greet also with reverence and affection all the people in the world. We regard them and love them as our brothers and sisters, since they are children of the same heavenly Father and brothers and sisters in Christ Jesus (cf. Mt. 23:8f)

We have begun this homily in Latin, because as is well known, it is the official language of the church and in an evident and effective way expresses its universality and unity.

The word of God that we have just been listening to has presented the church to us as in a crescendo, first, as prefigured and glimpsed by the prophet Isaiah (cf. Is. 2:2-5) in the form of the new temple with the nations streaming toward it from all sides, anxious to know the law of God and to observe it with docility, while the terrible weapons of war are transformed into instruments of peace.

But St. Peter reminds us that this mysterious new temple, the pole of attraction for the new humanity, has a cornerstone, a living, chosen and precious cornerstone (cf. 1 Pt. 2:4-9), which is Jesus Christ, who founded his church on the apostles and built it on blessed Peter, their leader (cf. Dogmatic Constitution *Lumen Gentium, 19*).

"You are Peter, and on this rock I will build my church" (Mt. 16:18) are the weighty, great and solemn words that Jesus speaks to Simon, son of John, after his profession of faith. This profession of faith was not the product of the Bethsaida fisherman's human logic or the expression of any special insight of his or the effect of some psychological impulse; it was rather the mysterious and singular result of a real revelation of the Father in heaven.

Jesus changes Simon's name to Peter, thus signifying the conferring of a special mission. He promises to build on him his church, which will not be overthrown by the forces of evil or death. He grants him the keys of the kingdom of God, thus appointing him the highest official of his church, and gives him the power to interpret authentically the law of God. In view of these privileges, or rather these superhuman tasks entrusted to Peter, St. Augustine points out to us: "Peter was by nature simply a man, by grace a Christian, by still more abundant grace one of the apostles and at the same time the first of the apostles" (St. Augustine, *In Ioannis Evang. Tract.*, 124, 5: Pl. 35, 1,973).

With surprised and understandable trepidation, but also with immense trust in the powerful grace of God and the ardent prayers of the church, we have agreed to become Peter's successor in the See of Rome, taking on us the yoke that Christ has wished to place on our fragile shoulders. We seem to hear as addressed to us the words that St. Ephrem represents Christ as speaking to Peter: "Simon, my apostle, I have made you the foundation of the holy church. I have already called you Peter because you will support all the edifices. You are the superintendent of those who will build the church on earth. . . . You are the source of the fountain from which my doctrine is drawn. You are the head of my apostles. . . . I have given you the keys of my kingdom" (St. Ephrem, *Sermones in Hebdomadam Sanctam,* 4,1:Lamy T.J., *S. Ephrem Syri Himni et Sermones,* 1,412).

From the moment we were elected, throughout the days that followed, we were deeply struck and encouraged by the warm manifestations of affection given by our sons and daughters in Rome and also by those sending us from all over the world the expression of their irrepressible jubilation at the fact that God has again given the church her visible head. Our mind re-echoes spontaneously the emotion-filled words that our great saintly predecessor, St. Leo the Great, addressed to the faithful of Rome: "Blessed Peter does not cease to preside over his See. He is bound to the eternal priest in an unbroken unity. . . . Recognize therefore that all the demonstrations of affection that you have given me because of fraternal amiability or filial devotion have with greater devotedness and truth been given by you and me to him whose See we rejoice to serve rather than preside over it" (St. Leo the Great, *Sermon V,* 4-5: Pl. 54, 155-156).

Yes, our presiding in charity is service. In saying this, we think not only of our Catholic brothers and sons and daughters but also of all those who endeavor to be disciples of Jesus Christ, to honor God, and to work for the good of humanity.

In this way we greet affectionately and with gratitude the delegations from other churches and ecclesial communities present here. Brethren not yet in full communion, we turn together to Christ our savior, advancing all of us in the holiness in which he wishes us to be and also in the mutual love without which there is no Christianity, preparing the paths of unity in faith with respect for his truth and for the ministry that he entrusted, for his church's sake, to his apostles and their successors.

Furthermore, we owe a special greeting to the heads of state and the members of the extraordinary missions. We are deeply touched by your presence, you who preside over the high destinies of your countries or represent your governments or international organizations, to which we are most grateful. In your participation we see the esteem and trust that you place in the Holy See and the church, that humble messenger of the Gospel for all the peoples of the earth, in order to help create a climate of justice, brotherhood, solidarity and hope, without which the world would be unable to live.

Let all here, great or small, be assured of our readiness to serve them according to the spirit of the Lord.

Surrounded by your love and upheld by your prayer, we begin our apostolic service by invoking, as a resplendent star on our way, the Mother of God, Mary, *Salus Populi Romani* and *Mater Ecclesiae,* whom the liturgy venerates in a special way in this month of September. May our Lady, who guided with delicate tenderness our life as a boy, as a seminarian, as a priest and as a bishop, continue to enlighten and direct our steps, in order that, as Peter's voice and with our eyes and mind fixed on her son Jesus, we may proclaim in the world with joyous firmness our profession of faith: "You are the Christ, the son of the living God" (Mt. 16:16). Amen.

POPE JOHN PAUL II'S
INSTALLATION HOMILY

"You are the Christ, the Son of the Living God."

These words were spoken by Simon, son of Jonah, in the district of Caesarea Philippi. Yes, he spoke them with his own tongue, with a deeply lived and experienced conviction — but it is not in him that they find their source, their origin: ". . .Because it was not flesh and blood that revealed this to you but my Father in heaven," they were the words of faith.

These words mark the beginning of Peter's mission in the history of salvation, in the history of the people of God. From that moment, from that confession of faith, the sacred history of salvation and of the people of God was bound to take on a new dimension: to express itself in the historical dimension of the church. This ecclesial dimension of the history of the people of God takes its origin, in fact is born, from these words of faith, and is linked to the man who uttered them: "You are Peter — the rock — and on you, as on a rock, I will build my church."

On this day and in this place these same words must again be uttered and listened to: "You are the Christ, the Son of the living God." Yes, brothers and sons and daughters, these words first of all. Their content reveals to our eyes the mystery of the living God, the mystery to which the Son has brought us close. Nobody, in fact, has brought the living God close to men and revealed him as he alone did. In our knowledge of God, in our journey toward God, we are totally linked to the power of these words: "He who sees me sees the Father." He who is infinite, inscrutable, ineffable, has come close to us in Jesus Christ, the only begotten Son of God, born of the Virgin Mary in the stable at Bethlehem.

All of you who already have the inestimable good fortune to believe, all of you who are still seeking God, and also you who are tormented by doubt: Please listen once again, today in this sacred place, to the words uttered by Simon Peter. In those words is the faith of the church. In those same words is the new truth, indeed, the ultimate and definitive truth about man: the Son of the living God — "You are the Christ, the Son of the living God."

Today the new bishop of Rome solemnly begins his ministry and the mission of Peter. In this city, in fact, Peter completed and fulfilled the mission entrusted to him by the Lord. The Lord addressed him with these words: ". . .When you were young you put on your own belt and walked where you liked, but when you grow old you will stretch out your hands and somebody else will put a belt round you and take you where you would rather not go." Peter came to Rome.

What else but obedience to the mandate received from the Lord guided him and brought him to this city, the heart of the empire? Perhaps the fisherman of Galilee did not want to come here. Perhaps he would have preferred to stay there, on the shores of the lake of Genesareth, with his boat and his nets. But guided by the Lord, obedient to his mandate, he came here.

According to an ancient tradition (given magnificent literary expression in a novel by Henryk Sienkiewicz), during Nero's persecution Peter wanted to leave Rome. But the Lord intervened: He went to meet him. Peter spoke to him and asked: *"Quo vadis, Domine?"* — "Where are you going, Lord?" And the Lord answered him at once: "I am going to Rome to be crucified again." Peter went back to Rome and stayed here until his crucifixion.

Yes, brothers and sons and daughters, Rome is the See of Peter. Down the centuries new bishops continually succeeded him in this See. Today a new bishop comes to the chair of Peter in Rome, a bishop full of trepidation, conscious of his unworthiness. And how could one not tremble before the greatness of this call and before the universal mission of his See of Rome?

To the See of Peter in Rome there succeeds today a bishop who is not a Roman. A bishop who is a son of Poland. But from this moment he too becomes a Roman. Yes — a Roman. He is a Roman also because he is the son of a nation whose history, from its first dawning, and whose thousand-year-old traditions are marked by a living, strong, unbroken and deeply felt link with the See of a nation which has ever remained faithful to this See of Rome. Inscrutable is the design of divine providence.

In past centuries, when the successor of Peter took possession of his See, the triregnum or tiara was placed on his head. The last pope to be crowned was Paul VI in 1963, but after the solemn coronation ceremony he never used the tiara again and left his successors free to decide in this regard.

Pope John Paul I, whose memory is so vivid in our hearts, did not wish to have the tiara, nor does his successor wish it today. This is not the time to return to a ceremony and an object considered — perhaps wrongly — to be a symbol of the temporal power of the popes. Our time calls us, urges us, obliges us to gaze on the Lord and immerse ourselves in humble and devout meditation on the mystery of the supreme power of Christ himself.

He who was born of the Virgin Mary, the carpenter's son (as he was thought to be), the Son of the living God (confessed by Peter), came to make us all "a kingdom of priests." The Second Vatican Council has reminded us of the mystery of this power and of the fact that Christ's mission as priest, prophet-teacher and king continues in the church. Everyone, the whole people of God, shares in this threefold mission.

Perhaps in the past the tiara, this triple crown, was placed on the pope's head in order to express by that symbol the Lord's plan for his church, namely that all the hierarchical order of Christ's church, all "sacred power" exercised in the church is nothing other than service, service with a single purpose: to ensure that all the people of God share in this threefold mission of Christ and always remain under the power of the Lord, power that has its source not in the powers of this world but in the mystery of the cross and resurrection.

The absolute and yet sweet and gentle power of the Lord responds to the whole depths of the human person, to his loftiest aspirations of intellect, will and heart. It does not speak the language of force but expresses itself in charity and truth.

The new successor of Peter in the See of Rome today makes a fervent, humble and trusting prayer: Christ, make me become and remain the servant of your unique power, the servant of your sweet power, the servant of your power that knows no eventide. Make me be a servant. Indeed, the servant of your servants.

Brothers and sisters, do not be afraid to welcome Christ and accept his power. Help the pope and all those who wish to serve Christ and with Christ's power to serve the human person and the whole of mankind. Do not be afraid. Open wide the doors for Christ. To his saving power open the boundaries of states, economic and political systems, the vast fields of culture, civilization and development. Do not be afraid. Christ knows "what is in man." He alone knows it.

So often today man does not know what is within him, in the depths of his mind and heart. So often he is uncertain about the meaning of his life on this earth. He is assailed by doubt, a doubt which turns into despair. We ask you therefore, we beg you with humility and trust, let Christ speak to man. He alone has words of life, yes, of eternal life.

Precisely today the whole church is celebrating World Mission Day, that is, she is praying, meditating and acting in order that Christ's words of life may reach all people and be received by them as a message of hope, salvation and total liberation. I thank all of you here present who have wished to participate in this solemn inauguration of the ministry of the new successor of Peter. I heartily thank the heads of state, the representatives of the authorities, and the government delegations for so honoring me with their presence.

Thank you, eminent cardinals of the Holy Roman Church.

I thank you, my beloved brothers in the episcopate. Thank you, priests. To you, sisters and brothers, religious of the orders and congregations, I give my thanks. Thank you, people of Rome. Thanks to the pilgrims who have come here from all over the world. Thanks to all of you who are linked with this sacred ceremony by radio and television.

I speak to you, my dear fellow-countrymen, pilgrims from Poland, brother bishops with your magnificent primate at your head, priests, sisters and brothers of the Polish religious congregations — to you representatives of Poland from all over the world. What shall I say to you who have come from my Cracow, from the See of St. Stanislaus of whom I was the unworthy successor for 14 years? What shall I say? Everything that I could say would fade into insignificance compared with what my heart feels, and your hearts feel, at this moment. So let us leave aside words. Let there remain just great silence before God, the silence that becomes prayer. I ask you: Be with me at Jasna Gora and everywhere. Do not cease to be with the pope who today prays with the words of the poet: "Mother of God, you who defend bright Czestochowa and shine at Ortrobrama." And these same words I address to you at this particular moment.

That was an appeal and a call to prayer for the new pope, an appeal expressed in my native language.

I make the same appeal to all the sons and daughters of the Catholic Church. Remember me today and always in your prayers.

I open my heart to all my brothers of the Christian churches and communities, and I greet in particular you who are here present, in anticipation of our coming personal meeting: But for the moment I express to you my sincere appreciation of your having wished to attend this solemn ceremony.

And I also appeal to all men — to every man (and with what veneration the apostle of Christ must utter this word, "man"):

—Pray for me.

—Help me to be able to serve you.

Amen.

CAMP DAVID ACCORDS

September 5-17, 1978

President Carter, Egyptian President Anwar al-Sadat and Israeli Prime Minister Menachem Begin emerged on Sept. 17 from 13 days of grueling negotiations to tell a surprised world that they had agreed on an outline for peace in the Middle East. Success at Camp David, the presidential retreat in the Maryland mountains, had not been expected.

The Camp David summit "exceeded our expectations," President Carter told a joint session of Congress on Sept. 18. "When this conference began, I said that the prospects for success were remote. Enormous barriers of ancient history, nationalism and suspicion would have to be overcome if we were to meet our objectives. But President Sadat and Prime Minister Begin have overcome those barriers, exceeded those expectations and signed two agreements that hold out the possibility of resolving issues that history had taught us could not be resolved."

The two agreements were "A Framework for Peace in the Middle East Agreed to at Camp David" and "A Framework for the Conclusion of a Peace Treaty Between Egypt and Israel." The former attempted to settle the issue of the West Bank and the Gaza Strip, which Israel seized in the June 1967 war. It called for negotiations over a five-year period among Egypt, Jordan, Israel and representatives of the Palestinian people living in the West Bank and Gaza — "or other Palestinians as mutually agreed" — to determine the future of the area. Before these negotiations would begin, "a self-governing authority" would be "freely elected" in the West Bank and Gaza, the Israeli military government would be withdrawn and the number of Israeli troops would be reduced and located at specific points away from the cities.

The second agreement provided for the total return of the Israeli-occupied Sinai to Egypt and the conclusion of an Egyptian-Israeli peace treaty within three months. Israel was to begin its withdrawal from the Sinai and complete the first phase of that withdrawal within three to nine months. At that time, "normal" relations between the two countries would be established. Final withdrawal would occur within three years. Israel's parliament, the Knesset, agreed on Sept. 28 to Sadat's demand that all military bases and civilian settlements be withdrawn from the Sinai.

West Bank-Gaza Uncertainties

A number of questions and problems dampened the euphoria that greeted the televised signing of the two agreements at the White House on Sept. 17. Carter referred to these problems in his address to Congress the next day: "The summit exceeded our expectations — but we know that it left many difficult issues still to be resolved. These issues will require careful negotiations in the months to come."

Most of the difficult issues concerned the future of the Gaza Strip and the West Bank territory of the Jordan River. Before leaving the United States for Israel, Begin challenged President Carter's contention that he had agreed to a moratorium on West Bank settlements during the five-year negotiating period and insisted that he had accepted only a three-month moratorium. Begin also described the agreement's recognition of "the legitimate rights of the Palestinian people" as "meaningless."

Israel was given a veto over the participation in the peace talks of any Palestinian representatives not living in the West Bank and Gaza. This opened the possibility that the Palestine Liberation Organization (PLO) would be excluded, since Israel had said repeatedly that it would never negotiate with the PLO.

Another uncertainty involved the participation in the peace talks of King Hussein of Jordan and Palestinians living in the West Bank and Gaza. Many Palestinian leaders in the occupied territories were supporters of the PLO and would be reluctant to take part in what PLO leader Yasir Arafat had called a "dirty deal."

Hussein made it clear that he would not join the negotiations unless the United States participated as a full partner and answered, to his satisfaction, about 25 questions he had sent to Washington concerning Jerusalem, Syria's Golan Heights, Israeli settlements, Palestinians outside the West Bank and Gaza and the issues of self-determination and sovereignty.

Hussein's questions for the United States touched on issues that could not be resolved at Camp David and were therefore left vague or completely omitted in the framework. After the summit, Begin stood firm on allowing Israeli troops to remain in the West Bank after five years, not dismantling Israeli settlements, keeping Jerusalem a united city under Israeli control and opposing an independent Palestinian state.

Responses

The reaction to the results of Camp David in the three countries participating in the summit was happiness and relief. While Begin was criticized by right-wing Israelis for not rejecting Sadat's demand for the dismantling of Jewish settlements in the Sinai, most Israelis seemed to feel that peace after 30 years and four wars was worth that price. And while Sadat's foreign minister, Mohammed Ibrahim Kamel, resigned in protest over the Camp David agreements, the vast majority of Egyptians seemed delighted with what their president had achieved. U.S. public opinion polls conducted after the summit showed a dramatic rise in President Carter's popularity.

While no Arab head of state praised the Camp David accords or spoke out in support of Sadat, the degree of opposition reflected the ideological position of the country. The more moderate nations, primarily Jordan and Saudi Arabia, expressed disappointment and listed a number of reservations they had about the agreements. On Sept. 19, an official Saudi communiqué concluded that "What has been reached at the Camp David conference cannot be considered a final acceptable formula for peace." The same day, Jordan disavowed any "legal or ethical commitment" to the accords.

Arab hard-liners were far less restrained. The most militant of Sadat's Arab opponents — Syria, Algeria, Libya, South Yemen and the PLO — met in Damascus soon after the Camp David summit to criticize Sadat for making what they termed a separate peace with Israel and for betraying the Arab cause.

Syria called the Camp David accords "a stab in the heart of the Arab nations and a flagrant deviation from the common Arab strategy, a contradiction of Arab summit resolutions and a denial of Palestinian rights." Syria was not specifically mentioned in the agreements but presumably could join the negotiations whenever it wished to do so.

Soviet leader Leonid Brezhnev also denounced the Camp David accords as an American attempt to split the Arab world and to force Arab nations to accept Israel's terms for peace in the area.

Carter had invited Sadat and Begin to Camp David to help regain the momentum that had been lost in the months following Sadat's peace initiative of November 1977, when he went to Jerusalem and addressed the Knesset. Begin in turn visited with Sadat at Ismailia, Egypt, Dec. 25-26, 1977. (Historic Documents of 1977, p. 827)

In recognition of their peace efforts, Sadat and Begin jointly received the Nobel Peace Prize on Dec. 10, 1978, in Oslo, Norway. Begin attended the award ceremony but Sadat, noting that a peace treaty had not been signed and that post-Camp David negotiations seemed to have reached a stalemate, sent a representative, Sayed Marei, to accept the prize.

Following are the texts of the Camp David accords, "A Framework for Peace in the Middle East Agreed to at Camp David" and "A Framework for the Conclusion of a Peace Treaty Between Egypt and Israel," that were signed by President Carter, President Sadat and Prime Minister Begin at the White House on Sept. 17; the remarks of the three leaders at the signing ceremony; Carter's address to a Joint Session of Congress on Sept. 18; Sadat's message to the Nobel Peace Prize ceremonies in Oslo, Norway, on Dec. 10 and Begin's speech there the same day. Sadat's message was delivered in English by his representative, Sayed Marei. (Boldface headings in brackets have been added by Congressional Quarterly to highlight the organization of the texts.):

A FRAMEWORK FOR PEACE IN THE MIDDLE EAST AGREED TO AT CAMP DAVID

Muhammad Anwar al-Sadat, President of the Arab Republic of Egypt, and Menachem Begin, Prime Minister of Israel, met with Jimmy Carter, President of the United States of America, at Camp David from September 5 to September 17, 1978, and have agreed on the following framwork for peace in the Middle East. They invite other parties to the Arab-Israeli conflict to adhere to it.

Preamble

The search for peace in the Middle East must be guided by the following:
●The agreed basis for a peaceful settlement of the conflict between Israel and its neighbors is United Nations Security Council Resolution 242, in all its parts.
●After four wars during 30 years, despite intensive human efforts, the Middle East, which is the cradle of civilization and the birthplace of three great religions, does not yet enjoy the blessings of peace. The people of the Middle East yearn for peace so that the vast human and natural resources of the region can be turned to the pursuits of peace and so that this area can become a model for coexistence and cooperation among nations.
●The historic initiative of President Sadat in visiting Jerusalem and the reception accorded to him by the Parliament, government and people of Israel, and the reciprocal visit of Prime Minister Begin to Ismailia, the peace proposals made by both leaders, as well as the warm reception of these missions by the peoples of both countries, have created an unprecedented opportunity for peace which must not be lost if this generation and future generations are to be spared the tragedies of war.
●The provisions of the Charter of the United Nations and the other

accepted norms of international law and legitimacy now provide accepted standards for the conduct of relations among all states.

● To achieve a relationship of peace, in the spirit of Article 2 of the United Nations Charter, future negotiations between Israel and any neighbor prepared to negotiate peace and security with it, are necessary for the purpose of carrying out all the provisions and principles of Resolutions 242 and 338.

● Peace requires respect for the sovereignty, territorial integrity and political independence of every state in the area and their right to live in peace within secure and recognized boundaries free from threats or acts of force. Progress toward that goal can accelerate movement toward a new era of reconciliation in the Middle East marked by cooperation in promoting economic development, in maintaining stability, and in assuring security.

● Security is enhanced by a relationship of peace and by cooperation between nations which enjoy normal relations. In addition, under the terms of peace treaties, the parties can, on the basis of reciprocity, agree to special security arrangements such as demilitarized zones, limited armaments areas, early warning stations, the presence of international forces, liaison, agreed measures for monitoring, and other arrangements that they agreed are useful.

Framework

Taking these factors into account, the parties are determined to reach a just, comprehensive, and durable settlement of the Middle East conflict through the conclusion of peace treaties based on Security Council Resolutions 242 and 338 in all their parts. Their purpose is to achieve peace and good neighborly relations. They recognize that, for peace to endure, it must involve all those who have been most deeply affected by the conflict. They therefore agree that this framework as appropriate is intended by them to constitute a basis for peace not only between Egypt and Israel, but also between Israel and each of its other neighbors which is prepared to negotiate peace with Israel on this basis. With that objective in mind, they have agreed to proceed as follows:

A. West Bank and Gaza

1. Egypt, Israel, Jordan and the representatives of the Palestinian people should participate in negotiations on the resolution of the Palestinian problem in all its aspects. To achieve that objective, negotiations relating to the West Bank and Gaza should proceed in three stages:

(a) Egypt and Israel agree that, in order to ensure a peaceful and orderly transfer of authority, and taking into account the security concerns of all the parties, there should be transitional arrangements for the West Bank and Gaza for a period not exceeding five years. In order to provide full autonomy to the inhabitants, under these arrangements the Israeli military government and its civilian administration will be withdrawn as soon as a self-governing authority has been freely elected by the inhabitants of these areas to replace the existing military government. To negotiate the details of a transitional arrangement, the Government of Jordan will be invited to join the negotiations on the basis of the framework. These new arrangements should give due consideration both to the principle of self-government by the inhabitants of these territories and to the legitimate security concerns of the parties involved.

(b) Egypt, Israel, and Jordan will agree on the modalities for establishing the elected self-governing authority in the West Bank and Gaza. The delegations of Egypt and Jordan may include Palestinians from the West Bank and Gaza or other Palestinians as mutually agreed. The parties will negotiate an agreement which will define the powers and responsibilities of the self-governing authority to be exercised in the West Bank and Gaza. A withdrawal of Israeli armed forces will take place and there will be a redeployment of the remaining Israeli forces into specified security locations. The agreement will also include arrangements for assuring internal and external security and public order. A strong local police force will be established, which may include Jordanian citizens. In addition, Israeli and Jordanian forces will participate in joint patrols and in the manning of control posts to assure the security of the borders.

(c) When the self-governing authority (administrative council) in the West Bank and Gaza is established and inaugurated, the transitional period of five years will begin. As soon as possible, but not later than the third year after the beginning of the transitional period, negotiations will take place to determine the final status of the West Bank and Gaza and its relationship with its neighbors, and to conclude a peace treaty between Israel and Jordan by the end of the transitional period. These negotiations will be conducted among Egypt, Israel, Jordan, and the elected representatives of the inhabitants of the West Bank and Gaza. Two separate but related committees will be convened, one committee, consisting of representatives of the four parties which will negotiate and agree on the final status of the West Bank and Gaza, and its relationship with its neighbors, and the second committee, consisting of representatives of Israel and representatives of Jordan to be joined by the elected representatives of the inhabitants of the West Bank and Gaza, to negotiate the peace treaty between Israel and Jordan, taking into account the agreement reached on the final status of the West Bank and Gaza. The negotiations shall be based on all the provisions and principles of UN Security Council Resolution 242. The negotiations will resolve, among other matters, the location of the boundaries and the nature of the security arrangements. The solution from the negotiations must also recognize the legitimate rights of the Palestinian people and their just requirements. In this way, the Palestinians will participate in the determination of their own future through:

1) The negotiations among Egypt, Israel, Jordan and the representatives of the inhabitants of the West Bank and Gaza to agree on the final status of the West Bank and Gaza and other outstanding issues by the end

of the transitional period.

2) Submitting their agreement to a vote by the elected representatives of the inhabitants of the West Bank and Gaza.

3) Providing for the elected representatives of the inhabitants of the West Bank and Gaza to decide how they shall govern themselves consistent with the provisions of their agreement.

4) Participating as stated above in the work of the committee negotiating the peace treaty between Israel and Jordan.

2. All necessary measures will be taken and provisions made to assure the security of Israel and its neighbors during the transitional period and beyond. To assist in providing such security, a strong local police force will be constituted by the self-governing authority. It will be composed of inhabitants of the West Bank and Gaza. The police will maintain continuing liaison on internal security matters with the designated Israeli, Jordanian, and Egyptian officers.

3. During the transitional period, representatives of Egypt, Israel, Jordan, and the self-governing authority will constitute a continuing committee to decide by agreement on the modalities of admission of persons displaced from the West Bank and Gaza in 1967, together with necessary measures to prevent disruption and disorder. Other matters of common concern may also be dealt with by this committee.

4. Egypt and Israel will work with each other and with other interested parties to establish agreed procedures for a prompt, just and permanent implementation of the resolution of the refugee problem.

B. Egypt-Israel

1. Egypt and Israel undertake not to resort to the threat or the use of force to settle disputes. Any disputes shall be settled by peaceful means in accordance with the provisions of Article 33 of the Charter of the United Nations.

2. In order to achieve peace between them, the parties agree to negotiate in good faith with a goal of concluding within three months from the signing of this Framework a peace treaty between them, while inviting the other parties to the conflict to proceed simultaneously to negotiate and conclude similar peace treaties with a view to achieving a comprehensive peace in the area. The Framework for the Conclusion of a Peace Treaty between Egypt and Israel will govern the peace negotiations between them. The parties will agree on the modalities and the timetable for the implementation of their obligations under the treaty.

C. Associated Principles

1. Egypt and Israel state that the principles and provisions described below should apply to peace treaties between Israel and each of its neighbors — Egypt, Jordan, Syria and Lebanon.

2. Signatories shall establish among themselves relations normal to

states at peace with one another. To this end, they should undertake to abide by all the provisions of the Charter of the United Nations. Steps to be taken in this respect include:

(a) full recognition;

(b) abolishing economic boycotts;

(c) guaranteeing that under their jurisdiction the citizens of the other parties shall enjoy the protection of the due process of law.

3. Signatories should explore possibilities for economic development in the context of final peace treaties, with the objective of contributing to the atmosphere of peace, cooperation and friendship which is their common goal.

4. Claims Commissions may be established for the mutual settlement of all financial claims.

5. The United States shall be invited to participate in the talks on matters related to the modalities of the implementation of the agreements and working out the timetable for the carrying out of the obligations of the parties.

6. The United Nations Security Council shall be requested to endorse the peace treaties and ensure that their provisions shall not be violated. The permanent members of the Security Council shall, be requested to underwrite the peace treaties and ensure respect for their provisions. They shall also be requested to conform their policies and actions with the undertakings contained in this Framework.

For the Government of the
Arab Republic of Egypt:

Al-Sadat

For the Government of Israel:

M. Begin

Witnessed by:

Jimmy Carter, President of the
United States of America

Annex

Text of United Nations Security Council
Resolution 242 of November 22, 1967

Adopted unanimously at the 1382nd meeting

The Security Council,

Expressing its continuing concern with the grave situation in the Middle East,

Emphasizing the inadmissibility of the acquisition of territory by war and the need to work for a just and lasting peace in which every State in the area can live in security,

Emphasizing further that all Member States in their acceptance of the

Charter of the United Nations have undertaken a commitment to act in accordance with Article 2 of the Charter,

1. *Affirms* that the fulfillment of Charter principles requires the establishment of a just and lasting peace in the Middle East which should include the application of both the following principles:

(i) Withdrawal of Israeli armed forces from territories occupied in the recent conflict;

(ii) Termination of all claims or states of belligerency and respect for and acknowledgement of the sovereignty, territorial integrity and political independence of every State in the area and their right to live in peace within secure and recognized boundaries free from threats or acts of force;

2. *Affirms further* the necessity

(a) For guaranteeing freedom of navigation through international waterways in the area;

(b) For achieving a just settlement of the refugee problem;

(c) For guaranteeing the territorial inviolability and political independence of every State in the area, through measures including the establishment of demilitarized zones;

3. *Requests* the Secretary-General to designate a Special Representative to proceed to the Middle East to establish and maintain contacts with the States concerned in order to promote agreement and assist efforts to achieve a peaceful and accepted settlement in accordance with the provisions and principles of this resolution.

4. *Requests* the Secretary-General to report to the Security Council on the progress of the efforts of the Special Representative as soon as possible.

Text of United Nations Security Council Resolution 338

Adopted by the Security Council at its 1747th meeting, on 21/22 October 1973

The Security Council

1. *Calls upon* all parties to the present fighting to cease all firing and terminate all military activity immediately, no later than 12 hours after the moment of the adoption of this decision, in the positions they now occupy;

2. *Calls upon* the parties concerned to start immediately after the cease-fire the implementation of Security Council Resolution 242 (1967) in all of its parts;

3 *Decides* that, immediately and concurrently with the cease-fire, negotiations start between the parties concerned under appropriate auspices aimed at establishing a just and durable peace in the Middle East.

FRAMEWORK FOR CONCLUSION OF
A PEACE TREATY BETWEEN EGYPT AND ISRAEL

In order to achieve peace between them, Israel and Egypt agree to negotiate in good faith with a goal of concluding within three months of the signing of this framework a peace treaty between them.

It is agreed that:

The site of the negotiations will be under a United Nations flag at a location or locations to be mutually agreed.

All of the principles of U.N. Resolution 242 will apply in this resolution of the dispute between Israel and Egypt.

Unless otherwise mutually agreed, terms of the peace treaty will be implemented between two and three years after the peace treaty is signed.

The following matters are agreed between the parties:

(a) the full exercise of Egyptian sovereignty up to the internationally recognized border between Egypt and mandated Palestine;

(b) the withdrawal of Israeli armed forces from the Sinai;

(c) the use of airfields left by the Israelis near El Arish, Rafah, Ras en Naqb, and Sharm el Sheikh for civilian purposes only, including possible commercial use by all nations;

(d) the right of free passage of ships of Israel through the Gulf of Suez and the Suez Canal on the basis of the Constantinople Convention of 1888 applying to all nations; the Strait of Tiran and the Gulf of Aqaba are international waterways to be open to all nations for unimpeded and nonsuspendable freedom of navigation and overflight;

(e) the construction of a highway between the Sinai and Jordan near Elat with guaranteed free and peaceful passage by Egypt and Jordan; and

(f) the stationing of military forces listed below.

Stationing of Forces

A. No more than one division (mechanized or infantry) of Egyptian armed forces will be stationed within an area lying approximately 50 kilometers (km) east of the Gulf of Suez and the Suez Canal.

B. Only United Nations forces and civil police equipped with light weapons to perform normal police functions will be stationed within an area lying west of the international border and the Gulf of Aqaba, varying in width from 20 km to 40 km.

C. In the area within 3 km east of the international border there will be Israeli limited military forces not to exceed four infantry battalions and United Nations observers.

D. Border patrol units, not to exceed three batallions, will supplement the civil police in maintaining order in the area not included above.

The exact demarcation of the above areas will be as decided during the peace negotiations.

Early warning stations may exist to insure compliance with the terms of the agreement.

United Nations forces will be stationed: (a) in part of the area in the Sinai lying within about 20 km of the Mediterranean Sea and adjacent to the international border, and (b) in the Sharm el Sheikh area to ensure freedom of passage through the Strait of Tiran; and these forces will not be removed unless such removal is approved by the Security Council of the United Nations with a unanimous vote of the five permanent members.

After a peace treaty is signed, and after the interim withdrawal is complete, normal relations will be established between Egypt and Israel, including: full recognition, including diplomatic, economic and cultural relations; termination of economic boycotts and barriers to the free movement of goods and people; and mutual protection of citizens by the due process of law.

Interim Withdrawal

Between three months and nine months after the signing of the peace treaty, all Israeli forces will withdraw east of a line extending from a point east of El Arish to Ras Muhammad, the exact location of this line to be determined by mutual agreement.

For the Government of the
Arab Republic of Egypt:

For the Government of Israel:

Witnessed by:
Jimmy Carter, President of the
United States of America

CARTER, BEGIN AND SADAT REMARKS
September 17, 1978

President Carter

When we first arrived at Camp David, the first thing upon which we agreed was to ask the people of the world to pray that our negotiations would be successful. Those prayers have been answered far beyond any expectations. We are privileged to witness tonight a significant achievement in the cause of peace, an achievement none thought possible a year ago, or even a month ago, an achievement that reflects the courage and wisdom of these two leaders.

Through 13 long days at Camp David, we have seen them display determination and vision and flexibility which was needed to make this agreement come to pass. All of us owe them our gratitude and respect.

They know that they will always have my personal admiration.

There are still great difficulties that remain and many hard issues to be settled. The questions that have brought warfare and bitterness to the Middle East for the last 30 years will not be settled overnight. But we should all recognize the substantial achievements that have been made.

One of the agreements that President Sadat and Prime Minister Begin are signing tonight is entitled, "A Framework For Peace in the Middle East." (Applause)

This framework concerns the principles and some specifics in the most substantive way which will govern a comprehensive peace settlement. It deals specifically with the future of the West Bank and Gaza, and the need to resolve the Palestinian problem in all its aspects. The framework document proposes a five-year transitional period in the West Bank and Gaza during which the Israeli military government will be withdrawn and a self-governing authority will be elected with full autonomy.

It also provides for Israeli forces to remain in specified locations during this period to protect Israel's security.

The Palestinians will have the right to participate in the determination of their own future, in negotiations which will resolve the final status of the West Bank and Gaza, and then to produce an Israeli-Jordanian peace treaty.

These negotiations will be based on all the provisions and all the principles of the United Nations Security Council Resolution 242. And it provides that Israel may live in peace within secure and recognized borders.

This great aspiration of Israel has been certified without constraint with the greatest degree of enthusiasm by President Sadat, the leader of one of the greatest nations on earth. (Applause)

The other document is entitled, "Framework For the Conclusion of a Peace Treaty," between Egypt and Israel.

It provides for the full exercise of Egyptian sovereignty over the Sinai. It calls for the full withdrawal of Israeli forces from the Sinai; and after an interim withdrawal which will be accomplished very quickly, the establishment of normal, peaceful relations between the two countries, including diplomatic relations. (Applause)

Together with accompanying letters, which we will make public tomorrow, these two Camp David agreements provide the basis for progress and peace throughout the Middle East.

There is one issue on which agreement has not been reached. Egypt states that the agreement to remove Israeli settlements from Egyptian territory is a prerequisite to a peace treaty. Israel states that the issue of Israeli settlements should be resolved during the peace negotiations. That is a substantial difference.

Within the next two weeks, the Knesset will decide on the issue of these settlements.

Tomorrow night, I will go before the Congress to explain these agreements more fully, and to talk about their implications for the United

States, and for the world. For the moment, and in closing, I want to speak more personally about my admiration for all of those who have taken part in this process, and my hope that the promise of this moment will be fulfilled.

During the last two weeks the members of all three delegations have spent endless hours, day and night, talking, negotiating, grappling with problems that have divided their people for 30 years. Whenever there was a danger that human energy would fail, or patience would be exhausted, or good will would run out — and there were such moments — these two leaders and the able advisers in all delegations found the resources within them to keep the chances for peace alive.

Well, the long days at Camp David are over. But many months of difficult negotiations still lie ahead.

I hope that the foresight and the wisdom that have made this session a success will guide these leaders and the leaders of all nations as they continue the process toward peace.

Thank you very much. (Applause)

President Sadat

Dear President Carter, in this historic moment, I would like to express to you my heartfelt congratulations and appreciation. For long days and nights, you devoted your time and energy to the pursuit of peace. You have been most courageous when you took the gigantic step of convening this meeting. The challenge was great, and the risks were high, but so was your determination.

You made a commitment to be a full partner in the peace process. I am happy to say that you have honored your commitment.

The signing of the framework for the comprehensive peace settlement has a significance far beyond the event. It signals the emergence of a new peace initiative with the American nation in the heart of the entire process.

In the weeks ahead, important decisions have to be made if we are to proceed on the road to peace. We have to reaffirm the faith of the Palestinian people in the ideal of peace.

The continuation of your active role is indispensable. We need your help and the support of the American people. Let me seize this opportunity to thank each and every American for his genuine interest in the cause of people in the Middle East.

Dear friend, we came to Camp David with all the good will and faith we possessed, and we left Camp David a few minutes ago with a renewed sense of hope and inspiration. We are looking forward to the days ahead with an added determination to pursue the noble goal of peace.

Your able assistants spared no effort to bring out this happy conclusion. We appreciate the spirit and dedication. Our hosts at Camp David and the State of Maryland were most generous and hospitable. To each one of them and to all those who are watching this great event, I say thank you.

Let us join in a prayer to God Almighty to guide our path. Let us pledge to make the spirit of Camp David a new chapter in the history of our nation.

Thank you, Mr. President. (Applause)

Prime Minister Begin

Mr. President of the United States, Mr. President of the Arab Republic of Egypt, ladies and gentlemen: The Camp David conference should be renamed. It was the Jimmy Carter Conference. (Applause)

The President took an initiative most imaginative in our time and brought President Sadat and myself and our colleagues and friends and advisers together under one roof. In itself it was a great achievement.

The President took a great risk on himself and did it with great civil courage, and it was a famous French field commander who said that it is much more difficult to show civil courage than military courage.

And the President worked. As far as my historic experience is concerned, I think that he worked harder than our forefathers did in Egypt, building the pyramids. (Laughter, applause)

Yes, indeed, he worked day and night, and so did we — (laughter) —

THE PRESIDENT: Amen.

PRIME MINISTER BEGIN: Day and night. We used to go to bed at Camp David between 3:00 and 4:00 o'clock in the morning, arise, as we are used to since our boyhood, at 5:00 or 6:00, and continue working.

The President showed interest in every section, every paragraph, every sentence, every word, every letter — (laughter) — of the framework agreements.

We had some difficult moments, as usually, there are some crises in negotiations; as usually, somebody gives a hint that perhaps he would like to pick up and go home. (Laughter) It is all usual. But ultimately, ladies and gentlemen, the President of the United States won the day. And peace now celebrates victory for the nations of Egypt and Israel and for all mankind.

Mr. President, we, the Israelis, thank you from the bottom of our hearts for all you have done for the sake of peace, for which we prayed and yearned more than 30 years. The Jewish people suffered much, too much. And therefore, peace to us is a striving, coming innermost from our heart and soul.

Now when I came here to the Camp David conference, I said perhaps as a result of our work, one day people will, in every corner of the world, be able to say "Habemus pacem" in the spirit of these days. Can we say so tonight? Not yet. We still have to go the road until my friend President Sadat and I sign the peace treaties.

We promised each other that we shall do so within three months.

Mr. President, tonight, at this celebration of the great historic event, let us promise each other that we shall do it earlier than within three months. (Laughter, applause)

Mr. President, you inscribed your name forever in the history of two ancient civilized peoples, the people of Egypt and the people of Israel.

Thank you, Mr. President.

THE PRESIDENT: Thank you very much. (Applause)

PRIME MINISTER BEGIN: I would like to say a few words about my friend, President Sadat. We met for the first time in our lives last November in Jerusalem. He came to us as a guest, a former enemy, and during our first meeting, we became friends.

In the Jewish teachings, there is a tradition that the greatest achievement of a human being is to turn his enemy into a friend, and this we do in reciprocity. Since then, we had some difficult days. (Laughter) I am not going now to tell you the saga of those days. Everything belongs to the past. Today, I visited President Sadat in his cabin because in Camp David you don't have houses, you only have cabins. (Laughter) He then came to visit me. We shook hands. And, thank God, we again could have said to each other, "You are my friend." (Applause)

And, indeed, we shall go on working and understanding, and with friendship and with good will. We will still have problems to solve. Camp David proved that any problem can be solved, if there is good will and understanding and some wisdom.

May I thank my own colleagues and friends, the Foreign Minister, the Finance Minister; Professor Barak who was the Attorney General. Now he is going to be His Honor, the Justice of the Supreme Court, the Israeli Brandeis and Dr. Rosenntz and our wonderful Ambassador to the United States, Mr. Simcha Dinitz, and all our friends, because without them, that achievement wouldn't have been possible.

I express my thanks to all the members of the American delegation, headed by the Secretary of State, a man whom we love and respect. So I express my thanks to all the members of the Egyptian delegation who worked so hard together with us, headed by Deputy Prime Minister, Mr. Touhamy, for all they have done to achieve this moment. It is a great moment in the history of our nations and indeed of mankind.

I looked for a precedent; I didn't find it. It was a unique conference, perhaps one of the most important since the Vienna Conference in the 19th century; perhaps.

Now, ladies and gentlemen, allow me to turn to my own people from the White House in my own native tongue.

(Brief remarks in Hebrew)

Thank you, ladies and gentlemen. (Applause)

President Carter

The first document that we will sign is entitled, "A Framework For Peace in the Middle East Agreed at Camp David," and the text of these two documents will be released tomorrow. The documents will be signed by President Sadat and Prime Minister Begin. It will be witnessed by me.

We have to exchange three documents, so we'll all sign three times for this one.

I might say that the first document is quite comprehensive in nature, encompassing a framework by which Israel can later negotiate peace treaties between herself and Lebanon, Syria, Jordan, as well as the outline of this document that we will now sign.

As you will later see, in studying the documents, it also provides for the realization of the hopes and dreams of the people who live in the West Bank and Gaza Strip and will assure Israel peace in the generations ahead.

This second document is the one relating to a framework for a peace treaty between Egypt and Israel. This is the document that calls for the completion of the peace treaty negotiations within three months. I have noticed the challenge extended by these two gentlemen to each other. They will complete within three months — I might say that this document encompasses almost all of the issues between the two countries and resolves those issues. A few lines remain to be drawn on maps and the question of the settlements is to be resolved. Other than that, most of the major issues are resolved already in this document.

We will now sign this document as well.

(Signing of document.)

THE PRESIDENT: Thank you very much. (Applause)

CARTER'S SPEECH
September 18, 1978

It has been more than 2,000 years since there was peace between Egypt and a free Jewish nation. If our present expectations are realized, this year we shall see such peace.

I would like to give tribute to the two men who have made this impossible dream now become a real possibility — the two great national leaders with whom I have met for the last two weeks at Camp David — President Anwar Sadat and Prime Minister Menachem Begin. At Camp David we sought a peace which is not only of vital importance to their own two nations, but to all the people of the Middle East — to all the people of the United States — indeed, to the rest of the world as well.

The world prayed for the success of our efforts, and those prayers have been answered.

I have come here tonight to discuss what these strong leaders have accomplished — and what it means for all of us. The United States has had no choice but to be concerned about the Middle East, and to use our influence and efforts to advance the cause of peace. For the last 30 years, through four wars, the people of this troubled region have paid a terrible price in suffering, division, hatred and bloodshed. No two nations have suffered more than Israel and Egypt. But the dangers and the costs of conflict in this region for our nation have been great as well. We have longstanding friendships with the nations and people of the region, and profound moral commitments which are deeply rooted in our values as a people.

'Vital to Our Nation'

The strategic location of these countries and the resources they possess mean that events in the Middle East directly affect people everywhere. We and our friends could not be indifferent if a hostile power were to establish domination there. In few areas of the world is there a greater risk that a local conflict could spread among other nations and then erupt into confrontation between the superpowers. Our people have come to understand that unfamiliar names — Sinai, Aqaba, Sharm el Sheikh, Ras en Naqb, Gaza, the West Bank of the Jordan — can have a direct and immediate bearing on our well-being as a nation and our hope for a peaceful world.

That is why we cannot be idle bystanders, why we have been full partners in the search for peace, and why it is so vital to our nation that these meetings have been a success.

Through the long years of conflict, four main issues have divided the parties.

One is the nature of peace — whether peace will mean simply that the guns are silenced, the bombs stop falling and the tanks cease to roll, or whether it will mean that the nations of the Middle East can deal with each other as neighbors and equals, with the full range of diplomatic, cultural, economic and human relations between them. The Camp David agreement has defined such relationships for Israel and her neighbors.

The second main issue is providing for the security of all the parties involved, including Israel, so that none of them need fear attack or military threats from any other. When implemented, the Camp David agreement will provide for such security.

Third is the question of an agreement on secure and recognized boundaries, the end of military occupation, and the granting of self-government or return to other nations of territories occupied by Israel during the 1967 conflict.

The Camp David agreement provides for the realization of these goals.

And finally, there is the painful human question of the fate of the Palestinians who live or who have lived in this disputed region. The Camp David agreement guarantees that the Palestinian people may participate in the resolution of the Palestinian problem in all its aspects.

Over the last 18 months there has been progress on some of these issues. Egypt and Israel came close to agreeing about the first issue — the nature of peace. They saw that the second and third — withdrawal and security — were intimately connected. But fundamental divisions remained in other areas — about the fate of the Palestinians, the future of the West Bank and Gaza, and the future of Israeli settlements in occupied Arab territories.

Sadat Initiative

We all remember the hopes for peace that were inspired by President Sadat's visit to Jerusalem last November, by the warm response of Prime

Minister Begin and the Israeli people and by the mutual promise that there would be no more war. Those hopes were sustained when Prime Minister Begin reciprocated by visiting Ismailia on Christmas Day.

That progress continued, at a slower and slower rate, through the early part of this year, but by early summer the negotiations had come to a standstill once again. It was this stalemate and the prospect of an even worse future that prompted me to invite both President Sadat and Prime Minister Begin to meet me at Camp David.

It is impossible to overstate the courage of these two men, or the foresight they have shown. Only through high ideals, through compromises of words and not of principle, and through a willingness to look deep into the human heart and to understand one another, can progress ever be made.

That is what these men and their wise and diligent advisers have done during these last 13 days.

When this conference began, I said that the prospects for success were remote. Enormous barriers of ancient history, nationalism and suspicion would have to be overcome if we were to meet our objectives.

But President Sadat and Prime Minister Begin have overcome those barriers, exceeded those expectations, and signed two agreements that hold out the possibility of resolving issues that history had taught us could not be resolved.

'Framework for Peace'

The first of the two documents is entitled "A Framework for Peace in the Middle East Agreed at Camp David." It deals with comprehensive settlement between Israel and all her neighbors, as well as the difficult question of the Palestinian people and the future of the West Bank and Gaza.

The agreement provides a basis for the resolution of issues involving the West Bank and Gaza over the next five years. It outlines a process of change which is in keeping with Arab hopes, while also respecting Israel's vital security interests. The Israeli military government over those areas will be withdrawn and will be replaced with a self-government with full autonomy. Israeli forces will also be withdrawn and redeployed into specified locations to protect Israel's security. The Palestinians will further participate in determining their own future through talks in which elected representatives of the inhabitants of the West Bank and Gaza will negotiate with Egypt, Israel and Jordan to determine the final status of the West Bank and Gaza.

Israel has agreed that the legitimate rights of the Palestinian people will be recognized. After the signing of this framework and during the negotiations concerning Palestinian self-government, no new Israeli settlements will be established in this area. The issue of future settlements will be decided among the negotiating parties.

The final status of the West Bank and Gaza will be decided by the end of the five-year transitional period, as part of a negotiation which will also produce a peace treaty between Israel and Jordan. These negotiations will be based on all the provisions and principles of U.N. Security Council Resolution 242. The agreement on the final status of these areas will be submitted to a vote by the representatives of the inhabitants of the West Bank and Gaza, and they will have the right, for the first time in their history, to decide how they will govern themselves. We also believe there should be a just settlement of the problems of displaced persons and refugees, which takes into account appropriate U.N. resolutions.

Finally, this document also outlines a variety of security arrangements to reinforce peace between Israel and its neighbors.

This is, indeed, a comprehensive and fair framework for peace in the Middle East.

'Framework for Treaty'

The second agreement is entitled "A Framework for the Conclusion of a Peace Treaty Between Egypt and Israel." It returns to Egypt the full exercise of its sovereignty over the Sinai peninsula and establishes several security zones for the protection of all parties. It also provides that Egypt will extend full diplomatic recognition to Israel at the time Israel withdraws her armed forces from most of the Sinai, which will take place between three and nine months after the conclusion of the peace treaty. The treaty is to be fully negotiated and signed no later than three months from now. Prime Minister Begin and President Sadat have now challenged each other to conclude the treaty even earlier. This will be a wonderful Christmas present for the world. Complete withdrawal of all Israeli forces will take place no more than three years after the treaty has been signed.

While both parties are in complete agreement on the goals I have just described, there is one issue on which agreement has not been reached. Egypt states that agreement to remove Israeli settlements from Egyptian territory is a prerequisite to a peace treaty. Israel states that the issue of the Israeli settlements should be resolved during the peace negotiations. Within two weeks the Knesset [Israeli parliament] will decide on the issue of the settlements. Our own government's position on this issue is well-known and has been consistent. It is my strong hope that the question of Israeli settlements on Egyptian territory will not be the final obstacle to peace.

None of us should underestimate the historic importance of what has been done. This is the first time that an Arab and an Israeli leader have signed a comprehensive framework for peace. It contains the seeds of a time when the Middle East, with all its vast potential, may be a land of human richness and fulfillment, rather than of bitterness and conflict. No region of the world has greater natural and human resources — and nowhere have they been more heavily weighed down by hatred and war. These agreements hold out the real possibility that this burden might be lifted.

Obstacles Remain

But we must also not forget the magnitude of the obstacles that remain. The summit exceeded our expectations — but we know that it left many difficult issues still to be resolved. These issues will require careful negotiation in the months to come.

The Egyptian and Israeli people must recognize the tangible benefits that peace will bring, and support the decisions their leaders have made so that a secure and peaceful future can be achieved. The American public must also offer its full support to those who have difficult decisions still to make.

What lies ahead for all of us is to recognize the statesmanship that President Sadat and Prime Minister Begin have shown and to invite others to follow their example. I have already invited the other leaders of the Arab world to help sustain progress toward a comprehensive peace.

We must also join in an effort to bring to an end the conflict and terrible suffering in Lebanon. We need to consult closely with the Arab leaders, and I am pleased to say that King Hussein of Jordan and King Khalid of Saudi Arabia have now agreed to receive Secretary [of State Cyrus R.] Vance, who will be leaving tomorrow to explain to them the terms of the Camp David agreement and to secure their support for the realization of the new hopes and dreams of the people of the Middle East.

For many years, the Middle East has been a textbook for pessimism, a demonstration that diplomatic ingenuity was no match for intractable human conflicts. Today we are privileged to see the chance for one of the bright moments in human history — a chance that may open the way to peace. We have a chance for peace because these two brave leaders found within themselves the willingness to work together to seek a lasting peace; for that, I hope you will share my prayer of thanks and my hope that the promise of this moment shall be fully realized.

The prayers at Camp David were the same as those of the shepherd King David who prayed in the 85th Psalm:

> *Wilt thou not revive us again that thy people may rejoice in thee?*
>
> *I will hear what God the Lord will speak: for he will speak peace unto his people, and to his saints: but let them not turn again to folly.*

SADAT MESSAGE
December 10, 1978

Your Majesty, Your Royal Highnesses, Mr. Prime Minister of Israel, Madam Chairman and members of the Nobel Peace Prize Committee, excellencies, distinguished guests, ladies and gentlemen:

I am very well aware that you would all have liked to see President al-Sadat here today. Circumstances, particularly those related to the negotiations, have required his presence in Cairo. I am deeply gratified to have been given the honor of representing on this privileged occasion my head of state, whom hundreds of millions of men of goodwill around the world recognize, along with you, as the man of peace. It is my lot to do this and I hope you are going to accept it.

It is of great honor to us to express Egypt's appreciation of the Norwegian people's support for the peace efforts — an appreciation that derives from Norway's tradition of supporting action for justice and humanity. Honoring President al-Sadat is a token of his recognition and encouragement for us all to follow in the path which the president has opened by his historic and unprecedented initiative. It is a path fraught with danger, difficulties and innumerable obstacles, but at the end of it the real prize awaits us all: peace based on justice; real, lasting and comprehensive peace in a blessed area where the people are longing to devote all their efforts for a future of prosperity and happiness.

[Reads Message]

Ladies and gentlemen, I have the honor to read to you the message of President Muhammad Anwar al-Sadat:

Your Majesty, Your Royal Highnesses, Mr. Prime Minister of Israel, Madam Chairman and members of the Nobel Prize Commitee, excellencies, distinguished guests, ladies and gentlemen: In the name of God, peace be with you. Peace be upon you. This is the traditional way in which every day we greet one another. It reflects our deepest feelings and hope. We always say it and we mean it.

Your Majesty, ladies and gentlemen, the decision of the Nobel Prize Committee to bestow upon me the peace award has been received by the people of Egypt not only as an honor but also as a confirmation of the universal recognition of our relentless efforts to achieve peace in an area in which God has chosen to bring to mankind — to Moses, Jesus and Muhammad — his message of wisdom and light.

Your Majesty, ladies and gentlemen, recognition is due to a man of high integrity — President Jimmy Carter — whose signal efforts to overcome obstacles in the way of peace deserves our keenest appreciation. The road to peace is one which, throughout its history, which coincides with the dawn of human civilization, the people of Egypt have considered as befitting their genius and their vocation. No people on earth have been more steadfastly faithful to the cause of peace and none more attached to the principles of justice which constitute the cornerstone of any real and lasting peace.

Do I need to remind such an august and distinguished gathering that the first recorded peace treaty in history was concluded more than 3,000 years ago between Ramses the Great and Hattusilis, prince of the Hittites, who resolved to establish good peace and good brotherhood? And since then through the ages, even when wars appeared as a necessary evil, the real genius of Egypt has been one of peace and its ambition has been to build, not to destroy; to create, not to annihilate; to coexist, not to eliminate, but the land of Egypt has always been cherished by God Almighty. Moses lived there. Jesus fled to it from injustice and foreign domination and the Holy Koran has blessed it. And Islam, which is the religion of justice, equality and moral values, has added new dimensions to the eternal spirit of Egypt.

We have always realized that the qualities of chivalry, courage, faith and discipline that were characteristic of a romantic concept of war should, in an era where war had become only synonymous with devastation to all, by a means of enriching life, not generating death. It is in this spirit that Alfred Nobel created the prize which bears his name and which is aimed at encouraging mankind to follow the path of peace, development, progress and prosperity.

Ladies and gentlemen, it is in the light of all this that I embarked a year ago upon my initiative aimed at restoring peace in an area where man received the words of God. Through me, it was the eternal Egypt that was expressing itself: Let us put an end to war. Let us reshape life on the solid bases of equity and truth. And it is this call which reflected the will of the Egyptian people, of the great majority of the Arab and the Israeli peoples and, indeed, of millions of men, women and children around the world that you are today honoring. And these hundreds of millions will judge to what extent every responsible leader in the Middle East has responded to the hope of mankind.

We have now come in the peace process to a moment of truth which requires each one of us to take a new look at the situation. I trust that you all know that when I made my historic trip to Jerusalem, my aim was not to strike a deal, as some politicians do. I made my trip because I am convinced that we owe it to this generation and the generations to come not to leave a stone unturned in our pursuit of peace. The deal is the greatest one in the history of men and we have accepted the challenge to translate it from a cherished hope into a living reality and to win through vision and imagination the hearts and minds of our people and enable them to look beyond the unhappy past.

[Recalls Knesset Speech]

Let me remind you of what I said in the Knesset more than 1 year ago. I said: "Let me tell you truthfully today we have a good chance for peace, an opportunity that cannot be repeated, if we are really serious in the quest for peace. If we throw or fritter away this chance, the curse of mankind and the curse of history will be for the one who plots against it."

I would like now on this most solemn and moving occasion to pledge again that we in Egypt, with the future rather than the past in mind, are determined to pursue in good faith, as we have always done, the road to peace and to leave no avenue unexplored to reach this cherished goal and to reconcile the sons of Isma'il and the sons of Isaac. In renewing this pledge, which I hope that the other parties will also adhere to, I again repeat what I said in the Knesset more than a year ago: "Any life lost in war is the life of a human being, irrespective of whether it is an Arab or an Israeli. The wife who becomes widow is a human being entitled to live in happy family, Arab or Israeli. Innocent children deprived of paternal care and sympathy are all our children, whether they live on Arab or Israeli soil and we owe them the biggest responsibility of providing them with a happy present and a bright future. For the sake of all this, for the sake of protecting the lives of all our sons and brothers, for our societies to produce in security and confidence, for the development of man, his well-being and his right to share in an honorable life, for responsibility towards the coming generations, for the smile of every child born on our land." This is our vision of peace which I repeat today, the day of human rights.

['Our Conception of Peace']

In the light of this, let me share with you our conception of peace:

First, the true essence of peace which insures its stability and durability is justice. Any peace not built on justice and on the recognition of the rights of the peoples would be a structure of sand which would crumble under the first blow.

The peace process comprises a beginning and steps toward this end. Reaching his end the process must achieve its projected goal; that goal is to bring security to the peoples of the area and the Palestinians in particular restoring to them all their right to a life of liberty and dignity. We are moving steadily towards this goal for all the peoples of the region. This is what it stands for, this is the letter and spirit of Camp David.

Second, peace is indivisible. To endure, it should be comprehensive and englobe all the parties in the conflict.

Third, peace and prosperity in our area are closely linked and interrelated. Our efforts should aim at achieving both because it is as important to save man from death by destructive weapons as it is to not abandon him to the evil of want and misery. And war is no cure for the problems of our area.

And last but not least, peace is a dynamic construction to which all should contribute, each adding a new brick. It goes far beyond a formal agreement or treaty. It transcends a word here or there. That is why it requires politicians who enjoy vision and imagination and who, beyond the present, look toward the future.

It is of this conviction deeply rooted in our history and our faith that the people of Egypt have embarked upon a major effort to achieve peace in the Middle East, an area of a paramount importance to the whole world. We will spare no effort. We will not tire or despair. We will not lose faith and we are confident that in the end our aim will be achieved.

I will ask you all to join me in a prayer that the day may soon come when peace will prevail on the basis of justice and the recognition of the rights of all the peoples to shape their own life, to determine their own future and to contribute to building a world of prosperity for all mankind.

Your Majesty, Your Royal Highnesses, Mr. Prime Minister of Israel, Madam Chairman and members of the Nobel Peace Prize Committee, excellencies, distinguished guests, ladies and gentlemen: Peace be upon you. [applause]

BEGIN SPEECH
December 10, 1978

Your Majesty, your Royal Highnesses, your Excellencies, Madam Chairlady and members of the Nobel Prize Committee, Mr. Marei, Representative of the President of Egypt, Ladies and Gentlemen.

I ask for permission first to pay tribute to Golda Meir, my predecessor, a great leader and Prime Minister, who strove with all her heart to achieve peace between Israel and her neighbors. Her blessed memory will live forever in the hearts of the Jewish people, and of all peace-loving nations.

I have come from the land of Israel, the land of Zion and Jerusalem, and here I stand in humility and with pride, as a son of the Jewish people, as one of the generation of the Holocaust and Redemption.

The ancient Jewish people gave the world the vision of eternal peace, of universal disarmament, of abolishing the teaching and learning of war. Two prophets, Yeshayahu Ben Amotz and Micha Hamorashti, having foreseen the spiritual unity of man under God — with his word coming forth from Jerusalem — gave the nations of the world the following vision expressed in identical terms:

> "And they shall beat their swords into ploughshares and
> their spears into pruning hooks.
> Nation shall not lift up sword against nation, neither shall
> they learn war anymore."

We mortals, who believe in divine providence, when recalling those sacred prophecies, ask ourselves, not whether, but when is this vision going to become reality? We remember the past, even in this century alone and we know. We look around and see. Millions of men of all nations are under arms. Intercontinental missiles deposited in the bowels of the earth or lying on the beds of oceans can destroy man and everything he has built. Not in Alfred Nobel's time, but in our own era, has mankind become capable of destroying itself and returning the earth to *tohu vevohu* [primordial chaos]. Under such circumstances, should we, can we, keep our faith in an eternal peace that will one day reign over mankind?

Yes, we should and we can. Perhaps, that very capability of total destruction of our little planet — achieved for the first time in the annals of mankind — will one day, God willing, become the origin, the cause and the prime mover for the elimination of all instruments of destruction from the face of the earth and ultimate peace, prayed for and yearned for by previous generations, will become portion of all nations. Despite the tragedies and disappointments of the past, we must never forsake that vision, that human dream, that unshakeable faith.

Peace is the beauty of life. It is sunshine. It is the smile of a child, the love of a mother, the joy of a father, the togetherness of a family. It is the advancement of man, the victory of a just cause, the triumph of truth. Peace is all of these and more and more.

[The Holocaust]

But in my generation, Ladies and Gentlemen, there was a time indescribeable. Six million Jews — men, women and children — a number larger than many a nation in Europe — were dragged to a wanton death and slaughtered methodically in the heart of the civilized continent.

It was not a sudden outburst of human, or rather inhuman cruelty that from time to time has happened in the history of mankind. It was a systematic process of extermination, which unfolded before the eyes of the whole world for more than six years. Those who were doomed, deprived of their human dignity, starved, humiliated, led away and ultimately turned into ashes, cried out for rescue, but in vain. Other than a few famous and unforgettable exceptions, they were left alone to face the destroyer.

At such a time, unheard of since the first generation, the hour struck to rise and fight — for the dignity of man, for survival, for liberty, for every value of the human image a man has been endowed with by his creator, for every known inalienable right for which he stands and lives. Indeed, there are days when to fight for a cause so absolutely just is the highest human command. Norway has known such days, and so have we. Only in honoring that command comes the regeneration of the concept of peace. You rise, you struggle, you make sacrifices to achieve and guarantee the prospect and hope of living in peace — for you and your people, for your children and their children.

Let it, however, be declared and known, stressed, and noted that fighters for freedom hate war. My friends and I learned this precept from Zeev Jabotinsky through his own example, and through the one he set for us from Giuseppe Garibaldi. Our brothers in spirit, wherever they dwell, learned it from their masters and teachers. This is our common maxim and belief — that if through your efforts and sacrifices you win liberty and with it the prospect of peace, then work for peace, because there is no mission in life more sacred.

And so reborn, Israel always strove for peace, yearned for it, made endless endeavours to achieve it.

My colleagues and I have gone in the footsteps of our predecessors, since the very first day we were called by our people to care for their future. We went any place, we looked for any avenue, we made any effort to bring about negotiations between Israel and her neighbors, negotiations without which peace remains an abstract desire.

[The Fruits of Peace]

We have labored long and hard to turn it into a reality — because of the blessing it holds for ourselves, our neighbors, the world. In peace, the Middle East, the ancient cradle of civilization, will become invigorated and transformed, throughout its lands, there will be freedom of movement of people, of ideas, of goods. Cooperation and development in agriculture will make the deserts blossom. Industry will bring the promise of a better life. Sources of water will be developed and the almost year-long sunshine will yet be harnessed for the common needs of all the nations. Yes, indeed, the Middle East, standing at the crossroads of the world, will become a peaceful center of international communication between East and West, North and South — a center of human advancement in every sphere of creative endeavor. This and more is what peace will bring to our region.

During the past year, many efforts for peace were made and many significant events took place. The President of the Arab Republic of Egypt expressed his readiness to come to Jerusalem, the eternal capital of Israel, and to address our Parliament, the Knesset. When that message reached me, I, without delay or hesitation, extended to President Sadat on behalf of Israel, an invitation to visit our country.

I told him: "You will be received with respect and cordiality." And, indeed, so he was received, cordially and respectfully, by the people, by the Parliament and by the Government of our nation.

We knew and learned that we have differences of opinion. But, whenever we recall those days of Jerusalem, we say always, that they were shining, beautiful days of friendliness and understanding.

It was in this same atmosphere, that the meetings in Ismailya were conducted. In the spirit of the Nobel Prize tradition, we gave to each other the most momentous pledge: "No more war. No more bloodshed. We shall negotiate and reach agreement."

Admittedly, there were difficult times as well. Let nobody forget, that we deal with a conflict of more than sixty years, with its manifold tragedies. These, we must put behind us, in order to establish friendship and make peace the beauty of our lives.

[Camp David Accord]

Many of the difficulties were overcome at Camp David, where the President of the United States, Mr. Jimmy Carter, unforgettably invested unsparing effort, untiring energy and great devotion, in the peace-making process. There, despite all the differences, we found solutions for problems, agreed on issues and the Framework for Peace was signed. With its signature, there was rejoicing in our countries and throughout the world. The path leading to peace was paved.

The phase that followed was the natural arduous negotiations to elaborate and conclude a peace treaty, as we promised each other to do at Camp David. The delegations of both countries worked hard and have, I believe, produced a draft document, that can serve, if and when signed and ratified, as a good treaty of peace between countries that decided to put an end to hostility and war and begin a new era of understanding and cooperation. Such a treaty can serve as the first indispensable step towards a comprehensive peace in our region.

If, because of all these efforts, President Sadat and I have been awarded the Nobel Peace Prize, let me from this rostrum, again congratulate him — as I did in a direct conversation between Jerusalem and Cairo, a few weeks ago on the morrow of the announcement.

Now, it is I who must express gratitude from the bottom of my heart, for the honor you do me.

[Protection of Human Rights]

But, Ladies and Gentlemen, before doing so, permit me to remind us all, that today is an important anniversary — the thirtieth anniversary of the adoption of the Universal Declaration of Human Rights. Let us always remember the magnificently written words of its first article. It expresses the essence of all the declarations of the rights of man and citizen, written throughout history. It says:

> "All human beings are born free and equal, in dignity and
> rights. They are endowed with reason and conscience and
> should act towards one another in a spirit of brotherhood."

Free women and men everywhere must wage an incessant campaign so that these human values become a generally recognized and practiced reality. We must regretfully admit that in various parts of the world, this is not yet the case. Without those values and human rights, the real peace of which we dream is jeopardized.

For reasons self-understood, but which every man and woman of goodwill accept, I must remind my honored listeners of my brethren and the prisoners who are deprived of one of their most basic rights: to go home. I speak about people of great courage, who deserve, not only the respect, but also the moral support of the free world. I speak about people who, even from the depths of their suffering, repeat the age-long prayer:

"Leshana Habaa BeYerusalem."

"Next Year in Jerusalem."

The preservation and protection of human rights are indispensable to give peace of nations and individuals its real meaning.

Allow me, now, to turn to you, Madame President of the Nobel Peace Prize Committee and to all its members and say, thank you. I thank you for the great distinction.

[Honor to Israel]

It does not, however, belong to me, it belongs to my people — the ancient people and renaissant nation that came back, in love and devotion, to the land of its ancestors, after centuries of homelessness and persecution. This prestigious recognition is due to this people, because they suffered so much, because they lost so many, because they love peace and want it, with all their hearts for themselves and for their neighbors. On their behalf, I humbly accept the award, and in their name, I thank you from the bottom of my heart.

And may I express to his Majesty, the King, our deep gratitude for the gracious hospitality his Majesty, on this occasion, bestowed upon my wife and myself.

Your Majesty, your Highnesses, Members of the Nobel Peace Prize Committee, Ladies and Gentlemen:

Seventy-seven years ago, the first Nobel Peace Prize was awarded. Jean Henri Dunant was its recipient. On December 10, 1901, the President of the Norwegian Parliament said:

> "The Norwegian people have always demanded that their independence be respected. They have always been ready to defend it. But at the same time, they have always had a keen desire and need for peace."

May I, Ladies and Gentlemen, on behalf of the people of Israel, respectfully subscribe to these true and noble words. Thank you.

INCIDENCE OF WORKPLACE CANCER
September 11, 15, 1978

Joseph A. Califano Jr., secretary of health, education and welfare, on Sept. 11 announced the completion of a study disclosing that at least 20 percent of the incidence of cancer in the United States was attributable to occupational exposure to cancer-causing agents. The major study, prepared by the National Cancer Institute, the National Institute of Environmental Health Sciences and the National Institute for Occupational Safety and Health, was released on Sept. 15.

Califano made the announcement at a National Conference on Occupational Safety and Health sponsored by the AFL-CIO, in Washington, D.C. The study raised sharply the estimate of the incidence of workplace-related cancer. Previously published estimates, according to the study, had been as low as 1 to 5 percent and no higher than 15 percent. Some health officials familiar with the study said that investigators had found that the incidence of occupational-related cancer could be as high as 40 percent of all cancer in the United States, according to The Washington Post.

Califano Speech

Califano told the conference that "at the turn of the century the big killers and cripplers were infectious diseases." He added, "Today, [they] are related to environment and lifestyle: heart disease, cancer, stroke and accidents." Stressing the need for prevention as well as treatment, Califano said, "The federal government will spend $48 billion on health care this year; of that amount, fully 96 percent is aimed at treatment; only four

633

percent — less than $2 billion — is earmarked for programs to prevent disease or promote health."

Califano asserted that it was "myopic" to consider occupational health and safety programs as inflationary. "It is time to take the blinders off: To count what these programs promise in ultimate savings," he said. " Which, after all, creates the greater burden: the cost of a program to protect workers from occupational hazards? Or the staggering costs of treating workers for the consequences of these hazards? Our economists must join with our scientists and find a new way to calculate inflation related to occupational health and safety."

Report

The 50-page report, entitled Estimates of the Fraction of Cancer in the United States Related to Occupational Factors, *said that earlier low estimates of work-related cancer resulted from incomplete documentation, an over-reliance on the "one effect-one cause" explanation of cancer incidence, complications because of the dependence of cancer incidence upon age and length of exposure, and the fluctuations in exposure to carcinogens over a worker's lifetime. The report said that cancer was thought to be a "disease of interactions," rarely caused by one substance or process and more likely attributable to two or more factors acting together or in tandem.*

Asbestos

The report cited previous studies of asbestos — the most analyzed work-related carcinogen — as ones in which estimates of cancer incidence had been "deceptively low." The report estimated that between 8 and 11 million workers had been exposed to asbestos since the beginning of World War II. Of the 4 million most heavily exposed asbestos workers still living, the study estimated that 1.6 million would die of asbestos-related cancers. The report stated, "The most important lesson to be learned from the asbestos story is that a major public health disaster can develop while its early manifestations are lost by being attributed to other factors."

Secretary Califano in his speech before the labor conference emphasized the need for public recognition of the dangers of such cancer-causing substances as asbestos. "This is of special importance," he said, "because the most serious diseases associated with asbestos take a long time to develop — from 15-35 years or more."

The study noted that five other cancer-producing substances prevalent on the job could cause as many cases of cancer as asbestos. These were arsenic, benzene, chromium, nickel (oxides) and petroleum fractions (including aromatics).

Smoking

The significance of smoking when it takes place in an occupational environment that already is hazardous was emphasized in the study and was underscored by Secretary Califano on Nov. 29. He ordered new federal standards to be drawn up which would tighten safety regulations on some manufacturers unless they required workers in certain jobs not to smoke. Califano said that the risk of cancer rose for smokers exposed to talc in the rubber industry, to decay products of the element radon in uranium mining and to fluorocarbons in the plastics industry. Those industries, he said, would be the initial targets of the standards.

Reaction

Spokesmen for a number of industrial firms were quick to challenge the study's estimates of the incidence of workplace-related cancer. Dr. Perry Gehring, the Dow Chemical Company's director of health and environmental research, said that "what it boils down to is that Califano is all wet. He doesn't have the data to support those findings." Dr. Gehring said that lower industry estimates of cancer related to occupations were drawn from studies by the International Agency for Research on Cancer in France and the American Health Foundation, an industry-supported organization.

Following are excerpts from a speech by Joseph A. Califano Jr., secretary of health, education and welfare, Sept. 11, 1978, at an AFL-CIO Conference on Occupational Safety and Health in Washington, D.C., and excerpts from a federal government report, Estimates of the Fraction of Cancer in the United States Related to Occupational Factors, *issued Sept. 15, 1978:*

CALIFANO SPEECH

I am delighted to be here; to join the first meeting of labor's new Division of Occupational Safety and Health as you consider a subject of increasing importance in our national life: the health of American workers and the safety of the American workplace.

Before passage of the Occupational Safety and Health Act of 1970, the federal government's involvement in this field was limited to federal employees, a few specific industries like mining, and firms holding federal contracts.

Today, largely because of your devotion to the cause, more than 85 million workers are protected by the Occupational Safety and Health Act. Because of you, employers generally are admonished by law to furnish each employee — and here I quote the Act — "a place of employment . . . free from recognized hazards that are . . . likely to cause death or serious physical harm."

We have made some progress toward that goal — but we have a long way yet to go. And just as the struggle has been marked by intense disagreements and controversies in the past, so it will be in the future.

But if there are still those who doubt the importance or question the necessity of this program, let them consider a few facts:

• Fourteen thousand people die each year from occupational accidents alone.

• The risks of occupational injury and illness are constantly growing. In the chemical industry alone, production has skyrocketed from one billion pounds of synthetic organic chemicals in 1940 to more than 300 billion pounds last year: many of them new and untested substances. And an estimated 390,000 new cases of work-related disease occur each year: a number equal to the population of Mobile, Alabama.

• The conventional judgment has been that the fraction of cancer incidence in the United States attributable to occupational exposure to cancer-causing agents is quite small, somewhere between 1 and 5 percent. However, a new study by scientists at the National Cancer Institute and the National Institute of Environmental Health Sciences is nearing completion; it will be delivered to OSHA later this week. This new study indicates for the first time that the percentage is many times higher. Indeed, the study concludes: "If the full consequences of occupational exposures in the present and the recent past are taken into account, estimates of at least 20 percent appear much more reasonable and may even be conservative." This means that at least 20 percent of all cancer in the United States — and perhaps more — may be work related.

The Importance of Prevention

Our great need in America today is not just for a vigorous program of occupational health and safety; we need a broad national strategy of prevention for all our citizens.

You and I know that the greatest lifesaving breakthroughs of this century have been breakthroughs in preventive, not curative, medicine: vaccines to eliminate diseases from smallpox to polio; pure water and pure food.

So successful have preventive public-health measures been that in this century, the pattern of crippling and killing diseases has shifted: At the turn of the century, the big killers and cripplers were infectious diseases. Today, the big killers and cripplers are related to environment and lifestyle: heart disease, cancer, stroke, and accidents.

Yet our health policies and health budgets are focused almost obsessively on treatment, not prevention. The federal government will spend $48 billion on health care this year; of that amount, fully 96 percent is aimed at treatment, only four percent — less than $2 billion — is earmarked for programs to prevent disease or promote health.

You and I know that a strategy of prevention in the workplace can make not only medical but economic sense. Some 25 million workdays, after all, are lost each year because of occupational injuries and disease; the cost to employers of the workers' compensation system was nearly $11 billion in 1976.

Yet most of the arguments against occupational health and safety measures, as you know, focus on costs. And these arguments seldom focus on the tremendous gain that these programs can provide.

It is, in my judgment, myopic to argue that programs to protect workers are inflationary — if we do not count in our calculations what those programs buy: safety, health and often greater productivity.

It is time to take the blinders off: to count what these programs promise in ultimate savings. Which, after all, creates the greater burden: the cost of a program to protect workers from occupational hazards? Or the staggering costs of treating workers for the consequences of these hazards? Our economists must join with our scientists and find a new way to calculate inflation related to occupational health and safety.

Finally, there is the matter of simple justice. We do not want an economy that buys goods at the expense of workers' health; an economy that asks workers to earn their livelihoods by endangering their lives. The workers of America are willing and able and eager to sweat on the job; we should not ask them to bleed.

So you and I have a job to do: a job of convincing the American public that programs of prevention and health promotion are not just an expense, but an investment; that they are worthwhile, desirable, economically feasible, and urgently needed — especially in the workplace. For it is in the workplace where many of the dangers are greatest.

And vigilance in the workplace is one way of detecting hazards that may otherwise spread from factory or laboratory to the world outside. We have learned, often by tragic experience, that Kepone, undetected in the workplace today, flows insidiously into our rivers and streams tomorrow. The occupational exposure to asbestos today is tomorrow's exposure of our families at home and our children in school. Today's chemical dumping ground may be tomorrow's subdivision or school playground. By protecting workers today, we are likely to make the greatest gains in our efforts to protect the rest of society.

So I would argue first that we should take a broad view of occupational health and safety programs: these are not programs which benefit workers alone — they are for all of us. So they belong at the center of a broad new national preventive-health strategy.

Action at HEW

What, then, are we at HEW doing to underscore these convictions with action? Over the past twenty months we have made major efforts in several areas.

The most important of these, as you know, is in the field of asbestos exposure.

Nearly two thousand years ago, Pliny the Elder and other ancient scholars recorded the first signs that asbestos might be harmful: a sickness of the lungs appeared in slaves who weaved asbestos into cloth.

Now scientific studies have demonstrated that asbestos creates an especially high risk of lung cancer and other serious lung diseases for workers heavily exposed to the substance.

But until last April, no systematic effort had ever been undertaken to notify physicians, former asbestos workers and others at risk of the hazards associated with asbestos exposure. Such notification is of special importance because the most serious diseases associated with asbestos take a long time to develop — from 15 to 35 years or more — and because recent studies have underscored that workers exposed in the past, especially during World War II, may just now be facing immediate, serious health threats.

We are dealing, as you know, with large numbers of workers: The total number exposed to asbestos just since the beginning of World War II is estimated at between 8 and 11 million.

And so last April 26, HEW launched a major campaign to inform doctors, workers, and others about the grave risks of asbestos exposure:

• We sent a letter from the Surgeon General to every one of the nation's physicians, describing the nature of the risk, and outlining steps doctors could take in diagnosing and treating patients.

• We put an Asbestos Education Task Force to work, developing aggressive public-education programs on asbestos.

• We produced and distributed public service announcements to radio and television stations across the nation. 182 television stations and 550 radio stations have committed themselves to airing these spots nearly 60,000 times. . . .

• We distributed 2.5 million brochures answering questions about asbestos.

• And on October 3 a warning flyer will be mailed to 30 million Social Security beneficiaries with their checks. By next January, 40 million people will have received notices. . . .

I cannot emphasize too strongly the importance of this effort. We are learning that the consequences of asbestos exposure are, if anything, even more serious than we originally suspected:

• An estimated 5 million American men and women — workers in asbestos plants, insulation workers, construction workers, steamfitters, carpenters, tile setters, auto mechanics, and the like — breathe significant amounts of asbestos fibers each day.

• On the basis of what we know today, it is estimated that 17 percent of all cancer deaths in the United States each year will be associated with previous exposure to asbestos.

• And the problem of protecting workers is not yet solved. A new study from Utah reveals that a group of construction workers exposed to asbestos dust developed breathing obstructions not within years — but within a few months of their exposure. And these workers were probably not as heavily exposed as other workers in the past.

Another problem to which we are directing increased attention is radiation. Last May, the President directed that I undertake, with the Secretaries of Defense and Energy and the Administrator of Veterans Affairs, an effort to measure and deal with the effects of radiation exposure on participants in nuclear tests and workers in nuclear projects. We have since expanded our effort to include not just nuclear, but all ionizing radiation.

The purpose of our program will be:

• To inform people who might have been affected by radiation, as well as the general public, of the probable risks;

• To ensure that persons adversely affected receive the benefits to which they may be or should be entitled; and finally,

• To take steps to minimize harmful exposures in the future.

This effort will necessarily be wide-ranging. Possible radiation sources include not only nuclear power plants, uranium mills, and gaseous diffusion plants but welding sites, medical settings and the transportation industry.

Our efforts will not be easy. The hazards of radiation exposure are still not precisely known. We must be careful — and we intend to take care — that our concern for safety be balanced with our concern for providing economically productive jobs, economic growth, and abundant energy and a strong national defense.

Let me mention one other area which is receiving increasing attention in HEW: occupational programs to deal with alcoholism and alcohol abuse.

Of the nation's more than 90 million employed workers, it is estimated that as many as 7 million have drinking problems. For this reason, occupational programs are among the most promising ways to identify, motivate and refer problem drinkers to treatment, especially early in their illness, before their work and job security are seriously affected.

Such programs are of particular value because they concentrate on job performance rather than on alcoholism or interference in private lives. They are available to all employees from the assembly line to the board room.

Along with George Meany [AFL-CIO president] and James Roche of GM [chairman of General Motors], who recently launched a joint labor-management alcohol program, we at HEW are strong believers in these efforts.

In the last fiscal year, the National Institute on Alcohol Abuse and Alcoholism provided more than a million dollars to the labor movement for occupational alcoholism programs.

I have called on Dr. Gerald L. Klerman, Administrator of HEW's Alcohol, Drug Abuse and Mental Health Administration, to review all our activities related to alcoholism — and to develop a series of recommendations in this critically important area. His effort is now underway. And I think it is safe to predict that occupational alcoholism programs will be a key part of our preventive-health efforts in the future.

Building Institutional Capacity

But our efforts at HEW to promote occupational health and safety can be no stronger, in the end, than our institutional machinery for dealing with these problems.

So I want to end by discussing very briefly the principal institutions at HEW that are working in this field.

The National Cancer Institute supports a wide range of work-related projects — from a study of cancer rates in workers exposed to benzidine to research on possible cancer-causing compounds in the metals industry. Many of the projects are epidemiological studies of cancer occurrence and death rates for specific jobs or in certain industries.

The National Institute of Environmental Health Sciences, though its mandate is a general one, is also deeply involved in the occupational field. Several current NIEHS studies, for example, deal with compounds such as PCB, PBB, vinyl chloride, and asbestos that are industrially used, as well as the chemicals such as Kepone to which workers have been accidently exposed.

Other NIEHS projects concern tests that could be used to screen workers, to screen new chemicals before workers are ever exposed to them, and to monitor work places for dangerous and possibly cancer-causing chemicals. Similarly, work on toxicology testing systems may be used to detect exposures to heavy metals and other dangerous chemicals and to determine their effects.

But the HEW agency most directly concerned with occupational hazards is, as you know, NIOSH — the National Institute for Occupational Safety and Health. NIOSH was created by the same 1970 law that created OSHA in the Labor Department; it is the leading agency in the federal government responsible for scientific research in the field of occupational safety and health. The Institute also has authority under the 1970 Act, for technical assistance and manpower development.

NIOSH has undertaken, in its relatively brief history, some large responsibilities:

● Since 1970, the NIOSH budget has increased from $10 million to $65 million; its staff has increased from 240 to over 900. Last year NIOSH was given additional responsibility under the Federal Mine Safety and Health Amendments Act for research on the occupational health problems of the approximately 500,000 miners in the United States.

● Its research projects include approximately 90 field studies of worker exposure to toxic substances, physical agents and safety hazards; approximately 70 studies conducted in NIOSH laboratories cover chemical and physical hazards to workers in the printing and painting trades; the plywood, pulp and paper industry; the steel industry; the effects of job stress on policemen and shift workers, and the reproductive effects of working with pesticides, anesthetic gases, and lead.

● NIOSH also conducts work place investigations. The results of these investigations, including recommendations for work practices, personal protective equipment, and engineering controls are reported back to workers, management, and the OSHA.

● NIOSH publishes intelligence bulletins on toxic substances. The NIOSH Clearinghouse for Occupational Safety and Health Information responds to nearly 200 requests a year for technical information, primarily on the health effects of chemical exposures. The Institute also publishes about 120 technical reports each year which are widely distributed in the occupational safety and health community.

● Finally, NIOSH provides research documents to OSHA which may be used in OSHA's enforcement and standard-setting. . . .

We are, in short, committed — at HEW and throughout this Administration — to a general strategy of prevention and health promotion. We intend to back that commitment with effective action on occupational health and safety. . . .

REPORT ON CANCER AND OCCUPATIONAL FACTORS

This statement addresses the question: "What is the best estimate of the fraction of cancer incidence (or deaths) in the United States that is reasonable to attribute to occupational exposure in the present, and in the foreseeable future?" Previously published estimates of this fraction have been as low as 1% to 5% for past data . . . and as high as 10% to 15%. . . . All these estimates are somewhat speculative and several were seriously incomplete or deficient. Most are now out of date. If recent evidence is considered and if the full consequences of occupational exposures in the present and recent past are taken into account, estimates of at least 20% appear much more reasonable, and may even be conservative. These estimates refer to the near term and to the future.

Four Pitfalls

Four general problems confound attempts to answer this question.

(a) *Incomplete data.* Few industries have been investigated adequately for evaluating the possible occurrence of occupationally related cancers. Because of the insensitivity of epidemiologic surveys and various difficulties in conducting them..., only agents and industrial processes which lead to rather large excess incidences have been identified to date. The International Agency for Research on Cancer (IARC) has an ongoing program to review data on chemicals for potential carcinogenic effects. To date, some 368 chemicals and industrial processes have been reviewed. According to a recent summary of the results of this program..., some 26 chemicals or industrial processes have been identified as associated with increased risk of cancer in man. . . . This list includes a number of drugs and chemicals to which there is little or no occupational exposure in the United States. Only 8 or 9 of the 26 substances and processes ... involve exposure to large numbers of workers. By way of contrast, some 221 chemicals or mixtures were identified in the same survey as carcinogenic to one or more animal species. Although there is some occupational exposure to the majority of these 221 substances, epidemiological and case studies were in all cases either lacking, or inadequate to determine whether or not the substances are associated with excess cancer incidence in exposed human populations.... Thus, adequate data are available for only a very small fraction of the substances and industrial processes which pose potential risks to exposed workers. Although it is possible that all the major hazards have already been identified, there is little reason to believe this without much more extensive epidemiologic investigations. In fact, many new processes and materials have been introduced in recent years. Some of these could be as hazardous or more hazardous than those used in the past.

(b) *The fallacy of "one effect-one cause" explanations....* The initiation and development of cancer is a multi-phased, multi-causal process in which both external and internal factors act, probably at each of several stages, before frank, clinical cancer appears. It is likely that many, if not most, cancers are influenced by two or more different external factors acting simultaneously or sequentially. Thus, alcohol by itself appears to be a minor cause of cancer — but alcohol combined with cigarette smoking leads to risks 15 times higher than those experienced by non-smoking non-drinkers. If a drinker smoker develops cancer of the oral cavity, to which "cause" should it be attributed? Drinking or smoking?... One of the best-studied examples of interaction between exogenous agents is that between asbestos and cigarette smoke in inducing lung cancer.... Most lung cancers "attributable to" asbestos are probably simultaneously "attributable to" smoking. If current theories of a multi-causal process are correct, it seems likely that a large fraction of cancers which at first appear to be "attributable to" smoking should also be "attributable to" asbestos, radiation, and/or other occupational factors.

(c) *Latent period, age, and duration of exposure.* Most occupational carcinogens are characterized by "latent periods" of 10 to 50 years between the onset of exposure and the clinical appearance of tumors.... This is consistent with a multi-stage process. When occupationally related cancers are detected, they usually reflect exposures which started one or more decades in the past. Accurate numerical assessment is futher complicated by the strong dependence of cancer incidence upon age and upon duration of exposure. Even in cases where and [sic] excess risk is detected within one or two decades, this dependence on age implies that most of the attributable cancers will not occur until later in the life span of the exposed workers, perhaps as much as 40 or 50 years after the first exposure. It is difficult to trace anyone for so long a time, and those epidemiological studies which do not follow people for a full lifetime are likely to underestimate lifetime risks. Most industrial-epidemiologic studies have not (and probably could not) follow a working population to its extinction.... [A] numerical example illustrates its importance. For many types of cancer, incidence increases approximately as the fourth or the fifth power of age...; hence the cumulative number of cancers occurring in a population over a lifetime increases as the fifth or sixth power of age. If exposure to a carcinogen results in a constant multiplicative increase in risk at all ages, then the number of cancers occurring in an exposed group will similarly increase as the fifth or sixth power of age. Thus, for example, the number of attributable cancers occurring by age 50 would be only about one-fifth or one-sixth of that expected by age 70. For this reason epidemiological studies often enumerate only a small fraction of the total excess cancers attributable to an agent. Any overall assessment of the importance of occupational carcinogenesis should take this into account.

(d) *Change in exposure patterns.* The dependence of cancer risk upon age and duration of exposure is further complicated by changes in patterns of exposure to potential carcinogens. Few, if any, workers are exposed throughout their entire working lives to the same chemical at similar concentrations. American workers change jobs fairly frequently; even within the same job, the chemicals to which a worker is exposed may be changed from time to time. By the time an occupationally related cancer develops, the workers will frequently have been exposed to different chemicals and may well have changed occupations. It is particularly difficult to make estimates of the consequences of present-day exposure, because the chemicals for which we have the best dose-response information are those which are generally recognized as carcinogenic. Several of them have been regulated, so that exposure to these chemicals has been reduced; this leaves other carcinogens that are not well controlled....

Re-formulating the Question

...Most [previous studies] appear to have been attempting to provide estimates of the fraction of present-day cancer incidence that is attributable to occupational exposures in the past, to agents that have already been demonstrated to be carcinogenic. However, such a question is of limited interest because the most important consequences of exposures in the recent past will not be manifested until some time in the future. The question that needs to be addressed is "What is the likely contribution of present-day occupational exposures to future cancer incidence?" An answer to this question must be somewhat speculative, because we do not know which of the chemicals in the present-day workplace will be identified sometime in the future as causing cancer. Accordingly, to provide a basis for making appropriate estimates, we will first attempt to estimate the contribution of occupational exposures to known carcinogens in the recent past to present and future cancer incidence. It is not particularly helpful merely to speculate about the possible existence of hazardous chemicals in present-day workplaces.

Asbestos as a Well-Studied Example

The consequences of occupational exposure to asbestos in the United States have only begun to be recognized in the recent past. . . . It has been estimated [several authors of the report were responsible for preparing those estimates] . . . that between 8 and 11 million workers have been exposed to asbestos in the U.S. since the beginning of World War II. Of that total, approximately 1.5 to 2.5 million are presently employed. Probably a million have already died, while the remainder — between 5.5 and 7.5 million workers — were formerly employed in environments with significant asbestos exposure, including the survivors among the 4.5 million who worked in shipyards during the 1940s. Of these and other asbestos workers, approximately 4 million are believed to have had heavy exposure to asbestos. . . . Epidemiological studies of workers . . . have indicated that, of heavily exposed workers who have already died, 20-25 percent have died of lung cancer, 7-10 percent of pleural or peritoneal mesothelioma, and 8-9 percent of gastrointestinal cancers, adding up to a total of 35-44%. These figures may be underestimates of lifetime cancer risks, because most of these workers have not been followed to the end of their life span.

Of the 4 million heavily exposed workers, at least 1.6 million are thus expected to die of the asbestos-related cancers listed above. . . . In the absence of exposure to asbestos, about 0.35 million (8-9 percent) would have been expected to die of cancers at these sites. . . . Assuming that the excess risk to the remaining less heavily exposed workers is one-quarter of that to the heavily exposed workers . . . the total number of cancers attributable to asbestos in the less-heavily exposed group would be expected to be in the range 0.4 to 0.7 million, raising the total to 2.0 to 2.3 million. Since most of these cancers will be manifested over a period of 30-35 years, the expected average number of cancer deaths associated with asbestos per year in that period will be between 58,000 to 75,000. . . . Such numbers would comprise 13-18% of all cancer deaths expected in the United States in the foreseeable future (assuming that total cancer deaths increase to 400,000 to 450,000 per year).

Three features of these estimates deserve emphasis:

1. Although most of the exposure to asbestos has been in the past, most of the predicted effects are expected to be in the future. An estimate of the present-day numbers of cancers attributable to asbestos would undoubtedly be smaller.

2. A large fraction of the asbestos-related cancers are also related to smoking (lung and esophagus) or are in the gastro-intestinal tract (esophagus, stomach, and colon), where cancers are usually assumed to be not occupationally related. . . . Hence, if the old one-effect, one-cause approach were used, the occupational origin of most of the asbestos-related cancers would be overlooked and they might be attributed to other or "unknown" factors.

3. Although the frequency of asbestos-related cancers is already substantial and is probably increasing rapidly, it has not yet been detected by examination of gross trends in cancer incidence (or mortality) in the general population. There are several reasons for this:

(a) two of the major types of asbestos-related cancer, pleural and peritoneal mesothelioma, are not classified as such in the national health statistics, but are usually listed as lung cancers or as various abdominal cancers, respectively;

(b) most asbestos-related lung cancers are also smoking-related, so that if one thinks one has the full explanation for the rise in lung cancer incidence in smoking, it is likely that no other causes will be looked for;

(c) any increase in asbestos-related cancers of the stomach and colon would be masked by the other long-term trends in cancer incidence at these sites (down in the stomach, probably up in the colon); these long-term trends are usually attributed to dietary or unknown factors.

Perhaps the most important lesson to be learned from the asbestos story is that a major public health disaster can develop while its early manifestations are lost by being attributed to other factors. This would support the argument that the earlier estimates for industrially related cancers may be deceptively low — having left out such information as the asbestos situation has now brought to our attention.

Comparison of Risks due to Asbestos with those due to Five Other High-Exposure Substances

...[W]e have tabulated data on carcinogenic risks associated with exposure to five other substances [arsenic, benzene, chromium, nickel (oxide) and petroleum fractions (including aromatics)] to which there is large-scale occupational exposure, for comparison with corresponding data on asbestos. The tabulation . . . is limited to the substances and cancer sites for which the best data are available on both exposure and relative risks. . . . Although these figures are crude projections of the numbers of excess cancers to be expected in the exposed workers, they are unlikely to be precise estimates of future cancer mortality. . . .

...[T]he figures should not be interpreted as precise estimates of future cancers, but it is reasonable to compare them with the data derived by the same method for asbestos-related cancers. At the least, the data . . . show that the five other agents together pose hazards similar to or greater than those posed by asbestos. The sum of the best projections . . . for the five compounds is about 33,000 cancers per year, versus 13,900 for asbestos. In presenting this comparison, it should be emphasized that the former figure includes only the primary sites of action [location of the cancer]. Inclusion of expected excess cancers at other sites would increase the estimates substantially.

It should be re-emphasized that many of the cancers considered here as attributable to occupational exposure would simultaneously be attributable to other factors, especially smoking. They are "attributable to" occupational exposure in the sense that most of them would not have occurred in the absence of exposure, so that they could have been prevented by prevention of occupational exposure.

Other Known and Potential Risks

In addition to the five major agents [discussed in previous section]..., a number of other agents and industrial processes are known or suspected to pose carcinogenic risks to exposed workers.

We omitted ... several agents listed as occupational carcinogens in [other studies]..., because we had difficulty matching data on relative risks to data on the number of workers exposed. These agents include cadmium, coal tar pitch volatiles, hematite, and vinyl chloride. The data we used on the number of workers exposed to carcinogenic petroleum fractions are probably conservative. The IARC ... has already reviewed 221 agents identified as capable of inducing cancer in experimental animals. Although some occupational exposure is known to occur for most of these chemicals, epidemiological and case studies of their possible association with cancer in humans were lacking or were judged to be "inconclusive." Other carcinogens have been reported in the literature. To date only a very small proportion of all the chemicals in use have been tested for carcinogenicity....

In addition to chemical carcinogens, occupational exposure to radiation is known to be a significant cause of cancer in U.S. workers. Groups at risk include radiologists, uranium miners, workers in the nuclear industry, military personnel exposed to radiation from nuclear explosions and to nuclear weapons, air crews, and persons working at high altitudes. Persons working outdoors such as farm workers and fishermen are subject to increased risks of skin cancer associated with solar radiation. We have not attempted to make numerical estimates of expected cancer incidence in these occupations although many millions of workers are at presumptive risk.

Consequences of Present-Day Exposures

...There is evidence that occupational exposure to several ... agents has been reduced.... Exposure to asbestos, benzene, coke oven emissions and vinyl chloride has been limited (although not eliminated) by recent OSHA regulations.

There is also evidence, however, that not all the major occupational carcinogens have been eliminated.... [T]here is today widespread exposure to arsenic, chromium, nickel, and many petroleum products. Most of the excess risks ... remain uncontrolled because the causative agents have not been identified. A number of important occupational groups (such as agricultural field workers) have not been adequately surveyed for excess cancer risks. Only a handful of the 221 chemicals found positive in experimental animals and reviewed by the IARC ... have been regulated as carcinogens in the U.S. workplace. Among those not regulated are a number of synthetic organic chemicals to which there is widespread occupational exposure, but which have not been in production for long enough periods for excess risks to have been identified by epidemiological studies.

For public policy purposes, it would be very desirable to make numerical estimates of the potential consequences of present-day exposure to carcinogens in the workplace. Such estimates would, however, require numerical data on the extent and intensity of exposure, and on dose-response relationships in experimental animals. If sufficient data were available, prediction of future consequences would require quantitative extrapolation from animal responses to man. In our view, existing methods for such extrapolation leave enough questions open concerning their precision so as to make us unwilling to attempt large scale estimates — particularly in the absence of exposure data. Hence, we can say nothing firm about the magnitude of future risks attributable to the unquantified present-day exposures.

There is no evidence, however, that these risks are substantially less than the risks resulting from exposures in the recent past. Although several of the most important known carcinogens have been controlled, others have not; many carcinogenic and potentially carcinogenic chemicals are still present in U.S. workplaces; the total volume of synthetic organic chemicals produced in the U.S. continues to increase rapidly. If only one of the thousands of chemicals introduced into commerce in the past 30 years proves to be as hazardous as asbestos, this could suffice to maintain comparable rates of occupationally-related cancer for decades into the future. In our view, any complacency about the future consequences of present-day exposure to uncharacterized chemicals would be unjustified.

Two Alternative Approaches

Other ways can be used to estimate the possible contribution of occupational exposures to human cancer incidence. Although none, to our knowledge, has been used formally to argue that occupationally-related cancers cannot be numerically important.

The first approach is to analyze trends in total cancer incidence (or mortality) in the U.S. population. The argument is made that if occupational factors were important causes of cancer, then total cancer incidence would be increasing rapidly, reflecting the rapid increase in the number and amount of synthetic organic chemicals produced in recent decades. In fact (the argument runs), the continued increase in cancer incidence and mortality is almost solely due to increases in lung cancer and other smoking-related cancers. If the "smoking-related" cancers are subtracted from the total, the argument is that the overall trend is constant or even slightly decreasing.

There are several fallacies in this argument:

1. Most of the increase in production of synthetic organic chemicals is too recent to be reflected in current cancer statistics.

2. The increase in production of synthetics (some of which are potential carcinogens) in the period 1940-1960 may well have been offset by reductions in the intensity of exposure to other chemicals, resulting from improvements in industrial controls stimulated, in part, by government regulation. Exposure to several major carcinogens has been reduced substantially in recent years. Exposure to other potential carcinogens (such as carbon tetrachloride) was reduced earlier, to reduce other types of toxic hazard. The predicted consequence of reduction in exposure to "old" carcinogens and increase in exposure to "new" carcinogens is consistent with what is observed: an increase in cancer at some sites and a decrease at others.

3. To subtract all the "smoking-related" cancers from the total is sophistry, because at least two of the sites in question are precisely those in which "occupationally-related" cancers are best recognized. Many of the smoking-related cancers should be simultaneously attributable to occupational factors. On a per-capita basis smoking among adults is declining and this should result in a decline in the smoking-related cancers — but none of this is factored in when all "smoking-related" cancers are removed from the total. If the smoking-related cancers are not subtracted, total age-adjusted cancer incidence in the U.S. is increasing at more than 1% per annum. . . .

4. Not all of the smoking-related cancers, i.e. those in the lung, pancreas, and bladder, are attributable to smoking. Even if a liberal figure is used for attributable risk, the fraction of lung cancer incidence not attributable to smoking is increasing and total cancers possibly industrially related have been increasing more rapidly in the last several years than in the two decades from 1950 to 1970. . . .

5. As pointed out earlier, the major public health impact of asbestos-related cancer is just beginning to be reflected in overall cancer statistics, despite 37 years of heavy exposure. One should hardly expect more recent additions to have shown a great effect already.

A second approach is to compare cancer incidence in men and women. To the extent that exposure to chemical carcinogens occurred in occupations in which most workers are (or were) male, this should be reflected in differences in overall cancer incidence (and trends in incidence) in the two sexes. This argument would tend to support the concept of industrial risk.

The predicted difference is in fact observed: age-adjusted cancer incidence is greater in males than in females at every common site except the gall bladder and thyroid. . . . In particular, incidence is much higher in males than in females in the key occupationally related sites: lung, liver, bladder, kidney, hematopoetic *[sic]* and lymphatic system and perhaps stomach and pancreas. . . .

Nonetheless, there are some flaws in this argument, too. Not only male workers have substantial exposure to carcinogens. Although male workers doubtless predominate in chemical manufacturing and heavy industry, women have long been employed in large numbers in light industry where there is substantial exposure to certain carcinogens, e.g. the radium dial painters. The fraction of occupationally related cancers in women may increase in future years due to increased employment of women in jobs where they are exposed to carcinogens. Even housewives have greater occupational exposure to some potential carcinogens than typical working men. . . .

It would clearly be valuable to make a rigorous comparison between employed and never employed women, but such a study would be difficult to conduct and interpret because of the many confounding variables. In our view, there is nothing in the gross cancer statistics for the U.S. population which is inconsistent with the hypothesis that up to 20-40% of all cancers are (or will be in the next several decades) attributable to occupational factors.

Relation between Occupational and Other Contributing Factors

These estimates do not diminish the importance of other contributing factors to cancer risk such as smoking, diet, and perhaps urban-rural differences. While much of the data on occupational cancer risk considered in this paper does not specifically consider factors such as smoking (except for asbestos) and diet, it is also fair to state that the prevailing body of data linking smoking and diet with cancer risk do not adequately consider the contribution of exposure to occupational carcinogens. This is largely because the available scientific methodologies do not facilitate adequate consideration of all contributing factors in any single study or approach. Until recently most scientists did not take into account the multiple etiologies and the multi-stage nature of cancer. In retrospect, it is likely that cancer risk is a function of multiple interacting factors. Past assessments, unfortunately, generally failed to consider adequately one of the most important, and preventable, risk factor[s], exposure to carcinogenic agents in the workplace.

Opportunities for Prevention

The estimates of cancer attributable to occupational exposure given here should be viewed as pointing up the opportunities that exist to prevent disease in future generations. The causes of cancer are multiple, with more than one factor contributing to cancer risk. In such a situation, any percentage accounting of contributing causes to cancer well exceeds 100%.

To prevent cancer, one must concentrate on causative factors that can be reduced so that we can decrease the burden of disease in future generations. It has been argued that present day asbestos workers are at lower risk than earlier workers. Opportunities to reduce risks and subsequent disease in other occupations are at hand.

Summary and Conclusions

1. The estimates that only 1% to 5% of total cancers in the United States are attributable to occupational factors have not been scientifically documented and have little meaning for estimating even short-term future risks.

2. Most cancers have multiple causes: it is a reductionist error and not in keeping with current theories of cancer causation to attempt to assign each cancer to an exclusive single cause.

3. Because cancer incidence is strongly dependent on age and upon duration of exposure, and because most cancer[s] occur late in life, many industrial epidemiological studies detect only a small fraction of cancers (i.e. those developing early).

4. Past exposure to asbestos is expected to result in up to 2 million excess cancer deaths in the next three decades: this would correspond to roughly 13-18% of the total cancer mortality expected in that period.

5. Reasonable projections of the future consequences of past exposure to established carcinogens suggests that at least five of them may be comparable in their total effects to asbestos.

6. These projections suggest that occupationally related cancers may comprise as much as 20% or more of total cancer mortality in forthcoming decades. Asbestos alone will probably contribute up to 13-18%, and the data [included in the study] . . . suggest at least 10%-20% more. These data do not include effects of radiation, nor effects of a number of other known chemical carcinogens.

7. Although exposure to some of the more important occupational carcinogens has been reduced in recent years, there are still many unregulated carcinogens in the U.S. workplaces; a number of occupations are characterized by excess cancer risks which have not yet been attributed to specific agents.

8. There is no sound reason to assume that the future consequences of present-day exposure to carcinogens in the workplace will be less than those of exposure in the recent past.

9. Patterns and trends in total cancer incidence (and mortality) in the U.S. are consistent with the hypothesis that occupationally-related cancers comprise a substantial and increasing fraction of total cancer incidence.

10. The conclusion that a substantial fraction of cancers in the United States are occupationally related is not inconsistent with conclusions that substantial fraction of cancers are also associated with other factors, such as cigarette smoking and diet.

11. Occupationally-related cancers offer important opportunities for prevention.

STUDY OF HUMAN EXPOSURE
TO P.B.B. IN MICHIGAN

September 23, 1978

As a result of a packaging and shipping error, several hundred pounds of a chemical used as a fire retardant, polybrominated biphenyls or P.B.B., were mixed with animal feeds in Michigan in May 1973. The feeds were then distributed to farms, especially in the state's Lower Peninsula. The Michigan Department of Agriculture called the feed contamination that resulted "the most costly and disastrous accidental contamination ever to occur in United States agriculture."

Because of the risk inherent in human consumption of the contaminated meat and dairy products, more than 30,000 head of cattle, 3,500 pigs and 1.5 million chickens were destroyed by health authorities. Persons living on the farms that were immediately involved or who had eaten produce from those farms were heavily exposed to the chemical. But later it became clear that thousands of other Michigan residents, especially those living in the Lower Peninsula, were also to some extent exposed. To assess the effects of the accident, eight investigators in Michigan conducted a random-sample survey of human breast milk.

Their findings, published in the Sept. 23 issue of The Lancet, *a prestigious British medical journal, were startling. Ninety-six percent of the samples from the Lower Peninsula and 43 percent of the samples from the Upper Peninsula in Michigan contained detectable levels of the chemical. The authors wrote, "These data indicate that about 8 million of Michigan's 9.1 million residents have detectable body burdens of P.B.B."*

The authors of the article were Lawrence B. Brilliant of the Department of Health Planning and Administration, School of Public Health, Univer-

sity of Michigan; George Van Amburg and Janet Eyster of the Office of Vital and Health Statistics of the Michigan Department of Public Health; and John Isbister, Harold Humphrey, Kenneth Wilcox, Arthur W. Bloomer and Harold Price of the Bureau of Disease Control and Laboratory Services of the state Department of Public Health.

Background

The chemical involved in the incident had been widely used as a flame retardant in the manufacture of plastics. In the 1973 accident, it was substituted for magnesium oxide, a nutritional supplement, in the cattle feed.

The effects of the consumption of the contaminated feed by livestock was quickly apparent, although it was a year before the poison was identified. Dairy cattle that had eaten the feed within days showed signs of loss of appetite, decreased milk production and weight loss. Stillbirths occurred among cows that had eaten the contaminated feed in the first trimester. The syndrome was in many cases fatal to the cattle.

Despite the destruction of the livestock by health authorities, a considerable amount of contaminated farm and dairy produce was consumed by people living in Michigan. There was, however, little information available that would have helped authorities to predict the consequences of human exposure to the chemical.

Random-Sample Survey

The random-sample survey of human breast milk was conducted by the Michigan investigators in an attempt to document the extent of the contamination of breast milk.

In their article in The Lancet, *the investigators wrote, "An estimated 10,000 to 12,500 persons who lived on contaminated farms or who had directly received the produce of those farms were heavily exposed to P.B.B., nearly all having detectable blood-levels of the chemical. . . . Human exposure to P.B.B. was initially assumed to be limited to this group."*

The article described in detail the random-sample survey of human breast milk. The authors wrote, "There is no reason to believe that P.B.B. consumption would have been limited to women who subsequently became pregnant, lactated, and were randomly chosen for this study. These data, therefore, are presumptive evidence that most people in Michigan have detectable levels of P.B.B."

They went on to say that "[t]here are many drawbacks to using these data for quantitative estimation of P.B.B. body-burdens in the entire population. . . . Despite such reservations, these are the only data on

P.B.B. exposure derived from a probability sample in the state of Michigan, and they may give a crude indication of the number of people with detectable P.B.B. in their bodies. Of the 1976 population of 9,104,000, 8,777,000 lived in the L.P. [Lower Peninsula] and 327,000 in the U.P. [Upper Peninsula]. Extrapolation of 85% confidence intervals to the general public yields an estimate of 7.9 to 8.7 million people in the Lower Peninsula with detectable P.B.B. — if the nursing mothers are representative of the total population. The estimate in the U.P. is 104,000-176,000 people. These calculations suggest that 9 out of 10 people in the state have been exposed to P.B.B."

Nursing Mothers

In their article, the authors wrote, "At the time of this study, there were no conclusive data on the toxicity of P.B.B. in man. We were therefore unable to specify a 'safe' level of P.B.B. in breast milk or otherwise advise mothers on the relative risks and benefits of breast feeding at various P.B.B. levels."

Dr. Isbister, one of the authors of the report, told a reporter that mothers who had been heavily exposed to P.B.B. (because, for example, they lived on farms immediately involved in the accident) were advised that they should not breast feed their babies. Other women, however, whose exposure had been far, far smaller, Dr. Isbister said, were advised to discuss the problem with their physicians. In cases where breast feeding seemed to be very important to those mothers, he said, the fact of the exposure probably should not rule out breast-feeding.

Following are excerpts from an article in the Sept. 23, 1978, issue of The Lancet, *"Breast-Milk Monitoring To Measure Michigan's Contamination with Polybrominated Biphenyls," by Lawrence B. Brilliant and colleagues:*

Summary

In 1973 and 1974, several thousand Michigan dairy farms were contaminated by polybrominated biphenyls (P.B.B.) as the result of an industrial accident. An unknown quantity of contaminated meat and dairy products entered the food chain before contaminated farms were quarantined. To determine the extent of human exposure, P.B.B. concentrations were measured in human breast milk, which was collected in a random-sample survey from nursing mothers throughout Michigan. 96% of 53 samples from Michigan's lower peninsula and 43% of 42 samples from the less densely populated upper peninsula contained detectable levels of P.B.B. These data indicate that about 8 million of Michigan's 9.1 million residents have detectable body burdens of P.B.B.

Introduction

The polybrominated biophenyls (P.B.B.) were widely employed until recently as flame retardants in the plastics industry. Commercial P.B.B. consists principally of hexa-brominated biphenyl, but also contains measurable quantities of the di- through octa-brominated isomers, as well as traces of brominated naphthalenes. In 1973 and 1974, as the result of a packaging and shipping error, several hundred pounds of P.B.B. were substituted for magnesium oxide, a dairy-cattle nutritional supplement, and distributed in cattle feed throughout Michigan. In exposed cattle a devastating and often fatal syndrome developed — anorexia, weight-loss, epidermal changes, decreased milk production, and increased fetal wastage. To limit human consumption of meat and dairy products contaminated with the chemical, 800 farms were quarantined and over 30,000 cattle, 3,500 swine, and millions of chickens and eggs were destroyed. The Michigan Department of Agriculture termed the event "the most costly and disastrous accidental contamination ever to occur in United States agriculture." An estimated 10,000 to 12,500 persons who lived on contaminated farms or who had directly received the produce of those farms were heavily exposed to P.B.B., nearly all having detectable blood-levels of the chemical. Some exposures were occupational, but most resulted from the ingestion of contaminated meat and dairy products. Human exposure to P.B.B. was initially assumed to be limited to this group.

In June, 1976, during a screening survey for pesticide residues, the laboratory of the Michigan Department of Public Health discovered that breast milk from 4 of 5 Michigan mothers, none of them from quarantined farms, contained P.B.B. The single woman with a Michigan address whose milk was negative for P.B.B. was a recent immigrant to the United States. She had arrived in Michigan after the bulk of P.B.B.-contaminated food had been removed from the state's food chain. 5 women from other states, tested at the same time, had no traces of P.B.B. in their milk. To document more fully the extent of human breast milk contamination, we collected milk specimens from a probability sample of nursing mothers throughout the state. Because of the highly lipophilic nature of P.B.B. and an apparently stable partition of the chemical in blood, adipose tissue, and milk fat, the survey would provide information about P.B.B. contamination in the state's general population.

Study Population and Methods

Our objectives were, first, to estimate the proportion of lactating women in Michigan with detectable P.B.B. in breast milk, and, second, to use the results of the breast-milk survey to estimate the levels of P.B.B. in the general population of the state.

The survey was designed to yield separate estimates for the state's two geographically distinct peninsulas, because the distribution of contaminated animals and quarantined farms suggested that P.B.B. were more widely distributed in the lower peninsula (L.P.) than in the upper peninsula (U.P.). To meet the first objective, we judged it adequate to make peninsula-wide inferences using an 85% confidence interval with width plus or minus 10%. On the assumption that 50% of lactating women in Michigan would have detectable P.B.B., the necessary sample sizes were reckoned at 41 in the U.P. and 55 in the L.P. The population in the L.P. from which the sample was drawn consisted of all lactating women who gave birth in hospitals during the week of Aug. 15-21, 1976. In the U.P., because of a much sparser population, all lactating women who gave birth during the month of August were included in the survey population. Since the distribution of P.B.B. levels was known to be highly skewed, we chose the population median and percentiles in preference to mean and standard deviation as measures for statistical comparison.

To obtain a random sample, hospitals throughout the state were asked to identify women who had given birth during the study period. Post-partum women were sequentially assigned numbers as hospitals were contacted. Since, at the time of sampling, the actual number of births could not be known, a high estimate of 3,400 births in the L.P. was derived, based on the previous year's data. Information was then collected only for women matching 330 numbers selected randomly from the integers 1 to 3,400. The actual number of live births in the L.P. for the study period was found later to be 2,537 (300 in the U.P.).

54% of women matched to random numbers decided not to breast-feed and they were not contacted again. An attempt was made to contact, screen, and enroll a random subset of the remaining matched women. This random subset contained 83 women; 21 were excluded because they too were not lactating. A further 3 had stopped breast-feeding before samples were collected. Of the 59 remaining women, 5 could not be contacted and 1 refused to participate. The 53 women who provided samples of milk represented a response-rate of 90%.

In the upper peninsula, through a similar process, a random sample of 49 lactating women were identified. 3 could not be contacted, 4 refused to participate, and 42 provided samples — a response rate of 86%.

Women who agreed to participate were sent a questionnaire and a kit containing supplies and instructions for obtaining breast-milk samples by manual expression and for storing them until collection by local health departments. Results were sent to each participant's physician.

Chemical Analysis

Breast-milk samples were tested for P.B.B. by the Michigan Department of Public Health. The method was that of the Food and Drug Administration for pesticides in milk, on a micro-scale, omitting the acetonitrile partitioning step to improve recoveries of P.B.B.

Results

51 (96%) of 53 breast-milk samples from women in the L.P. contained detectable P.B.B. The median was 0.068 p.p.m. [parts per million], the

highest 1.2 p.p.m. In the U.P., 43% of samples had detectable P.B.B. The highest value in the U.P. was 0.320 p.p.m. — about a quarter the highest value found in the lower peninsula. . . .

At the time of this study, there were no conclusive data on the toxicity of P.B.B. in man. We were therefore unable to specify a "safe" level of P.B.B. in breast milk or otherwise to advise mothers on the relative risks and benefits of breast-feeding at various P.B.B. levels. Charts . . . were distributed to all physicians in the state, and these helped to put individual values in the general context.

Discussion

There is no reason to believe that P.B.B. consumption would have been limited to women who subsequently became pregnant, lactated, and were randomly chosen for this study. These data, therefore, are presumptive evidence that most people in Michigan have detectable levels of P.B.B.

There are many drawbacks to using these data for quantitative estimation of P.B.B. body-burdens in the entire population. First, the study included only women 15-45 years old. It is possible that lactating women have dietary preferences which affect the quantity or type of food consumed. Women who breast feed may have different socioeconomic status and therefore differential risk of dietary exposure to P.B.B. And physiological changes during pregnancy or lactation may influence the mobilisation of P.B.B. between body compartments and thus distort the relationship between total body burden and P.B.B. concentration in milk relative to other tissues.

Despite such reservations, these are the only data on P.B.B. exposure derived from a probability sample in the state of Michigan, and they may give a crude indication of the number of people with detectable P.B.B. in their bodies. Of the 1976 population of 9,104,000, 8,777,000 lived in the L.P. and 327,000 in the U.P. Extrapolation of 85% confidence intervals to the general public yields an estimate of 7.9 to 8.7 million people in the lower peninsula with detectable P.B.B. — if the nursing mothers are representative of the total population. The estimate in the U.P. is 104,000-176,000 people. These calculations suggest that 9 out of 10 people in the state have been exposed to P.B.B. . . .

IMF-WORLD BANK CONFERENCE
September 24-28, 1978

"Free world" financial leaders attending a joint meeting of the International Monetary Fund (IMF) and the World Bank in Washington, D.C., Sept. 24-28 confidently predicted a return of stability to foreign exchange markets. But even as the finance ministers and central bankers were speaking, the U.S. dollar continued its decline against such "stronger" currencies as the West German mark, the British pound and the Japanese yen. Because the dollar was the world's principal reserve asset, declines in its value, described by the Wall Street Journal *as "often tumultuous" in 1978, had become a problem of growing concern.*

Addressing the international gathering on Sept. 25, President Carter reiterated his determination "to maintain a sound dollar." Currency traders, however, looking for solid evidence, were not easily convinced that a turning point for the dollar had arrived. In the first eight months of the year the price of gold had soared from about $175 to more than $200 an ounce as nervous investors tried to hedge against the dollar's depreciation. Central banks in a number of countries had intervened by making massive purchases of dollars, but that rate-propping tactic had had only limited success.

Reasons for Decline

The sliding dollar was widely viewed by currency traders and others as a consequence of a lack of will or incapacity on the part of the United States to bring about improvements in its balance-of-payments position and its high rate of inflation.

Jacques de Larosiere, the managing director of the IMF, addressing the delegates on the same day as President Carter, said that greater stability in the foreign exchange markets would come about only with a "convergence" of the inflation rates, economic growth rates and balance-of-payments positions of the United States and its major trading partners. "In the case of the United States," he said, "a growth rate well below that of 4 to 5 percent experienced in recent years is clearly suitable."

Monetary System

The IMF was established in 1944 as part of the post-World War II monetary system devised at the Bretton Woods (N.H.) conference. The Bretton Woods system was based on the concept of fixed rates of exchange, pegged to the value of gold.

As the years passed, the fixed-rate system proved inadequate. Since 1973, the major world currencies had "floated," a condition recognized in an agreement reached by the Monetary Fund's Interim Committee at a meeting in Jamaica on Jan. 8, 1976. Under a revision of the IMF's Article IV proposed at Jamaica and later adopted, member nations would collaborate with the IMF to "assure orderly exchange arrangements and to promote a stable system of exchange rates." (Jamaica meeting, Historic Documents of 1976, p. 30) In his Sept. 23 address, de Larosiere said that the amended Article IV "has made it possible to address ourselves to the basic aspects of members' economic policies and to bring into force principles and procedures for firm surveillance over exchange rate policies."

Carter Speech

In his address before the delegates, Carter noted that two months earlier, at the economic summit conference in Bonn, West Germany, he had "pledged that the United States will fight inflation, will reduce oil imports, will expand exports." (Bonn summit, see p. 533) "Let there be no doubt in your mind about how seriously I take these pledges that have been made on my own word of honor and on behalf of the people of the United States," he said. Carter added that he would soon announce an effort which U.S. officials hoped would help reduce the nation's huge international payments deficit, and he spoke of his confidence that Congress would pass measures "comprising a strong package of energy legislation."

Reaction

In making predictions of the dollar's eventual recovery, financial leaders at the Washington meeting pointed to a probable convergence of the most disruptive extremes in the economies of the Western democracies. Convergence was seen by Denis Healey, Britain's chancellor of the exchequer and chairman of the IMF's Interim Committee, as "substantially reducing currency instability in the next 12 months."

But currency dealers, many of them located in London and other European financial centers, went their own way, and, in the days immediately following the finance ministers' and central bankers' departure from Washington, the dollar plunged to new lows.

Following are excerpts from speeches delivered Sept. 25, 1978, at a joint meeting of the International Monetary Fund and the International Bank for Reconstruction and Development (World Bank) by President Carter and by Jacques de Larosiere, managing director of the IMF:

PRESIDENT CARTER'S REMARKS

. . .Three decades of existence of the Fund and the Bank have brought progress and a better life for the people of the world. Like you, I want to build on that record to achieve still further economic cooperation, progress, and a better life. Since your meeting here last year, our countries acting together have made tangible progress on world economic problems.

The issues that remain, as you and I well know, are very difficult. But they, like other difficult questions, are not insoluble.

You assembled in this room are the economic leaders of the world. The task before you is to consolidate past gains and then to push ahead in ways that will foster economic growth in both developing and the industrialized nations.

Our goal is to achieve progress for all peoples, not just a few. The basic strategy has already been agreed. In Mexico City, at the IMF Interim Committee, agreement was reached on the general directions that economic policy should take.

Progress on those agreements has been made. The outlook for improvement is good. We must not falter. A contribution to this strategy is needed from every country represented here, no matter how great nor small, no matter how weak nor powerful.

In this effort, the United States has a major responsibility. Two months ago at Bonn, I made specific promises to our major trading partners about the actions that my country will take to this end. I pledged that the United States will fight inflation, will reduce oil imports, will expand exports.

Let there be no doubt in your mind about how seriously I take these pledges that have been made on my own word of honor and on behalf of the people of the United States. Taken together, they encompass the most urgent priorities of my own administration; my own reputation is at stake as a leader. And they are commitments that I am most fully determined to fulfill.

I've come here today to underline that determination and to describe the next steps that we will take.

I will soon announce the first phase of a long-term program to expand American exports. Removing disincentives to exports and encouraging exports are overriding tasks for my own administration. As you know, compared to many nations represented here, the export commitment has not been as great in our own country as it has perhaps among some of you.

I've also intensified my efforts, which were already great, to obtain legislation that will curtail United States imports of oil, imports which are entirely too high.

The United States Senate is scheduled to vote this week, day after tomorrow, on the key bill, natural gas regulation and pricing. This is one of the most complicated and difficult and challenging assignments that the United States Congress has ever faced.

This particular bill is expected to save 1.4 million barrels of imported oil per day by 1985. I am confident that the Senate and then the House of Representatives will do their duty to our Nation by approving this bill. I hope to have other bills comprising a strong package of energy legislation enacted before the Congress adjourns, probably, hopefully, less than a month from now.

This is essential, we know, to a sound American dollar. I intend very shortly to announce a further series of important and specific and tough measures to strengthen our fight against inflation.

These next steps will certainly not be the end of our effort, only the renewed beginning and commitment, part of a sustained effort to control these very serious problems for our own people in this country, and our relationship with your countries as well.

Every nation represented in this room understands how difficult this struggle against inflation is and what sustained commitment it demands. My administration will continue that struggle on a wide variety of fronts until we succeed. There will be obstacles and objections from special interest groups all along the way. But I will not shrink from the hard decisions and the persistent efforts that are needed.

I'm determined to maintain a sound dollar. This is of primary importance to us, and I know it is of great interest and importance to you as well. We recognize that our currency plays an international role, and we accept the responsibilities which this involves. Our countries are acting to meet our responsibilities to the system, consistent with the directives set at the IMF meeting in Mexico and as was pledged again by seven of us national leaders at the Bonn summit. The United States will do the same.

Through programs which I have just described, we will achieve the strong U.S. economy and noninflationary U.S. growth that must underlie a sound dollar and a stable international monetary system.

The outlook for progress is good. Some of the causes of our large trade deficit have already been removed. Others are now being removed. Our current account position should improve significantly next year. The United States will remain an open and vigorous economy, and an attractive place to invest.

Other steps are also required to achieve the economic progress that we all seek. In these steps, the IMF and the World Bank have, of course, a vital role to play. These two institutions are the core and the symbol of the international economic order that was built after World War II. They've shown a high capacity to adapt to new and rapidly changing needs. Strengthening and enlarging them, both institutions, is a prime goal of United States policy.

The United States is firmly committed to a strong International Monetary Fund, exercising effective surveillance over the system and with adequate resources to meet official financing needs. The United States has supported and will continue to support an increase in IMF quotas and a new allocation of special drawing rights.

STATEMENT BY J. DE LAROSIERE

...Another problem of the world economy concerns the international adjustment process, which has not been working satisfactorily. Mainly as a result of divergent rates of growth of domestic demand among the industrial countries, balances of payments on current account have become badly out of line. Especially important and troublesome is the contrast between the deficit of the United States and the surpluses of the Federal Republic of Germany, Japan, and Switzerland. Taken together, the surpluses of the latter three countries in 1978 will substantially exceed the combined surplus of the major oil exporting countries. Now estimated at $18 billion, the oil exporters' surplus has declined by some $50 billion since 1974, when it was the major source of concern with respect to the international adjustment process.

Because of the maldistribution of current account balances among the industrial countries, and also because of concern over the policies that have led to it, foreign exchange markets for major currencies have been quite unstable during several prolonged periods in the past year. This instability — through effects on prices, confidence, and investment — has doubtless exacerbated the various economic problems confronting national authorities. . . .

The problems facing the world economy are both severe and complex. It would be naive to suppose that they could be overcome in a short period. This consideration makes it all the more urgent to take steps to alleviate the problems. In the main, we need to achieve:

—more convergence in growth rates around a higher average level,
—more success in the fight against inflation,
—more stability in exchange markets, and
—a strengthening of the economies of the developing countries.

Improvement and Convergence in Growth Rates

Since the divergence in rates of economic growth is one of the main causes of the present external imbalances, it is essential to achieve more coordination in this field. This is increasingly understood, and the growth rates of the major countries constituted a central topic at the July Bonn Conference.

In our recent discussions in the Fund on the world economic situation and outlook, we have paid particular attention to a medium-term strategy of coordinated growth and balance of payments adjustment for the industrial countries. Our calculations show that the very marked changes in exchange rates that have taken place over the past year and a half could yield large volume effects by 1980. These would lead to a substantial improvement in the pattern of current account balances among the industrial countries. But this finding is subject to an essential condition, namely, that adequate internal measures are taken to offset the effects of the exchange rate changes on output. It is crucial that surplus countries take the measures necessary to counteract the deflationary effects of their exchange rate appreciations. Without such measures, the effects on current account balances expected to result from these appreciations could be partly or wholly dissipated. Similarly, it is fundamental that countries incurring exchange rate depreciations, such as the United States, be ready to counteract the resulting expansionary effects.

It must be realized that the domestic effects of exchange rate changes will make it more difficult to bring about a pattern of growth rates conducive to substantial improvement in current account balances over the next few years. Still, let me stress that a pattern of growth rates differing significantly from the one we have seen in recent years is needed to make a sizable contribution to the desired evolution of current account balances. Without such an adaptation of growth rates, excessive weight would be placed on further changes in exchange rates to bring about adjustment.

Let me be a little more specific. In the case of the United States, a growth rate well below that of 4½-5 per cent experienced in recent years is clearly suitable in light of the prospects for domestic prices and the current high level of resource utilization. Moreover, it would also have the effect of constraining the size of the U.S. current account deficit. On the other hand, I believe that most industrial countries other than the United States — and especially the major surplus countries — should aim for growth rates in 1979-80 significantly higher than the actual rates for 1977 and those now seen for 1978. The pace of economic expansion in the surplus countries has not been commensurate with the strength of their economic positions. The international adjustment process has therefore functioned in an asymmetrical fashion. These countries will have to accept a lasting shift from external to domestic demand and to adopt appropriate policies — especially in the fiscal areas — for the achievement of higher growth rates.

More Success in the Fight Against Inflation

But to advocate a "scenario" of convergent growth rates would be a vain exercise if it consisted only of advice for expansionary measures by the countries in relatively strong positions. Lasting success can only be achieved if it is also based on strong and persistent action by the "weaker" countries to bring down their rates of inflation.

Countries with relatively high inflation rates usually have weak or vulnerable external positions. In such deficit countries, whether developed or developing, recovery of economic activity cannot be achieved merely by expanding domestic demand. The fundamental weaknesses of their economies need to be tackled first. Demand expansion in such circumstances leads rapidly to still greater inflation and to further balance of payments difficulties. It therefore makes the ultimate task of adjustment all the more difficult and painful. Instead, in order to lay the basis for sustained future growth, it is essential that deficit countries undertake corrective actions of a fundamental nature. Depending on individual situations, such actions may need to include reduction in the growth of government expenditures, moderation of rates of increase in wages and other incomes, restoration of incentives to invest, measures in the field of energy, and a turning away from devices that undermine economic efficiency, such as subsidies, artificial prices, and import restrictions. A program of corrective actions along these lines is likely to bring about a sharp improvement in a country's situation over the medium term, provided that the country has the determination to stay with the program through a difficult initial period. In this context, the Fund stands ready to provide financing needed to carry the member through this period, if it is satisfied that the member's program constitutes a constructive answer to its problems. The function of the Fund's conditionality is basically a simple, and also an indispensable, one: to make sure that the member's program meets this test.

In present circumstances, a strategy of encouraging noninflationary growth in the industrial countries would clearly require adaptations in fiscal and monetary policies. It might also require more emphasis on incomes policy, to try to affect some of the special causes of upward pressures on prices. Obviously, the broad range of approaches encompassed by the term "incomes policy" must be geared in each country to its own institutions, traditions, and other aspects of the social and political setting. But attempts by countries to do whatever they can in this difficult field are especially relevant because of the predominance of cost-push factors in the current inflation.

More Stability in Exchange Markets

In recent discussions in the Executive Board of the Fund on the subject of exchange rates, many members have stressed the disadvantages of too great a variability in exchange rate movements. They have indicated their concern about the unsettling effects of such movements: in deficit countries, they stir up inflation through import prices; in all countries, they can discourage investment. The developing countries are particularly concerned about the implications of these phenomena on world trade, and on their problems of exchange rate management. The deep interest that has recently been expressed in the European Community in measures that could bring about greater stability of exchange rates is a manifestation of similar concerns.

It is well understood — and the Fund's new Article IV makes this understanding explicit — that greater exchange market stability has to be based primarily on the correction of imbalances in the domestic economy, and that monetary arrangements and intervention can play a useful role only if the more fundamental policies are appropriate. In this regard, it is worth noting that the surveillance principles of the Fund not only permit intervention in the exchange markets, but also obligate members to intervene in order to counter disorderly conditions. But decisions on the appropriate scale of intervention raise difficult issues of judgment. Given the overwhelming size of balances free to move, there is a danger of stimulating such movements, rather than containing them, if intervention is interpreted as reluctance to face the problems posed by underlying conditions. This is an added reason for placing emphasis on measures that will give confidence that basic factors — particularly inflation control in the United States and domestic demand expansion in Germany and Japan — are being addressed. With such confidence, only limited and occasional intervention might suffice to smooth the market satisfactorily. Without such confidence, even huge amounts of intervention would do little good. Intervention serves its purpose best in an environment of sound domestic policies in the countries concerned. . . .

October

REPORT TO CALIFANO
ON SWINE FLU PROGRAM
October 21, 1978

Two Harvard professors, one an expert on government decision-making and the other on public health, reported in June to Joseph A. Califano Jr., secretary of health, education and welfare, on the controversial swine flu immunization program that had been conducted by the federal government in 1976. The report, with an introduction by Califano, was released by the Department of Health, Education and Welfare on Oct. 21.

Strongly promoted by President Ford, the $134 million swine flu program had the unprecedented goal of inoculating almost all Americans against an influenza strain that many scientists thought might become as deadly as the great flu epidemic of 1918. The program was hurriedly launched in response to the alarming discovery that Army recruits in New Jersey had contracted a flu virus similar to the one in the World War I epidemic. Before the program was suspended by Ford in December 1976, more than 40 million civilians had been inoculated — at least twice as many as ever before in a single flu season.

The abrupt suspension of the swine flu program was directly related to a serious side-effect, the Guillain-Barre syndrome, which had turned up in a few of the persons who had been vaccinated. But the program was plagued with troubles from the start, and no swine flu epidemic, either in the United States or anywhere else in the world, developed.

Looking back on the swine flu program, the authors of the report wrote that it was generally recalled as a "fiasco," a "disaster" or a "tragedy."

669

They were able to say, however, that the program "chalked up a number of accomplishments which give it weight historically," and they predicted that the program "may go down as a qualified success."

Neustadt-Fineberg Report

The report, The Swine Flu Affair: Decision-Making on a Slippery Disease, *was commissioned by Secretary Califano who asked the authors to reconstruct the events associated with the swine flu program so as to suggest lessons for future decision-making in the government.*

The 189-page report was written by Richard E. Neustadt, a professor at the John F. Kennedy School of Government, and Dr. Harvey V. Fineberg, an assistant professor at the Harvard School of Public Health. Neustadt was the author of Presidential Power *and other studies of governmental decision-making.*

In tone, the Neustadt-Fineberg report was analytical rather than accusatory. It made clear that in the author's view there were neither heroes nor villains in the swine flu affair. Yet it included a vivid account of the bureaucratic processes involved in the launching of the program.

Go-Ahead Decision

A number of recruits at Fort Dix, N.J., became sick with influenza in January and February 1976. One of them died. New Jersey public health officials determined that the Victoria flu strain was responsible for most of the sickness. But in some cases they found another virus which they could not identify. Cultures were sent to the federal government's Center for Disease Control (CDC) in Atlanta, Ga., and on Feb. 13 the CDC reported that in four cases, including the fatality, the virus was swine flu.

The CDC finding was a matter of grave concern to a number of the nation's leading experts in virology and public health. The disease had been transmitted by humans — not pigs. Furthermore, recent theories advanced by experts linked outbreaks of influenza to cycles. An epidemic of Asian flu occurred in 1957 and of Hong Kong flu in 1968. Was 1976-77 the time for a return of the deadly swine flu? Some scientists believed so, and they knew that since swine flu had not turned up in an epidemic for almost 50 years only older persons would possess natural protection against it.

The Neustadt-Fineberg report identified Dr. David J. Sencer, the respected director of the CDC, as the mainspring of the immunization program. The report quoted an "action-memorandum" written by Sencer which went not only to David Mathews, then secretary of health, education and welfare, but on up to the Office of Management and Budget, to the

Domestic Council and finally to President Ford. As quoted by Neustadt and Fineberg, Sencer wrote that the new strain of influenza virus was "antigenically related to the . . . [one] implicated as the cause of the 1918-19 pandemic which killed 450,000 people — more than 400 of every 100,000 Americans. . . . The entire U.S. population under the age of 50 is probably susceptible to this new strain. . . . The situation is one of 'go or no go.'"

Neustadt and Fineberg related that on March 22, 1976, the government's top health officials met with Ford to recommend mass immunization. In recalling his decision, Ford told the authors, "I think you ought to gamble on the side of caution. I would always rather be ahead of the curve than behind it." Nevertheless, on March 24, 1976, Ford assembled a group of distinguished scientists from outside the government to seek their advice. According to the report, "At some point in the meeting, Ford asked for a show of hands on whether to proceed. All hands went up." Among the scientists at that meeting were Dr. Jonas E. Salk and Dr. Albert B. Sabin, well-known to the public for having developed vaccines for immunization against poliomyelitis.

Persuaded by his advisers, Ford decided to go ahead. Neustadt and Fineberg were convinced that Ford did not try to use the immunization program to advance his chances in an election year. They wrote, "President Ford wanted to protect the public health."

Lessons in Program

Even while the program was being developed the chances against a swine flu epidemic were always greater than the chances for one, according to the authors. In analyzing the decisions leading to the program, they concluded that "doctors, at least of the older generation, rarely think in probabilistic terms and, if asked, dislike it. . . . As scientists accustomed to thinking about experiments and 'truth,' they were uncomfortable expressing subjective estimates, even if based on expert knowledge and experience. They resented having to quantify their judgments." The result of those attitudes, they suggested, was an "all-or-nothing" approach to immunization.

More specifically, Neustadt and Fineberg pointed to the perils lurking for administrators in dealing with such a "slippery" disease as flu. It was "slippery," they said, because so little was known about it. "To the degree research unravels . . . dilemmas [posed by flu], influenza will become a far less slippery disease."

Following are excerpts from The Swine Flu Affair: Decision-Making on a Slippery Disease, by Richard E. Neustadt and Harvey V. Fineberg, a report released by the Department of Health, Education and Welfare on Oct. 21,

1978. (Boldface headings in brackets have been added by Congressional Quarterly to highlight the organization of the text.):

Foreword

The swine flu program of the Federal government was launched in March 1976 with a White House announcement by President Gerald R. Ford. The program was finally set aside in March 1977, when HEW Secretary Joseph A. Califano, Jr. stated influenza prospects for the coming year. These did not include swine flu. The program thus outlasted, although not for long, the Ford Administration.

The National Influenza Immunization Program, the official title for this venture, was unprecedented in intended timing and in scope among American immunization efforts. It aimed at inoculating everyone before December 1976 against a new flu strain that might conceivably become as big a killer as the flu of 1918, the worst ever. The program was funded by Congress through a $135 million appropriation, and it was later buttressed by special legislation in the field of liability. It was conducted through state health departments, with technical assistance from health agencies in HEW. Inoculations started late, October 1, 1976. They had been slowed somewhat by difficulties in deciding children's dosages and seriously stalled by liability issues. On December 16, the program was suspended to assess statistical evidence of a serious side-effect. Mass immunization never started up again. As a full-scale operation, the program's life was thus not twelve months but two and a half.

The killer never came. The fact that it was feared is one of many things to show how little experts understand the flu, and thus how shaky are the health initiatives launched in its name. What influenza needs, above all, is research.

Decision-making for the swine flu program had seven leading features. To simplify somewhat, they are:

● Overconfidence by specialists in theories spun from meagre *[sic]* evidence.

● Conviction fueled by a conjunction of some preexisting personal agendas.

● Zeal by health professionals to make their lay superiors do right.

● Premature commitment to deciding more than had to be decided.

● Failure to address uncertainties in such a way as to prepare for reconsideration.

● Insufficient questioning of scientific logic and of implementation prospects.

● Insensitivity to media relations and the long-term credibility of institutions.

...One thing we are convinced the program was not. Whatever the contemporary notions from outside, it wasn't party politics; President Ford wanted to protect the public health.

In the year of its formal existence from March to March, the swine flu program chalked up numbers of accomplishments which give it weight historically. In these terms it may go down as a qualified success. More than 40 million civilians were inoculated, twice the number ever reached before in one flu season. A notable surveillance system was developed, better than anything before. A serious side-effect of influenza vaccination, Guillain-Barre syndrome, occasionally fatal, was tracked by that system and remains under investigation. A critical policy problem for all public health interventions and research, the problem of liability, was brought into sharp focus for the first time; it is now being addressed at policy levels both in HEW and in Congress. The flu as a disease and shots as a preventive were dramatized sufficiently so that a permanent program aimed at high risk groups is now in view. With that comes what the influenza specialists in public health have long desired, recognition for the flu alongside polio or measles among Federally-supported immunization initiatives.

While media attention focused on the troubles of the swine flu program — which were many — net effects on general public consciousness seem small. Possibly, indeed, they will turn out on balance to have been more positive than negative for public health. Swine flu may have a bad ring in public ears, but millions may have heard of flu shots for the first time. On this nobody has good information.

Yet to attentive publics in and near the Washington community, to doctors in the country's schools of medicine and public health, to professionals in print and electronic journalism, to members of Congress and the Carter Administration, also to most members of the Ford Administration, the swine flu program was once widely seen and now is overwhelmingly recalled as a "fiasco," a "disaster," or a "tragedy."

More interesting still, it was and is a trauma to the government officials most involved and to their scientific advisers. A year and more later, cheeks flush, brows furrow, voices crack. . . .

[Center for Disease Control]

. . .[A]t the March 10 ACIP [Advisory Committee on Immunization Practices of the Public Health Service (in practice, of the Center for Disease Control, Atlanta, Ga., an agency of the Public Health Service)] meeting, staff spelled out the situation. . . . It was an open meeting, though with minimal press attendance. After hours of discussion a consensus emerged:

First the possibility of pandemic existed. None thought it negligible. Kilbourne [Dr. Edwin D. Kilbourne, a respected influenza specialist] thought it very likely. Most seem to have thought privately of likelihoods within a range from two to twenty percent; each was prepared to bet, however, with nobody but himself. These probabilities, after all, were based on personal judgment, not scientific fact. . . .

Second, while severity could not be estimated, one death in a dozen was worrisome. Besides, somewhere in everybody's mind lurked 1918. No one thought there literally could be a repetition; antibiotics would hold down the death rate. Deaths aside, few thought the virus would be so severe. When last seen in the '20's it was mild. But nobody could bring himself to argue that such mildness was assured. It wasn't.

Third, traditional definition of high-risk groups did not apply. People under 50 had no natural protection, and young adults had suffered unusually high mortality in the 1918 pandemic. This argued for producing enough vaccine to inoculate them all before the next flu season. All meant all, or as many as possible, because one could not count on "herd" immunity to stifle epidemic spread. In influenza nothing on this scale had ever been attempted. But not since 1957 had the timing of discovery allowed for it. And then we did not have vaccines as safe or as effective as the ones developed since. Nor did we have the guns for swift injection. With a decision now the manufacturers could buy their eggs and make the vaccine fast enough so that inoculations could begin in summer, when the chance of flu was slightest and the risk of panic least. Meanwhile plans could be made for mass immunization.

Predisposition buttressed that consensus. It reflected the agendas several ACIP members drew from other aspects of their working lives. Kilbourne, for one, not only championed his theories, but was keen to make the country see the virtues of preventive medicine. Swine flu seemed to him a splendid opportunity. Others also saw the chance to demonstrate the value of public health practice. . . . Consensus . . . might have dissolved over one issue which at this meeting was never joined: should one move automatically from ordering the vaccine and preparing for its use to using it? If so, what evidence about the spread of the disease would make one stop and stockpile it instead? If not, what evidence would make one move from stockpiling into mass immunization? . . .

[The White House]

[L]ike [HEW Secretary David] Mathews before him he [President Gerald R. Ford] had been told that a swine flu pandemic, shades of 1918, was "possible," but that the probability remained "unknown." . . . If those words meant what Ford took them to mean, justifying an unprecedented Federal action, he wanted to be sure the experts felt the same, or know if some did not, and why, and wanted to hear it from them at first hand. Lacking a science adviser (the post was in abeyance then), he asked, as he recalls, that the "best" scientists (along with experts on such things as manufacturing) be brought together with him two days hence. Others recall his asking for "a full spectrum" of scientific views. Either way, he ended this first meeting [March 22] on that note. . . .

On March 24, at 3:30 p.m., Ford met his scientists and some others from the states, the AMA and so forth, in the Cabinet Room. He was accompanied by a full complement of aides and HEW officials. [The director of the Center for Disease Control, Dr. David J.] Sencer opened with a briefing. The president then turned to [Dr. Jonas E.] Salk who strongly urged mass immunization. In back rows aides sighed with relief. Salk recalled for us:

> When the President asked for comment I made the points that influenza was indeed an important disease, and that the program was an opportunity to educate the public and to justify further research. . . . I don't think I then said but I certainly thought of it as a great opportunity to fill part of the "immunity gap" [between antigens in our environment and populations without antibodies]. We should close the gap whenever we can. Here was a chance. . . . That's what I saw in the program, so of course I supported it.

[Dr. Albert B.] Sabin followed Salk . . . and then the President asked others to chime in. He went around the table seeking views as if he really wanted them, which indeed he did. His respondents saw that and it gratified them but it also puzzled them. Summoned to the White House on short notice, many for the first time, ushered into a large, formal meeting, watching Ford call first on one and then another, most of those we've interviewed took it to be "programmed," a "stage set" and they "players" . . . "the decision taken" . . . "we were used." . . .

At some point in the meeting, Ford asked for a show of hands on whether to proceed. All hands went up. He then asked whether there were any dissents or objections on the other side. A long silence ensued. One of the experts present tells us now:

> Later, I regretted not having spoken up and said, "Mr. President, this may not be proper for me to say, but I believe we should not go ahead with immunization until we are sure this is a real threat."

However that may be, it wasn't said. . . .

. . . [Ford] stopped by the Cabinet Room, collared both Sabin and Salk, waved good-bye to the others, and continued to the Press Room, over the old swimming pool, with its facilities for instant briefing. Then and there with Salk and Sabin flanking him, he announced his decision:

> I have been advised that there is a very real possibility that unless we take effective counteractions, there could be an epidemic of this dangerous disease next fall and winter here in the United States.
>
> Let me state clearly at this time: no one knows exactly how serious this threat could be. Nevertheless, we cannot afford to take a chance with the health of our nation. Accordingly, I am today announcing the following actions.
>
> . . . I am asking the Congress to appropriate $135 million, prior to their April recess, for the production of sufficient vaccine to inoculate every man, woman, and child in the United States.

Sabin spoke up also. Mathews and [Assistant Secretary for Health Theodore] Cooper then took questions. . . .

[Program Suspension]

From mid-October on, polls showed a downward drift of persons who intended to be immunized. Absolute numbers of those actually inoculated rose for a while as state plans took hold. During "Pittsburgh week" [when the program received adverse publicity following the Oct. 11,1976, deaths of three elderly persons inoculated at a Pittsburgh clinic] and despite it, 2.4 million people were immunized. A month later those numbers rose to 6.4 million for the second week of November. A month after that, however, they had dropped back to 2.3 million for the second week of December. . . .

And then, of course, there was no swine flu, or almost none. One case, not directly traceable to pigs, showed up in Concordia, Missouri. That was all. Millions came down with other respiratory ailments passed from human to human that fall. But with this one exception there were none the swine flu virus could have caused, or vaccine cured.

Between October 1 and December 16, more than 40 million Americans received swine flu shots through Sencer's program. (Defense and VA programs accounted for some millions more.) This is twice the number ever immunized before for any influenza virus in a single season. Considering the obstacles it is an impressive number. It also is a number oddly distributed. Some states, albeit small ones, inoculated 80 percent of their adults in that time period. Others immunized not more than 10 percent. Delaware was at the top of that range, New York City near the bottom. Variations in between are striking: Houston, Texas inoculated only 20 percent of its adults, while San Antonio, Texas immunized nearly one-third. Despite coincident deaths, Pittsburgh, Pennsylvania vaccinated nearly 43 percent while Philadelphia, home of Legionnaire's Disease, managed but 23 percent. . . .

One state that was conscientious in its conduct of the national program was Minnesota, where nearly two-thirds of the eligible adults were immunized. In the third week of November, a physician there reported to his local health authorities a patient who had contracted an ascending paralysis, called Guillain-Barre syndrome, following immunization. The physician said he had just learned of this possible side-effect from a cassette-tape discussion of flu vaccination prepared for the continuing education of family practitioners by a California specialist. The Minnesota immunization program officer, Denton R. Peterson, dutifully called CDC and spoke to one of the surveillance physicians there. The latter expressed no interest in this single case, but Peterson was sufficiently bothered to conduct a literature search and did indeed discover previous case reports. "We felt we were sitting on a bomb," he told us. Within a week three more cases, one fatal, were reported to Peterson. Two came from a single neurologist who remarked that he had observed this complication of flu vaccine during his residency training. More anxious than ever, Peterson again called CDC, where the surveillance center was just being told by phone of three more cases in Alabama. The next day they learned of an additional case in New Jersey. By then CDC was taking the problem seriously. Center staff surveyed neurologists in eleven states to ascertain the relative risk of this rare disease (estimated at 5000 cases annually) among vaccinated and unvaccinated. When the preliminary results suggested an increased risk among the vaccinated, Sencer sought advice from usual sources, NIAID [National Institute of Allergy and Infectious Diseases], BoB [Bureau of Biologics in the Food and Drug Administration], ACIP and his own people. The statistical association did not convince them all.

But what struck everybody, sensitized by their long summer, was the thought: until the risk (if any) is established, it cannot be put into a consent form! The statistical relationship would have to be reviewed and immunization halted in the interim. After everything that had already happened, everybody took that to mean virtual termination. Even the least imaginative could conjure up the television shots of victims in their beds, wheel chairs, and respirators. . . .

[Probabilities]

For purposes of sharpening assumptions and distinguishing them, nothing beats an exercise in probability. Deciding on a swine flu program is like placing a bet without knowing the odds. A serious stake in the outcome ought to concentrate the mind on breaking down the issue and scrounging for anything that might inform judgment. If one has "scientific" evidence from laboratory tests, one need not scrounge, but swine flu decisions are not like that. Expertise counts for a lot, but only by way of informing subjective judgment. To assign a number to the likelihood that something will occur is to expose one's judgment for comparison with that of others. This leads to explicitness about everyone's reasons. If two people assign different numbers, the question becomes, why? That starts them digging into the detail of their own — and each other's — reasoning.

But doctors, at least of the older generation, rarely think in probabilistic terms and, if asked, dislike it. Some of the scientists involved with the swine flu decision did participate in an exercise to estimate the probabilities of an epidemic and its severity. This was not done as part of any decision-making deliberation, but as an academic exercise, a favor for a colleague writing a paper. . . . As scientists accustomed to thinking about experiments and "truth," they were uncomfortable expressing subjective estimates, even if based on expert knowledge and experience. They resented having to quantify their judgments.

Indeed, they think that it is unprofessional to express judgments in terms they cannot call scientific, worse still to express them in the presence of laymen. They see placing precise numbers on uncertainties as an incitement to public misunderstanding. . . .

Doctors, like other people, often think simplistically when, as so often happens, they must judge despite themselves on grounds other than laboratory evidence. . . .

The best of expert panels should be supplemented by separate scientific advice. In a swine flu case when evidence is thin — with unobserved phenomena vastly outweighing observations from the three pandemic years of 1918, 1957, 1968 — it is not only the assumptions but appraisal of their scientific quality that top decision-makers need. Panels tend toward "group think" and over-selling, tendencies nurtured by longstanding interchanges and intimacy, as in the influenza fraternity. Other competent scientists, who do not share their group identity or vested interests, should be able to appraise the scientific logic applied to available evidence. In medicine, as in law, there are rules of evidence by which argument can be tested. . . .

['Slippery Disease']

We have called influenza a "slippery" disease. Five features combine to make it so.

First is the changing character of the influenza virus, with spreading and timing mortgaged to the processes of antigenic change [changes in the surface proteins, antigens, that distinguish one virus from another] about which there are painfully few documented observations. As for severity, the specialists are almost wholly in the dark. Nothing is sure, not even the reasons why 1918 was the worst flu of all.

Second, the effectiveness of influenza vaccine is relatively short-lived. Its effectiveness may be compromised by minor antigenic drifts in the virus, which are frequent. Moreover, most experts believe that, even in the absence of drift, effective protection lasts only for about a year.

Third, influenza symptoms are widely misunderstood. Millions of Americans, and perhaps half the doctors in the country, use the term for a variety of gastrointestinal troubles, "stomach flu," which no flu virus causes and no flu vaccine cures. Influenza is found in the respiratory tract and there alone.

Fourth, although it resides in the respiratory tract, it is by no means the only virus likely to be lurking there and may not be the major source of flu-like aches and fever. If not, then immunization against influenza, even assuming that the vaccine fits the strain and that it actually immunizes, safeguards nobody from identical symptoms caused by other viruses.

Fifth, the multitude of causes of flu-like illness make it difficult to estimate the year-to-year impact of the influenza virus on the public health. Especially in non-epidemic years, the proportion of flu-like illness actually caused by the flu virus is unknown. . . .

Contrast influenza's features with those of well-established Federal immunization targets, measles and polio, or smallpox in its day. For the established targets, causes, symptoms, treatments, risks are understood alike by doctors and laymen. Immunization "immunizes": it prevents the symptoms for all time, or for several years at least. From decade to decade there are no antigenic shifts. Compared to the slippery flu, these are stable targets indeed. Medical and public health professionals, congressmen, administrators, parents, children, journalists and citizens at large all know what they are shooting at.

The comparative aspect is critical. All diseases are slippery in some degree. All interventions risk, to some degree, the credibility of institutions. But to treat swine flu as though it were the polio of twenty years ago is to beg for trouble. The two diseases have some tempting likenesses but in these key respects they are at opposite ends of the spectrum. When this country started on its campaign against polio it confronted a well understood disease with methods that worked as advertised. Contrast the swine flu program. It oversold a method of ostensible protection from the paradigm of slippery diseases. The risk to credibility was rendered as extreme as was the combination of its five slippery features.

Up to 1976, the Federal government had drawn a line, perhaps unconsciously, between stable and such slippery diseases. Swine flu represented the first Federally sponsored and financed mass immunization at the slippery end of the spectrum. Diseases at the stable end had been an exclusive company. Its members shared an inferential base of medical knowledge, public understanding, and support, far beyond that now accorded influenza. . . .

Technical Afterword

Policy decisions regarding influenza rest on judgments about the behavior of the virus, the impact of the disease and our ability to interdict its course. But the virus is capricious, the disease elusive, and our remedies imperfect. The technical dilemmas discussed in this Afterword reflect what we know, what we think we know and what we do not know. They run from matters of definition, to matters of measurement, to matters of substantive understanding. We hope they convey the nature of technical limitations in contending with the influenza problems. . . .

The term influenza applies both to a particular virus and to a clinical disease, consisting of fever, headache, muscle aches, prostration and, frequently, cough, watery eyes, nasal stuffiness. The influenza virus can cause this syndrome, although not always exactly the same symptoms, and the severity of the disease ranges from very mild to fatal; death usually comes from rapidly progressive pneumonia. . . .

Many other infectious agents, mostly viruses, can produce illness resembling that caused by the influenza virus. . . . Influenza-the-virus certainly predominates as a cause of influenza-the-disease during epidemic periods, but other viruses are relatively more prominent as producers of year-in and year-out influenza-like illness. Persons who are vaccinated and protected against the influenza virus remain susceptible to "flu" when caused by other organisms.

Public understanding thus is constantly at risk. To virologists and influenza experts, "influenza" means the influenza virus and only the disease produced by that virus. To members of the public, "flu" is the disease regardless of viral cause. Many people also speak colloquially of "intestinal flu," a misnomer to the specialist since influenza is not a gastrointestinal ailment.

For public policy, therefore, the problem of influenza-the-disease is analytically distinct from problems produced by the influenza virus. This applies to any assessment of the health and economic magniture [sic] of the "influenza" problem, to the development of short and long term strategies to address the "influenza" problem, and to the presentation and promotion of "influenza" programs. . . .

Vaccination strategies differ for different diseases. In smallpox eradication, for example, the idea was to contain disease by vaccinating people in the immediate vicinity of any new cases. In another instance, children are vaccinated against rubella (German measles) so they will not carry disease to their pregnant mothers. Some vaccination programs aim at herd immunity, achieved by vaccinating enough people to suppress epidemic spread in a population. Some have advocated this approach for influenza. . . . However, herd immunity does not seem reliable for influenza at achievable levels of immunization in the population. . . . Outbreaks have spread in boarding schools, even when more than 95 percent had been vaccinated. . . . Therefore, advocates of influenza vaccination usually stress protection for the individual against the virus and its consequences, without regard for herd effect. This was the prevailing view at CDC in 1976 and is so now. Civilian immunization programs typically focus on the groups at increased risk of death, for example, the elderly and the chronically ill. Military forces try to prevent illness in large numbers of their troops at the same time.

Both live and killed virus vaccines are used in different countries to prevent influenza. Live vaccine has certain theoretical advantages, including protection more akin to that from natural infection and lower volume of virus required for immunization, but questions about its dependability, safety and acceptability (it must be inhaled) have thus far discouraged its use in the United States. . . . Over the near term, killed virus vaccine will probably remain the key element in programs to control influenza in the United States.

Insofar as scientists can more quickly produce more potent vaccines against a broader spectrum of strains, longer-lasting and with fewer side effects, we will strengthen our hand against the influenza virus. No strategy against the virus, no matter how successful, copes with the whole "influenza" disease problem. . . .

Rare side effects can be detected only by a comprehensive and sensitive surveillance system. These are unlikely to reveal themselves during field trials. Whether side effects such as Guillain-Barre syndrome are related only to swine flu vaccines, or to any influenza vaccine, or to any vaccine of any kind, is not now known.

The effectiveness of flu vaccines in the general population remains uncertain. Despite administration of millions of doses of vaccine, there have been no direct measures of the extent to which immunization reduces mortality. In terms of ability to prevent disease, the measured effectiveness of influenza vaccines has ranged in different studies from zero to 100 percent. . . . The expert consensus is that present influenza vaccines would be about 60 to 80 percent effective in the general population. . . . By this is meant that compared to an unvaccinated group, 60 to 80 percent fewer people in a similar but vaccinated group will contract influenza. . . .

Finally, observed vaccine effectiveness in one population may not apply to others. Findings in the military may not apply to civilian populations; findings in nursing homes may not apply to the elderly living on their own; and findings in one age group may not apply to another.

Taken together, the foregoing comments elaborate, selectively, the five features of influenza . . .: first, a capricious virus; second, short-lived (and partial) protection against it; third, attribution to it of assorted other ailments; fourth, a mimicking by others of its symptoms; and as a consequence, the fifth, entanglement of influenza-the-virus with influenza-the-disease, causing confusion in the measurement of impact. These are the features that, taken together, give influenza standing in our eyes as an extremely slippery phenomenon.

Regarding swine flu, one question remains to be asked. In 1918, something extraordinary happened: Why? What accounts for the most devastating influenza pandemic history records? Why were young, healthy adults carried off as surely as the elderly and infirm? Epidemiologists have debated for sixty years. Theories abound, but nobody knows. Perhaps concomitant bacterial or other infection played a major role, perhaps the stress of war or other environmental factors made a difference. If so, well and good, for the times have changed and today we have potent antibiotics. But conceivably a large part of that pandemic mortality was due to some intrinsic feature of the virus, a characteristic that may be harbored even today on a gene fragment somewhere in the animal kingdom, a gene that could just possibly combine with human virus.

Despite impressions left by the swine flu affair, this remains a possibility. Ford could not accurately predict the killer and was thus severely limited in seeking to guard everyone against it. Mathews, Cooper and Sencer could not do so either. Neither could their scientific advisers. Nor can anyone in 1978. Only research, perhaps, someday will manage that.

CARTER, FED ACTIONS
ON DOLLAR AND INFLATION
October 24; November 1, 1978

President Jimmy Carter's three predecessors had grappled, as would Carter himself, with the problem of relentless inflation. The roots of the inflation, most economists agreed, went back to 1966 when the costs of a rapidly escalating Vietnam war and Lyndon Johnson's expensive Great Society programs "overheated" the economy.

By mid-1978 the seeming inability of the United States to get a grip on the rising rate of inflation and on related economic problems was causing the U.S. dollar to decline sharply against other major currencies. Carter, at an economic summit meeting in Bonn, Germany, on July 18 and again at a meeting of the International Monetary Fund (IMF) in Washington, D.C., on Sept. 27, had pledged that he would take the actions needed to strengthen the U.S. dollar and reduce the rate of inflation. (Economic summit, p. 533; IMF meeting, p. 659.) But the response of currency dealers on major international exchanges had been one of little confidence in the president's will to adopt a tough policy.

The bold U.S. monetary move the traders had been looking for came Nov. 1, and its effect was stunning. The monetary package set in motion included a full percentage point increase in the Federal Reserve discount rate and massive intervention by the U.S. Treasury in the currency markets.

The joint administration-Federal Reserve Board announcement came at a moment when the dollar was falling precipitously on international exchanges and when other financial markets were in tumult. It also came at a moment when U.S. policy-makers were alarmed by the lukewarm reception that had been accorded the administration's new anti-inflation program, announced by Carter only eight days earlier. The Nov. 1 dollar support program was seen as essential not only to bolster the dollar but also to make the president's anti-inflation program more credible.

Anti-Inflation Plan

In a somber television address Oct. 24, Carter called inflation "our most serious domestic problem" and declared, "We must face a time of national austerity." The president reiterated his opposition to compulsory wage and price controls and said that he did not intend his new program, which he outlined, to be a step in that direction.

Carter asked that annual wages and fringe benefits not be increased in any company by more than 7 percent. The average would be calculated separately for each company's executives, unionized workers and nonunion workers. Workers earning less than $4 an hour would be exempt from the pay standard as would be workers with existing contracts calling for raises in excess of 7 percent.

The president asked companies to keep their price increases half a percentage point below their average increases in 1976 and 1977. If that standard were met, Carter said, overall annual price increases would be 5.75 percent.

Though termed voluntary, the wage and price program contained limited government sanctions. If unions or companies exceeded the voluntary standards for wages and prices, various government actions would be triggered. Among them were the relaxation of import quotas, a reduction in rates regulated industries were allowed to charge and a modification of wages paid on federal projects. Moreover, the president said that to the extent practicable government agencies would limit their purchases to companies observing the pay and price guidelines.

The most novel idea in Carter's anti-inflation program, and the only provision requiring congressional action, was a system of tax rebates to workers who abided by the 7 percent pay standard if the inflation rate exceeded 7 percent. Together with the wage-price plan, Carter pledged that he would hold the federal budget deficit below $30 billion. The entire program included virtually no mention of monetary policy.

Reporting Oct. 26 on reaction to the president's program, The Wall Street Journal said, "While many [in the business and labor communities] expressed their intent to help the president fight inflation to the utmost, few believed that the Carter plan would win the battle." That reaction, and the grave weakness of the dollar, provided the context for the strong monetary policy announced Nov. 1.

Dollar Support Program

The principal figures in the successful effort to persuade President Carter to adopt the tough policy were W. Michael Blumenthal, secretary of the Treasury; G. William Miller, chairman of the Federal Reserve Board; and Charles L. Schultze, chairman of the Council of Economic Advisers.

Described as "dismayed" by the reaction of the financial markets to the president's anti-inflation program, Blumenthal on Oct. 27 saw Carter alone and urged strong action. Schultze produced new information showing that over the previous 18 months the depreciation of the dollar had been responsible for as much as one-third of the accelerating inflation. Many of the details of the emergency package were worked out at a Saturday night meeting Oct. 28 in the White House basement map room, which Carter attended.

The actions announced Nov. 1 included these elements:

● The Federal Reserve Board raised the discount rate charged member banks from 8.5 percent to 9.5 percent. The previous time the bellwether rate was raised by so large an amount was in the 1920s.

● The Fed also moved to tighten credit by requiring U.S. banks to keep on reserve an additional 2 percent of their time deposits in denominations of $100,000 or more. The reserve requirement was money that banks had to keep on hand or on deposit with a Federal Reserve bank without interest. In addition to leaving the banks less money to lend, an increase in the reserve requirement was expected to induce banks to borrow surplus dollars overseas.

● The government announced plans to exchange $15 billion for marks, yen and Swiss francs under so-called "swap" arrangements that existed among governments for currency-support operations. The United States would then use those other currencies to buy dollars abroad.

● The Treasury said that it would sell up to $10 billion worth of U.S. government securities in foreign denominations to private holders of marks, yen and Swiss francs. Again, the government would use those currencies to buy dollars.

● The government also announced plans to draw $3 billion in foreign currencies from its reserves at the IMF and to sell another $2 billion of its IMF Special Drawing Rights for foreign currencies. Special Drawing Rights were international reserve assets used in monetary exchange.

● The Treasury said that it would expand its monthly sale of gold from 300,000 to 1.5 million ounces to gather surplus dollars and help improve the U.S. trade deficit.

The immediate reaction to the strong U.S. moves was gratifying to U.S. policy-makers. After its long slide downward, the dollar shot upward on currency exchanges. The price of gold plummeted, the U.S. stock market soared and other financial markets responded favorably. For the short term, at least, the assault on the dollar was repelled.

Recession Fears

Most private economists believed that by choking off credit with high interest rates the Nov. 1 actions would bring on a mild recession, perhaps by mid-1979. A number of black leaders and spokesmen for the nation's cities expressed concern over the possibility of rising unemployment.

Carter, however, told reporters Nov. 3 that he did not "think there is going to be a recession because the economy is strong enough to withstand it." He added, "There would have been a recession if we hadn't acted strongly and decisively to support the dollar with a strong anti-inflation program."

Following are the texts of President Carter's Oct. 24, 1978, nationally televised speech in which he outlined his anti-inflation program; an Oct. 24 "fact sheet" distributed by the White House containing details of the program; Carter's Nov. 1 statement supporting the dollar; and the Nov. 1 joint statement by Treasury Secretary W. Michael Blumenthal and Federal Reserve Board Chairman G. William Miller. (Boldface headings in brackets have been added by Congressional Quarterly to highlight the organization of the text.):

CARTER SPEECH ON INFLATION
Oct. 24, 1978

Good evening.

I want to have a frank talk with you tonight about our most serious domestic problem. That problem is inflation. Inflation can threaten all the economic gains we have made, and it can stand in the way of what we want to achieve in the future.

This has been a long-time threat.

For the last ten years, the annual inflation rate in the United States has averaged 6.5 percent, and during the three years before my inauguration, it had increased to an average of 8 percent.

Inflation has, therefore, been a serious problem for me ever since I became President. We have tried to control it, but we have not been successful. It is time for all of us to make a greater and a more coordinated effort.

If inflation gets worse, several things will happen. Your purchasing power will continue to decline, and most of the burden will fall on those who can least afford it. Our national productivity will suffer. The value of our dollar will continue to fall in world trade.

We have made good progress in putting our people back to work over the past 21 months. We have created more than 6 million new jobs for American workers. We have reduced the unemployment rate by about 25 percent, and we will continue our efforts to reduce unemployment further, especially among our young people and minorities.

But I must tell you tonight that inflation threatens this progress. If we do not get inflation under control, we will not be able to reduce unemployment further, and we may even slide backward.

[No Simple Solution]

I do not have all the answers. Nobody does.

Perhaps there is no complete and adequate answer, but I want to let you know that fighting inflation will be a central preoccupation of mine during the months ahead, and I want to arouse our Nation to join me in this effort.

There are two simplistic and familiar answers which are sometimes proposed — simple, familiar, and too extreme. One of these answers is to impose a complicated scheme of Federal government wage and price controls on our entire free economic system.

The other is a deliberate recession, which would throw millions of people out of work.

Both of these extreme proposals would not work and they must be rejected.

I have spent many hours in the last few months reviewing with my own advisors and with a number of outside experts every proposal, every suggestion, every possibility for eliminating inflation.

If there is one thing I have learned beyond any doubt, it is that there is no single solution for inflation.

What we have, instead, is a number of partial remedies. Some of them will help, others may not. But we have no choice but to use the best approaches we have — and to maintain a constant search for additional steps which may be effective.

I want to discuss with you tonight some of the approaches we have been able to develop. They involve action by government, business, labor and every other sector of our economy. Some of these factors are under my control as President — especially government actions — and I will insist that the government does its part of the job.

But whether our efforts are successful will finally depend on you as much as on me. Your decisions — made every day at your service station or your grocery store, in your business, in your union meetings — will determine our nation's answer to inflation as much as decisions made here in the White House or by the Congress on Capitol Hill.

I cannot guarantee that our joint effort will succeed. In fact, it is almost certain not to succeed if success means quick or dramatic changes. Every free government on earth is wrestling with this problem of inflation, and every one of them knows that a long-term disease requires long-term treatment. It is up to us to make the improvements we can, even at the risk of partial failure, rather than to ensure failure by not trying at all.

[Government Must Set Example]

I will concentrate my efforts within the government. We know that government is not the only cause of inflation. But it is one of the causes, and government does set an example. Therefore, it must take the lead in fiscal restraint.

We are going to hold down Government spending, reduce the budget deficit, and eliminate Government waste.

We will slash Federal hiring and cut the Federal work force.

We will eliminate needless regulations.

We will bring more competition back to our economy.

And we will oppose any further reduction in Federal income taxes until we have convincing prospects that inflation will be controlled.

Let me explain what each one of these steps means.

The Federal deficit is too high. Our people are simply sick and tired of wasteful Federal spending and the inflation it brings with it.

We have already had some success. We have brought the deficit down by one-third since I ran for President — from more than $66 billion in fiscal year 1976, to about $40 billion in fiscal year 1979 — a reduction of more than $25 billion in the Federal deficit in just three years.

It will keep going down. Next year with tough restraints on Federal spending and moderate economic growth in prospect, I plan to reduce the budget deficit to less than one-half what it was when I ran for office — to $30 billion or less.

The Government has been spending too great a portion of what our Nation produces. During my campaign I promised to cut the Government's share of our total national spending from 23 percent, which it was then, to 21 percent in fiscal year 1981.

We now plan to meet that goal one year earlier.

Reducing the deficit will require difficult and unpleasant decisions.

We must face a time of national austerity. Hard choices are necessary if we want to avoid consequences that are even worse.

I intend to make those hard choices. I have already vetoed bills that would undermine our fight against inflation, and the Congress has sustained those vetoes. I know that the Congress will continue to cooperate in the effort to meet our needs in responsible, non-inflationary ways.

[Will Use Veto]

I will use the administrative and the budgetary powers of my office, including the veto, if necessary, to keep our Nation firmly on the path of fiscal restraint.

Restraint involves tax policy as well as spending decisions. Tax reduction has never been more politically popular than it is today. But if future tax cuts are made rashly, with no eye on the budget deficits, they will hurt us all by causing more inflation.

There are tax cuts which could directly lower costs and prices and help in the fight against inflation. I may consider ways to reduce those particular taxes while still cutting the budget deficit, but until we have a convincing prospect of controlling inflation, I will oppose any further reductions in Federal income taxes.

To keep the government a manageable size, I am ordering tonight a reduction in Federal hiring. This order will mean a reduction of more than 20,000 in the number of permanent Federal employees already budgeted for this fiscal year and will cut the total size of the Federal work force.

I have already placed a 5.5 percent cap on the pay increase for Federal employees, and Federal executive officers are receiving no pay increases at all.

It is not enough just to control government deficits, spending and hiring. We must also control the costs of government regulations.

In recent years, Congress has passed a number of landmark statutes to improve social and environmental conditions. We must and we will continue progress toward protecting the health and safety of the American people.

But we must also realize that everything has a price — and that consumers eventually pick up the tab. Where regulations are essential, they must be efficient. Where they fight inflation, they should be encouraged. Where they are unnecessary, they should be removed.

[Reduced Regulation]

Early this year, I directed Federal agencies to eliminate unnecessary regulations and to analyze the costs and benefits of new ones. Today, for instance, the Occupational Safety and Health Administration, sometimes called OSHA, eliminated nearly 1,000 unnecessary regulations.

Now we can build on this progress.

I have directed a council of my regulatory departments and agencies to coordinate their regulations, to prevent overlapping and duplication.

Most important, the council will develop a unified calendar of planned major regulations. The calendar will give us, for the first time, a comprehensive list of regulations the Federal Government is proposing, with their costs and objectives.

As President, I will personally use my authority to ensure that regulations are issued only when needed and that they meet their goals at the lowest possible cost.

We are also cutting away the regulatory thicket that has grown up around us, and giving our competitive free enterprise system a chance to grow up in its place.

Last year we gave the airline industry a fresh shot of competition. Regulations were removed. Free market forces drove prices down, record numbers of passengers traveled — and profits went up. Our new airline deregulation bill will make these benefits permanent. For the first time in decades, we have actually deregulated a major industry.

Next year, we will work with Congress to bring more competiticn to others, such as the railroad and trucking industries.

Of all our weapons against inflation, competition is the most powerful. Without real competition, prices and wages go up — even when demand is going down.

We must therefore work to allow more competition wherever possible so that powerful groups — Government, business, labor — must think twice before abusing their economic power.

We will redouble our efforts to put competition back into the American free enterprise system.

Another reason for inflation is the slowdown in productivity growth. More efficient production is essential if we are to control inflation, make American goods more competitive in world markets, add new jobs, and increase the real incomes of our people.

We have made a start toward improving productivity. The tax bill just passed by the Congress includes many of the investment incentives that I recommended last January. Federal support for research and development will continue to increase, especially for basic research. We will coordinate and strengthen Federal programs that support productivity improvements throughout our economy.

[Inflation in the Essentials]

Our Government efforts will attack the inflation that hurts most — inflation in the essentials: Food, housing, and medical care.

We will continue to use our agricultural policies to sustain farm production, to maintain stable prices, and to keep inflation down.

Rising interest rates have always accompanied inflation. They add further to the costs of business expansion and to what consumers must pay when they buy houses and other consumer items.

The burden of controlling inflation cannot be left to monetary policy alone, which must deal with the problem through tight restrictions on money and credit that push interest rates up.

I will work for a balanced, concerted, and sustained program under which tight budget restraint, private wage and price moderation, and responsible monetary policy support each other.

If successful, we should expect lower inflation and lower interest rates for consumers and businesses alike.

As for medical care, where costs have gone up much faster than the general inflation rate, the most important step we can take is to pass a strong bill to control hospital costs. This year, the Senate passed one. Next year, I will try again, and I believe the whole Congress will act to hold down hospital costs — if your own Members of Congress hear from you.

Between now and January, when the new Congress convenes, I will be preparing a package of specific legislative proposals to help fight inflation.

The government will do its part, but in a country like ours, government cannot do the job alone.

In the end, the success or failure of this effort will also rest on whether the private sector will accept — and act on — the voluntary wage and price standards I am announcing tonight.

['Standards Are Fair']

These standards are fair. They are standards that everyone can follow. If we do follow them, they will slow prices down — so that wages will not have to chase prices just to stay even.

And they point the way toward an eventual cure for inflation, by removing the pressures that cause it in the first place.

In the last ten years, in our attempts to protect ourselves from inflation, we have developed attitudes and habits that actually keep inflation going once it has begun. Most companies raise their prices because they expect costs to rise.

Unions call for large wage settlements because they expect inflation to continue. Because we expect it to happen, it does happen, and once it is started, wages and prices chase each other up and up.

It is like a crowd standing at a football stadium. No one can see any better than when everyone is sitting down — but no one is willing to be the first to sit down.

Except for our lowest paid workers, I am asking all employees in this country to limit total wage increases to a maximum of 7 percent per year. From tonight on, every contract signed and every pay raise granted should meet this standard.

My price limitation will be equally strict. Our basic target for economy-wide price increases is 5.75 percent. To reach this goal, I am tonight setting a standard for each firm in the Nation to hold its price increases at least one-half of one percentage point below what they averaged during 1976 and 1977.

Of course, we have to take into account binding commitments already in effect, which will prevent an absolute adherence to these standards.

But this price standard is much lower than this year's inflation rate — and more important, it is less than the standard for wage increases. That difference is accounted for by rising productivity — and it will allow the income of America's workers to stay ahead of inflation.

This is a standard for everyone to follow — everyone. As far as I am concerned, every business, every union, every professional group, every individual in this country, has no excuse not to adhere to these standards. If we meet these standards, the real buying power of your paycheck will rise.

The difficulty with a voluntary program is that workers fear that if they cooperate with the standards while others do not, then they will suffer if inflation continues.

[Rebate Program]

To deal with this concern, I will ask the Congress next January to enact a program that workers who observe the standards would be eligible for a tax rebate if the inflation rate is more than 7 percent. In other words, they would have a real wage insurance policy against inflation which might be caused by others.

This will give our workers an additional incentive to observe the program — and will remove their only legitimate reason not to cooperate.

Because this is not a mandatory control plan, I cannot stop an irresponsible corporation from raising its prices, or a selfish group of employees from using its power to demand excessive wages. But then if that happens, the Government will respond — using the tools of Government authority and public opinion.

Soon after they raise prices or demand pay increases that are excessive, the company or the union will feel the pressure that the public can exert, through new competition to drive prices down, or removal of Government protections and privileges which they now enjoy.

We will also make better use of the $80 billion worth of purchases the Government makes from private industry each year. We must be prudent buyers. If costs rise too fast, we can delay those purchases as your family would — or switch to another supplier. We may not buy a fleet of cars this year, for example, if cars cost too much, or we may channel our purchases to suppliers who have observed our wage and price standards rather than to buy from those who have not.

We will require firms that supply goods and services to the government to certify their compliance with the wage and price standards. We will make every effort, within legal limits, to deny government contracts to companies that fail to meet our wage and price standards.

We will use our buying power more effectively — to make price restraint and competition a reality.

The government now extends economic privileges to many parts of the private economy — special franchises, protected wages and prices, subsidies, protection from foreign competition. If wages or prices rise too fast in some industry, we will take that as a sign that those privileges are no longer needed — and that this protection should be removed.

We will make sure that no part of our economy is able to use its special privilege or its concentrated power to victimize the rest of us.

[Public Cooperation Needed]

This approach I have outlined will not end inflation. It simply improves our chances of making it better rather than worse.

To summarize the plan I am announcing tonight:

We will cut the budget deficit.

We will slash federal hiring and reduce the federal work force.

We will restrain federal pay.

We will delay further tax cuts.

We will remove needless regulations.

We will use Federal policy to encourage more competition. We will set specific standards for both wages and prices throughout the economy. We will use all the powers at our disposal to make this program work. And we will submit new anti-inflation proposals to the Congress next January, including the real wage insurance proposal I have discussed tonight.

I have said many times that these steps will be tough — and they are. But I also said they will be fair — and they are. They apply equally to all groups. They give all of us an equal chance to move ahead.

And these proposals, which give us a chance, also deserve a chance. If tomorrow, or next week, or next month, you ridicule them, ignore them, pick them apart before they have a chance to work, then you will have reduced their chance of succeeding.

These steps can work, but that will take time, and you are the ones who can give them that time. If there is one thing I am asking of every American tonight, it is to give this plan a chance to work — a chance to work for us.

You can help give it that chance by using your influence.

Business and labor must know that you will not tolerate irresponsible price and wage increases. Your elected officials must know how you feel as they make difficult choices.

Too often the only voices they hear are those of special interests, supporting their own narrow cause. If you want government officials to cut inflation, you have to make sure that they hear your voice.

I have heard you with unmistakable clarity.

Nearly 40 years ago, when the world watched to see whether his nation would survive, Winston Churchill defied those who thought Britain would fall to the Nazi threat. Churchill replied by asking his countrymen, "What kind of people do they think we are?"

There are those today who say that a free economy cannot cope with inflation, and that we have lost our ability to act as a nation rather than as a collection of special interests. And I reply, "What kind of people do they think we are?"

I believe that our people, our economic system, and our government are equal to this task. I hope that you will prove me right.

Thank you, and good night.

ANTI-INFLATION FACT SHEET

Federal Government Actions

The Federal government alone cannot solve the inflation problem, but it must take the lead. The Administration will do everything in its power to ensure that its actions are consistent with the objectives of the anti-inflation program.

Budgetary Policy

• Substantial progress has been made in reducing the rate of unemployment. But further progress in reducing unemployment will depend on our success in reducing the rate of inflation. The budget that will be submitted in January will give top priority to moderating inflation. To achieve that goal the President will:

—Put a tight rein on the growth of Federal spending. He has pledged to cut the share of Gross National Product accounted for by Federal spending from 23 percent in FY 1976 to about 21 percent in FY 1980, one year ahead of his previously announced schedule.

—Reduce the Federal deficit. In fiscal year 1976, the Federal deficit was $66 billion. In just three years, by 1979, the deficit will be cut to below $40 billion. In the 1980 budget, the deficit will be reduced still further — to less than one-half the 1976 deficit.

• In order to contribute to these goals, the President has imposed severe limits on the hiring of Federal employees. Effective immediately, for an indefinite period, Federal agencies will be permitted to fill only one out of two vacancies as they occur.

Regulatory Policy

• Programs to protect the environment and the health and safety of workers and consumers are vital. But the achievement of these critical objectives should not place unnecessary burdens on the economy. Regulatory agencies are now required to analyze major new regulations to identify and compare benefits and costs. In addition, the President has:

—Directed the formation of a Regulatory Council. This Council will include all regulatory departments and agencies. The Council will have the important task of coordinating duplicative and overlapping regulations, in concert with the Office of Management and Budget's efforts to enforce the regulatory-process Executive Order 12044.

—Directed the new Regulatory Council to develop a unified *calendar* of major regulations. The calendar will provide, for the first time, a comprehensive list of major regulations to be proposed by the various agencies of the Federal government. This calendar will facilitate a comprehensive and consistent approach to the evaluation of costs and benefits of proposed regulations. The Council will help to ensure that regulatory objectives are achieved at the lowest possible cost.

—Pledged to use his authority to ensure that regulations are issued only when necessary and that they achieve their goals at the lowest possible cost.

—Directed each Executive branch regulatory agency to include additional regulations that have a major economic impact in the "sunset" reviews that are required by E.O. 12044.

Private Sector Actions

Success of this anti-inflation effort will depend upon the cooperation of the private sector. To this end, the President has set forth explicit numerical standards of behavior for pay and prices in the year ahead.

Pay Standard

• Annual increases in wages and private fringe benefits should not exceed *7 percent*.

—Workers earning less than $4.00 per hour will be exempt as well as wage contracts already signed.

—In new collective bargaining situations, a contract in which wage and fringe benefit increases average no more than 7 percent annually over the life of the contract will be consistent with the standard. In evaluating a contract for consistency with the standard, cost-of-living clauses will be evaluated using a 6 percent per year rate of price inflation over the life of the contract.

—No more than an 8 percent pay increase should be included in the first year of a multi-year contract.

—Increases above the standard will be acceptable to the extent that they reflect changes in work rules and practices that show demonstrable productivity improvements.

—The standard does *not* apply to individual workers. The standard applies to *average* pay increases for *groups* of workers. Firms will be expected to divide their work force into three categories:

(a) management employees, (b) groups of employees covered by separate collectively bargained contracts, and (c) all other employees.

Price Standard

• Individual firms are expected to limit their price increases over the next year to *one-half of one percentage point* below their average annual rate of price increase during 1976-77.

—If wage-rate increases for a firm decelerate by more than one-half percentage point from the 1976-77 base period, greater deceleration in prices will be required in order to ensure that savings are reflected in prices.

—The standard does not apply to specific products, but to a firm's overall average price.

—Firms unable to meet the one-half percent deceleration standard due to *unavoidable* cost increases must demonstrate, as an alternative, that their before-tax profit margins are no higher than in the best two of the last three years.

Objectives for the Program

• The pay and price standards have been developed to be consistent with one another.

—The deceleration standard for prices can be related to the wage standard by adding 0.5 percentage point to the 7 percent wage standard to reflect scheduled increases in legislatively mandated payroll costs and deducting 1.75 percentage points for productivity growth. The result is a 5.75 percent economy-wide rate of increase in unit labor costs. If firms reduce their average price increases by the price standard — that is, if they reduce their average price increase by one-half percentage point below the average rate of price increase in 1976-77 — the result would be a 5.75 percent increase in prices of nonfood commodities and services. The pay and price standards are thus consistent with one another.

—Because of the allowances necessary to deal with a complex economy — such as the treatment of wage contracts already signed and the existence of some uncontrollable cost increases — widespread observance of the standards would lead to an overall rate of inflation of 6 to 6.5 percent in the year ahead, well below the rate of inflation in 1978 to date.

Real Wage Insurance

● The President will recommend to the Congress a program of "real wage insurance." Under this program, workers who are members of groups that meet the pay standard would receive a tax rebate if the rate of inflation in the year ahead exceeds 7 percent. The program will be developed for submission to the Congress in January. Although final decisions remain to be made, the broad outlines of the program are as follows:

—The amount of the rebate would be equal to the difference between the actual rate of inflation and 7 percent, multiplied by an individual worker's pay, up to some reasonable limit.

—Workers who are members of groups that meet the 7 percent pay limitation would be eligible for the real wage insurance.

—The rebate would be paid *only* if the rate of inflation in the year ahead actually exceeds 7 percent.

Incentives for Compliance

The Administration will interpret wage and price increases above the standards as indications of inflationary conditions, such as shortages, excessive market power, or shelter from competition. Thus, increases in excess of the standards will trigger actions by the government such as:

—Reexamining various restrictions on imports and, where possible and appropriate, relaxing them.

—Asking regulatory agencies to review rate levels and other rules in light of the standards for wages and prices.

—Seeking modification in those regulations that set minimum levels for prices or wages in specific situations.

Government Purchases

● The Federal government itself is a major purchaser of goods and services. By channeling its procurement to those firms whose price and wage decisions meet the standards, it can realize long-term savings in its procurement budget and simultaneously take the lead in fighting inflation.

—To the extent consistent with legal requirements and ensuring national security, the President will direct government agencies to limit purchases to those firms observing the pay and price standards.

—After January 1, the government will require firms awarded contracts in excess of $5 million to certify that they are observing the standards.

—This program will be administered by the Office of Federal Procurement Policy (OFPP) of the OMB.

—Specific procedures to carry out this policy will be announced soon by OFPP and by The Council on Wage and Price Stability (CWPS).

Monitoring

● The Council on Wage and Price Stability will be expanded by about 100 persons to monitor the adherence to the wage and price standards by firms and employee groups.

—CWPS has the authority to obtain, where necessary, required information on prices, profits and wage rates. It will publicly identify areas of the economy and firms that are not complying with the standards.

—In addition CWPS will monitor on a regular basis wage and price developments of individual firms whose annual sales exceed $500 million. It will also monitor individually all major collective bargaining settlements.

CARTER STATEMENT ON DOLLAR

Last week, I pledged my Administration to a balanced, concerted and sustained program to fight inflation. That program requires effective policies to assure a strong dollar.

The basic factors that affect the strength of the dollar are heading in the right direction. We now have an energy program; our trade deficit is declining; and last week I put in place a strong anti-inflation program. The continuing decline in the exchange value of the dollar is clearly not warranted by the fundamental economic situation. That decline threatens economic progress at home and abroad and the success of our anti-inflation program.

As a major step in the anti-inflation program, it is now necessary to act to correct the excessive decline in the dollar which has recently occurred. Therefore, pursuant to my request that strong action be taken, the Department of the Treasury and the Federal Reserve Board are today initiating measures in both the domestic and international monetary fields to assure the strength of the dollar.

The international components of this program have been developed with other major governments and central banks, and they intend to cooperate fully with the United States in attaining our mutual objectives.

Secretary Blumenthal and Chairman Miller are announcing detailed measures immediately.

BLUMENTHAL-MILLER STATEMENT

Recent movement in the dollar exchange rate has exceeded any decline related to fundamental factors, is hampering progress toward price stability and is damaging the climate for investment and growth. The time has come to call a halt to this development. The Treasury and Federal Reserve are today announcing comprehensive corrective actions.

In addition to domestic measures being taken by the Federal Reserve, the United States will, in cooperation with the governments and central banks of Germany and Japan, and the Swiss National Bank, intervene in a forceful and coordinated manner in the amounts required to correct the situation. The U.S. has arranged facilities totaling $30 billion in the currencies of these three countries for its participation in the coordinated market intervention activities. In addition, the Treasury will increase its gold sales to at least 1-1/2 million ounces monthly beginning in December.

The currency mobilization measures, described in the attached annex, include drawings on the U.S. reserve tranche [shares] in the IMF [International Monetary Fund], for part of which we contemplate that the General Arrangements to Borrow will be activated; sales of Special Drawing Rights; increases in central bank swap facilities, and issuance of foreign currency denominated securities by the U.S. Treasury.

Fundamental economic conditions and growth trends in the four nations are moving toward a better international balance. This will provide an improved framework for a restoration of more stable exchange markets and a correction of recent excessive exchange rate movements.

The annex:

A. Actions in the International Monetary Fund:

    1. Drawing of U.S. reserve tranche, $3 billion.

(U.S. would draw DM [deutsche-marks] and yen totaling the equivalent of $2 billion immediately. An additional $1 billion equivalent drawing would be made shortly thereafter, for which GAB activation would be contemplated.)

    2. Sale of SDR, $2 billion.

B. Actions increasing Federal Reserve swap lines:

    1. Increase in swap lines with Bundesbank to $6 billion.

    2. Increase in swap line with Bank of Japan to $5 billion.

    3. Increase in swap line with Swiss National Bank to $4 billion.

C. Issuance of foreign currency denominated securities up to $10 billion.

TOTAL, $30 billion. (Of this total, approximately $1.8 billion has been utilized in earlier operations under Fed swap lines, but the total excludes Treasury swap facility with Bundesbank.)

U.S. POLICY AND IRAN'S CRISIS
October-December 1978

When 1978 ended, Shah Mohammed Reza Pahlevi was still in power. But he had just chosen a member of the opposition to head a new civilian government, presumably one that would run Iran if the shah were forced to leave the country — as shortly was to happen.

In White House and State Department statements from October through December, the Carter administration had been unstinting in its support of the shah. At year's end, it found itself in a debate over whether to express support for Shahpur Bakhtiar, whom the shah had selected on Dec. 29 to form a new civilian cabinet. Part of the administration's indecision could have been caused by previous criticism that blamed the administration's continued and unflagging support of the shah for contributing to Iran's failure to resolve its crisis.

Other criticism of the administration, both from within and without, centered around the U.S. intelligence community's apparent failure to accurately predict the outcome of the year-long demonstrations in opposition to the shah. The trouble in Iran had become so critical by Sept. 8 that the shah considered it necessary to impose martial law. President Carter viewed the situation grave enough that the White House announced on Sept. 10 that Carter had telephoned the shah to assure him he still had U.S. support. As late as Sept. 28, it was revealed later, the Central Intelligence Agency was predicting the shah would remain actively in power through the 1980s. A feud reportedly waged within the White House for the next three months over whether the intelligence was insufficient or the administration simply ignored what it had been told.

699

In any case, White House and State Department statements on the situation in Iran remained strongly supportive of the shah throughout the fall and up to the moment when the shah said he would appoint Bakhtiar to eventually take over. The tone of support during the period hardened if it changed at all. In an Oct. 10 news conference, Carter said, "The strategic importance to . . . the entire Western World, of a good relationship with a strong and independent Iran is crucial. We have historic friendships with Iran." In a Dec. 14 interview, Carter noted that Iran had its "ups and downs" and added, "But there's a certain stability there, a certain inclination and capability of the Iranians to govern themselves that I think is a stabilizing factor." And he said U.S. support for the shah was not limited to verbal support. "We obviously support him fully. . . . We have treaty agreements with Iran. We have strong defense agreements with Iran. We look on Iran, as do their neighbors, as being a stabilizing factor."

Religious, Political Influences

Moslem influence in Iran dated back to the religion's founding by Mohammed in the seventh century. Today, 90 percent of the 35 million Iranians belong to the Moslem Shi'ite faith. The monarchy in Iran dates back 2,500 years but it has not always been in the same family line. In fact, Shah Mohammed Reza Pahlevi was the son of the first shah of his family line, Reza Khan, an army colonel who had taken over the government in 1921, although the shah at that time stayed on the throne. Khan had the Iranian parliament depose the shah in 1925 and elect him in his place as Reza Shah Pahlevi. The new shah was a student of the reforms of Ataturk and set about westernizing his nation. One of his reforms was a change of the ancient name of Persia to Iran.

Despite the opposition of the conservative Moslem sects, the shah brought about other reforms including ending the customary wearing of veils by Arab women. Mohammedan priests resisted but the shah was persistent. His downfall, however, came not from Moslems, but from foreigners. He was friendly with the Axis powers at the advent of World War II. Britain and Russia invaded Iran to protect the key Iranian oil fields from the Germans. The shah abdicated in 1941 in favor of his son, Mohammed Reza Pahlevi.

Modernizing Reforms

The son inherited his father's passion for westernization but adopted a pro-Allies policy. After the war, he outlawed the communist Tudeh (Masses) party. The 1950s brought economic problems to Iran, leading to political unrest. After less than a year as premier, Gen. Ali Razmara was assassinated in 1951. Mohammed Mossadegh, leader of the National Front party, became premier and promptly nationalized the oil industry. The following year he led a revolution that for a brief time toppled the shah from the throne. The United States and its CIA, with the backing of Iranian Moslem leaders, came to the shah's aid and restored him to power in 1953.

In 1963, again over Moslem objections, the shah instituted his "White Revolution" that brought about even more modernizing reforms, including land reform, nationalization and many other social reforms. The same year he sent a Moslem leader (or ayatollah), Ruholla Khomeini, into exile in neighboring Iraq. By that time the shah and the United States had become so close that an unwritten agreement emerged whereby the CIA would not have any contact with the shah's opponents — a fact later attributed as a factor in U.S. intelligence failures in assessing the Iranian situation. The shah's critics increasingly accused him of wielding power ruthlessly, primarily through his secret police force, SAVAK, which the CIA helped him establish.

Mossadegh's National Front party remained outlawed but joined the Moslem sects, primarily the Shi'ites, in encouraging opposition to the shah. Early in 1978, not long after a New Year's visit by President Carter, the unrest built to the point of riots in two of the nation's holiest cities, Qum and Tabriz. The unrest continued, fed in part by complaints with the way the shah put down the riots in Qum and Tabriz. Universities in Iran were closed in June, not to reopen again in 1978, and their students demonstrated. Outbreaks occurred with increasing frequency and intensity. Khomeini took an active part in fomenting the demonstrations from his exile in Iraq until his ouster from there Oct. 6. Khomeini moved to near Paris and continued calling for demonstrations.

The Shah's Downfall

In September the violence increased to the point that the government imposed a ban on unauthorized rallies on Sept. 6. In defiance an estimated 100,000 persons marched in Tehran the following day. On Sept. 8 violent demonstrations were held throughout Iran and the shah responded by declaring martial law. The violence continued and hundreds lost their lives. The government continued its crackdown and the Carter administration stepped up its announcements of support for the shah. Khomeini criticized Carter for expressing that support. On Nov. 6 the shah installed a military government and renewed his pledge to hold national elections in June 1979. Later in November various groups of Iranian workers staged strikes, the most important of them the oil workers who brought about a fuel shortage, causing serious damage to the economy of the beleaguered nation. The shah made several attempts at appeasement, trying to mollify those accusing him and his government of lavish spending and corruption. The shah even granted amnesty to Khomeini. But the shah also pledged to continue his controversial reforms.

In a last act of 1978 appeasement, the shah appointed Bakhtiar to form a new civilian government. Two weeks later, on Jan. 16, 1979, the shah left

Iran on an indefinite "vacation," stopping first in Egypt for what was widely expected to become a permanent exile, perhaps in the United States. On Jan. 17 President Carter pledged U.S. support for the Bakhtiar government, which faced serious threats to its survival, particularly from supporters of Khomeini.

The 78-year-old ayatollah ended his 14-year exile from Iran on Feb. 1, staging a triumphant return to Tehran on the heels of a massive show of force in the capital city by the pro-shah military. Khomeini's supporters vowed to wipe out all traces of U.S. influence in Iran and predicted that the Bakhtiar government would soon fall.

Meanwhile, the Carter administration ordered Americans in Iran to leave for their own safety. Most of the 41,000 Americans who had been living in Iran already had left as a "voluntary action" that the Carter administration had recommended on Dec. 31, while it was still refusing to publicly recognize the futility of the shah's chances of survival.

Following are excerpts from White House and State Department interviews and news conferences October through December 1978 and the text of Soviet leader Leonid Brezhnev's remarks on the Iranian situation as transmitted Nov. 18, 1978, by the Soviet news agency, Tass: (Boldface headings in brackets have been added by Congressional Quarterly to highlight the organization of the text.):

CARTER NEWS CONFERENCE
Oct. 10, 1978

. . .**Q.** Mr. President, I'd like to ask you about Iran. How do we view the situation involving the Shah there now? Is he secure? How important is it to U.S. interests that the Shah remain in power? And what, if anything, can the United States Government do to keep him in power?

THE PRESIDENT. The strategic importance to our country, I think to the entire Western World, of a good relationship with a strong and independent Iran is crucial. We have historic friendships with Iran. I think they are a great stabilizing force in their part of the world. They are a very important trade partner. They've acted very responsibly.

My own belief is that the Shah has moved aggressively to establish democratic principles in Iran and to have a progressive attitude towards social questions, social problems. This has been the source of much of the opposition to him in Iran.

We have no inclination to try to decide the internal affairs of Iran. My own hopes have been that there could be peace there, an end to bloodshed, and an orderly transformation into more progressive social arrangements and, also, increased democratization of the government itself, which I believe the Shah also espouses. He may not be moving fast enough for some; he may be moving too fast for others. I don't want to get involved in that specifics. . . .

STATE DEPARTMENT NEWS BRIEFING
Nov. 6, 1978

[By Jill A. Schuker, special assistant to the
assistant secretary for public affairs]

. . .**Q:** Have you got any reading on the situation in Iran for us?

A: Our embassy reports that conditions are calmer in Tehran today. Although there are reports of scattered incidents, reports from our Consulates say that the situation in other cities is calm. . . .

Q: How do you view the latest development of the Shah appointing a military government?

A: We support the Shah in his decision. . . . [Reads statement] The Shah moved to appoint a military government under his authority when it became apparent that another civilian government could not be formed to restore the public order essential to moving toward elections.

For some time previous to his decision, he actively explored the possibility of a new civilian government, including one that would be joined by members of the opposition. When those persons refused to join in a coalition cabinet, and there appeared to be no alternative, the Shah asked the military to form a cabinet.

The Shah has emphasized that military rule is only temporary, and he intends as rapidly as possible to move the country toward free elections and a new civilian-directed government. . . .

Q: Last week, the Department was saying that it thought that the Shah's problems were manageable. Since then, the situation appears to have deteriorated.

I wonder if the Department still believes that the problems are manageable?

A: Yes, we do.

Q: Do you have any indication that the Shah may call for elections before June 1979?

A: Any indications? I believe that the Shah has said that that is what he intends to do, and we have no indications other than that.

Q: Does the United States intend to continue to press for liberalization during this period from now until the time elections are held?

A: Yes, we do. I believe the Secretary [Cyrus R. Vance, secretary of state] addressed this on Friday in a couple of questions.

Q: That was before the military government came into being?

A: I believe in the statement that was just read, we talk about pursuing liberalization, as well.

Q: Does the United States support the Shah's move to have appointed the military government?

A: I think in the statement that I just read, we support it in the sense that it seems to be the only alternative after he attempted to put together a civilian government.

Q: Jill, has Ambassador [William H.] Sullivan been in direct contact? I mean, has he seen the Shah personally over the weekend?

A: I believe so, yes.

Q: Has the President been in touch with the Shah over the weekend?

A: I would refer you to the White House on that, but I don't know of any contact the President has had.

Q: Could I just continue on your statement, two points? You are suggesting that the reason that there was no alternative to a military government is that certain unnamed persons, the opposition, refused to join the coalition government. Can you tell us who you are talking about?

A: I don't have anything further on it, no.

Q: Secondly, on your statement, do you foresee the formation of a civilian government prior to elections, or will that come only after elections?

A: I have no timetable for you. I would say that we hope there will be a return to civilian government, as I believe the Shah has said, as well.

Q: Have you got any reading on the impact of the chaos in Iran on the American oil supply and on Israel's oil supply and on the possibility of an OPEC price increase?. . . First of all, what do you know about the impact of the strike on American oil supplies to date, beyond what Hodding [Hodding Carter III, chief State Department spokesman] had last week, if anything?

A: I don't think I have anything beyond what Hodding had last week. We know that production is still considerably reduced, but we don't have precise figures. Some workers have gone back, but the strike continues. I really don't have any better figures for you.

Q: Do you have anything on what impact the oil production halt might have on Israeli oil supplies, and whether the United States has any plans to make up for the supply of Iranian oil which generally goes to Israel?

A: On the first part of your question, we have seen press reports on the subject, but I have nothing to offer you. And on the second part, I am not prepared to address it. . . .

Q: I just wondered about your explanation of why the Shah had no alternative to a military government. Was that what he told Ambassador Sullivan?

A: I think on the basis of what I have already said, some time previous to his decision to form a military government, that he had actively explored the possibility of a civilian government. However, when those persons refused to join in a coalition cabinet, there appeared to be no alternative, and he asked the military to form a cabinet. . . .

Q: Jill, does the U.S. Government believe that the Shah's position is now in jeopardy?

A: No. . . .

Q: What is the Embassy there telling Americans in Iran?

A: On November 4, the Embassy advised all Americans to remain at home until further notice. On November 6, the Embassy, in consultation with a representative committee of Americans, told Americans in Iran they could plan on returning to work on November 7, tomorrow.

The Embassy recommended that Americans continue to exercise caution in moving about the city. The Embassy has also recommended that all non-essential travel to Iran be postponed until security improves.

We are monitoring the situation closely and do not believe other measures are required at this time. As of November 6, there were no reports of any injuries to Americans.

Q: Do you have anything on what sort of an impact the situation in Iran would have on the Trucial States' future, the states of the Persian Gulf, or whatever?

A: No, I don't have anything on that.

Q: The second question would be, don't you see that as a contradiction between this Administration's stand on human rights and backing a military government in a turbulent Iran?

A: No.

Q: All of the reports that people have been reading over the weekend suggest that the Shah's position is in jeopardy. And so I would like to ask you, as the representative of the State Department, since you came in with a flat "no," what is your confidence based on?

A: The confidence is based on the fact that we expect that the moves that the Shah has undertaken in Iran will prove successful.

Q: To do what?

A: To both bring order and to move continually in the direction of liberalization. . . .

Q: Would an amnesty for exile, such as Ayatollah Khomeini, be considered liberalization? Is that something you are pressing for?

A: I think a lot of things come under the rubric of liberalization. Exactly what our position is, in terms of elaboration of it, I am not going to get into.

Q: Can you take a question on that, though, because he's right. We do continually get this phrase used — the Secretary used it at his press conference the other day — we keep talking vaguely about "liberalization," but it's not clear what this Government has in mind when it uses the word.

A: I think the Shah has said that he hoped to move toward elections and such, and there are certain measures that he has undertaken over the past few weeks that we would consider movements in that direction. Whatever else I can get you on that I will try, but I don't really know whether there will be anything.

Q: Will you take a question? Have you discussed with the Shah what you consider an agenda for liberalization is?

A: I don't really think I can get into diplomatic contacts or what our discussions with the Shah have been now.

Q: Does your support for the Shah's steps include support for the reported plan to begin firing on demonstrators if they don't disperse?

A: I don't think that our hope is that there will be any escalation of violence; and hopefully, that will not be a result of the measures that he has taken now.

Q: But the military government has indicated its intention to use force to break up these demonstrations and so on. I assume that you support that intention.

A: I think what we have supported is what I've said we support. I wouldn't extend our support beyond what I've said.

Q: You stated support for the Shah's establishing a military government; you've stated support for the Shah's continuing to move in a direction of liberalization. Do you see the establishing of a military government as moving in the direction of liberalization?

A: We see the establishment of the military government as an interim step, as something temporary. As the Shah has emphasized, it is only temporary, and we hope and trust that it will be that.

Q: Do you see it as an interim or temporary interruption of the movement toward liberalization?

A: We see it as, hopefully, a parallel movement. . . .

Q: Did I understand you to say that the Shah notified this Government prior to the imposition of these measures?

A: No. I believe that the question was raised as to when we were notified, and I said I would try to find out. But in terms of the diplomatic contacts, I'm not sure what I would be able to get you on it.

Q: Do you know whether or not any attempt was made to dissuade the Shah from implementing these harsh measures of punishment for demonstrators?

A: I don't know what our discussions with the Shah have been in that regard. . . .

Q: Jill, why do you feel compelled to comment or approve or disapprove when the Shah forms a military government? Why do you feel compelled to approve or disapprove when he moves toward liberalization or does not? Why is it your business?

A: I think the Secretary made very clear on Friday, as has the President, our interest in Iran, and I think anything that is said falls under that rubric of interest.

Q: You don't consider it meddling in their internal affairs?

A: No. We see it as commenting. . . .

Q: Jill . . . one simple question for you: Are you expecting calm in Iran tomorrow?

A: Am I expecting —

Q: Calm, the return of calm?

A: I don't know what we're expecting. We hope that it will be calm.

Q: Why would you, then, ask the Americans in Iran to go back to normal work on November 7?

A: I would say, based on the reports that we have, we feel that it would be appropriate for them to go back to work. If the situation changes, there may be a different directive or advisory to the American population there.

Q: Jill, does the Department consider that the support for the Shah — whatever reasons there are, and there must be good reasons for it — weakens the human rights policy in other areas? I mean, how are you going to tell government X which you criticized for having a military government or for imposing a state of seige that you don't like that when you have supported it somewhere else? Could you sort of address that?

A: I think what we have expressed in relation to the Iranian Government is the stated policy of the Government, and we'll just have to deal with each situation as it comes up. . . .

STATE DEPARTMENT REPLIES
TO REPORTERS' QUESTIONS

[Reply Posted Nov. 6]

Q: Is Ambassador Sullivan returning to Washington for consultations on the situation in Iran?

A: There are no plans for Ambassador Sullivan to come to Washington at this time.

Q: Who is heading the State Department working group on Iran?

A: Henry Precht, Director for Iranian Affairs.

Q: Did the Shah contact the U.S. on forming the military government?

A: We have frequent contact with Iran's leaders, but we are not prepared to discuss the content of our talks.

[Replies Posted Nov. 13]

Q: Exactly what crowd control equipment have we sold to Iran? What are the dates it was ordered and when was it shipped? Was it requested before the martial law was imposed in September?

A: We have provided crowd control and police equipment to Iran for a number of years. This year in the spring, summer, and as recently as last month, we approved licenses for commercial firms to sell Iran a total of about 25,000 cannisters of tear gas, 20,000 police batons, a supply of protective vests and similar equipment. (A cannister of tear gas costs about $5 as does a police baton.) Most of these orders were made before martial law was declared. Generally speaking, it takes about 1 month to process a request for a license within the Department of State and associated agencies.

Q: Were three homes of Americans fire bombed in Tehran? How much damage was done? When did these incidents occur?

A: The homes of two Americans and one Swede were fire bombed in the early evening of November 7. The fires were quickly extinguished and no serious damage was done.

Q: Have we asked for Iranian police protection for Americans living outside of Tehran?

A: Extra police protection is already being provided in areas where numbers of Americans live in Tehran and other cities. When the fire bombings occurred in a particular district of Tehran, the Embassy asked for and received additional protection in that area.

Q: When was Ambassador Sullivan or another senior Embassy officer last in touch with the Shah?

A: The Ambassador has seen the Shah frequently. We believe the last conversation was Monday.

Q: Did U.S. military cargo planes arrive in Tehran last Saturday, and if so were they carrying riot equipment?

A: USAF cargo aircraft regularly fly to Tehran carrying supplies for American residents there — i.e. mail, commissary items, etc.

—Crowd control items purchased by Iran have been shipped by commercial carriers, not by military aircraft.

CARTER INTERVIEW
Nov. 13, 1978

[By Bill Moyers on Public Television]

. . .MR. MOYERS. Let me apply the multiple-choice, difficult options equation to a couple of other contemporary and very live issues. One is Iran. What are the options facing you there?

THE PRESIDENT. Well, we look on the Shah, as you know, as a friend, a loyal ally, and the good relationship that Iran has had and has now with ourselves and with the other democracies in the world, the Western powers as being very constructive and valuable. Also, having a strong and independent Iran in that area is a very stabilizing factor, and we would hate to see it disrupted by violence and the government fall with an unpredictable result.

The Shah has been primarily criticized within Iran because he has tried to democratize the country and because he's instituted social reforms in a very rapid fashion. Some of his domestic adversaries either disagree with the way he's done it, or thinks he hasn't moved fast enough or too fast, and deplore his breaking of ancient religious and social customs as Iran has become modern.

MR. MOYERS. But he was also criticized, Mr. President, for running a police state — political prisoners —

THE PRESIDENT. That's exactly right. I think the Shah has had that criticism, sometimes perhaps justified — I don't know the details of it. But I think there's no doubt that Iran has made great social progress and has moved toward a freer expression of people. Even in recent months, for instance, the Shah has authorized or directed, I guess, the parliament to have all of its deliberations open and televised, something that we don't even do in our country here.

MR. MOYERS. You think this is all too late?

THE PRESIDENT. Well, I hope not. I don't know what will come eventually. I would hope that a coalition government could be formed rapidly. At the present time there's a quasi-military government. The Shah has reconfirmed his commitment to have open and democratic elections, maybe within 6 months or 8 months. I hope that would be possible.

Our inclination is for the Iranian people to have a clear expression of their own views and to have a government intact in Iran that accurately expresses a majority view in Iran.

MR. MOYERS. But can we do anything to encourage that, or are our hands tied?

THE PRESIDENT. No, we don't try to interfere in the internal affairs of Iran.

MR. MOYERS. We did put the Shah in, but you're saying we can't keep him in.

THE PRESIDENT. I think that's a decision to be made by the people of that country.

MR. MOYERS. Does it hurt you sometimes to have to sit back and do nothing when you know there are large stakes in a part of the world beyond your influence?

THE PRESIDENT. Well, we don't have any inclination to be involved in the internal affairs of another country unless our own security should be directly threatened. And that's a philosophy that I have espoused ever since I've been in the national political realm.

I just think we've learned our lessons the hard way, in Vietnam and in other instances, and we've tried to be loyal to our allies and loyal to our friends, to encourage one person-one vote, majority rule, the democratic processes, the protection of human rights. Obviously, we have not always succeeded in encouraging other people to measure up to our own standards, but I think we've been consistent in our effort.

MR. MOYERS. . . .But if we take the position that you're espousing, we'll sit back and do nothing when we should be in there covertly or clandestinely or overtly, taking a tough stand, saying that we may not like the Shah but we need him in power. You're saying that day is over, that we cannot do that.

THE PRESIDENT. No, we have made it clear through my own public statements and those of Secretary Vance that we support the Shah and support the present government, recognizing that we don't have any control over the decisions ultimately made by the Iranian people and the stability of that region. The absence of the success of terrorism, of violence, the anarchy that might come with the complete disruption of their government is a threat to peace.

We don't have any evidence that the Soviets, for instance, are trying to disrupt the existing government structure in Iran nor that they are a source of violence in Iran. I think they recognize — they have a very long mutual border with Iran, and a stable government there, no matter who its leaders might be, is valuable to them.

This might change. If it becomes obvious that the Shah is very vulnerable and that other forces might come into power, the Soviets might change their obvious posture. But that's the observation that we have now. . . .

BREZHNEV'S REMARKS
Nov. 18, 1978

[Question by *Pravda* Correspondent]

Q: How do you assess foreign press reports on interference by Western powers, especially the USA, in the events in Iran and even the possibility of military intervention by them?

A: Yes, there have been such reports, including reports on the possibility of military intervention by certain powers. What puts one on guard is the fact that officials of the states concerned actually do not deny such reports. If they deny attempts to interfere in Iran's internal affairs — as was done recently by the U.S. president — they right away make reservations which do not exclude the possibility of such interference under an appropriate excuse.

The Soviet Union, which maintains traditional good-neighbour relations with Iran, states resolutely that it is against any foreign interference in the internal affairs of Iran by anyone, in any form and under any pretext. The events taking place in that country constitute a purely internal affair and the questions involved in them should be decided by the Iranians themselves. All states should abide in this matter by the principles recorded in the U.N. charter and in a number of other basic international documents, should respect the sovereignty and independence of Iran and the Iranian people.

It must be also clear that any interference, especially military interference in the affairs of Iran — a state which directly borders on the Soviet Union — would be regarded by the USSR as a matter affecting its security interests.

STATE DEPARTMENT STATEMENT
Nov. 19, 1978

As President Carter has indicated, the United States does not intend to interfere in the internal affairs of any other country, and reports to the contrary are totally without foundation.

We expect other countries to conduct themselves in similar fashion, and we note that the Soviet Union has said yesterday that it will not interfere in the affairs of Iran and will respect its territorial integrity, sovereignty, and independence.

As we have said, we firmly support the Shah in his efforts to restore domestic tranquility in Iran, and have confidence that Iran can solve its own problems. We intend to preserve and pursue with Iran our strong bilateral political, economic, and security relationship.

CARTER NEWS CONFERENCE
Nov. 30, 1978

. . .**Q:** Mr. President, is there any reason that you feel that the Shah is justifiably in trouble with his people?

THE PRESIDENT: Well, I think the Shah understands the situation in Iran very clearly and the reasons for some of the problems that he has experienced recently. He has moved forcefully and aggressively in changing some of the ancient religious customs of Iran, for instance, and some of the more conservative or traditional religious leaders deplore this change substantially. Others of the Iranian citizens who are in the middle class, who have a new prosperity brought about by enhanced oil prices and extra income coming into the country, I think, feel that they ought to have a greater share of the voice in determining the affairs of Iran. Others believe that the democratization of Iran ought to proceed more quickly.

The Shah, as you know, has offered the opposition groups a place in a coalition government. They have rejected that offer and demand more complete removal from the Shah of his authority.

We trust the Shah to maintain stability in Iran, to continue with the democratization process, and also to continue with the progressive change in the Iranian social and economic structure. But I don't think either I or any other national leader could ever claim that we have never made a mistake or have never misunderstood the attitudes of our people. We have confidence in the Shah, we support him and his efforts to change Iran in a constructive way, moving toward democracy and social progress. And we have confidence in the Iranian people to make the ultimate judgments about their own government.

We do not have any intention of interfering in the internal affairs of Iran, and we do not approve any other nation interfering in the internal affairs of Iran. . . .

CARTER BREAKFAST WITH NEWSMEN
Dec. 7, 1978

Q: Mr. President . . . I find it a little difficult to reconcile your statements about the Shah's concern for human rights, democracy, and liberalization with the pretty well documented record of his regime.

. . .I'm wondering if you could enlighten us on that, both points, and anything else on the issue?

THE PRESIDENT: I'll try.

There are several basic premises on which our relationship with Iran is postulated. First of all, our bilateral relationships with Iran have been constructive for both countries. We consider the Iranian people's relationship with the West to be very important. Iran has been a stabilizing factor around the Persian Gulf. This stability is valuable in the region. It's valuable in the surrounding territory, reaching certainly as far as Israel and the Mediterranean, and it's important for world peace. Iran has been very helpful to us in economic matters concerning OPEC, and we have a good and longstanding relationship between Presidents, myself and my predecessors, and the Shah himself.

The Shah has attempted, in my opinion, while maintaining order in a very difficult period, to move toward social liberalization, sometimes directly in conflict with the desires of the more traditional religious leaders, and has on several occasions, increasingly, lately, offered to form coalition governments encompassing his political opponents there. These offers have been rejected.

I don't have any apology to offer for the difference in human rights values that our own Nation espouses and those that have been accomplished by the Shah in Iran. There have been abuses. There have been incarcerations of people without formal charge and trial under the Shah's government that would not be acceptable in our own country.

But I think the trend has been, under the Shah, toward democratic principles and social liberalization. Some have thought he moved too fast; some have thought he has moved not long enough — not strongly and rapidly enough, rather. And, of course, there have been instances when human rights violations have occurred as measured by any objective standard. But I might hasten to add that we have those kinds of violations in our own country as well.

Q: Mr. President, I was going to ask you about the Shah. Do you think he could survive now, and how?

THE PRESIDENT: I don't know. I hope so. This is something that is in the hands of the people of Iran. We have never had any intention and don't have any intention of trying to intercede in the internal political affairs of Iran.

We primarily want an absence of violence and bloodshed, and stability. We personally prefer that the Shah maintain a major role in the government, but that's a decision for the Iranian people to make.

Q: Do you think there's still any chance that he'll form a civilian coalition government?

THE PRESIDENT: I think he has offered that publicly. And as you know, yesterday, I believe, he released two of his top political opponents. And I think, I would guess, surmise, that one of the reasons for those political leaders being released was to encourage them and their followers to join in some form of coalition government. That's the Shah's desire that's expressed to me personally by him and through his own Ambassador here, and I take him at his word. . . .

CARTER NEWS CONFERENCE
Dec. 12, 1978

. . .**Q:** Mr. President, what will be the domestic and international effect if the Shah fails to maintain power in Iran?

THE PRESIDENT: I fully expect the Shah to maintain power in Iran and for the present problems in Iran to be resolved. Although there have been certainly deplorable instances of bloodshed which we would certainly want to avoid, or see avoided, I think the predictions of doom and disaster that came from some sources have certainly not been realized at all. The Shah has our support and he also has our confidence.

We have no intention of interfering in the internal affairs of Iran, and we have no intention of permitting others to interfere in the internal affairs of Iran. The difficult situation there has been exacerbated by uncontrolled statements made from foreign nations that encourage bloodbaths and violence. This is something that really is deplorable, and I would hope would cease after this holy season passes.

I think it's good to point out that the Iranian people for 2,500 years, perhaps as long as almost any nation on Earth, have had the ability for stable, self-government. There have been changes in the government, yes, sometimes violence, but they have a history of an ability to govern themselves. And because of that and other factors which I've just described, I think the situation in Iran will be resolved successfully. . . .

CARTER INTERVIEW
Dec. 14, 1978

[By Barbara Walters, American Broadcasting Co.]

MS. WALTERS: Mr. President, there are reports that you've recently sent messages to the Soviet Union, warning them to keep hands off of Iran. Can you confirm these, and can you tell us if you have any information on Russian involvement in Iran?

THE PRESIDENT: Yes, that's accurate.

MS. WALTERS: You have sent the letters?

THE PRESIDENT: Yes. President Brezhnev and I exchanged messages.

MS. WALTERS. Recently?

THE PRESIDENT. Within the last few weeks, a couple of weeks. And I made it very clear to them, to the Soviets, that we have no intention of interfering in the internal affairs of Iran and that we have no intention of permitting others to interfere in the internal affairs of Iran.

I think it's good to point out, Barbara, that Iran has a 2,500-year history of statecraft, of managing their own affairs properly. Obviously, they've had ups and downs, as we have in our own country. But there's a certain stability there, a certain inclination and capability of the Iranians to govern themselves that I think is a stabilizing factor. We don't know what changes will take place.

MS. WALTERS: Have the Russians been involved, sir, that you know of?

THE PRESIDENT: As far as we know, they have not. We monitor the situation closely. Obviously, there is a communist party there, the Tudeh party, which perhaps is inclined to encourage violence or disruption in order to change the existing government. But the Shah is communicating with opposition leaders. He is committed to a broader base for the government. He is working toward democratic principles and social change. And he has been embattled lately. And we obviously support him fully.

MS. WALTERS: When we talk about support, what do we mean today, 1978, post-Vietnam, by support? For example, if the Shah does fall, it threatens our oil supply, it threatens Israel's oil supply, it threatens Saudi Arabia, it threatens the whole Persian Gulf. At what point would support turn into action and what kind of action, if any?

THE PRESIDENT: I am not prepared to answer that question.

MS. WALTERS: Because there is no answer, or because —

THE PRESIDENT: Well, the answer is difficult. But I think just conjecturing on something that's hypothetical like that, assuming all the catastrophes that might possibly occur in the Persian Gulf, is something on which I don't want to comment. I don't think it's going to happen. And if I were to surmise that if it happens, we would do this, it would be interpreted by some as an actual prediction by me that it's going to happen, and I don't think it's going to happen.

MS. WALTERS: Is support primarily verbal support?

THE PRESIDENT: No. We have treaty agreements with Iran. We have strong defense agreements with Iran. We look on Iran, as do their neighbors, as being a stabilizing factor. Even the Soviet Union shares a long border with Iran. I'm sure they want stability there on their border. Exactly the formation of the government — I can't speak for the Soviets, but I think that for world peace and for the Soviets, and for us, certainly for the entire Middle East-Persian Gulf region, a stability is desirable, and that's what we want, also. . . .

STATE DEPARTMENT NEWS BRIEFING
Dec. 26, 1978

[By Hodding Carter III, assistant secretary
for public affairs]

...**Q:** Does the U.S. Government still give its full support to the Shah?

A: Marvin [Kalb, CBS], I have no change in the position that has been expressed publicly by the Secretary and the President in recent days and weeks.

Q: That answer still leaves me a bit puzzled because the President on one occasion, as I recall, said he really doesn't know whether the Shah will survive, and two or three days later he gave his full blessings to the Shah — and that was about two weeks ago. Since that time the situation appears to have deteriorated further. There are major political developments under way in Iran.

Does the United States, as a Government, continue to give its full support to the Shah?

A: The answer is yes, and to his efforts to promote stability.

Q: What are his efforts?

A: In that respect I would have to ask you to refer that question to the Iranian Government.

We have seen several reports on the subject which we are following, but I don't have an assessment of them right now.

Q: Do you feel that the Shah has been successful in his efforts to promote stability — in light, at least, of what you've just told us?

A: I think that the situation is as I have described it; and, therefore, there are clearly problems involved in Iran. The efforts continue, however, as we understand it — that is, to promote stability — and we do support those efforts. The logic of the situation is that there are significant problems.

Q: Could you tell us, please, in what way the American position of full support for the Shah at this point enhances the national interests of the United States — which embraces both oil and other factors, which you've run through with us before?

A: Well, the fundamental perception has been that the stability of Iran was of importance to the United States on several counts — both on a geopolitical count because of the location of the country, and on the basis of its major contribution to the industrialized world's economy.

It is on that basis that we continue to support the efforts of the Shah to produce a more stable situation. None of that has changed perceptibly. . . .

STATE DEPARTMENT NEWS BRIEFING
Dec. 29, 1978

[By Hodding Carter III, assistant secretary
for public affairs]

. . .**Q:** Your answer "A" we have heard over the last month, and it stands — and that is that the United States Government supports the Shah fully. With that in mind and in light of what has been happening in Iran, do you believe that the Shah can succeed in his effort to restore stability?

A: Our position on that question as well, Marvin, is unchanged.

Q: Do you believe that he can succeed in restoring stability?

A: Our position on that is yes.

Q: And on what basis do you have that belief, in light of all of the evidence that we have — and probably a good bit more that you have?

A: It is based on several things, including obviously the steps that he announces he intends to take and on our own assessments of the situation, which involve a number of factors that I'm really not going to be able to run down on a list. It is, however, simply a position that reflects the assessment of this Government. . . .

November

FIRESTONE 500 RECALL
November 29, 1978

The largest product recall in history was initiated Nov. 29 when the federal government and Firestone Tire & Rubber Co. signed a "final agreement" that committed the company to recall 10 million "Firestone 500" and similar steel-belted radial tires the government claimed contained a "safety-related defect." Firestone, the nation's second-largest tire maker (Goodyear Tire and Rubber Co. was larger), had made the tires since 1972.

The agreement, estimated by the company to cost it as much as $234 million, did not end Firestone's troubles over the tires. More than 270 individual and class-action civil suits seeking billions of dollars were pending at year's end. One of the suits, in New York City, asked $1.1 billion for 147 plaintiffs, and another, in Ohio, sought $1,000 for every Ohioan who had bought one of the tires involved in the dispute.

At issue were 13 million five-rib and seven-rib "steel-belted radial 500 tires" bearing the Firestone brand, the TPC brand or any of 14 private brand labels for whom Firestone had made the tires. Three million tires were estimated to have been worn beyond use by that time, 2.5 million still in the delivery chain and not yet purchased by car owners and another 7.5 million estimated to still be in service and the subject of Firestone notifications telling owners to return them to the dealer for replacement. Involved were five-rib tires sold since Sept. 1, 1975, but manufactured before Jan. 1, 1977, and seven-rib tires sold since Sept. 1, 1975, but made before May 1, 1976. The notifications, pamphlets and advertising required by the agreement provided serial numbers and other identifying data that tire owners could check to determine if their tires qualified for the recall.

The agreement also committed Firestone to offer to exchange at half price six million of the 500s sold before Sept. 1, 1975, and therefore too old for mandatory recall under the Federal Traffic Safety Act. A press release from the National Highway Traffic Safety Administration (NHTSA) announcing the agreement noted, "The agency had urged Firestone to recall these tires even though the statute requires only notification, but the company would offer only the adjustment arrangement."

The private brands included in the recall were Wards Grappler II Steel Radial, Shell Steel Radial, National Steel Radial, Seiberling RT 78 Steel Belt Radial, Holiday Supreme Steel Belt Radial, LeMans Steel Belted Radial, Atlas Goldenaire II, Caravelle Supreme & Caravelle Double Steel Radial, Wards Grappler Steel Radial, K Mart Radial 40, Union Steel Radial, Zenith Supreme Steel Belt Radial, JTW Ferrari Supreme Steel Radial and JTW Ferrari Steel Radial.

Victory for Firestone?

The agreement contained a non-admission-of-guilt clause for Firestone: "Nothing contained in this Final Agreement nor any actions undertaken by Firestone pursuant to this agreement are intended to constitute an admission by Firestone of a safety-related defect, nor a concession by NHTSA that a safety-related defect does not exist."

The NHTSA settlement with Firestone drew fire from several consumer activists who had pressed the recall. Clarence Ditlow, director of the Center for Auto Safety, for example, said, "Firestone won a major victory in the 500 case." He said 24 million "defective tires" were manufactured by Firestone, yet the NHTSA had not explained why the recall involved only tires manufactured before 1977. The tires apparently weren't phased out of production until the spring of 1978. Firestone had said that before 1975 it had remedied production problems with the "500" tires, but Montgomery Ward Co., for whom Firestone manufactured the tires under the brand "Grappler Radial 8000," told the NHTSA that the 1975 tires caused higher adjustment rates than those made in previous years.

Joan Claybrook, NHTSA administrator, criticized Firestone's actions in the case, which she said "gave American industry a black eye. This is an example of a company that was knowledgeable of the problem for a long time and attempted to divert the agency from an investigation." She added, "This is an example of corporate values which give great weight to the saving of dollars with virtually no regard for the safety of the public."

Firestone stood fast. Bernard W. Frazier, its spokesman, said, "There is no evidence to substantiate the claim that we manufactured defective 500s. The NHTSA has not identified any specific defect in the tire." The company called the agreement "a voluntary recall."

Background

Secret internal Firestone memos that came to light only a few months before the agreement was reached showed that in 1972 and 1973 nearly 30 percent of the tires were being returned by customers. Over the next few years authorities began associating the tires with many traffic accidents and early in 1978 the NHTSA began an investigation of the steel-belted radials. Half the Firestone customers surveyed as part of the investigation complained about their tires. Firestone got a restraining order in March to prevent the results of the survey from being made public, but the Center for Auto Safety divulged its contents in April.

The NHTSA investigation continued and on July 8 it made an "initial determination" that the tires had a "safety-related defect" leading them to blow out or suffer tread separation. It cited 14,000 tire failures causing 50 injuries and 29 deaths. The House Interstate and Foreign Commerce Subcommittee on Oversight and Investigations conducted its own probe and in an Aug. 31 report confirmed the NHTSA findings and urged Firestone to recall the tires.

The NHTSA already had begun negotiations with Firestone after its "initial determination" and on Oct. 20 the two parties reached an "agreement in principle." The agreement was that there would be a massive recall of the tires but the two parties continued to negotiate the details. On Nov. 29 they reached a "final agreement" that included a commitment by Firestone to mail recall notices to tire purchasers in December and place advertisements in 242 Sunday newspapers serving the top 200 markets in the country on Dec. 17. A quirk in the law freed Firestone from having to use massive television advertising to announce the recall. By the end of the year, Firestone announced it had replaced more than 750,000 tires and was producing 400,000 of the replacements a month to make the switch.

Following are excerpts from the "Final Agreement" negotiated by Firestone Tire & Rubber Co. and the National Highway Traffic Safety Administration, leading to the massive recall on Nov. 29, 1978, of Firestone 500 steel-belted tires and similar radial tires sold under other brand names:

Final Agreement

The National Highway Traffic Safety Administration ("NHTSA") and The Firestone Tire & Rubber Company ("Firestone" or "the Company") hereby agree to conclude NHTSA's investigation of the Company's steel belted radial tires (ODI Case No. C8-18), initiated pursuant to the National Traffic and Motor Vehicle Safety Act of 1966, as amended ("the Act").

1. Firestone will issue a notification pursuant to this agreement and provide a free replacement for all 5-rib 500 steel belted radial tires (including private brands of the same or similar internal construction) manufactured in the United States or Canada and sold for the first time on or after September 1, 1975 and manufactured prior to January 1, 1977.

2. Firestone will issue a notification pursuant to this agreement and provide a free replacement for all 7-rib 500 steel belted radial tires (including private brands of the same or similar internal construction) manufactured in the United States or Canada and TPC tires that were manufactured in the United States or Canada and which were sold for the first time on or after September 1, 1975 and manufactured prior to May 1, 1976.

3. Tires subject to notification and recall under paragraphs 1 and 2 above shall be considered "sold for the first time on or after September 1, 1975," if *anyone* of the following conditions is met: (a) the DOT identification numbers indicate that the tire was manufactured after September 1, 1975; or (b) the purchasers or owners of the tires produce with the tires a proof of purchase on or after September 1, 1975; or (c) with respect to Firestone steel belted radial 500 tires and private brand tires of the same or similar internal construction (i.e., replacement tires), the DOT identification numbers indicate that the tires were manufactured on or after March 1, 1975 but before September 1, 1975, and the tires are not mounted on 1975 model passenger cars. Tires mounted on 1975 model vehicles may be included in the recall only if either condition (a) or (b) above is met.

4. Proof of purchase for replacement tires, if required, shall be either the purchasers or owner's recall notification letter from Firestone or the new tire invoice or other evidence of tire purchase date. Proof of purchase for original equipment tires, if required, shall be the purchaser or owner's recall notification letter or new vehicle invoice or title or other evidence of vehicle purchase date. In all cases, including those where proof of purchase is required, the eligible tire must be presented for replacement.

5. "Owners and purchasers" is used herein to describe those persons presenting tires for replacement of tires pursuant to this agreement and who were first purchasers of those tires and still have possession of them, or those persons who are currently using the tires on their vehicles, or have used the tires on their vehicles and still have possession of them. Firestone may exclude from those eligible the following: manufacturers or retreaders of tires, tire dealers, and persons engaged in the sale of used or scrapped tires. Eligible tires shall not include tires which have previously been retreaded, adjusted or scrapped. Tires which fail to meet the NHTSA standards set forth in 49 C.F.R. §570.9(a)(1) and are not currently being used on vehicles shall also be ineligible for replacement. Tires which would otherwise be eligible but do not meet the standards of 49 C.F.R. §570.9 (a)(1) shall be replaced if presented for replacement by the owner-purchaser. Firestone shall have the right to ensure that the individual presenting such tires is the actual owner-purchaser of the vehicle (or his authorized agent) on which such tires are being used.

6. If the tire to be replaced under any provision of this agreement is a Firestone steel belted radial 500 (5 and 7-rib) or TPC, replacement shall be made with a new Firestone steel belted radial 721, TPC or comparable tire. The owner-purchaser shall have his choice from among the comparable tires which may be available, or may elect to wait for that choice to become available. If the owner-purchaser so chooses, he may select a lower priced non-comparable, radial tire as the replacement tire. Because of the hazard of mixing radial and non-radial tires on the same vehicle, non-radial tires may be selected for replacement if all tires on the vehicle are eligible for replacement or if the owner-purchaser replaces the non-eligible radial tires for non-radials at his own cost. Firestone shall have the right, if a selection is made by the owner-purchaser of a replacement tire which is not comparable to the steel belted radial 721 or TPC, to require that the owner-purchaser sign a document indicating that he has made such a selection of his own free will and that he is satisfied that Firestone has met its obligation to him under this recall. If the tire to be replaced is a private brand tire of the same or similar internal construction as the Firestone steel belted radial 500 tire (5 or 7-rib), replacement may be made, if the private brand marketer, rather than Firestone, has elected to effect the replacement, with a comparable private brand tire manufactured by Firestone and currently being sold by the private brand marketer. If the owner-purchaser so chooses, he may select a lower-priced, non-comparable, radial or non-radial private brand tire as the replacement tire under the conditions described above relating to Firestone brand tires.

7. Firestone will issue a notification pursuant to this agreement and offer to owners and purchasers who were sold a 5-rib Firestone 500, a 7-rib Firestone 500, the same or similar private brand, or a TPC, prior to September 1, 1975, the opportunity to exchange that tire for a new Firestone 721 tire, TPC tire, or at the choice of owners and purchasers, other comparable tires manufactured by Firestone at one-half of the regular retail price of the replacement tire. Such owner-purchasers shall have the opportunity to select a lower-price, non-comparable radial or non-radial tire as the exchange tire subject to the conditions described in paragraph 6 above. Firestone may exclude from those eligible for this one-half price program the following: manufacturers or retreaders of tires, tire dealers, and persons engaged in the sale of used or scrapped tires. Eligible tires shall not include tires which have previously been retreaded, adjusted or scrapped, or tires which fail to meet the NHTSA standards set forth in 49 C.F.R. §570.9(a)(1).

8. Firestone agrees to use its best efforts, including employment of overtime and other feasible methods of accelerating production, to manufacture and distribute replacement tires as soon as possible in order to complete the recall.

9. Nothing contained in this Final Agreement nor any actions undertaken by Firestone pursuant to this agreement are intended to constitute an admission by Firestone of a safety-related defect, nor a concession by NHTSA that a safety-related defect does not exist.

10. In an effort to notify those persons whose tires are subject to recall, for whom no record of purchase may exist, and those persons for whom notice is required pursuant to paragraph 7 above, but whose tires are outside the statutory recall period, Firestone will undertake a nationwide media campaign to provide notification and explain the recall and the procedures to be followed in its implementation.

A. Print Media

(1) Because of the complexity of the information to be communicated, print media will be primarily relied upon to effect public notice. Firestone will place in a position normally used by Firestone in its national tire advertising a 1000-line advertisement in the Sunday editions of 242 major daily newspapers in the top 200 markets in the United States. Such newspaper notices shall notify the reader of the NHTSA's initial determination and shall, to the degree possible, substantially incorporate the terms of the notification letter to be sent to individual purchasers of tires subject to the recall and will, in addition, provide information on the two additional Firestone programs set forth in paragraphs 7 and 18 of this Final Agreement. The notice shall also state that tires purchased prior to September 1, 1975, but not subject to recall, are covered by the initial determination. . . .

(2) These public notices will first appear in print as soon as production and scheduling of the TV commercials hereinafter referred to will permit. In order to provide maximum impact and to coincide with the commencement of the nationwide mailing of notices, Firestone plans to run the majority of said print notices simultaneously, although availability of replacement tires in specific geographic markets and ad placement procedures may alter this schedule to some degree.

(3) Since the vast majority of the tires involved in the recall are Firestone brand tires, the print notice will primarily refer to such tires. Unless the private brand marketer shall prefer an alternative method of public notice, Firestone will include at the bottom of the print notice a list of the private brand tires that are also subject to the recall.

(4) Firestone will supplement the above newspaper advertising program by utilizing the services of a news release syndication group which will process a detailed Firestone press release on the recall to 3800 daily and weekly newspapers throughout the country. Previous experience by Firestone indicates that the utilization of such a release by the local newspapers subscribing to this service will provide effective supplemental notice.

B. Broadcast Media

Firestone will prepare a 30-second TV message with Firestone Chairman Richard A. Riley, or another appropriate Company spokesman, announcing that Firestone has entered into an agreement with NHTSA to recall certain steel belted radial 500 tires, private brand tires and TPC tires. The message will announce that NHTSA made an initial determination that a safety-related defect exists in Firestone 500 steel belted radials and private brands of the same or similar construction. The message shall refer consumers to the print media notification for details of the recall and exchange programs under this agreement, and will notify registered consumers who have purchased tires within the statutory recall period that they will receive notification of the recall by mail. The message shall also state that tires purchased prior to September 1, 1975, will be treated under the Firestone 50% exchange program as described in paragraph 7. Because of time and communications limitations, no other private brand information will be provided in the messages and the viewer will be referred to the individual mail notices and print media for further details. The general purpose of this message will be to alert people to the fact of the recall and to obtain the public's cooperation in its orderly implementation. The TV message will be shown at least once on two of the three major networks on programs and at times normally used by Firestone in its national tire advertising.

11. Firestone shall agree with NHTSA on the language of a dealer instruction letter concerning the mechanics of the implementation of this recall. Additionally, Firestone and NHTSA shall jointly prepare a consumer information booklet explaining in as simple and concise a manner as possible the consumer's rights and remedies under this recall. Such an information booklet will be made readily available by Firestone to the consumer through Firestone stores and dealers.

12. Firestone shall further agree with NHTSA on the language of the print and broadcast media announcements detailed in paragraph 10 above.

13. Recall of private brand tires will be accomplished in the following manner:

 A. Firestone shall be responsible for the recall of Firestone-produced private brand tires subject to this recall and may, if the private brand marketer so agrees, implement the recall through the facilities of the private brand marketers.

 B. . . .The private brand tires subject to the recall shall be returned to the private brand marketer, if he so agrees, for replacement with a comparable private brand tire manufactured by Firestone.

14. Firestone and NHTSA shall agree upon the written notification to be provided to owners of the affected tires. This notification . . . (1) will state that NHTSA has made an initial determination of defect and will refer to that determination, (2) may state that Firestone's negotiated recall plan which is the subject of this agreement is undertaken to resolve this matter, (3) with respect to all notification provisions, shall refer to statements of NHTSA, rather than Firestone, and (4) shall not contain any statements by Firestone contesting NHTSA's initial determination.

15. Individual notification will be accomplished in the following manner:

 A. Firestone will endeavor to notify or cause to be notified by mail all persons registered in accordance with applicable laws as having purchased new a replacement tire subject to free replacement under this recall. Firestone will endeavor to notify or cause to be notified all persons which Firestone original equipment manufacturing customers identify as having purchased a new vehicle equipped with new Firestone tires that may be subject to free replacement under this recall. The NHTSA recognizes that the original equipment vehicle manufacturers do not maintain records which identify the serial numbers of tires applied to individual vehicles and that Firestone must, necessarily, rely upon such records as are kept by the original equipment manufacturers for notification purposes. . . .

B. Firestone maintains registration lists of tire purchases from private brand marketers only for Montgomery Ward Co. and brands marketed by Firestone's Seiberling Division. These purchasers will receive notification letters processed by R. L. Polk similar to the procedures hereinafter described. All other private brand marketers maintain their own registration lists and notification either by Firestone or the private brand marketer will rely on those lists.

C. The individual notification by mail of the owner-purchasers covered by the recall shall be accomplished, to the degree possible, in accordance with the following schedule:

(1) By November 9, 1978, the Firestone Computer Center will have compiled a list of microfilm and frame numbers containing registrations of trade tires subject to the recall and will have forwarded those lists to R. L. Polk & Co. By November 15, 1978, the Des Moines Tire Registration Center will deliver to R. L. Polk & Co. the microfilm reels containing registrations of tires subject to the recall. R. L. Polk & Co. will immediately thereafter begin the process of compiling the lists of names and most recent addresses of registered purchasers of the tires.

(2) Automobile manufacturers, at Firestone's request, will develop lists of vehicle identification numbers for automobiles which their records indicate may have been equipped with new Firestone tires subject to the recall. Thereafter, Firestone will provide R. L. Polk & Co. with the information obtained from the automobile manufacturers and R. L. Polk & Co. will obtain the name and most recent address of the current owner of each affected vehicle.

(3) The number of letters to be mailed each week will be dependent upon the availability of replacement tires based upon a production rate of 400,000 tires per month for the recall and related programs. Firestone will regularly review the recall replacement demand by size and type of tire and will make such adjustments in production schedules and

notification schedules as are reasonably feasible in order to expedite accomplishment of the recall program.

16. NHTSA reserves the right to initiate and disseminate media notices and other information relating to the recall campaign, apart from Firestone's efforts, but any such activity by NHTSA shall not release or discharge Firestone from its aforementioned obligations to undertake media advertising and news releases.

17. No sale or resale of whatever nature, kind or description of tires covered by the recall will be made by Firestone, its agents, servants, or employees or anyone under its direction or control, except for non-motor vehicle use.

18. Although not a part of this agreement, Firestone will offer refunds to those customers who have received an adjustment during the period from September 1, 1975 until the date of this agreement on tires that would otherwise have been subject to recall and a free replacement under this agreement.

19. Within five days of the signing of this Final Agreement, Firestone shall file the report agreed to be filed pursuant to 15 U.S.C. §1414(c) and 49 C.F.R. §573.4. As soon as administratively practical after Firestone files such report, but not later than December 15, 1978, NHTSA shall close Defect Investigation Case Number C8-18 and seek no penalties or additional remedies under the National Traffic and Motor Vehicle Safety Act of 1966, as amended, based upon facts presently known to NHTSA. Firestone shall thereafter provide NHTSA with the quarterly reports pursuant to 49 C.F.R. §573.5.

20. The parties recognize that in a recall of the duration, complexity and scope contemplated by this Final Agreement, some misinformation and complaints will undoubtedly occur. The NHTSA agrees promptly to forward to Firestone's Consumer Affairs Department ... any complaints received concerning the recall and Firestone will endeavor promptly to investigate and satisfy those complaints. . . .

21. It is further understood and agreed by the parties that all terms of the Final Agreement and any subsequent modifications, extensions and additions to this agreement will be made public.

David I. Granger	Joseph J. Levin, Jr.

Attorney for
  The Firestone Tire &
  Rubber Company
	Chief Counsel
	  National Highway Traffic
	  Safety Administration

Dated: November 29, 1978

▼▼▼

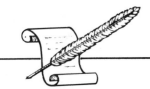

December

CARTER'S PRESERVATION
OF ALASKA'S FEDERAL LANDS
December 1, 1978

President Carter on Dec. 1 acted to preserve 56 million acres of federal land in Alaska from mining, logging or commercial development. Using the authority in a 1906 law, the president signed proclamations designating the lands as national monuments, thus placing them within the National Park System.

In a statement, Carter said, "Because of the risks of immediate damage to these magnificent areas, I felt it was imperative to protect all of these lands and preserve for the Congress an unhampered opportunity to act next year." The president said that among "the treasures to be preserved are the nation's largest pristine river valley, the place where man may first have come into the New World, a glacier as large as Rhode Island and the largest group of peaks over 15,000 feet in North America."

National Monuments

Of the 17 national monuments created by the proclamations, 13 were to be managed by the National Park Service. These included Aniakchak (350,000 acres), Bering Land Bridge (2.6 million acres), Cape Krusenstern (560,000 acres), Denali (3.9 million acres), Gates of the Arctic (8.2 million acres), a 550,000-acre enlargement of Glacier Bay, a 1.4-million-acre enlargement of Katmai, Kenai Fjords (570,000 acres), Kobuk Valley (1.7 million acres), Lake Clark (2.5 million acres), Noatak (5.8 million acres), Wrangell-St. Elias (11 million acres) and Yukon Charley (1.7 million acres). Hunting, road building, mineral development and human settle-

ment will be prohibited in these areas except for some subsistence hunting and fishing by Eskimos, Indians and Aleuts.

The Fish and Wildlife Service was charged with managing the Yukon Flats (10.6 million acres) and Becharof (1.2 million acres). Hunting and fishing would be permitted in these areas. Two other monuments were to be managed by the Forest Service: Admiralty Island (1.1 million acres) and Misty Fjords (2.2 million acres). Mineral exploration and the cutting of timber was to be prohibited in these areas.

The president acted after the Senate had failed to pass the administration's Alaska lands bill (HR 39). That legislation, which had been approved by the House, would have set aside more than 100 million acres as national recreation areas, wildlife refuges and wilderness areas. Congressional failure to act meant that restrictions on the use of federal land under the Alaska Native Claims and Settlement Act of 1971 would have expired on Dec. 17 and that many of the areas would then have been open for state claims or for oil and mineral exploration.

Carter used the Antiquities Act of 1906 to protect what he termed "Alaska's extraordinary Federal lands." Section 2 of that act provided that the president "is authorized, in his discretion, to declare by public proclamation historic landmarks, historic and prehistoric structures and other objects of historic or scientific interest that are situated upon the lands owned or controlled by the Government of the United States to be national monuments, and may reserve as part thereof parcels of land, the limits of which in all cases shall be confined to the smallest area compatible with the proper care and management of the objects to be protected." National monuments are identical to national parks except for the fact that they are created by the president rather than by the Congress.

Action by Andrus

On Nov. 16, Secretary of the Interior Cecil D. Andrus withdrew 110 million acres — about 170,000 square miles — of Alaska's federal lands from development. Andrus cited the Land Policy and Management Act of 1976 as his authority for protecting the 110 million acres. Section 204(e) of that law allowed the Secretary of the Interior to place restrictions on development if he determined that an "emergency situation" threatened the natural state of the land.

Two weeks after Andrus' action, the president selected 56 million of the 110 million acres for "permanent protection." The 1976 law merely froze development for three years, while the 1906 statute had no time limitation and would require an act of Congress for any of the protected areas to be opened. Administration officials were also concerned that the 1976 law might allow the state of Alaska to take part of the 110-million-acre area. The Alaska Statehood Act of 1959 gave the state the right to "select" 104 million acres of federal land for its own use.

Reaction

Alaskans favoring development, including Gov. Jay S. Hammond (R), Sen. Mike Gravel (D) and Sen. Ted Stevens (R), were quick to criticize Carter's and Andrus' actions. The state of Alaska had filed suit in federal court in Anchorage on Oct. 30 to prevent the administration from using the 1906 law to create national monuments on federal lands. Alaska claimed that there was no legal basis for using either the 1976 or the 1906 statute.

To avoid a battle in the courts, President Carter expressed the hope in his Dec. 1 statement that "the 96th Congress will act promptly to pass Alaska lands legislation." He said that he would submit a new bill in January 1979. "Passing legislation to designate National Parks, Wildlife Refuges, Wilderness Areas and Wild and Scenic Rivers in Alaska is the highest environmental priority of my Administration," he said.

Following are the texts of President Carter's statement on Dec. 1, 1978, setting aside certain federal lands in Alaska, and Dec. 1 Interior Department releases on Proclamations Under Antiquities Act of 1906 and on the New Alaska National Monuments:

CARTER STATEMENT

Our nation has been uniquely blessed with a vast land of great natural beauty and abundant resources. Once these gifts seemed limitless. As our people have spread across the continent and the needs for development reach once distant frontiers, we realize how urgent it is to preserve our heritage for future generations.

Today I have taken several actions to protect Alaska's extraordinary Federal lands. Because of the risks of immediate damage to these magnificent areas, I felt it was imperative to protect all of these lands and preserve for the Congress an unhampered opportunity to act next year.

Passing legislation to designate National Parks, Wildlife Refuges, Wilderness Areas and Wild and Scenic Rivers in Alaska is the highest environmental priority of my Administration. There is strong support for such legislation in the Congress. In the 95th Congress, the House of Representatives overwhelmingly passed an Alaska bill. A bill was reported out of the Senate Committee, but time ran out and the Senate was unable to finally pass a bill. Because existing "d-2" land withdrawals under the 1971 Alaska Native Claims Settlement Act expire on December 17, much of the land to be protected by legislation would be unprotected and perhaps irrevocably lost if I did not act now.

Accordingly, along with Secretaries [Cecil D.] Andrus [Department of Interior] and [Bob] Bergland [Department of Agriculture], I have taken the following actions:

—I have signed proclamations under the Antiquities Act of 1906 designating as National Monuments 17 of the most critical areas proposed for legislative designation — 13 proposed National Parks, two proposed Wildlife Refuges and two proposed National Forest Wilderness areas.

These areas, totaling approximately 56 million acres, contain resources of unequalled scientific, historic and cultural value, and include some of the most spectacular scenery and wildlife in the world. The Antiquities Act has been used in the past to preserve such treasures, for example by President Teddy Roosevelt who designated the Grand Canyon in this way. The Monuments I have created in Alaska are worthy of the special, permanent protections provided by the Antiquities Act. They will remain permanent Monuments until the Congress makes other provisions for the land.

—I have directed Secretary Andrus to proceed with necessary steps to designate National Wildlife Refuges for the remaining twelve proposed refuge areas, an additional 40 million acres.

—Secretaries Andrus and Bergland have already taken steps under Section 204 of the Federal Land Policy and Management Act to withdraw or segregate all of the areas covered by either Congressional or Administration proposals from mineral entry and selection by the State of Alaska. I have directed that these withdrawals remain in place.

Each of the areas protected by these actions is exceptional and valuable. Among the treasures to be preserved are the nation's largest pristine river valley, the place where man may first have come into the New World, a glacier as large as the State of Rhode Island and the largest group of peaks over 15,000 feet in North America. Breeding areas of the Great Alaska brown bear, caribou and Dall sheep, and of ducks, geese and swans that migrate through the other 49 States each year will also be protected.

In addition to preserving these natural wonders, historical sites and wildlife habitats, our actions will ensure that Alaskan Eskimos, Indians and Aleuts can continue their traditional way of life, including hunting and fishing.

In Alaska we have a unique opportunity to balance the development of our vital resources required for continued economic growth with protection of our natural environment. We have the imagination and the will as a people to both develop our last great natural frontier and also preserve its priceless beauty for our children and grandchildren.

The actions I have taken today provide for urgently-needed permanent protections. However, they are taken in the hope that the 96th Congress will act promptly to pass Alaska lands legislation.

PROCLAMATIONS UNDER
ANTIQUITIES ACT OF 1906

1. *Provisions of the Act.* Section 2 of the Act of June 8, 1906 (34 Stat. 225; 16 U.S.C. 431), provides as follows:

"The President of the United States is authorized, in his discretion, to declare by public proclamation historic landmarks, historic and prehistoric structures, and other objects of historic or scientific interest that are situated upon the lands owned or controlled by the Government of the United States to be national monuments, and may reserve as a part thereof parcels of land, the limits of which in all cases shall be confined to the smallest area compatible with the proper care and management of the objects to be protected."

2. *History.* Under this authority 66 units of the National Park System have been created by proclamations of various Presidents. One of the earlier proclamations created Grand Canyon National Monument, Arizona, of 273,145 acres; the most recent exercise of this authority was Proclamation 4346 of February 1, 1975, whereby President Ford added 30 acres of Federal submerged lands to Buck Island Reef National Monument, Virgin Islands.

3. *Application to Alaska.* Proclamations reserving Federal lands in Alaska as national monuments have been issued as follows:

Katmai National Monument —
Proclamation No. 1487 of September 24, 1918 (Wilson) created 1,700 square mile national monument
Proclamation No. 1950 of April 24, 1931 (Hoover) added certain lands.
Proclamation No. 2564 of August 4, 1942 (Roosevelt) added certain offshore islands.

Glacier Bay National Monument —
Proclamation No. 1733 of February 26, 1925 (Coolidge) created 1,820 square mile national monument.
Proclamation No. 2330 of April 18, 1939 (Roosevelt) added 904,960 acres; including lands 3 miles offshore. (Lands were excluded from Tongass National Forest in this proclamation and made part of the national monument).

Sitka National Monument —
Proclamation No. 959 of March 23, 1910 (Taft) established 57-acre national monument.

NEW ALASKA NATIONAL MONUMENTS

New Alaska National Monuments and new areas of existing units managed by the National Park Service except Kenai Fjords will be open to continued subsistence hunting and fishing under appropriate regulations. There is no record of contemporary subsistence hunting on shore at Kenai Fjords.

Aniakchak National Monument. The monument includes 350,000 acres located on the Alaska Peninsula. A prime feature of the monument is the Aniakchak Crater, one of the world's largest dry calderas, covering a 30-square mile area. The interior of the crater contains volcanic features such as lava flows, cinder cones, and explosion pits, as well as the unusual and aptly named Surprise Lake. This lake is the source of the Aniakchak River, which cascades through a 1,500 foot gash in the caldera wall and flows on to the Pacific Ocean. The flanks of the crater provide a geological and biological continuum for the study of significant processes of plant and animal succession, as life returns to an area devastated by the volcano in 1931.

Denali National Monument. Mount McKinley National Park, established in 1917, would be enlarged by a 3.89 million acre national monument and the additions named in recognition of the ancient Alaska Native name for North America's highest peak (20,320 feet). The addition would protect the entire Mount McKinley geological formation, including forelands, glacial features, and scenic resources. It would also ensure the preservation of important ecological values, among them habitat of large mammal species.

Critical caribou wintering grounds and wolf dens are found in the monument. Moose, black bear, grizzly bear, foxes, lynxes, beavers, wolverines, and a multiplicity of bird life, including longtailed jaegers, whimbrels, surfbirds, and wandering tattlers are all resident species.

The existing 1.9 million-acre park is on the Anchorage-Fairbanks highway, 240 miles north of Anchorage. In 1976, the park drew more than half-a-million visitors.

Katmai National Monument Enlargement. The existing Katmai National Monument was created in 1918 to preserve the site of the 1912 volcanic eruption that formed the Valley of Ten Thousand Smokes and subsequently was enlarged to include prime scenic, recreation and wildlife values. It would be enlarged by 1.37 million acres.

The additions would round out Katmai by adding critical habitat necessary to protect populations of brown bear and preserve pristine watersheds necessary for red salmon fisheries.

Once isolated 300 miles southwest of Anchorage, Katmai now has 9,000 to 12,000 visits a year. More than 2,500 overnight stays are recorded annually.

Cape Krusenstern National Monument. This National Monument of 560,000 acres borders the Chukchi Sea, 600 miles northwest of Anchorage. Its succession of 114 lateral-beach ridges, extending three miles inland, tells of Eskimo communities of every known cultural period in Arctic Alaska, going back over 4,000 years. The area also may yield archeological discoveries concerning the Bering Land Bridge. It would bring into the National Park System not only internationally significant archeological sites but also a type of ecosystem not now represented — a segment of the Arctic coastal tundra. Walrus and occasional polar bears are among the coastal wildlife.

The unique geologic process of erosion and sediment transport from the rivers in the northern portion of the area created and continues to create the beach ridges in which is preserved the archeological record.

Bering Land Bridge National Monument. This 2.6 million acre monument takes in remains of the land bridge which once linked Asia and North America. On the north side of the Seward Peninsula, it lies only 50 miles from Siberia, about 30 minutes by air north from Nome, Alaska. The archeological and paleontological resources of the area are its most important attribute, but it also contains valued natural resources.

The diversity of soils, topography, permafrost action, and climate within the monument leads to an excellent representation of varied tundra plant communities. Their proximity and diversity make the area a prime outdoor laboratory.

The monument has polar bear, grizzly bear, wolves, wolverines, arctic foxes, and 21 other land mammal species co-existing in a relatively undisturbed ecosystem. Adjoining waters contain four threatened species of whales. Bird life includes 112 known species, some varieties of which migrate to one or more of six continents. A prehistoric ecosystem has been preserved here under a blanket of ashes from volcanic eruptions, and scores of archeological sites also lie within the proposed boundaries.

Reindeer are an important food source and cultural element of native communities on the Seward Peninsula, and carefully managed herding could continue as a valid existing right.

Kenai Fjords National Monument. This National Monument would preserve 570,000 acres of the interrelated Harding Icefield fjord system on the Kenai peninsula in federal ownership.

Located only 20 miles from Seward, glaciers spin off from the Harding icefield in four directions, many flowing into the monument's Gulf of Alaska waters. The fjords, containing richly varied rain forest habitats, are an illustration of tectonic movement and the subsiding of mountains over geologic time.

Noatak National Monument. The Noatak River basin is the largest mountain-ringed river basin in the Nation still virtually unaffected by technological human activity. This monument of 5.8 million acres contains landforms and ecological variations of scientific interest, including the northwestern most fringe of boreal forest in North America, the 65 mile long Grand Canyon of the Noatak, a transition zone and migration route for plants and animals between subarctic and arctic environments, and an array of flora which is among the most diverse anywhere in the earth's northern latitudes. This freely functioning ecosystem includes a rich variety of animal life; two-thirds of the Western Arctic caribou herd migrate through the monument. Nearly 200 arecheological sites, dating as far back in time as 5,000 years, are within the area. They give promise of future discoveries leading to a deeper understanding of Early Man's first arrival in the New World from Asia.

Lake Clark National Monument. This monument includes 2.5 million acres at the head of the Alaska Peninsula, bordering on Cook Inlet. The monument would serve to protect and interpret for public benefit an exceptionally diverse, scenic array of natural features. The area is about one hour, flying time, southwest of Anchorage. This plan would also preserve the headwaters of the Kivichak River as a freeflowing stream system, thereby protecting the Bristol Bay red salmon fishery.

The rugged mountain and valley systems encompassed in the monument provide habitat for grizzly bear, black bear, wolves, wolverine, mink, marten, lynxes, red foxes, otter, and muskrat. Caribou graze on the western slopes and Dall sheep reach the southern limits of their range here. A 50-mile segment along the Cook Inlet has some 100 bird species, including bald eagles, the endangered peregrine falcon, concentrations of swans, and 11 varieties of ducks. The coastal Chigmit Mountains contain two active volcanoes over 10,000 feet high within the monument. The area already attracts several thousand visitors annually for fishing and wilderness recreation and has very high potential for greatly increased visitation in the near future.

Glacier Bay National Monument Enlargement. Established in 1925, Glacier Bay National Monument would be expanded from its 2.8 million acres to 3.35 million acres with the 558,000 acre addition.

The monument contains great tidewater glaciers, a dramatic range of plant communities from rocky terrain recently covered by ice to lush temperate rain forest, and a surprising variety of wild animals, including brown and black bears, mountain goats, whales, seals, and eagles. The additional 558,000 acres would protect and interpret the northwest slope of Mount Fairweather, the U.S. portion of the Alsek River, mountain-flaked sand beaches, and associated animal habitat and migration routes.

Glacier Bay, about 100 miles west of Juneau, can be reached by boat or by plane from Juneau.

Yukon-Charley National Monument. Encompassing 1.72 million acres along the Yukon and Charley Rivers in east-central Alaska along the Canadian border. This monument would preserve the Charley River basin and its wildlife and protect and interpret the area's internationally significant geological and paleontological resources. The area also includes a large concentration of nesting endangered peregrine falcons and historic resources from the gold rush era.

The monument encompasses a 115-mile stretch of the 1,800-mile Yukon River as well as the 88-mile Charley.

Wrangell-St. Elias National Monument. This monument would preserve a wilderness of more than 18,000 square miles — an area so vast and wild that non-natives have not yet visited many of its remote mountains and valleys. The Wrangell-St. Elias National Monument contains 10.95 million acres. The Wrangell Mountains in the north and the Chugach Range in the south contain the country's greatest collection of peaks over 16,000 feet and the continent's largest assemblage of glaciers. Among the peaks are Mount St. Elias, 18,008 feet, second highest in North America.

Wildlife includes the grizzly and black bear, the rare glacier bear along the Gulf of Alaska coast, wolverines, wolves, moose, Dall sheep, mountain goats, mink, foxes, otter and other fur-bearers.

The monument is a day's drive east of Anchorage.

Gates of the Arctic National Monument. Lying wholly north of the Arctic Circle, the 8.22 million acre Gates of the Arctic National Monument preserves an area containing a wide variety of interior Arctic geological and biological forms. The essence of the geology of the area is its great diversity. Included in the area is the bladelike Arrigetch Peaks and the turreted Mount Igikpuk, which are in contrast to the immense open valleys of the central Brooks Range. Plant communities and wildlife species are also varied; wildlife inhabiting this tundra environment includes the exceedingly important migrant arctic caribou of the Western Arctic herd, grizzly bear, Dall sheep, moose, wolves, and raptors. Walter Lake, an exceptional geologic and ecologic area, is among the variety of large lakes and untamed streams found in the monument. Wilderness explorer Bob Marshall named the eastern part of the area Gates of the Arctic because of the remarkable terrain found there. The archeological and historical significance of the area is demonstrated by evidence of human habitation for approximately 7,000 years.

Kobuk Valley National Monument. Situated in northeastern Alaska between the Baird Mountains on the north and the Waring Mountains on the south, the Kobuk Valley National Monument contains 1.71 million acres. It embraces the central valley of the Kobuk River which flows west to the coast. The placid and easily navigable Kobuk has been a major transportation route for centuries. The monument would protect the northwestern limits of the boreal forest and the Arctic tundra which contains several important caribou migration routes and the northern portion of the Arctic herd's winter range. Moose, black and grizzly bear, and wolves are indigenous. The protection of archeological resources, including Onion Portage, would be a major objective of the monument. An Arctic rarity, the geologically significant Great Kobuk Sand Dunes, lies within the area.

The Secretary of the Interior plans to designate the Fish and Wildlife Service to manage the Becharof and Yukon Flats National Monuments. These monuments will be open to sport hunting and fishing as well as subsistence hunting and fishing, all under appropriate regulation.

Becharof National Monument. Jutting into the Pacific Ocean from the southwest corner of Alaska is the Alaska Peninsula. Near its northern end, the Becharof National Monument, (1.2 million acres) contains one of the major brown bear habitats in Alaska. The giant peninsula brown bear are free-ranging, feeding in salmon streams and coastal marshes over a wide area and hibernating in mountain dens. Some 232 dens have been located in mountain sides and on islands in the Becharof area.

Caribou and large numbers of moose range through the refuge ...;

streams abound with salmon, rainbow trout and Arctic grayling; and rocky seacliffs host tens of thousands of seabirds of several species.

The area is also interesting and significant geologically, as it contains one of Alaska's most recent volcanically active areas, the Gas Rocks under Mount Peulik. Scientific studies here of recent volcanism may contribute to the growing understanding of this powerful geological force.

Yukon Flats National Monument. The Yukon Flats National Monument of 10.6 million federal acres is the largest and most complete example of a scientifically significant interior Alaskan solar basin with its associated ecosystem. The mountain-ringed physiography of this basin, coupled with the continuous sunlight of the summer months, results in the climatic phenomenon in the basin of warmer summer temperatures and other factors which produce a lush wetland area. The Yukon Flats is one of North America's most productive wildlife habitats. The area contains 40,000 lakes, oxbows and potholes which are recharged when the Yukon River floods across the vast basin. This basin contributes an annual flight of 2,100,000 ducks and 16,500 geese as well as 11,000 sandhill cranes, 15,000 loons and 100,000 grebe to flyways touching all parts of the Lower 48, Canada and Mexico. Major populations of wolves, black and grizzly bears, moose, furbearers and production of over a quarter of a million salmon also contribute to the fish and wildlife values of the Yukon Flats.

▼▼▼

NEW EUROPEAN MONETARY SYSTEM

December 4, 5, 1978

The nine member nations of the European Economic Community (Common Market) decided Dec. 4 and 5 at Brussels, Belgium, to set up a new monetary system to compete with the U.S. dollar and the Japanese yen in the world markets. Underlining the difficulty of obtaining agreement among that many nations on a complex common action was the fact that by year end the future of the embryonic European Monetary System (EMS) already was clouded.

Great Britain, Italy and Ireland at first said they would not participate in the new system. Great Britain remained out, but Italy and Ireland soon changed their minds and joined. Then on Dec. 29, France, a linchpin nation in the agreement, abruptly pulled out, delaying for at least several weeks the start of the system that had been set to begin on Jan. 1, 1979. France demanded an end to agricultural subsidies that allowed food products from all European Community (EC) nations to compete within the community at the same prices. France felt its farmers were being adversely affected by subsidies granted other EC countries, especially to West Germany, the richest of the EC nations.

Ironically, France was quarreling with the very nation it had joined in getting the EMS started. West German Chancellor Helmut Schmidt and French President Valery Giscard d'Estaing had seemingly put aside traditional enmity between the two nations to get the EC started on the EMS plan centered around what they termed "a zone of monetary stability in Europe." After the groundwork had been laid in a series of other meetings of EC representatives, the European Council consisting of the heads of the nine member governments met at Brussels to reach agreement

741

on the new pact. Schmidt and Giscard had continued to be the staunchest supporters of the EMS plan right up through agreement.

Goal of Stability

The impetus for the plan was a European recession encouraged in part by the constant fluctuation, or float, of the EC currencies against each other. Under the common money system, they would float as a bloc, a near-equal force against the dominating dollar and yen. As the member nations saw it, monetary union was needed to end the recession, reduce inflation and unemployment, restore business confidence and international trade growth, set the EC nations up collectively as an influential world body and at the same time create economic and political unity in the Common Market.

For bookkeeping purposes, the common means of settlement under the EMS plan would be the European Currency Unit, whose acronym, ECU, spelled the dominant currency in France from the 13th to 18th centuries, identified by its display of a shield. Until the French-inspired delay in the birth of EMS, the plan had been to freeze the currencies of the participants at the exchange rates as of 2:30 p.m., Jan. 2, 1979. After that time, each currency would be allowed to float no more than 2.25 percent up or down from that rate, a value of so many ECUs. An exception was granted the weak Italian lira, which could float by as much as 6 percent either side of the ECU. Each participating nation would contribute up to 20 percent of its gold and dollar reserves to a European Monetary Cooperative Fund, giving it an estimated $33 billion. The fund would provide the backing for the ECU exchange mechanism and protect it from the incursion of speculators. With such backing, the ECU could gain the status of a major reserve, as gold and the dollar had been.

Jenkins' Speech

Roy Jenkins, president of the Commission of the European Communities, explained the plan to U.S. journalists in a speech at the National Press Club in Washington, D.C., on Dec. 15. ". . .A common market without a common money system would make little sense," he told his audience. He suggested that they envision a situation in the United States similar to that plaguing the Common Market. How would Americans like it, he asked rhetorically, if there were "some exchange controls on every frontier between every American state, and state currencies, some strong, some weak, which constantly fluctuated against each other."

That movement of European currencies, Jenkins said, was having "evil effects . . . on our ability to run our economies as we wish. . . ." He said, "Community countries with strong currencies have found themselves hurt by lack of demand in countries with weak currencies, and weak currency countries have been unable to achieve the growth they so badly need through the risk of running exchange rate crises. Never has the need for the convergence of our European economies and the reduction — and evening out — of inflation rates among us been more apparent."

As Jenkins noted in his address, there was apprehension within the United States about the effect of the EMS on the U.S. dollar. *"I believe that those fears have been exaggerated,"* he said. *"The European Monetary System is designed not only to establish a zone of monetary stability in Europe but also to contribute to greater stability in the world monetary system as a whole."* The creation of the ECU, he said, could not *"be a threat to the dollar, the strength of which is as much in our interest as yours, the stability of which is made even more necessary to us by this immediate, major and delicate task we are now undertaking."*

Background

On July 1, 1944, as light began to shine at the end of the World War II tunnel, representatives of 44 nations gathered at a New Hampshire vacation resort known as Bretton Woods. The gathering, called the United Nations Monetary and Financial Conference, lasted three weeks and led to an agreement to base world currencies on the U.S. dollar. The agreement set exchange rates for the currencies of all the nations involved. The rates could be adjusted if a country's economy fluctuated erratically.

In 1958, Belgium, France, Italy, the Netherlands, Luxembourg and West Germany agreed to form the European Economic Community to promote their own collective economic welfare. Basically, the EC eliminated trade barriers among the participating nations and established common import duties on goods from other countries. Other European nations joined later until there were nine. There was speculation at the end of 1978 that Greece, Spain and Portugal might also join soon.

The decade of the 1960s dominated by the Vietnam War spelled the doom of the Bretton Woods agreement. America's war spending was so vast that the world was flooded with dollars. Adjustments of currencies of the Bretton Woods signators became so frequent that participating nations began ignoring the established rates. Finally, on Aug. 15, 1971, President Richard M. Nixon announced a new U.S. economic policy that had the effect of ending the Bretton Woods agreement. European nations, however, wanted to continue the Bretton Woods setup and adopted it for their own use in 1972. It became known as the "snake" because of the appearance of the relative values of the currencies involved when displayed on a graph. European countries joined and dropped out over the years until only six nations belonged — West Germany, Belgium, Luxembourg, Denmark, the Netherlands and Norway.

Giscard and Schmidt agreed during the Western economic summit at Rambouillet, France, on April 2 on some overall monetary objectives that would encompass a larger version of the "snake." They outlined a broad

*concept to a meeting of the European Council in Copenhagen, Denmark,
April 7 and 8. On June 23, Schmidt and Giscard met at Hamburg,
Germany, and reached a surprise agreement on a detailed proposal they
submitted to another European Council meeting at Bremen, Germany,
July 6 and 7. The plan received wider discussion July 16 and 17 at the
seven-nation economic summit at Bonn, Germany. On Nov. 20, the finance
ministers of the Common Market nations approved the EMS plan and it
was presented in its final form to the European Council again on Dec. 4 at
Brussels.*

*Following are the text of the resolution creating the European
Monetary System, approved by the European Council at a
meeting in Brussels Dec. 4 and 5, 1978; and excerpts from a
Dec. 15, 1978, speech by Roy Jenkins, president of the
Commission of the European Communities, to the National
Press Club in Washington, D.C.:*

EUROPEAN COUNCIL
RESOLUTION

A.

1.) Introduction —

In Bremen we discussed a "scheme for the creation of closer monetary
cooperation leading to a zone of monetary stability in Europe." We
regarded such a zone "as a highly desirable objective" and envisaged "a
durable and effective scheme."

Today, after careful examination of the preparatory work done by the
Council and other Community bodies, we are agreed as follows: A
European Monetary System (EMS) will be set up on 1 January 1979.

We are firmly resolved to ensure the lasting success of the EMS by
policies conducive to greater stability at home and abroad for both deficit
and surplus countries.

The following chapters deal primarily with the initial phase of the EMS.

We remain firmly resolved to consolidate, not later than two years after
the start of the scheme, into a final system the provisions and procedures
thus created. This system will entail the creation of the European
Monetary Fund as announced in the conclusions of the European Council
meeting at Bremen on 6/7 July 1978, as well as the full utilization of the
ECU as a reserve asset and a means of settlement. It will be based on
adequate legislation at the Community as well as the national level.

2.) The ECU and its functions —

A European Currency unit (ECU) will be at the center of the EMS; the
value and the composition of the ECU will be identical with the value of

the EUA* at the outset of the system.

The ECU will be used —

a.) As the denominator (numeraire) for the exchange rate mechanism

b.) As the basis for a divergence indicator

c.) As the denominator for operation in both the intervention and the credit mechanism

d.) As a means of settlement between monetary authorities of the EC.

The weights of currencies in the ECU will be reexamined and if necessary revised within six months of the entry into force of the system and thereafter every five years or, on request, if the weight of any currency has changed by 25 per cent.

Revisions have to be mutually accepted. They will, by themselves, not modify the external value of the ECU. They will be made in line with underlying economic criteria.

3.) The exchange rate and the intervention mechanism —

Each currency will have an ECU-related central rate. These central rates will be used to establish a grid of bilateral exchange rates.

Around these exchange rates fluctuation margins of 2.25 per cent will be established. EC countries with presently floating currencies may opt for wider margins up to 6 per cent at the outset of EMS. These margins should be gradually reduced as soon as economic conditions permit to do so.

A member state which does not participate in the exchange rate mechanism at the outset may participate at a later date.

Adjustments of central rates will be subject to mutual agreement, a common procedure which will comprise all countries participating in the exchange rate mechanism and the Commission. There will be reciprocal consultation in the Community framework about important decisions concerning exchange rate policy between countries participating and any country not participating in the system.

In principle, interventions will be made in participating currencies. Intervention in participating currencies is compulsory when the intervention points defined by the fluctuation margins are reached.

An ECU basket formula will be used as an indicator to detect divergences between Community currencies. A "threshold of divergence" will be fixed at 75 per cent of the maximum spread of divergence for each currency. It will be calculated in such a way as to eliminate the influence of weight on the probability to reach the threshold.

---

*The European Unit of Account (EUA) is a composite basket of fixed amounts of currencies of the nine Member States as follows:

0.028	German marks,	3.66	Belgian francs,
1.15	French francs	0.140	Luxembourg francs,
0.0885	Pounds sterling,	0.217	Danish crowns,
109	Italian lira,	0.00759	Irish pounds.
0.286	Dutch florins,		

The equivalent of the EUA in any currency is equal to the sum of the equivalents of these amounts in that currency.

When a currency crosses its "threshold of divergence," this results in a presumption that the authorities concerned will correct this situation by adequate measures, namely:

a.) Diversified intervention,
b.) Measures of domestic monetary policy,
c.) Changes in central rates,
d.) Other measures of economic policy.

In case such measures, on account of special circumstances, are not taken, the reasons for this shall be given to the other authorities, especially in the "concertation between central banks." Consultations will, if necessary, then take place in the appropriate Community bodies, including the Council of Ministers.

After six months these provisions shall be reviewed in the light of experience. At that date the questions regarding imbalances accumulated by divergent creditor or debtor countries will be studied as well.

A very short-term facility of an unlimited amount will be established. Settlements will be made 45 days after the end of the month of intervention with the possibility of prolongation for another 3 months for amounts limited to the size of debtor quotas in the short-term monetary support.

To serve as a means of settlement, an initial supply of ECU will be provided by the European Monetary Cooperation Fund (EMCF) against the deposit of 20 per cent of gold and 20 per cent of dollar reserves currently held by central banks.

This operation will take the form of specified, revolving swap arrangements. By periodical review and by an appropriate procedure it will be ensured that each central bank will maintain a deposit of at least 20 per cent of these reserves with EMCF. A member state not participating in the exchange rate mechanism may participate in this initial operation on the basis described above.

4.) The credit mechanism —

The existing credit mechanisms with their present rules of application will be maintained for the initial phase of the EMS. They will be consolidated into a single fund in the final phase of the EMS.

The credit mechanisms will be extended to an amount of 25 billion ECU of effectively available credit. The distribution of this amount will be as follows:

| Short-term monetary support | 14 billion ECU |
| Medium-term financial assistance | 11 billion ECU |

The duration of the short-term monetary support will be extended for another 3 months on the same conditions as the first extension.

The increase of the medium-term financial assistance will be completed by 30 June 1979. In the meantime, countries which still need national legislation are expected to make their extended medium-term quotas available by an interim financing agreement of the central banks concerned.

5.) Third countries and international organizations —

The durability of EMS and its international implications require coordination of exchange rate policies vis-a-vis third countries and, as far as possible, a concertation with the monetary authorities of those countries.

European countries with particularly close economic and financial ties with the European Communities may participate in the exchange rate and intervention mechanism.

Participation will be based upon agreements between central banks. These agreements will be communicated to the Council and the Commission of the EC.

EMS is and will remain fully compatible with the relevant articles of the International Monetary Fund agreement.

6.) Further procedure —

To implement the decision taken under (A), the European Council requests the Council to consider and to take a decision on 18 December 1978 on the following proposals of the Commission:

(A) Council regulation modifying the unit of account used by the European Monetary Cooperation Fund, which introduces the ECU in the operations of the European Monetary Cooperation Fund and defines its composition.

(B) Council regulation permitting the EMCF to receive monetary reserves and to issue ECUs to the monetary authorities of the member states which may use them as a means of settlement.

(C) Council regulation on the impact of the European Monetary System on the Common Agricultural Policy. The European Council considers that the introduction of the EMS should not of itself result in any change in the situation obtaining prior to 1 January 1979 regarding the expression in national currencies of agricultural prices, monetary compensatory amounts (MCAs) and all other amounts fixed for the purposes of the Common Agricultural Policy.

The European Council stresses the importance of henceforth avoiding the creation of permanent MCAs and progressively reducing present MCAs in order to reestablish the unity of prices of the Common Agricultural Policy, giving also due consideration to price policy.

It requests the Commission to submit in good time a proposal to amend the Council decision of 22 March 1971 on the introduction of a mechanism for the medium-term financial support to enable the Council of Economics and Finance Ministers to take a decision on such proposal at their session of 18 December 1978.

It requests the central banks of member states to modify their agreement of 10 April 1972 on the reduction of margins of fluctuation between the currencies of member states in accordance with the rules set forth above (see paragraph 3).

It requests the central banks of member states to modify as follows the rules on short-term monetary support by 1 January 1979 at the latest:

a.) The total of debtor quotas available for drawings by the central banks of member states shall be increased to an aggregate amount of 7.9 billion ECU.

b.) The total of creditor quotas made available by the central banks of member states for financing the debtor quotas shall be increased to an aggregate amount of 15.8 billion ECU.

c.) The total of the additional creditor amount as well as the total of the additional debtor amount may not exceed 8.8 billion ECU.

d.) The duration of credit under the extended short-term monetary support may be prolonged twice for a period of 3 months.

B. Measures designed to strengthen the economies of the less prosperous member states of the European Monetary System

We stress that, within the context of a broadly-based strategy aimed at improving the prospects of economic development and based on symmetrical rights and obligations of all participants, the most important concern should be to enhance the convergence of economic policies toward greater stability. We request the Council (Economic and Finance Ministers) to strengthen its procedures for coordination in order to improve that convergence.

We are aware that the convergence of economic policies [sic] and that steps must be taken to strengthen the economic potential of the less prosperous countries of the Community. This is primarily the responsibility of the member states concerned. Community measures can and should serve a supporting role.

The European Council agrees that, in the context of the European Monetary system, the following measures in favor of the less prosperous member states effectively and fully participating in the exchange rate and intervention mechanisms will be taken.

The European Council requests the Community institutions by the utilization of the new financial instrument and the European Investment Bank to make available for a period of 5 years loans of up to 1 billion EUA per year to these countries on special conditions.

The European Council requests the Commission to submit a proposal to provide interest-rate subsidies of 3 per cent for these loans, with the following elements: The total cost of this measure, divided into annual tranches of 200 million EUA each over a period of 5 years shall not exceed 1 billion EUA.

Any less prosperous member country which subsequently effectively and fully participates in the mechanisms would have the right of access to this facility within the financial limits mentioned above. Member states not participating effectively and fully in the mechanisms will not contribute to the financing of the scheme.

The funds thus provided are to be concentrated on the financing of selected infrastructure projects and programs, with the understanding that any direct or indirect distortion of the competitive position of specific industries within member states will have to be avoided.

The European Council requests the Council (Economic and Finance Ministers) to take a decision on the above mentioned proposals in time so that the relevant measures can become effective on 1 April 1979 at the latest. There should be a review at the end of the initial phase of the EMS.

The European Council requests the Commission to study the relationship between greater convergence in economic performance of the member states and the utilization of Community instruments, in particular the funds which aim at reducing structural imbalances. The results of these studies will be discussed at the next European Council.

JENKINS' SPEECH

...We are now half way between the Western Economic Summit of Bonn which took place in July this year, and that which is generally expected to be held in Tokyo in June next year. In my talks with members of the United States Administration I have therefore been able to conduct a sort of mid-term review of general developments in our economies, how these compare with our expectations in Bonn, and what are the prospects for Tokyo. Although it is too early to say exactly how and whether the various specific commitments into which the Summit participants entered will be met, I think that the results so far are not at all bad. At least the trends are right in every participating country — although not necessarily the same for some of the problems are different. Too much should not be expected of Summits, but one of the valuable things about them is that, at least temporarily, they concentrate the minds of the participants on a recognition of common problems, and on the need for the major industrial countries of the world to support each other in dealing with them.

In the last few years we in the European Community have put on a relatively poor economic performance in comparison with our major industrial partners in the United States and Japan. For a Community dedicated to economic integration and enjoying rich and diversified economies this may seem strange. It is indeed one of the curiosities of the Treaty of Rome that it catered for freer movement of goods, services, people and capital but set no objectives in the monetary field. Yet in the long run a common market without a common money system would make little sense. In the stable monetary conditions of the 50s and early 60s, perhaps this gap among our objectives was not of crucial importance. But when the cracks appeared in the Bretton Woods system and inflation began to accelerate, the Member States of the Community realised with greater clarity than before that the European union towards which they were striving could scarcely exist without a common monetary system. It was Raymond Barre, then Vice-President of the European Commission and now Prime Minister of France, who produced the first scheme for a European economic and monetary union.

It is perhaps worth asking how you would like to run your economy if you had a common tariff barrier round the United States, a common agricultural policy, even a common energy policy, but some exchange controls on every frontier between every American state, and state currencies, some strong, some weak, which constantly fluctuated against each other. Europe of the Community is not the same as America of the United States, and our evolution is following its own particular course. But it is no coincidence that those who are dedicated to the construction of Europe are dedicated also to the construction of an economic and monetary union.

In spite of an immense effort and acceptance of a commitment to economic and monetary union, the work set in train by Raymond Barre and carried forward by Pierre Werner, Prime Minister of Luxembourg, had disappointingly meagre results. The combined shocks of the collapse of the Bretton Woods system in 1971, the energy crisis of 1973 and their aftermath of monetary confusion made it very difficult for the European governments concerned to give effect to the undertakings into which they had entered. Indeed when I tried to re-launch the idea in a speech at Florence just over a year ago I was told that I was trying to resuscitate a very dead duck. I am glad to say that the duck turned out to be no more than asleep. Indeed, to pursue the analogy, it is beginning to spread its wings and will fly from the first of January next year.

How and why has this remarkable change taken place? First I think that we in Europe have become better aware of the evil effects which the movement of European currencies against each other has had on our ability to run our economies as we wish and continue the upward trend which only countries of broad geographical spread have managed in difficult circumstances to achieve. Community countries with strong currencies have found themselves hurt by lack of demand in countries with weak currencies, and weak currency countries have been unable to achieve the growth they so badly need through the risk of running exchange rate crises. Never has the need for the convergence of our European economies and the reduction — and evening out — of inflation rates among us been more apparent.

Second there has been the decline in the value of the US dollar, the continuing pivot of the international monetary system, systematically until 1971, unsystematically since then, which has obliged Europeans to take in more dollars than they want or need, and thus lose control of an essential element of economic management: their own money supply. The idea of creating a zone of monetary stability in Europe has therefore become a common objective about which there has been no dispute among any of us.

In the last nine months we have come a long way. I pay tribute to the inspiration, energy, and determination of Chancellor Schmidt of Germany and President Giscard d'Estaing of France who have provided the essential motor of the work which led to the agreement to create a European Monetary System at the beginning of last week. What we then did could well turn out to be the most important event in the building of Community Europe since the early days of the Treaty of Rome. It merits more than a careful examination; and if you will forgive me for being a little technical, I think it would be right for me to say a word or two about it now.

NEW EUROPEAN MONETARY SYSTEM

The essential features of the European Monetary System are first the creation of a system of fixed but adjustable exchange rates between member currencies; second the creation of a European Currency Unit or ECU, a basket of Community currencies, which will be used as an indicator of divergence between them; third the creation of a Community reserve asset, beginning with the deposit by Member States of 20 per cent of their gold and dollar reserves in exchange for credits denominated in ECUs; and last the provision of credit facilities of around 25 billion ECUs (or at the present rate of exchange 33 billion dollars).

I want to emphasise that Member States of the Community unanimously agreed to set up the European Monetary System on 1 January 1979. It is perhaps surprising when governments stick to the deadlines they set themselves, but this time the deadlines were fully respected. Yet as you know our success was not unqualified. To my own regret the British Government while supporting the system felt unable to participate in the exchange rate mechanism and the arrangements made for intervention. The governments of Italy and Ireland wanted more time to consider their position, and so were not able to commit themselves on the spot. Since then we have all heard of the courageous decision of the Italian Government to join the system, and now today that the Irish Government will do likewise. I warmly welcome this. Perhaps the essential point for the Community and the Commission over which I preside is that the system we have created is a Community system which will take its place alongside the other institutions of the Community and will be designed to serve the interests of all. The fact that it is such a system and includes in some form all members of the Community, even the one which has chosen not to participate in the exchange rate mechanism, should make it easier for it to join in all aspects of its work later on.

It has sometimes been suggested that the European Monetary System is in fact little more than an enlarged version of the exchange rate arrangement commonly known as the snake. The snake, which is in some ways an historic remnant of previous attempts to bring European currencies together, is in fact a very different animal. In the mechanisms of the snake there was no basket to indicate divergence between the currencies. There was no acceptance of the presumption of action by governments or central banks when the threshold of divergence was approached. The credits available were less than half those of the new system. No serious account was taken of the need for economic convergence. There was no accompanying provision for transfer of resources (which in the case of the European Monetary System will amount to 5 billion ECUs (or 6-1/2 billion dollars) in interest reduced loans to be taken up over five years). There was no real political commitment. Finally — most important of all — it was not a Community system and in its later years essentially a deutschmark zone.

I shall be very ready to answer any questions you may have about the European Monetary System. I hope in particular you will give me the opportunity to say more about its place among our wider objectives. It is true to the best traditions of the European Community, established since the early post-war activity of Jean Monnet [French statesman who helped establish and served as first president of the European Coal and Steel Community, forerunner of the European Economic Community], an economic weapon, valid in itself, but also serving a wider political aim, that of underpinning and developing our unity, so that we may be more effective partners with you in discharging our world responsibilities.

There have been some apprehensions in the United States about the effect of the system on the international monetary system and the US dollar which continues as its essential pivot. I believe that those fears have been exaggerated, and I was delighted to find during my visit here that they were not shared by members of the Administration. Indeed I was greatly heartened by the welcome which the Administration has given to the creation of the European Monetary System, a welcome which President Carter repeated to me yesterday. The European Monetary System is designed not only to establish a zone of monetary stability in Europe but also to contribute to greater stability in the world monetary system as a whole. If it is true that one of the external factors which weighed in the creation of the system was the decline in the value of the dollar earlier this year, it is equally true that we have a vital interest in a stable dollar if the system is to be properly born and well-nurtured in its infancy. To try to set the system in place at a time of international monetary storm and confusion would make our task much more difficult. Some people have suggested that the creation of the ECU and the eventual establishment of a European monetary fund could precipitously and dangerously weaken the role of the dollar as a medium of international exchange. Let me therefore emphasise that although we shall be creating a new reserve unit in the ECU, its use will be limited to transactions between the central banks of the Community. It cannot therefore be a threat to the dollar the strength of which is as much in our interest as yours, the stability of which is made even more necessary to us by this immediate, major and delicate task we are now undertaking.

There are many other aspects of the life of the Community about which I could have spoken today. There is the now imminent prospect of its enlargement to include Greece, and then Portugal and Spain, and the need to strengthen its central institution to carry the additional weight. There is also the prospect of the first direct elections to the European Parliament next June. But you have heard enough from me today on what is, I think the central most important event in our development. Throughout its history the Community has always moved forward unevenly. It is no easy task to bring together the nations of Europe with their differences of history, traditions, civilization and national outlook. But I believe that the friends and well-wishers whom we have in the United States should take heart from what we have achieved. Pray continue to encourage us with your understanding and your cooperation.

COURT ON SEARCHES AND EVIDENCE
December 5, 1978

In a 5-4 ruling Dec. 5, the Supreme Court held that passengers did not have the right to challenge at a trial the introduction of evidence seized by police in a warrantless search of a car in which they were riding.

The case of Rakas v. *Illinois came to the court after state courts rejected the efforts of two men, convicted of armed robbery on the basis of evidence seized from a car in which they were riding, to have that evidence suppressed. The two men argued that because police had not had a search warrant authorizing their examination of the car, the evidence taken from it — a rifle and shells — was illegally seized and should not be used in court.*

The state courts and the Supreme Court rejected that claim, holding that because the men owned neither the car nor the gun they lacked legal standing to ask a court to suppress the evidence.

The Supreme Court majority based its rejection of the challenge in this case on the fact that the men attempting to win suppression of the evidence neither owned the automobile nor demonstrated any legitimate expectation of privacy in it. The Fourth Amendment right to be secure against unreasonable search and seizure is a personal right, wrote Justice William H. Rehnquist for the majority: "A person who is aggrieved by an illegal search and seizure only through the introduction of damaging evidence secured by a search of a third person's premises or property has not had any of his Fourth Amendment rights infringed."

Rehnquist, joined in the majority by Chief Justice Warren E. Burger, Justices Potter Stewart, Lewis F. Powell Jr. and Harry A. Blackmun, also indicated a reluctance to expand the group of persons who could invoke the so-called "exclusionary rule" to suppress illegally obtained evidence, regardless of its validity, simply because it was obtained in violation of the Fourth Amendment or other constitutional provision.

But in 1960 the court had allowed a person legitimately present in someone else's apartment to challenge, and win exclusion of, evidence seized in an illegal search of that apartment. In that opinion the court stated that "anyone legitimately on premises where a search occurs may challenge its legality." The case was Jones v. United States.

That statement was too broad, wrote Rehnquist, and did not apply to the passengers in the automobile in this case. "Jones had a legitimate expectation of privacy in the premises he was using and therefore could claim the protection of the Fourth Amendment with respect to a governmental invasion of those premises," he continued, but the two men in this case demonstrated no such legitimate expectation of privacy in the interior of the car in which they were passengers.

In Dissent

"Insofar as passengers are concerned, the Court's opinion today declares an 'open season' on automobiles," wrote Justice Byron R. White for the four dissenters. He was joined in that opinion by Justices William J. Brennan Jr., Thurgood Marshall and John Paul Stevens.

They criticized the majority for tying the Fourth Amendment guarantee to property law concepts: "The court today holds that the Fourth Amendment protects property, not people." The ruling, continued White, "has no support in the Court's controlling decisions, in the logic of the Fourth Amendment, or in common sense. . . ."

Suggesting that the real impetus behind the majority's ruling was its dissatisfaction with "the practical impact of the exclusionary rule," White recommended that the court "face the issue of that rule's continued validity squarely instead of distorting other doctrines in an attempt to reach what are perceived as the correct results in specific cases."

Following are excerpts from the Supreme Court ruling in Rakas v. Illinois, *delivered Dec. 5, 1978, that broadened police search power:*

No. 77-5781

Frank L. Rakas and Lonnie L. King, Petitioners, v. State of Illinois.	On Writ of Certiorari to the Appellate Court of Illinois, Third District.

[December 5, 1978]

MR. JUSTICE REHNQUIST delivered the opinion of the Court.

Petitioners were convicted of armed robbery in the Circuit Court of Kankakee County, Ill., and their convictions were affirmed on appeal. At their trial, the prosecution offered into evidence a sawed-off rifle and rifle shells that had been seized by police during a search of an automobile in which petitioners had been passengers. Neither petitioner is the owner of the automobile and neither has ever asserted that he owned the rifle or shells seized. The Illinois Appellate Court held that petitioners lacked standing to object to the allegedly unlawful search and seizure and denied their motion to suppress the evidence. We granted certiorari in light of the obvious importance of the issues raised to the administration of criminal justice . . . and now affirm.

I

Because we are not here concerned with the issue of probable cause, a brief description of the events leading to the search of the automobile will suffice. A police officer on a routine patrol received a radio call notifying him of a robbery of a clothing store in Bourbonnais, Ill., and describing the getaway car. Shortly thereafter, the officer spotted an automobile which he thought might be the getaway car. After following the car for some time and after the arrival of assistance, he and several other officers stopped the vehicle. The occupants of the automobile, petitioners and two female companions, were ordered out of the car and after the occupants had left the car, two officers searched the interior of the vehicle. They discovered a box of rifle shells in the glove compartment, which had been locked, and a sawed-off rifle under the front passenger seat. . . . After discovering the rifle and the shells, the officers took petitioners to the station and placed them under arrest.

Before trial petitioners moved to suppress the rifle and shells seized from the car on the ground that the search violated the Fourth and Fourteenth Amendments. They conceded that they did not own the automobile and were simply passengers; the owner of the car had been the driver of the vehicle at the time of the search. Nor did they assert that they owned the rifle or the shells seized. The prosecutor challenged petitioners' standing to object to the lawfulness of the search of the car because neither the car, the shells nor the rifle belonged to them. The trial court agreed that petitioners lacked standing and denied the motion to suppress the evidence. . . . In view of this holding, the court did not determine whether there was probable cause for the search and seizure. On appeal after petitioners' conviction, the Appellate Court of Illinois, Third Judicial District, affirmed the trial court's denial of petitioners' motion to suppress because it held that "without a proprietary or other similar interest in the automobile, a mere passenger therein lacks standing to challenge the legality of the search of the vehicle.". . . The court stated:

"We believe that defendants failed to establish any prejudice to their own constitutional rights because they were not persons aggrieved by the unlawful search and seizure. . . . They wrongly seek to establish prejudice only through the use of evidence gathered as a consequence of a search and seizure directed at someone else and fail to prove an invasion of their own privacy. . . ."

The Illinois Supreme Court denied petitioners leave to appeal.

II

Petitioners first urge us to relax or broaden the rule of standing enunciated in *Jones* v. *United States* . . . (1960), so that any criminal defendant at whom a search was "directed" would have standing to contest the legality of that search and object to the admission at trial of evidence obtained as a result of the search. Alternatively, petitioners argue that they have standing to object to the search under *Jones* because they were "legitimately on [the] premises" at the time of the search.

The concept of standing discussed in *Jones* focuses on whether the person seeking to challenge the legality of a search as the basis for suppressing evidence was himself the "victim" of the search or seizure. . . . Adoption of the so-called "target" theory advanced by petitioners would in effect permit a defendant to assert that a violation of the Fourth Amendment rights of a third party entitled him to have evidence suppressed at his trial. If we reject petitioners' request for a broadened rule of standing such as this, and reaffirm the holding of *Jones* and other cases that Fourth Amendment rights are personal rights that may not be asserted vicariously, we will have occasion to re-examine the "standing" terminology emphasized in *Jones*. For we are not at all sure that the determination of a motion to suppress is materially aided by labeling the inquiry identified in *Jones* as one of standing, rather than simply recognizing it as one involving the substantive question of whether or not the proponent of the motion to suppress has had his own Fourth Amendment rights infringed by the search and seizure which he seeks to challenge. We shall therefore consider in turn petitioners' target theory, the necessity for continued adherence to the notion of standing discussed in *Jones* as a concept that is theoretically distinct from the merits of a defendant's Fourth Amendment claim, and finally, the proper disposition of petitioners' ultimate claim in this case.

A

We decline to extend the rule of standing in Fourth Amendment cases in the manner suggested by petitioners. As we stated in *Alderman* v. *United States* . . . (1969), "Fourth Amendment rights are personal rights which, like some other constitutional rights, may not be asserted vicariously.". . . A person who is aggrieved by an illegal search and seizure only through the introduction of damaging evidence secured by a search of a third person's premises or property has not had any of his Fourth Amendment rights infringed. . . . And since the exclusionary rule is an attempt to effectuate the guarantees of the Fourth Amendment . . . it is proper to permit only defendants whose Fourth Amendment rights have been violated to benefit from the rule's protections. . . . There is no reason to think that a party whose rights have been infringed will not, if evidence is used against him, have ample motivation to move to suppress it. . . . Even if such a person is not a defendant in the action, he may be able to recover damages for the violation of his Fourth Amendment rights . . . or seek redress under state law for invasion of privacy or trespass.

In support of their target theory, petitioners rely on the following quotation from *Jones:*

"In order to qualify as a 'person aggrieved by an unlawful search and seizure' one must have been a victim of a search or seizure, *one against whom the search was directed,* as distinguished from one who claims prejudice only through the use of evidence gathered as a consequence of a search or seizure directed at someone else.". . .

The above-quoted statement from *Jones* suggests that the italicized language was meant merely as a parenthetical equivalent of the previous phrase "a victim of a search or seizure." To the extent that the language might be read more broadly, it is dictum which was impliedly repudiated in *Alderman* v. *United States* . . . and which we now expressly reject. In *Jones,* the Court set forth two alternative holdings: it established a rule of "automatic" standing to contest an allegedly illegal search where the same possession needed to establish standing is an essential element of the offense charged; and second, it stated that "anyone legitimately on premises where a search occurs may challenge its legality by way of a motion to suppress.". . . Had the Court intended to adopt the target theory now put forth by petitioners, neither of the above two holdings would have been necessary since Jones was the "target" of the police search in that case. . . .

. . .Each time the exclusionary rule is applied it exacts a substantial social cost for the vindication of Fourth Amendment rights. Relevant and reliable evidence is kept from the trier of fact and the search for truth at trial is deflected. . . . Since our cases generally have held that one whose Fourth Amendment rights are violated may successfully suppress evidence obtained in the course of an illegal search and seizure, misgivings as to the benefit of enlarging the class of persons who may invoke that rule are properly considered when deciding whether to expand standing to assert Fourth Amendment violations.

B

Had we accepted petitioners' request to allow persons other than those whose own Fourth Amendment rights were violated by a challenged search and seizure to suppress evidence obtained in the course of such police activity, it would be appropriate to retain *Jones'* use of standing in Fourth Amendment analysis. Under petitioners' target theory, a court could determine that a defendant had standing to invoke the exclusionary rule without having to inquire into the substantive question of whether the challenged search or seizure violated the Fourth Amendment rights of that particular defendant. However, having rejected petitioners' target theory and reaffirmed the principle that the "rights assured by the Fourth Amendment are personal rights, [which] . . . may be enforced by exclusion of evidence only at the instance of one whose own protection was infringed by the search and seizure," . . . the question necessarily arises whether it serves any useful analytical purpose to consider this principle a matter of standing, distinct from the merits of a defendant's Fourth Amendment claim. We can think of no decided cases from this Court that would have come out differently had we concluded, as we do now, that the type of standing requirement discussed in *Jones* and reaffirmed today is more properly subsumed under substantive Fourth Amendment doctrine. Rigorous application of the principle that the rights secured by this Amendment are personal, in place of a notion of "standing," will produce no additional situations in which evidence must be excluded. The inquiry under either approach is the same. But we think the better analysis forthrightly focuses on the extent of a particular defendant's rights under the Fourth Amendment, rather than on any theoretically separate, but invariably intertwined concept of standing. The Court in *Jones* also may have been aware that there was a certain artificiality to analyzing this question in terms of standing because in at least three separate places in its opinion the Court placed that term within quotation marks. . . .

It should be emphasized that nothing we say here casts the least doubt on cases which recognize that, as a general proposition, the issue of standing involves two inquiries: first, whether the proponent of a particular legal right has alleged "injury in fact," and, second, whether the proponent is asserting his own legal rights and interests rather than basing his claim for relief upon the rights of third parties. . . . But this Court's long history of insistence that Fourth Amendment rights are personal in nature has already answered many of these traditional standing inquiries, and we think that definition of those rights is more properly placed within the purview of substantive Fourth Amendment law than within that of standing. . . .

Analyzed in these terms, the question is whether the challenged search or seizure violated the Fourth Amendment rights of a criminal defendant who seeks to exclude the evidence obtained during it. That inquiry in turn requires a determination of whether the disputed search and seizure has infringed an interest of the defendant which the Fourth Amendment was designed to protect. We are under no illusion that by dispensing with the rubric of standing used in *Jones* we have rendered any simpler the determination of whether the proponent of a motion to suppress is entitled to contest the legality of a search and seizure. But by frankly recognizing that this aspect of the analysis belongs more properly under the heading of substantive Fourth Amendment doctrine than under the heading of standing, we think the decision of this issue will rest on sounder logical footing.

C

Here petitioners, who were passengers occupying a car which they neither owned nor leased, seek to analogize their position to that of the defendant in *Jones* v. *United States.* . . . In *Jones,* petitioner was present at the time of the search of an apartment which was owned by a friend. The friend had given Jones permission to use the apartment and a key to it, with which Jones had admitted himself on the day of the search. He had a suit and shirt at the apartment and had slept there "maybe a night," but his home was elsewhere. At the time of the search, Jones was the only occupant of the apartment because the lessee was away for a period of several days. . . . Under these circumstances, this Court stated that while one wrongfully on the premises could not move to suppress evidence obtained as a result of searching them, "anyone legitimately on premises where a search occurs may challenge its legality.". . . Petitioners argue that their occupancy of the automobile in question was comparable to that of Jones in the apartment and that they therefore have standing to contest the legality of the search — or as we have rephrased the inquiry, that they, like Jones, had their Fourth Amendment rights violated by the search.

We do not question the conclusion in *Jones* that the defendant in that case suffered a violation of his personal Fourth Amendment rights if the search in question were unlawful. Nonetheless, we believe that the phrase "legitimately on premises" coined in *Jones* creates too broad a gauge for measurement of Fourth Amendment rights. For example, applied literally, this statement would permit a casual visitor who has never seen, or been permitted to visit the basement of another's house to object to a search of the basement if the visitor happened to be in the kitchen of the house at the time of the search. Likewise, a casual visitor who walks into a house one minute before a search of the house commences and leaves one minute after the search ends would be able to contest the legality of the search. The first visitor would have absolutely no interest or legitimate expectation of privacy in the basement, the second would have none in the house, and it advances no purpose served by the Fourth Amendment to permit either of them to object to the lawfulness of the search.

We think that *Jones* on its facts merely stands for the unremarkable proposition that a person can have a legally sufficient interest in a place other than his own home so that the Fourth Amendment protects him from unreasonable government intrusion into that place. . . . In defining the scope of that interest, we adhere to the view expressed in *Jones* and echoed in later cases that arcane distinctions developed in property and tort law between guests, licensees, invitees, and the like, ought not to control. . . . But the *Jones* statement that a person need only be "legitimately on premises" in order to challenge the validity of the search of a dwelling place cannot be taken in its full sweep beyond the facts of that case.

Katz v. *United States,* . . . (1967), provides guidance in defining the scope of the interest protected by the Fourth Amendment. . . . [T]he Court in *Katz* held that capacity to claim the protection of the Fourth Amendment depends not upon a property right in the invaded place but upon whether the person who claims the protection of the Amendment has a legitimate expectation of privacy in the invaded place. . . . Viewed in this manner, the holding in *Jones* can best be explained by the fact that Jones had a legitimate expectation of privacy in the premises he was using and therefore could claim the protection of the Fourth Amendment with respect to a governmental invasion of those premises, even though his "interest" in those premises might not have been a recognized property interest at common law. . . .

D

Judged by the foregoing analysis, petitioners' claims must fail. They asserted neither a property nor a possessory interest in the automobile, nor an interest in the property seized. And as we have previously indicated, the fact that they were "legitimately on [the] premises" in the sense that they were in the car with the permission of its owner is not determinative of whether they had a legitimate expectation of privacy in the particular areas of the automobile searched. It is unnecessary for us to decide here whether the same expectations of privacy are warranted in a car as would be justified in a dwelling place in analogous circumstances. We have on numerous occasions pointed out that cars are not to be treated identically with houses or apartments for Fourth Amendment purposes. . . . But here petitioners' claim is one which would fail even in an analogous situation in a dwelling place since they made no showing that they had any legitimate expectation of privacy in the glove compartment or area under the seat of the car in which they were merely passengers. Like the trunk of an automobile, these are areas in which a passenger *qua* passenger simply would not normally have a legitimate expectation of privacy. . . .

Jones v. *United States* . . . (1960) and *Katz* v. *United States* . . . (1967) involved significantly different factual circumstances. Jones not only had permission to use the apartment of his friend, but had a key to the apartment with which he admitted himself on the day of the search and kept possessions in the apartment. Except with respect to his friend, Jones had complete dominion and control over the apartment and could exclude others from it. Likewise in *Katz,* the defendant occupied the telephone booth, shut the door behind him to exclude all others and paid the toll, which "entitled him to assume that the word he utter[ed] into the mouthpiece would not be broadcast to the world.". . . Katz and Jones could legitimately expect privacy in the areas which were the subject of the search and seizure they sought to contest. No such showing was made by these petitioners with respect to those portions of the automobile which were searched and from which incriminating evidence was seized.

IV

The Illinois courts were therefore correct in concluding that it was unnecessary to decide whether the search of the car might have violated the rights secured to someone else by the Fourth and Fourteenth Amendments to the United States Constitution. Since it did not violate any rights of these petitioners, their judgment of conviction is

Affirmed.

MR. JUSICE WHITE, with whom MR. JUSTICE BRENNAN, MR. JUSTICE MARSHALL, and MR. JUSTICE STEVENS join, dissenting.

The Court today holds that the Fourth Amendment protects property, not people, and specifically that a legitimate occupant of an automobile may not invoke the exclusionary rule and challenge a search of that vehicle unless he happens to own or have a possessory interest in it. Though professing to acknowledge that the primary purpose of the Fourth Amendment's prohibition of unreasonable searches is the protection of privacy — not property — the Court nonetheless effectively ties the application of the Fourth Amendment and the exclusionary rule in this situation to property law concepts. Insofar as passengers are concerned, the Court's opinion today declares an "open season" on automobiles. However unlawful stopping and searching a car may be, absent a possessory or ownership interest, no "mere" passenger may object, regardless of his relationship to the owner. Because the majority's conclusion has no support in the Court's controlling decisions, in the logic of the Fourth Amendment, or in common sense, I must respectfully dissent. If the Court is troubled by the practical impact of the exclusionary rule, it should face the issue of that rule's continued validity squarely instead of distorting other doctrines in an attempt to reach what are perceived as the correct results in specific cases. . . .

Two interesting doctrines long established in this Court's opinions control here. The first is the recognition of some cognizable level of privacy in the interior of an automobile. Though the reasonableness of the expectation of privacy in a vehicle may be somewhat weaker than that in a home . . . "[a] search, even of an automobile, is a substantial invasion of privacy. To protect that privacy from official arbitrariness, the Court has always regarded probable cause as the minimum requirement for a lawful search." *United States* v. *Ortiz* . . . [1975] So far, the Court has not strayed from this application of the Fourth Amendment.

The second tenet is that when a person is legitimately present in a private place, his right to privacy is protected from unreasonable governmental interference even if he does not own the premises. . . .

These two fundamental aspects of Fourth Amendment law demand that petitioners be permitted to challenge the search and seizure of the automobile in this case. It is of no significance that a car is different for Fourth Amendment purposes from a house, for if there is some protection for the privacy of an automobile then the only relevant analogy is between a person legitimately in someone else's vehicle and a person legitimately in someone else's house. If both strands of the Fourth Amendment doctrine adumbrated above are valid, the Court must reach a different result.

Instead, it cho[o]ses to eviscerate the *Jones* principle, an action in which I am unwilling to participate.

. . .The proposition today overruled was stated most directly in *Mancusi* v. *DeForte* . . . (1968): "the protection of the Amendment depends not upon a property right in the invaded place but upon whether the area was one in which there was a reasonable expectation of freedom from governmental intrusion. . . .

In sum, one consistent theme in our decisions under the Fourth Amendment has been, until now, that "the Amendment does not shield only those who have title to the searched premises.". . . Though there comes a point when use of an area is shared with so many that one simply cannot reasonably expect seclusion . . . short of that limit a person legitimately on private premises knows the others allowed there and, though his privacy is not absolute, is entitled to expect that he is sharing it only with those persons and that governmental officials will intrude only with consent or by complying with the Fourth Amendment. . . .

It is true that the Court asserts that it is not limiting the Fourth Amendment bar against unreasonable searches to the protection of property rights, but in reality it is doing exactly that. Petitioners were in a private place with the permission of the owner, but the Court states that that is not sufficient to establish entitlement to a legitimate expectation of privacy. . . . But if that is not sufficient, what would be? We are not told, and it is hard to imagine anything short of a property interest that would satisfy the majority. Insofar as the Court's rationale is concerned, no passenger in an automobile, without an ownership or possessory interest and regardless of his relationship to the owner, may claim Fourth Amendment protection against illegal stops and searches of the automobile in which he is rightfully present. The Court approves the result in *Jones,* but it fails to give any explanation why the facts in *Jones* differ, in a fashion material to the Fourth Amendment, from the facts here. More importantly, how is the Court able to avoid answering the question why presence in a private place with the owner's permission is insufficient? If it is "tautological to fall back on the notion that those expectations of privacy which are legitimate depend primarily on cases deciding exclusionary rule issues in criminal cases,". . . then it surely must be tautological to decide that issue simply by unadorned fiat.

As a control on governmental power, the Fourth Amendment assures that some expectations of privacy are justified and will be protected from official intrusion. That should be true in this instance, for if protected zones of privacy can only be purchased or obtained by possession of property, then much of our daily lives will be unshielded from unreasonable governmental prying, and the reach of the Fourth Amendment will have been narrowed to protect chiefly those with possessory interests in real or personal property. I had thought that *Katz* firmly established that the Fourth Amendment was intended as more than simply a trespass law applicable to the government. Katz had no possessory interest in the public telephone booth, at least no more than petitioners had in their friend's car;

Katz was simply legitimately present. And the decision in *Katz* was based not on property rights but on the theory that it was essential to securing "conditions favorable to the pursuit of happiness" that the expectation of privacy in question be recognized.

At most, one could say that perhaps the Constitution provides some degree less protection for the personal freedom from unreasonable governmental intrusion when one does not have a possessory interest in the invaded private place. But that would only change the extent of the protection; it would not free police to do the unreasonable, as does the decision today. And since the accused should be entitled to litigate the application of the Fourth Amendment where his privacy interest is merely arguable, the failure to allow such litigation here is the more incomprehensible. . . .

The Court's holding is contrary not only to our past decisions and the logic of the Fourth Amendment, but also to the everyday expectations of privacy that we all share. Because of that, it is unworkable in all the various situations that arise in real life. If the owner of the car had not only invited petitioners to join her but had said to them, "I give you a temporary possessory interest in my vehicle so that you will share the right to privacy that the Supreme Court says that I own," then apparently the majority would reverse. But people seldom say such things, though they may mean their invitation to encompass them if only they had thought of the problem. If the nonowner were the spouse or child of the owner, would the Court recognize a sufficient interest? If so, would distant relatives somehow have more of an expectation of privacy than close friends? What if the nonowner were driving with the owner's permission? Would nonowning drivers have more of an expectation of privacy than mere passengers? What about a passenger in a taxicab? *Katz* expressly recognized protection for such passengers. Why should Fourth Amendment rights be present when one pays a cabdriver for a ride but be absent when one is given a ride by a friend?

The distinctions the Court would draw are based on relationships between private parties, but the Fourth Amendment is concerned with the relationship of one of those parties to the government. Divorced as it is from the purpose of the Fourth Amendment, the Court's essentially property-based rationale can satisfactorily answer none of the questions posed above. That is reason enough to reject it. The *Jones* rule is relatively easily applied by police and courts; the rule announced today will not provide law enforcement officials with a bright line between the protected and the unprotected. Only rarely will police know whether one private party has or has not been granted a sufficient possessory or other interest by another private party. Surely in this case the officers had no such knowledge. The Court's rule will ensnare defendants and police in needless litigation over factors that should not be determinative of Fourth Amendment rights.

More importantly, the ruling today undercuts the force of the exclusionary rule in the one area in which its use is most certainly justified — the deterrence of bad-faith violations of the Fourth Amendment. . . . This decision invites police to engage in patently unreasonable searches every time an automobile contains more than one occupant. Should something be found, only the owner of the vehicle, or of the item, will have standing to seek suppression, and the evidence will presumably be usable against the other occupants. The danger of such bad faith is especially high in cases such as this one where the officers are only after the passengers and can usually infer accurately that the driver is the owner. The suppression remedy for those owners in whose vehicles something is found and who are charged with crime is small consolation for all those owners *and* occupants whose privacy will be needlessly invaded by officers following mistaken hunches not rising to the level of probable cause but operated on in the knowledge that someone in a crowded car will probably be unprotected if contraband or incriminating evidence happens to be found. After this decision, police will have little to lose by unreasonably searching vehicles occupied by more than one person.

Of course, most police officers will decline the Court's invitation and will continue to do their jobs as best they can in accord with the Fourth Amendment. But the very purpose of the Bill of Rights was to answer the justified fear that governmental agents cannot be left totally to their own devices, and the Bill of Rights is enforceable in the courts because human experience teaches that not all such officials will otherwise adhere to the stated precepts. Some policemen simply do act in bad faith, even if for understandable ends, and some deterrent is needed. In the rush to limit the applicability of the exclusionary rule somewhere, anywhere, the Court ignores precedent, logic, and common sense to exclude the rule's operation from situations in which, paradoxically, it is justified and needed.

DEMOCRATIC MIDTERM CONFERENCE
December 8-10, 1978

Those of the 1,633 delegates to the Democratic Party's midterm confer-ence who showed up in Memphis, Tenn., Dec. 8-10, voted to require an equal split of men and women delegates to the 1980 nominating convention and to ban the last remaining type of winner-take-all primary.

Other than those votes, cast on the first day of the three-day conference, it was generally agreed that little else of substance occurred. The confer-ence was required as one of the reforms adopted by the party in 1972. President Carter had not even wanted it to be held. Part of the criticism for holding the conference was its cost — $640,000 to a party that began the year with a $2.5 million debt.

The central attention of the conference thus focused on the austerity budget drafted by Carter and on a speech by Sen. Edward M. Kennedy, D-Mass., attacking it. Inevitable comparisons were made between Kennedy and Carter, comparisons that linked them as possible opponents for the 1980 presidential nomination. Kennedy's speech to a second-day workshop on national health insurance contrasted sharply to Carter's low-key and highly partisan keynote address the previous day. Neither speaker stayed around for the debate on issues held the final day of the midterm conference.

Only a few fights developed over policy resolutions and the White House managed to maintain control. It had to make only a few concessions, primarily on the budget resolution. But that compromise had been worked out between Carter and Kennedy before the conference began.

Carter's Speech

Carter's keynote address Dec. 8 had all the usual earmarks of opening speeches to a national convention. He attacked the past of the Republicans and praised the work of the Democrats.

In defense of his austerity budget and the criticism he knew was coming, Carter said that inflation was robbing "working families, the pensioner, the widow and the poor." He said it was "an illusion to believe we can preserve a commitment to compassionate and progressive government if we fail to bring inflation under control." To obtain that control, Carter was proposing across-the-board cuts in federal spending, including cuts in welfare programs. But defense spending cuts were expected either to be smaller or funding itself increased.

The only sustained applause Carter received during his speech came when he called on the delegates to "join forces to wipe out discrimination based on sex and make the equal rights amendment the law of the land, and give voting rights to the people of the District of Columbia."

Kennedy's Speech

In widely noted contrast, Kennedy brought the delegates to their feet Dec. 9 when he pounded with his fist and attacked the proposed cuts in welfare spending. He warned, "The party that tore itself apart over Vietnam in the 1960s cannot afford to tear itself apart today over budget cuts in basic social programs."

He said, "We cannot accept a policy that cuts spending to the bone in areas like jobs and health, but allows billions of dollars in wasteful spending for tax subsidies to continue, and adds even greater fat and waste through inflationary spending for defense." Kennedy demanded that a national health insurance plan be acted upon promptly.

Resolutions Adopted

Before the conference, Kennedy had wanted a resolution that said it was the policy of the Democratic Party to have a vote on a national health insurance plan immediately. Carter favored a slower approach and did not want a timetable included in the resolution. A compromise stating that Congress should pass the legislation by the end of the 96th Congress finally was adopted.

The closest vote, 822 to 521, occurred on a resolution praising Carter's proposed budget, over a more critical compromise offered by Douglas A. Fraser, president of the United Auto Workers. The compromise attacked the military spending plans and called for a budget at least equal to "the current services budget for human and social services for 1980."

Also voted was a resolution calling on Congress to approve whatever strategic arms limitation agreement is reached with the Soviet Union.

Rules Changes

Rules changes adopted were expected to have an important effect on the 1980 Democratic presidential nomination. Chief among them was one that would require state delegations to be equally divided between men and women.

Another would ban single-member delegate districts, criticized as a last bastion of winner-take-all primaries that the party had intended to be outlawed in previous years. Thus, every delegate district regardless of size will have to elect several delegates and award some to any candidate who garners a respectable share of the primary vote. Another rules change set a time limit during which nominating caucuses, conventions and primaries can be held during a presidential nominating year.

Those three rules changes, plus others that received little conference debate, were the outgrowth of recommendations made by a commission formed after the 1976 convention to study possible improvements in the nominating system. Formally known as the Democratic National Committee's special Commission on Presidential Nomination and Party Structure, it was more commonly known as the Winograd Commission, after its chairman, Michigan party chief Morley A. Winograd.

> *Following are the texts of Carter's keynote address Dec. 8, 1978, and of Kennedy's speech Dec. 9, 1978, to a health workshop and the resolutions and rules changes adopted at the Democratic midterm conference in Memphis, Tenn., Dec. 8-10, 1978. (Boldface headings in brackets have been added by Congressional Quarterly to highlight the organization of the text.):*

CARTER KEYNOTE ADDRESS

...I have to say that I've not been to very many, and I don't know what I will experience in the future, but so far I like Democratic conventions very much.

It is an honor for me to speak before the most open, honest, progressive, compassionate political organization in the world today, our Democratic Party. And we are also the oldest continuing political party in the world. And after the American people spoke so clearly last month, we are still the majority political party in the United States, and we're going to stay that way.

Ours is a party of practical dreamers. Thomas Jefferson conceived of the United States of America as no other nation had ever tried to be —

dedicated to human fulfillment, where individual liberty was guaranteed. But Thomas Jefferson also founded a university; he collected a national library; he planned beautiful cities; he mapped the wilderness; and as a farmer, he invented a better plow — typical of Democrats. Time and again in our history, the Democratic Party has given new life and new meaning to our Nation's oldest dreams.

When a generation of hard-working Americans was robbed by the Depression of a lifetime of savings, the New Deal restored economic security and vision and brought new hope because of the vision of Franklin D. Roosevelt.

When a devastated Europe was threatened by economic chaos, political fragmentation, and alien ideologies, the Marshall plan and NATO sustained and strengthened our crucial alliance because of the courage of Harry Truman.

And when an uncontrolled arms race threatened the devastation of nuclear war, a test ban treaty took the first crucial steps toward peace under the bold leadership of John F. Kennedy.

When black Americans challenged our Nation's conscience to fulfill the historic pledge of equal rights, a nation finally answered, "We Shall Overcome," and Democrats wrote the promise of equal opportunity in law, led by and inspired by a great Texan, Lyndon B. Johnson.

I'm proud to be a member of the Democratic Party. And I'm also proud to be a member of a party of others who should have been President, like Adlai Stevenson and Hubert Humphrey.

We Democrats share with the founders of this Nation a faith in the good sense and the decency of average Americans. We are a pioneer people who learned early that survival and our dreams depended on hard work and courage and caring for one another. America's founding principle remains the most revolutionary idea in the world today — that all people are born free.

The dreams, the courage, the ideals of the American people have never been lost. But for too many years, some of our leaders did not reflect that faith. The challenge of government in America is to tap the greatness of a free people, but, for a long time, government failed that challenge.

We have passed through a painful decade — a tragic war abroad and bitter division at home; millions in unemployment lines and the highest inflation since the War Between the States; break-ins and buggings, and our Nation's highest public trust betrayed. Democrats will never permit such anguish and embarrassment to happen in the Nation which we love.

[Party Record]

For too many years, the most open society in history had a government that operated in secrecy. We pledged an open government in 1976 which the American people could trust.

When government operates in the shadow and is complicated, bloated, and impossible to understand, the best financed, the most powerful and often the most selfish lobbies have the advantage. Average citizens, the poor and the weak, who seek no special favors, are denied their rightful voice. We are tearing down the barriers between Americans and our Government. We've already passed new ethics legislation. The Government of the United States today belongs to the people of the United States, and not to the power brokers. And we're going to keep it that way. And you can depend on it.

Under this administration, we have restricted the use of wiretaps. No law-abiding American should ever have to live in fear that our Government will open mail, break in a home, or eavesdrop on private conversations. Under this administration, we will honor personal privacy.

Instead of leadership by veto and government by stalemate we now have a new Democratic partnership: President and Congress, Governors and mayors, legislators and local officials. The Congress has rarely had a more able and respected leadership, and certainly no President has ever had two better allies than Speaker Tip O'Neill [D-Mass.] and Majority Leader Robert Byrd [D-W.Va.].

For the first time in 200 years, the Nation's second highest office is a position of full responsibility. The Vice President is my eyes and my ears. His wisdom and his rapidly increasing experience have benefited our country time and again, at home and abroad. And I know that each one of you share my deep respect and gratitude for the leadership of Vice President Fritz Mondale.

Two years ago, the most productive people in the world were governed by a wasteful and an inefficient bureaucracy. Republican Presidential candidates said they wanted to run government in the worst possible way, and that's exactly what they did. We Democrats pledged to have government as good as the American people, and that's exactly what we are doing.

Democrats do not believe that government should solve every problem or substitute for private initiative. But I have seen the power of rural electrification programs transform the life of a young farmboy in the rural South. And I know what it meant to my own people to eliminate typhoid and malaria, polio and cholera. And I've seen, as has my own wife, Rosalynn, retarded youngsters come alive with excitement and pride, learning new skills because a mental health program run by the Government reached out to them with love.

When government fails to deliver promised services, when redtape, paperwork, bureaucratic waste of time and tax dollars, those who suffer most — those who suffer most — are the ones who depend on government the most. We are cutting redtape, throwing out ridiculous regulations, reorganizing government, and eliminating millions of hours of paperwork. We've breathed new energy and initiative into the Federal civil service for the first time in a hundred years. We Democrats are trying to make government competent so that it can be truly compassionate, and we will achieve both those goals together, competence and compassion.

Those who rob from government with waste, theft, fraud, abuse, steal precious resources that could have helped a child get out of poverty with a head start, trained an unemployed youngster for a job, built a decent home for a family, provided legal services for the poor, or nursed an older American back to health. The stolen tax dollars come from every steelworker, every store clerk, every teacher, every farmer. This administration — and the new Inspectors General will help — will continue to root out every instance of fraud and theft and abuse, and we will prosecute the guilty to the full extent of the law.

[Jobs and Economy]

For too many years, our free enterprise system was hobbled by massive unemployment, inflation, and an energy crisis that grew worse every year. Harry Truman spoke for every Democrat when he said, "We do not propose, like some people, to meet today's problems by saying that they do not exist, and tomorrow's problems by wishing tomorrow would never come."

We have been willing to confront the difficult and the complicated energy problem, and we are now getting it under control. If we join together as a people, I see an America of the future, strong and secure and free of the fear of energy shortages. I see American genius and technology harnessing solar power for millions of homes and buildings and creating thousands of new jobs. And I see America's achievements offering new hope to an energy-starved world.

In the last 2 years, we have created more than 6-1/2 million new jobs, an all-time record. And we're not through yet. We've cut unemployment by more than 25 percent. The Republicans say they favor work, not welfare. But we Democrats have reduced the welfare rolls by 1.3 million Americans, by giving them new jobs. We have already saved more than $20 billion in welfare payments and unemployment compensation. We still have much more to do. Our Democratic partnership will continue to put America back to work.

After a Republican recession and a housing depression, our economy has grown 9-1/2 percent. Last year we built 2 million new homes. Corporate profits have increased, in 2 years, 37 percent. Alben Barkley said, "If you want to live like a Republican, be sure to vote Democratic."

A Republican administration squeezed us farmers — the most productive in the world — by boosting the profits of middlemen, by embargoing shipments of American grain overseas, and by dictating the decisions that farmers should make themselves.

We have ended grain embargoes, once and for all. The Congress has passed a superb new farm bill, and our Democratic Congress and new legislation has untied the farmers' hands. Farm exports, so vital to our balance of trade, broke all records year before last. They're breaking all records this year, and farm income, net farm income is up 25 percent. We Democrats are committed to what they have long deserved and are now beginning to get — a decent and fair income for American farmers.

And for the first time in 40 years, we have actually deregulated a major industry. Now the airlines are making more money, more Americans are flying, and they are paying less. Now, that's what I call free enterprise under Democrats. And next year — next year — we'll bring similar benefits to Americans by deregulating the surface transportation industry.

Republicans promise tax cuts. We Democrats have cut taxes nearly $25 billion. The Republicans left us the biggest budget deficit in American history. We have added new resources for human needs, strengthened the American dollar overseas, and cut that deficit $30 billion. Large deficits fuel the flames of inflation, so we must cut them even more, and we will. For inflation threatens all our gains and all our hopes for continued growth.

[Inflation]

Inflation is robbing those whom we most want and need to help — working families, the pensioner, the widow, and the poor. It breeds a narrow politics of fear. It's an illusion to believe we can preserve a commitment to compassionate and progressive government if we fail to bring inflation under control.

Each of us must do our part, but government must lead. I have set my budget goals. I am determined to meet them. Short-term sacrifices must be made. But we will balance those sacrifices fairly. And if we err in this balance, it will be on the side of those who are most in need. That's the way Democrats govern.

By joining together to control inflation now, we can lay the foundation for an extended era of growth and prosperity which all Americans can share — with more stable prices, with new jobs and opportunity, with new security and hope. And as President, I have no alternative except to bring inflation under control. As Democrats and as partners, we will meet this challenge, and we will meet it successfully.

[Education and Health]

Now, most of us have dreams, the same dreams for our children and our grandchildren — the opportunity to learn in schools that are challenging and which nurture them, to be protected against disease, to grow up in good neighborhoods, to know the taste of clean water and the smell of fresh air and the pleasure of beauty, natural beauty around them. We want a nation, as our Constitution promises, where the only limits on our children are the talents God gave them and their own determination and hard work.

In the past 2 years, we have added more new resources to educate America's children than ever before in our history. Across this country, 500,000 more handicapped children, 200,000 more children of migrant workers, 125,000 children who do not speak English as their native language — all children who have lived on the outskirts of hope too long — will start life now with a better chance because of our Democratic partnership. And for the first time, every young person in our country, everyone who wants to go to college or vocational school is now eligible for a grant or a loan.

No American family should be reduced to poverty, or bankruptcy, or go without needed health care because they cannot afford the cost. We have begun the fight for hospital cost containment. Next year we're going to win that fight. This is one of the essential steps toward reaching the goal that we all have — to protect every American through a comprehensive system of national health care.

People in every American city are struggling to raise their children in safe neighborhoods and safe homes, where teenagers can go to a good job, instead of to a bad street corner, where there is sunlight and open spaces and green parks. These formerly hopeless and lonely children are no longer struggling alone.

[Aid to Cities]

Federal resources are not unlimited, but we are targeting new aid, and we have forged a new urban policy. Our Nation's largest city is putting its finances in order and now facing its future with hope because the Democratic Party kept faith with the people of New York. And I'm thankful we did.

We have also begun the fight to bring billions of dollars of private enterprise, private investment to America's cities and also to our rural centers through a National Development Bank. Next year, we're going to win that fight.

Let me say that our national heritage, our natural heritage, is a gift to each generation. We have finally enacted long-awaited strip mining protection. We have strengthened standards for clean water and clean air. And last week, we guaranteed the protection of 114 million acres of our land in Alaska, our most precious wilderness. This doubled our system of national parks. And with your help, this administration will continue to keep faith with the next generation by protecting our environment.

The civil rights revolution liberated both black and white, North and South. My commitment as President will never be in doubt. I will continue to uphold and vigorously to enforce the spirit and the letter of the laws of this land to ensure equal justice and opportunity for the people of America. I know you share that commitment.

We will not close our eyes to 200 years of systematic discrimination. We will promote effective affirmative action programs. We have already extended the time limits for ratifying the equal rights amendment. Now let us join forces to wipe out discrimination based on sex and make the equal rights amendment the law of the land, and give voting rights to the people of the District of Columbia.

The experience and the wisdom of our older citizens is a priceless resource. Our Democratic partnership has struck down discrimination based on age. Retired Americans deserve a life of dignity and not fear. The social security checks of all Americans are now guaranteed, not only for today but for the rest of the century.

For too many years, the most idealistic people in the world saw our highest ideals betrayed.

Woodrow Wilson spoke for every American when he said: "I would rather belong to a poor nation that was free than to a rich nation that had ceased to be in love with liberty."

[Human Rights]

Our Nation, conceived in liberty, is standing in defense of human rights. We do not claim easy victories; but brave people around the world who are struggling to taste the freedom that we now enjoy, they now know that they are no longer alone. Thousands of prison doors which once held innocent people have swung open. And as long as I'm President, America will continue to lead the worldwide struggle for basic human rights.

For many years I dreaded the autumn sessions of the United Nations General Assembly, because I knew that the country which I loved would be vilified and castigated by scores of nations in the developing world. But the peoples of many of those nations now look to America with fresh eyes and new friendship, because we are struggling with them for justice and economic development, for democracy, and for peace.

In our own hemisphere, we have initiated a new era of mutual respect and cooperation with our neighbors. And I am proud that the United States Senate had the courage and vision to demonstrate to the world the greatness and the strength of our Nation by ratifying the Panama Canal treaties.

And I'm also proud that while I have been President, no American has fought or died in combat anywhere on Earth. My deepest prayer is to be able to say when I leave this office, "My country lived in peace."

With its great strength, America is a continuing and it is a persistent force for peace in Cyprus, in Nicaragua, in Namibia, in Rhodesia, and elsewhere. We've seen the President of Egypt and the Prime Minister of Israel, two long-term enemies, stand in the White House and before the Congress and clasp hands in a genuine gesture of peace.

No single individual in our life time gave more of her life and her energies and her devotion to the cause of peace than did Golda Meir. The world has lost one of its great, good hearts.

The road to permanent peace in the Middle East, God knows, is difficult and frustrating, with many deadlocks and delays. But after 4 wars, and 3,000 years of hatred, I am confident that our prayers will be answered and Golda Meir's dream will come true, and we will see a treaty of just and durable peace between the nations of Israel and Egypt signed, and signed very soon.

We want peace. And we are reducing our sales of conventional arms and trying to convince other nations to join with us in this commitment. America does not enjoy and does not want the title "Arms Merchant of the

World." I would rather the peoples of other nations see the letters "USA" printed on a bag of American wheat than I would on the butt of a rifle.

As President, I know that many depend upon the strength of America for their peace and for their freedom. I am committed to a strong defense. My first career was military, in the submarine force. My greatest responsibility as President is to maintain the security of our Nation. I will continue to keep that commitment. NATO and our other alliances are being strengthened. Under this administration, America's defense forces will remain so strong and well prepared that no nation will ever be tempted to test them and destroy the peace we love.

[Nuclear Arms Race]

But we know that even strong defenses cannot give us true security as long as the awesome power of the atom remains a weapon of war. At the end of World War II, the United States was the only nation that possessed an atomic weapon. Today at least five nations share this sobering responsibility. We dare not permit the ability to produce nuclear explosives to become available to dozens of nations, large and small, led either by responsible leaders or perhaps by madmen.

We acted in the Congress last year to halt the spread of weapons-grade uranium and plutonium. Fifty nations led by us are now working together on this program and on this problem. We must and we will continue to prevent the proliferation of nuclear weapons throughout the world.

And finally, let me say that the nuclear arms race matches super power against super power. It is an unending, unwinnable, ever more costly contest. It escalates the risk of ultimate confrontation. It increases the danger that a fatal miscalculation, a tragic accident, or an act of madness could propel the world into nuclear war and wipe out life as we know it on Earth. I am dedicated to bring the nuclear arms race under control.

We have been negotiating daily and we are now negotiating daily with the Soviet Union on a new treaty to limit strategic arms. We hope soon to sign a SALT agreement which will strengthen the security of the United States, will provide for accurate verification, and will substantially reduce the threat of nuclear war.

Once the SALT II treaty is signed — and I believe it will be soon — I will depend on your help to ensure that it is ratified. We have no more urgent responsibility to the next generation of Americans than to act now to reduce the danger of nuclear holocaust. When the history of our time is written, it will be said that you and I, the American people met that responsibility.

Well, we face these and other serious challenges as Democrats and as Americans. But as a party and as a people we have met and we have overcome great challenges before. We will stay true to the promise of the Democratic Party. We will meet our urgent responsibilities. We will strive for competence. We will act with compassion. And we will continue to dream great dreams — and to make those dreams come true.

With the courage and the common sense of the American people as our guide, we will make this Nation what our founders envisioned — a land of liberty and opportunity, proud of its heritage of hope and human dignity, with the potential for greatness that only a free people can fulfill, a symbol of peace and a symbol of liberty to all the world.

Thank you very much.

KENNEDY'S SPEECH

I am proud to be here with all of you today. I am proud of our country, proud of the Democratic Party, and proud of the dream we have for America and our future.

Since the time of Jefferson and Jackson, the Democratic Party has always held its standard high. As a party, we have stood for action, hope and progress in meeting the people's basic needs. We are not a party of reaction or retreat. We are not the party of McKinley or Harding. We are not the party of Coolidge or Hoover.

At our best, we have had leaders with both the vision to see the path, and the skill to guide the nation forward, to bring us closer to our historic goals:

—Woodrow Wilson saw a world at peace.

—Franklin Roosevelt lit a candle in the darkness of the depression.

—Harry Truman raised Europe to its feet after the devastation of war.

—John Kennedy touched the hearts of youth and launched the longest period of economic growth and price stability in our history.

—Lyndon Johnson and Hubert Humphrey brought the dream of equality closer to reality.

—And Jimmy Carter has led us to the threshold of peace in the Middle East and given America world leadership in the cause of human rights.

We meet, however, at a time of caution and uncertainty in the land. The hopes and dreams of millions of citizens are riding on our leadership.

Sometimes a party must sail against the wind. We cannot afford to drift or lie at anchor. We cannot heed the call of those who say it is time to furl the sail.

We know that some things in America today are wrong. It is wrong that prices are rising as rapidly as they are.

But it is also wrong that millions of our fellow citizens are out of work. It is wrong that cities are struggling against decay. It is wrong that women and minorities are denied their equal rights. And it is wrong that millions who are sick cannot afford the care they need.

I support the fight against inflation. But no fight against inflation can be effective or successful unless the fight is fair. The party that tore itself apart over Vietnam in the 1960's cannot afford to tear itself apart today over budget cuts in basic social programs.

There could be few more divisive issues for America and for our party than a Democratic policy of drastic slashes in the federal budget at the expense of the elderly, the poor, the black, the sick, the cities and the unemployed.

There must be sacrifice if we are to bring the economy back to health. But the burden must be fairly shared by all. We cannot accept a policy that asks greater sacrifice from labor than from business. We cannot accept a policy that cuts spending to the bone in areas like jobs and health, but allows billions of dollars in wasteful spending for tax subsidies to continue, and adds even greater fat and waste through inflationary spending for defense.

[Health Care]

Our workshop here on health care will clarify this crucial point about priorities in spending federal dollars. One of the most shameful things about modern America is that in our unbelievably rich land, the quality of health care available to many of our people is unbelievably poor, and the cost is unbelievably high.

That is why national health insurance is the great unfinished business on the agenda of the Democratic Party. Our party gave Social Security to the nation in the 1930's. We gave Medicare to the nation in the 1960's. And we can bring national health insurance to the nation in the 1970's.

One of the saddest ironies in the worldwide movement for social justice in the twentieth century is that America now stands virtually alone in the international community on national health insurance. It seems that every nation is out of step but Uncle Sam. With the sole exception of South Africa, no other industrial nation in the world leaves its citizens in fear of financial ruin because of illness.

A generation after Franklin Roosevelt set the noble goals of freedom from want and freedom from fear, large numbers of Americans are deprived of decent health care and are fearful of the bills they may be forced to pay.

For a very few, for whom the need is least, we have already made a start on national health insurance.

—We've got national health insurance for the rich, who deduct the cost of major illness on their income tax returns. And the richer you are, the higher the percentage of your health bill you can charge to the IRS.

—We've got national health insurance for members of the Senate and House of Representatives. They give their speeches and cast their votes in Congress. And then they go out to Walter Reed Army Hospital or Bethesda Naval Hospital for the free medical and dental care that Uncle Sam provides.

That isn't fair. If national health insurance is good enough for the wealthy and good enough for Congress, then it is good enough for every American citizen in every city, town and village and on every farm throughout this land.

There are some who say we cannot afford national health insurance. They say it has become an early casualty of the war against inflation. But the truth is, we cannot afford not to have national health insurance.

Health care in 1978 has become the fastest-growing failing business in America. Costs are out of control. If we do nothing, if all we do is drift with the present system, the cost of health care in America will climb from $175 billion this year to $250 billion in 1981.

The rising cost of health is not just a crisis that afflicts the poor and helpless. It has hit the suburbs, too. Millions of middle income citizens face the Hobson's choice of cutting back on health or other family needs.

The average worker is lucky if his paycheck barely holds its own against inflation. Yet the cost of health in recent years has been rising twice as rapidly as the Consumer Price Index. There is not enough money to go around. Something has to give. And it is often the family's budget for health that is the first to go.

Every day, parents are deciding whether they can afford the $25 doctor office charge and the $25 laboratory bill when their child is sick. Elderly citizens are deciding whether to spend for food or rent or health. Young Americans are gambling on their health, signing up for cut-rate, fly-by-night insurance schemes because their budgets cannot afford the premium for a decent health insurance policy.

Only through national health insurance can we achieve the effective controls on costs that will bring inflation down and bring adequate health care within financial reach of every citizen.

More than most Americans, I know what it means to have serious illness in the family. My father was crippled by a stroke and required constant care for years. My son was stricken with cancer, and is well today because of the miracle of American medicine. A decade ago, I myself was hospitalized for several months, my back broken in many places.

Fortunately, our family could afford to pay for all the care we needed. And so the tragedy of serious illness for those we loved was not compounded by the additional tragedy of a heavy financial burden.

Together, we can lift that financial burden from all the families of America. Through national health insurance, we can provide a decent health care system for the benefit of the people of this land. We can make health care a basic right for all, not just an expensive privilege for the few.

But to achieve the reform we need, we must have genuine leadership by the Democratic Party. We are heirs of a great tradition in American public life. Our party took up the cause of jobs for the unemployed in the Great Depression. Our party took up the cause of civil rights for black and brown Americans, and the cause of equal rights for women in America and the people of the District of Columbia.

In that same tradition of leadership, it is time for the Democratic Party now to take up the cause of health.

If we care about our party, if we care about the future of our nation, let us honor the commitment of our platform. Let us pledge in Memphis, at this convention of our party, to make health care a right for all our people now.

PRELIMINARY CALL FOR 1980

To Whom It May Concern:

By authority of the Democratic National Committee, the National Convention of the Democratic Party is hereby called to meet, at a time and place in 1980 to be designated at a later date, to select nominees for the Offices of President and Vice President of the United State of America, to adopt and promulgate a platform and to take such other actions with respect to any other matters as the Convention may deem advisable.

I. Distribution of Delegate Votes

Notice is hereby given that the following resolutions have been approved by the Democratic National Committee, acting under authority of the Charter of the Democratic Party of the United States, with respect to the distribution of votes, delegates and alternates to the 1980 Democratic National Convention shall be in accordance with the following:

(1) The total number of Convention votes for the delegates to the Convention shall be 3,317. . . .

(2) 2,974 delegate votes are distributed among the 50 states and the District of Columbia according to a formula giving equal weight to the vote for the Democratic candidates in the three most recent Presidential elections and population as measured by electoral votes.

(3) The Virgin Islands, Guam, the Canal Zone and Democrats Abroad will receive 3 delegate votes each. Puerto Rico will receive 24 delegate votes.

(4) Ten percent of the delegate votes distributed pursuant to paragraphs 2 and 3 above shall be added to the number of votes allocated for the purpose of representing party and elected official delegates.

(4) Each state, the District of Columbia, Puerto Rico, the Virgin Islands, Guam, the Canal Zone and Democrats Abroad may select a number of alternates equivalent to the sum of: (i) one alternate for each of the first 20 Convention votes received by it pursuant to paragraphs (2), (3) and (4) hereof, (ii) one alternate for each two Convention votes in excess of 20 but less than 101 Convention votes received by it pursuant to paragraphs (2), (3) and (4) hereof, and (iii) one alternate for each three Convention votes in excess of 100 Convention votes received by it pursuant to paragraphs (2), (3) and (4) hereof. . . .

II. Qualifications of State Delegations

(a) Notice is hereby given that delegates and alternates to the 1980 Democratic National Convention shall be selected in accordance with the Delegate Selection Rules for the 1980 Democratic National Convention adopted by the Democratic National Committee on June 9, 1978, except that Rule 12, section (c), the second sentence of the aforesaid delegate selection rules, is hereby repealed and the following is substituted in its place:

"Under no circumstances shall the use of single member delegate districts be permitted."

(b) Notice is hereby given that the Democratic National Committee has adopted the following resolutions with regard to Affirmative Action in selecting the delegates to the 1980 Democratic National Convention.

BE IT RESOLVED by the Democratic National Committee that in order to assure that requirements of Rule 6 of the Delegate Selection Rules are carried out each State Democratic Party shall adopt and implement an Affirmative Action program. . . . The State Affirmative Action program shall be sufficiently detailed to establish compliance with this resolution; and

BE IT FURTHER RESOLVED by the Democratic National Committee, pursuant to the specific direction of the 1976 Democratic National Convention, that State Affirmative Action programs include a specific plan to help defray the expenses of those delegates otherwise unable to participate in the Convention and that the Democratic National Committee provide all necessary aid to carry out this resolution.

(c) It is understood that a State Democratic Party, in selecting and certifying delegates to the Democratic National Convention, thereby undertakes to assure that voters in the State, regardless of economic status, sex, race, age, color, national origin or creed will have the opportunity to participate fully in Party affairs and that voters in the State will have the opportunity to cast their election ballots for the Presidential and Vice Presidential nominees selected by said Convention, and for electors pledged formally and in good conscience to the election of these Presidential and Vice Presidential nominees, under the Democratic Party label and designation, and that the delegates it certifies will not publicly support or campaign for any candidates for President or Vice President other than the nominees of the Convention.

(d) It is understood that the Delegates to the Democratic National Convention, when certified by the State Democratic Party, are bona fide Democrats who have the interests, welfare and success of the Democratic Party at heart, and will participate in the Convention in good faith and therefore no additional assurances shall be required of Delegates to the Democratic National Convention in the absence of credentials contest or challenge.

(e) Pursuant to the mandate of the 1976 Democratic National Convention State Parties and Territories in selecting delegates shall promote equal division between delegate men and delegate women from each State and Territory. In fulfillment of this mandate the Democratic National Committee hereby requires that State Delegate Selection Plans provide for equal division between Delegate men and Delegate women and Alternate men and Alternate women in the Convention Delegation.

III. Delegates to be Selected Not Later Than June 23, 1980

Notice is hereby given that the Democratic National Committee has adopted the following resolution:

BE IT RESOLVED by the Democratic National Committee that all state parties are requested to take all steps necessary and appropriate to complete the process of selecting delegates to the 1980 Democratic National Convention no later than June 23, 1980. . . .

'NORMALIZATION' OF U.S.-CHINA RELATIONS

December 15, 1978

The United States and the People's Republic of China crossed a 30-year diplomatic gulf Jan. 1, 1979, when each formally recognized the other for the first time. The breakthrough had been announced on Dec. 15 by Chinese officials in Peking and by President Carter in a nationally televised speech. Carter also disclosed that Chinese Deputy Premier Teng Hsiao-ping planned to visit the United States early in 1979.

Besides withdrawing its recognition of the Republic of China (Taiwan), the United States served notice that it would terminate its mutual defense treaty with that nation at the end of 1979 and would remove the 753 non-combat U.S. troops remaining on Taiwan. The treaty permitted either party to terminate it with one year's notice.

Since 1949, when communist forces completed the takeover of the mainland, the United States had recognized the nationalist regime on Taiwan as the sole government of China. In deciding to shift that policy, Carter told the American people, "we are recognizing simple reality" that the People's Republic was the single government of a nation comprising "about one-fourth of the total population of the earth...."

"Normalization — and the expanded commercial and cultural relations that it will bring — will contribute to the well-being of our own nation, to our own national interest, and it will also enhance the stability of Asia," Carter said in the Dec. 15 speech. "The normalization of relations between the United States and China has no other purpose than this — the advancement of peace."

Reaction

Although eventual normalization had been taken for granted since President Nixon's trip to China in 1972, the sudden announcement caught most of the world by surprise. (Peking summit, Historic Documents of 1972, p. 183)

Among those most surprised by Carter's speech were members of Congress, who thought the president had promised to consult with them before changing the status of the Taiwan treaty. The most vocal reaction was the anguish of conservatives who had faithfully stood by Taiwan for decades. They spoke of the betrayal of Taiwan, and threatened political retaliation against Carter. But many of those conservatives admitted Carter had the legal right to take the actions he did.

On Taiwan itself, the initial reaction was one of shock and violence. Cars carrying U.S. officials were pelted with eggs and rocks as they passed through mobs of angry demonstrators. However, President Chiang Ching-kuo, son of nationalist government founder Chiang Kai-shek, criticized the U.S. action in moderate tones and spoke of the need to "strengthen the friendship and mutual interests" between Taiwan and its largest trading partner, the United States.

Despite the long-standing animosity between the Soviet Union and its communist neighbor, President Carter said that Soviet Leader Leonid I. Brezhnev responded with a "very positive" message about the U.S. rapprochement with China. However, the Kremlin later pointed out that Brezhnev had criticized U.S. acceptance of China's "anti-hegemony" language in the joint communiqué. The Soviets had long opposed such language as a Chinese effort to thwart Russia's legitimate status as a power in the Pacific area. Soviet objections to almost identical wording had delayed for several years a China-Japan peace treaty completed Oct. 23. (Treaty, p. 585)

Concessions

The breakthrough in U.S.-China relations was made possible by the willingness of both sides to make concessions. Each side claimed that the other side had made the greater sacrifice. For its part, U.S. willingness to 1) drop recognition of Taiwan, 2) end the mutual defense treaty and 3) withdraw its troops satisfied the conditions that the Chinese had insisted must be met. The Chinese also made three major concessions when they: 1) tacitly agreed not to oppose continued American sales of arms to Taiwan, 2) agreed that the United States could terminate its defense treaty with Taiwan on one year's notice rather than immediately, and 3) agreed not to object to an American declaration of continued interest in the future of Taiwan.

Conservative critics argued that the Chinese concessions were merely rhetorical and that the United States essentially gave in to Peking's demands. But the Carter administration orchestrated a chorus of high-level officials who insisted that the United States had won essential points that would ensure Taiwan's independence for the foreseeable future. The officials made clear that U.S. arms sales to Taiwan would continue.

The impetus for the breakthrough was a trip to China in May by Carter's national security adviser Zbigniew Brzezinski, who impressed Chinese officials with his anti-Soviet rhetoric. In July Leonard Woodcock, chief of the U.S. delegation in Peking, began serious negotiations with Chinese Foreign Minister Huang Hua.

Anxious to modernize China and strengthen its hand against the Soviet Union, Chinese leaders pressed for the normalization of U.S.-China relations. Apparently with official sanction, wall posters suddenly began appearing throughout China expressing favorable thoughts toward the United States and questioning the closed-China ideology of Mao Tse-tung, who died in 1976.

On Sept. 19 President Carter met with Chai Tse-min, the new Chinese liaison officer in Washington, and laid out the American considerations for normalized relations. Negotiations then proceeded rapidly, with the two sides secretly exchanging draft statements and proposals up until the day before the public announcement of recognition on Dec. 15.

> *Following are the texts of President Carter's Dec. 15, 1978, address, as delivered, announcing establishment of full diplomatic relations between the United States and the People's Republic of China; a United States statement released Dec. 15; a People's Republic of China statement read by Chairman Hua Kuo-feng Dec. 15; and an unofficial translation of a statement by Nationalist Chinese President Chiang Ching-kuo Dec. 16:*

CARTER'S SPEECH

Good evening.

I would like to read a joint communiqué which is being simultaneously issued in Peking at this very moment by the leaders of the People's Republic of China:

"Joint Communiqué on the Establishment of Diplomatic Relations Between the United States of America and the People's Republic of China, January 1, 1979

"The United States of America and the People's Republic of China have agreed to recognize each other and to establish diplomatic relations as of January 1st, 1979.

"The United States recognizes the Government of the People's Republic of China as the sole legal government of China. Within this context, the people of the United States will maintain cultural, commercial and other unofficial relations with the people of Taiwan.

"The United States of America and the People's Republic of China reaffirm the principles agreed on by the two sides in the Shanghai Communiqué of 1972 and emphasize once again that:

"—Both sides wish to reduce the danger of international military conflict.

"—Neither should seek hegemony [that is a dominance of one nation over the other*] in the Asia-Pacific region or in any other region of the world and each is opposed to efforts by any other country or group of countries to establish such hegemony.

"—Neither is prepared to negotiate on behalf of any other third party or to enter into agreements or understandings with the other directed at other states.

"—The Government of the United States of America acknowledges the Chinese position that there is but one China and Taiwan is part of China.

"—Both believe that normalization of Sino-American relations is not only in the interest of the Chinese and American peoples but also contributes to the cause of peace in Asia and in the world.

"—The United States of America and the People's Republic of China will exchange Ambassadors and establish embassies on March 1, 1979."

Yesterday, our country and the People's Republic of China reached this final historic agreement.

On January 1, 1979, a little more than two weeks from now, our two governments will implement full normalization of diplomatic relations.

As a nation of gifted people who comprise about one-fourth of the total population of the earth, China plays, already, an important role in world affairs — a role that can only grow more important in the years ahead.

We do not undertake this important step for transient tactical or expedient reasons. In recognizing the People's Republic of China, that it is the single government of China, we are recognizing simple reality. But far more is involved in this decision than just recognition of a fact.

Before the estrangement of recent decades, the American and the Chinese people had a long history of friendship. We have already begun to rebuild some of those previous ties. Now, our rapidly expanding relationship requires the kind of structure that only full diplomatic relations will make possible.

The change that I am announcing tonight will be of great long-term benefit to the peoples of both our country and China — and, I believe, to all the peoples of the world.

Normalization — and the expanded commercial and cultural relations that it will bring — will contribute to the well-being of our own Nation, to our own national interest, and it will also enhance the stability of Asia.

These more positive relations with China can beneficially affect the world in which we live and the world in which our children will live.

We have already begun to inform our allies and other nations and the members of the Congress of the details of our intended action. But I wish also tonight to convey a special message to the people of Taiwan — I have

* Not in official communiqué.

already communicated with the leaders in Taiwan — with whom the American people have had and will have extensive, close and friendly relations.

This is important between our two peoples.

As the United States asserted in the Shanghai Communiqué of 1972, issued on President Nixon's historic visit, we will continue to have an interest in the peaceful resolution of the Taiwan issue.

I have paid special attention to ensuring that normalization of relations between our country and the People's Republic will not jeopardize the well-being of the people of Taiwan.

The people of our country will maintain our current commercial, cultural, trade and other relations with Taiwan through nongovernmental means. Many other countries in the world are already successfully doing this.

These decisions and these actions open a new and important chapter in our country's history, and also in world affairs.

To strengthen and to expedite the benefits of this new relationship between China and the United States, I am pleased to announce that Vice Premier Teng has accepted my invitation and will visit Washington at the end of January. His visit will give our governments the opportunity to consult with each other on global issues and to begin working together to enhance the cause of world peace.

These events are the final result of long and serious negotiations begun by President Nixon in 1972, and continued under the leadership of President Ford. The results bear witness to the steady, determined and bipartisan effort of our country to build a world in which peace will be the goal and the responsibility of all nations.

The normalization of relations between the United States and China has no other purpose than this — the advancement of peace.

It is in this spirit, at this season of peace, that I take special pride in sharing this good news with you tonight.

UNITED STATES STATEMENT

As of January 1, 1979, the United States of America recognizes the People's Republic of China as the sole legal Government of China. On the same date, the People's Republic of China accords similar recognition to the United States of America. The United States thereby establishes diplomatic relations with the People's Republic of China.

On that same date, January 1, 1979, the United States of America will notify Taiwan that it is terminating diplomatic relations and that the Mutual Defense Treaty between the United States and the Republic of China is being terminated in accordance with the provisions of the Treaty. The United States also states that it will be withdrawing its remaining military personnel from Taiwan within four months.

In the future, the American people and the people of Taiwan will maintain commercial, cultural, and other relations without official Government representation and without diplomatic relations.

The Administration will seek adjustments to our laws and regulations to permit the maintenance of commercial, cultural, and other nongovernmental relationships in the new circumstances that will exist after normalization.

The United States is confident that the people of Taiwan face a peaceful and prosperous future. The United States continues to have an interest in the peaceful resolution of the Taiwan issue and expects that the Taiwan issue will be settled peacefully by the Chinese themselves.

The United States believes that the establishment of diplomatic relations with the People's Republic will contribute to the welfare of the American people, to the stability of Asia where the United States has major security and economic interests and to the peace of the entire world.

PEOPLE'S REPUBLIC OF CHINA STATEMENT

As of January 1, 1979, the People's Republic of China and the United States of America recognize each other and establish diplomatic relations, thereby ending the prolonged abnormal relationship between them. This is an historic event in Sino-United States relations.

As is known to all, the Government of the People's Republic of China is the sole legal Government of China and Taiwan is a part of China. The question of Taiwan was the crucial issue obstructing the normalization of relations between China and the United States. It has now been resolved between the two countries in the spirit of the Shanghai Communiqué and through their joint efforts, thus enabling the normalization of relations so ardently desired by the people of the two countries.

As for the way of bringing Taiwan back to the embrace of the motherland and reunifying the country, it is entirely China's internal affair.

At the invitation of the U.S. Government, Teng Hsiao-ping, Deputy Prime Minister of the State Council of the People's Republic of China, will pay an official visit to the United States in January 1979, with a view to further promoting the friendship between the two peoples and good relations between the two countries.

TAIWAN STATEMENT

The decision by the United States to establish diplomatic relations with the Chinese Communist regime has not only seriously damaged the rights and interests of the Government and the people of the Republic of China, but has also had a tremendously adverse impact upon the entire free world. For all the consequences that might arise as a result of this move, the United States Government alone should bear full responsibility.

In the past few years, the United States Government has repeatedly reaffirmed its intention to maintain diplomatic relations with the Republic of China and to honor its treaty commitments. Now that it has broken the assurances and abrogated the treaty, the United States Government cannot be expected to have the confidence of any free nation in the future.

The United States, by extending diplomatic recognition to the Chinese Communist regime, which owes its very existence to terror and suppression, is not in conformity with its professed position of safeguarding human rights and strengthening the capability of democratic nations to resist the totalitarian dictatorship.

The move is tantamount to denying the hundreds of millions of enslaved peoples on the Chinese mainland of their hope for an early restoration of freedom. Viewed from whatever aspect, the move by the United States constitutes a great setback to human freedom and democratic institutions. It will be condemned by all freedomloving and peaceloving peoples all over the world.

Recent international events have proven that the United States' pursuance of the "normalization" process with the Chinese Communist regime did not protect the security of free Asian nations, has further encouraged Communist subversion and aggressive activities and hastened the fall of Indochina into Communist hands. The Government and the people of the Republic of China firmly believe lasting international peace and security can never be established on an unstable foundation of expediency.

Regardless of how the international situation may develop, the Republic of China, as a sovereign nation will, with her glorious tradition, unite all her people, civilian and military, at home and abroad, to continue her endeavors toward progress in the social, economic and political fields. The Chinese Government and the people, faithful to the national objectives and their international responsibilities, have full confidence in the future of the Republic of China.

The late President Chiang Kai-shek repeatedly instructed the Chinese people to be firm with dignity and to complete the task of national recovery and reconstruction. The Government and the people of the Republic of China have the determination and the faith, which they will exert their utmost, to work together with other free peoples in democratic countries to conquer Communist tyrannical rule and its aggressive policy. Henceforth, we shall be calm and firm, positive and hardworking. It is urged that all citizens cooperate fully with the Government, with one heart and one soul, united and determined to fight at this difficult moment. Under whatever circumstances, the Republic of China shall neither negotiate with the Communist Chinese regime, nor compromise with Communism, and it shall never give up its sacred task of recovering the mainland and delivering the compatriots there. This firm position shall remain unchanged.

OPEC OIL PRICE RISE
December 17, 1978

Ending an 18-month freeze on its crude oil prices, the Organization of Petroleum Exporting Countries (OPEC) Dec. 17 announced a 14.49 percent price increase for 1979. The increase would boost the price of Arabian light, the benchmark grade for the cartel, from $12.70 to $14.54 per 42-gallon barrel. (Previous increase, Historic Documents of 1976, p. 937)

The 13-member cartel is responsible for about half the oil produced in the world. The price hike was expected to spur similar increases by other producers, including U.S. producers of oil not restricted by federal price controls. Mexico, considered a potential supplier of future U.S. needs, already had announced a 10 to 12 percent increase for 1979.

Effect of Increase

The increase could add .3 to .4 percentage point to what the U.S. inflation rate would have been without any price increase. The rate in 1978 was expected to exceed 9 percent.

However, U.S. consumers were shielded from the full brunt of the OPEC move by federal controls that keep the price of about 35 percent of domestically produced oil at less than $6 a barrel. Averaging the price of domestic oil with the OPEC hike means prices would increase at the gasoline pump by about 3 cents a gallon, instead of the full 4.4 cents they would if the OPEC increase applied to all oil consumed domestically.

The increase voted by OPEC in the price of Arabian light was to be implemented in four stages, starting with a 5 percent increase on Jan. 1,

1979, which would bring the price to $13.335 a barrel. Then, on April 1, the price would be increased another 3.809 percent, to $13.843. That increase would be followed on July 1 by a 2.294 percent increase, bringing the price to $14.161. On Oct. 1, the scheduled increase of 2.691 percent would bring the price to $14.542 a barrel. The total $1.84 price rise was an increase of 14.49 percent.

The official OPEC communiqué called the increase "an amount of 10 percent, on average, over the year 1979." A volume of oil bought from OPEC in 1978 would cost 10 percent more in 1979 because the full price increase would not be in place until October. However, the total price increase for the year would be 14.49 percent.

The phased-in schedule meant the United States would pay another $4 billion for foreign oil in 1979, according to Federal Reserve Board Chairman G. William Miller. In 1980, when the full increase would apply for the whole year, imports would cost an additional $7 billion. The U.S. bill for foreign oil could be as high as $50 billion in 1979, an estimate that factors in both the higher OPEC prices and an expected increase in consumption. That was a sharp increase over the estim. ted bill for 1978 of about $42.7 billion, a figure that contributed substantially to the 1978 U.S. trade deficit of about $34.9 billion.

Response to OPEC Decision

In response to the OPEC decision, the White House Dec. 17 issued a statement asking for reconsideration of the increase. "We regret OPEC's decision and hope that it will be reconsidered before the next steps take effect," the statement said. "This large price hike will impede the programs to maintain world economic recovery and reduce inflation. Responsibility for the success of these programs is shared by the oil producing countries."

The OPEC oil ministers said the increase was designed to recoup some of the decline in OPEC purchasing power caused by inflation and the decline of the dollar. The dollar is the currency on which the OPEC pricing system is based.

The increase ended a price freeze in effect since mid-1977. An oil surplus had prevented OPEC from raising prices during that time. But political turmoil in Iran in late 1978 disrupted oil production, reducing the surplus. Production from Iran dropped from normal output of six million barrels a day to as low as one million barrels a day. The reduction drove up prices.

"We believe this is a responsible increase that the world economy can absorb without problems," said Sheik Manae Said al-Oteiba of Kuwait, who was elected president of OPEC. "We believe the increase represents the minimum we should get to compensate for some of our losses over the last two years."

Saudi Arabia's oil minister, Sheik Ahmed Zaki Yamani, said that the 14.5 percent figure "was a medium solution representing the best we could do under the circumstances."

"I wanted something lower than that," he said. "I was hoping for 5 percent in fact, but when you look at what happens in the market, and particularly at the shortage caused by the Iranian situation, it is very difficult to hold the prices down under such circumstances." Libya and Iraq had called for increases of 20 percent or more.

The members of OPEC are Algeria, Iraq, Kuwait, Libya, Qatar, Saudi Arabia, the United Arab Emirates, Ecuador, Gabon, Indonesia, Iran, Nigeria and Venezuela.

Following is the final statement of the OPEC Ministerial Counsel issued in Abu Dhabi, United Arab Emirates, Dec. 17, 1978, as reported by the Emirates News Agency and reprinted by the Foreign Broadcast Information Service; and the White House statement Dec. 17 on the price increase:

OPEC STATEMENT

Abu Dhabi, 17 December — The 52d meeting of OPEC convened in Abu Dhabi in the United Arab Emirates from 16-17 December 1978. The conference unanimously elected His Highness Dr. Mani' Sa'id al-'Utaybah, UAE [United Arab Emirates] minister of petroleum and natural resources and head of it delegation, as chairman of the conference. Dr. Dubroto, Indonesian minister of mining and energy and head of Indonesia's delegation, was elected alternate chairman.

The meeting reviewed the report of the economic council and observed with great concern the high inflation rate and the decline of the dollar during the last 2 years, and the resulting large decrease in the revenues of the oil member-states as well as the negative effect of all this on the economic and social development of these states.

Despite this and out of a desire to help world economy toward further development and in order to back up the current efforts aimed at strengthening the U.S. dollar and curbing the inflation trends, the conference has decided the following:

To introduce a partial rectification of oil prices at the average of 10 percent throughout the year 1979. In addition to that and as a gesture of good will, the conference has decided to divide this rectification on a quarterly basis in accordance with the following ratios:

5 percent on 1 January 1979

3.809 percent on 1 April 1979

2.294 percent on 1 July 1979

2.691 percent on 1 October 1979

If, for instance, we apply these rectifications to the price of crude oil, the result will be the following prices:

$13.335 as of 1 January 1979

$13.843 as of 1 April 1979

$14.161 as of 1 July 1979

$14.542 as of 1 October 1979

In another development, the conference noted that if inflation and the current instability continue to negatively affect the oil revenues of the member-states in a manner encouraging the squandering of this significant source, which is tending toward exhaustion, the conference will be forced to adopt measures compatible with this inflation and the drop in the dollar.

The conference fully supports the OPEC finance ministers in setting up a joint fund in its capacity as a basic tool to achieve the objectives agreed upon in the unified program for commodities.

Considering the progress made at the final negotiations meeting held in Geneva in November, the conference expressed the sincere hope that the outstanding issues will be solved in a satisfactory manner.

The conference approved the 1979 OPEC budget.

The conference appointed 'Abdallah Isma'il, UAE representative in the board of governors, as chairman of the board for 1979. The conference also appointed (Jose Manuel Benio), Venezuela representative, as deputy chairman for 1979.

The conference appointed Rene Ortiz from Ecuador as OPEC secretary general for 2 years, effective 1 January 1979. The conference expressed its appreciation for the excellent services that current Secretary General 'Ali Jidah [of Qatar] has rendered during his term of service.

The conference expressed its appreciation to the UAE for the generous hospitality and for the efficient way the conference was arranged.

The conference adopted resolutions which will be issued on 17 January after being approved by member-states.

The OPEC ordinary meeting will be held in the first half of June 1979.

WHITE HOUSE STATEMENT

We regret the OPEC decision and hope that it will be reconsidered before the next steps take effect.

Market conditions do not warrant a price increase of this magnitude, since the current tightness in the world oil market is a temporary situation that does not reflect underlying demand forces.

This large price hike will impede programs to maintain world economic recovery and to reduce inflation. Responsibility for the success of these programs is shared by the oil-producing countries.

FAA FLIGHT SAFETY PLAN
December 27, 1978

The nation's worst air disaster, over San Diego, Calif., three months earlier led the Federal Aviation Administration Dec. 27 to propose sweeping changes in the conduct of airplane traffic at and near most of the country's commercial airports. Associations representing the airline pilots and scheduled airlines praised the FAA's safety proposals, but a group representing private plane owners and pilots denounced them as impositions of unnecessary restrictions.

The FAA proposals went beyond a simple reaction to the San Diego collision of an airliner and a private plane that claimed 144 lives. FAA Administrator Langhorne M. Bond announced several changes, some of which could be accomplished administratively, others through a longer rule-making procedure. The net effect, though, was to place more of the nation's airspace under FAA control and to require installation of more electronic signaling equipment on more aircraft and more sophisticated radar equipment at more airports.

In a joint statement with Transportation Secretary Brock Adams, Bond said the primary purpose of the proposed program was to increase the level of safety for the nation's airline passengers, who totaled 280 million during 1978. He said that figure was expected to increase to about 500 million by the end of 1980. In addition to the announced proposals, Bond said, the FAA was studying whether practice instrument approach procedures were adequate, whether transfer of communications from one controller to another was being handled properly and whether pilots were sufficiently informed about the use of standards for keeping their aircraft separated from others in terminal areas.

The increased protection to cover airports serving 97 percent of all scheduled airline travelers, Bond said, was expected to reduce the number of near collisions involving airlines above 10,000 feet by 80 percent. Beyond the Dec. 27 announced changes, Bond said, the FAA would propose later that an altitude-reporting transponder, a signaling device activated in a plane to identify the craft on the air controller's radar screen along with an indication of the airplane's altitude, be required by July 1981 for all aircraft operating in the control areas. It also would propose that all airliners and air taxi planes carry collision avoidance systems by January 1985.

The immediate plan outlined by Bond would offer radar services at 80 commercial airports — in addition to the 105 where the service already was available — and bring pilots flying inside an additional 44 locations under the mandatory control of the air controllers. There were only 21 such areas in early 1979, estimated to cover about 67 percent of all airline passengers within the United States. The expansion to 65 would increase that protection to cover 87 percent of the passengers, the FAA estimated. In addition, the FAA proposed to lower the minimum altitude at which aircraft come under direct air traffic control and add more sophisticated equipment at eight airport control towers. To relieve some of the commercial airports of pilot training traffic, the FAA planned to install 24 instrument landing systems at non-airline airports in the large metropolitan areas.

Because the plans would bring more air traffic under direct supervision of the FAA controllers, the number of FAA personnel would have to be increased, Bond said, at an estimated cost of $11 million for the first year alone. The equipment Bond proposed adding would cost another $43 million. The first of the improved radar display devices the FAA proposed to add would be installed at Lindbergh Field at San Diego.

Background

At about 9 a.m. on a clear day, Sept. 25, 1978, a Boeing 727 jet belonging to Pacific Southwest Airlines (PSA), which had never had a fatal crash, was approaching San Diego's Lindbergh Field for a landing. At the same time, a Cessna 172, capable of carrying four persons, was practicing landings under instrument landing conditions, meaning it was operating as if there were little or no visability. The airliner was under the control of the tower at Lindbergh; the private airplane containing a student pilot and his instructor was in radio contact with nearby Miramar Naval Air Station. The air controller at Lindbergh could see that the two aircraft were in the same area but could not tell on his equipment that they were near the same altitude. He warned the PSA pilot of a small airplane in his area.

The PSA pilot acknowledged the warning and later said he has "passed" the small plane moments previous. He apparently hadn't passed the one the controller was referring to, however, and the Cessna struck the right wing tip of the jetliner just as it was banking for a turn at about 2,600 feet above the ground. The PSA wing burst into flames and disintegrated and the jetliner plummeted to the ground, the Cessna dropping behind it. There were 135 persons, including crew, aboard the jetliner. All persons aboard both craft and seven persons on the ground died as the debris of the planes destroyed or set fire to at least 16 houses.

The danger of flight collisions had long been a source of controversy in the aviation industry. Several studies had been performed and in recent years the FAA had taken steps to encourage greater candor in reporting near collisions in the interest of gathering better statistics. Between January 1976 and September 1978, then, the FAA was able to report that 1,006 near collisions of aircraft had occurred below the altitude of 18,000 feet. Thirty-five of the near misses occurred above 13,000 feet and 79 between 10,000 and 12,900 feet. The rest occurred below 9,900 feet. Extrapolating from its proposed expansion of controlled airspace, the FAA said that 327 of the 1,006 reported near misses occurred within that additional controlled space. The implication was that had its proposals been in effect during the study period, nearly one-third of the near misses would not have occurred. There had never been a fatal collision involving an airliner within such areas and the type of control envisioned was not present at Lindbergh Field.

Following are excerpts from the Federal Aviation Administration's "Plan For Enhanced Safety of Flight Operations in the National Airspace System" released Dec. 27, 1978:

Preface

As a part of the investigation of the recent midair collision over San Diego, we directed a review of the Federal Aviation Administration's air traffic control system and procedures to determine what actions could be taken in the near future to reduce the probability of midair collisions. This report outlines the planned and proposed actions that we have determined necessary to implement the outcomes of this review. . . .

Analysis

A recent analysis of near midair collision data recorded by FAA for a 33-month period (January 1976 through September 1978), revealed some 1,006 near midair collisions recorded below 18,000 feet within the contiguous 48 states. Of this number, 95 percent (948) involved visual flight rules (VFR) aircraft. Twenty-six percent (257) involved air carrier flights, and of those, 83 percent (212) involved an encounter with a VFR aircraft.

When the total numbers are segregated by various altitude strata, they disclose that there were 35 near midair collisions of record between 13,000 feet and 17,900 feet. Of these, 91 percent (32) involved a VFR aircraft, and

46 percent (16) involved air carrier flights. Ninety-three percent (15) of the incidents involving air carriers involved a VFR aircraft.

Between the altitudes of 10,000 feet through 12,900 feet, there were 79 near midair collisions recorded of which 91 percent (72) involved a VFR aircraft, and 57 percent (45) involved air carrier flights. Of the incidents involving air carriers, 87 percent (39) resulted from an encounter with a VFR aircraft. Sixty-two percent (24) of the air carrier near midair collisions reported involved a VFR encounter while operating in the en route environment. The remaining 38 percent (15) at these altitudes involved an encounter with a VFR aircraft while operating within 30 miles of an airport at which at least one of the aircraft involved had either departed or intended to land.

At 9,900 feet and below, 892 near midair collisions were recorded of which 94 percent (844) involved a VFR aircraft, and 22 percent (196) involved air carrier flights. Of the incidents involving air carrier aircraft, 86 percent (168) resulted from an encounter with a VFR aircraft. Twenty-three percent (39) of the air carrier near midair collisions involved an encounter with a VFR flight while operating in the en route environment, and 77 percent (129) of the air carrier near midair collisions involved an encounter with a VFR aircraft while operating within 30 miles of an airport at which at least one of the aircraft had departed or intended to land.

Further analysis reveals that there were 327 midair collisions recorded below 13,000 feet within 30 miles of those airports being considered for the establishment of a Terminal Control Area [TCA] or Terminal Radar Service Area [TRSA]. Of these 327, 94 percent (306) involved a VFR aircraft, and 32 percent (106) involved an air carrier aircraft. Of these air carrier incidents, 87 percent (92) involved an encounter with a VFR aircraft. . . .

Airport Area Operations

The takeoff and landing phases of flight result in the concentration of inflight aircraft in a relatively limited volume of airspace surrounding an airport. The number of aircraft per unit volume of airspace at a specific instant of time is a function of the number of aircraft using that airport and its proximity to one or more adjacent airports that share or abut that airspace. As air traffic activity at an airport increases, the need for increasingly precise control of aircraft and protection of airspace from unknown aircraft becomes essential for continued safe operations. The FAA has developed a spectrum of air traffic procedures which, when coupled with precision navigational aids, airport surveillance radar facilities, automated radar data processing capability, and a highly skilled work force, form a comprehensive system to provide safe and efficient flight operations at all controlled airports.

The scope of services range from simple suggested airport traffic flows at lowest density airports, to terminal control areas at the busiest airports which provide positive controlled airspace. Within the latter, all aircraft are subject to specific operating rules and avionics equippage.

The FAA is taking action or proposing to take action to extend or enhance the application of these proven control techniques and hardware subsystems to more airports to assure greater protection of air traffic in the airspace regions most commonly used by passenger-carrying aircraft.

Terminal Control Areas

A Terminal Control Area (TCA) is a volume of airspace around a major airport(s) that is designated and charted for the pilot in which certain airborne equipments and operational requirements must be met. A pilot must receive authorization from air traffic control before flight into this airspace may be conducted. The purpose of the TCA is to provide positive separation between all flights within that designated airspace.

Preceding the establishment of the first TCA at the Atlanta Airport in June of 1970, this agency had conducted extensive studies on the near midair and actual midair collision problem. These efforts culminated with the publication of our Near Midair Collision Study (1968). On September 30, 1969, a Notice of Proposed Rulemaking was issued which proposed 22 TCAs at locations determined most prone to terminal area hazard. Subsequently, a series of public meetings were held throughout the country to discuss the proposal and obtain user input. Significant objections were voiced and a modified proposal which categorized the classification of TCAs into groups was issued on March 11, 1970.

During the ensuing 5 years a total of 9 Group I and 12 Group II TCAs were established individually following extensive public involvement in planning and supplemental rulemaking. The last TCA established was at the Kansas City, Missouri, Airport on August 1, 1975.

Today these 21 TCA locations provide a positive control environment around a total of 23 of our busiest airports serving approximately 67 percent of all air carrier passengers. These 23 airports are:

GROUP I	GROUP II
Atlanta, Georgia	Cleveland, Ohio
Boston, Massachusetts	Denver, Colorado
Chicago, Illinois	Detroit, Michigan
Dallas-Fort Worth, Texas	Houston, Texas
Los Angeles, California	Kansas City, Missouri
Miami, Florida	Las Vegas, Nevada
New York (Kennedy, LaGuardia,	Minneapolis, Minnesota
Newark)	New Orleans, Louisiana
San Francisco, California	Philadelphia, Pennsylvania
Washington, D.C.	Pittsburgh, Pennsylvania
	Seattle, Washington
	St. Louis, Missouri

The basic difference in the groups of TCAs for the operators are equipment and operational requirements. A Group I TCA requires two-way radio, VOR or TACAN [navigation equipment], altitude encoding transponder, and a private pilot rating or better. The Group II requires all of the above except the altitude encoder and the private pilot rating. There are no Group III TCAs although provisions for this category are contained in the Federal Aviation Regulations.

The existing criteria for the two groupings is as follows:

Group I —   3.5 million enplaned passengers
                  300,000 instrument operations count
                  60 percent of all operations must be air carrier

Group II —   1 percent of the nationally enplaned passengers

The effectiveness of TCAs is readily evident, particularly from a safety standpoint. During a 2-year period prior to their establishment (1968-69), there were 376 reported near midair collisions within the 9 Group I TCA airspace. Following implementation of these TCAs, during the 1975-76 period, there were 23 reported. At the 12 Group II TCA locations, there was also a substantial reduction in reported near midair collisions after implementation of the TCAs. More important, there has *never* been a fatal air carrier collision in TCA airspace.

Now, in the interest of increased safety, particularly for the airline passenger, and with due consideration of system capability and the growth of aviation activity, a Notice of Proposed Rulemaking has been prepared extending the Group II TCA establishment criteria to include those airports accommodating at least .25 percent of the total passenger enplanements (approximately 650,000 passengers each year).

This action adds the following 41 airports as eligible for TCA establishment in a 3-phase effort, based on resource availability (i.e., display, remoting, and ancillary equipment can be made available and controllers trained).

Phase I

Memphis, Tennessee	Tulsa, Oklahoma
Orlando, Florida	El Paso, Texas
Portland, Oregon	Tucson, Arizona
Des Moines, Iowa	Salt Lake City, Utah
Spokane, Washington	San Diego, California
Sacramento, California	Albuquerque, New Mexico
Rochester, New York	San Antonio, Texas
Jacksonville, Florida	Albany, New York

(Established within 1 year of the enabling rule)

Phase II

San Juan, Puerto Rico	Omaha, Nebraska
Fort Lauderdale, Florida	Windsor-Locks, Connecticut
Buffalo, New York	Dulles, Virginia
Baltimore, Maryland	Columbus, Ohio
Cincinnati, Ohio	Dayton, Ohio

Charlotte, North Carolina
Kahului, Hawaii
Nashville, Tennessee
Louisville, Kentucky
Oklahoma City, Oklahoma

Norfolk, Virginia
Syracuse, New York
Raleigh-Durham, North Carolina
Birmingham, Alabama

(Established within 18 months of the enabling rule)

Phase III

Milwaukee, Wisconsin
Lihue, Hawaii
Indianapolis, Indiana

Anchorage, Alaska
West Palm Beach, Florida
Reno, Nevada

(Established through 1983)

Additionally, Honolulu, Hawaii, Tampa, Florida, and Phoenix, Arizona, which meet existing Group II criteria, have commenced action toward formal implementation of their TCAs. These 3 TCAs are expected to be in place by September 1979.

The additional 44 TCA locations extend the existing positive control environment to an additional 56,000,000 airline passengers annually. When this program is completed, a total of 87 percent of all airline passenger enplanements will occur at TCA airports.

Terminal Radar Service Areas

Long before the more stringent Terminal Control Area had become a reality, FAA recognized the need for a more organized means of handling the mix of high performance and other aircraft in and around airports.

Late in the 1950's busier radar terminal facilities were encouraged to establish procedures for the previously "uncontrolled" aircraft operating solely under the "see and avoid" concept to contact the radar facility before contacting the control tower. The purpose of this earlier contact was to permit the radar facility to assist in much of the last minute adjustments to landing sequence done by the tower by using radar to establish an organized arrival flow. Obviously, this procedure also enhanced safety by merely establishing order in the busy and complex terminal area.

In October 1962, the first version of a TRSA was established at Atlanta, Georgia. This effort provided enhanced separation in a defined and charted area of lateral and vertical dimension around the airport except for those aircraft operated under visual flight rules that specifically declined the service. In other words, separation was provided by the system to all users that desired it.

A national requirement was stated in 1974 that all operational automated radar terminal facilities provide a TRSA level of service as a minimum. This requirement has been satisfied. TRSAs have since been established at 86 locations serving 105 airports. One of the most recent being at Peoria, Illinois, in October of this year.

Although the mandatory aspect of the TCA is not levied on the pilot in the TRSA, we have found that systemwide approximately 90 percent of the aircraft using these airports avail themselves of our TRSA separation service.

In addition to the 105 existing TRSA airports, we now require radar terminal facilities to provide this service to all airports used by scheduled air carriers within their radar coverage area. This action will create 80 additional TRSA airports. Some of these airports have very few air carrier operations as compared to their total number of operations. Nonetheless, at those locations where the radar capability exists, we intend to provide this increased level of aviation safety.

The following list identifies the 80 new TRSA airports. Lindbergh Field, San Diego, California, will have an operational TRSA by May 1, 1979. The remaining locations will be implemented in three phases, based on resource availability, as follows:

Phase I

Fairbanks, Alaska
Boise, Idaho
Waterloo, Iowa
Allentown, Pennsylvania
Erie, Pennsylvania
Wilkes-Barre, Pennsylvania
Huntington, West Virginia
Utica, New York
Islip, New York
Sioux City, Iowa
Springfield, Missouri
Cedar Rapids, Iowa
Bangor, Maine
Tri-Cities, Tennessee
Jackson, Mississippi
Lexington, Kentucky
Greer, South Carolina
Ashville, North Carolina
Wilmington, North Carolina
Oakland, California
Billings, Montana
(To be implemented by December 1979)

Lincoln, Nebraska
Gulfport, Mississippi
Fayetteville, North Carolina
St. Thomas, Virgin Islands
Amarillo, Texas
Fort Smith, Arkansas
Lake Charles, Louisiana
Longview, Texas
Monroe, Louisiana
Midland, Texas
Beaumont, Texas
Corpus Christi, Texas
Lubbock, Texas
Austin, Texas
Monterey, California
Augusta, Georgia
Palm Springs, California
Tallahassee, Florida
Sioux Falls, South Dakota
Fargo, North Dakota
Great Falls, Montana

Phase II

Binghamton, New York
Patrick-Henry, Virginia
Baton Rouge, Louisiana
Reno, Nevada
Casper, Wyoming
Duluth, Minnesota

Harrisburg, Pennsylvania
Portland, Maine
Lafayette, Louisiana
Pueblo, Colorado
Midway, Illinois
Rockford, Illinois

Saginaw, Michigan
Anchorage, Alaska
(To be implemented by August 1981)

Youngstown, Ohio
Sarasota, Florida

Phase III

Hobby (Houston), Texas
Fresno, California
Muskegon, Michigan
Santa Ana, California
Long Beach, California
Kinston, North Carolina
Melbourne, Florida
Myrtle Beach, South Carolina
Panama City, Florida
Valdosta, Georgia
Hilo, Hawaii
(To be implemented through 1983)

Elmira, New York
Evansville, Indiana
Daytona Beach, Florida
San Jose, California
Love Field, Texas
Dothan, Alabama
Minot, North Dakota
Rapid City, South Dakota
Grand Forks, North Dakota
Abilene, Texas

Control Tower Radar Display and Alphanumerics

Since December of 1967, the FAA has had an ongoing program to provide a television display of the approach control radar in certain control towers. The purpose of this equipment is to assist the tower controller in carrying out his assigned responsibilities.

Current programs provide for remoting this televised radar data to a total of 116 airports without radar data, but within the radar coverage of radars located at adjacent airports. This program is well underway with 23 of the systems presently operational.

As the processing of radar data became increasingly automated, it became evident that tower controllers could be more effective if the alphanumeric information associated with the parent automated radar facility were available. This has been accomplished at over 50 locations including all airport control towers located on the same airport as the automated radar air traffic control facility.

Additionally, we will provide the alphanumerics and its associated controller tools; i.e., conflict alert and minimum safe altitude warning, to all TCA airport towers regardless of their location, and to airport towers serving air carrier operations whenever the total operations count for the airport exceeds 500,000 per year. These efforts involve 70 locations. These actions will be completed by December 1980.

Terminal Procedures Review

A number of procedural areas have come under question as a result of the San Diego accident. Specifically, the areas of concern are:

Visual Separation — Within the air traffic control system visual separation may be accomplished in either of two ways: (1) The controller sees the aircraft involved and assures that separation is maintained, or (2) a pilot sees the other aircraft involved and is instructed to avoid it, or follow it by visual reference. Visual separation may only be employed in the terminal area.

Visual separation, as used in air traffic control, is not the same as the commonly called "see and be seen" concept. When visual separation is employed, the pertinent aircraft have been observed and are required to remain in an observed status until visual separation is no longer required.

To substantially reduce air traffic control use of visual separation would greatly impact system efficiency, capacity, and airport usage. At some airports, because of runway configuration, arrival capacity could be reduced as much as 50 percent if visual separation was not employed.

Practice Approaches — Practice instrument approaches are and will continue to be an ongoing requirement in the National Airspace System. Practice approaches are approved on a low priority basis as system and airport activity will allow. Practice approaches should not disrupt transit operations. Controllers are required to ensure separation until the practicing aircraft has completed its approach procedure. If the aircraft is operating within a TRSA or TCA, separation service will continue after completion of the practice procedure while the aircraft remains in that airspace.

Communication Transfer Practices — Communications transfer is the process of a controller instructing an aircraft to change radio frequency — usually for the purpose of communicating with another controller. Two aircraft may be in the same general area but each in radio communications with different controllers. A communication transfer is not a control transfer.

Controllers are required to ensure that separation will continue to exist after communications transfer as long as an aircraft remains in their area of jurisdiction. A receiving controller is not permitted to alter an aircraft's clearance (instructions) until the aircraft enters the airspace for which the receiving controller has jurisdiction.

Action — An existing task force composed of FAA/DOD air traffic elements is studying terminal area operations and procedures. The study of the three foregoing procedural questions has been assigned to that group and their effort is well underway.

As a part of their background data, this group will analyze all Aviation Safety Reports compiled by NASA that may relate to these three areas of concern. The final recommendations for any needed changes will be transmitted to all elements of the aviation user community for comment prior to any procedural change.

In conjunction with the foregoing effort, we are looking into pilot awareness of their particular roles and responsibilities related to separation in the terminal area. We have initiated the following immediate actions to increase the pilot's awareness in collision avoidance and reemphasize scan procedures:

1. Visual scanning procedures have been incorporated into the pilot examiner clinic program. Every examiner is encouraged to place special emphasis upon pilot scanning techniques on all flight tests.

2. Guidance has been provided industry organizations conducting flight instructor refresher clinics to place emphasis on scan techniques in their flight instructor clinics.

3. An operations bulletin will be issued to all FAA inspectors stressing added emphasis on scanning techniques on all FAA-conducted flight tests. Inspectors are to ensure that scanning techniques are included as part of FAA approved school training programs and aviation educational programs.

4. An air carrier operations bulletin has been prepared requiring all principal operations inspectors to review their assigned carriers training programs to ensure the inclusion of scanning techniques.

5. We are instructing our inspector work force, pilot examiner, and flight instructors to emphasize scanning techniques during the conduct of the biennial flight review.

6. We are negotiating with the Aircraft Owners and Pilots Association (AOPA) to obtain copies of their scanning program "Take Two and See," and will produce copies for our district offices to use in pilot education clinics and dissemination to industry organizations.

7. We are updating Advisory Circular 90-48, Pilot's Role in Collision Avoidance, and will widely disseminate it in the general aviation sector.

8. We have requested our accident prevention specialists and accident prevention counselors to place special emphasis upon visual scanning techniques in accident prevention clinics.

We will continue to explore the potential benefits derived from pilot education efforts regarding scan procedures for use during visual flight conditions.

En Route Flight Operations

The en route phase of flight encompasses all inflight activities conducted outside of airport traffic areas while the aircraft are in transit between points of origin and destination. The aircraft may be operating at any altitude ranging from the minimum en route altitude to 60,000 feet or above while in this phase of flight. . . .

Since the majority of air carriers fly at the higher altitudes in the continental United States, FAA has long required all aircraft operating above 18,000 feet mean sea level [MSL] to be under the "control" of the air traffic system. This means that any airplane operating above that level must be properly equipped as provided for in published regulations . . . and provided positive separation by air traffic control. The FAA operates a modern, highly effective automated en route air traffic control complex at its 20 air route traffic control centers in the contiguous 48 states. In conjunction with airplane avionics, this system determines aircraft identity, position, altitude, and ground speed to facilitate separation.

As an additional en route control advisory feature, aircraft operating above 12,500 feet mean sea level have for several years been required to be equipped with an air traffic control radar beacon transponder having an automatic altitude reporting function. However, positive separation has not been provided to aircraft operating under visual flight rules at altitudes lower than 18,000 feet mean sea level.

We have now concluded that added safety benefits can be provided airline passengers by lowering this positive control airspace floor and providing additional aircraft separation services as outlined in the following paragraphs.

Positive Control Areas and Controlled Visual Flight

The airspace presently defined as Positive Control Area concerns the en route phase of flight. In this airspace, which extends upward from 18,000 feet MSL through 60,000 feet MSL, all aircraft are controlled and provided positive separation. This volume of designated airspace and the attendant safety, have been in existence since August 1971.

When one considers the extensive activity in the past, and presently underway, regarding the expansion of TCAs and TRSAs, it becomes apparent that a positive control void exists for the air carrier passenger in that airspace between the top of the terminal area and the 18,000 foot base of the Positive Control Area.

Although this area represents a relatively small potential for mishap, the possibility of an encounter between an uncontrolled aircraft and a controlled air carrier flight is real.

Presently, the only restriction placed on the uncontrolled flight below 18,000 feet is to carry and operate an altitude encoding transponder when flying at or above 12,500 feet MSL. If we were to lower the floor of the Positive Control Area, we would virtually eliminate the potential for an uncontrolled encounter with an air carrier aircraft in that airspace.

In consideration of the risk and safety benefits, we are proposing to lower the Positive Control Area floor to 10,000 feet MSL east of the Mississippi River and in the coastal and western valley areas of the State of California. Elsewhere in the 48 states, we propose a floor altitude of 12,500 feet MSL, excluding airspace within 2,500 feet of terrain. . . .

Within this newly designated airspace, both controlled visual flight and instrument flights can operate with positive separation provided by the air traffic system. Controlled visual flight for en route aircraft is a new concept although the handling of these aircraft will be similar to flights within the Terminal Control Area. Equipment requirements for controlled visual flight consist of carriage of an altitude encoding transponder, VOR or TACAN receiver, and a two-way radio. Additionally, the pilot would be expected to file a flight plan, obtain authorization to enter the Positive Control Area, adhere to controller instructions, and, of course, comply with all Federal Aviation Regulations relevant to visual flight. These are the only requirements imposed on the pilot conducting controlled visual flight.

The newly described airspace was selected as best for Positive Control Area expansion and the introduction of controlled visual flight for several reasons. Most important is that this area, statistically, as discussed earlier in this paper, is the most fertile for reduction of the potential for a midair collision within the system's capability.

Another obvious safety benefit becomes evident when the Positive Control Area is adjusted downward so that it enjoins the TCA. When this situation exists, the air carrier passenger remains in a positive control environment from "takeoff to touchdown."

En Route Radar Service Areas

As previously addressed, FAA has established TRSAs at more than 100 moderately busy airports to enhance safety of flight operations and traffic flow efficiency. The same concept is proposed to be extended to the en route environment below the floor of the Positive Control Area. This service would be directed to the en route airspace that contain an insufficient volume of air carrier enplaned passengers or near midair collision potential to warrant designation of Positive Control Area. It would be implemented within areas where radar and radio coverage are adequate to ensure continuous surveillance and communications. Pilot participation would be encouraged but voluntary, and air traffic control provision of the service mandatory, once it is undertaken. As with TRSAs, the En Route Radar Service Areas would produce a higher level of safety with a minimum opposition from airspace users. Moreover, it would make available a higher level of safety for those who desire it without imposing the procedural constraints associated with Positive Control Areas.

Collision Avoidance Systems

Collision avoidance systems detect conflicts in the flight paths of two aircraft on a potential collision course and provide instructions necessary to avert the collision. These systems may be airborne or ground based.

The development of systems began in the mid-1950's and has been the subject of intense research and development by the FAA, private companies, and industry groups since that time.

As an output of this effort, the FAA has developed a dual approach to collision avoidance. This approach provides for a ground-based primary system, backed up by an airborne system. These two systems work together to provide coverage to the greatest number of people in flight at a comparatively low overall cost.

Each of these systems is made up of parts. Some of the parts are currently operational, some are planned for implementation, some remain in development.

The Ground-Based System

The ground-based system is made up of four parts. All of these utilize air traffic control computer systems and are time sequential ranging from approximately 20 minutes and progressing to 20 to 25 seconds in advance of a potential conflict.

Conflict Probe is designed to analyze the flight plan data filed by the pilots and project possible conflicts approximately 20 minutes before the potential conflict. The appropriate air traffic controller is advised. He determines corrective action and notifies the aircraft. Conflict Probe is under development.

Conflict Alert analyzes radar and beacon data and altitude information to determine possible conflicts approximately 2 minutes before expected conflict in the en route system, and 40 seconds before expected conflict in the terminal system. The appropriate air traffic controller is advised. He determines corrective action and notifies the aircraft. Conflict Alert is currently operating in all en route facilities and at major airports. Developments are underway to extend this capability to other airports.

Conflict Resolution is an extension of Conflict Alert in the en route system to provide resolution advisories to the controller. Conflict Resolution is under development.

Automated Traffic Advisory and Resolution Service (ATARS) provides the pilot of equipped aircraft with cockpit displayed resolution advisories when the potential conflict is not resolved by approximately 1 minute before expected conflict in the en route system, and approximately 20 seconds before expected conflict in the terminal system. The ATARS requires implementation of a data link between ground-based computers and aircraft. Development of ATARS is currently nearing completion and implementaion is planned to begin in 1984.

The Airborne System

The airborne system is built around the Beacon Collision Avoidance System (BCAS). This system utilizes air traffic control radar beacon equipment as its base. This equipment currently provides radar position data, aircraft identification, and altitude on properly equipped aircraft. Two versions of the BCAS are planned.

The active BCAS provides a cockpit-displayed warning to pilots of equipped aircraft of potential conflicts with any other aircraft equipped with an altitude encoding beacon system. Service is limited to airspace having a moderate number of aircraft. Resolution advisories provided to the pilot are limited to climb or dive instructions. Anticipated proposals will require all airlines and air taxis to be equipped by 1985.

The full BCAS will provide a cockpit-displayed warning to pilots of equipped aircraft of a potential conflict with any other aircraft equipped with a beacon system in all airspace. Resolution service provides for both horizontal and vertical maneuvering instructions.

Future Avionics Requirements

These proposals require the acquisition of avionics equipment, particularly radar beacon transponders, on certain aircraft not currently equipped.

In the long term, collision avoidance equipment will be required for some aircraft. The following is a summary of those proposed requirements.

Radar Beacon transponders, navigation equipment (VOR or TACAN), encoding and communications equipment proposed for aircraft operating in the TCAs and positive control areas.

Altitude encoding transponder in all Terminal Control Areas and Terminal Radar Service Areas by July 1981.

Discrete Address Beacon System (DABS) transponders for all aircraft installations, new or replacement, made after July 1982, and require data link carriage in all air carrier, air taxi, and military aircraft by January 1985.

Active Beacon Collision Avoidance Systems equipment in all air carrier, air taxi, and military aircraft by January 1985.

SPANISH DEMOCRATIC CONSTITUTION
December 29, 1978

Spain's first constitution in nearly 40 years, its 11th in 170, went into effect on Dec. 29, creating a democracy known as a parliamentary monarchy and embodying many basic liberties Spaniards had never officially enjoyed. The constitution became effective when it was published in the official state gazette two days after King Juan Carlos I signed it.

In a national referendum Dec. 6, the Spanish people overwhelmingly approved the constitution that their parliament (Cortes) had spent the month of October writing. Copies of the document had been distributed to all households and were written in six of the Spanish dialects. The charter, which the Cortes ratified Oct. 31 by overwhelming votes in both houses, was the product of compromises fashioned by Spain's primary political factions, including the Union of the Democratic Center, the governing party, and the Socialist Workers, Communist and Popular Alliance parties. The constitution was considered the most liberal in Europe.

Low Turnout

Of the 17.9 million Spaniards who voted, 88 percent approved of the constitution. The vote was clouded somewhat by the large number of abstentions encouraged by dissidents ranging from the autonomous-minded Basque nationalists to right-wingers still loyal to Generalissimo Francisco Franco, who as dictator ruled with his list of "fundamental laws" from 1939 until his death on Nov. 20, 1975. Thus, only 68 percent of the 26.8 million eligible voters cast ballots, disappointing government leaders who had spent an estimated $8 million on a campaign to win approval for the document.

Some members of the Roman Catholic hierarchy in Spain, who disapproved of the constitution's embodiment of the principle of separation of church and state, also encouraged abstention or at least casting blank ballots. Until the constitution was adopted, the church had been the official religion of Spain. That the constitution was the work of compromise to satisfy as many factions as possible was evident in article 16, which said, "There shall be no State religion. The public authorities shall take the religious beliefs of Spanish society into account and shall maintain the consequent relations of cooperation with the Catholic Church and the other confessions." But the church's influence was to be reduced somewhat by the creation of a public school system to exist alongside the parochial system and the transfer of the matters of marriage and divorce from exclusive church control to civil government. Ordering provisions for divorce thus became the first official recognition of the legality of dissolving marriages in Spain.

Individual Rights

The 169-article document guaranteed most of the basic individual rights enjoyed in other democracies, including ones similar to those in the U.S. Bill of Rights. In addition, the constitution abolished the death penalty, allowed trade unions to be formed (but also allowed the right not to join them) and protected workers' right to strike, allowed political parties, lowered the legal age to 18 and made universities autonomous, no longer run by the state. The constitution also outlawed discrimination on the basis of "birth, race, sex, religion, opinion or any other condition or personal or social circumstance." And it embodied many of the arrest procedures worked out in the United States only in the past few decades, such as the right of an individual to be "informed immediately, and in a manner understandable to him, of his rights and of the reasons for his arrest, and . . . not be compelled to make a statement." A broad social security system also was embodied in the constitution.

In contrast to the guarantee of rights to the citizens, the king lost some of his powers with the constitution's adoption. What he could do as king was proscribed in title II, "Concerning the Crown." His duties and powers are similar to those enjoyed by the British monarchy, including the power to dissolve the Cortes and call new elections. Much of the section, however, dealt with the route of succession to the crown, beginning with Juan Carlos as a member of the Bourbon dynasty.

The next title set down provisions for the Cortes Generales, the bicameral parliament. It established a Senate of four senators from each province and a larger body, the Congress of Deputies, composed of 300 to 400 members elected by proportional representation. All members of the Cortes would serve four-year terms and operate with many of the same privileges as members of the U.S. Congress or British Parliament. Other titles established the makeup of the administration run by a president nominated by the king every four years, subject to the approval of the Congress of Deputies. And the king would appoint the president of the Supreme Court, who also would serve as the head of the 21-member General Council of the Judiciary. Its members, in turn, had to be qualified for the job and could serve only five years.

Concessions to Basques

The compromise, reached in an attempt to satisfy the demands of the Basques and other nationalists who wanted autonomy from the central government, arranged for "self-governing communities" to serve those areas in addition to the normal municipal and provincial governments. Self-governing communities could be comprised of "bordering provinces with common historic, cultural and economic characteristics, island territories and provinces with historic regional status...." The constitution barred self-governing communities from joining in a federation of such bodies and spelled out the jurisdictions the communities had to yield to the national government.

As indicated by their campaign for abstention or casting blank ballots in the Dec. 6 referendum, however, the Basques and others were not satisfied with the provisions for their regions. In another compromise of demands by the several nationalistic groups, the constitution settled on Castillian as the official Spanish language. Castillian is commonly spoken in the northern two-thirds of Spain, in some areas along with a more localized dialect. "All Spaniards have the duty to know it and the right to use it," article 3 of the constitution said, but added, "The other languages of Spain shall also be official in the respective Self-Governing Communities...."

Even after the constitution became official, the country faced other momentous decisions, including holding national elections to elect the first Cortes under the new constitution. It was estimated that the new Cortes would have to enact 50 laws over the next three years to implement the constitutional provisions.

Background

The Borbon line of the Spanish monarchy began in 1700 with Philip V, grandson of Louis XIV of France. Philip was willed the throne on the death of Charles II, the last of the Hapsburg dynasty in Spain. The Borbon kings and queens were constantly beset with revolution over the next 200 years. The final blow came in 1923 when Gen. Miguel Primo de Rivera headed a military coup that gained control of the government. Alfonso XIII remained as king but his powers were subjugated to those of Rivera. Rivera later served as prime minister until he resigned in 1930.

In 1931 the king left Spain when a national election forced on him resulted in creation of a republic. On Dec. 9, 1931, a republican constitu-

tion was promulgated, bearing many of the designs of the current constitution. But supporters of the exiled king, who by this time was forbidden to return to Spain, grew increasingly fearful of what were considered socialist actions on the part of the republican government. In 1936 Gen. Franco began a military revolt from Morocco on behalf of the royalists. The civil war raged until the last cities fell to Franco's troops in March 1939. The exiled king's rights were restored, but not his crown. Franco, although favoring the monarchy, elected instead to keep absolute authority. In March 1947, Spain officially was re-established as a monarchy, but with Franco serving as chief of state for the rest of his life. It was that 1947 provision, approved in a national referendum, that allowed Don Juan Carlos de Borbon y Borbon, Franco's hand-picked successor and grandson of the last king, to become king upon Franco's death in 1975.

But Carlos himself led the three-year transition from Franco's dictatorship to the formation of a parliamentary democracy culminating in the promulgation of the 1978 constitution. He already had instituted many of the freedoms that were to be spelled out in that document.

> *Following are excerpts from the Spanish Constitution (unofficial translation), which became effective Dec. 29, 1978:*

PREAMBLE

The Spanish Nation, desirous of establishing justice, liberty and security and promoting the good of its members, by virtue of its sovereignty, proclaims its will to:

—guarantee democratic co-existence within the Constitution and the law consistent with a just social and economic order;

—consolidate a State of Law which assures the rule of law as an expression of the popular will;

—protect all Spaniards and peoples of Spain in the exercise of human rights, of their cultures and traditions, and of their languages and institutions;

—promote the progress of culture and of the economy in order to ensure a worthy quality of life for all;

—establish a democratic and advanced society, and

—collaborate in the strengthening of peaceful relations and effective co-operation amongst all the peoples of the World.

Therefore, the Cortes adopts and the Spanish people ratify the following

CONSTITUTION
PRELIMINARY TITLE

Article 1.

1. Spain constitutes a social and democratic State of Law, advocating as

higher values of its legal order, liberty, justice, equality and political pluralism.

2. National sovereignty is vested in the Spanish people, from whom emanate the powers of the State.

3. The political form of the Spanish State is that of Parliamentary Monarchy.

Article 2.

The Constitution is based on the indissoluble unity of the Spanish Nation, the common and indivisible country of all Spaniards, and recognizes and guarantees the right to self-government of the nationalities and regions of which it is composed and solidarity amongst them all.

Article 3.

1. Castillian is the official Spanish language of the State. All Spaniards have the duty to know it and the right to use it.

2. The other languages of Spain shall also be official in the respective Self-Governing Communities in accordance with their Statutes.

3. The wealth of the different language variations of Spain is a cultural heritage which shall be the object of special respect and protection.

Article 4.

1. The flag of Spain consists of three horizontal stripes: red, yellow and red, the yellow stripe being double the width of the red ones.

2. The Statutes may recognize flags and ensigns of the Self-Governing Communities. These shall be used together with the flag of Spain on and in their public buildings and in their official ceremonies.

Article 5.

The capital of the State is the City of Madrid.

Article 6.

The political parties are the expression of political pluralism, cooperate in the formation and expression of the will of the people and are a basic instrument for political participation. Their creation and the exercise of their activity are free in so far as they are compatible with respect for the Constitution and the law. Their internal structure and operation must be democratic.

Article 7.

Trade unions and employers' associations contribute to the defence and promotion of the economic and social interests proper to them. Their creation and the exercise of their activity are free in so far as they are compatible with respect for the Constitution and the law. Their internal structure and operation must be democratic.

Article 8.

1. The Armed Forces, comprising the Army, the Navy and the Air Force, have as their mission the guaranteeing of the sovereignty and indepen-

dence of Spain and of defending her territorial integrity and the Constitutional order.

2. An organic law shall regulate the bases of military organization in
conformity with the principles of the present Constitution.

Article 9.

1. Citizens and public authorities are bound by the Constitution and the
rest of the legal order. . . .

TITLE I

Concerning fundamental rights and duties

Article 10.

1. Human dignity, man's inviolable and inherent rights, the free development of his personality, respect for the law and for the rights of others
are fundamental to political order and social peace.

2. The standards relative to the fundamental rights and liberties recognized by the Constitution shall be interpreted in conformity with the
Universal Declaration of Human Rights and the international treaties and
agreements thereon ratified by Spain.

Chapter One

Concerning Spaniards and aliens

Article 11.

1. Spanish nationality is acquired, retained and lost in accordance with
the provisions of the law.

2. No person of Spanish origin may be deprived of his nationality.

3. The State may negotiate dual-nationality treaties with Ibero-Ameri-
can countries or with those which have special links with Spain. In these
countries, Spaniards may become naturalized without losing their nationality of origin, even if said countries do not recognize the reciprocal right of
their own citizens.

Article 12.

Spaniards are legally of age at the age of eighteen.

Article 13.

1. Aliens shall enjoy the public freedoms guaranteed by the present
Title, under the terms to be laid down by treaties and the law. . . .

3. Extradition shall be granted only in compliance with a treaty or with
the law, on the basis of the principle of reciprocity. Not subject to
extradition are political offences; acts of terrorism are not regarded as such.

4. The law shall establish the terms under which citizens from other
countries and stateless persons may enjoy the right of asylum in Spain.

Chapter Two

Concerning Rights and Liberties

Article 14.

Spaniards are equal before the law and may not in any way be discriminated against on account of birth, race, sex, religion, opinion or any other condition or personal or social circumstance.

SECTION 1

Concerning fundamental rights and public liberties

Article 15.

Every person has the right to life and physical and moral integrity, and may under no circumstances be subject to torture or to inhuman or degrading punishment or treatment. The death penalty shall be abolished, except as provided for by military criminal law in wartime.

Article 16.

1. Freedom of ideology, religion and worship of individuals and communities is guaranteed, with no more restrictions on their expression as may be necessary in order to maintain the public order protected by law.

2. Nobody may be compelled to make declarations regarding his religion, beliefs or ideologies.

3. There shall be no State religion. The public authorities shall take the religious beliefs of Spanish society into account and shall maintain the consequent relations of cooperation with the Catholic Church and the other confessions.

Article 17.

1. Every person has a right to freedom and security. Nobody may be deprived of his freedom except as laid down in this article and in the cases and in the manner provided by the law.

2. Preventive detention may last no longer than the time strictly necessary in order to carry out the necessary investigations aimed at establishing the facts and in any case the person arrested must be set free or handed over to the judicial authorities within a maximum period of seventy-two hours.

3. Any person arrested must be informed immediately, and in a manner understandable to him, of his rights and of the reasons for his arrest, and may not be compelled to make a statement. The arrested person shall be guaranteed the assistance of a lawyer for police or legal enquiries, under the terms to be laid down by the law.

4. A *habeas corpus* procedure shall be regulated by law in order to secure the immediate handing over to the judicial authority of any person arrested illegally. Likewise, the maximum period of provisional imprisonment shall be determined by law.

Article 18.

1. The right to honour, to personal and family privacy and to personal reputation is guaranteed.

2. The home is inviolable. No entry or search may be made without the consent of the occupant or a legal warrant, except in case of *flagrante delicto.*

3. Secrecy of communications is guaranteed, particularly of postal, telegraphic and telephonic communications, except in the event of a legal ruling.

4. The law shall limit the use of data processing in order to guarantee the honour and personal and family privacy of citizens and the full exercise of their rights.

Article 19.

Spaniards have the right to choose their place of residence freely, and to move about freely in the National territory.

Likewise, they have the right to freely enter and leave Spain under the terms to be laid down by the law. This right may not be restricted for political or ideological reasons.

Article 20.

1. The following rights are recognized and protected:

a) the right to freely express and disseminate thoughts, ideas and opinions by word, in writing or by any other means of divulgation;

b) the right to literary, artistic, scientific and technical production and creation;

c) the right to professorial freedom;

d) the right to freely communicate or receive truthful information by any means of dissemination whatsoever. The law shall regulate the right to invoke the clause of conscience and that of professional secrecy in the exercise of these freedoms.

2. The exercise of these rights may not be restricted by any kind of prior censorship.

3. The law shall regulate the organization and Parliamentary control of the social communications media dependent upon the State or upon any public agency and shall guarantee access to such media by significant social and political groups, respecting the pluralism of society and of the various languages of Spain.

4. These freedoms are limited by respect for the rights recognized in this Title, by the precepts of the laws implementing it, and especially by the right to honour, to privacy, to personal reputation and to the protection of youth and childhood.

5. The confiscation of publications and recordings and other information media may only be granted by virtue of a legal ruling.

Article 21.

1. The right to· peaceful assembly without arms is recognized. The exercise of this right shall not require previous authorization.

2. In cases of meetings in places of public transit and of demonstrations, prior notification shall be given to the authorities, who may ban them only when there are well-founded reasons to expect a breach of public order, with danger to persons or property.

Article 22.

1. The right to association is recognized.

2. Associations which pursue ends or use means classified as criminal offences are illegal.

3. Associations set up on the basis of this article must be recorded in a register for the sole purpose of public knowledge.

4. The associations may only be dissolved or have their activities suspended by virtue of a considered judicial ruling.

5. Secret and paramilitary associations are prohibited.

Article 23.

1. Citizens have the right to participate in public affairs, directly or through their representatives freely elected in periodic elections by universal suffrage.

2. They likewise have the right to accede on equal terms to public functions and offices, in accordance with the requirements to be prescribed by law.

Article 24.

1. Every person has the right to obtain the effective protection of the Judges and Courts in the exercise of his legitimate rights and interests, and in no case may he go undefended.

2. Likewise, all persons have the right to access to the Ordinary Judge predetermined by law, to the defence and assistance of a lawyer, to be informed of the charges brought against them, to a public trial without undue delays and with full guarantees, to the use of the evidence pertinent to their defence, not to make declarations against themselves, not to confess themselves guilty, and to the presumption of innocence.

The law shall regulate the cases in which, for reasons of family relationship or professional secrecy, it shall not be obligatory to make declarations regarding presumed criminal offences.

Article 25.

1. No-one may be convicted or sentenced for any act or omission which at the moment it was committed did not constitute a criminal offence, misdemeanour or administrative infringement according to the law in force at that time.

2. Punishments entailing deprivation of liberty and security measures shall be oriented towards re-education and social reintegration and may not consist of forced labour. The person sentenced to a prison term shall, during his imprisonment, enjoy the fundamental rights contained in this Chapter except those expressly limited by the content of the conviction, the meaning of the sentence and the penitentiary law. In any case, he shall

be entitled to paid employment and to the corresponding Social Security benefits, as well as to access to culture and the full development of his personality.

3. The Civil Administration may not impose sanctions which directly or in a subsidiary manner imply deprivation of freedom.

Article 26.

Honour Courts are prohibited within the framework of the Civil Administration and of professional societies.

Article 27.

1. Everyone is entitled to education. Freedom of instruction is recognized.

2. Education shall have as its objective the full development of the human personality compatible with respect for the democratic principles of co-existence and for the fundamental rights and liberties.

3. The public authorities guarantee the right of parents to ensure that their children receive religious and moral instruction compatible with their own convictions.

4. Basic education is compulsory and gratuitous. . . .

10. The autonomy of the Universities is recognized, under the terms to be laid down by the law.

Article 28.

1. Everyone has the right to freely join a trade union. The law may limit the exercise of this right or make an exception to it in the case of the Armed Forces or Institutes or other Corps subject to military discipline, and shall regulate the special features of its exercise by public officials. Trade union freedom includes the right to found trade unions to form confederations and found international trade union organizations, or to become members of same. Nobody may be compelled to join a trade union.

2. The right of workers to strike in defence of their interests is recognized. The law regulating the exercise of this right shall establish the guarantees necessary to ensure the maintenance of essential community services. . . .

SECTION 2

Concerning the rights and duties of citizens

Article 30.

1. Citizens have the right and the obligation to defend Spain.

2. The law shall determine the military obligations of Spaniards and shall regulate, with the proper safeguards, conscientious objection as well as other causes of exemption from compulsory military service; it may also, when appropriate, impose a substitutional form of social service. . . .

Article 31.

1. Everyone shall contribute to bearing public expenditure in accordance with his financial means, through a just system of taxation based on

principles of equality and progress, which in no case shall be confiscatory in character.

2. Public expenditure shall be incurred in such a way that an equitable allocation of public resources may be achieved, and its planning and execution shall comply with criteria of efficiency and economy.

3. Personal or property contributions of a public nature may only be imposed in accordance with the law.

Article 32.

1. Men and women are entitled to enter into marriage on a basis of full legal equality.

2. The law shall regulate the forms of marriage, the age at which it may be entered into and the required capacity therefor, the rights and duties of the spouses, the grounds for separation and dissolution, and their consequences.

Article 33.

1. The right to private property and inheritance is recognized.

2. The social function of these rights shall determine their content, in accordance with the law.

3. No-one may be deprived of his property and rights, except on justified grounds of public utility or social interest in return for proper compensation in accordance with the provisions of the law.

Article 34.

1. The right of foundation for reasons of general interest is recognized, in conformity with the law.

2. The provisions of clauses 2 and 4 of article 22 shall be applicable to foundations.

Article 35.

1. All Spaniards have the duty to work and the right to employment, to free choice of profession or trade, to advancement through their work, and to sufficient remuneration for the satisfaction of their needs and those of their families, while in no case may they be discriminated against on account of their sex. . . .

Article 36.

The law shall regulate the special features of the legal status of the Professional Colleges and the exercise of the degree professions. The internal structure and operation of the Colleges must be democratic.

Article 37.

1. The law shall guarantee the right to collective labour bargaining between workers' and employers' representatives, as well as the binding force of the agreements. . . .

Article 38.

Free enterprise is recognized within the framework of a market economy. . . .

Chapter Three

Concerning the governing principles of economic and social policy

Article 39.

1. The public authorities guarantee the social, economic and legal protection of the family.

2. The public authorities likewise guarantee full protection of children, who shall be equal before the law, irrespective of their filiation, and of mothers, whatever their civil status. The law shall allow for the investigation of paternity.

3. Parents must provide their children, whether born within or outside wedlock, with assistance of every kind while they are still under age, and in other cases which are legally applicable.

4. Children shall enjoy the protection provided in the international agreements which safeguard their rights. . . .

Article 41.

The public authorities shall maintain a public Social Security system for all citizens which will guarantee adequate social assistance and benefits in needy situations, especially in cases of unemployment. Complementary assistance and benefits shall be optional. . . .

Article 43.

1. The right to protection of health is recognized.

2. It is incumbent upon the public authorities to organize and safeguard public health through preventive measures and the necessary benefits and services. The law shall establish the rights and duties of all concerned to this effect.

3. The public authorities shall foster health education, physical education and sports. Likewise, they shall encourage the proper use of leisure. . . .

Article 47.

All Spaniards are entitled to enjoy fitting and adequate housing. . . .

Article 49.

The public authorities shall carry out a policy of preventive care, treatment, rehabilitation and integration of the physically, sensorially and mentally handicapped. . . .

Article 50.

The public authorities shall guarantee, through adequate and periodically updated pensions, sufficient financial means for citizens during old age. . . .

Article 51.

1. The public authorities shall guarantee the protection of consumers and users and shall, by means of effective measures, safeguard their safety, health and legitimate economic interests. . . .

Chapter Four

Concerning the guaranteeing of fundamental rights and liberties

Article 54.

1. An organic law shall regulate the institution of Defender of the People, who shall be the supreme instrument of the Cortes Generales, appointed by them to defend the rights contained in this Title; for this purpose he may supervise Administration activities, reporting thereon to the Cortes Generales.

Chapter Five

Concerning the suspension of rights and liberties

Article 55.

1. The rights recognized in articles 17 and 18, clauses 2 and 3, articles 19 and 20, clause 1, sub-clauses a) and d) and clause 5, articles 21 and 28, clause 2, and article 37, clause 2, may be suspended when the declaration of a state of emergency or siege is decided upon under the terms provided in the Constitution. Clause 3 of article 17 is excepted from the foregoing provisions in the event of the declaration of a state of emergency. . . .

TITLE II

Concerning the Crown

Article 56.

1. The King is the Head of the State, the symbol of its unity and permanence. He arbitrates and moderates the regular working of the institutions, assumes the highest representation of the Spanish State in international relations, especially with those nations belonging to the same historic community, and exercises the functions expressly conferred on him by the Constitution and the law.

2. His title is King of Spain, and he may use the other titles belonging to the Crown.

3. The person of the King is inviolable and is not subject to liability. His acts shall always be countersigned in the manner established in article 64. Without such countersignature they shall lack validity, except as provided for in article 65, 2.

Article 57.

1. The Crown of Spain is hereditary with respect to the successors of H. M. Juan Carlos I de Borbon, legitimate heir of the historic dynasty. Succession to the throne shall follow the regular order of primogeniture and representation, with preference always being given to the earlier line over the later ones; within the same line, to the closer degree over the more

distant one; within the same degree, to the male over the female; and for the same sex, to the older person over the younger.

2. The Crown Prince, from the time of his birth or the event giving rise to his claim, shall hold the title of Prince of Asturias and the other titles traditionally linked to the heir of the Crown of Spain.

3. Should all the lines designated by law become extinct, the Cortes Generales shall provide for the succession to the Crown in the manner most suited to the interests of Spain.

4. Those persons with a right of succession to the Throne who should enter into marriage against the express prohibition of the King and the Cortes Generales, shall be excluded from succession to the Crown, both with regard to themselves and their descendants.

5. Abdications and renunciations and any doubt concerning a fact or the law that may arise in connection with the succession to the Crown shall be resolved by an organic law.

Article 58.

The Queen Consort, or the Queen's consort, may not assume any constitutional functions, except as provided for by the Regency.

Article 59.

1. In the event of the King being under age, the father or mother of the King or, in their default, the relative of legal age who is nearest in succession to the Crown, according to the order established in the Constitution, shall immediately assume the office of the Regency, which he shall exercise during the King's minority.

2. If the King becomes incapacitated for the exercise of his authority, and this incapacity is recognized by the Cortes Generales, the Crown Prince shall immediately assume the power of the Regency, if he is of age. If he is not, the procedure outlined in the foregoing clause shall be followed until the coming of age of the Prince.

3. If there is no person entitled to assume the Regency, the latter shall be appointed by the Cortes Generales and shall consist of one, three or five persons.

4. In order to exercise the Regency, it is necessary to be Spanish and legally of age.

5. The Regency shall be exercised by constitutional mandate, and always on behalf of the King. . . .

Article 61.

1. The King, on being proclaimed before the Cortes Generales, shall take oath to discharge his functions faithfully, to abide by the Constitution and the law and ensure that they are abided by, and respect the rights of citizens and the Self-Governing Communities.

2. The Crown Prince, on coming of age, and the Regent or Regents, on assuming their functions, shall take the same oath, as well as that of loyalty to the King.

Article 62.

It is incumbent upon the King:

a) to sanction and promulgate the laws;

b) to summon and dissolve the Cortes Generales and to call elections upon the terms provided for in the Constitution;

c) to call a referendum in the cases provided for in the Constitution;

d) to propose a candidate for President of the Government and, as the case may be, appoint him or remove him from office, under the terms provided in the Constitution.

e) to appoint and dismiss members of the Government at the proposal of its President;

f) to issue the decrees agreed upon by the Council of Ministers, to confer civil and military employments and award honours and distinctions in conformity with the law;

g) to keep himself informed about the affairs of State and to preside, for this purpose, [over] the meetings of the Council of Ministers when he deems opportune, at the request of the President of the Government;

h) to exercise supreme command of the Armed Forces;

i) to exercise the right to grant pardons in accordance with the law, which may not authorize general pardons.

j) to exercise the High Patronage of the Royal Academies.

Article 63.

1. The King accredits ambassadors and other diplomatic representatives. Foreign represetatives in Spain are accredited to him.

2. It is incumbent on the King to express the State's assent to make international commitments through treaties, in conformity with the Constitution and the law.

3. It is incumbent on the King, following authorization by the Cortes Generales, to declare war and make peace.

Article 64.

1. The King's acts shall be countersigned by the President of the Government and, where appropriate, by the competent ministers. The nomination and appointment of the President of the Government, and the dissolution provided for in article 99, shall be countersigned by the President of the Congress.

2. Those countersigning the King's acts shall be liable for them.

Article 65.

1. The King receives an overall amount from the State Budget for the upkeep of his Family and Household and distributes it freely.

2. The King freely appoints and dismisses the civil and military members of his Household.

TITLE III

Concerning the Cortes Generales

Chapter One

Concerning the Chambers

Article 66.

1. The Cortes Generales represent the Spanish people and consist of the Congress of Deputies and the Senate.

2. The Cortes Generales exercise the legislative power of the State, approve its Budgets, control Government action and hold all the other powers vested in them by the Constitution.

3. The Cortes Generales are inviolable.

Article 67.

1. No one may be a member of both Chambers simultaneously, nor be a representative in the Assembly of a Self-Governing Community at the same time that he is a Deputy to Congress. . . .

Article 68.

1. Congress consists of a minimum of three hundred and a maximum of four hundred deputies, elected by universal, free, equal, direct and secret suffrage on the terms laid down by the law.

2. The electoral district is the province. . . . The total number of Deputies shall be distributed in accordance with the law, each electoral district being assigned a minimum initial representation and the rest being distributed in proportion to the population.

3. The election in each electoral district shall be conducted on the basis of proportional representation.

4. Congress is elected for four years. The term of office of the Deputies ends four years after their election or on the day that the Chamber is dissolved. . . .

6. Elections shall take place between thirty and sixty days after the end of the term of office. Congress-elect must be summoned within twenty-five days after the holding of elections.

Article 69.

1. The Senate is the Chamber of territorial representation.

2. In each province, four Senators shall be elected by universal, free, equal, direct and secret suffrage by the voters in each of them, on the terms to be contained in an organic law. . . .

5. The Self-Governing Communities shall moreover nominate one Senator and a further Senator for each million inhabitants in their respective territories. . . .

6. The Senate is elected for four years. The Senators' term of office shall end four years after their election or on the day that the Chamber is dissolved. . . .

Article 71.

1. Deputies and Senators shall enjoy inviolability for opinions expressed in the exercise of their functions.

2. During their terms of office, Deputies and Senators shall likewise enjoy immunity and may only be arrested in the event of *delicto flagrante*. They may neither be indicted nor tried without prior authorization of the respective Chamber.

3. In actions brought against Deputies and Senators, the competent court shall be the Criminal Division of the Supreme Court.

4. Deputies and Senators shall receive a salary to be fixed by the respective Chambers.

Article 72.

1. The Chambers establish their own Standing Orders, adopt their budgets autonomously and, in common agreement, regulate the Personnel Statutes of the Cortes Generales. The Standing Orders and any alteration thereof shall be subject in their entirety to a final vote, which shall require an absolute majority.

2. The chambers choose their respective Presidents and the other members of their Steering Committees. . . .

3. The Presidents of the Chambers exercise on behalf of the latter all administrative powers and disciplinary functions within their respective Chambers.

Article 73.

1. The Chambers shall meet annually for two ordinary sessions: the first from September to December, and the second from February to June.

2. The Chambers may meet in extraordinary assembly at the request of the Government, of the Standing Committee ("Deputation") or of the absolute majority of members of either of the Chambers. Extraordinary meetings must be convened with a specific agenda and shall be adjourned once it has been covered.

Article 74.

1. The Chambers shall meet in joint assembly in order to exercise the non-legislative powers expressly conferred upon the Cortes Generales by Title II.

2. The decisions of the Cortes Generales outlined in articles 94, 1, 145, 2 and 158, 2 shall be adopted by majority of each of the Chambers. In the first case, the procedure shall be initiated by Congress, and in the other two by the Senate. In both cases, if an agreement is not reached between the Senate and Congress, an attempt to reach agreement shall be made by a Mixed Commission consisting of an equal number of Deputies and Senators. The Commission shall submit a text which shall be voted on by both Chambers. If this is not passed in the established manner, Congress shall decide by absolute majority.

Article 75.

1. The Chambers shall function in Plenary Assembly and in Committee.

2. The Chambers may delegate to the Standing Legislative Committees the passing of Government or non-Government bills. However, the Plenum may at any time demand debate and a vote on any Government or non-

Government bill which has been the object of this delegation.

3. Excluded from the provisions of the foregoing paragraph are constitutional reform, international affairs, organic and basic laws and the General State Budgets.

Article 76.

1. Congress and the Senate and, when appropriate, both Chambers jointly, may appoint fact-finding committees on any matter of public interest. Their conclusions shall not be binding on the Courts, nor shall they affect judicial decisions, notwithstanding the fact that the results of investigations may be transmitted to the Public Prosecutor for him to take appropriate action when necessary.

2. It shall be compulsory to appear when summoned by the Chambers. Penalties which may be imposed for failure to comply with this obligation shall be established by law.

Article 77.

1. The Chambers may receive individual and collective petitions, always in writing, while direct submittal by citizens' demonstration is prohibited.

2. The chambers may refer the petitions that they receive to the Government. The Government is obliged to provide an explanation regarding their content, when required to do so by the Chambers.

Article 78.

1. In each Chamber there shall be a Standing Committee consisting of a minimum of twenty-one members who shall represent the Parliamentary groups in proportion to their numerical importance. . . .

Article 79.

1. In order to adopt decisions, the Chambers must have met in a statutory manner, with a majority of their members present.

2. In order to be valid, said decisions must be passed by the majority of the members present, without prejudice to the special majorities that may be established by the Constitution or the organic laws and those which are established by the Standing Orders of the Chambers.

3. The votes of Senators and Deputies are personal and may not be delegated.

Article 80.

The plenary meetings of the Chambers shall be public, except in case of agreement to the contrary on the part of each Chamber, adopted by absolute majority, or in accordance with the Standing Orders.

Chapter Two

Concerning the Drafting of Bills

Article 81.

1. The organic laws are those relative to the development of fundamen-

tal rights and public liberties, those which adopt Statutes of Self-Government and the general electoral system, and the others provided for in the Constitution.

2. The passing, amendment or repeal of the organic laws shall require an absolute majority of the members of Congress in a final vote on the bill as a whole.

Article 82.

1. The Cortes Generales may delegate to the Government the power to issue rules with the status of law on specific matters not included in the foregoing article. . . .

Article 83.

The basic laws may in no case:
a) authorize the modification of the basic law itself;
b) grant power to enact retroactive legal rules.

Article 84.

In the event that a non-Government bill or amendment is contrary to currently valid legislative delegation, the Government may oppose its passage. In this case, a non-Government bill may be submitted for the total or partial repeal of the delegation law. . . .

Article 86.

1. In cases of extraordinary and urgent need, the Government may issue temporary legislative provisions which shall take the form of Decree-Laws and which may not affect the regulation of the basic State institutions, the rights, duties and liberties of citizens contained in Title 1, the system of the Self-Governing Communities, nor the General Electoral Law.

2. The Decree-Laws must immediately be submitted to the Congress of Deputies, which must be summoned for this purpose if not already in session. They must be debated and voted upon in their entirety within thirty days after their promulgation. Congress must expressly declare itself in favour of ratification or repeal within said period of time, for which purpose the Standing Orders shall establish a special summary procedure. . . .

Article 87.

1. The Government, the Congress and the Senate are competent to propose legislation, in accordance with the Constitution and the Standing Orders of the Chambers.

2. The Assemblies of the Self-Governing Communities may request the Government to adopt a bill or refer a non-Government bill to the Congressional Steering Committee, delegating a maximum of three Assembly members to defend it.

3. An organic law shall establish the manner in which popular initiative relative to the submitting of non-Government bills shall be regulated, as well as the requirements therefor. In any case, no fewer than 500,000 authorized signatures shall be required; this initiative may not touch on

matters concerning organic laws, taxation, international affairs or the prerogative of granting pardons. . . .

Article 89.

1. The passage of non-Government bills shall be regulated by the Standing Orders of the Chambers, in such a way that the priority owing to Government bills shall not prevent the exercise of the right to propose legislation under the terms laid down in article 87. . . .

Article 90.

1. Once an ordinary or organic bill has been passed by the Congress of Deputies, the President thereof shall immediately report on it to the President of the Senate, who shall submit it to the latter for its deliberation.

2. Within two months of receiving the text, the Senate may, by means of a considered opinion, veto it or introduce amendments into it. The veto must be passed by an absolute majority. The bill may not be submitted to the King for his sanction unless, in case of veto, Congress has ratified the initial text by an absolute majority, or by simple majority if two months have elapsed since its introduction, or has reached a decision relative to the amendments, accepting them or not by simple majority.

3. The period of two months allowed to the Senate for vetoing or amending a bill shall be reduced to twenty calendar days for bills declared by the Government or the Congress of Deputies to be urgent.

Article 91.

The King shall, within a period of fifteen days, sanction the laws passed by the Cortes Generales, and shall promulgate them and order their immediate publication. . . .

Chapter Three

Concerning International Treaties

Article 93.

By means of an organic law, authorization may be granted for concluding treaties by which powers from the Constitution shall be vested in an international organization or institution. . . .

Article 94.

1. Before contracting obligations by means of treaties or agreements, the State shall require the prior authorization of the Cortes Generales in the following cases:

    a) treaties of a political nature;

    b) treaties or agreements of a military nature;

    c) treaties or agreements affecting the territorial integrity of the State or the fundamental rights and duties established in Title I;

    d) treaties or agreements which imply financial obligations for the Public Treasury.

e) treaties or agreements which involve amendment or repeal of some law or require legislative measures for their execution.

2. Congress and the Senate shall immediately be informed regarding the conclusion of other treaties or agreements. . . .

Article 96.

1. Validly concluded international treaties, once officially published in Spain, shall form part of the internal legal order. Their provisions may only be repealed, amended or suspended in the manner provided in the treaties themselves or in accordance with the general rules of international law.

2. The same procedure shall be used for denouncing international agreements as that, contained in Article 94, for adopting them.

TITLE IV

Concerning the Government and the Administration

Article 97.

The Government directs domestic and foreign policy, civil and military administration and the defence of the State. It exercises the executive function and statutory authority in accordance with the Constitution and the law.

Article 98.

1. The Government comprises the President, Vice-Presidents, when applicable, Ministers and other members as may be laid down by law.

2. The President directs Government action and coordinates the functions of the other members thereof, without prejudice to the competence and direct responsibility of the latter in the discharge of their functions.

3. Members of the Government may not exercise representative functions other than those derived from their Parliamentary mandate, nor any other public function not derived from their office, nor engage in any professional or commercial activity whatever. . . .

Article 99.

1. After each renewal of the Congress of Deputies, and in other cases provided for in the Constitution, the King, after consultation with the representatives appointed by the political groups with Parliamentary representation, and through the President of the Congress, shall put forward a candidate for President of the Government.

2. The candidate put forward in accordance with the provisions of the foregoing paragraph shall submit to the Congress of Deputies the political programme of the Government that he intends to form and shall seek the confidence of the Chamber.

3. If the Congress of Deputies, by vote of the absolute majority of its members, grants its confidence to said candidate, the King shall appoint him President. If said majority is not obtained, the same proposal shall be submitted for a fresh vote forty-eight hours after the previous vote, and it

shall be considered that confidence has been obtained if it passes by simple majority.

4. If, after said voting, confidence for the investiture has not been obtained, successive proposals shall be voted upon in the manner provided in the foregoing paragraphs.

5. If within two months from the first vote for investiture no candidate has obtained the confidence of Congress, the King shall dissolve Congress and call new elections, following endorsement by the President of Congress.

Article 100.

The other members of the Government shall be appointed and dismissed by the King at the proposal of its President.

Article 101.

1. The Government shall resign after the holding of general elections, in the event of loss of Parliamentary confidence as provided in the Constitution, or on account of the resignation or death of its President.

2. The outgoing Government shall continue to exercise its functions until the new Government takes office.

Article 102.

1. The President of the Government and other members of the Government shall be held criminally liable, should the occasion arise, before the Criminal Division of the Supreme Court.

2. If the charge is of treason or of any offence against the security of the State committee in the exercise of their functions, it may only be brought at the initiative of one quarter of the members of Congress and with the approval of the absolute majority thereof.

3. The Royal prerogative of pardon shall not be applicable in any of the cases contained in the present article. . . .

TITLE V

Concerning the relations between the
Government and the Cortes Generales

Article 108.

The Government is jointly answerable to the Congress of Deputies for its political management.

Article 109.

The Chambers and their Committees may, through their respective Presidents, request whatever information and help they may need from the Government and its Departments and from any authorities of the State and of the Self-Governing Communities.

Article 110.

1. The Chambers and their Committees may require the presence of members of the Government.

2. Members of the Government are entitled to attend meetings of the Chambers and their Committees and to be heard in them, and may request that officials from their Departments submit information to them.

Article 111.

1. The Government and each of its members are subject to interpellations and questions put to them in the Chambers. The Standing Orders shall establish a minimum weekly period for this type of debate.

2. Any interpellation may give rise to a motion in which the Chamber makes known its position.

Article 112.

The President of the Government, after deliberation by the Council of Ministers, may ask Congress for a vote of confidence in favour of his programme or of a general policy statement. Confidence shall be considered obtained when a simple majority of the Deputies votes in favour.

Article 113.

1. The Congress of Deputies may challenge Government policy by means of the adoption by an absolute majority of its members of a motion of censure.

2. The motion of censure must be proposed by at least one tenth of the Deputies, including a candidate for the office of President of the Government.

3. The motion of censure may not be voted until five days after it has been submitted. During the first two days of this period, alternative motions may be submitted.

4. If the motion of censure is not passed by Congress, its signatories may not submit another during the same session.

Article 114.

1. If Congress withholds its confidence from the Government, the latter shall submit its resignation to the King, whereafter a President of the Government shall be nominated in accordance with the provisions of article 99.

2. If Congress adopts a motion of censure, the Government shall submit its resignation to the King, while the candidate proposed in the motion of censure shall be considered to have the confidence of the Chamber for the purposes provided in article 99. The King shall appoint him President of the Government.

Article 115.

1. The President of the Government, after deliberation by the Council of Ministers, and under his own exclusive responsibility, may propose the dissolution of the Congress, the Senate or the Cortes Generales, which shall be decreed by the King. The decree of dissolution shall set the date of the elections.

2. The proposal for dissolution may not be submitted while a motion for censure is in process.

3. There shall be no further dissolution until a year has elapsed since the previous one, except as provided for in article 99, clause 5.

Article 116.

1. An organic law shall regulate the states of alarm, emergency and siege and the corresponding powers and restrictions.

2. The state of alarm shall be declared by the Government, by means of a decree decided upon by the Council of Ministers, for a maximum period of fifteen days. The Congress of Deputies shall be informed and must convene immediately in this connection. Without their authorization the said period may not be prolonged. The decree shall specify the territorial area to which the effects of the declaration shall apply.

3. The state of emergency shall be declared by the Government by means of a decree decided upon by the Council of Ministers, after prior authorization by the Congress of Deputies. The authorization for and proclamation of the state of emergency must specifically determine the effects thereof, the territorial area to which it is to apply and its duration, which may not exceed thirty days, subject to prolongation for a further thirty-day period, with the same requirements.

4. The State of siege shall be declared by absolute majority of the Congress of Deputies, exclusively at the proposal of the Government. Congress shall determine its territorial extension, duration and terms.

5. Congress may not be dissolved while any of the states contained in the present article remain in operation, and if the Chambers are not in session, they must automatically be convened. Their functioning, as well as that of the other constitutional State authorities may not be interrupted while any of these states is in operation.

In the event that Congress has been dissolved or its term has expired, if a situation giving rise to any of these states occurs, the powers of the Congress shall be assumed by its Standing Committee.

6. Declaration of states of alarm, emergency and siege shall not modify the principle of responsibility of the Government or its agents as recognized in the Constitution and the law.

TITLE VI

Concerning the judicial power

Article 117.

1. Justice emanates from the people and is administered on behalf of the King by Judges and Magistrates of the Judiciary who shall be independent, irremovable, liable and subject only to the rule of law.

2. Judges and Magistrates may only be dismissed, suspended, transferred or retired for one of the reasons, and with the guarantees, provided by law.

3. Exercise of jurisdictional power in any kind of action, both in passing judgment and having judgments executed, lies exclusively within the competence of the Courts and Tribunals laid down by the law....

Article 118.

It is compulsory to execute the sentences and other final judgments of Judges and Courts, as well as to collaborate with them as they may require during the course of trials and execution of judgments.

Article 119.

Justice shall be gratuitous, when thus provided by law, and shall in any case be so in respect of those who have insufficient means to litigate.

Article 120.

1. Judicial proceedings shall be public, with the exception of those provided for in the laws of procedure.

2. Proceedings shall be predominantly oral, especially in criminal cases.

3. Sentences shall always be justified, and they shall be delivered in a public hearing.

Article 121.

Damages caused by judicial errors, as well as those arising from irregularities in the administration of Justice, shall be subject to compensation by the State, in accordance with the law. . . .

Article 122.

....

3. The General Council of the Judiciary shall consist of the President of the Supreme Court, who shall preside [over] it, and of twenty members appointed by the King for a five-year period, amongst whom shall be twelve Judges and Magistrates of all judicial categories, under the terms established by the organic law; four nominated by the Congress of Deputies and four by the Senate, elected in both cases by three-fifths of their members from amongst lawyers, and other jurists of acknowledged competence and over fifteen years' experience in the exercise of their profession.

Article 123.

1. The Supreme Court, with jurisdiction over the whole of Spain, is the highest judicial body in all branches of justice, except with regard to the provisions concerning Constitutional guarantees.

2. The President of the Supreme Court shall be appointed by the King, on being proposed by the General Council of the Judiciary, in the manner to be laid down by the law.

Article 124.

1. The Office of the Public Prosecutor, without prejudice to the functions entrusted to other bodies, has as its mission that of promoting the working of justice in the defence of the rule of law, of citizens' rights and of the public interest as safeguarded by the law, whether *ex officio* or at the request of interested parties, as well as that of protecting the independence of the Courts and securing through them the satisfaction of social interest. . . .

4. The State Public Prosecutor shall be appointed by the King on being proposed by the Government, after consultation with the General Council of the Judiciary.

Article 125.

Citizens may engage in popular action and participate in the administration of justice through the establishment of the Jury, in the manner and with respect to those criminal actions as may be determined by law, as well as in consuetudinary and traditional courts.

Article 126.

The judiciary police are responsible to the Judges, the Courts and the Public Prosecutor when discharging their duties of crime detection and the discovery and apprehension of criminals, under the terms to be laid down by the law.

Article 127.

1. Judges and Magistrates, as well as Public Prosecutors, whilst on active service, may not hold other public office, nor belong to political parties or trade unions. The law shall lay down the system and methods of professional association for Judges, Magistrates and Prosecutors.

2. The law shall establish the system of incompatibilities for members of the Judiciary, which must assure their total independence.

TITLE VII

Economy and Finance

Article 128.

1. All the wealth of the country in its different forms, by whosoever it may be owned, is subordinate to the general interest.

2. Public initiative in economic activity is recognized. Essential resources or services may be restricted by law to the public sector, especially in the case of monopolies. Likewise, intervention in companies may be decided upon when the public interest so demands. . . .

Article 130.

1. The public authorities shall attend to the modernization and development of all economic sectors and, in particular, those of agriculture, livestock raising, fishing and handicrafts, in order to bring the standard of living of all Spaniards up to the same level.

2. With the same object in view, special treatment shall be given to mountainous areas. . . .

Article 132.

1. The legal system governing public domain and community property shall be regulated by law, based on the principles of inalienability and imprescriptibility; they shall not be subject to attachment, nor be put to other uses.

2. Considered property of the state public domain is that determined by the law which shall, in any case, include the coastal area, the beaches, the territorial sea and the natural resources of the economic zone and the continental shelf. . . .

Article 133.

1. The original power to raise taxes is vested exclusively in the State by law.

2. The Self-Governing Communities and local Corporations may establish and levy taxes, in accordance with the Constitution and the law. . . .

Article 134.

1. It is incumbent upon the Government to prepare the General State Budgets and upon the Cortes Generales to examine, amend and approve them.

2. The General State Budgets shall be prepared annually and shall include the entire expenditure and income of the State public sector and in them shall be recorded the amount of the fiscal benefits affecting State taxes.

3. The Government must submit the General State Budgets to the Congress of Deputies at least three months before the expiration of those of the previous year.

4. If the Budget Law is not approved before the first day of the corresponding financial year, the budgets of the previous year shall be considered automatically prolonged until the new ones have been approved.

5. Once the General State Budgets have been approved, the Government may submit bills involving increases in public expenditure or decreases in the revenue corresponding to the same budgetary year.

6. Any non-Government bill or amendment which involves an increase in credit or a decrease in budget revenue shall require previous approval of the Government before its passage.

7. The Budget Law may not establish new taxes. It may modify them if a substantive tax law makes provision therefor. . . .

Article 136.

1. The Court of Audit is the supreme body charged with auditing the State's accounts and financial management, as well as those of the public sector.

It shall be directly responsible to the Cortes Generales and shall discharge its functions by delegation of the latter when examining and verifying the General Accounts of the State. . . .

TITLE VII

Concerning the territorial organization of the State

Chapter One

General Principles

Article 137.

The State is organized territorially into municipalities, provinces and any Self-Governing Communities that may be constituted. All these bodies shall enjoy self-government for the management of their respective interests.

Article 138.

1. The State guarantees the effective implementation of the principle of solidarity consecrated in Article 2 of the Constitution, safeguarding the establishment of a just and adequate economic balance between the different areas of Spanish territory and taking into special consideration the circumstances pertaining to the situation of the islands.

2. The differences between the Statutes of the different Self-Governing Communities may in no case imply economic or social privileges.

Article 139.

1. All Spaniards have the same rights and obligations in any part of the State territory.

2. No authority may adopt measures which directly or indirectly obstruct freedom of movement and settlement of persons and free movement of goods throughout the Spanish territory.

Chapter Two

Concerning Local Administration

Article 140.

The Constitution guarantees the autonomy of the municipalities, which shall enjoy full legal personality. Their government and administration shall be incumbent on their respective Town Councils consisting of Mayors and Councillors. The Councillors shall be elected by the residents of the municipalities by universal, equal, free and secret suffrage, in the manner laid down by the law. The Mayors shall be elected by the Councillors or by the residents. The law shall regulate the terms under which an open Council System shall be applicable.

Article 141.

1. The province is a local entity, with its own legal personality, determined by the grouping of municipalities as well as a territorial division, in order to carry out the activities of the State. Any alteration of the provincial boundaries must be approved by the Cortes Generales by means of an organic law. . . .

Chapter Three

Concerning the Self-Governing Communities

Article 143.

1. In the exercise of the right to self-government recognized in article 2 of the Constitution, bordering provinces with common historic, cultural and economic characteristics, island territories and provinces with historic regional status may accede to self-government and form Self-Governing Communities in conformity with the provisions contained in this Title and in the Respective Statutes.

2. The right to initiate the process towards self-government . . . lies with all the Provincial Councils concerned or with the corresponding inter-island body and with two-thirds of the municipalities whose populations represent at least the majority of the electorate of each province or island. These requirements must be met within six months from the initial agreement adopted to this effect by any of the local corporations concerned.

3. If this initiative should not be successful, it may only be repeated after five years have elapsed. . . .

Article 145.

1. Under no circumstances shall the federation of Self-Governing Communities be allowed.

2. The Statutes may provide for the cases, requirements and terms under which the Self-Governing Communities may reach agreements amongst themselves for management and the rendering of services relative to matters pertaining to them, as well as the nature and effects of the corresponding communication to the Cortes Generales. In all other cases, cooperation agreements between the Self-Governing Communities shall require the authorization of the Cortes Generales. . . .

Article 147.

1. Within the terms of the present Constitution, the Statutes shall constitute the basic institutional rules of each Self-Governing Community and the State shall recognize and protect them as an integral part of its legal order. . . .

Article 149.

1. The State holds exclusive jurisdiction over the following matters:

i) regulation of the basic conditions guaranteeing the equality of all Spaniards in the exercise of their rights and in the fulfilment of their constitutional duties;

ii) nationality, immigration, emigration, alienage, and right of asylum;

iii) international relations;

iv) defence and the Armed Forces;

v) Administration of Justice;

vi) commercial, penal and penitentiary legislation; procedural legislation, without prejudice to the necessary special applications in these fields derived from the peculiar features of the substantive law of the Self-Governing Communities;

vii) labour legislation, without prejudice to its execution by the agencies of the Self-Governing Communities;

viii) civil legislation, without prejudice to the preservation, modification and development by the Self-Governing Communities of their civil rights, "fueros" or special rights, whenever these exist; in any case, the rules relative to the application and effectiveness of legal rules, legal-civil codes relative to the forms of marriage, the keeping of records and drawing up of public instruments, bases of contractual obligations, rules for resolving conflicts of law and determination of the sources of law in conformity, in this last case, with the rules of the "fueros" or with those of special laws.

ix) legislation on intellectual and industrial property;

x) customs and tariff regulations; foreign trade;

xi) monetary system; foreign currency, exchange and convertibility, bases for the regulations concerning credit, banking and insurance;

xii) legislation on weights and measures, determination of the official time;

xiii) bases and coordination of general planning of economic activity;

xiv) General Finances and the State Debt;

xv) promotion and general coordination of scientific and technical research;

xvi) External health measures; bases and general coordination of health matters; legislation on pharmaceutical products;

xvii) basic legislation and financial system of the Social Security, without prejudice to the implementation of its services by the Self-Governing Communities;

xviii) the bases of the legal system of Public Administrations and the statutes of their public officials which shall, in any case, guarantee that the administered will receive equal treatment from them; the common administrative procedure, without prejudice to the special features of the Self-Governing Communities' own organizations; legislation on forced expropriation; basic legislation on contracts and administrative concessions and the system of liability of all the Public Administrations;

xix) sea fishing, without prejudice to the powers which, in the regulations governing this sector, shall be conferred on the Self-Governing Communities;

xx) the Merchant Navy and the registering of ships; lighting of coasts and signals at sea; general-purpose ports; general-purpose airports; control of the air space, air traffic and transport; meteorological services and registration of aircraft;

xxi) railways and land transport passing through the territory of more than one Self-Governing Community; general system of communications; motor vehicle traffic; Post Office services and telecommunications; air and underwater cables and radiocommunications;

xxii) legislation, regulation and concession of hydraulic resources and development when the waters flow through more than one Self-Governing Community, and authorization for hydroelectrical installations when their development affects another Community or when energy transport leaves its territorial area;

xxiii) basic legislation on environmental protection, without prejudice to the powers of the Self-Governing Communities to establish additional protective measures; basic legislation on woodlands, forestry, and cattle trails;

xxiv) public works of general benefit or whose execution affects more than one Self-Governing Community;

xxv) bases of the oganization of mining and energy;

xxvi) system of production, sale, possession and use of arms and explosives;

xxvii) basic rules relating to the organization of the press, radio and television and, in general, all the means of social communication, without prejudice to the powers vested in the Self-Governing Communities relative to their development and implementation;

xxviii) protection of Spain's cultural and artistic heritage and national monuments against exportation and exspoliation [sic]; museums, libraries and archives belonging to the State, without prejudice to their management by the Self-Governing Communities;

xxix) public safety, without prejudice to the possibility of the creation of police forces by the Self-Governing Communities, in the manner to be laid down in their respective Statutes and within the framework to be established by an organic law;

xxx) regulation of the conditions relative to the obtaining, issuing and standardization of academic degrees and professional qualifications and basic rules for the development of article 27 of the Constitution, in order to guarantee the fulfilment of the obligations of the public authorities in this matter;

xxxi) statistics for State purposes;

xxxii) authorization for popular consultations through the holding of referendums. . . .

3. Matters not expressly assigned to the State by virtue of the present Constitution may fall under the jurisdiction of the Self-Governing Communities by virtue of their respective Statutes. Matters for which jurisdiction has not been assumed by the Statutes of Self-Government shall fall within the jurisdiction of the State, whose rules shall prevail, in case of conflict, over those of the Self-Governing Communities regarding all matters over which exclusive jurisdiction has not been conferred upon the latter. State law shall, in all cases, be supplementary to that of the Self-Governing Communities. . . .

Article 156.

1. The Self-Governing Communities shall enjoy financial autonomy for the development and exercising of their powers, in conformity with the principles of coordination with the State Treasury and solidarity amongst all Spaniards.

2. The Self-Governing Communities may act as delegates or collabora-

tors of the State for the collection, management and settlement of the latter's tax resources, in conformity with the law and the Statutes.

Article 157.

1. The resources of the Self-Governing Communities shall comprise:

a) taxes wholly or partially made over to them by the State; surcharges on State taxes and other shares in State revenue;

b) their own taxes, rates and special levies;

c) transfers from an inter-territorial clearing fund and other allocations to be charged to the General State Budgets;

d) revenues accruing from their property and private law income;

e) the yield from credit operations.

2. The Self-Governing Communities may under no circumstances adopt measures to raise taxes on property located outside their territory or likely to hinder the free movement of goods or services.

3. The exercise of the financial powers enumerated in clause 1, above, the rules for settling the conflicts which may arise, and the possible forms of financial collaboration between the Self-Governing Communities and the State, may be regulated by an organic law.

Article 158.

1. In the General State Budgets, an allocation may be made to the Self-Governing Communities in proportion to the volume of State services and activities for which they have assumed responsibility and to their guarantee to provide a minimum level of basic public services throughout Spanish territory.

2. With the object of correcting inter-territorial economic unbalances and implementing the principle of solidarity, a clearing fund shall be set up for investment expenditure, whose resources shall be distributed by the Cortes Generales amongst the Self-Governing Communities and the provinces, as the case may be.

TITLE IX

Concerning the Constitutional Court

Article 159.

1. The Constitutional Court consists of twelve members appointed by the King. Of these, four shall be nominated by Congress by a majority of three-fifths of its members, four shall be nominated by the Government, and two by the General Council of the Judiciary.

2. The members of the Constitutional Court shall be appointed from among Magistrates and Prosecutors, University professors, public officials and lawyers, all of whom must be jurists of acknowledged competence with at least fifteen years' experience in the exercise of their professions.

3. The members of the Constitutional Court shall be appointed for a period of nine years and shall be renewed by thirds every three years.

4. The office of member of the Constitutional Court is incompatible:

with any representative function, with a management role in a political party or trade union or any employment in their service, with a career as a Judge or Prosecutor, and with any professional or commercial activity whatsoever.

In other cases, the incompatibilities relative to the judicial power shall also be applicable to the members of the Constitutional Court.

5. The members of the Constitutional Court shall be independent and irremovable during their term of office.

Article 160.

The President of the Constitutional Court shall be appointed by the King from among its members, on the recommendation of the Plenum of the Court itself, for a period of three years.

Article 161.

1. The Constitutional Court holds jurisdiction over the whole of Spanish territory and is competent to hear:

a) unconstitutionality appeals against laws and regulations having the force of law. A declaration of unconstitutionality of a legal rule with the status of law, interpreted by jurisprudence, shall also affect the latter, although an overturned sentence or sentences shall not lose the validity of a judgment;

b) individual appeals against violation of the rights and liberties contained in Article 53.2 of this Constitution, in the cases and forms to be laid down by law;

c) conflicts of jurisdiction between the State and the Self-Governing Communities or between the Self-Governing Communities themselves;

d) other matters assigned to it by the Constitution or by organic laws.

2. The Government may contest before the Constitutional Court the provisions and resolutions adopted by the agencies of the Self-Governing Communities, which shall bring about the suspension of the contested provisions or resolutions, but the Court must either ratify or lift the suspension, as the case may be, within a period of not more than five months.

Article 162.

1. The following are eligible to:

a) lodge an appeal of unconstitutionality: the President of the Government, the Defender of the People, fifty Deputies, fifty Senators, the executive corporate bodies of the Self-Governing Communities and, when applicable, their Assemblies;

b) lodge an individual appeal (recurso de amparo): any individual or corporate body with a legitimate interest, as well as the Defender of the People and the Office of the Public Prosecutor.

2. In all other cases, the organic law shall determine which persons and agencies are eligible.

Article 163.

If a judicial body considers, in some action, that a regulation with the status of law which is applicable thereto and upon the validity of which the judgment depends, may be contrary to the Constitution, it may bring the matter before the Constitutional Court in the cases, manner and with the consequences to be laid down by law, which in no case shall be suspensive.

Article 164.

1. The verdicts of the Constitutional Court shall be published in the Official State Gazette *(Boletin Oficial del Estado)*, with the dissenting votes, if any. They have the validity of a judgment as from the day following their publication, and no appeal may be brought against them. Those which declare the unconstitutionality of a law or of a rule with the force of law, and all those which are not limited to the subjective evaluation of a right, shall be fully binding on everybody.

2. Unless the verdict rules otherwise, that part of the law not affected by unconstitutionality shall remain in force.

Article 165.

An organic law shall regulate the functioning of the Constitutional Court, the statutes of its members, the procedure to be followed before it, and the conditions governing actions brought before it.

TITLE X

Concerning Constitutional amendment

Article 166.

The right to propose a Constitutional amendment shall be exercised under the terms contained in clauses 1 and 2 of Article 87.

Article 167.

1. Bills on Constitutional amendment must be approved by a majority of three-fifths of the members of each Chamber. If there is no agreement between the Chambers, an effort to reach it shall be made by setting up a Joint Commission of Deputies and Senators which shall submit a text to be voted on by the Congress and the Senate.

2. If adoption is not obtained by means of the procedure outlined in the foregoing clause, and provided that the text has been passed by an absolute majority of the members of the Senate, Congress may pass the amendment by a two-thirds vote in favour.

3. Once the amendment has been passed by the Cortes Generales, it shall be submitted to ratification by referendum, if so requested by one tenth of the members of either Chamber within fifteen days after its passage.

Article 168.

1. If a total revision of the Constitution is proposed, or a partial revision thereof, affecting the Preliminary Title, Chapter Two, Section 1 of Title I, or Title II, the principle shall be approved by a two-thirds majority of the members of each Chamber, and the Cortes shall immediately be dissolved.

2. The Chambers elected must ratify the decision and proceed to examine the new Constitutional text, which must be approved by a two-thirds majority of the members of both Chambers.

3. Once the amendment has been passed by the Cortes Generales, it shall be submitted to ratification by referendum.

Article 169.

The process of Constitutional amendment may not be initiated in time of war or when any of the states outlined in Article 116 are in operation. . . .

KOREAN INFLUENCE INVESTIGATION
December 29, 1978

The House Committee on Standards of Official Conduct Dec. 29 released a report that concluded the South Korean government had made a concerted effort to buy the influence of members of Congress in the early 1970s and probably succeeded. But the panel had no proof it could reveal and it closed the books on an investigation that had begun in January 1977 with charges that as many as 115 members of Congress had taken illegal gifts from agents of the Republic of South Korea (ROK). (Earlier hearings, Historic Documents of 1977, p. 769)

The final report said, "The investigation established that the early press reports of involvement of up to 115 members were greatly exaggerated. The efforts made by the ROK were substantial, however." Although it had plenty of proof that such efforts were made, the report said, it was unable because of several obstacles to obtain proof other than from sacrosanct intelligence sources that any members actually took money in exchange for using their influence on behalf of South Korea.

Three Members Reprimanded

The only charges the panel brought against sitting congressmen were to accuse three California Democrats of accepting campaign contributions from South Korean rice dealer Tongsun Park and failing to report it. The three were John J. McFall, Charles H. Wilson and Edward R. Roybal. McFall received $3,000, the report said, and the others $1,000 each. In addition, the committee said Roybal twice "had been found to have deliberately lied under oath to the committee." In October, when it had *taken all the testimony it could, the panel recommended to the full House that it reprimand McFall and Wilson and censure Roybal. On Oct. 13, the House voted to reprimand all three and censure no one. "Statements of Alleged Violation" also had been filed against a fourth member, Edward J. Patten, D-N.J., but he was exonerated by the committee.*

The report went into great detail in describing the schemes of the South Korean government through Park, its embassy in Washington, D.C., its ambassador Kim Dong Jo and through various Korean Central Intelligence Agency (KCIA) operatives to buy the influence of members of Congress. "The ROK caused money to be paid to members of Congress," the report said, but added: "Key witnesses are beyond the jurisdiction of the Congress; and some recipients of ROK money remain unidentified."

Incomplete Probe

It was unable to complete several areas of the investigation, the committee said, because it could not force key witnesses to testify under oath. That meant they couldn't be cross-examined by the accused and fair play dictated the panel should not rely on such testimony. The report indicated the committee had evidence it could have used to cite congressmen for taking "large gifts of money" from officials of the Korean government, but decided not to do so because it would have to reveal secret intelligence information. "Release and use of intelligence information would not, in the committee's opinion nor that of its chief counsel, make up this deficiency . . . ," the report said. "This being the case, it is the committee's conclusion that the benefits to be gained by publicizing the information in the possession of the intelligence community are outweighed by the costs of the disclosure of intelligence sources and methods which would necessarily be involved."

The panel, headed by John J. Flynt Jr., D-Ga., who retired at the end of the Congress, reported that the Korean government began its scheme at least as early as 1972. The details centered on three former congressmen who figured prominently in the South Korean efforts. They also were the subject of Justice Department investigations into the influence-buying scheme. The three were Richard T. Hanna, D-Calif. (1963-74), who went to prison in 1978 after admitting guilt in the scheme, and Otto E. Passman, D-La. (1947-77), and Cornelius E. Gallagher, D-N.J. (1959-73). Involved to lesser extents were Edwin W. Edwards, D-La. (1965-72), and William E. Minshall, R-Ohio (1955-75), also former members. The report also outlined the connection the Koreans had with Suzi Park Thomson, who during the operation of the scheme was on the staff of Speaker Carl Albert, D-Okla. (1947-77), also retired.

Reforms Urged

The report detailed congressional trips to South Korea during that time and the inflated practice of the South Koreans of giving honorary degrees to members of Congress who would be flown to that country at South Korean expense. The committee said it had "only one substantive proposal" to make regarding congressional rules of conduct. It said the House should adopt a rule "forbidding the receipt of trips by members, officers or employees of the House of Representatives to and from a foreign country paid for by foreign nationals or foreign organizations, unless the particular trip is specifically exempted in writing by action of the Committee on Standards of Official Conduct."

The committee also suggested reforms in House disciplinary procedures, including a strong recommendation that members and staffers be required to report any improper conduct they become aware of. Although they may find it distasteful to be informers, the committee said, this is necessary if the House wants to discipline itself. "If not," it said, "then the House should not ask 12 of its members to do the job without the support of the House."

Jaworski Criticism

The inability of the committee to force the testimony under oath by the KCIA agents and former ambassador Kim Dong Jo led to a great deal of notoriety for the committee. Special Counsel Leon Jaworski continually prodded the House leadership to use whatever power it had to persuade the South Korean government to hand over the people he wanted to interview. He suggested without success that the Congress and administration withhold aid from South Korea until the witnesses were produced.

Eventually Jaworski and Flynt came to a parting of the ways as Jaworski kept up his campaign. He withdrew from active participation as special counsel on Aug. 2, questioning Flynt's commitment to investigate the influence-peddling and criticizing the House's ability to investigate itself and the Justice Department's role in the inquiry. Public hearings began on Sept. 14 on the charges against the four sitting members and wound up with the final arguments Sept. 27 in which Committee Counsel John W. Nields Jr. accused Roybal of lying to the committee.

Following are excerpts from the report to the House by the Committee on Standards of Official Conduct on its Korean influence investigation, dated Dec. 22, 1978, and released Dec. 29, 1978:

I. INTRODUCTION

On February 9, 1977, citing "information" alleging "that Members of the House of Representatives have been the object of efforts by . . . the Government of the Republic of Korea [ROK] to influence the Members' official conduct by conferring things of value on them," the House of

Representatives unanimously adopted House Resolution 252. House Resolution 252 imposed three obligations on this committee. First, it directed the committee to conduct a "full and complete inquiry and investigation" into the allegation set forth above that Members of Congress accepted things of value from the ROK Government. Second, it directed the committee to make "findings, conclusions and recommendations" with respect to the adequacy of the existing rules of conduct to prevent actual and apparent exertion of improper influence by foreign governments on Members of Congress. Third, it directed the committee to report its recommendations to the House of Representatives regarding disciplinary action to be taken against any Member of the House of Representatives found, as a result of the investigation, to have violated any applicable standard of conduct.

Although there was, at the time of the adoption of House Resolution 252, already an ongoing investigation by the Department of Justice into the allegations of influence buying by the ROK, the reasons for its adoption are manifest. Certain Members of the House of Representatives were the objects of the allegations and the integrity of the House of Representatives had been publicly questioned. This committee viewed House Resolution 252 as an attempt by the House of Representatives to establish that it has the will to conduct a thorough and uninhibited investigation of itself and to judge and discipline its Members where warranted.

Thus, in addition to conducting the Korean influence investigation and fulfilling the tasks assigned to it under House Resolution 252, the committee believed that it had a second responsibility, namely, to establish that the House is serious about the very unpleasant but extremely important job of self-investigation and self-discipline. The results of the committee's efforts are set forth in this report.

The Investigation

In parts II through VI of this report, the committee sets forth the results of its investigative task.

Structure

In order to insure that its own investigation would be thorough and impartial in both appearance and fact, the committee adopted, on February 8, 1977, a resolution — contingent on the adoption by the House of House Resolution 252 — under which the investigation would be conducted by an outside independent special counsel and a special staff picked by the special counsel himself. The committee retained as special counsel, Philip Lacovara, of the firm Hughes, Hubbard & Reed. Mr. Lacovara previously had acted as counsel to the Special Prosecutor during the Watergate investigation and had been tentatively employed by the chairman and ranking minority member in the fall of 1976.

Mr. Lacovara recruited a special staff of attorneys, investigators, and support staff to carry out the Korean influence inquiry investigation.

He was given total independence in his selection of staff. To supervise the work of this staff, Lacovara appointed John W. Nields Jr., senior law clerk to Supreme Court Justice Byron White and former Chief of the Civil Division of the Office of the U.S. Attorney, Southern District of New York. In addition, five other attorneys, nine investigators, three paralegals and seven secretaries were hired. The attorneys and investigators appointed to the special staff were experienced in law enforcement, financial investigations, and congressional investigations. Special staff investigators came largely from federal law enforcement agencies and local units investigating official corruption.

On July 15, 1977, Philip Lacovara resigned as special counsel. On July 19, 1977, the committee retained as the new special counsel, former Watergate Special Prosecutor Leon Jaworski. Mr. Jaworski brought with him as Deputy Special Counsel Peter A. White, a member of the firm of Fulbright and Jaworski. John W. Nields Jr. remained as chief counsel directly in charge of the daily conduct of the investigation. The entire special staff recruited by Lacovara remained with the committee. During this change, the work of the special staff continued without interruption.

Methods

At the outset of the investigation, the information available to the staff consisted of diffuse and unspecific press reports that the Korean Government had adopted plans to influence Congress through three private citizens of Korean extraction, Tongsun Park, Hancho Kim, and Suzi Park Thomson, and through direct payments from ROK Embassy officials in Washington, D.C. In order to give the investigation more focus, attempts were made at the outset to determine the scope of efforts by the Government of the Republic of Korea to influence Members of Congress. There were two possible sources of information concerning the scope of such efforts: the ROK Government and the U.S. Congress.

The committee had no access to the officials of the ROK Government at the outset of the investigation, and it was determined that the most fruitful way to gather information about the outlines and scope of any lobbying effort would be to canvass both present and former Members of the House of Representatives. Thus, the committee issued a questionnaire to each person who served as a Member of the House of Representatives since January 3, 1970. The questionnaire inquired about a variety of contacts with representatives of the ROK, including the offer or receipt of gifts of over $100 in value. Specific questions were asked about contacts with five individuals: Tongsun Park, Suzi Park Thomson, Kim Dong Jo, Hancho Kim, and Kim Sang Keun. The questionnaire inquired about innocuous contacts, such as attendance at parties hosted by the named individuals and travel to Korea, as well as about gifts of substantial value. An accompanying letter explained that the purpose of the questionnaire was not only to learn of any improper activities, but to determine the extent of Korean lobbying activities, including legal activities.

The response by the Members to this questionnaire was viewed as an important first test of the willingness of the entire House to give assistance and support to the investigation. Notwithstanding the resulting inconvenience to the Members, the questionnaire, or a followup set of interrogatories, was answered by every sitting Member of the House except one, Representative Henry B. Gonzalez of Texas.

The committee also sought information at early stages of the investigation from other branches of the Federal Government: the Department of Justice, the Department of Agriculture, the Department of the Treasury, the Department of State, and agencies in the intelligence community. However, the committee operated on the assumption that it would only be satisfied with its work if it did the actual investigating itself. Thus, with rare exceptions, the committee utilized information received from other agencies for lead purposes only. Research was conducted on legislation of interest to the ROK Government. Individuals who were knowledgeable about the activities of Tongsun Park, Hancho Kim, Suzi Park Thomson, and officials of the ROK Government in Washington, D.C., and who were subject to the committee's jurisdiction were interviewed and deposed.

Information gathered in this manner persuasively demonstrated that a scheme or schemes had existed under which the Government of the Republic of Korea had attempted to influence Members of Congress. The committee held hearings disclosing this information on October 19, 20, and 21, 1977. The hearings did not identify the Members who at that time appeared to have been the targets of the scheme.

The committee then began to focus its investigative efforts on specific Members of Congress who, for a variety of reasons, appeared to have been likely or actual targets of ROK influence efforts. Most of these individual investigations centered on sitting Members of Congress. Some former Members who appeared to be important elements in a ROK scheme, however, were also investigated. The committee had no jurisdiction to discipline these former Members, but the obtaining of information about their roles was necessary to an understanding of the influence scheme, particularly as it related to Tongsun Park.

Then in January 1978, the Department of Justice questioned Tongsun Park in Seoul, Korea, about his activities involving Members of the Congress of the United States. Information obtained from Park in Seoul was made available to the committee. In March 1978, Park traveled to the United States pursuant to an agreement among the U.S. Department of Justice, this committee and the ROK Government and was questioned by the committee under oath in executive session. In April 1978, the committee held open hearings at which Park was questioned again. He described payments to a number of Congressmen. Richard Hanna, a former Member of Congress to whom Park gave substantial sums of money, also testified. Corroboration of Park's testimony was provided by ledgers and other documents, some of which had been removed from Park's home by Federal agents during his absence from the country, and by other witnesses who testified about Park's activities and about the activities of the Members of

Congress to whom he had paid money.

The investigation was far flung, thorough and unimpeded; 718 witnesses were interviewed. Depositions under oath were taken of 165 persons, of which 25 were depositions of sitting Members of Congress, and 10 were depositions of former Members. Over 40,000 documents were obtained, most of them by subpena. The committee authorized the taking of 19 depositions under grants of immunity, 11 of these depositions were in fact taken.

The committee pursued its investigative task much as does a grand jury. Initially, evidence was gathered and evaluated in executive session. Only after the committee finished a portion of its work was its information made public. Thus, publication of suspicious but unreliable information was avoided, as was publication of irrelevant matters. In the committee's judgment, this method also improved its ability to obtain information from reluctant witnesses.

The investigation was substantially facilitated by a provision of House Resolution 252 which authorized the committee to take depositions before a single member of the committee. . . . This permitted the committee to avoid the normal requirement of two member quorums for going into executive session. The committee believes that in light of the number of depositions taken and the other business which members of the committee had to conduct during this investigation, section 4(a) (1) (A) was essential to the conduct of the investigation. In part VII of this report, we recommend that this become a part of the Standing Rules of the House applicable to the Committee on Standards of Official Conduct.

Evidence relating to the overall activities of the ROK Government, Tongsun Park, and to the four Members of Congress against whom charges were filed, was eventually presented in open session. The committee's responsibility to present the facts uncovered by the investigation to the public and to publicize evidence of misconduct made this essential.

Results

The investigation established that the early press reports of involvement of up to 115 Members were greatly exaggerated. The efforts made by the ROK were substantial, however. The committee finds that the ROK Government adopted at least three plans the purpose of which was to influence Members of Congress through payments of money. Two were to utilize private individuals of Korean extraction — Tongsun Park and Hancho Kim. The third was to be carried out by ROK Government officials stationed in Washington, D.C.

The committee reports that the investigation into the implementation of the plan involving Tongsun Park has been completed. It is described in part II of this report. While it is impossible to know with certainty whether Mr. Park withheld information about payments as to which the committee has no evidence, the judgment of the committee is that Tongsun Park's testimony relating to his payments to sitting and former Members was substantially true and complete.

The results of the investigation into the implementation of the plan involving Hancho Kim is described in part III of this report. The committee found convincing evidence that Mr. Kim received $600,000 from the ROK Government for this purpose. The committee found no evidence, however, that any of this money was actually paid to any Members of Congress; and it has some evidence that the money paid to Kim was put to his personal use. The investigation relating to Hancho Kim, however, is incomplete. Although Kim answered questions relating to his contacts with Members of Congress, he refused even after he was granted immunity to answer questions relating to whether he received the $600,000 from the KCIA. Without an admission or denial by Mr. Kim that he received the money and an explanation of what he did with it, this aspect of the investigation remains somewhat unsatisfactory and incomplete.

The results of the investigation into the implementation of the plan involving officials of the ROK Embassy is described in part IV of this report. The committee must also report that while this aspect of the Korean Influence Inquiry is incomplete, the committee has done everything possible to obtain the information and complete the investigation. The committee has information indicating that representatives of the ROK Embassy in Washington, and other officials of the ROK Government offered to make and made large gifts of money to Members of Congress. However, the committee has been unable to obtain the cooperation of the Government of the Republic of Korea in investigating allegations relating to its official representatives in Washington, D.C. Testimony has been obtained from none of them.

The committee, through its chairman and ranking minority member, the chief counsel and the efforts of the Speaker and minority leader of the House, has done everything feasible to obtain from the ROK Government the cooperation necessary to determine the truth with respect to charges that ROK officials made offers and gifts of cash to Members of Congress. In the absence of such cooperation, the committee reluctantly reports that these allegations remain unresolved.

The committee also investigated allegations that Suzi Park Thomson, a congressional staff member of Korean extraction, was utilized by the ROK Government as an agent of influence. The committee finds that she was used by the ROK Government. However, the committee has found no hard evidence that she was involved in arranging or making illegal payments of money to Members of Congress. The results of the investigation with respect to Ms. Thomson are set forth in part V of this report.

Finally, the committee investigated allegations that trips to Korea were used in the ROK lobbying effort and that such trips may have constituted improper gifts from a foreign State. The results of this aspect of the committee's investigation are set forth in part VI of this report.

In summary, the investigation conducted by the committee convincingly establishes that the allegations on which House Resolution 252 was predicated are true. The ROK caused money to be paid to Members of Congress. The investigation is, however, incomplete. Key witnesses are beyond the jurisdiction of the Congress; and some recipients of ROK money remain unidentified.

The committee believes, however, that the investigation was an exceptionally thorough one. It involved direct investigation of a large number of present and former Members. It was carried on in a professional manner with little or no resistance from or interference by the House of Representatives or its Members. To the extent that it failed, the committee does not believe that the failure resulted from any unwillingness of the House to investigate itself. . . .

II. TONGSUN PARK

. . .When the investigation began, Tongsun Park was not subject to the jurisdiction of the committee. There was considerable doubt whether he ever would be available to testify and even more doubt whether his testimony, if obtained, would disclose the whole truth regarding his payments to Members of Congress. In the early phases, therefore, the investigation consisted of interviewing all of Park's employees, business associates and major congressional contacts; and obtaining records which would reveal a total picture of Park's finances. A vast amount of information was obtained demonstrating the existence of a plan under which Park would use money, earned as commissions on purchases of rice by the ROK, to pay Members of Congress. Information was gathered indicating that Park knew certain Members of Congress, that some had helped him in his efforts to become the middle man in the rice purchases, and that some had helped him in efforts to lobby for the ROK. Also a fairly complete picture of his finances was developed establishing the availability to him of large quantities of cash. There was, however, little first hand information regarding the actual transfer of cash from Park to Members of Congress and there would never have been such information if Park had remained unavailable to the committee as a witness. However, in January 1978, following intensive efforts by the Department of Justice, the Department of State, and this committee, which are recounted in further detail in Part IV C(2) of this report, the ROK Government agreed to produce Park in this country for testimony before this committee. In March 1978, Park did testify in executive session, and in April 1978, he testified at a public hearing. In September, 1978, Park gave public testimony in three of four disciplinary proceedings which had been brought against sitting Members of Congress of his earlier testimony.

It is the judgment of the committee, based on a study of Park's testimony, his demeanor, the manner in which Park's testimony is supported by the documentary and other evidence gathered in the earlier phase of the investigation, and the fact that Park willingly testified to some transactions of which the committee had no previous information, that with respect to payments to Members of Congress Park's testimony was substantially truthful and complete. On the question whether Park, in making payments to Members of Congress, was acting as part of a plan adopted by the ROK Government to influence Congress in its policies toward the ROK, the committee does not believe Mr. Park's testimony was substantially truthful and complete. Park studiously denied any discussion with any ROK Government official of his payments to Members of Congress; he denied that he agreed to use the commissions earned on rice purchases by the ROK to pay Congressmen or to make contributions to their campaigns, and he denied that he reported to ROK officials with respect to such payments or campaign contributions.

The committee finds, based on both direct and extremely convincing circumstantial evidence, that Park's testimony regarding the relationship between the ROK Government and his payments to Congressmen is false. The committee finds that Park proposed a plan to the ROK Government under which the ROK Government would force U.S. rice sellers to name Park as their agent in connection with rice purchases by the ROK; under which Park would then earn very large commissions on such purchases (in fact amounting to over $9 million during the period 1969-75); and under which he would give part of the proceeds to Members of Congress so that they would become supporters of Korea on important issues such as military and economic aid. The committee finds that on two occasions — once in 1968 and again in 1972 — Park persuaded the Director of the KCIA to adopt such a plan and to cause Park to become the agent on such rice purchases. The committee finds that Park received the commissions, gave part of the proceeds to Members of Congress and made reports to the ROK Government detailing money given to such Members. However, the committee finds that on these reports Park exaggerated the number of the Congressmen to whom he gave money and minimized the amount that he gave a few key Congressmen who were helping him in his efforts to become rich on rice commissions. Although Park to some degree made efforts to influence Congress on legislation affecting the ROK and undoubtedly made some payments in part for that purpose, it appears that he was far more interested in paying Congressmen who would help him maintain his status as a rice agent rather than help the ROK on legislative issues affecting it. . . .

. . .The Lobbying Plan. . .

Prior to his appointment in 1968 as agent for the sale of U.S. rice to the ROK, Tongsun Park was by his own admission, a "struggling business-man" in the United States. . . . Although the committee has heard testimony that he had inherited substantial wealth in Korea, Korean currency laws prevented him from taking his wealth outside Korea. A financial investigation done by the special staff revealed that, in 1968, Park was in debt and almost insolvent in this country. Indeed, even the George Town Club during the early years was losing money.

In late 1967, Park devised a proposal for cooperation between himself and the ROK Government. It was this scheme that eventually made him a wealthy man in the United States, and also enabled him to meet and influence important political figures.

Park was aware that, in the year 1968, Korea needed to import substantial quantities of rice in order to feed its people. He also knew that it had decided for the first time that the rice would be imported and purchased by a Government agency — Office of Supply of the Republic of Korea (OSROK) — and not by private companies as had been done previously. Park was further aware that the United States grew and produced more rice than it consumed, that Congressmen in rice growing districts in this country had a keen political interest in finding a market for their constituents' surplus rice and that under Public Law 480 money would be loaned by the United States on favorable terms to foreign governments so that they would purchase the excess rice. Park saw in this a business opportunity for himself — a Korean living in the United States who had contacts in Government in both the buying and selling countries — and a chance to help his country obtain military and economic aid. He decided to encourage Korea to buy its rice from the United States and to attempt to become a middleman in connection with such purchases. It was Park's concept, which he later reduced to writing in a Korean language plan found in his house, entitled "Plan for Korea's Foreign Policy Toward the United States" and marked in Park's handwriting "Prepared by TSP", . . . that his plan would help Korea in two ways — first, Congressmen whose constituents grew rice would be grateful to the ROK for buying the surplus; and second, the Congressmen would further be grateful to the ROK if commissions on such purchases were given back to the Congressmen by Park as campaign contributions. Park considered himself to be in a position to make the contributions as a result of his friendships with Congressmen and his social activities through the George Town Club.

Park's initial move was to seek assistance from his friend Representative Richard Hanna, then a Member of the House of Representatives representing the 34th District of California. Hanna was at that time uniquely well situated to provide such assistance. He had become interested in Korea prior to becoming a Congressman as a result of his participation in a "sister cities" program; had considerable contact with Korea as a Congressman before meeting Tongsun Park; and had met several Korean officials while in Korea. . . . Hanna and Park met in 1966 . . . and became close friends in 1967. By 1968 Hanna's interest in Korea had increased and from then until he retired from Congress he gave advice to certain officials in Korea about the importance of the role of Congress in the United States Government and the need for Korea to improve its lobbying efforts. The Korean officials were anxious to receive this advice because Korea was very dependent upon U.S. military and economic support, and they were anxious about the attitude which the incoming Nixon Administration would take toward Korea. Hanna and Park discussed Park's plan and Hanna informed various officials over a period of time that Korea should purchase products produced by businessmen in specified congressional districts — thereby making the Congressmen in those Districts friendly toward Korea. He also told them that campaign funds should be routed to Congressmen through people "associated" with Korea. . . .

More specifically, in August 1968, Park asked Hanna to go with him to Korea to help him obtain a position as agent in the impending purchase of rice by OSROK. Park offered Hanna a share of the proceeds of the commissions if they were successful in obtaining them. Park arranged a meeting among himself, Hanna and General Kim Hyung Wook, the Director of the Korean Central Intelligence Agency. Park's mentor in the ROK was a family friend, Chung Il Kwon, the Prime Minister of ROK. Through Chung's efforts, the meeting was arranged. Before the meeting, Park asked Hanna to emphasize that Park had many congressional friends and considerable influence in Washington, D.C., and to tell General Kim that he would be better able to take advantage of his contacts in Washington for the benefit of Korea if he had more money, and indeed that he would use part of the commissions received on any rice sales to make campaign contributions to Congressmen. . . .

According to Hanna's testimony, Hanna first told General Kim at the meeting that it would be in the ROK's interest to buy rice from California rather than from Japan. Hanna then emphasized that Park had contacts in Washington, would be a good agent on such a purchase, that he was anxious to help his country and that Park intended to use part of the commissions earned as a rice agent to make campaign contributions. . . .

Park received $200,000 in commissions in 1969 and in excess of $500,000 in 1970 on rice purchases negotiated through him. . . . In 1970 he contributed by checks, in amounts ranging from $100 to $1,000, to the campaigns of 20 Congressmen. In addition, cash campaign contributions of $5,000 to Hanna, $5,000 to William Minshall, $2,000 to John Rooney, and $13,000 to Cornelius Gallagher were also made in 1970, according to Park and his contemporaneously maintained ledger. . . .

On November 5, 1970, Hanna wrote to the then-KCIA Director Kim Kae Won as follows in part:

> It was an incident of some significance to have our mutual good friend Tongsun Park visit my district to bring greetings, encouragement and some needed assistance to our efforts. We certainly appreciated the thoughtfulness and the support. *It is our understanding that Tongsun has been helpful to other of our friends in Congress. Such efforts should assure a warm consideration and a high regard for the programs which mean much for the future relations of our two countries.* (Emphasis added.). . . .

Park, therefore, appears to have fulfilled the part of the plan calling for him to make campaign contributions to Members of Congress and saw to it that this fact was reported back to the KCIA Director by Congressman Hanna together with Hanna's thanks for the KCIA's role in the contributions, and Hanna's promise of Congressional support for the ROK.

That Tongsun Park in fact functioned in part as a lobbyist for the ROK during this period of time is clear. A document received by the committee from Jay Shin Ryu, a former employee of Park, after its April 1978, public hearings contains a list of Congressmen followed by visits to their offices and an explanation of the reason for the visit. Park has conceded that the document is substantially accurate. . . . There are, for example, some 28 recorded visits to the offices of Congressmen in connection with military aid at a time in December 1969, when a military aid bill calling for $50 million in specially earmarked funds for the ROK was pending before the Congress. Other lobbying efforts are also recorded on this document.

Park apparently reduced the plan to writing in October 1970. A document was found in Park's house in the fall of 1976 after Park had fled this country. The document was in the Korean language, bore a red "secret" stamp and stated "Prepared by TSP, October 1970." in the upper right hand corner. . . . Park denied writing or knowing about this document. . . . However, handwriting samples were taken from Park and a handwriting expert in the employ of the Federal Bureau of Investigation gave his positive opinion that Park wrote the words "Prepared by TSP, October 1970" in English and also at least one of the English names — that of "Gallagher" — in the body of the document. The document is a blue print for a lobbying effort by the ROK in the House of Representatives, the Senate, the intelligence community and the American press. . . .

In early 1971, Tongsun Park learned that he was no longer the agent, and that his job had been given instead to a Korean businessman in the United States who knew ROK Ambassador to the United States Kim Dong Jo. The reason for this change is not entirely clear. However, Park, in attempting to learn of its cause, discovered that Kim Dong Jo had been sending messages back to Korea that Park was conducting himself in a way that was injurious to the ROK. It is Park's belief that Kim Dong Jo continuously resented Park's intrusion into what Ambassador Kim viewed as his domain. Park learned that U.S. Ambassador to the ROK, Philip Habib, and Representative William Broomfield were also saying derogatory things about him to ROK officials. He later learned that Representative Otto Passman, Chairman of the Subcommittee on Foreign Operations of the House Committee on Appropriations, had also spoken against him. The circumstances surrounding Park's efforts to retain his position as agent further confirm the fact that the payment of part of the commissions to Members of Congress was a key part of the plan under which the ROK Government made Park the intermediary in its rice purchases. . . .

Park set about to disprove the claims that he was ineffective in Congress and indeed injurious to the ROK's interests. From June 17, 1971, until July 16, 1971, Park caused 14 letters from Senators and Representatives praising him to be sent to ROK President Park Chung Hee. . . .

Then Park turned for special assistance to former Representative Cornelius Gallagher, then chairman of the Subcommittee on Asian and Public Affairs of the House Foreign Affairs Committee. Park had already given Gallagher $13,000 in cash during 1970. On August 3, 1971, just 6 days before Gallagher went to Korea with a large congressional delegation, Park, according to his testimony, gave Gallagher $30,000 in cash. The $30,000 payment to Gallagher, which Park testified to, is recorded twice in Park's ledger. . . . Where the money Park said he paid to Gallagher came from is unclear. At the end of June 1971, Park's combined bank accounts in this country totaled $786. On July 2, 1971, Park left the United States for Korea. Then his ledger reflects, at p. 107, at [sic] receipt of $450,000 from "Angels" on July 20, 1971, at a time when Park was still in Korea. . . . The committee has not determined with certainty what "Angels" referred to. When Park was asked under oath, he first said "I don't recall.". . . When it was pointed out to him that the $450,000 was a lot of money, that it was essential to his solvency and that he would surely remember who gave it to him, he said "Angels" "could have" referred to his brother Ken. Then he said that it referred to a super tanker owned by Ken's company called "Angel Park." Then he said "Angels" was a code word for his brother. He conceded he may never have referred to his brother as "Angels" except on his ledger. Then he said "if you met my brothers you would call them Angels." Finally, he stated "this is another matter where you must accept my word.". . .

In any event, whatever the source of the money, Park returned from Korea on July 29, 1971. He had lunch with Gallagher 1 hour after he returned. . . . Then Park testified he gave Representative Gallagher $30,000 in cash on August 3rd. Of the $450,000, $350,000 was deposited in cash in Park's bank on August 4, 1971. . . . On August 9, Representative Gallagher traveled to Korea. Park also traveled to Korea. The committee has no direct proof of what Representative Gallagher did in Korea to help Park. However, the committee is in possession of a letter from Representative Gallagher to Park Chung Hee dated November 9, 1971, less than 3 months after he returned from Korea, in which Representative Gallagher refers to difficulties with the foreign aid bill for Korea and then states:

> It is therefore essential that our friend whom we discussed when we last met have full support that you indicated so that a meaningful result can be brought about to strengthen the relationship of the Republic of Korea and the United States. . . .

The letter continues, praising "our mutual friend Tongsun Park's" lobbying efforts and reiterating that it is "vital that he has the kind of support that you indicated to me when we talked."

On November 23, 1971, Park withdrew $25,000 in cash from his account at the Equitable Trust Co. . . . He gave Representative Gallagher $25,000 on the same day, according to his testimony, and recorded the payment in his ledger. . . . On January 3, 1972, Park gave Representative Gallagher $5,000 in cash to pay for a trip to Korea which he and Representative Gallagher took on January 5, 1972. . . . Park's diary reflects that Representative Gallagher met both with President Park and KCIA Director Lee Hu Rak during his trip. . . . Park attended neither meeting. . . .

Park apparently then turned his attention toward influencing Representative Otto Passman who, as recently as December 1971, had cabled Philip Habib and attacked Park's integrity and questioned his support in Congress. . . . Representative Passman and Park met in Hong Kong in mid-January 1972. The meeting was probably arranged through Edwin Edwards, then a Representative from Louisiana, now Governor of that State, by rice miller Gordon Dore who was traveling with Passman. . . . In Hong Kong, Park, who was again out of funds in U.S. currency, borrowed $5,000 from Dore, gave $5,000 in cash to Representative Otto Passman and p:omised to give him $50,000 more each year. . . . Representative Passman then traveled to Korea, and according to Park's diary, met with President Park. . . . A cable from Representative Passman to Tongsun Park after Passman returned to the United States, dated January 24, 1972, clearly suggests that Park's promise of money caused Representative Passman to support Park as the agent. . . .

Nonetheless Park apparently had not immediately regained his agency. In spite of repeated and threatening demands by Representative Passman for Park to return home during February, Park did not do so until March 22. . . .

It is not entirely clear why Park did not return home. He claims that the question whether he would be reinstated as the intermediary had already been resolved in his favor. There are indications that the question had not yet been resolved — these indications are set forth below. In any event, however, Park seems to have been confronted with another problem. Park had promised Representative Passman $50,000 per year. Park, however, had little money in the United States. His total bank holdings in February 1972, was *[sic]* just over $5,000. Park, therefore, was attempting to obtain United States dollars before returning to the United States. Park himself testified that he sought approximately $200,000 from those in the ROK Government who had benefited from his being removed as the rice agent. He described this money as being in the nature of damages for a wrongful injury to him. In fact, Park received a decision in his favor on this issue in late March 1972. . . . He returned to the United States, sent Jay Shin Ryu to Switzerland where Ryu caused $190,000 to be transferred to Park's account from a Swiss account controlled by an aide to Park Chong Kyu, Chief of the Presidential Protective Force. . . . The money was deposited in Park's Equitable Trust account on March 29, 1972. . . . Park used it and other moneys to pay Passman $40,000 in late March and early April 1972. . . .

On February 16, 1972, Park called his assistant, Jay Shin Ryu in Washington. According to Ryu's diary, Park dictated a letter which he wanted Gallagher to send — Ryu's diary contains the following proposed letter:

All of our friends in Washington had expected that the *commitment* which was made during my last visit should have been fulfilled now. I don't have to reiterate the importance and urgency involved. Stop. It is most essential that your side make special effort to see to the *commitment* become (sic) materialized as quickly as possible. (Emphasis added.). . .

On February 26, 1972, Park dictated a similar letter which Ryu was to get Edwin Edwards to send. . . .

Shortly after Gallagher's letter would have been received, Tongsun Park wrote in his diary on March 21, 1972:

"Saw Director" [Lee Hu Rak, Director of the KCIA].

"Riviera resolved" [Riviera is Park's code word for rice].

"Saw OSROK — Letter". . . .

Park returned to the United States the following day.

The Committee has no direct evidence of the full nature of the "Commitment" to Mr. Gallagher which Tongsun Park referred to in his messages to Jay Ryu. Park told the committee nothing except that there was a commitment to make him the rice agent. . . . However, the evidence available to the committee points persuasively to the conclusion that the "commitment" included a plan similar to the one hatched in 1968 with Lee Hu Rak's predecessor — namely that Tongsun Park would use part of the rice commissions to pay certain Congressmen. Gallagher's letter of March 9 is devoid of any reference to Park — who claims he was the sole beneficiary of the "commitment" — and instead refers to his "colleagues" as the apparently interested parties. The letter refers to the fact that the entire House of Representatives is running for reelection. It seems likely that Park and the ROK Government would, on making him the rice agent, have reactivated his "plan" to pay Congressmen as he had written it in October of 1970 and as he had proposed it to General Kim both in 1968 and again in 1972. Indeed, the proof in the committee's possession persuasively establishes that this time the KCIA attempted to keep close tabs on how Park spent the commissions.

The committee is in possession of a document entitled the "T.S. Report" which was taken from Park's house by Jay Ryu in October of 1972. . . . The report is dated September 30, 1972 — some 6 months after Park wrote "Riviera resolved" in his diary — and presumably 6 months after the "commitment" to Mr. Gallagher was fulfilled. The report concludes:

> Within a short and tumultuous period of 6 months since the task started, he [Tongsun Park] was able to put the persons with influence over the issue of military aid to Korea into his organization of restoration, including senators and representatives, high-ranking administration officials and White House staffers. The evaluation is that he has performed his duties without committing serious mistakes. It seems necessary to continue to use him under supervision.

The T.S. Report is, on its face, a report of Tongsun Park's lobbying activities including a list of Congressmen to whom he supposedly made campaign contributions out of the rice commissions. The Report contains a section describing Park's background and his virtues as a lobbyist, referring briefly to the incentive supplied by his "competition" with "D.J." (Dong Jo Kim). It contains a section on the George Town Club. It contains a section on the rice commissions. It contains a section on the results of Park's lobbying efforts; actions of Congressmen Passman and Gallagher and the defeat in the Senate of a bill damaging to Korea. Finally, it refers to "political funds" for 30 Members of the House "who have influence over the Korean issues." There is a list attached to the Report of the Congressmen who have supposedly received the contributions together with comments describing the significance of their roles in Congress and the manner in which they have helped Korea in the past.

Park has admitted under oath that the T.S. Report contains so much accurate detail about him that it must have been prepared by someone with intimate knowledge of his life and activities. He denied any knowledge of the Report, however, and denied that it was prepared in order to show the KCIA. . . . The Committee does not accept these denials. The committee does accept Park's claim that most of the contributions listed on the report are fictitious. . . .

The committee is also in possession of one other list found in Park's house and one which was found in his briefcase by a Customs Inspector in December of 1973 when he was in Anchorage, Alaska, on his way back from Korea. These lists record or purport to record campaign contributions to Members of Congress. . . . Park has testified under oath that these lists did not purport to be reports to his Government of contributions made. It seems clear, based on the committee's investigation as well as Park's own testimony, that most of the contributions listed were never made. The committee can think of no reason for Park to make up a list of fictitious contributions unless it was to show to the KCIA to convince them that he was doing his job. Indeed, it is possible that the Alaska list had been taken to Korea with Park, because Park had it in his possession when returning from Korea. Park claims, however, that the lists were all of proposed payments and are inaccurate solely because he never carried out his proposals. Park offered no reason for his failure to carry out his intentions. Further, the Alaska list was for 1972 and was clearly made up after the 1972 election because it records the 1973 committee assignments of the Members on the list. Finally, the Customs Inspector who asked Park about the list has testified that Park told him it was a list of payments already made. . . . The committee finds it is much more likely that these lists were made up to show to officials of the KCIA to impress them with Park's work on behalf of the ROK, than that they were proposed lists Park made up to show himself.

In summary, the committee finds that Park became an agent on purchases of U.S. rice by the ROK Government and consequently received over $9 million in commissions as a result of his agreement to use part of the commissions to pay Members of Congress. It was part of this agreement that Park would attempt to influence Congressmen to support the ROK on legislative matters of importance to the ROK. The committee believes, based on the evidence set forth in this subsection as well as the evidence set forth in the subsections to follow, that Park paid money to Congressmen principally so that they would help him earn rice commissions, rather than so that they would help the ROK on legislative matters. However, the committee has direct evidence that Park did lobby for legislation helpful to the ROK Government. . . .

...The Plan in Operation...

1. Richard Hanna

Representative Richard Hanna was a Congressman whose interest in Korea and the whole of the Far East predated his acquaintance with Tongsun Park and even his election to Congress. By the time Hanna met Park, he had traveled to Korea several times. He believed that the interests of the United States, and particularly the commercial interests of his own State of California, were closely allied to those of the Far East. His work on the House Banking and Currency Committee took him to a number of meetings of the Asia Development Bank. He had many friends in Korea, other than Tongsun Park. . . .

Through Tongsun Park, however, Hanna acquired a direct, personal financial interest in the sale of U.S. rice to Korea. He agreed to use and did use his influence as a Member of Congress to further his interest.

Hanna testified that he met Tongsun Park in late 1966. . . . Park sought Hanna's advice about the George Town Club, which was then in financial difficulty. Hanna, who quickly became close friends with Park, assisted him by joining the club, advising Park on the recruitment of new members who could be useful to the club, inviting some of his own friends from the business community to join the club, and hosting a number of parties with Park designed to attract favorable publicity for the club. . . . The committee found no evidence, however, that Hanna offered the club any financial assistance, or that he was involved in any way in assistance or efforts to obtain assistance for the club from the ROK Government. . . .

In late 1967, Park went to Hanna with a new problem. According to Hanna, Park approached him with the idea that he wanted to become the seller's agent for the sale of rice to Korea by growers in the United States. Park then asked Hanna to help him in two ways: by promoting Park's candidacy as rice agent with ROK officials in a position to help him, and by introducing Park to sellers of rice in the United States. In return Park promised to share with Hanna any profits he might make as rice agent. According to Hanna, these promises were oral and nonspecific. He said that as a result of these promises, however, he did expect to share in the rice sales commissions. . . .

. . .Hanna's role with regard to ROK officials was to (1) suggest to the Koreans that they should cultivate the goodwill of Members of Congress; (2) describe how this could be done, including the purchase of products produced by the constituents of Congressmen, specifically rice, and the making of campaign contributions; (3) endorse Tongsun Park's plan to become agent for the sale of U.S. rice to Korea and use the resulting commissions to make campaign contributions.

In the United States, Hanna introduced Park to Joseph Alioto, counsel and former President of the Rice Growers Association of California, and advised Alioto that the Korean Government would prefer Park as rice sellers' agent. . . .

Shortly after Park's appointment as agent for RGA's rice sales to the

ROK, Park and Hanna began work on a trip to Korea for a large delegation of Members of the House, to be led by then House Majority Leader Carl Albert. Hanna corresponded with KCIA Director Kim Hyung Wook on this subject, referring to Park as "liaison" for the trip. . . . As a result of State Department objections, Park's role in the trip was curtailed however, and his attempts to be included as a passenger on the delegation plane failed. But it appears that this trip represented Park's first efforts to carry out his promise to the Korean Government to work to improve Korean-United States relations in return for his designation as rice agent.

Richard Hanna was in Seoul to make arrangements for the Congressional delegation January 22-25, 1969. He returned to Korea on February 28, 1969, shortly before the delegation arrived. Just before his departure from the United States in February, Hanna received a check for $3,000 from Park, which Hanna testified was compensation for his time and travel expenses in attending the Fall, 1968, meeting with Alioto. . . .

Less than a year after this trip, in a letter dated December 11, 1969, Hanna wrote to Tongsun Park's friend, Prime Minister Chung Il Kwon, about the status of legislation to appropriate $50 million in earmarked funds for military assistance to the Republic of Korea. . . . In the letter, Hanna noted that members of the House Committee on Appropriations who had traveled to Korea in February on the Albert delegation, "did staunchly support funds for Korea." Hanna also noted the efforts of Tongsun Park to have funds earmarked for Korea included in the bill. He wrote:

> Last week, Tongsun Park and I conferred on this matter on several occasions. Pursuant to my request, he made several calls to all of his friends in the Congress and also arranged to come to the United States to aid in our efforts.

Hanna testified that he included references to Park in this letter at Park's request. He said that the letter exaggerated Park's contribution to getting the House to vote to earmark the ROK funds. . . .

Between 1968 and his departure from Congress at the end of 1974, Hanna wrote a number of letters to high officials in the Korean Government, including President Park Chung Hee. In each he noted the successful efforts which Tongsun Park was making to further the interests of the ROK in the United States. He said that Park was repeatedly making demands that he [Hanna] recommend Park to ROK officials in this way. . . . Hanna was aware that this was necessary because Park's continuation as a rice agent was contingent on his work in Washington, D.C., to improve relations between the ROK and the United States, and specifically to insure continued U.S. military aid.

In spite of Park's vague promises to share his rice commissions with Hanna and Hanna's efforts to improve Park's standing with the ROK Government so that his income from the commissions would be insured. Hanna received no more money from Park until August 1970. . . .

In August 1970, Park gave Hanna a cash campaign contribution of

$5,000. This contribution was not reported. Hanna testified that this payment was not in pursuance of the agreement to share in the rice commissions. . . . It was a campaign contribution and not the profits of a personal business venture. Park made another cash contribution to Hanna in November 1970, which Hanna testified was around $2,000. . . . A ledger contemporaneously maintained by Park shows a November 1970 entry by the name "Dick" for $16,000 [referring to Hanna]. While Hanna in other instances confirmed the accuracy of this ledger, he said that he was certain that the November 1970 contribution was not nearly that large, and that in fact he never received a single payment from Park in so large an amount. . . . If these payments were not a part of the Hanna-Park agreement to share the profits of the rice business, they would seem clearly to be a part of the General Kim Hyung Wook-Park agreement to use the commissions — in part — to make campaign contributions to Congressmen helpful to the ROK.

Indeed, on November 5, 1970, Hanna wrote a letter to General Kim Kae Won who succeeded Kim Hyung Wook as Director of the KCIA, including the following passage related to the just completed election campaign:

> It was an incident of some significance to have our mutual good friend Tongsun Park visit my district to bring greetings, encouragement and some needed assistance to our efforts. We certainly appreciated the thoughtfulness and the support. It is our understanding that Tongsun had been helpful to other of our friends in Congress. Such efforts should assure a warm consideration and a high regard for the programs which mean much for the future relations of our two countries. . . .

According to Hanna, he was referring in this letter to the cash contributions which Park had made to his campaign and other assistance that Park had given him in arranging campaign events. Hanna said that he included the reference to Park's helpfulness to other Members of Congress because Park had told him that he had made campaign contributions to other Congressmen. Hanna testified that Park either asked him to write this letter to Director Kim, or asked him to include the references to his campaign assistance. . . . Hanna's letter confirmed to the ROK Government that Tongsun Park was in fact investing the rice commissions as promised, in contributions to congressional campaigns.

In 1971 the business relationship between Park and Hanna changed. In late 1970 and 1971, Park's position as agent for the sale of rice from the United States to the ROK was in jeopardy. Influential elements in the Korean Government were favoring another Korean firm for this role. On February 26, 1971, in response to agitation in the ROK against Tongsun Park, Congressman Hanna wrote to the KCIA Director, Lee Hu Rak, the following two-sentence letter:

> I believe we need continuity on the rice sales matter. Suggest involvement of Tongsun Park as agent in negotiations. . . .

At about this same time, according to Hanna, Tongsun Park informed him that he was badly in need of credit in order to maintain his position as rice agent. In response to Park's request, Hanna agreed to provide collateral for a line of credit to Park at the Equitable Trust Co. in Baltimore. Hanna put up his shares of stock in a California corporation called Spectra Strip, in return for which a $25,000 line of credit was established at Equitable in Hanna's name. Funds borrowed on the line of credit were deposited into the account of Tongsun Park, and Park repaid the loans. . . .

In return for undertaking this financial risk, however, Hanna asked Park for a firmer commitment for a share of the rice commissions. In a letter dated April 26, 1971 . . . , Hanna wrote to Park with regard to the credit agreement made at Equitable Trust. In his closing paragraph he wrote, "I hope you will continue to bring on all fronts so that the agreed upon division of commission on the rice sale can be implemented as soon as possible." Hanna later testified that this agreed upon division provided that he receive one fourth of the net profits received by Park on the rice sales. This agreement formally established Congressman Hanna's financial interest in Park's rice agency.

The same day that Hanna wrote this letter to Park, he also wrote again to Lee Hu Rak of the KCIA, noting the good relationship which then existed between the ROK and the House of Representatives and the part which Tongsun Park had played in establishing this relationship. Hanna went on to say:

"It is of primary importance that Koreans have a solid and appreciated reputation for keeping commitments. I have already indicated to mutual friends where I feel that a singular problem in this regard has developed,". . . Hanna testified that he referred to the problems of Tongsun Park and his rice agency. . . .

In June 1971, at Park's request and in a further effort to salvage the rice agency of Tongsun Park, Hanna wrote to Korean President Park Chung Hee, outlining his own accomplishments on behalf of the ROK and noting the importance of the work of Tongsun Park. . . .

It is significant that Hanna in his testimony described Park's problem in losing his rice agency as resulting in part from a perception in the ROK that Park "did not know the kind of people that he said he knew, and that people in Washington didn't like Tongsun Park.". . . In short, Park's position as rice agency was related to his position as a person of influence in Washington, a person in a position to lobby on the ROK's behalf. For this reason, it appears that Hanna in his letters to ROK officials stressed Park's successful efforts to improve relations between the ROK and the United States, often at the request of Park and even in letters originally drafted by Park himself. The fact that these letters also reported on Hanna's activities suggests that it was important to Park that ROK officials perceive Hanna as someone who could wield influence on their behalf. In addition, Hanna's letters stressed, over and over, the importance of Congress, as opposed to the executive branch, to future relations between the ROK and the United States. The message conveyed by these letters was that Congress was important to the ROK, that Tongsun Park was influential with Congress, Hanna was an important man in Congress, who was helpful to the ROK, and that Hanna endorsed Tongsun Park. . . .

In 1971, however, it became clear that mere letter writing on Park's behalf by Hanna and other Members of Congress was not enough to retain for Park his rice agency. By November, Park had not regained his appointment as rice agent. In addition, the possibility had again arisen that the ROK would purchase rice from Japan, rather than the United States. Hanna, at Tongsun Park's request and expense, then traveled to Korea to do what he could to salvage the situation.

By this time, ROK deliberations on U.S. rice purchases centered on "Southern" rice from Louisiana, Texas, and Arkansas, as well as rice from California. Hanna took with him letters from Senator Allen Ellender of Louisiana, designating him as Louisiana's representative in connection with any purchase of rice by the ROK. . . .

These letters were obtained for Hanna by Tongsun Park. Hanna was also designated as the representative of the California congressional delegation by letter from Congressman Chet Holifield. . . .

In Korea, Hanna met with KCIA Director Lee Hu Rak, a meeting that is referenced in a letter from Hanna to Lee dated December 8, 1971. . . . At that meeting, Hanna pressed the interests of United States rice producers, and, specifically, the interest of Tongsun Park in regaining his position as rice agent. Hanna's December 8 letter indicates, and his own testimony confirms . . ., that he believed that Lee was receptive to his presentation, and that the rice negotiations would be resolved in favor of the U.S. producers and Tongsun Park.

A few months after Hanna's November 1971 trip to Korea, Tongsun Park's rice agency was indeed restored. It is important to note, however, that it was not solely or even principally the intervention of Hanna that brought this about; by this time, other Members of Congress were becoming involved in the rice negotiations and in the efforts of Park to regain his agency.

Hanna never received the promised one fourth or one half of Park's rice commissions. In return for his financial backing and his efforts in the ROK on Park's behalf, however, Hanna did receive income from Park. Between the time of the first Equitable Trust loan and Hanna's retirement from Congress at the end of 1974, he received from Park about $75,000 by check and $10,000 in cash. . . . The fact that the money was paid by check evidences that, although Hanna had unquestionably used his office to obtain money from Park, he viewed the money not as a bribe, but as his share of a joint business venture. In addition, Hanna received from Park $26,000 to $40,000 in cash, which he described as campaign contributions and spending money. . . .

2. *Cornelius E. Gallagher*

According to Tongsun Park, he first met Cornelius Gallagher shortly before Gallagher traveled to the ROK as part of a Congressional delegation headed by the Majority Leader, Carl Albert, in March of 1969 — a delegation for which Park was in large measure responsible. . . . Indeed, the document on which Park's assistant recorded his lobbying efforts reflects a visit by Park to Gallagher's office on February 28, 1969, in order to invite him to travel to the ROK. . . . The document also reflects a visit to Gallagher's office in connection with a proposed ROK constitutional amendment, and on October 14, 1969, Gallagher, at Park's request did place a statement in the Congressional Record supporting a proposed ROK constitutional amendment permitting President Park Chung Hee to run for a third term. Congressmen Thomas Kleppe, Thomas P. O'Neill and Richard Hanna offered similar statements into the record on the same day. The constitutional amendment was approved by referendum on October 17, 1969. On December 11, 1969, Gallagher was visited by Park . . . in connection with the then pending bill calling for an appropriation on $50 million in earmarked funds for military aid to the ROK.

There is no indication that Park paid any money to Mr. Gallagher during 1969. However, according to Park's ledger, and according to Park, he paid Gallagher $13,000 in cash in 1970. The committee has no proof that Gallagher did or agreed to do anything in return for this money.

In 1971, however, Gallagher became chairman of the Subcommittee on Asian and Pacific Affairs of the House Committee on Foreign Affairs. . . . Park's ledger reflects that $30,000 in cash went to Cornelius Gallagher on August 3, 1971. . . . Jay Shin Ryu's diary confirms a meeting with Gallagher both on August 2 and August 3, 1971. . . . This gift occurred, according to Park, for no reason other than that Gallagher asked for it. It occurred, however, the day before Gallagher went to the ROK. The committee has no direct evidence of whom Gallagher saw in the ROK or what he said. However, on November 9, 1971, about 3 months after he returned from Korea, Gallagher wrote a letter to President Park Chung Hee at Tongsun Park's request. . . . The letter refers to the then pending foreign aid bill; it refers to "our friend whom we discussed when we last met" urging that he have "full support that you indicated;" mentions Park by name later on and praises his efforts in both the House and the Senate.

The letter then goes on pointedly to state that Foreign Aid will be decided on a "country to country basis"; and to point out that Israel, with "the most effective lobby group in the United States," is the only country for which aid has recently increased. The letter states:

I believe there is a lesson to be learned in the way they handled their activities. This is one of the things that you should discuss with our friend. For I have briefed him fully.

Finally the letter states:

He presently has a commitment from his friends in the Senate that will coincide with those in the House that should bring about a meaningful result. It makes it easier when both parties have access to the others [sic] thinking. It is vital that he has the kind of support that you indicated to me when we talked.

I have taken the liberty of suggesting that he should return shortly to Korea in order that he may privately brief you on this and several other matters that I am certain you will find of interest.

Then on November 18, 1971, Gallagher wrote another letter to Park Chung Hee claiming that the Foreign Aid issue had been resolved favorably to the ROK and giving Tongsun Park credit for this achievement. . . .

Then, according to Park's testimony, he gave Gallagher $25,000 in cash on November 23, 1971. His testimony on this score is well corroborated. On November 23, 1971, Park withdrew $25,000 in cash from his account at the Equitable Trust Co., in Baltimore. . . . His ledger at p. 110 reflects a $25,000 payment to "Neil" on November 23. . . . Finally, Park recalled going to Gallagher's house in northern New Jersey for Thanksgiving at some time when Gallagher was still a Congressman. . . .

Toward the end of the year, Park again asked Gallagher to go to the ROK to help Park in his efforts to regain his position as agent. Park gave Gallagher $5,000 on January 3, 1972, and recorded this fact in his ledger. . . . According to Park's diary, Gallagher was with him in Hong Kong in mid-January 1972, when Park made his accommodation with Otto Passman. Finally, when Park became anxious that his plan to regain his position as middleman might not succeed — or having succeeded temporarily the success might be reversed through the efforts of others — he called Jay Shin Ryu on the telephone from the ROK and asked Ryu to get Gallagher to send a letter on his behalf. The call was made on February 16, 1972, and Jay Shin Ryu wrote down in his diary the substance of the letter as requested by Park. It states:

All of our friends in Washington had expected that the commitment which was made during my last visit should have been fulfilled now. I don't have to reiterate the importance and urgency involved. It is most essential that your side make special effort to see to it that the commitment become materialized as quickly as possible.

Ryu notes in his diary on February 24, 1972, that Gallagher met with Lee (i.e., Lee Sang Ho, then KCIA Station Chief in Washington). In a letter dated March 9, 1972, Gallagher wrote to Lee Hu Rak, Director of the KCIA. The letter clearly is the one which Park had requested in his phone call to Ryu of February 16, 1972. . . .

On March 21, 1972, Park, according to his testimony and his diary, finally obtained a meeting with Director Lee and was shown the letter which designated him as the intermediary on all Korean-United States rice purchases.

It is reasonable to infer from these events that Gallagher — acting at

Park's request or in concert with him — was extremely influential in helping Park regain his position as agent. It is reasonable to infer that Gallagher's substantial efforts on Park's behalf were related to the fact that Park had given him $60,000 in cash from August 1971 to January 1972. Finally, it is reasonable to infer that Gallagher believed that it was in his financial interest to have Park named the rice agent. Shortly after Park returned from Korea on April 25, 1972, he gave Gallagher $8,000 in cash . . .; and he gave him $6,000 more on June 12, 1972.

The March 9, 1972, letter to Lee Hu Rak broadly hints that both Gallagher and other colleagues were waiting impatiently for the ROK Government to arrange commissions for Park so that he could help them in their upcoming elections, and that Gallagher was fully expecting the money which Park gave him.

3. Otto E. Passman and Edwin W. Edwards.

(a) Edwin W. Edwards

As noted . . . Tongsun Park lost his position as middleman on the ROK's rice purchases from the United States during the year 1971. One person from whom he sought help in regaining that position was Edwin Edwards. Edwin Edwards was a Member of Congress from October 1965 until May 1972. He represented a district in Louisiana which is one of the largest rice producing districts in the United States. Park and Edwards became acquainted during Edwards' service as a Member of Congress.

Although Edwards was still a Member of Congress in 1971, he spent most of his time that year campaigning for the governorship of Louisiana. He ran in the primary in the fall and then won a hotly contested run off against J. Bennett Johnston in January of 1972.

Edwards wrote a letter for Tongsun Park to President Park Chung Hee in June 1971. . . . Then on November 2, 1971, Park travelled to Louisiana and after Edwin Edwards rebuffed his offer of a campaign contribution, gave the $10,000 in cash which he had brought for Representative Edwards instead to his wife, Elaine Edwards, in the coffee shop of the Monteleone Hotel in New Orleans. Then on November 19, 1971, Park delivered $5,000 in cash to Marion Edwards, Edwin Edwards' brother. . . .

Shortly after the November contribution, Park left for the Far East on what proved to be his successful push to have himself reinstated as rice agent. While out of the country, Park instructed his assistant, Jay Shin Ryu, to deliver another $5,000 cash contribution to the Edwards campaign. Ryu went to New Orleans on December 18, 1971. . . .

Then on January 28, 1972, on the eve of the primary runoff, Ryu delivered another $5,000 in cash to Marion Edwards at Park's direction.

Edwin Edwards testified under oath before this committee. He denied being present for the December delivery of cash or any other delivery of cash from Park. He claims to have first learned about the $10,000 cash delivery to his wife in 1974 when the IRS investigated him. Finally, while Marion Edwards testified that he told his brother about money he received from Park at the time of its receipt, Edwin Edwards claims that he remembers no such conversations. . . .

. . .In 1971 Edwards counseled Park that it was important to have Otto Passman as a friend in order for Park to regain the rice agency. In July 1971, Edwards wrote to President Park and praised Tongsun Park. Edwards then asked Gordon Dore, who was traveling to Korea with Passman in December 1971, to try to act as an intermediary between Passman and Park. Dore met with Park the night before he and Passman left the United States. Dore thereafter suggested to Passman that he be more friendly toward Park. In early 1972 Edwards again wrote to President Park on Tongsun Park's behalf. In February 1972 Tongsun Park asked Edwards to send a cable asking Park to return to the United States immediately and resume his activities as rice agent. The June 1971 letter and the January 1972 letter were both based on drafts that Park supplied to Edwards. It was during this very period that Park contributed $25,000 to Edwards' campaign.

An understanding of the Edwards-Park relationship is somewhat complicated by the widely publicized allegations of a former Edwards confidant, Clyde Vidrine. Vidrine said he was present on two occasions when Park handed Edwards $10,000 in cash. Vidrine's testimony that he was present is contradicted by Park, by Edwards and by Ryu. The committee has concluded that Vidrine has not told the truth in this respect. It remains unclear how Vidrine learned that Park did, in fact, make some contributions to Edwards' campaign.

It was difficult to investigate this matter further because Edwards' campaign received between $500,000 and $1 million in cash, kept no records and maintained the cash in a safe deposit box. . . .

(b) Otto E. Passman

Representative Otto Passman and Tongsun Park first met during a trip Passman took to the ROK in December 1970 for the purpose in part, of persuading the ROK to purchase U.S. rice instead of Japanese rice and to purchase Louisiana rice in addition to California rice. Shortly thereafter, Park lost his position as rice agent. Park later learned that Passman had taken a position antagonistic to him as the rice agent. Approximately 1 year later, in January 1972, Otto Passman scheduled an around-the-world trip. The itinerary included stops in Geneva, Bangkok, Hong Kong, and Seoul. Traveling with Passman was Gordon Dore, the rice miller from Crowley, La. His trip was paid for by the Agency for International Development, an agency whose appropriation was controlled by the subcommittee that Passman chaired.

Prior to departing Edwards asked Dore to meet with Park to try to work out an accommodation between Park and Passman. Passman was very antagonistic to Park at this time. For example, on December 3, 1971, Passman cabled the U.S. Ambassador to the ROK, Philip Habib, and said in part,

We may be having trouble with Tongsun Park who is a commissioned lobbyist representing certain American Congressmen who are in Korea at this time as possessing influence they do not have. This is very disadvantageous to the highly ethical procedure we are now following on the aid bill and the rice sale. I, personally, will have nothing to do with any deal involving excessive commissions and favors. Tongsun Park knows this very well. Help us keep this matter regular and on an ethical business basis, discounting Park's claims of great influence in Washington and insist that all interested parties deal with the Korean Ambassador to Washington who is a strict operator. . . .

Dore had dinner with Park at the George Town Club the night before he departed with Passman. In mid-January the Passman party arrived in Hong Kong. Tongsun Park was also in Hong Kong. According to Park, he (Park) had two private meetings with Passman in Hong Kong. During these meetings Passman told Park that he (Passman) had annual campaign expenses of about $150,000. Passman wanted Park to take care of $50,000 that year. Park agreed. Park also borrowed $5,000 from Dore in Hong Kong and gave Passman $5,000 in cash. Park stated this $5,000 was payment for watches he bought from Passman. Finally, Park agreed to buy a quantity of dehydrated yams from a factory in Passman's district.

From Hong Kong, Passman and Park went to Seoul, Korea, where among other people Passman saw President Park on January 21, 1972. This meeting is recorded in Park's diary, although Park was not present at the meeting. . . . The committee has no direct evidence of what was said at the meeting. However, it is reasonable to assume that Passman supported Park. . . .

Between December 3, 1971 . . . and January 24, 1972 . . . Passman went from Park's enemy to his friend. During this period Park made a $5,000 payment to Passman in Hong Kong, promised Passman $50,000 per year and promised to buy Louisiana yams. For Park, who was still desperately trying to regain his rice agency, the recruitment of Passman as a friend was of monumental importance.

Park did finally regain the rice agency on March 21, 1972. . . .

Park's rice agency was to prove very lucrative. In 1972 he received $586,000 in rice commissions from Connell Rice & Sugar. In 1973, $682,000. In 1974 the commissions soared to $3,705,000. In 1975 they were $3,581,000. In 1976 Park's commissions were $19,000. . . .

The day after Park returned to the United States, on March 23, 1972, he met, as is reflected in his diary, with Otto Passman and Gordon Dore. . . . On March 25 or 27 Park delivered $5,000 to Passman according to his reconstruction based upon an entry in his ledger. . . . On March 28 Park delivered $10,000 in cash to Passman. On March 29 he delivered another $10,000 in cash to Passman. These payments are memorialized in Park's diary by an entry of the 28th, "(Passman 10 copies)" and of the 29th, "Passman (10 L. Copies)." . . . .

Passman's concern about Park's pledge to buy dehydrated yams was quieted by April 1, 1972, when Passman issued a press release stating that, "(h)e has arranged for Korean Ambassador Tung-son [sic] Park to fly to Louisiana for the purpose of visiting sweet potato or yam canning plant in the State.". . . On April 4, 1972, Park did go to St. Francisville, La., where he purchased 1,000 cases of dehydrated yams from the Joan of Arc Co. On hand for the ceremony were, among others, Edwin Edwards, Gordon Dore, and John Breaux, a staff member of Edwards who had announced his intention to run for Congress to succeed Edwards. Within 1 week of this event the President of Joan of Arc, one Mr. Truitt, handed Gordon Dore a $2,000 campaign contribution for Passman. Dore, during public hearings, conceded receiving the contribution and that it was for Passman, but testified that "I wouldn't want my testimony to reflect that the campaign contribution was based on the one sale of yams to Korea.". . . Dore went on to explain that in addition to this purchase, Passman was able to get dehydrated yams included in the school lunch program.

On April 3, 1972, the day before Park went to St. Francisville, La., Park gave Passman another $10,000 in cash. His ledger for 1972 supports this. . . . On May 1 Park delivered $5,000 in cash to Passman. However, based upon Park's diary entry which reads "2.5 + 2.5," . . . Park suspects that this payment represented in part a watch transaction. During this period Park's ledger contained the entry "Otto's F.S. — 2.". . . Park cannot recall whether this represented a $2,000 contribution to Passman or possibly a watch sale.

In the Spring of 1972 because of Park's rice agency, Passman and Grover Connell became friends. Connell was chief executive officer of Connell Rice & Sugar headquartered in Westfield, N.J. Connell Rice & Sugar bought almost all of the U.S. rice which was to go to the ROK and then resold it to the ROK. Connell bought some of this rice from the California RGA and some from Louisiana. A vice president of Connell Rice & Sugar was headquartered in Crowley, La.

In order fully to understand Passman's relationship with Park it is necessary to understand the role played by Grover Connell and also Gordon Dore. When OSROK wrote to Connell on March 21, 1972, stating that Park's services as intermediary would be required on all rice trade with the ROK, Grover Connell was angry. An agent on such a sale is the agent of the seller (in this case Connell) and Connell did not want the buyer nominating the seller's agent. On March 30, 1972, Connell wrote to U.S. Department of Agriculture ("USDA") and complained.

On April 13, 1972, Park went to New Jersey and met with Connell. They argued over the rice agency question and Park walked out. Connell objected both to the commissions demanded by Park and to the fact that Park was being forced on him by OSROK. The very next day, April 14, Park's diary reflects the fact that Otto Passman called Park and told him he must go back and talk to Connell. The following day, April 15, Park again went to see Connell to discuss the situation. . . .

On April 17, 1972, Connell cabled USDA to ask if they were going to approve Park as an agent. . . . The USDA was in fact considering disqualifying Park on the ground that, in light of the letter from OSROK, Park could never qualify as a "bona fide" agent of the seller. . . . Park learned of the problem and announced his withdrawal. USDA advised Connell on April 21, 1972, that Park had withdrawn as rice agent. . . .

During April and May 1972, Connell offered to sell rice to the ROK without an agent, thereby avoiding altogether the payment of any commissions. These offers, although lowest in price, were rejected by OSROK ostensibly because Connell had no agent. . . . Shortly thereafter Connell agreed to accept a Korean company known as the Daihan Nongsan Co., as their agent, . . . which was in fact acting solely as a front for Tongsun Park. On June 16, 1972, after a Passman cable to Ambassador Kim Dong Jo on June 8, 1972, which read,

> Korea's stubbornness on rice purchase is on the verge of bringing about my defeat for re-election to Congress. After releasing a statement that the rice sale had been made, opponent now finds that Korea is now dragging its feet. This information is hitting all newspapers in my district. Please call President Park and ask him to get this thing off dead center, otherwise, I could be defeated. Will you act today Mr. Ambassador. . . .

Connell signed a contract to sell rice to the ROK with Daihan Nongsan acting as Connell's agent.

Park has testified that Daihan Nongsan was a company in whose name he received rice commissions after he had "withdrawn" as the nominated rice agent due to objections made by USDA. Grover Connell testified that he did not know Park was involved with Daihan Nongsan. . . . The Committee has evidence that Park met with Connell's lawyer and later Grover Connell met with and spoke to Park and Ryu about where and when commissions would be paid to Daihan Nongsan. Connell's testimony to the Department of Justice on this subject gave rise to a false declarations indictment presently pending against Grover Connell.

On June 23, 1972, a week after the rice contract was signed, Park, as reflected in his diary, gave Passman $7,000. . . . Then on August 9, 1972, the day after the first $40,000 rice commission was forwarded to Park's Daihan Nongsan account in Washington by Connell, Park gave Passman $15,000 . . . of that $40,000. This brought Park's total payments to Passman in 1972 to $69,000.

In December 1972 Passman again travelled to the Far East. This trip included a stop in the ROK. In addition to Dore, Passman was accompanied by Governor Edwards' brother Marion and newly elected Congressman John Breaux who succeeded Edwin Edwards. Tongsun Park was in Seoul at the same time the Passman party was there. Park testified . . . and his records indicate . . . that he gave Dore a $5,000 check to cash to help Breaux make up his campaign deficit. This check was subsequently cashed in Crowley, La., the hometown of Breaux, Dore, and Marion Edwards. All three have denied under oath ever receiving or transacting that check.

In February 1973, a month during which Park gave Passman $3,000 . . . Park asked Passman to write to President Park. Similar requests were made and letters written by Richard Hanna, John J. McFall, William E. Minshall and Senator Joseph Montoya. . . .

The event that triggered Park to request these letters was the resignation of Secretary of Defense Melvin Laird, who through William Minshall, Park had portrayed as a person over whom he had influence. . . .

In late April of 1973 Passman traveled to the Far East again. During his trip to the ROK Tongsun Park was at Passman's side most of the time. Park has testified that just prior to departing on this trip he gave Otto Passman $50,000 on April 11, 1973. . . . On that same occasion he gave Passman another $75,000 intended for Dore as a premium for certain rice Dore sold during a period of short supply. . . . Dore testified that he did not receive $75,000 from Passman at that or any subsequent time. . . .

In June 1973, as reflected on two check stubs, Park cashed checks of $20,000 and $28,000 respectively. The proceeds were given to Passman and this fact was noted on the stubs. . . . These payments were made in 1973. The $3,000 in February, $50,000 in April and $48,000 in June bring the 1973 total to $101,000. If Passman retained the $75,000 given him in April for Dore the 1973 total was $176,000.

By the fall of 1973, Park had ceased to rely on other Members of Congress for assistance. Passman, as a solid friend, was sufficient to insure Park's position with his Government. Park, when asked whether he was exclusively relying on Passman said,

> I think this is a fair statement yes. I felt that I finally found somebody powerful enough and brazen enough to protect my interest, and I was very grateful to Mr. Passman.

Prior to Park's departure for Korea in December 1973, Passman provided Park with a letter beginning, "My dear T.P." This letter complimented Park and urged the ROK to buy rice. Four days later Passman sent Park a cable urging the ROK to buy rice. Passman concluded, "I am limiting my intervention to Gordon Dore and Grover Connell only, because they are reliable and likewise appreciate Korea's rice purchases in former years. . . .

Why Passman sought to limit his intervention to Dore and Connell is unclear. Several facts, however, are well established. Dore, Connell and Passman were good personal friends. Much of the money Passman received from Park came from commissions Park received from Connell. . . .

Passman . . . [went] to the ROK in January 1974. He met with KCIA Director Shin Jik Soo. The purpose of the meeting was, according to Tongsun Park, to discuss rice. Passman received a commitment from the KCIA Director that Korea would buy a large quantity of U.S. rice in 1974. This fact is confirmed by Passman in a letter to the KCIA Director some six months later. Passman wrote:

> I have fond memories of the very pleasant meeting I had in your office with our mutual wonderful friend, Tongsun Park, back in

January when you indicated you would buy a large quantity of rice from my country during 1974. . . .

The symbiotic relationship enjoyed by Park and Passman is best demonstrated by two documents which were written in 1974. On June 2, 1974, Park wrote to Passman to inform him that Korea had decided to purchase a large quantity of U.S. rice. . . .

This letter makes it clear that Park needed Passman's support to continue as rice agent and that the KCIA was the key Korean Government agency on rice. Passman on the other hand issued a press release a week and a half later announcing the sale of rice and stating that the sale represented the fulfillment of a personal promise made to him by President Park. The unmistakable impression created is that without Passman Louisiana rice would not be sold to the ROK.

Passman acted on Park's advice and wrote to the KCIA Director on June 18, 1974. His praise of Park was effusive. For example,

> Mr. Director, you can imagine how pleased I was when I was informed by your fellow countrymen, including our energetic and dynamic friend, Tongsun Park, that you were going to buy 100,000 tons of United States rice.
>
> I marvel at the effective and professional manner in which Tongsun Park operates. He was in rare form in persuading the exporters to reduce substantially the price of the rice that you had authorized to be purchased. He did a very effective job, and I anticipate working with Tongsun in the future. . . .

Passman stated that he was going to have this letter delivered by Park and went on to say, "At Tongsun's request, I am also enclosing a letter for your personal information.". . .

The committee has uncovered the letter enclosed for the KCIA Director's personal information. . . . It is a letter dated June 6, 1974 written by the Acting Undersecretary of State for Security Assistance, George S. Vest, to Passman and details the Security Assistance Program (military aid) for Korea for fiscal 1974. Passman may have had good reason for omitting any description of this letter. For if this letter included information not generally available to the public, Passman may have been guilty of espionage.

Undersecretary Vest's letter was sent to Passman when requested of Vest during his testimony before Passman on the foreign aid bill. . . .

Vest and others at State were interviewed and no one was able to tell the Committee whether the information included in the letter was public as of the date Passman sent it to the KCIA Director. Likewise, Admiral Raymond Peet was interviewed but was of no assistance on this matter. However, all parties agree that the usual method of publicizing funding levels is for the State Department to inform the embassy of the country involved. If this had already happened here there would have been no reason for Park to have requested Passman to get this information. Further, there would have been no need for Passman to be so veiled in his letter to the KCIA Director. At a minimum this incident is an example of Tongsun Park acting as an agent of the Korean Government and not merely as a businessman.

KCIA Director Shin acknowledged receipt of Passman's letter on June 30, 1974. . . . Passman sent copies of the KCIA Director's letter to Connell and Dore. . . .

In October 1974, Passman cabled Park to report on the *military situation* (emphasis added) with regard to aid for the ROK. . . . In November, Passman made his annual pitch to Park to the effect that the ROK better place its rice order soon. . . .

Passman learned in early December 1974 that the ROK had agreed to purchase 400,000 tons of rice. Passman immediately cabled the KCIA Director to express his extreme gratification for the ROK's purchase having been so informed "through your (the KCIA Director's) special negotiator and my (Passman's) personal friend, T. S. Park.". . . Later in December there is a letter to the KCIA Director in a similar vein. . . . The Committee has in its possession a partial draft of this December letter which was probably supplied to Passman by Tongsun Park. . . . However, Passman added a paragraph to Park's draft in which he suggests that Connell is prepared to sell rice under Public Law 480 without an agent.

Park's 1975 commissions were generated, as previously explained, from the 400,000 ton sale of rice to the ROK in December 1974. Also as previously noted 1975 was Park's last big year of commissions. In 1975, the ROK purchased rice from Connell, without an agent.

As previously mentioned Otto Passman had a fascination for watches and jewelry. In this regard there is one transaction in February 1976 which bears mention. Early in the morning of February 27, 1976, Passman appeared in the jewelry store of G. J. Somavilla in Alexandria, Va. Passman had done business with Somavilla in the past and had in fact sold watches to Somavilla on credit, for which Somavilla always paid eventually.

On the morning in question Passman told Somavilla that he had about $7,000 in cash and asked Somavilla to take the cash and issue Passman a check. When Somavilla explained that he didn't have enough money in his account to cover such a check Passman told him to take the cash he (Passman) had to the bank and deposit it and then write Passman a check. Somavilla deposited $7,100 and then wrote Passman a check for $7,000. Somavilla explained that Passman allowed him to retain $100 for his trouble. The check Somavilla gave Passman has a notation on it that this check is for the purchase of watches from Passman. This was not true and Somavilla's check stub records the true facts. . . . This was an attempt by Passman to conceal the fact that he had received $7,100 in hundred dollar bills from a source still unknown.

Lastly while on the subject of watches, Passman used the diplomatic pouch to have watches shipped to him in Washington. Jules Bassin, the Deputy Chief of Mission in Geneva, who dared question this unauthorized use (which included double wrapping the package so it would not be readily apparent that Passman was the ultimate addressee) received the following letter dated October 10, 1969, from Passman:

Thank you very much for calling the State Department via long distance to ascertain if I was pulling a fast one in having some antique watches, as well as three other watches I returned to Geneva from Washington for bracelet adjustments, sent to me.

May I assure you politely, factually, and to the point that I consider myself an ethical operator. It certainly goes without saying that the two stickers that I mailed to one of your co-workers to be used in returning my watches was for no reason other than to expedite their return.

I have been in Congress 23 years, and on the Committee on Appropriations 21 years, and I think my reputation for integrity would stand a fair test, so may I assure you again that my specialty is not pulling tricks. If you need any additional information, write to your own Secretary of State, Mr. Rogers, who is a personal friend of mine, or for that matter, to John Rooney, whom I am sure you know. . . .

Passman's activities with Tongsun Park are the subject of two indictments naming Passman as a defendant. On March 31, 1978, Passman was indicted for conspiracy, bribery and receipt of illegal gratuities. Shortly thereafter Passman was indicted for income tax evasion. He is awaiting trial on both indictments which have been consolidated for trial.

4. William E. Minshall

Tongsun Park's relationship with former Congressman William E. Minshall evolved for two reasons: Minshall's prominent position among Republican Members of the House and on the Defense Subcommittee of the Appropriations Committee, and Minshall's friendship with Secretary of Defense Melvin R. Laird. Minshall first became friendly with Park in 1968 or 1969, during the period between the November 1968 elections and the January 1969 inauguration when President Nixon selected his cabinet and Laird became Secretary of Defense. . . . The relationship between Park and Minshall progressed to the point that, in 1970, Park suggested that Minshall visit Korea. Minshall claims that the trip he eventually took to Korea in September of 1970 was planned and proposed by Chairman George Mahon of the Committee on Appropriations in connection with committee business. Mahon's August 13 letter asking Minshall to travel to Korea shows that there may well have been committee business for Minshall to conduct, and the Appropriations Committee did in fact pay for his travel and per diem expenses.

Other evidence, however, suggests that Minshall may have used the committee business as a public excuse to travel to Korea at the behest of Tongsun Park. Minshall says that he and Park spoke about the trip before the committee authorized it and even before Minshall asked Mahon for the letter. Furthermore, Park gave Minshall $5,000 in cash on August 26, shortly before Minshall's departure on September 3. Minshall characterized that cash as a campaign contribution, but Park claims that he gave it to Minshall for travel expenses and indicated that Minshall could use whatever remained in the campaign. Minshall himself testified that Park may have paid his bill at the Chosun Hotel in Seoul during that trip. Minshall claims that the purpose of the trip, which lasted from September 3 to September 5, was primarily "congressional" and incidentally to help Tongsun Park. Nevertheless, Minshall admits feeling at the time that Park "wanted me [Minshall] there to show the influence that he [Park] had with the Congress of the United States."

Minshall apparently agreed, in April of 1972, to make a second trip to Korea this time at Tongsun Park's request and expense. Tongsun Park's records show a payment to Minshall of $5,000 in April 1972. Minshall claims this was not received by him, and Park apparently feels that this payment noted in his records in April may have, in fact, been paid in August. Minshall claims that Park promised him $10,000 for his 1972 campaign but that he only received between $4,000 and $6,000. According to Minshall, this campaign contribution appeared to be the same as Park's ledger entry of a $5,000 payment for travel expenses in April. . . .

Shortly after the Republican Convention in August, 1972, Minshall went to Korea. He travelled on a commercial airline ticket purchased by Park and stayed in Korea from August 28 to September 4-5, 1972. Minshall acknowledges that his expenses in the ROK were paid by Park but does not recall receiving any spending money from Park. Park, however, has testified to giving — and his records reflect that he gave — $500 to Minshall on or after August 17 at Minshall's request. . . .

Tongsun Park claims that, shortly before the 1972 Presidential election, he delivered to Minshall at Minshall's request an envelope containing between $20,000 and $25,000 in cash which was to be contributed to President Nixon's campaign committee, the Committee to Re-elect the President. Minshall agrees that he received an envelope containing an unknown sum of cash from Tongsun Park in the Rayburn House Office Building. According to Minshall, he then placed the envelope in his jacket and went immediately to the office of Clark MacGregor, Nixon's campaign director. Minshall testified that he delivered the unknown quantity of cash to MacGregor and said merely that it was from Tongsun Park. MacGregor agrees that, within ten days before the election, he received an envelope from Minshall which contained a cash contribution. MacGregor, however, claims that he did not know the amount of the contribution and that Minshall told him the contribution was from the "officers of the George Town Club." MacGregor testified that he thereafter delivered the contribution to the campaign headquarters. . . .

The campaign committee's records at the time do not reflect any such receipt and this Committee has been unable to determine the eventual disposition of the cash.

Park has testified to one payment to Minshall in addition to the payments described above. This was a $1,000 payment for "spending money", and his 1972 ledger records the date as August 6, 1971. . . .

Minshall denies receiving this payment. . . .

While Minshall was in the Republic of Korea both in 1970 and 1972, he spoke with ROK officials and mentioned Tongsun Park's name favorably. Minshall also introduced Park to Secretary of Defense Melvin Laird and facilitated Park's visits with the Secretary at the Department of Defense. Minshall wrote at least six letters to the President of the ROK, the Prime Minister of the ROK, and the Director of the KCIA at Tongsun Park's request. Each of the letters praised Tongsun Park's representation of the ROK in the United States, and, at least to Minshall's knowledge, exaggerated Tongsun Park's influence with United States officials. This Minshall correspondence claimed that Tongsun Park discussed the military security of the Republic of Korea with Secretary of Defense Laird and further that Laird planned to use Minshall and Park as a conduit for sharing information between the Department of Defense and the President of the Republic of Korea. Minshall testified that the letters, which were probably either presented to his office in draft form by Park or one of his employees, or the content of which was suggested by Park, did "puff" and that Laird did not communicate with Minshall as described in the letters. Minshall was further aware of the fact that Park would use the letters, which were either mailed or given to Park or one of his employees for delivery to the addressee, to influence members of the government of the Republic of Korea in favor of Tongsun Park. Minshall claims, that despite the statements contained in these letters he never thought of Park as an agent of the ROK but merely as a businessman and "good friend of Korea and the United States."

Minshall testified before this committee under a grant of immunity — only after the Department of Justice had indicated that its criminal investigation of Minshall was closed. Minshall's testimony admitting receipt of large sums of cash in even years only, sums which he now says were campaign contributions, conflicts with Park's testimony. Minshall does not admit to receiving any payments during off-election years. Nevertheless, he accepted cash from Tongsun Park which Minshall characterizes as the largest single contributions to his campaigns of 1970 and 1972. Furthermore, Minshall failed to report either of the two cash receipts or to detail their use in reports to the Ohio State Election commission or the House of Representatives. Minshall has testified that he used Park's contributions solely for campaign purposes and says he placed the money in his desk and afterwards transferred it to his office safe, from which he personally disbursed it. The Committee has been unable to determine whether he used the money for campaign purposes or for personal purposes, but, in either case, Minshall's treatment of the contributions gives some indication that he himself found them suspect. . . .

5. Sitting Members as to whom the committee instituted disciplinary proceedings

Park gave cash under differing circumstances to Congressmen Edward R. Roybal, John J. McFall, Charles H. Wilson and Edward J. Patten. After a full investigation of the circumstances surrounding these payments, the committee on July 13, 1978, filed Statements of Alleged Violation (Statements) against each of these Members. None of the Statements charged that the Members has been influenced or agreed to be influenced in return for the gifts; and none of the Statements charged that the Members knew that Park was acting on behalf of the ROK Government when he made the gifts. The charges dealt in the main with the manner in which the gifts were handled or disclosed.

Roybal was charged with failure to report the contribution; conversion of the contribution to his personal use; and two counts of giving deliberately false testimony under oath.

McFall was charged with accepting the gifts under circumstances which a reasonable person might construe as influencing him in his official duties; failing to report a campaign contribution; and converting the contribution to his personal use.

Wilson was charged with falsely denying that he had received a $1,000 cash wedding present from Park.

Patten was charged with passing off two contributions from Park to the Middlesex County Democratic Organization as his own.

After public hearings, the committee sustained all charges against Representative Roybal except for one of the two false testimony charges; sustained only the charge against Representative McFall that he had failed to report the campaign contribution; sustained the charge against Representative Wilson; and exonerated Representative Patten. It recommended censure for Roybal and reprimands for McFall and Wilson. The House voted to reprimand all three. Full printed reports on all four cases were submitted to the House and they are hereby incorporated into this report by reference.

6. Sitting Members who were investigated as to whom the committee did not institute disciplinary proceedings

Park made campaign contributions to seven other sitting Members: Representatives John Brademas, Eligio de la Garza, Thomas Foley, John J. Murphy, Melvin Price, Frank Thompson, and Morris K. Udall. He also gave two parties for Thomas P. O'Neill Jr., then majority leader. The results of the committee's investigative efforts with respect to these contributions and parties were released on July 13, 1978. . . . In each case, the committee concluded that the receipt and handling of those contributions involved no impropriety. The committee noted that the contributions were by check and therefore traceable; that they were reported where required; that there was no evidence that these Members agreed to be influenced in return for the contributions; that there was no evidence that these Members knew or should have known that Tongsun Park was an agent of the ROK; that the contributions were made prior to January 1, 1975, when it became illegal to accept a campaign contribution from a foreign national; and that there was no evidence that the receipt of these contributions was otherwise improper. In addition, Tongsun Park gave

Representative Broomfield a check for $1,000 which was returned to him with a thank you note from Representative Broomfield on November 13, 1970.

7. Other former Members

Park testified that he also made cash contributions to five additional former Members: Nick Galifianakis — $10,000 in 1972; John R. Rarick — $1,000 in 1974; Albert Johnson — $1,000 in 1974; John J. Rooney — $2,000 each in 1972 and 1974; and Donald Lukens — $500 each in 1968 and 1970. . . . Since these men are no longer Members of the House and are accordingly beyond the jurisdiction of the House, and because none appeared to be active participants in the scheme, the committee went no further than to attempt to ascertain whether money had in fact been paid to them. Albert Johnson disclosed on his questionnaire and during a subsequent deposition that he received $1,000 from Park in 1974. John Rooney is dead. Galifianakis and Rarick testified that they had not received cash contributions from Park. Their testimony, together with Park's testimony to the contrary and other evidence supporting it was sent to the Department of Justice on July 13, 1978, for consideration by the Department of Justice whether perjury had been committed. Lukens denied in an interview with a member of the special staff that he had received any cash from Park. There is no evidence supporting Park's testimony that he gave Lukens money and, when pressed, Park was not sure whether he gave money to Lukens or not. . . .

Park testified that he gave small checks to some former Congressmen or candidates for Congress in the year 1970, ranging in amounts from $300 to $1,000. The checks were given to Ross Adair ($500); William H. Ayers ($500); Peter Frelinghuysen ($500 — this check was never cashed or deposited); Seymour Halpern ($500); Lawrence J. Hogan ($500); Thomas E. Kleppe ($500); Spark Matsunaga ($500); Cole McMartin ($1,000); Chester L. Mize ($500); Robert A. Reveles ($300), and Nelson Gross ($100). The committee has copies of all of these checks. . . .

III. HANCHO KIM

. . .From 1970 through 1976, Kim Sang Keun was an agent of the Korean Central Intelligence Agency (the "KCIA") stationed at the Korean Embassy in Washington, D.C. In November, 1976, he defected to the United States. After his defection, Kim Sang Keun (KSK) told the story of how in September 1974 and June 1975 he had given a total of $600,000 in cash to Hancho C. Kim, a Korean-born American citizen residing in Lanham, Md. This money was to be used to influence, among others, Members of the House of Representatives. KSK testified that Hancho Kim reported to KSK the identity of five Representatives referred to by the code name of "Advance Guard," to whom KSK said Hancho Kim had told him (KSK) that he had paid money: Representatives Tennyson Guyer, Guy Vander Jagt, Benjamin A. Gilman, Larry Winn Jr., and Robert J. Lagomarsino. . . .

After comprehensive investigative efforts . . . the committee found no evidence that Hancho Kim had done what KSK said Hancho Kim claimed he had done; that is, there is no evidence that Hancho Kim paid any money to any Members of Congress. . . .

The Plan

1. *KSK's evidence*

KSK had the title of "First Secretary" and later "Counsellor" at the Korean Embassy in Washington, D.C., during the period October, 1970 until November, 1976. In fact, since 1961, he had been an agent for the Korean Central Intelligence Agency. In November of 1976, KSK defected after having been warned by a Korean official that he might have to spend 1 year in jail as a result of his participation in the "Koreagate scandal.". . .

After his defection, KSK was questioned before a Federal Grand Jury, by FBI agents, and later by this committee. In October 1977, he testified in public before this committee. . . .

In his public testimony and in his discussion with the staff, KSK told the following story:

In late August 1974, Hancho Kim called KSK at the ROK Embassy in Washington. Up until that time, KSK barely knew Hancho Kim and had had no official contact with him. Hancho Kim told KSK that KSK had been designated by the KCIA headquarters in Seoul to work with Hancho Kim on an important project. . . . On September 3, 1974, KSK received a formal instruction from General Yang Doo Won, Director of Planning and Coordination, at KCIA headquarters in Seoul. . . .

On September 11, 1974, KSK was visited at his apartment by the accounting section chief of the KCIA, who was visiting the United States from the ROK. He handed KSK $256,000 in $100 bills wrapped in brown paper. . . . At the same time, KSK withdrew an additional $44,000 from his personal checking account at the Dupont Circle branch of the Riggs National Bank. . . . This money came from a deposit of $100,000 he had made previously. That deposit consisted of a check drawn on the account of Tongsun Park. The check had been forwarded to KSK in the summer of 1974 by General Yang Doo Won. . . . The next day, September 12, 1974, KSK delivered the total of $300,000 in $100 bills to Hancho Kim's home in Lanham, Md. . . .

At the time, KSK received a receipt from Hancho Kim in Korean handwriting which translates as follows:

Receipt
September 12, 1974, 8:00 p.m.
    (I) duly received at my home the sum of $300,000 and promise

definitely to deliver it to the designated person(s) by tomorrow (September 12).

Kim Han-Cho. . . .

KSK's information about Hancho Kim's activities on behalf of Yang Doo Won came from Hancho Kim himself, when Hancho Kim asked KSK to send reports of Hancho Kim's activities (as reported to him by Hancho Kim) to Yang Doo Won. KSK viewed his own function as ministerial and assumed that Hancho Kim and Yang had had conversations to which he was not privy. Hancho Kim told KSK at that time that he was embarking on an important operation to gain influence with, among others, Members of Congress on behalf of the Seoul regime. He said that the money was to be spent to expand his activities in the Congress. . . . KSK said that Hancho Kim said he had to help Representative Tennyson Guyer and, through him, four other Members of the House. Later, Hancho Kim referred to this group as the "Advance Guard." The general objective of the "Advance Guard" was to gain support for the ROK in the Congress. More specifically, it was to counter the activities of the Fraser Subcommittee of the International Relations Committee, which was critical of the ROK Government. . . .

According to KSK, though Hancho Kim never said so in so many words, he implied to KSK repeatedly that he was dispensing cash to Congressman Guyer and other members of the "Advance Guard." KSK said Kim told him he did this principally before short recesses of the House when the Congressmen were ready to return to their districts. . . . In describing the payments to KSK, Hancho Kim used a Korean analogy: he was handing out cash and gifts, he said, like a father marrying off three daughters all at once. KSK explained that he believed that Hancho Kim meant that he was spending money busily and beyond his means. . . . It was not until the spring of 1975, however, that KSK saw for the first time the list of the "Advance Guard." Hancho Kim brought the list from Korea. KSK was under the impression that the list was prepared by KCIA officials in Seoul. . . . On the list were the same five names.

At the time, all were members of the International Relations Committee.

. . .Toward the end of 1974 and through the early part of 1975, Hancho Kim repeatedly told KSK he had spent more than $600,000 to $700,000 for the "operation" and asked for more money. . . .

. . .On April 21, 1975, Hancho Kim related to KSK that he had met with Secretary of State Henry Kissinger and President Ford on April 17. Thereupon, the two drafted a cable report of the event, the language of which KSK recorded in his diary which he later gave to the committee: "Dr. H[ancho Kim], together with Congressman [Tennyson Guyer] got together with Secretary Henry Kissinger, and met with the President." The following day, Hancho Kim asked KSK to send a written report to Yang Doo Won in the diplomatic pouch in which Kim stated he was spending a lot of money maintaining his contacts with the Congress. . . .

From May through the first part of June 1975, Hancho Kim visited

Korea again, and upon returning, Hancho Kim told KSK that additional funds for the operation would be forthcoming. KSK received another $300,000 in cash in the diplomatic pouch soon afterward. In early June 1975, KSK delivered this money to Hancho Kim at his home. . . .

Hancho Kim traveled to the ROK in August of 1975. This trip coincided with a Korean visit by a congressional delegation led by Representative Lester Wolff. Hancho Kim told KSK that three members of the "Advance Guard" were in the group. After returning to Washington, Hancho Kim told KSK that while in Seoul he had spent some $100,000 . . . and "took good care" of the visiting Congressmen. . . .

As time went by, KSK began to doubt the truthfulness of what Hancho Kim told him. Indeed on April 22, 1975, KSK described Hancho Kim in his diary as "A liar.". . .

In mid-August 1976, Hancho Kim angrily told KSK that the Korean Ambassador at the time, Hahm Pyong Choon, either had given or attempted to give $20,000 in cash to Representative Guyer. Hancho Kim complained because he thought Representative Guyer was his contact. Hancho Kim told KSK that Representative Guyer had told him of Ambassador Hahm's offer. At Hancho Kim's direction, KSK reported these events to Yang Doo Won. . . .

KSK saw Hancho Kim in September 1976 for the last time. . . . The Korean scandal had then received some press coverage. In November, 1976, after having been informed that he might have to spend a year in jail in Korea to make it appear that the Korean Government was doing something about the Korean scandal, KSK defected. After consulting with a former KCIA Director, General Kim Hyung Wook, KSK met with agents of the FBI on November 26, 1976, and turned over to them copies of some of the letters from Yang Doo Won and the receipt from Hancho Kim he had retained. . . .

3. The Investigation of the "Advance Guard"

(a) Congressman Tennyson Guyer

The committee conducted an in-depth investigation of Congressman Tennyson Guyer, which included a detailed investigation of Guyer's finances. The committee found no evidence that Guyer received cash from Hancho Kim. The committee decided early in its inquiry to focus its attention on Congressman Guyer. Guyer was clearly the Member of Congress whom Hancho Kim knew the best and perhaps the only one whom he knew at all. If Representative Guyer was not paid by Hancho Kim, it is unlikely that any others were.

In an investigation that took a year and a half, the staff took sworn testimony from Congressman Guyer, obtained boxes of financial and other records, took testimony from Mrs. Guyer, and conducted lengthy interviews with Representative Guyer, his wife and members of his staff. The staff also conducted an in-depth analysis of Representative Guyer's finances. The result of the investigation was that there were none of the indicia which one would expect to find in the case of a Congressman who has received cash from an illegitimate source; there was no particular need for money uncovered; no unusual expenditures uncovered; no unusual or unexplained deposits of cash; and no indication that the expenditures of which we have records are insufficient to maintain the Guyers at their standing of living. . . .

As a member of the Subcommittee for Future Foreign Policy Development, Representative Guyer went to Korea on the delegation led by Representative Wolff in August 1975. Hancho Kim was also there, and they met twice briefly. . . .

Representative Guyer inserted several items with respect to the ROK in the Congressional Record. He testified that he inserted them on his own initiative and testified that Hancho Him had neither asked him to nor offered him compensation to make the entries. Some of what the entries contained was based on information Representative Guyer got from Kim, however, in conversation or from Kim's articles on the "Op-Ed" page of the New York Times. Kim did not bring Representative Guyer material to be inserted or supporting documents. Representative Guyer would tell Kim that he or the ROK was in the Record, but Guyer believed Kim received the Record and read it on his own. Representative Guyer personally drafted the entries he made in the Record. His secretary helped write them occasionally and typed them. . . .

Former Congressman Vernon Thomson made an entry in the Congressional Record, November 11, 1974, following a Korean border incident. Representative Guyer had written the statement, based in part on information he got from Kim and asked Representative Thomson to insert it. The statement refers to a meeting the week before of a few members, including Representative Thomson, with Hancho Kim. Representative Guyer said that meeting was the luncheon in the Capitol Dining Room mentioned earlier. According to Representative Guyer, Representative Thomson did not have a clear recollection of the luncheon, but in inserting remarks in the Record took Guyer's word about the circumstances of the meeting.

Representative Thomson, now a member of the Federal Election Commission, told the staff and later testified at the trial of Hancho Kim that he was quite certain that he had never met Hancho Kim. . . . Asked about the statement in the Record to the contrary, he said that Representative Guyer had drafted the statement and that he had not reviewed it carefully before inserting it in the Record.

Representative Guyer seemed to remember press statements that he had issued on January 28 or January 29, 1975, in response to press criticism of ROK President Park Chung Hee's Emergency Decree No. 5. He did not remember if anyone else signed the statement. He did not recall who had initiated or drafted the statement. He did not think Kim had a hand in it. . . .

Representative Guyer also sent a memo to and made an oral request of Vern Loen and Max Friedersdorf, White House Congressional liaison, to arrange a meeting between President Ford and Hancho Kim. The White House denied the request. He also sent a letter along to the White House that Kim wanted delivered to President Ford. . . .

(b) Representative Guy Adrian Vander Jagt

The committee conducted an in-depth investigation of Representative Vander Jagt. The result was that the committee found no evidence that Vander Jagt received any money from Hancho Kim.

Congressman Vander Jagt, at a deposition before a member of the committee, testified that he did not recall having met Kim. . . . Hancho Kim testified that, if he had met Vander Jagt, it was only briefly. . . . Moreover, interviews of Congressman Vander Jagt's staff and others disclosed no contact between Hancho C. Kim and Congressman Vander Jagt.

Congressman Vander Jagt's appointment books reflect one meeting in 1970, five meetings in 1971, one meeting in 1972 and one meeting in 1975 with a "Mr. Kim." Independent investigation identified that "Mr. Kim" who appears in Congressman Vander Jagt's appointment books is Kim Young-ho, a Korean-American who met Congressman Vander Jagt through Edward Frederick, a mutual friend. Staff interviews revealed that Mr. Frederick knew Congressman Vander Jagt when the Congressman was a Michigan State Senator, and Kim Young-ho was Mr. Frederick's language instructor at the Foreign Service Institute.

Congressman Vander Jagt's campaign, office and personal finances were examined in minute detail in the same manner as Congressman Guyer's. The investigation uncovered no unexplained deposits or other uses of cash, and there is no evidence that Vander Jagt received any money from Hancho Kim.

(c) Representative Benjamin A. Gilman

The committee conducted an in-depth investigation of Representative Gilman. The result was that the committee uncovered no evidence that Gilman received any money from Hancho Kim. As in the case of the other alleged members of the "Advance Guard," the committee made an extensive request for documents from Representative Benjamin Gilman, and he provided the committee with voluminous records. An exhaustive review was made of these documents, which included but was not limited to appointment books, visitor cards, visitor log sheets, campaign records, correspondence, public statements, Congressional Record entries, and Federal income tax returns and other financial records. In addition, numerous interviews of present and former staff members both in Washington, D.C., and Mr. Gilman's Congressional District were conducted.

At one of his depositions, Hancho Kim, was shown a photograph of Representative Gilman. He testified that to the best of his recollection he had never met Representative Gilman, either in the United States or the Republic of Korea. . . . This testimony is consistent with that of Congressman Gilman, his wife and the information obtained from the members of his staff. Moreover, it is not contradicted by any of the records obtained by the committee.

(d) Representative Larry Winn

The committee conducted an in-depth investigation of Representative Larry Winn. The result was that the committee uncovered no evidence that Winn received any money from Hancho Kim. In an effort to determine what, if any contacts Mr. Winn had with Hancho Kim, a request was made of Representative Larry Winn that he provide the committee with certain documents. He provided the committee with the documents he had available, and a review was made of this material. This review included but was not limited to the analysis of appointment books, guest registers, correspondence, personal calendars, invitations, campaign records, and financial records.

At his deposition on November 23, 1977, Hancho Kim stated he did not recall ever meeting Congressman Winn. Kim was shown Winn's photograph and responded that he had never met Winn. . . .

(e) Congressman Robert J. Lagomarsino

The committee conducted an in-depth investigation of Representative Robert Lagomarsino. The result was that the committee uncovered no evidence that Lagomarsino received any money from Hancho Kim. Representative Lagomarsino, Representative Guyer, and Hancho Kim were all questioned about Representative Lagomarsino's relationship to Hancho Kim. Similar interviews were held with members of Representative Lagomarsino's staff and documentary evidence was obtained as with other members of the "Advance Guard." The testimony of all of them is, in substance, consistent and establishes that Representative Lagomarsino's contacts with Hancho Kim were fleeting. Indeed, from the evidence gathered by the staff it appears that Representative Lagomarsino was not with Hancho Kim alone at any time and that, accordingly, there was no opportunity for a transfer of cash to take place. . . .

IV. PAYMENTS. . .BY OFFICIALS OF THE KOREAN GOVERNMENT

In addition to the activities of Tongsun Park and Hancho Kim, both private citizens, the committee is convinced that the Government of the Republic of Korea adopted and implemented a plan to influence the policy of Congress towards the Republic of Korea by paying, directly through officials of the ROK Government, large amounts of U.S. currency to Members of the House of Representatives. The basis for this judgment follows.

A. Publicized Information

Dr. Jai Hyon Lee was employed by the Korean Embassy in Washington, D.C., from February 1970 through June 1973. He worked under Kim Dong

Jo who was the ROK Ambassador to the United States from 1967 until December 1973. In June 1973, Lee resigned his post in the Embassy to seek political asylum in this country, and is presently an associate professor of Journalism at Western Illinois University. He testified under oath in public session in October 1977, that in the spring of 1973 he and about 10 other officials in the ROK Embassy attended a series of meetings called by Ambassador Kim Dong Jo and presided over by KCIA station chief Le Sang Ho. These meetings were attended by officials at the Embassy, including Jai Hyon Lee, who were not members of the KCIA; and part of the purpose of the meetings was to enlist support from non-KCIA officials for KCIA programs. Dr. Lee did not know to what extent these programs had been in operation previously. At the meetings, documents were distributed by the KCIA station chief to each person present for discussion purposes. The documents were serially numbered and were re-collected at the end of the meeting. One such document recalled by Dr. Lee contained a number of proposals for action, one of which was a proposal for "seduction and buying off of American leaders, particularly in the Congress." The KCIA Station Chief referred briefly to this proposal, saying that its implementation would be left to the Ambassador and the KCIA people so that the other Embassy employees need not know about it.

At or about the same time, Dr. Lee, who was one of five or so people in the Embassy who had access to Kim Dong Jo's office, walked into the Ambassador's office unannounced. He saw Kim Dong Jo stuffing $100 bills into envelopes and saw him putting the envelopes into his pockets and into his attache case. According to Lee, Kim explained that he had to deliver "these things" and that he was on his way to "the Capitol.". . .

Dr. Lee's testimony was originally viewed with some skepticism by both the staff and the committee. It was not easy to picture an Ambassador personally delivering envelopes full of money to Members of Congress. However, Nan Elder, personal secretary to Representative Larry Winn, Jr., testified under oath in public session in October 1977, that in September 1972, Kim Dong Jo, whom she identified positively from a photographic spread, dropped in to Mr. Winn's office without an appointment and handed him an envelope containing a stack of $100 bills about 1-inch thick. Ms. Elder testified that she returned the money to Ambassador Kim a few minutes later at Winn's direction. . . . Ms. Elder's testimony was later corroborated under oath by Representative Larry Winn, Jr.

Although this event occurred before the series of meetings testified to by Dr. Lee, and before Dr. Lee saw Kim Dong Jo go "to the Capitol" with envelopes filled with cash, in the committee's opinion it establishes the reliability of Dr. Lee's testimony. It also suggests that Kim Dong Jo carried envelopes of cash "to the Capitol" on more than one occasion.

Further credibility was lent indirectly to Dr. Lee's testimony by the testimony of the wives of two Congressmen who were traveling in Korea in August of 1975, at a time when Kim Dong Jo was no longer Ambassador but was the ROK Minister of Foreign Affairs. Mrs. Kika de la Garza and Mrs. John T. Myers were visited in their hotel rooms on the same night by a Korean lady who gave each of them envelopes containing stacks of U.S. currency. Mrs. Myers did not know the lady who delivered the money. Mrs. de la Garza did. It was the wife of Kim Dong Jo. The money was returned the next day, in each case by the Congressmen. The exact amount of money offered in each case is unknown. However, Representative de la Garza, when returning the money to Kim Dong Jo, the then Korean Minister of Foreign Affairs, suggested that the money be given to a school in the ROK in which the Congressman had taken an interest. Mr. de la Garza furnished the committee with a letter he subsequently received from the head of the Korean school confirming receipt of $2,000 from the Korean Ministry of Foreign Affairs, and thanking Mr. de la Garza for his efforts. Mrs. Myers was told by her husband that the currency in the envelope was in $100 bills, and Representative Myers subsequently told committee investigators that he believes that envelope to have contained $10,000. . . .

Kim Dong Jo's penchant for distributing cash to U.S. politicians was further demonstrated by the fact that two honorary Korean Consuls — Donald Clark of Atlanta, Ga., and Dwight Hamilton of Englewood, Colo. — were each given $3,000 in cash by Kim Dong Jo, then ROK Foreign Minister in October 1974, while at a conference of Honorary Consuls in Washington, D.C.

Each was asked by Kim Dong Jo to distribute the money to pro-Korean candidates for State or Federal office. Each did so, one making extremely small contributions to each such candidate, the other giving the money to the State Republican Party, and concealing from such candidates the true source of the money. . . .

In addition to the information set forth above pertaining to Kim Dong Jo, the committee has also considered information about Row Chin Hwan, a member of the Korean National Assembly who had once lived in this country. Row offered to make a campaign contribution to Congressman Charles Wiggins, with whom he had previously become acquainted, in 1972 or 1974. Congressman Wiggins provided the committee with this information but was not sure of the year. The offers were made on behalf of "people in Korea." When Wiggins told Row that it was illegal to accept contributions from a foreign national, Row suggested that the money could be routed through an intermediary. Wiggins persisted in declining the offer. . . .

Row also approached John Nidecker, then a special assistant to President Nixon, in June 1974, during a visit by Row to Washington, D.C. Row offered to contribute $5,000 to the campaign of Members of the House designated by Nidecker and from $10,000 to $30,000 to Members of the Senate so designated. Nidecker also refused. . . .

B. Non-Publicized Information

The committee has had access to information in the possession of the intelligence community. The information indicates that during the period after Kim Dong Jo became Minister of Foreign Affairs (following his

Ambassadorship to the United States), others operating from the ROK Embassy in Washington, D.C., made payments of money in four figure amounts to four current Members of Congress whose names were reported to the committee, and planned to pay to two other Members of Congress money in five figure amounts. In some cases, the information is specific and detailed. In others, the information is much less so. . . .[T]his information is not sufficient to support a disciplinary charge against any Member, and the committee's considerable efforts to corroborate this information, set forth below, also was insufficient to support such a charge. It is not known whether these Congressmen are the same or in addition to those to whom Kim Dong Jo allegedly paid money.

In addition, a document entitled "1976 Plan for Operations in the United States," obtained by the Subcommittee on International Organizations of the House Committee on International Relations from a confidential source, was identified by a KCIA defector, Sohn Ho Young, who in sworn testimony linked this document to the KCIA Station Chief in Washington, Kim Yung Hwan. The document, which bears a notation that it had been processed through the office of the Director of the KCIA on December 15, 1975, clearly indicates that the KCIA had a plan to continue its efforts as late as 1976 to influence the U.S. Congress through payments of money. According to Mr. Sohn, the 1976 plan accurately reflected the operational objectives of the KCIA in the United States. Mr. Sohn explained that "there was great concern in Korea" at this time that the United States might withdraw from the ROK in the same way that it had from Vietnam; he said that the 1976 plan "was drafted in order to get the firm support of the United States for Korea.". . .

One section of the 1976 plan is entitled "Operations in the Congress." It describes the Koreans' "targets" for their lobbying in the Congress and, in a column headed "The Plan To Be Promoted," it outlines the strategy for achieving these goals. In the "Remarks" column, cost estimates are provided for many of the operations outlined. According to Mr. Sohn, these planned expenditures had to be approved in Seoul because the money came from the KCIA budget. . . .

One planned expenditure involved a $5,000 campaign contribution to a Member of Congress in connection with a fundraising dinner. The Member had only one such fundraising dinner — in August 1976. All available records relating to the dinner were reviewed; other campaign records of the Member were reviewed for the 1976 election and the Member's deposition was taken. The committee found no evidence that this proposed contribution was ever made or offered. . . .

D. Conclusions

The committee finds that the ROK Government adopted a plan or series of plans at least as early as 1972 under which persons stationed in the Embassy in Washington, D.C., notably Ambassador Kim Dong Jo and KCIA operatives stationed here were to obtain influence in Congress by making gifts of cash to U.S. Congressmen. The committee believes that the plan was implemented. However, the committee is unable to produce evidence which would substantiate charges against any individual Member of Congress for receipt of such a gift. The reason for this inability is as follows.

The committee believes that any gifts of money were made directly to the Member of Congress with no one else present except the ROK official making the gift. This was the almost unvarying pattern followed by Tongsun Park; it was the pattern followed by Kim Dong Jo in the one case of which we have direct proof; and it makes sense as a matter of prudence and Korean custom. Koreans view the giving of cash gifts as a very personal and intimate event.

The Congressmen who received the gifts — assuming that some did — have not admitted such receipt. The ROK officials who made the gifts — assuming that some did — have either refused to testify or — in the case of Kim Dong Jo — given written answers not under oath not subject to cross-examination which the committee views as wholly unreliable. Thus, the committee has available to it no direct testimony from anyone with first-hand knowledge of a payment. Principles of fundamental fairness almost always require that adjudications of misconduct be based, at least in part, on testimony under oath and subject to cross-examination by someone with first-hand knowledge of the misconduct. Under our legal system, statements by people who cannot be confronted and cross-examined by an accused are almost always an insufficient basis on which to bring a charge of misconduct. Release and use of intelligence information would not, in the committee's opinion nor that of its chief counsel, make up this deficiency — that is, the deficiency created by the absence of any live witnesses to testify to payments to Congressmen. This being the case, it is the committee's conclusion that the benefits to be gained by publicizing the information in the possession of the intelligence community are outweighed by the costs of the disclosure of intelligence sources and methods which would necessarily be involved.

V. SUZI PARK THOMSON

The activities of Suzi Park Thomson, as reported by the media, were among the reasons an investigation was authorized pursuant to House Resolution 252. A review of newspaper accounts indicated that she had widespread social contacts among Congressmen and was also in contact with ROK Embassy officials including KCIA officers. The implication of this media coverage was that she may have been utilized by the ROK Government to unduly influence Congressmen in connection with their decisions regarding legislation involving the ROK. It was therefore decided to include a specific question concerning Suzi Park Thomson in the questionnaire to Congressmen in connection with attendance at parties hosted by her. In response to the questionnaire, 44 sitting Members and eight former members reported that they had attended parties hosted by Suzi Park Thomson. However, no Congressman reported any gifts or offers of gifts from Suzi Park Thomson.

Suzi Park Thomson ... was employed by Congressman Lester Wolff from 1968 until January 1971, after which time she became employed by Speaker Carl Albert at a salary of $12,500 a year. She remained with Speaker Albert's staff until he left Congress in 1976. Her top pay during this period was a little less than $15,000 a year. ...

Suzi Park Thomson's bank records were reviewed to determine whether her assets as therein reflected were commensurate with her known sources of income. This review revealed that prior to 1971 she experienced financial difficulties from time-to-time as established by the fact that her bank on occasions refused to honor her checks because of an insufficiency of funds. She frequently made deposits to her savings account in amounts as low as $2. Judging from those financial records which were made available, it appears that until 1971 her banking records were about as expected given her stated income. However, a sudden change in her financial affairs occurred in 1971. Her $2 savings deposits ceased and deposits in even figures ranging from $200 to $600 appeared. These deposits, some of which were in cash, continued until 1976. The committee could not determine whether any of them were by check or what the source of these were. It should be noted that this apparent change in her financial status coincided with her employment by Mr. Albert and the separation from her husband, both of which occurred in January 1971.

The committee has determined that there were certain years after 1971 during which Suzi Park Thomson had income from sources other than her congressional salary and alimony. For example in 1975 she made two deposits to two different savings accounts on the same day totaling almost $5,400. One of $3,250 was made to her account at the Jefferson Federal Savings & Loan Association and one of $2,145 to her account at the Wright Patman Congressional Credit Union. Both deposits were made on October 6, 1975. None of this money was reported on her income tax return for 1975. When questioned under oath Ms. Thomson said she could not recall the source of those deposits. ...

Suzi Park Thomson's parties ranged from informal, pot luck dinners for 6 to 10 people in her apartment, to New Year's celebrations at nearby restaurants with 200 to 300 people in attendance. There were also other parties with attendance ranging between 50 to 100 people at other places such as in the recreation room in her apartment building: Her parties were often described as being informal and relaxing. Suzi Park Thomson became well known for her culinary expertise. A number of people who attended her parties stated that there were frequently two or three Koreans in attendance at parties which also included Congressmen and congressional employees. On occasion the guests brought food or drink to the parties. On other occasions when Suzi Park Thomson hosted parties in honor of certain Congressmen's birthdays, the Congressman whose birthday was being celebrated reimbursed her for the expense. There were other times, however, when witnesses have stated that an unidentified Korean male paid the restaurant bill.

In sworn testimony, Suzi Park Thomson explained that she enjoyed entertaining and frequently held parties at which Congressmen and congressional staff members were in attendance. She said that she frequently included Koreans in such affairs because she wanted them to learn about U.S. democracy. She stated that Ambassador Kim Dong Jo, KCIA officers Col. Kim Kyu Il, Col. Choi Yae-Heun, and Minister Kim Yung Hwan attended her parties. The last named three have been identified as KCIA agents. She stated that her relationship with Ambassador Kim Dong Jo evolved through a distant family relationship which she has with the Ambassador's wife. She denied receiving any money or liquor in quantity from the Korean Embassy or from any Korean to be utilized in connection with these parties or in any other respect. She did admit receiving some liquor and Korean food from Mrs. Kim Dong Jo every few months. . . .

Suzi Park Thomson denied any official or unofficial involvement with the ROK Government. She denied that anyone from the ROK Embassy or any Korean consulted with her with regard to which Congressman should be invited to her affairs or on how any Congressmen should be approached or lobbied in regard to Korean interests. She denied ever paying any Congressmen any money and denied having knowledge of any such gifts or offers to any Congressmen by any Korean. She stated that she was never employed by the Korean Government or by the KCIA. She further denied that she was ever asked by the KCIA to work as an agent. She denied ever receiving any money from any Korean Government official or officer other than from her late father, who was at one time a Korean official. She insisted that she gave a great number of parties because she enjoyed cooking and Congressmen came to her parties because they were fun and relaxing. She stated it did not occur to her that the Koreans were using her to meet Congressmen.. . . .

However, Chung In Shik, Information Officer, Embassy of Korea, Washington, D.C., July 1973 to July 1975, testified that he recalled accompanying KCIA Station Chief Kim Yung Hwan to a small party in Suzi Park Thomson's apartment between 1973 and 1975. He recalled that approximately five Congressmen and five young girls were in attendance. He and Kim were the only two Koreans in attendance and they left about an hour later. After leaving, Kim told Chung that the KCIA paid Suzi Park Thomson $300 to $400 for each party she held. . . .

Margaret Jean Heffron, who served as secretary to Ambassador Kim Dong Jo from 1970 to 1973, advised that Speaker Albert and Suzi Park Thomson were entertained frequently by Mrs. Kim. Mrs. Heffron also stated that Kim Dong Jo visited Congressmen in their offices. Prior to such meetings, Suzi Park Thomson would call and ask for the Ambassador and he would then go to the Hill. Suzi Park Thomson attended most Embassy parties and was escorted on various occasions by Mr. Albert, former Representative Hugh Carey or Representative Lester Wolff. Mrs. Heffron stated that she would send invitations to Congressmen for Embassy affairs and later Ms. Thomson would call and tell her which Congressmen would attend. . . .

Kim Sang Keun, former KCIA agent stationed in the Korean Embassy in Washington from 1970 to 1976, recalled accompanying Colonel Lim, a senior KCIA officer stationed in Washington, to Suzi Park Thomson's apartment in 1971, at which time he delivered one or two cases of liquor to her. He recalled that in 1972, at Lim's instruction, he delivered a case of liquor to Ms. Thomson in the basement of the Rayburn Building. He transferred the case from his car to the car of Suzi Park Thomson. Lim once complained to Kim that he had a problem controlling Suzi Park Thomson as she was continually asking for more liquor and that her connection with Mrs. Kim Dong Jo reduced Lim's control over her. Kim received the impression from these comments of Colonel Lim, who handled congressional liaison for the KCIA, that Lim, in speaking of "control" was referring to his efforts to utilize her in connection with his duties. Kim Sang Keun recalled once stopping at Lim's apartment and departing shortly thereafter when he discovered that Ms. Thomson was visiting. He recalled that Suzi Park Thomson maintained a close relationship with KCIA Station Chief Kim Yung-Hwan (1974-1976). Kim Sang Keun recalled that Kim Yung Hwan once told him that he had to, or was going to, give Suzi Park Thomson liquor. Kim Sang Keun further recalled that shortly after the first delivery to Suzi Park Thomson, Colonel Lim took him to a party in a building in Southwest Washington near Hogates Restaurant. He recalled that about 70 to 80 people were present. The only Congressman he recognized as being present was Carl Albert. Colonel Lim and Kim Sang Keun were the only Korean guests. They did not mix with the others and left after a short while. . . .

Ms. Thomson testified to six trips she took to Korea while employed by the House of Representatives. The first was in 1970, and she paid her own expenses for this trip. The five trips subsequent to 1970 were either at U.S. Government expense, or at the expense of an organization in Taiwan or a Korean veterans organization. She traveled with Members of Congress on all five of these trips. . . .

The wife of one Congressman reported that while in Korea on one such trip in August 1975, Suzi Park Thomson, who was also a member of the delegation, gave her a gold bracelet and said it was from Mrs. Kim Dong Jo who had entertained the congressional wives during the visit. (Mrs. Norman Mineta interview, Dec. 7, 1977) Mrs. Mineta and another Congressman's wife who had also been on the trip, recalled that a few months after this trip, Suzi Park Thomson invited the two Congressmen and the wives to a dinner at a Chinese restaurant in Virginia. (Mrs. Norman Mineta interview, Dec. 7, 1977; Mrs. Paul Simon interview, Nov. 1, 1977) The dinner was apparently in honor of a visiting Korean Congresswoman and her husband, 10 or 11 persons, including Koreans from the ROK Embassy, attended. The bill was paid by one of the individuals from the Embassy. Mrs. Mineta recalled another party subsequently hosted by Suzi Park Thompson in honor of another visiting Korean Congressman at which at least two U.S. Congressmen were present. She could not recall who paid the bill for this party.

Representative Charles Wiggins told the staff that Suzi Park Thomson urged him to introduce Ambassador Hahm to Representative Morris Udall in August 1974. . . . Representative Udall said that such a meeting took place August 2, 1974. The discussion with Ambassador Hahm dealt with hearings then being held by a subcommittee of the Committee on International Relations which concerned alleged violations of human rights in the ROK. The specific topic of interest was a joint statement by Representative Udall and Representative Lloyd Meeds which eventually was presented on August 5, 1974, at the hearing and which criticized repression by the ROK regime. Representative Udall said that Ambassador Hahm unsuccessfully made the usual arguments in defense of the regime in the ROK. Mr. Udall said the Ambassador's conduct was correct and proper and there was no intimation or offer of any money or support. . . .

Finally, in the 1976 KCIA Plan of Operations . . . , Sue Thomson of the House of Representatives is mentioned as a person who was utilized in the past and who was targeted for utilization in 1976.

In summary, this investigation has established that starting about 1971 Suzi Park Thomson entertained Congressmen extensively, that the Korean Embassy, through the KCIA agents stationed therein, supported her activities with liquor and probably with cash, and attempted to control her activities.

VI. TRIPS

Because of considerable publicity surrounding trips to Korea taken by Congressmen and congressional staff members, the committee from the outset sought to determine whether or not any such trips were illegal or improper. The first part of the committee questionnaire of June 1977 inquired specifically about travel to Korea by Congressmen, their families, or their staff members since 1970. The special staff also conducted a thorough search of the Congressional Record, the Congressional Quarterly, and records maintained by the Clerk of the House, the State Department and various committees of the House. From the questionnaire responses and this research, the committee was able to compile an extensive chronology of congressional trips to Korea from the end of 1967 through 1976. These trips fall into two categories: (1) those arranged through and funded by the U.S. Government; and (2) those sponsored and funded at least partially by such non-U.S. Government sources as foreign governments, foreign universities and private organizations. The committee felt that a complete study and analysis of all such trips was an essential ingredient of an accurate and thorough investigation.

The committee has found no reason to question most of these trips by Members of the House of Representatives. Obviously, it is not improper for a Member of the House of Representatives to take a trip sponsored, approved, and paid for by the U.S. Government. Also, existing laws and rules of the House have never forbidden trips sponsored by foreign universities or foreign private organizations and, prior to 1974, did not even forbid trips sponsored and paid for by foreign governments. As there were no such prohibitions and as for most of the trips, the committee has found no evidence of illegal or unethical acts committed by Members of the House of Representatives or staff members visiting the Republic of Korea, trips made by Members of the House of Representatives to Korea generally did not differ from congressional trips to any other country.

In the course of the investigation, however, the committee obtained several KCIA reports which claimed, in part, that the Government of Korea formulated and attempted to implement plans to influence Members of the House and staff members by extending hospitality while such Members and staff members were visiting in the Republic of Korea. The KCIA reports described these plans as "Invitation Diplomacy" and claimed that such diplomacy had succeeded in prior years. Although the evidence suggests that some parts of the KCIA reports are either unfounded or exaggerated, the Committee has been able to determine that the ROK Government did to a certain extent embark upon a form of "Invitation Diplomacy" which the ROK Government undoubtedly felt, would augment the overall efforts of the ROK to win support in the Congress of the United States. Thus, this section of the report centers upon this "Invitation Diplomacy" as it relates to trips funded both by the U.S. Government and to those sponsored by diplomatic and/or foreign private organizations and universities.

A. Congressional Delegations Sponsored by the U.S. Government

Among the documents seized in Tongsun Park's house in Washington were three Korean language reports which significantly dwell upon Congressional travel to Korea. Two of these are the reports (referred to in this section as the Plan Reports) described earlier, which, the Committee has concluded, outline Tongsun Park's lobbying plan to use his rice agency to influence the Congress, the intelligence community, and the American press. . . . The notation in Park's handwriting on one plan report and the similar content of the other suggest that the two were prepared either by Park or with his knowledge in late 1970. The third Korean language report dealing with Congressional travel is entitled "The U.S. Congressional Delegation's visit to Korea" (referred to in this section as the O'Neill Delegation Report) and was apparently prepared shortly before April 1974, when the then House Majority Leader Thomas P. O'Neill Jr., led a large Congressional delegation to Korea. . . . Although Park denies he wrote the O'Neill Delegation Report, he suggested in executive session that Steve Kim — a KCIA agent who periodically lived with Park — knew enough to have prepared the Report and might have written it to impress his superiors in the KCIA. . . . In public testimony, however, Park refrained from naming Kim and instead suggested that someone had planted the Report in his house "to zing" or discredit him. . . .

Despite denying authorship of all three reports, Park has acknowledged they reflect his belief that encouraging and bringing Congressmen to visit the ROK would aid efforts to win their support of the ROK. . . . This belief the two plan reports call "Invitation Diplomacy." They state that congressional leaders are "of vital necessity" to the ROK's foreign policy toward the United States and that "Invitation Diplomacy" provides "opportunities to persuade [Congressmen] effectively." Furthermore, the reports claim "Invitation Diplomacy" has enjoyed "almost 100 percent successful" results in the past.

In discussing the past successes of "Invitation Diplomacy," the three Reports elaborate on only two types of trips by Congressmen. One type includes trips taken individually by the Congressmen with whom Tongsun Park was most involved financially. These trips and their importance to Tongsun Park's lobbying plan are discussed elsewhere in this report. The other type of congressional trips elaborated on by the reports are the so-called Speaker's trips — the three large delegations of 1969, 1971, and 1974 led in each instance by a member of the House leadership. The reports do not allege that the Speaker's trips themselves were improper or illegal, and the evidence gathered by the Committee in its investigation of all the trips funded by the U.S. Government indicates that, during most of them, no improper or illegal activity occurred. The Reports, however, claim that the Speaker's trips — particularly the first trip in 1969 — resulted from the "Invitation Diplomacy" which Tongsun Park incorporated into the lobbying plan proposed to and adopted by the ROK Government. The Committee's investigation of the Speaker's trips establishes that Tongsun Park, although only superficially involved in the final two trips, was in fact involved in bringing about the first one in 1969. Because the Speaker's trips traveled at U.S. Government expense and because many similar, large delegations customarily travel to other countries around the world, the committee concludes that this "Invitation Diplomacy" was an entirely acceptable means of lobbying.

(i) Speaker's Trips — 1969 Albert Delegation

In its investigation of the three Speaker's trips the committee found much evidence that both Park and former Representative Hanna played active, though not necessarily improper, roles in the planning of the delegation which then-Majority Leader Carl Albert led in 1969. Park testified before the committee that, because of his long-standing desire to enhance Korean relations with the United States, he felt in 1968 that a congressional delegation should visit Korea. Consequently, he suggested to Hanna and other Representatives the idea of such a delegation. . . .

For his part, Hanna acknowledged discussing such a trip with Park and other Korean officials. Hanna testified before the committee that, on March 2, 1967, he wrote a letter to then-Korean Prime Minister Chung Il Kwon in which he sought Chung's advice on improving Korean-American relations through the U.S. Congress. The 1969 Albert Delegation, Hanna stated, grew out of his subsequent discussions with Chung and other Korean politicians about exchanges between U.S. and Korean Parliamentarians. . . .

Although he claims he withdrew from the planning, Park clearly worked through Hanna's office to involve himself once again. Mike Reed, the majority leader's administrative assistant who handled many of the details of the trip, recalls attending a luncheon in January 1969 with Hanna's administrative assistant, Frank Gailor, at which Gailor introduced Reed to Park. During the luncheon, Park and Gailor discussed which Members should be invited and the agenda for the trip. Reed, however, did not participate in the conversation. Later, Majority Leader Albert, Hanna, and the aides working on the trip held a planning meeting in the Majority Leader's office. Park showed up uninvited but was not admitted to the meeting. . . . Park's diary records the date of this meeting as January 8, 1969. In addition to these direct approaches to those planning the trip, Park's 1969 diary bears at least four entries pertaining to the delegation including two telephone calls to Gailor. The last of the four entries is dated January 15, but, as former Representative Minshall's records indicate, Park invited Minshall on February 19 to accompany the delegation. Park apparently continued his efforts to become involved. . . .

Park also did not wish the ROK Government to think he was removed from the planning of the trip. In his February 24 cable to Vice-Speaker Chang, Park informs Chang that Hanna has agreed to precede the delegation and assist in the final preparations and ask [sic] Chang to inform Majority Leader Albert that Park will be delivering brochures and educational material for the delegation. Park also asks Chang to decide whether Park should accompany Hanna or the delegation. The committee has found no evidence that Chang contacted Majority Leader Albert about either the brochures or Park's travel arrangements. . . .

The delegation which eventually visited Korea included 23 Representatives and, except for Hanna, arrived on March 2, 1969. Hanna arrived the previous day, he said, to make final arrangements. . . . Park, who testified he never intended to travel with the delegation, arrived separately and met the delegation at the Seoul airport. During the delegation's visit, however, Park was unable to entertain the Congressmen and, indeed, could get no closer to them than the "fringes," according to staff aides who went. . . . The visit lasted until March 7, and the Representatives attended briefings, ceremonies, and official functions. They also met many Korean officials and attended several informal dinners for small groups. Although the Korean National Assembly had offered through Vice-Speaker Chang to pay the delegation's expenses in the ROK, the U.S. Government instead paid for all the travel and in-Korea expenses. . . .

Tongsun Park, then, actively involved himself in proposing the first Speaker's trip to Hanna and other Representatives and indirectly, through his relationship with Hanna and the ROK Government, helped to bring about the trip. The committee has uncovered no evidence that any undue lobbying or other improper activity occurred.

(ii) Speaker's Trips — 1971 Albert Delegation

On July 27, 1971, Paik Too Chin, the Speaker of the Korean National Assembly, wrote then-Speaker of the House Carl Albert and invited Speaker Albert to head a second parliamentary delegation to Korea. Consequently, from August 9 to August 13, 1971, a delegation of 24 Representatives visited Korea. As it had in 1969, the Korean legislature offered to pay all the in-country expenses of the delegation. The United States Government, however, again paid for the entire trip and all the in-country expenses. . . .

Unlike the committee's investigation of the 1969 Albert delegation, the investigation of the 1971 Albert delegation uncovered no evidence of Tongsun Park's involvement during the planning of the trip. In fact, Speaker Albert had tentatively agreed at the time of that first trip to send a second delegation. . . .

In 1971, Tongsun Park had fallen out of favor with the ROK Government and had lost his rice agency. Thus, it is not surprising that there is little evidence showing that Park was to any degree involved with the 1971 Albert delegation. Even the intelligence reports which were seized from Park's house and which so prominently discuss the 1969 Albert delegation barely mention the 1971 delegation. The committee did, however, find evidence that former Representative Gallagher and perhaps Hanna had tried and failed to include Kim Kwang on the delegation airplane. A relative of Tongsun Park, Kim was working on Representative Gallagher's staff in 1971 after having worked on Representative Hanna's staff. Intelligence sources also indicate that Kim was reporting to Tongsun Park and the KCIA, particularly about matters relating to the Foreign Affairs Committee on which Representative Gallagher sat. According to the evidence, Gallagher had insisted to Speaker Albert that Kim be allowed to travel on the delegation airplane and the Speaker tentatively agreed. Speaker Albert, though, asked the State Department for its views and, when he learned they were disapproved, asked a Department official to impress those views on Gallagher. According to the former Speaker, Representative Gallagher eventually relented when the official indicated that a foreign national could not travel on the official plane. . . . Kim nevertheless met the delegation at the Seoul airport, but the Members hardly came into contact with him. Suzi Park Thomson, by then a member of Speaker Albert's staff, accompanied the delegation. Participants in the trip stated, though, that her involvement was limited to assisting and translating for the wives of the delegation members. . . .

Overall, the committee found no evidence suggesting that the ROK Government used the 1971 Albert delegation to influence any Representatives. Tongsun Park, Suzi Park Thomson, and Kim Kwang were present in Korea during the delegation's visit, but only Thomson came in regular contact with the delegation and then only as an interpreter. As none of the delegation members interviewed by the staff recall any instances of improper lobbying or other activities during the trip, then, the 1971 Speaker's trip appears to have been a normal parliamentary exchange which resulted from the precedent of the first Speaker's trip and not from any specific Korean effort at the time of the second one.

(iii) Speaker's Trips — 1974 O'Neill Delegation

From April 15 to April 17, 1974, then-Majority Leader Thomas P. O'Neill Jr. led a third and final Speaker's delegation to Korea. The O'Neill delegation report found in Tongsun Park's house implies that Park played a significant part in arranging the delegation's visit. According to the document, the oil shortage crisis, the Watergate scandals and the election campaigns delayed the trip four times. Nevertheless, "through our persuasion" and with the help of "the most ardent pro-Korean Congressmen, such as Patten, de la Garza, Hanna, Wolff, (and) Speaker Albert," the trip took place.

When first shown this report, Speaker O'Neill immediately and emphatically denied that Patten, de la Garza, Hanna, Wolff or any other person had influenced his planning of the trip. Former Speaker Albert was initially involved, but only because the ROK Government formally issued the invitation to the Speaker of the House. According to Speaker O'Neill, former Speaker Albert merely suggested to then Majority Leader O'Neill that he head the delegation and use it for purposes stemming from his position in the House leadership. . . .

Because there had been a 2-year interval between the previous Speaker's trips, the O'Neill delegation was originally scheduled for 1973. Speaker O'Neill's testimony indicates that only the 2-year interval, and not some third party, dictated the original date. The Speaker verified that the oil crisis had delayed the delegation once, but he emphasized that only those political purposes mentioned earlier by Speaker Albert motivated him to reschedule the delegation's trip. Otherwise, Speaker O'Neill said, he had no interest in heading the delegation. . . .

As in the previous years, the Korean legislature offered to pay the in-country expenses of the delegation. . . . Once again, though, the American Government paid all travel and in-country expenses. By all accounts, the O'Neill delegation did not differ from any of the previous parliamentary exchanges and was entirely proper. Tongsun Park's involvement in the trip was apparently limited to a party he hosted at his home before the delegation left. The committee is therefore unable to find any evidence to substantiate the claims of outside influence on the trip which are contained in the O'Neill delegation report and instead concludes that the idea of the third Speaker's trip grew out of the precedent of the first two such delegations.

B. Privately Sponsored Trips to Korea

From information gathered primarily from responses to the committee questionnaire of June 1977, the committee was able to compile a list of several trips funded by non-U.S. Government sources. The chronology of these trips clearly shows that most of these trips were sponsored by foreign private organizations and universities. These organizations and universities began noticeably to sponsor congressional trips at the end of 1974 and during 1975. The committee's investigation of these privately sponsored trips increasingly focused on two organizations — the Pacific Cultural Foundation ("PCF"), which is based in the Republic of China; and the Korean-U.S. Economic Council ("KUSEC"), which is based in Seoul, Korea — for the committee uncovered evidence linking Tongsun Park, the KCIA and the ROK Government to the trips sponsored by the two organizations. The committee, however, looked as well into trips involving honorary degrees bestowed by ostensibly private Korean universities, and the evidence again indicates ROK Government complicity. In addition, several of the privately sponsored trips, which increased so noticeably in 1975, closely resemble the congressional trips described in a document recounting KCIA operations during that year.

The committee has concluded that the Representatives and staff members who went on the trips had no reason to suspect the ROK Government and the KCIA were so involved and therefore did not violate any applicable law or Rule of the House. As the sponsoring organizations and universities are located overseas, the committee has no means of determining — either that the ROK Government actually financed the trips or that it did not finance those trips. After mid-1974, though, Congressmen and staff members could not accept trips paid for by foreign governments. . . .

(ii) Trips involving honorary degrees

Evidence collected by the committee shows that, at the time a program of congressional trips to Korea sponsored by private organizations was beginning in 1975, another program intended to bring Congressmen to Korea by offering them honorary degrees began simultaneously. The evidence further indicates that, as they had with the trips sponsored by the private organizations, the ROK Government and the KCIA encouraged and participated in the honorary degree program. Overall, though, the honorary degree program enjoyed only limited success.

According to the committee's evidence, the bestowal of honorary degrees upon Congressmen visiting Korea occurred only sporadically until 1974. Of the universities bestowing such degrees before then, none bestowed a degree upon more than one Congressman, either in that period or afterward. Until late 1974, the recipients of these degrees were all traveling to Korea on U.S. Government funds, and the universities apparently did not pay any of the expenses. The universities also passed up opportunities to give degrees to other Congressmen traveling with the delegations. Moreover, the committee has found no evidence suggesting that either the Embassy or the Korean Government had any direct participation in the granting or offering of the degrees. The only evidence that any one not affiliated with the universities had anything to do with the degrees comes from former Representative Thomas Morgan's recollection that, on three or four occasions, former Representative Cornelius Gallagher — himself a frequent traveler to Korea and a close associate of Tongsun Park — urged Morgan to visit Korea and accept an honorary degree. Morgan declined.

At the end of 1974, the incidence of both offers and grants of honorary degrees to Congressmen increased markedly. Within 8 months (late December 1974 to mid-August 1975), Hanyang University alone bestowed degrees upon four Representatives and offered to bestow a degree on one other Member. As for all Korean universities including Hanyang, the committee has evidence that, in all, six Representatives received degrees between December 1974 and early 1976 and another six refused offers during the same period. Of these 12 offers of degrees, 7 were accompanied by offers either of trips or in-Korea expenses.

Not only did the number of offers of trips to receive degrees increase markedly between the end of 1974 and early 1976, but the involvement of Korean officials and certain Koreans figuring in the committee's entire investigation — Ambassador Hahm, KCIA Station Chief Kim Yung Hwan, KCIA Congressional Liaison Choi Yae-Heun and Korean Assemblyman Row Chin Hwan — increased noticeably. In various combinations, these Korean officials participated in 5 of the 12 offers of degrees. All five offers included offers of trips.

The committee's evidence, then, shows that, at the end of 1974, the Korean universities in general and Hanyang University in particular began a program to bring Congressmen to Korea to receive honorary degrees. The committee has uncovered no evidence proving that the ROK Government either paid or offered to pay any of the expenses resulting from this program, but the evidence clearly shows that the Government did in fact involve itself in this program. Although the program did not attract as many Representatives to Korea as the trips sponsored by private organizations, it nevertheless succeeded in bringing three Representatives to Korea who otherwise would not have gone.

VII. RECOMMENDATIONS [ON] RULES OF CONDUCT

In Parts II through VI, the committee has set forth its conclusion that the ROK Government adopted and implemented plans to influence Members of Congress by giving things of value to them, and the information on which that conclusion is based. The acceptance by a Member of Congress of things of value from a foreign state is illegal.

A. Criminal Statutes — Bribery

18 U.S.C. Sec. 201 makes it a crime, punishable by up to 5 years in prison, for a public official, including a Member of Congress, to accept anything of value in return for an agreement to be influenced in his official duties. This statute plainly applies to gifts of things of value from foreign

states and officials and representatives thereof. There are difficulties in
enforcing this statute, however, because it is difficult to prove an agreement to be influenced even where there is one. This difficulty is aggravated
in prosecutions of Members of Congress because the speech or debate
clause of the U.S. Constitution (which is by its terms inapplicable to an
investigation or disciplinary proceeding brought by the Congress or a
committee thereof) prevents proof in court of much of the official conduct
which a Member may have agreed to perform in return for the money. See,
U.S. v. *Brewster,* 408 U.S. 506 (1972).

Campaign laws

Since 1966 there has been a prohibition against the receipt of campaign
contributions from an agent of a foreign government (18 U.S.C. Sec. 613)
without regard to any agreement on the part of the recipient to be
influenced by the contribution. Since foreign governments can act only
through agents, this effectively prohibits campaign contributions by foreign governments. Effective January 1, 1975, this statute was amended so
that it also prohibited receipt of campaign contributions from any foreign
national — that is, a foreign citizen not admitted in this country for
permanent residence. (2 U.S.C. sec. 441 (e)) A violation of this provision
could, if more than $1,000 is involved, result in imprisonment of the
recipient for up to 1 year, a fine of $25,000 and a forfeiture of three times
the amount of the contribution. (2 U.S.C. sec. 441 (j)) Thus, the criminal
law prohibits even the possibility of foreign influence resulting from gifts
from foreign governments or individuals if the influence results from
campaign gifts. With respect to gifts to Members of Congress from foreign
governments or nationals that are not campaign contributions, the criminal law proscribes them only if it can be proved that the Member agreed to
be influenced in return.

B. The Constitutional Prohibition

The U.S. Constitution, however, forbids receipt of any gift from a foreign
state unless consented to [by] the Congress without regard to any agreement to be influenced.

The U.S. Constitution contains a flat prohibition against the receipt by a
Member of Congress of a "present" from a "foreign state," without the
consent of Congress (article I, section 9, clause 8). Congress has consented
by statute only to the receipt of gifts valued at less than $100 (22 C.F.R.
sec. 33(3)). Other gifts may be received only if immediately turned over to
the U.S. Government. Of course a foreign State operates only through its
representatives, and the Constitutional prohibition applies to the receipt of
gifts from a foreign state delivered by any representative thereof. See
"Manual of Offenses and Procedures, Korean Influence Investigation," p.
6; 5 U.S.C. sec. 7342(a) (2). The committee concluded that no Member
should be disciplined for receipt of a gift from a representative of a foreign
State, however, unless the Member knew or should have known that the

903

gift came from the foreign state. "Manual of Offenses and Procedures," supra, at pp. 33-36.

C. House Rules

Clause 4 of the Code of Official Conduct ... was amended on March 2, 1977, to forbid the receipt by a Member of the House of a gift of any kind worth more than $100 in any calendar year from a foreign national.

D. Evaluation

The committee believes that the existing substantive rules are, on the whole, adequate. The existing laws prohibit receipt of gifts of more than minimal value directly or indirectly from a foreign state, thus removing almost all opportunity for improper influence by a foreign government both real and apparent; and existing laws penalize criminally more serious examples of influence buying. The existing laws, however, require proof of some degree of knowledge on the part of a recipient of a gift that the gift came from a foreign state. This created a serious problem for the committee in this investigation. The committee, for example, has evidence that Hanna suggested, and the Koreans adopted, a plan to influence Members of Congress without apparently violating the law by delivering money to them indirectly, that is, through Tongsun Park. Money was then paid in the form of campaign contributions to a number of Members of Congress ... by Tongsun Park in pursuance of this plan. Absent proof that Park acted as an agent of the ROK Government and absent knowledge of that fact by the Member who received the contribution, actionable violations of law could not be proved. This problem has been substantially ameliorated by the change in the law, applicable January 1, 1975, prohibiting receipt of campaign contributions from foreign nationals, and a change in the House rules, applicable March 2, 1977, prohibiting receipt of other kinds of gifts from foreign nationals regardless of whether or not the foreign national is acting as an agent of his Government.

Thus, the committee has only one substantive proposal.

The committee proposes a rule forbidding the receipt of trips by Members, officers or employees of the House of Representatives to and from a foreign country paid for by foreign nationals or foreign organizations, unless the particular trip is specifically exempted in writing by action of the Committee on Standards of Official Conduct.

The committee has information described in part VI of this report that the ROK sought to use trips to Korea by Congressmen and congressional staff members as a method of influencing Congress and that it caused "private" organizations in the ROK to pay for these trips. However, as these organizations are headquartered overseas, there was no way for the committee to prove this fact and no way for the recipient of the trip to learn it. In any event, the committee is of the opinion that there is seldom reason to permit foreign travel funded by a foreign private organization. All foreign travel useful to the United States should be paid for by the U.S. Government unless expressly exempted.

It is worth emphasizing that this proposed change in the rules is an extremely modest one. As set forth above, the difficulties in preventing serious efforts to influence Congressmen arise not from loopholes in the law but from the difficulties in enforcing the law — that is, in obtaining evidence of violations even where they occur.

The committee also has one procedural proposal. The committee proposes that section 4(a) (1) (A) of House Resolution 252 authorizing the committee to take depositions before a single member of the committee be made a part of the standing Rules of the House applicable to the Committee on Standards of Official Conduct. The committee believes that its ability to gather facts will be substantially impaired if every time a witness' testimony is taken it must convene a quorum of the committee which would otherwise be necessary in order to hold an investigative hearing in executive session.

VIII. DISCIPLINARY RECOMMENDATIONS

After a little more than a year of investigating, the committee concluded that there was sufficient evidence of unethical conduct by four present Members of Congress to warrant the bringing of charges against them. Thus, on July 13, 1978, the committee served on each of these four Members a "Statement of Alleged Violation" (Statement) briefly describing the conduct alleged to be unethical and the applicable provision alleged to have been violated. The service of these Statements followed months of investigation done in secret so that apparently incriminating evidence would not be publicized until its reliability had been tested. This investigation included the taking of testimony from the Member involved, so that his version of the facts would be before the committee when it made its decision whether or not to bring charges.

Following the service of the statements, the committee adopted a resolution which granted to the respondent-Members the kind of discovery of the evidence against them which is available to litigants in Federal courts. The attorneys for the respondent-Members then received transcripts of relevant depositions, memoranda of informal witness interviews, documentary evidence and other materials to assist them in preparing their defenses. Answers and motions were then received from the respondent-Members. After considering these answers and motions; after hearing argument in executive session by attorneys for the respondents and for the staff; and after the extraordinary step of hearing from the respondent-Members in executive session not under oath; the committee made its decision whether to proceed to a public disciplinary hearing to resolve the charges in the Statement. In each case, the committee decided to proceed to a public hearing.

Each public hearing was conducted much like the trial of a case in court. The attorney for the staff made an opening statement; the attorney for the respondent was permitted but not required to do so. The attorney for the staff then called witnesses and introduced documents in evidence. The witnesses were subject to cross-examination by the attorney for the respondent-Member; and evidentiary objections were made and ruled on by the chairman subject to an appeal to a majority of the committee members present. The rules of evidence in civil and criminal trials in Federal courts were followed subject to the overriding provision of committee rule 11(a):

> Rule 11. Admissibility of Evidence. — (a) The object of the hearing shall be to ascertain the truth. Any evidence that is relevant and probative shall be admissible, unless privileged or unless the Constitution otherwise requires its exclusion. Objections going only to the weight that should be given to evidence will not justify its exclusion.

The provision of the committee's rules authorizing use at the hearing of "depositions, interrogatories and sworn statements" in lieu of a witness live testimony was never utilized. . . .

The committee sustained one or more charges against Representatives Roybal, Wilson, and McFall. It sustained no charge against Representative Patten. It recommended that Roybal be censured and that McFall and Wilson be reprimanded.

Reports for the House were then prepared in each of the four cases. Only the House can actually impose discipline. The reports described the procedures followed and contained the evidence and arguments of counsel for each side. The reports were not distributed to the offices of the Members of Congress prior to the time when they were called up in the House. Instead, they were made available to any Member who asked for one prior to the time they were called up, and were available on the House floor during the debate.

When the reports were discussed on the floor of the House, some Members criticized the committee's work generally; some criticized its procedures; no Member not on the committee referred in any way to the facts of the cases; many members of the committee remained silent; and those members of the committee who did speak expressed their dislike for the task of investigating and judging their peers. The House rejected the committee's recommendation in one case — amid statements that the committee "appeared" to have recommended the higher sanction for racial reasons, and without any discussion or evaluation of the facts, which were substantially uncontradicted.

The committee believes that much needs to be done to improve the procedures for bringing the committee's recommendations to the House floor. If the House is unwilling to support the committee, it should assign this task elsewhere.

A. Recommended Procedural Reforms

Some of the criticisms of the committee's procedures voiced on the floor of the House were valid. If the House is to accept or reject the committee's recommendations as to discipline for reasons having to do with the facts rather than for political considerations, the committee must communicate the facts to the other members in a useful way. To this end the committee recommends that the following provisions be made part of the House rules in each case in which the Committee on Standards of Official Conduct recommends to the House that it discipline a Member:

(1) The report to the House shall, with respect to each Count of the Complaint or Statement of Alleged Violation which the committee has found to have been proven, contain a statement of that count, a brief but complete statement of the evidence on which the finding is based, together with transcripts of all testimony and copies of all exhibits presented at the disciplinary hearing;

(2) The report to the House shall contain a brief but complete statement of the reasons for the sanction recommended by the committee;

(3) A copy of the report shall be delivered to the office of every Member of the House no less than 3 full days before the report is considered by the House;

(4) With respect to each report, the House will debate on all of the committee's findings of fact and vote on such findings count by count. Then, if the House has adopted the committee's findings with respect to one or more counts, it will debate and vote on the proposed sanction; and

(5) At the outset of the first debate contemplated in proposal (4), supra, the count or counts which the committee found to have been proved will be read together with the committee's statement of the evidence which supported the count. If the House votes to sustain the committee's finding with respect to any count, the committee's statement of reasons for the sanction recommended by it will be read by the clerk at the outset of the debate on sanction.

B. Recommended Substantive Reforms

The committee commenced this investigation into allegations of ROK Government payments to Members of Congress with the determination of ascertaining the truth. The committee expected that if any evidence of such payments existed, it might be obtained from one or more of three sources: former officials and agents of the ROK Government; the intelligence community; and congressional employees. This report details elsewhere the information obtained from the first two sources, the limitations thereof and the reasons for those limitations. It is striking, however, that the committee received virtually no evidence of misconduct from congressional employees. Indeed, the committee filed a statement against one employee alleging that she had testified falsely and otherwise obstructed the investigation of her employer; and the committee, in sustaining a charge against one member implicitly found unworthy of belief the testimony of his former employee in defense of the charge. It may be that there are no congressional employees with knowledge of wrongdoing relevant to House Resolution 252. But we believe it is probable that congressional employees in general, like the two described above, hold personal loyalty to the Members for whom they work to be more important than their loyalty to this institution itself.

The committee believes that the support of the Members, officers and employees of the House for the work of this committee is crucial to its continuing effectiveness.

Accordingly, the committee proposes adoption of the following additions to the Code of Official Conduct:

(1) It shall be the duty of every Member, officer and employee of the House of Representatives, who becomes aware of any violation or evidence of a violation of a provision of the Code of Official Conduct, or any other standard of conduct to report such violation or evidence thereof promptly in writing to the Committee on Standards of Official Conduct; and

(2) The committee shall, consistent with the fulfillment of its duties, maintain the confidentiality of information communicated to it pursuant to (1) above, and the identity of the person who communicated it, until such time as a Complaint or a Statement of Alleged Violation is filed with respect to the information. The information shall be kept confidential, both from the public and from the subject of the information until a complaint or statement of Alleged Violation is filed.

The committee is aware of the difficulties both moral and practical of a rule requiring every Member, officer and employee to become an informer on his or her colleagues. These are, however, difficulties inherent in any effort at self-discipline. The Committee on Standards of Official Conduct should not be asked to make this effort alone. Either it must be the effort of every person in this institution, or the effort should not be made at all.

The resolution of this problem is not easy. The committee believes that now is as good a time as any to confront the problem, and to decide whether the House of Representatives wants to discipline itself. If so, it should be the job of every Member, officer and employee. If not, then the House should not ask 12 of its Members to do the job without the support of the House. . . .

ASSASSINATIONS COMMITTEE CONCLUSION
December 31, 1978

The House Select Committee on Assassinations Dec. 31 ended a two-year, $5.8 million investigation with a conclusion that President John F. Kennedy and the Rev. Martin Luther King Jr. were assassinated probably as a result of conspiracies. The committee could not identify the conspirators other than assassins Lee Harvey Oswald in the case of Kennedy and James Earl Ray in the case of King. But its conspiracy theory was a marked departure from previous federal investigations that concluded that each assassin had acted alone.

A summary of its conclusions, a prelude to a two-volume final report to follow in 1979, also criticized several government bodies for their handling of the slayings and recommended that Congress and the executive branch make changes for preventing or prosecuting future assassinations. It also urged the Justice Department to follow up on at least two aspects of the committee's investigation and review the entire inquiry to determine "whether further official investigation is warranted in either case."

Kennedy Assassination

The committtee's summary said that "scientific acoustical evidence establishes a high probability that two gunmen fired at President John F. Kennedy" in Dallas on Nov. 22, 1963. Although other scientific evidence was not supportive, the committee said it believed that Kennedy "was probably assassinated as a result of a conspiracy. The committee is unable to identify the other gunman or the extent of the conspiracy."

Previous federal investigations had determined that Oswald, crouched in a sixth-floor window of the Texas School Book Depository at the rear of the presidential motorcade, had fired only three shots at Kennedy as he rode by in a limousine. But on Dec. 29, the committee wrapped up its hearings by taking testimony from Mark Weiss and Ernest Aschkenasy, Queens College professors expert in acoustics. Based on their examination of a recording of sounds from the scene, they said, they were at least 95 percent certain that four shots were fired, one of them from a grassy knoll ahead of the limousine. That shot apparently went astray.

The theory that two gunmen were involved had been advanced by numerous conspiracy buffs since the 1963 slaying. Some of the theories put the blame on other governments or on U.S. government agencies, but the committee concluded that neither the Soviet nor the Cuban government was involved. It also said that neither "anti-Castro Cuban groups" nor "the national syndicate of organized crime, as a group," was involved, although "individual members may have been involved." Also uninvolved, it said, were the Secret Service, FBI and CIA.

The summary did conclude, however, that each agency and the Justice Department and the 1964 Warren Commission were guilty of failures in connection with the assassination or the investigation of it. "President Kennedy did not receive adequate protection," the report said, and "the investigation into the possibility of a conspiracy in the assassination was inadequate. The conclusions of the investigations were arrived at in good faith, but presented in a fashion that was too definitive."

King Assassination

The committee also said it believed "there is a likelihood that James Earl Ray assassinated Dr. Martin Luther King as a result of a conspiracy." Again, it could not identify conspirators other than Ray and it said no other government agencies were involved in the April 4, 1968, slaying. But, the report said, the Justice Department and the FBI also were guilty of failures in the King case. It cited the FBI's "COINTELPRO campaign against Dr. King [which] grossly abused and exceeded its legal authority and failed to consider the possibility that actions threatening bodily harm to Dr. King might be encouraged by the program." (Review of King Investigations, Historic Documents of 1977, p. 113.)

Although the committee believed in the likelihood of a conspiracy, it did not accept Ray's contention that a man named "Raoul" was involved. The summary said that "and other allegedly exculpatory evidence" offered by Ray "are not worthy of belief."

Recommendations

The committee said the Justice Department should review the panel's findings in each case, "analyze whether further official investigation is warranted in either case" and report to the House Judiciary Committee. It specifically asked the Justice Department to examine an amateur's film of the assassination and join with the National Science Foundation in "a study of the theory and application of the principles of acoustics to forensic questions, using materials available in the assassination of President John F. Kennedy as a case study."

The committee also recommended that the Judiciary Committee make the assassination of any chief of state a federal offense if there is a U.S. connection. It also should revise federal homicide laws, "paying special attention to assassinations," and consider "extending the protection of federal law" to Supreme Court justices and Cabinet officers, the committee said.

The Justice Department, the committee said, should re-examine its contingency plans for handling homicides under federal jurisdictions.

Background

The one-million-word report of the 1964 commission headed by Chief Justice Earl Warren encountered resistance almost from the moment it was issued. It concluded that Oswald acted alone and that no conspiracy was involved in the Kennedy assassination. One of those unconvinced was lawyer Mark Lane, who said so in a 1966 best-selling book, Rush To Judgment, *which denounced the commission's findings.*

Partly at the urging of Lane and partly as a result of his own suspicions, Rep. Henry B. Gonzalez, D-Texas, who had been in the Dallas motorcade when Kennedy was shot, introduced a bill on Feb. 19, 1975, calling for a House inquiry into the assassination. His effort made little headway, however, until the Senate Select Committee to Study Governmental Operations issued a 1976 report citing CIA and FBI failures to carry out all of their responsibilities in the case. (Historic Documents of 1976, p. 235)

Rep. Thomas N. Downing, D-Va. (1959-77), was convinced the case should be reopened. He joined Gonzalez' cause. In the aftermath of revelations of past FBI hostility toward King, the Congressional Black Caucus joined the cause by suggesting the proposed inquiry be expanded to reopen the investigation of the King assassination. The Gonzalez bill was then approved on Sept. 17, 1976, and Downing, although a lame duck, was appointed chairman.

Richard Sprague, former assistant district attorney in Philadelphia, was chosen as chief counsel. He promptly proposed a $6.5 million budget for the first year. It proved to be a near-fatal proposal when the new Congress seated in 1977 took up the matter. It fueled the already-existing doubts about the advisability of such a committee, so that on Feb. 2 the House voted to extend the panel only until March 31. Gonzalez was appointed the new chairman to replace the retired Downing. Richardson Preyer, D-N.C.,

*was named to head the Kennedy half of the panel's assignment and Del.
Walter E. Fauntroy, D-D.C., the King inquiry.*

*Part of the reason for the limited duration of the committee resulted
from deteriorating relations between Gonzalez and Sprague. Their squab-
bling erupted into the open and Gonzalez fired Sprague. But the rest of the
committee countermanded Gonzalez' action and after another snub the
chairman went home to San Antonio. He then declared on March 1 that
either he or Sprague had to leave the committee. Gonzalez' resignation was
accepted March 8 and Rep. Louis Stokes, D-Ohio, was named to replace
him. Gonzalez continued to wage a public campaign against Sprague, who
in late March resigned to remove controversy from the committee. The
House on March 30 voted 230-181 to extend its life for the rest of the 95th
Congress.*

*In April the House approved a $2.5 million budget for the committee for
1977. On June 20, G. Robert Blakey, a former Senate staffer, law professor
and director of the Cornell Institute on Organized Crime, was named
Sprague's replacement. The same day, he said his first press conference
would be his last. A lid of secrecy was clamped on the committee's
activities from then until public hearings began on Aug. 14, 1978.*

*The committee received another $3.3 million during its life, took public
testimony from former President Gerald R. Ford, who as House GOP
leader had served on the Warren Commission, and tape recorded testimony
from Cuban Prime Minister Fidel Castro, who denied any part in the
Kennedy assassination.*

*The panel later was the subject of live television coverage when it heard
Ray's testimony in the King case. Ray was represented during the often
stormy hearings by Mark Lane, whose conspiracy emphasis had shifted
from the Kennedy to the King assassination.*

Following is the text of the Summary of Findings and
Recommendations of the House Select Committee on Assassinations, dated Dec. 29, 1978, and released to the public Dec.
31, 1978:

U.S. House of Representatives
Select Committee on Assassinations
Washington, D.C., December 29, 1978

Hon. Edmond L. Henshaw, Jr.
Clerk of the House
U.S. Capitol
Room H105
Washington, D.C. 20515

Dear Mr. Henshaw:

On behalf of the Select Committee on Assassinations, and pursuant to the mandate of House Resolutions 222 and 433, I am filing for presentation to the House of Representatives the enclosed Summary of Findings and Recommendations of the Select Committee on Assassinations.

As has been agreed upon with the Speaker of the House, the Committee is filing this Summary of Findings and Recommendations while the preparation of the complete volumes of its Final Report continues under your auspices. The complete Final Report will include Volume I, the Findings and Recommendations of the Select Committee with an analysis of the evidence concerning each finding and recommendation; and Volumes II and sequential volumes, which will contain the Committee's hearings, scientific reports, and other materials pertinent to the Committee's investigation. These volumes will be presented to the House as soon as they can be suitably prepared for publication, including, where appropriate, the declassification of classified information. It is anticipated that the entire Final Report will be published by March 30, 1979.

Sincerely,

Louis Stokes
Chairman

Table of Contents

  I. Findings of the Select Committee on Assassinations in the Assassination of President John F. Kennedy in Dallas, Texas, November 22, 1963.

   A. Lee Harvey Oswald fired three shots at President John F. Kennedy. The second and third shots he fired struck the President. The third shot he fired killed the President.

      1. President Kennedy was struck by two rifle shots fired from behind him.

      2. The shots that struck President Kennedy from behind him were fired from the sixth floor window of the southeast corner of the Texas School Book Depository Building.

3. Lee Harvey Oswald owned the rifle that was used to fire the shots from the sixth floor window of the southeast corner of the Texas School Book Depository Building.

4. Lee Harvey Oswald, shortly before the assassination, had access to and was present on the sixth floor of the Texas School Book Depository Building.

5. Lee Harvey Oswald's other actions tend to support the conclusion that he assassinated President Kennedy.

B. Scientific acoustical evidence establishes a high probability that two gunmen fired at President John F. Kennedy. Other scientific evidence does not preclude the possibility of two gunmen firing at the President. Scientific evidence negates some specific conspiracy allegations.

C. The Committee believes, on the basis of the evidence available to it, that President John F. Kennedy was probably assassinated as a result of a conspiracy. The Committee is unable to identify the other gunman or the extent of the conspiracy.

1. The Committee believes, on the basis of the evidence available to it, that the Soviet Government was not involved in the assassination of President Kennedy.

2. The Committee believes, on the basis of the evidence available to it, that the Cuban Government was not involved in the assassination of President Kennedy.

3. The Committee believes, on the basis of the evidence available to it, that anti-Castro Cuban groups, as groups, were not involved in the assassination of President Kennedy, but the available evidence does not preclude the possibility that individual members may have been involved.

4. The Committee believes, on the basis of the evidence available to it, that the national syndicate of organized crime, as a group, was not involved in the assassination of President Kennedy, but the available evidence does not preclude the possibility that individual members may have been included.

5. The Secret Service, Federal Bureau of Investigation and Central Intelligence Agency were not involved in the assassination of President Kennedy.

D. Agencies and departments of the United States Government performed with varying degrees of competency in the fulfillment of their duties. President John F. Kennedy did not receive adequate protection. A thorough and reliable investigation into the responsibility of Lee Harvey Oswald for the assassination of President John F. Kennedy was conducted. The investigation into the possibility of conspiracy in the assassination was inadequate. The conclusions of the investigations were arrived at in good faith, but presented in a fashion that was too definitive.

1. The Secret Service was deficient in the performance of its duties.

   (a) The Secret Service possessed information that was not properly analyzed, investigated or used by the Secret Service in connection with the President's trip to Dallas; in addition, Secret Service agents in the motorcade were inadequately prepared to protect the President from a sniper.

   (b) The responsibility of the Secret Service to investigate the assassination was terminated when the Federal Bureau of Investigation assumed primary investigative responsibility.

2. The Department of Justice failed to exercise initiative in supervising and directing the investigation by the Federal Bureau of Investigation of the assassination.

3. The Federal Bureau of Investigation performed with varying degrees of competency in the fulfillment of its duties.

   (a) The Federal Bureau of Investigation adequately investigated Lee Harvey Oswald prior to the assassination and properly evaluated the evidence it possessed to assess his potential to endanger the public safety in a national emergency.

   (b) The Federal Bureau of Investigation conducted a thorough and professional investigation into the responsibility of Lee Harvey Oswald for the assassination.

   (c) The Federal Bureau of Investigation failed to investigate adequately the possibility of a conspiracy to assassinate the President.

   (d) The Federal Bureau of Investigation was deficient in its sharing of information with other agencies and departments.

4. The Central Intelligence Agency was deficient in its collection and sharing of information both prior to and subsequent to the assassination.

5. The Warren Commission performed with varying degrees of competency in the fulfillment of its duties.

   (a) The Warren Commission conducted a thorough and professional investigation into the responsibility of Lee Harvey Oswald for the assassination.

(b) The Warren Commission failed to investigate adequately the possibility of a conspiracy to assassinate the President. This deficiency was attributable in part to the failure of the Commission to receive all the relevant information that was in the possession of other agencies and departments of the government.

(c) The Warren Commission arrived at its conclusion, based on the evidence available to it, in good faith.

(d) The Warren Commission presented the conclusions in its Report in a fashion that was too definite.

II. Findings of The Select Committee on Assassinations in the Assassination of Dr. Martin Luther King, Jr. in Memphis, Tennessee, April 4, 1968.

A. James Earl Ray fired one shot at Dr. Martin Luther King, Jr. The shot killed Dr. King.

1. Dr. King was killed by one rifle shot fired from in front of him.

2. The shot that killed Dr. King was fired from the bathroom window at the rear of a rooming house at 422-1/2 Main Street, Memphis, Tennessee.

3. James Earl Ray purchased the rifle used to shoot Dr. King and transported it from Birmingham, Ala., to Memphis, Tenn., where he rented a room at 422-1/2 South Main Street, and moments after the assassination, he dropped it near 424 South Main Street.

4. It is highly probable that James Earl Ray stalked Dr. King for a period immediately preceding the assassination.

5. James Earl Ray fled the scene of the crime immediately after the assassination.

6. James Earl Ray's alibi for the time of the assassination, his story of "Raoul," and other allegedly exculpatory evidence are not worthy of belief.

7. James Earl Ray knowingly, intelligently, and voluntarily pleaded guilty to the first degree murder of Dr. King.

B. The Committee believes, on the basis of the circumstantial evidence available to it, that there is a likelihood that James Earl Ray assassinated Dr. Martin Luther King as a result of a conspiracy.

C. The Committee believes, on the basis of the evidence available to it, that no private organizations or individuals, other than those discussed under Section B, were involved in the assassination of Dr. King.

D. No federal, state or local government agency was involved in the assassination of Dr. King.

E. The Department of Justice and the Federal Bureau of Investigation performed with varying degrees of competency and legality in the fulfillment of their duties.

   1. The Department of Justice failed to supervise adequately the Domestic Intelligence Division of the Federal Bureau of Investigation. In addition, the Federal Bureau of Investigation, in the Domestic Intelligence Division's COINTELPRO campaign against Dr. King, grossly abused and exceeded its legal authority and failed to consider the possibility that actions threatening bodily harm to Dr. King might be encouraged by the program.

   2. The Department of Justice and Federal Bureau of Investigation performed a thorough investigation into the responsibility of James Earl Ray for the assassination of Dr. King, and conducted a thorough fugitive investigation, but failed to investigate adequately the possibility of conspiracy in the assassination. The Federal Bureau of Investigation manifested a lack of concern for constitutional rights in the manner in which it conducted parts of the investigation.

III. Recommendations of the Select Committee on Assassinations

I. *Legislative Recommendations on Issues Involving the Prohibition, Prevention and Prosecution of Assassinations and Federally Cognizable Homicides*

A. Prohibition and Prevention

   1. The Judiciary Committee should process for early consideration by the House legislation that would make the assassination of a Chief of State of any country, or his political equivalent, a federal offense, if the offender is an American citizen or acts on behalf of an American citizen, or if the offender can be located in the United States.

   2. The Judiciary Committee should process for early consideration by the House comprehensive legislation that would codify, revise and reform the federal law of homicide, paying special attention to assassinations. The Judiciary Committee should give appropriate attention to the related offenses of

conspiracy, attempt, assault and kidnapping in the context of assassinations. Such legislation should be processed independently of the general proposals for the codification, revision or reform of the Federal criminal law. The Committee should address the following issues in considering the legislation:

(a) Distinguishing between those persons who should receive the protection of federal law because of the official positions they occupy and those persons who should receive protection of federal law only in the performance of their official duties.

(b) Extending the protection of federal law to persons who occupy high judicial and executive positions, including Justices of the Supreme Court and Cabinet officers,

(c) The applicability of these laws to private individuals in the exercise of constitutional rights,

(d) The penalty to be provided for homicide and the related offenses, including the applicability and the constitutionality of the death penalty,

(e) The basis for the exercise of federal jurisdiction, including domestic and extraterritorial reach,

(f) The pre-emption of state jurisdiction without the necessity of any action on the part of the Attorney General where the President is assassinated,

(g) The circumstances under which federal jurisdiction should pre-empt state jurisdiction in other cases,

(h) The power of federal investigative agencies to require autopsies to be performed,

(i) The ability of federal investigative agencies to secure the assistance of other federal or state agencies, including the military, other laws notwithstanding,

(j) The authority to offer rewards to apprehend the perpetrators of the crime,

(k) A requirement of forfeiture of the instrumentalities of the crime,

(l) The condemnation of personal or other effects of historical interest,

(m) The advisability of providing, consistent with the first amendment, legal trust devices to hold for the benefit of victims, their families, or the general treasury, the profits realized from books, movie rights, or public appearances by the perpetrator of the crime, and

(n) The applicability of threat and physical zone of protection legislation to persons under the physical protection of federal investigative or law enforcement agencies.

3. The appropriate Committees of the House should process for early consideration by the House charter legislation for the Central Intelligence Agency and Federal Bureau of Investigation. The Committees should address the following issues in considering the charter legislation:

(a) The proper foreign and domestic intelligence functions of the intelligence and investigative agencies of the United States,

(b) The relationship between the domestic intelligence functions and the interference with the exercise of individual constitutional rights,

(c) The deliniation of proper law enforcement functions and techniques including:

(i) the use of informants and electronic surveillance,

(ii) guidelines to circumscribe the use of informants or electronic surveillance to gather intelligence on, or investigate, groups that may be exercising first amendment freedoms, and

(iii) the proper response of intelligence or investigative agencies where information is developed that an informant has committed a crime.

(d) Guidelines to consider the circumstances, if any, when an investigative agency or a component of that agency should be disqualified from taking an active role in an investigation because of an appearance of impropriety growing out of a particular intelligence or investigative action,

(e) Definitions of the legislative scope and extent of "sources and methods" and the "informant privilege" as a rationale for the executive branch withholding information in response to Congressional or judicial process or other demand for information,

(f) Institutionalizing efforts to coordinate the gathering, sharing, and analysis of intelligence information,

(g) Insuring those agenies that primarily gather intelligence perform their function so as to serve the needs of other agencies that primarily engage in physical protection, and

(h) Implementing mechanisms that would permit inter-agency tasking of particular functions.

B. Prosecution

1. The Judiciary Committee should consider the impact of the provisions of law dealing with third-party records, bail and speedy trial as it applies to both the investigation and prosecution of federally cognizable homicides.

2. The Judiciary Committee should examine recently passed special prosecutor legislation to determine if its provisions should be modified to extend them to presidential assassinations and the circumstances, if any, under which they should be applicable to other federally cognizable homicides.

II. *Administrative Recommendations to the Executive*

The Department of Justice should re-examine its contingency plans for the handling of assassinations and federally cognizable homicides in light of the record and findings of the Committee. Such an examination should consider the following issues:

A. Insuring that its response takes full advantage of inter- and intra-agency task forces and the strike force approach to investigations and prosecutions,

B. Insuring that its response takes full advantage of the advances of science and technology, and determining when it should secure independent panels of scientists to review or perform necessary scientific tasks, or secure qualified independent forensic pathologists to perform a forensic autopsy,

C. Insuring that its fair trial/free press guidelines, consistent with an alleged offender's right to a fair trial, allow information about the facts and circumstances surrounding an assassination promptly be made public, and promptly be corrected when erroneous information is mistakening *[sic]* released, and

D. Entering at the current time into negotiations with representatives of the media to secure voluntary agreements providing that photographs, audio tapes, television tapes and related matters, made in and around the site of assassinations, be made available to the government by consent immediately following an assassination.

III. *General Recommendations for Congressional Investigations*

A. The appropriate Committees of the House should consider amending the Rules of the House to provide for a right to appointive counsel in investigative hearings where a witness is unable to provide counsel from private funds.

B. The appropriate Committees of the House should examine the Rules of the House governing the conduct of counsel in legislative and investigative hearings and consider delineating guidelines for professional conduct and ethics, including guidelines to deal with conflicts of interest in the representation of multiple witnesses before a Committee.

C. The Judiciary Committee should examine the adequacy of federal law as it provides for the production of federal and state prisoners before legislative or investigative committees under a writ of habeas corpus ad testificandum.

D. The appropriate Committees of the House should examine and clarify the applicability to Congressional subpoenas of recently enacted legislative restrictions on access to records and other documents.

E. The appropriate Committees of the House should consider legislation that would authorize the establishment of a legislative counsel to conduct litigation on behalf of committees of the House incident to the investigative or legislative activities and confer jurisdiction on the United States District Court for the District of Columbia to hear such lawsuits.

F. The appropriate committees of the House should consider if Rule 11 of the House should be amended, so as to restrict the current access by all Members of the House to the classified information in the possession of any committee.

IV. *Recommendations for Further Investigation*

A. The Department of Justice should contract for the examination of a film taken by Charles L. Bronson to determine its significance, if any, to the assassination of President Kennedy.

B. The National Institute of Law Enforcement and Criminal Justice of the Department of Justice and the National Science Foundation should make a study of the theory and application of the principles of acoustics to forensic questions, using the materials available in the assassination of President John F. Kennedy as a case study.

C. The Department of Justice should review the Committee's findings and report in the assassinations of President John F. Kennedy and Dr. Martin Luther King, Jr., and after completion of the recommended investigation enumerated in Sections A and B, analyze whether further official investigation is warranted in either case. The Department of Justice should report its analysis to the Judiciary Committee.

CUMULATIVE INDEX, 1974-78

CUMULATIVE INDEX, 1974-78

A

State of the Union, 42, 50, 53, 56-57 *(1974)*; 20 *(1975)*; 13, 18-19 *(1976)*; 51 *(1977)*; 12 *(1978)*

BUREAU OF ECONOMIC ANALYSIS, 68 *(1976)*

BUREAU OF NARCOTICS AND DANGEROUS DRUGS, 433 *(1975)*

BURGER, WARREN E. *See also* Supreme Court.
  Abortion, 483 *(1976)*
  Campaign Finance Law, 73, 104 *(1976)*
  Capital Punishment, 495-507 *(1978)*
  Confinement of Mentally Ill, 476-480 *(1975)*
  Corporate Spending in Referendum Campaigns, 315-317 *(1978)*
  Criminal Procedures, 221, 229 *(1977)*
  Cross-District Busing, 639-648 *(1974)*
  Death Penalty for Murder, 400 *(1977)*
  Death Penalty for Rape, 525 *(1977)*
  Drug Advertising, 351 *(1976)*
  Endangered Species, 433-446 *(1978)*
  Gag Orders, 464 *(1976)*
  Gilmore Execution, 918 *(1976)*
  Kent State Parents' Suit, 265 *(1974)*
  Legislative Redistricting, 152, 164 *(1977)*
  Nixon Tapes Ruling, 622-637 *(1974)*; 493 *(1977)*
  Parochial School Aid, 440 *(1977)*
  Pensions for Men and Women, 301-303 *(1978)*
  Proposed New Appeals Court, 456 *(1975)*
  Right to Reply Law, 524-527 *(1974)*
  School Desegregation, 457 *(1977)*
  Search and Seizure, 527 *(1976)*

BURNS, ARTHUR F.
  Fight Against Inflation, 67 *(1976)*
  Ford Economic Summit, 862 *(1974)*
  Inflation Speech, 419-425 *(1974)*; 635-642 *(1975)*
  Joint Economic Report, 718-733 *(1977)*

BUSINESS AND INDUSTRY. *See also* Foreign Trade. Small Business.
  Aerosol Sprays, Fluorocarbon Uses, 443-445 *(1975)*
  Carter on Lawyers and Doctors, 327 *(1978)*
  Democratic Platform, 555, 558 *(1976)*
  Economic Report, 85, 91 *(1974)*; 107-110 *(1975)*; 45-70 *(1976)*; 78 *(1977)*; 77-93 *(1978)*
  Firestone 500 Recall, 719-728 *(1978)*
  Ford Economic Summit, 862 *(1974)*
  Joint Economic Report, 717-733 *(1977)*
  Rail Reorganization, 529-542 *(1975)*
  Report on Workplace Cancer, 633 *(1978)*
  Supreme Court on Corporate Spending in Referendum Campaigns, 307 *(1978)*
  Supreme Court on Drug Advertising, 351 *(1976)*; 313 *(1977)*
  Supreme Court on Safety Inspections, 339 *(1978)*

Supreme Court on Water Pollution, 131-141 *(1977)*

BUSING
  Coleman Desegregation Report, 613-633 *(1975)*
  Court on School Desegregation, 447-464 *(1977)*
  Court on School Zones, 413 *(1976)*
  Supreme Court Cross-District Ruling, 639-654 *(1974)*

BUTLER, M. CALDWELL (R Va.)
  Impeachment Report, 733, 760, 762 *(1974)*

BUTTERFIELD, ALEXANDER P.
  White House Tapes, 24 *(1974)*; 658 *(1975)*

BYRD, ROBERT C. (D W.Va.)
  Nixon Pardon, 812 *(1974)*

BYRNE, W. MATTHEW JR.
  Fielding Break-in Case, 37, 39, 208, 1000 *(1974)*

C

CABINET. *See* Executive Branch.

CALIFANO, JOSEPH A. JR.
  Incidence of Workplace Cancer, 633 *(1978)*
  Swine Flu Program, 669 *(1978)*

CALIFORNIA
  Asilomar Conference on Genetic Engineering, 319 *(1975)*
  Farm Labor Law, 377-399 *(1975)*
  Offshore Oil Ruling, 167 *(1975)*
  Proposition 13, 397-402 *(1978)*
  School Zones Decision (Pasadena Plan), 413 *(1976)*

CALLAGHAN, JAMES, 533 *(1978)*

CALLEY, WILLIAM L. JR.
  Conviction Reversal, 857-860 *(1974)*

CAMBODIA
  Ford Foreign Policy Address, 223, 227, 230 *(1975)*
  Mayaguez Affair, 311-318 *(1975)*; 754 *1976*
  Missing Americans Report, 925 *(1976)*; 214 *(1977)*
  Secret Bombing
    Final Impeachment Report, 728, 742, 747 *(1974)*
    Nixon-Frost Interviews, 346 *(1977)*
    Nixon on National Security Wiretaps, 161 *(1976)*

CAMPAIGN FINANCE
  Carter Reform Proposals, 203 *(1977)*; 33 *(1978)*
  Court on Federal Financing of Elections, 71-111 *(1976)*
  Final Watergate Report, 681-688 *(1975)*
  ITT and Milk Fund, 3-21 *(1974)*
  Korean Influence Investigation, 845-908 *(1978)*

937

G

I

L

O

P

Q

R

954

T

U

XYZ